Corporate Finance and Investment

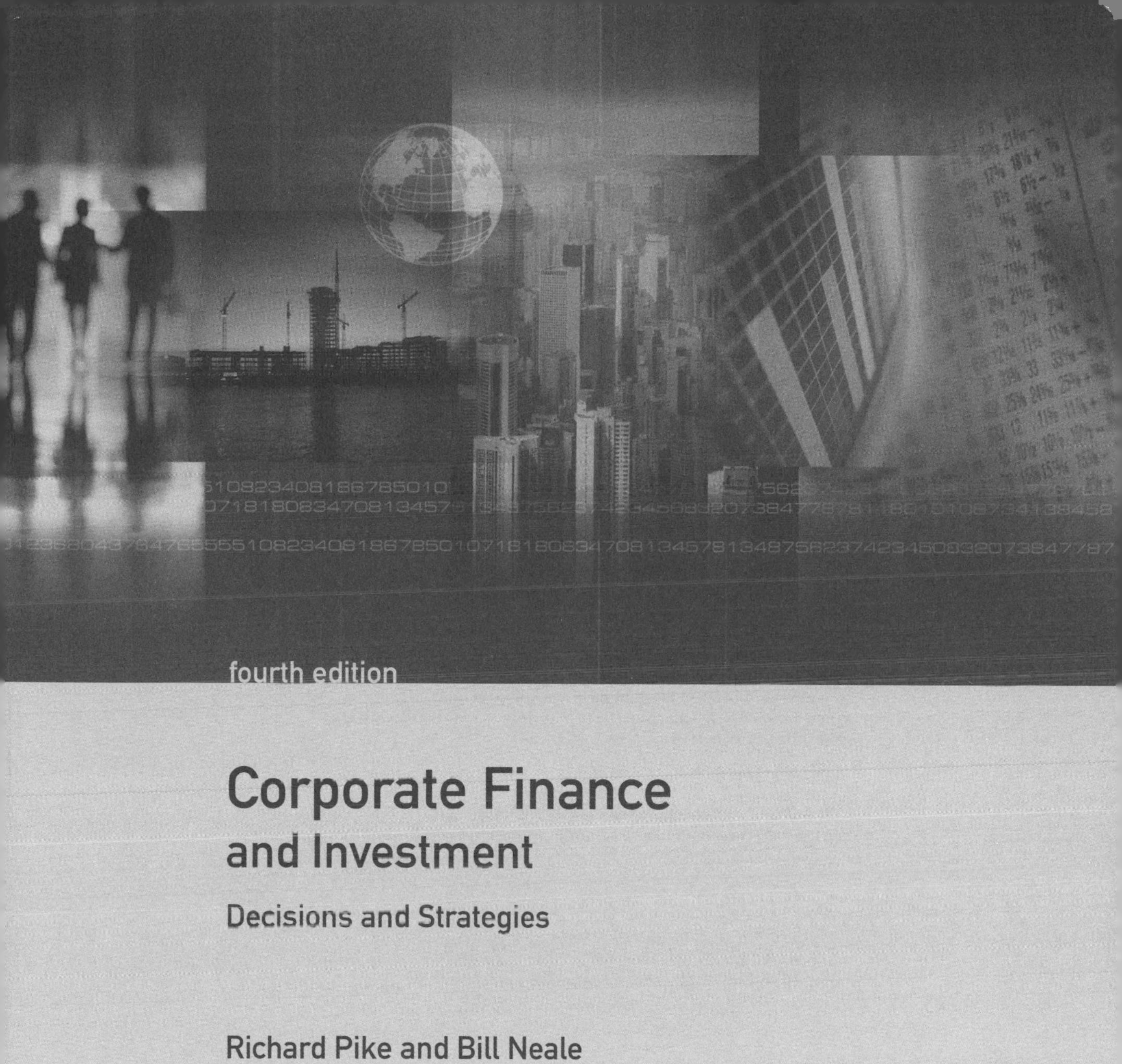

fourth edition

Corporate Finance
and Investment
Decisions and Strategies

Richard Pike and Bill Neale

FT Prentice Hall
FINANCIAL TIMES

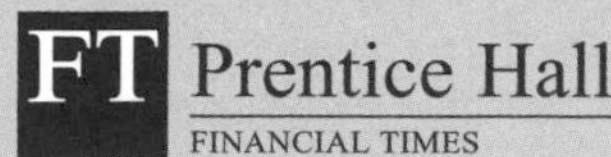

An imprint of Pearson Education
Harlow, England • London • New York • Boston • San Francisco • Toronto • Sydney • Singapore • Hong Kong
Tokyo • Seoul • Taipei • New Delhi • Cape Town • Madrid • Mexico City • Amsterdam • Munich • Paris • Milan

Pearson Education Limited
Edinburgh Gate
Harlow
Essex CM20 2JE
England

and Associated Companies throughout the world

Visit us on the World Wide Web at:
www.pearsoneduc.com

First published 1993
Fourth edition published 2003

ISBN 0 273 65138 2

British Library Cataloguing-in-Publication Data
A catalogue record for this book can be obtained from the British Library.

10 9 8 7 6 5 4 3 2
07 06 05 04 03

Typeset in Palatino 10/12.5 by 68
Printed and bound by Ashford Colour Press Ltd, Hampshire

To our wives, Carol and Jean

Contents

List of figures		xvii
List of tables		xx
Preface to Fourth Edition		xxiii
Acknowledgements		xxix
Guided Tour		xxxii
Part I	**A framework for financial decisions**	**1**
1	An overview of financial management	3
1.1	Introduction	4
1.2	The finance function	6
1.3	Investment and financial decisions	7
1.4	Cash – the lifeblood of the business	8
1.5	The emergence of financial management	9
1.6	The finance department in the firm	11
1.7	The financial objective	12
1.8	The agency problem	13
1.9	Managing the agency problem	14
1.10	Social responsibility and shareholder wealth	16
1.11	The corporate governance debate	17
1.12	The risk dimension	18
1.13	The strategic dimension	19
1.14	The underlying principles of finance	23
	Summary	27
	Key points	28
	Further reading	28
	Questions	29

2 The financial environment 33

2.1 Introduction 34
2.2 Financial markets 34
2.3 The financial services sector 37
2.4 The London Stock Exchange (LSE) 41
2.5 Are financial markets efficient? 46
2.6 A new perspective – Chaos Theory 55
2.7 Short-termism in the City 57
2.8 Reading the financial pages 58
2.9 Taxation and financial decisions 61
Summary 62
Key points 62
Further reading 62
Appendix Financial statement analysis 63
Questions 74

3 Present values and financial arithmetic 78

3.1 Introduction 79
3.2 Measuring wealth 79
3.3 Time-value of money 81
3.4 Financial arithmetic for capital growth 81
3.5 Present value 84
3.6 Present value arithmetic 89
3.7 Valuing bonds 92
3.8 Net present value 94
Summary 99
Key points 99
Further reading 99
Appendix I The Term Structure of Interest Rates and the Yield Curve 100
Appendix II The investment–consumption decision 102
Appendix III Present value formulae 107
Questions 109

4 Valuation of assets, shares and companies 112

4.1 Introduction 113
4.2 The valuation problem 113
4.3 Valuation using published accounts 115
4.4 Valuing the earnings stream 122
4.5 EBITDA – a half-way house 124
4.6 Valuing cash flows 125
4.7 The DCF approach 127
4.8 Valuation of unquoted companies 131

4.9 Valuing shares: the Dividend Valuation Model 131
4.10 Problems with the Dividend Growth Model 135
4.11 Shareholder Value Analysis 138
Summary 143
Key points 143
Further reading 144
Questions 145

Part II Investment decisions and strategies 151

5 Investment appraisal methods 153

5.1 Introduction 154
5.2 Cash flow analysis 154
5.3 Investment techniques – net present value 156
5.4 Internal rate of return 158
5.5 Profitability index 161
5.6 Payback period 162
5.7 Accounting rate of return 163
5.8 Ranking mutually exclusive projects 165
5.9 Investment evaluation and capital rationing 170
Summary 174
Key points 175
Further reading 175
Appendix I Modified IRR 176
Appendix II Multi-period capital rationing and mathematical programming 177
Questions 182

6 Project appraisal – applications 187

6.1 Introduction 188
6.2 Incremental cash flow analysis 188
6.3 Replacement decisions 192
6.4 Inflation cannot be ignored 194
6.5 Taxation is a cash flow 196
6.6 Use of DCF techniques 200
6.7 Traditional appraisal methods 202
Summary 206
Key points 206
Further reading 207
Appendix The problem of unequal lives: Allis plc 207
Questions 210

7	Investment strategy and process	220
7.1	Introduction	221
7.2	Strategic considerations	221
7.3	Advanced manufacturing technology (AMT) investment	225
7.4	Environmental aspects of investment	228
7.5	The capital investment process	229
7.6	Post-auditing	237
	Summary	240
	Key points	240
	Further reading	240
	Questions	241
8	Foreign investment decisions	243
8.1	Introduction	244
8.2	Advantages of MNCs over national firms	245
8.3	Foreign market entry strategies	246
8.4	The incremental hypothesis	248
8.5	Complexities of foreign investment	250
8.6	Should firms worry about exchange rate changes?	252
8.7	Evaluating FDI	255
8.8	Exposure to foreign exchange risk	259
8.9	How MNCs manage operating exposure	263
8.10	Political and country risk	264
8.11	Managing political and country risk (PCR)	267
	Summary	269
	Key points	269
	Further reading	269
	Questions	271
Part III	**Investment risk and return**	**275**
9	Analysing investment risk	277
9.1	Introduction	278
9.2	Expected net present value (ENPV): Betterway plc	279
9.3	Attitudes to risk	280
9.4	The many types of risk	281
9.5	Measurement of risk	283
9.6	Risk description techniques	288
9.7	Adjusting the NPV formula for risk	292
9.8	Risk analysis in practice	295
	Summary	298
	Key points	298

	Further reading	299
	Appendix Multi-period cash flows and risk	299
	Questions	303
10	**Relationships between investments: portfolio theory**	**308**
10.1	Introduction	309
10.2	Portfolio analysis: the basic principles	310
10.3	How to measure portfolio risk	313
10.4	Portfolio analysis where risk and return differ	316
10.5	Different degrees of correlation	319
10.6	Worked example: Gerrybild plc	320
10.7	Portfolios with more than two components	323
10.8	Can we use this for project appraisal? Some reservations	325
	Summary	326
	Key points	326
	Further reading	327
	Questions	329
11	**Setting the risk premium: the Capital Asset Pricing Model**	**331**
11.1	Introduction	332
11.2	Security valuation and discount rates	332
11.3	Concepts of risk and return	333
11.4	The relationship between different equity markets	338
11.5	Systematic risk	339
11.6	Completing the model	344
11.7	Using the CAPM: assessing the required return	345
11.8	The underpinnings of the CAPM	350
11.9	Portfolios with many components: the capital market line	351
11.10	How it all fits together: the key relationships	353
11.11	Reservations about the CAPM	355
11.12	Testing the CAPM	356
11.13	The Arbitrage Pricing Theory	358
11.14	Issues raised by the CAPM: some food for managerial thought	359
	Summary	362
	Key points	362
	Further reading	362
	Appendix Analysis of variance	363
	Questions	365

12 The required rate of return on investment and Shareholder Value Analysis 367

12.1 Introduction 368
12.2 The required return in all-equity firms: the DGM 368
12.3 The required return in all-equity firms: the CAPM 374
12.4 Using value drivers – Shareholder Value Analysis (SVA) 376
12.5 Worked example: Safa plc 378
12.6 Using 'tailored' discount rates 381
12.7 Another problem: taxation and the CAPM 388
12.8 Problems with 'tailored' discount rates 389
12.9 A critique of divisional hurdle rates 390
12.10 The discount rate for Foreign Direct Investment (FDI) 392
Summary 393
Key points 393
Further reading 394
Questions 394

13 Identifying and valuing options 398

13.1 Introduction 399
13.2 Share options 399
13.3 Option pricing 407
13.4 Application of option theory to corporate finance 413
13.5 Capital investment options 414
13.6 Why conventional NPV may not tell the whole story 419
Summary 421
Key points 421
Further reading 421
Appendix Black–Scholes option pricing formula 422
Questions 423

Part IV Short-term financing and policies 427

14 Treasury management and working capital policy 429

14.1 Introduction 430
14.2 The treasury function 430
14.3 Funding 433
14.4 Banking relationships 436
14.5 Risk management 436
14.6 Working capital management 445
14.7 Predicting corporate failure 448
14.8 Cash operating cycle 450
14.9 Working capital policy 451
14.10 Overtrading problems 456
14.11 How firms can use the yield curve 458

	Summary	460
	Key points	460
	Further reading and website	461
	Questions	462
15	**Short-term asset management**	**466**
15.1	Introduction	467
15.2	Managing trade credit	467
15.3	Inventory management	478
15.4	Cash management	484
15.5	Cash management models	490
	Summary	492
	Key points	492
	Further reading	492
	Appendix Miller–Orr cash management model	493
	Questions	495
16	**Short- and medium-term finance**	**500**
16.1	Introduction	501
16.2	Trade credit	501
16.3	Bank credit facilities	504
16.4	Factoring and invoice discounting	508
16.5	Using the money market: bill finance	511
16.6	Hire purchase (HP)	514
16.7	Leasing	516
16.8	Lease evaluation: a simple case	518
16.9	Motives for leasing	522
16.10	Allowing for Corporation Tax in lease evaluation	524
16.11	Financing international trade	529
	Summary	533
	Key points	533
	Further reading	534
	Questions	535
17	**Managing currency risk**	**539**
17.1	Introduction	540
17.2	The structure of exchange rates: spot and forward rates	542
17.3	Foreign exchange exposure	543
17.4	Economic theory and exposure management	546
17.5	Exchange rate forecasting	553
17.6	Devising a foreign exchange management (FEM) strategy	557
17.7	Internal hedging techniques	560
17.8	External hedging techniques	563

17.9	Hedging the risk of foreign projects	571
17.10	Conclusions	573
	Summary	573
	Key points	573
	Further reading	574
	Questions	575

Part V Strategic financial decisions **581**

18 Long-term finance 583

18.1	Introduction	584
18.2	Guiding lights: corporate aims and corporate finance	584
18.3	How companies raise finance in practice	586
18.4	Shareholders' funds	587
18.5	Methods of raising equity finance	590
18.6	Debt instruments: debentures, bonds and notes	606
18.7	Leasing and sale-and-leaseback (SAL)	618
	Summary	620
	Key points	620
	Further reading	621
	Questions	622

19 Returning value to shareholders: the dividend decision 626

19.1	Introduction	627
19.2	The strategic dimension	628
19.3	The legal dimension	629
19.4	The theory: dividend policy and firm value	630
19.5	Objections to dividend irrelevance	638
19.6	The information content of dividends: dividend smoothing	645
19.7	Alternatives to cash dividends	647
19.8	The dividend puzzle	651
19.9	Conclusions	654
	Summary	655
	Key points	655
	Further reading	656
	Appendix Home-made dividends	656
	Questions	658

20 Capital structure and the required return 662

20.1	Introduction	663
20.2	Measures of gearing	665
20.3	Operating and financial gearing	670
20.4	Financial gearing and risk: Lindley plc	673

20.5 The 'traditional' view of gearing and the required return 677
20.6 The cost of debt 680
20.7 The overall cost of capital 682
20.8 Worked example: Damstar plc 685
20.9 International financing 687
20.10 The WACC for foreign investment projects 690
20.11 Financial distress 690
20.12 Two more issues: signalling and agency costs 695
20.13 Conclusions 696
Summary 698
Key points 698
Further reading 699
Appendix Slipping down the credit ratings 699
Questions 701

21 Does capital structure really matter? 706

21.1 Introduction 707
21.2 The Modigliani–Miller message 708
21.3 MM's propositions 710
21.4 Impediments to arbitrage 714
21.5 MM with corporate income tax 715
21.6 Capital structure theory and the CAPM 719
21.7 MM with financial distress 721
21.8 Calculating the WACC 722
21.9 The adjusted present value method (APV) 725
21.10 Applying the APV to foreign direct investment 728
21.11 Which discount rate should we use? 729
Summary 730
Key points 730
Further reading 731
Appendix I Derivation of MM's Proposition II 732
Appendix II MM's Proposition III: the cut-off rate for new investment 732
Appendix III Allowing for personal taxation: Miller's revision 733
Questions 735

22 Acquisitions and restructuring 741

22.1 Introduction 742
22.2 Takeover waves 743
22.3 Motives for takeover 750
22.4 Financing a bid 756
22.5 Evaluating a bid: the expected gains from takeovers 757
22.6 Worked example: ML plc and CO plc 759
22.7 The importance of strategy 762

22.8	The strategic approach	763
22.9	Post-merger activities	768
22.10	Assessing the impact of mergers	773
22.11	Value gaps	780
22.12	Corporate restructuring to create value	782
	Summary	790
	Key points	791
	Further reading	791
	Questions	793

Appendix A Solutions to selected questions 801

Appendix B Present value interest factor (PVIF) 838

Appendix C Present value interest factor for an annuity (PVIFA) 842

Glossary 846

References 861

Index 873

A Companion Website accompanies *Corporate Finance and Investment*, 4th edition by Pike and Neale

Visit the ***Corporate Finance and Investment*** Companion Website at www.booksites.net/pikeneale to find valuable teaching and learning material including:

For students:

- Study material designed to help you improve your results
- Multiple choice questions to test and reinforce your learning
- Links to relevant sites on the Internet
- An online glossary
- A search facility for specific information within the companion website

For lecturers:

- A secure, password protected site with teaching material
- A downloadable Instructor's Manual
- Extra problems and answers
- Cases section with questions and model answers
- Downloadable PowerPoint presentations to assist in lecturing
- A syllabus manager that will build and host a course web page

List of figures

1.1 The Finance function in a large organisation 6
1.2 Cash – the lifeblood of the business 8
1.3 The risk–return trade-off 19
1.4 Main elements in strategic planning 21
1.5 Factors influencing the value of the firm 22
2.1 Financial markets, institutions, suppliers and users 36
2.2 Chart showing breakout beyond resistance line 49
3.1 The relationship between present value of £1 and interest over time 88
3.2 Investment appraisal elements 95
3.3 The term structure of interest rates 100
3.4 Investment opportunities for Platt Enterprises 103
3.5 Investment and financing opportunities for Platt Enterprises 105
3.6 Investment decisions in imperfect capital markets 107
4.1 Calculating Free Cash Flow (FCF) 129
4.2 Shareholder value analysis framework 139
5.1 Lara proposal: NPV–IRR graph 160
5.2 NPV and IRR compared 169
7.1 McKinsey–GE portfolio matrix 222
7.2 Normal progression of product over time 223
7.3 Investment strategy 223
7.4 A simple capital budgeting system 231
8.1 The spectrum of foreign market service modes 246
8.2 Exporting vs. FDI 249
8.3 Classification of firms by extent of operating exposure 259
9.1 Risk profiles 280
9.2 Investor's risk-averse utility function 281
9.3 Variability of project returns 284
9.4 Mean–variance analysis 287
9.5 Sensitivity graph 288
9.6 Simulated probability distributions 292
9.7 How risk is assumed to increase over time 294

10.1 Equal and offsetting fluctuations in returns 310
10.2 Available portfolio risk–return combinations when both assets' risks and expected returns are different 318
10.3 The effect on the efficiency frontier of changing correlation 319
10.4 Gerrybild's opportunity set 322
10.5 Portfolio combinations with three assets 323
10.6 Portfolio combinations with four assets 328
11.1 Specific vs. market risk of a portfolio 335
11.2 The effect of international diversification on portfolio risk 338
11.3 The characteristics line: no specific risk 341
11.4 The characteristics line: with specific risk 341
11.5 The security market line 344
11.6 The capital market line 351
11.7 The CAPM: the three key relationships 354
11.8 Theoretical and empirical SMLs 357
11.9 Alternative characteristics lines 363
12.1 Risk premiums for activities of varying risk 382
12.2 The Beta pyramid 383
13.1 Payoff lines for shares and share options in Enigma Drugs plc 400
13.2 BP call option 404
13.3 BP put option 406
13.4 Option transactions 407
13.5 Option and share price movements for Bradford plc 409
13.6 The value of the options to delay investments: Cardiff Components Ltd 416
14.1 Financing working capital: the matching approach 435
14.2 Financing working capital needs: an aggressive strategy 435
14.3 Cash conversion cycle 451
14.4 Helsinki plc working capital strategies 453
14.5 Optimal level of working capital for a 'relaxed' strategy 455
14.6 Optimal level of working capital for an 'aggressive' strategy 456
14.7 Yield curves 459
15.1 The credit management process 469
15.2 Ordering and debt collection cycle 475
15.3 The inventory cycle 481
15.4 Cash flow activity for main stakeholders 485
15.5 Miller–Orr cash management model 493
16.1 How hire purchase works 515
17.1 Interlocking theories in international economics 552
17.2 Flow chart demonstrating a logical approach towards devising a foreign exchange management strategy 558
17.3 Illustration of multilateral netting 561
17.4 Achieving the swap 570
18.1 How an SPV works 609
19.1 The impact of a permanent dividend cut 634
19.2 Dividends as a residual 636
20.1 How gearing affects the ROE 675
20.2 The 'traditional' view of capital structure 679
21.1 MM's Propositions I and II 712

21.2	The MM thesis with corporate income tax	716
21.3	The two components of the geared Beta	720
21.4	Optimal gearing with liquidation costs	721
21.5	A simple APV model	729
22.1	Who does what? – merger flow chart	748
22.2	A strategic framework	763
22.3	Type of acquisition and integrative complexity	768

List of tables

2.1	Leading Stock Exchanges (based on 2000 statistics)	46
2.2	Share performance for the food retail sector	60
2.3	*Foto-U* plc	64
2.4	*Foto-U* key ratios	67
2.5	*Foto-U* annual corporate performance report	72
3.1	Annual percentage rates for a loan with interest payable at 22 per cent per annum	83
3.2	Present value of a single future sum	89
4.1	Balance Sheet for DS Smith plc as at 28 April 2001	115
4.2	How earnings and dividends grow in tandem (figures in £m)	134
5.1	Net present value calculations	157
5.2	Why NPV makes sense to shareholders	157
5.3	IRR calculations for Lara proposal	159
5.4	Payback period calculation	163
5.5	Calculation of the ARR on total assets	164
5.6	Comparison of various appraisal methods	165
5.7	Comparison of mutually exclusive projects	168
5.8	Investment opportunities for Mervtech plc	172
5.9	NPV vs. PI for Mervtech plc	173
5.10	Modified IRR for Lara	176
5.11	Atherton plc: planned investment schedule (£000)	178
5.12	Projects accepted based on LP solution	179
6.1	Profitability of Sevvie's project	193
6.2	Sevvie plc solution	194
6.3	The money terms approach	195
6.4	The real terms approach	196
6.5	Project Tiger 2000 (assuming no capital allowances)	197
6.6	Woosnam plc – Tiger 2000 tax reliefs	199
6.7	Woosnam plc Tiger 2000 with tax relief	199
6.8	Capital investment evaluation methods in 100 large UK firms	200
6.9	Relationship between ARR and IRR	202
6.10	Allis plc cash flows for two projects	208

6.11 Profit projection for CNC milling machine (£000) 217
8.1 Sparkes and Zoltan: project details 256
8.2 Evaluation of the Zoltan project 257
8.3 Alternative evaluation of Zoltan project 258
8.4 Country risk scores for selected locations 266
9.1 Betterway plc: expected net present values 279
9.2 Effects of cost structure on profits (£000) 282
9.3 Snowglo plc project data 284
9.4 Project risk for Snowglo plc 285
9.5 UMK cost structure 289
9.6 Risk analysis in 100 large UK firms 295
9.7 Bronson project payoffs with independent cash flows 300
10.1 Returns under different states of the economy 314
10.2 Calculating the covariance 315
10.3 Differing returns and risks 317
10.4 Portfolio risk–return combinations (%) 317
10.5 Returns from Gerrybild 320
10.6 Calculation of standard deviations of returns from each investment 321
10.7 Calculation of the covariance 321
11.1 The annual TSRs on Pilkington shares 334
11.2 How to remove portfolio risk 336
11.3 Possible returns from Walkley Wagons 340
11.4 Beta values of the constituents of the FT 30 Share Index 343
11.5 Equity-gilts relative returns 348
12.1 The return on Tomkins plc shares 370
12.2 Cash flow profile* for Safa, plc (ungeared) 380
12.3 Divisional Betas for Tomkins plc 385
12.4 The effect of operating gearing (£m) 386
12.5 Subjective risk categories 388
13.1 Option on BP shares (current price 397p) 402
13.2 Returns on BP shares and options 404
13.3 Valuing a call option in Riskitt plc 412
13.4 Harlequin plc: call option valuation 419
14.1 Helsinki plc: profitability and risk of working capital strategies 454
15.1 Trade credit policy in large UK firms (145 firms) 476
15.2 Credit management practices in large UK firms (145 firms) 476
15.3 Total inventory levels and stockholding periods 479
15.4 Thorntons plc consolidated cash flow statement 487
15.5 Mangle Ltd: production and sales 488
15.6 Mangle Ltd: cash budget for six months to June (£) 488
16.1 Tax relief on an HP contract (£) 515
16.2 Hardup plc's leasing analysis 519
16.3 The behaviour of the equivalent loan (£m) 520
16.4 Hardup's leasing decision with tax 526
16.5 Interest charges on a lease contract (figures in £m) 527
16.6 Changes in tax-allowable lease costs (figures in £m) 527
17.1 Twelve-month forecasts to November 1 2000 556
17.2 Oilex's internal currency flows 561
18.1 European corporate asset-backed deals, Jan.–June 2001 610

19.1 Kelda Group plc Financial Calendar 627
19.2 Rawdon plc 642
19.3 BAA plc: dividend smoothing 646
19.4 Analysis of a share repurchase 650
20.1 Financial data for BAA plc 668
20.2 How gearing affects shareholder returns in Lindley plc 673
20.3 How gearing affects the risk of ordinary shares 674
20.4 How gearing can affect share price 676
20.5 British Airways plc borrowings (£m) 689
21.1 Key definitions in capital structure analysis 709
21.2 The tax shield with finite-life debt 727
22.1 The scale and financing of takeover activity of UK firms by UK firms 744
22.2 Acquisition according to status of acquiree 745
22.3 Cross-border acquisitions involving UK companies 746
22.4 Hawk and Vole 755
22.5 Strategic opportunities 765
22.6 Pre- and post-bid returns 775
22.7 The gains from mergers 776

Preface to Fourth Edition

Not all text-books survive to a fourth edition. As one of the lucky survivors, we wish to preface this edition with a 'thank you' – thank you to the lecturers who have recommended our book and also to the students who have purchased and used it. Hopefully, you have all obtained good value from it.

We first began work on this project around 1990, well over a decade ago. Over this period, there have been many changes in the financial arena. For example, a radical downshift in inflationary expectations, the formation of the World Trade Organisation, increasing integration of world financial markets, powered by the ongoing revolution in communications, the end of the 'Japanese Miracle', and the introduction of the Euro. We have seen several financial meltdowns – at the national level, the 'Asian Crisis', and more recently in Argentina, and at the micro-level, the 'dotcom' boom and bust and the crisis in corporate governance.

It is not surprising that financial issues increasingly dominate the news bulletins, emphasizing the need for both students of business and also business practitioners to have at least a working knowledge of finance. Yet academic courses are becoming increasingly fragmented, for example, with the move to semesterization. At the same time, within academic courses, the emphasis now placed on formal mathematical and statistical training is also being reduced.

These considerations reinforce our view that finance should be about developing, explaining and, above all, **applying** key concepts and techniques to a broad range of contemporary management and business policy concerns and challenges. It is becoming more appropriate, certainly at the undergraduate level, to demonstrate the role finance has to play in explaining and shaping business development rather than concentrating on rigorous, quantitative aspects.

The focus of the fourth edition, as in previous ones, is distinctly corporate, examining financial issues from a managerial standpoint. To simplify greatly, we have tried, wherever possible, to present the reader with the question 'OK, but how does this help the managerial decision-maker?' and also to provide a few answers, or at least pointers.

Some might say we should include chapters on other financial issues deemed to have a degree of importance equivalent to those covered here. Yet we believe, as ever, that there is a trade-off between comprehensiveness and manageability. Admittedly, this edition has grown a little but it is directed at those issues, which in our experience are regarded as the central issues in finance.

Distinctive features

The fourth edition retains a set of distinctive features, including the following:

- *A strategic focus*. Students often regard financial management as a subject quite distinct from management and business policy. We attempt to relate the subject to these matters, emphasizing the integration of the finance function within the context of managerial decision-making and corporate planning, and to the wider external environment.
- *A practical approach*. Financial theory increasingly dominates some texts. Theory has its place, and this text covers an appreciable amount; however, we seek to blend theory and practice: to ask why they sometimes differ, and to assess the role of less-sophisticated financial approaches. In other words, we do not elevate theory above common sense and intuition.
- *A clear and accessible style*. Personal experience and feedback suggests that much of our target readership prefers a more descriptive, rather than heavily mathematical, approach but appreciates worked examples and illustrations. There is a place for formulae, proofs and quantitative analysis; however, where possible, an alternative narrative explanation is provided. Appendices are often used to deal with rather more complex mathematical aspects.
- *An international perspective*. Although emanating from the UK, our text uses, where appropriate, examples drawn from other regions and countries, especially Europe and the USA.

Teaching and learning features

A range of teaching and learning features is provided, including the following:

- *Mini-case studies*. Topical cameos, applying financial management principles to well-known companies, are presented at the start of chapters and elsewhere within the text.
- *Learning objectives*. Specified early in each chapter, these highlight what the reader should achieve in terms of concepts, terminology and skills.
- *Worked examples*. Integrated throughout the text to illustrate the key principles.
- *Extracts from the press*. Each chapter includes an article from either the *Financial Times* or the *Economist* focusing on one of the key issues addressed in the chapter (new).
- *Key revision points*. Provided at the end of each chapter to summarize the main concepts covered.
- *Annotated further reading*. At the end of each chapter, a number of key books and articles are suggested to offer additional perspectives and enable subjects to be studied in more depth. Full details of all books and articles are given in the References at the end of the book.
- A quick reference *glossary* of simple definitions (new).

Assessment features

Flexible study and assessment is facilitated by a variety of activities:

- *Self-assessment Activities (SAAs)*. These include both short questions and simple numerical exercises designed to reinforce a point made in the text or to encourage the reader to pursue a particular line of thought. However, they are presented differently and consistently in this edition. Questions are inserted in the text at appropriate points and the answers are packaged together at the end of each chapter.
- *Questions*. These test a mix of numerical, analytical and descriptive skills, offering a spread of difficulty. A selection of solutions is also provided in Appendix A at the end of the text, making these suitable for self-assessment, tutorial or examination purposes.
- *Practical assignments*. These provide the opportunity to look beyond the confines of the text to consider the application of concepts to a company or organization, or to publish financial reports and data, and are suitable where group or individually assessed coursework is set.

Readership

The text has proved successful both for newcomers to finance and also for students with a prior knowledge of the subject. It is particularly relevant to undergraduate, MBA and other postgraduate and post-experience courses in corporate finance or financial management. Students seeking a professionally accredited qualification will also find it especially relevant to the financial management papers of the Chartered Association of Certified Accountants, Institute of Chartered Secretaries and Administrators, Certified Diploma in Finance and Accounting, Chartered Institute of Management Accountants and the Institute of Chartered Accountants in England and Wales.

Changes to the fourth edition

As with previous editions, our revisions are based on extensive market research including reviewers' questionnaires and direct feedback from adopters and users. Feedback, while always interesting and helpful, was sometimes contradictory. Some wished for a more comprehensive, and sometimes more rigorous treatment, while others expressed concern that we might lean too far in the direction of strategy. Hopefully, we have achieved a balance between academic rigour and practical application.

In preparing this edition, we have battled with two opposing forces. We wanted to avoid expanding the text to an unmanageable size, yet we have been aware of several gaps in our coverage in previous editions, and the need for 'infill'.

The main changes to this edition can be divided into format and content changes.

Changes in format

- We have tried to shorten the introductory cameos at the start of each chapter to sharpen the focus. Many of these have been updated, although some old favourites (of ours, at least) remain, for example the Pearson cameo in Chapter 10.

- Each chapter now includes a relevant article reproduced from the financial press.
- Some useful website addresses are provided where appropriate.
- More 'Self-assessment Activities' (SAAs) have been provided with answers collected at the end of each chapter. Many more of these are quantitative in nature, helping to supplement the assessment materials.
- Key points are highlighted with icons in the margin.

Changes in content

- Chapter 2 now has an appendix on how to read financial statements.
- Chapter 3 now includes the term structure of interest rates, and the yield curve.
- Strategic investment considerations now form part of Chapter 7, while investment practices, formerly in Chapter 7, moves to Chapter 6 (Project Appraisal – Applications).
- Chapter 8 is now wholly devoted to analysing foreign investment decisions. This also provides a foretaste of the problems of dealing with foreign exchange variations covered in more detail in Chapter 17. However, whereas in Chapter 8, the focus is on operating exposure, Chapter 17 deals with transactions exposure to a far greater degree.
- Chapter 10 now includes a section on multi-asset portfolios, brought forward from Chapter 11.
- Chapter 16 now includes material on financing international trade, e.g. forfaiting.
- Chapter 17 now includes a section on forecasting exchange rates.
- Chapter 18 has been extensively rewritten and updated, for example, to include Floating Rate Notes and Asset-Backed Securities.
- Chapter 19 has been extensively rewritten.
- Chapter 22 includes a revised section on investigation of mergers.
- The material in the old Chapter 23 has been transferred to the website.

The international material

As noted, this edition substantially extends the treatment of issues of international finance. However, unlike many other texts, we decided not to offer a single chapter on international aspects but to present much of this material side by side with material discussing financial issues in a domestic context This may not be to the taste of all, but we have found that students do tend to struggle with international finance. Consequently, our approach allows an opportunity to absorb this material in a more digestible fashion as well as enabling an ongoing contrast with financial issues viewed from a purely domestic perspective.

It may help to set out the location and hence, the progression of the coverage of international aspects:

- Chapter 8 analyses foreign investment decisions. It covers Purchasing Power Parity in the context of whether a firm should worry about foreign exchange rate movements. The primary focus is on long-term operating/strategic exposure and how to manage it. It also covers political and country risk.
- Chapter 11 contains a section (11.4) discussing the relationship between international equity and the scope for reducing market risk by international portfolio diversification.

- Chapter 12 contains a section (12.10) on identifying the appropriate Beta to use in selecting the discount rate for evaluating all-equity financed foreign investment projects.
- Chapter 16 includes a section (16.11) on methods of financing and insuring international trade.
- Chapter 17 looks at different forms of foreign exchange rate exposure and analyses the Four-Way Model of international economics. It looks at ways of hedging FX risk, both internally and using the external markets. There is also a section on approaches to forecasting FX rates (17.5).
- Chapter 20 contains a section (20.9) on financing foreign investment projects, with particular reference to the case for borrowing, and the implications for the required rate of return on new projects.
- Chapter 21 contains a section (21.10) on applying the Adjusted Present Value Method to foreign investment projects, following a discussion of the appropriate rate of discount to use in cases where risk and financing may differ from existing activities.
- Chapter 22 has a small sub-section on international/European regulation of takeovers as at the time of writing.

Structure and outline

The structure of the text is illustrated below.

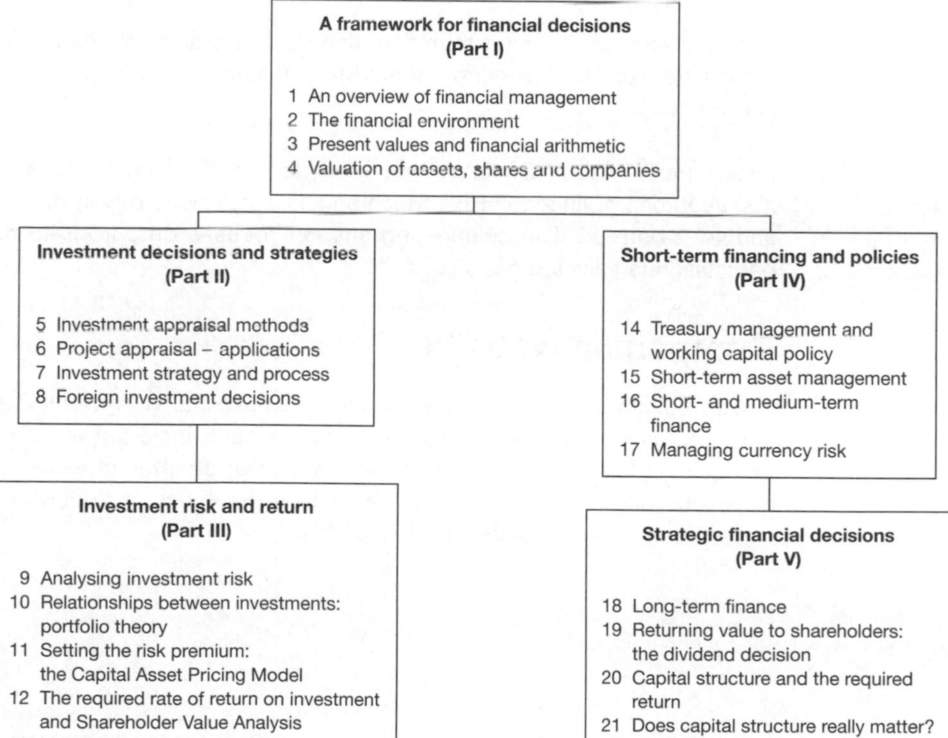

An outline of the text is given below; however, a further description of the purpose and content of each section is given in the introduction to each.

Part I considers the underlying framework for corporate financing and investment decisions; key aspects of this part are the financial objectives of business, the financial environment within which firms operate, the time value of money and the concept of value.

Part II addresses investment decisions and strategies within firms. Emphasis is placed on evaluation procedures, including treatments of taxation, inflation and capital rationing. Because, in practice, investment decision-making often bears little relationship to the theoretical approaches outlined in some texts, we persist in our attempt to promote an understanding of the practical evaluation of investment decisions by firms, with particular emphasis on foreign investment decisions.

The importance of risk management is examined in Part III. Five chapters are devoted to analysing and managing investment risk: the first considers the investment project in isolation, while other chapters view risk more from a shareholder perspective. Fundamental to this section and to the whole of financial management is the rate of return on investment required by shareholders. The rapidly developing and exciting field of options analysis is also explored.

Part IV discusses the short-term financing decisions and policies for acquiring assets. It covers treasury and working capital management and the alternatives for managing currency risk.

Finally, Part V addresses long-term, strategic financing and policy issues. What are the main sources of finance? How much should a company pay in dividends? How much should it borrow? The culminating chapter focuses on corporate restructuring with particular reference to acquisitions.

Companion website

This edition is supported by a companion website, at **www.booksites.net/pikeneale**. This contains much of the material that we have included in previous instructors' manuals. It provides answers to all the end-of-chapter questions, plus additional questions and answers. The case exercises previously included in Chapter 23 also appear there. It also reproduces the glossary.

Acknowledgements

All textbooks include 'acknowledgements' but, on reflection, this seems too weak a word to use when assistance has so often been so freely given. *Roget's Thesaurus* offers as a synonym, 'the act of admitting to something', suggesting rather grudging recognition!

Our recognition of the wide range of people and organizations is anything but grudging. We extend our warm appreciation of the helpful comments provided by you over the years, and also for consent to use your material.

To the existing roll of honour, we wish to add the following names and organizations, whom we sincerely hope will be happy to be associated with our efforts:

Sue Matthews and Charles Macey of Barclays Capital
Richard Miller of the Factors & Discounters Association
John Leaning of the Office of Fair Trading
Mark Thompson
Alex Ludecke, Paul Cannon, Peter Walsh, Jon Ridge (who will not mind being grouped together!)
Steve Letza
David Holmes

As ever, we apologise for any omissions.

Finally, we are especially grateful to the ever-patient, ever-tolerant editorial staff at Pearson Education, and to the anonymous contributors to the market research conducted by the publisher. We hope that you will agree that your comments have led to an improvement in the quality of the final product. Naturally, we claim sole responsibility for any remaining errors.

Richard Pike, University of Bradford
Bill Neale, University of Leicester

Publisher's Acknowledgements

We are grateful to the following for permission to reproduce copyright material:

Figure 8.1 from *Contemporary Strategic Analysis*, Blackwell Publishing Ltd., (Grant, R.M. 1998).

We are grateful to the Financial Times Limited for permission to reprint the following material:

Marrying in haste, © *Financial Times*, 12 April, 2000; The subtle art of getting paid: late payment, © *Financial Times*, 26 April, 2001; A superjumbo investment, © *Financial Times*, 2 November, 2000; BT's £2.3 billion UK property sale cheers market, © *Financial Times*, 14 June, 2002; Table 2.2 Share performance for the food retail sector from The dividend cover and market capitalisation value, © *Financial Times*, 2 January, 2002.

We are grateful to the Association of Chartered Certified Accountants (ACCA) and the Chartered Institute of Management Accountants (CIMA) for permitting the reproduction of examination questions throughout the book.

The publishers are grateful to all the copyright owners whose material appears in this book.

Guided Tour

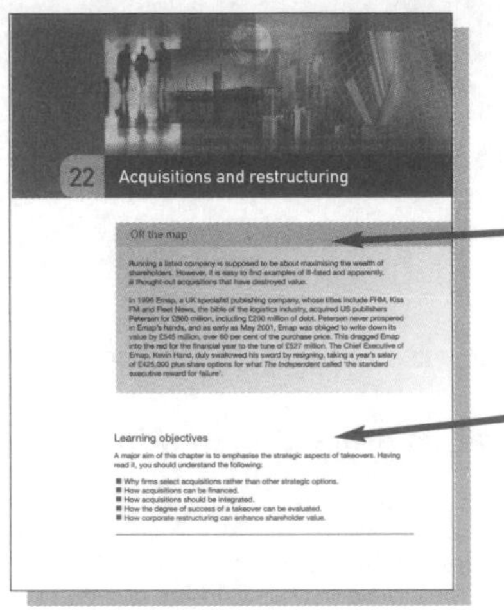

Topical Cameos open each chapter, applying financial management principles to well-known companies. Mini-cases also appear elsewhere within the text.

Learning Objectives highlight what you should expect to achieve from each chapter in terms of concepts, terminology and skills.

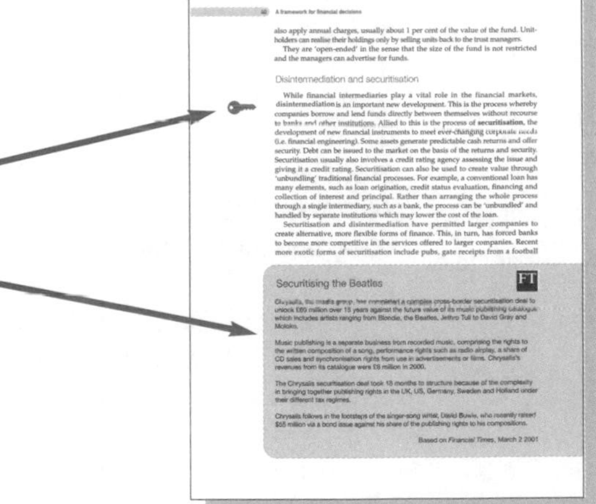

Key Points are highlighted by the key icon in the margin, with definitions appearing in the glossary.

Topical Articles on real-world examples taken from the financial press bring the subject to life.

Self-Assessment Activities reinforce points made in the text, and encourage self-learning. Answers are found at the end of each chapter.

Summaries and Key Points appear at the end of each chapter to give a reminder of main concepts covered.

Further Reading suggestions are made to enable topics to be studied in more depth.

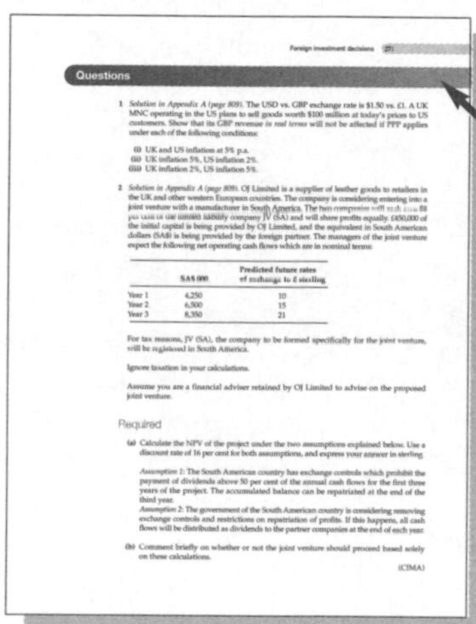

Questions test a mix of numerical, analytical and descriptive skills. Selected answers can be found in Appendix A at the end of the book.

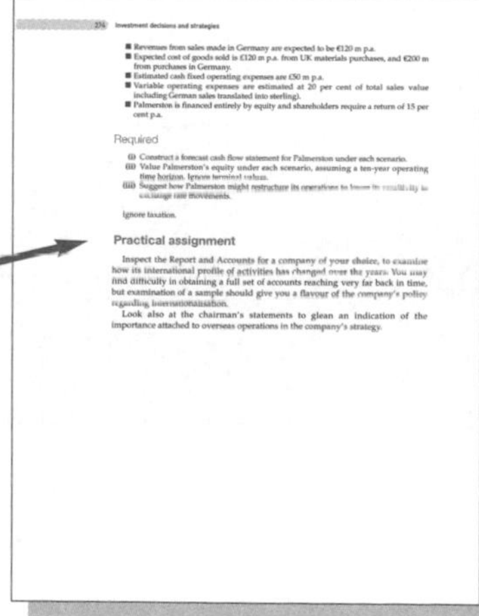

Practical Assignments consider the application of concepts to a company, organisation or published report.

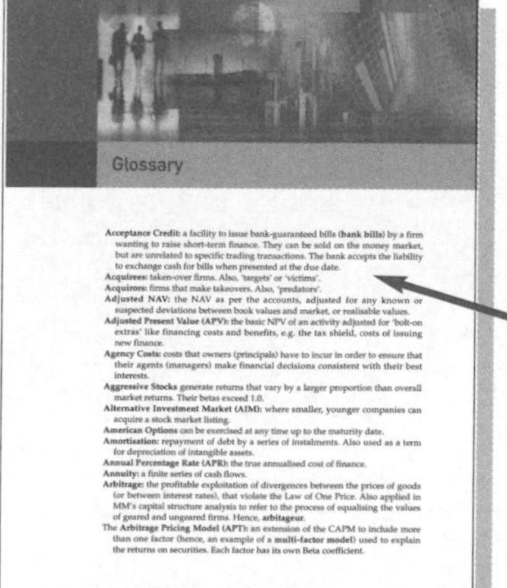

Glossary new for this fourth edition, provides explanations of key terms.

PART I

A framework for financial decisions

Business financial decisions are not made in a vacuum. An 'obvious' decision may often have to be tempered by an appreciation of the restrictions imposed by the prevailing environment. Although it is beyond our scope to consider the full social, political and economic complexity of the financial decision-making context, we provide an overview of the key features of the UK financial and economic system. A sound grasp of the framework for financial decisions is essential if the reader is to appreciate fully the issues discussed in subsequent chapters of this book.

Part I provides an introduction to the scope and the fundamental concepts of financial management, Chapter 1 provides a broad picture of the subject and the important role it plays in business. It examines the nature of financing and investment decisions, the role of the financial manager and the fundamental objective for corporate financial management. This leads on, in Chapter 2, to consideration of the financial and tax environment in which businesses operate. Particular attention is devoted to the characteristics and operation of the London Stock Exchange, which provides a barometer of the success of financial decisions via the market's valuation of the company's shares. The extent to which any market can provide 'accurate' valuations is also considered.

Central concepts in financial management are the time-value of money and present value, which are discussed in Chapter 3. These ideas are developed in Chapter 4 to provide an understanding of valuation. Concepts of value and its measurement play important roles in subsequent chapters, where investment, financing and other key decisions are discussed.

3 An overview of financial management

33 The financial environment

78 Present values and financial arithmetic

112 Valuation of assets, shares and companies

1 An overview of financial management

Working for shareholders

Tomkins plc, the international engineering and manufacturing group, has enjoyed one of the fastest growth rates over the past thirty years. What are the main objectives for such a company? The chairman, in his statement on the 2001 accounts, makes it clear:

> 'Tomkins is committed to enhancing shareholder value through increasing the economic value of its businesses by concentrating in product and geographic markets in its chosen sectors where the businesses have sustained competitive advantage, and which offer prospects for profitable growth.'

The key elements of its strategy are:

- to focus on those businesses where sustainable long-term value can be created
- to provide value to customers through product innovation and development
- to achieve superior execution of business and operational processes
- to maintain a low cost position through simplifying the business, outsourcing low-value-added functions, relocating to low-cost areas, the standardisation of products, business process improvements and the use of internet technology.

Learning objectives

By the end of this chapter, you should understand the following:

- What corporate finance and investment decisions involve.
- How financial management has evolved.
- The finance function and how it relates to its wider environment and strategic planning.
- The central role of cash in business.

- The goal of shareholder wealth-creation and how investors can encourage managers to adopt this goal.
- The underlying principles of finance.

1.1 Introduction

The Tomkins' mission statement, summarised at the start, suggests that its management has a clear idea of its purpose and key objectives. Its mission is to deliver value to its shareholders in the form of dividend and capital growth. An organisation such as Tomkins, with a broad range of products, understands the importance of meeting the requirements of its existing and potential customers. But it also recognises that the most important 'customers' are the shareholders – the owners of the business. Its objectives, strategies and decisions are all directed towards creating value for them.

One of the challenges in any business is to make investments that consistently yield rates of return to shareholders in excess of the cost of financing those projects and better than the competition. This book centres on that very issue: how can firms create value through sound investment decisions and financial strategies?

This chapter provides a broad picture of financial management and the fundamental role it plays in achieving financial objectives and operating successful businesses. First, we consider where financial management fits into the strategic planning process for a new business. This leads to an outline of the finance function and the role of the financial manager, and what objectives he or she may follow. Central to the subject is the nature of these financial objectives and how they affect shareholders' interests. Finally, we introduce the underlying principles of finance, which are developed in later chapters.

Starting a business: Brownbake Ltd

Ken Brown, a recent business graduate, decides to set up his own small bakery business. He recognises that a clear business strategy is required, giving a broad thrust to be adopted in achieving his objectives. The main issues are market identification, competitor analysis and business formation. He identifies a suitable market with room for a new entrant and develops a range of bakery products that are expected to stand up well, in terms of price and quality, against the existing competition.

Brown and his wife become the directors of a newly formed limited company, Brownbake Ltd. This form of organisation has a number of advantages not found in a sole proprietorship or partnership:

- *Limited liability*. The financial liability of the owners is limited to the amount they have paid in. Should the company become insolvent, those with outstanding claims on the company cannot compel the owners to pay in further capital.
- *Transferability of ownership*. It is generally easier to sell shares in a company, particularly if it is listed on a stock market, than to sell all or part of a partnership or sole proprietorship.

- *Permanence*. A company has a legal identity quite separate from its owners. Its existence is unaffected by the sale of shares or death of a shareholder.
- *Access to markets*. The above benefits, together with the fact that companies enable large numbers of shareholders to participate, mean that companies can enjoy financial economies of scale, giving rise to greater choice and lower costs of financing the business.

Brown should have a clear idea of why the business exists and its financial and other objectives. He must now concentrate on how the business strategy is to be implemented. This requires careful planning of the decisions to be taken and their effect on the business. Planning requires answers to some important questions. What resources are required? Does the business require premises, equipment, vehicles and material to produce and deliver the product?

The key to industrial capitalism: limited liability

Shares were first issued in the 16th century, by Europe's new joint-stock companies, led by the Muscovy Company, set up in London in 1553 to trade with Russia. (Bonds, from the French government, made their debut in 1555.) Equity's popularity waxed and waned over the next 300 years or so, soaring with the South Sea and Mississippi bubbles, then slumping, after both burst in 1720. But share-owning was mainly a gamble for the wealthy few, though by the early 19th century in London, Amsterdam and New York trading had moved from the coffee houses into specialised exchanges. Yet the key to the future was already there. In 1811, from America, came the first limited-liability law. In 1854, Britain, the world's leading economic power, introduced similar legislation.

The concept of limited liability, whereby the shareholders are not liable, in the last resort, for the debts of their company, can be traced back to the Romans. But it was rarely used, most often being granted only as a special favour to friends by those in power.

Before limited liability, shareholders risked going bust, even into a debtors' prison maybe, if their company did. Few would buy shares in a firm unless they knew its managers well and could monitor their activities, especially their borrowing, closely. Now, quite passive investors could afford to risk capital – but only what they chose – with entrepreneurs. This unlocked vast sums previously put in safe investments; it also freed new companies from the burden of fixed-interest debt. The way was open to finance the mounting capital needs of the new railways and factories that were to transform the world.

Based on *The Economist*, December 31 1999

Once these issues have been addressed, an important further question is: how will such plans be funded? However sympathetic his bank manager, Brown will probably need to find other investors to carry a large part of the business risk. Eventually, these operating plans must be translated into financial plans, giving a clear indication of the investment required and the intended sources of finance. Brown will also need to establish an appropriate finance and accounting function (even if he does it himself), to keep informed of financial progress in achieving plans and ensure that there is always sufficient cash to pay the bills and to implement plans. Such issues are the principal concern of financial management, which applies equally to small businesses, like Brownbake Ltd, and large multinational corporations, like Tomkins plc.

1.2 The finance function

In a well-organised business, each section should arrange its activities to maximise its contribution towards the attainment of corporate goals. The finance function is very sharply focused, its activities being specific to the financial aspects of management decisions. Figure 1.1 illustrates how the accounting and finance functions may be structured in a large company. This book focuses primarily on the role of finance director and treasurer.

It is the task of those within the finance function to plan, raise and use funds in an efficient manner to achieve corporate financial objectives. Two central activities are as follows:

1 Providing the link between the business and the wider financial environment.
2 Investment and financial analysis and decision-making.

Link with financial environment

The finance function provides the link between the firm and the financial markets in which funds are raised and the company's shares and other financial instruments are traded. The financial manager, whether a corporate treasurer in a multinational company or the sole trader of a small business, acts as the vital link between financial markets and the firm. Corporate finance is therefore as much about understanding financial markets as it is about good financial management within the business. We examine financial markets in Chapter 2.

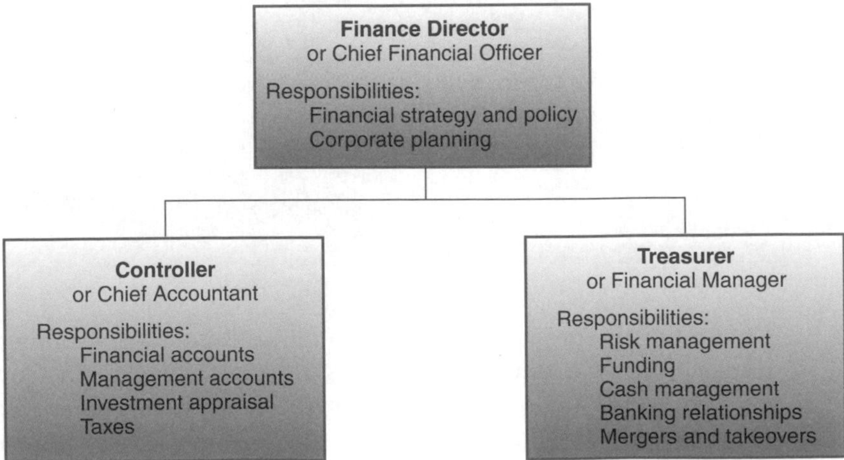

Figure 1.1 The Finance function in a large organisation

1.3 Investment and financial decisions

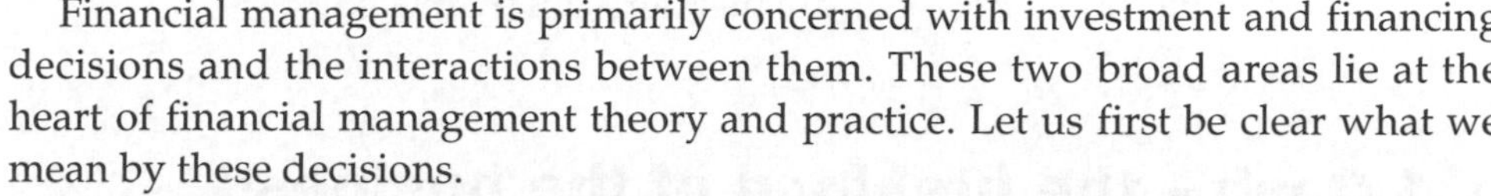

Financial management is primarily concerned with investment and financing decisions and the interactions between them. These two broad areas lie at the heart of financial management theory and practice. Let us first be clear what we mean by these decisions.

The **investment decision**, sometimes referred to as the capital budgeting decision, is the decision to acquire assets. Most of these assets will be *real assets* employed within the business to produce goods or services to satisfy consumer demand. Real assets may be tangible (e.g. land and buildings, plant and equipment, and stocks) or intangible (e.g. patents, trademarks and 'know-how'). Sometimes a firm may invest in *financial assets* outside the business, in the form of short-term securities and deposits.

The basic problems relating to investments are as follows:

1 How much should the firm invest?
2 In which projects should the firm invest (fixed or current, tangible or intangible, real or financial)? Investment need not be purely internal. Acquisitions represent a form of external investment.

The **financing decision** addresses the problems of how much capital should be raised to fund the firm's operations (both existing and proposed), and what the best mix of financing is. In the same way that a firm can hold financial assets (e.g. investing in shares of other companies or lending to banks), it can also sell claims on its own real assets, by issuing shares, raising loans, undertaking lease

Self-assessment Activity 1.1

Take a look at the balance sheet of Brownbake Ltd.

Assets employed	£
Machinery and equipment	15,000
Vehicles	8,000
Patents	12,000
Stocks	10,000
Debtors	3,000
Cash and building society deposit	4,000
	52,000
Liabilities and shareholders' funds	
Trade creditors	12,000
Loans	8,000
Shareholders' equity	32,000
	52,000

Identify the tangible real assets, intangible assets and financial assets. Who has financial claims on these assets?

(answer at end of chapter)

obligations etc. A financial security, such as a share or bond, gives the holder a claim on the future profits, the dividend or interest due. Financing and investment decisions are therefore closely related.

1.4 Cash – the lifeblood of the business

Central to the whole of finance is the generation and management of cash. Figure 1.2 illustrates the flow of cash for a typical manufacturing business. Rather like the bloodstream in a living body, cash is viewed as the 'lifeblood' of the business, flowing to all essential parts of the corporate body. If at any point the cash fails to flow properly, a 'clot' occurs that can damage the business and, if not addressed in time, can prove fatal!

Good cash management therefore lies at the heart of a healthy business. Let us now consider the major sources and uses of cash for a typical business.

Sources of cash

Shareholders' funds

The largest proportion of long-term finance is usually provided by shareholders and is termed **equity capital**. By purchasing a portion of, or shares in, a company, almost anyone can become a shareholder with some degree of control over a company.

Ordinary share capital is the main source of new money from shareholders. They are entitled both to participate in the business through voting in general meetings and to receive dividends out of profits. As owners of the business, the ordinary shareholders bear the greatest risk, but enjoy the main fruits of success in the form of dividends and share price growth.

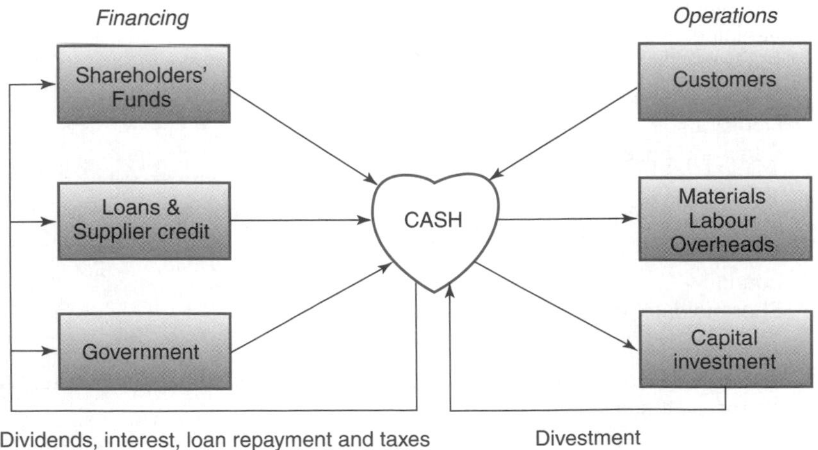

Figure 1.2 Cash – the lifeblood of the business

Retained profits

For an established business, the majority of equity funds will normally be internally generated from successful trading. Any profits remaining after deducting operating costs, interest payments, taxation and dividends are reinvested in the business (i.e. ploughed back) and regarded as part of the equity capital. As this is not an external source of finance, it is not shown in Figure 1.2. But as the business reinvests its cash surpluses, it grows and creates value for its owners. The purpose of the business is to do just that – create value for the owners.

Loan capital

Money lent to a business by third parties is termed **debt finance** or **loan capital**. Most companies borrow money on a long-term basis by issuing loan stocks (or debentures). The terms of the loan will specify the amount of the loan, rate of interest and date of payment, redemption date, and method of repayment. Loan stock always carries a lower risk than equity capital and, hence, offers a lower return.

The finance manager will monitor the long-term financial structure by examining the relationship between loan capital, where interest and loan repayments are contractually obligatory, and ordinary share capital, where dividend payment is at the discretion of directors. This relationship is termed **gearing** (known in the USA as leverage).

Government

Governments and the European Union (EU) provide various financial incentives and grants to the business community. A major cash outflow for successful businesses will be taxation. Types of finance are discussed further in Chapters 16 and 18.

We now turn from longer-term sources of cash to the more regular cash flows from business operations. The main source of cash will be from customers for cash sales or cash collected from credit sales. The main uses of cash are to pay:

1 Suppliers for goods and services received.
2 Employees for wages and other benefits.
3 Lenders who receive interest and eventual repayment of principal.
4 Government for taxes levied on profits, etc.
5 Shareholders for dividends on their investment.

1.5 The emergence of financial management

While aspects of finance, such as the use of compound interest in trading, can be traced back to the Old Babylonian period (c. 1800 BC), the emergence of financial management as a key business activity is a far more recent development. During the 20th century, financial management has evolved from a peripheral to a central aspect of corporate life. This change has been brought about largely through the need to respond to the changing economic climate.

With continuing industrialisation in the UK and much of Europe in the first quarter of the century, the key financial issues centred around forming new businesses and raising capital for expansion. Legal and descriptive consideration was given to the types of security issued, company formations and mergers.

As the focus of business activity moved from growth to survival during the depression of the 1930s, finance evolved by focusing more on business liquidity, reorganisation and insolvency.

Successive Companies Acts, Accounting Standards and other regulations have been designed to increase investors' confidence in published financial statements and financial markets. However, the US accounting scandals in 2002, involving such giants as Enron and Worldcom, have dented this confidence.

Recent years have seen the emergence of financial management as a major contributor to the analysis of investment and financing decisions. The subject continues to respond to external economic and technical developments:

1 The move to floating exchange rates, high interest rates and inflation during the 1970s focused attention on interest rate and currency management, and the impact of inflation on business decisions. For example, in September 1992, following intense pressure by currency speculators, the UK government was forced to suspend its membership of the Exchange Rate Mechanism, leading to devaluation of sterling. New ways of coping with these uncertainties have been developed to allow investors to hedge, or cover, such risks. It is argued that countries adopting the euro as their currency will remove some of these uncertainties.
2 Successive waves of merger activity over the past forty years have increased our understanding of valuation and takeover tactics. With governments committed to freedom of markets and financial liberalisation, acquisitions, mega-mergers and management buy-outs have become a regular part of business life. A wave of cross-border mergers took place during 2000, the largest of which was the £113 billion takeover of the German engineering and telecoms company Mannesmann by Vodafone.
3 Technological progress in communications has led to the globalisation of business. The single European market has created a major financial market with generally unrestricted capital movement. Modern computer technology not only makes globalisation of finance possible, but also brings complex financial calculations and financial databases within easy reach of every manager.
4 Complexities in taxation and the enormous growth in new financial instruments for raising money and managing risk have made some aspects of financial management highly specialised. The collapse in 1995 of Barings, the highly respected merchant bank, resulted from a lack of internal controls in the complex derivatives market.
5 Deregulation in the City is an attempt to make financial markets more efficient and competitive. For example, the London Stock Market was deregulated ('Big

Bang') in 1986, while in 1998, the London International Financial Futures and Options Exchange (LIFFE) was forced by competition from Frankfurt to move away from the trading floor to computerised transactions.

6 Greater awareness of the need to view all decision-making within a strategic framework is moving the focus away from purely technical to more strategic issues. For example, a good deal of corporate restructuring has taken place, breaking down large organisations into smaller, more strategically compatible, businesses.
7 The full adoption of the Euro in 2002 for most European countries has reduced the risk and cost of doing business between such nations.

1.6 The finance department in the firm

The organisation structure for the finance department will vary with company size and other factors. The board of directors is appointed by the shareholders of the company. Virtually all business organisations of any size are limited liability companies, thereby reducing the risk borne by shareholders and, for companies whose shares are listed on a stock exchange, giving investors a ready market for disposal of their holdings or further investment.

Self-assessment Activity 1.2

What are the financial manager's primary tasks?

(answer at end of chapter)

The financial manager can help in the attainment of corporate objectives in the following ways:

1 *Strategic investment and financing decisions*. The financial manager must raise the finance to fund growth and assist in the appraisal of key capital projects.
2 *Dealing with the capital markets*. The financial manager, as the intermediary between the markets and the company, must develop good links with the company's bankers and other major financiers, and be aware of the appropriate sources of finance for corporate requirements.
3 *Managing exposure to risk*. The finance manager should ensure that exposure to adverse movements in interest and exchange rates is adequately managed. Various techniques for hedging (a term for reducing exposure to risk) are available.
4 *Forecasting, coordination and control*. Virtually all important business decisions have financial implications. The financial manager should assist in and, where appropriate, coordinate and control activities that have a significant impact on cash flow.

1.7 The financial objective

For any company, there are likely to be a number of corporate goals, some of which may, on occasions, conflict. In finance, we assume that the objective of the firm is to **maximise shareholder value**. Put simply, this means that managers should create as much wealth as possible for the shareholders. Given this objective, any financing or investment decision expected to improve the value of the shareholders' stake in the firm is acceptable. You may be wondering why shareholder wealth maximisation is preferred to profit maximisation. Quite apart from the problems associated with profit measurement, it ignores the *timing* and *risks* of the profit flows. As will be seen later, value is heavily dependent on when costs and benefits arise and the uncertainty surrounding them.

The Quaker Oats Company was one of the first firms to adopt this goal:

> Our objective is to maximise value for shareholders over the long term . . . Ultimately, our goal is the goal of all professional investors – to maximise value by generating the highest cash flow possible.

However, many practising managers might take a different view of the goal of their firm. In recent years, a wide variety of goals have been suggested, from the traditional goal of **profit** maximisation to goals relating to earnings per share, sales, employee welfare, manager satisfaction, survival and the good of society. It has also been questioned whether management attempts to maximise, by seeking optimal solutions, or to 'satisfice', by seeking merely satisfactory solutions.

Managers often seem to pursue a **sales** maximisation goal subject to a minimum profit constraint. As long as a company matches the average rate of return for the industry sector, the shareholders are likely to be content to stay with their investment. Thus, once this level is attained, managers will be tempted to pursue other goals. As sales levels are frequently employed as a basis for managerial salaries and status, managers may adopt goals that maximise sales subject to a minimum profit constraint.

A popular performance target is **earnings per share** (EPS). It focuses on the shareholder, rather than the company's performance, by calculating the earnings (i.e. profits after tax) attributable to each equity share.

Other subsidiary targets may be employed, often more in the form of a constraint ensuring that management does not threaten corporate survival in its pursuit of shareholder goals. Examples of such secondary goals which are sometimes employed include targets for:

1 *Profit retention*. For example, 'distributable profits must always be at least three times greater than dividends (i.e. a dividend cover of three or more)'.
2 *Borrowing levels*. For example, 'long-term borrowing should not exceed 50 per cent of total capital employed (i.e. a gearing ratio of 50 per cent)'.
3 *Profitability*. For example, 'return on capital employed (ROCE), the profit before interest and tax as a percentage of capital employed by the company, should be at least 18 per cent'.

4 *Non-financial goals*. These take a variety of forms but basically recognise that shareholders are not the only group interested in the company's success. Other stakeholders include trade creditors, banks, employees, the government and management. Each stakeholder group will measure corporate performance in a slightly different way. It is therefore to be expected that the targets and constraints discussed above will, from time to time, conflict with the overriding goal of shareholder value, and management must seek to manage these conflicts.

The financial manager has the specific task of advising management on the financial implications of the firm's plans and activities. The shareholder wealth objective should underlie all such advice, although the chief executive may sometimes allow non-financial considerations to take precedence over financial ones. It is not possible to translate this objective directly to the public sector or not-for-profit organisations. However, in seeking to create wealth in such organisations, the 'value for money' goal perhaps comes close.

Self-assessment Activity 1.3

The past ten years have seen a much greater emphasis on investor-related goals, such as earnings per share and shareholder wealth. Why do you think this has arisen?

(answer at end of chapter)

1.8 The agency problem

Potential conflict arises where ownership is separated from management. The ownership of most larger companies is widely spread, while the day-to-day control of the business rests in the hands of a few managers who usually have a relatively small proportion of the total shares issued. This can give rise to what is termed **managerialism** – self-serving behaviour by managers at the shareholders' expense. Examples of managerialism include pursuing more perquisites (splendid offices and company cars, etc.) and adopting low-risk survival strategies and 'satisficing' behaviour. This conflict has been explored by Jensen and Meckling (1976), who developed a theory of the firm under agency arrangements. Managers are, in effect, agents for the shareholders and are required to act in their best interests. However, they have operational control of the business and the shareholders receive little information on whether the managers are acting in their best interests.

A company can be viewed as simply a set of contracts, the most important of which is the contract between the firm and its shareholders. This contract describes the **principal–agent** relationship, where the shareholders are the principals and the management team the agents. An efficient agency contract allows full delegation of decision-making authority over use of invested capital to management without the risk of that authority being abused. However, left to themselves, managers cannot be expected to act in the shareholders' best interests, but require appropriate incentives and controls to do so. **Agency costs** are the difference between the return expected from an efficient agency contract and the actual return, given that managers may act more in their own interests than the interests of shareholders.

Self-assessment Activity 1.4

Identify some potential agency problems that may arise between shareholders and managers.

(answer at end of chapter)

1.9 Managing the agency problem

To attempt to deal with such agency problems, various incentives and controls have been recommended, all of which incur costs. Incentives frequently take the form of bonuses tied to profits (profit-related pay) and share options as part of a remuneration package scheme.

Managerial incentives: Blanco plc

Relating managers' compensation to achievement of owner-oriented targets is an obvious way to bring the interests of managers and shareholders closer together. A group of major institutional shareholders of Blanco plc has expressed concern to the chief executive that management decisions do not appear to be fully in line with shareholder requirements. They suggest that a new remuneration package is introduced to help solve the problem. Such packages have increasingly been introduced to encourage managers to take decisions that are consistent with the objectives of the shareholders.

The main factors to be considered by Blanco plc might include the following:

1. Linking management compensation to changes in shareholder wealth, where possible reflecting managers' contributions.
2. Rewarding managerial efficiency, not managerial luck.
3. Matching the time horizon for managers' decisions to that of shareholders. Many managers seek to maximise short-term profits rather than long-term shareholder wealth.
4. Making the scheme easy to monitor, inexpensive to operate, clearly defined and incapable of managerial manipulation. Poorly devised schemes have sometimes 'backfired', giving senior managers huge bonuses.

Two performance-based incentive schemes that Blanco plc might consider are rewarding managers with shares or with share options.

Continued

1 *Long-term incentive plans (LTIPs)*. Such schemes typically incentivise performance over a period of three or more years, with the manager receiving the award at the end of the period. Shares are allotted to managers on attaining performance targets. Commonly employed performance measures are growth in earnings per share, return on equity and return on assets. Managers are allocated a certain number of shares to be received on attaining prescribed targets. While this incentive scheme offers managers greater control, the performance measures may not be entirely consistent with shareholder goals. For example, adoption of return on assets as a measure, which is based on book values, can inhibit investment in wealth-creating projects with heavy depreciation charges in early years.
2 *Executive share option schemes*. These are long-term compensation arrangements that permit managers to buy shares at a given price (generally today's) at some future date (generally 3–10 years). Subject to certain provisos and tax rules, a share option scheme usually entitles managers to acquire a fixed number of shares over a fixed period of time for a fixed price. The shares need not be paid for until the option is exercised – normally 3–10 years after the granting of the option. For example, a manager may be granted 20,000 share options. She can purchase these shares at any time over the next three years at £1 a share. If she decides to exercise her option when the share price has risen to £4, she would have gained £60,000 (i.e. buying 20,000 shares at £1, now worth £80,000).

Share options only have value when the actual share price exceeds the option price; managers are thereby encouraged to pursue policies that enhance long-term wealth-creation. At least a quarter of UK companies now operate share option schemes, which are spreading to managers well below board level. The figure is far higher for companies recently coming to the stock market: virtually all of them have executive share option schemes, and many of these operate an all-employee scheme. However, a major problem with these approaches is that general stock market movements, due mainly to macroeconomic events, are sometimes so large as to dwarf the efforts of managers. No matter how hard a management team seeks to make wealth-creating decisions, the effects on share price in a given year may be undetectable if general market movements are downward. A good incentive scheme gives managers a large degree of control over achieving targets. Chief executives in a number of large companies have recently come under fire for their 'outrageously high' pay resulting from such schemes.

Executive compensation schemes, such as those outlined above, are imperfect, but useful, mechanisms for retaining able managers and encouraging them to pursue goals that promote shareholder value.

Another way of attempting to minimise the agency problem is by setting up and **monitoring** managers' behaviour. Examples of these include:

1 Audited accounts of the company,
2 Management audits and additional reporting requirements, and
3 Restrictive covenants imposed by lenders, such as ceilings on the dividend payable or the maximum borrowings.

To what extent does the agency problem invalidate the goal of maximising the value of the firm? In an efficient, highly competitive stock market, the share price is a 'fair' reflection of investors' perceptions of the company's expected future performance. So agency problems in a large publicly quoted company will, before long, be reflected in a lower than expected share price. This could lead to an *internal* response – the shareholders replacing the board of directors with others more committed to their goals – or an *external* response – the company being acquired by a better-performing company where shareholder interests are pursued more vigorously.

Not such a Daft idea

Douglas Daft, Coca Cola's chairman and chief executive, received a compensation package worth nearly $92 m in 2000. Much of the compensation – about $87.3 m – is in the form of a restricted stock award tied to the future earnings performance of the soft drinks group.

In an unusual move, the board of directors granted 1 million restricted stock to ensure Mr Daft achieved 'significant wealth only in the presence of significant performance'.

Mr Daft is to receive the 1 million restricted shares if the company achieves average annual per share growth of 20 per cent in the next five years. If earnings per share (EPS) rises 15 per cent in the same period, only half the shares will be granted. The board further noted if earnings fell short, Mr Daft would receive none of the award. Last year, EPS actually fell 10 per cent and the board of directors, unhappy with the performance of the company under the previous chief executive, did not award bonuses to any senior executives.

Based on *Financial Times*, March 5 2001

1.10 Social responsibility and shareholder wealth

Is the shareholder wealth maximisation objective consistent with concern for social responsibility? In most cases it is. As far back as 1776, Adam Smith recognised that, in a market-based economy, the wider needs of society are met by individuals pursuing their own interests: 'It is not from the benevolence of the butcher, the brewer, or the baker, that we expect our dinner, but from their regard to their own interest.' The needs of customers and the goals of businesses are matched by the 'invisible hand' of the free market mechanism.

Of course, the market mechanism cannot differentiate between 'right' and 'wrong'. Addictive drugs and other socially undesirable products will be made available as long as customers are willing to pay for them. Legislation may work, but often it simply creates illegal markets in which prices are much higher than before legislation. Other products have side-effects adversely affecting individuals other than the consumers, e.g. passive smoking and car exhaust emissions.

There will always be individuals in business seeking short-term gains from unethical activities. But, for the vast majority of firms, such activity is counter-productive in the longer term. Shareholder wealth rests on companies building long-term relationships with suppliers, customers and employees, and promoting a reputation for honesty, financial integrity and corporate social responsibility. After all, a major company's most important asset is its good name.

Not all large businesses are dominated by shareholder wealth goals. The John Lewis Partnership, which operates department stores and Waitrose supermarkets, is a partnership with its staff electing half the board. The Partnership's ultimate aim, as described in its constitution, 'shall be the happiness in every way of all its members'. The Partnership rule book makes it clear, however, that pursuit of happiness shall not be at the expense of business efficiency.

Some authors have questioned the strong emphasis on shareholder goals, preferring shareholders to be regarded more like financial guardians, keeping a watchful eye on business and not selling out for short-term gains. Certainly, Japanese companies seem to place less emphasis on shareholder returns than UK or US companies, typically paying out far less in dividends than UK companies.

Environmental concerns have in recent years become an important consideration for the boards of large companies, including the source of supplies, such as timber and paper from 'managed forests'. Investors are also becoming more socially aware and many are channelling their funds into companies that employ environmentally and socially responsible practices.

1.11 The corporate governance debate

In recent years, there has been considerable concern in the UK about standards of corporate governance, the system by which companies are directed and controlled. While, in company law, directors are obliged to act in the best interests of shareholders, there have been many instances of boardroom behaviour difficult to reconcile with this ideal.

There have been numerous examples of spectacular collapses of companies, often the result of excessive debt financing in order to finance ill-advised takeovers, and sometimes laced with fraud. Many companies have been criticised for the generosity with which they reward their leading executives. The procedures for remunerating executives have been less than transparent, and many compensation schemes involve payment by results in one direction alone. Many chief executives have been criticised for receiving pay increases several times greater than the increases awarded to less exalted staff.

In the train of these corporate collapses and scandals, a number of committees have reported on the accountability of the board of directors to their stakeholders and risk management procedures (e.g. The Cadbury, Hampel and Turnbull reports). The Principles of Good Governance and Code of Best Practice, which apply to all listed companies from 1999 onwards, are summarised below:

1 *Directors and the Board*
An effective board is required to lead and control the company.

It should have a balance of executive and non-executive directors. No individual or group must dominate the board.
Running the board and running the business are separate activities. No individual has unfettered powers.
Timely and quality information is given to the board.
Clear procedures for appointments. Re-election at least every three years.

2 *Directors' remuneration*
Executive remuneration is linked to corporate and individual performance.
Directors are not involved in deciding their own remuneration.

3 *Relations with shareholders*
Encourage dialogue on objectives with institutional shareholders.
Use the AGM to communicate with shareholders and encourage participation.

4 *Accountability*
Reports influencing share price to give a balanced, understandable assessment of the company's position and prospects.
A sound system of internal control to safeguard shareholders' interests and company assets.

The main reservations centre on the issues of compliance and enforcement. These changes in the rules and responsibilities of directors and auditors are non-statutory. The Stock Exchange will not withdraw the listings of companies that fail to comply, although it hopes that any adverse publicity will whip offenders into line. This lack of 'teeth' has raised suspicions that determined wrong-doers can still exert their influence on weak boards of directors, to the detriment of the relatively ill-informed private investor in particular.

1.12 The risk dimension

Some financial decisions incur very little risk (e.g. investing in government stocks, since the interest is known); others may carry far more risk (e.g. investing in shares). Risk and expected return tend to be related: the greater the perceived risk, the greater the return required by investors. This is seen in Figure 1.3.

When the finance manager of a company seeks to raise funds, potential investors take a view on the risk related to the intended use of the funds. This can best be measured in terms of a **risk premium** above the risk-free rate (R_f) obtainable from, say, government stocks to compensate investors for taking risk. The capital market offers a host of investment opportunities for private and corporate investors, but in all cases there exists a clear relationship between the perceived degree of risk involved and the expected return. For example, R_f in Figure 1.3 represents the return on three-month Treasury Bills; point A represents a long-term fixed interest corporate bond; point B, a portfolio of ordinary shares in major listed companies; and point C, a more speculative investment, such as non-quoted shares. Studies indicate that the long-term average return on an investment portfolio consisting of the market index (e.g. the FTSE-100) is up to 6 percentage points higher than that from holding risk-free government securities.

One task of the financial manager is to raise funds in the capital markets at a cost consistent with the perceived risk, and to invest such funds in wealth-creating

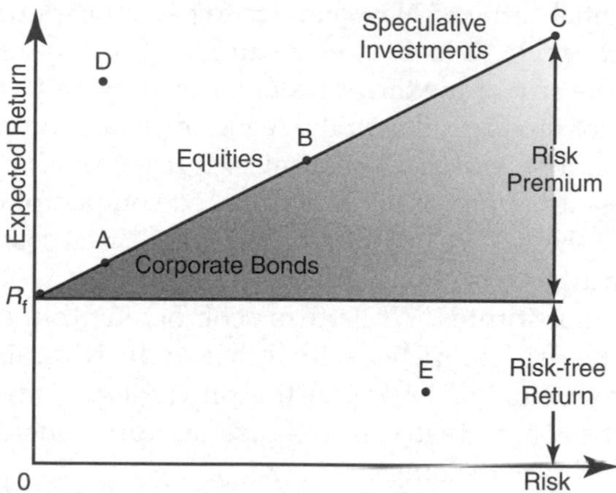

Figure 1.3 The risk–return trade-off

opportunities in the business. Here it is quite possible – because of a firm's competitive advantage, or possession of superior brand names – to make highly profitable capital projects with relatively little risk (see D in diagram). It is also possible to find the reverse, such as project E. If the goal is to deliver cash flows to shareholders at rates above their cost of capital, managers should seek to invest in projects, such as D, that offer returns better than those obtainable on the capital market for the same degree of risk (A in the diagram).

1.13 The strategic dimension

To enhance shareholder value, managers could adopt a wide range of strategies. Strategic management may be defined as a systematic approach to positioning the business in relation to its environment to ensure continued success and offer security from surprises. No approach can guarantee continuous success and total security, but an integrated approach to strategy formulation, involving all levels of management, can go some way.

Strategy can be developed at three levels:

1 *Corporate strategy* is concerned with the broad issues, such as the types of business the company should be in. Strategic finance has an important role to play here. For example, the decision to enter or exit from a business – whether through corporate acquisitions, organic growth, divestment or buy-outs – requires sound financial analysis. Similarly, the appropriate capital structure and dividend policy form part of strategic development at the corporate level.
2 *Business or competitive strategy* is concerned with how strategic business units (SBUs) compete in particular markets. Business strategies are formulated which influence the allocation of resources to these units. This allocation may be based on the attractiveness of the markets in which SBUs operate and the firm's competitive strengths. Porter (1985) identifies five competitive forces determining the profitability of an industry:

(a) Threat of potential entrants. New entrants to the industry will increase total productive capacity, which can result in price wars and reduced profitability. The size of the threat is determined by entry barriers such as differentiation of products, the capital requirement and economies of scale.

(b) Competition among existing companies. Intense rivalry is the result of factors such as numerous or equally balanced competitors, slow industry growth and a high level of fixed charges in the cost structure, i.e. operating gearing.

(c) Pressure from substitutes. While firms compete within an industry, the industry itself also competes with other industries that can deliver substitute products. For example, the oil industry offers a substitute product for the coal industry. In the case of a price increase, customers may shift from one to the other.

(d) Bargaining power of buyers. Buyers can exert downward pressure on prices, negotiating for higher quality or better service, and playing off one competitor against another, at the expense of the industry's profitability.

(e) Bargaining power of suppliers. Suppliers can exert considerable pressure on an industry by threatening to raise prices or cut the quality of goods and services delivered.

Careful analysis of these factors enables managers to understand the major competitive forces that shape the industry structure and to determine the company's potential levels of profitability. A business strategy stands little chance of success unless developed with a clear understanding of the firm's competitive setting. Each of the five competitive forces will vary in intensity and importance according to the industry involved. For example, the privatised UK water industry is virtually free from these competitive forces, whereas another former publicly owned company, Rolls-Royce, is intensely affected by most of them since it operates in a global market.

3 *Operational strategy* is concerned with how functional levels contribute to corporate and business strategies. For example, the finance function may formulate strategies to achieve a new dividend policy identified at the corporate strategy level. Similarly, a foreign currency exposure strategy may be developed to reduce the risk of loss through currency movements. A typical strategic planning process is shown in Figure 1.4.

Strategic planning and value creation

The importance of the five competitive forces in determining shareholder wealth cannot be overestimated. They largely determine the price at which goods and services can be sold, the quantities sold, the cost of production, the level of required investment and the risks inherent in the business.

However, individual companies can develop strategies leading to long-term financial performance well above the industry average. A study of the consequences of business strategies on financial performance concluded that market share, quality, capacity utilisation and capital investment strategies had the greatest impact on shareholder wealth (Gale and Swire, 1988).

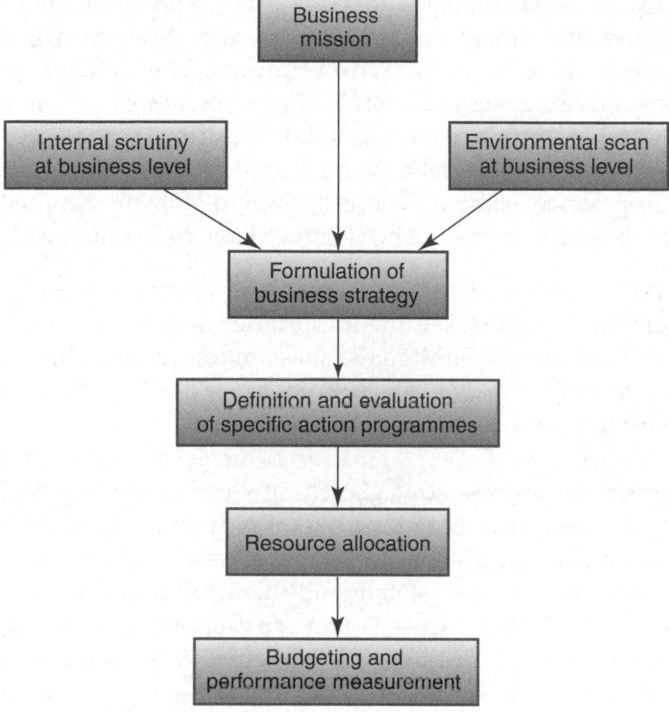

Figure 1.4 Main elements in strategic planning

Figure 1.5 illustrates the main factors influencing the value of the firm. In any industry, all firms will be subject to much the same underlying economic conditions. Rates of inflation, interest and taxation and competitive forces in the industry will affect all businesses, although not necessarily to the same degree. The firm will develop corporate, business and operating strategies to exploit economic opportunities and to create sustainable competitive advantage. We are mainly

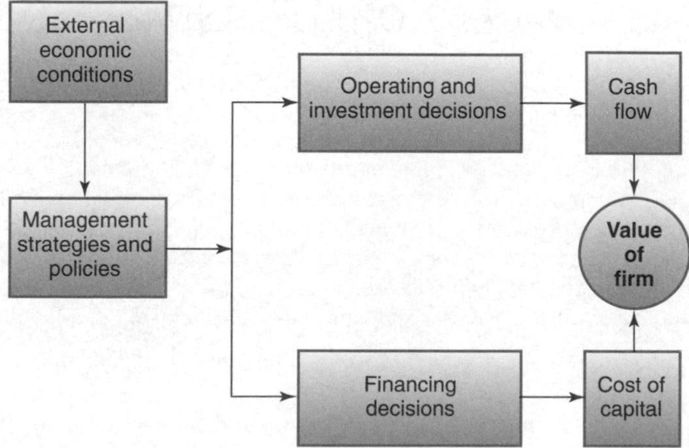

Figure 1.5 Factors influencing the value of the firm

concerned with those strategies affecting investment, financing and dividends. Operating and investment decisions create cash flows for the business, while financing decisions influence the cost of capital. The value of the firm depends upon the cash flows generated from business operations – their size, timing and riskiness – and the firm's cost of capital. Depending on the success of the firm's strategies and decisions, the value of the firm will increase or shrink.

While, in practice, some decisions appear to lack any rational process, most approaches to decisions of a financial nature have five common elements:

1 *Clearly defined goals*. It is particularly noticeable how, in recent years, corporate managements have realised the importance of defining and communicating their declared mission and goals, some more quantifiable than others, and some more relevant to financing decisions. For Cadbury Schweppes the goal is growth in shareholder value.
2 *Identifying courses of action to achieve these objectives*. This requires the development of business strategies from which individual decisions emanate. Cadbury Schweppes refer to focusing on growth markets, developing brands, innovation and acquisitions as key approaches to goal attainment.

   The search for new investment and financing opportunities for any organisation is far better focused and cost-effective when viewed within well-defined financial objectives and strategies. Most decisions have more than one possible solution. For instance, the requirement for an additional source of finance to fund a new product launch can be satisfied by a multitude of possible financial options.
3 *Assembling information relevant to the decision*. The financial manager must be able to identify what information is relevant to the decision and what is not. Data gathering can be costly, but good, reliable information greatly facilitates decision analysis and confidence in the decision outcome.

Goals and strategies in Cadbury Schweppes

Cadbury Schweppes' objective is growth in shareholder value. The strategy by which we will achieve this objective is:

- Focusing on our core growth of beverages and confectionery
- Developing robust, sustainable market positions which are built on a platform of strong brands with supported franchises
- Expanding our market share through innovation in products, packaging and route to market where economically profitable
- Enhancing our market positions by acquisitions or disposals.

Managing for Value is the process which supports the achievement of our strategy.

Source: Annual Report, 2000

4 *Evaluation*. Analysing and interpreting assembled information lies at the heart of financial analysis. A large part of this book is devoted to techniques of appraising financial decisions.

5 *Monitoring the effects of the decision taken*. However sophisticated a firm's financial planning system, there is no real substitute for experience. Feedback on the performance of past decisions provides vital information on the reliability of data gathered, the efficacy of the method employed in decision appraisal and the judgement of decision-makers.

Self-assessment Activity 1.5

Compare Cadbury's objectives and strategies with those of Tomkins provided at the start of the chapter.

1 What do they have in common and how do they differ?
2 What issues discussed in the chapter do they focus upon?

1.14 The underlying principles of finance

This chapter has provided an overview of financial management. We want to conclude by introducing the reader to the main principles of finance underpinning the rest of the book; these will be developed more fully later.

Most readers will be familiar with the popular board game 'Monopoly'. There is more than a passing resemblance between this game and corporate finance. Both are about maximising investors' wealth in risky environments, making investment decisions with uncertain payoffs, raising finance and managing cash flow. Players and managers must stick to the rules and seek to devise appropriate investment and financing strategies to gain competitive advantage.

While rules and procedures may be adequate for routine financial decisions, good managers look for something more. They seek to understand:

1 Why managers behave as they do.
2 Why firms behave as they do.
3 Why markets behave as they do.

Theories of finance provide explanations for the behaviour of individuals, firms and markets. The better the theory, the better we understand how finance operates. Throughout the book we seek to combine the 'why' with the 'how', in the theory and practice of finance. For the present, we will introduce readers to a few basic financial principles.

Understanding individual behaviour

To understand how organisations function we must first understand individual behaviour. There are many models of human behaviour (e.g.

sociological, psychological and political); we shall restrict our examination to two models of most relevance to finance.

The first is the **traditional economic model** of human behaviour. Here the manager is seen as a short-run wealth maximiser. The model is a useful starting point in studying finance because it offers a simple approach to model building, using only the pursuit of wealth as a goal. Much of the argument underlying the theories discussed in this book is based on such a model. But we all know that this is a poor explanation of human behaviour. Money may not come before morality, honesty, love, altruism or having fun.

This leads us to develop a more realistic model of human behaviour which Jensen and Meckling (1994) term the **resourceful, evaluative, maximising model** (or REMM). This model assumes that people are resourceful, self-interested maximisers, but rejects the notion that they are only interested in making money. They also care about respect, power, quality of life, love and the welfare of others. Individuals respond creatively to opportunities presented, seeking out opportunities, evaluating their likely outcomes, and working to loosen constraints on their actions.

To sum up, money is not the only, or even the most important, thing in life. But when all else is equal, we act in a rational economic manner, choosing the course of action that best benefits us financially. Two fundamental concepts naturally follow.

Managers should only consider present and future costs and benefits in making decisions

This is the principle of **incrementalism** – only the additional costs or benefits resulting from a choice of action should be considered. For example, expenditures already incurred are not relevant to the decision in hand; they are **sunk costs**.

Choices often involve trade-offs, denying the possibility of other alternatives. The opportunity cost of making one decision is the difference between that choice and the next best alternative. If you sell the contents of your attic to the local junk shop for £20, when the 'junk' contained some valuable antiques that could have been auctioned to raise £2,000, there is a sizeable **opportunity cost** (i.e. the income forgone). These principles are discussed more fully in Chapter 6.

Most managers are risk averse

Most managers are **risk averse**: given two investments offering the same return, they would choose the one with least risk. Unlike the risk-seeker or gambler, most managers try to avoid unnecessary risks. Risk aversion is a measure of a manager's willingness to pay to reduce exposure to risk. This could be in the form of insurance or other 'hedging' devices, discussed in Chapter 14. Alternatively, it could be by preferring a lower-return investment because it also has a lower risk.

As we have already seen, in business, risk and the expected return are usually related. Rational managers do not look for more risk unless the likely benefits are commensurately greater. This principle of **risk aversion** is further discussed in Chapter 9.

One way in which investors can reduce risk is by spreading their capital across a range (portfolio) of investments. This is the principle of **diversification** (or not putting all your eggs in one basket), discussed more fully in Chapter 10.

Understanding corporate behaviour

A firm may be viewed as a collection of individuals and resources. More precisely, it is a set of contracts that bind individuals together, each with his or her own interests and goals. As we have seen, **agency theory** explores the relationship between the principal (e.g. owner) and the agents responsible for taking actions on his or her behalf (e.g. board of directors). It follows that, to understand how firms behave, we must understand the nature of the contracts and monitoring procedures.

Information is not usually available to all parties in business in equal measure. For example, the board of directors will know more about the future prospects of the business than the shareholders, who have to rely on published information. This **information asymmetry** means that investors not only listen to the board's rhetoric and confident projections, but also examine the **information content** in its corporate actions. This **signalling effect** is most commonly seen in the reaction to dividend declaration and share dealings by the board. An increase in dividends signals that the company is expected to be able to sustain that level of cash distribution in the future. Chapter 19 discusses this topic.

Value is created by investing in wealth creating opportunities. The firm should invest in those areas in which it has some competitive advantage giving rise to superior returns or **positive net present value**. This vitally important concept is discussed in Chapters 3 to 5.

Options have value. We devote the whole of Chapter 13 to the fascinating theory of **options**. Here we can simply state than an option is the right, but not the obligation, to do something – usually to buy or sell assets. A firm will only exercise its right if it adds value to the business. This time, the more risky the option, the more valuable it is, because only the 'good news' is taken up. The convertible loan stock instrument is one example of an option in business. 'Convertibles' begin as a loan, but at some point may be converted into equity shares. The investor can decide at that point whether to take up the option to convert, and this option has a value.

Understanding how markets behave

To make sound financial decisions consistently, we need to understand how financial markets operate. This is the subject of Chapter 2, where we consider the nature of the money and capital markets.

Money has a time-value

Fundamental to the study of financial management is the principle of the **time-value of money**. Put simply, we cannot add current and future money together in a meaningful way without first converting into a common currency. This currency can be either present (i.e. today's) value or future value. The value of money changes with time because it has an alternative use (opportunity cost): it can be invested in financial markets to earn a rate of interest. We discuss the time-value of money more fully in Chapter 3.

Capital markets are efficient

In an efficient market, financial asset prices, such as those of stocks and shares, reflect all available information and adjust quickly to new information. There are degrees of market efficiency and, in Chapter 2, we consider the efficiency of the London Stock Exchange together with its implications. Many of the theories discussed in the book assume that capital markets are reasonably efficient in reflecting all available information.

Financial theory and practice

A good finance theory is one which offers useful explanations of existing behaviour and provides a guide to future behaviour. We frequently find that rather restrictive assumptions are made in developing financial models. For example:

1 All markets – not just capital markets – are perfectly competitive.
2 Information is perfect and costless and transaction costs are zero.
3 No taxes exist.

These assumptions lead naturally to certain propositions. First, only shareholders are interested in the firm. A perfect labour market implies that managers and workers can always find another equally attractive job. Second, shareholders are only interested in maximising the market value of their shareholdings. Given perfect, costless information, managers are perfectly controlled by the shareholders to implement value-maximising strategies. Third, the pursuit of shareholder wealth is achieved by instructing managers to invest only in those projects that are worth more than they cost. Financing strategies, whether concerning dividends, capital structure or leasing, are largely irrelevant as they do little to increase shareholders' wealth.

The assumptions underlying the theory of finance appear to be at odds with reality. Information is imperfect; transaction costs and information costs may be sizeable. Markets are frequently highly imperfect; management will usually have a good deal of interest in the firm – interest which may well conflict with that of shareholders. Managers have far from complete knowledge of the set of feasible financing strategies available, their cash flow patterns and impact on market values. Shareholders are even less well informed. Taxation policy, bankruptcy costs and other factors can have a major influence on financial strategies.

Throughout this book, we shall attempt to allow for such practical, real-world considerations when considering appropriate financial policy decisions. However, we hope that a clearer understanding of the concepts, together with an awareness of the degree of realism in their underlying assumptions, will enable the reader to make sound and successful investment and financial decisions in practice.

The following advertisement recently appeared in a major newspaper.

Shareholder value

We are seeking a manager to join a small management team to develop concepts in our organisation. This is an important role with exposure to all levels of management, both centrally and within our business units.

You will communicate shareholder value concepts to decision makers and assist in piloting the implementation of a value based perspective.

A highly motivated qualified accountant or MBA, you should have at least 3 years' post qualification experience – what's more important will be an impressive track record.

With excellent communication and influencing skills, you should have a high degree of numeracy, be pragmatic and open to new ideas and concepts.

You will preferably have an excellent knowlege of shareholder value concepts in a corporate environment or working as a consultant.

Having read this chapter the reader should have a clearer idea of the shareholder value concepts involved (and how to obtain jobs like this!).

Summary

This chapter has provided an overview of strategic financial management and the critical role it plays in corporate survival and success. We have examined how financial management has evolved over the years, its main functions and objectives. The chapter concludes by introducing readers to the underlying principles of finance.

Key points

- It is the task of the financial manager to plan, raise and use funds in an efficient manner to achieve corporate financial objectives. This implies (1) involvement in investment and financing decisions, (2) dealing with the financial markets, and (3) forecasting, coordinating and controlling cash flows.
- Cash is the lifeblood of any business. Financial management is concerned with cash generation and control.
- Financial management evolved during the last century, largely in response to economic and other external events (e.g. inflation and technological developments), making globalisation of finance a reality and the need to concentrate on more strategic issues essential.
- The distinction should be drawn between accounting – the mere provision of relevant financial information for internal and external users – and financial management – the utilisation of financial and other data to assist financial decision-making.
- In finance, we assume that the primary corporate goal is to maximise value for the shareholders.
- The agency problem – managers pursuing actions not totally consistent with shareholders' interests – can be reduced both by managerial incentive schemes and also by closer monitoring of actions.
- Investors require compensation for taking risks in the form of enhanced potential returns.
- Most of the assumptions underlying pure finance theory are not particularly realistic. In practice, market and other imperfections must also be considered in practical financial decision-making.
- Financial management has an essential role in strategic development and implementation at strategic, business and operational levels. Competitive forces, together with business strategy, influence the value drivers that impact on shareholder value.

Further reading

Students should get into the habit of reading the *Financial Times* and relevant pages of the *Economist* and *Investors Chronicle*.

Most finance texts have helpful introductory chapters, for example Brealey and Myers (2000). For a fuller discussion on managerial compensation, see Lambert and Larcker (1985). Jensen and Meckling (1976) provide the best article on agency costs while Brickley *et al*. (1994) give a useful insight into organisational ethics and social responsibility. Grinyer (1986) provides an alternative to the shareholder wealth goal while Doyle (1994) argues for a 'stakeholder' approach to goal setting. On the other hand, Copeland *et al*. (1996) argue that shareholder wealth creation is good for all stakeholders, productivity and employment. Details on these and other references are provided at the end of the book.

Useful websites

Financial Times: **www.FT.com**
Guardian: **www.guardian.co.uk/money**
The Economist: **www.economist.com**

Self-assessment Answers

1.1 Tangible real assets: machinery and equipment, vehicles, stock
Intangible assets: patents
Financial assets: debtors, cash and building society deposits
Financial claims: trade creditors, loans, shareholders' equity

The financial manager has two broad responsibilities:

1.2 (1) Providing financial information and advice for internal and external users. The financial accountant prepares the statutory financial accounts and deals with the auditors; the management accountant provides information for decision-making, planning and control. Other departments, such as taxation, may also report to the controller (or chief accountant).

(2) Managing cash and raising finance at the best possible rate. This is the responsibility of the treasurer or financial manager. Typical functions within the treasury area are raising finance, the management of cash, credit and inventory, foreign currency management and financial risk management.

1.3 (1) The past ten years have seen a much greater emphasis on investor-related goals, such as earnings per share and shareholder wealth. This is mainly attributed to the growth in shareholdings by institutional investors (e.g. pension funds). The recognition that profitability is not necessarily the same as shareholder wealth has led to greater emphasis on shareholder goals.

1.4 (1) The goal of maximising owners' wealth is the normally accepted economic objective for resource allocation decisions. Rather than concentrate on the organisation, it evaluates investments from the viewpoint of the organisation's owners – usually shareholders. Any investment that increases their stock of wealth (the present value of future cash flows) is economically acceptable.
In practice, many of the assumptions underlying this goal do not always hold (e.g. shareholders are only interested in maximising the market value of their shareholdings). In addition, owners are often far removed from managerial decision-making, where capital investment takes place. Accordingly, it is common to find that more easily measurable criteria are used, such as profitability and growth goals. There are also non-economic considerations, such as employee welfare and managerial satisfaction, which can be important for some decisions.

(2) Separation of ownership from management can give rise to managerialism – self-serving behaviour by managers at the shareholders' expense, e.g. pursuing managerial 'perks' (company cars etc.), adopting low-risk survival strategies, settling for less than the best.

Questions

1 *Solution in Appendix A (page 801).* Why is the goal of maximising owners' wealth helpful in analysing capital investment decisions? What other goals should also be considered?

2 Go4it plc is a young dynamic company which became listed on the stock market three years ago. Its management is very keen to do all it can to maximise shareholder value

and, for this reason, has been advised to pursue the goal of maximising earnings per share. Do you agree?

(Solution on Companion website www.booksites.net/pikeneale)

3 **(a)** 'Managers and owners of businesses may not have the same objectives.' Explain this statement, illustrating your answer with examples of possible conflicts of interest.
(b) In what respects can it be argued, that companies need to exercise corporate social responsibility?
(c) Explain the meaning of the term 'Value for Money' in relation to the management of publicly owned services/utilities.

(ACCA)

4 Discuss the importance and limitations of ESOPs (executive share option plans) to the achievement of goal congruence within an organisation.

(ACCA)

5 **(a)** A group of major shareholders of Zedo plc wishes to introduce a new remuneration scheme for the company's senior management. Explain why such schemes might be important to the shareholders. What factors should shareholders consider when devising such schemes?
(b) Eventually a short-list of three possible schemes is agreed. All pay the same basic salary plus:
(i) A bonus based upon at least a minimum pre-tax profit being achieved.
(ii) A bonus based upon turnover growth.
(iii) A share option scheme.

Briefly discuss the advantages and disadvantages of each of these three schemes.

(ACCA)

6 The primary financial objective of companies is usually said to be the maximisation of shareholders' wealth. Discuss whether this objective is realistic in a world where corporate ownership and control are often separate, and environmental and social factors are increasingly affecting business decisions.

7 The main principles of financial management may be applied to most organisations. However, the role of the financial manager may be affected by the type of organisation in which he or she works.

Required

Describe the key characteristics of the financial management function and the role of the financial manager in each of the following types of organisation.

(a) Quoted high-growth company
(b) Quoted low-growth company
(c) Unquoted company aiming for a stock exchange listing
(d) Small family-owned business
(e) Non-profit-making organisation, for example a charity
(f) Public sector, for example a government department

(CIMA)

8 **(a)** The Cleevemoor Water Authority was privatised in 2000, to become Northern Water plc (NW). Apart from political considerations, a major motive for the privatisation was to allow access for NW to private sector supplies of finance. During the 1990s, central government controls on capital expenditure had resulted in relatively low levels of investment, so that considerable investment was required to enable the company to meet more stringent water quality regulations. When privatised, it was valued by the merchant bankers advising on the issue at £100 million and was floated in the form of 100 million ordinary shares (par value 50p), sold fully paid for £1 each. The shares reached a premium of 60 per cent on the first day of stock market trading.

Required

In what ways might you expect the objectives of an organisation like Cleevemoor/NW to alter following transfer from public to private ownership?

(b) Selected biannual data from NW's accounts are provided below relating to its first six years of operation as a private sector concern. Also shown, for comparison, are the pro forma data as included in the privatisation documents. The pro forma accounts are notional accounts prepared to show the operating and financial performance of the company in its last year under public ownership as if it had applied private sector accounting conventions. They also incorporate a dividend payment based on the dividend policy declared in the prospectus.

The activities of privatised utilities are scrutinised by a regulatory body which restricts the extent to which prices can be increased. The demand for water in the area served by NW has risen over time at a steady 2 per cent per annum, largely reflecting demographic trends.

Required

Using the data provided, assess the extent to which NW has met the interests of the following groups of stakeholders in its first six years as a privatised enterprise.

Key financial and operating data for year ending 31 December (£m)

	2000 (pro forma)	2002 (actual)	2004 (actual)	2006 (actual)
Turnover	450	480	540	620
Operating profit	26	35	55	75
Taxation	5	6	8	10
Profit after tax	21	29	47	65
Dividends	7	10	15	20
Total assets	100	119	151	191
Capital expenditure	20	30	60	75
Wage bill	100	98	90	86
Directors' emoluments	0.8	2.0	2.3	3.0
Employees (number)	12,000	11,800	10,500	10,000
P:E ratio (average)	–	7.0	8.0	7.5
Retail Price Index	100	102	105	109

If relevant, suggest what other data would be helpful in forming a more balanced view.

(i) shareholders
(ii) consumers
(iii) the workforce
(iv) the government, through NW's contribution to the achievement of macroeconomic policies of price stability and economic growth.

(ACCA)

Practical assignment

Examine the annual report for a well-known company, particularly the chairman's statement. Are the corporate goals clearly specified? What specific references are made to financial management? What does it say about corporate governance and risk management?

2 The financial environment

City fumes over Marconi share suspension

FT

On July 4 2001, investors in the City of London were seething over Marconi's decision, approved by the London Stock Exchange and Financial Services Authority, to suspend trading in its shares ahead of its profit warning.

Having signed a deal to sell its medical systems business to Philips Electronics for $1.1 billion during the night, both companies felt obliged to put out a statement next morning. However, Marconi and its brokers feared it would be problematic to allow investors to trade on the basis of a successful disposal at the same time as the company was preparing to issue a profits warning only hours later. When trading in the shares resumed after the profit warning, Marconi's shares tumbled by 57 per cent from 245p to a 20-year low of 104p, valuing the company at £2.91 billion – less than 10 per cent of its worth ten months earlier.

Angry shareholders called for top management changes in the wake of the severe profit warning when, just a month before, management were issuing bullish statements despite evidence of a global slowdown in the sector.

Efficient financial markets imply that investors are informed on all price-sensitive matters. So what does this case tell us about market efficiency, and what are the implications for corporate finance?

Based on *Financial Times*, July 5–7 2001

Learning objectives

By the end of this chapter, the reader should understand the nature of financial markets and the main players within them. Particular focus is placed on the following topics:

- The functions of financial markets.
- The operation of the Stock Exchange.
- The extent to which capital markets are efficient.
- How taxation affects corporate finance.

Improved ability to read financial statements and the financial pages in a newspaper should also be achieved.

2.1 Introduction

The corporate financial manager has the important task of ensuring that there are sufficient funds available to meet all the likely needs of the business. To do this properly, he or she requires a clear grasp both of the future financial requirements of the business and of the workings of the financial markets. This chapter provides an overview of these markets, and the major institutions within them, paying particular attention to the Stock Exchange.

2.2 Financial markets

A **financial market** is any mechanism for trading financial assets or claims. Frequently, there is no physical market-place, transactions being conducted via telephone or computer. London is widely regarded as the pre-eminent European financial centre. Its main financial markets are as follows:

1. The **money market** channels wholesale funds, usually for less than one year, from lenders to borrowers. The market is largely dominated by the major banks and other financial institutions, but local government and large companies also use it for short-term lending and borrowing purposes.
2. The **securities** or **capital market** deals with long-dated securities such as shares and loan stock. The London Stock Exchange is the best-known institution in the capital market, but there are other important markets, such as the bond market (for long-dated government and corporate borrowing) and the Eurobond market.
3. The **foreign exchange market** is a market for buying and selling one currency against another. Deals are either on a **spot** basis (for immediate delivery) or on a **forward** basis (for future delivery).
4. The **London International Financial Futures and Options Exchange** (LIFFE) provides various means of hedging (i.e. protecting) or speculating against

movements in currencies and interest rates. These are called **derivatives**. A **future** is an agreement to buy or sell an asset (e.g. foreign currency, shares etc.) at an agreed price at some future date. An **option** is the right, but not the obligation, to buy or sell such assets at an agreed price at, or within, an agreed time period.

The financial markets provide mechanisms through which the corporate financial manager has access to a wide range of sources of finance and instruments.

Capital markets have two important functions:

1 *Primary market* – providing new capital for business and other activities, usually in the form of share issues to new or existing shareholders (equity), or loans.

2 *Secondary market* – trading existing securities, thus enabling share or bond holders to dispose of their holdings when they wish. An active secondary market is a necessary condition for an effective primary market, as no investor wants to feel 'locked in' to an investment that cannot be realised when necessary.

Imagine what business life would be like if these capital markets were not available to companies. New businesses could start up only if the owners had sufficient personal wealth to fund the initial capital investment; existing businesses could develop only through re-investing profits generated; and investors could not easily dispose of their shareholdings. In many parts of the world where financial markets are embryonic or even non-existent this is exactly what does happen. *The development of a strong and healthy economy rests very largely on efficient, well-developed financial markets.*

Financial markets promote savings and investment by providing mechanisms whereby the financial requirements of lenders (suppliers of funds) and borrowers (users of funds) can be met. Figure 2.1 shows in simple terms how businesses finance their operations.

Financial institutions (e.g. pension funds, insurance companies, banks, building societies, unit trusts and specialist investment institutions) act as **financial intermediaries**, collecting funds from savers to lend to their corporate and other customers through the money and capital markets, or directly through loans, leasing and other forms of financing.

Businesses are major users of these funds. The financial manager raises cash by selling claims to the company's existing or future assets in financial markets (e.g. by issuing shares, debentures or Bills of Exchange) or borrowing from financial institutions. The cash is then used to acquire fixed and current assets. If those investments are successful, they will generate positive cash flows from business operations. This cash surplus is used to service existing financial obligations in the form of dividends, interest etc., and to make repayments. Any residue is re-invested in the business to replace existing assets or to expand operations.

We focus in this chapter on the financial institutions and financial markets shown in Figure 2.1.

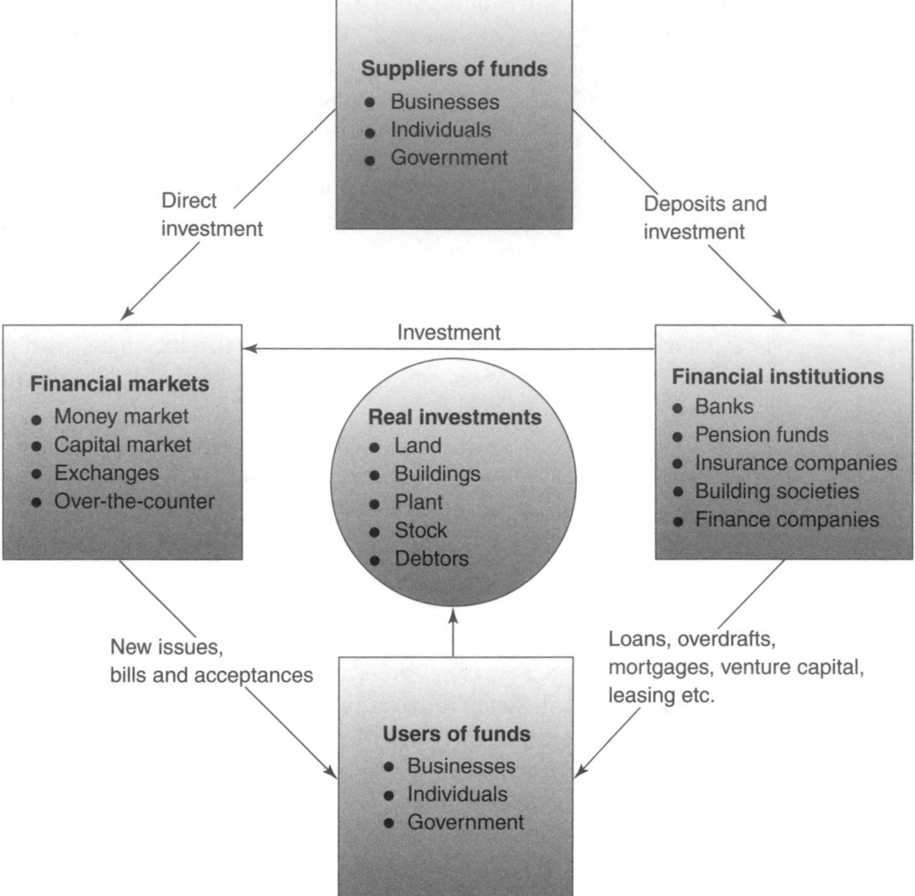

Figure 2.1 Financial markets, institutions, suppliers and users

Financial institutions provide essential services

The needs of lenders and borrowers rarely match. Hence, there is an important role for financial intermediaries, such as banks, if the financial markets are to operate efficiently:

1 *Re-packaging finance*: gathering small amounts of savings from a large number of individuals and re-packaging them into larger bundles for lending to businesses. The banks have an important role here.
2 *Risk reduction*: placing small sums from numerous individuals in large, well-diversified investment portfolios, such as unit trusts.
3 *Liquidity transformation*: bringing together short-term savers and long-term borrowers (e.g. building societies and banks). Borrowing 'short' and lending 'long' is acceptable only where relatively few savers will want to withdraw funds at any given time. The history of banking failures in the USA shows that this is not always the case.

4 *Cost reduction*: minimising transaction costs by providing convenient and relatively inexpensive services for linking small savers to larger borrowers.
5 *Financial advice*: providing advisory and other services for both lender and borrower.

2.3 The financial services sector

The financial services sector can be divided into three groups: institutions engaged in (1) deposit-taking, (2) contractual savings and (3) other investment funds.

Deposit-taking institutions

Clearing banks have three important roles: they operate nationwide networks of High Street branches and on-line facilities; they effect a national payments system by clearing cheques and by receiving and paying out notes and coins; and they accept deposits in varying amounts from a wide range of customers. Hence, these operations are often called **retail banking**. As well as being the dominant force in retail banking, the clearing banks have diversified into wholesale banking and are continuing, to expand their international activities. (Useful websites: **www.bba.org.uk, www.bcsb.co.uk**)

The Balance Sheet of any clearing bank reveals that the main sterling assets are advances to the private sector, other banks, the public sector in the form of Treasury Bills and government stock, local authorities and private households. Nowadays, the main instruments of lending by retail banks are overdrafts, term loans and mortgages.

Wholesale banks

Wholesale banking (or merchant banking) developed out of the need to finance the enormous growth in world trade in the 19th century. **Accepting houses** were formed whose main business was to accept Bills of Exchange (promising to pay a sum of money at some future date) from less well-known traders, and from **discount houses** which provided cash by discounting such bills. **Merchant banks** nowadays concentrate on dealing with institutional investors, large corporations and governments. They have three major activities, frequently organised into separate divisions: corporate finance, mergers and acquisitions, and fund management.

Merchant banks' activities include *giving financial advice to companies and arranging finance* through syndicated loans and new security issues. Merchant banks are also members of the Issuing Houses Association, an organisation responsible for the *flotation of shares* on the Stock Exchange. This involves advising a company on the correct mix of financial instruments to be issued and on drawing up a prospectus and underwriting the issue. They also play a leading role in the *development of new financial products*, such as swaps, options and other derivative products, which have become very popular in recent years.

Another area of activity for wholesale banks is advising companies on corporate *mergers, acquisitions and restructuring*. This involves both assisting in the negotiation of a 'friendly' merger of two independent companies and also developing strategies for 'unfriendly' takeovers, or acting as an adviser for a company defending against an unwanted bidder.

Finally, merchant banks fulfil a major role as *managers of the investment portfolios* of some pension funds, insurance companies, investment and unit trusts, and various charities. Whether in arranging finance, advising on takeover bids or managing the funds of institutional investors, merchant banks exert considerable influence on both corporate finance and the capital market.

The growth of *overseas banking* has been closely linked to the development of Euro-currency markets and to the growth of multinational companies. Over 300 foreign banks operate in London. A substantial amount of their business consists of providing finance to branches or subsidiaries of foreign companies.

Building societies (www.buildingsociety.html, www.bsa.org.uk) are a form of savings bank specialising in the provision of finance for house purchase in the private sector. As a result of deregulation of the financial services industry, building societies now offer an almost complete set of private banking services, and the distinction between them and the traditional banks is increasingly blurred. Indeed, many societies, have given up their mutual status to become public limited companies.

Self-assessment Activity 2.1

What are financial intermediaries and what economic service do they perform?

(answer at end of chapter)

Institutions engaged in contractual savings

Pension funds accumulate funds to meet the future pension liabilities of a particular organisation to its employees. Funds are normally built up from contributions paid by the employer and employees. They can be divided into **self-administered schemes**, where the funds are invested directly in the financial markets; and **insured schemes**, where the funds are invested by, and the risk is covered by, a life assurance company. Pension schemes have enormous and rapidly growing funds available for investment in the securities markets. Pension funds enjoy major tax advantages. Subject to certain restrictions, individuals enjoy tax relief on their subscriptions to a fund. In turn, the fund's income and capital gains are tax-free. Together with insurance companies, pension funds comprise the major purchasers of company securities.

Insurance companies' activities (**www.abi.org.uk**) can be divided into long-term and general insurance. Long-term insurance business consists mainly of *life assurance* and *pension provision*. Policyholders pay premiums to the companies and are guaranteed either a lump sum in the event of death, or a regular annual income for some defined period. With a guaranteed premium inflow and predictable aggregate future payments, there is no great need for liquidity, so life assurance funds are able to invest heavily in long-term assets.

General insurance business (e.g. fire, accident, motor, marine and other insurance) consists of contracts to cover losses within a specified period, normally 12 months. As liquidity is important here, a greater proportion of funds is invested in short-term assets, although a considerable proportion of such funds is invested in securities and property.

The investment strategy of both pension fund managers and insurance companies tends to be long-term. They invest in **portfolios** of company shares and government stocks, direct loans and mortgages.

Other investment funds: unit and investment trusts

As we shall see in Section 2.4, private investors, independently managing their own investment portfolios, are a dying breed. Increasingly, they are being replaced by financial institutions that manage widely diversified portfolios of securities, such as unit trusts and investment trusts (**www.investmentfunds.org.uk**). These pool the funds of large numbers of investors, enabling them to achieve a degree of diversification not otherwise attainable owing to the prohibitive transactions costs and time required for active portfolio management. However, there are important differences between these institutions.

Investment trusts

Investment trusts are limited companies, whose shares are usually quoted on the Stock Exchange, and set up specifically to invest in securities. The company's share price depends on the value of the securities held in the trust, and also on supply and demand. As a result, these shares often sell at values different from their net asset values, usually at a discount.

They are traditionally 'closed-ended' in the sense that the company's articles restrict the number of shares, and hence the amount of share capital, that can be issued. However, several open-ended investment trust companies have now been launched. To realise their holdings, shareholders can sell their shares on the stock market.

Unit trusts

Unit trusts are investment syndicates, established by trust deed and regulated by trust law. Investors' funds are pooled into a portfolio of investments, each investor being allocated tranches or 'units' according to the amount of the funds they subscribe. They are mainly operated by banks and insurance companies, which appoint managers whose conduct is supervised by a set of trustees.

Unit prices are fixed by the managers, but reflect the value of the underlying securities. Prices reflect the costs of buying and selling, via an initial charge. Managers also apply annual charges, usually about 1 per cent of the value of the fund. Unit-holders can realise their holdings only by selling units back to the trust managers.

They are 'open-ended' in the sense that the size of the fund is not restricted and the managers can advertise for funds.

Disintermediation and securitisation

While financial intermediaries play a vital role in the financial markets, **disintermediation** is an important new development. This is the process whereby companies borrow and lend funds directly between themselves without recourse to banks and other institutions. Allied to this is the process of **securitisation**, the development of new financial instruments to meet ever-changing corporate needs (i.e. financial engineering). Some assets generate predictable cash returns and offer security. Debt can be issued to the market on the basis of the returns and security. Securitisation usually also involves a credit rating agency assessing the issue and giving it a credit rating. Securitisation can also be used to create value through 'unbundling' traditional financial processes. For example, a conventional loan has many elements, such as loan origination, credit status evaluation, financing and collection of interest and principal. Rather than arranging the whole process through a single intermediary, such as a bank, the process can be 'unbundled' and handled by separate institutions which may lower the cost of the loan.

Securitisation and disintermediation have permitted larger companies to create alternative, more flexible forms of finance. This, in turn, has forced banks to become more competitive in the services offered to larger companies. Recent more exotic forms of securitisation include pubs, gate receipts from a football

Securitising the Beatles

Chrysalis, the media group, has completed a complex cross-border securitisation deal to unlock £60 million over 15 years against the future value of its music publishing catalogue which includes artists ranging from Blondie, the Beatles, Jethro Tull to David Gray and Moloko.

Music publishing is a separate business from recorded music, comprising the rights to the written composition of a song, performance rights such as radio airplay, a share of CD sales and synchronisation rights from use in advertisements or films. Chrysalis's revenues from its catalogue were £8 million in 2000.

The Chrysalis securitisation deal took 18 months to structure because of the complexity in bringing together publishing rights in the UK, US, Germany, Sweden and Holland under their different tax regimes.

Chrysalis follows in the footsteps of the singer-song writer, David Bowie, who recently raised $55 million via a bond issue against his share of the publishing rights to his compositions.

Based on *Financial Times*, March 2 2001

club, future income from a pop star's recordings, and even the World Cup competitions for 2002 and 2006.

2.4 The London Stock Exchange (LSE)

The capital market is the market where long-term capital is raised and traded. The London Stock Exchange is the principal trading market for long-dated securities in the UK (**www.londonstockexchange.com**).

A stock exchange has two principal economic functions: to enable companies to *raise new capital* (the primary market), and to *facilitate the trading of existing shares* (the secondary market) through the negotiation of a price at which title to ownership of a company is transferred between investors. Secondary trading dwarfs the issue of new ordinary shares. In 2000, secondary turnover was £3,520 billion. By contrast, new money raised by UK companies in the same year was only £126 billion.

A brief history of the London Stock Exchange

The world's first joint-stock company – the Muscovy Company – was founded in London in 1553. With the growth in such companies there was the need for shareholders to be able to sell their holdings, leading to a growth in brokers acting as intermediaries for investors. In 1760, after being ejected from the Royal Exchange for rowdiness, a group of 150 brokers formed a club at Jonathan's Coffee House to buy and sell shares. By 1773, the club was renamed the Stock Exchange.

The Exchange developed rapidly, playing a major role in financing UK companies during the Industrial Revolution. New technology began to have an impact in 1872, when the Exchange Telegraph tickertape service was introduced.

For over a century, the Exchange continued to expand and become more efficient, but fundamental changes did not arise until 27 October 1986 – 'Big Bang' – the most important of which were:

1. All firms became broker/dealers able to operate in a dual capacity – either buying securities from, or selling them to, clients without the need to deal through a third party. Firms could also register as market makers committed to making firm bid (buying) and offer (selling) prices at all times.
2. Ownership of member firms by an outside corporation was permitted, enabling member firms to build a large capital base to compete with competition from overseas.
3. Minimum scales of commission were abolished to improve competitiveness.
4. Trading moved from being conducted face-to-face on a single market floor to being performed via computer and telephone from separate dealing rooms. Computer-based systems were introduced to display share price information, such as SEAQ (Stock Exchange Automated Quotations).

The Alternative Investment Market (AIM) was introduced, in 1995, to provide a market that is accessible to both investors and companies from a wide range of backgrounds, including start-ups and established firms. Over 500 companies had listings on AIM in 2001.

In 1997, the settlement service for exchanging shares and associated payment moved to the CREST electronic settlement system. In the same year, the Stock Exchange Electronic Trading Service (SETS) was launched to bring greater speed and efficiency to the market. Today, the London Stock Exchange is viewed as one of the leading and most competitive places to do business in the world, second only to New York in total market value terms.

The LSE has two tiers. The main market is the **Official List**, providing a quotation for nearly 3,000 companies. To obtain a full listing, companies have to satisfy rigorous criteria laid down in the Stock Exchange's 'Listing Rules' (or 'Yellow Book'). These relate to size of issued capital, financial record, trading history and acceptability of board members. These details are set out in a document called the company's 'listing particulars'.

The second tier is the **Alternative Investment Market (AIM)** with over 500 companies listed. It attempts to minimise the cost of entry and membership by keeping the rules and application process as simple as possible. A nominated

Mini case

When do you take AIM?

In December 1996, Oxford BioMedica – the gene therapy company wanting to test its developments on cancer and AIDS treatments – floated on the Alternative Investment Market. Investors paid 88p a share and the company was given a market value of £50 million even though the company had virtually no assets or staff – just a highly promising drug in late-stage animal trial development and some highly talented researchers. The trouble is that the industry rule of thumb suggests that only one in a hundred drugs at this stage makes it to market. Gene therapy is a very high-risk business.

Fifteen months after flotation, in March 1998, the company was in need of a further cash injection of £6 million – small beer compared with the initial equity issue. By now, however, the biotechnology sector was somewhat depressed following a number of disappointing drug trial results and other setbacks. To raise the necessary finance, Oxford BioMedica was forced to price the issue at just 10p; this despite the fact that it had now established new laboratories, recruited top-level research staff, agreed collaboration with a leading pharmaceutical company and brought forward clinical trials by a year.

Like many things in life, success is all about getting the timing right. But as Professor Kingsmann, BioMedica's chief executive observed, 'If we are too early for AIM, then AIM has no role for a biotechnology company. If it's too early for AIM, then what the hell is AIM for?'

Questions

1 Explain to Professor Kingsmann what AIM is for.
2 Suggest to him where he might have gone wrong.

adviser firm (typically a stock broker or bank) both introduces the new company to the market and acts as a mentor, ensuring that it complies with market rules. Although the majority of companies are capitalised at between £2 million and £20 million, it also includes start-up operations at one end and companies capitalised at over £200 million at the other. However, the requirement to observe existing obligations in relation to publication of price-sensitive information and annual and interim accounts remains. The AIM is unlikely to appeal to private investors unless they are prepared to invest in relatively high-risk businesses.

While the vast majority of share trading takes place through the Stock Exchange, it is not the only trading arena. For some years, there has been a small, but active **Over-The-Counter (OTC) Market**, where organisations trade their shares, usually on a 'matched bargain' basis, via an intermediary.

Self-assessment Activity 2.2

What type of company would be most likely to trade on:

(a) the Official Listed Securities Market?
(b) the Alternative Investment Market?
(c) The Over-The-Counter Market?

(answer at end of chapter)

A game of two halves at Manchester United

It seems that football at Manchester United is still very much a game of two halves – the half that takes place on the Old Trafford turf, and the other half on the far bumpier business playing surface, where success is in terms of financial goals and the stock market 'Footsie'. Once upon a time, Manchester United was just a great football club. Now it is a major listed company exploiting the UK's most powerful sporting brand.

Success on the field has been matched only by its success in the business field – two-thirds of all revenues in 2000 came from sponsorship, merchandise sales and TV revenues. It has now set up its own television channel, MUTV, in a joint venture with satellite broadcaster BSkyB and media group Granada. The Annual Report 2000 states, 'We strive to ensure that shareholders, loyal supporters, customers and key commercial partners alike benefit from our performance'. (website: **www.manutd.com**)

Regulation of the market

Investor confidence in the workings of the stock market is paramount if it is to operate effectively. Even in deregulated markets there is still a requirement to provide strong regulation to safeguard against unfair or incompetent trading and to ensure that the market operates as intended. The mechanism for regulating the whole UK financial system was established by the Financial Services Act 1986 (FSA86), which provided a structure based on 'self-regulation within a statutory framework'.

In 1997, statutory powers were vested in a supervisory body, the **Financial Services Authority** (FSA), responsible to the Treasury. Its objectives are to sustain confidence in the UK's financial services industry and monitor, detect and prevent financial crime (**www.fsa.gov.uk**). This involves the regulation of the financial markets, investment managers and investment advisors.

The FSA also takes on additional responsibilities for monitoring the Bank of England and money markets, building societies and the insurance market. The hope is that, by having a single regulator covering all financial markets, there will be greater efficiency, lower costs, clearer accountability and a single point of service for customer enquiries and complaints.

In an attempt to enhance London's reputation for clean and fair markets, the FSA has introduced new powers, effective from 2000, to deal with insider dealing and attempts to distort prices. It is a criminal offence to undertake 'investment business' without due authorisation. A **Recognised Investment Exchange** (RIE), of which the London Stock Exchange is one, may also receive authorisation. Recognition exempts an exchange (but not its members) from needing authorisation for any activity constituting investment business.

The Stock Exchange discharges its responsibilities by:

- vetting new applicants for membership
- monitoring members' compliance with its rules
- providing services to aid trading and settlement of members' business
- supervising settlement activity and management of settlement risk
- investigating suspected abuse of its markets

Market abuse includes three strands:

(a) Market distortion – acting in such a manner as to force up a company's share price.

(b) Misuse of information – e.g. buying or selling shares on the basis of privileged information.

(c) Creating false information – e.g. putting false information on to a website.

FSA86 also gave the Exchange responsibility for regulating both the admission of companies to the Official List and their ongoing compliance with the listing requirements. Companies violating the Exchange's rules of conduct can have their listings removed.

Other bodies also keep a watchful eye on the workings of capital markets. These include the Bank of England (**www.bankofengland.co.uk**), the Competition Commission (CC), the Panel on Takeovers and Mergers, the Office of Fair Trading, the press and various government departments.

Self-assessment Activity 2.3

To what extent does an effective primary capital market depend on a healthy secondary market?

(answer at end of chapter)

Share ownership in the UK

Back in 1963, over half (54 per cent) of all UK equities were held by private individuals. Today, share ownership is dominated by the investing institutions (the pension funds, insurance groups and investment and unit trusts). Together, they own around 80 per cent of the value of UK traded companies. These impersonal bodies, acting for millions of pensioners and employees, policy-holders and small investors, have vast power to influence the market and the companies they invest in. Institutional investors employ a variety of investment strategies, from passive index-tracking funds, which seek to reflect movements in the stock market, to actively managed funds.

Institutional investors have important responsibilities, and this can create a dilemma: on the one hand, they are expected to speak out against corporate management policies and decisions that are deemed unacceptable environmentally, ethically or economically. But public opposition to the management could well adversely affect share price. Institutions therefore have a conflict between their responsibilities as major shareholders and their investment role as managers seeking to outperform the markets.

A further indication of changing patterns of share ownership is the proportion of the adult population that holds shares. Successive governments have promoted a 'share-owning democracy', particularly through privatisation programmes. However, individuals tend to hold small, undiversified portfolios – over half of private investors hold just one security – which exposes them to a greater degree of risk than from investing in a diversified investment portfolio.

Towards a European stock market

The European Union is meant to be about removing barriers and providing easier access to capital markets. Until recently, this was still a pipe dream, with some 30 stock exchanges within the EU, most of which had different regulations. With the introduction of a single currency, there will undoubtedly be strong pressure towards a single capital market. But does this mean a single European stock exchange, with one set of rules for share listing and trading?

Euronext was formed in 2000 as a result of the merger of the Amsterdam, Brussels and Paris stock exchanges. As the first pan-European stock exchange, it is looking to agree further mergers with other smaller exchanges in Europe, which will create more pressure on the London and Frankfurt exchanges. These two exchanges attempted, but failed, to merge in 2000. The New York Stock

Table 2.1 Leading Stock Exchanges (based on 2000 statistics)

	Domestic equity market valuation £bn	Number of companies	
		Domestic	International
New York	7,659	2,035	433
London	1,725	2,428	501
Tokyo	2,113	2,055	41
Nasdaq	2,395	4,239	487
Germany	850	744	245
Euronext	1,519	1,416	426

Based on *London Stock Exchange* Fact File (2001)

Exchange is easily the largest in terms of market value, while Nasdaq, the US exchange for young growth companies, has the most companies listed.

2.5 Are financial markets efficient?

If financial managers are to achieve corporate goals, they require well-developed financial markets where transfers of wealth from savers to borrowers are efficient in both pricing and operational cost.

Efficiency can mean many things. The *economist* talks about **allocative efficiency** – the extent to which resources are allocated to the most productive uses, thus satisfying society's needs to the maximum. The *engineer* talks about **operating** or **technical efficiency** – the extent to which a mechanism performs to maximum capability. The *sociologist* and *the political scientist* talk about **social efficiency** – the extent to which a mechanism conforms to accepted social and political mores and values. The most important concept of efficiency for our purposes is **pricing** or **information efficiency**. This refers to the extent to which available information is built into the structure of share prices. If information relevant for assessing a company's future earnings prospects (including both past information and relevant information relating to future expected events) is widely and cheaply available, then this will be impounded into share prices by an efficient market. As a result, the market should allow all participants to compete on an equal basis in a so-called **fair game**.

We often hear of the shares of a particular company being under- or over-valued, the implication being that the stock market pricing mechanism has got it wrong and that analysts know better. *In an efficient stock market, current market prices fully reflect available information* and it is impossible to outperform the market consistently, except by luck.

Consider any major European stock market. On any given trading day, there are hundreds of analysts – representing the powerful financial institutions which dominate the market – closely tracking the daily performance of the share price of, say, Wimpey, the construction company. They each receive at the same time new information from the company – a major order, a labour dispute or a revised profits forecast. This information is rapidly evaluated and reflected in the share price by their decisions to buy or sell Wimpey shares. *The measure of efficiency is seen in the extent and speed with which the market reflects new information in the share price.*

The Law of One Price suggests that equivalent securities must be traded at the same price (excluding differences in transaction costs). If this is not the case, **arbitrage** opportunities arise whereby a trader can buy a security at a lower price and simultaneously sell it at a higher price, thereby making a profit without incurring any risk. In an efficient market, arbitrage activity will continue until the price differential is eliminated.

The Efficient Market Hypothesis (EMH)

Information can be classified as historical, current or forecast. Only current or historical information is certain in its effect on price. The more information that is available the better the situation. Informed decisions are more likely to be correct, although the use of inside information to benefit from investment decisions (insider dealing) is illegal in the UK.

Company information is available both within and without the organisation. Those within the organisation will obviously be better informed about the state of the business. They have access to sensitive information about future investment projects, contracts under negotiation, forthcoming managerial changes, etc. The additional knowledge will vary according to a person's level of responsibility and place in the organisational hierarchy.

Outsider investors fall into two categories: **individual investors** and the **institutions**. Of these two groups, the institutions are the better informed, as they have greater access to senior management, and may be represented on the board of directors.

Different amounts of financial information are available to different groups of people. There is **unequal** access to the information, which may affect a company's share price. If you are one of the well-informed, this gives you the opportunity to keep one step ahead of the market. Otherwise, you may lose out. The share price reflects who knows what about the company. You should note, however, that in the UK, share dealings by company directors are tightly circumscribed; for example, they can only buy and sell at specific times, and details of all such trades must be publicly disclosed.

Market efficiency evolved from the notion of perfect competition, which assumes free and instantly available information, rational investors and no taxes or transaction costs. Of course, such conditions do not exist in capital markets, so just how do we assess their level of efficiency? Market efficiency, as reflected by the Efficient Markets Hypothesis (EMH), may exist at three levels:

1 The **weak form** of the EMH states that current share prices fully reflect *all information contained in past price movements*. If this level of efficiency holds, there is no value in trying to predict future price movements by analysing trends in past price movements. Efficient stock market prices will fluctuate

more or less randomly, any departure from randomness being too expensive to determine. Share prices are said to follow a **random walk**.

2 The **semi-strong form** of the EMH states that current market prices reflect not only all past price movements, but *all publicly available information*. In other words, there is no benefit in analysing existing information, such as that given in published accounts, dividend and profits announcements, appointment of a new chief executive or product breakthroughs, after the information has been released. The stock market has already captured this information in the current share price.

3 The **strong form** of the EMH states that current market prices reflect *all relevant information* – even if privately held. The market price reflects the 'true' or intrinsic value of the share based on the underlying future cash flows. The implications of such a level of market efficiency are clear: no one can consistently beat the market and earn abnormal returns. Few would go so far as to argue that stock markets are efficient at this level.

You will have noticed that as the EMH strengthens, the opportunities for profitable speculation reduce. Competition between well-informed investors drives share prices to reflect their intrinsic values.

The EMH and fundamental and technical analysis

Investment analysts who seek to determine the **intrinsic worth** of a share based on underlying information undertake **fundamental analysis**. The EMH implies that fundamental analysis will not identify under-priced shares unless the analyst can respond more quickly to new information than other investors, or has inside information. Chapter 4 adopts a fundamental analysis approach in its examination of share valuation.

Another approach is often termed **technical analysis**, its advocates being labelled **chartists** because of their reliance upon graphs and charts of price movements. Chartists are not interested in estimating the intrinsic value of shares, preferring to develop trading rules based on patterns in share price movement over time, or breakout points of change. Charts are used to predict 'floors' and 'ceilings', marking the end of a share price trend. Figure 2.2 shows how charts are used to detect patterns of 'resistance' (for shares on the way up) and 'support' (for shares on the way down). This approach can often prove to be a 'self-fulfilling prophecy'. In the short term, if analysts predict that share prices will rise, investors will start to buy, thus creating a bull market and resulting in upward prices.

Even in its weak form, the EMH questions the value of technical analysis; future price changes cannot be predicted from past price changes. However, the fact that many analysts, using fundamental or technical analysis, make a comfortable living from their investment advice, suggests that many investors find comfort in the advice given.

Considerable empirical tests on market efficiency have been conducted over many years. In the USA and the UK, until the 1987 stock market crash, the evidence broadly supported the semi-strong form of efficiency. More specifically, it suggests the following:

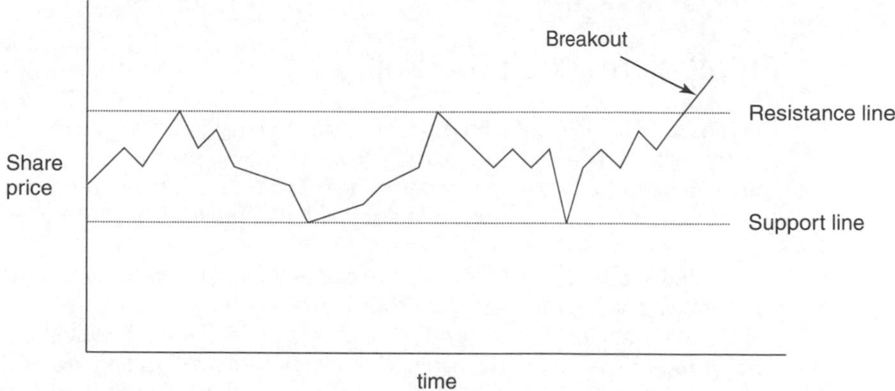

Figure 2.2 Chart showing breakout beyond resistance line

1 *There is little benefit in attempting to forecast future share price movements by analysing past price movements.* As the EMH seems to hold in its weak form, the value of charts must be questioned.
2 For quoted companies that are regularly traded on the stock market, analysts are *unlikely to find significantly over- or under-valued shares through studying publicly held information.* Studies indicate (e.g. Ball and Brown 1968) that most of the information content contained in annual reports and profit announcements is reflected in share prices anything up to a year before release of the information, as investors make judgements based on press releases and other information during the year. However, analysts with specialist knowledge, paying careful attention to smaller, less well-traded shares, may be more successful. Equally, analysts able to respond to new information slightly ahead of the market may make further gains. The semi-strong form of the EMH seems to hold fairly well for most quoted shares.
3 The strong form of the EMH does not hold, so superior returns can be achieved by those with 'inside knowledge'. However, it is the duty of directors to act in the shareholders' best interests, and it is a criminal offence to engage in insider trading for personal gain. The fact that cases of insider trading have led to the conviction of senior executives shows that market prices do not fully reflect unpublished information.

Recent governments have encouraged greater market efficiency in several ways:

- Stock market deregulation and computerised dealing have enabled speedier adjustment of share prices in response to global information.
- Mergers and takeovers have been encouraged as ways of improving managerial efficiency. Poorly performing companies experience depressed share prices and become candidates for acquisition.
- Governments have seen privatisation of public utilities as a means of subjecting previously publicly-owned organisations to market pressures.

An efficient stock market?

The Big Bang in 1986 gave the London Stock Exchange a huge advantage over most of its competitors. The result was strong growth in trading activity and international participation. But Big Bang was only a partial revolution – automating the distribution of price information, but stopping short of automating the trading function itself.

Since 1986, global equity markets have become increasingly complex, with investors constantly looking for greater choice and lower costs. The London Stock Exchange made various attempts to retain its reputation as one of the most efficient stock markets. In 1997, it took a major step by moving from a quote-based trading system, under which share dealing is conducted by telephone, to order-driven trading, termed SETS – the Stock Exchange Electronic Trading Service. The aim was to improve efficiency and reduce costs by automating trading and narrowing the spread between buying and selling prices. This it achieves by the automatic matching of orders placed electronically by prospective buyers and sellers.

The system, which initially only applies to heavily traded shares, works as follows. Instead of agreeing to trade at a price set by a market maker, prospective buyers and sellers can:

(a) advertise through their broker the price at which they would like to deal, and wait for the market to move, or
(b) execute immediately at the best price available.

An investor wishing to buy or sell will contact his or her broker and agree a price at which the investor is willing to trade. The broker enters the order in the order book, which is then displayed to the entire market along with other orders. Once the order is executed, the trade is automatically reported to the Exchange. Time will tell whether it does lead to greater efficiency, but it is hoped that it will offer users more attractive, transparent and flexible trading opportunities.

Heads, shoulders and broadening bottoms

The popularity of business television channels such as CNBC has done wonders for the careers of Wall Street's technical analysts, who claim to be able to predict future share prices by spotting trends in past prices. Their market charts, showing descriptively named patterns such as 'head and shoulders' – a big peak surrounded by two smaller peaks – or 'broadening bottoms' – a series of troughs, each lower than the preceding one – make ideal graphics for television producers in need of something pretty for viewers to watch while the glamorous reporters are busy off-camera, catching up on the latest market gossip. The simple trading advice conveyed by charts is, for CNBC's stock-tip-hungry viewers, manna from heaven.

Continued

But technical analysis is not merely for gullible CNBC-watchers. It has been around a long time, dating back a century to Charles Dow, the founder of Dow Jones, who invented the 'Dow theory' for identifying trends in share prices. Charts are used by some of the world's most successful investors.

Nevertheless, economists who study financial markets have long regarded technical analysis as mumbo jumbo, bearing much the same relationship to rigorous economic 'fundamental analysis' that astrology does to astronomy. Since the 1960s, economists have believed, more or less, in 'efficient-market theory'. In an efficient market, prices reflect all available information, and so scouring past prices for patterns can tell you nothing useful about whether in future prices will go up or down. Instead, prices will move unpredictably, in a 'random walk'.

In the past decade some economists have challenged efficient-market theory, by finding numerous examples of apparently predictable movements in share prices. But there is still a fierce debate about whether these movements are predictable enough for investors to make money trading on the basis of expected price changes. The evidence was described at length in 'A Non-Random Walk Down Wall Street' (Princeton University Press, 1999), a book by Craig MacKinlay, of the Wharton School, and Andrew Lo, of the Massachusetts Institute of Technology.

Mr Lo and two new co-authors have now come to the defence of technical analysis.* Using American share prices during 1962–96, they investigated the predictive ability of five pairs of widely-used technical patterns. The results showed that the various technical patterns mostly occurred far more frequently than they would have done if they were truly random events. The most common patterns were double tops and bottoms – two peaks (or two troughs) at similar prices to each other – followed by head and shoulders and inverted head and shoulders. In general, the charts contained useful information about future share prices. The study does not test whether this information was useful enough to allow investors to make sufficient profit trading on it to justify the extra risk.

Since investors have been using charts for 100 years or so and they still seem to work, the patterns may be so deeply ingrained that their predictive powers will persist come what may.

Based on *The Economist*, August 19 2000

* Foundations of technical analysis by Lo, Mamaysky and Wang, *Journal of Finance*, August 2000

Implications of market efficiency for corporate managers

In quoted companies, managers and investors are directly linked through stock market prices, corporate actions being rapidly reflected in share prices. This indicates the following:

1 Investors are not easily fooled by glossy financial reports or 'creative accounting' techniques, which boost corporate reported earnings but not underlying cash flows.

2 Corporate management should endeavour to make decisions that maximise shareholder wealth.
3 The timing of new issues of securities is not critical. Market prices are a 'fair' reflection of the information available and rationally evaluate the degree of risk in shares.
4 Where corporate managers possess information not yet released to the market, there is an opportunity for influencing prices. For example, a company may retain information so that, in the event of an unwelcome takeover bid, it can offer positive signals.

Self-assessment Activity 2.4

Consider why a dealing rule like 'Always buy in early December' should be doomed to failure. This rule is designed to exploit the so-called 'end of year effect' claiming that share prices 'always' rise at the end of the year.

(answer at end of chapter)

Surfing towards greater stock market efficiency

One of the essential requirements of stock market efficiency is that all participants have roughly equal access to price-sensitive information. In the past, the big players – with online databases – were able to obtain information, and thereby enjoy a competitive advantage, well before the small investors who may have had to rely on the daily paper to keep abreast of recent events and price movements.

The Internet offers enormous scope for narrowing the information gap between big and small market participants. This arises in various ways.

1 *Company information*. Electronic reporting of company information will result in a significant enfranchisement of shareholders and enable greater accountability and corporate governance. The electronic information revolution should also give rise to a movement away from conventional accounting-based information to more user-friendly shareholder information which focuses on the key value drivers. For example, customer satisfaction and market penetration may be regular information as part of a 'balanced scorecard' performance measurement system. Videos of AGMs, analysts' presentations and information on ethical/environmental investment will become standard, enabling all investors to be kept up-to-date on corporate progress.
2 *Market information*. There are already thousands of Web pages devoted to investment and personal finance information, much of which was hitherto only available to professional users. Although a charge is made for real-time information, those with share prices on a 20 minute delay are often free.

The following websites may be of interest:

Yahoo! (**finance.yahoo.co.uk**) focuses on providing share information for London, Frankfurt and Paris, with links to the US exchanges.

Moneyworld (**www.moneyworld.co.uk**) covers a much wider range of financial services as well as share prices.

However much information efficiency may improve through surfing the Web's financial pages, remember that the market is renowned for its occasional catastrophic share price waves, which few can predict and even fewer ride.

Self-assessment Activity 2.5

Share prices of takeover targets invariably rise before the formal announcement of a takeover bid. What does this suggest for the EMH?

(answer at end of chapter)

Criticisms of the EMH

Michael Jensen, a leading financial economist, argued in 1978 that 'the efficient markets hypothesis is the best-established fact in all of social science'. Why then is the EMH debate still hotly disputed? The main issue is whether investors react correctly to new information or whether they make systematic errors by over- or under-reacting. The **overreaction hypothesis** argues that share prices tend to overshoot the true value due to excessive optimism or pessimism by investors in their initial reactions to new information. There is some evidence for this in UK financial markets (Dissanaike 1997).

Much criticism of the EMH is misplaced because it is based on a misconception of what the hypothesis actually says. For example, it does not mean that financial expertise is of no value in stock markets and that a share portfolio might as well be selected by sticking a pin in the financial pages. This is clearly not the case. It does suggest, however, that in an efficient market, after adjusting for portfolio risk, fund managers will not, on average, achieve returns higher than that of a randomly selected portfolio. Roll (see Ross *et al.* 1991, p. 324) makes the point that publicly-available information need not be reflected in share prices. Instead, the link 'between unreflected information and prices is too subtle and tenuous to be easily or costlessly detected'.

Market efficiency also suggests that share prices are 'fair' in the sense that they reflect the value of that stock given the available information. So shareholders need not be unduly concerned with whether they are paying too much for a particular share.

The fact that many investors have done very well through investing on the stock market should not surprise us. For much of the last century the market generated positive returns. Most investment advice, if followed over a long period of time, is likely to have done well; the point is that, in efficient markets, investors cannot consistently achieve above-average returns except by chance.

A few apparent anomalies in the EMH

There appear to be two main anomalies in the EMH, the effects of size and timing.

Size effects

Market efficiency seems to be less in evidence among smaller firms. Shares of smaller companies tend to yield higher average returns than those of larger companies of comparable risk. Dimson and Marsh (1986) found that in the UK, on average, smaller firms outperformed larger firms by around 6 per cent per annum. Some of the difference can be accounted for by the higher risk and trading costs involved in dealing with smaller companies. Another explanation is institutional neglect. Financial institutions dominating the stock market often neglect small firms offering what appear to be high returns because the maximum investment is relatively small (if they are not to exceed their normal 5 per cent maximum stake). The costs of monitoring and trading may not warrant the sums involved.

Timing effects

In the longer term, disparities in share returns seem to correct themselves. A share performing poorly in one year is likely to do well the following year. Seasonal effects have also been observed. At the other extreme, it has been observed that share performance is related to the day of the week or time of the day. Prices tend to rise during the last fifteen minutes of the day's trading, but the first hour of Monday trading is generally characterised by heavy selling. Investors may evaluate their portfolios over the weekend and decide what to sell first thing on Monday, but are more cautious in their buying decisions, preferring to take their broker's advice.

Stock market surges and bubbles

An investor holding a wide portfolio of shares (e.g. the FTA All-Share Index) for, say, 25 years, would have been rewarded handsomely. But the capital growth was not a steady monthly appreciation; the bulk of it came in just a fraction of the investment period through stock market surges. In an efficient market, few – if any – are clever enough to be able to predict short-term stock market surges.

The famous South Sea Bubble of 1729 was one of the early speculative stock market 'bubbles' where investors adopt the 'herd' instinct and drive up prices well above any rational valuation based on economic fundamentals. The economist J.M. Keynes described this in terms of a 'beauty contest' where investors are not following their own judgments but trying to guess how other investors are going to behave. The Internet Bubble of 1999 shows that speculative bubbles are still with us and the cost of following the trend can be considerable.

Black Monday

In October 1987, on 'Black Monday', share prices fell by 30 per cent or more on most of the world's stock markets. Had this collapse been triggered by some cataclysmic event, shareholders' reactions could be easily explained as the efficient market reacting to new information. However, Black Monday was not a reaction to external events, but rather a recognition that the prolonged bull market had ended and that the speculative share price bubble had burst. This brings into question the validity of the simple EMH, which implies that share prices cannot rise to the artificially high levels observed prior to the 1987 crash. The newly introduced computer trading methods, which automatically sell shares when they fall below a predetermined level, were unable to cope with such an adverse situation. It is now generally accepted that the EMH failed to explain why the Dow Jones Industrials index plummeted 23 per cent in just a few hours.

This enigma has led to a re-evaluation of the simple EMH and the assumption that there is a single 'true' value for shares; there may be a very wide range of plausible values. The EMH, if it operates at all, does so in the weakest of forms and is most efficient when conditions are stable.

Black Monday's crash adds credence to the Speculative Bubble theory. Stock market behaviour is based on inflating and bursting speculative bubbles, rather than fundamental analysis based on new information. Investors buy shares because they believe that others will pay yet more for them later, thus creating a bull market. Eventually, the bubble bursts and the market corrects itself or crashes, depending on the size of the bubble.

Self-assessment Activity 2.6

If the stock market is efficient, can no one beat the market average?

(answer at end of chapter)

2.6 A new perspective – Chaos Theory

The EMH is based on the assertion that rational investors rapidly absorb new information about a company's prospects, which is then impounded into the share price. Any other price variations are attributable to random 'noise'. This implies that the market has no memory – it simply reacts to the advent of each new information snippet, registers it accordingly and settles back into equilibrium; in other words, all price-sensitive events occur randomly and independently of each other.

The crash of 1987, possibly attributed to the market's realisation that shares were over-valued and triggered by the collapse of a relatively minor management buy-out deal, has provoked more detailed scrutiny of the pattern of past share prices. This has uncovered evidence that share price movements do not always conform to a 'random walk'. For example, significant downturns happen more frequently than significant upturns.

A new branch of mathematics, chaos theory, has been harnessed to help explain such features. Observations of natural systems such as weather patterns and river systems often give a chaotic appearance – they seem to lurch wildly from one extreme to another. However, chaos theorists suggest that apparently random, unpredictable patterns are governed by sets of complex sub-systems that react interdependently. These systems can be modelled, and their behaviour forecast, but predictions of the behaviour of chaotic systems are very sensitive to the precise conditions specified at the start of the estimation period. An apparently small error in the specification of the model can lead to major errors in the forecast.

Edgar Peters (1991) has suggested that stock markets are chaotic in this sense. Markets have memories, are prone to major price swings and do not behave entirely randomly. For example, in the UK, he found that today's price movement is affected by price changes that occurred several years previously. The most recent changes, however, have the biggest impact. In addition, he found that price moves were persistent, i.e. if previous moves in price were upwards, the subsequent price move was more likely to be up than down. Yet chaos theory also suggests that persistent uptrends are also more likely ultimately to result in major reversals!

Peters' work suggests that world stock markets exhibit patterns that are overlaid with substantial random noise. The more noise, the less efficient the market. In this respect, the US markets appear to be more efficient than those in the UK and Japan. Other observers suggest that markets are essentially rational and efficient, but succumb to chaos on occasions, with bursts of chaotic frenzy being attributed to speculative activity. This suggests some scope for informed insiders to outperform the market during such periods.

Which view is right? Are stock markets efficient, chaotic or somewhere in between? Pending the results of further research, it seems that corporate financial managers cannot necessarily regard today's market price as a fair assessment of company value, but that the market may well correctly value a company over a period of years. Examination of long-term trends gives more insight than consideration of short-term oscillations. For example, if a company's share price persistently underperforms the market, then perhaps its profitability really is low, or its management poor, or it has failed to release the right amount of information.

To conclude, it seems that the Efficient Markets Hypothesis does not hold, except perhaps in its very weakest form, in today's capital markets. Evolving from both the EMH and chaos theory is a promising successor termed the Coherent Market Hypothesis (CMH) based on a combination of fundamental factors and market sentiment or technical factors (see Vaga 1991). The CMH argues that capital markets are, at any point in time, in one of the following states, depending on a combination of economic fundamentals and 'crowd behaviour' in the market:

- Random walks – market efficiency with neutral fundamentals
- Unstable transition – market inefficiency with neutral fundamentals
- Coherence – crowd behaviour with bullish fundamentals
- Chaos – crowd behaviour with bearish fundamentals.

We will have to wait to see how well it helps explain stock market behaviour.

Self-assessment Activity 2.7

Q List three important changes to the London Stock Exchange brought about by the 'Big Bang' in 1986 and discuss their impact on market efficiency.

(answer at end of chapter)

2.7 Short-termism in the City

Pressure to perform well has not only led fund managers to increase their activity in managing funds, but may also have led to a more short-term perspective regarding capital investment. The argument is that fund managers focus on the short-term performance of companies in arriving at a valuation of their worth, placing excessive emphasis on current profit performance and dividend payments. Such apparent behaviour is said to have two consequences. First, management, in order to keep up the price of its stock, will tend to focus on producing the short-term results that it thinks the market wants to see. This results in management failing to undertake important long-term investment in resources and research and development. Second, the volatility of short-term corporate results will be exaggerated in securities markets, producing undesirable fluctuations in stock prices.

This chain of argument gained support from a survey carried out by the Department of Trade and Industry's Innovation Advisory Board (1990), which suggested the City placed too high a priority on short-term profits and dividends at the expense of R&D and other innovative investment.

The argument was supported by a Confederation of British Industry (CBI) survey of major companies in 1987, in which 35 per cent doubted that financial institutions take a long-term and strategic evaluation of their companies. As a result, the CBI set up a task force to investigate the whole issue. Its report concluded that many UK companies have given insufficient weight to long-term development, but that this does not arise primarily from City pressure. It arises mainly from underlying economic and political factors, including inadequate profitability (Ferguson 1989).

The problem of short-termism has also been addressed by US researchers (e.g. Graves 1988), who argue that the increasing shareholder power of institutional investors has had a damaging effect on R&D expenditure among US firms.

The EMH argues that rational investors will approve of any long-term investments that make sound economic sense. They will not sell the stock of a fundamentally sound firm undertaking long-term investments that promise remarkably high future cash flows just because that firm has reported one bad trading period. Such short-term stock shuttling is viewed as irrational behaviour.

The City rejects most allegations of short-termism, arguing that much of the responsibility for the lack of long-term innovative investment is attributable to managers' preference for growth by acquisition, their poor record of commercial development and their reward systems based on short-term targets. This view is advocated by Marsh (1990), who claims that:

> There is no evidence that shares are priced in a way which emphasises their short- rather than long-run prospects. Nor is there any evidence that the market penalises long-term investments or expenditure on R&D by awarding the shares of the company in question a lower rating – indeed, quite the contrary.

He identifies 'managerial short-termism' as a key force behind poor investment in the UK. When it comes to making plans for the future, managers' perceptions are influenced by their organisational systems and contexts, including the way they are remunerated and rewarded; their time-horizons within the jobs; the role played by the internal performance measurement and management accounting systems; and the internal capital budgeting and project appraisal systems.

There is broad consensus among all parties to the debate that action is required to improve communication between the City and industry. Emerging very clearly from the debate on short-termism is that UK companies need to improve the information they provide to the capital markets on their R&D activity and other strategic investments if they are to achieve a market rating appropriate to their future expected profitability.

2.8 Reading the financial pages

Corporate finance is changing so quickly that it is essential for students of finance to read the financial pages in newspapers on a regular basis. In this section, we explain the main information contained in the Share Service pages of the *Financial Times*, and other newspapers.

The FT-SE Index

Every day shares move up or down with the release of information from within the firm, such as a revised profits forecast, or from an external source, such as the latest government statistics on inflation or unemployment. To indicate how the whole share market has performed, a share index is used, the most common being the **FT-SE 100** – familiarly known as 'Footsie'. This index is based on the share prices of the 100 most valuable UK quoted companies, (sometimes termed 'blue chips') mostly those with capitalisations above £3 billion, with each company weighted in proportion to its total market value. All the world's major stock markets have similar indices (for example, the Nikkei index in Japan, the Dow Jones index in the USA and the CAC-40 in France).

Every share index is constructed on a base date and base value. The FT-SE 100 started with a base value of 1000 at the end of 1983. By January 2002 the index had increased to 5218, an annual compound growth rate of 18 per cent, well above the rate of inflation over the same period.

The FT-SE Actuaries Share Indices reveal share movements by sector. Their total gives the **All-Share Index**, representing the more frequently traded quoted companies.

Other FT indices

In recent years, the Stock Exchange has introduced several new indices.

- **FT-SE 250** covers medium-sized companies too small to enter the FT-SE 100, with capitalisations in the range £350 million – £3 billion, and accounting for some 25 per cent of market trading. It is calculated both including and excluding investment trusts.
- **FT-SE Actuaries 350** provides the benchmark for investors who wish to focus on the more actively traded large and medium-sized UK companies, and covers 95 per cent of trading by value. It thus combines the FT-SE 100 and the FT-SE 250.
- **FT-SE Small Cap** offers investors a daily measure of the performance of about 500 smaller companies, accounting for about 7 per cent of market trading. Whereas the previous indices are calculated continuously, this is computed only at the close of trading.
- **FT-SE Fledgling** covers some 700 smaller companies taken from the main listing and the Alternative Investment Market (AIM).
- **FT-SE techMARK 100** covers 100 technology stocks.

Using the published information

Financial managers and investors need to study the performance of the shares of their company, both against the appropriate sector as a whole and also against competitors within that sector. Two performance statistics that are most commonly reported are the **dividend yield** and **price:earnings ratio**.

Dividend yield

This is the gross, or pre-tax, dividends of the companies in the sector in the last year as a percentage of the total value of the sector. Generally, sectors with low dividend yields are those with companies where the market expects high growth. The dividend yield for the 300 largest European firms (FTSE Eurotop 300) on 1 January 2002 was just 2.3 per cent – well below the return investors could currently earn on a safe investment in Treasury Bills. This is because shareholders are looking to a capital gain on top of the dividend yield to recompense them for the higher risks involved.

Price:earnings (P:E) ratio

The P:E ratio is a much-used performance indicator. It is the share price divided by the current earnings per share. So for the sector, it is the total market value of the companies represented divided by total sector earnings. The P:E ratio is a measure of the market's confidence in a particular company or industry. A high P:E usually indicates that investors have confidence that profits will grow strongly in future, perhaps after a short-term setback, although irregular events like a rumoured takeover bid will raise the P:E ratio if they lead to a higher share price.

Let us now turn to the performance of individual companies. Table 2.2 is an extract from the London Share Service pages in the *Financial Times*, giving the Food and Drug Retailing sector on 2 January 2002. Different information is provided on Mondays than on other days of the week. We will focus on a major supermarket chain, Tesco Group. Bold names indicate FT-SE 100 stock.

Transactions and prices of stocks are published continuously through SEAQ (the Stock Exchange Automatic Quotation). Quoted prices assume that shareholders buying a share are entitled to any forthcoming dividend (cum div) unless this is expressly precluded. The symbol 'xd' (ex div, i.e. excluding dividends) means that new investors are too late to qualify for it. The share price will accordingly be lower to reflect the forgone dividend.

Tesco's closing share price of 249p is up 1½p from the previous day's trading with over 2.2 million shares traded in the day. The current price is about mid way between its highest and lowest prices over the past year. Every Monday the *Financial Times* publishes the dividend cover and market capitalisation value (i.e. number of issued shares times current share price).

Table 2.2 Share performance for the food retail sector

	Share price[1]	Change since previous day	52-week price range high	low	Trades per day 000s	Dividend yield	P:E
Alldays	7¾	...	20½	7¼	33	–	–
Budgens	99½	+¼	110¾	66¼	113	2.6	13.6
Caffe Nero	36	...	54½	34½	–	–	–
Coffee Republic	7¾	...	30	6¼	65	–	–
Dairy Farm $	45	...	49¾	24	–	–	–
Donatantonio	66½	...	71½	48½	–	4.5	13.2
Greggs	3062½	...	3492½	2387½	–	2.0	15.6
Iceland	178xd	+1½	322½	134½	1,226	0.6	–
John Lusty	1¾	...	3¼	1¼	47	–	3.6
Le Riche	555	...	560	485	–	5.7	13.3
Morrison (W)	201¾	−1¾	220	167¼	219	0.9	21.2
Safeway	320xd	+4¼	421	285¼	564	2.9	13.8
Sainsbury (J)	366xd	+3¾	452¾	318	596	3.9	21.1
Somerfield	84½	+¼	149	77¼	489	–	–
T & S Stores	313½	...	358½	265½	–	3.7	10.9
Tesco	249	+1½	285½	218	2,205	2.1	20.6
Thorntons	102	+1	104	68½	44	6.7	14.4
Whittard of Chelsea	27½	...	38½	20	–	–	–

[1] Share price based on mid price (between selling and buying price) at the end of previous day's trading.

Source: *Financial Times* Wednesday January 2nd 2002

The **Yield** of 2.1 per cent is the pre-tax dividend yield, i.e. the dividend expressed as a proportion of the current share price. The **price:earnings** (P:E) ratio of 20.6 suggests that it would take over 20 years for an investor to get her money back in profit terms. Why should anyone be willing to wait that long? Remember that the calculation compares the last reported earnings per share with the current share price. Investors expect the payback period to be far quicker than 20 years because they anticipate strong earnings growth for Tesco.

2.9 Taxation and financial decisions

Few financial decisions are immune from taxation considerations. *Corporate and personal taxation affects both the cash flows received by companies and the dividend income received by shareholders*. Consequently, financial managers need to understand the tax consequences of investment and financing decisions. Taxation may be important in three key areas of financial management:

1 *Raising finance*. There are clear tax benefits in raising finance by issuing debt rather than capital. Interest on borrowings attracts tax relief, thereby reducing the company's tax bill, while a dividend payment on equity capital does not attract tax relief. The tax system is thereby biased in favour of debt finance.
2 *Investment in fixed assets*. Spending on certain types of fixed asset attracts a form of tax relief termed **capital allowances**. This is intended to stimulate certain types of investment, such as in industrial plant and machinery. The taxation implications of an investment decision can be very important. We discuss capital allowances and tax implications for investment decisions in Chapter 6.
3 *Paying dividends*. Until 1973, in the UK, company profits were effectively taxed twice – first on the profits achieved and then again on those profits paid to shareholders in the form of dividends. Such a 'classical' tax system (which still exists in certain countries, including the USA) is clearly biased in favour of retaining profits rather than paying out large dividends. The UK taxation system is more neutral, the same tax bill being paid (for companies making profits) regardless of the dividend policy.

Finally, the corporate financial manager should understand not only how taxation affects the company, but also how it affects the company's shareholders (**www.inlandrevenue.gov.uk**). For example, some financial institutions (e.g. pension funds) pay no tax; some shareholders pay tax at 20 per cent, while others pay higher-rate income tax at 40 per cent. Some may prefer capital gains to dividends.

Self-assessment Activity 2.8

Explain why it is important to consider the tax implications of financial and investment decisions.

(answer at end of chapter)

Summary

This chapter has introduced readers to the financial and tax environment within which financial and investment decisions take place.

Key points

- Financial markets consist of numerous specialist markets where financial transactions occur (e.g. the money market, capital market, foreign exchange market, derivatives markets).
- Financial institutions (e.g. banks, building societies, pension funds) provide a vital service by acting as financial intermediaries between savers and borrowers.
- Securitisation and disintermediation have permitted larger companies to create alternative, more flexible forms of finance.
- The Stock Exchange operates two tiers: the Official List for larger established companies, and the Alternative Investment Market which mainly caters for very young companies.
- An efficient capital market is one where investors are rational and share prices reflect all available information. The Efficient Markets Hypothesis has been examined in its various forms (weak, semi-strong and strong). In all but the strong form, it seems to hold up reasonably well, but it is increasingly unable to explain 'special' circumstances.
- The problem of 'short-termism' may stem more from managerial attitudes than those of investors.
- Taxation can play a key role in financial management, particularly in raising finance, investing in fixed assets and paying dividends.

Further reading

Brett (1995) provides a clear explanation on how to read the financial pages in the press. Clear and more extensive introductions to capital markets are found in Foley (1991), Weston and Copeland (1988), O'Shea (1986) and Redhead (1990).

The Stock Exchange Fact Book is published annually by the Stock Exchange. Two classic review articles on market efficiency were written by Fama (1970 and 1992), while Rappaport (1987) examines the implications for managers. Tests of capital market efficiency are found in Copeland and Weston (1988) and Keane (1983), while some exceptions to efficiency are found in the June 1977 special issue of *Journal of Financial Economics*. Peters (1991, 1993) applies Chaos Theory to stock markets. Discussion on short-termism in the City is found in Marsh (1990) and Ball (1991). *Mastering Finance* (Pitman 1998) offers useful articles on securitisation, financial intermediaries, the role of financial markets, market efficiency and short-termism.

Useful websites

www.moneyfactor.co.uk
www.moneysupermarket.com
www.moneyextra.com
www.find.co.uk
www.moneynet.co.uk
www.ftourmoney.co.uk

Appendix

Financial statement analysis

Most readers will previously have undertaken a module in accounting and be familiar with financial statements. This appendix provides a summary of the key elements in analysing financial statements and the main ratios involved in interpreting accounts.

Investors, whether shareholders or bank managers, ask three basic questions when they examine the accounts of a business:

Position – what is the current financial position, or state of affairs, of the business? This question is addressed by examining the **balance sheet**, sometimes referred to as the **position statement**.

Performance – how well has the business performed over the period of time we are interested in, for example, the past year? This question is addressed by looking at the **profit and loss account**, otherwise termed the **income statement**.

Prospects – what are the likely prospects of the business for which we are considering investment? A bank manager would probably request a cash flow forecast, showing the expected cash receipts and payments for the coming year. However, published accounts are historical documents and the shareholder will have to settle for the **cash flow statement** for the past year. Clues as to the expected future prospects may be found in the Chairman's Statement frequently published with the accounts.

We will examine the three financial statements, drawing on the abridged accounts of a fictitious company called *Foto-U*, a business specialising in offering instant photographs through photo booths in public places throughout Europe.

The balance sheet

Imagine it is possible to take a financial snapshot of *Foto-U* on the 31 March 2003, the end of its trading year. What we would see are the very things we find in the **balance sheet**. Looking at *Foto-U*'s balance sheet in Table 2.3, we see three main categories – assets, creditors (or liabilities) and capital and reserves. This statement is the accounting equation: the money invested in the business by shareholders and creditors is represented by the assets in which they have been invested.

Table 2.3 *Foto-U* plc

Balance Sheet as at 31 March		
	2003 £m	**2002 £m**
Fixed assets		
Intangible assets	15	10
Tangible assets	117	92
	132	**102**
Current assets		
Stocks	25	24
Debtors	29	25
Investments and short-term deposits	3	–
Cash at bank and in hand	9	5
	66	**54**
Creditors amounts falling due within one year	**(60)**	**(62)**
Net current assets (liabilities)	**6**	**(8)**
Total assets less current liabilities	**138**	**94**
Creditors* amounts falling due after more than one year	(60)	(23)
Net assets	**78**	**71**
Capital and reserves		
Called-up share capital	2	2
Reserves	76	69
Shareholders' funds	**78**	**71**
* The creditors figures includes trade creditors	40	42

Profit and Loss Account for the year ended 31 March		
Turnover – continuing operations	**200**	**190**
Cost of sales (including depreciation of £27 m)	(157)	(160)
Gross profit	**43**	**30**
Administration expenses	(21)	(20)
Operating profit (Earning before interest and taxes)	**22**	**10**
Interest payable	(2)	(2)
Profit before taxation	**20**	**8**
Tax on profit	(6)	(4)
Profit after tax attributable to shareholders	**14**	**4**
Dividends	(7)	(3)
Retained profit for year	**7**	**1**

Cash Flow Statement for the year ended 31 March 2003		
Net cash inflow from operations	36	43
Servicing of finance	(2)	(2)
Taxation	(6)	(4)
Capital expenditure	(57)	(33)
Dividends paid	(7)	(3)
Financing	37	2
Increase in cash in the year	**13**	**6**

Other data: *Foto-U* has 200 million shares in issue.
Share price at 31 March 2003 is 120p (50p for 2002).

Where the cash came from = *Where the cash went*
(*sources of funds*) (*uses of funds*)

Shareholder's funds £78 m + Creditors £60 m = Assets £138 m

The more permanent assets (typically with a life beyond a year) are termed **fixed assets** while the less permanent are termed **current assets**. For *Foto-U*, **intangible** fixed assets refer to patents and goodwill, the latter arising from acquiring another company and paying more for it than the value of its underlying assets. **Tangible** fixed assets include land and buildings, photo booths, plant and machinery, vehicles and fixtures and fittings. Their values are not stated at what they could be sold for, but at their **net book value** – what they originally cost less an estimate of the extent to which they have depreciated in value with use or age.

Current assets represent the less permanent items (typically less than a year) the business owns at the balance sheet date. Our financial snapshot for *Foto-U* captures four items – stocks, debtors, investments and cash. Unlike fixed assets, these items are continuously changing as trading takes place. Trade creditors and bank overdraft, where the amount has to be settled within one year, are deducted from the current assets to give the **net current assets** figure, commonly termed **working capital**. This is the amount of money likely to be turned into cash over the coming weeks. Creditors to be paid after more than a year are typically in the form of medium/long-term loans. Finally, **shareholders' funds** represent the capital originally paid in by shareholders plus any reserves created since then. The most common reserve will be the profit retained in the business rather than paid to the shareholders as dividends.

Does the balance sheet show the worth of the business?

Although the shareholders' funds for *Foto-U* of £78 million is the difference between what it *owns*, in the form of various assets, and what it *owes* to third parties, it would not be correct to say that this is what their investment is worth. The market value for the company is based on what investors are willing to pay for it. But the assets and liabilities are valued according to **generally accepted accounting principles (GAAP)**. We cannot explore them all here, but one principle is that assets are usually valued at their historical cost less a provision for such things as depreciation, in the case of fixed assets, and bad or doubtful debts, in the case of debtors. The key difference is that book values, based on GAAP, are backward-looking, while market values are forward-looking, based on expected future profits and cash flows.

To get some idea of the difference between the market and book values of the shareholders' funds we can look at the share price listed on the Stock Exchange on the balance sheet date. For *Foto-U* the share price at the balance sheet date was 120p. There are 200 million issued shares so the **market capitalisation** is:

200 million shares × 120p a share = £240 million

Comparing the market value with the book value for shareholders' equity, we find a ratio of approximately 3:1 (240 m/78 m). We should not be surprised to find that the market value is so much higher. Successful businesses are much more than a collection of assets less liabilities. They include creative people, successful trading strategies, profitable brands and much more. Generally, we can say that the greater the market-to-book value ratio, the more successful the business.

The profit and loss account

To gain an impression of how well *Foto-U* has performed over the past year we need to turn to the **profit and loss account** or **income statement**. This shows the sales income less the costs of trading. Shareholders are primarily interested in the **profit after tax (PAT)** available for distribution to them in the form of dividends. *Foto-U* has made a **PAT** of £14 million of which half has or will be paid to shareholders in the form of **dividend**, the remainder being **retained profit**, reinvested in the business, hopefully to earn a higher profit next year.

Investors also want to know how much profit has been made from its trading, before the cost of financing is deducted. **Earnings before interest and taxes (EBIT)** for *Foto-U* is:

EBIT = total revenues − operating costs (including depreciation)
= £200 m − £178 m
= £22 m

This is also termed **operating profit**.

Profit is not the sole consideration for investors. They are perhaps more interested in how much cash has been created through successful trading. This can be estimated by adding back the depreciation (a non-cash cost) previously deducted in calculating EBIT. This is termed **earnings before interest, taxes, depreciation and amortisation** (amortisation is just a fancy name for depreciating intangible assets) or **EBITDA**. For our company this is:

EBITDA = EBIT + Depreciation
= £22 m + £27 m
= £49 m

The cash flow statement

The third and final financial statement in a published set of accounts is the **cash flow statement**. This statement is valuable because it reveals the main sources of cash and how it has been applied. For *Foto-U*, the main two sources of cash during the year are additional finance raised from new loans and net cash from operations (basically the EBITDA referred to above plus a few other adjustments for non-cash items). The main applications of this cash generated from trading are investment in capital expenditure and dividends. The final line on this statement shows that, during the year, cash has increased by £7 million.

A financial health check using ratios

Accountants and bank managers have formulated dozens of financial ratios to help diagnose the financial health of the business, its position, performance and prospects. We shall restrict our focus to those key financial ratios that every finance manager and investor should be acquainted with. These are summarised in Table 2.4 and discussed briefly below.

Profitability ratios

To assess the performance of *Foto-U*, we study a number of profitability ratios.

Profit margin

This ratio shows how much profit is generated from every £ of sales. It can be considered at both the gross and net profit levels.

Table 2.4 *Foto-U* key ratios

Ratio		2003	2002
Profitability			
Gross profit margin	%	21.5	15.8
Net profit margin	%	11.0	5.3
Return on capital employed (ROCE)	%	15.9	10.6
Activity ratios			
Net asset turnover	times	1.4	2.0
Debtor days	days	53	48
Stock	days	58	54
Supplier credit period	days	93	96
Liquidity and financing ratios			
Current ratio	times	1.1	0.9
Quick (acid test) ratio	times	0.7	0.5
Gearing	%	43.5	24.5
Interest cover	times	11	5
Investor ratios			
Return on shareholders' funds	%	17.9	5.6
Dividend per share	pence	3.5	1.5
Earnings per share	pence	7	2
Dividend cover	times	2	1.3
Price:earnings	times	17.1	25
Dividend yield	%	2.9	3

Gross profit margin

$$\frac{\text{Gross profit}}{\text{Sales}} \times 100 = \frac{43}{200} \times 100$$
$$= 21.5\% \quad (15.8\% \text{ last year})$$

Net profit margin

$$\frac{\text{EBIT}}{\text{Sales}} \times 100 = \frac{22}{200} \times 100$$
$$= 11\% \quad (5.3\% \text{ last year})$$

(EBIT is earnings before interest and tax, i.e. operating profit.)

Return on capital employed (ROCE)

This ratio, also termed the primary ratio, examines the rate of profit the business makes on the long-term capital invested in it. *Foto-U* has shareholders' funds of £78 million and long-term creditors of £60 million giving long-term capital of £138 million. This is represented by the total assets less current liabilities figure on the balance sheet.

$$\text{ROCE} = \frac{\text{EBIT}}{\text{Long-term capital}} \times 100 = \frac{22}{138} \times 100$$
$$= 15.9\% \quad (10.6\% \text{ last year})$$

Activity ratios

Here we examine how efficiently *Foto-U* manages its assets in terms of the level of sales obtained from the assets invested.

Asset turnover

$$\frac{\text{Sales}}{\text{Total assets} - \text{current liabilities}} = \frac{200}{138}$$
$$= 1.45 \text{ times} \quad (2 \text{ times last year})$$

This can also be expressed in terms of each type of asset, but here we usually express it in terms of days. For example, the average number of days it takes for debtors to pay is given by debtor days.

Debtor days

$$\frac{\text{Debtors}}{\text{Credit sales}} \times 365 = \frac{29}{200} \times 365$$
$$= 53 \text{ days} \quad (48 \text{ days last year})$$

Note also that we have used the asset figure at the year-end. A more accurate picture is given by finding the average asset value based on the values at the start and end of the year.

Similar calculations can be made for stock and creditors, but with one important difference. Stock and trade creditors are valued in the balance sheet at original cost so instead of using sales, we use cost of sales.

Stockholding period

$$\frac{\text{Stock}}{\text{Cost of sales}} \times 365 = \frac{25}{157} \times 365$$

$$= 58 \text{ days} \quad \text{(54 days last year)}$$

Supplier credit days

$$\frac{\text{Trade creditors}}{\text{Cost of sales}} \times 365 = \frac{40}{157} \times 365$$

$$= 93 \text{ days} \quad \text{(96 days last year)}$$

Liquidity and Financing ratios

To assess whether the company is able to meet its financial obligations as they fall due, we need to compare short-term assets with short-term creditors. Two such ratios are commonly employed.

Current ratio

$$\frac{\text{Current assets}}{\text{Current liabilities}} = \frac{66}{60}$$

$$= 1.1 \text{ times} \quad \text{(0.9 times last year)}$$

Quick assets

For most firms, the stock is not easy to convert into cash over the next month or so. The quick assets (or acid-test ratio) is a more prudent liquidity ratio which excludes stock entirely.

$$\frac{\text{Current assets} - \text{stock}}{\text{Current liabilities}} = \frac{66 - 25}{60}$$

$$= 0.7 \text{ times} \quad \text{(0.5 times last year)}$$

As a general rule-of-thumb we would typically expect the current ratio to be 2 and the quick assets to match creditors (i.e. a quick ratio 1). However, this guide may differ from industry to industry depending on the trade credit periods granted to customers and claimed from suppliers.

Gearing

A rather different question asks how the capital employed in the business is financed. The gearing ratio shows the proportion of capital employed funded by long-term borrowings.

$$\frac{\text{Long-term borrowings}}{\text{Dept + Equity capital}} \times 100 = \frac{60}{138} \times 100$$
$$= 43.5\% \quad (24.5\% \text{ last year})$$

An equally acceptable way of expressing the gearing ratio is by the Debt/Equity ratio.

$$\frac{\text{Long-term borrowings}}{\text{Shareholders' funds}} = \frac{60}{78} = 0.77 : 1$$

Interest cover

Another way of considering gearing is to look to the profit and loss account by assessing the degree of profits cover the firm has to meet its interest payments.

$$\frac{\text{Earnings before interest and taxes}}{\text{Interest payable}} = \frac{22}{2}$$
$$= 11 \text{ times (5 times last year)}$$

An interest cover of 11 times is very safe. But were it to fall to, say, below three there may well be concern given that taxation and dividends have not yet been paid.

Investor ratios

Shareholders are more interested in the return they obtain on *their* investment rather than the return the company makes on the total business.

Return on shareholders' funds (return on equity)

This indicates how profitable the company has been for its shareholders.

$$\frac{\text{Earnings after tax and preference dividends} \times 100}{\text{Shareholders' funds}} = \frac{14}{78} \times 100$$
$$= 17.9\% \quad (5.6\% \text{ last year})$$

Shareholders will also be interested in the dividend per share and earnings per share for the year.

Dividend per share

$$\frac{\text{Total ordinary dividend}}{\text{Number of ordinary shares in issue}} = \frac{7}{200}$$
$$= 3.5 \text{ pence per share} \quad (1.5 \text{ pence last year})$$

Earnings per share (EPS)

$$\frac{\text{Earning after tax and preference dividends}}{\text{Number of ordinary shares in issue}} = \frac{14}{200}$$

$$= 7 \text{ pence per share} \quad \text{(2 pence last year)}$$

In practice, the EPS calculation is usually more complex than this, but the notes to the accounts will explain the calculation.

Dividend cover

$$\frac{\text{Earnings per share}}{\text{Divident per share}} = \frac{7}{3.5}$$

$$= 2 \text{ times} \quad \text{(1.3 times last year)}$$

The final two ratios relate earnings and dividends to stock market performance as reflected in the current share price. If the current share price for *Foto-U* is 120p, we can calculate the price:earnings ratio and dividend yield.

Price:earnings ratio (P:E)

$$\frac{\text{Current share price}}{\text{Earnings per share}} = \frac{120}{7}$$

$$= 17.1 \text{ times} \quad \text{(25 times last year)}$$

The share price, of course, is based on investors' expectations of *future* profits. A high P:E ratio indicates that investors expect future profits to grow – the higher the P:E, the greater the profit growth expectation.

Dividend yield

$$\frac{\text{Dividend per share}}{\text{Share price}} \times 100 = \frac{3.5}{120} \times 100$$

$$= 2.9\% \quad \text{(3\% last year)}$$

In the UK, income tax has effectively been deducted at source, so the calculation should therefore be based on the gross dividend.

Interpretation of the accounts and ratios

The financial manager or investor needs to put together all the clues suggested by ratio analysis and reading the accounts to gain insights into the financial position, performance and prospects of the company. This will probably involve looking at the trend of financial indicators, not simply comparison with the previous year, together with comparison with industry and competitor data. It certainly requires a reasonable grasp of the business, its objectives and strategies. Table 2.5 offers a brief report to senior management of *Foto-U* by the finance manager on the company's published accounts.

Table 2.5 *Foto-U* annual corporate performance report

To: Senior Management of *Foto-U*
From: Finance Manager

Subject: Annual corporate performance
30 April 2003

I have reviewed the published accounts for the past year to establish how successful *Foto-U* was in financial terms.

Profitability. The Return on Capital Employed has improved over the year from 10.6% to 16%. This is a significant improvement and well above the risk-free return we would expect from investing in say building society deposits, but we need also to compare the return against that achieved by our competitors. ROCE is a combination of two subsidiary ratios – net profit margin and asset turnover:

	ROCE	=	**Net profit margin**	×	**Asset turnover**
2002	10.6%	=	5.3%	×	2 times
2003	15.9%	=	11%	×	1.45 times

Both the gross and net profit margins have improved significantly as a result of the £10 million growth in sales over the year without any increase in costs. However, this growth has come at the expense of a poorer utilisation of our assets, as reflected in the significant decline in asset turnover. This is mainly attributable to a major capital expenditure programme during the year, the benefits of which will not be fully experienced for at least another year. A further factor is the increase in working capital. Last year, we actually managed to have negative working capital (i.e. our trade creditors and overdraft financed more than our current assets). This year, there has been a slight deterioration in all elements of working capital:

- We take five more days to collect cash from customers
- Stockholding period has increased by four days
- We pay suppliers a little quicker.

Liquidity. Our current and quick asset ratios are both well below the typical level for the industry of 1.8 and 1.0 respectively. However, this is largely due to the fact that our suppliers have been willing to grant us extended credit periods of about three months. Realistically, we cannot expect this to continue. Were they to demand payment within say, 45 days, it is difficult to see where we would be able to find the cash. It is not good financial management for us to rely on the generous credit of suppliers over whom we have no control, and we need to address this issue urgently. Linked to this, we have just raised a large medium-term loan in order to fund our capital expenditure in the coming year. Our gearing ratio has now nearly doubled and we will have to find cash both for additional interest payments and, eventually, the loan repayments. Unless the new investment very rapidly produces higher profits and cashflow, I am concerned that we could be in serious financial difficulty, despite the strong level of profits. Perhaps it is time to consider asking shareholders to invest more capital in the business or to reduce dividend payments.

Investment attractiveness. The company's share price has progressed from 50 pence to 120 pence over the year. No doubt this is due to the growth in sales, profits and dividends in the year. Many of the investment performance indicators have improved, particularly earnings per share and return on shareholders' funds, the latter looking much healthier at nearly 18%. However, the price:earnings ratio has slipped a little, suggesting that investors do not expect the company's profits and share price to continue to grow at quite the same rate as this year.

In summary, *Foto-U* has improved its performance over the past year, but there remain concerns regarding its liquidity. Management is urged to give urgent attention to this matter.

Self-assessment Answers

2.1 (1) Financial intermediaries are the various financial institutions, such as pension funds, insurance companies, banks, building societies, unit trusts and specialist investment institutions. Their role is to accept deposits from personal and corporate savers to lend to customers (e.g. companies) via the capital and money markets.

Financial intermediaries perform a vital economic service:

(a) Re-packaging finance: collecting small amounts of finance and re-packaging into larger bundles for specific lending requirements (e.g. banks).
(b) Risk reduction: investing sums, on behalf of individuals and companies, into large, well-diversified investment portfolios (e.g. pension funds and unit trusts).
(c) Liquidity transformation: bringing together short-term lenders and long-term borrowers (e.g. building societies).
(d) Cost reduction and advice: minimising transaction costs and providing low-cost services to lenders and borrowers.

2.2 Companies using the main Listed Securities Market are generally those with a lengthy track record (i.e. a history of stable/growing sales and profits), seeking large amounts of capital, where the board is prepared to release a sizeable proportion of its controlling interest.

AIM is designed to appeal to smaller and growing companies which seek access to risk capital or where the board wishes to sell some of its holding, but cannot meet all the requirements for a full listing and prefers less regulation.

The OTC market is for the remaining, smaller companies where shareholders occasionally wish to dispose of shares. This is performed on a 'matched bargain' basis, using facilities offered by authorised securities dealers.

2.3 A major function of an active capital market is to provide a mechanism whereby investors can realise their holdings by selling securities, and, obviously, for every seller, there has to be a buyer. Investors will be reluctant to commit their funds to the capital market by subscribing to new share issues if they doubt their ability to find a willing buyer as and when they decide to sell their holdings. The more liquid the market, the greater its ability to entice firms to make new share issues and investors to subscribe to them. Where market liquidity is poor, companies will have to offer much higher returns, making share issues uneconomic.

2.4 If these rules ever applied, investors would have soon realised the potential, and would have bought in November rather in advance of the expected price increase in December, thus creating a 'November effect', and so on.

Try the same argument on the old stock market advice 'Sell in May, and go away, and come back on St. Leger Day' (the date of a horse race in the UK).

Many statistical tests have shown that all such dealing rules are usually inferior, and never superior, to a simple 'buy and hold' strategy.

2.5
- On the face of it, this represents insider dealing, by people in the know.
- It could represent speculation and rumour. If the company is known to be weak, then it is a candidate for takeover and people begin to speculate about how much the company may be worth in the hands of an alternative owner.

- Most bidders build up a 'strategic stake' in a takeover target prior to formal announcement. The present UK rules *(The Take-over Code)* allow a holding of up to 3% without declaration of beneficial ownership. The upward movement could simply be due to this buying pressure. In reality, 'abnormal' buying also promotes speculation.

2.6 **(1)** Some people are simply lucky.
(2) Some people stay lucky for several time periods, although shrewd ones remember to get out while ahead!
(3) In any time period, 50 per cent of investors ought to beat the market average.
(4) Some people deliberately assume high levels of risk for which a relatively high return is appropriate. We should therefore talk about 'risk-adjusted returns' rather than simple returns.
(5) Some people have access to inside information. This, of course, contravenes strong-form efficiency but it happens, although such information is unlikely to arrive in a steady stream over time.

2.7 **(1)** Admission of corporate and overseas membership with access to larger sources of capital.
(2) Introduction of Stock Exchange Automated Quotation System (SEAQ) hastening the movement of trading away from the floor of the Exchange to dealing by telephone and computer. This has led to quicker dissemination of information, enabling it to be incorporated more rapidly into share prices. Thus the market has become more information-efficient in the semi-strong form.
(3) Abolition of minimum commission and the expansion of membership have led to greater competition for business among market makers. As a result, commission rates have fallen markedly.

2.8 The reader is refered to Section 2.9

Questions

1 When a company seeks a listing for its shares on a stock exchange, it usually recruits the assistance of a merchant bank.

(a) Explain the role of a merchant bank in a listing operation with respect to the various matters on which its advice will be sought by a company.
(b) Identify the conflicts which might arise if the merchant bank were part of a group providing a wide range of financial services.

(CIMA)

2 **(a)** Briefly outline the major functions performed by the capital market and explain the importance of each function for corporate financial management. How does the existence of a well-functioning capital market assist the financial management function?
(b) Describe the Efficient Markets Hypothesis and explain the differences between the three forms of the hypothesis which have been distinguished.
(c) *Solution in Appendix A (page 801).* Company A has 2 million shares in issue and company B 6 million. On day 1 the market value per share is £2 for A and £3 for B. On day 2, the management of B decides, at a private meeting, to make a cash

takeover bid for A at a price of £3.00 per share. The takeover will produce large operating savings with a value of £3.2 million. On day 4, B publicly announces an unconditional offer to purchase all shares of A at a price of £3.00 per share with settlement on day 15. Details of the large savings are not announced and are not public knowledge. On day 10, B announces details of the savings which will be derived from the takeover.

Required

Ignoring tax and the time-value of money between days 1 and 15, and assuming the details given are the only factors having an impact on the share prices of A and B, determine the day 2, day 4 and day 10 share prices of A and B if the market is:

1 semi-strong form efficient, and
2 strong form efficient

in each of the following separate circumstances:

(i) the purchase consideration is cash as specified above, and
(ii) the purchase consideration, decided upon on day 2 and publicly announced on day 4, is one newly issued share of B for each share of A.

(ACCA)

3 You are an accountant with a practice, which includes a large proportion of individual clients, who often ask for information about traded investments. You have extracted the following data from a leading financial newspaper.

(i)

Stock	Price	P:E ratio	Dividend yield (% gross)
Buntam plc	160p	20	5
Zellus plc	270p	15	3.33

(ii) Earnings and dividend data for Crazy Games plc are given below:

	1993	1994	1995	1996	1997
EPS	5p	6p	7p	10p	12p
Div. per share (gross)	3p	3p	3.5p	5p	5.5p

The estimated before tax return on equity required by investors in Crazy Games plc is 20%.

Required

Draft a report for circulation to your private clients which explains:

(a) the factors to be taken into account (including risks and returns) when considering the purchase of different types of traded investments.
(b) the role of financial intermediaries, and their usefulness to the private investor.
(c) the meaning and the relevance to the investor of each of the following:
  (i) Gross dividend (pence per share)
  (ii) EPS
  (iii) Dividend cover

Your answer should include calculation of, and comment upon, the gross dividends, EPS and dividend cover for Buntam plc and Zellus plc, based on the information given above.

(ACCA)

4 Beta plc has been trading for twelve years and during this period has achieved a good profit record. To date, the company has not been listed on a recognised stock exchange. However, Beta plc has recently appointed a new chairman and managing director who are considering whether or not the company should obtain a full Stock Exchange listing.

Required

(a) What are the advantages and disadvantages which may accrue to the company and its shareholders, of obtaining a full stock exchange listing?

(b) What factors should be taken into account when attempting to set an issue price for new equity shares in the company, assuming it is to be floated on a stock exchange?

(Certified Diploma)

5 Collingham plc produces electronic measuring instruments for medical research. It has recorded strong and consistent growth during the past 10 years since its present team of managers bought it out from a large multinational corporation. They are now contemplating obtaining a stock market listing.

Collingham's accounting statements for the last financial year are summarised below. Fixed assets, including freehold land and premises, are shown at historic cost net of depreciation. The debenture is redeemable in two years although early redemption without penalty is permissible.

Profit and Loss Account for the year ended 31 December 1994

£m	
Turnover	80.0
Cost of sales	(70.0)
Operating profit	10.0
Interest charges	(3.0)
Pre-tax profit	7.0
Corporation tax (after capital allowances)	(1.0)
Profits attributable to ordinary shareholders	6.0
Dividends	(0.5)
Retained earnings	5.5

Balance Sheet as at 31 December 1994

£m Assets employed		
Fixed: Land and premises	10.0	
Machinery	20.0	30.0
Current: Stocks	10.0	
Debtors	10.0	
Cash	3.0	23.0
Current liabilities: Trade creditors	(15.0)	
Bank overdraft	(5.0)	(20.0)
Net current assets		3.0
Total assets less current liabilities		33.0

14% Debentures	(5.0)
Net assets	28.0
Financed by:	
Issued share capital (par value 50p):	
Voting shares	2.0
Non-voting 'A' shares	2.0
Profit and Loss Account	24.0
Shareholders' funds	28.0

The following information is also available regarding key financial indicators for Collingham's industry.

Return on (long-term) capital employed	22% (pre-tax)
Return on equity	14% (post-tax)
Operating profit margin	10%
Current ratio	1.8:1
Acid test	1.1:1
Gearing (total debt/equity)	18%
Interest cover	5.2
Dividend cover	2.6
P:E ratio	13:1

Required

(a) Briefly explain why companies like Collingham seek stock market listings.

(b) Discuss the performance and financial health of Collingham in relation to that of the industry as a whole.

(c) In what ways would you advise Collingham:

  (i) to restructure its balance sheet prior to flotation,

  (ii) to change its financial policy following flotation?

Practical assignment

Select two companies from one sector in the Financial Times share information service. Analyse the share price and other data provided and compare with the FT All-Share Index data for the sector. Suggest why the P:E ratios for the companies differ.

3 Present values and financial arithmetic

An investment parable

A man, going off to another country, called together his servants and loaned them money to invest for him while he was gone. He gave £500 to one, £200 to another and £100 to the last – dividing it in proportion to their abilities – and then left on his trip. The man who received the £500 began immediately to buy and sell with it and soon earned another £500. The man with £200 went right to work, too, and earned another £200. But the man who received the £100 dug a hole in the ground and hid the money for safe keeping.

After a long time their master returned from his trip and called them to him to account for his money. The man to whom he had entrusted the £500 brought him £1,000. His master praised him for good work. 'You have been faithful in handling this small amount,' he told him, 'so now I will give you many more responsibilities.' Next came the man who had received £200, with the report, 'Sir, you gave me £200 to use, and I have doubled it.' 'Good work', his master said. 'You have been faithful over this small amount, so now I will give you much more.'

Then the man with the £100 came and said, 'Sir, I knew you were a hard man, and I was afraid you would rob me of what I earned, so I hid your money in the earth and here it is!'

But his master replied, 'You lazy rogue! Since you knew I would demand your profit, you should at least have put my money into the bank so I could have some interest.'

Matthew, Chapter 25, *Living Bible*

Learning objectives

Having completed this chapter, you should have a sound grasp of the time-value of money and discounted cash flow concepts. In particular, you should understand the following:

- The time-value of money.
- The financial arithmetic underlying compound interest and discounting.
- Present value formulae for single amounts, annuities, perpetuities and bonds.
- The net present value approach and why it is consistent with shareholder goals.

Skills developed in discounted cash flow analysis, using both formulae and tables, will help enormously in subsequent chapters.

3.1 Introduction

The above investment parable, taken from business life in 1st century Palestine, is equally appropriate to present times. Managers are expected to make sound long-term decisions and to manage resources in the best interests of the owners. To do otherwise is to risk the wrath of an unmerciful stock market! Rather like the lazy servant in the parable, Eurotunnel put the £10 billion entrusted to it by shareholders and bankers into a 'hole in the ground' stretching from Dover to Calais. From an investment perspective they would have done better letting it earn interest in a bank.

To assess whether investment ideas are wealth-creating, we need to have a clear understanding of cash flow and the time-value of money. Capital investment decisions, security and bond value analyses, financial structure decisions, lease vs. buy decisions and the tricky question of the required rate of return can be addressed only when you understand exactly what the old expression 'time is money' really means.

In this chapter we will consider the measurement of wealth and the fundamental role it plays in the decision-making process; the time-value of money, which underlies the discounted cash flow concept; and the net present value approach for analysing investment decisions.

3.2 Measuring wealth

'Cash flow is King' seems to be the message for businesses today. Spectacular business collapses in recent years demonstrate that reliance on profits or earnings per share as measures of performance can be dangerous.

The chairman of Rockwood Holdings stated in an annual report: 'Last year, we delivered a 425% increase in turnover from £19.9 million to £109.8 million.' But when Rockwood was placed into the hands of the receiver the following year, it was not the lack of sales or even profits that put it there. It was the lack of cash. Businesses go 'bust' because they run out of the cash required to fulfil their financial obligations. Of course, there are always reasons why this happens – recession, an over-ambitious investment programme, rapid growth without adequate long-term finance – but basically corporate survival and success come down to cash flow and value creation.

Boo.com, the internet fashion retailer, thought it had a promising future at the start of 2000. It had raised $135 million to set up the new business and invest in marketing to break into the competitive fashion retail sector. But less than six months later, it had virtually run out of cash and was forced into liquidation.

Recall from Chapter 1 that the assumed objective of the firm is to create as much wealth as possible for its shareholders. A successful business is one that creates value for its owners. Wealth is created when the market value of the outputs exceeds the market value of the inputs, i.e. the benefits are greater than the costs. Expressed mathematically:

$$V_j = B_j - C_j$$

The value (V_j) created by decision j is the difference between the benefits (B_j) and the costs (C_j) attributable to the decision. This leads to an obvious decision rule: accept only those investment or financing proposals that enhance the wealth of shareholders, i.e. accept if $B_j - C_j > 0$.

Nothing could be simpler in concept – the problems emerge only when we probe more deeply into how the benefits and costs are measured and evaluated. One obvious problem is that benefits and costs usually occur at different times and over a number of years. This leads us to consider the **time-value of money**.

Boo.com collapses as investors refuse funds

Boo.com, the online sportswear retailer, last night became Europe's first big internet casualty when the refusal of its backers to continue funding its heavy losses forced it into liquidation. The company – one of the highest profile internet retailers in Europe – appointed KPMG as liquidator, having spent all but $500,000 of the $135 million it had raised since early last year.

Boo's founders, including former model Kajsa Leander and Ernst Malmsten, chief executive, own about 40 per cent of the equity. Ernst Malmsten said last night: 'It could be a big blow for the internet in Europe and frighten investors from investing in start-ups because they could lose their reputation as well as their funding. We have been too visionary. We wanted everything to be perfect, and we have not had control of costs. My mistake has been not to have a counterpart who was a strong financial controller'.

After a high-profile launch, the company was dogged by technical problems that delayed the site going live by five months. Boo needed $430 million to implement an emergency restructuring plan that would have seen redundancies among the 300-strong workforce and closure of some overseas offices. But investors were not prepared to back the plan with more money.

Based on *Financial Times*, May 18 2000

3.3 Time-value of money

An important principle in financial management is that the value of money depends on *when* the cash flow occurs – £100 *now* is worth more than £100 at some *future* time. There are a number of reasons for this:

1 *Risk*. One hundred pounds now is certain, whereas £100 receivable next year is less certain. This 'bird-in-the-hand' principle affects many aspects of financial management.
2 *Inflation*. Under inflationary conditions, the value of money, in terms of its purchasing power over goods and services, declines.
3 *Personal consumption preference*. Most of us have a strong preference for immediate rather than delayed consumption.

More fundamental than any of the above, however, is the time-value of money. Money – like any other desirable commodity – has a price. If you own money, you can 'rent' it to someone else, say a banker, and earn interest. A business which carries unnecessarily high cash balances incurs an opportunity cost – the lost opportunity to earn money by investing it to earn a higher return. The investor's return, which reflects the time-value of money, therefore comprises:

(a) the risk-free rate of return rewarding investors for forgoing immediate consumption, plus
(b) compensation for risk and loss of purchasing power.

Self-assessment Activity 3.1

Imagine you went to your bank manager asking for a £50,000 loan, for five years, to start up a burger bar under a McDonald's franchise. Which of the considerations in the previous paragraph would the bank manager consider?

(answer at end of chapter)

Before proceeding further, we need to understand the essential financial arithmetic for the time-value of money. This will stand readers in good stead not only in analysing capital and financial investments in the remainder of this book, but also in handling their personal finances. For example, it will provide a better understanding of how interest is calculated for credit cards, bank loans, repayment mortgages and hire purchase arrangements.

3.4 Financial arithmetic for capital growth

Simple and compound interest

The future value (FV) of a sum of money invested at a given annual rate of interest will depend on whether the interest is paid only on the original investment (**simple interest**), or whether it is calculated on the original investment plus accrued interest (**compound interest**). In the case of compound interest, another factor also affects the future value, namely the frequency with which interest is paid (e.g. monthly, quarterly or annually). We examine these below.

With simple interest, the future value is determined by:

$$FV_n = V_o(1 + in)$$

where FV_n is the future value at time n, V_o is the original sum invested, sometimes termed the principal (note that the o subscript refers to the time period, i.e. today), and i is the annual rate of interest.

Suppose you win £1,000 on the National Lottery and decide to invest it at 10 per cent for five years, simple interest. The future value will be the original £1,000 capital plus five years' interest of £100 a year, giving a total future value of £1,500.

$$FV_5 = £1{,}000[1 + (0.10)(5)] = £1{,}500$$

With compound interest, the interest is paid on the original capital plus accrued interest. The process of compounding provides a convenient way of adjusting for the time-value of money. An investment made now in the capital market of V_o gives rise to a cash flow of $V_o(1 + i)^2$ after two years, and so on. In general, the future value of V_o invested today at a compound rate of interest of i per cent for n years will be:

$$FV_{(i,n)} = V_o(1 + i)^n$$

Suppose your £1,000 investment were put into a building society paying a fixed 10 per cent a year compound interest. What will your investment be worth after five years?

In one year's time, the investment will be worth

$$£1{,}000(1 + 0.10) = £1{,}100$$

After two years it will be worth $£1{,}000(1 + 0.10)^2 = £1{,}210$ and after five years, it will be worth:

$$FV_5 = £1{,}000(1 + 0.10)^5 = £1{,}610$$

Note that the effect of compound interest yields a much higher value than simple interest, which yielded only £1,500.

In practice, the situation is frequently more complex. Adjustment to the formula is required in two main areas: namely, where the interest rate changes and when interest is paid more frequently than annually.

Interest rate changes

Building societies and banks usually offer variable, rather than fixed, rates of interest. Assume the rate of 10 per cent remains for the first two years then falls to 8 per cent for years 3 to 5. The calculation now has two elements:

$$FV_5 = £1{,}000(1 + 0.10)^2(1 + 0.08)^3 = £1{,}524$$

More frequent compounding and annual percentage rates

Unless otherwise stated, it is assumed that compounding or discounting is an annual process; cash payments of benefits arise either at the start or the end of the year. Frequently, however, the contractual payment period is less than one year. Building societies and government bonds pay interest semi-annually or quarterly. Interest charged on credit cards is applied monthly. To compare the true costs or benefits of such financial contracts, it is necessary to determine the **annual percentage rate** (APR), or effective annual interest rate.

Returning to our earlier example of £1,000 invested for five years at 10 per cent compound interest, we now assume 5 per cent payable every six months.

After the first six months, the interest is £50, which is reinvested to give interest for the second half year of (£1,050 × 5%) = £52. The end-of-year value is therefore (£1,050 + £52) = £1,102. We can still use the compound interest formula, but with i as the six-monthly interest rate and n the six-monthly, rather than annual, interval:

$$\begin{aligned}\text{After 1 year, } FV_1 &= £1{,}000(1 + 0.05)^2\\ &= £1{,}102\\ \text{After 5 years, } FV_5 &= £1{,}000(1 + 0.05)^{10}\\ &= £1{,}629\end{aligned}$$

Note that this value is higher than the £1,610 value based on the earlier annual interval calculation. In converting the annual compounding formula to another interest payment frequency, the trick is simply to divide the annual rate of interest (i) and multiply the time (n) by the number of payments each year.

If, in the above example, interest is calculated at weekly intervals over five years, the future value will be:

$$FV_5 = £1{,}000\left(1 + \frac{0.10}{52}\right)^{52(5)} = £1{,}648$$

Table 3.1 calculates the APRs based on a range of interest payment frequencies for a 22 per cent per annum loan. By charging compound interest on a daily

Table 3.1 Annual percentage rates for a loan with interest payable at 22 per cent per annum

Annually	$(1 + 0.22) - 1$	$= 0.22$ or 22%
Semi-annually	$\left(1 + \frac{0.22}{2}\right)^2 - 1$	$= 0.232$ or 23.2%
Quarterly	$\left(1 + \frac{0.22}{4}\right)^4 - 1$	$= 0.239$ or 23.9%
Monthly	$\left(1 + \frac{0.22}{12}\right)^{12} - 1$	$= 0.244$ or 24.4%
Daily	$\left(1 + \frac{0.22}{365}\right)^{365} - 1$	$= 0.246$ or 24.6%

basis, the effective annual rate is 24.6 per cent, some 2.6 per cent higher than on an annual basis. It is now a legal requirement for many financial contracts that the lender clearly states the APR.

Continuous compounding

Taking compounding to its limit, we can adopt a continuous compounding approach. When the number of compounding periods each year approaches infinity, the future value is found by:

$$FV_n = V_o e^{in}$$

where i is the annual interest rate, n is the number of years and e is the value of the exponential function. Using a scientific calculator, this is shown as 2.71828 (to five decimal places).

To illustrate the above, we find the future value of £1,000 invested at a continuously compounded rate of 10 per cent p.a. for four years:

$$FV_4 = V_o e^{in} = £1,000\ e^{(0.1)4}$$
$$= £1,491.82$$

This compares with annual compounding of £1,000$(1.10)^4$ = £1,464.

3.5 Present value

An alternative way of assessing the worth of an investment is to invert the compounding process to give the **present value** of the future cash flows. This process is called **discounting**.

The time-value of money principle argues that, given the choice of £100 now or the same amount in one year's time, it is always preferable to take the £100 now because it could be invested over the next year at, say, a 10 per cent interest rate to produce £110 at the end of one year. If 10 per cent is the best available annual rate of interest, then one would be indifferent to (i.e. attach equal value to) receiving £100 now or £110 in one year's time. Expressed another way, the *present value* of £110 received one year hence is £100.

We obtained the present value (PV) simply by dividing the future cash flow by 1 plus the rate of interest, i, i.e.

$$PV = \frac{£110}{(1 + 0.10)} = \frac{£110}{(1.1)} = £100$$

Discounting is the process of adjusting future cash flows to their present values. It is, in effect, compounding in reverse.

Recall that earlier we specified the future value as:

$$FV_n = V_o(1 + i)^n$$

Dividing both sides by $(1 + i)^n$:

$$\text{Present value} = \frac{FV_n}{(1 + i)^n}$$

which can be read as the present value of future cash flow FV receivable in n years' time given a rate of interest i. This is the process of discounting future sums to their present values.

Let us apply the present value formula to compute the present value of £133 receivable three years hence, discounted at 10 per cent:

$$PV_{(10\%, 3 \text{ yrs})} = \frac{£133}{(1 + 0.10)^3} = \frac{£133}{1.33} = £100$$

The message is: do not pay more than £100 today for an investment offering a certain return of £133 after three years, assuming a 10 per cent market rate of interest.

Calculator tip

Your calculator should have a power function key, usually x^y. Try the following steps for the previous example.

Input	1.1
Press	x^y function key
Input	3
Press	=
Display	1.331
Press	1/x
Multiply	133
Press	=
Answer	99.9

Self-assessment Activity 3.2

Calculate the present value of £623 receivable in eight years' time plus £1,092 receivable eight years after that, assuming an interest rate of 7 per cent.

(answer at end of chapter)

Discount tables

Much of the tedium of using formulae and power functions can be eased by using discount tables or computer-based spreadsheet packages. In the previous example, the **discount factor** for £1 for a 10 per cent discount rate in three years' time is:

$$\frac{1}{(1.10)^3} = \frac{1}{1.33} = 0.751$$

Damned usurers

The lending of money at interest goes back, at least, to the Babylon of Hammurabi in 1775 BC. So does its regulation. For much of our millennium, in many societies that meant condemnation. The Torah goes half-way, instructing Jews that:

> *to a foreigner thou mayest lend upon interest, but unto thy brother thou shalt not.*

The Koran damns interest outright:

> *They say, "Interest is like trade". But God has permitted trade and forbidden interest.*

The Christian church had long viewed interest-taking as a sin, and a council of bishops held in France in 1312 hardened this into a threat of excommunication for those who did it, or even rulers who allowed them to. Dante, writing about that time, put usurers amid the fiery sand of the seventh circle of Hell.

In practice, as commerce developed, Muslims and Christians alike sidestepped these rules; Jews happily lent, at interest, to both, as their own selective prohibition allowed. Yet as late as 1571 an English law banned interest-taking afresh, with special penalties for rates above 10 per cent. And though such bans, always flouted, in time were dropped, regulation of maximum rates went on, for consumer credit, until 1974 in Britain, and to this day in parts of the United States and elsewhere. Even Adam Smith supported this limitation, to stop capital being lavished at high rates on 'prodigals and projectors': so much for market choice.

And in the past 20 years some Islamic states, notably Iran and Pakistan, have tried to reimpose the Koranic ban – in practice, that is, to make bankers find ways round it.

Based on *The Economist*, December 31 1999

This can be found in Appendix B by locating the 10 per cent column and the 3 year row. We call this the **present value interest factor** (PVIF) and express it as $\text{PVIF}_{(10\%,3\text{ yrs})}$ or $\text{PVIF}_{(10,3)}$.

Multiplying the cash flow of £133 by the discount factor yields the same result as before:

$$\text{PV} = £133 \times 0.751 = £100 \text{ (subject to rounding)}$$

With a constant annual cash flow, termed an **annuity**, we can short-cut the discounting operation. Appendix C provides the **present value interest factor for an annuity** (PVIFA). Thus, if £133 is to be received in each of the next three years, the present value is:

$$\begin{aligned}\text{PV} &= £133 \times \text{PVIFA}_{(10\%,\ 3\text{ yrs})}\\ &= £133 \times 2.4868 = £331\end{aligned}$$

It is standard practice to write interest factors as: Interest factor(rate, period).

Examples:

$PVIF_{(8,10)}$ is the present-value interest factor at 8 per cent for ten years.
$PVIFA_{(10,4)}$ is the present-value interest factor for an annuity at 10 per cent for four years.

Example of present values: Soldem Pathetic plc

Soldem Pathetic Football Club has recently been bought up by a wealthy businessman who intends to return the club to its former glory days. He also wants to pay a good dividend to the shareholders of the newly-formed quoted company by making sound investments in quality players. One such player the manager would dearly like in his squad is Bryan Riggs, currently on the market for around £9 million. The chairman reckons that, quite apart from the extra income at the turnstiles from buying him, he could be sold for £11 million by the end of the year, given the way transfer prices are moving. Should he bid for Riggs?

Assuming a 10 per cent rate of interest as the reward that the other shareholders demand for accepting the delayed payoff, the present value (PV) of £11 million receivable one year hence is:

$$PV = \text{discount factor} \times \text{future cash flow} = \frac{1}{1.10} \times £11 \text{ million}$$
$$= £10 \text{ million}$$

How much better off will the club be if it buys Riggs? The answer is, in present value terms:

£10 million − £9 million = £1 million

We call this the **net present value** (NPV). The decision to buy the player makes economic sense; it promises to create wealth for the club and its shareholders, even excluding the likely additional gate receipts. Of course, Riggs could break a leg in the very first game for his new club and never play again. In such an unfortunate situation, the club would achieve a negative NPV of £9 million, the initial cost. Alternatively, he could be insured against such injury, in which case there would be premiums to pay, resulting in a lower net present value.

Another way of looking at this issue is to ask whether the investment offers a return greater than could have been achieved by investing in financial, rather than human, assets. The return over one year from acquiring Riggs' services is:

$$\text{Return} = \frac{\text{Profit}}{\text{investment}} = \frac{£11\text{ m} - £9\text{ m}}{£9\text{ m}} \times 100 = 22.2\%$$

If the available rate of interest is 10 per cent, the investment in Riggs is a considerably more rewarding prospect.

In this highly simplified example, we assumed that the future value was certain and the interest rate known. Of course, a spectrum of interest rates is listed in the financial press.

Continued

This variety of rates arises predominantly because of uncertainty surrounding the future and imperfections in the capital market. To simplify our understanding of the time-value of money concept, let us 'assume away' these realities. The lender knows with certainty the future returns arising from the proposal for which finance is sought, and can borrow or lend on a perfect capital market. The latter assumes the following:

1 Relevant information is freely available to all participants in the market.
2 No transaction costs or taxes are involved in using the capital market.
3 No participant (borrower or lender) can influence the market price for funds by the scale of its activities.
4 All participants can lend and borrow at the same rate of interest.

Under such conditions, the corporate treasurer of a major company like Shell can raise funds no more cheaply than the chairman of Soldem Pathetic. A single market rate of interest prevails. Borrowers and lenders will base time-related decisions on this unique market rate of interest. The impact of uncertainty will be discussed in later chapters; for now, these simplistic assumptions will help us to grasp the basics of financial arithmetic.

The effect of discounting

Figure 3.1 shows how the discounting process affects present values at different rates of interest between 0 and 20 per cent. The value of £1 decreases very significantly as the rate and period increase. Indeed, after 10 years, for an interest rate of 20 per cent, the present value of a cash flow is only a small fraction of its nominal value.

Table 3.2 summarises the discount factors for three rates of interest. It is useful to develop a 'feel' for how money changes with time for these rates of interest. The 15 per cent discount rate is particularly useful, because investment surveys (e.g. Pike 1988) suggest that this is a popular discount rate for evaluating capital projects. It also happens to be easy to remember: every five years the discounted value halves. Thus, with a 15 per cent discount rate, after five years the value of £1 is 50p, after 10 years 25p, etc.

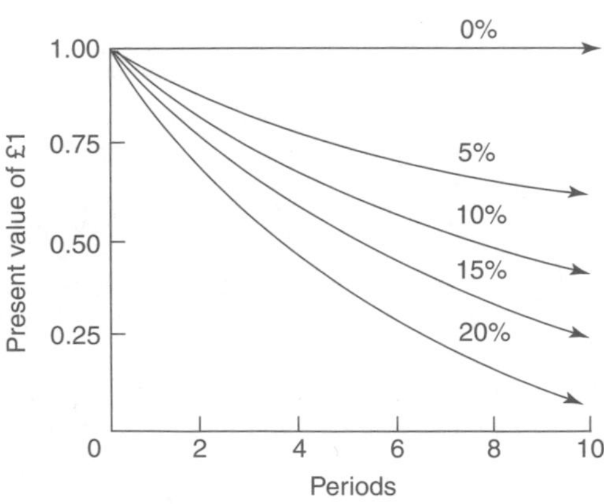

Figure 3.1 The relationship between present value of £1 and interest over time

Table 3.2 Present value of a single future sum

Year	10%	15%	20%
0	£1.00	£1.00	£1.00
5	0.60	0.50	0.40
10	0.40	0.25	0.16
15	0.24	0.12	0.06
20	0.15	0.06	0.03
25	0.09	0.03	0.01

Self-assessment Activity 3.3

Your company is just about to sign a deal to purchase a fleet of lorries for £1 million. The payment terms are £500,000 down payment and £500,000 at the end of five years. No one present has a calculator or discount tables to hand. If the cost of capital for the company is 15 per cent, what is the present value cost of the purchase?

(answer at end of chapter)

3.6 Present value arithmetic

We have seen that the present value of a future cash flow is found by multiplying the cash flow by the present value interest factor. The present value concept is not difficult to apply in practice. This section explains the various present value formulae, and illustrates how they can be applied to investment and financing problems. Throughout, we shall use the symbol X to denote annual cash flow in pounds and i to denote the interest, or discount, rate (expressed as a percentage).

Present value

We know that the present value of X receivable in n years is calculated from the expression:

$$PV_{(i,n)} = \frac{X_n}{(1 + i)^n}$$
$$= X \text{ times } PVIF_{(i,n)}$$

Example

Calculate the present value of £1,000 receivable in 10 years' time, assuming a discount rate of 14 per cent:

$$PVIF_{(14,10)} = \frac{1}{(1.14)^{10}} = 0.26974$$

Alternatively, the table in Appendix B provides PVIF of 0.26974 for $n = 10$ and $i = 14$ per cent:

$$PV = £1{,}000 \times 0.26974 = £269.74$$

The present value of £1,000 receivable ten years hence, discounted at 14 per cent, is thus £269.74.

Self-assessment Activity 3.4

Calculate the present value of £1,000 receivable 12 years hence, assuming the discount rate to be 12 per cent.

(answer at end of chapter)

Valuing perpetuities

Frequently, an investment pays a fixed sum each year for a specified number of years. A series of annual receipts or payments is termed an **annuity**. The simplest form of annuity is the infinite series or **perpetuity**. For example, certain government stocks offer a fixed annual income, but there is no obligation to repay the capital. The present value of such stocks (called **irredeemables**) is found by dividing the annual sum received by the annual rate of interest:

$$\text{PV perpetuity} = \frac{X}{i}$$

Example

Uncle George wishes to leave you in his will an annual sum of £10,000 a year, starting next year. Assuming an interest rate of 10 per cent, how much of his estate must be set aside for this purpose? The answer is:

$$\text{PV perpetuity} = \frac{£10{,}000}{0.10} = £100{,}000$$

Suppose that your benevolent uncle now wishes to compensate for inflation, estimated to be at 5 per cent per annum. The formula can be adjusted to allow for growth at the rate of g per cent p.a. in the annual amount. (The derivation of the present value of a growing perpetuity is found in Appendix II at the end of the chapter.)

$$PV = \frac{X}{i - g}$$

As long as the growth rate is less than the interest rate, we can compute the present value required:

$$PV = \frac{£10{,}000}{0.10 - 0.05} = £200{,}000$$

This formula plays a key part in analysing financial decisions and will be developed further in Chapter 4, when we consider the valuation of assets, shares and companies.

Valuing annuities

An annuity is an investment paying a fixed sum each year for a specified period of time. Examples of annuities are many credit agreements and house mortgages.

The life of an annuity is less than that of a perpetuity, so its value will also be somewhat less. In fact, the formula for calculating the present value of an annuity of £*A* is found by calculating the present value of a perpetuity and deducting the present value of that element falling beyond the end of the annuity period. This gives the somewhat complicated formula (see Appendix II at the end of chapter for the derivation) for the present value of an annuity (PVA):

$$\begin{aligned} \text{PVA}_{(i,n)} &= A\left(\frac{1}{i} - \frac{1}{i(1+i)^n}\right) \\ &= A \times \text{PVIFA}_{(i,n)} \end{aligned}$$

In words, the present value of an annuity for n years at i per cent is the annual sum multiplied by the appropriate present value interest factor for an annuity.

Suppose an annuity of £1,000 is issued for 20 years at 10 per cent. Using the table in Appendix C, we find the present value as follows:

$$\begin{aligned} \text{PVA}_{(10,20)} &= £1{,}000 \times \text{PVIFA}_{(10,20)} \\ &= £1{,}000 \times 8.5136 = £8{,}513.60 \end{aligned}$$

Self-assessment Activity 3.5

Calculate the present value of £250 receivable annually for 21 years plus £1,200 receivable after 22 years, assuming an interest rate of 11 per cent.

(answer at end of chapter)

Calculating interest rates

Sometimes, the present values and future cash flows are known, but the rate of interest is not given. A credit company may offer to lend you £1,000 today on condition that you repay £1,643 at the end of three years. To find the compound rate of interest on the loan, we solve the present value formula for i:

$$\text{PV}_{(i,n)} = \text{PVIF}_{(i,n)} \times \text{FV}$$

Rearranging the formula,

$$\text{PVIF}_{(i,3)} = \frac{\text{PV}}{\text{FV}} = \frac{£1{,}000}{£1{,}643} = 0.60864$$

Turning to the tables in Appendix B and looking for 0.6086 under the year 3 column, we find the rate of interest is 18 per cent. As we shall see in Chapter 5, this calculation is fundamental to investment and finance decisions and is termed the **internal rate of return**.

It is also possible to solve the present value formula for i:

$$PV = \frac{FV}{(1 + i)^n}$$

$$(1 + i)^n = FV/PV$$

$$i = (FV/PV)^{1/n} - 1$$

In the above example:

$$i = (1{,}643/1{,}000)^{1/n} - 1 = 0.18 \text{ or } 18\%$$

Who wants to be a millionaire?

An advertisement in the financial press read: 'How to become a millionaire? Invest £9,138 in the M&G Recovery unit trust in 1969 and wait for 25 years.' So, for those of us who missed out on this investment, let us grudgingly calculate its annual return:

$$i = (FV/PV)^{1/n} - 1$$
$$= (£1 \text{ million}/£9{,}138)^{1/25} - 1$$
$$= 20.66\%$$

By investing in a unit trust earning an annual rate of return of around 21 per cent, £9,138 turns you into a millionaire in 25 years' time. All you have to do is find an investment giving 21 per cent for 25 years!

3.7 Valuing bonds

DCF has long been used to help value financial securities. We consider share valuation in the next chapter, but deal here with the valuation of bonds. A bond is a long-term loan which promises to pay interest and repay the loan in accordance with the agreed terms. Governments, local authorities, companies and other organisations frequently seek to raise funds by issuing bonds, sometimes termed loan stock.

Once issued, bonds are traded in the secondary bond markets. Although a bond has a par, or nominal, value – typically £100 – its actual value will vary according to the cash flows it pays (interest and repayments) and the prevailing rate of interest for this type of bond. The fair price is the present value of the future interest and repayments.

$$V_o = PV \text{ (interest payments)} + PV \text{ (redemption value)}$$

Valuing a bond in Millie Meter plc

Some time ago you purchased an 8 per cent bond in the fashion chain, Millie Meter. Today, it has a par value of £100 and two years to maturity. Interest is payable half-yearly. What is it worth? Assuming the current comparable rate of interest is 8 per cent, the value should equal the par value of £100.

$$V_o = \frac{4}{(1.04)} + \frac{4}{(1.04)^2} + \frac{4}{(1.04)^3} + \frac{4}{(1.04)^4} + \frac{100}{(1.04)^4} = £100$$

Notice that because payments are made half-yearly, both the interest and discount rate are half the annual figures.

In reality, the required rate of return demanded by investors may be different from the original coupon rate. Let us say it is 10 per cent. As this is higher than the coupon rate, the bond value for Millie Meter will fall below its par value:

$$V_o = \frac{4}{(1.05)} + \frac{4}{(1.05)^2} + \frac{4}{(1.05)^3} + \frac{4}{(1.05)^4} + \frac{100}{(1.05)^4} = £96.45$$

This example shows that an investor would have to pay £96.45 for a bond offering a 4 per cent coupon rate (i.e. based on the par value of £100) plus the redemption value in two years' time, assuming that the market rate of interest for this security is 10 per cent.

For actively traded bonds there is little need to value them in this way because, if the bond market is efficient, it has already done it for you. All you need do is to look at the latest quoted price. However, the required rate of return is less easy to obtain. Who says, in the above example, that 10 per cent is the return expected by the market for this type of bond? The answer is simple.

The *Financial Times* quotes yields and prices for fixed-interest securities. We quote below one of the long-dated government gilt-edged securities.

	Yield		
	Int	**Red**	**Price £**
Five to fifteen years			
Exch 9pc 2002	8.11	6.19	111

We see for this Exchequer stock:
Coupon rate is 9%, paid as a percentage of the face value.
Bond redemption date is 2002.
Interest yield is 8.11%, the interest payment as a percentage of the closing price.
Redemption yield – the yield if held to maturity is 6.19%
Current price at close of business is £111.

Based on *Financial Times*, April 23 1998

If we know the current bond price, we put this in the above equation to find that discount rate which equates price with the discounted future cash flows – 10 per cent in the previous example. Although it is somewhat cumbersome to do this manually by trial and error, most spreadsheets offer this as a standard feature.

Factors affecting interest rates

It is common in financial management to talk about the interest rate ruling in the money market. However, it is important to realise that there is never a single prevailing rate. At any time, there is a spectrum of interest rates on offer – along this spectrum the rates depend on the identity of the borrower e.g. firm or government, and hence, the degree of risk faced by the lender, the amount lent or borrowed and the period over which the loan is made available. The last of these aspects is referred to as the **term structure of interest rates**. This shows how the yields offered for loans of different maturities vary as the term of the loan increases. We discuss this, together with the Yield Curve, in Appendix I to this chapter.

3.8 Net present value

We have assumed that the paramount objective of the firm is to create as much wealth as possible for its owners through the efficient use of existing and future resources. To create wealth, the present value of all future cash inflows must exceed the present value of all anticipated cash outflows. Quite simply, *an investment with a positive net present value increases the owners' wealth*. The elements of investment appraisal are shown in Figure 3.2.

Most decisions involve both costs and benefits. Usually, the initial expenditure incurred on an investment undertaken is clear-cut: it is what we pay for it. This includes the cash paid to the supplier of the asset plus any other costs involved in making the project operational. The problems start in measuring the worth of the investment project. What an asset is worth may have little to do with what it cost or what value is placed on it in the firm's Balance Sheet. A machine standing in the firm's books at £20,000 may be worth far more if it is essential to the manufacture of a highly profitable product, or far less than this if rendered obsolete through the advent of new technology. To measure its worth, we need to consider the *value of the current and future benefits less costs* arising from the investment. Wherever possible, these benefits should be expressed in terms of *cash flows*. Sometimes (as will be discussed later) it is impossible to quantify benefits so conveniently. Typically, investment decisions involve an initial capital expenditure followed by a stream of cash receipts and disbursements in subsequent periods. The net present value (NPV) method is applied to evaluate the desirability of investment opportunities. NPV is defined as:

$$\text{NPV} = \frac{X_1}{(1+k)} + \frac{X_2}{(1+k)^2} + \frac{X_3}{(1+k)^3} + \cdots + \frac{X_n}{(1+k)^n} - I$$

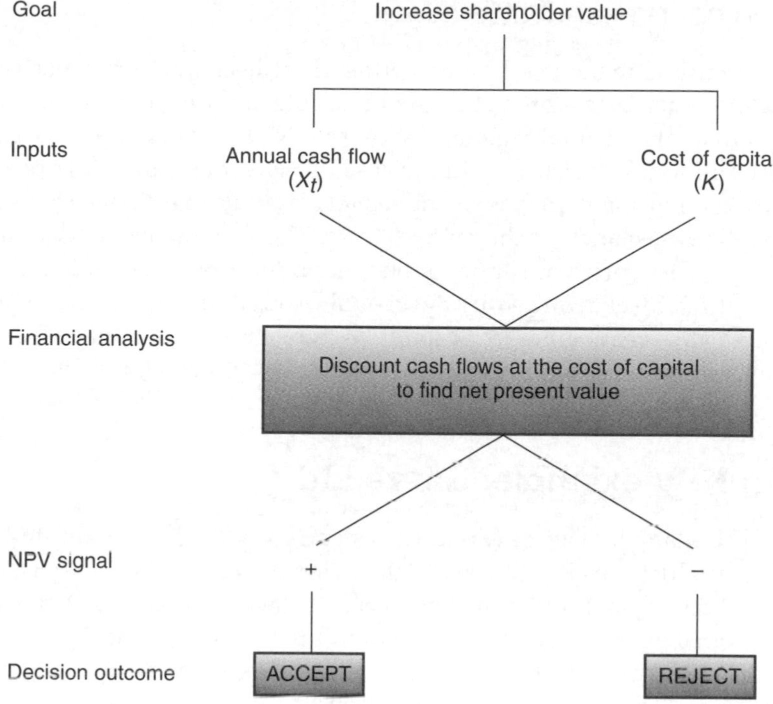

Figure 3.2 Investment appraisal elements

which may be summarised as:

$$NPV = \sum_{t=1}^{n} \frac{X_t}{(1 + k)^t} - I$$

where X_t is the net cash flow arising at the end of year t, I is the initial cost of the investment, n is the project's life, and k the minimum required rate of return on the investment (or discount rate). (The Greek letter Σ, or sigma, denotes the sum of all values in a particular series.)

Note that we have introduced a subtle change in notation, replacing i, which denoted the general market rate of interest, by k, which refers to the rate of return that must be achieved by the firm in question. As we shall see, k may vary significantly from firm to firm.

A project's net present value (NPV) is determined by summing the net annual cash flows, discounted at a rate that reflects the cost of an investment of equivalent risk on the capital market, and deducting the initial outlay.

Self-assessment Activity 3.6

Define the main elements in the capital budgeting decision.

(answer at end of chapter)

The net present value rule

Wealth is maximised by accepting all projects that offer positive net present values when discounted at the required rate of return for each investment.

Most of the main elements in the NPV formula are largely externally determined. For example, in the case of investment in a new piece of manufacturing equipment, management has relatively little influence over the price paid, the life expectancy or the discount rate. These elements are determined, respectively, by the price of capital goods, the rate of new technological development and the returns required by the capital market. Management's main opportunity for wealth creation lies in its ability to implement and manage the project so as to generate positive net cash flows over the project's economic life.

An NPV example: Gazza Ltd

The management of Gazza Ltd is currently evaluating an investment in hair dye products costing £10,000. Anticipated net cash inflows are £6,000 received at the end of year 1 and a further £6,000 at the end of year 2. Assuming a discount rate of 10 per cent, calculate the project's net present value.

We can compute the NPV for Gazza using three different approaches, all of which will be employed in later chapters.

1 *Formula approach*

$$\begin{aligned} NPV &= \frac{£6{,}000}{1.1} + \frac{£6{,}000}{(1.1)^2} - £10{,}000 \\ &= £5{,}454 + £4{,}959 - £10{,}000 \\ &= £413 \end{aligned}$$

This approach is particularly useful with few cash flows or where discount factors are not available in tables.

2 *Present value tables* (using Appendix B)

Year	*Cash flow £*		*Discount factor at 10%*		*Present value £*
1	6,000	×	0.90909	=	5,454
2	6,000	×	0.82645	=	4,959
			1.73554		10,413
		Less initial cost			(10,000)
			NPV		413

3 *Present value annuity tables* (using Appendix C)

$$\begin{aligned} NPV &= (£6{,}000 \times PVIFA_{(10,2)}) - £10{,}000 \\ &= (£6{,}000 \times 1.7355) - £10{,}000 \\ &= £413 \end{aligned}$$

This approach is appropriate only when annual cash flows are constant. Notice that the present-value interest factor for an annuity at 10 per cent for two years (taken from Appendix C) is simply the cumulative total of the individual factors in the previous approach.

How would the net present value differ if the perceived project risk were greater? The risk-averse management of Gazza would probably require a higher return from the project, reflected in a higher discount rate. Let us repeat the exercise using 13 per cent (average risk) and 16 per cent (high risk).

Using 13 per cent:

$$\begin{aligned} \text{NPV} &= (\pounds 6{,}000 \times \text{PVIFA}_{(13,2)}) - \pounds 10{,}000 \\ &= (\pounds 6{,}000 \times 1.6681) - \pounds 10{,}000 \\ &= \pounds 8 \text{ (i.e. approximately zero)} \end{aligned}$$

Using 16 per cent:

$$\begin{aligned} \text{NPV} &= \pounds 6{,}000 \times 1.6052 - \pounds 10{,}000 \\ &= (369) \end{aligned}$$

Looking at the net present values, what interpretation can be made? With a 10 per cent discount rate, the project offers a *positive* NPV of £413. If the projected cash flows are generally expected to be achieved, the market value of the firm should rise by £413. Hence, the project should be accepted. On the other hand, if the project is classified as high risk, the cash inflows are discounted at a rate of 16 per cent and the NPV is estimated at −£369. Its acceptance would reduce the firm's market value by £369. Hence, the project should not be accepted. Clearly, it would not be wise to exchange £10,000 today for future cash flows having a present value of less than this amount.

If the project is classified as having average risk, the discount rate used is 13 per cent, yielding an NPV of £8. The project is just acceptable; it yields 13 per cent, which is the required rate of return. We can draw two important conclusions:

1 Project acceptability depends upon cash flows and risk.
2 The higher the risk of a given set of expected cash flows (and the higher the discount rate), the lower will be its present value. In other words, the value of a given expected cash flow *decreases* as its risk *increases*.

Why NPV makes sense

In Appendix I to this chapter, we examine more rigorously the rationale for the NPV approach and how the net present value concept permits efficient separation of ownership and corporate management.

The main rationale for the net present value approach may be summarised as follows:

1 Managers are assumed to act in the best interests of the owners or shareholders, even if agency costs – in the form of incentives or controls – have to be incurred. They seek to increase shareholders' wealth by maximising cash flows through time. The market rate of exchange between current and future wealth is reflected in the current rate of interest.

Mini case

How NPV is used in debt relief to the poorest nations

The International Monetary Fund (IMF) and World Bank have designed a framework to provide special assistance for heavily indebted poor countries. It entails coordinated action by the international financial community, including banks and multinational companies, to reduce and reschedule the debt burden to levels that countries can service through exports and aid.

Net Present Value is central to the calculation of the sustainable debt level. The face value of debt stock is not a good measure of a country's debt burden if a significant part of it is contracted on concessional terms, for example with an interest rate below the prevailing market rate. The net present value of debt is used to find the sum of all future debt-service obligations (interest and principal) on existing debt, discounted at the market interest rate. Whenever the interest rate on the loan is lower than the market rate, the resulting NPV of debt is smaller than its face value, with the difference reflecting the grant element.

In June 1999, the IMF, World Bank and other creditors agreed to provide debt relief to Mozambique totalling US$3 billion in nominal terms, which, after adjustment for the lower rate of interest, becomes US$1.4 billion in NPV terms. This assistance represents over 70 per cent of Mozambique's gross domestic product. Mozambique is the sixth country to benefit under the scheme, raising total debt relief of US$3 billion in NPV terms by 2000.

Question

Explain to a government official from one of the world's poorest countries why the NPV approach is an appropriate method for calculating the sustainable debt level.

2 Managers should undertake all projects up to the point at which the marginal return on the investment is equal to the rate of interest on equivalent financial investments in the capital market. This is exactly the same as the net present value rule: accept all investments offering positive net present values when discounted at the equivalent market rate of interest. The result is an increase in the market value of the firm and thus in the market value of the shareholders' stake in the firm.

3 Management need not concern itself with shareholders' particular time patterns of consumption or risk preferences. In well-functioning capital markets, shareholders can borrow or lend funds to achieve their personal requirements. Furthermore, by carefully combining risky and safe investments, they can achieve the desired risk characteristics for those consumption requirements. This argument is discussed more fully in Appendix I.

Self-assessment Activity 3.7

Why should managers seek to maximise net present value? Is business not about maximising profit?

(answer at end of chapter)

Summary

We have examined the meaning of wealth and its fundamental importance in financial management. Given that for most capital projects there is a time-lag between the initial investment outlay and the receipt of benefits, consideration must be given to both the timing and size of the costs and benefits. Whenever there is an alternative opportunity to use funds committed to a project (e.g. to invest in the capital market or in other capital projects), cash today is worth more than cash received tomorrow.

Key points

- Money, like any other scarce resource, has a cost. We allow for the time-value of money by discounting. The higher the interest cost for a future cash flow, the lower its present value.
- Discount tables take away much of the tedium of discounting – but computer spreadsheets eliminate it altogether.
- Standard discount factors are:

  PVIF = the present value interest factor,
  PVIFA = the present value interest factor for an annuity.

  Conventional shorthand is:
  Interest factor (rate of interest, number of years)
  e.g. $PVIFA_{(10,3)}$ reads 'the present value interest factor for an annuity at 10 per cent for three years'.
- The net present value (NPV) of a project is found by (1) discounting a project's future net cash flows at the minimum required rate of return for the project; and (2) deducting the initial investment outlay from the total present values over the project's life.
- Where the corporate goal is to maximise the wealth of its shareholders, the simple decision rule is:
  When the NPV is positive, accept the investment.
  When the NPV is negative, reject the investment.

Further reading

Brealey and Myers (2000) provides a good theoretical case for net present value. The work of Hirshleifer (1958) and Tobin (1958) provides the background to the approach adopted in Appendix I.

website: www.investinginbonds.com

Appendix I

The Term Structure of Interest Rates and the Yield Curve

We saw in Section 3.7 that the interest rate depends on a number of factors, one of which is duration of the investment or loan. This is called the **term structure of interest rates**. It shows how the yields offered for loans of different maturities vary as the term of the loan increases.

Relating this to bonds issued by the state, or **government stock**, the term structure shows the rate of return expected, or yield, by today's purchaser of stock who plans to hold to **maturity**, or **redemption** i.e. when the stock will be repaid, or redeemed, by the government. It also shows how the yield varies for different lengths of time to maturity. In graphical terms, it is shown by a relationship called **the Yield Curve**.

Normally, we find that yields to maturity increase as the term increases, as Figure 3.3 shows. Notice that the relevant yield is the Gross Redemption Yield, which includes both interest payments and any capital gain or loss at redemption.

By tradition, short-dated stocks, with up to further five years to maturity are called *shorts, mediums* have between five and 15 years before repayment and *longs* will be paid beyond 15 years. Notice that *longs* include a number of **irredeemables** or **perpetuities** which quite literally will never be repaid but will attract interest forever. These are also called **undated** stocks.

Explaining the shape of the Yield Curve

Three theories have been proposed to explain the shape of the Yield Curve – the Expectations Theory, the Liquidity Preference Theory and the Market Segmentation Theory. These are not mutually exclusive explanations – the influences incorporated in each theory all tend to operate at any one time but

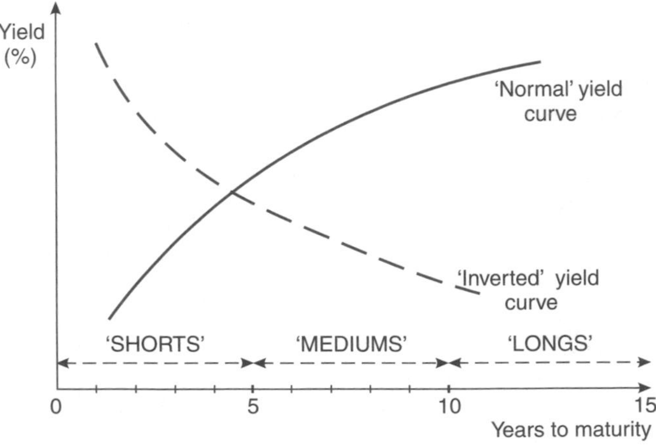

Figure 3.3 The term structure of interest rates

with different degrees of pressure. Sometimes, investors' expectations (e.g. about future inflation) are predominant, while, at other times, investors' desire for liquidity may govern the shape of the curve.

Expectations theory

This theory asserts that investors' expectations about future interest rates exert the dominant influence. When the curve rises with years to maturity, this suggests that people expect interest rates to rise in the future. This is reflected in the relative demand for short-dated and long-dated securities – investors expect to be able to earn higher rates in the future so they defer buying long-dated stocks, preferring to invest in shorts. This pushes up the yield on shorts, and thus lowers the yields on them, and conversely, for longer-dated stock.

Liquidity preference theory

Most investors, being risk-averse, prefer to hold cash rather than securities – cash is effectively free of risk (although banks do go bust!), while even the shortest-dated government stocks carry a degree of risk. Here, by risk, we mean not the risk of default, but the risk of not being able to find a willing buyer of the stock at an acceptable price, i.e. liquidity risk. Consequently, investors need to be compensated for having to wait for the return of their money. Preference for liquidity now, and risk avoidance thus explains the shape of the yield curve. The longer the time to maturity, the greater the risk of illiquidity and the higher the compensation required.

Market segmentation theory

In developed markets, there is a wide range of investors with different needs and time horizons who, therefore, focus on different segments of the yield curve. For example, some financial institutions, such as banks, are anxious to protect their ability to allow investors to withdraw their deposits freely – for them, shorts are very attractive as they need liquidity. Conversely, pension funds have far longer-term liabilities and wish to match the maturity stream of their assets to these quite predictable liabilities. For them, longs are more suitable.

According to this view, the 'short' market is quite distinct from the 'long' market and the two ends could behave quite differently under similar conditions. For example, if the government is expected to be a net repayer of its debt in the future, this suggests a shortage of longs – as applied in the UK during 2000. This is likely to increase the demand for those stocks presently available and thus reduce their yields. This would explain the case of the 'inverted' i.e. downward-sloping, yield curve, shown by the dotted line in Figure 3.3.

In Chapter 18, we will examine how firms can use the information contained in the yield curve for their financial planning.

Appendix II

The investment–consumption decision

Theoretical case for NPV

We have suggested that managers should base investment decisions on the net present value criterion: accept all projects that offer a positive net present value. We will now justify this claim by presenting the theoretical case for the NPV rule.

There are three fundamental financial decisions facing individuals and shareholders:

1 *Consumption decisions*: how much of my available resources should I spend on immediate consumption?
2 *Investment decisions*: how much of the resources available should I forgo now in the expectation of increased resources at some time in the future? How should such decisions be made?
3 *Financing decisions*: how much cash should I borrow or lend to enable me to carry out these investment and consumption decisions?

Clearly, these decisions are interrelated and should not be viewed in isolation.

Individuals are faced with the choice of how much of their wealth should be consumed immediately, and how much should be invested for consumption at a later date. This applies equally to young children with their pocket money, undergraduates with their grants, professionals with their capital, and shareholders with their investment portfolios. All these cases involve a trade-off between immediate and delayed consumption.

We are primarily concerned with how managers should reach investment decisions. Cash generated from business operations can be utilised in two ways: it can be distributed to the shareholders in the form of a dividend, or reinvested within the business. Periodically, the directors decide how much of the shareholders' wealth to distribute in the form of dividends and how much to withhold for investment purposes, such as building up stock levels or purchasing new equipment. The shareholders will only be willing to forgo a higher present level of consumption (in the form of dividends) if they expect an even greater future level of consumption. This willingness to give up consumption now in order to increase future consumption characterises investment decisions.

Graphical example

Derek Platt is the sole proprietor of Platt Enterprises, a new business with just one asset of £4 million in cash. He has a number of interesting investment ideas (all lasting just a year), but before investing his capital within the business, he asks the following key questions:

1 What return could I earn by investing my capital (or some part of it) in the capital market?

2 How much should I invest within the business?
3 What is the net present value of the business?

Before addressing these issues and in order to present a conceptual framework for the NPV rule, it is first necessary to make certain simplifying assumptions that allow us to portray in two-dimensional form the essential features of the investment–consumption decision model. The basic assumptions are as follows:

1 Investors are wealth-maximisers.
2 Only two periods are considered – the present period (t_0) and the next period (t_1). This two-period model implies that investments involve an immediate cash outlay in t_0 in return for a cash benefit in the following period, t_1.
3 All information for decision-making is known with certainty.
4 Investment projects are entirely independent of each other and are divisible.

These assumptions are clearly unrealistic in the setting within which investment decisions are taken in practice. Nonetheless, they serve as a useful guide to the relevance and limitations of the net value approach.

Let us assume that Platt Enterprises has £4 million available for investment but there are only two possible projects, each costing £2 million and having a one-year life. Figure 3.4 illustrates the investment opportunities line for the two projects, showing the cost of investing this year and the payoffs arising next year. Platt could invest £4 million, in both projects, producing a £4 million payoff next year. But he would probably prefer to invest only in project A, costing £2 million, but giving a payoff of £3 million. Project B is unprofitable, offering only £1 million from £2 million investment. If there are no opportunities to invest surplus cash externally, say by putting it on deposit with a bank or investing in short-term securities, Platt would have to pay a dividend to shareholders of the £2 million unused cash.

In this example, the choice was fairly straightforward. But if Platt had hundreds of potential projects, it would be far harder to know where the cut-off

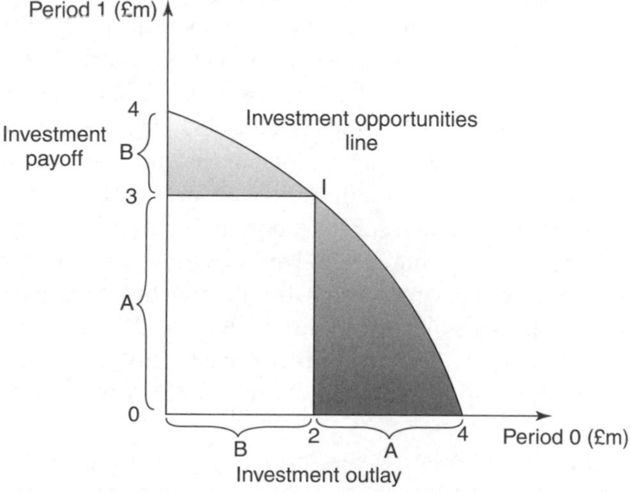

Figure 3.4 Investment opportunities for Platt Enterprises

point for investment should be drawn. He requires a criterion for judging between cash today and cash receivable next year. In effect, he requires a rate of exchange for the transfer of wealth across time. Suppose he requires a minimum of £115 receivable next year to induce him to give up £100 now, the rate of exchange would be £115$_{t_0}$:£100$_{t_1}$ or £1.15:£1. This represents a premium for delayed consumption of one year of

$$\frac{£115}{£100} - 1 = 0.15, \quad \text{or} \quad 15\%$$

This exchange rate between today's money and tomorrow's money varies with the level of present consumption sacrificed. Platt may be willing to forgo the first £100 of potential dividend in return for an additional 15 per cent next year, but to persuade him to delay the consumption of a further £100 will probably require something in excess of 15 per cent. This variable exchange rate for the transfer of wealth across time at various levels of investment is termed the marginal rate of time preference, and differs from individual to individual.

The investment opportunities line is concave to the origin rather than a straight line. This indicates the decreasing returns to scale of each subsequent investment opportunity. As a wealth-maximiser, Platt will first select those investment projects offering the greatest return and work down towards those offering the least return. Point I represents the marginal project beyond which it ceases to be worthwhile to invest – the marginal return from the next £1 in investment would not be sufficient to compensate for the sacrifice involved in giving up a further £1 in dividends. For Platt, I represents the point where the marginal return on investment equals his marginal rate of time preference.

Borrowing and lending opportunities

So far, under our highly simplistic assumptions, our owner-manager, Platt, is given only two decisions – consumption and investment. The more he invests, the less he can consume now, and vice versa. This ignores the third choice open to him, namely the financing decision. Where capital markets exist, individuals and firms can buy and sell not only real assets (i.e. fixed and current), but also financial assets. As we saw earlier in this chapter, when perfect capital markets are introduced (i.e. no borrower can influence the interest rate, all traders have equal and costless access to information, no transaction costs or taxes), there will be a single market rate of interest for both borrowing and lending.

The existence of a capital market permits owners to transfer wealth across time in a manner different from the investment–consumption pattern of the firm. This is shown by the interest rate line in Figure 3.5, which represents the exchange rate between current and future cash flows under perfect capital market conditions. Its slope is $(1 + i)$, where i denotes the single period rate of interest.

In our example, the interest rate is found by relating present wealth to next year's wealth at any point on the graph. At the extremes, this is £6 million/£5 million = 1.20. The interest rate is therefore 20 per cent.

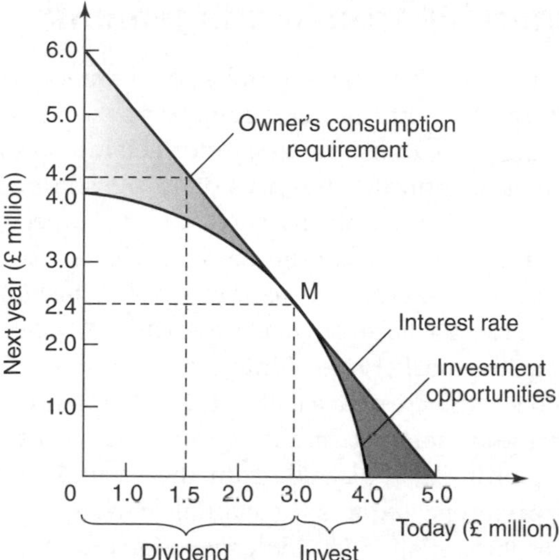

Figure 3.5 Investment and financing opportunities for Platt Enterprises

With the introduction of financing opportunities afforded by the capital market, Platt can now identify the appropriate level of corporate investment. He should continue to invest until project M – where the interest rate line is tangential to the investment opportunities line. At this point, all investments offering a return at least as high as the market rate of interest are accepted, since they all offer positive net present values. Reading off the graph in Figure 3.5, we find that investment as far as M would mean a dividend of £3 million today and an investment of £1 million (i.e. £4 million – £3 million). It is not worth investing further as the projects offer negative NPVs. It would be more beneficial for Platt to withdraw the £3 million from the business and to invest it in the capital market at 20 per cent p.a.

What then is the net present value of the £1 million investment programme envisaged by Platt? Reading off the investment opportunities curve, we find that the capital outlay will produce cash flows of £2.4 million next year. The NPV is therefore £1 million:

$$\text{NPV} = \frac{£2.4 \text{ m}}{1.2} - £1 \text{ m} = £2 \text{ m} - £1 \text{ m} = £1 \text{ m}$$

The new value of the business becomes £5 million (starting capital of £4 million plus NPV of investment programme).

We suggested earlier that the £3 million not invested by the firm would be paid out as a dividend. An alternative would be for the firm to invest all or part of it on behalf of the owners in the capital market until such time as investment opportunities offering positive NPVs arise. Suppose Platt is only looking for a dividend of £1.5 million. The extra £1.5 million can be invested in the capital market to earn £1.8 million next year (i.e. £4.2 m – £2.4 m, or £1.5 m × 1.20). Platt's cash flow next year will then be the £2.4 million from capital investments plus the £1.8 million from financial investments.

Separating ownership from management

Most firms are characterised by a large number of shareholders (owners), few of whom are actively involved in the management of the firm. It is obviously impossible for managers to evaluate investment decisions on the basis of the personal investment–consumption preferences of all the shareholders. Happily, the existence of capital markets renders any such attempt unnecessary. Managers do not need to select an investment programme whose cash flows exactly match shareholders' preferred time patterns of consumption. The task of the manager is to maximise present value by accepting all investment proposals offering a return at least as good as the market rate of interest.

This criterion maximises the current wealth of the shareholders, who can then transform that wealth into whatever time pattern of consumption they require. They can do this by lending or borrowing on the capital market until their marginal rate of time preference equals the capital market rate of interest. This **Separation Theorem**, as it is usually termed, leads to the following decision rules:

1 Corporate management should invest in projects offering positive net present values when discounted at the capital market rate.
2 Shareholders should borrow or lend on the capital market to produce the wealth distribution which best meets their personal time pattern of consumption requirements.

Capital market imperfections

Based on the assumptions laid down at the start of the chapter, managers should undertake investments up to the point at which the marginal return on investment is equal to the rate of return in the capital market. You will recall that two important assumptions were the existence of perfect capital markets and the absence of risk. When these assumptions are relaxed, the argument in favour of the net present value rule becomes weaker. For one thing, there is no longer a unique rate of interest in the capital market, but a range of interest rates varying with the status of the borrower, the amount required and the perceived riskiness of the investment. A detailed analysis of investment under risk is the subject of subsequent chapters, but at this stage we can say that a project's return should be compared with the rate of return on investments in the capital market of equivalent risk – the greater the investment risk, the higher the required rate of return.

A major concern involves the particular capital market imperfections where the borrowing rate is substantially higher than the lending rate. In this case, the two-period investment model will resemble Figure 3.6. The steeper line represents the interest rate for the borrower and the flatter line represents the lending rate. The existence of two different interest rates gives rise to two different points on the investment opportunities line CD. Prospective borrowers, having to pay a higher rate of interest for funds, would prefer the company to invest only BD this year (i.e. up to project *Y*). However, prospective lenders will require the company to discount at the lower lending rate, leading to a much greater investment of *AD*, with investment *X* being the marginal project.

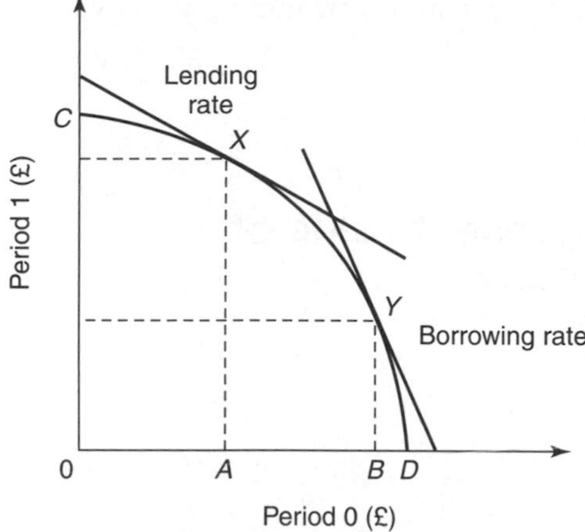

Figure 3.6 Investment decisions in imperfect capital markets

There is no simple solution to the investment–consumption decision when capital market imperfections prevail. Fortunately, in the UK, USA, Japan and much of Western Europe, capital markets are highly competitive and function fairly well, so that differences between lending and borrowing rates are minimised, but significant differentials can be found in emerging capital markets such as that in Turkey.

Appendix III

Present value formulae

1 Formula for the present value of a perpetuity

This formula derives from the present value formula:

$$PV = \frac{X}{1 + i} + \frac{X}{(1 + i)^2} + \frac{X}{(1 + i)^3} + \cdots$$

Let $X/(1 + i) = a$ and $1/(1 + i) = b$. We now have:

(i) $PV = a(1 + b + b^2 + \cdots)$

Multiplying both sides by b gives us:

(ii) $PVb = a(b + b^2 + b^3 + \cdots)$

Subtracting (ii) from (i) we have:

$$PV(1 - b) = a$$

Substituting for a and b,

$$PV\left(1 - \frac{1}{1 + i}\right) = \frac{X}{1 + i}$$

Multiplying both sides by $(1 + i)$ and rearranging, we have:

$$PV = \frac{X}{i}$$

2 Formula for the present value of a growing perpetuity

In 1 above, we obtained:

$$PV(1 - b) = a$$

Redefining $b = (1 + g)/(1 + i)$ and keeping $a = X/(1 + i)$:

$$PV\left(1 - \frac{1 + g}{1 + i}\right) = \frac{X}{1 + i}$$

Multiplying both sides by $(1 + i)$ and rearranging, we have:

$$PV = \frac{X}{i - g}$$

3 The present value of annuities

The above perpetuities were special cases of the annuity formula. To find the present value of an annuity, we can first use the perpetuity formula and deduct from it the years outside the annuity period. For example, if an annuity of £100 is issued for 20 years at 10 per cent, we would find the present value of a perpetuity of £100 using the formula:

$$PV = \frac{X}{i} = \frac{100}{0.10} = £1,000$$

Next, find the present value of a perpetuity for the same amount, starting at year 20, using the formula:

$$PV = \frac{X}{i(1 + i)^t} = \frac{£100}{0.10(1 + 0.10)^{20}} = £148.64$$

The difference will be:

$$\text{PV of annuity} = \frac{X}{i} - \frac{X}{i(1 + i)^t}$$
$$= £1,000 - £148.64 = £851.36$$

The present value of an annuity of £100 for 20 years discounted at 10 per cent is £851.36.

The formula may be simplified to:

$$\text{PV of annuity} = X\left(\frac{1}{i} - \frac{1}{i(1 + i)^t}\right)$$

Self-assessment Answers

3.1 Most likely, the banker would wish to reflect on the rate of interest required:

(a) the rate of interest available from a risk-free investment,
(b) the expected changes in purchasing power over the five years, and
(c) the risk that you may not be able to repay.

We consider other factors a banker will consider in a later chapter.

3.2 $\text{PV} = \dfrac{£623}{(1.07)^8} + \dfrac{£1{,}092}{(1.07)^{16}} = £732$

3.3 Discounting at 15 per cent, a pound halves in value every five years. The present value of the purchase cost is therefore £750,000 (£500,000 today and £250,000 in year 5).

3.4 $\text{PV} = \dfrac{£1{,}000}{(1.12)^{12}} = £257$

3.5 Using the tables:

$$\text{PV} = (£250 \times 8.0751) + (£1{,}200 \times 0.10067) = £2{,}140$$

3.6 The main elements in the capital budgeting decision are found in the formula

$$\text{NPV} = \frac{X_1}{1+k} + \frac{X_2}{(1+k)^2} + \cdots + \frac{X_n}{(1+k)^n} - I$$

where X is the net cash flow arising at the end of year, k is the minimum required rate of return (or discount rate), I is the initial cost of the investment and n is the project's life.

3.7 The net present value rule states that a project is acceptable if the present value of anticipated cash flows exceeds the present value of anticipated cash flows. Wealth is maximised by accepting all projects offering positive net present values when discounted at the required rate of return.

Questions

1 *Solution in Appendix A (page 803).* Explain the difference between accounting profit and cash flow.

2 *Solution in Appendix A (page 803).* Calculate the present value of a ten-year annuity of £100, assuming an interest rate of 20 per cent.

3 *Solution in Appendix A (page 803).* A firm is considering the purchase of a machine which will cost £20,000. It is estimated that annual savings of £5,000 will result from the machine's installation, that the life of the machine will be five years, and that its residual value will be £1,000. Assuming the required rate of return to be 10 per cent, what action would you recommend?

4 *Solution in Appendix A (page 803).* (Based on Appendix I to this chapter.) Ron Bratt decides to commence trading as a sportswear retailer, with initial capital of £6,000 in cash. The capital market and investment opportunities available are shown below:

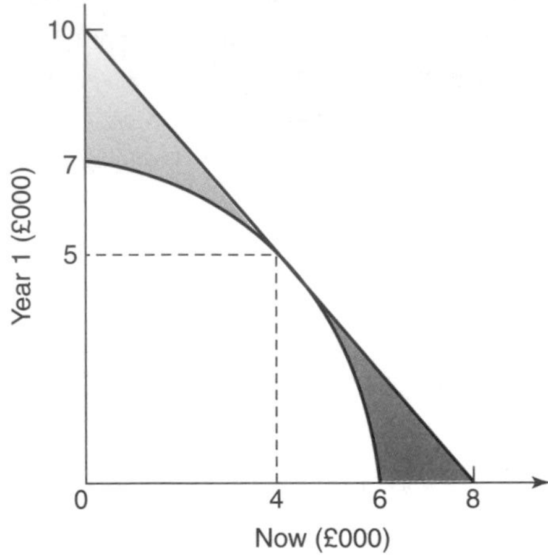

You are required to calculate:

(a) How much the firm should invest in real assets.
(b) The market rate of interest for the business.
(c) The average rate of return on investment.
(d) The net present value of the investment.
(e) The value of the firm after this level of investment.
(f) Next year's dividend if Bratt only requires a current dividend of £3,000.

5 The gross yield to redemption on gilts are as follows:

Treasury 8.5% 2000	7.00%
Exchequer 10.5% 2005	6.70%
Treasury 8% 2015	6.53%

(a) Examine the shape of the yield curve for gilts, based upon the information above, which you should use to construct the curve.
(b) Explain the meaning of the term 'gilts' and the relevance of yield curves to the private investor.

6 Calculate the net present value of projects A and B, assuming discount rates of 0 per cent, 10 per cent and 20 per cent.

	A (£)	B (£)
Initial outlay	1,200	1,200
Cash receipts:		
Year 1	1,000	100
Year 2	500	600
Year 3	100	1,100

Which is the superior project at each level of discount rate? Why do they not all produce the same answer?

7 The directors of Yorkshire Autopoints are considering the acquisition of an automatic car-washing installation. The initial cost and setting-up expenses will amount to about £140,000. Its estimated life is about seven years, and estimated annual accounting profit is as follows:

Year	1	2	3	4	5	6	7
Operations cash flow (£)	30,000	50,000	60,000	60,000	30,000	20,000	20,000
Depreciation (£)	20,000	20,000	20,000	20,000	20,000	20,000	20,000
Accounting profit (£)	10,000	30,000	40,000	40,000	10,000	–	–

At the end of its seven-year life, the installation will yield only a few pounds in scrap value. The company classifies its projects as follows:

Required rate of return	
Low risk	20 per cent
Average risk	30 per cent
High risk	40 per cent

Car-washing projects are estimated to be of average risk.

(a) Should the car-wash be installed?

(b) List some of the popular errors made in assessing capital projects.

Practical assignment

List three decisions in a business with which you are familiar where cash flows arise over a lengthy time period and where discounted cash flow (DCF) may be beneficial. To what extent is DCF applied (formally or intuitively)? What are the dangers of ignoring the time-value of money in these particular cases?

4 Valuation of assets, shares and companies

Must do better . . .

Provision of training courses and learning materials for students preparing for professional accounting exams is now big business, with a number of listed companies involved. In June 1998, the first quoted operator, Nord Anglia plc, acquired EW Fact, a leading accountancy training firm, for £19 million. After the acquisition, Nord Anglia was dismayed to find that restructuring costs were much higher than expected.

In May 1999, Nord Anglia announced a profits warning and also that it was considering legal action against EW Fact for 'materially overstating' profits for the year before acquisition. Nord Anglia's chairman alleged that pre-tax profits in 1997, posted at £1.4 million, should have been just £80,000. This knowledge would presumably have affected the sum that Nord Anglia would have paid to acquire EW Fact. Shares in Nord Anglia fell from 230 p to 187 p on the announcement.

The *Daily Telegraph* quipped: 'The sort of mistake any student can make, of course. But not what should be expected from auditors – if properly trained'.

Learning objectives

The ultimate effectiveness of financial management is judged by its contribution to the value of the enterprise. This chapter aims:

- To provide an understanding of the main ways of valuing companies and shares, and of the limitations of these methods.
- To stress that valuation is an imprecise art, requiring a blend of theoretical analysis and practical skills.
- To introduce the dividend valuation model, an important underpinning of the analysis of dividend policy in Chapter 19.

A sound grasp of the principles of valuation is essential for many other areas of financial management.

4.1 Introduction

The concept of value is at the heart of financial management, yet the introductory case demonstrates that valuation of companies is by no means an exact science. Inability to make precisely accurate valuations complicates the task of financial managers.

The financial manager controls capital flows into, within and out of the enterprise to achieve maximum value for shareholders. The test of his/her effectiveness is the extent to which these operations enhance shareholder wealth. He/she needs a thorough understanding of the determinants of value to anticipate the consequences of alternative financial decisions. If there is an active and efficient market in the company's shares, it should provide a reliable indication of value. However, managers may feel that the market is unreliable, and may wish to undertake their own valuation exercises. Indeed, some managers behave as though they doubt the Efficient Markets Hypothesis (EMH), as outlined in Chapter 2.

In addition, there are specific situations where financial managers must undertake valuations, for example, when valuing a proposed acquisition, or assessing the value of their own company when faced with a takeover bid. Directors of unquoted companies may also need to apply valuation principles, if they intend to invite a takeover approach from a larger firm or if they decide to obtain a market quotation.

Valuation skills thus have an important strategic dimension. In order to advise on the desirability of alternative financial strategies, the financial manager needs to assess the value to the firm of pursuing each option. This chapter examines the major difficulties in valuation and explains the main methods available.

4.2 The valuation problem

Anyone who has ever attempted to buy or sell a second-hand car or house will appreciate that value, like beauty, is in the eye of the beholder. Value is whatever the highest bidder is prepared to pay. With a well-established market in the asset concerned, and if the asset is fairly homogeneous, valuation is relatively simple. *So long as the market is reasonably efficient, the market price can be trusted as a fair assessment of value.*

Problems arise in valuing unique assets, or assets that have no recognisable market, such as the shares of most unquoted companies. Even with a ready market, valuation may be complicated by a change of use or ownership. For example, the value of an incompetently-managed company may be less than the same enterprise after a shake-up by replacement managers. But by how much would value increase? Valuing the firm under new management would require access to key financial data not readily available to outsiders. Similarly, a conglomerate that has grown haphazardly may be worth more when broken up and sold to the highest bidders. But who are the prospective bidders, and how much might they offer? Undoubtedly, valuation in practice involves considerable informed guesswork. (Inside information often helps as well!)

Regarding the introductory case, we do not know how the valuation was arrived at, but we can see that even the 'experts' can get it wrong. This illustrates an important lesson – the only certain thing about a valuation is that it will be 'wrong'! However, this is no excuse for hand-wringing. A key question is whether the valuations were reasonable in the light of the information then available.

The three basic valuation methods are **net asset value, price–earnings multiples** and **discounted cash flow.** None of these is foolproof, and they often give different answers. Moreover, different approaches may be required when valuing whole companies from those appropriate to valuing part shares of companies. In addition, the value of a whole company (i.e. the value of its entire stock of assets) may differ from the value of the shareholders' stake. This applies when the firm is partly financed by debt capital.

Enterprise value vs. equity value: Coats Viyella plc

To persuade the present owners to sell, a bidder has to offer an acceptable price for their equity and expect to take on responsibility for the company's debt. Consider the purchase in 1995 by Coats Viyella, the textiles company, of the US precision engineer Bace Manufacturing. This formed part of Coats' strategy of re-focusing its activities away from traditional activities such as yarns and carpets and into core sectors such as textile engineering. The deal was valued at £65 million, comprising £51 million cash paid to the owners and £14 million of Bace debt.

Bace's stock of assets was financed partly by equity and partly by debt. To obtain ownership of all the assets, i.e. the whole company, Coats was obliged to offer £51 million to the shareholders to induce them to sell, *and* either pay off the debt or assume responsibility for it. Although Coats chose the latter route, either course of action would increase the cost of the acquisition to £65 million.

Obviously, to make the acquisition worthwhile to Coats, its own (undisclosed) valuation would presumably have exceeded £65 million. We thus encounter several different concepts of value:

Value of company to the buyer:	probably more than £65 million
Cost of acquiring company:	£65 million
Value of equity stake required to clinch sale:	£51 million
Value of equity stake perceived by owners:	possibly below £51 million

The distinction between company value and the value of the owners' stake is clarified by considering the first method of valuation, the **net asset value approach**, which is based on scrutiny of company accounts.

Self-assessment Activity 4.1

Distinguish between the value of a whole company and the value of the equity stake. When do these two measures coincide?

(answer at end of chapter)

4.3 Valuation using published accounts

Using the asset value stated in the accounts has obvious appeal for those impressed by the apparent objectivity of published accounting data. The Balance Sheet shows the recorded value for the total of fixed assets (sometimes, but not invariably, including intangible assets) and current assets, namely stocks and work-in-progress, debtors, and other holdings of liquid assets such as cash and marketable securities. After deducting the debts of the company, both long- and short-term, from the total asset value (i.e. the value of the whole company) the residual figure is the **net asset value (NAV),** i.e. the value of net assets or the book value of the owners' stake in the company, or simply, 'owners' equity'.

The Balance Sheet for D S Smith plc, the paper and packaging group, is shown in Table 4.1. The Balance Sheet in its modern vertical form pinpoints the NAV, the net assets figure, £508.4 million, which, by definition, must coincide with shareholders' funds, i.e. the value of the shareholders' stake net of all liabilities (and, in this case, net of a small minority item, i.e. residual ownership in an acquired firm). (The book value of the whole company, i.e. its total assets, is fixed assets plus current assets = (£587.6 m + £519.1 m) = £1,106.7 m.) However, the NAV is a very unreliable indicator of value in most circumstances. Most crucially, it derives from a valuation of the separate assets of the

Table 4.1 Balance Sheet for DS Smith plc as at 28 April 2001

Assets employed	**£m**	**£m**
Fixed assets (net)		587.6
Current assets:		
Stocks	155.2	
Debtors	334.6	
Cash and investments	29.3	
Creditors falling due within one year	(356.1)	
Net current assets		163.0
Total assets less current liabilities		750.6
Creditors falling due after one year (inc. provisions)		(237.2)
Minority interests		(5.0)
Net assets (NAV)		508.4
Financed by:		
Called-up share capital		32.1
Share premium account		188.0
Profit and loss account		278.8
Revaluation reserve		9.5
Shareholders' funds (NAV)		508.4

Source: D S Smith plc, Annual Report 2001 (www.dssmith.uk.com)

Continued

enterprise, although the accountant will assert that the valuation has been made on a 'going concern basis', i.e. as if the bundle of assets will continue to operate in their current use. Such a valuation often, but not invariably, understates the earning power of the assets, particularly for profitable companies.

In the third edition of this book, the market value (or 'capitalisation') of D S Smith's equity at the Balance Sheet date was greatly in excess of the Balance Sheet value, because its net assets, when combined with its workforce and strategies, were at that time worth far more than the bare assets alone. However, repeating this analysis in 2001, we find capitalisation of £480 million, some 5 per cent less than the NAV. Possibly, D S Smith was going through a bad patch or the market was depressed at this time, but the question of future profitability and the break-up value of the firm arises. If the profit potential of a company is suspect, however, then break-up value assumes greater importance. The value of the assets in their best alternative use (e.g. selling them off) might then exceed the market value of the business, providing a signal to the owners to disband the enterprise and shift the resources into those alternative uses. Sometimes, then we may be able to adjust the NAV to take into account more up-to-date, or more relevant information, thus obtaining the **Adjusted NAV**.

Self-assessment Activity 4.2

For D S Smith plc, identify:

(i) the value of the whole firm, i.e. enterprise value
(ii) the value of its total liabilities
(iii) the value of the owners' equity.

(answer at end of chapter)

Problems with the NAV

The NAV, even as a measure of break-up value, may be defective for three main reasons.

1 Fixed asset values are based on historical cost

Book values of fixed assets, e.g. £587.6 million for D S Smith, are expressed net of depreciation, the result of writing down asset values over their assumed useful lives. Depreciating an asset, however, is not an attempt to arrive at a market-oriented assessment of value but an attempt to spread out the historical cost of an asset over its expected lifetime so as to reflect the annual cost of using it. It would be an amazing coincidence if the historical cost less accumulated depreciation were an accurate measure of the value of equipment to the owners, especially at times of generally rising prices. Some companies try to overcome this problem by periodic valuations of assets, especially freehold property. However, few companies do this annually, and even when they do, the resulting estimate is valid only at the stated dates. Whichever way we look at it, fixed asset values are always out-of-date!

A more sophisticated approach (but thus far stoutly resisted by the accounting profession) is to adopt **current cost accounting (CCA)**. Under CCA, assets are valued at their **replacement cost**, i.e. what it would cost the firm now to obtain assets of similar vintage. For example, if a machine cost £1 million five years ago, and asset prices have inflated at 10 per cent p.a., the cost of a new asset would be about £1.6 million (i.e.) £1 m $\times$ $(1.10)^5$. The historical cost less five years' depreciation on a straight-line basis, and assuming a ten-year life, would be £0.5 million. However, the cost of acquiring an asset of similar vintage, would be around £0.8 million.

There are obvious problems in applying CCA. For example, estimating current cost requires knowledge of the rate of inflation of identical assets, and of the impact of changing technology on replacement values. Nevertheless, the replacement cost measure is often far closer to a market value than historical cost less depreciation. Ideally, companies should revalue assets annually, but the time and costs involved are generally considered prohibitive.

Asset values may also fall. Directors are legally required to state in the annual report if the market value of assets is materially different from book value. It is better to 'bite the bullet' and actually reduce the value of poorly-performing assets in the accounts. This was done by BT in September 2001 when it announced a charge of £500 million in its first-half results to reflect the reduced value of its disastrous 9 per cent holding in AT&T Canada and its 20 per cent holding in Impsat of Argentina.

2 Stock values are often unreliable

Generally accepted accounting practice (GAAP) values stocks at the lower of cost or net realisable value. Such a conservative figure may hide appreciation in the value of stocks, e.g. when raw material and fuel prices are rising. Conversely, in some activities, fashions and tastes change rapidly, and although the recorded stock value might have been reasonably accurate at the Balance Sheet date, it may look inflated some time later.

3 The debtors figure may be suspect

Similar comments may apply to the recorded figure for debtors. Not all debtors can be easily converted into cash, since debtors may include an element of dubious or bad debts, although some degree of provision is normally made for these.

The debtor collection period, supplemented by an ageing profile of outstanding debts, should provide clues to the reliability of the debtors position.

4 A further problem: valuation of intangible assets

Even if these problems can be overcome, the resulting asset valuation is often less than the market value of the firm. 'People businesses' typically have few fixed assets and low stock levels. Based on the accounts, several leading quoted advertising agencies and consultancies have tiny or even negative NAVs.

Vanishing stock values (USA: stock inventory)

In March 2000, shares in New Economy powerhouse Cisco Systems Inc. peaked at $80, and its founder, Larry Ellison, became (briefly) the richest man in the world. Cisco, whose remarkable growth was founded on making gear to power the Internet, was now planning to re-focus on selling equipment to new-world telecoms companies planning to supplant 'dinosaurs' like AT&T.

Yet its customers were beginning to complain about long lead times for products. So Cisco entered into long-term supply contracts with suppliers and manufacturers to ensure the availability of customised components. But, already, the US economy was slowing down, reducing demand for Cisco's products. In April 2001, Cisco announced that sales for the current quarter were set to drop by 30 per cent, driving the share price down to a 52-week low of $13.63.

In May 2001, Cisco announced a third quarter loss of $2.7 billion, a loss struck after a write-down of excess stock by $2.2 billion, 70 per cent of this involving telecom gear and parts. The amount and the timing of the write-down surprised many. Cisco's inventory, valued at $4.1 billion for the quarter ending April 2001, was 65 per cent higher than the previous quarter's $2.5 billion, itself up from $1.3 billion a year earlier. Over the whole year, Cisco was clearly adding inventory that it knew it could not sell, given weak demand and rapid technological change. This raised the issue of why it had not disclosed any similar write-downs in previous quarters. The Cisco case clearly illustrates the folly of rapid stock-building of high-tech products based on suspect demand forecasts.

Mini case

Phantom debtors

Numerous 'phantom' debtors were found by the electronics and defence contractor Ferranti when it consolidated the accounts of its 1987 acquisition, US armaments manufacturer International Signal Corporation (ISC). ISC had carried some highly questionable debtors in its accounts for several years. As a result of this revelation, and allowing also for significant over-valuation of work-in-progress, in 1990 Ferranti was forced to write off £215 million of shareholder funds.

The former chairman of ISC was jailed for 15 years in 1991 for fraud, accused of misrepresenting ISC's true financial position. Ferranti never recovered from this fiasco, being forced to sell off its radar division to GEC for £310 million, and then experiencing a severe reduction in orders due to the ending of the Cold War. Mounting losses, worsening liquidity and the failure to secure a defence contract in Bahrain that would have yielded a much-needed advance payment, forced it to call an emergency general meeting (EGM) of shareholders in October 1993, when net worth fell below half of its

Continued

share capital. Shortly afterwards, it received a bid for a nominal 1p per share from GEC. This valued the equity at a mere £10 million compared with a mighty £845 million just before the ISC scandal was revealed. GEC was attracted by the sonar division, a joint venture with the French company, Thomson, a substantial pension fund surplus and unutilised tax losses. The bid, pitched well below the current market price of 9p, was probably designed to fail, but to draw more attention to Ferranti's parlous position. The shares were quickly re-rated by the market to around 3p.

The bid was recommended by the Ferranti board, reckoning that the alternative was liquidation, but in the face of mounting shareholder opposition, it became clear to GEC that it could not achieve the 90 per cent acceptances that they demanded. GEC withdrew the bid, and Ferranti was duly placed into receivership. GEC subsequently purchased a range of Ferranti's defence interests for less than it would have had to pay for the whole business, allowing for the Ferranti debt that it would have had to assume (about £100 million, dating back to the ISC acquisition).

There is a tailpiece to this story. The Ferranti purchase had been audited by accounting firm KPMG (then Peat Marwick) who paid Ferranti £40 million in 1991 in an out-of-court settlement in a negligence action. Following this, the Joint Disciplinary Scheme, which investigates cases of alleged professional misconduct and incompetence, began an examination of KPMG's due diligence studies conducted at the time of the takeover. In July 1996, the JDS concluded that KPMG had no case to answer as they were 'among those comprehensively deceived by a fraud which was designed and executed with extraordinary care and skill'.

It transpired that ISC had operated a money-laundering scheme involving the creation of front companies and fictitious contracts designed to inflate ISC's profits. Two missile contracts in particular, worth some £290 million, with the UAE and Pakistan, involved front companies supposedly representing South African and Chilean arms suppliers, yet apparently were not investigated by KPMG.

However, they often have substantial market values because the people they employ are 'assets' whose interactions confer earning power – the quality that ultimately determines value. This may be seen most clearly in the case of professional football clubs, few of which place a value for players on their Balance Sheets. Manchester United led the way in this respect when it valued its players prior to flotation on the market in 1991. The reader will find details of 17 quoted football companies in the Financial Times listings, 16 English and one Scottish (Celtic). Is your club there?

However, some other companies have attempted to close the gap between economic value and NAV by valuing certain intangible assets under their control, such as brand names.

Valuation of brands

The brand valuation issue came to the fore in 1988 when the Swiss confectionery and food giant Nestlé offered to buy Rowntree, the UK chocolate manufacturer, for more than double its then market value. This generated considerable discussion about whether and why the market had undervalued Rowntree and perhaps other companies that had invested heavily in brands, either via internal product development or by acquisition. Later that year, Grand Metropolitan Hotels (now Diageo) decided to capitalise acquired brands in their accounts, and were followed by several other owners of 'household name' brands, such as Rank-Hovis-McDougall, which capitalised 'home-grown' brands.

Decisions to enter the value of brands in Balance Sheets were partly a consequence of the prevailing official accounting guidelines, relating to the treatment of assets acquired at prices above book value, often termed 'goodwill'. These guidelines enabled firms to write off goodwill directly to reserves, thus reducing capital, rather than carrying it as an asset to be depreciated against income in the Profit and Loss Account, as in the USA and most European economies. UK regulations allowed companies to report higher earnings per share, but with reduced shareholder funds, thus raising the reported return on capital, especially for merger-active companies. Such write-offs have now been stopped by a new accounting standard, FRS10, which also prevents capitalisation of 'home-grown' brands.

Brand valuation raises the value of the intangible assets in the Balance Sheet and thus the NAV. Some chairpeople have presented the policy as an effort to make the market more aware of the 'true value' of the company. Under strong-form capital market efficiency, the effect on share price would be negligible, since the market would already be aware of the economic value of brands. However, under weaker forms of market efficiency, if placing a Balance Sheet value on brands provides genuinely new information, it may become an important vehicle for improving the stock market's ability to set 'fair' prices.

Methods of brand valuation

Many methods are available for establishing the value of a brand, all of which purport to assess the value to the firm of being able to exploit the profit potential of the brand.

1 Cost-based methods

At its simplest, the value of a brand is the historical cost incurred in creating the intangible asset. However, there is no obvious correlation between expenditure on the brand and its economic value, which derives from its future economic benefits. For example, do failed brands on which much money has been spent have high values? Replacement cost could be used, but it is difficult to estimate the costs of re-creating an asset without measuring its value initially. Alternatively, one may look at the cost of maintaining the value of the brand, including the cost of advertising and quality control. However, it is difficult to differentiate between expenditure incurred in maintaining the value of an asset and investment expenditure which enhances its value.

2 Methods based on market observation

Here, the value of the brand is determined by looking at the prices obtained in transactions involving comparable assets, for example, in mergers and acquisitions. This may be based on a direct price comparison, or by separating the market value of the company from its net tangible assets or by looking at the P:E multiple at which the deal took place, compared to similar unbranded businesses. Although the logic is more acceptable, the approach suffers from the infrequency of transactions involving similar brands, given that individual brands are supposedly unique.

3 Methods based on economic valuation

In general, the value of any asset is its capitalised net cash flows. If these can be readily identified, this approach is viable, but it requires separation of the cash flows associated with the brand from other company cash inflows. The 'brand contribution method' looks at the earnings contributed by the brand over and above those generated by the underlying or 'basic' business. The identification, separation and quantification of these earnings can be done by looking at the financial ratios (e.g. profit margin, ROI), of comparable non-branded goods and attributing any differential enjoyed by the brand itself as stemming from the value of the brand, i.e. the incremental value over a standard or 'generic' product.

For example, if a brand of chocolates enjoys a price premium of £1 per box over a comparable generic product, and the producer sells ten million boxes per year, the value of the brand is imputed as (£1 × 10 m) = £10 m p.a., which can then be discounted accordingly to derive its capital value. Alternatively, looking at comparative ROIs as between the branded manufacture and the generic, we may find a 5 per cent differential. If capital employed by the former is £100 million, this implies a profit differential of £5 million, which is then capitalised accordingly.

Such approaches beg many questions about the comparability of the manufacturers of branded and non-branded goods, the life span assumed, and the appropriate discount rate. Adjustments should also be made for brand maintenance costs, such as advertising, that result in cash outflows.

4 Brand strength methods

Other, more intuitive, methods have been devised which purport to capture the 'strength' of the brand. This involves assessing factors like market leadership, longevity, consumer esteem, recall and recognition, and then applying a subjectively determined multiplier to brand earnings in order to derive a value. Although appealing, the subjectivity of these approaches divorces them from commercial reality.

No broad measure of agreement has yet been reached about the best method to use in brand valuation, or whether the whole exercise is meaningful. Indeed, a report commissioned by the ICAEW (1989), which rejected brand valuation for Balance Sheet purposes, was said to have been welcomed by its sponsors. The report claimed that brand valuation 'is potentially corrosive to the whole basis of financial reporting', arguing that Balance Sheets do not purport to be statements of value!

Mini case

How Cadbury Schweppes valued its brands

In February 1990, Cadbury Schweppes, the confectionery and soft drinks group, placed a Balance Sheet value of £307 million on the main brands it had acquired during the previous five years. These included Canada Dry, Bassetts and Trebor. Its finance director argued that the prior practice of writing off goodwill purchased when companies were acquired at prices above asset values, and of writing off to Profit and Loss Account the ongoing expenditure on 'nurturing and succouring' brands 'to make them grow and be more valuable', had led to serious understatement of shareholder funds in the accounts. The valuation was based on the cost of the brands, assessed by their imputed earning power at the time of acquisition. The effect was to double the Balance Sheet value of shareholder funds. However, the market was indifferent. On the announcement day, Cadbury shares actually fell from 317p to 315p (less than 1 per cent) against a similar fall in the market. But had the market anticipated this announcement after other brand-owners had previously adopted similar policies?

The role of the NAV

Generally speaking, the NAV, even when based on reliable accounting data, only really offers a guide to the lower limit of the value of owners' equity, but even so, some form of adjustment is often required. Assets are often revalued as a takeover defence tactic. The motive is to raise the market value of the firm and thus make the bid more expensive and difficult to finance. However, the impact on share price will be minimal unless the revaluation provides new information, which largely depends on the perceived quality and objectivity of the 'expert valuation'.

We conclude that while the NAV may provide a useful reference point, it is unlikely to be a reliable guide to valuation. This is largely because it neglects the capacity of the assets to generate earnings. We now consider the commonest of the earning-based methods of valuation, the use of price-to-earnings multiples.

4.4 Valuing the earnings stream

It is well known that accounting-based measures of earnings are suspect for several reasons, including the arbitrariness of the depreciation provisions (usually based on the historic cost of the assets) and the propensity of firms to designate unusually high items of cost or revenue as 'exceptional' (i.e. unlikely to be repeated in magnitude in future years). Yet we find that one of the commonest methods of valuation in practice is based on accounting profit. This method uses the **price-to-earnings multiple** or **P:E** ratio.

The meaning of the P:E ratio

As we saw in Chapter 2, the P:E ratio is simply the market price of a share divided by the last reported earnings per share (EPS). P:E ratios are cited daily in the financial press and vary with market prices. A P:E ratio measures the price that the market attaches to each £1 of company earnings, and thus superficially (at least) is a sort of payback period. For example, for its financial year 2000–01, Severn Trent Water plc reported EPS of 53p. Its share price in late September 2001 was 730p producing a P:E ratio of 13.8. Allowing for daily variations, the market seemed to indicate that it was prepared to wait about 14 years to recover the share price, on the basis of the 2001 earnings. So would a higher P:E ratio signify a willingness to wait longer? Not necessarily, because companies that sell at relatively high P:E ratios do so because the market values their perceived ability to grow their earnings from the present level. Contrary to some popular belief, a high P:E ratio does not signify that a company has done well, but that it is *expected* to do better in the future. (Not that they always do – witness the very high P:E ratios among 'dotcom' companies in 1999–2000.)

The P:E ratio varies directly with share price, but it also *derives from* the share price, i.e. from market valuation, so how does this help with valuation? Investment analysts typically have in mind what an 'appropriate' P:E ratio should be for particular share categories and individual companies, and look for disparities between sectors and companies. If, for example, BP is selling at a P:E ratio of 15 with EPS of 45p, and Shell whose EPS is 40p has a P:E ratio of 20, then their share values may look out of line. Assuming Shell's shares are correctly valued at (20 × 40p) = £8, then BP's shares, priced at (15 × 45p) = £6.75, might appear undervalued.

Of course, there is a circularity here – this conclusion relies on the assumption that Shell rather than BP is correctly valued. Moreover, despite the apparent similarity of these two oil majors, there may be very good reasons why they should be valued differently. BP's earnings may be far more variable – it operates further 'upstream' (away from the final consumer) than Shell, and hence turbulence in the primary oil markets hits its profits harder.

Using P:E ratios to detect under- or over-valuation implies that markets are slow or inefficient processors of information, but there are reliable rough benchmarks that can be utilised. The industry benchmark is established by one or more transactions, against which other deals in the same industry can be judged, and exceptions identified. In some industries, analysts use benchmarks other than the earnings figure implicit in the P:E ratio. Some examples are multiples of billings in advertising, sale price per room in hotels, price per subscriber in mail order businesses, price per bed in nursing homes, and the more grisly 'stiff ratio' (value per funeral) in the undertaking business. At the height of the 'dotcom boom', some analysts attempted to explain the stratospheric valuations of internet companies in terms of number of 'hits' or visits to the site in question. More analysts are now utilising multiples based on cash flow. This development hints at the major problem with using P:E ratios – it relies on accounting profits rather than the expected cash flows which confer value on any item. We now consider cash-flow-oriented approaches to valuation.

Self-assessment Activity 4.3

XYZ plc, which is unquoted, earns profit before tax of £80 million. It has issued 100 million shares. The rate of Corporation Tax is 30 per cent.
A similar listed firm sells at a P:E ratio of 15:1. What value would you place on XYZ's shares?

(answer at end of chapter)

4.5 EBITDA – a half-way house

Cash flows and profits differ due to application of accruals accounting principles, but value depends upon cash generating ability rather than 'profitability'. An intermediate concept currently in vogue is that of **EBITDA**, an unattractive acronym standing for **Earnings Before Interest, Taxes, Depreciation and Amoritisation.** EBITDA is equivalent to operating profit with depreciation and amoritisation (the writing-down of intangible assets) added back. As such, it is a measure of the basic operating cash flow before deducting tax, but ignoring working capital movements.

Many companies use EBITDA as a measure of performance, especially when related to capital employed. For example, E.On AG, the German utility and chemicals group, evaluates the performance of both the whole firm and its business units by using a measure known as **Cash Flow Return on Investment (CFROI).** This is essentially a cash-based measure of return on capital employed, which is not influenced by the capital structure. In other words, being expressed before interest and tax, it is independent of financing policy, and thus the 'share-out' of the operating profit as between interest payments, taxation and profits for shareholders. According to E.On, EBITDA has the merit of being '. . . net of one-off and rare effects, which mainly include book gains from divestments and expenses for re-structuring and cost management. EBITDA thus represents the sustainable return on capital employed'.

However, EBITDA is essentially a *performance* measure. It can only be used in valuation if we look at the way in which the market values other companies' EBITDAs. As with P:E ratios, comparison with other companies is needed as a reference point. For example, in late 2000, when Coca-Cola was evaluating Quaker as an acquisition candidate, observers noted that Coke was prepared to pay some 16 times Quaker's EBITDA, which appeared expensive, being well above recent deals in the US food sector. Attempting to explain this, the *Financial Times* suggested that if the Quaker food division were valued at the then prevailing industry average of ten times EBITDA, then the bid price implied an EBITDA multiple of 25 times for the real jewel in Quaker's crown, the fast-growing Gatorade sports drink.

In July 2001, the US oil firm Amerada Hess acquired Triton Energy in order to acquire its upstream capability and exploration skills. The price paid per share was $45 cash, a premium of 50 per cent to Triton's previous share price. The comment was made that it was paying 'top dollar'. Including some $500 million of debt, Amerada was laying out 9 times 2001 EBITDA, in line with similar deals involving acquisition of proven reserves but ahead of valuations for oil companies oriented more towards downstream activities.

Like a P:E multiple, an EBITDA multiple used in valuation stems from the value which the market attaches to other companies' EBITDAs, which invites the question of how it values those other companies, i.e. the EBITDA multiple is led by the valuation. Moreover, even when used crudely as a rough-and-ready comparison of value, one should appreciate that it is still based on accounting earnings. Although gross of depreciation and special items, it is still subject to different accounting practices between firms at the operating level, e.g. stock valuation.

Continuing to focus on income-generating methods, we now examine the genuine article, Discounted Cash Flow.

4.6 Valuing cash flows

The value of any asset depends upon the stream of benefits that the owner expects to enjoy from his or her ownership. Sometimes these benefits are intangible, as in the case of Van Gogh's 'Sunflowers', which simply gives pleasure from looking at it. In the case of financial assets, the benefits are less subjective. Ownership of ordinary shares, for example, entitles the holder to receive a stream of future cash flows in the form of dividends plus a lump sum when the shares are sold on to the next purchaser, or if held until the demise of the company, a liquidating dividend when it is finally wound up. In the case of an all-equity financed company, the earnings over time should be compared on an equivalent basis by discounting them at the minimum rate of return required by shareholders or the **cost of equity capital** (which we henceforth denote as k_e).

Valuing a newly created company: Navenby plc

Navenby plc is to be formed by public issue of one million £1 shares. It proposes to purchase and let out residential property in a prime location. It has been agreed that, after five years, the company will be liquidated and the proceeds returned to shareholders. The fully-subscribed book value of the company is £1 million, the amount of cash offered for the shares. However, this takes no account of the investment returns likely to be generated by Navenby. In the prospectus inviting investors to subscribe, the company announced details of its £1 million investment programme. It has concluded a deal with a builder to purchase a block of properties on very attractive terms, as well as instructing a letting agency to rent out the properties at a guaranteed income of £130,000 p.a. Based upon past property price movements, Navenby's management estimate 70 per cent capital appreciation over the five-year period. All net income flows (after management fees of £30,000 p.a.) will be paid out as dividends.

Continued

In the absence of risk and taxation, Navenby is easy to value. Its value is the sum of discounted future expected cash flows (including the residual asset value) from the project i.e. (£130,000 – £30,000) p.a., plus the eventual sales proceeds:

	Year				
	1	2	3	4	5
Net rentals p.a. (£m)	+0.1	+0.1	+0.1	+0.1	+0.1
Sales proceeds (£m)					+1.7

If shareholders require, say, a 12 per cent return for an activity of this degree of risk, the present value (PV) of the project is found using the relevant annuity (PVIFA) and single payment (PVIF) discount factors, introduced in Chapter 3, as follows:

$$\begin{aligned} PV &= (£0.1\text{ m} \times PVIFA_{(12,5)}) + (£1.7\text{ m} \times PVIF_{(12,5)}) \\ &= (£0.1\text{ m} \times 3.6048) + (£1.7\text{ m} \times 0.5674) \\ &= (£0.361\text{ m} + £0.964\text{ m}) = £1.325\text{ m} \end{aligned}$$

The value of the company is £1.325 million and shareholders are better off by £0.325 million. In effect, the managers of Navenby are offering to convert subscriptions of £1 million into cash flows worth £1.325 million. If there is general consensus that these figures are reasonable estimates, and if the market efficiently processes new information, then Navenby's share price should be £1.325 m/1 m = £1.325 when information about the project is released. If so, Navenby will have created wealth of £0.325 million for its shareholders.

Self-assessment Activity 4.4

Navenby has a value of £1.325 million, but a major part of this reflects the eventual resale value of the assets. What final asset value would enable investors to just break even?

(answer at end of chapter)

The general valuation model (GVM)

In analysing Navenby, we applied the **general valuation model,** which states that the value of any asset is the sum of all future discounted net benefits expected to flow from the asset:

$$V_o = \sum_{t=0}^{n} \frac{X_t}{(1 + k_e)^t}$$

where X_t is the net cash inflow or outflow in year t, k_e is the rate of return required by shareholders and n is the time period over which the asset is expected to generate benefits.

It should be noted that for a newly-formed company, such as Navenby, the valuation expression can be written in two ways:

value = cash subscription + NPV of proposed activities

or

value = present value of all future cash inflows less outflows

These are equivalent expressions. The value of Navenby is £1.325 million, and the net value of the investment is £0.325 million, i.e. it would be rational to pay up to £0.325 million to be allowed to undertake the investment opportunity. Valuation of Navenby is relatively straightforward partly because the company has only one activity, but primarily because most key factors are known with a high degree of precision (although not the residual value). In practice, future company cash flows and dividends are far less certain.

The oxygen of publicity

Many corporate managers are somewhat parsimonious in their release of information to the market. Their motives are often understandable, such as reluctance to divulge commercially-sensitive information. As a result, many valuations are largely based on inspired guesswork. The value of a company quoted on a semi-strong efficient share market can only be the product of what information has been released, supplemented by intuition.

Yet company chairpeople are often heard to complain that the market persistently undervalues 'their' companies. Some, for example Richard Branson (Virgin) and Andrew Lloyd-Webber (Really Useful Group), in exasperation, even mounted buy-back operations to re-purchase publicly held shares. The 'problem', however, is often of their own making. The market can only absorb and process that information which is offered to it. Indeed, information-hoarding may even be interpreted adversely. If information about company performance and future prospects is jealously guarded, we should not be surprised when the valuation appears somewhat enigmatic.

4.7 The DCF approach

The previous section implies that we should rely on a discounted cash flow approach. After all, it is rational to attach value to future cash proceeds rather than to accounting earnings, which are based on numerous accounting conventions, including the deduction of a largely notional charge for depreciation. Given that depreciation is a non-cash item, surely all we need do is to take the reported profit after tax (PAT) figure and add back depreciation to arrive at cash flow and then discount accordingly?

As a first approximation, we could thus value a company by valuing the stream of annual cash flows as measured by:

Cash flow = (operating profit + depreciation)
= (cash revenues – cash operating costs)

The depreciation charge is added back because it is merely an accounting adjustment to reflect the fall in value of assets. If firms did replace capacity as it expired, in principle, this investment should equate to depreciation. In practice, however, only by coincidence does the annual depreciation charge accurately measure the annual capital expenditure required to maintain production, and thus earnings capacity. Moreover, most companies need investment funds for growth purposes as well as for replacement. The value of growing companies depends not simply on the earning power of their existing assets, but also on their growth potential; in other words, the NPV of the cash flows from all future non-replacement investment opportunities.

This suggests a revised concept of cash flow. To obtain an accurate assessment of value, we should assess total ongoing investment needs and set these against anticipated revenue and operating cost flows; otherwise we might over-value the company.

Valuation and free cash flow (FCF)

The inflow remaining net of investment outlays is referred to as **free cash flow** (i.e. 'free' of investment expenditure).

Free cash flow = [revenues − operating costs] + [depreciation] − [investment expenditure]

Using this measure, the value of a company is the sum of future discounted free cash flows:

$$V_o = \sum_{t=1}^{n} \frac{FCF}{(1 + k_e)^t}$$

This approach removes the problem of confining investment financing to retentions, as in the **Dividend Growth Model** (see below). However, we encounter significant forecasting problems in having to assess the growth opportunities and their financing needs in all future years.

Unfortunately, the accounting data for revenues and operating costs upon which this approach is based may fail to reflect cash flows due to movements in the various items of working capital. For example, a sales increase may raise reported profits, but if made on lengthy credit terms, the effect on cash flow is delayed. Indeed, the net effect may be negative if suppliers of additional raw materials insist on payment before debtors settle.

It is important to mention another distortion. Stock-building, either in advance of an expected sales increase or simply through poor inventory control, can seriously impair cash flow, although the initial impact on profit reflects only the increased stockholding costs.

For these and similar reasons, accurate estimation of cash flow involves forecasting not merely all future years' sales, relevant costs and profits, but also all movements in working capital and taxation payments. Alternatively, one may assume that these factors will have a net cancelling effect, which may be reasonable for longer-term valuations but much less appropriate for short time-horizon valuations, as in the case of high-risk activities. Figure 4.1 provides a schema to show the calculation of FCF, and how it relates to other cash flow concepts.

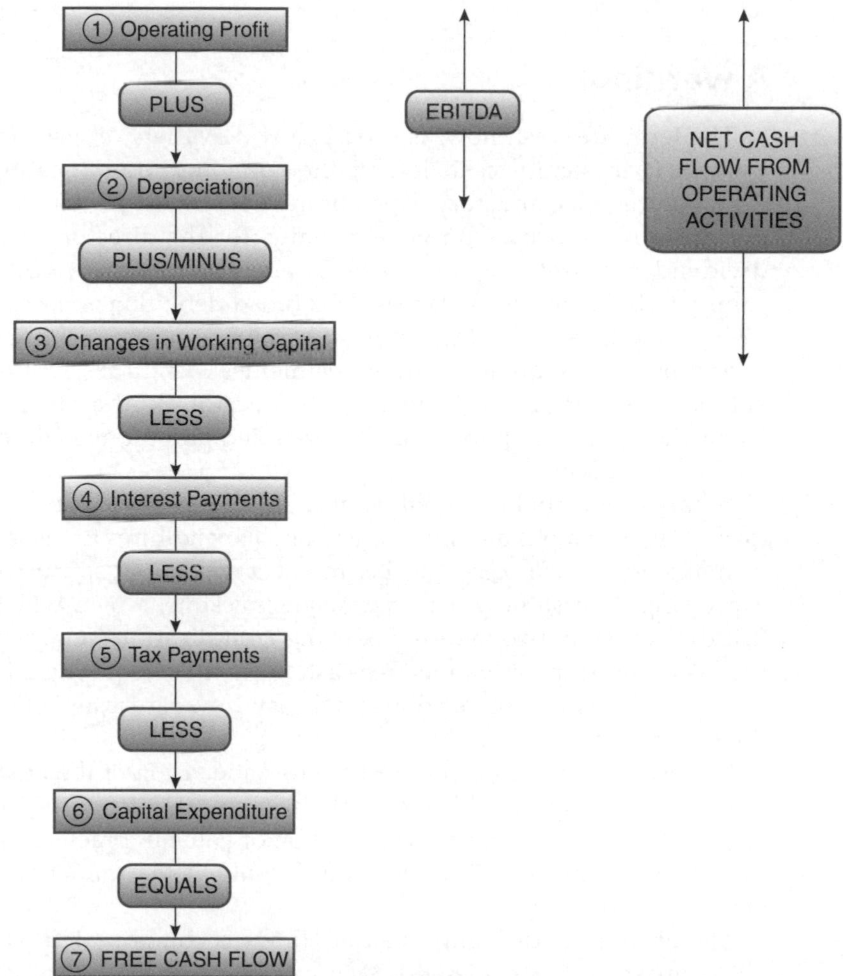

Notes: 1 ①+② is roughly equivalent to EBITDA.

2 ①+②+③ corresponds to 'Net Cash Flow from Operating Activities' found on a UK firm's Cash Flow Statement.

3 Item ⑥ is sometimes confined to Replacement Capital Expenditure.

Figure 4.1 Calculating Free Cash Flow (FCF)

Self-assessment Activity 4.5

What is the free cash flow for the following firm?

Operating Profit (after depreciation of £2 m)	= £25 m
Interest paid	= £1 m
Tax rate	= 30%
Investment expenditure	= £3 m

(answer at end of chapter)

A warning!

The term 'free cash flow' is used in a wide variety of ways in practice. Here, we use it to signify cash left in the company after meeting all operating expenditures, all mandatory expenditures such as tax payments, and investment expenditure. It focuses on what remains for the directors to spend either as dividend payments, repayment of debts, acquisition of other companies or simply to build up cash balances. This broad definition is necessary because the cash inflow figure is defined to include revenues from both existing and future operations. Consequently, the investment expenditure required to generate enhancements in revenue must be allowed for. By the same token, a growth factor should be incorporated in the operating profit figures to reflect the returns on this investment.

A narrower definition could be used to confine cash inflows to those relating to existing operations and investment, and expenditures to those required simply to make good wear and tear, i.e. replacement outlays. This has the merit of expressing the cash flow before strategic investment, over which directors have full discretion. It also avoids financing complications, e.g. where a company wishes to invest more than its free cash flows, thus requiring additional external finance, which may distort the actual cash flow figure, as reflected in the cash flow statement.

However, this yields a very restricted, static vision of the business, neglecting the strategic opportunities and their costs and benefits, which are truly responsible for imparting a major portion of value in practice. Failure to capture these longer-term strategic opportunities could yield a valuation well short of the market's assessment.

The problem of defining free cash flows is compounded by examination of UK company reports. Listed UK companies are obliged to present cash flow statements which report the net change in cash and near cash holdings over the year. This is a backward-looking statement which says more about past liquidity changes than future cash flows. Some firms do report a figure for 'free cash flow', but often without defining it. Jupe and Rutherford (1997) analysed the reports of 222 of the 250 largest listed UK companies. They found that just 21 disclosed a free cash flow figure, although only 14 used the term itself, and few of these supplied either a definition or a breakdown. Analysis of the comments of 13 companies appeared to reveal the use of 13 different definitions. Clearly, this is an area where care is required in definition and usage.

4.8 Valuation of unquoted companies

The inexact science of valuing a company or its shares is made considerably simpler if the firm's shares are traded on a stock market. If trading is regular and frequent, and if the market has a high degree of information efficiency, we may feel able to trust market values. If so, the models of valuation merely provide a check, or enable us to assess the likely impact of altering key parameters such as dividend policy or introducing more efficient management.

With unquoted companies, the various models have a leading rather than a supporting role, but give by no means definitive answers. Attempts to use the models inevitably suffer from information deficiencies, which may be only partially overcome. For example, in using a P:E multiple, a question arises concerning the appropriate P:E ratio to apply. Many experts advocate using the P:E ratio of a 'surrogate' quoted company, one that is similar in all or most respects to the unquoted subject. One possible approach is to take a sample of 'similar' quoted companies, and find a weighted average P:E ratio using market capitalisations as weights.

However, the shares of a quoted company are, by definition, more marketable than those of unquoted firms, and marketability usually attracts a premium, suggesting a lower P:E ratio for the unquoted company. Any adjustment for this factor is bound to be arbitrary, and different valuation experts might well apply quite different adjustment factors.

Furthermore, a major problem in valuing and acquiring unquoted companies is the need to tie in the key managers for a sufficient number of years to ensure the recovery of the investment. The cost of such 'earn-outs', or '**golden handcuffs**', could be a major component of the purchase consideration.

In principle, all the valuation approaches explained in this chapter are applicable to valuing unquoted companies, so long as suitable surrogates can be found, or if reliable industry averages are available. If surrogate data cannot be used, valuation becomes even more subjective. In these circumstances, it is not unusual to find valuers convincing themselves that company accounts are objective and reliable indicators of value. While accounts may offer a veneer of objectivity, we need hardly repeat the pitfalls in their interpretation.

4.9 Valuing shares: the Dividend Valuation Model

The Navenby example (discussed in Section 4.6) demonstrates why investors purchase and hold ordinary shares. Shareholders attach value to shares because they expect to receive a stream of dividends and hope to make an eventual capital gain. However, Navenby was a special case because it proposed to pay out all its earnings as dividend – few companies do this in reality. Although shareholders are legally entitled to the earnings of a company, in the case of a company with a dispersed ownership body, their influence on the dividend payout is limited by their ability to exert their voting power on the directors. Other things being equal, shareholders prefer higher to lower dividends, but issues such as capital investment strategy and taxation may cloud the relationship between dividend policy and share value. With this reservation in mind, we now develop the **Dividend Valuation Model (DVM)**. This is appropriate for valuing part shares of companies rather than whole enterprises. This is because minority shareholders have little or no control over dividend policy and thus it is reasonable to project past dividend policy, especially as companies are known to prefer a steadily rising dividend pattern rather than more erratic payouts. Conversely, if control changes hands, the new owner can appropriate the earnings as it chooses.

Valuing the dividend stream

The DVM states that the value of a share now, P_o, is the sum of the stream of future discounted dividends plus the value of the share as and when sold, in some future year, n:

$$P_o = \frac{D_1}{(1 + k_e)} + \frac{D_2}{(1 + k_e)^2} + \frac{D_3}{(1 + k_e)^3} + \cdots + \frac{D_n}{(1 + k_e)^n} + \frac{P_n}{(1 + k_e)^n}$$

However, since the new purchaser will, in turn, value the stream of dividends after year n, we can infer that the value of the share at any time may be found by valuing all future expected dividend payments over the lifetime of the firm. If the lifespan is assumed infinite and the annual dividend is constant, we have:

$$P_o = \sum_{t=1}^{\infty} \frac{D_t}{(1 + k_e)^t} = \frac{D_1}{k_e}, \quad \text{where} \quad D_1 = D_2 = D_3 \text{ etc.}$$

This is an application of valuing a perpetuity, the mathematics of which were explained in Appendix III to Chapter 3.

For example, the shares of a company whose owners require a return of 15 per cent, and which is expected to pay a constant annual dividend of 30p per share through time would be valued thus:

$$P_o = \frac{30\text{p}}{0.15} = £2.00 \text{ per share}$$

In reality, the assumptions underlying this basic model are suspect. The annual dividend is unlikely to remain unchanged indefinitely, and it is difficult to forecast a varying stream of future dividend flows. To a degree, the forecasting problem is moderated by the effect of applying a risk-adjusted discount rate because more distant dividends are more heavily discounted. For example, discounting at 20 per cent, the present value of a dividend of £1 in 15 years' time is only 6p, while £1 received in 20 years adds only 3p to the value of a share. In other words, for a plausible cost of equity, we lose little by assuming a time-horizon of, say, 15 years. Even so, reliable valuations still require estimates of dividends over the intervening years, and by the same token, any errors will have a magnified effect during this period.

Allowing for future dividend growth

Dividends fluctuate over time, largely because of variations in the company's fortunes, although most firms attempt to grow dividends more or less in line with the company's longer-term earnings growth rate. For reasons explained in Chapter 19, financial managers attempt to 'smooth' the stream of dividends. For companies operating in mature industries, the growth rate will roughly correspond to the underlying growth rate of the whole economy. For companies operating in activities with attractive growth opportunities, dividends are likely to grow at a faster rate, at least over the medium term.

Allowing for dividend growth: the DGM

The constant dividend valuation model can be extended to cover constant growth thus becoming the Dividend Growth Model (DGM). This states that the value of a share is the sum of all discounted dividends, growing at the annual rate g:

$$P_o = \frac{D_o(1+g)}{(1+k_e)} + \frac{D_o(1+g)^2}{(1+k_e)^2} + \frac{D_o(1+g)^3}{(1+k_e)^3} + \cdots + \frac{D_o(1+g)^n}{(1+k_e)^n}$$

If D_o is this year's dividend, recently been paid, $D_o(1 + g)$ is the dividend to be paid in one year's time (D_1), and so on.

Appendix II to Chapter 3 shows that such a series growing to infinity has a present value of:

$$P_o = \frac{D_o(1+g)}{(k_e - g)} = \frac{D_1}{(k_e - g)}$$

The growth version of the model is often used in practice by security analysts (it is popularly known as 'the dividend discount model'), at least as a reference point, but it makes some key assumptions. Dividend growth is assumed to result from earnings growth, generated solely by new investment financed by retained earnings. Such investment is, of course, worthwhile only if the anticipated rate of return, R, is in excess of the cost of equity, k_e. Furthermore, it is assumed that the company will retain a constant fraction of earnings and invest these in a continuous stream of projects all offering a return of R. It also breaks down if g exceeds k_e. (Problems with the DGM are discussed in Section 4.10)

Navenby again

To illustrate the growth model, we return to the Navenby example but assume an infinite project and thus business life, which requires removal of the asset sale at the end of year 5. Suppose further that, at the end of the first year, it will retain 50 per cent of its earnings and reinvest these at an expected annual return of 20 per cent, comfortably above the required 12 per cent. In the next year, earnings would grow at 10 per cent to reach a new level of:

'original' cash flow + return on reinvested earnings =
new earnings level of £0.1 m + 20% (50% × £0.1 m) = (£0.1 m + £0.01 m) = £0.11 m

If further retentions of 50 per cent are made at the end of the second year and also reinvested in further projects offering annual returns of 20 per cent, earnings after three years will be:

£0.11 m + 20% (50% × £0.11 m) = (£0.11 m + £0.011 m) = £0.121 m

and so on. The policy of retention and reinvestment has launched Navenby on an exponential growth path. The dividend growth rate of 10 per cent is a compound of the retention ratio, denoted by b, and the return on reinvested earnings, R:

$$g = (b \times R) = (50\% \times 20\%) = 10\%$$

Table 4.2 shows the future behaviour of both earnings and dividends assuming b and R are constant. Clearly, both magnitudes grow in tandem, so long as the company maintains the same retention ratio (50 per cent).

Table 4.2 How earnings and dividends grow in tandem (figures in £m)

	Year				
	1	**2**	**3**	**4**	**etc.**
Earnings	0.10	0.11	0.121	0.1331	etc.
Dividends (50%)	0.05	0.055	0.0605	0.06655	etc.

In Chapter 19, we examine more fully the issues of whether and how a change in dividend policy can be expected to alter share value. For the moment, we are mainly concerned with the mechanics of the DGM and rely simply on the assumption that any retained earnings are used for worthwhile investment. If this applies, the value of the equity will be higher with retentions-plus-reinvestment than if the investment opportunities were neglected, i.e. the decision to retain earnings benefits the shareholders because of company access to projects offering returns higher than the owners could otherwise obtain.

Self-assessment Activity 4.6

XYZ plc earns 16p per share. It retains 75 per cent of its profits to reinvest at an average return of 18 per cent. Its shareholders require a return of 15 per cent. What is the ex-dividend value of XYZ's shares? What happens to this value if investors suddenly become more risk-averse by seeking a return of 20 per cent?

(answer at end of chapter)

4.10 Problems with the Dividend Growth Model

The Dividend Growth Model, while possessing some convenient properties, also has some major limitations.

What if the company pays no dividend?

The company may be faced with highly attractive investment opportunities that cannot be financed in other ways. According to the model, such a company would have no value at all! Total retention is fairly common, either because the company has suffered an actual or expected earnings collapse, or because, as in some European economies (e.g. Switzerland), the expressed policy of some firms is to pay no dividends at all. The American computer software firm Microsoft has only recently begun to pay dividends, while two other computer firms, Dell and Compaq, have yet to pay dividends. In these cases, we observe that shares in such companies do not have zero values. Indeed, nothing could be further from the truth.

In the case of Dell, $100 invested in its initial public offering in June 1988, would have been worth $28,360 by February 2001 following 100 per cent profits retention. After seven stock splits, 100 shares of Dell was equivalent to 9,600 shares. In 1998, it was reported that Bill Gates, co-founder of Microsoft and still the main shareholder, had become the world's richest man with a personal fortune of over $50 billion. Even after the September 2001 terrorist attacks, Gates' stake in Microsoft stood at $53 billion, according to *Forbes* magazine.

A distressed company would have a positive value so long as its management were thought capable of staging a corporate recovery, i.e. the market is valuing more distant dividends on hopes of a turn-around in earnings. If recovery is thought unlikely, the company is valued at its break-up value.

For inveterate non-dividend payers, the market is implicitly valuing the liquidating dividend when the company is ultimately wound up. Until this happens, the company is adding to its reserves as it reinvests, and continually enhancing its assets, its earning power and its value. In effect, the market is valuing the stream of future earnings that are legally the property of the shareholders.

Will there always be enough worthwhile projects in the future?

The DGM implies an ongoing supply of attractive projects to match the earnings available for retention. It is most unlikely that there will always be sufficient attractive projects available, each offering a constant rate of return, R, sufficient to absorb a given fraction, b, of earnings in each future year. While a handful of firms do have very lengthy lifespans, corporate history typically parallels the marketing concept of the product life cycle – introduction, (rapid) growth, maturity, decline and death – with paucity of investment opportunities a very common reason for corporate demise. It is thus rather hopeful to value a firm over a perpetual lifespan. However, remember that the discounting process compresses most of the value into a lifespan of, say, 15 years.

What if the growth rate exceeds the discount rate?

The arithmetic of the model shows that if $g > k_e$, the denominator becomes negative and value is infinite. Again, this appears nonsensical, but, in reality, many companies do experience periods of very rapid growth. Usually, however, company growth settles down to a less dramatic pace after the most attractive projects are exploited, once the firm's markets mature and competition emerges. There are two ways of redeeming the model in these cases. First, we may regard g as a long-term average or 'normal' growth rate. This is not totally satisfactory, as rapid growth often occurs early in the life cycle and the value computed would thus understate the worth of near-in-time dividends. Alternatively, we could segment the company's lifespan into periods of varying growth and value these separately. For example, if we expect fast growth in the first five years and slower growth thereafter, the expression for value is:

$$P_o = \text{[Present value of dividends during year 1–5]} + \text{[Present value of all further dividends]}$$

Note that the second term is a perpetuity beginning in year 6, but we have to find its present value. Hence it is discounted down to year zero as in the following expression:

$$P_o = \frac{D_o(1+g_f)}{(1+k_e)} + \frac{D_o(1+g_f)^2}{(1+k_e)^2} + \cdots + \frac{D_o(1+g_f)^5}{(1+k_e)^5} + \left(\frac{D_5(1+g_s)}{(k_e - g_s)} \times \frac{1}{(1+k_e)^5}\right)$$
$$= \sum_{t=1}^{5} \frac{D_o(1+g_f)}{(1+k_e)^t} + \sum_{t=6}^{\infty} \frac{D_5(1+g_s)}{(1+k_e)^t}$$

where g_f is the rate of fast growth during years 1–5 and g_s is the rate of slow growth beginning in year 6, (i.e. from the end of year 5.)

The DGM may be used to examine the impact of changes in dividend policy, i.e. changes in b. Detailed analysis of this issue is deferred to Chapter 19.

Example: the case of unequal growth rates

Consider the case of dividend growth of 25 per cent for years 1–5 and 7 per cent thereafter. Assuming shareholders require a return of 10 per cent, and that dividend in year zero is 10p, the value of the share is calculated as follows:

For years 1–5			
Year	**Dividend (p)**	**Discount factor at 10%**	**PV (p)**
1	10(1.25) = 12.5	0.909	11.4
2	$12.50(1.25)^2$ = 15.6	0.826	12.9
3	etc. = 19.5	0.751	14.6
4	= 24.4	0.683	16.7
5	= 30.5	0.621	18.9
		Total =	74.5

For later years, we anticipate a perpetual stream growing from the year 5 value at 7 per cent p.a. The present value of this stream as at the end of year 5 is:

$$\frac{D_6}{k_e - g_s} = \frac{D_5(1 + 7\%)}{(10\% - 7\%)} = \frac{30.5\text{p}(1.07)}{0.03} = \frac{32.64\text{p}}{0.03} = £10.88$$

This figure, representing the PV of all dividends following year 5, is now converted into a year zero present value:

$PV = £10.88\ (PVIF_{10,5}) = (£10.88 \times 0.621) = £6.76$

Adding in the PV of the dividends for the first five years, the PV of the share right now is:

$PV = (£0.745 + £6.76) = £7.51$

However, we may note here that valuation of the dividend stream implies a known dividend policy. Because dividends are not controlled by shareholders, but by the firm's directors, the DGM is more applicable to the valuation of investment stakes in companies than to the valuation of whole companies, as in takeover situations. When company control changes hands, control of dividend policy is also transferred. It seems unrealistic, therefore, to assume an unchanged dividend policy when valuing a company for takeover.

The P:E ratio and the Constant Dividend Valuation Model

If we examine the P:E ratio more closely, we find it has a close affinity with the growth version of the DVM. The P:E ratio is defined as price per share (PPS) divided by earnings per share (EPS). In its reciprocal form, it measures the **earnings yield** of the firm's shares:

$$\frac{1}{\text{P:E}} = \frac{\text{EPS}}{\text{PPS}} = \frac{\text{Earnings}}{\text{Company value}} = \frac{E}{V}$$

This equals the dividend yield plus retained earnings (bE) per share. As in the DGM, the growth version of the DVM, we define the fraction of earnings retained as b. We can then write:

$$\frac{E}{V} = \frac{D}{V} + \frac{bE}{V}$$

The ratio E/V is the overall rate of return *currently* achieved. If this equals R, the rate of return on reinvested funds, then bE/V is equivalent to the growth rate g in the DGM. In other words, the earnings yield, E/V, comprises the dividend yield plus the growth rate or 'capital gains yield' for a company retaining a constant fraction of earnings and investing at the rate R. The two approaches thus look very similar. However, this apparent similarity should not be over-emphasised for three important reasons:

1 The earnings yield is expressed in terms of the current earnings, whereas the DGM deals with the *prospective* dividend yield and growth rate, i.e. the former is historic in its focus, while the latter is forward-looking.
2 The DGM relies on discounting cash returns, while the earnings figure is based on accounting concepts. It does not follow that cash flows will coincide with accounting profit, not least due to depreciation adjustments.
3 For the equivalence to hold, the current rate of return, E/V, would have to equal the rate of return expected on future investments.

Despite these qualifications, it is still common to find the earnings yield presented as the rate of return required by shareholders, and hence the cut-off rate for new investment projects. Unfortunately, this confuses a historical accounting measure with a forward-looking concept.

4.11 Shareholder Value Analysis

During the 1980s, based on the work of Rappaport (1986), an allegedly new approach to valuation emerged, called **shareholder value analysis (SVA)**. In fact, it is not really novel, but a rather different way of looking at value, based on the NPV approach.

The key assumption of SVA is that a business is worth the net present value of its future cash flows, discounted at the appropriate cost of capital. Many leading US corporations (e.g. Westinghouse, Pepsi and Disney) and a growing number of European companies (e.g. Philips, Siemens) have embraced SVA because it provides a framework for linking management decisions and strategies to value creation. The focus is on how a business can plan and manage its activities to increase value for shareholders and, at the same time, benefit other stakeholders.

How is this achieved? Figure 4.2 shows the relationship between decision-making and shareholder value. Key decisions – whether strategic, operational, investment or financial – with important cash flow and risk implications are specified. Managers

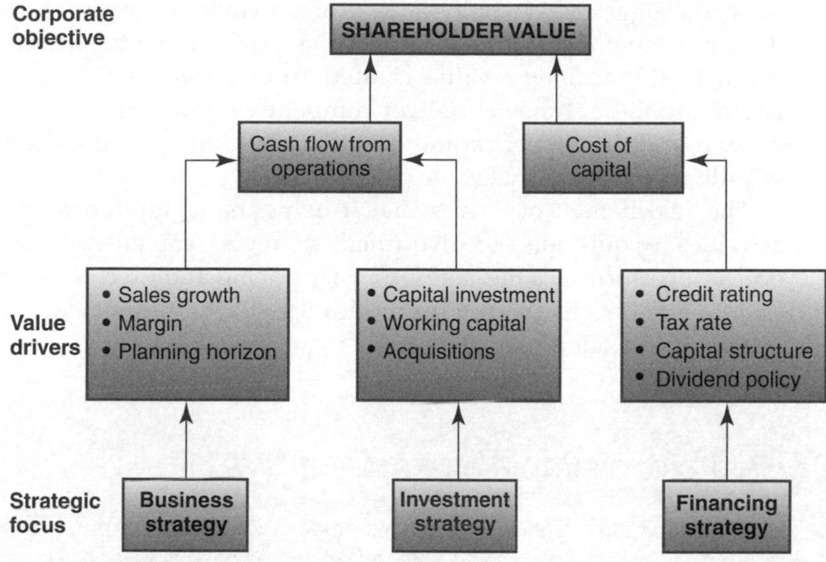

Figure 4.2 Shareholder value analysis framework

should focus on decisions influencing the **value drivers,** the factors that have greatest impact on shareholder value. Typically, these include the following:

1 *Sales growth and margin*. Chapter 1 showed how sales growth and margins are influenced by competitive forces (e.g. threat of new entrants, power of buyers and suppliers, threat of substitutes and competition in the industry). The balance between sales, growth and profits should be based not only on profit impact, but also on value impact.
2 *Working capital and fixed capital investment*. Over-emphasis on profit, particularly at the operating level, may result in neglect of working capital and fixed asset management. In Section 4.7, the free cash flow approach advocated using cash flows after meeting fixed and working capital requirements.

3 *The cost of capital*. A firm should seek to make financial decisions that minimise the cost of capital, given the nature of the business and its strategies. As will be seen later, this does not simply mean taking the source of finance that is nominally the cheapest.
4 *Taxation* is a fact of business life, especially as it affects cash flows and the discount rate. Managers need to be aware of the main tax impact on both investment and financial decisions.

SVA requires specification of a planning horizon, say, of five or ten years, and forecasting the cash flows and discount rates based on the underlying plans and strategies. Various strategies can then be considered to assess the implications for shareholder value.

A particular problem with SVA is specifying the terminal value at the end of the planning horizon. One approach is to try to predict the value of all cash flows beyond the planning horizon, based on that of the final year. Another is to simply take the value of the net assets predicted at the end of the horizon. None of the methods suggested is wholly satisfactory. It could be argued, however, that SVA does not have to be used to obtain the value of the business – rather, it can estimate the *additional* value created from implementing certain strategies. Assuming these strategies deliver competitive advantage, and therefore returns in excess of the cost of capital over the planning horizon, there is no need to wrestle with the terminal value problem.

The real benefit of SVA is that it helps managers focus on value-creating activities. Acquisition and divestment strategies, capital structure and dividend policies, performance measures, transfer pricing and executive compensation are seen in a new light. Short-term profit-related activities may actually be counter-productive in value-creation terms.

Balti plc: a simple example of SVA

Balti plc is a food manufacturer with a stock market listing. Its shareholders require a return of 12 per cent. It has just determined its free cash flow for the year at £100,000, as shown in the first table below.

The free cash flows for years 2–5 of its five-year planning horizon are predicted at £150,000, £170,000, £230,000 and £250,000 respectively. Its net asset value after five years is predicted to be £300,000.

The calculation of the value of the firm to its shareholders (i.e. SV) is shown in the second table. The SV is the NPV of all future free cash flows, calculated at £2,036,500

Forecast data for Year 1		**£000**	**Value drivers**
	Sales	900	Sales growth
less	Operating costs	(600)	
	Pre-tax profit	300	Margin
less	Tax paid	(100)	Tax rate
	Net operating profit after tax	200	
add	Depreciation	75	
less	Fixed capital investment	(125)	Capital expenditure
less	Additional working capital	(50)	Working capital investment
	Free cash flow	100	

Calculation of shareholder value

		Forecast cash flows £000					
		Yr1	**Yr2**	**Yr3**	**Yr4**	**Yr5**	**Terminal Value**
		100	150	170	230	250	300
NPV@12%	£617,900 ←						
PV terminal value	£1,418,600 ←						2,500
Total NPV	£2,036,500 = Shareholder Value						

Self-assessment Activity 4.7

Determine the impact on Balti's SV if it is able to invest £0.3 now in order to extend its competitive advantage period to ten years. Assume Free Cash Flow for years 6–10 is £250,000, and that the terminal value in year 10 is £4 million.

(answer at end of chapter)

Economic value added (EVA)

Closely related to SVA is the concept of **economic value added**, or **EVA**. If the primary financial goal of a company is to maximise shareholder wealth, and if net present value is the decision-making tool best suited to guide actions and strategies to that end, managers need to know how to manage operations to achieve this. EVA seeks to determine a company's true economic profit. It is the residual income, after charging the cost of using capital required to produce the profit.

$$\text{EVA} = \text{NOPAT} - (k \times \text{ Net Assets})$$

where NOPAT is the net operating profit after tax, k is the cost of capital and Net Assets is the book value of equity.

In the example below, two companies have equity capital employed of £100 million and a cost of capital of 15 per cent:

	Company A (£m)	Company B (£m)
After-tax operating profit	20	10
Total capital × cost of capital	(15)	(15)
EVA	5	(5)

While Company A makes a positive EVA of £5 million, Company B has a negative EVA of £5 million. Many companies find that the correlation between EVA and shareholder returns is very high.

Mini case

How much would you pay for Rolls-Royce?

In October 1997, Vickers, the defence and industrial group, put its luxury cars subsidiary, Rolls-Royce Motor Cars, up for sale. But what should the price tag have been?

Continued

In the 93 years since Henry Royce and Charles Rolls first got together to make cars, the owners of the company have experienced a much rougher financial ride than the owners of the cars. In 1971, the Rolls-Royce parent aerospace company went into liquidation following heavy overspending on the development of the RB–211 engine. Vickers then bought the car operation out of receivership for £38 million, but demand for luxury cars is known to rise and fall with business cycles, and Rolls-Royce had its fair share of both. Things recovered well until 1980, when the market for luxury cars collapsed leading to seven years of losses. The late 1980s witnessed a recovery, only for it to collapse again with the global economic recession of the early 1990s.

More recently, the company has concentrated on reducing production costs (bringing down the breakeven level from 2,500 to around 1,400 cars a year) and has made heavy investment in developing new models.

Vickers' chairman claimed that the sale was in the best interests of both its shareholders and the car industry. The decision was part of the group's strategic repositioning and its attempt to maximise shareholder value:

> We have taken this great business . . . from the low days of the last recession through to the present high level of investment, to a stage where we are confident its value to shareholders has been maximised.

The decision to sell Rolls-Royce was part of Vickers' strategy of reorganising the business to focus on its core businesses of armoured vehicles and propulsion technology.

So what price-tag should Vickers put on Rolls-Royce? The physical assets are worth about £250 million, but the prestigious name led analysts to predict that the eventual price could be double that figure – all this for a company with operating profits of less than £20 million in a boom year. The stock market clearly thought that disposing of the famous name made good sense, as Vickers' share price rose 13p on a day when the London Stock Market slumped by over 300 points in response to even greater nose dives on other global markets such as Wall Street in America and the Hang Seng in Hong Kong.

BMW immediately registered an interest in acquiring Rolls-Royce, arguing that it would be a good strategic fit, but others, including Volkswagen, also made positive noises. Volkswagen launched its initial bid of £310 million in March 1998. BMW then mounted a counter-bid valuing Rolls-Royce at £340 million, which the Vickers board agreed to put to its shareholders in June. VW then increased its offer with a £479 million bid, after concluding that developing its own luxury model was a more expensive and riskier option than acquiring Rolls-Royce. It also declared its intention to invest up to £2 billion in Rolls-Royce, increasing production five-fold, setting up a British management board and securing a British engine, probably from Cosworth.

At the June 1998 shareholders' meeting, both bids were considered, with Volkswagen receiving final investor approval. A Vickers spokesman said: 'We have managed to make a sale at a much higher price for our shareholders and we have obtained better shareholder value than anyone had considered possible'. However, proud Rolls-Royce owners who tried to mount a British bid were lamenting the end of an era and the creation of a 'Rollswagen'.

Continued

Volkswagen shareholders assumed that the famous name and the silver lady emblem now belonged to Volkswagen. But this gift lay in the hands of Rolls-Royce plc, the aero-engine maker, who had made it clear that they preferred BMW. Rather than go through a drawn-out legal battle, after extensive discussions, it was agreed that BMW would pay Rolls-Royce £40 million to use the name and bonnet badge. Volkswagen would keep the Rolls-Royce factory at Crewe and the Bentley name (Bentley being part of Rolls-Royce), while BMW would become the sole manufacturer of Rolls-Royces from 2003 after building a new factory in England.

Questions

1. What were the main considerations for Vickers in selling Rolls-Royce and for BMW and Volkswagen in bidding for it?
2. To what extent did shareholders' interests and financial considerations dominate their actions?
3. Why should Volkswagen offer almost twice as much for Rolls-Royce as the book value of the physical assets?

Summary

We have discussed the reasons why financial managers may wish to value their own and other enterprises, the problems likely to be encountered and the main valuation techniques available.

Given the uncertainties involved in valuation, it seems sensible to compare the implications of a number of valuation models and to obtain valuations from a number of sources. A pooled valuation is unlikely to be correct, but armed with a range of valuations, managers should be able to develop a likely consensus valuation. This consensus is, after all, what a market value represents, based upon the views of many times more market participants. There should be no stigma attached to obtaining more than one opinion – medical experts do not hesitate to call for second opinions when unsure about diagnoses.

Key points

- An understanding of valuation is required to appreciate the likely effect of investment and financial decisions, to value other firms for acquisition, and to organise defences against takeover.
- Valuation is easier if the company's shares are quoted. The market value is 'correct' if the EMH applies, but managers may have withheld important information.
- Using published accounts is fraught with dangers, e.g. under-valuation of fixed assets.

- Some companies attempt to value the brands they control. An efficient capital market will already have valued these, but not necessarily in a fully informed manner.
- The economic theory of value tells us that the value of any asset is the sum of the discounted benefits expected to accrue from owning it.
- A company's earnings stream can be valued by applying a P:E multiple, based upon a comparable, quoted surrogate company.
- Valuing a company on a DCF basis requires us to forecast all future investment capital needs, tax payments and working capital movements.
- Valuation of unquoted companies is highly subjective. It requires examination of similar quoted companies and applying discounts for lack of marketability.
- The value of a share can be found by discounting all future expected dividend payments.
- The retention of earnings for worthwhile investment enhances future earnings, dividends and, therefore, the current share price.
- The Dividend Valuation Model must be treated with caution. It embodies many critical assumptions.
- The two main lessons of valuation are: use a variety of methods (or consult a variety of experts) and don't expect to get it exactly right.

Further reading

Comprehensive treatments of share and company valuation are quite rare: Copeland *et al.* (1994) is probably the best available. A good overview can be found in Chapter 15 (the contribution by Davies) of Firth and Keane (1986).

The brand valuation issue is addressed by Murphy (1989) and Barwise *et al.* (1989).

Young (1997) provides a practical application of the EVA concept.

Self-assessment Answers

4.1 The value of a whole company, or enterprise value, is the value of all its assets, whether measured at book value or market value. The value of the equity is the value of the owners' investment in the firm, or shareholders' funds. These are equal only when the firm is financed entirely by equity.

4.2 **(i)** DS Smith's enterprise value is the total value of its assets, i.e. £1,106.7 million.

(ii) Total liabilities are creditors falling due within one year plus those payable after one year, valued at £356.1 million and £237.2 million respectively, total £593.3 million. Minority interests represent remaining shares in firms previously taken over by Smiths. These are neither Smiths' liabilities nor Smiths' owners' equity. They represent 'outsiders' share of the total assets. Strictly, the figure given for total assets in (i) should be adjusted for this small item.

(iii) The value of owners' equity = shareholders' funds = net assets = NAV = £508.4 million. These four terms are synonymous.

4.3 Profit after tax = [1 − 30%] × £80 m = £56 m
EPS = (£56 m/100 m) = 56p
Implied share value = EPS × surrogate P:E ratio = (56p × 15) = £8.40.

4.4 Break-even value is £1 million, of which £0.361 represents the PV of the rental income. To break even, the resale value must have a PV of (£1 m − £0.361 m) = £0.639 m. Reversing the discounting process, this is a value of £0.639 × $(1.12)^5$ = £1.126 m. Hence, the property must rise in value by about 13% to prevent investors from losing out.

4.5 Taxation = 30% × (£25 m − £1 m) = £7.2 m
Free cash flow = Operating Profit + depreciation − interest − tax − expenditure investment
(£25 m + £2 m − £1 m − £7.2 m − £3 m) = £15.8 m.

4.6 Price per share $= \dfrac{D_1}{k_e - g} = \dfrac{D_o(1 + g)}{k_e - g}$
D_o = (25% × 16p) = 4p
growth = (0.75 × 0.18) = 0.135 i.e. 13.5%

Share price $= \dfrac{4\text{p}}{(0.15 - 0.135)} = £2.67\text{p}$

With shareholders seeking a 20% return, share price reduces to:

$$\frac{4\text{p}}{(0.2 - 0.1350)} = 61\text{p}$$

Because the return on reinvestment now is less than the cost of equity the firm should stop reinvesting, at least in the short term.

4.7 The effects are:

(i) lower SV by the investment outlay, i.e. £0.3 million.
(ii) higher SV by a five year annuity delayed by five years, *viz.*
(£0.25 m × 5-year annuity factor × 5-year present value factor)
= (£0.25 m × 3.6048 × 0.5674) = £0.51 m.
(iii) lower SV by the postponed terminal value, i.e.
(−£2.5 m × 5-year PV factor) + (£3.0 m × 10-year PV factor)
= (−£2.5 m × 0.5674) + (£3.0 m × 0.3220)
= −£1.42 m + £1.29 m = −£0.13 m.

The net effect is thus a marginal increase of:
(£0.51 m − £0.3 m − £0.13 m) = +£0.08 m.

Questions

1 Amos Ltd has operated as a private limited company for 80 years. The company is facing increased competition and it has been decided to sell the business as a going concern.

The financial situation is as shown on the balance sheet:

Balance Sheet as at 30 June 1999

	£	£	£
Fixed assets			
Premises			500,000
Equipment			125,000
Investments			50,000
			675,000
Current assets			
Stock	85,000		
Debtors	120,000		
Bank	25,000		
		230,000	
Creditors: amounts due within one year			
Trade creditors	(65,000)		
Dividends	(85,000)		
		(150,000)	
Net current assets			80,000
Total assets less current liabilities			755,000
Creditors: amounts due after one year			
Secured loan stock			(85,000)
Net assets			670,000
Financed by			
Ordinary shares (50p par value)			500,000
Reserves			55,000
Profit and loss account			115,000
Shareholders' funds			670,000
The current market values of the fixed assets are estimated as:			
Premises			780,000
Equipment			50,000
Investments			90,000
Only 90 per cent of the debtors are thought likely to pay			

Required

Prepare valuations per share of Amos Ltd using:

(i) Book value basis
(ii) Adjusted book value

2 The Board of Directors of Rundum plc are contemplating a takeover bid for Carbo Ltd, an unquoted company which operates in both the packaging and building materials industries. If the offer is successful, there are no plans for a radical restructuring or divestment of Carbo's assets.

Carbo's Balance Sheet for the year ending 31 December 1991 shows the following:

	£m	£m
Assets employed		
Freehold property		4.0
Plant and equipment		2.0
Current assets:		
stocks	1.5	
debtors	3.0	
cash	0.1	4.6
Total assets		10.6
Creditors payable within one year		(3.0)
Total assets less current liabilities		7.6
Creditors payable after one year		(1.0)
Net assets		6.6
Financed by		
Ordinary share capital (25p par value)		2.5
Revaluation reserve		0.5
Profit and loss account		3.6
Shareholders' funds		6.6

Further information:

(a) Carbo's pre-tax earnings for the year ended 31 December 1991 were £2.0 million.
(b) Corporation Tax is payable at 33 per cent.
(c) Depreciation provisions were £0.5 million. This was exactly equal to the funding required to replace worn-out equipment.
(d) Carbo has recently tried to grow sales by extending more generous trade credit terms. As a result, about a third of its debtors have only a 50 per cent likelihood of paying.
(e) About half of Carbo's stocks are probably obsolete with a resale value as scrap of only £50,000.
(f) Carbo's assets were last revalued in 1980.
(g) If the bid succeeds, Rundum will pay off the presently highly overpaid Managing Director of Carbo for £200,000 and replace him with one of its own 'high-flyers'. This will generate pre-tax annual savings of £60,000 p.a.
(h) Carbo's two divisions are roughly equal in size. The industry P:E ratio is 8:1 for packaging and 12:1 for building materials.

Required

(a) Value Carbo using a net asset valuation approach.
(b) Value Carbo using a price:earnings ratio approach.

3 *Solution in Appendix A (page 804)*. Lazenby plc has been set up to exploit an opportunity to import a new product from overseas. It has issued two million ordinary shares of par value 25p, sold at a 25 per cent premium. Its projected accounts show the following annual operating figures:

Sales revenue	£500,000
Operating costs	(£300,000)
(after depreciation of £50,000)	
Operating profit	£200,000
Taxation @ 30%	(£60,000)
Profit after tax	£140,000

Notes:

(i) Shareholders require a return of 10 per cent p.a.
(ii) Replacement investment is financed out of depreciation provisions and is fully tax-allowable.
(iii) 2% of sales should be written off as bad debts.
(iv) Bad debt write-offs are 50 per cent tax-allowable.

Required

Value each share in Lazenby:

(a) assuming perpetual life
(b) over a ten-year horizon.

4 *Solution in Appendix A (page 804).* Brosnan plc generates free cash flows of £5 million p.a. after allowing for tax and depreciation, which is used for reinvestment. It has issued 10 million shares. Shareholders require a 12 per cent return.

Required

Value each share:

(i) assuming all free cash flows are distributed as dividend.
(ii) assuming 50 per cent of FCFs are retained, with a return on retained earnings of 15 per cent.
(iii) as for (ii), but assuming 10 per cent return on reinvestment.
(iv) assuming that FCFs grow at 7.5 per cent for each of the first three future years, then at 5 per cent thereafter.

Note: assume all cash flows are perpetuities.

5 *Solution in Appendix A (page 804).* Insert the missing values in the following table:

	P_o	D_o	D_1	g	b	R	k_e
(i)	£8.44	£0.35	?	8.5%	0.5	17%	13%
(ii)	£4.98	£0.20	£0.219	?	0.6	16%	14%
(iii)	?	£0.10	£0.108	8%	0.4	20%	15%
(iv)	£2.75	?	£0.220	10%	0.5	20%	18%
(v)	£10.20	£0.60	£0.610	2%	?	10%	8%
(vi)	£0.60	£0.05	£0.054	8%	0.8	20%	?
(vii)	£1.47	£0.12	£0.133	10.5%	0.7	?	19.5%

Note: answers may have some minor rounding errors.

6 Leyburn plc currently generates profits before tax of £10 million, and proposes to pay a dividend of £4 million out of cash holdings to its shareholders. The rate of Corporation Tax is 30 per cent. Recent dividend growth has averaged 8 per cent p.a. It is considering retaining an extra £1 million in order to finance new strategic investment. This switch in dividend policy will be permanent, as management believe that there will be a stream of highly attractive investments available over the next few years, all offering returns of around 20 per cent after tax. Leyburn's shares are currently valued 'cum-dividend'. Shareholders require a return of 14 per cent. Leyburn is wholly equity-financed.

Required

(a) Value the equity of Leyburn assuming no change in retention policy.
(b) What is the impact on the value of equity of adopting the higher level of retentions? (Assume the new payout ratio will persist into the future.)

7 The most recent Balance Sheet for Vadeema plc is given below. Vadeema is a stock market-quoted company that specialises in researching and developing new pharmaceutical compounds. It either sells or licenses its discoveries to larger companies, although it operates a small manufacturing capability of its own, accounting for about half of its turnover:

Balance Sheet as at 30 June 1996

Assets employed	£m	£m	£m
Fixed assets			
Tangible	50		
Intangible	120		170
Current assets			
Stock and work in progress	80		
Debtors	20		
Bank	5	105	
Current liabilities			
Trade creditors	(10)		
Bank overdraft	(20)	(30)	
Net current assets			75
10% loan stock			(40)
Net assets			205
Financed by			
Ordinary shares capital (25p par value)			100
Share premium account			50
Revenue reserves			55
Shareholders' funds			205

Further information:

1 1995–96, Vadeema made sales of £300 million, with a 25 per cent net operating margin (i.e. after depreciation but before tax and interest).
2 The rate of corporate tax is 33 per cent.
3 Vadeema's sales are quite volatile, having ranged between £150 million and £350 million over the previous five years.
4 The tangible fixed assets have recently been revalued (by the directors) at £65 million.

5 The intangible assets include a major patent (responsible for 20 per cent of its sales) which is due to expire in April 1997. Its book value is £20 million.
6 50 per cent of stocks and work-in-progress represents development work for which no firm contract has been signed (potential customers have paid for options to purchase the technology developed).
7 The average P:E ratio for quoted drug research companies at present is 22:1 and for pharmaceutical manufacturers is 14:1. However, Vadeema's own P:E ratio is 20:1.
8 Vadeema depreciates tangible fixed assets at the rate of £5 million p.a. and intangibles at the rate of £25 million p.a.
9 The interest charge on the overdraft was 12 per cent.
10 Annual fixed investment is £5 million, none of which qualifies for capital allowances.

Required

(a) Determine the value of Vadeema using each of the following methods:
- **(i)** net asset value
- **(ii)** price:earnings ratio
- **(iii)** discounted cash flow (using a discount rate of 20 per cent)

(b) How can you reconcile any discrepancies in your valuations?
(c) To what extent is it possible for the Stock Market to arrive at a 'correct' valuation of a company like Vadeema?

Practical assignment

Obtain the latest annual report and accounts of a company of your choice.* Consult the Balance Sheet and determine the company's net asset value.

- What is the composition of the assets, i.e. the relative size of fixed and current assets?
- What is the relative size of tangible fixed and intangible fixed assets?
- What proportion of current assets is accounted for by stocks and debtors?
- What is the company's policy towards asset revaluation?
- What is its depreciation policy?

Now consult the financial press to assess the market value of the equity. This is the current share price times the number of ordinary shares issued. (The notes to the accounts will indicate the latter.)

- What discrepancy do you find between the NAV and the market value?
- How can you explain this?
- What is the P:E ratio of your selected company?
- How does this compare with other companies in the same sector?
- How can you explain any discrepancies?
- Do you think your selected company's shares are under- or over-valued?

*Most large companies post their Annual Reports and Accounts on their websites. The commonest address forms of UK companies are: **companyname.co.uk**. or **companyname.com**.

PART II

Investment decisions and strategies

Chapters 5 to 8 examine in depth the investment decision and how it is evaluated. The concepts of time-value of money and present value are extensively applied. The available methods for assisting the financial manager to evaluate investment proposals are examined in Chapter 5, both when capital is freely available and when it is in short supply. Methods of appraisal that do not utilise discounting procedures are also examined.

In Chapter 6, investment appraisal procedures are applied to practical situations, incorporating the impact of both taxation and inflation. Consideration is given to identifying the relevant information for project evaluation, particularly for replacement decisions.

Chapter 7 sets the whole project appraisal system in a strategic perspective and explores the wider aspects of the investment appraisal system within companies. It dispels the notion that investment analysis hinges solely on methods of appraisal, and it reveals how companies approach their project evaluations in practice. Chapter 8 considers the strategic motives for foreign investment and how firms should evaluate overseas projects.

153 Investment appraisal methods

187 Project appraisal – applications

220 Investment strategy and process

243 Foreign investment decisions

5 Investment appraisal methods

Cigarettes can damage your wealth

Cigarette companies have for years looked for the Holy Grail of a smokeless cigarette. R. J. Reynolds Tobacco, US maker of Camel and other cigarette brands, launched a smokeless cigarette called Premier. It spent £210 million developing and marketing the new product, which had vast wealth-creating potential and was socially more acceptable to passive smokers.

After test marketing it for several months, the company finally recognised that it had created one of the biggest new product flops on record. With 400 brands of cigarette in the USA, launching a new product is costly and risky. But the idea of a smokeless cigarette was still seen by the company as worth pursuing and it recently began trials on a new smokeless cigarette brand, Eclipse. Since the earlier flop, however, the market has changed, with passive smoking becoming a bigger issue. Time will tell whether the Eclipse cigarette brand is launched successfully and generates a positive net present value.

Learning objectives

Having read this chapter, you should have a good grasp of the investment appraisal techniques commonly employed in business, and have developed skills in applying them. Particular attention will be devoted to the following:

- The three discounted cash flow approaches – net present value, internal rate of return and profitability index.
- The underlying strengths and limitations of the above methods.
- How net present value and internal rate of return methods can be reconciled when they conflict.
- Non-discounting methods.
- Analysing investments when capital availability is an important constraint.

5.1 Introduction

We saw in Chapters 3 and 4 how investing in capital projects that offer positive net present values creates additional wealth for the business and its owners. Quaker Oats provides a clear statement in its Annual Report of how it employs the NPV approach in assessing capital projects:

> We measure all potential projects by their cash flow merit. We then discount projected cash flows back to present value in order to compare the initial investment cost with a project's future returns to determine if it will add incremental value after compensating for a given level of risk.

There are, however, a number of alternative techniques to the NPV method. The aim of this chapter is to present the main methods of investment appraisal and to consider their strengths and limitations. In a later chapter, we consider their practical application in business, large and small.

5.2 Cash flow analysis

The investment decision is the decision to commit the firm's financial and other resources to a particular course of action. Confusingly, the same term is often applied to both real investment, such as buildings and equipment, and financial investment, such as investment in shares and other securities. While the principles underlying investment analysis are basically the same for both types of investment, it is helpful for us to concentrate here on the former category, usually referred to as capital investment. Our particular emphasis on strategic capital projects concentrates on the allocation of a firm's long-term capital resources.

Self-assessment Activity 5.1

Investment projects do not only include investment in plant and equipment or buildings. Think of some other types of capital projects.

(answer at end of chapter)

Generally accepted accounting practice would recommend that many expenditures are not 'capitalised' but 'expensed' (i.e. charged against profits rather than viewed as assets). This may well be the prudent treatment for accounting purposes, but we are primarily concerned with the analysis of decisions rather than their accounting treatment. Wherever a course of action is considered that has longer-term implications, it makes sense to treat it as a 'capital' project regardless of the accounting treatment.

Cash flow not profit

Managers in business usually view profit as the best measure of performance. It might, therefore, be assumed that capital project appraisal should seek to assess whether the investment is expected to be 'profitable'. Indeed, many firms do use such an approach.

There are, however, many problems with the profit measure for assessing future investment performance. Profit is based on accounting concepts of income and expenses relating to a particular accounting period, based on the *matching* principle. This means that income receivable and expenses payable, but not yet received or paid, along with depreciation charges, form part of the profit calculation. Consider the case of the Oval Furniture Company with expected annual sales from its new factory of £400,000 and profits of £60,000. In order to stimulate demand, customers are offered two years' credit. While this decision has no impact on the reported profit, it certainly affects the cash position – no cash flow being received for two years. Cash flow analysis considers all the cash inflows and outflows resulting from the investment decision. Non-cash flows, such as depreciation charges and other accounting policy adjustments, are not relevant to the decision. We seek to estimate the stream of cash flows arising from a particular course of action and the period in which they occur.

Timing of cash flows

Project cash flows will usually arrive throughout the year. For example, if we acquire a machine with a four-year life on 1 January 2003, the subsequent cash flows related to it may involve the monthly payment of creditors for purchases and expenses and daily receipt of cash from customers throughout each year. Strictly speaking, these cash flows should be identified on a monthly, even daily, basis and discounted using appropriate discount factors.

In practice, to facilitate the use of annual discount tables, cash flows arising during the year are treated as occurring at the year end. Thus, while the initial outlay is assumed to occur at the start of the project (frequently termed Year 0), subsequent cash flows are deemed to arrive later than they actually arise. This has the effect of producing an NPV slightly lower than the true NPV, given that subsequent cash flows are positive.

Decision-making can be viewed as an *incremental* activity. Businesses generally operate as going concerns with fairly clear strategies and well-established management processes. Decisions are part of a sequence of actions seeking to move the organisation from its current to its intended position. The same idea is apparent in analysing projects – the decision-maker must assess how the business changes as a direct result of selecting the project. Every project can be either accepted or rejected, and it is the difference between these two alternatives in any time period, t, expressed in cash flow terms (CF_t), that is taken into the appraisal.

Incremental analysis

Project CF_t = CF_t for firm *with* project – CF_t for firm *without* project

5.3 Investment techniques – net present value

Discounted cash flow (DCF) analysis is a family of techniques, of which the NPV method is just one variant. Two other DCF methods are the internal rate of return (IRR) and the profitability index (PI) approaches. Many managers prefer to use non-discounting approaches such as the payback and return on capital methods; others use both approaches. The following example illustrates the various approaches to investment appraisal.

Example: appraising the Lara and Carling projects

Sportsman plc is a manufacturer of sports equipment. The firm is considering whether to invest in one of two automated processes, the Lara or the Carling, both of which give rise to staffing and other cost savings over the existing process. The relevant data relating to each are given below:

	Lara (£)	Carling (£)
Investment outlay (payable immediately)	(40,000)	(50,000)
Year 1 Annual cost savings	16,000	17,000
2 Annual cost savings	16,000	17,000
3 Annual cost savings	16,000	17,000
4 Annual cost savings	12,000	17,000
The required return is 14 per cent p.a.		

The investment outlays are obviously additional cash outflows, while the annual cost savings are cash flow benefits because total annual expenditures are reduced as a result of the investment.

Should the company invest in either of the two proposals and if so, which is preferable?

The NPV solution

The net present value for the Lara machine is found by multiplying the annual cash flows by the present-value interest factor (PVIF) at 14 per cent (using the tables) and finding the total, as shown in Table 5.1. An immediate cash outlay (treated as Year 0) is not discounted as it is already expressed in present value terms. The same factors could be applied to evaluate the Carling proposal. However, as the annual savings are constant, it is far simpler to use the present value interest factor for an annuity (PVIFA) at 14 per cent for four years.

Comparison of the two proposals reveals the following:

1. The Lara machine offers a positive NPV of £4,252, and would increase shareholder wealth.
2. The Carling machine offers a negative NPV of £467 and would reduce value.
3. Given that the proposals are mutually exclusive (i.e. only one is required), the Lara proposal should be accepted.

Continued

Table 5.1 Net present value calculations

Year		Cash flow (£)	PVIF at factor 14%	Present value (£)
Lara proposal				
0	Outlay	(40,000)	1	(40,000)
1	Cost savings	16,000	0.87719	14,035
2	Cost savings	16,000	0.76947	12,312
3	Cost savings	16,000	0.67497	10,800
4	Cost savings	12,000	0.59208	7,105
		Net present value at 14%		4,252
Carling proposal				
	Cost savings	£17,000 × $PVIFA_{(14,4)}$ 2.9137		49,533
	Outlay			(50,000)
		Net present value at 14%		(467)

What does an expected NPV of £4,252 from the Lara proposal really mean? The project's future cash flows are sufficient for the firm to pay all costs associated with financing the project and to provide an adequate return to shareholders. From the shareholders' viewpoint, it means that the firm could borrow £44,252 (the cost plus the NPV) to purchase the machine and pay out a dividend today of £4,252, and still have sufficient funds from the project to pay off the interest at 14 per cent p.a. and annual repayments (see Table 5.2).

Table 5.2 Why NPV makes sense to shareholders

			£
Year 0	Borrow: machine	£40,000	
	Pay NPV as dividend	£4,252	44,252
1	Interest: £44,252 at 14%		6,195
			50,447
	Less: repayment (through annual savings)		(16,000)
			34,447
2	Interest: £34,447 at 14%		4,822
			39,269
	Less: repayment		(16,000)
			23,269
3	Interest: £23,269 at 14%		3,257
			26,526
	Less: repayment		(16,000)
			10,526
4	Interest: £10,526 at 14%		1,474
			12,000
	Less: repayment		(12,000)
			–

Continued

In practice, it is unlikely that the lender will agree to a repayment schedule that exactly matches the expected annual cash flows of the project. It is also somewhat imprudent to pay as a dividend the whole of the expected NPV before the project commences! However, in theory at least, the proposal creates wealth of £4,252 and the shareholders are that much better off than they were prior to the decision. Note that we assume that borrowing and lending rates of interest are the same. We discuss in later chapters how the discount rate is estimated; suffice it to say that it is the required rate of return that investors can expect on comparable alternative investment in the market-place.

5.4 Internal rate of return

Managers frequently ask: 'What rate of return am I getting on my investment?' To calculate the correct return, or yield, requires us to find the rate that equates the present value of future benefits to the initial cash outlay. We call this the **internal rate of return (IRR),** or **DCF yield.**

The IRR is that discount rate, r, which, when applied to project cash flows (X_t), produces a net present value of zero. It is found by solving the equation for r:

$$\sum_{t=0}^{n} \frac{X_t}{(1 + r)^t} = 0$$

Where the IRR exceeds the required rate of return ($r > k$), the project should be accepted.

Suppose a savings scheme offers a plan whereby, for an initial investment of £100, you would receive £112 at the year end. The IRR is thus:

$$\left(\frac{£112 - £100}{£100}\right) \times 100 = 12\%$$

If another scheme offered a single payment of £148 in three years' time, from an initial investment of £100, the IRR is found by solving:

$$£100\,(1 + r)^3 = £148$$

or

$$\frac{1}{(1 + r)^3} = \frac{£100}{£148} = 0.6757$$

Turning to the present-value interest factor (PVIF) table (Appendix B) for three years and looking for the rate that comes closest to 0.6757, we find that the IRR for the investment is approximately 14 per cent. The same approach is used to find the IRR for capital investment, but here the annual cash flows may differ. We find the IRR by solving for the rate of return at which the present value of the cash inflows equals the present value of the cash outflows. That is, we have to solve for

$$I_o = \frac{X_1}{1 + r} + \frac{X_2}{(1 + r)^2} + \cdots + \frac{X_n}{(1 + r)^n}$$

This is the same as finding the rate of return that produces an NPV of zero.

Table 5.3 IRR calculations for Lara proposal

Year	Cash flow (£)	PVIF at 18%	PV (£)	PVIF at 20%	PV (£)
0	(40,000)	1.0	(40,000)	1.0	(40,000)
1	16,000	0.84746	13,559	0.83333	13,333
2	16,000	0.71818	11,490	0.69444	11,111
3	16,000	0.60863	9,738	0.57870	9,259
4	12,000	0.51579	6,189	0.48225	5,787
NPV			976		(510)

$$\text{IRR} = 18\% + \left(\frac{976}{976 + 510} \times 2\%\right) = 19.31\%$$

In our earlier example, the Lara produced an NPV of £4,252 at 14 per cent. Given a 'normal' pattern of cash flows, i.e. an outlay followed by cash inflows, we can see that as the discount rate increases, the NPV falls. Trial and error will give us the discount rate that yields a zero NPV.

Trying 18 per cent, as shown in Table 5.3, gives a positive NPV of £976. Trying 20 per cent gives a negative NPV of £510. Clearly the IRR giving a zero NPV falls between 18 and 20 per cent, probably closer to 20 per cent. Using linear interpolation, we estimate the IRR by applying the formula:

$$\text{IRR} = r_1 + \left(\frac{N_1}{N_1 + N_2} \times (r_2 - r_1)\right)$$

where r_1 is the rate of interest and N_1 the NPV for the first guess, and r_2 and N_2, the NPV for the second guess. Applying the formula:

$$\text{IRR} = 18\% + \left(\frac{£976}{£976 + £510} \times 2\%\right) = 19.31\%$$

Note that the calculation includes the class interval, in this case (20% – 18%) = 2%.

If we had chosen two discount rates further apart, such as 10 and 25 per cent, the linear approximation would be less accurate:

at 10%, NPV = +£7,972
at 25%, NPV = −£3,860

$$\text{IRR} = 10\% + \left(\frac{£7,972}{£7,972 + £3,860} \times 15\%\right) = 20.1\%$$

Even over a range of 15 per cent the accuracy is to within 1 per cent of the true IRR.

In the Lara example, the NPV at various rates of interest is shown in Figure 5.1. The graph shows a clearer relationship between IRR and NPV. We also have an idea of the break-even rate of interest – or IRR – at around 19–20 per cent, as calculated earlier. The IRR of 19.31 per cent is well above the required rate of 14 per cent and the project is, therefore, wealth-creating.

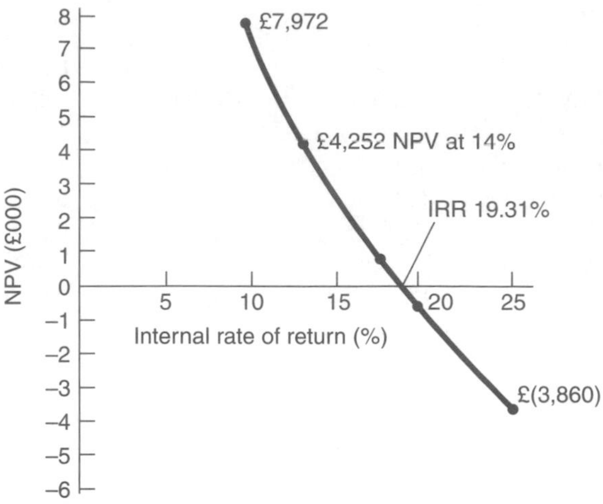

Figure 5.1 Lara proposal: NPV–IRR graph

Most managers have access to computer spreadsheets that solve the equation in a fraction of a second and avoid tedious manual effort. However, our analysis explains the logic behind the computer calculation.

For the Carling proposal, the IRR calculation is much more straightforward as the annual cash flows are constant.

$$\pounds 17{,}000 \times \text{PVIFA}_{(r,4)} = \pounds 50{,}000$$

$$\text{PVIFA}_{(r,4)} = \frac{\pounds 50{,}000}{\pounds 17{,}000} = 2.9411$$

Prince makes 500% profit on Canary Wharf

Prince Al Waleed Bin Talal Bin Abdul Aziz, the Saudi prince said to be the richest businessman outside the US, yesterday revealed that he had realised 500 per cent profit by selling most of his stake in Canary Wharf.

The Prince was one of a group of investors who funded Canary Wharf chairman Paul Reichmann to buy back the 85-acre estate in London's docklands from its bankers in 1995 for £800 million.

When Canary Wharf emerged from administration in 1993, it had attracted interest from few potential tenants and most investors gave it little chance of success.

On Tuesday the Prince completed the sale of two-thirds of his stake, raising £122 million. The Prince calculates that the internal rate of return, over the five years of the investment, has been a healthy 47.7 per cent per year. He will retain the remaining third of his investment. 'He likes it', a spokesman said. Asked how the money will be reinvested, a spokesman said, 'Very wisely'.

Based on Norma Cohen, *Financial Times*, January 18 2001

Referring to annuity tables (Appendix C), we find that for four years at 13 per cent, the factor is 2.9745 and at 14 per cent, it is 2.9137. The IRR is therefore between 13 and 14 per cent. This return falls just below the 14 per cent requirement, making it an uneconomic proposal.

5.5 Profitability index

Another method for evaluating capital projects is the **profitability index** (PI), sometimes called the benefit–cost ratio.

The profitability index

The profitability index is the ratio of the present value of project benefits to the present value of initial costs. The decision rule is that projects with a PI greater than 1.0 are acceptable.

Referring back to the present values calculated in Table 5.1, we can find for the Lara proposal:

$$PI = \frac{\text{PV benefits}}{\text{PV outlay}} = \frac{£44,252}{£40,000} = 1.1063$$

while for the Carling proposal:

$$PI = \frac{£49,533}{£50,000} = 0.9906$$

From this we see that the Lara is acceptable on financial grounds. The higher the PI, the more attractive the project. For *independent* projects, the PI gives the same advice as NPV and IRR methods, although there are important reservations when projects are 'mutually exclusive' (see Section 5.8).

The PI can also be expressed as the net present value per £1 invested, i.e.

$$PI = \frac{\text{NPV}}{\text{PV of outlays}}$$

If NPV per £1 invested exceeds zero, then PV per £1 exceeds 1.0 and the project should be accepted.

Self-assessment Activity 5.2

What are the three main DCF methods and how do you know when to accept a capital project with each?

(answer at end of chapter)

5.6 Payback period

Over the years, managers have come to rely upon a number of rule-of-thumb approaches to analyse investments. Two of the most popular methods are the payback period and the accounting rate of return.

The **payback period** (PB) is the period of time taken for the future net cash inflows to match the initial cash outlay.

Table 5.4 gives the cumulative cash flows for the two projects in our earlier example. After two years, the cumulative cash flow for Lara has reduced to –£8,000; but by the end of the third year it has improved to +£8,000. The project therefore breaks even, or pays back, in two and a half years. Similarly, the Carling pays back in 2.9 years. Many companies set payback requirements for capital projects. For example, if all projects are required to pay back within three years, both the Lara and Carling are acceptable.

A number of modifications to simple payback are possible. **Discounted payback** addresses the problem of comparing cashflows in different time periods. It calculates how quickly discounted cash flows recoup the initial investment. Referring back to the NPV calculation for the Lara, the discounted payback period at 14 per cent interest is approximately three and a half years (see below). The cumulative present values recoup the initial outlay only in the final year.

Year	Present value @14%	Cumulative PV
0	(40,000)	(40,000)
1	14,035	(25,965)
2	12,312	(13,653)
3	10,800	(2,853)
		Payback period 3.5 years
4	7,105	4,252
NPV	4,252	

Bail-out payback period recognises that there is usually a residual value at the end of each year for which the asset could be sold. Suppose that in the Lara proposal the residual values for each year were as below:

Year-end	Net cash flow (£)	Residual value (£)	Cumulative including Residual value (£)
1	16,000	15,000	31,000
2	16,000	10,000	42,000
3	16,000	5,000	53,000
4	12,000	–	60,000

Table 5.4 Payback period calculation

Year		Lara cash flow		Carling cash flow	
		Annual	Cumulative	Annual	Cumulative
0	Cost	(40,000)	(40,000)	(50,000)	(50,000)
1	Cost savings	16,000	(24,000)	17,000	(33,000)
2	Cost savings	16,000	(8,000)	17,000	(16,000)
3	Cost savings	16,000	8,000	17,000	1,000
4	Cost savings	12,000	20,000	17,000	18,000

Payback: Lara $2 + \frac{8{,}000}{16{,}000}$ years = 2.5 years

Carling $2 + \frac{16{,}000}{17{,}000}$ years = 2.9 years

If we sold the equipment after one year, the total cash flow would be £16,000 + £15,000 = £31,000. This is not sufficient to cover the initial outlay of £40,000. However, after the second year, the cash flow would be £32,000 in operating cash flows plus £10,000 residual value, which would recover the initial cost. The bail-out payback period is, therefore, within two years, which is slightly quicker than the payback period calculated earlier. This method is feasible only where there is an active second-hand market for the assets.

A fuller discussion of the popularity of the payback period will be given in Chapter 7. However, we should note that this approach has some serious problems as a measure of investment worth:

1. The time-value of money is ignored (except in the case of discounted payback).
2. Cash flows arising after the payback period are ignored.
3. The payback period criterion that firms stipulate for assessing projects has little theoretical basis. How do firms justify setting, say, a two-year payback requirement?

5.7 Accounting rate of return

A key ratio in analysing accounts is the **return on capital employed**, or ROCE. This is calculated as:

$$\frac{\text{Profit before interest and tax}}{\text{Capital employed}} \times 100$$

This indicates a company's efficiency in generating profits from its asset base. All new investment should at least match existing assets in terms of its earning power. However, the annual ROCE on a project will change each year. Typically, it is less profitable in the early years but improves over time as the project's sales build up and as the book value of the asset (i.e. cost less depreciation) declines.

The **accounting rate of return** (ARR) seeks to provide a measure of project profitability over the entire asset life. It compares the average profit of the project with the book value of the asset acquired. The ARR can be calculated on the *original* capital invested or on the *average* amount invested over the life of the asset.

Accounting rate of return

$$\text{ARR (total investment)} = \frac{\text{Average annual profit}}{\text{Initial capital invested}} \times 100$$

$$\text{ARR (average investment} = \frac{\text{Average annual profit}}{\text{Average capital invested}} \times 100$$

Returning to our example, suppose the depreciation policy is to depreciate assets over their useful lives on a straight-line basis. The annual depreciation for the Lara will be £10,000 (i.e. £40,000 over four years) and for the Carling, £12,500. The annual profit from the proposals will be the annual cash saving less the annual depreciation. The ARRs based on initial capital invested for the two proposals are shown in Table 5.5.

Alternatively, we could base the calculation of ARR on the average investment, found by summing the opening and closing asset values and dividing by 2. This would yield answers for the Lara and Carling of 25 per cent and 18 per cent, respectively, double the returns based on the initial capital. (In our case, the residual values are zero.)

A benefit of this profitability measure is that managers feel they understand it. It makes sense to use an investment evaluation measure that is broadly consistent with return on capital employed, which is the primary business ratio. However, the ARR has some definite drawbacks. Suppose the Lara proposal is expected to continue into Year 5, yielding a profit of £1,000 in that year. Common

Table 5.5 Calculation of the ARR on total assets

	Year					
	1	**2**	**3**	**4**	**Average**	**ARR**
Project						
Lara						
Cash flow (£)	16,000	16,000	16,000	12,000	–	
Depreciation* (£)	(10,000)	(10,000)	(10,000)	(10,000)	–	
Accounting profit (£)	6,000	6,000	6,000	2,000	5,000	5,000/40,000 = 12½%
Carling						
Cash flow (£)	17,000	17,000	17,000	17,000	–	
Depreciation* (£)	(12,500)	(12,500)	(12,500)	(12,500)	–	
Accounting profit (£)	4,500	4,500	4,500	4,500	4,500	4,500/50,000 = 9%

* Straight-line depreciation is used in each case.

sense suggests that this would make the proposal more attractive. However, the new ARR actually declines from 25 to 21 per cent as a result of averaging over five rather than four years.

$$\text{ARR} = \frac{(£6{,}000 + £6{,}000 + £6{,}000 + £2{,}000 + £1{,}000)/5}{(£40{,}000 + 0)/2} \times 100 = 21\%$$

It also takes no account of the size and life of the investment, or the timing of cash flows. Moreover, this approach is based on profits rather than cash flows, the significance of which we discuss in the next chapter. Such important weaknesses make ARR inappropriate as a main investment appraisal method, particularly when comparing projects.

Self-assessment Activity 5.3

List four capital budgeting methods for evaluating project proposals. Identify the main strengths and drawbacks of each.

(answer at end of chapter)

5.8 Ranking mutually exclusive projects

Suppose the manufacturers of the Lara also make the Bruno – a larger, more powerful, but more erratic model – offering a further 50 per cent in cost savings each year, but costing a further 50 per cent to purchase. The NPV will be 50 per cent greater than the Lara, but the other measures of performance – based on ratios or percentages – will be the same, as shown in Table 5.6.

In ranking mutually exclusive capital projects, we can reject the Carling for having a negative NPV and performance indicators that are consistently inferior to the alternatives. While the Bruno and Lara are, pound-for-pound, identical, the Bruno creates £2,126 additional wealth and is preferred.

Under the conditions typically found in business, no single method is ideal, which is why three or four different measures are often calculated. The ready availability of spreadsheet packages with graphics facilities makes this

Table 5.6 Comparison of various appraisal methods

	Lara	Bruno	Carling
Net present value (£)	4,252	6,378	(467)
Internal rate of return (%)	19.3	19.3	13.5
Profitability index	1.1	1.1	0.99
Payback period (years)	2.5	2.5	2.9
Accounting rate of return (%)	25.0	25.0	18.0

a straightforward and inexpensive procedure. Investment appraisal techniques are tools to assist managers in assessing the worth of a given project.

NPV or IRR?

In many cases, the choice of DCF method has no effect on the investment advice, and it is simply a matter of personal preference. In certain circumstances, however, the choice does matter. We shall consider three such situations:

1 Mutually exclusive projects.
2 Variable discount rates.
3 Unconventional cash flows.

Mutually exclusive projects

The decision to accept or reject a project cannot always be separated from other investment projects. For example, a company may have a spare plot of land that could be used to build a warehouse or a sports centre. In such cases, the problem is to evaluate mutually exclusive alternatives.

A first-glass investment decision

Pilkington, the St Helens-based glass manufacturer, was evaluating sites for a new £100 million float glass plant. Four sites, three in southern England, were considered. The south-east was considered particularly attractive as it was then the fastest growing market in Europe. Pilkington was also anxious to increase its market share in the area from half to the 65 per cent it enjoyed in the UK overall. Expecting stronger rivalry in the coming years, it wanted a southern presence to counteract European competitors. It already had three plants in Germany and one in Sweden.

Despite the strategic attractions of the south-east site at Thanet in Kent, the vote went to a site at the St Helens headquarters. Two key factors were the anticipated additional cost of some £20 million for the Thanet location over the St Helens site, and the support that the local St Helens labour force and township had displayed for Pilkington when it was subject to a takeover bid from BTR a few years earlier.

This is an excellent example of mutual exclusivity, and also demonstrates the subtle blend of economic and socio-political issues that often determines strategic investment decisions.

The earlier worked examples comparing the Lara, Carling and Bruno proposals are mutually exclusive. Recall that, while the Lara and Bruno offered the same IRR, the latter offered a much higher NPV because it was on a larger scale. The weakness of IRR is that it ignores the scale of the project. It assumes that firms would prefer to make a 60 per cent IRR on an investment of £1,000 than a 30 per cent return on a £1 million project. Clearly, project scale should be taken into consideration, which is why we recommend the NPV method when assessing mutually exclusive projects of different size or duration.

Variable discount rates

It is common to discount cash flows at a constant rate of return throughout a project's life. But this may not always be appropriate. The required rate of return is linked to underlying interest rates and cash flow uncertainties, both of which can change over time.

This presents little difficulty in the case of NPV: different discount rates can be set for each period. The IRR method, however, is compared against a single required rate of return and cannot handle variable rates.

Unconventional cash flows

There are three basic cash flow profiles:

Type	Cash flow pattern	Example
Conventional	Outlay followed by inflows (−+++)	Capital project
Reverse	Inflow followed by outflow (+−−−)	Loan
Unconventional	More than one change of sign (−+−+)	Two-stage development project

For a reverse cash flow pattern, such as a loan where cash is received and interest paid in subsequent periods, the IRR can be usefully applied. But in interpreting the result, remember that the lower the rate of return the better, so the decision rule is to accept the loan proposal if the IRR is below the required rate of return.

Unconventional cash flow patterns create particular difficulty for the IRR approach. Consider the following project cash flows and NPV calculation at 10 per cent required rate of return.

		£	PVIF at 10%	PV (£000)
Initial outlay	0	−100,000	1.00	−100
Year	1	+360,000	0.909	327
	2	−432,000	0.826	−357
	3	+173,000	0.751	130
		NPV		0

With an NPV of zero, the IRR is, by definition, 10 per cent. But if you try various other rates, such as 20 per cent and 30 per cent, the NPV is still zero!

Multiple solutions may occur where there are multiple changes of sign. In our example there are three changes in sign – from negative cash flow at the start to positive in Year 1, negative in Year 2 and positive in Year 3. While a conventional project has only one IRR, unconventional projects may have as many IRRs as there are changes in the cash flow sign.

Self-assessment Activity 5.4

Why do problems arise in evaluating mutually exclusive projects? What approach would you recommend in such circumstances?

(answer at end of chapter)

To summarise, the use of NPV and IRR is a matter of personal preference in most instances. But where the evaluation is for mutually exclusive projects, where the discount rate is not constant throughout the project's life, or where an unconventional cash flow pattern is suspected, we recommend use of the net present value approach. To underline the superiority of NPV we need to examine the respective reinvestment assumptions of the two methods.

The NPV method assumes that all cash flows can be reinvested at the firm's cost of capital. This is entirely sensible, since the discount rate is an opportunity cost of capital that should reflect the alternative use of funds. The IRR method assumes that a project's annual cash flows can be reinvested at the project's internal rate of return. Thus, a project offering a 30 per cent IRR, given a 12 per cent cost of capital, assumes that interim cash flows are compounded forward at the project's rate of return (30 per cent) rather than at the cost of capital (12 per cent). In effect, therefore, the IRR method includes a bonus of the assumed benefits accruing from the reinvestment of interim cash flows at rates of interest in excess of the cost of capital. This is a serious error for projects with IRRs well above the cost of capital.

Consider the mutually exclusive investment proposals given in Table 5.7. X and Y each cost £18,896. Project rankings reveal that X has the higher internal rate of return but the lower net present value. Figure 5.2 shows

Table 5.7 Comparison of mutually exclusive projects

	Cash flows (£)							
Proposal	Year 0	Year 1	Year 2	Year 3	Year 4	Undiscounted cash flow	IRR	NPV at 10%
X	−18,896	8,000	8,000	8,000	8,000	13,104	25%	6,463
Y	−18,896	0	4,000	8,000	26,164	19,268	22%	8,290

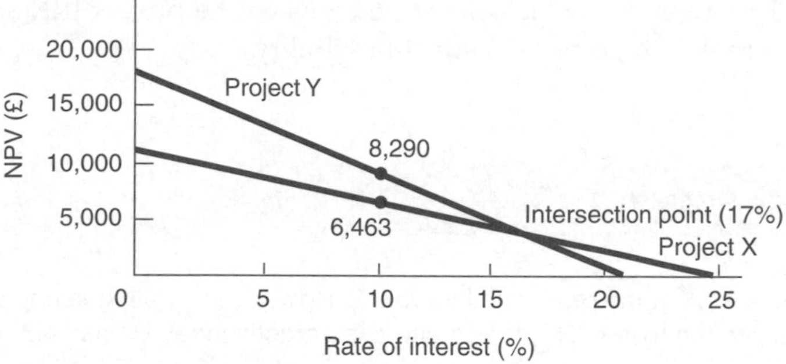

Figure 5.2 NPV and IRR compared

how this apparent anomaly occurs. (Strictly speaking, the graphs should be curvilinear.)

While Project Y has the higher NPV when discounted at 10 per cent, it has the lower IRR, the two projects intersecting in the graph at around 17 per cent.

Harry Potter and the global sales hopes of Coca-Cola

When the long-awaited *Harry Potter* movie opened in November 2001, one of the biggest stars was not even seen on film. As millions enjoy *Harry Potter and the Philosopher's Stone,* Coca-Cola is assuming the role of exclusive marketing partner.

Never has so much been poured into one movie by one company. Since lengthy negotiations with Warner Bros Pictures for exclusivity last year, the beverage group has sunk $150 million into a global marketing programmes usually preserved for world sporting events such as the Olympics.

In many ways, *Harry Potter* is able to do what Coca-Cola has been attempting for many years – to reach out to a younger audience while not alienating adults. That is crucial as Coca-Cola reinvents itself as an all-beverage company, offering from fun juice drinks to gourmet coffees.

But *Harry Potter* also serves another purpose: instantly elevating the Coke brand by its sheer popularity worldwide, something its own advertising campaigns have failed to do.

Such a powerful platform seems to justify spending nearly 10 per cent of the group's global marketing budget on *Harry Potter*.

The biggest critics Coke has to worry about are its shareholders. Its share price has been relatively flat since the announcement of the *Harry Potter* campaign. 'Investors are simply looking for Coke to meet volume goals. That would be enough,' says Ms. Levy, a spokesperson for the firm. 'If this can help re-establish the brand in the hearts of consumers, then putting 10 per cent of the budget into *Harry Potter* won't be a bad investment'.

Based on *Financial Times,* November 15 2001

Wherever there is a sizeable difference between the project IRR and the discount rate, this problem becomes a distinct possibility.

Self-assessment Activity 5.5

Take another look at the graphs in Figure 5.2. How would you explain to a manager that Project X, with the higher IRR, is actually less attractive than Project Y?

(answer at end of chapter)

5.9 Investment evaluation and capital rationing

We have seen that, under the somewhat limiting assumptions specified, the wealth of a firm's shareholders is maximised if the firm accepts all investment proposals that have positive net present values. Alternatively, the NPV decision rule may be restated as: accept investments that offer rates of return in excess of their opportunity costs of capital. The opportunity cost of capital is the return shareholders could obtain for the same level of risk by investing their capital elsewhere. Implicit in the NPV decision rule is the notion that capital is always available at some cost to finance investment opportunities.

In this section, we relax another assumption of perfect capital markets to include the situation where firms are restricted from undertaking all the investments offering positive net present values. Although individual projects cannot be accepted/rejected on the basis of the NPV rule, the essential problem remains: namely, to determine the package of investment projects that offers the highest total net present value to the shareholders.

The nature of constraints on investment

In imperfect markets, the capital budgeting problem may involve the allocation of scarce resources among competing, economically desirable projects, not all of which can be undertaken. This **capital rationing** applies equally to non-capital, as well as capital, constraints. For example, the resource constraint may be the availability of skilled labour, management time or working capital requirements. Investment constraints may even arise from the insistence that top management appraise and approve all capital projects, thus creating a backlog of investment proposals.

Hard and soft rationing

Capital rationing may arise either because a firm cannot obtain funds at market rates of return, or because of internally imposed financial constraints by management. Externally imposed constraints are referred to as hard rationing and internally imposed constraints as soft rationing.

The Wilson Committee (1980) found no evidence of any general shortage of finance for industry at prevailing rates of interest and levels of demand. A survey of managers (Pike 1983) found that:

1 The problem of low investment essentially derives not from a shortage of finance but from an inadequate demand for funds.
2 Capital constraints, where they exist, tend to be internally imposed rather than externally imposed by the capital market.
3 Capital constraints are more acutely experienced by smaller, less profitable and higher-risk firms.

Soft rationing

Why should the internal management of a company wish to impose a capital expenditure constraint that may actually result in the sacrifice of wealth-creating projects? Soft rationing may arise because of the following:

1 Management sets maximum limits on borrowing and is unable or unwilling to raise additional equity capital in the short term. Investment is restricted to internally generated funds.
2 Management pursues a policy of stable growth rather than a fluctuating growth pattern with its attendant problems.
3 Management imposes divisional ceilings by way of annual capital budgets.
4 Management is highly risk-averse and operates a rationing process to select only highly profitable projects, hoping to reduce the number of project failures.

The capital budget forms an essential element of the company's complex planning and control process. It may sometimes be expedient for capital expenditure to be restricted – in the short term – to permit the proper planning and control of the organisation. Divisional investment ceilings also provide a simple, if somewhat crude, method of dealing with biased cash flow forecasts. Where, for example, a division is in the habit of creating numbers to justify the projects it wishes to implement, the institution of capital budget ceilings forces divisional management to set its own priorities and to select those offering highest returns.

It is clear that capital rationing can be explained, in part, by imperfections in both the capital and labour markets and agency costs arising from the separation of ownership from management. Of particular relevance are the problems of **information asymmetry** and **transaction costs**.

Information asymmetry

Shareholders and other investors in a business do not possess all the information available to management. Nor do they always have the necessary expertise to appreciate fully the information they do receive. Capital rationing may arise because senior managers, convinced that their set of investment proposals is wealth-creating, cannot convince a more sceptical group of potential investors who have far less information on which to make an assessment and who may be influenced by the company's recent performance record.

Transaction costs

The issuing and other costs associated with raising long-term capital do not vary in direct proportion to the amount raised. Corporate treasurers in large organisations will not want to go to the capital market each year for relatively small sums of money if the costs can be significantly reduced by raising much larger sums at less frequent intervals. Capital rationing is therefore a distinct possibility in the intervening years, although this usually means delaying the start date for investments rather than outright rejection.

One-period capital rationing in Mervtech plc

The simplest form of capital rationing arises when financial limits are imposed for a single period. For that period of time, the amount of funds available becomes the limiting factor. The manufacturing division of Mervtech plc has been set an upper limit on capital spending for the coming year of £20 million. It is not normal practice for the group to set investment ceilings, and it is anticipated that the capital constraint will not extend into future years. Assuming a cost of capital of 10 per cent, which of the investment opportunities set out in Table 5.8 should divisional management select?

In the absence of any financial constraint, projects A–D, each with positive net present values, would be selected. Once this information has been communicated to investors, the total stock market value would, in theory at least, increase by £44 million – the sum of their net present values.

However, a financial constraint may prevent the selection of all profitable projects. If so, it becomes necessary to select the investment package that offers the highest net present value within the £20 million expenditure limit. A simple

Table 5.8 Investment opportunities for Mervtech plc

Project	Initial cost (£m)	Cash flows (£m)		Present value at 10% (£m)	NPV at 10% (£m)
		Year 1	Year 2		
A	−15	+17	+17	30	15
B	−5	+5	+10	13	8
C	−12	+12	+12	21	9
D	−8	+12	+11	20	12
E	−20	+10	+10	17	−3

method of selecting projects under these circumstances is the profitability index. Recall that this measure is defined as:

$$\text{Profitability index} = \frac{\text{Present value}}{\text{Investment outlay}}$$

Project selection is made on the basis of the highest ratio of present value to investment outlay. This method is valuable under conditions of capital rationing because it focuses attention on the net present value of each project relative to the scarce resource required to undertake it. Appraising projects according to the NPV per £1 of investment outlay can give different rankings from those obtained from application of the NPV rule. For example, while in the absence of capital rationing, project A ranks highest (using the NPV rule), project B ranks highest when funds are limited, as shown in Table 5.9. Assuming project independence and infinite divisibility, divisional management will obtain the maximum net present value from its £20 million investment expenditure permitted by accepting projects B and D in total and £7,000 or 7/15 of project A.

However, the profitability index rarely offers optimal solutions in practice. First, few investment projects possess the attribute of divisibility. Where it is possible for projects to be scaled down to meet expenditure limits, this is frequently at the expense of profitability. Let us suppose that projects are not capable of division. How would this affect the selection problem? The best combination of projects now becomes A and B, giving a total net present value of £23 million. Project D, which ranked above A using the profitability index, is now excluded. Even more fundamental than this, however, is the limitation that the profitability index is appropriate only when capital rationing is restricted to a single period. This is not usually the case. Firms experiencing either hard or soft capital rationing tend to experience it over a number of periods.

In summary, the profitability index provides a convenient method of selecting projects under conditions of capital rationing when investment projects are divisible and independent, and when only one period is subject to a resource constraint. Where, as is more commonly the case, these assumptions do not hold, investment selections should be made after examining the total net present

Table 5.9 NPV vs. PI for Mervtech plc

Project	Profitability index	Outlay (£m)	Outlay (£m)	NPV (£m)
B	2.6	5 accept	5	8
D	2.5	8 accept	8	12
A	2.0	15 accept 7/15	7	7
C	1.7	12 reject	–	–
E	0.8	20 reject	–	–
		60	38	27

values of all the feasible alternative combinations of investment opportunities falling within the capital outlay constraints.

Self-assessment Activity 5.6

What do you understand by 'soft' and 'hard' forms of capital rationing? Give two approaches available to resolve capital rationing problems.

(answer at end of chapter)

Multi-period capital rationing

Many business problems have similar characteristics to those exhibited in the capital rationing problem, namely:

1 Scarce resources have to be allocated between competing alternatives.
2 An overriding objective that the decision-maker is seeking to attain.
3 Constraints, in one form or another, imposed on the decision-maker.

As the number of alternatives and constraints increases, so the decision-making process becomes more complex. In such cases, mathematical programming models are particularly valuable in the evaluation of decision alternatives, for two reasons:

1 They provide descriptive representations of real problems using mathematical equations. Because they capture the critical elements and relationships existing in the real system, they provide insights about a problem without having to experiment directly on the actual system.
2 They provide optimal solutions – that is, the best solution for a given problem representation.

A mathematical programming approach to solving more complex capital rationing problems is provided in Appendix II to this chapter.

Summary

We have examined a number of commonly employed investment appraisal techniques and asked the question: to what extent do they assist managers in making wealth-creating decisions? The primary methods advocated involve discounting the incremental cash flows resulting from the investment decision, although non-discounting techniques are useful secondary methods for evaluating capital projects.

Key points

- The net present value (NPV) method discounts project cash flows at the firm's required return and then sums the cash flows. The decision rule is: accept all projects whose NPV is positive.
- The internal rate of return (IRR) is that discount rate which, when applied to project cash flows, produces a zero NPV. Projects with IRRs above the required return are acceptable.
- The profitability index (PI) is the ratio of the present value of project benefits to the present value of investment costs. The decision rule is to accept projects with a PI greater than 1.
- The NPV, IRR and PI methods give the same investment advice for independent projects. But where projects are mutually exclusive, differences can arise in rankings.
- The NPV approach is viewed as more sound than the IRR method because it assumes reinvestment at the required return rather than the project's IRR.
- The modified IRR (MIRR) is that rate of return which, when the initial outlay is compared with the terminal value of the project's cash flows reinvested at the cost of capital, gives an NPV of zero. This method provides a rate of return consistent with the NPV approach. This is discussed in Appendix I.
- Payback in its various forms (simple, discounted and bail-out) is a useful method, but ignores cash flows beyond the payback period. Simple payback also ignores the time-value of money.
- Accounting rate of return (ARR) compares the average profit of the project against the book value of the asset acquired. Its main merit is that, as a measure of profitability, it can be related to the accounts of the business. However, it takes no account of the timing of cash flows or of the size and life of the investment.
- Capital rationing, where it exists, tends to be of the 'softer' form where management voluntarily imposes investment ceilings in the short term.
- Single-period capital rationing is resolved by ranking projects according to their profitability index. More complex multi-period capital rationing problems demand a mathematical programming approach.

Further reading

Most good finance texts cover the topic of investment appraisal well, including, Brealey and Myers (2000). These texts also address the capital rationing problem. More detailed treatment of capital rationing is found in Pike (1983), Elton (1970), Lorie and Savage (1955) and Weingartner (1977). For a fuller discussion on the modified IRR, see McDaniel *et al.* (1988).

Appendix I
Modified IRR

Most managers prefer the IRR to the NPV method. The modified IRR seeks to adjust the IRR so that it has the same reinvestment assumption as the NPV approach.

The modified internal rate of return (MIRR)

MIRR is that rate of return which, when the initial outlay is compared with the terminal value of the project's net cash flows reinvested at the cost of capital, gives an NPV of zero.

This involves a two-stage process:

1 Calculate the terminal value of the project by compounding forward all interim cash flows at the cost of capital to the end of the project.
2 Find that rate of interest that equates the terminal value with the initial cost.

Table 5.10 Modified IRR for Lara

Year	Cash flow (£)	Future value factor @14%	Terminal value (£)
(a) Find the terminal value			
1	16,000	$(1.14)^3$	23,704
2	16,000	$(1.14)^2$	20,794
3	16,000	1.14	18,240
4	12,000	1.00	12,000
			74,738

(b) Find the rate of interest (denoted by x) which equates the terminal value with initial cost: $PVIF_{(x\%,4yrs)} = £40,000/£74,738 = 0.535$

Using tables (Appendix B) for four years we find that 17 per cent gives a PVIF of 0.534.

	£
To check: £74,738 × 0.534 =	39,910
less initial investment	(40,000)
NPV	(90) i.e. close to zero

The modified IRR is approximately 17 per cent compared with the IRR of 19.3 per cent.

Self-assessment Activity 5.7

Describe how the modified IRR is calculated. What advantages does the MIRR have over the IRR in assessing capital investment decisions?

(answer at end of chapter)

We established earlier that the Lara proposal offered an NPV of £4,252 (Table 5.1) and an IRR of approximately 19 per cent (Table 5.3). Table 5.10 shows that by compounding the interim cash flows at 14 per cent to the end of Year 4, the project offers a terminal value of £74,738. To find the Year 4 present value factor that comes closest to equating the terminal value with the initial outlay, we divide the initial outlay by the terminal value and look up the interest rate that gives this factor in Year 4 (see Appendix B). For the Lara, the MIRR is approximately 17 per cent, a good 2 per cent below the IRR figure. For more profitable projects, the deviation would be greater.

Appendix II
Multi-period capital rationing and mathematical programming

Where an overriding financial objective exists (such as maximising shareholder wealth) and financial constraints are expected to operate over a number of years, the allocation of capital resources to investment projects is best solved by the mathematical programming approach.

Many programming techniques have been developed. We shall concentrate on the most common technique: linear programming. The assumptions and limitations underlying the LP approach will be discussed in a subsequent section. Problem-solving using the LP approach involves four basic steps:

1 *Formulate the problem*. This requires specification of the objective function, input parameters, decision variables and all relevant constraints. Take a firm that produces two products, A and B, with contributions per unit of £5 and £10 respectively. The firm wishes to determine the product mix that will maximise its total contribution. The objective function may be expressed as follows:

   maximise contribution: £5A + £10B

   A and B are the decision variables representing the number of units of products A and B that should be produced. The input values £5 and £10 specify the unit contribution values for products A and B respectively. Constraint equations may also be determined to describe any limitations on resources, whether imposed by managerial policies or the external environment.

2 *Solve the LP problem*. Simple problems can be solved using either a graphical approach or the simplex method. More complex problems require a computer-based solution algorithm.

3 *Interpret the optimal solution*. Examine the effect on the total value of the objective function if a binding constraint were marginally slackened or tightened.

4 *Conduct sensitivity analysis*. Assess, for each input parameter, the range of values for which the optimal solution remains valid.

These four stages in the LP process are illustrated in the following example.

Example: multi-period capital rationing in Atherton plc

Atherton's five-year planning exercise shows that the cost of its six major projects, forming the basis of the firm's investment programme, exceeds the planned finance available. Atherton is already highly geared and control is in the hands of a few shareholders who are reluctant to introduce more equity funds. Accordingly, the main source of funds is through cash generated from existing operations, estimated to be £300,000 p.a. over the next five years. The six projects are independent and cannot be delayed or brought forward. Each project has a similar risk complexion to that of the existing business. If necessary, projects are capable of division but no more than one of each is required. The planned investment schedule and associated cash flows are given in Table 5.11.

The six projects, if implemented, are forecast to produce a total NPV of £857,000. However, the annual capital constraint of £300,000 means that for the next three years the required investment expenditure exceeds available investment finance, i.e. there is a capital rationing problem.

The solution sequence is as follows.

1. Specify the problem

The objective function seeks to maximise the NPV from the given set of projects available.

Max NPV: $130A + 184B + 35C + 42D + 186E + 280F$

However, given the capital expenditure constraints over the coming years, we must express for each year the capital required for each project and the maximum capital available each year (i.e. £300,000):

Year 0 $200A + 220C + 110D + 24E \leq 300$
Year 1 $220A + 220B + 100C + 150D + 48E \leq 300$
Year 2 $66B + 50C + 500F \leq 300$
Year 3 $200E \leq 300$

Table 5.11 Atherton plc: planned investment schedule (£000)

	Project outlays						Total	Available
Year	A	B	C	D	E	F	outlay	capital
0	−200	–	−220	−110	−24	–	−554	300
1	−220	−220	−100	−150	−48	–	−718	300
2		−66	−50			−500	−616	300
3					−200		−200	300
NPV	130	184	35	42	186	280		
Total NPV = £857,000								

In addition to the capital constraints, we need to define the bounds for each variable. As no more than one of each project is required and projects are divisible, we can specify the bounds as:

$A, B, C, D, E, F \geq 0 \leq 1$

This linear programming formulation tells us to find the mix of projects producing the highest total net present value, given the constraint that only £300,000 can be spent in any year and that not more than one of each project is permitted.

2. Solve the problem

Using a linear program on the computer gives the solution in Table 5.12. Atherton plc should accept investment proposals B and E in full plus 14.5 per cent of project A and 46.8 per cent of project F. This will produce the highest possible total net present value available, £520,000. This is significantly less than the £857,000 total NPV if no constraints are imposed.

3. Interpret the optimal solution

Table 5.12 shows that only in Years 1 and 2 is the full £300,000 utilised. These years then impose binding constraints – their existence limits the company's freedom to pursue its objective of NPV maximisation because it restricts the investment finance available to the firm in those years. Conversely, Years 0 and 3 are non-binding: they do not constrain the firm in its efforts to achieve its objective. Hence while there is no additional opportunity cost (besides that already incorporated in the discount rate), for non-binding periods there is an additional opportunity cost attached to the use of investment finance in the two years where constraints are binding. These additional opportunity costs are termed shadow prices (or dual values). Shadow prices show how much the

Table 5.12 Projects accepted based on LP solution

Project	Proportion accepted	NPV (£000)	Capital outlay (£000) Year 0	Year 1	Year 2	Year 3
A	0.145	19	−29	32	–	–
B	1	184		220	66	
C	0	–				
D	0	–				
E	1	186	−29	−48	–	−200
F	0.468	131	–	–	−234	–
		520	−58	−300	−300	−200

decision-maker would be willing to pay to acquire one additional unit of each constrained resource. In this case, computer analysis reveals that the shadow prices are:

Year	Shadow price (£)	Constraint
0	0	non-binding
1	0.59	binding
2	0.56	binding
3	0	non-binding

A £1 increase (reduction) in capital spending in Year 1 would produce an increase (reduction) in total NPV of £0.59. Similarly, for Year 2 a £1 change in investment expenditure would result in a £0.56 change in total NPV. Because the capital constraints in Years 0 and 3 are non-binding, their shadow prices are zero and a marginal change in capital spending in those years will have no impact on the NPV objective function. Shadow prices, while of value in indicating the additional opportunity cost, can be used only within a specific range. In addition, it is desirable to ascertain the effect of changes in input parameters on the optimal solution. These issues require some form of sensitivity analysis.

4. Perform sensitivity analysis

The computer output provides two additional pieces of information. First, it tells the decision-maker the maximum variation for each binding constraint. In our example, the shadow price for the Year 1 constraint has a range of −36 to +188. In other words, the shadow price of £0.59 would hold up to an increase in capital expenditure for that year of £188,000, or a reduction of £36,000.

The program also indicates the margin of error permitted for input parameters before the optimal solution differs. In our example, the actual NPV for the optimal investment mix could fall as indicated below and still not change the optimal solution:

Project	Maximum permitted fall in NPV (£000)
A	−68
B	−17
E	−158
F	−280

This facility is particularly appropriate as a means of assessing the margin of error permitted for risky projects under conditions of capital rationing.

LP assumptions

In order to assess the value of the basic linear programming approach, we must consider the assumptions underlying its application. These are as follows:

1 All input parameters to the LP model are certain.
2 There is a single objective to be optimised.
3 The objective function and all constraint equations are linear.
4 Decision variables are continuous (i.e. divisible).
5 There is independence among decision variables and resources available.

Most, if not all, of these limiting assumptions can be relaxed by using more complex mathematical programming. For example, uncertainty, multiple objectives and non-linearity can be better addressed by other approaches such as stochastic LP, goal programming and quadratic programming respectively.

For most businesses, the LP assumption that projects are divisible is unrealistic. Even if a project could be operated on a reduced scale, it is unlikely that the NPV would reduce *pro rata* because many of the fixed costs would remain while the benefits of sale would be reduced. *Integer programming* is more appropriate when projects are non-divisible. This is a special case of linear programming where variables can take only the values 0 (reject the project) or 1 (accept it *in toto*).

Applying integer programming to Atherton plc requires only one change in the problem specification. The bounds become:

$A, B, C, D, E, F, = 0$ or 1

The solution, provided by an integer programming computer application, shows that only two projects should be accepted: projects B and E. These offer a combined NPV of £370,000, which is the best available given the capital constraints. This is well under half the £857,000 total NPV achievable in the absence of capital rationing (see Table 5.11). Were the shareholders of Atherton plc aware of these lost wealth-creating opportunities, they might well be concerned and ask the chairman whether the capital constraints were really as fixed as they appeared to be!

Self-assessment Answers

5.1 Your answer could include the costs of developing a new product; a marketing campaign designed to increase long-term brand awareness; investment in training and management development; acquisition of other businesses; reorganisation and rationalisation costs (frequently in the form of redundancy payments), or research costs incurred in developing a strategic advantage.

5.2

	Accept when
Net Present Value	NPV > 0
Internal Rate of Return	IRR > *k*
Profitability Index	PI > 1 (or PI > 0 if based on NPV)

5.3

For	Against
Payback period	
Simple to calculate	Ignores time-value of money
Easily understood	Ignores cash flows beyond payback period
Crude measure of profitability	Problems in setting payback requirement
Emphasises liquidity	
Net present value	
Theoretically sound	Not well understood by non-financial managers
Based on cash flows	
Incorporates the time-value of money	Estimating the appropriate discount rate is difficult in practice
Internal rate of return	
Based on cash flows	Can incorrectly rank projects
Incorporates the time-value of money	Difficult to calculate without a computer
Accounting rate of return	
Can be related to accounts	Ignores time-value of money
Based on profits not cash flows	Problems in setting the required return

5.4 Evaluation of mutually exclusive projects using IRR and NPV approaches can produce different recommendations. This is particularly the case where projects are very different in scale or where the cash flow profiles of the various alternatives differ significantly. In such circumstances, the NPV approach is the better method.

5.5 Project Y offers the highest NPV for all discount rates up to 17 per cent. At the 12 per cent cost of capital, it offers a better cash return than Project X.

5.6 Soft capital rationing is internally imposed by the firm. This may be because management is unwilling to borrow or wishes to pursue a policy of stable growth. Hard rationing is externally imposed by the capital market. No additional external finance is available to the firm. Capital for a single period may be resolved by applying the profitability index to investment cash flows. Multi-period rationing requires a form of mathematical programming.

5.7 The modified IRR is that rate of return which, when the initial outlay is compared with the terminal value of the project's cash flows reinvested at the cost of capital, gives an NPV of zero. Whereas the IRR method implicitly assumes that cash flows generated by the project are reinvested at the project's internal rate of return, the modified IRR assumes reinvestment at the cost of capital. This means that it gives the same investment advice as the NPV approach.

Questions

1 *Solution in Appendix A (page 805).* Microtic Ltd, a manufacturer of watches, is considering the selection of one from two mutually exclusive investment projects, each with an estimated five-year life. Project A costs £1,616,000 and is forecast to generate annual cash flows of £500,000. Its estimated residual value after five years is £301,000. Project B, costing £556,000 and with a scrap value of £56,000, should generate annual

cash flows of £200,000. The company operates a straight-line depreciation policy and discounts cash flows at 15 per cent p.a.

Microtic Ltd uses four investment appraisal techniques: payback period, net present value, internal rate of return and accounting rate of return (i.e. average accounting profit to initial book value of investment).

Make the appropriate calculations and give reasons for your investment advice.

2 *Solution in Appendix A (page 806).* Mace Ltd is planning its capital budget for 19_7 and 19_8. The company's directors have reduced their initial list of projects to five, the expected cash flows of which are set out below:

Project	19_7	19_8	19_9	19_0	NPV
1	−60,000	+30,000	+25,000	+25,000	+1,600
2	−30,000	−20,000	+25,000	+45,000	+1,300
3	−40,000	−50,000	+60,000	+70,000	+8,300
4	0	−80,000	+45,000	+55,000	+900
5	−50,000	+10,000	+30,000	+40,000	+7,900

None of the five projects can be delayed and all are divisible. Cash flows arise on the first day of the year. The minimum return required by shareholders of Mace Ltd is 10 per cent p.a. Which projects should Mace Ltd accept if the capital available for investment is limited to £100,000 on 1 January 19_7, but readily available at 10 per cent p.a. on 1 January 19_8 and subsequently?

3 The directors of Mylo Ltd are currently considering two mutually exclusive investment projects. Both projects are concerned with the purchase of new plant. The following data are available for each project:

	Project	
	1 (£)	2 (£)
Cost (immediate outlay)	100,000	60,000
Expected annual net profit (loss)		
Year 1	29,000	18,000
2	(1,000)	(2,000)
3	2,000	4,000
Estimated residual value	7,000	6,000

The company has an estimated cost of capital of 10 per cent and employs the straight-line method of depreciation for all fixed assets when calculating net profit. Neither project would increase the working capital of the company. The company has sufficient funds to meet all capital expenditure requirements.

Required

(a) Calculate for each project:

(i) the net present value

(ii) the approximate internal rate of return

(iii) the profitability index

(iv) the payback period

(b) State which, if any, of the two investment projects the directors of Mylo Ltd should accept, and why.

(c) State, in general terms, which method of investment appraisal you consider to be most appropriate for evaluating investment projects and why.

(Certified Diploma)

4 Mr Cowdrey runs a manufacturing business. He is considering whether to accept one of two mutually exclusive investment projects and, if so, which one to accept. Each project involves an immediate cash outlay of £100,000. Mr Cowdrey estimates that the net cash inflows from each project will be as follows:

Net cash inflow at end of:	Project A (£)	Project B (£)
Year 1	60,000	10,000
Year 2	40,000	20,000
Year 3	30,000	110,000

Mr Cowdrey does not expect capital or any other resource to be in short supply during the next three years.

Required

(a) Prepare a graph to show the functional relationship between net present value and the discount rate for the two projects (label the vertical axis 'net present value' and the horizontal axis 'discount rate').

(b) Use the graph to estimate the internal rate of return of each project.

(c) On the basis of the information given, advise Mr Cowdrey which project to accept if his cost of capital is (i) 6 per cent; (ii) 12 per cent.

(d) Describe briefly any additional information you think would be useful to Mr Cowdrey in choosing between the two projects.

(e) Discuss the relative merits of net present value and internal rate of return as methods of investment appraisal.

Ignore taxation.

(ICAEW)

5 The directors of XYZ plc wish to expand the company's operations. However, they are not prepared to borrow at the present time to finance capital investment. The directors have therefore decided to use the company's cash resources for the expansion programme.

Three possible investment opportunities have been identified. Only £400,000 is available in cash and the directors intend to limit the capital expenditure over the next 12 months to this amount. The projects are not divisible (i.e. cannot be scaled down) and none of them can be postponed. The following cash flows do not allow for inflation, which is expected to be 10 per cent per annum constant for the foreseeable future.

Expected net cash flows (including residual values)

Project	Initial investment £	Year 1 £	Year 2 £	Year 3 £
A	−350,000	95,000	110,000	200,000
B	−105,000	45,000	45,000	45,000
C	−35,000	−40,000	−25,000	125,000

The company's shareholders currently require a return of 15 per cent nominal on their investment.
Ignore taxation.

Required

(a) (i) Calculate the expected net present value and profitability indexes of the three projects; and

(ii) comment on which project(s) should be chosen for the investment, assuming the company can invest surplus cash in the money market at 10 per cent. (Note: you should assume that the £400,000 expenditure decision not to borrow, thereby limiting investment expenditure, is in the best interests of its shareholders.)

(b) Discuss whether the company's decision not to borrow, thereby limiting investment expenditure, is in the best interests of its shareholders.

(CIMA)

6 Raiders Ltd is a private limited company financed entirely by ordinary shares. Its effective cost of capital, net of tax, is 10 per cent p.a. The directors are considering the company's capital investment programme for the next two years, and have reduced their initial list of projects to four. Details of the projects' cash flows (net of tax) are as follows (in £000):

Project	Immediately	After 1 year	After 2 years	After 3 years	NPV (at 10%)	IRR (to nearest 1%)
A	−400	+50	+300	+350	+157.0	26%
B	−300	−200	+400	+400	+150.0	25%
C	−300	+150	+150	+150	+73.5	23%
D	0	−300	+250	+300	+159.5	50%

None of the projects can be delayed. All projects are divisible; outlays may be reduced by any proportion and net inflows will then be reduced in the same proportion. No project can be undertaken more than once. Raiders Ltd is able to invest surplus funds in a bank deposit account yielding a return of 7 per cent p.a., net of tax.

Required

(a) Prepare calculations showing which projects Raiders Ltd should undertake if capital for immediate investment is limited to £500,000, but is expected to be available without limit at a cost of 10 per cent p.a. thereafter.

(b) Provide a mathematical programming formulation to assist the directors of Raiders Ltd in choosing investment projects if capital available immediately is limited to £500,000, capital available after one year is limited to £300,000, and capital is available thereafter without limit at a cost of 10 per cent p.a.

(c) Outline the limitations of the formulation you have provided in (b).

(d) Comment briefly on the view that in practice capital is rarely limited absolutely, provided that the borrower is willing to pay a sufficiently high price, and in consequence a technique for selecting investment projects that assumes that capital is limited absolutely is of no use.

(ICAEW)

Practical assignment

Either drawing on your own experience, or by asking someone you know in management, find out the primary investment appraisal techniques employed in an organisation. How well does the appraisal system appear to operate?

6 Project appraisal – applications

Virgin investment decisions

There is a danger that investment analysis can become bogged down in unnecessary detail. So how does an entrepreneur like Richard Branson, inventor of the Virgin brand, make investment decisions?

Like many other top managers, Branson places more reliance on experience and 'hunch' in decision making than detailed financial analyses. However, he also works through the risks involved and whether they can be managed. In his autobiography, Branson claims to make up his mind about whether a business proposal excites him within about thirty seconds of looking at it. He relies more on gut instinct than researching huge quantities of statistics. The idea of operating a Virgin airline grabbed his imagination, but he had to work out in his own mind what the potential risks were. (Branson 1998, p. 216).

Branson also argues that fun is at the core of the way he likes to do business and the main secret of Virgin's success. He observes that the idea of business being fun and creative goes right against the grain of convention, and it's certainly not how they teach it at some of those business schools, where, as he puts it, 'business means hard grind and lots of discounted cash flows and net present values!' (Branson 1998, p. 490).

Learning objectives

Having read this chapter, you should be well equipped to handle most capital investment decision problems found either on examination papers or in business.

Skills should develop in the following areas:

- Identifying the relevant information in investment analysis.
- Evaluating replacement and other investment decisions.
- Handling inflation.

- Assessing the effects of taxation on investment decisions.
- Investment appraisal practices, strengths and limitations.

6.1 Introduction

In the previous chapter, we examined a variety of approaches to assessing investment projects. The focus was almost exclusively on the appropriate appraisal method. But even the best appraisal method is of little use unless we can first identify the relevant information.

Investment decisions, particularly larger ones with strategic implications, are not usually made on 'the spur of the moment'. The whole process, from the initial idea through to project authorisation, usually takes many months, or even years. A vital part of this process is gathering information to identify the *incremental cash flows* pertaining to the investment decision. In this chapter, we consider the principles underlying economic feasibility analysis and apply them to particular situations. We pay particular attention to the treatment of inflation and taxation in project evaluation.

Need for relevant information

In financial management, as with all areas of management, an effective manager needs to identify the right information for decision-making. In the case of capital investment decisions, committing a substantial proportion of the firm's funds to non-routine, largely irreversible actions can be risky and demands a careful examination of all the relevant information available.

Information on the likely costs and benefits of an investment proposal, its expected economic life, appropriate inflation rates and discount rates should be gathered to provide a clearer picture of the project's economic feasibility. Frequently, we find that the reliability of the information source varies. For example, a demand forecast from a marketing executive with a track record of making wildly inaccurate forecasts will be viewed differently from an official quote for the cost of a machine. The accounting system and formal reports provide a part of the relevant information, the remainder coming through informal channels, frequently more qualitative than quantitative in nature.

In identifying and analysing information, managers should remember that effective information should, wherever possible, be relevant, reliable, timely, accurate and cost-efficient.

6.2 Incremental cash flow analysis

We stressed in the previous chapter that the financial input into any investment decision analysis should be based on the incremental cash flows arising as a consequence of the decision. These can be found by calculating the differences between the forecast cash flows from going ahead with the project and the forecast cash flows from not accepting the project.

This is not always easy. To illustrate this point, we consider how investment analysis handles opportunity costs, sunk costs, associated cash flows, working capital changes, interest costs and fixed overheads.

Self-assessment Activity 6.1

What do you understand by the term 'incremental cash flow'?

(answer at end of chapter)

Remember opportunity costs

Capital projects frequently give rise to opportunity costs. For example, a company has developed a patent to produce a new type of lawnmower. If it makes the product, the expected NPV is £70,000. However, this ignores the alternative course of action: to sell the patent to another company for £90,000. This opportunity cost is a fundamental element in the investment decision to manufacture the product and should be deducted from the £70,000, giving a negative NPV of £20,000. The in-house production option is not wealth-creating – and the sale of the patent appears to be more attractive.

Opportunity cost example: Belfry plc

We often see opportunity costs in replacement decisions. In Belfry plc, an existing machine can be replaced by an improved model costing £50,000, which generates cash savings of £20,000 each year for five years, after which it will have a £5,000 scrap value. The equipment manufacturers are prepared to give an allowance on the existing machine of £15,000, making a net initial cash outlay of £35,000. But in pursuing this course of action, we terminate the existing machine's life, preventing it from yielding £3,000 scrap value in three years. The prospective scrap value denied is the opportunity cost of replacing the existing machine. The cash flows associated with the replacement decision are therefore:

Year 0	Net cost	(£35,000)
Years 1–5	Annual cash savings	£20,000
Year 3	Opportunity cost (scrap value forgone on old machine)	(£3,000)
Year 5	Scrap value on new machine	£5,000

Ignore sunk costs

By definition, any costs incurred or revenues received prior to a decision are not relevant cash flows; they are sunk costs. This does not necessarily imply that previously-incurred costs did not produce relevant information. For example, externally conducted feasibility studies are often undertaken to provide important, technical, marketing and cost data prior to a major new investment. However, the costs of the study are excluded from project analysis. We are concerned with future cash flows arising as a particular consequence of the course of action.

Look for associated cash flows

Investment in capital projects may have company-wide cash flow implications. Those involved in forecasting cash flows may not realise how the project affects other parts of the business – senior management should therefore carefully consider whether there are any additional cash flows associated with the investment decision. The decision to produce and launch a new product may influence the demand for other products within the product range. Similarly, the decision to invest in a new manufacturing plant in Eastern Europe, or to take over existing facilities, may have an adverse effect on the company's exports to such countries.

Self-assessment Activity 6.2

Waxo plc has developed a new wonder earache drug. The management is currently putting together an investment proposal to produce and sell the drug, but is not sure whether to include the following:

1. The original cost of developing the drug.
2. Production of the new product will have an adverse effect on the sale of related products in another division of Waxo.
3. Instead of producing the drug internally, the patent could be sold for £10 million.

How would you advise Waxo on the relevant costs?

(answer at end of chapter)

Include working capital changes

It is easy to forget that the total investment for capital projects can be considerably more than the fixed asset outlay. Normally, a capital project gives rise to increased stocks and debtors to support the increase in sales. This increase in working capital forms part of the investment outlay and should be included in project appraisal. If the project takes a number of years to reach its full capacity, there will probably be additional working capital requirements in the early years, especially for new products where the seller may have to tempt purchasers by offering more than usually generous credit terms. The investment decision implies that the firm ties up fixed and working capital for the life of the project. At the end of the project, whatever is realised is returned to the firm. For fixed assets, this will be scrap or residual value – usually considerably less than the original cost, except in the case of land and some premises. For working capital, the whole figure – less the value of damaged stock and bad debts – is treated as a cash inflow in the final year, because the finance tied up in working capital can now be released for other purposes.

Occasionally, the introduction of new equipment or technology reduces stock requirements. Here the stock reduction is a positive cash flow in the start year; but an equivalent negative outflow at the end of the project should be included only if it is assumed that the firm will revert to the previous stock levels. A more realistic assumption may be that any replacement would at least maintain existing stock levels, in which case no cash flow for stock in the final year is necessary.

Separate investment and financing decisions

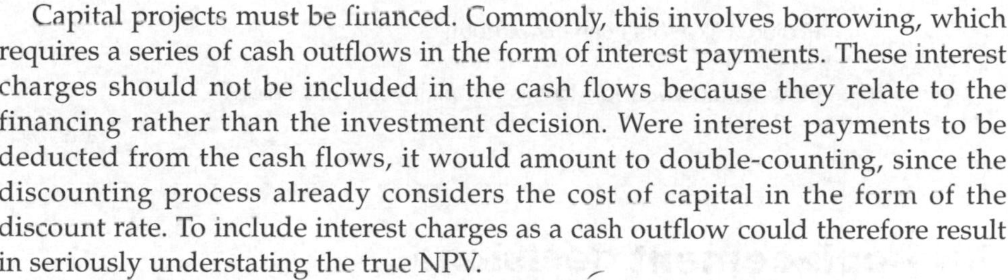

Capital projects must be financed. Commonly, this involves borrowing, which requires a series of cash outflows in the form of interest payments. These interest charges should not be included in the cash flows because they relate to the financing rather than the investment decision. Were interest payments to be deducted from the cash flows, it would amount to double-counting, since the discounting process already considers the cost of capital in the form of the discount rate. To include interest charges as a cash outflow could therefore result in seriously understating the true NPV.

Some companies include interest on short-term loans (such as for financing seasonal fluctuations in working capital) in the project cash flows. If so, it is important that both the timing of the receipt and the repayment of the loan are also included. For example, the NPV on a 15 per cent one-year loan of £100,000, assuming a 15 per cent discount rate, must be zero: £100,000 cash received today less the present value of interest and loan repaid after a year (i.e. £115,000/1.15).

Fixed overheads can be tricky

Only additional fixed overheads incurred as a result of the capital project should be included in the analysis. In the short term, there will often be sufficient factory space to house new equipment without incurring additional overheads, but ultimately some additional fixed costs (for rent, heating and lighting, etc.) will be incurred. Most factories operate an accounting system whereby all costs, including fixed overheads, are charged on some agreed basis to cost centres. Investment in a new process or machine frequently attracts a share of these overheads. While this may be appropriate for accounting purposes, only *incremental* fixed overheads incurred by the decision should be included in the project analysis.

Self-assessment Activity 6.3

Rick Faldo – the marketing manager of a manufacturer of golf equipment – has recently submitted a proposal for the production of a range of clubs for beginners. He has just received the following response from the managing director:

To: Rick Faldo

From: Sid Torrance

I have examined your proposal for the new 'Clubs for Beginners' range which you say promises a three-year payback and a 30 per cent DCF return. Some hope! You seem to have forgotten the following relevant points.

1 We have a policy that all investment is subject to a depreciation charge of 25 per cent on the reducing balance.
2 The accounting department will need to recover factory fixed overheads on the new machine.
3 We need to charge against the project the £8,000 marketing research conducted to assess the size of the market for the new range.
4 I'd have to pay 15 per cent to finance the project.

Projects like this I can do without!

How would you reply to this e-mail if you were Faldo?

(answer at end of chapter)

6.3 Replacement decisions

The decision to replace an existing machine which has yet to reach the end of its useful life is often necessary because of developments in technology and generous trade-in values offered by manufacturers. In analysing replacement decisions, we assess the additional costs and benefits arising from the replacement, rather than the attractiveness of the new machine in isolation.

Example of replacement analysis: Sevvie plc

Sevvie plc manufactures components for the car industry. It is considering automating its line for producing crankshaft bearings. The automated equipment will cost £750,000. It will replace equipment with a residual value of £80,000 and a written-down book value of £200,000. It is anticipated that the existing machine has a further five years to run, after which its scrap value would be £5,000.

At present, the line has a capacity of 1.25 million units per annum but, typically, it has only been run at 80 per cent of capacity because of the lack of demand for its output. The new line has a capacity of 1.4 million units per annum. Its life is expected to be five years and its scrap value at that time £105,000. The main benefits of the new proposal are a reduction in staffing levels and an improvement in price due to its superior quality.

The accountant has prepared the cost estimates shown in Table 6.1 based on output of 1 million units p.a. Fixed overheads include depreciation on the old machine of £40,000 p.a. and £130,000 for the new machine. It is considered that for the company overall, other fixed overheads are unlikely to change.

Continued

Table 6.1 Profitability of Sevvie's project

	Old line (per unit) (p)	New line (per unit) (p)
Selling price	150	155
Materials	(40)	(36)
Labour	(22)	(15)
Variable overheads	(14)	(14)
Fixed overheads	(34)	(40)
Profit per unit	40	50

The introduction of the new machine will enable the average level of stocks held to be reduced by £160,000. After five years, the machine will probably be replaced by a similar one.

The company uses a 10 per cent discount rate. We shall ignore taxation.

The solution is given in Table 6.2. Several comments are worthy of note:

1 It has been assumed that no benefits can be obtained from the additional capacity due to the sales constraints. In reality, it would be useful to explore whether – for example, by investing in advertising – demand could be increased.
2 Fixed costs are not relevant. Depreciation is not a cash flow, and we are told that other fixed costs will not alter with the decision. The incremental cash flow per unit is therefore 16p, giving £160,000 (i.e. 1 million units at 16p) additional cash each year on the expected sales.
3 In addition to the scrap values of £80,000 in Year 0 and £105,000 in Year 5 on the old and new machines respectively, there is a £5,000 opportunity cost in Year 5. This is the scrap value no longer available as a consequence of the replacement decision.
4 Working capital will be reduced by £160,000 for the period of the project and it therefore appears as a benefit in Year 0.
5 The book value of the existing machine represents the undepreciated element of the original cost, a sunk cost which is not relevant to the decision. The book value of assets, however, may be important in practice, as it can sometimes mean a heavy accounting loss in the year of acquisition. In this case, the loss would be £120,000 (i.e. book value of £200,000 less £80,000 residual value). This is not a cash flow, but, in practice, it may still be regarded as undesirable to depress reported profit figures in this way. This, of course, raises issues of market efficiency – will the market see through the accounting adjustment?

The replacement decision is a wealth-creating opportunity offering an NPV of £157,000, although the cumulative present value calculation in Table 6.2 shows that the project does not come into surplus, in net present value terms, until the final year.

Continued

Table 6.2 Sevvie plc solution

	Old line (pence per unit)	New line (pence per unit)
Selling price	150	155
Less:		
Materials	(40)	(36)
Labour	(22)	(15)
Variable overheads	(14)	(14)
Variable costs	(76)	(65)
Cash contribution	74	90
Incremental cash flow per unit (90–74)		16p
Total incremental cash flow on 1 million unit sales		£160,000

Year (£000)	0	1	2	3	4	5
Cost savings		160	160	160	160	160
New machine	(750)					105
Scrap old machine	80					(5)
Working capital reduction	160					
Net cash flow	(510)	160	160	160	160	260
Net present value						
10% discount factor	1.000	0.909	0.826	0.751	0.683	0.621
Present value	(510)	145	132	120	109	161
Cumulative present value	(510)	(365)	(233)	(113)	(4)	157
NPV	157					

6.4 Inflation cannot be ignored

Inflation can have a major impact on the ultimate success or failure of capital projects. In considering how it should be treated in discounted cash flow analysis, two problems arise: first, how does inflation affect the estimated cash flows from the project; and second, how does it affect the discount rate?

For example, a machine costs £18,000 and is projected to produce, in current prices, cash flows of £6,000, £10,000 and £7,000 respectively over the next three years. The expected rate of inflation is 6 per cent and the firm's cost of capital is 16.6 per cent.

We can adopt one of two approaches:

1. Forecast cash flows in *money* terms and discount at the nominal or *money* cost of capital including inflation (i.e. 16.6 per cent), or
2. Forecast cash flows in *constant* (i.e. current) money terms and discount at the *real* cost of capital.

Table 6.3 The money terms approach

Year	Cash flow current prices (£)	Actual money prices (£)	Discount factor @ 16.6%	Present value (£)
0	(18,000) × 1.0	(18,000)	1	(18,000)
1	6,000 × 1.06	6,360	$\frac{1}{1.166}$	5,454
2	10,000 × $(1.06)^2$	11,236	$\frac{1}{(1.166)^2}$	8,264
3	7,000 × $(1.06)^3$	8,337	$\frac{1}{(1.166)^3}$	5,259
			NPV	977

'Money terms' here means the actual price levels that are forecast to obtain at the date of each cash flow; 'constant terms' means the price level prevailing today; and 'real cost of capital' means the net of inflation cost.

In Table 6.3 cash flows expressed at constant prices are converted to actual money cash flows by compounding at $(1 + I)$, where I is the inflation rate. These cash flows are then discounted in the normal manner at the money discount factor (the reason for such an awkward rate will become apparent later) to give a positive NPV of £977. Had we not adjusted cash flows for inflation, the NPV would have been incorrectly expressed as a negative value.

In this example, we undertook both compounding and discounting. The process could be simplified by multiplying the two elements. For example, in Year 2 we could multiply $(1.06)^2$ by $1/(1.166)^2$ to obtain a net of inflation discount factor of 0.8264 which, when multiplied by the cash flow in current prices, gives a present value of £8,264, as stated above. This gives rise to the formula for the real cost of capital, denoted by P.

Calculating the real cost of capital

$$(1 + P) = \frac{1 + M}{1 + I}$$

or

$$P = \frac{1 + M}{1 + I} - 1$$

where M is the money cost of capital, I is the inflation rate and P is the real cost of capital.

In our example, this gives us a real cost of capital of:

$$P = \frac{1.166}{1.06} - 1 = 0.10, \text{ i.e. a rate of 10 per cent.}$$

Table 6.4 The real terms approach

Year	Cash flow current prices (£)	Real discount rate @ 10%	PV (£)
0	(18,000)	1	(18,000)
1	6,000	$\frac{1}{1.1}$	5,454
2	10,000	$\frac{1}{(1.1)^2}$	8,264
3	7,000	$\frac{1}{(1.1)^3}$	5,259
		NPV	977

Applying the real cost of capital gives the same NPV as before, as shown in Table 6.4.

While the latter approach may be simpler, it is not without difficulties. In business, the use of a single indicator of the rate of inflation, such as the Retail Price Index, may be inappropriate. Selling prices, wage rates, material costs and overheads rarely change at exactly the same rate each year. Rent may be fixed for a five-year period; selling prices may be held for more than a year. Furthermore, when taxation is introduced into the analysis, we find that tax relief on capital investment is not subject to inflation. Such complexities lead us to recommend that both cash flows and discount rates should include inflation.

Self-assessment Activity 6.4

What is the impact of firms not adjusting their investment 'hurdle' rates for changing levels of inflation? How would you advise a company which employs a 20 per cent discount rate which was based on a calculation made when inflation was twice the current level?

(answer at end of chapter)

6.5 Taxation is a cash flow

In Chapter 2, we introduced the subject of taxation and its broad implications for financial management. In this section, we examine in greater depth the taxation considerations for capital investment projects.

Recall that in the UK, Corporation Tax is assessed by the Inland Revenue on the profits of the company after certain adjustments. While it is not calculated on a project basis by the Inland Revenue, the actual tax bill will increase with every new project offering additional profits and reduce with every project offering losses. Corporation Tax is charged on the profits, gains and income of an accounting period, usually the period for which accounts are made up annually. In arriving at taxable profits, a deduction is made for capital allowances on certain types of capital investment. Following the principle outlined earlier of identifying the incremental cash flow, we need to ask: by how much will the Corporation Tax bill for the company change each year as a result of the decision? To answer this, we must consider the tax charged on project operating profits and the tax relief obtained on the capital investment outlay.

Taxation implications of Tiger 2000 for Woosnam plc

Woosnam plc invests in a new piece of equipment, the Tiger 2000, costing £40,000 on 1 January 2000. It intends to operate the equipment for four years when the scrap value will be zero. Expected net cash flows from the project are £10,000 in the first year and £20,000 for each of the next three years. The discount rate is 15 per cent and the rate of Corporation Tax is 30 per cent.

No tax position

If we ignore taxation (perhaps Woosnam is making losses and is unlikely to pay tax for some time), the net present value of the project's pre-tax cash flows is £8,390, as shown in Table 6.5. The positive NPV suggests that, on economic grounds, it should be accepted.

With Corporation Tax but no capital allowances

Most companies have to pay Corporation Tax, and a large company, like Woosnam plc, will pay at the rate of 30 per cent of taxable profits. A recent change is that this tax is now paid in the same year as the related profits, usually by quarterly instalments. Hitherto, companies enjoyed a tax delay of at least a year, which meant that the tax payment would typically lag a full year behind the investment cash flows to which they relate. Most investments attract a capital allowance (equivalent to a depreciation charge) which reduces the tax bill. At this stage, we assume that the Tiger 2000 does not attract any capital allowance.

Table 6.5 Project Tiger 2000 (assuming no capital allowances)

Year	(1) Pre-tax cash flows £	(2) Tax @ 30%	(3) After-tax cash flows £	(4) Discount factor @ 15%	(1 × 4) PV pre-tax £	(3 × 4) PV post-tax £
0	(40,000)	–	(40,000)	1.0	(40,000)	(40,000)
1	10,000	(3,000)	7,000	0.869	8,690	6,083
2	20,000	(6,000)	14,000	0.756	15,120	10,584
3	20,000	(6,000)	14,000	0.657	13,140	9,198
4	20,000	(6,000)	14,000	0.572	11,440	8,008
				NPV	8,390	(6,127)

Table 6.5 shows that after deducting tax to be paid, the NPV for the project falls sharply to –£6,127. It is no longer economically viable.

With Corporation Tax and capital allowances

For many types of capital investment, tax relief is granted on capital expenditure incurred. In the United Kingdom, this is in the form of a **first-year allowance** and subsequent **annual writing-down allowances (WDAs)**. The first-year allowance is a government incentive to encourage firms to invest and has in the past been as high as 100 per cent. Currently, for large companies, it is the same as the writing-down allowance as follows:

Plant and machinery	25 per cent on the reducing balance
Industrial buildings	4 per cent on the initial cost

So for expenditure on machinery of £1,000, the allowance would be as follows:

Year	Tax allowance (£)	Written-down value at year-end (£)
1	25% × 1,000 = 250	750
2	25% × 750 = 188	562
3	25% × 562 = 141, etc.	422, etc.

Clearly, the tax allowances diminish over time. Companies are allowed to write assets down for tax purposes to their disposal value. Any discrepancy between written-down value (WDV) and disposal value may trigger a tax liability (balancing charge) or qualify for tax relief (balancing allowance). In the above example, disposal of the asset for £500 after three years would mean that the capital allowances have been over-generous to the extent of £78 (i.e. disposal value of £500 – WDV of £422). This **balancing charge** of £78 would then be subject to Corporation Tax. Disposal for, say, £300 would qualify the company for a **balancing allowance** of £122 (i.e. £422 – £300), a loss that would be set against the taxable profits.

Let us return to the Woosnam plc example, this time assuming that the Tiger 2000 attracts a 25 per cent writing-down allowance. Table 6.6 calculates the WDAs. Tax is payable in the same year as the investment cash flows to which they relate.

The difference between what the investment finally sold for (in this case zero) and the balance at the start of the year is a balancing allowance, which is treated in the same way as the writing-down allowance. (We will not introduce further complications such as the election to pool plant and machinery in this book.) A useful check is to see that the total WDA (column 3) equals the initial investment, and the tax benefit (column 4) on this total corresponds, in this case £40,000 at 30% = £12,000.

These cash flows can then be added to the earlier example, as in Table 6.7, showing that the investment offers a positive NPV of £2,185 after tax.

Table 6.6 Woosnam plc – Tiger 2000 tax reliefs

End of accounting year	Tax written-down value £	Writing-down allowance £	30% tax relief £
1 Initial outlay	40,000		
WDA at 25%	10,000	10,000	3,000
	30,000		
2 WDA at 25%	7,500	7,500	2,250
	22,500		
3 WDA at 25%	5,625	5,625	1,688
	16,875		
4 Sales proceeds	–		
Balancing allowance	16,875	16,875	5,062
		40,000	12,000

How would the after-tax NPV differ were Woosnam plc a small or medium-size company? Such firms currently have a further tax incentive to invest by attracting a 40 per cent initial allowance, rather than 25 per cent. The effect is to reduce the tax bill in the early years, deferring it to later years. Because later cash flows are less valuable, this means that the NPV will increase.

Taxation therefore affects cash flows from investments. It is payable on taxable profits arising from the investment decision after deduction of capital allowances.

Self-assessment Activity 6.5

Your boss says: 'We only assess capital projects before tax. Every firm has to pay tax, so we can ignore it'. Do you agree?

(answer at end of chapter)

Table 6.7 Woosnam plc Tiger 2000 with tax relief

Year	Pre-tax cash flows £	Tax at 30%	Tax relief on WDA £	Net cash flow £	Discount factor 15%	PV £
0	(40,000)	–		(40,000)	1.000	(40,000)
1	10,000	(3,000)	3,000	10,000	0.869	8,690
2	20,000	(6,000)	2,250	16,250	0.756	12,285
3	20,000	(6,000)	1,688	15,688	0.657	10,307
4	20,000	(6,000)	5,062	19,062	0.572	10,903
						2,185

6.6 Use of DCF techniques

It is a common misconception that the discounted cash flow approach is a relatively recent phenomenon. Historical records reveal an understanding of compound interest (upon which discounted cash flow techniques are based) as far back as the Old Babylonian period (c. 1800–1600 BC) in Mesopotamia. The earliest manuscripts setting out compound interest tables date back to the 14th century, while the first recorded reference to the net present value rule is found in a book by Stevin published in 1582.

In these early days, the application of discounted cash flow methods was restricted to financial investments such as loans and life assurance, where either the cash flows were known or their probabilities could be determined based on actuarial evidence. Only in the 19th century, with the Industrial Revolution well established, did the scale of capital investments lead some engineering economists to begin to apply discounted cash flow concepts to capital assets. However, in practice, these concepts were largely ignored until the early 1950s in the USA and the early 1960s in the UK.

Surveys between 1975 and 1997 provide a clearer picture of the changing trends in the practices of larger firms in the UK. Table 6.8 shows that, while all firms surveyed conduct financial appraisals on capital projects, the choice of method varies considerably, and most firms employ a combination of appraisal techniques.

The use of DCF methods in larger firms increased greatly from 58 per cent in 1975 to 100 per cent by 1997. Hitherto, the IRR method enjoyed much greater popularity than the theoretically preferred NPV approach. However, in recent years, there has been a marked acceleration in adoption of the NPV method, with virtually all large firms now employing it.

The payback method has declined in popularity in recent years, but remains more popular with smaller firms. It is clear that firms do not normally rely on any single appraisal measure, but prefer to employ a combination of simple and more sophisticated techniques. DCF methods therefore complement, rather than substitute for, traditional approaches.

Table 6.8 Capital investment evaluation methods in 100 large UK firms

Firms using:	1975 (%)	1981 (%)	1986 (%)	1992 (%)	1997 (%)
Payback	73	81	92	94	66
Average accounting rate of return	51	49	56	50	55
DCF methods (IRR or NPV)	58	68	84	88	100
Internal rate of return	44	57	75	81	84
Net present value	32	39	68	74	97

Sources: Pike (1988, 1996), Arnold and Hatzopoulos (2000)

Dangers with DCF

While we have argued that DCF analysis offers a conceptually sound approach for appraising capital projects, a word of caution is appropriate.

From the emphasis devoted by most textbooks to advanced capital budgeting methods, one might be forgiven for assuming that successful investment is exclusively attributable to the correct evaluation method. However, DCF methods often create an illusion of exactness that the underlying assumptions do not warrant. As top management places more weight on the quantifiable element, there is a danger that the unquantifiable aspects of the decision, which frequently have a critical bearing on a project's success or failure, will be devalued. The human element is particularly important with regard to the project sponsor. The margin between a project's success or failure often hinges on the enthusiasm and commitment of the person sponsoring and implementing it.

Managers cannot afford to treat investment decisions in a vacuum, ignoring the complexities of the business environment. Any attempt to incorporate such complexities, however, will at best consist of abstractions from reality relying on generalised and simplified assumptions concerning business relationships and environments. A fundamental assumption underlying DCF methods is that decision-makers pursue the primary goal of maximising shareholders' wealth. For many firms, this may not be the case.

Critical errors may often be seen in the way DCF theory is applied by managers. Usually, these errors are biased against investment. For example, many firms do not adjust their operating cash flows for inflation, but discount them at the money cost of capital, rather than the real rate of return before inflation. The effect is that cash flows in later years (typically the strong positive cash flows) are unduly deflated by the high discount factor, giving a lower net present value than should be the case.

Perhaps even more important, DCF methods ignore the value of investment options. This key topic is the subject of Chapter 13.

Common errors in applying DCF

- Discount rates are calculated on a pre-tax basis, while operating cash flows are calculated after tax.
- Discount rates are increased to compensate for non-economic statutory and welfare investments.
- Cash flows are reduced 'to allow for depreciation'.
- Cash flows are specified in today's money (excluding inflation), while hurdle rates are based on the money cost of capital (including inflation).
- Managerial aversion to uncertainty frequently results in conservative project life and terminal value assumptions.
- Use of a single cut-off rate instead of a rate reflecting project risk. This often leads to rejection of low-risk/low-return replacement projects.
- Failure to include scrap values.
- Neglect of working capital movements.

6.7 Traditional appraisal methods

Managers have developed and come to rely upon simple rule-of-thumb approaches to analysing investment worth. Two of the most popular traditional methods are the **payback period** and the **accounting rate of return**, both of which were described in earlier chapters. Our present concern is to ask whether they have a valuable role to play in the modern capital budgeting process. Do they offer anything to the decision-maker that cannot be found in the DCF approaches?

Accounting rate of return (ARR)

We discussed the basic application of the ARR approach in Chapter 5. Table 6.8 reports that a little over half the companies surveyed employ the accounting rate of return approach in assessing investment decisions. This is not altogether surprising, given that the rate of return on capital is a very important financial goal in practice.

The ARR can be criticised on at least two counts: it uses accounting profits rather than cash flows, and it ignores the time-value of money. Nevertheless there has been a certain amount of support for the ARR in the literature. The absence of ARR leads to an inconsistency between the methods commonly used to *report* a firm's results and the techniques most frequently employed to *appraise* investment decisions. This is most acutely experienced where the divisional manager of an investment centre is expected to use a DCF approach in reaching investment decisions, while his or her short-term performance is being judged on a return on investment basis. Little wonder, then, that the divisional manager generally shows a marked reluctance to enter into any profitable long-term investment decisions that produce low returns in the early years.

A common assumption among managers is that the accounting rate of return and the internal rate of return produce much the same solutions. But while there is a relationship between a project's discounted return and the ARR, the relationship is not simple. Consider an investment costing £10,000 and generating an annual stream of net cash flows of £3,000. Assuming straight-line depreciation, the relationship between the internal rate of return and the accounting rate of return calculated on both the total investment and the average investment is as shown in Table 6.9.

From this example we can see that the accounting rate of return on *total* investment consistently *understates*, and the accounting rate of return on *average*

Table 6.9 Relationship between ARR and IRR

Project duration (years)	5	10	20	25
IRR (%)	15.2	27.3	29.8	30
ARR on total investment (%)	10	20	25	27.5
Deviation from IRR	−5.2	−7.3	−4.8	−2.5
ARR on average investment (%)	20	40	50	55
Deviation from IRR	+4.8	+12.7	+20.2	+25

investment *overstates*, the internal rate of return. The case for retaining the accounting rate of return is, therefore, valid only when applied as a secondary criterion to highlight the likely impact on the organisation's profitability upon which the divisional manager is judged.

Residual income approach: Pluto Electronics

While the average accounting return can be a misleading decision indicator for capital projects, it is possible to employ a profit-based approach that is in line with net present value. This involves calculating the **Residual Income** (RI), the profit less a cost of capital charge based on the book value of the assets employed.

Pluto Electronics has acquired the rights to manufacture a product for three years and has set up a new division to do so. The investment outlay is £60 million and annual cash flows are forecast to be £30 million. The company operates a straight-line depreciation policy and has a cost of capital of 10 per cent.

We can calculate the NPV (£m) as:

$$\text{NPV} = -60 + 30 \cdot \text{PVIFA}_{10,3} = -60 + (30 \times 2.4868) = £14.6\text{ m}$$

The same answer is given by calculating the residual income for each year and discounting at the cost of capital, as shown below. The annual profit is £10 million (i.e. £30 million cash flow less £20 million depreciation).

	£m		PV @ 10% (£m)
Yr 1 profit	10		
Investment outlay: £60 m			
10% capital charge on investment	(6)		
Residual income	4	× 0.909 =	3.636
Yr 2 profit	10		
Book value of assets: £40 m			
10% capital charge	(4)		
	6	× 0.826 =	4.956
Yr 3 profit	10		
Book value of assets: £20 m			
10% capital charge	(2)		
	8	× 0.751 =	6.008
Net present value			14.600

Payback period

Most finance texts have condemned the use of the payback period as potentially misleading in reaching investment decisions. However, Table 6.8 shows that it continues to flourish, being employed by most firms surveyed. Typically, the payback period required by firms is within 2–4 years (Arnold & Hatzopoulos 2000). Why is payback so popular? Does it possess certain qualities not so apparent in more sophisticated approaches?

The two main objections to payback (PB)

1 It ignores all cash flows beyond the payback period.
2 It does not consider the profile of the project's cash flows within the payback period.

Although such theoretical shortcomings could fundamentally alter a project's ranking and selection, the payback criterion possesses a number of merits.

1 PB estimates DCF return

The payback period provides a crude measure of investment profitability. When the annual cash receipts from a project are uniform, the payback reciprocal is the internal rate of return for a project of infinite life, or a good approximation to this rate for long-lived projects.

$$\text{IRR} = \frac{1}{\text{payback period}}$$

In the case of *very* long-lived projects where the cash inflows are, on average, spread evenly over the life of the project, the payback reciprocal is a reasonable proxy for the internal rate of return. For example, a project offering permanent cash savings and giving a four-year payback period with relatively stable annual cash returns will have approximately a 25 per cent internal rate of return (i.e. the reciprocal of payback period). However, if the project life is only ten years, the IRR would fall to 21 per cent – some four percentage points below the payback reciprocal. In fact, the payback reciprocal consistently *overstates* the true rate of return for finite project lives.

2 PB considers uncertainty

Whereas more sophisticated techniques attempt to model the uncertainty surrounding project returns, payback assumes that risk is time-related; the longer the period, the greater the chance of failure. General economic uncertainty makes the task of forecasting cash flows extremely difficult; but for the most part, cash flows are correlated over time. If the operating returns are below the expected level in the early years, they will probably also be below plan in the later years.

Discounted cash flow, as practised in most firms, ignores this increase in uncertainty over time. Early cash flows, therefore, have an important information content on the degree of accuracy of subsequent cash flows. By concentrating on the early cash flows, the payback approach analyses the data where managers have greater confidence. If such evaluation provides a different signal from DCF methods, it highlights the need for a more careful consideration of the project's risk characteristics.

3 PB as a screening device

Payback provides a relatively efficient method for ranking projects when constraints prevail. The most obvious constraint is the time that managers can devote to initial product screening. Only a handful of the investment ideas may stand up to serious and thorough financial investigation. Payback period serves as a simple, first-level screening device which, in the case of marginal projects, tends to operate in their favour and permits them to go forward for more thorough investigation.

Many firms also resort to payback period when experiencing liquidity constraints. Such a policy may make sense when funds are constrained and better investment ideas are in the pipeline. The attractiveness of investment proposals considered during the interim period will be a function more of their ability to pay back rapidly than of their overall profitability. This does not necessarily lead to optimal solutions.

4 PB assists communication

Managers feel more comfortable with payback period than with DCF. In the first place, it is simple to calculate and understand. The non-quantitative manager is reluctant to rely on the recommendations of 'sophisticated' models when he or she lacks both the time and expertise to verify such outcomes. Confidence in and commitment to a proposal depend to some degree on how thoroughly the evaluation model is comprehended. The payback method offers a convenient shorthand for the desirability of each investment that is understandable at all levels of the organisation: namely, how quickly will the project recover its initial outlay? Some firms use a project classification system in which the payback period indicates how rapidly proposals should be processed and put into operation.

Ultimately, it is the manager – not the method – who makes investment decisions and is appraised on their outcome. Payback period is particularly attractive to managers not only because it is convenient to calculate and communicate, but also because it signals good investment decisions at the earliest opportunity.

While the payback concept may lack the refinements of its more sophisticated evaluation counterparts, it possesses many endearing qualities that make it irresistible to most managers; hence its resilience.

Self-assessment Activity 6.6

The following reasons for using payback were made by finance executives from three different companies:

> 'We use payback in support of other methods. It is not a sufficiently reliable tool to be used in isolation.'
>
> 'When liquidity is under pressure, payback is particularly relevant.'
>
> 'Payback helps to give some idea of the riskiness of the project – a long time to get one's money back is obviously more risky than a short time.'

To what extent do you agree with these views?

Investing in biotech drugs

Sanofi-Synthelabo, the French pharmaceutical group, is to invest up to $528 million in the late-stage development and commercialisation of 20 cancer drugs belonging to Paris-based biotech company, Immuno-Designed Molecules.

IDM has developed therapeutic drugs to target cancer cells either by directly destroying tumour cells or by inducing a specific immune response. Its most advanced product, an ovarian cancer drug, is in its third-phase clinical trials and four products are in phase two. Sanofi will have first refusal for the first five years of the deal and then on two drugs a year for the last five. It will pay an upfront fee of $2 million per drug with further payments at each stage of clinical testing, as well as a success fee; totalling $30 million for each drug.

Over the past two years, biotechnology companies have been able to strike better deals because of the problems that large drugs companies have in developing their known products.

Bristol Myers Squibb of the US signed a deal in September for up to $2 billion for a cancer drug being developed by ImClone. However, the Food and Drug Administration rejected ImClone's licence application in December, which caused the company's share price to plunge 64 per cent.

Based on Jo Johnson, *Financial Times*, January 22 2002

Summary

One of the most difficult aspects of capital budgeting is identifying and gathering the relevant information for analysis. This chapter has examined the incremental cash flow approach to project analysis. Specific attention has been paid to the replacement decision and to the impact of inflation and taxation on investment decisions.

Key points

- Include only future, incremental cash flows relating to the investment decision and its consequences. This implies the following:

  1. Only additional fixed overheads are included.
  2. Depreciation (a non-cash item) is excluded.
  3. Sunk (or past) costs are not relevant.
  4. Interest charges are financing (not investment) cash flows and are therefore excluded from the cash flow profile.
  5. Opportunity costs (e.g. the opportunity to rent or sell premises if the proposal is not acceptable) are included.

- Replacement decision analysis examines the change in cash flows resulting from the decision to replace an existing asset with a new asset.
- Inflation can have important effects on project analysis. Two approaches are possible: (1) specify all cash flows at 'money-of-the-day' (i.e. including inflation) prices and discount at the money cost of capital, or (2) specify cash flows at today's prices and discount at the real (i.e. net of inflation) cost of capital. We recommend the former in most cases.
- Taxation is for most organisations a cash flow. Tax is calculated by deducting any cash benefits from tax relief on the initial capital expenditure from tax payable on additional cash flows. Care should be taken in estimating the timing of tax cash flows.
- In practice, most firms, particularly larger companies, employ a combination of DCF and traditional appraisal methods.

Further reading

Most finance texts are not particularly strong on the applied aspects of capital budgeting. Levy and Sarnat (1996) and Brigham and Gapenski (1991) have useful chapters, but the US tax system is employed. For a discussion on the investment appraisal criteria under low inflation, see the Bank of England (1994). Pointon (1980) examines the effect of capital allowances on investment, while Hodgkinson (1989) surveys tax treatment in corporate investment appraisal.

Studies on the investment practices of UK firms are well worth reading. See, for example, Pike (1982, 1988, 1996), McIntyre and Coulthurst (1985), Mills (1988), Pike and Wolfe (1988) and Arnold and Hatzopoulos (2000). Useful references on the capital budgeting process are Cooper (1975), Pinches (1982) and Neale and Holmes (1991). Tomkins (1991) and Butler *et al.* (1993) explore the strategic and organisational aspects in greater depth.

Appendix

The problem of unequal lives: Allis plc

In the earlier example, both existing and new machines had five-year project lives. Comparing mutually exclusive projects – such as retaining the old asset or replacing it with a new one – frequently involves the problem of assessing projects with different economic lives.

Allis plc is seeking to modernise and speed up its production process. Two proposals have been suggested to achieve this: the purchase of a number of forklift trucks and the acquisition of a conveyor system. The accountant has produced cost savings figures for the two proposals using a 10 per cent discount rate, shown in Table 6.10.

At first sight, the more expensive conveyor system appears more wealth-creating. But it is not appropriate to compare projects with different lives without making some adjustment. Two approaches can be employed for this: the replacement chain approach and the equivalent annual annuity approach.

Table 6.10 Allis plc cash flows for two projects

Year	Forklift trucks	Conveyor system
0	(30,000)	(66,000)
1	10,000	12,000
2	15,000	20,000
3	18,000	20,000
4		18,000
5		15,000
6		15,000
NPV at 10%	5,010	6,538

The **replacement chain approach** recognises that while, for convenience, we usually consider only the time-horizon of the proposal, most investments form part of a replacement chain over a much longer time-period. We therefore need to compare mutually exclusive projects over a common period. In the example, this period is six years, two forklift truck proposals (one following the other) being equivalent to one conveyor system proposal. Assuming the cash flows for the original forklift trucks also apply to their replacements in Year 4 (a pretty big assumption, given inflation, improvements in technology etc.), the replacement will produce a further NPV of £5,010 at the start of Year 4.

To convert this to the present value (i.e. Year 0) we must discount this figure to the present using the discount factor for 10 per cent for a cash flow three years hence:

$$PV = £5{,}010 \times PVIF_{(10,3)} = £5{,}010 \times 0.7513 = £3{,}764$$

The NPV for the forklift truck proposal, assuming like-for-like replacement after three years, is therefore £5,010 + £3,764 = £8,774. This is well in excess of the NPV of the conveyor system proposal (£6,538) over the same time-period.

Allis plc NPV comparison

Year		Forklift trucks £	Conveyor system £
1–3		5,010	
4–6	£5,010 × 0.7513	3,764	
1–6		8,774	6,538

A second approach, the **equivalent annual annuity (EAA)** approach, is easier than its name suggests. It seeks to determine the constant annual cash flow that offers the same present value as the project's NPV. This is found by dividing the project's NPV by the relevant annuity discount factor (i.e. 10 per cent over three years):

Continued

$$EAA = \frac{NPV}{PVIFA_{(10,3)}}$$

For the forklift proposal:

$$EAA = \frac{£5,010}{2.4869} = £2,015$$

For the conveyor system proposal:

$$EAA = \frac{NPV}{PVIFA_{(10,6)}} = \frac{£6,538}{4.3553} = £1,501$$

The forklift proposal offers the higher equivalent annual annuity and is to be preferred. Assuming continuous replacement at the end of their project lives, the NPVs for the projects over an infinite time-horizon are found by dividing the EAA by the discount rate:

NPV forklift truck = £2,015/0.10 = £20,150
NPV conveyor = £1,501/0.10 = £15,010

Self-assessment Answers

6.1 Incremental cash flows, applied to capital budgeting, are the additional cash flows created as a direct result of making an investment decision. Frequently, identifying these is not as straightforward as one might think, particularly where replacement decisions are involved or where decisions in one part of the business have ramifications for other parts.

6.2 The original cost of developing the drug is a sunk cost and should not form part of the analysis. Any adverse effects on other parts of the business resulting from the decision to manufacture the product are an associated cash flow and should be included in the analysis. The external sale value of the patent is an opportunity cost of proceeding with production. The £10 million cost should be deducted from the project's cash flows.

6.3 To: Sid Torrance

From: Rick Faldo

Clubs for Beginners Proposal

I have re-examined the points raised in your e-mail and discussed them with our accountant.

In analysing capital projects, only future investment cash flows incremental to the business are relevant to the decision.

1. Depreciation is not a cash flow – it is a charge against profits. By comparing operating cash flows against initial outlay, the need for depreciation becomes unnecessary.

2 Only additional fixed costs resulting from the introduction of the new project should be charged. I have checked that no extra overheads are incurred.
3 The market research is a past cost. Its existence is not dependent upon the outcome of the decision, so it should not be included.
4 I agree that finance costs are important, but the cost of finance has already been accounted for within the discount rate.

My 'Clubs for Beginners' proposal is, I suggest, an attractive one, from which the business should benefit considerably.

6.4 Many companies have failed to take account of the relatively low inflation and interest rates when calculating the required return on investment projects. For example, a nominal rate of 20 per cent, which many firms use, may not be unreasonable during times of relatively high inflation, but is probably excessive during periods of low inflation. This makes it more difficult for economically attractive projects to be accepted.

6.5 Tax is a cash flow and shareholders want firms to maximise their after-tax cash flows. It affects companies in different ways, depending on their tax situations and the capital allowances available to them. Some types of business attract more generous allowances than others. However, for the majority of capital projects, the tax effect will have a relatively minor impact on the project outcome. Good projects are usually viable both before and after tax.

Questions

1 *Solution in Appendix A (page 806).* Most capital budgeting textbooks strongly recommend NPV, but most firms prefer IRR. Explain.

2 *Solution in Appendix A (page 806).* A project costing £20,000 offers an annual cash flow of £5,000 over its life.

(a) Calculate the internal rate of return using the payback reciprocal assuming an infinite life.
(b) Use tables to test your answer assuming the project life is (i) 20 years, (ii) eight years.
(c) What conclusions can be drawn as to the suitability of the payback reciprocal in measuring investment profitability?

3 Your firm uses the IRR method and asks you to evaluate the following mutually exclusive projects:

	Year				
Cash flows (£)	**0**	**1**	**2**	**3**	**4**
Proposal L	−47,232	20,000	20,000	20,000	20,000
Proposal M	−47,232	0	10,000	20,000	65,350

Using the appropriate IRR method, evaluate these proposals assuming a required rate of return of 10 per cent. Compare your answer with the net present value method.

4 *Solution in Appendix A (page 806).* State two ways in which inflation can be handled in investment analysis. Which way would you recommend and why?

5 *Solution in Appendix A (page 806).* Bramhope Manufacturing Co. Ltd has found that, after only two years of using a machine for a semi-automatic process, a more advanced model has arrived on the market. This advanced model will not only produce the current volume of the company's product more efficiently, but allow increased output of the product. The existing machine had cost £32,000 and was being depreciated straight-line over a ten-year period, at the end of which it would be scrapped. The market value of this machine is currently £15,000 and there is a prospective purchaser interested in acquiring it.

The advanced model now available costs £123,500 fully installed. Because of its more complex mechanism, the advanced model is expected to have a useful life of only eight years. A scrap value of £20,500 is considered reasonable.

A comparison of the existing and advanced model now available shows the following:

	Existing machine	**Advanced model**
Capacity p.a.	200,000 units	230,000 units
	£	£
Selling price per unit	0.95	0.95
Production costs per unit		
Labour	0.12	0.08
Materials	0.48	0.46
Fixed overheads (allocation of portion of company's fixed overheads)	0.25	0.16

The sales director is of the opinion that additional output could be sold at 95p per unit.

If the advanced model were to be run at the old production level of 200,000 units per annum, the operators would be freed for a proportionate period of time for reassignment to the other operations of the company.

The sales director has suggested that the advanced model should be purchased by the company to replace the existing machine.

The required return is 15 per cent.

(i) You are required to calculate:
  (a) payback period
  (b) the net present value
  (c) the internal rate of return (to the nearest per cent)

(ii) What recommendation would you make to the sales director? What other considerations are relevant?

6 Argon Mining plc is investigating the possibility of purchasing an open-cast coal mine in South Wales at a cost of £2.5 million which the British Government is selling as part of its privatisation programme. The company's surveyors have spent the last three months examining the potential of the mine and have incurred costs to date of £0.2 million. The surveyors have prepared a report which states that the company will require equipment and vehicles costing £12.5 million in order to operate the mine and that these assets can be sold for £2.5 million in four years time when the coal reserves of the mine are exhausted.

The assistant to the Chief Financial Officer of the company has prepared the following projected profit and loss accounts for each year of the life of the mine.

Projected Profit and Loss Accounts

	Year			
	1 £m	2 £m	3 £m	4 £m
Sales	9.4	9.8	8.5	6.3
less Wages and salaries	(2.3)	(2.5)	(2.6)	(1.8)
Selling and distribution costs	(1.3)	(1.2)	(1.5)	(0.6)
Materials and consumables	(0.3)	(0.4)	(0.4)	(0.2)
Depreciation and equipment	(2.5)	(2.5)	(2.5)	(2.5)
Head office expenses	(0.6)	(0.6)	(0.6)	(0.6)
Survey costs	(0.4)			
Interest charges	(1.2)	(1.2)	(1.2)	(1.2)
Net profit (loss)	0.8	1.4	(0.3)	(0.6)

In his report to the Chief Financial Officer, the assistant recommends that the company should not proceed with the acquisition of the mine as the profitability of the proposal is poor.

The following additional information is available:

(i) The project will require an investment of £0.5 million of working capital from the beginning of the project until the end of the useful life of the mine.
(ii) The wages and salaries expenses include £0.5 million of working capital in Year 1 for staff who are already employed by the company but who would be without productive work until Year 2 if the project does not proceed. However, the company has no intention of dismissing these staff. After Year 1, these staff will be employed on another project of the company.
(iii) One-third of the head office expenses consists of amounts directly incurred in managing the new project and two-thirds represents an apportionment of other head office expenses to the project to ensure that it bears a fair share of these expenses.
(iv) The survey costs include those costs already incurred to date, and which are to be written off in the first year of the project, as well as costs to be incurred in the first year if the project is accepted.
(v) The interest charges relate to finance required to purchase the equipment and vehicles necessary to carry out the project.
(vi) After the mine has been exhausted, the company will be required to clean up the site and to make good the damage to the environment resulting from its mining operations. The company will incur costs of £0.4 million in Year 5 in order to do this.

The company has a cost of capital of 12 per cent.
Ignore taxation.

Required

(a) Using what you consider to be the most appropriate investment appraisal method, prepare calculations which will help the company to decide whether or not to proceed with the project.
(b) State, giving reasons, whether you think the project should go ahead.
(c) Explain why you consider the investment appraisal method selected in (a) above to be most appropriate for evaluating investment projects.

7 Consolidated Oilfields plc is interested in exploring for oil near the west coast of Australia. The Australian government is prepared to grant an exploration licence to the company for a five-year period for a fee of £300,000 p.a. The option to acquire the rights must be taken immediately, otherwise another oil company will be granted the rights. However, Consolidated Oilfields is not in a position to commence operations immediately, and exploration of the oilfield will not start until the beginning of the second year. In order to carry out the exploration work, the company will require equipment costing £10,400,000, which will be made by a specialist engineering company. Half of the equipment cost will be payable immediately and half will be paid when the equipment has been built and tested to the satisfaction of Consolidated Oilfields. It is estimated that the second instalment will be paid at the end of the first year. The company commissioned a geological survey of the area and the results suggest that the oilfield will produce relatively small amounts of high-quality crude oil. The survey cost £250,000 and is now due for payment.

The assistant to the project accountant has produced the following projected Profit and Loss Accounts for the project for Years 2–5 when the oilfield is operational.

	Year							
		2		3		4		5
	£000	£000	£000	£000	£000	£000	£000	£000
Sales		7,400		8,300		9,800		5,800
Less expenses								
Wages and salaries	550		580		620		520	
Materials and consumables	340		360		410		370	
Licence fee	600		300		300		300	
Overheads	220		220		220		220	
Depreciation	2,100		2,100		2,100		2,100	
Survey cost written off	250		–		–		–	
Interest charges	650		650		650		650	
		4,710		4,210		4,300		3,160
Profit		2,690		4,090		5,500		2,640

The following additional information is available:

1 The licence fee charge appearing in the accounts in Year 2 includes a write-off for all the annual fee payable in Year 1. The licence fee is paid to the Australian government at the end of each year.
2 The overheads contain an annual charge of £120,000, which represents an apportionment of head office costs. This is based on a standard calculation to ensure that all projects bear a fair share of the central administrative costs of the business. The remainder of the overheads relate directly to the project.
3 The survey costs written off relate to the geological survey already undertaken and due for payment immediately.
4 The new equipment costing £10,400,000 will be sold at the end of the licence period for £2,000,000.
5 The project will require a specialised cutting tool for a brief period at the end of Year 2, which is currently being used by the company in another project. The manager of

the other project has estimated that he will have to hire machinery at a cost of £150,000 for the period the cutting tool is on loan.

6 The project will require an investment of £650,000 working capital from the end of the first year to the end of the licence period.

The company has a cost of capital of 10 per cent.
Ignore taxation.

Required

(a) Prepare calculations that will help the company to evaluate further the profitability of the proposed project.
(b) State, with reasons, whether you would recommend that the project be undertaken.
(c) Explain how inflation can pose problems when appraising capital expenditure proposals, and how these problems may be dealt with.

(Certified Diploma)

8 You are the chief accountant of Deighton plc, which manufactures a wide range of building and plumbing fittings. It has recently taken over a smaller unquoted competitor, Linton Ltd. Deighton is currently checking through various documents at Linton's head office, including a number of investment appraisals. One of these, a recently rejected application involving an outlay on equipment of £900,000, is reproduced below. It was rejected because it failed to offer Linton's target return on investment of 25 per cent (average profit-to-initial investment outlay). Closer inspection reveals several errors in the appraisal.

Evaluation of profitability of proposed project NT17 (all values in current year prices)

Item (£000)	0	1	2	3	4
Sales		1,400	1,600	1,800	1,000
Materials		(400)	(450)	(500)	(250)
Direct labour		(400)	(450)	(500)	(250)
Overheads		(100)	(100)	(100)	(100)
Interest		(120)	(120)	(120)	(120)
Depreciation		(225)	(225)	(225)	(225)
Profit pre-tax		155	255	355	55
Tax at 33%		(51)	(84)	(117)	(18)
Post-tax profit		104	171	238	37
Outlay					
Stock	(100)				
Equipment	(900)				
Market research	(200)				
	(1,200)				

$$\text{Rate of return} - \frac{\text{Average profit}}{\text{Investment}} = \frac{£138}{£1,200} = 11.5\%$$

You discover the following further details:

1 Linton's policy was to finance both working capital and fixed investment by a bank overdraft. A 12 per cent interest rate applied at the time of the evaluation.

2 A 25 per cent writing-down allowance (WDA) on a reducing balance basis is offered for new investment. Linton's profits are sufficient to utilise fully this allowance throughout the project.
3 Corporation Tax is paid a year in arrears.
4 Of the overhead charge, about half reflects absorption of existing overhead costs.
5 The market research was actually undertaken to investigate two proposals, the other project also having been rejected. The total bill for all this research has already been paid.
6 Deighton itself requires a nominal return on new projects of 20 per cent after taxes, is currently ungeared and has no plans to use any debt finance in the future.

Required

Write a report to the finance director in which you:

(a) Identify the mistakes made in Linton's evaluation.
(b) Restate the investment appraisal in terms of the post-tax net present value to Deighton, recommending whether the project should be undertaken or not.

(ACCA)

9 **(a)** Explain how inflation affects the rate of return required on an investment project, and the distinction between a real and a nominal (or 'money terms') approach to the evaluation of an investment project under inflation.
(b) Howden plc is contemplating investment in an additional production line to produce its range of compact discs. A market research study, undertaken by a well-known firm of consultants, has revealed scope to sell an additional output of 400,000 units p.a. The study cost £0.1 million, but the account has not yet been settled.

The price and cost structure of a typical disc (net of royalties) is as follows:

	£	£
Price per unit		12.00
Costs per unit of output		
Material cost per unit	1.50	
Direct labour cost per unit	0.50	
Variable overhead cost per unit	0.50	
Fixed overhead cost per unit	1.50	
		(4.00)
Profit		8.00

The fixed overhead represents an apportionment of central administrative and marketing costs. These are expected to rise in total by £500,000 p.a. as a result of undertaking this project. The production line is expected to operate for five years and require a total cash outlay of £11 million, including £0.5 million of materials stocks. The equipment will have a residual value of £2 million. Because the company is moving towards a JIT stock management policy, it is expected that this project will involve steadily reducing working capital needs, expected to decline at about 3 per cent p.a. by volume. The production line will be accommodated in a presently empty building for which an offer of £2 million has recently been received from another company. If the building is retained, it is expected that property price inflation will increase its value to £3 million after five years.

While the precise rates of price and cost inflation are uncertain, economists in Howden's corporate planning department make the following forecasts for the average annual rates of inflation relevant to the project:

Retail Price Index	6% p.a.
Disc prices	5% p.a.
Material prices	3% p.a.
Direct labour wage rates	7% p.a.
Variable overhead costs	7% p.a.
Other overhead costs	5% p.a.

Note: You may ignore taxes and capital allowances in this question.

Required

(a) Given that Howden's shareholders require a real return of 8.5 per cent for projects of this degree of risk, assess the financial viability of this proposal.

(b) Briefly discuss how inflation may complicate the analysis of business financial decisions.

(ACCA)

Practical assignment

Engineering Products case study

The following case study brings together many of the issues raised in Part 2 of this book on the analysis of strategic investment decisions. In answering certain parts the student should also read Chapters 7 and 8.

Roger Davis, the newly appointed financial analyst of the Steel Tube division of Engineering Products plc, shut his office door and walked over to his desk. He had just 24 hours to re-examine the accountant's profit projections and come up with a recommendation on the proposed new computer numerically controlled (CNC) milling machine.

At the meeting he had just left, the managing director made it quite clear: 'If the project can't pay for itself in the first three years, it's not worth bothering with.' Davis was unhappy with the accountant's analysis which showed that the project was a loss maker. But as the MD said, 'Unless you can convince me by this time tomorrow that spending £240,000 on this capital project makes economic sense, you can forget the whole idea.'

His first task was to re-examine the accountant's profitability forecast (Table 6.11) in the light of the following facts that emerged from the meeting:

1 Given the rapid developments in the market, it was unrealistic to assume that the product had more than a four-year life. The machinery would have no other use and could not raise more than £20,000 in scrap metal at the end of the project.
2 The opening stock in Year 1 would be acquired at the same time as the machine. All other stock movement would occur at the year ends.
3 This type of machine was depreciated over six years on a straight-line basis.
4 Within the 'other production expenses' were apportioned fixed overheads equal to 20 per cent of labour costs. As far as could be seen, none of these overheads were incurred as a result of the proposal.
5 The administration charge was an apportionment of central fixed overheads.

Table 6.11 Profit projection for CNC milling machine (£000)

	Year			
	1	**2**	**3**	**4**
Sales	400	600	800	600
Less costs				
Materials				
Opening stock	40	80	80	60
Purchases	260	300	360	240
Closing stock	(80)	(80)	(60)	–
Cost of sales	220	300	380	300
Labour	80	120	120	80
Other production expenses	80	90	92	100
Depreciation	40	40	40	40
Administrative overhead	54	76	74	74
Interest on loans to finance the project	22	22	22	22
Total cost	496	648	728	616
Profit (loss)	(96)	(48)	72	(16)

Later that day, Davis met the production manager, who explained that if the new machine was installed, it would have sufficient capacity to enable an existing machine to be sold immediately for £20,000 and to create annual cash benefits of £18,000. However, the accountant had told him that, with the machine currently standing in the books at £50,000, the company simply could not afford to write off the asset against this year's slender profits. 'We'd do better to keep it operating for another four years, when its scrap value will produce about £8,000,' he said.

Davis then raised the proposal with the marketing director. It was not long before two new pieces of information emerged:

(a) To stand a realistic chance of hitting the sales forecast for the proposal, marketing would require £40,000 for additional advertising and sales promotion at the start of the project and a further £8,000 a year for the remainder of the project's life. The sales forecast and advertising effort had been devised in consultation with marketing consultants whose bill for £18,000 had just arrived that morning.

(b) The marketing director was very concerned about the impact on other products within the product range. If the investment went ahead, it would lead to a reduction in sales value of a competing product of around £60,000 a year. 'With net profit margins of around 10 per cent and gross margins (after direct costs) of 25 per cent on these sales, this is probably the "kiss of death" for the CNC proposal,' Davis reflected.

The Steel Tube division was a profitable business operating within an attractive market. The investment, which employed new technology, had recently been identified as part of the group's core activities. The chief engineer felt that once they had got to grips with the new technology it should deliver improved product quality, and greater flexibility, enabling shorter production runs and other benefits.

The latest accounts for the division showed a 16 per cent return on assets, but the MD talked about a three-year payback requirement. His phone call to the finance director at head office, to whom this proposal would eventually be sent, was distinctly unhelpful: 'We have, in the past, found that whenever we lay down a hurdle rate for divisional capital projects, it merely encourages unduly optimistic estimates from divisional executives eager to promote their pet proposals. So now we give no guidelines on this matter.'

Davis decided to use 10 per cent as the required rate of return, made up of 6 per cent currently obtainable from risk-free government securities plus a small element to compensate for risk. Davis went home that evening with a very full briefcase and a number of unresolved questions.

1 How much of the information which he had gathered was really relevant to the decision?
2 What was the best approach to assessing the economic worth of the proposal? The company used payback and return on investment, but he felt that discounted cash flow techniques had some merit.
3 Cash was particularly limited this year and acceptance of this project could mean that other projects would have to be deferred. How should this be taken into consideration?
4 How should the strategic factors be assessed?
5 What about tax? Engineering Products plc pays Corporation Tax at 30 per cent and annual writing-down allowances of 25 per cent on the reducing balance may be claimed. The existing machine has a nil value for tax purposes and tax is payable in the same year as the cash flows to which it relates.

Required

Prepare the case, with recommendations, to be presented by Davis at tomorrow's meeting. The report should address points 1–5 above.

7 Investment strategy and process

A Mickey Mouse investment?

The Euro Disney theme park opened with all the razzmatazz of a Disney spectacular. However, from an investment perspective, it was a spectacular flop in its first few years of operation. It planned to make a profit in its opening year. Instead, Euro Disney produced losses in each of its first three years, with the second year producing a staggering loss of FFr 5.3 billion.

The park simply failed to attract sufficient visitors to cover its initial costs. The northern French climate, rising franc, economic recession, Gallic hostility to American culture and high admission cost all contributed to the lack of visitors.

There were rumours that the Walt Disney Corporation would abandon its Euro Disney investment. It summoned the banks to tell them that, unless a rescue package was agreed, it would pull the plug and Euro Disney would close. Such a package was eventually agreed, but with rival parks opening in Spain and Germany, the prospects of success were not looking good.

This seemed a far cry from its initial public offer for shares launched on many of the stock exchanges throughout Europe. The offer document indicated an internal rate of return of 13.3 per cent between 1992 and 2017 based on an inflation assumption of 5 per cent per annum. A fairytale start to Euro Disney life, followed by a financially delinquent adolescence – but would Euro Disney ever produce the returns to make investors happy ever after? They are still waiting.

Learning objectives

This chapter examines strategic issues in investment and the investment process:

- How strategy shapes investment decisions.
- Evaluating new technology and environmental projects.

- The investment decision and control process.
- Post-audit reviews.

7.1 Introduction

A company's ability to succeed in highly competitive markets depends to a great extent on its ability to regenerate itself through wealth-creating capital investment decisions compatible with business strategy. In recent years, most of the combined internal and external funds generated by UK firms have been committed to fixed capital investment. Applying such resources to long-term capital projects in anticipation of an adequate return – although a hazardous step – is essential for the vitality and well-being of the organisation.

7.2 Strategic considerations

Where do positive NPV projects come from? By definition, a positive NPV means that a project offers returns superior to those obtainable in the capital market on investments of comparable risk. In the short run, it is quite feasible to find capital projects that do just this, but in a competitive market it will not be long before other firms make similar investments, thereby ensuring that any superior returns are not perpetuated.

Selecting wealth-creating capital projects is no different from picking undervalued shares on the stock market. Earlier discussion on market efficiency argued that this is possible only if there are capital market imperfections that prevent asset prices reflecting their equilibrium values.

Companies that consistently create projects with high NPVs have developed a sustainable competitive advantage arising from imperfections in the product and factor markets. These imperfections generally take the form of entry barriers that discourage new entrants. Successful investments are therefore investments that help create, preserve or enhance competitive advantage.

Porter (1985) argues that there are really only three coherent strategies for strategic business units:

1 To be the lowest-cost producer.
2 To focus on a niche or segment within the market.
3 To differentiate the product range so that it does not compete directly with lower-cost products.

Investment expenditure that helps achieve the appropriate strategy is likely to generate superior returns. For example, Coca-Cola invests enormous sums into its product differentiation strategy through its brand support.

Capital projects should be viewed not simply in isolation, but within the context of the business, its goals and strategic direction. This approach is often termed **strategic portfolio analysis**.

The attractiveness of investment proposals coming from different sectors of the firm's business portfolio depends not only on the rate of return offered, but also on the strategic importance of the sector. Business strategies are formulated that involve the allocation of resources (capital, labour, plant, marketing support etc.) to these business units. The allocation may be based on analysis of the market's attractiveness and the firm's competitive strengths, such as the **McKinsey–General Electric portfolio matrix** outlined in Figure 7.1.

The attractiveness of the market or industry is indicated by such factors as the size and growth of the market, ease of entry, degree of competition and industry profitability for each strategic business unit. Business strength is indicated by a firm's market share and its growth rate, brand loyalty, profitability, and technological and other comparative advantages. Such analysis leads to three basic strategies:

1 Invest in and strengthen businesses operating in relatively attractive markets. This may mean heavy expenditures on capital equipment, working capital, research and development, brand development and training.
2 Where the market is somewhat less attractive and the business less competitive (the diagonal unshaded boxes), the business strategy is to get the maximum out of existing resources. The financial strategy is therefore to maximise or maintain cash flows, while incurring capital expenditures mainly of a replacement nature. Tight control over costs and management of working capital lead to higher levels of profitability and cash flow.
3 The remaining businesses have little strategic quality and may, in the longer term, be run down or divested unless action can be taken to improve their attractiveness.

Market Attractiveness \ Business Strength	High	Medium	Low
High	INVEST & GROW	INVEST & GROW	IMPROVE & DEFEND (Selective Investment)
Medium	INVEST & GROW	IMPROVE & DEFEND (Selective Investment)	HARVEST OR DIVEST
Low	IMPROVE & DEFEND (Selective Investment)	HARVEST OR DIVEST	HARVEST OR DIVEST

Figure 7.1 McKinsey–GE portfolio matrix

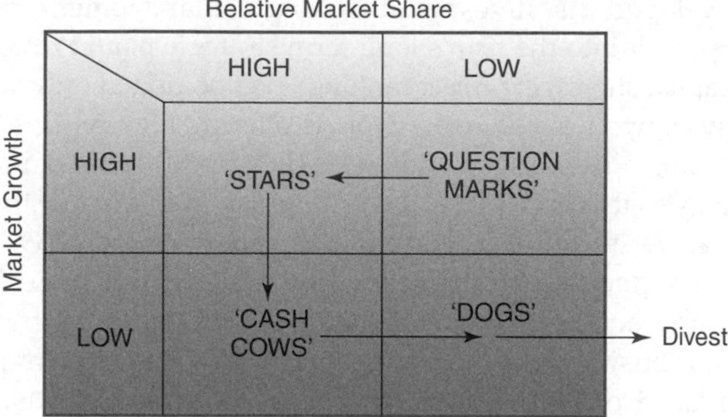

Figure 7.2 Normal progression of product over time

An alternative is the **Boston Consulting Group approach**, which describes the business portfolio in terms of relative market share and rate of growth (see Figure 7.2). This matrix identifies four product markets within which a firm may operate: (1) 'stars' (high market share, high market growth), (2) 'cash cows' (high market share, low market growth), (3) 'question marks' (low market share, high market growth) and (4) 'dogs' (low market share, low market growth). The normal progression starts with the potentially successful product ('question mark') and moves in an anticlockwise direction, eventually to be withdrawn (divested).

From this strategic analysis of the firm's business portfolio, we suggest the pattern of resource allocation outlined in Figure 7.3. Businesses offering high growth and the possibility of acquiring market dominance are the main areas of investment ('stars' and 'question marks'). Once such dominance is achieved, the growth rate declines and investment is necessary only to maintain market share. These 'cash cows' become generators of funds for other growth areas. Business areas that have failed to achieve a sizeable share of the market during their growth phase ('dogs') become candidates for divestment and should be evaluated accordingly. Any cash so generated should be applied to high-growth sectors.

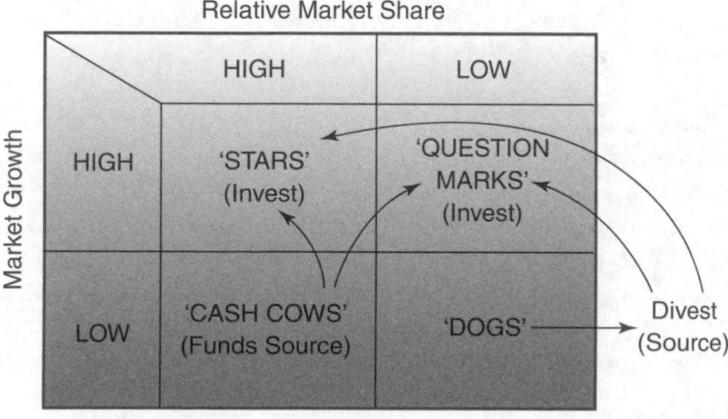

Figure 7.3 Investment strategy

Having developed its investment strategy, management can assess how individual projects fit into the firm's long-term strategic plan. Project appraisal – or, in the case of capital shortage, project ranking – is not judged only according to rates of return. Many companies will reject projects offering high returns because projects fall outside strategic thinking. Ultimately, the capital budget must tie up with corporate strategy so that each project contributes to an element of that strategy.

In Chapter 4, we introduced Shareholder Value Analysis (SVA) as a valuable planning tool and guide for strategic decision making. It is basically an extension of the NPV approach where the focus is on business units, strategies and financial goals. A business is viewed as a portfolio of investment projects, but the emphasis is placed on maximising the value of strategic business units, not merely that of the capital projects within them.

Rather than dwell on short-term measures, such as annual earnings per share or return on capital, SVA manages cash flows over time. It is this long-term cash flow that determines the long-term value of the business. The value of adopting a new strategy is assessed in terms of the difference in the value of the business before and after implementation.

Self-assessment Activity 7.1

Why is it important to view capital budgeting within a strategic framework?

(answer at end of chapter)

Corporate mortality at Microsoft

Bill Gates is the world's richest man and head of Microsoft, arguably the world's most successful company. Yet he is brutally aware of his company's vulnerability, even when most people regard the business as an indomitable near monopolist at the heart of the software industry. As he said recently: 'Someday Microsoft will go out of business, it's only a matter of time. Will it happen in my lifetime, while I am still deeply involved in the company? I hope not. I wake up every day working hard to reduce the probability of this. Companies are mortal' (Bennet, 2001).

Gates realises that it is this awareness of corporate mortality that forces the company to continue its punishing innovation cycle.

Over the years, there has been talk that Microsoft will use its vast cash resources and market capitalisation to diversify into other industries such as banking and telecoms. Gates rejects this. So why has it been so successful? Of course, at one level, the main reason is its ability to innovate and keep ahead of the competition. But Gates explains why the company has the highest market capitalisation in terms of its high-volume, low-cost products.

Project finance

Large-scale strategic projects, such as the construction of tunnels, roads and power stations, are often funded through project finance. Here the operation is financed and controlled separately from the operations of the constructor or user. The obvious benefit to the company is that creditors of the project only have claims on the project's cash flows, not those of the companies involved in the construction process. Following the Private Finance Initiative (PFI), which was introduced in the UK in 1992, many public sector projects have been funded in this manner.

7.3 Advanced manufacturing technology (AMT) investment

An area where strategic decision-making is often required is the evaluation of advanced manufacturing technology projects. Strategic investment appraisal links corporate strategy to the costs and benefits associated with AMT and other strategic decisions. Frequently, it is insufficient to consider only financial issues; many of the benefits are less tangible and hard to quantify.

The past 20 years have seen growth in new technology capital projects, creating different problems for the decision-maker. AMT projects offer a range of less tangible benefits: for example, greater flexibility with reduced 'downtime' on production changeover. Greater flexibility enables businesses to meet the challenge of increasing competition, shorter product life cycles and satisfying customers'specific requirements. AMT offers a flexible manufacturing system (FMS), in which a sequence of production operations are computer-controlled to respond to ever-changing production and design requirements.

AMT terminology

AMT investment helps companies achieve competitive advantage through a number of technologies:

- **Computer-aided design** (CAD) helps the engineer test and modify a design from any viewpoint.
- **Computer-integrated manufacture** (CIM) brings together the manufacturing process and the computer.
- **Computer-numerically controlled** (CNC) machines can be easily reprogrammed to perform different tasks.
- **Flexible manufacturing systems** (FMS) enable the firm to produce a far greater variety of components quickly.
- **Direct numerical control** (DNC) systems connect a number of numerically controlled machines by computer.

AMT example: Foster Engineering Ltd

Foster Engineering Ltd is considering introducing a flexible manufacturing system (FMS) to modernise production in a department currently using conventional metal-working machinery. The declining market and the awareness that its main competitors have recently introduced new technology have made the need to modernise plant facilities an urgent priority.

An AMT proposal has been put forward, offering an FMS capable of producing the present output. It involves two machining centres with CNC lathes, a conveyor system for transferring components and a computer for scheduling, tooling and overall control. The total investment would cost £2.4 million, half being incurred at the start and the other half after one year, at which point the existing machinery could be sold for £50,000. Any benefit would arise from Year 2 onwards for five years. The two quantified benefits are as follows:

1 A reduction in the number of skilled workers from 50 to 15. The annual cost of a skilled worker is £20,000 (savings of 35 × £20,000 = £700,000 p.a.).
2 Savings in scrap and re-work of £50,000 p.a.

The company requires all projects to offer a positive net present value discounted at 15 per cent.

The accountant produces the following evaluation showing that the FMS proposal has a negative NPV of £159,000 and fails to meet corporate investment criteria:

FMS proposal

Annual benefit		(£000)	
PV at Year 1	£700,000 × $\text{PVIFA}_{(15,5)}$		
	£700,000 × 3.352	2,346	
PV at Year 0	£2,346 × $\text{PVIF}_{(15,1)}$		
	£2,346 × 0.87		2,041
Initial investment			
Year 0		(£1,200)	
Year 1 (£1,200 − 50) × 0.87		(£1,000)	(2,200)
NPV			(159)

An incensed production engineer in Foster Engineering, on hearing that the proposal is unacceptable, points to the 'intangible' benefits that the FMS will offer:

- Improved quality leading to a significant, but unknown, reduction in sales returns through faulty workmanship.
- Reduced stock and work-in-progress, enabling improved shopfloor layout, greater space and a lower working capital requirement.
- Lower total manufacturing time, enabling the company to respond more quickly to customer orders and to reduce work-in-progress further.
- Significantly improved machine utilisation rates, although the actual degree of improvement is difficult to quantify.
- Increased capacity with the option to operate unmanned night workings.
- Greater flexibility, enabling shorter production runs and faster re-tooling and re-scheduling.

CIM involves the computerisation of functions and their integration into a system that regulates the manufacturing process. It brings together the individual manufacturing techniques referred to earlier under unified computer control.

Many of these benefits could be quantified, at least in part (e.g. the savings in working capital), although the degree of confidence in the underlying assumptions may not be high. But even so, there will still be a large intangible element that cannot be quantified. This has led to the charge that conventional methods of investment appraisal are biased against AMT investments.

Kaplan (1986) raises the question of whether AMT projects must be 'justified by faith alone'. Should managers in Foster Engineering replace the DCF approach with a belief that AMT is the key to the future and that strategic positioning must override economic analysis?

The answer is not to dismiss DCF analysis, but to see it within a wider strategic context. We advocate a three-stage approach to analysing AMT capital projects:

1 Does the project fit well within the company's overall corporate strategy?
2 Does the DCF analysis, based on the quantifiable elements of the decision, justify the investment outlay?
3 Where the net present value calculated in stage 2 is negative, examine the shortfall. Does management believe that the 'value' of the intangible benefits exceeds the shortfall? This last stage is a somewhat subjective process whereby managers consider the strategic and operational benefits. No one can put an accurate value on flexibility, for example, but it would be wrong to exclude such a major benefit from consideration in the decision process.

Can firms afford not to invest?

Henry Ford once claimed: 'If you need a new machine and don't buy it, you pay for it without getting it.' The price paid is the loss in competitiveness from not taking advantage of new technology.

In evaluating proposed investments, managers have turned increasingly to sophisticated techniques. Their goal has been greater rationality in making investment decisions, yet their accomplishment has often been quite different – serious under-investment in the capital stock (the productive capacity, technology and worker skills) on which their companies rest. As a result, they have unintentionally jeopardised their companies' futures.

Ingersoll Milling Machine Company took a strategic view that it needed to invest in the latest technology. Each production department manager annually had to write a justification to keep any machine that was over seven years old. The only generally accepted reason for not replacing equipment was that a new machine did not offer any significant improvements over older models.

Based on Hayes and Garvin (1982); Kaplan (1986)

7.4 Environmental aspects of investment

Much like AMT investment, many environmental capital projects have substantial costs or benefits which may not be wholly reflected in conventional net present value analysis. It should be recalled, from Chapter 1, that shareholders are not the only stakeholders in the company and the needs of other stakeholders, including the wider community, should also be incorporated into decisions. Environmental considerations have many dimensions, including economic, political, technological and social.

Pollution issues will be covered by legislation and regulation, but often the directors will want to go beyond the statutory requirements. While costs are not difficult to determine, the benefits are harder to quantify. For example, a greater sense of social responsibility may be costly but could have long-term benefits if the enhanced corporate image results in more business and improved shareholder value.

The steps involved in evaluating projects with environmental implications are:

1 Evaluate the projects using conventional capital appraisal methods.

2 Identify and incorporate statutory environmental costs as part of the evaluation.

3 Assess the costs and benefits of other environmental measures. For example, introducing anti-pollution measures should help reduce compensation claims.

4 Specify the internal controls to be introduced to ensure that pollution etc. is minimised during construction and implementation.

5 Assess the impact of the decision on shareholder wealth, ethical and social responsibility goals.

Does Shell take the longer view?

The Royal Dutch Shell group operates in 140 countries and invests over £8 billion annually in oil exploration, refining and other capital projects. Most of its capital projects have sustainable environmental implications.

Take a look at Shell's annual report (**www.shell.com**) to examine the level of environmental capital investment and provisions for cost of decommissioning and site restoration. What is its policy on environmental investment and sustainable development? To what extent does Shell take a long-term view on investment and consider wider social and environmental aspects?

Mattel boss wants you to be a Barbie girl in a Barbie world

Not many grown men will admit to playing with dolls. For Robert Eckert, chairman and chief executive of Mattel, it is a daily activity.

But then Mr Eckert has been trying to develop ways of keeping his brands fresh instead of diversifying into new ones.

It is a sign that Mattel is keeping up with the times. This month, the world's biggest toy company is gearing up to launch its latest Barbie doll. The Multi-Ethnic Barbie is the most politically correct doll to be launched yet and comes at a sensitive time for the US following the war in Afghanistan.

Barbie is set to feature in *Barbie as Rapunzel*, her second animated feature film, in the hope of repeating the success of last year's *Barbie in the Nutcracker*. The film earned Barbie more than $150 million in video sales, dolls and other related merchandise last year.

When Eckert arrived at the helm last year, Mattel had been struggling with poor earnings, senior management defections and the botched acquisition of the Learning Company, a software group. Eckert says, 'But every time Mattel has strayed from toys, it has done poorly. We are a toy brand, that is what we know and that is our business'.

Mattel's shareholders find it difficult to argue against this strategy. Like Mr Eckert, the business unit managers are on performance-related incentive schemes, all of which are linked to stock. 'If the company does well, we all do well. Otherwise we don't.' he says.

Based on Lina Saigol, the *Financial Times*, February 15 2002

7.5 The capital investment process

So far we have focused on investment *appraisal*. Similar emphasis is found in much of the capital budgeting literature, the assumption being that application of theoretically correct methods leads to optimal investment selection and, hence, maximises shareholders' wealth. The decision-maker is viewed as having a passive role, acting more as a technician than as an entrepreneur. Somehow, investment ideas come to the surface; various assumptions and cash flow estimates are made; and risk is incorporated within the discounting formula to produce the project's net present value. If this is positive, the proposal becomes part of the admissible set of investment possibilities. This set is then further refined by the evaluation of mutually exclusive projects and the appraisal of projects under capital rationing, where appropriate.

Inherent in this approach to capital budgeting are the following assumptions, few of which bear much relevance to the world of business:

1 Investment ideas simply emerge and land on the manager's desk.
2 Projects can be viewed in isolation, i.e. projects are not interdependent.

3 Risk can be fully incorporated within the net present value framework.
4 Non-quantifiable or intangible investment considerations are unimportant.
5 Cash flow estimates are free from bias.

Increasingly, it has become apparent that the emphasis on investment appraisal rather than on the whole capital investment process is misplaced and will not necessarily produce the most desirable investment programme. Investment decision-making could be improved significantly if the emphasis were placed on asking the appropriate strategic question rather than on increasing the sophistication of measurement techniques. Managers need to re-evaluate the investment procedures within their organisations, not to determine whether they are aesthetically and theoretically correct, but to determine whether they allow managers to make better decisions.

Capital budgeting may best be understood as a process with a number of distinct stages. Decision-making is an incremental activity, involving many people throughout the organisational hierarchy, over an extended period of time. While senior management may retain final approval, actual decisions are effectively taken much earlier at a lower level, by a process that is still not entirely clear and that is not the same in all organisations.

Figure 7.4 shows the key stages in the capital budgeting process. The primary aim of such a process is to ensure that available capital resources are distributed to wealth-creating capital projects that make the best contribution to corporate goals. A second goal is to see that good investment ideas are not held back and that poor or ill-defined proposals are rejected or further refined. We shall explore the following four stages:

1 Determination of the budget.
2 Search for, and development of, projects.
3 Evaluation and authorisation.
4 Monitoring and control.

Determination of the budget

In theory at least, all capital projects could be put to the capital market for funding (individually or collectively as investment programmes), the availability of funds for projects and rate required being a function of the market's perception of the prospective returns and associated risks. In practice, multi-divisional organisations operate an internal capital market in which senior management is better informed than the external capital market to assess capital proposals and allocate scarce resources.

If the investment decision-making body is a sub-unit of a larger group, the budget may be more or less rigidly imposed on it from above. However, for quasi-autonomous centres (divisions of larger groups with capital-raising powers) and/or independent units, the amount to be spent on capital projects is largely under their control, subject, of course, to considerations of corporate control and gearing.

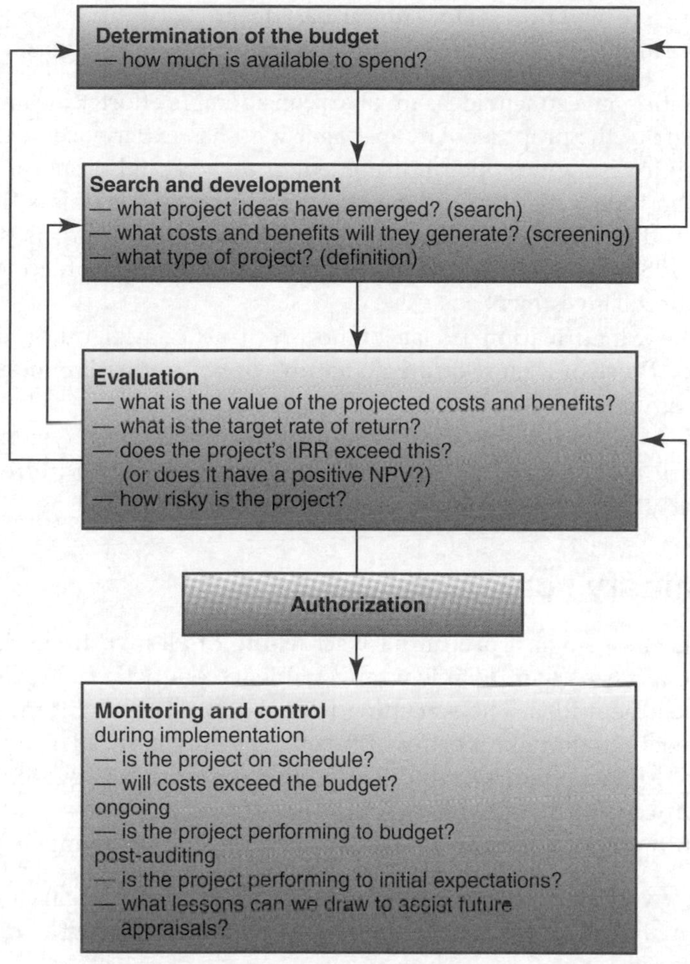

Figure 7.4 A simple capital budgeting system

Search for, and development of, projects

Economic theory views investment as the interaction of the supply of capital and the flow of investment opportunities. It would be wrong, however, to assume that there is a continuous flow of investment ideas. In general, the earlier an investment opportunity is identified, the greater is the scope for reward.

Possibly the most important role which top management can play in the capital investment process is to cultivate a corporate culture that encourages managers to search for, identify and sponsor investment ideas. Questions to be asked at the identification stage include the following:

1 How are project proposals initiated?
2 At what level are projects typically generated?

3 Is there a formal process for submitting ideas?
4 Is there an incentive scheme for identifying good project ideas?

Generating investment ideas involves considerable effort, time and personal risk on the part of the proposer. Any manager who has experienced the frustration of having an investment proposal dismissed, or an accepted proposal fail, is likely to develop an inbuilt resistance to creating further proposals unless the organisation culture and rewards are conducive to such activity. There is some evidence (Larcker 1983) that firms adopting long-term incentive plans tend to increase their level of capital investment.

For the identification phase of non-routine capital budgeting decisions, especially those of a more strategic nature, to be productive, managers need to conduct environmental scanning, gathering information that is largely externally oriented. We should not expect the formal information system within most organisations, which is set up to help control short-term performance, to be particularly helpful in identifying non-routine investment ideas.

Preliminary screening

At this early stage, a **preliminary screening** of all investment ideas is usually conducted. It is neither feasible nor desirable to conduct a full-scale evaluation of each investment idea. The screening process is an important means of filtering out projects not thought worthy of further investigation. Ideas may not fit with strategic thinking, or may fall outside business units designated for growth or maintenance.

Screening proposals address such questions as the following:

1 Is the investment opportunity compatible with corporate strategy? Does it fall within a section of the business designated for growth, maintenance or divestment?
2 Are the resources required by the project available (expertise, finance, etc.)?
3 Is the idea technically feasible?
4 What evidence is there to suggest that it is likely to provide an acceptable return?
5 Are the risks involved acceptable?

As the quality of data used at the screening stage is generally poor, it makes little sense to apply sophisticated financial analysis. Accordingly, the simple payback method is frequently used at this stage because it offers a crude assessment of project profitability and risk.

Project definition

Any investment proposal is vague and shapeless until it has been properly defined. At the definition stage of the capital investment process, detailed specification of the investment proposal involves the collection of data describing its technical and economic characteristics. For each proposal, a number of alternative options should be generated, defined and, subsequently, appraised in order to create the project offering the most attractive financial characteristics.

Even at this early stage, proposals are gaining commitment. The very act of collecting information necessitates communicating with managers who may either lend support or seek to undermine the proposal. The danger is that, in this process, commitments are accumulated such that investment becomes almost inevitable. The amount of information gathered for evaluation is largely determined by the following:

- The data perceived as desirable to gain a favourable decision.
- The ease and cost of its development.
- The extent to which the proposer will be held responsible for later performance related to the data.

Top management should seek to ensure that the most suitable projects are submitted by managers through establishing mechanisms that induce behaviour congruence. The accounting information system, reward system and capital budgeting procedures should all encourage managers to put forward the proposals that top management is looking for. For many firms, however, the accounting information system and reward mechanism encourage divisional managers to promote their own interests at the expense of those of the organisation, and to emphasise short-term profit performance at the expense of the longer term. Capital budgeting then becomes a 'game', with the accounting and reward systems as its rules. Cash flow estimates are biased to maximise the gains to individuals within such rules.

Self-assessment Activity 7.2

Outline the important stages in the capital budgeting process.

(answer at end of chapter)

Project classification

The information required and method of analysis will vary according to the nature of the project. A suggested investment proposal classification is given below under the headings replacement, cost reduction, expansion or improvement, new products, strategic, and statutory and welfare.

Replacement proposals are justified primarily by the need to replace assets that are nearly exhausted or have excessively high maintenance costs. Little or no improvement is expected from the replacement, but the expenditure is essential to maintain the existing level of capacity or service (e.g. replacement of vehicles). Engineering analysis plays an important role in these proposals.

Cost reduction proposals (which may also be replacement proposals) are intended to reduce costs through addition of new equipment or modification to existing equipment. Line managers and specialists (such as industrial engineers and work study groups) should conduct a continuous review of production operations for profit improvement opportunities.

Expansion or improvement proposals relate to existing products, and are intended to increase production, service and distribution capacity, to improve product quality, or to maintain and improve the firm's competitive position.

New product proposals refer to all capital expenditures pertaining to the development and implementation of new products.

Strategic proposals are generated at senior management level and involve expenditure in new areas, or where benefits extend beyond the investment itself. A project may appear to offer a negative net present value and yet still create further valuable strategic opportunities. Three examples demonstrate this point:

1 Diversification projects may have the effect of bringing the company into a lower risk category.
2 A patent may be acquired not for use within the firm, but to prevent its use by competitors.
3 Where information is difficult to obtain, such as in overseas markets, it may make sense to set up a small plant at a loss because it places the firm in a good position to build up information and to be ready for minor investment at the appropriate time.

Statutory and welfare proposals do not usually offer an obvious financial return, although they may contribute in other ways, such as enhancing the contentment, and hence productivity, of the labour force. The main consideration is whether standards are met at minimum cost.

Each proposal should be ranked within each category in terms of its effect on profits, its degree of urgency, and whether or not it can be postponed.

Evaluation and authorisation

Evaluation

The evaluation phase involves appraisal of the project and decision outcome (accept, reject, request further information etc.). Project evaluation, in turn, involves the assembly of information (usually in terms of cash flows) and the application of specified investment criteria. Each firm must decide whether to apply rigorous, sophisticated evaluation models, or simpler models that are easier to grasp yet capture many of the important elements in the decision.

The capital appropriation request forms the basis for the final decision to commit financial and other resources to the project. Typical information included in an appropriation request is given below:

1 *Purpose of project* – why it is proposed and the fit with corporate strategy and goals.
2 *Project classification* – e.g. expansion, replacement, improvement, cost saving, strategic, research and development, safety and health, legal requirement.

3 *Finance requested* – amount and timing, including net working capital, etc.
4 *Operating cash flows* – amount and timing, together with the main assumptions influencing the accuracy of the cash flow estimates.
5 *Attractiveness of the proposal* – expressed by standard appraisal indicators, such as net present value, DCF rate of return and payback period calculated from after-tax cash flows.
6 *Sensitivity of the assumptions* – effect of changes in the main investment inputs. Other approaches to assessing project risk should also be addresssed (e.g. best/worst scenarios, estimated range of accuracy of DCF return, discussed in Chapter 9) .
7 *Review of alternatives* – why they were rejected and their economic attractiveness.
8 *Implications of not accepting the proposal* – some projects with little economic merit according to the appraisal indicators may be 'essential' to the continuance of a profitable part of the business or to achieving agreed strategy.
9 *Non-financial considerations* – those costs and benefits that cannot be measured.

Following evaluation, larger projects may require consideration at a number of levels in the organisational hierarchy before they are finally approved or rejected. The decision outcome is rarely based wholly on the computed signal derived from financial analysis. Considerable judgement is applied in assessing the reliability of data underlying the appraisal, fit with corporate strategy, and track record of the project sponsor. Careful consideration is required regarding the influence on the investment of such key factors as product markets, the economy, production, finance and people.

Authorisation

Following evaluation, the proposal is transmitted through the various authorisation levels of the organisational hierarchy until it is finally approved or rejected. The driving motive in the decision process is the willingness of the manager to make a commitment to sponsor a proposal. This is based not so much on the grounds of the proposal itself as on whether or not it will enhance the manager's reputation and career prospects. Sometimes those involved in the preliminary investigation and appraisal of major projects are promoted into head office decision-making positions in time to support and assist the approval of the same projects!

In larger organisations, the authorisation of major projects is usually a formal endorsement of commitments already given. Complete rejection of proposals is rare, but proposals are, on occasions, referred back. The approval stage appears to have a twofold purpose:

1 *A quality control function*. As long as the proposals have satisfied the requirements of all previous stages, there is no reason for their rejection other than on political grounds. Only where the rest of the investment planning process is inadequate will the approval stage take on greater significance in determining the destiny of projects.

2 *A motivational function*. An investment project and its proposer are inseparable. The decision-maker, in effect, forms a judgement simultaneously on both the proposal and the person or team submitting it.

Sometimes the costs associated with rejection of capital projects, in terms of managerial motivation, far exceed the costs associated with accepting a marginally unprofitable project. The degree of commitment, enthusiasm and drive of the management team implementing the project is a major factor in determining the success or failure of marginal projects.

Mini case

How SmithKline Beecham makes investments

In recent years, with more projects successfully reaching late-development stage, the demands for funding at SmithKline Beecham (now merged with Glaxo) were considerable. The pharmaceutical group, which invests more than half a billion dollars annually, had to create more value from its investments to help meet its tough earnings targets.

A new decision-making process was introduced, designed to identify those development projects likely to create the most value and reflect the complexity and risk of its investments. Each project team was asked to develop four alternatives: its current plans, a 'buy-up' option and a 'buy-down' option (where they explored the effects of increasing and reducing the investment outlay) and a minimum plan, where the project was abandoned at minimum cost. These alternatives were generated and valued before a decision was taken.

A variety of decision approaches were taken, focusing on creating net present value. These included decision tree analysis, probability analysis, options analysis and sensitivity analysis (discussed in the following chapters) . However, management soon discovered that equally important were softer issues such as information quality, credibility and trust.

It was their initial intention that this new resource allocation process would be useful in cutting the development budget. But they now saw investment decisions in a new light and recognised that the investment portfolio was worth far more than expected. The net result was an increase in capital spending by more than 50 per cent.

Based on Sharpe and Keelin, *Harvard Business Review*, March–April 1998

Self-assessment Activity 7.3

Read the above article and discuss the impact that a new resource allocation system can have on capital investment creation, evaluation and decision-making.

Monitoring and control

The capital budgeting control process can be classified in terms of pre-decision and post-decision controls. **Pre-decision controls** are mechanisms designed to influence managerial behaviour at an early stage in the investment process. Examples are setting authorisation levels and procedures to be followed, and influencing the proposals submitted by setting goals, hurdle rates and cash limits and identifying strategic areas for growth. **Post-decision controls** include monitoring and post-audit procedures.

Major investment projects may justify determining the critical path (i.e. a set of linked activities) in the delivery and installation schedule. The critical path is defined as the longest path through a network. Control is established by accounting procedures for recording expenditures. Progress reports usually include actual expenditure; amounts authorised to date; amounts committed against authorisations; amounts authorised but not yet spent; and estimates of further cost to completion.

The case of the disappearing projects

Ameritech, a major US company operating in the electronics industry, invests over $2 billion a year, mostly in thousands of relatively small-scale projects. When the company announced that it proposed to monitor and audit capital projects, that year's budgets had already been submitted. But the company told every division to take back their submissions, think about the fact that everyone who worked on the project was going to be 'tracked', and then resubmit the estimates. Seven hundred projects never came back – they just disappeared. Many others had much lower estimates. We will never know just how many of those 700 projects could have been investment 'winners'.

This illustrates just how influential capital budgeting controls can be on managerial investment behaviour.

Based on Weaver *et al*. (1989)

7.6 Post-auditing

The final stage in the capital budgeting decision-making and control sequence is the post-completion audit. UK firms have been considerably more hesitant in appreciating the need to post-audit than their North American counterparts, although there is evidence that this is changing. In a survey conducted in 1985, Neale and Holmes (1988) found that 48 per cent of large quoted UK companies had adopted post-audits. By 1997, the use of post-audits among large firms had risen to 100 per cent (Arnold and Hatzopoulos, 2000), although mainly for major projects.

A **post-audit** aims to compare the actual performance of a project after, say, a year's operation with the forecast made at the time of approval, and ideally also with the revised assessment made at the date of commissioning. The aims of the exercise are twofold: first, post-audits may attempt to encourage more thorough and realistic appraisals of future investment projects; and second, they may aim to facilitate major overhauls of ongoing projects, perhaps to alter their strategic focus. These two aims differ in an important respect. The first concerns the overall capital budgeting system, seeking to improve its quality and cohesion. The second concerns the control of existing projects, but with a broader perspective than is normally possible during the regular monitoring procedure when project adjustments are usually of a 'fire-fighting' nature.

Self-assessment Activity 7.4

What are the main benefits from post audits?

(answer at end of chapter)

Problems with post-auditing

There are many problems with post-audits:

1 *The disentanglement problem*. It may be difficult to separate out the relevant costs and benefits specific to a new project from other company activities, especially where facilities are shared and the new project requires an increase in shared overheads. Newly developed techniques of overhead cost allocation may prove helpful in this respect.
2 *Projects may be unique*. If there is no prospect of repeating a project in the future, there may seem little point in post-auditing, since the lessons learned may not be applicable to any future activity. Nevertheless, useful insights into the capital budgeting system as a whole may be obtained.
3 *Prohibitive cost*. To introduce post-audits may involve interference with present management information systems in order to generate flows of suitable data. Since post-auditing every project may be very resource-intensive, firms tend to be selective in their post-audits.
4 *Biased selection*. By definition, only accepted projects can be post-audited, and often only the underperforming ones are singled out for detailed examination. Because of this biased selection mechanism, the forecasting and evaluation expertise of project analysts may be cast in an unduly bad light – they might have been spot on in evaluating rejected and acceptably performing projects.
5 *Lack of cooperation*. If the post-audit is conducted in too inquisitorial a fashion, project sponsors are likely to offer grudging cooperation to the review team and be reluctant to accept and act upon their findings. The impartiality of the review team is paramount – for example, it would be inviting resentment to draw post-auditors from other parts of the company that may be competitors

for scarce capital. Similarly, there are obvious dangers if reviews are undertaken solely by project sponsors. A balanced team of investigators needs to be assembled.

6 *Encourages risk-aversion*. If analysts' predictive and analytical abilities are to be thoroughly scrutinised, they may be inclined to advance only 'safe' projects where little can go awry and where there is less chance of being 'caught out' by events.

7 *Environmental changes*. Some projects can be devastated by largely unpredictable swings in market conditions. This can make the post-audit a complex affair, as the review team is obliged to adjust analysts' forecasts to allow for 'moving of the goalposts'.

The conventional wisdom

Studies conducted in North America and the UK have generated a conventional wisdom about corporate post-auditing practices. Its main elements are as follows:

- Few firms post-audit every project, and the selection criterion is usually based on size of outlay.
- The commonest time for a first post-audit is about a year after project commissioning.
- The most effective allocation of post-audit responsibility is to share it between central audit departments and project initiators to avoid conflicts of interest, while using relevant expertise.
- The 'threat' of post-audit is likely to spur the forecaster to greater accuracy, but it can lead to excessive caution, possibly resulting in suppression of potentially worthwhile ventures.

When does post-auditing work best?

What guidelines can we offer to managers who wish to introduce post-audit from scratch or to overhaul an existing system? Here are some key points:

1 When introducing and operating post-audit, emphasise the learning objectives and minimise the likelihood of its being viewed as a 'search for the guilty'.

2 Clearly specify the aims of a post-audit. Is it to be primarily a project control exercise, or does it aim to derive insights into the overall project appraisal system?

3 When introducing post-audits, start the process with a small project to reveal as economically as possible the difficulties that need to be overcome in a major post-audit.

4 Include a pre-audit in the project proposal. When the project is submitted for approval, the sponsors should be required to indicate what information would be required to undertake a subsequent post-audit.

Summary

We have examined the strategic framework for investment decisions, paying particular attention to new technology and environmental projects.
The resource allocation process is the main vehicle by which business strategy can be implemented. Investment decisions are not simply the result of applying some evaluation criterion. Investment analysis is essentially a search process: a search for ideas, for information and for decision criteria. The prosperity of a firm depends more on its ability to create profitable investment opportunities than on its ability to appraise them.

Key points

- Investments form part of a wider strategic process and should be assessed both financially and strategically.
- New technology projects are often particularly difficult to evaluate because of the many non-financial values.
- The four main stages in the capital budgeting process are:
  1 Determine the budget.
  2 Search for and develop projects.
  3 Evaluation and authorisation.
  4 Monitoring and control.
  Once a firm commits itself to a particular project, it should regularly and systematically monitor and control the project through its various stages of implementation.
- Post-audit reviews, if properly designed, fulfil a useful role in improving the quality of existing and future investment analysis and provide a means of initiating corrective action for existing projects.

Further reading

Further reading on AMT investment evaluation is found in Finnie (1988), Pike *et al*. (1989) and Kaplan (1986).

Self-assessment Answers

7.1 The attractiveness of any project depends, in large measure, on how well it helps the business implement agreed strategies to achieve agreed goals. Investment is one of the main vehicles for implementing strategy.

It is quite possible for capital projects to be rejected because they are not compatible with long-term corporate intentions. An important element of the investment decision process is to ensure that there is a good 'fit' between projects proposed and corporate strategy.

7.2 Stages in the investment process:

Search for opportunities
Screening (is it worth evaluating further?)
Defining the project
Evaluation
Transmission through the organisation
Authorisation
Monitoring
Post-audit

7.4 Post-auditing may confer substantial benefits on the firm. Among these are the following:

1. The enhanced quality of decision-making and planning, which may stem from more carefully and rigorously researched project proposals.
2. Tightening of internal control systems.
3. The ability to modify or even abandon projects on the basis of fuller information.
4. The identification of key variables on whose outcome the viability of the current and similar future projects may depend.

Questions

1 *Solution in Appendix A (page 807).* 'Capital budgeting is simply a matter of selecting the right decision rule.' How true is this statement?

2 *Solution in Appendix A (page 807).* What are the aims of post-audits?

3 *Solution in Appendix A (page 808).* AMT plc is increasing the level of automation of a production line dedicated to a single product. The options available are total automation or partial automation. The company works on a planning horizon of five years and either option will produce the 10,000 units which can be sold annually.

Total automation will involve a total capital cost of £1 million. Material costs will be £12 per unit and labour and variable overheads will be £18 per unit with this method.

Partial automation will result in higher material wastage and an average cost of £14 per unit. Labour and variable overhead are expected to cost £41 per unit. The capital cost of this alternative is £250,000.

The products sell for £75 each, whichever method of production is adopted. The scrap value of the automated production line, in five years' time, will be £100,000, while the line which is partially automated will be worthless. The management uses straight-line depreciation and the required rate of return on capital investment is 16 per cent p.a. Depreciation is considered to be the only incremental fixed cost.

In analysing investment opportunities of this type the company calculates the average total cost per unit, annual net profit, the break-even volume per year and the discounted net present value.

Required

(a) Determine the figures which would be circulated to the management of AMT plc in order to assist their investment analysis.

(b) Comment on the figures produced and make a recommendation with any qualifications you think appropriate.

(Certified Diploma)

4 Bowers Holdings plc has recently acquired a controlling interest in Shaldon Engineering plc, which produces high-quality machine tools for the European market. Following this acquisition, the internal audit department of Bowers Holdings plc examined the financial management systems of the newly acquired company and produced a report that was critical of its investment appraisal procedures.

The report summary stated:

> Overall, investment appraisal procedures in Shaldon Engineering plc are very weak. Evaluation of capital projects is not undertaken in a systematic manner and post-decision controls relating to capital projects are virtually non-existent.

Required

Prepare a report for the directors of Shaldon Engineering plc, stating what you consider to be the major characteristics of a system for evaluating, monitoring and controlling capital expenditure projects.

(Certified Diploma)

What procedures should a business adopt for approving and reviewing large capital expenditure projects?

Practical assignment

Read the *Harvard Business Review* article (Sept.–Oct. 1989) 'Must finance and strategy clash?' by Barwise, Marsh and Wensley. Summarise and comment on their views on the question.

8 Foreign investment decisions

Cut or Shut

In early 2001, Japanese motor firm Nissan, 37 per cent owned by its French strategic partner, Renault, was mulling over whether to locate its new Micra assembly plant in Sunderland, UK, or at Renault's Flins plant, near Paris. In the 1990s, Nissan had spent several hundred million pounds building the Sunderland site into a world-class manufacturing plant, reputedly the most efficient in Europe. A European base to get behind the EU's tariff wall, the flexible working attitudes, low labour costs and less onerous social welfare overheads made the UK an attractive location.

By 2001, things had changed. Despite Sunderland's productivity advantage, Flins had become a serious contender for the new plant due to the 27 per cent appreciation of sterling against European currencies. A Nissan executive claimed: 'A currency movement of 20 per cent or more cancels out all the gross margin on a B-class (small) car'. The sterling appreciation had already put paid to car assembly at Dagenham (Ford) and at Luton (Vauxhall), as well as scuppering Siemens' semi-conductor plant near Sunderland.

In the event, Sunderland won the day, but only after management pledged a 30 per cent cut in costs over three years. Meanwhile Nissan announced that it would henceforth increase its components sourcing in euros from 25 per cent to 65 per cent.

Learning objectives

This chapter focuses on foreign investment decisions by multinational corporations (MNCs). It will:

- study the advantages of MNCs.
- discuss different ways of entering foreign markets.
- consider the complexities of foreign direct investment (FDI).

- analyse the appraisal of foreign FDI.
- consider the impact of foreign exchange variations on foreign projects.
- analyse ways of insulating projects against foreign exchange risk.
- study political and country risk, and how to cope with it.

8.1 Introduction

Foreign investment may be divided into **portfolio** and **direct** investment. Portfolio investment involves the purchase of shares or loan stock in an overseas organisation, usually without control over the running of the business. Foreign direct investment (FDI) is a lasting interest in an enterprise in another economy where the investor's purpose is to have an effective voice in the management of the enterprise. Such direct investment may arise from the acquisition of a controlling interest in an overseas business or from setting up an overseas branch or subsidiary. Firms such as Nissan that invest in foreign countries are examples of multinational corporations (MNCs).

The multinational corporation

A working definition of a multinational corporation is: a firm that owns production, sales and other revenue-generating assets in a number of countries (although a wider definition would include firms that simply sell home-produced goods overseas). Foreign direct investment by MNCs includes establishment and acquisition of overseas raw material and component operations, production plants and sales subsidiaries. This occurs because of potentially greater cost-effectiveness and profitability in sourcing inputs and servicing markets through a direct presence in a number of locations, rather than relying solely on a single 'home' base and on imports and exports to support operations. A global firm is one that trades *and* invests abroad.

It is tempting to think of MNCs as western firms that invest in developing countries. Not so: over 80 per cent of cross-border investment occurs between developed countries. In 2000, the United Nations Conference on Trade and Development (UNCTAD) (**www.unctad.org**) estimated that direct investment flows to developing countries amounted to $240 billion out of a global total of $1.3 trillion. Moreover, acquisitions of firms in developed countries by those in developing countries are not unknown. The acquisition of the UK's Tetley tea operation by the Tata Corporation of India was a recent example (2001).

Self-assessment Activity 8.1

What is meant by a multinational corporation?

(answer at end of chapter)

8.2 Advantages of MNCs over national firms

The MNC may be in a position to enhance its competitive position and profitability in four main ways:

1 It can take advantage of differences in country-specific circumstances. In a world where countries are at different stages of economic evolution (some industrially advanced, others mainly primary producers), certain advantages in a country may have knock-on effects that the MNC can exploit on a global basis. For example, the MNC may locate its R&D establishments in a technologically advanced country in order to draw on local scientific and technological infrastructure and skills. Similarly, it may locate its production plants in a less developed country in order to take advantage of lower input costs, especially cheap labour. Alternatively, it may continue to produce its outputs in its 'home' country, but seek to remain competitive by sourcing key components from subsidiary plants based abroad.

2 MNCs can choose the appropriate mode of serving a particular market. For example, exporting may provide an entry route into a low-price, commodity-type market, with the MNC taking advantage of marginal pricing and the absence of set-up costs; licensing may be an appropriate mode if market size is limited or market niches are being targeted; direct investment in production and sales subsidiaries may be a more effective way of capturing a large market share where proximity to customers is important, or where market access via exporting is limited by tariffs. These various routes enable an MNC to pursue a complex global market servicing strategy. For example, Ford makes car engines in its UK plants and gearboxes in its German factories, which are shipped (along with other parts) to Spain for assembly into complete cars. These are then exported to other European markets.

3 'Internalisation' of the MNC's operations by foreign direct investment provides a unique opportunity for the firm to maximise its global profits by using transfer pricing policies. While a national, vertically integrated firm needs to establish transfer prices for components and finished products being transferred between component and assembly plants, and between assembly plants and sales subsidiaries, the greater scale and cross-frontier nature of such transactions by MNCs makes these transfer prices more significant.

4 An international network of production plants and sales subsidiaries enables an MNC to protect component supplies. The Swedish/Swiss engineering conglomerate Asea Brown Boveri (ABB) has built up a network of component-manufacturing subsidiaries in the Baltic region, including the former Soviet bloc, in order to diversify sources of supply. Networks also help in the simultaneous introduction of new products in several markets. This is important (where products have a relatively short life cycle and/or patent protection) in order to maximise sales potential. Equally importantly, it spreads the risk of consumer rejection across a diversified portfolio of overseas markets, so that failure in one market may be offset (or perhaps more

than compensated by) rapid acceptance in another. Additionally, it enables the MNC to develop a 'global brand' identity (e.g. Coca-Cola, Levis and McDonalds) or to 'customise' a product more effectively to suit local demand preferences.

8.3 Foreign market entry strategies

Firms enter foreign markets in pursuit of incremental profits and cash flows by exploiting advantages over local producers and other MNCs. The two basic vehicles for foreign market entry are, first, via transactions, and second, via Foreign Direct Investment (FDI). Each mode can be pursued in a number of ways. Figure 8.1 shows the spectrum of entry modes arranged by degree of commitment.

At one extreme, exporting (one-off or 'spot' transactions) involves least commitment, as it is relatively inexpensive and withdrawal is easy. At the other extreme, establishing a fully-owned foreign operating subsidiary involves managing a range of complex functions including production, marketing and distribution. This is relatively expensive and requires substantial long-term commitment.

Exporting includes both indirect export of products from the home country via independent agents or distributors, and direct export of products through the firm's own export division to foreign markets. With exporting, the bulk of value-adding activities take place in the home country, while FDI transfers many of these activities to the foreign location. Both exporting and FDI involve **internalisation**, i.e. retaining value-adding activities within the firm (although to different degrees).

Licensing is often a half-way house that results in **externalising** most of these activities. It involves transferring to a licensee the right to use corporate

TRANSACTIONS				
Exporting: Spot Transactions	Exporting: Long-Term Contracts	Exporting: Foreign Agent or Distributor	Licensing Technology and Trademarks	Franchising

VERSUS

FOREIGN DIRECT INVESTMENT			
Joint Venture		Wholly-Owned Subsidiary	
Marketing and Distribution only	Fully-integrated	Marketing and Sales only	Fully-integrated

Figure 8.1 The spectrum of foreign market service modes
Source: Grant (1998)

assets, such as a brand name, and often the sale of intermediate goods for the licensee to use in production. Licensing enables a firm to gain rapid overseas market penetration when it lacks the resources to set up overseas operations.

Choosing between entry modes: the determinants

The choice of entry mode hinges on several factors:

1 Whether the firm's source of competitive advantage is based on location-specific factors, e.g. low labour costs. If so, the firm is more likely to export. If managerial skills are transferable to other locations, FDI is more likely.

2 Whether the product is tradable, and whether barriers to trade exist. If import restrictions such as tariff barriers and government-imposed regulations make trade infeasible, licensing or FDI becomes more likely.

3 Whether the firm possesses the required skills and resources to build and exploit competitive advantage abroad. Marketing and distribution capabilities are essential for foreign operation, which argues in favour of appointing a distributor or agent when these skills are lacking. If a wider range of manufacturing and/or marketing skills is needed, the firm may license its product and/or technology to a local operator.

   In marketing-intensive industries, MNCs may offer their brands to local firms by trademark **licensing**. Licensing involves assigning production and selling rights to producers located in foreign locations in return for royalty payments. If tighter control over operations is required, a joint venture with a local firm may be set up.

4 Whether the resources are 'appropriable' – can the technology be stolen? In some industries, technology can be closely guarded via **patents**, but in more service-oriented activities such as computer software, ownership rights are far more difficult to enforce. In the former case, FDI involves less risk, while in the latter case, exporting may be preferred. When licensing a foreign partner, the firm must consider any potential damage to the reputation of its brand resulting from poor quality or service provided by a local operator.

   Where a firm wants to exert close control over the use of its trademarks, technologies or trade secrets, **franchising** may be chosen as a way of licensing a fully-packaged business system, as in the international fast food business.

5 What transactions costs are involved? These are the costs of negotiating, monitoring and enforcing the terms of such agreements as compared with internationalisation via a fully-owned subsidiary. With low or no transactions costs, exporting would usually be preferred.

Factors favouring foreign direct investment (FDI)

International expansion through FDI is an alternative to growth focused on the firm's domestic market. A firm may choose to expand horizontally on a global basis by replicating its existing business operations in a number of countries, or via international vertical integration, backwards by establishing raw material/components sources and forwards into final production and distribution. Firms may also choose product diversification to develop their international business interests. Firms may expand internationally by greenfield (new 'start-up') investments in component and manufacturing plants etc.; takeover of, and merger with, established suppliers; or forming joint ventures with overseas partners. In the case of foreign market servicing, the MNC may also choose to complement direct investment with some exporting and licensing.

FDI also provides opportunities for exploiting its competitive advantages over rival suppliers. A firm may possess advantages in the form of patented process technology, know-how and skills, or a unique branded product that it can better exploit and protect by establishing overseas production or sales subsidiaries. A production facility in an overseas market may enable a firm to reduce its distribution costs and keep it in closer touch with local market conditions – customer tastes, competitors' actions etc. Moreover, direct investment enables a firm to avoid government restrictions on market access, such as tariffs and quotas, and the problems of currency variation. For example, the growth of protectionism by the European Union and the rising value of the yen were important factors behind increased Japanese investment in the EU, especially in the UK motor and electronics sectors.

Firms may benefit from grants and other subsidies by 'host' governments to encourage inward investment. Much Japanese investment (e.g. Nissan's plant near Sunderland) was attracted into the UK by regional selective assistance. In the case of sourcing, direct investment allows the MNC to take advantage of some countries' lower labour costs or provides them with access to superior technological know-how, thereby enhancing their international competitiveness.

Moreover, direct investment, by internalising input sourcing and market servicing within one organisation, enables the MNC to avoid various transaction costs: the costs of finding suppliers and distributors and negotiating contracts with them; and the costs associated with imperfect market situations, such as monopoly surcharges imposed by input suppliers, unreliable sources of supply and restrictions on access to distribution channels. It also allows the MNC to take advantage of the internal transfer of resources at prices that enable it to minimise its tax bill ('transfer pricing') or practise price discrimination between markets.

Finally, for some products (e.g. flat glass, metal cans, cement), decentralised local production rather than exporting is the only viable way an MNC can supply an overseas market because of the prohibitive costs of transporting a bulky product or one which, for competitive reasons, has to be marketed at a low price.

8.4 The incremental hypothesis

Johanson and Wiedersheim-Paul (1975) observed that firms tend to progress through several stages of foreign market servicing, typically beginning with exporting to obtain a 'bridgehead' and eventually graduating to FDI. A major factor in the progression is the relative cost of servicing mode, which is a function of market size.

This thesis can be illustrated with a simple break-even model, using Buckley and Casson's (1981) model. Two possible entry modes, exporting and FDI, are displayed in Figure 8.2.

These activities have quite different cost structures:

- Exporting involves relatively low fixed costs (OA) and relatively high unit variable costs, witness the steeper Total Cost profile.
- FDI involves relatively high investment fixed costs (OB) and relatively low variable costs due to lower production and distribution costs, reflected in a flatter TC profile.

For relatively low volumes, exporting may be more appropriate but the firm will eventually encounter a 'crossover' point where it becomes cheaper to switch to FDI. The switchover occurs at market size OQ. Below this, exporting involves lower operating costs, but beyond OQ, a switch to FDI becomes preferable.

In practice, the switch decision is less clear-cut. Switchover costs would 'step' the FDI function, and most firms would wait a while before switching to ascertain whether the market expansion was permanent. Moreover, some firms 'jump' the intermediate stages if the foreign market size is already deemed sufficiently large.

Self-assessment Activity 8.2

Consider how licensing would fit into Figure 8.2 – i.e. what is its likely cost structure relative to exporting and FDI?

(answer at end of chapter)

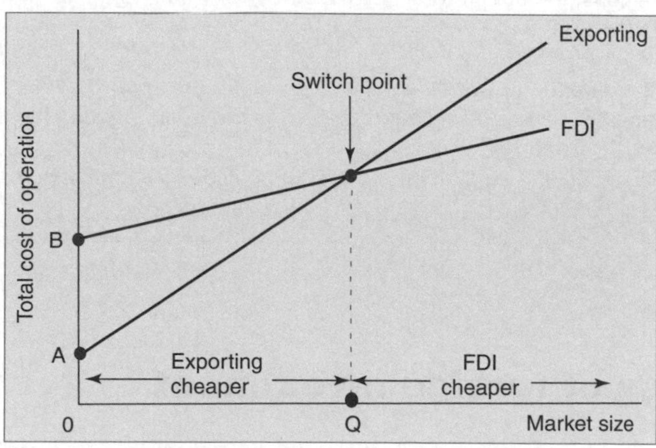

Figure 8.2 Exporting vs. FDI
Source: Buckley and Casson (1981)

Nalco plans $2 billion smelter in Qatar

India group's first overseas venture

National Aluminum Company, India's state-owned metals group, is in advanced talks with the government in Qatar and Japanese investors to set up a $2 billion smelter in the Gulf state.

The project, which will be finalised this year, would be Nalco's first overseas venture.

It would use its surplus alumina from India and Qatar's cheap and abundant supply of gas-based power to make aluminium for export.

The talks come as the company is preparing for privatisation this summer.

Initially, 30 per cent of the group will be sold through an issue of depository receipts, expected to raise between $250 million and $300 million.

This will be followed about 18 months later by the sale of another 30 per cent stake to a strategic partner, possibly to Pechiney of France, cutting the government's holding from 87.1 per cent to 26 per cent.

China refinery

Separately, Nalco executives will this week visit China, where the company is considering building a refinery.

China's domestic aluminium market is growing by 10–15 per cent a year, fuelled by restructuring of businesses and fast economic growth.

Nalco wants to capture this demand by exporting its surplus alumina to refine at a smelter it would build in China, possibly with Pechiney.

The company is already working on expanding its mines, alumina refinery and smelter in Orissa in a plan designed to lift total alumina capacity from 1.57 million tonnes to 2.1 million tonnes a year.

Some of the increased output of the finished metal will be absorbed in India, where the aluminium market is growing but could weaken as the economy continues to lose pace.

Based on Khozem Merchant and Kunal Bose, *Financial Times*, March 21 2002

8.5 Complexities of foreign investment

Evaluation of foreign direct investment decisions is not fundamentally different from the evaluation of domestic investment projects, although the political structures, economic policies and value systems of the host country may cause certain analytical problems. There is evidence (Robbins and Stobaugh 1973; Wilson 1990; Neale and Buckley 1992) that the majority of MNCs use essentially similar methods for evaluation and control of capital investment projects for overseas subsidiaries and for domestic operations, although they may well apply different discount rates.

Appraising foreign investment involves complexities not encountered in evaluating domestic projects. Here are the main ones:

1 Fluctuations in exchange rates over lengthy time periods are largely unpredictable. On the one hand, these may enhance the domestic currency value of project cash flows, but depreciation of the currency of the host country will reduce the domestic currency proceeds. This aspect is further examined in Section 8.6.
2 A foreign investment project may involve levels of risk quite different from those of the equivalent project undertaken in the domestic economy. This poses the problem of how to estimate a suitable required rate of return for discounting purposes.
3 Once up-and-running, the foreign investment is exposed to variations in economic policy by the host government (e.g. tax changes), which may reduce net cash flows.
4 Investment incentives provided by the host country government; e.g. in Ireland, the rate of Corporation Tax faced by inward manufacturing investors is only 10 per cent.
5 Overspill effects on the firm's existing operations; e.g. goods produced overseas may displace some existing sales.
6 The host government may block the repatriation of profits to the home country. A project that is inherently profitable may not be worth undertaking if the earnings cannot be remitted. This raises the issue of whether the evaluation should be conducted from the standpoint of the subsidiary (i.e. the project itself), or from that of the parent company. But for a company pursuing shareholder value, the relevant evaluation is from the parent's standpoint. Some companies have adopted ingenious ways of repatriating profits. Pepsico, which invested in a bottling plant in Hungary, found it difficult to repatriate profits from this operation. To overcome this problem, it financed the local shooting of a motion picture (*The Ninth Configuration*), which was then exported to the West. (It was not a box-office hit).

Usually, only remittable cash flows (whether or not they are actually repatriated) should be considered, and the project accepted only if the NPV of the cash flows available for investors exceeds zero. Thus items like management fees, royalties, interest on parent company loans, dividend remittances, and loan and interest payments to the parent should all be included. In effect, a two-stage analysis is applied:

(i) specify the project's own cash flows.
(ii) isolate the cash flows remittable to the parent.

Due allowance should be made for taxation in the foreign location.

Overcoming exchange controls

Possible ways of minimising the impact of controls over cash repatriation include:

(i) paying interest on loans or dividends on equity. Maximising dividend flows may involve 'creative accounting' to inflate the local profits, although this may be counter-productive if local tax rates exceed those in the home country. It may also antagonise local interests.

(ii) paying royalty fees where the foreign project utilises any process over which the parent claims proprietary rights, e.g. control of a patent or trade mark, such as Levis.

(iii) transfer pricing policies that involve charging the overseas subsidiary high prices for components and other supplies.

(iv) applying a management charge if the senior managers are seconded from the parent. Similar charges can be used to make the foreign subsidiary pay for other services provided by the parent, e.g. IT and treasury costs. However, this may provoke close scrutiny by the host authorities.

Self-assessment Activity 8.3

How does FDI differ from domestic investment?

(answer at end of chapter)

8.6 Should firms worry about exchange rate changes?

According to the theory of Purchasing Power Parity (PPP), the answer to this question is 'no'.

PPP says that the purchasing power of any currency should be equivalent in any location. It is based on the **Law of One Price**, which asserts that identical goods must sell at the same price in different markets, after adjusting for the exchange rate. For example, if the market rate of exchange between USD and GBP is \$1.6 : £1, a microcomputer could not sell for very long at simultaneous prices of, say, £1,500 in London and \$2,000 (i.e. £1,250) in New York. People would buy in the 'cheap' market (New York) and ship the goods to London, thus tending to equilibrate the two prices at, say, a London price of £1,300 and a New York price of \$2,080 (£1,300). (In reality, transport and other transaction costs may prevent the precise operation of PPP.)

The Law of One Price states that, for tradeable goods and services, the

(£ price of a good × \$/£ exchange rate) = USD price of a good

Exchange rate changes

If relative price levels change, for example, UK prices inflate at 10 per cent p.a. and US prices inflate at 3 per cent p.a., the Law of One Price states that there should be a fall in the value of the £ against the USD of about 7 per cent, in order to restore PPP.

Taking our microcomputer example, after one year, the £ price will rise to £1,300 (1.1) = £1,430, while the US price becomes \$2,080 (1.03) = \$2,142. This implies that the \$/£ exchange rate should move to:

$$\frac{\$2{,}142}{£1{,}430} = \$1.5{:}£1$$

which represents a depreciation in GBP of 6.4 per cent.

If foreign exchange markets operate freely without government intervention, goods that can be easily traded on international markets, such as oil, are highly likely to obey the Law of One Price, although transport costs between markets may explain a continued price discrepancy. However, not all goods can be easily transported. Most notably, with land and property, which are physically impossible to shift, a sustained price discrepancy may apply between markets. In the longer term, however, even these differentials may close as investors and property speculators perceive that one market is cheap relative to the other.

PPP may be expected to operate broadly in the longer term for most goods and services, although it can be distorted by government intervention in the foreign exchange markets and the formation of currency blocs. The authorities in these cases are attempting to smooth out the effects and hence minimise the dislocation to business activity that sudden swings in currency values might cause. However, while exchange controls and official intervention can delay any adjustment necessary to reflect differential rates of inflation, the required change will eventually take place.

Accepting PPP and the Law of One Price, we arrive at a remarkable conclusion regarding the need to hedge FX risks – there is no need to worry!

Example: Stonewall plc

Stonewall plc has a factory in Baltimore, USA. It plans to produce and sell goods to generate a net cash inflow of \$180 million at today's prices over the coming trading year. For simplicity, we assume all transactions are completed at year-end, and that any price adjustments resulting from inflation also occur at year-end.

At the current exchange rate of US\$1.50 *vs.* £1, the sterling value of its planned sales = (\$180 m/1.50) = £120 m. Stonewall is worried about the \$US falling due to the annual rate of inflation in the US of 6 per cent compared to 3 per cent in the UK.

Continued

Concern about exposure to foreign exchange risk seems justified – with these inflation rates, PPP predicts the \$US will decline to:

$1.50 × (1.06/1.03) = $1.544 after one year.

At this exchange rate, the sterling value of the \$US cash flow is (\$180 m/1.544) = £116.58 m, a fall of about 3 per cent on the start-year valuation. But should sleep be lost over this?

The answer is 'yes' if selling prices within the USA remained static. However, prices within the USA are not static – the reason why the FX rate will change is due to inflation at a higher rate in the USA relative to the UK.

With US prices rising at 6 per cent, the \$US cash flow *ought* to rise to \$180 m (1.06) = \$190.8 m. Converted to sterling at the year-end rate, this is worth (\$190.8 m/1.544) = £123.6 m. This is precisely equal to its sterling-denominated value at the end of one year with UK price inflation at 3% (£120 m × 1.03 = £123.6 m).

So what has been lost from inflation affecting the relative value of sterling and \$US? The answer is nothing if PPP operates! Should the firm take precautions against FX exposure? The answer is 'no' – why should it bother when it is automatically protected by market adjustments? Should the firm try to forecast future rates of exchange, e.g. by comparing the respective inflation rates? It could, but again, it is a waste of time, at least in theory, as the rate of \$1.544 should already be quoted in the market for one-year forward deals (see Chapter 17).

However, it is not always this simple. In reality, prices rise in a continuous process rather than in a series of end-year adjustments. The policy of benign neglect only works if prices of the traded goods are adjusted *pari passu* as prices in general alter and the exchange rate 'crawls' in the appropriate direction, by the appropriate amount and if the movement is synchronised.

In reality, FX rates adjust in response to relative inflation rates at the national level, as measured by a basket of goods. The basket may well inflate at a different rate from the goods traded. Indeed, competitive conditions may be so powerful that firms may be unable to raise prices even to compensate for inflation. For these reasons, most firms seek protection against FX movements.

Self-assessment Activity 8.4

The C\$ *vs*. sterling exchange rate is C\$2.20 *vs*. £1. A UK MNC operating in Canada plans to sell goods worth C\$100 million at today's prices to Canadian customers. Show that its sterling income will not be affected if PPP applies, and if both the UK and Canada have 5 per cent inflation.

(answer at end of chapter)

8.7 Evaluating FDI

Under certain conditions, analysing foreign project cash flows will yield the same result as analysing the cash flows to the parent. The key conditions are:

(i) Exchange rates adjust to reflect inflation differences between the parent country and the foreign location, i.e. PPP applies.
(ii) Project cash inflows and outflows move in line with prices in general in both locations.
(iii) No tax differentials between the two countries.
(iv) No exchange controls.

Because these conditions probably will not apply in practice, the following steps are generally recommended:

1. Predict local cash flows in money terms, i.e. including local inflation.
2. Allow for any 'overspill' effects like the 'cannibalisation' of existing exports. The opportunity cost is neither the sales revenue nor indeed the profit lost, but the gross margin or contribution.
3. Calculate the project's NPV using a discount rate reflecting the cost of finance in host country terms.
4. Allow for any management charges and royalties.
5. Estimate parent company cash flows by applying the expected future exchange rate to host country cash flows if there are no blocks on remittances, or to net remittable cash flows if exchange controls operate.
6. Allow for both local and parent country taxation.
7. Calculate the project's NPV.

Differences between host and parent country taxation

Quite apart from different tax rates, taxation issues can complicate FDI in several ways, most notably, if there are different systems of investment incentives in the two countries, and whether or not a Double Taxation Agreement (DTA) operates. Under a DTA, tax paid in the host country is credited in calculating tax in the parent country. The generally-recommended procedure is to:

1. Allow for host country investment incentives before applying the local tax rate to local cash flows.
2. Apply the relevant UK rate of tax to remitted cash flows only.
3. Adjust stage 2 for any double tax rules. For example, with a DTA and host country tax payable at 15 per cent and where the rate of tax applicable in the UK is 30 per cent, the relevant rate of tax to apply to remittances is (30% – 15%) = 15%.

Self-assessment Activity 8.5

A UK MNC earns cash flow (all taxable) of $100 million in the USA. What is its overall tax bill if the rate of tax on profits in both the USA and the UK is 30 per cent and a DTA applies?

(answer at end of chapter)

A full examination of the complexities of FDI is beyond our scope. However, several of these features are brought out in the example below.

Example – Sparkes plc and Zoltan Kft

A UK company, Sparkes plc, is planning to invest £5 million in the Zoltan consumer electronics factory in Hungary. The project will generate a stream of cash flows in the local currency, Forints, which have to be converted into sterling as in Table 8.1. Should Sparkes invest?

First, we must consider the time dimension. The project is capable of operating for ten years, but the host government has expressed its desire to buy into the project after four years. This may signal to Sparkes the possibility of more overt intervention, possibly extending to outright nationalisation, perhaps by a successor government. It seems prudent to confine the analysis to a four-year period and to include a terminal value for the project based on net book values. If we assume a ten-year life, straight-line depreciation and ignore investment in working capital, the NBV after four years will be 60 per cent of Ft1,000 m = Ft600 m. Half of this can be treated as a cash inflow paid by the host government and half as a (perhaps conservative) assessment of the value of Sparkes' continuing stake in the enterprise.

In practice, we often encounter complications in assessing terminal values. For example, the assets may include land, which may appreciate in value at a rate faster than general

Table 8.1 Sparkes and Zoltan: project details

- Expected net cash flows from Zoltan in millions of Forints (at current prices):

Year	0	1	2	3	4
	−1,000	+400	+400	+400	+400

- The project may operate for a further six years, but the local government has expressed its desire to purchase a 50 per cent stake at the end of Year 4. The purchase price will be based on the net book value of assets.
- The spot exchange rate between sterling and Forints is 200 per £1. The present rates of inflation are 25 per cent in Hungary and 5 per cent for the UK. These rates are expected to persist for the next few years.
- For this level of risk, Sparkes requires a return of 10 per cent in real terms.

Continued

price inflation. If so, there may be holding gains to consider, gains which may well be taxable by the host government. However, it is unwise to rely overmuch on terminal values – if project acceptance hinges on the terminal value, it is probably unwise to proceed with this sort of project.

Second, how should we specify the cash flows? Here, we have two problems: first, divergence between UK and Hungarian rates of inflation; and second, the need to convert locally-denominated cash flows into sterling. To be consistent, we should discount nominal cash flows at the nominal cost of capital or real cash flows at the real cost. Each will give the same answer, but we initially conduct the analysis in nominal cash flows, thus incorporating the effect of inflation. Hence all cash flows are inflated at the anticipated Hungarian rate of inflation of 25 per cent.

The discount rate also has to be adjusted for inflation – if the UK shareholders require a return of P per cent in real terms, the nominal rate, M, under I per cent inflation (as we found in Chapter 6) is:

$$\begin{aligned} M = (1 + P)(1 + I) - 1 &= (1.10)\,(1.25) - 1 \\ &= 1.375 - 1, \text{ i.e. } 37.5\% \end{aligned}$$

Finally, we need to adjust for the exchange rate. We will see in Chapter 17 that in perfect world financial markets, exchange rates adjust to take into account movements in interest rates and inflation rates. If so, the exchange rate between the Forint and sterling will adjust by the discrepancy in their inflation rates so as to preserve their relative purchasing power. Hence there is no need to adjust the exchange rate at the outset of the project. If we calculate the net present value of the project in Forints in real terms, it is sufficient to adjust at the current exchange rate and allow international capital markets to produce the predicted real sterling values.

The calculations shown in Table 8.2 suggest that Sparkes should invest. Meanwhile, you may have spotted that we would have obtained the same answer (allowing for rounding) by discounting at 10 per cent the cash flows expressed in sterling, using the current rate of exchange, as shown in Table 8.3.

Table 8.2 Evaluation of the Zoltan project

Year	Uninflated cash flow in Forints (m)	Inflated at 25%	37.5% discount factor	Present value in Forints (m)
0	(1,000)	(1,000)	1,000	(1,000)
1	400	500	0.727	364
2	400	625	0.529	331
3	400	781	0.385	301
4	400	977	0.280	273
	Terminal value			
4	600	1,465	0.280	410
Net present value				679

= +679 (i.e.) Ft679 m = £679 m/200 = £3.40 m

Continued

Table 8.3 Alternative evaluation of Zoltan project

Year	Cash flow in Forints (m)	Value (£m)	PV at 10% (£m)
0	(1,000)	(5.0)	(5.0)
1	400	2.0	1.82
2	400	2.0	1.65
3	400	2.0	1.50
4	400	2.0	1.50
			NPV = £3.39

The two equivalent approaches: which is best?

Say we are looking at a UK firm investing in Canada. The two approaches are:

A The cash flows denominated in C$ are discounted at the local Canadian discount rate to generate a C$ NPV. This is then converted at the current spot rate for C$ against sterling to yield a sterling NPV.

B The predicted C$ cash flows are converted to sterling cash flows, using expected future spot rates. These sterling cash flows are discounted at the sterling discount rate to yield a sterling NPV, numerically the same as in Approach A.

Each approach has the same departure point, i.e. the C$ cash flows, and ends up at the same place, i.e. the sterling NPV. Which approach is 'better'? This depends on what information is available. Both approaches require forecasting cash flows in C$, so forecasts of Canadian inflation are required. Beyond this, it depends whether the financial manager is happier in forecasting future FX rates than in forecasting the required return in local currency terms. Approach A requires merely a one-year forecast of FX rates to derive the required return in C$ terms, whereas Approach B requires forecasts of FX rates over all future years of the project.

Remember that the equivalence of each approach depends on several factors, in particular, operation of PPP and the existence of project inflation rates similar to those experienced at the national economy level. PPP ensures that if, say, the Canadian inflation rate exceeds the UK rate, the exchange rate of C$ *vs.* sterling will deteriorate, i.e. sterling will strengthen to ensure the parity of purchasing power of each currency in each country.

Either approach is acceptable, although the first is preferable as it has the advantage of allowing cash flows to be adjusted at inflation rates specific to the project where these may differ from the national rate, although this does require more detailed forecasting.

8.8 Exposure to foreign exchange risk

You may appreciate now that FX variations are not always disastrous. The extent of FX exposure, and thus the urgency of dealing with it, depends on the structure of the firm's net cash flows in terms of its FX denomination. Firms with naturally-hedged cash flows may be relatively unconcerned by FX variations. In Chapter 17, we look at FX risk in more detail, but, as a prelude, it may be useful to look at a four-way classification of firms based on the extent of their exposures.

The four-way classification

Figure 8.3 shows a schema for classifying the extent of a firm's exposure to FX variations. Essentially, this depends on the sensitivity of their domestic currency cash flows to FX movements. Net cash inflows are broken down into their revenue and operating cost components, in order to focus on firms' net exposure. Classified by corresponding sensitivity, the four types of firm are:

Domestics generate little or no income from abroad and source mainly from local suppliers. Their net exposure is indirect and usually low, stemming from the exposure suffered by their competitors on the UK markets and by their local suppliers.

Exporters source mainly from their own country, have high direct net exposures as their cash inflows, and whose outflows are not naturally hedged, being in different currencies. They might consider adjusting their operating and/or financial strategies to achieve more insulated positions.

Importers are in a similar position to exporters but in reverse – their net exposure is high because they source from abroad and sell on domestic markets.

Globals have the lowest, and often minimal, net exposure. They have structured their operations so as to match as far as possible the currencies in which their inflows are denominated with those in which they incur costs. The match may not be perfect, given the indivisibility of some types of operation, e.g. production facilities, but regarding the overall profile of activities, their

Sensitivity of cash inflows to FX variations	Sensitivity of cash outflows to FX variations:	
	HIGH	LOW
HIGH	*GLOBALS* – LOW EXPOSURE	*EXPORTERS* – HIGH EXPOSURE
LOW	*IMPORTERS* – HIGH EXPOSURE	*DOMESTIC TRADERS* – LOW EXPOSURE

Figure 8.3 Classification of firms by extent of operating exposure

portfolios of cash inflow currencies should correlate highly with their portfolios of outflow currencies. At the group level, global firms should have little concern about FX exposures.

This is a powerful set of distinctions, but is counter-intuitive to many people. Firms heavily engaged in foreign operations may actually have low net exposures while many domestics, blissfully thinking they are insulated from overseas-generated exposures may in reality, be more highly exposed. A high indirect exposure could conceivably outweigh a low direct exposure.

Operating/economic/strategic exposure

If PPP always worked, forecasting FX rates would be very simple – in practice, prolonged uncertainty over future exchange rates and thus the effect on the firm's future cash flows in domestic currency terms greatly concerns many financial managers. The longer the time horizon that the firm works to, the greater is its concern. Continuing exposure over a period of years is called **economic exposure.** This refers to the effect of changing FX rates on the value of a firm's operations, generally the result of changing economic and political factors, hence the alternative label **operating exposure**. Because these variations will also affect the firm's competitive position, and because protecting or enhancing that position often provokes a change in strategy, it is also called **strategic exposure**.

These three terms are often used as synonyms. Whatever we call it, the impact is felt on the present value of the firm's operating cash flows over time, and thus the value of the whole enterprise. To prevent or mitigate damage, the firm can adopt various strategies to protect its inherent value. Measurement of exposure is the first step.

Measuring operating exposure

Operating exposure is both direct and indirect. Firms are concerned not only about how FX changes affect their own cash flows, but also how their competitors are affected by these changes. If the Chinese yuan declines against the US dollar, this may seem of no great consequence to a UK firm that sources in the US. However, it becomes important if, for example, competitors in the US that import from China see their import costs fall. These indirect effects are part of a firm's overall exposure.

Measurement of operating exposure thus involves identification and analysis of all future exposures both for the individual firm and also its main competitors, actual and even potential ones, bearing in mind that FX changes may even entice new entrants into existing markets.

It is worth repeating that operating exposure is concerned less with *expected* changes in FX rates, because, in efficient financial markets, both managers and investors will have already incorporated these into their anticipation of parent company currency cash flows. If the markets expect sterling to decline *vs.* the US dollar, the likely higher future sterling cash inflows of UK firms that export to the USA will have been factored into share valuations. In this situation, it is generally advisable to incorporate the forward rate of exchange into projections for future planning purposes. The damage is done when expectations are not fulfilled and/or when changes result from totally unexpected factors.

Example: Pitt plc

Pitt plc produces half its output in the USA, valued at today's exchange rate (US$1.50 *vs.* £1) at £100 million. The other half is sold in the UK. About 25 per cent of Pitt's supplies are sourced from the USA, valued at £15 million. Labour costs are £10 million per annum, and cash overheads are £5 million per annum. Shareholders require a return of 12 per cent per annum.

Required

(a) Determine the present value of Pitt's operating cash flows in sterling terms over a 10-year time horizon.
(b) Identify Pitt's direct and indirect operating exposures.
(c) What is the effect on Pitt's PV if the sterling/dollar exchange rate changes to US$1.40 *vs.* £1?

Solution

(a) At the present exchange rate, Pitt's cash flows are:

■ Cash inflows: 2 × £100 m p.a.	= £200 m
■ Cash outflows:	
Supplies (4 × £15 m p.a.)	= (£60 m)
Labour	= (£10 m)
Overheads	= (£5 m)
Net Cash Flow	£125 m

Present value = (£125 m × ten year annuity factor at 12%)
= (£125 m × 5.650) = £706 m.

(b) Direct exposures:

- 50 per cent of cash inflows are exposed.
- 25 per cent of payments to suppliers are exposed.
- Any US$ content of labour input and cash overheads would also be exposed.

Indirect exposures stem from the extent to which:

- US competitors are exposed to currency fluctuations.
- US suppliers are exposed.
- UK competitors are exposed.
- UK suppliers are exposed.

As discussed, it is important to realise that overall exposures transcend variations in the US$/£ rate. If, for example, suppliers in the UK import from India, they face exposure from the exchange rate of the rupee *vs.* sterling. Adverse variations are likely to spur them to recoup cost increases from their customers. Obviously, the extent to which they can achieve this depends on their own market power, e.g. the number and relative size of their own competitors and the importance of the components to customers like Pitt plc.

Continued

(c) Sterling depreciation to US$1.40 *vs.* £1 will increase the sterling value of the net cash inflows, because, at present, annual USD cash inflows exceed USD cash outflows. At the current exchange rate of US$1.50 *vs.* £1, the annual difference is (£100 m – £15 m) = £85 m p.a.

Revised valuation:

- Inflows: [£100 m + (£100 m × 1.50/1.40)] = £207 m pa
- Outflows:

Supplies: (3 × £15 m) + (£15 m × 1.50/1.40)	= (£61 m)
Labour	= (£10 m)
Overheads	= (£5 m)
Net Cash Inflow	= £131 m

- PV @ 12% = (£131 m × 5.650) = £740 m

In this example, depreciation of sterling by (1 – 1.40/1.50) = 7% has resulted in an increase in firm value of about 5 per cent. The sensitivity of a firm's value will depend on the structure of the firm's cash inflows and outflows – the greater the net foreign currency component, the greater the sensitivity of firm value.

Comment

The result is somewhat oversimplified for several reasons:

It assumes no change in the volumes of US-generated business in response to sterling depreciation. In reality, Pitt may lower the US$ price to stimulate sales as it can now afford a price cut of up to 7 per cent and still achieve the same sterling cash inflow, after converting US$ into sterling at the more favourable rate.

The effect will depend on:

(i) the extent of the price cut, i.e. whether Pitt matches the 7 per cent fall in sterling or takes some or all of this as windfall profit.
(ii) the elasticity of US demand for the product, i.e. the extent to which demand is stimulated by a price cut
(iii) whether Pitt can produce enough to satisfy the demand increase.
(iv) the extent to which US competitors follow a price cut.

Consequently, a full answer would depend on more rigorous strategic evaluation of the various consequences of the sterling depreciation. Similar comments apply to the increased sterling costs of supplies. Will Pitt try to absorb these costs? Will it try to pass them on wholly or partly? Will it seek alternative UK suppliers? In addition, there may be wider effects – will Pitt win sales from US competitors in the UK and elsewhere? How will fellow UK rivals respond to the sterling depreciation? How will non-exporting UK firms that import from the USA respond?

Self-assessment Activity 8.6

A UK-owned MNC produces in the USA and also exports to South American countries directly from the UK where it is paid in $US. Its US revenue is $50 million and its operating costs are $30 million. Export sales to South America are $100 million. What is its exposure to the $US/sterling exchange rate?

(answer at end of chapter)

8.9 How MNCs manage operating exposure

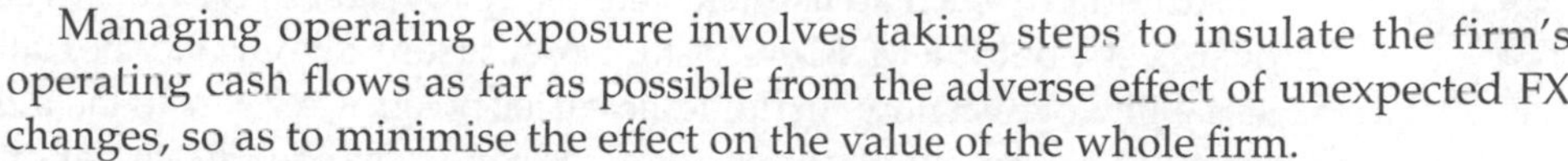

Managing operating exposure involves taking steps to insulate the firm's operating cash flows as far as possible from the adverse effect of unexpected FX changes, so as to minimise the effect on the value of the whole firm.

In Chapter 17, we explain a number of theories of the operation of FX markets. The upshot of these is that, if they are valid, firms need not worry about FX variations. However, because foreign exchange markets cannot always be relied upon to move quickly to new equilibria, it is often considered prudent to safeguard against the adverse impact of future contingencies. Moreover, given the strongly competitive nature of many international markets, it is sensible to anticipate how competitors are likely to behave in dis-equilibrium situations.

There are two broad ways in which operating exposure can be minimised. The first involves structuring the firm's operations to insulate it from damage, and the second, structuring its financial policy to this end. As we cover international financing in Chapter 20, primary attention is given here to operating policy.

The general aim is to construct a **natural hedge.** This occurs when there is little or no exposure because the adverse impact on cash inflows is exactly offset by the beneficial impact on cash outflows. A British firm producing and selling in the USA has a high degree of protection against sterling/dollar variations. If sterling appreciates, thus reducing the sterling value of dollar inflows, the adverse effect is largely counter-balanced by the corresponding fall in the sterling value of its US$-denominated inputs. Only the profit element is unhedged.

Firms that service only one overseas location can achieve this 'self-hedging' effect in various ways:

- Source components and other inputs in the country where sales are made
- Open an operating subsidiary there to manufacture or assemble the product.
- Borrow in the same currency as that of cash inflows. The stream of outflows (interest and capital repayments) will help to match the series of inflows.
- The firm may pay suppliers in other countries with the currency received from sales. If it sells in US$, and sources from Poland, it can pay the Polish suppliers in US$ rather than zlotys. This is called **currency switching**.

The hedge constructed may not be a match in the same currency. As some currencies tend to move together due to the interdependence of the associated economies, e.g. Canada and the USA, the MNC could offset, say, a $US revenue stream with a C$ cost stream. This is termed **parallel matching**.

Where several locations are serviced, the key is diversification of operations. A diversified firm is better placed both to recognise dis-equlibrium situations in foreign exchange markets and also to adapt accordingly. For example:

- If relative costs in sterling terms alter as between different locations, a diversified MNC can arrange to reschedule production between locations.
- If product prices change in different markets, the MNC may strengthen its marketing efforts to exploit greater profit opportunities where prices are higher.
- If raw material prices alter as between different locations, the MNC can alter its sourcing policy.

Admittedly such adjustments are likely to trigger certain conversion or switch-over costs, but the MNC may still benefit from favourable 'portfolio effects'. The variability of cash flows in domestic currency terms is likely to fall if the firm receives income in a variety of currencies – foreign exchange rate variations may increase competitiveness in some markets to offset lower competitiveness in others. This, of course, underpins the diversification motive for foreign investment, mentioned earlier in the chapter. Portfolio diversification is considered more fully in Chapter 10.

Self-assessment Activity 8.7

Revisit SAA 8.6.
Suggest three ways for this firm to lower its exposure.

(answer at end of chapter)

8.10 Political and country risk

According to *Euromoney*, which conducts a regular analysis of political risk: 'Political Risk is the risk of non-payment or non-servicing of payment for goods and services, or trade-related finance and dividends, and the non-repatriation of capital.'

The definition and the above discussion imply a distinction between economic and political risk, the former resulting from governmental interference and the latter from general economic turbulence. But because these are usually inter-twined, the two risks are often grouped under the heading of **country risk.**

It is not surprising that FDI by MNCs involves strong elements of political risk. Their very size and strength in relation to host countries creates the possibility of politically-inspired action, whether favourable, e.g. granting generous incentives, or adverse, e.g. expropriation of assets. Where the goals of the host government and the MNC conflict, the political risk escalates. Political risk is heightened where political and social instability prevails, and host government objectives are unclear.

The task of the MNC's planners is to define, identify and predict these sources of instability. Instability results from internal pressures or civil strife that may be caused by factors such as inequities, actual or perceived, between internal factions (whether racial, religious, tribal, etc.), extremist political programmes, forthcoming independence or impending elections.

An MNC that is considering FDI may observe the signals of political instability, but to measure its extent is a complex task. A major cause of political and social instability is due to economic influences. Factors such as oscillating oil prices, banking crises, foreign exchange crises and rampant inflation all promote instability.

As in Argentina, Turkey and Egypt in the early 2000s, economic instability often necessitates heavy overseas borrowing to finance reconstruction. Because reforms take time to implement, risk of default is ever-present. Default risk can be gauged by factors such as debt service ratio (debt service payments relative to exports) and the debt age profile. The political risks of such pressures can provoke actions such as:

- exchange controls.
- restrictions on registration of foreign companies
- restrictions on local borrowing
- expropriation or nationalisation
- tax discrimination
- import controls
- limitation on access to strategic sectors of the economy.

Expropriation – confiscation of corporate assets with or without compensation –, asset freezing – loss of control over asset management – and outright nationalisation represent the greatest political threat to foreign investors. The main risk is less that of expropriation *per se*, but the risk that compensation will be inadequate or delayed.

'Creeping' expropriation may also occur where mounting restrictions on prices, issue of work permits, transfer of shares, imports and dividends become likely when a nation feels threatened by the size and influence of MNCs. Hence, prior to deciding whether to operate in a new country, a pertinent question to consider is whether the MNC, either individually, or collectively with other MNCs, will dominate the industry, as occurs when oligopolistic rivals follow the strategic entry of a leader. If this is a strong probability, the political risk is greater than when penetration is low.

Assessing political and country risk (PCR)

There are several ways of assessing PCR:

1 Scoring systems

The magazines *Institutional Investor* and *Euromoney* produce country risk ratings on a regular basis. *Euromoney*'s ratings are based on a weighted average method, using the following scoring system, based on percentages:

- Political risk – 25 per cent
- Economic performance – 25 per cent

- Debt indicators – 10 per cent
- Debt in default or re-scheduled – 10 per cent
- Credit ratings – 10 per cent
- Access to bank finance – 5 per cent
- Access to short-term finance – 5 per cent
- Access to capital markets – 5 per cent
- Discount on forfaiting (see Chapter 16) – 5 per cent

Scores and rankings for selected countries as at September 2001 are shown in Table 8.4.

Although there is a high element of arbitrariness and subjectivity in such systems, there appears to be a strong degree of correlation between competing league tables. Given the subjectivity, consideration of movements of countries up and down the tables over time is worth study, e.g. Vietnam has been rapidly upwardly mobile in recent years.

2 Delphi techniques, or 'Consulting the oracle', involve canvassing a panel of experts for their opinions, via questionnaires or direct personal or telephone contact, and then aggregating the replies. The *Euromoney* analysis is actually a combination of check-listing and the Delphi technique.

Table 8.4 Country risk scores for selected locations

Rank	Country	Score out of 100
1.	Luxembourg	99.21
2.	Switzerland	98.20
3.	Norway	95.27
4.	Denmark	94.70
5.	USA	93.50
12.	UK	92.09
18.	Australia	88.42
29.	Cyprus	76.41
38.	Saudi Arabia	67.16
48.	Poland	59.56
57.	India	54.95
76.	Kazakhstan	43.59
81.	Vietnam	40.72
129.	Nigeria	28.78
164.	Zimbabwe	23.18
181.	Cuba	6.73
182.	Democratic Rep. of Congo	6.48
183.	North Korea	3.88
184.	Iraq	3.35
185.	Afghanistan	1.30

Source: *Euromoney*, September 2001 (**www.euromoney.com**).

3 Inspection visits – key staff from the MNC's Head Office make a 'Grand Tour' to the prospective host country, often accompanied by local embassy officials.

4 Using local intelligence – consulting local experts e.g. official insiders and credit analysts from banks to advise on prevailing local trends.

8.11 Managing political and country risk (PCR)

Protection against the adverse consequences of changes in the political or economic complexion of a host country can be achieved in four ways:

- Pre-investment negotiation
- Laying down operating strategies
- Preparation of a contingency crisis plan
- Insurance

These aspects are now considered in turn.

Pre-investment negotiation

The best approach to PCR management is to anticipate problems and negotiate an understanding beforehand. Different countries apply different codes of ethics regarding the honouring of prior contracts, especially if concluded under a previous regime. Nevertheless, pre-negotiation does provide a better basis for subsequent wrangling.

An investment agreement sets out respective rights and obligations on both the MNC and the host government. It could cover aspects such as:

- The basis whereby financial flows, such as dividends, management fees, royalties, patent fees and loan repayments may be remitted back to the home country.
- The basis for setting transfer prices used for costing inputs delivered from the home country.
- Rights relating to third-country markets, i.e. who can serve them.
- Obligations to build or fund social infrastructure like schools and hospitals.
- Methods of taxation – rates and calculation procedures.
- Requirements for **offset**, i.e. local sourcing.
- Access to host country financial markets.
- Employment practices, especially regarding openings for nationals. This is very common in the Middle East, e.g. Oman.

Operating strategies

Flexible, risk-averting strategies that enhance the MNC's bargaining position can be devised in several areas.

Production and logistics

- Local sourcing increases local employment and may head off trouble if local interests would be damaged thereby.
- Siting production facilities to minimise risk, e.g. siting oil refineries in low-risk locations.
- Retaining control of transportation facilities like oil tankers and pipelines.
- Control of technology embodied in patents and the appointment of home country staff to manage complex technological processes. Coca Cola has never divulged its magic formula, reputedly locked in a bank vault in Atlanta, Georgia.

Marketing

- Controlling markets by eliminating competition – locals are often happy to sell out.
- Controlling brand names and trademarks. McDonalds only franchises operations to local entrepreneurs.

Financial

- Issuing equity on the local stock market to extend ownership to locals. A Joint Venture is also an effective way to promote local participation.
- Restricting parental equity input – local debt financing is preferable to equity funding as it creates a hedge to offset local inflation and exchange rate depreciation, and also exerts leverage on local politicians if local banks stand to suffer from political intervention.
- Multi-source borrowing – raising loans from banks in several countries, and perhaps international development agencies, will build a wide nexus of vested interests in keeping the MNC healthy.

Preparation of a contingency crisis plan

Contingency planning helps in two ways, first, by providing an action plan to implement if things do go wrong, and second, it forces managers to think about the contingencies to which their foreign operation is most vulnerable.

Investment insurance

MNCs may be able to shift risk to a home country agency that specialises in accepting international risks. In the UK, the Export Credit Guarantee Department (ECGD) offers confiscation cover for new overseas investments and Lloyds offers insurance facilities for existing and new investments in a comprehensive and non-selective form. In the USA, the government-owned Overseas Private Investment Corporation (OPIC) will cover risks relating to inability to convert overseas earnings into dollars, expropriation, war and revolution, and loss of business income arising from events of political violence that damage MNC assets.

Self-assessment Activity 8.8

List eight ways in which MNCs can lower political risk.

(answer at end of chapter)

Summary

This chapter has examined the strategic motivations that drive firms to enter foreign markets, and methods of effecting entry, in particular direct investment. Evaluating FDI is a complex process that differs in several important respects from evaluation of home country investment, not least the exposure to FX rate variations. As a result, FDI evaluation is more art than science, especially as it involves so many un-quantifiable aspects such as the prevailing political mood of the host country, assessing political and other country risks and devising appropriate safeguards. Clearly, this topic transcends purely *financial* strategy.

Key points

- Foreign direct investment (FDI) may be undertaken for a variety of strategic reasons: for example, globalisation of component sources or meeting the threat of a competitor already based overseas.
- FDI is generally undertaken when exporting (with relatively high variable costs, but low fixed costs) becomes more expensive than overseas production (with relatively high fixed costs but low variable costs).
- In principle, the evaluation of FDI is similar to the evaluation of 'domestic' investment.
- In practice, FDI may be complicated by factors such as concessionary access to local finance, difficulties in repatriating profits and differential inflation rates.

Further reading

Tomkins (1991) and Butler *et al.* (1993) explore the strategic aspects of investment. Interesting and comprehensive texts on international business strategy and operations are Daniels and Radebaugh (1989) and Rugman *et al.* (1985). The texts by Eiteman *et al.* (1995), Shapiro (1989) and Madura (1995) all focus more closely on multinational business finance, each devoting several chapters to foreign investment. Special issues of *Managerial Finance* (Wilson 1990; Shao 1996) were devoted to the evaluation of overseas investment, while Holland's contribution to Firth and Keane (1986) is clear and concise. Prasad

(1987) reports on a survey of MNC motivations to invest in Ireland, while Madura and Whyte (1990) discuss the diversification benefits of foreign direct investment.

The most comprehensive text devoted to evaluating FDI is Buckley (1996).

Self-assessment Answers

8.1 Broadly, an MNC is a firm whose activities span national borders, but the term usually applies to firms that invest in foreign locations. A global firm both trades and invests abroad.

8.2 Licensing tends to have very low variable costs. Its fixed costs depend on the degree of supervision applied to the overseas operator (the agency costs). Fixed costs are probably higher than for exporting but lower than for FDI.

8.3 FDI differs from domestic investment for many reasons:

- Exposure to FX risk
- Likelihood of inflation abroad occurring at rates different from home inflation
- Risk of political intervention, leading to blocked funds, etc.
- Access to concessionary finance and grants
- Overspill effects on existing operations.

8.4 Sterling income will be unaffected because both countries experience the same rate of inflation so that the C$ *vs*. sterling exchange rate will be unaffected.

Canadian income will be: C$100 m (1.05) = C$105 m
Value in sterling terms: (C$105 m/2.20) = £47.7 m

8.5 The firm will pay tax only in the US, i.e. (US$100 m × 30%) = US$30 m, which is allowable in full against UK tax liability.

8.6

Exposure of US operations = US$(50 m − 30 m) =	US$20 m
Exposure in South America =	US$100 m
Total exposure	US$120 m

8.7 The net exposure could be reduced by:

- Producing more output in the US and shipping direct to South America.
- Sourcing more US$-denominated inputs to support UK production.
- Borrowing in US$.

8.8
- Source materials and services from local suppliers.
- Employ locals in key management posts.
- Invest in training programmes for locals.
- Invest in sports and health facilities, open to the wider population.
- Sponsor local cultural events.
- Undertake joint ventures with local firms.
- Reinvestment rather than repatriation of profits.
- Use local sources of finance.

Questions

1 *Solution in Appendix A (page 809).* The USD vs. GBP exchange rate is \$1.50 vs. £1. A UK MNC operating in the US plans to sell goods worth \$100 million at today's prices to US customers. Show that its GBP revenue *in real terms* will not be affected if PPP applies under each of the following conditions:

(i) UK and US inflation at 5% p.a.
(ii) UK inflation 5%, US inflation 2%.
(iii) UK inflation 2%, US inflation 5%.

2 *Solution in Appendix A (page 809).* OJ Limited is a supplier of leather goods to retailers in the UK and other western European countries. The company is considering entering into a joint venture with a manufacturer in South America. The two companies will each own 50 per cent of the limited liability company JV (SA) and will share profits equally. £450,000 of the initial capital is being provided by OJ Limited, and the equivalent in South American dollars (SA\$) is being provided by the foreign partner. The managers of the joint venture expect the following net operating cash flows which are in nominal terms:

	SA\$ 000	**Predicted future rates of exchange to £ sterling**
Year 1	4,250	10
Year 2	6,500	15
Year 3	8,350	21

For tax reasons, JV (SA), the company to be formed specifically for the joint venture, will be registered in South America.

Ignore taxation in your calculations.

Assume you are a financial adviser retained by OJ Limited to advise on the proposed joint venture.

Required

(a) Calculate the NPV of the project under the two assumptions explained below. Use a discount rate of 16 per cent for both assumptions, and express your answer in sterling.

Assumption 1: The South American country has exchange controls which prohibit the payment of dividends above 50 per cent of the annual cash flows for the first three years of the project. The accumulated balance can be repatriated at the end of the third year.
Assumption 2: The government of the South American country is considering removing exchange controls and restrictions on repatriation of profits. If this happens, all cash flows will be distributed as dividends to the partner companies at the end of each year.

(b) Comment briefly on whether or not the joint venture should proceed based solely on these calculations.

(CIMA)

3 *Solution in Appendix A (page 810)*. PC plc is considering investing in a new project in Canada that will have a life of four years. Initial investment is C$150,000, including working capital. The net cash flows that the project will generate are C$60,000 per annum for years 1, 2 and 3 and C$45,000 in year 4. The terminal value of the project is estimated at C$50,000, net of tax.

The current spot rate for C$ against the pound sterling is 1.70. Economic forecasters expect the pound to strengthen against the Canadian dollar by 5 per cent per annum over the next four years. The company evaluates UK projects of similar risk at 14 per cent per annum.

Required

Calculate the NPV of the Canadian project using the following two methods:

(i) Convert the foreign currency cash flows into sterling and discount at a sterling discount rate.

(ii) Discount the cash flows in C$ using an adjusted discount rate that incorporates the 12-month forecast spot rate.

(CIMA)

4 *Solution on website*. Kay plc, a UK-based chemical firm but with plants in Germany and the Netherlands, manufactures man-made fibres. It would like to expand its exports to Latin America and the country of Copacabana, in particular. However, Copacabana is unable to pay in Western currency and its own currency, the poncho, is subject to rapid depreciation, due to high local inflation. One solution to this problem is an arrangement whereby Kay manages and pays for the construction of a fibres plant and accepts payment in the form of the finished product of fibres (a so-called buyback).

Construction will take two years and expenditures can be treated as four equal half-yearly payments of 10 million ponchos at today's prices, beginning in six months' time. The plant will have a fifteen-year life, but will attract no local investment incentives. The inflation rate in Copacabana is expected to average 20 per cent p.a. over the construction period. The current exchange rate of the poncho *vs.* sterling is 1:4 and inflation in the UK has recently averaged 5 per cent.

The fibres produced and taken as payment can be traded on world markets, probably in Europe, where the present price is €500 per tonne. Kay is not prepared to accept payment in this way for more than five years. The expected production rate of the plant is 20,000 tonnes per annum, and Kay would take 40 per cent of this in payment.

The current euro *vs.* sterling rate is €1.60 per £1, and sterling is expected to depreciate by 5 per cent per annum prior to joining the euro bloc.

Further information

- The project will be financed by equity only.
- Kay is at present debt-free. Its shareholders seek a return of 20 per cent p.a. for projects of this degree of risk.
- Profits from the operation will be taxed at 30 per cent when repatriated to the UK. Assume no delay in tax payment. All development costs will qualify for UK tax relief.
- Any losses will be carried forward to qualify for tax relief.
- There will be no tax liability in Copacabana.

Required

Determine whether Kay should undertake this project.

5 *Solution on website*. Brighteyes plc manufactures medical and optical equipment for both domestic and export sale. It is investigating the construction of a manufacturing plant in Lastonia, a country in the former Soviet bloc. Initial discussions with the Ministry of Economic Development in Lastonia have met with favourable response, providing the project can generate a 10 per cent pre-tax return. Shareholders look for a return of 15 per cent in real terms.

The investment will be partly import-substituting and partly export-based, selling to neighbouring countries. The project has been offered a local tax holiday, exempting it from all taxes for the first ten years, except for cash remittances, for which a 20 per cent withholding tax will apply. Modern factory premises on an industrial estate with convenient road and rail links have been offered at a reasonable rent.

The initial investment will be £10 million in plant, machinery and set-up costs, all payable in sterling by the parent company. Additional funds will come from a bank loan of 20 million latts, the local currency (4 latts = £1), negotiated with a local bank, at a concessionary rate of interest of 10 per cent p.a. This will be used to finance working capital. Operating cash flows, the basis for calculating tax, are estimated at L10 million in Year 1 and L22 million thereafter until year 5.

The whole of the parent's earnings after payment of local interest and taxation will be repatriated to the UK. The Lastonia withholding tax is to be allowed as a deduction before calculating the UK Corporation Tax, currently at the rate of 30 per cent. All transfers can be treated as occurring on the final day of each accounting period, when all taxes become due.

The new venture is expected to 'cannibalise' exports that Brighteyes would otherwise have made to neighbouring countries, resulting in post-tax cash flow losses of £0.5 million in each of years 2 to 5. For planning purposes, year 5 is the cut-off year, when the realisable value of the plant and equipment is estimated at L24 million. The working capital will be realised, subject to losses of L2 million on stocks and L2 million on debtors. Funds realised will be used to repay the local borrowing, and the balance transferred to the UK without further tax penalty or restriction.

The exchange rate is forecast to remain at L4 *vs.* £1 until year 2, when the Latt is expected to fall to L5 *vs.* £1.

Required

(i) Is the project acceptable from the Lastonian Ministry's point of view?
(ii) Is it worthwhile from the viewpoint of the foreign subsidiary?
(iii) Does it create wealth for Brighteyes' shareholders?

6 *Solution in Appendix A (page 810)*. Palmerston Plc operates in both the UK and Germany. In attempting to assess its economic exposure, it compiles the following data:

- UK sales are influenced by the euro's value as it faces competition from German suppliers. It forecasts annual UK sales based on three possible scenarios:

Euro:sterling exchange rate	Revenue from UK business
1.65:1	£200 m
1.60:1	£215 m
1.55:1	£220 m

- Revenues from sales made in Germany are expected to be €120 m p.a.
- Expected cost of goods sold is £120 m p.a. from UK materials purchases, and €200 m from purchases in Germany.
- Estimated cash fixed operating expenses are £50 m p.a.
- Variable operating expenses are estimated at 20 per cent of total sales value including German sales translated into sterling).
- Palmerston is financed entirely by equity and shareholders require a return of 15 per cent p.a.

Required

(i) Construct a forecast cash flow statement for Palmerston under each scenario.
(ii) Value Palmerston's equity under each scenario, assuming a ten-year operating time horizon. Ignore terminal values.
(iii) Suggest how Palmerston might restructure its operations to lower its sensitivity to exchange rate movements.

Ignore taxation.

Practical assignment

Inspect the Report and Accounts for a company of your choice, to examine how its international profile of activities has changed over the years. You may find difficulty in obtaining a full set of accounts reaching very far back in time, but examination of a sample should give you a flavour of the company's policy regarding internationalisation.

Look also at the chairman's statements to glean an indication of the importance attached to overseas operations in the company's strategy.

PART III

Investment risk and return

The preceding analysis of investment decisions has implied that future returns from investment can be forecast with certainty. Clearly, this is unlikely in practice. In Part III we examine the impact of uncertainty on the investment decision, and the various approaches available to decision-makers to cope with this problem.

In Chapter 9, we discuss a number of methods that may assist the decision-maker when looking at the risky investment project in isolation. In Chapter 10, we look at how more desirable combinations of risk and return can be achieved by forming a portfolio of investment activities. In Chapter 11, we examine the contribution to risk analysis of the Capital Asset Pricing Model, which offers a guide to setting the premium required for risk. The earlier study of how capital markets behave is particularly important here. Chapter 11 is highly important because it links the behaviour of individual investors, buying and selling securities, to the behaviour of the capital investment decision-maker. This focus is further developed in Chapter 12, which discusses how to alter the discount rate when faced by projects of degrees of risk that differ from the company's existing activities. Finally, in Chapter 13, we look at the contribution to investment appraisal under risk promised by the rapidly developing field of options analysis.

277 Analysing investment risk

308 Relationships between investments: portfolio theory

331 Setting the risk premium: the Capital Asset Pricing Model

367 The required rate of return on investment and Shareholder Value Analysis

398 Identifying and valuing options

9 Analysing investment risk

Eurotunnel investors discover a black hole

In 1802, Napoleon turned down French mining engineer Matthieu Favier's proposal for a Channel tunnel, rising in the centre to a man-made island allowing for a change of horses for the stage-coach traffic. Many other schemes were subsequently rejected until, in 1986, the Anglo-French Treaty was signed, authorising the construction, financing and operation of a twin rail tunnel system by Eurotunnel. The company is, effectively, a one-project business.

The 1986 preliminary prospectus provided forecasts upon which expected returns and sensitivities could be prepared. Potential investors and lenders were asked to invest in a highly risky venture that would not pay a dividend for at least eight years and where the expected annual return was around 14 per cent. *The Economist* commented at the time that the Tunnel was 'a hole in the ground that will either make or lose a fortune' for its investors. Throughout its much-publicised history, Eurotunnel has struggled to raise the necessary finances. The project's construction costs have more than doubled the original estimate, while delays in completion and late delivery of trains have held up revenue growth. On top of this, a major fire on the supposedly safe freight carriages put it out of operation and dented public confidence.

It hit rock bottom in 1995, when this giant black hole had sucked in over £12 billion from 225 banks and over 700,000 private investors. Nine years after the original decision to go ahead, it was still a highly risky project for investors.

By 2000, things were looking a little better. The chairman announced that the first dividend was expected in 2006. However, closer questioning revealed that this was the 'upper case scenario'. In the 'lower case scenario' dividend payments do not begin until 2010. Those first investors who took a risk on either making or losing a fortune saw Eurotunnel's share price plummet from 900p to 53p, and may have to wait a quarter of a century before they receive their first dividend!

Learning objectives

The main learning objectives are the following:

- To understand how uncertainty affects investment decisions.
- To explore managers' risk attitudes.
- To appreciate the levels at which risk can be viewed.
- To be able to measure the expected NPV and its variability.
- To appreciate the main risk-handling techniques and apply them to capital budgeting problems.

9.1 Introduction

The Channel Tunnel is one of many cases where investment decisions turn out to be far riskier than originally envisaged. The finance director of a major UK manufacturer for the motor industry remarked, 'We know that, on average, one in five large capital projects flops. The problem is: we have no idea beforehand which one!'

Stepping into the unknown – which is what investment decision-making effectively is – means that mistakes will surely occur. Entrepreneurs, on average, have nine failures for each major success. Similarly, on average, nine empty oil wells are drilled before a successful oil strike. Richard Branson, head of Virgin Atlantic, once said, 'the safest way to became a millionaire is to start as a billionaire and invest in the airline industry.'

This does not mean that managers can do nothing about project failures. In this and subsequent chapters, we examine how project risk is assessed and controlled. The various forms of risk are defined and the main statistical methods for measuring project risk within single-period and multi-period frameworks are described. A variety of risk analysis techniques will then be discussed. These fall conveniently into methods intended to describe risk and methods incorporating project riskiness within the net present value formula. The chapter concludes by examining the extent to which the methods discussed are used in business organisations.

Defining terms

At the outset, we need to clarify our terms:

- *Certainty*. Perfect certainty arises when expectations are single-valued: that is, a particular outcome will arise rather than a range of outcomes. Is there such a thing as an investment with certain payoffs? Probably not, but some investments come fairly close. For example, an investment in three-month Treasury Bills will, subject to the Bank of England keeping its promise, provide a precise return on redemption.
- *Risk and uncertainty*. Although used interchangeably in everyday parlance, these terms are not quite the same. Risk refers to the set of unique consequences for a given decision that can be assigned probabilities, while uncertainty implies that it is not fully possible to identify outcomes or to assign probabilities. Perhaps the

worst forms of uncertainty are the 'unknown unknowns' – outcomes from events that we did not even consider.

The most obvious example of risk is the 50 per cent chance of obtaining a 'head' from tossing a coin (but this did not stop the England Cricket Captain losing the toss eleven times in a row in 2001!). For most investment decisions, however, empirical experience is hard to find. Managers are forced to estimate probabilities where objective statistical evidence is not available. Nevertheless, a manager with little prior experience of launching a particular product in a new market can still subjectively assess the risks involved based on the information he or she has. Because subjective probabilities may be applied to investment decisions in a manner similar to objective probabilities, the distinction between risk and uncertainty is not critical in practice, and the two terms are often used interchangeably.

Investment decisions are only as good as the information upon which they rest. Relevant and useful information is central in projecting the degree of risk surrounding future economic events and in selecting the best investment option.

Self-assessment Activity 9.1

Why is risk assessment important in making capital investment decisions?

(answer at end of chapter)

9.2 Expected net present value (ENPV): Betterway plc

To what extent is the net present value criterion relevant in the selection of risky investments? Consider the case of Betterway plc, contemplating three options with very different degrees of risk. The distribution of possible outcomes for these options is given in Table 9.1. Notice that A's cash flow is totally certain.

Table 9.1 Betterway plc: expected net present values

Investment	NPV outcomes (£)		Probability		Weighted outcomes (£)
A	9,000	×	1	=	9,000
	−10,000	×	0.2	=	−2,000
B	10,000	×	0.5	=	5,000
	20,000	×	0.3	=	6,000
			1.0	ENPV =	9,000
	−55,000	×	0.2	=	−11,000
C	10,000	×	0.5	=	5,000
	50,000	×	0.3	=	15,000
			1.0	ENPV =	9,000

Clearly, while the NPV criterion is appropriate for investment option A, where the cash flows are certain, it is no longer appropriate for the risky investment options B and C, each with three possible outcomes. The whole range of possible outcomes may be considered by obtaining the **expected net present value** (ENPV), which is the mean of the NPV distribution when weighted by the probabilities of occurrence. The ENPV is given by the equation:

$$\overline{X} = \sum_{i=1}^{N} p_i X_i$$

where $\overline{X}$ is the expected value of event X, X_i is the possible outcome i from event X, p_i is the probability of outcome i occurring and N is the number of possible outcomes.

The NPV rule may then be applied by selecting projects offering the highest expected net present value. In our example, all three options offer the same expected NPV of £9,000. Should the management of Betterway view all three as equally attractive? The answer to this question lies in their attitudes towards risk, for while the *expected* outcomes are the same, the *possible* outcomes vary considerably. Thus, although the expected NPV criterion provides a single measure of profitability, which may be applied to risky investments, it does not, by itself, provide an acceptable decision criterion.

9.3 Attitudes to risk

Business managers prefer less risk to more risk for a given return. In other words, they are *risk-averse*. In general, a business manager derives less **utility** from gaining an additional £1,000 than he or she forgoes in losing £1,000. This is based on the concept of diminishing marginal utility, which holds that, as wealth increases, marginal utility declines at an increasing rate. Thus the utility function for risk-averse managers is concave, as shown in Figure 9.1. As long as the utility function of the decision-maker can be specified, this approach may be applied in reaching investment decisions.

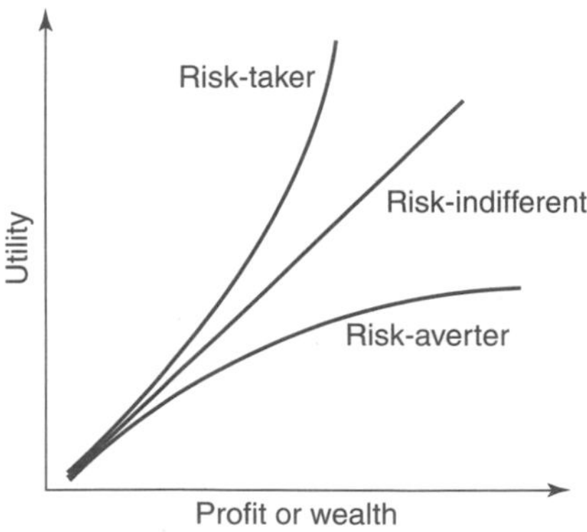

Figure 9.1 Risk profiles

Example: Carefree plc's utility function

Mike Cool, the managing director of Carefree plc, a business with a current market value of £30 million, has an opportunity to relocate its premises. It is estimated that there is a 50 per cent probability of increasing its value by £12 million and a similar probability that its value will fall by £10 million. The owner's utility function is outlined in Figure 9.2. The concave slope shows that the owner is risk-averse. The gain in utility (ΔU_F) as a result of the favourable outcome of £42 million, is less than the fall in utility (ΔU_A) resulting from the adverse outcome of only £20 million.

The conclusion is that, although the investment proposal offers £1 million expected additional wealth (i.e. 0.5 × £12 m + 0.5 × (−£10 m)), the project should not be undertaken because total expected utility would fall if the factory were relocated.

While decision-making based upon the expected utility criterion is conceptually sound, it has serious practical drawbacks. Mike Cool may recognise that he is risk-averse, but is unable to define, with any degree of accuracy, the shape of his utility function. This becomes even more complicated in organisations where ownership and management are separated, as is the case for most companies. Here, the agency problem discussed in Chapter 1 arises. Thus, while utility analysis provides a useful insight into the problem of risk, it does not provide us with operational decision rules.

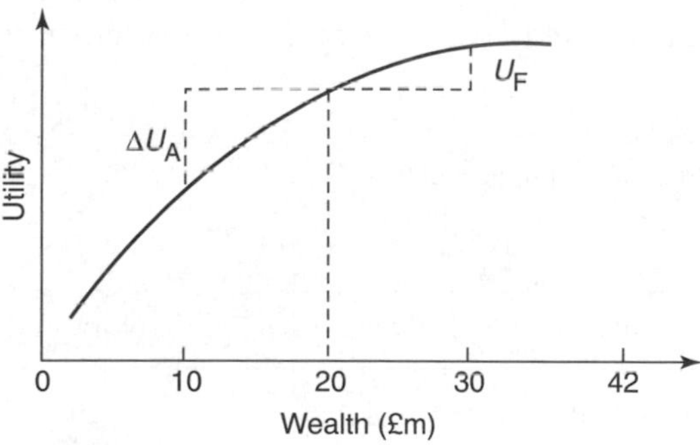

Figure 9.2 Investor's risk-averse utility function

9.4 The many types of risk

Risk may be classified into a number of types. A clear understanding of the different forms of risk is useful in the evaluation and monitoring of capital projects:

1 *Business risk* – the variability in operating cash flows or profits before interest. A firm's business risk depends, in large measure, on the underlying economic environment within which it operates. But variability in operating cash flows can be heavily affected by the cost structure of the business, often termed its **operating gearing**. A company's break-even point is reached when sales

revenues match total costs. These costs consist of **fixed costs** – that is, costs that do not vary much with the level of sales – and **variable costs**. The decision to become more capital-intensive generally leads to an increase in the proportion of fixed costs in the cost structure. This increase in operating gearing leads to greater variability in operating earnings.

Operating gearing example: Hifix and Lofix

Hifix and Lofix are two companies identical in every respect except cost structure. While Lofix pays its workforce on an output-related basis, Hifix operates a flat-rate wage system. The sales, costs and profits for the two companies are given under two economic states, normal and recession, in Table 9.2. While both companies perform equally well under normal trading conditions, Hifix, with its heavier fixed cost element, is more vulnerable to economic downturns. This can be measured by calculating the degree of operating gearing:

$$\text{Operating gearing} = \frac{\text{percentage change in profits}}{\text{percentage change in sales}}$$

$$\text{For Hifix} = \frac{-200\%}{-40\%} = 5$$

$$\text{For Lofix} = \frac{-80\%}{-40\%} = 2$$

The degree of operating gearing is far greater for the firm with high fixed costs than for the firm with low fixed costs. (Chapter 20 further discusses operating gearing.)

Table 9.2 Effects of cost structure on profits (£000)

	Hifix		Lofix	
	Normal	**Recession**	**Normal**	**Recession**
Sales	200	120	200	120
Variable costs	−100	−60	−160	−96
Fixed costs	−80	−80	−20	−20
Profit/loss	20	−20	20	4
Change in sales		−40%		−40%
Change in profits		−200%		−80%

2 *Financial risk* – the risk, over and above business risk, that results from the use of debt capital. **Financial gearing** is increased by issuing more debt, thereby incurring more fixed-interest charges and increasing the variability in net earnings. Financial risk is considered more fully in later chapters.
3 *Portfolio or market risk* – the variability in shareholders' returns. Investors can significantly reduce their variability in earnings by holding carefully selected investment portfolios. This is sometimes called 'relevant' risk, because only

this element of risk should be considered by a well-diversified shareholder. Chapters 10 and 11 examine such risk in greater depth.

Project risk can be viewed and defined in three different ways: (1) in isolation, (2) in terms of its impact on the business, and (3) in terms of its impact on shareholders' investment portfolios. One survey (Pike and Ho 1991) found that 79 per cent of managers in larger UK firms use project-specific risk and 61 per cent consider the impact of business risk, but only 26 per cent consider the impact on shareholder portfolios.

In this chapter, we assess project risk in isolation before moving on to estimate its impact on investors' portfolios (i.e. market risk) in Chapter 11.

Self-assessment Activity 9.2

Which type of risk do the following describe:

1 Risks associated with increasing the level of borrowing?
2 The variability in the firm's operating profits?
3 Variability in the cash flows of a proposed capital investment?
4 Variability in shareholders' returns?

(answer at end of chapter)

9.5 Measurement of risk

A well-known politician (not named to protect the guilty) once proclaimed, 'Forecasting is very important – particularly when it involves the future!' Estimating the probabilities of uncertain forecast outcomes is difficult. But with the little knowledge the manager may have concerning the future, and by applying past experience backed by historical analysis of a project and its setting, he or she may be able to construct a probability distribution of a project's cash outcomes. This can be used to measure the risks surrounding project cash flows in a variety of ways. If we assume that the range of possible outcomes from a decision is distributed normally around the expected value, risk-averse investors can assess project risk using expected value and standard deviation. We shall consider three statistical measures: the standard deviation, semi-variance and coefficient of variation for single-period cash flows.

Measuring risk for single-period cash flows: Snowglo plc

Table 9.3 shows the information on two projects for Snowglo plc.

Table 9.3 Snowglo plc project data

State of economy	Probability of outcome	Cash flow (£) A	Cash flow (£) B
Strong	0.2	700	550
Normal	0.5	400	400
Weak	0.3	200	300

Standard deviation

We have seen that expected value overlooks important information on the dispersion (risk) of the outcomes. We also know that different people behave differently in risky situations. Figure 9.3 shows the NPV distributions for projects A and B. Both projects have the same expected NPV, indicated by *M*, but project A has greater dispersion. The risk-averse manager in Snowglo will choose B since he or she wants to minimise risk. The risk-taker will choose A because the NPV of project A has a chance (*W*) of being higher than *X* (which project B cannot offer), but also a chance (*L*) of being lower than *Y*. Hereafter we make the reasonable assumption that most people are risk-averse.

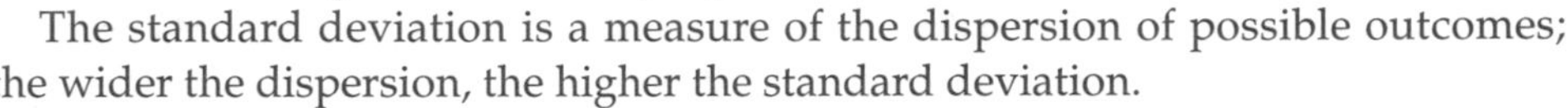

The standard deviation is a measure of the dispersion of possible outcomes; the wider the dispersion, the higher the standard deviation.

The expected value of cash flows is given by the equation:

$$\overline{X} = \sum_{i=1}^{N} p_i X_i$$

and the standard deviation of the cash flows by:

$$\sigma = \sqrt{\sum_{i=1}^{N} p_i (X_i - \overline{X})^2}$$

Table 9.4 provides the workings for projects A and B.

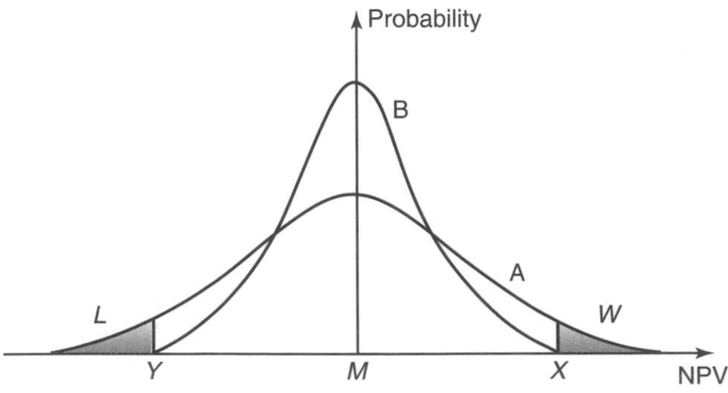

Figure 9.3 Variability of project returns

Table 9.4 Project risk for Snowglo plc

Economic state	Probability (a)	Outcome (b)	Expected value ($c = a \times b$)	Deviation ($d = b - \overline{X}$)	Squared deviation ($e = d^2$)	Variance ($f = a \times e$)
Project A						
Strong	0.2	700	140	300	90,000	18,000
Normal	0.5	400	200	0	0	0
Weak	0.3	200	60	−200	40,000	12,000
		$\overline{X}_A$ =	400		Variance = σ_A^2 =	30,000
				Standard deviation = σ_A =		173.2
Project B						
Strong	0.2	550	110	150	22,500	4,500
Normal	0.5	400	200	0	0	0
Weak	0.3	300	90	−100	10,000	3,000
		$\overline{X}_B$ =	400		Variance = σ_B^2 =	7,500
				Standard deviation = σ_B =		86.6

Alternatively:

$\overline{X}_A = 700\ (0.2) + 400\ (0.5) + 200\ (0.3) = 400$

$\sigma_A = \sqrt{[0.2\ (700 - 400)^2 + 0.5\ (400 - 400)^2 + 0.3\ (200 - 400)^2]}$
$= 173.2$

$\overline{X}_A = 550\ (0.2) + 400\ (0.5) + 300\ (0.3) = 400$

$\sigma_B = \sqrt{[0.2\ (550 - 400)^2 + 0.5\ (400 - 400)^2 + 0.3\ (300 - 400)^2]}$
$= 86.6$

Applying the formulae, we obtain an expected cash flow of £400 for both project A and project B. If the decision-maker had a neutral risk attitude, he or she would view the two projects equally favourably. But as the decision-maker is likely to be risk-averse, it is appropriate to examine the standard deviations of the two probability distributions. Here we see that project A, with a standard deviation twice that of project B, is more risky and hence less attractive. This could have been deduced simply by observing the distribution of outcomes and noting that the same probabilities apply to both projects. But observation cannot tell us by how much one project is riskier than another.

Semi-variance

While deviation above the mean may be viewed favourably by managers, only 'downside risk' (i.e. deviations below expected outcomes) is really considered in the decision process. Downside risk is best measured by the semi-variance, a special case of the variance, given by the formula:

$$SV = \sum_{j=1}^{K} p_j(X_j - \overline{X})^2$$

where SV is the semi-variance, j is each outcome value less than the expected value, and K is the number of outcomes that are less than the expected value.

Applying the semi-variance to the example in Table 9.4, the downside risk relates exclusively to the 'weak' state of the economy:

$SV_A = 0.3(200 - 400)^2 = £\,12{,}000$
$SV_B = 0.3\,(300 - 400)^2 = £\,3{,}000$

Once again project B is seen to have a much lower degree of risk. In both cases, the semi-variance accounts for 40 per cent of the project variance.

Coefficient of variation (CV)

Where projects differ in scale, a more valid comparison is found by applying a relative risk measure such as the coefficient of variation. The lower the CV, the lower the relative degree of risk. This is calculated by dividing the standard deviation by the expected value of net cash flows, as in the expression:

$$CV = \sigma/\overline{X}$$

The Snowglo example (Table 9.4) gives the following coefficients:

	Standard deviation (1)	Expected value (2)	Coefficient of variation (1 ÷ 2)
Project A	£173.2	£400	0.43
Project B	£86.6	£400	0.22

Both projects have the same expected value, but project B has a significantly lower degree of risk. Next, we consider the situation where the two projects under review are different in scale:

	Standard deviation		Expected value		Coefficient of variation
Project F	£1,000	÷	£10,000	=	0.10
Project G	£2,000	÷	£40,000	=	0.05

Although the absolute measure of dispersion (the standard deviation) is greater for project G, few people in business would regard it as more risky than project F because of the significant difference in the expected values of the two investments. The coefficient of variation reveals that G actually offers the lower amount of risk per £1 of expected value.

Self-assessment Activity 9.3

Project X has an expected return of £2,000 and a standard deviation of £400. Project Y has an expected return of £1,000 and a standard deviation of £400. Which project is more risky?

(answer at end of chapter)

Mean–variance rule

Given the expected return and the measure of dispersion (variance or standard deviation), we can formulate the **mean–variance rule.** This states that one project will be preferred to another if either of the following holds:

1 Its expected return is *higher* and the variance is *equal* to or *less* than that of the other project.
2 Its expected return *exceeds* or is *equal* to the expected return of the other project and the variance is *lower*.

This is illustrated by the mean–variance analysis depicted in Figure 9.4. Projects A and D are preferable to projects C and B respectively because they offer a higher return for the same degree of risk. In addition, A is preferable to B because for the same expected return, it incurs lower risk. These choices are applicable to all risk-averse managers regardless of their particular utility functions. What this rule cannot do, however, is distinguish between projects where both expected returns and risk differ (projects A and D in Figure 9.4). This important issue will be discussed in Chapters 10 and 11.

So far, our analysis of risk has assumed single-period investments. We have conveniently ignored the fact that, typically, investments are multi-period. The analysis of project risk where there are multi-period cash flows is discussed in the appendix to this chapter.

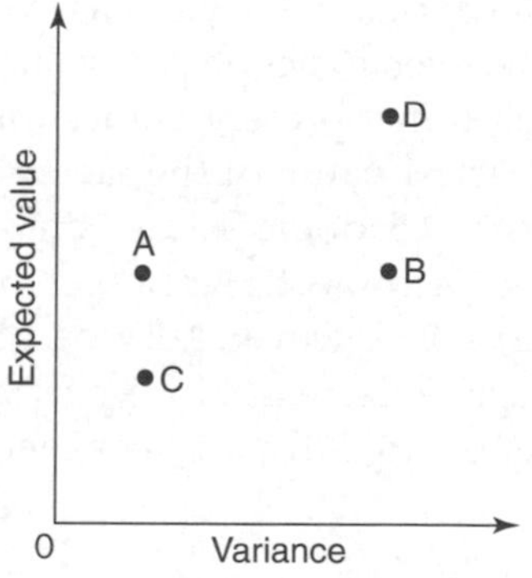

Figure 9.4 Mean–variance analysis

Risk-handling methods

There are two broad approaches to handling risk in the investment decision process. The first attempts to *describe* the riskiness of a given project, using various applications of probability analysis or some simple method. The second aims to *incorporate* the investor's perception of project riskiness within the NPV formula.

We turn first to the various techniques available to help describe investment risk.

Self-assessment Activity 9.4

What do you understand by the following?

(a) risk
(b) uncertainty
(c) risk-aversion
(d) expected value
(e) standard deviation
(f) semi-variance
(g) mean–variance rule

(answer at end of chapter)

9.6 Risk description techniques

Sensitivity analysis

In principle, sensitivity analysis is a very simple technique, used to locate and assess the potential impact of risk on a project's value. It aims not to quantify risk, but to identify the impact on NPV of changes to key assumptions. Sensitivity analysis provides the decision-maker with answers to a whole range of 'what if' questions. For example, what is the NPV if selling price falls by 10 per cent? What is the IRR if the project's life is only three years, not five years as expected? What is the level of sales revenue required to break even in net present value terms?

Sensitivity graphs permit the plotting of net present values (or IRRs) against the percentage deviation from the expected value of the factor under investigation. The sensitivity graph in Figure 9.5 depicts the potential impact of deviations from the expected values of a project's variables on NPV. When everything is unchanged, the NPV is £2,000. However, NPV becomes zero when market size decreases by 20 per cent or price decreases by 5 per cent. This shows that NPV is very sensitive to price changes. Similarly, a 10 per cent increase in the

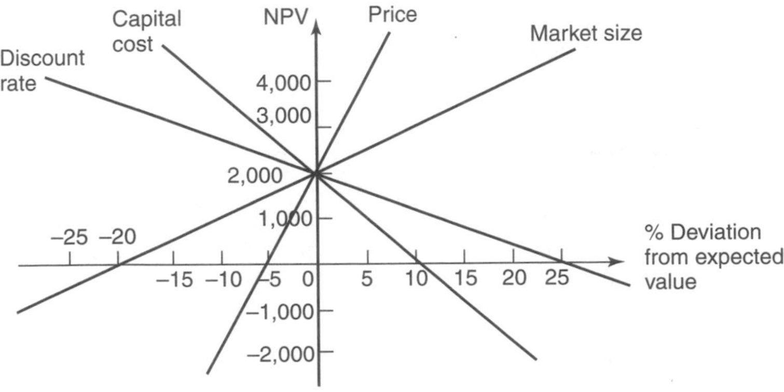

Figure 9.5 Sensitivity graph

capital cost will bring the NPV down to zero, while the discount rate must increase to 25 per cent in order to render the project uneconomic. Therefore, the project is more sensitive to capital investment changes than to variations in the discount rate. The sensitivity of NPV to each factor is reflected by the slope of the sensitivity line – the steeper the line, the greater the impact on NPV of changes in the specified variable.

Sensitivity analysis is widely used because of its simplicity and ability to focus on particular estimates. It can identify the critical factors that have greatest impact on a project's profitability. It does not, however, actually *evaluate* risk; the decision-maker must still assess the likelihood of occurrence for these deviations from expected values.

Break-even sensitivity analysis: UMK plc

The accountant of UMK plc has put together the cash flow forecasts for a new product with a four-year life, involving capital investment of £200,000. It produces a net present value, at a 10 per cent discount rate, of £40,920. His basic analysis is given in Table 9.5. Which factors are most critical to the decision?

Table 9.5 UMK cost structure

Unit data	£	£
Selling price		20
Less: Materials	(6)	
Labour	(5)	
Variable costs	(1)	
		(12)
Contribution		8
Annual sales (units)	12,000	
Total contribution		96,000
Less: Additional fixed costs		(20,000)
Annual net cash flow		76,000
Present value (4 years at 10%)		
76,000 × 3.17		240,920
Less: Capital outlay		(200,000)
Net present value		40,920

Investment outlay

This can rise by up to £40,920 (assuming all other estimates remain unchanged) before the decision advice alters. This is a percentage increase of

$$\frac{£40,920}{£200,000} \times 100 = 20.5\%$$

Continued

Annual cash receipts

The break-even position is reached when annual cash receipts multiplied by the annuity factor equal the investment outlay. The break-even cash flow is therefore the investment outlay divided by the annuity factor:

$$\frac{£200,000}{3.17} = £63,091$$

This is a percentage fall of

$$\frac{£76,000 - £63,091}{£76,000} = 17.0\%$$

Annual fixed costs could increase by the same absolute amount of £12,909, or

$$\frac{£12,909}{£20,000} \times 100 = 64.5\%$$

Annual sales volume the break-even annual contribution is £63,091 + £20,000 = £83,091. Sales volume required to break even is £83,091/£8 = 10,386, which is a percentage decline of

$$\frac{12,000 - 10,386}{12,000} \times 100 = 13.5\%$$

Selling price can fall by:

$$\frac{£96,000 - £83,091}{12,000} = £1.07 \text{ per unit}$$

a decline of

$$\frac{£1.07}{£20} \times 100 = 5.4\%$$

Variable costs per unit can rise by a similar amount:

$$\frac{£1.07}{£12} \times \; = 8.9\%$$

Discount rate

The break-even annuity factor is £200,000/£76,000 = 2.63. Reference to the present value annuity tables for four years shows that 2.63 corresponds to an IRR of 19 per cent. The error in cost of capital calculation could be as much as nine percentage points before it affects the decision advice.

Sensitivity analysis, as applied in the above example, discloses that selling price and variable costs are the two most critical variables in the investment decision. The decision-maker must then determine (subjectively or objectively) the probabilities of such changes occurring, and whether he or she is prepared to accept the risks.

Scenario analysis

Sensitivity analysis considers the effects of changes in key variables only one at a time. It does not ask the question: 'How bad could the project look?' Enthusiastic managers can sometimes get carried away with the most likely outcomes and forget just what might happen if critical assumptions – such as the state of the economy or competitors' reactions – are unrealistic. Scenario analysis seeks to establish 'worst' and 'best' scenarios, so that the whole range of possible outcomes can be considered.

Simulation analysis

An extension of scenario analysis is simulation analysis. **Monte Carlo simulation** is an operations research technique with a variety of business applications. The computer generates hundreds of possible combinations of variables according to a pre-specified probability distribution. Each scenario gives rise to an NPV outcome which, along with other NPVs, produces a probability distribution of outcomes.

One of the first writers to apply the simulation approach to risky investments was Hertz (1964), who described the approach adopted by his consultancy firm in evaluating a major expansion of the processing plant of an industrial chemical producer. This involved constructing a mathematical model that captured the essential characteristics of the investment proposal throughout its life as it encountered random events.

A simulation model might consider the following variables, which are subject to random variation.

Market factors	Investment factors	Cost factors
Market size	Investment outlay	Variable costs
Market growth rate	Project life	
Selling price of product	Residual value	Fixed costs
Market share captured by the firm		

Comparison is then possible between mutually exclusive projects whose NPV probability distributions have been calculated in this manner (Figure 9.6). It will be observed that project A, with a higher expected NPV and lower risk, is preferable to project B.

In practice, few companies use this risk analysis approach, for the following reasons:

1 The simple model described above assumes that the economic factors are unrelated. Clearly, many of them (e.g. market share and selling price) are statistically dependent. To the extent that dependency exists among variables, it must be specified. Such interrelationships are not always clear and are frequently complex to model.

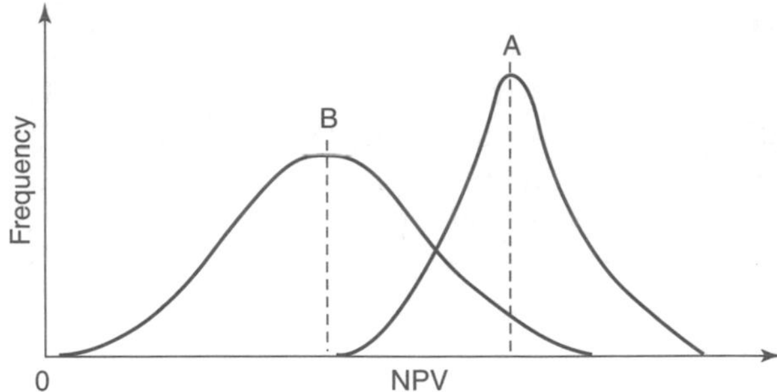

Figure 9.6 Simulated probability distributions

2 Managers are required to specify probability distributions for the exogenous variables. Few managers are able or willing to accept the demands required by the simulation approach.

Self-assessment Activity 9.5

What do you understand by Monte Carlo simulation? When might it be useful in capital budgeting?

(answer at end of chapter)

9.7 Adjusting the NPV formula for risk

Two approaches are commonly used to incorporate risk within the NPV formula.

Certainty equivalent method

This conceptually appealing approach permits adjustment for risk by incorporating the decision-maker's risk attitude into the capital investment decision. The certainty equivalent method adjusts the numerator in the net present value calculation by multiplying the expected annual cash flows by a certainty equivalent coefficient. The revised formula becomes:

Certainty equivalent method

$$\overline{\text{NPV}} = \sum_{t=1}^{N} \frac{\alpha \overline{X}_t}{(1+i)^t} - I_o$$

where: $\overline{\text{NPV}}$ is the expected net present value; α is the certainty equivalent coefficient, which reflect's management's risk attitude; $\overline{X}_t$ is the expected cash flow in period t; i is the riskless rate of interest; n is the project's life; and I_o is the initial cash outlay.

The numerator ($\alpha \overline{X}_t$) represents the figure that management would be willing to receive as a certain sum each year in place of the uncertain annual cash flow offered by the project. The greater is management's aversion to risk, the nearer the certainty equivalent coefficient is to zero. Where projects are of normal risk for the business, and the cost of capital and risk-free rate of interest are known, it is possible to determine the certainty equivalent coefficient.

Example

Calculate the certainty equivalent coefficient for a normal risk project with a one-year life and an expected cash flow of £5,000 receivable at the end of the year. Shareholders require a return of 12 per cent for projects of this degree of risk and the risk-free rate of interest is 6 per cent.

The present value of the project, excluding the initial cost and using the 12 per cent discount rate, is:

$$PV = \frac{£5{,}000}{1 + 0.12} = £4{,}464$$

Using the present value and substituting the risk-free interest rate for the cost of capital, we obtain the certainty equivalent coefficient:

$$\frac{\alpha \times £5{,}000}{1 + 0.06} = £4{,}464$$

$$\alpha = \frac{(£4{,}464)(1.06)}{£5{,}000}$$

$$= 0.9464$$

The management is, therefore, indifferent as to whether it receives an uncertain cash flow one year hence of £5,000 or a certain cash flow of £4,732 (i.e. £5,000 × 0.9464).

Risk-adjusted discount rate

Whereas the certainty equivalent approach adjusted the numerator in the NPV formula, the risk-adjusted discount rate adjusts the denominator:

Risk-adjusted discount rate method

$$\overline{NPV} = \sum_{t=1}^{N} \frac{\overline{X}_t}{(1 + k)^t} - I_o$$

where k is the risk-adjusted rate based on the perceived degree of project risk.

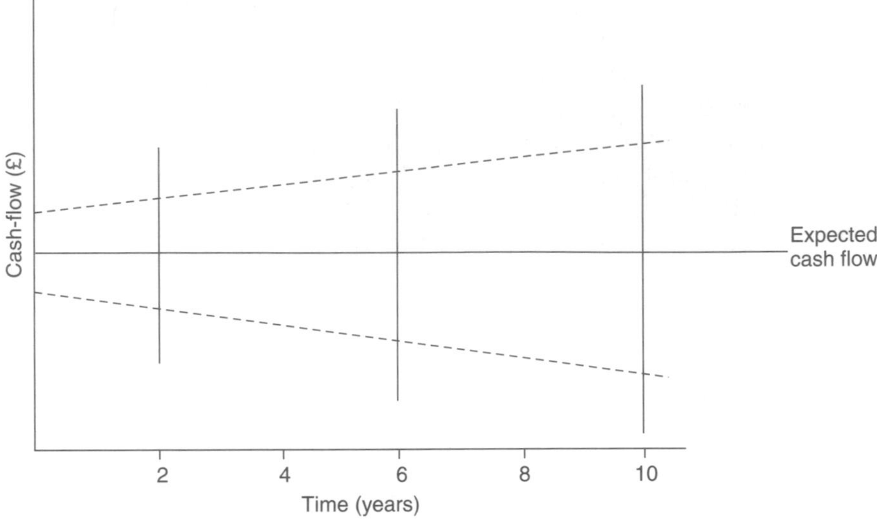

Figure 9.7 How risk is assumed to increase over time

The higher the perceived riskiness of a project, the greater the risk premium to be added to the risk-free interest rate. This results in a higher discount rate and, hence, a lower net present value.

Although this approach has a certain intuitive appeal, its relevance depends very much on how risk is perceived to change over time. The risk-adjusted discount rate involves the impact of the risk premium growing over time at an exponential rate, implying that the riskiness of the project's cash flow also increases over time. Figure 9.7 demonstrates this point. Although the expected cash flow from a project may be constant over its ten-year life, the riskiness associated with the cash flows increases with time. However, if risk did not increase with time, the risk-adjusted discount rate would be inappropriate.

Adjusting the discount rate: Chox-Box Ltd

Chox-Box Ltd is a manufacturer of confectionery currently appraising a proposal to launch a new product that has had very little pre-launch testing. It is estimated that this proposal will produce annual cash flows in the region of £100,000 for the next five years, after which product profitability declines sharply. As the proposal is seen as a high-risk venture, a 12 per cent risk premium is incorporated in the discount rate. The risk-adjusted cash flow, before discounting at the risk-free discount rate, is therefore £89,286 in Year 1 (£100,000/1.12), falling to £56,742 in Year 5 (£100,000/1.12^5).

To what extent does this method reflect the actual riskiness of the annual cash flows for Years 1 and 5? Arguably, the greatest uncertainty surrounds the initial launch period. Once the initial market penetration and subsequent repeat orders are known, the

Continued

subsequent sales are relatively easy to forecast. Thus, for Chox-Box, a single risk-adjusted discount rate is a poor proxy for the impact of risk on value over the project's life, because risk does not increase exponentially with the passage of time, and, in some cases, actually declines over time. The Eurotunnel project provides another illustration of this. By far the greatest risks were in the initial tunnelling and development phases.

A deeper understanding of the relationship between the certainty equivalent and risk-adjusted discount rate approaches may be gained by reading the appendix to this chapter.

9.8 Risk analysis in practice

To what extent do companies employ the techniques discussed in this chapter? Table 9.6 shows changes over the past twenty-five years.

Sensitivity analysis and best/worst case (or scenario) analysis are conducted in almost all larger UK companies. Approximately one half of larger firms adjust the discount rate for risk. Less common, however, are techniques requiring managers to assign probabilities to possible outcomes; managers prefer to assess the likelihood of outcomes in a more subjective manner. Finally, there is little real evidence that Beta analysis (based on the Capital Asset Pricing Model and discussed in Chapter 11) is used extensively in industry.

Table 9.6 Risk analysis in 100 large UK firms

	1975 (%)	1980 (%)	1986 (%)	1992 (%)	1997 (%)
Sensitivity analysis	28	42	71	86	89
Best/worst case analysis	n.a.	n.a.	93	95	n.a
Reduced payback period	25	30	61	59	11
Risk-adjusted rate	37	41	61	64	50
Probability analysis	9	10	40	47	42
Beta analysis	–	–	16	20	5

Source: Pike (1996), Arnold and Hatzopoulos (2000)

Mini case

A dead canary finds new life

In July 1987, at the height of the property boom, Olympia and York obtained the rights to develop the Canary Wharf site in London's Docklands. The project involved the construction of luxury office accommodation within the next five years, the

Continued

government providing a link road and the Docklands Light Railway at a cost of £700 million.

The Canary Wharf development was successfully implemented, being completed ahead of schedule and within the budget. Yet, in May 1992, Canary Wharf filed for insolvency, having failed to raise a required £500 million new loan facility. In many ways, it was a victim of largely uncontrollable circumstances: a prolonged economic recession, a downward spiral in office rents, government abolition of generous tax allowances to the Docklands, and inadequate road and rail infrastructure.

By 1998, however, the picture was rather different. Properties were 96 per cent occupied, with many banks and government departments having relocated to Canary Wharf and the Jubilee Line extension easing the earlier travel problems. Canary Wharf Ltd bought the failed company out of administration for £800 million, approximately half the original cost, and has since managed one of the most successful recoveries in business history. The chief executive of the new company observed: 'When the company went into administration I had so much trust that the project was of good quality that I decided to stay. It was purely a matter of time.'

Question

Compare this case with the Eurotunnel case presented at the start of the chapter, both of which commenced in the late 1980s.

1 Identify and contrast the risks for the two projects at the time of the decisions.
2 With hindsight, how could these risks have been reduced or better managed?

A superjumbo investment

Airbus's A300 is about to become a reality. But constructing the world's largest passenger aircraft will require shrewd financing and logistical solutions.

Potential customers have shown sufficient commitment for the final go-ahead by Airbus's two shareholders, European Aeronautic Defence and Space and BAE Systems, to be a foregone conclusion in Toulouse. Airbus has already secured 32 firm orders – the most important of which was one last month from Singapore Airlines for 10 aircraft, with an option on a further 15.

The A300 will define the fight between Airbus and Boeing, the titan of the US aerospace and defence sector, for domination of the world jetliner market. It is expected to set new standards in aerospace technology and to provide work for as many as 96,000

Continued

employees in the supply chain. That is why the European aerospace industry is preparing to gamble $10.7 billion on it.

But success is far from assured. Despite the firm orders Airbus has received, Boeing believes it is grossly overestimating the likely demand for such an aircraft. 'There is not a groundswell of orders for big planes. Airlines walk a fine line. You want the biggest plane you can get but you have to be able to fill it,' says Alan Mulally, head of Boeing's commercial aircraft division.

As well as defying Boeing's pessimism about the size of the potential market, Airbus has to show it can make money. It will have to finance nearly half of the development cost itself and estimates that the project will break even in cashflow terms only after it has sold 250 aircraft. Boeing has portrayed the project as a grand European vision that makes no commercial sense – like Concorde before it.

Airbus has offered airlines a vision of how the A300 could help their own strained profitability. It has promised to cut 15 to 20 per cent off the direct operating cost of the Boeing 747-400. The A300 would also have 35 per cent more seats than the 747-400-555 compared with 416. Of these, 232 would be 'profit seats' – the number left after selling enough tickets to break even on a flight – compared with 123 on the 747-400. It would also have a 10 per cent greater range: 8,150 nautical miles. It is a daunting ambition. Not only will Airbus use new technology, but it must also show that the A300 can operate within existing fleets. The A300 must use existing runways and taxiways. It has to create no more air turbulence than the 747-400, allowing air traffic controllers to use the same separation distances between aircraft in flight.

Robert Lafontan, vice-president for engineering and product development in the Airbus large aircraft division, says its engineers always intended to establish a technological lead over Boeing. 'You cannot make the big breakthroughs by copying existing technology. When you are the challenger you have to be innovative,' he says.

Much of the technological edge will come from new, weight-saving materials. Better aerodynamics and lower airframe weight should allow the aircraft to burn less fuel, reducing emissions and lowering operating costs. Airbus claims it will save between 10 and 15 tonnes on a similar-sized aircraft using existing 747 technology, giving it a weight of about 240 tonnes. An estimated 40 per cent of the aircraft's structure and components will be made from new carbon composites and metal alloys.

Instead of the customary aluminium, the upper fuselage shell is to be made from Glare, a laminate with alternate layers of aluminium and glass-fibre reinforced adhesive. This is 10 per cent less dense than aluminium and Airbus claims it is tougher. Innovation in hydraulic systems should also cut weight by about 1 tonne, while improved air-conditioning should also reduce fuel consumption.

Final assembly of the aircraft will be carried out in Toulouse. The wings will be made in Britain, while the fitting out of the fuselage and interior customisation will take place in Hamburg. The tailplanes will be made in Spain. Bringing the parts together will pose unique logistical challenges.

Continued

Yet such technical challenges are less daunting than the financial one. Andreas Sperl, Airbus's finance director, puts on a brave face. 'There are rumours that this programme could kill Airbus, but that is not the case. This is a huge amount to finance, but we are in a good position to do it,' he says.

Of the $10.7 billion financing cost, $2.5 billion should come from government loans and $3.1 billion from risk-sharing partners and subcontractors, leaving Airbus to finance $5.1 billion, an investment that depends on Airbus's winning a 50 per cent share of what it expects to be a global market of about 1,500 very large aircraft by 2020.

Mr Sperl insists Airbus can be confident. It has made a 'bottom-up calculation' of development costs with its partners and suppliers and is not merely hoping for the best. 'This is not the result of some eggheads in Toulouse saying "let's make a figure." Much of my professional life will be determined by this.'

Based on Kevin Done, *Financial Times,* November 2 2000

Required

Identify the risks in this investment and suggest how they should be assessed and managed.

Summary

Risk is an important element in virtually all investment decisions. Because most people in business are risk-averse, the identification, measurement and, where possible, reduction of risk should be a central feature in the decision-making process. The evidence suggests that firms are increasingly conducting risk analysis. This does not mean that the risk dimension is totally ignored by other firms; rather, they choose to handle project risk by less objective methods such as experience, feel or intuition.

We have defined what is meant by risk and examined a variety of ways of measuring it. The probability distribution, giving the probability of occurrence of each possible outcome following an investment decision, is the concept underlying most of the methods discussed. Measures of risk, such as the standard deviation, indicate the extent to which actual outcomes are likely to vary from the expected value.

Key points

- The expected NPV, although useful, does not show the whole picture. We need to understand managers' attitudes to risk and to estimate the degree of project risk.
- Three types of risk are relevant in capital budgeting: project risk in isolation, the project's impact on corporate risk and its impact on market risk. The last two are addressed more fully in the following two chapters.

- The standard deviation, semi-variance and coefficient of variation each measure, in slightly different ways, project risk.
- Sensitivity analysis and scenario analysis are used to locate and assess the potential impact of risk on project performance. Simulation is a more sophisticated approach, which captures the essential characteristics of the investment that are subject to uncertainty.
- The NPV formula can be adjusted to consider risk. Adjustment of the cash flows is achieved by the certainty equivalent method. The risk-adjusted discount rate increases the risk premium for higher-risk projects.

Further reading

A fuller treatment of risk is found in Levy and Sarnat (1994). Useful research studies on the use of risk analysis are given in Pike (1988, 1996), Pike and Ho (1991), Mao and Helliwell (1969) and Bierman and Hass (1973).

Appendix
Multi-period cash flows and risk

For simplicity, we have so far assumed single-period investments and conveniently ignored the fact that investments are typically multi period. As risk is to be specifically evaluated, cash flows should be discounted at the risk-free rate of interest, reflecting only the time-value of money. To include a risk premium within the discount rate, when risk is already considered separately, amounts to double-counting and typically understates the true net present value. The expected NPV of an investment project is found by summing the present values of the expected net cash flows and deducting the initial investment outlay. Thus, for a two-year investment proposal:

$$\overline{\text{NPV}} = \frac{\overline{X}_1}{1+i} + \frac{\overline{X}_2}{(1+i)^2} - I_o$$

where $\overline{\text{NPV}}$ is the expected NPV, $\overline{X}_1$ is the expected value of net cash flow in Year 1, $\overline{X}_2$ is the expected value of net cash flow in Year 2, I_o is the cash investment outlay and i is the risk-free rate of interest.

A major problem in calculating the standard deviation of a project's NPVs is that the cash flows in one period are typically dependent, to some degree, on the cash flows of earlier periods. Assuming for the present that cash flows for our two-period project are statistically independent, the total variance of the NPV is equal to the discounted sum of the annual variances.

For example, the Bronson project, with a two-year life, has an initial cost of £500 and the possible payoffs and probabilities outlined in Table 9.7. Applying the standard deviation and expected value formulae already discussed, we obtain an expected NPV of £268 and standard deviation of £206.

Table 9.7 Bronson project payoffs with independent cash flows

Probability	Year 1 cash flow (£)	Year 2 cash flow (£)
0.1	100	200
0.2	200	400
0.4	300	600
0.2	400	800
0.1	500	1,000
Expected value	£300	£600
Standard deviation	£109	£219

Assuming a risk-free discount rate of 10 per cent, the expected NPV is:

$$\overline{\text{NPV}} = \frac{300}{(1.10)} + \frac{600}{(1.10)^2} - 500 = £268$$

The standard deviation of the entire proposal is found by discounting the annual variances to their present values, applying the equation:

$$\sigma = \sqrt{\sum_{t=1}^{N} \frac{\sigma_t^2}{(1+i)^2}}$$

In our simple case, this is:

$$\sigma = \sqrt{\frac{\sigma_1^2}{(1+i)^2} + \frac{\sigma_2^2}{(1+i)^4}} = \sqrt{\frac{12{,}000}{(1.1)^2} + \frac{48{,}000}{(1.1)^4}} = £206$$

The project therefore offers an expected NPV of £268 and a standard deviation of £206.

Perfectly correlated cash flows

At the other extreme from the independence assumption is the assumption that the cash flows in one year are entirely dependent upon the cash flows achieved in previous periods. When this is the case, successive cash flows are said to be perfectly correlated. Any deviation in one year from forecast directly affects the accuracy of subsequent forecasts. The effect is that, over time, the standard deviation of the probability distribution of net present values increases. The standard deviation of a stream of cash flows perfectly correlated over time is:

$$\sigma = \sum_{t=1}^{N} \frac{\sigma_t}{(1+i)^t}$$

Returning to the example in Table 9.7, but assuming perfect correlation of cash flows over time, the standard deviation for the project is:

$$\sigma = \frac{£109}{1.1} + \frac{£219}{(1.1)^2}$$
$$= £280$$

Thus the risk associated with this project is £280, assuming perfect correlation, which is higher than that for independent cash flows. Obviously, this difference would be considerably greater for longer-lived projects.

In reality, few projects are either independent or perfectly correlated over time. The standard deviation lies somewhere between the two. It will be based on the formula for the independence case, but with an additional term for the covariance between annual cash flows.

Interpreting results

While decision-makers are interested to know the degree of risk associated with a given project, their fundamental concern is whether the project will produce a positive net present value. Risk analysis can go some way to answering this question. If a project's probability distribution of expected NPVs is approximately normal, we can estimate the probability of failing to achieve at least zero NPV. In the previous example, the expected NPV was £268. This is standardised by dividing it by the standard deviation using the formula:

$$Z = \frac{X - \overline{NPV}}{\sigma}$$

where X in this case is zero and Z is the number of standardised units X lies away from the mean. Thus, in the case of the independent cash flow assumption, we have:

$$Z = \frac{0 - £268}{£206}$$
$$= -1.30 \text{ standardised units}$$

Reference to normal distribution tables reveals that there is a 0.0968 probability that the NPV will be zero or less. Accordingly there must be a (1 − 0.0968) or 90.32 per cent probability of the project producing an NPV in excess of zero.

It is probably unnecessary to attempt to measure the standard deviation for every project. Even the larger European companies tend to use probability analysis sparingly in capital project analysis. Unless cash flow forecasting is wildly optimistic, or the future economic conditions underlying all investments are far worse than anticipated, the bad news from one project should be compensated by good news from another project.

Sometimes, however, a project is of such great importance that its failure could threaten the very survival of the business. In such a case, management should be fully aware of the scale of its exposure to loss and the probability of occurrence.

Probability of failure: Microloft Ltd

Microloft Ltd, a local family-controlled company specialising in attic conversions, is currently considering investing in a major expansion giving wider geographical coverage. The NPV from the project is expected to be £330,000 with a standard deviation of £300,000. Should the project fail (perhaps because of the reaction by major competitors), the company could afford to lose £210,000 before the bank manager 'pulled the rug' and put in the receiver. What is the probability that this new project could put Microloft out of business?

We need to find the value of Z where X is the worst NPV outcome that Microloft could tolerate:

$$Z = \frac{X - \overline{NPV}}{\sigma}$$

$$= \frac{-£210 - £330}{£330} = -1.8$$

Assuming the outcomes are normally distributed, probability tables will show a 3.6 per cent chance of failure from accepting the project. A family-controlled business, like Microloft, may decide that even this relatively small chance of sending the company on to the rocks is more important than the attractive returns expected from the project.

Self-assessment Answers

9.1 While a capital project may have a high expected return, the risks involved may mean that there is the possibility that it will be unsuccessful – even to the extent of putting the whole business in jeopardy.

9.2 **(1)** Financial risk; **2** Business risk; **3** Project risk; **4** Portfolio or market risk.

9.3 X has the lower degree of risk relative to the expected returns.

Coefficient of variation: X = 400/2,000 = 0.2
Y = 400/1,000 = 0.4

9.4 **(a)** Risk – a set of outcomes for which probabilities can be assigned.
(b) Uncertainty – a set of outcomes for which accurate probabilities cannot be assigned.
(c) Risk-aversion – a preference for less risk rather than more.
(d) Expected value – the sum of the possible outcomes from a project each multiplied by their respective probability.
(e) Standard deviation – a statistical measure of the dispersion of possible outcomes around the expected value.
(f) Semi-variance – a special case of the variance which considers only outcomes less than the expected value.
(g) Mean–variance rule – Project A will be preferred to Project B if either the expected return of A exceeds that of B and the variance is equal to or less than that of B, or the expected return of A exceeds or is equal to the expected return of B and the variance is less than that of B.

9.5 Monte Carlo simulation involves constructing a mathematical model which captures the essential characteristics of the proposal throughout its life as it encounters random events. It is useful for major projects where probabilities can be assigned to key factors (e.g. selling price or project life) which are essentially independent.

Questions

1 *Solution in Appendix A (page 811).* Explain the importance of risk in capital budgeting.

2 *Solution in Appendix A (page 811).* Explain the distinction between project risk, business risk, financial risk and portfolio risk.

3 *Solution in Appendix A (page 811).* The 'wood pulp' project has an initial cost of £13,000 and the firm's risk-free interest rate is 10 per cent. If certainty equivalents and net cash flows (NCF) for the project are as below, should the project be accepted?

Year	Certainty equivalents	Net cash flows (£)
1	0.90	9,000
2	0.85	7,000
3	0.80	7,000
4	0.75	5,000
5	0.70	5,000
6	0.65	5,000
7	0.60	5,000

4 *Solution in Appendix A (page 811).* Mystery Enterprises has a proposal costing £800. Using a 10 per cent cost of capital, compute the expected NPV, standard deviation and coefficient of variation, assuming independent interperiod cash flows.

Probability	Year 1 net cash flow (£)	Year 2 net cash flow (£)
0.2	400	300
0.3	500	400
0.3	600	500
0.2	700	600

5 Mikado plc is considering launching a new product involving capital investment of £180,000. The machine has a four-year life and no residual value. Sales volumes of 6,000 units are forecast for each of the four years. The product has a selling price of £60 and a variable cost of £36 per unit. Additional fixed overheads of £50,000 will be incurred. The cost of capital is 12.5 per cent p.a. Present a report to the directors of Mikado plc giving:

(a) the net present values
(b) the percentage amount each variable can deteriorate before the project becomes unacceptable
(c) a sensitivity graph

6 Devonia (Laboratories) Ltd has recently carried out successful clinical trials on a new type of skin cream, which has been developed to reduce the effects of ageing. Research and development costs in relation to the new product amount to £160,000. In order to gauge the market potential of the new product, an independent firm of market research consultants was hired at a cost of £15,000. The market research report submitted by the consultants indicates that the skin cream is likely to have a product life of four years and could be sold to retail chemists and large department stores at a price of £20 per 100 ml container. For each of the four years of the new product's life sales demand has been estimated as follows:

Number of 100 ml containers sold	Probability of occurrence
11,000	0.3
14,000	0.6
16,000	0.1

If the company decides to launch the new product, production can begin at once. The equipment necessary to make the product is already owned by the company and originally cost £150,000. At the end of the new product's life, it is estimated that the equipment could be sold for £35,000. If the company decides against launching the new product, the equipment will be sold immediately for £85,000 as it will be of no further use to the company.

The new skin cream will require two hours' labour for each 100 ml container produced. The cost of labour for the new product is £4.00 per hour. Additional workers will have to be recruited to produce the new product. At the end of the product's life the workers are unlikely to be offered further work with the company and redundancy costs of £10,000 are expected. The cost of the ingredients for each 100 ml container is £6.00. Additional overheads arising from the product are expected to be £15,000 p.a.

The new skin cream has attracted the interest of the company's competitors. If the company decides not to produce and sell the skin cream, it can sell the patent rights to a major competitor immediately for £125,000.

Devonia (Laboratories) Ltd has a cost of capital of 12 per cent.

Ignore taxation.

Required

(a) Calculate the expected net present value (ENPV) of the new product.

(b) State, with reasons, whether or not Devonia (Laboratories) Ltd should launch the new product.

(c) Discuss the strengths and weaknesses of the expected net present value approach for making investment decisions.

(Certified Diploma)

7 Plato Pharmaceuticals Ltd has invested £300,000 to date in developing a new type of insect repellent. The repellent is now ready for production and sale and the marketing director estimates that the product will sell 150,000 bottles per annum over the next five years. The selling price of the insect repellent will be £5 per bottle and the variable costs are estimated to be £3 per bottle. Fixed costs (excluding depreciation) are expected to be £200,000 per annum. This figure is made up of £160,000 additional fixed costs and £40,000 fixed costs relating to the existing business which will be apportioned to the new product.

In order to produce the repellent, machinery and equipment costing £520,000 will have to be purchased immediately. The estimated residual value of this machinery and equipment in five years time is £100,000. The company calculates depreciation on a straight-line basis.

The company has a cost of capital of 12 per cent. Ignore taxation.

Required

(a) Calculate the net present value of the product.

(b) Undertake sensitivity analysis to show by how much the following factors would have to change before the product ceased to be worthwhile:

  (i) the discount rate

  (ii) the initial outlay on machinery and equipment

  (iii) the net operating cash flows

  (iv) the residual value of the machinery and equipment

(c) Discuss the strengths and weaknesses of sensitivity analysis in dealing with risk and uncertainty.

(d) State, with reasons, whether or not you feel the project should go ahead.

(Certified Diploma)

8 The managing director of Tigwood Ltd believes that a market exists for 'microbooks'. He has proposed that the company should market 100 best-selling books on microfiche, which can be read using a special microfiche reader that is connected to a television screen. A microfiche containing an entire book can be purchased from a photographic company at 40 per cent of the average production cost of best-selling paperback books.

The average cost of producing paperback books is estimated at £1.50, and the average selling price of paperbacks is £3.95 each. Copyright fees of 20 per cent of the average selling price of the paperback books would be payable to the publishers of the paperbacks plus an initial lump sum that is still being negotiated, but is expected to be £1.5 million. No tax allowances are available on this lump-sum payment. An agreement with the publishers would be signed for a period of six years. Additional variable costs of staffing, handling and marketing are 20p per microfiche, and fixed costs are negligible.

Tigwood Ltd has spent £100,000 on market research, and expects sales to be 1,500,000 units per year at an initial unit price of £2.

The microfiche reader would be produced and marketed by another company.

Tigwood would finance the venture with a bank loan at an interest rate of 16 per cent per year. The company's money (nominal) cost of equity and real cost of equity are estimated to be 23 per cent p.a. and 12.6 per cent p.a., respectively. Tigwood's money weighted average cost of capital and real weighted average cost of capital are 18 per cent p.a. and 8 per cent p.a., respectively. The risk-free rate of interest is 11 per cent p.a. and the market return is 17 per cent p.a.

Corporation Tax is at the rate of 35 per cent, payable in the year the profit occurs. All cash flows may be assumed to be at the year end, unless otherwise stated.

Required

(a) Calculate the expected net present value of the microbooks project.

(b) Explain the reasons for your choice of discount rate in the answer to part (a). Discuss whether this rate is likely to be the most appropriate to use in the analysis of the proposed project.

(c) **(i)** Using sensitivity analysis, estimate by what percentage each of the following would have to change before the project was no longer expected to be viable:

initial outlay
annual contribution
the life of the agreement
the discount rate

(ii) What are the limitations of this sensitivity analysis?

(d) What further information would be useful to help the company decide whether to undertake the microbook project?

(ACCA)

9 The general manager of the nationalised postal service of a small country, Zedland, wishes to introduce a new service. This service would offer same-day delivery of letters and parcels posted before 10 a.m. within a distance of 150 km. The service would require 100 new vans costing $8,000 each and 20 trucks costing $18,000 each. One hundred and eighty new workers would be employed at an average annual wage of $13,000, and five managers on average annual salaries of $20,000 would be moved from their existing duties, where they would not be replaced.

Two postal rates are proposed. In the first year of operation letters will cost $0.525 and parcels $5.25. Market research undertaken at a cost of $50,000 forecasts that demand will average 15,000 letters per working day and 500 parcels per working day during the first year, and 20,000 letters per day and 750 parcels per day thereafter. There is a five-day working week. Annual running and maintenance costs on similar new vans and trucks are estimated to be $2,000 per van and $4,000 per truck, respectively, in the first year of operation. These costs will increase by 20 per cent p.a. (excluding the effects of inflation). Vehicles are depreciated over a five-year period on a straight-line basis. Depreciation is tax-allowable and the vehicles will have negligible scrap value at the end of five years. Advertising in Year 1 will cost $500,000 and in Year 2 $250,000. There will be no advertising after Year 2. Existing premises will be used for the new service, but additional costs of $150,000 per year will be incurred.

All the above cost data are current estimates and exclude any inflation effects. Wage and salary costs and all other costs are expected to rise because of inflation by approximately 5 per cent p.a. during the five-year planning horizon of the postal service. The government of Zedland will not permit annual price increases within nationalised industries to exceed the level of inflation.

Nationalised industries are normally required by the government to earn at least an annual after-tax return of 5 per cent on average investment and to achieve, on average, at least zero net present value on their investments.

The new service would be financed half by internally generated funds and half by borrowing on the capital market at an interest rate of 12 per cent p.a. The opportunity cost of capital for the postal service is estimated to be 14 per cent p.a. Corporate taxes in Zedland, to which the postal service is subject, are at the rate of 30 per cent for annual profits of up to $500,000 and 40 per cent for the balance in excess of $500,000. Tax is payable one year in arrears. All transactions may be assumed to be on a cash basis and to occur at the end of the year, with the exception of the initial investment, which would be required almost immediately.

Required

(a) Acting as an independent consultant, prepare a report advising whether the new postal service should be introduced. Include a discussion of other factors that might need to be taken into account before a final decision was made. State clearly any assumptions that you make.

(b) Monte Carlo simulation has been suggested as a possible method of estimating the net present value of a project. Briefly assess the advantages and disadvantages of using this technique in investment appraisal.

(ACCA)

Practical assignment

Describe the types of risks associated with investment decisions in a firm known to you. (If necessary, read the Annual Report of a major company, like BP Amoco plc, to familiarise yourself with a company.) Suggest how these risks should be formally assessed within their investment appraisal process.

10 Relationships between investments: portfolio theory

Pearson's diversification

The following extract from an article in *The Guardian* illustrates the experience of Pearson plc, a company that had grown by extensive diversification. Although dating back to the recession of the early 1980s, the message still packs a powerful punch.

> Even secure diversified groups like Pearson are not immune from the recession. There, the downturn has been particularly marked at the Pearson Longman subsidiary, underlining both the cyclical nature of the publishing business, and the particular pressure on some sections of it, like Penguin. But the more fundamental point must be that diversification alone is no real protection – in this case, the bits of the business that are doing better are too small a proportion to help the total very much. While some bits – like Midhurst Corporation in the US, and the London merchant bank Lazard – are virtually recession-proof, the body of the business has to move in line with the economy as a whole. And recent diversification into things like Madame Tussaud's hardly helps as that is affected by just the same strong pound as the publishing trade.

To discover how Pearson has changed over the years, visit its website – **www.pearson.com**. Do you think the lessons have been learned?

Learning objectives

This chapter is designed to explore the financial equivalent of the maxim 'don't put all your eggs in one basket'. In particular, it aims:

- To give the reader an understanding of the rationale behind the diversification decisions of both shareholders and companies.
- To illustrate the mechanics of portfolio construction with a user-friendly approach to statistics, using several numerical examples.

- To explain that optimal portfolio selection is a matter of personal choice.
- To examine the drawbacks of portfolio analysis as an approach to project appraisal.

A good grasp of the principles of portfolio analysis is an essential underpinning to understanding the Capital Asset Pricing Model, to be covered in Chapter 11.

10.1 Introduction

This chapter deals with the theory underlying **diversification** decisions. Diversification is a strategic device for dealing with risk. Whereas the previous chapter examined methods of risk analysis that focused on individual projects, here we study how the financial manager can exploit interrelationships between projects to adjust the risk–return characteristics of the whole enterprise. In the process, we will show why many firms develop a wide spread of activities or **portfolios**. The term 'portfolio' is usually applied to combinations of securities, but we will show that the principles underlying security portfolio formation can be applied to combinations of any type of asset, including investment projects.

Many firms diffuse their efforts across a range of products, market segments and customers in order to spread the risks of declining trade and profitability. If a firm can reduce its reliance on particular products or markets, it can more easily bear the impact of a major reverse in any single market. However, firms do not reduce their exposure to the threat of new products or new competitors for entirely negative reasons. Diversification can generate some major strategic advantages: for example, the wider the spread of activities, the greater the access to star-performing sectors of the economy. Imagine an economy divided into five sectors, with one star-performer each year whose identity is always random. A company operating in a single sector is likely to miss out in four years out of five. In such a world, it is prudent to have a stake in every sector by building a portfolio of all five activities.

Spreading the marmalade too thinly?

Tomkins plc built up a diverse range of activities in the 1980s and 1990s, although it is currently re-defining its strategy into a far more focused portfolio of operations. A statement in its 1994 Report encapsulated the risk-reducing properties of diversification:

> We deliberately spread shareholders' risk by investing in businesses which operate across a broad range of products, customers, markets, cycles and countries. We are not dependent on the fortunes of any single company, industry or economy. Tomkins' products range from lawnmowers to cakes, plumbing equipment to control instrumentation, snowblowers to marmalade.

Visit the Tomkins website to learn how it has pruned its activities – **www.tomkins.co.uk**.

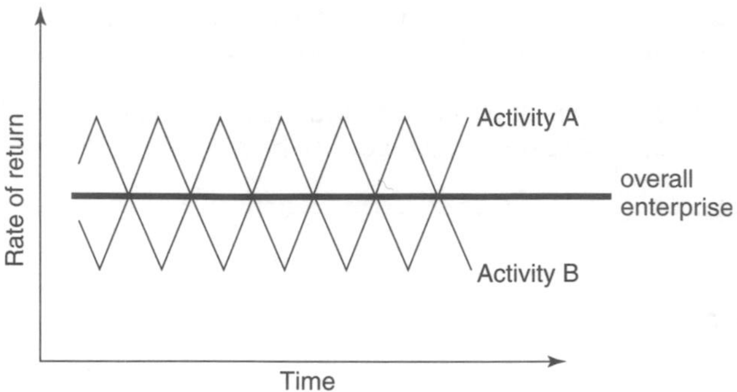

Figure 10.1 Equal and offsetting fluctuations in returns

Diversification is designed to even out the bumps in the time profile of profits and cash flows. The ideal form of diversification is to engage in activities that behave in exactly opposite ways. When sales and earnings are relatively low in one area, the adverse consequences can be offset by participation in a sector where sales and profits are relatively high. With perfect synchronisation, the time profile of overall returns will describe the pattern shown in Figure 10.1. This shows the returns from two activities: A, which moves in parallel with the economy as a whole; and B, which moves in an *exactly* opposite way. The equal and opposite fluctuations in the returns from these two activities would result in a perfectly level profile for a diversified enterprise comprising both activities. In generally adverse economic conditions, the returns from activity A, closely following the economy as a whole, will be depressed, but involvement in activity B has an exactly compensating effect. The reverse applies when the economy is expanding. The returns from B are said to be **contra-cyclical**, and the dampening effect on the variability of returns is called a **portfolio effect**.

In the case of Pearson (and maybe Tomkins), there are two important messages. First, it is not enough simply to spread your activities. Different activities are subject to different types of risk, which are not always closely related. The factors affecting the profitability of publishing operations, such as the price of newsprint, are rather different from those that determine the returns from major tourist attractions like Madame Tussauds, such as the £/$ exchange rate. If changes in these influences are random and relatively uncorrelated, diversification may significantly reduce the variability of company earnings. Second, to generate an appreciable impact on overall returns, diversification must usually be substantial in relation to the whole enterprise. Hence, the key messages of portfolio diversification are: *look for unrelated activities, and engage in significant diversification*.

10.2 Portfolio analysis: the basic principles

The theory of diversification was developed by Markowitz (1952) but can be reduced to the maxim 'don't put all your eggs in one basket'. This is a simple motto, but one that many investors persistently ignore. How often do we read heart-rending stories of small investors who have lost their savings in some shady venture or other? Why do more than 50 per cent of private investors persist in holding a single security in their investment portfolios? Perhaps they are unaware of the advantages of spreading their risks, or have not understood the arguments. Perhaps they are not risk-averse or are simply irrational.* Rational, risk-averse investors appreciate that not all investments perform well at the same time, that some may never perform well, and that a few may perform spectacularly well. Since no one can predict which investments will fall into each category in any one period, it is rational to spread one's funds over a wide set of investments.

A simple example will illustrate the remarkable potential benefits of diversification.

Achieving a perfect portfolio effect

An investor can undertake one or both of the two investments, Apple and Pear. Apple has a 50 per cent chance of achieving an 8 per cent return and a 50 per cent chance of returning 12 per cent. Pear has a 50 per cent chance of generating a return of 6 per cent and a 50 per cent chance of yielding 14 per cent. The two investments are in sectors of the economy that move in direct opposition to each other. The investor expects the return on Apple to be relatively high when that on Pear is relatively low, and vice versa. What portfolio should the investor hold?

First of all, note that the expected value (EV) of each investment's return is identical:

Investment Apple: EV = (0.5 × 8%) + (0.5 × 12%) = 4% + 6% = 10%
Investment Pear: EV = (0.5 × 6%) + (0.5 × 14%) = 3% + 7% = 10%

At first glance, it may appear that the investor would be indifferent between Apple and Pear or, indeed, any combination of them. However , there is a wide variety of possible expected returns according to how the investor 'weights' the portfolio. Moreover, a badly-weighted portfolio can offer wide variations in returns in different time periods.

For example, when Pear is the star performer, a portfolio comprising 20 per cent of Apple and 80 per cent of Pear will offer a return of:

$$\frac{\text{Apple} \qquad \text{Pear} \qquad \text{Portfolio}}{(0.2 \times 8\%) + (0.8 \times 14\%) = (1.6\% + 11.2\%)} = 12.8\%$$

When Apple is the star, the return is only:

$$(0.2 \times 12\%) + (0.8 \times 6\%) = (2.4\% + 4.8\%) = 7.2\%$$

* The real reason is probably that they have applied for shares in a privatisation, or been given shares in a building society demutualisation!

Although there should be as many good years for Apple as for Pear, resulting over the long-term in an average return of 10 per cent, *in the shorter term*, the investor would be over-exposed to the risk of a series of bad years for Pear. Happily, there is a portfolio which removes this risk entirely.

Consider a portfolio invested two-thirds in Apple and one-third in Pear. When Apple is the star, the return on the portfolio, R_p, is a weighted average of the returns from the two components:

$$R_p = (2/3 \times 12\%) + (1/3 \times 6\%) = (8\% + 2\%) = 10\%$$

Conversely, when Pear is the star, the portfolio offers a return of:

$$R_p = (2/3 \times 8\%) + (1/3 \times 14\%) = (5.33\% \times 4.67\%) = 10\%$$

With this combination, the risk-averse investor cannot go wrong! The portfolio completely removes variability in returns as there are only two possible states of the economy. Any rational risk-averse investor should select this combination of Apple and Pear to eliminate risk for a guaranteed 10 per cent return. Here, the portfolio effect is perfect, similar to that shown in Figure 10.1. However, not every investor would necessarily opt for this particular balanced portfolio. Super-optimists might load their funds entirely on to Pear, hoping for 14 per cent returns every year. This may work for a year or two, but the chances of achieving a consistent return of 14 per cent year after year are very low. The chance of achieving 14 per cent in the first year is 50 per cent, but the chance of getting 14 per cent in *each* of the first two years is (50 per cent) × (50 per cent) = 25 per cent and so on. Diversification is usually the safest (and often the most profitable) policy. We will study later in the chapter how different portfolio weightings affect the risk and return.

In this example, the opportunity to eliminate all risk arises from the *perfect negative correlation* between the two investments, but this attractive property can only be exploited by weighting the portfolio in a particular way.

Regrettably, cases of perfect negative correlation between the returns from securities are rare. Most investment returns exhibit varying degrees of positive correlation, largely according to how they depend on overall economic trends. This does not rule out risk-reducing diversification benefits, but suggests they may be less pronounced than in our example. As we will see, *the extent to which portfolio combination can achieve a reduction in risk depends on the degree of correlation between returns*. Later in the chapter, we will examine rather more realistic cases, but first we need to explore more fully the nature and measurement of portfolio risk.

Self-assessment Activity 10.1

What are the two required conditions for total elimination of portfolio risk?

(answer at end of chapter)

10.3 How to measure portfolio risk

We have just seen the importance of the degree of correlation between the returns from two investments. We saw also how the return from a portfolio could be expressed as a weighted average of the individual asset returns, the weights being the proportions of the portfolio accounted for by each of the various components. A similar relationship applies before the event: that is, if we consider the *expected value* of the return from the portfolio. The expected return on a portfolio (ER_p) comprising two assets, A and B, whose individual expected returns are ER_A and ER_B respectively, is given by:

$$ER_p = \alpha ER_A + (1 - \alpha)\, ER_B \qquad (10.1)$$

where α and $(1 - \alpha)$ are the respective weightings of assets A and B, with $\alpha + (1 - \alpha) = 1$.

The riskiness of the portfolio expresses the extent to which the actual return may deviate from the expected return. This may be expressed by the variance of the return, σ^2_p, or by its standard deviation, σ_p.

Portfolio risk

The (rather fearsome!) expression for the standard deviation of a two-asset investment portfolio, σ_p, is:

$$\sigma_p = \sqrt{[\alpha^2\sigma^2_A + (1 - \alpha)^2\sigma^2_B + 2\alpha(1 - \alpha)\mathrm{cov}_{AB}]} \qquad (10.2)$$

where

α = the proportion of the portfolio invested in asset A.
$(1 - \alpha)$ = the proportion of the portfolio invested in asset B.
$\sigma_A{}^2$ = the variance of the return on asset A.
$\sigma_B{}^2$ = the variance of the return on asset B.
cov_{AB} = the covariance of the returns for A and B.

We need now to explain the meaning of the covariance. The **covariance**, like the correlation coefficient, is a measure of the interrelationship between random variables, in this case, the returns from the two investments A and B. In other words, it measures the extent to which their returns move together, i.e. their **co-movement** or **covariability**. When the two returns move together, it has a positive value; when they move away from each other, it has a negative value; and when there is no covariability at all, its value is zero. However, unlike the correlation coefficient, whose value is restricted to a scale ranging from −1 to +1, the covariance can assume any value. It measures co-movement in *absolute* terms, whereas the correlation coefficient is a *relative* measure.

The correlation coefficient between the return on A and the return on B, r_{AB}, is simply the covariance, normalised or standardised, by the product of the two relevant standard deviations:

$$\text{Correlation coefficient between A and B's returns} = r_{AB} = \frac{\mathrm{cov}_{AB}}{\sigma_A \times \sigma_B}$$

Table 10.1 Returns under different states of the economy

State of the economy	Probability	Return from A	Return from B
E_1	0.25	−10%	+60%
E_2	0.25	−10%	−20%
E_3	0.25	+50%	−20%
E_4	0.25	+50%	+60%

Self-assessment Activity 10.2

With the figures in Table 10.1 check that the expected values for both A and B are 20 per cent, and that their respective standard deviations are 30 per cent and 40 per cent, using the formulae presented in Chapter 9.

(answer at end of chapter)

The covariance, cov_{AB}, between the returns on the two investments, A and B, is given by:

$$\text{cov}_{AB} = \sum_{i=1}^{N} [pi(R_A - ER_A)(R_B - ER_B)] \quad (10.3)$$

where R_A is the realised return from investment A, ER_A is the expected value of the return from A, R_B is the realised return from investment B, ER_B is the expected value of the return from B, and *pi* is the probability of the *i*th pair of values occurring.

Equation (10.3) tells us to calculate, for each pair of simultaneously occurring outcomes, their deviations from their respective expected values; next, to multiply these deviations together and then to weight the resulting product by the relevant probability for each pair. Finally, the sum of all weighted products of paired divergences between expected and actual outcomes defines the covariance. This relationship is more easily understood with a numerical example. Table 10.1 shows possible returns from two assets under four different economic conditions, with associated probabilities. First, do Self-assessment Activity 10.2. Then, check through the calculation in Table 10.2.

In this case, there is no covariability at all between the returns from the two assets. If the return from A increases, it is just as likely to be associated with a fall in the return from B as a concurrent increase. If the covariance (which measures the degree of co-movement in absolute terms) is zero, we should expect to find

Table 10.2 Calculating the covariance

R_A	ER_A	R_B	ER_B	$(R_A - ER_A)$	$(R_B - ER_A)$	Product	Probability	Weighted product
−10	20	+60	20	−30	+40	−1200	0.25	−300
−10	20	−20	20	−30	−40	+1200	0.25	+300
+50	20	−20	20	+30	−40	−1200	0.25	−300
+50	20	+60	20	+30	+40	+1200	0.25	+300
								$\text{covariance}_{AB} = 0$

Note: Although the rate of return figures are percentages, they have been treated as integers to clarify exposition.

the correlation coefficient (the relative measure of co-movement) is also zero. We may now demonstrate this:

$$\text{Correlation coefficient between A and B's returns} = r_{AB} = \frac{\text{cov}_{AB}}{(\sigma_A \times \sigma_B)} = \frac{0}{(30 \times 40)} = 0$$

The case of zero covariance is a convenient one, as we can see from looking at the expression for portfolio risk, σ_p.

$$\sigma_p = \sqrt{[\alpha^2\sigma_A^2 + (1 - \alpha)^2\sigma_B^2 + 2\alpha(1 - \alpha)\text{cov}_{AB}]}$$

When the covariance is zero, the third term is zero, and portfolio risk reduces to:

$$\sigma_p = \sqrt{[\alpha^2\sigma_A^2 + (1 - \alpha)^2\sigma_B^2]}$$

With zero covariance, portfolio risk is thus smaller for any portfolio compared to cases where the covariance is positive. Even better, when the covariance is negative, the third term becomes negative and risk falls even further. In general, the lowest achievable portfolio risk declines as the covariance diminishes: if it is negative, all the better. There is, however, no limit on the covariance value. If we re-express portfolio risk in terms of the correlation coefficient, we can be more specific about the greatest achievable degree of risk reduction. The formula relating covariance and correlation coefficient (Equation 10.3) can be rewritten as:

$$\text{cov}_{AB} = (r_{AB} \times \sigma_A \times \sigma_B)$$

Substituting into the general expression for portfolio risk (Equation 10.2), we derive:

$$\sigma_p = \sqrt{[\alpha^2\sigma_A^2 + (1 - \alpha)^2\sigma_B^2 + 2\alpha(1 - \alpha)r_{AB}\sigma_A\sigma_B]}$$

Clearly, when the correlation coefficient is negative, risk is reduced, but since the limit to negative correlation is minus one, this places a lower limit on σ_p. As we saw in the Apple and Pear example, this may fall to zero if the portfolio is appropriately weighted. Whether one works in terms of the covariance or the correlation coefficient is generally a matter of preference, but, sometimes, it is dictated by the information available.

The optimal portfolio

An obvious question to ask is: which is the best portfolio to hold? In this example, the two investments have the same expected values, so any portfolio we construct by combining them will also offer this expected value. The optimal portfolio is simply the one that offers the lowest level of risk. Although very few decision-makers are outright risk minimisers, any rational risk-averse manager will adopt the risk-minimising action where every alternative offers an equal expected payoff.

The minimum risk portfolio with two assets

The expression for finding the weighting required to minimise the risk of a portfolio comprising two assets, A and B, where α_A^* = the proportion invested in asset A is:

$$\alpha_A^* = \frac{\sigma_B^2 - \text{cov}_{AB}}{\sigma_A^2 + \sigma_B^2 - 2\text{cov}_{AB}} \tag{10.4}$$

Substituting the figures for the AB example into Equation 10.4, we find:

$$\alpha_A^* = \frac{40^2}{30^2 + 40^2} = \frac{1{,}600}{2{,}500} = 0.64$$

This formula tells us that, to minimise risk, we should place 64 per cent of our funds in A and 36 per cent in B.

Self-assessment Activity 10.3

Verify that the standard deviation of this portfolio is 24%.

(answer at end of chapter)

In the next section, we analyse the more likely, and more interesting, case where both the risks and expected returns of the two components differ.

10.4 Portfolio analysis where risk and return differ

Suppose we are offered the two investments, Z and Y, whose characteristics are shown in Table 10.3. Which should we undertake? Or should we undertake some combination? To answer these questions, we need to consider the possible combinations of risk and return.

Let us assume that the two assets can be combined in any proportions, i.e. the two assets are perfectly divisible, as with security investments. There is an infinite number of possible combinations of risk and return. However, for

Table 10.3 Differing returns and risks

Asset	Expected return	Standard deviation
Z	15%	20%
Y	35%	40%

Correlation coefficient$_{ZY}$ = −0.25; Covariance$_{zy}$ = (−0.25) × (20) × (40) = −200

Table 10.4 Portfolio risk–return combinations (%)

Z Weighting	Y Weighting	Expected return	Standard deviation
100	0	15	20
75	25	20	16
50	50	25	20
25	75	30	29
0	100	35	40

simplicity, we confine our attention to the restricted range of portfolios whose risk and return characteristics are shown in Table 10.4.

If we wanted to minimise risk, we would invest solely in asset Z, since this has the lowest standard deviation. However, as we move from the all-Z portfolio to the 75 per cent of Z plus 25 per cent of Y combination, the risk of the whole portfolio diminishes and the expected return increases. Eventually, though, for portfolios more heavily weighted towards Y, the effect of Y's higher risk outweighs the beneficial effect of negative correlation, resulting in rising overall risk.

Figure 10.2 traces the range of available opportunities (or **opportunity set**), shaped rather like the nose cone of an aircraft. The profile ranges from point A, representing total investment in Y, through to point C, representing total investment in Z, having described a U-turn at B.

Self-assessment Activity 10.4

Verify that the portfolio at B, involving 75 per cent of Z and 25 per cent of Y, is the minimum risk combination.

Not all combinations are of interest to the rational risk-averse manager. Comparing segment AB with the segment BC, we find that combinations lying along the latter are inefficient. For any combination along BC, we can achieve

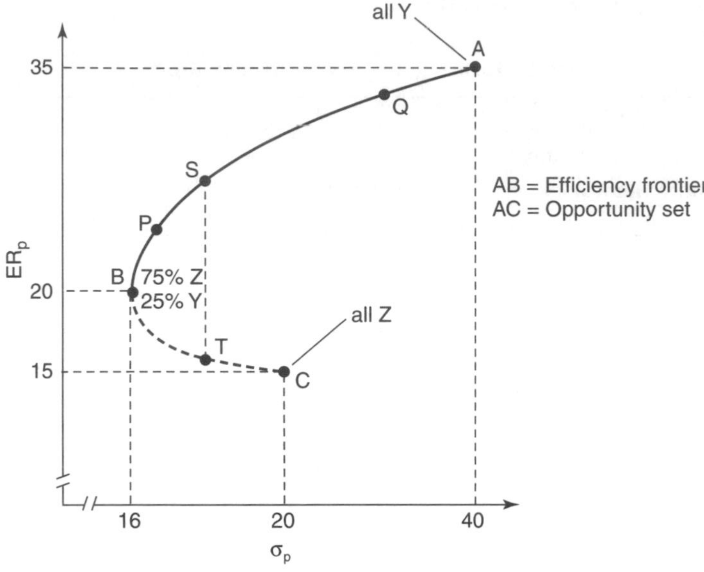

Figure 10.2 Available portfolio risk–return combinations when both assets' risks and expected returns are different

a higher return for the same risk by moving to the combination vertically above it on AB. Point S is clearly superior to T and, applying similar logic to the whole of BC, we are left with the segment AB summarising all efficient portfolios, i.e. those that maximise return for a given risk. AB is thus called the **efficiency frontier**.

However, we cannot specify an **optimal portfolio**, except for the outright risk-minimiser, who would select the portfolio at B, and for the maximiser of expected return, who would settle at point A (all Y). A risk-averse person might select any portfolio along AB, depending on his or her degree of risk aversion: that is, what additional return they would require to compensate for a specified increase in risk. For example, a highly risk-averse person might locate at point P, while the less cautions risk-averting person might locate at point Q.

This is a crucial result. The most desirable combination of risky assets depends on the decision-maker's attitude towards risk. If we know the extent of their risk-aversion – that is, how large a premium is required for a given increase in risk – we can specify the best portfolio.

Self-assessment Activity 10.5

What is meant by an efficient frontier in portfolio analysis?

(answer at end of chapter)

10.5 Different degrees of correlation

Using arbitrary values for the correlation coefficient, we have found that negative correlation offers a handsome portfolio effect, and, to a lesser degree, also with zero correlation. It is useful now to consider more carefully the general relationship between risk, correlation and return. To do this, we look at the full range of possible degrees of correlation, extending from perfect negative to perfect positive.

Say we are dealing with two investments, A and B, with Asset A offering the higher expected return but also carrying greater risk. These are shown in Figure 10.3.

Consider the following degrees of correlation:

1 *Perfect positive.* In this case, it is not possible to achieve a portfolio effect at all. Combinations of A and B locate along the straight line AB. To achieve lower risk levels, we would simply invest more in asset B, while the risk-minimising 'portfolio' is simply asset B alone.

2 *Perfect negative.* With the returns from the two assets moving in perfect opposition to each other, it is possible to eliminate risk by adding B to A, but only by weighting the portfolio correctly is it possible to fully exploit the beneficial effect of correlation. Maximum risk-reduction is achieved at point X where the portfolio risk is zero. Combinations along XB are clearly inefficient.

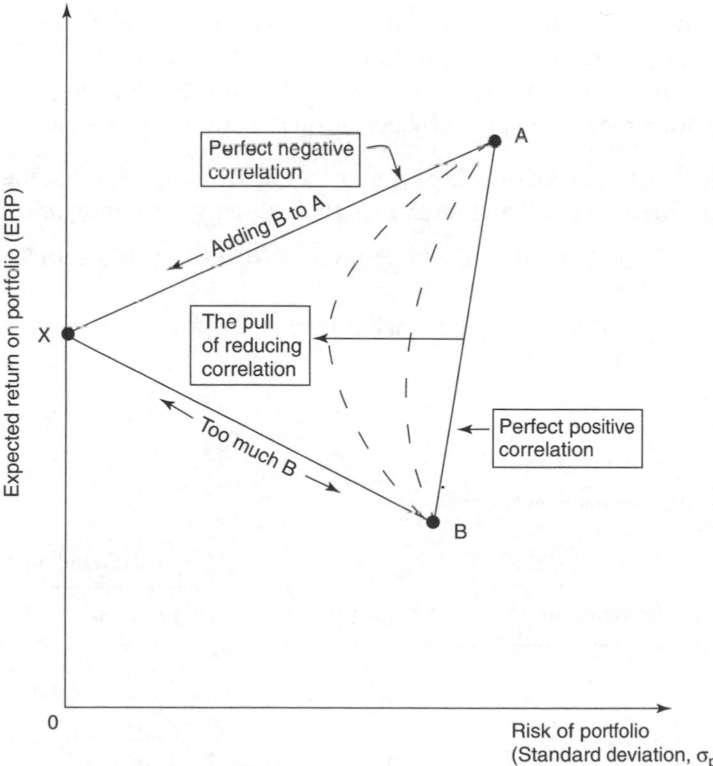

Figure 10.3 The effect on the efficiency frontier of changing correlation

3 *Intermediate values*. For correlation coefficients between +1 and −1, it is still possible to generate a portfolio effect. The lower the correlation, i.e. the further away from +1, the greater the portfolio effect achievable. Two examples are shown in Figure 10.3 as dotted lines between A and B. The characteristic 'bow' shapes result from progressively lower correlation bending the profile from its original position until we start observing the 'nose cones' identified earlier.

10.6 Worked example: Gerrybild plc

Gerrybild plc is a firm of speculative housebuilders that builds in advance of firm orders from customers. It has a given amount of capital to purchase land and raw materials and to pay labour for development purposes. It is considering two design types – a small two-bedroomed terraced town house and a large four-bedroomed 'executive' residence. The project could last a number of years and its success depends largely on general economic conditions, which will influence the demand for new houses. Some information is available on past sales patterns of similar properties in roughly similar locations – the demand is relatively higher for larger properties in buoyant economic conditions and for smaller properties in relatively depressed states of the economy. Since there appears to be a degree of inverse correlation between demand, and, therefore, net cash flows, from the two products, it seems sensible to consider diversified development. Table 10.5 shows annual net cash flow estimates for various economic conditions.

To analyse this decision problem, we need, first, to calculate the risk–return parameters of the investment, and, second, to assess the degree of correlation. This information may be obtained by performing a number of statistical operations:

1 *Calculation of expected values*. A shortcut is available, since some outcomes may occur under more than one state of the economy. Grouping data where possible:

EV_L = Expected value of a large house = (0.5 × £2,000) + (0.5 × £4,000) = £3,000

EV_S = Expected value of a small house = (0.6 × £2,000) + (0.4 × £3,000) = £2,400

Table 10.5 Returns from Gerrybild

		Estimated NPV (£) per:	
State of the economy	**Probability**	**Large house**	**Small house**
E_1	0.2	2,000	2,000
E_2	0.3	2,000	3,000
E_3	0.4	4,000	3,000
E_4	0.1	4,000	3,000

Table 10.6 Calculation of standard deviations of returns from each investment

Outcome (£)	Probability	EV (£)	Deviation (£)	Squared deviation (£)	Weighted squared deviation (£)
Large houses					
2,000	0.5	3,000	−1,000	1 m	0.5 m
4,000	0.5	3,000	+1,000	1 m	0.5 m
				$\sigma_L^2 =$ Variance =	1 m
				hence $\sigma_L =$	$\sqrt{1\text{ m}}$
					= 1,000
Small houses					
2,000	0.6	2,400	−400	160,000	96,000
3,000	0.4	2,400	+600	360,000	144,000
				$\sigma_S^2 =$ Variance =	240,000
				hence $\sigma_S =$	$\sqrt{240{,}000}$
					= 489

2 *Calculation of project risks.* We now apply the usual expression for the standard deviation. The calculations for each activity are shown in Table 10.6. Clearly, the relative money-spinner, the large house project, is also the more risky activity.
3 *Calculation of covariability.* Table 10.7 presents the calculation of the covariance in tabular form, following the steps itemised in Section 10.3.

The covariance of −£200,000 suggests a strong element of inverse association. This is confirmed by the value of the correlation coefficient:

$$r_{LS} = \frac{\text{cov}_{LS}}{\sigma_L \times \sigma_S} = \frac{-200{,}000}{(1{,}000)(489)} = -0.41$$

There are clearly significant portfolio benefits to exploit. To offer concrete advice to the builder, we would require information on his risk–return preferences, but we can specify the available set of portfolio combinations. Rather than compute the full set of opportunities, we will identify the minimum risk portfolio, to enable construction of the overall risk–return profile.

Table 10.7 Calculation of the covariance

Outcomes (£)						
R_L	R_S	Probability	$(EV_L - R_L)$ (£)	$(EV_S - R_S)$ (£)	Product (£)	Weighted product (£)
2,000	2,000	0.2	−1,000	−400	+400,000	+80,000
2,000	3,000	0.3	−1,000	+600	−600,000	−180,000
4,000	2,000	0.4	+1,000	−400	−400,000	−160,000
4,000	3,000	0.1	+1,000	+600	+600,000	+60,000
					$COV_{LS} =$	−200,000

The minimum risk portfolio

Using Equation (10.4), and defining $\alpha_L{}^*$ as the proportion of the portfolio (i.e. of the available capital) devoted to large houses and that minimises risk, we have:

$$\alpha_L{}^* = \frac{(\sigma_S{}^2 - \text{cov}_{LS})}{(\sigma_S{}^2 + \sigma_L{}^2 - 2\,\text{cov}_{LS})} = \frac{240{,}000 + 200{,}000}{240{,}000 + 1\text{ m} + 400{,}000}$$

$$= \frac{440{,}000}{1{,}640{,}000} = 0.27$$

If Gerrybild wanted to minimise risk, it would have to invest 27 per cent of its capital in developing large houses and 73 per cent in developing small houses.

Self-assessment Activity 10.6

Verify that the lowest achievable portfolio standard deviation is £349 and the expected NPV per house built from the minimum risk portfolio is £2,562.

(answer at end of chapter)

The opportunity set

We now have assembled sufficient information to display the full range of opportunities available to Gerrybild. The opportunity set ABC is shown on Figure 10.4 as the familiar nose cone shape. If Gerrybild risk-averts, only segment AB is of interest, but precisely where along this segment it will choose to locate depends on its attitude towards risk.

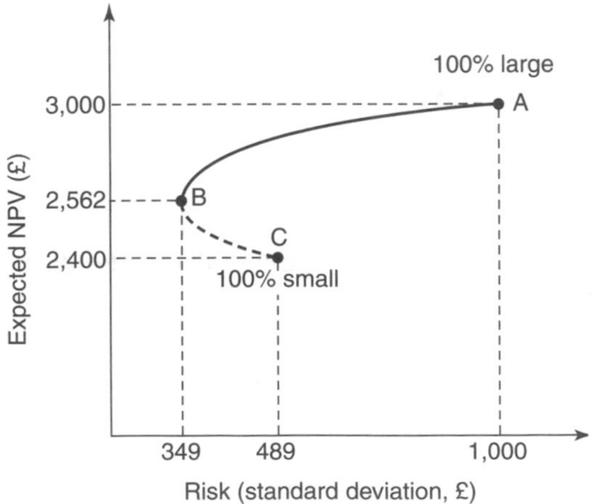

Figure 10.4 Gerrybild's opportunity set

Self-assessment Activity 10.7

Using Figure 10.4, distinguish between risk minimisation and risk aversion.

(answer at end of chapter)

10.7 Portfolios with more than two components

Having so far looked only at simple two-asset portfolios, it is now useful to extend the analysis to more comprehensive combinations (see Figure 10.5). Imagine three assets are available, A, B and C, for each of which we have estimates of expected return and standard deviation, and also the covariance (and hence correlation) between each pair of assets. Imagine further that, whereas A and B are quite closely correlated, B and C are less so, and that correlation between A and C is even weaker.

Using a technique called Quadratic Programming, developed by Sharpe (1963), we can specify all available portfolios comprising one, two or three assets. Although there are only seven possible combinations of whole investments (A, B and C alone, A plus B, B plus C, A plus C and all three together), there are

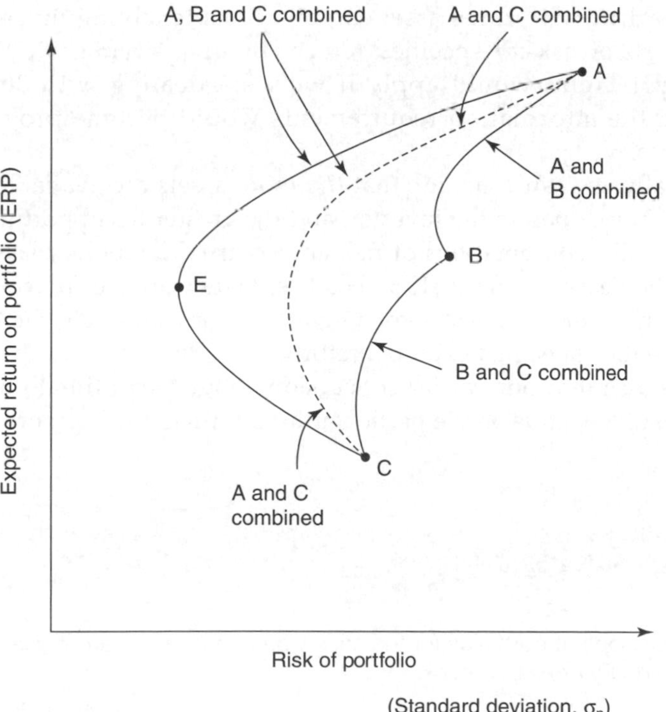

Figure 10.5 Portfolio combinations with three assets

myriads of combinations if we allow for divisibility of assets. The full range of available portfolios, i.e. risk–return combinations, is shown by the opportunity set in the form of an envelope, or 'bat-wing'.

The corners represent individual assets, while two-asset combinations are shown by the solid lines AB and BC and the dotted profile AC. Notice that by combining A and C, the investor can exploit the relative lack of correlation by accessing relatively more attractive portfolios in terms of their respective returns for particular levels of risk. The opportunity set thus moves inwards as assets with lower correlation are included. However, he can now access even more attractive combinations of A and C by combining all three assets. Points inside the envelope, or along the outer boundary, represent all possible combinations of A, B and C.

Notice that the investor now has access to a far wider range of investment combinations. If he is limited to combinations of only two assets, say A and B, as we saw in earlier analyses, he is restricted to risk–return combinations along AB or BC, depending on which two assets are combined. However, if access is opened up to include a third asset, the expanded range of combinations now available allows him to select far superior mixes of risk and return. For example, combinations within the envelope and on its upper bound, AEC, are superior to most of the two-asset portfolios available along AB and BC.

As before, we can apply the concept of dominance to differentiate between efficient and inefficient combinations. Clearly, all points lying beneath the upper edge AE and those along the segment EC are inefficient. The efficient set is therefore AE, identical in shape to our earlier profile, except that we are dealing with three asset combinations (enabling investors to achieve lower levels of risk for specified returns by diversifying away yet more risk). Similar principles would apply if we were dealing with 30 or 300 assets, although the information requirements would become progressively more formidable.

Generally, we can conclude that the more assets are available, the wider the range of choice open to the investor, and the greater his opportunities to achieve more desirable combinations of risk and return. The more assets under consideration, the nearer to the vertical axis lies the envelope of portfolios. Hence, the higher is the return achievable for a given risk, or conversely, the lower is the risk achievable for a specified expected return.

Notice also that our earlier conclusion about the optimal portfolio remains valid – it still depends on the particular investor's risk–return preferences.

Self-assessment Activity 10.8

Draw an envelope of portfolios for the case where four assets are available to invest in, either individually or as portfolios.

(answer at end of chapter)

10.8 Can we use this for project appraisal? Some reservations

The Gerrybild example illustrates some drawbacks with the portfolio approach to handling project risk.

1. Most projects can be undertaken only in a very restricted range of sizes or even on an 'all-or-nothing' basis. This does not entirely undermine the portfolio approach – it simply means that the range of combinations available is much narrower. Besides, enterprises are often undertaken on a joint venture basis (e.g. in large, high-risk activities like Eurotunnel and Airbus and many cross-border automobile operations), where the various parties had some freedom to select the extent of their participation.
2. A more severe problem is the implication of constant returns to scale. Our analyses imply that if a smaller version of a project is undertaken, the percentage returns, or the absolute return per pound invested, will remain unchanged. For example, if the return on a whole project is 20 per cent, the return from doing 30 per cent of the same project is still 20 per cent. This may apply for investment in securities, but is unlikely for investment projects, where there is often a minimum size below which there are zero or negative returns, and, thereafter, increasing returns to scale.
3. We should be wary of any approach that relies on subjective assessments of probabilities, or at least wary of the probabilities themselves. In the case of repetitive activities, such as replacement of equipment, about which a substantial data bank of costs and benefits has been compiled, the probabilities may have some basis in reality. In other cases, such as major new product developments, probabilities are largely based on inspired guesswork. Different decision analysts may well formulate different 'guesstimates' about the chances of particular events occurring. However, the subjective nature of probabilities used in practice need not be a deterrent if the estimates are well supported by reasoned argument, and therefore instil confidence.
4. Since attitudes to risk determine choice, we need to know the decision-maker's utility function, which summarises his or her preferences for different monetary amounts. The difficulties of obtaining information about an individual manager's utility function (let alone for a group) are formidable, as Swalm (1966) has shown. Besides, we should really be seeking to apply the risk–return preferences of shareholders rather than those of managers.
5. The portfolio approach to analysing project risk seems unduly management-oriented. Managers formulate the assessments of alternative payoffs, assess the relevant probabilities and determine what combinations of activities the enterprise should undertake. Managers are considerably less mobile and less well diversified than shareholders, who can buy and sell securities more or less at will. Managers can hardly shrug off a poor investment outcome if it jeopardises the future of the enterprise or, more pertinently, their job security. Most managers are more risk-averse than shareholders, resulting in the likelihood of sub-optimal investment decisions. Here, we see another

manifestation of the agency problem – how do we get managers to accept the levels of risk that owners are prepared to tolerate?

These may appear to be highly damaging criticisms of the portfolio approach, especially as it applies to investment decisions. However, although having limited operational usefulness for many investment projects, it provides the infrastructure of a more sophisticated approach to investment decision-making under risk, the **Capital Asset Pricing Model** (CAPM). This is based on an examination of the risk–return characteristics and resulting portfolio opportunities of securities, rather than physical investment opportunities.

The CAPM explains how individual securities are valued, or priced, in efficient capital markets. Essentially, this involves discounting the future expected returns from holding a security at a rate that adequately reflects the degree of risk incurred in holding that security. A major contribution of the CAPM is the determination of the premium for risk demanded by the market from different securities. This provides a clue as to the appropriate discount rate to apply when evaluating risky projects. The CAPM is analysed in the next chapter.

Summary

This chapter has examined some reasons why firms diversify their activities, and has considered the extent to which the theory of portfolio analysis can provide operational guidelines for diversification decisions.

Key points

- Both firms and individuals diversify investments – firms build portfolios of business activities and individuals build portfolios of securities.
- An important motive for business diversification is to reduce fluctuations in returns.
- Variations in returns can be totally eliminated only if the investments concerned have perfect negative correlation and if the portfolio is weighted so as to minimise risk.
- The expected return from a portfolio is a weighted average of the returns expected from its components, the weights determined by the proportion of capital invested in each activity or security. For a portfolio comprising the two assets, A and B:

  $$ER_p = \alpha ER_A + (1 - \alpha)ER_B$$

- Portfolio risk, however, is given by a square-root formula:

  $$\sigma_p = \sqrt{[\alpha^2\sigma_A^2 + (1 - \alpha)^2\sigma_B^2 + 2\alpha(1 - \alpha)\,\text{cov}_{AB}]}$$

- The degree of covariability between the returns expected from the components of the portfolios can be measured by the covariance, cov_{AB}, or by the correlation coefficient, r_{AB}. The lower the degree of covariability, the lower is the risk of the portfolio (for given weightings).
- The available risk–return combinations for mixing investments are shown by the opportunity set.

- Some combinations can be rejected as inefficient. Rational risk-averting investors focus only on the efficient set.
- The optimal portfolio for any investor depends on their attitude to risk: that is, how risk-averse they are.
- In practice, there are serious difficulties in applying the portfolio techniques to physical investment decisions.

Further reading

The classic works on portfolio theory are by Markowitz (1952), Sharpe (1964) and Tobin (1958) (all of whom have won Nobel Prizes for Economics). See also Fama and Miller (1972), Sharpe and Alexander (1990), Levy and Sarnat (1984) and Copeland and Weston (1988) for more developed analyses, and also proofs and derivations of the formulae used in this chapter. Finally, Markowitz's Nobel address (1991) is well worth reading. Dobbins *et al.* (1994) offer an up-to-date survey of empirical work in this area.

Self-assessment Answers

10.1 To eliminate the risk of, say, a two-asset portfolio, there would have to be perfect negative correlation between the returns from the two assets, and also the portfolio would have to be 'correctly' weighted.

10.2 Expected values:

A: EV = (0.5 × −10%) + (0.5 × 50%) = 20%
B: EV = (0.5 × −20%) + (0.5 × 60%) = 20%

Standard deviations

$$\begin{aligned} \text{A: } \sigma_A &= \sqrt{[(0.5)(-10\% - 20\%)^2 + (0.5)(50\% - 20\%)^2]} \\ &= \sqrt{[(0.5 \times 900) + (0.5 \times 900)]} \\ &= \sqrt{900} = 30 \text{ (i.e. 30\%)} \end{aligned}$$

$$\begin{aligned} \text{B: } \sigma_B &= \sqrt{[(0.5)(60\% - 20\%)^2 + (0.5)(-20\% - 20\%)^2]} \\ &= \sqrt{[(0.5 \times 1600) + (0.5 \times 1600)]} \\ &= \sqrt{1600} = 40 \text{ (i.e. 40\%)} \end{aligned}$$

10.3 To minimise portfolio risk, let α^* = the proportion invested in asset Z. Using the risk-minimising formula 10.4:

$$\alpha^* = \frac{\sigma_y^2 - COV_{zy}}{\sigma_z^2 + \sigma_y^2 - 2COV_{zy}}$$

$$= \frac{40^2 - (-200)}{200^2 + 40^2 - (2 \times -200)}$$

$$= \frac{1600 + 200}{400 + 1600 + 400}$$
$$= 1800/2400 = 0.75, \text{ i.e. } 75\%$$

10.5 An efficient frontier is a schedule tracing out all the available portfolio combinations that either minimise risk for a given expected return or maximise expected return for a given risk.

10.6 Expected NPV = (0.27 × £3,000) + (0.73 × £2,400)
= £2,562

$$\text{Standard deviation} = \sqrt{[0.27)^2 (1{,}000)^2 + (0.73)^2 (489)^2 + 2(0.27)(0.73)(-200{,}000)]}$$
$$= \sqrt{72{,}900 + 127{,}428 - 78{,}840}$$
$$= \sqrt{121{,}288}$$
$$= £349$$

10.7 The outright risk-minimiser locates at point B, the portfolio with minimum possible risk. However, risk-averters are willing to accept higher levels of risk if offered sufficient additional rewards, i.e. higher returns. Hence, any portfolio along AB is consistent with risk aversion. The lower the investor's concern with risk, the nearer to point A he/she will locate.

10.8 With four separate assets to choose from, the investor faces a wider array of available portfolios. The envelope that summarises his/her opportunities has the same basic shape as in the text, but with an extra 'corner' representing the fourth asset, denoted by point D in Figure 10.6. Notice that all sorts of configurations of the envelope are possible, depending on the location of the four assets.

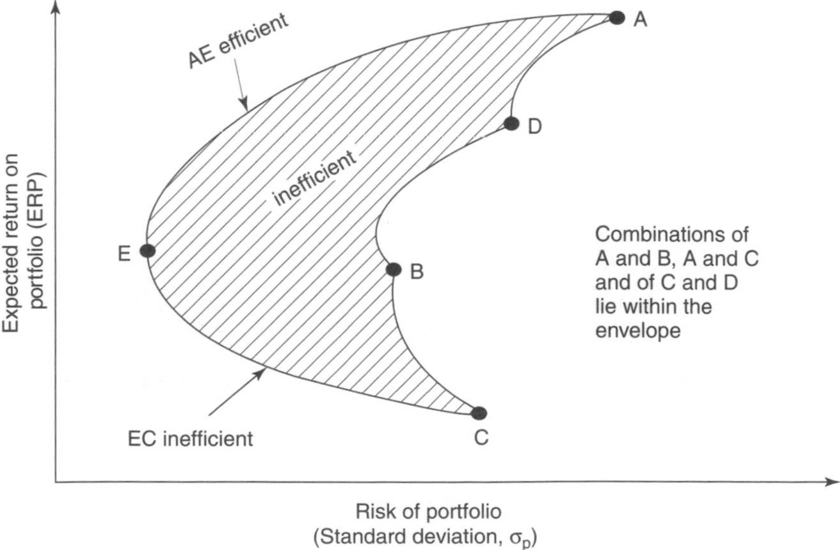

Figure 10.6 Portfolio combinations with four assets

Questions

1 *Solution in Appendix A (page 812).* The returns on investment in two projects, X and Y, have standard deviations of 30 per cent and 45 per cent respectively. The correlation coefficient between the returns on the two investments is 0.2. What is the standard deviation of a portfolio containing *equal* proportions of the two investments?

2 *Solution in Appendix A (page 812).* Determine the risk-minimising portfolios for the following two asset portfolios.

(i) $ER_A = 20\%$; $ER_B = 12\%$; $\sigma_A = 12\%$; $\sigma_B = 6\%$; $r_{AB} = +½$
(ii) $ER_A = 11\%$; $ER_B = 5\%$; $\sigma_A = 15\%$; $\sigma_B = 1\%$; $r_{AB} = -1$
(iii) $ER_A = 11\%$; $ER_B = 5\%$; $\sigma_A = 15\%$; $\sigma_B = 1\%$; $r_{AB} = 0$
(iv) $ER_A = 8\%$; $ER_B = 10\%$; $\sigma_A = 3\%$; $\sigma_B = 7\%$; $r_{AB} = +1$

3 *Solution in Appendix A (page 812).* Tomb-zapper plc manufactures computer video games. It is considering whether to expand production at its existing site in 'Silicon Glen' in Scotland, or to start production in a 'greenfield site' in China, where labour costs are considerably lower than in Europe. The IRRs for each project depend on average rates of growth in the world economy over the ten-year life span of the project. These are expected to be:

World Growth	Probability	IRR China	IRR Scotland
Rapid	0.3	50%	10%
Stable	0.4	25%	15%
Slow	0.3	0%	16%

Tomb-zapper wants to exploit the less than perfect correlation between the returns from the two projects, without over-committing itself to the China investment.

Required

(a) What is the expected return and standard deviation of return for each separate project?
(b) Determine the expected return and standard deviation of an expansion programme that involves 25 per cent of available funds in China and 75 per cent in the Scottish location.

4 *Solution in Appendix A (page 813).* Nissota, a Japanese-based car manufacturer, is evaluating two overseas locations for a proposed expansion of production facilities at a site in Ireland and another on Humberside. The likely future return from investment in each site depends to a great extent on future economic conditions. Three scenarios are postulated, and the internal rate of return from each investment is computed under each scenario. The returns with their estimated probabilities are shown below:

	Internal rate of return (%)	
Probability	Ireland	Humberside
0.3	20	10
0.3	10	30
0.3	15	20

There is zero correlation between the returns from the two sites.

Required

(a) Calculate the expected value of the IRR and the standard deviation of the return from investment in each location.

(b) What would be the expected return and the standard deviation of the following split investment strategies:

(i) committing 50 per cent of available funds to the site in Ireland and 50 per cent to Humberside

(ii) committing 75 per cent of funds to the site in Ireland and 25 per cent to the Humberside site

5 The management of Gawain plc is evaluating two projects whose returns depend on the future state of the economy as shown below:

Probability	**IRR_A (%)**	**IRR_B (%)**
0.3	27	35
0.4	18	15
0.3	5	20

The project (or projects) accepted would double the size of Gawain.

Required

(a) Explain how a portfolio should be constructed to produce an expected return of 20 per cent.

(b) Calculate the correlation between projects A and B, and assess the degree of risk of the portfolio in (a).

(c) Gawain's existing activities have a standard deviation of 10 per cent. How does the addition of the portfolio analysed in (a) and (b) affect risk?

Practical assignment

Select a company with a reasonably wide portfolio of activities. Such companies do not always give segmental earnings figures, but they usually divulge sales figures for their component activities. By looking at the annual reports for three or four years you can obtain a series of annual sales figures for each activity.

Assess the degree of past volatility of the sales of each sub-unit and their degree of inter-correlation. Also, see whether you can assess the extent of the correlation between each segment and the overall enterprise. How well diversified does your selected company appear to be? What qualifications should you make in your analysis?

11 Setting the risk premium: the Capital Asset Pricing Model

Target practice does not make perfect

Efficient capital markets should generate an upward-sloping risk–return frontier on which all securities locate – the higher the risk, the higher the required return. The Capital Asset Pricing Model (CAPM) explains how great a premium is required for specified risks. Although companies acknowledge the need to discount returns expected from risky activities at higher rates, surveys conducted by the Confederation of British Industry (CBI) reveal some alarming information about how firms approach capital investment decisions.

In 1998, the CBI surveyed 326 firms with turnovers above £20 million and with capital expenditures ranging from rather less than £1 million to well over £25 million. Two points stood out:

1 Firms tended to apply much higher rates than appear warranted by theoretical best practice, with those using IRR setting higher hurdle rates than users of the NPV method.

2 Firms tend not to adjust their hurdle rates when inflation rates change. Only 60 per cent of respondents conducted a regular review of hurdle rates, and there was little evidence that targets had fallen since the previous study in 1994, despite lower inflation.

Setting too high a cut-off rate for investment projects carries two dangers. First, it may curtail the volume of capital expenditure to the detriment of business growth. Second, setting too high a target may lead to over-investment in high risk, speculative projects (albeit potentially lucrative ones) at the expense of more secure 'bread and butter' capital projects.

Source: *Target Practice,* Confederation of British Industry, 1998

Learning objectives

This chapter deals with the rate of return required by shareholders of an all-equity financed company building on portfolio theory. Its specific aims are:

- To explain what type of risk is relevant for valuing capital assets.
- To explain what a 'Beta coefficient' is.
- To determine the appropriate risk premium to incorporate into a discount rate, whether for investment in securities or in capital projects.
- To examine the case for *corporate* diversification.
- To examine some criticisms of the CAPM.

An understanding of the significance of Beta coefficients is particularly important in appreciating how financial managers should view risk.

11.1 Introduction

In Chapters 9 and 10, we examined various methods of handling risk and uncertainty in project appraisal, ranging from sensitivity analysis to diversification, to exploit the less than perfect correlation between the returns from risky investments. Most of these approaches aim to identify the sources and extent of project risk and to assess whether the expected returns sufficiently compensate investors for bearing the risk. Utility theory suggests that, as risk increases, rational risk-averse people require higher returns, justifying the common practice of adjusting discount rates for risk. However, none of these approaches offers an explicit guide to measuring the precise reward investors should seek for incurring a particular level of risk.

The CAPM is a theory originally devised by Sharpe (1964) to explain how the capital market sets share prices. It now provides the infrastructure of much of modern financial theory and research and offers important insights into measuring risk and setting risk premiums. In particular, it shows how the study of security prices can help in assessing required rates of return on investment projects. However, as we shall see, the CAPM has not gone unchallenged.

11.2 Security valuation and discount rates

Asset value is governed by two factors – the stream of expected benefits from holding the asset and their 'quality', or likely variability. For example, the value of a single-project company is assessed by discounting future project cash flows at a discount rate reflecting their risk. The value, V_o, of a company newly formed by issuing one million shares to exploit a one-year project offering a single net cash flow of £10 million, at a 25 per cent discount rate, is:

$$V_o = \frac{£10\text{ m}}{(1.25)} = £8\text{ m}$$

This suggests a market price per share of £8 m/1 m shares = £8. This would be the value established by an efficient capital market taking account of all known information about the company's future prospects.

Sometimes, the 'correct' discount rate is unclear to the firm. A major contribution of the CAPM is to explain how discount rates are established and hence how securities are valued. However, from the capital market value of a company, we can 'work backwards' to infer what discount rate underlies the market price. In the example, if we observe a market price of £8 this suggests a required return of 25 per cent.

By implication, if the market sets a value on a security that implies a particular discount rate, it is reasonable to conclude that any further activity of similar risk to current operations should offer at least the same rate. This argument depends critically on market prices being unbiased indicators of the intrinsic worth of companies, i.e. that the Efficient Markets Hypothesis applies.

Any discount rate is an amalgam of three components:

1 Allowance for the time value of money – the compensation required by investors for having to wait for their payments.

2 Allowance for price level changes – the additional return required to compensate for the impact of inflation on the real value of capital.

3 Allowance for risk – the promised reward that provides the incentive for investors to expose capital to risk.

Ignoring expected inflation (or assuming that it is 'correctly' built into the structure of interest rates), discount rates have two components – the rate of return required on totally risk-free assets, such as government securities, and a risk premium.

11.3 Concepts of risk and return

In this section, we examine risk and return concepts relevant for security valuation.

The returns from holding shares

Investors hold securities because they hope for positive returns. Purchasers of ordinary shares are attracted by two elements: first, the anticipated dividend(s) payable during the holding period; and second, the expected capital gain. Taken together, there elements make up the **Total Shareholder Return (TSR)**.

Total shareholder return (TSR)

In general, for any holding period, t, and company, j, the TSR is the percentage return, R_{jt}, from holding its shares:

$$R_{jt} = \frac{D_{jt} + (P_{jt} - P_{jt-1})}{P_{jt-1}} \times 100$$

Table 11.1 The annual TSRs on Pilkington shares

Year	Return (%)	Year	Return (%)
1992–93	+3.2	1997–98	+6.7
1993–94	+49.6	1998–99	−28.3
1994–95	−8.1	1999–2000	−5.5
1995–96	+30.5	2000–01	+52.1
1996–97	−40.2		
Arithmetic mean*			6.7%
Standard deviation			30.3%

*Note: Strictly, the geometric mean should be used here as we are dealing with proportions. This is 2.2%.

where D_{jt} is the dividend per share paid by company j in period t, P_{jt} is the share price for company j at the end of period t and P_{jt-1} is the share price for company j at the start of period t.

To illustrate this calculation (and to show that returns are not always positive!), consider the following figures for Pilkington plc for 1996–97:

Share price at end of March 1996 = 209p
Share price at end of March 1997 = 120p
Net dividend paid during 1996–97 = 5p per share

The percentage return over this year was:

$$\frac{5p + (120p - 209p)}{209p} \times 100 = \frac{-84p}{209p} \times 100 = -40.2\%$$

Table 11.1 shows the annual returns and how they varied for the period 1992–2001.

If we regard past returns on Pilkington shares as a good guide to likely future returns and also believe that future annual returns will be randomly distributed about the mean, we might assess the expected value of holding Pilkington shares for a given year as 6.7 per cent. However, the actual return in any one year may diverge considerably from this average, as indicated by the substantial standard deviation. The variability in return would suggest that investors should seek a high return to compensate for this risk. However, not all risk is relevant in setting the required return. Let us now see why.

Self-assessment Activity 11.1

Determine the TSR for the year 200X in the following case:

- Share price January 1st: £2.20
- Share price December 31st: £2.37

- Interim dividend paid: £0.035 per share
- Final dividend paid: £0.065 per share

(answer at end of chapter)

The risks of holding ordinary shares

In Chapter 10, we saw the power of portfolio combination in reducing the risk of a collection of investments. Risk was measured by the variance or standard deviation of the return on the combination. This measure can also be applied to portfolios of securities, with some remarkable results, as shown in Figure 11.1.

As the number of securities held in the portfolio increases, the overall variability of the portfolio's return, measured by its standard deviation, diminishes very sharply for small portfolios, but falls more gradually for larger combinations. This reduction is achieved because exposure to the risk of volatile securities can be offset by the inclusion of low-risk securities or even ones of higher risk, so long as their returns are not closely correlated.

Self-assessment Activity 11.2

How many shares would an investor have to hold in order to totally eliminate specific risk?

(answer at end of chapter)

Specific and systematic risk

Not all the risk of individual securities is relevant for assessing the risk of a portfolio of risky shares. The CAPM separates the total risk of securities (and also of portfolios) into two components:

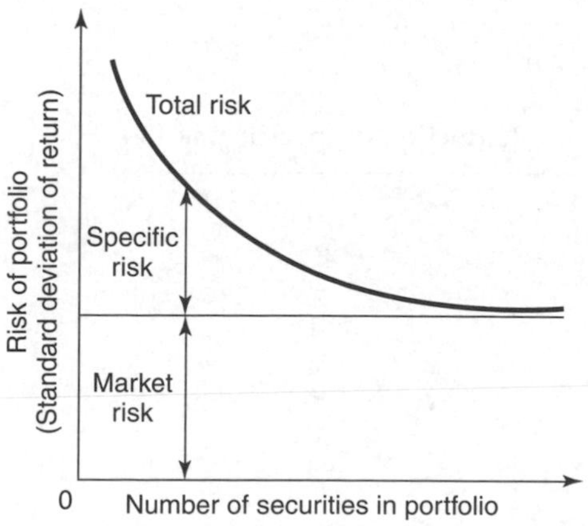

Figure 11.1 Specific vs. market risk of a portfolio

1 *Specific risk*: the variability in return due to factors unique to the individual firm.
2 *Systematic risk*: the variability in return due to dependence on factors that influence the return on all securities traded in the market.

Specific risk refers to the expected impact on sales and earnings of random events – industrial relations problems, equipment failure, R&D achievements etc. In a portfolio of shares, such factors tend to cancel out as the number of securities included increases. **Systematic risk** refers to the impact of movements in the macroeconomy, such as fiscal changes, swings in exchange rates and interest rate movements, all of which cause reactions in security markets. These are captured in the movement of an index reflecting security prices in general, such as the FTSE in the UK or the DAX index in Germany. No firm is entirely insulated from these factors, and even portfolio diversification cannot provide total protection. Because these factors affect all firms in the market, such risk is often called 'market-related' (or just 'market') risk.

Returning to Figure 11.1, we see that the reduction in the total risk of a portfolio is achieved by gradual elimination of the risks unique to individual companies, leaving an irreducible, undiversifiable, risk floor. The extent to which specific risk declines for a portfolio comprising *N* equally weighted and randomly selected securities is also shown in Table 11.2.

Substantial reductions in specific risk can be achieved with quite small portfolios, and the main scope for risk reduction is achieved with a portfolio of around 30 securities. To eliminate unique risk totally would involve holding a vast portfolio comprising all the securities traded in the market. This construct, called the '**market portfolio**', has a pivotal role in the CAPM, but for the individual investor, it is neither practicable nor cost-effective, in view of the dealing fees required to construct and manage it. However, since relatively small portfolios can capture the lion's share of diversification benefits, it is only a minor simplification to use a well-diversified portfolio as a proxy for the overall market, such as the FTSE-100, which covers over 80 per cent of the market capitalisation of UK quoted companies.

Table 11.2 How to remove portfolio risk

Number of securities (*N*)	Reduction in specific risk (%)
1	0
2	46
4	72
8	81
16	93
32	96
64	98
500	99

Source: Fosback (1985)

Implications

Three major implications now follow:

1. *It is clear that risk-averse investors should diversify*. Yet in reality, over half of UK investors hold just one security (usually, shares in a privatised company or a former building society). However, the major players in capital markets, holding well over 60 per cent of all quoted UK ordinary shares, are financial institutions such as pension funds and insurance companies, which do hold highly diversified portfolios.
2. *Investors should not expect rewards for bearing specific risk*. Since risk unique to particular companies can be diversified away, the only relevant consideration in assessing risk premiums is the risk that cannot be dispersed by portfolio formation. If bearing unique risk was rewarded, astute investors prepared to build portfolios would snap up securities with high levels of unique risk to diversify it away, while still hoping to enjoy disproportionate returns. The value of such securities would rise and the returns on them would fall until only systematic risks were rewarded.
3. *Securities have varying degrees of systematic risk*. Few securities exhibit patterns of returns rising or falling exactly in line with the overall market. This is partly because in the short term, unique random factors affect particular companies in different ways. Yet even in the long term, when such factors tend to even out, very few securities track the market. Some appear to outperform the market by offering superior returns and some appear to underperform it. However, performance relative to the market should not be too hastily judged, because the returns on different securities do not always depend on general economic factors in the same way.

For example, in an expanding economy, retail sales tend to increase sharply, but sales in less responsive sectors like water and defence are barely altered. Share prices of retailers usually increase quite sharply in an expanding economy, but the share prices of water companies and armaments suppliers respond far less dramatically. Retail sales are said to be 'more highly geared to the economy'. Systematic or market risk varies between companies, so we find different companies valued by the market at different discount rates. Already, we begin to see that the CAPM, based on the premise that rational investors can and do hold efficiently diversified portfolios, may show us how these discount rates might be assessed. Clearly, we need to measure systematic risk, which is covered in Section 11.5.

Self-assessment Activity 11.3

Give three examples of systematic and unique factors that cause the returns on holding ordinary shares to vary over time.

(answer at end of chapter)

11.4 The relationship between different equity markets

Investors have tended to prefer to invest in their own national stock markets, although this is changing. Reasons for this past parochialism include:

- relative lack of research into overseas markets and firms
- transactions costs, especially connected with foreign exchange
- fear of foreign exchange risk
- legal barriers, e.g. custody regulations
- political risk.

Several studies have shown that international diversification can generate even greater portfolio benefits than investing in purely domestic shares. Recall that the reason that portfolio risk reduces as the number of component shares increases was low correlation between investments, enabling investors to reduce specific risks. However, if foreign stock markets are less than perfectly correlated, it may be possible to lower risk below the level of market risk that defines the floor of the risk profile relating to purely domestic investment.

Indeed, studies pioneered by Solnik (1974) have shown that international markets are not all closely correlated. Kaplanis (1997), for example, showed that between 1990 and 94, London had the following cross-national correlation coefficients: USA (0.7), Germany (0.4), Italy (0.2), Japan (0.3) and Australia (0.5). However, European markets tended to have higher correlations, e.g. Germany/France (0.7), Netherlands/Germany (0.7), due presumably to closer European integration.

Astute investors could exploit these less than perfect correlations by combining investments in two or more markets, thus achieving a bodily shift downwards in the risk profile. The effect is shown in Figure 11.2.

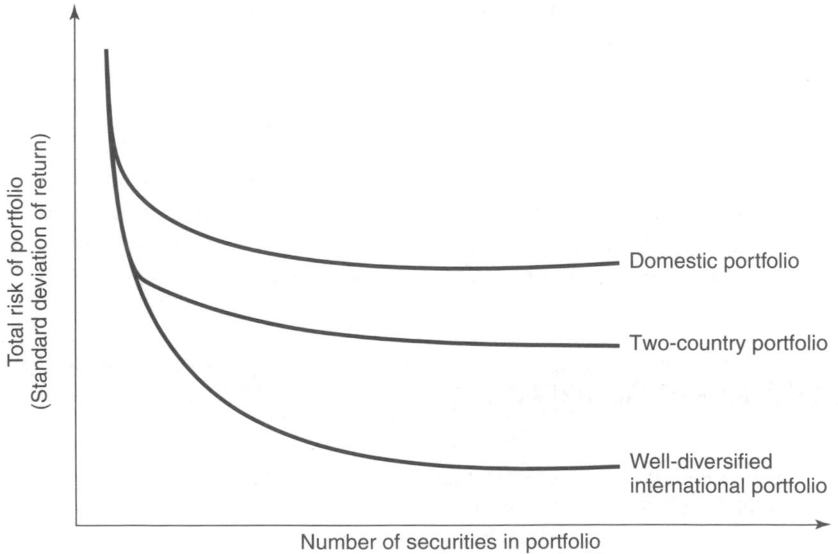

Figure 11.2 The effect of international diversification on portfolio risk

However, these opportunities may be disappearing. By the mid-1990s, the correlation between changes in US and European share price movements was estimated at around 0.4 – Wall Street movements would 'explain' 40 per cent of movement in the main European indices. But Brooks and Catao (2000) showed that rapid technical and institutional change had raised the correlation to 0.8 by 2000.

They suggested several reasons for this convergence:

- removal of controls on capital movements.
- more efficient trading systems.
- greater cross-border trading volumes.
- more large companies obtaining listings on several markets.
- more cross-border mergers and acquisitions with foreign activities accounting for higher proportions of company profits.
- easier access to information on foreign firms via the internet.

Due to these changes, equity markets have become more integrated, so that changes in prices in one market are more easily and quickly transmitted to others, e.g. good news for US banking shares is increasingly likely to lead to higher share prices for banking shares across the world. This means that industry membership rather than location has become a more important determinant of market value. In other words, investors should diversify more by industry than by country to achieve optimal diversification benefits.

Brooks and Catao also showed that the most important factor explaining increased correlation was developments in information technology. They found an overall correlation between European IT stocks and US IT stocks at May 2000 of 0.85, but for non-IT stocks, it was only 0.54. This implies that high-tech stocks now constitute a channel whereby shocks in one market are spread throughout the world, e.g. in 2001, the information announced in the US about the reduced prospects and the stock write-downs by internet technology suppliers Cisco, had a rapid impact not just on US technology shares, but throughout the world stock markets.

11.5 Systematic risk

As specific risk can be diversified away by portfolio formation, rational investors expect to be rewarded only for bearing systematic risk. Since systematic risk indicates the extent to which the expected return on individual shares varies with that expected on the overall market, we have to assess the extent of this co-movement. This is given by the slope of a line relating the expected return on the share, ER_j, to the return expected on the market, ER_m. It is important to appreciate that 'returns' in this context include both changes in market price and also dividends as we saw in the Pilkington example. For the overall market, dividend returns may be measured by the average dividend yield on the market index.

Example: Walkley Wagons

The case of Walkley Wagons is shown in Table 11.3. Investors anticipate four possible future states of the economy. For every percentage point increase in the expected market return (ER_m), the expected return on Walkley shares (ER_j) rises by 1.2 percentage points. Walkley thus outperforms a rising market. The graphical relationship between ER_j and ER_m, shown in Figure 11.3, is known as the **characteristics line**. Its slope of 1.2 is the **Beta coefficient**. Beta indicates how the return on Walkley is *expected* to vary alongside given variations in the return on the overall stock market.

Table 11.3 Possible returns from Walkley Wagons

State of economy	ER_m(%)	ER_j(%)
E_1	10	12
E_2	20	24
E_3	5	6
E_4	15	18

The market model

In practice, because it is not possible to record people's expectations, the measurement of Beta cannot be done looking forward. We have to measure Beta using *past* observations of the actual values of both the return on the individual company's shares, and also for the overall market, i.e. R_j and R_m respectively. So long as the past is accepted as a reliable indication of likely future events (i.e. people's expectations are moulded by examination of the frequency distribution of past recorded outcomes), observed Betas can be taken to indicate the extent to which R_j may vary for specified variations in R_m. A regression line is fitted to a set of recorded relationships, as in Figure 11.4. The hypothesized relationship is:

$$R_j = \alpha_j + \beta_j R_m$$

and the fitted line is given by:

$$R_j = \hat{\alpha}_j + \hat{\beta}_j R_m + u$$

where $\hat{\alpha}_j$ and $\hat{\beta}_j$ are estimates of the 'true' values of α and β, and u is a term included to capture random influences, that are assumed to average zero. This regression model is called the **market model**.

The intercept term, α_j, deserves explanation. This is the return on security j when the return on the market is zero, i.e. the return on j with the impact of market or systematic risk stripped out. Consequently, it indicates what return the security offers for unsystematic risk. We might expect this to average out at zero over time, given the random character of sources of specific risk. However, it is by no means uncommon empirically to record non-zero values for α.

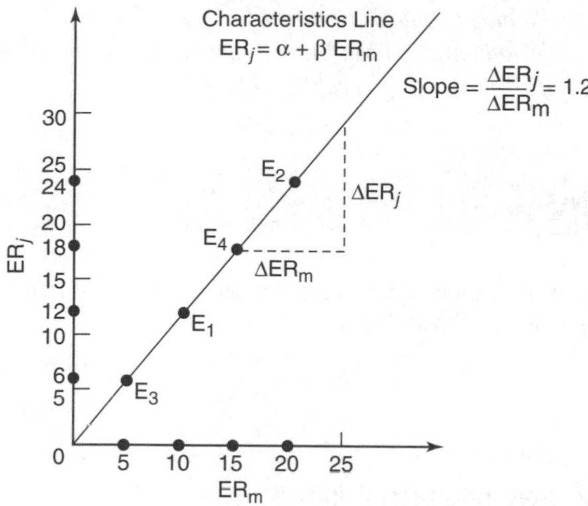

Figure 11.3 The characteristics line: no specific risk

Systematic and unsystematic returns

Figure 11.4 shows an imaginary set of monthly observations relating to a given year, say 1998, to which has been fitted a regression line. Clearly, unlike the *expected* values displayed in Figure 11.3, most values actually lie off the line of best fit. These divergences are due to the sort of random, unsystematic factors suggested in Section 11.3. For example, observation Z relates to the returns in May 1998. The overall return on security j in this month, XZ, can be broken down into the market-related return, XY, due to co-movement with the overall market, and the non-market return, or 'excess return' YZ, due to unsystematic factors, which, in this month, have operated favourably. The opposite appears to have applied in June 1998, indicated by point H. The market-related return 'should' have been FG, but the actual return of GH was dampened by unfavourable random factors represented by FH. *This analysis implies that variations in R_j* ***along***

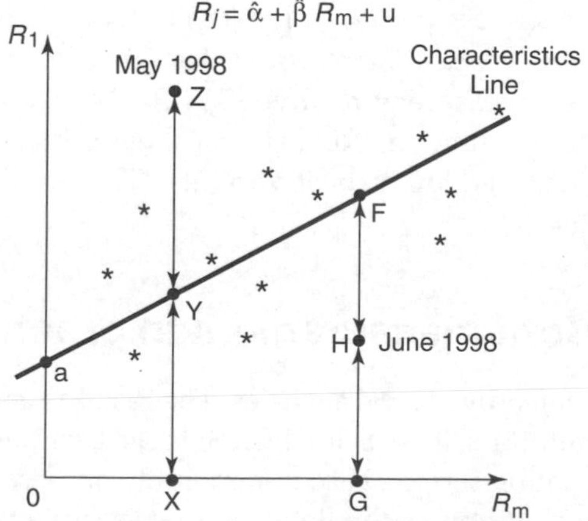

Figure 11.4 The characteristics line: with specific risk

the characteristics line stem from market-related factors, which systematically affect all securities, and that variations around the line represent the impact of factors specific to company j. The systematic relationship is captured by β.

Self-assessment Activity 11.4

What is the significance of variations around the characteristics line? Relate this to a particular company, say, British Airways.

(answer at end of chapter)

Beta values: the key relationships

Beta is the slope of a regression line. The slope coefficient relating R_j to R_m equals the covariance of the return on security j with the return on the market (cov_{jm}) divided by the variance of the market return (σ^2_m):

$$\text{Beta}_j = \frac{cov_{jm}}{\sigma^2_m}$$

Since the covariance is equal to the correlation coefficient times the product of the respective standard deviations ($r_{jm}\sigma_j\sigma_m$) (see Chapter 10), Beta is also equivalent to:

$$\text{Beta}_j = \frac{r_{jm}\sigma_j\sigma_m}{\sigma^2_m} = \frac{r_{jm}\sigma_j}{\sigma_m}$$

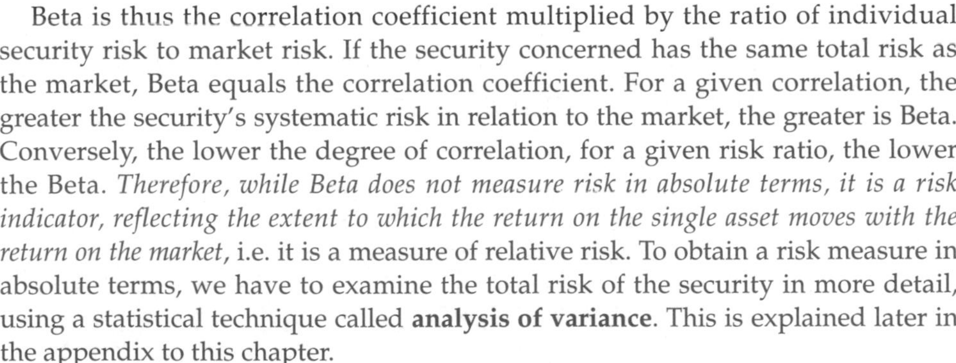

Beta is thus the correlation coefficient multiplied by the ratio of individual security risk to market risk. If the security concerned has the same total risk as the market, Beta equals the correlation coefficient. For a given correlation, the greater the security's systematic risk in relation to the market, the greater is Beta. Conversely, the lower the degree of correlation, for a given risk ratio, the lower the Beta. *Therefore, while Beta does not measure risk in absolute terms, it is a risk indicator, reflecting the extent to which the return on the single asset moves with the return on the market*, i.e. it is a measure of relative risk. To obtain a risk measure in absolute terms, we have to examine the total risk of the security in more detail, using a statistical technique called **analysis of variance**. This is explained later in the appendix to this chapter.

Systematic risk: Beta measurement in practice

Betas are regularly calculated by several agencies. The Risk Measurement Service (RMS) operated by the London Business School (LBS) is the best known in the UK. The RMS is a quarterly updating service, based on monthly observations extending back over five years, which computes the Betas of all constituents of the FT All-Share Index. For each of the preceding 60 months, R_j is calculated for every security and regressed against R_m. An extract from the RMS showing the components of the FT 30 Index of leading industrial shares is given in Table 11.4.

The Beta values of securities fall into three categories: 'defensive', 'neutral' and 'aggressive'. An aggressive security has a Beta greater than 1. Its returns move by a greater proportion than the market as a whole. In the case of GKN, with a Beta of 1.17, for every percentage point change in the market's return, the return on GKN's shares changes by 1.17 points. Such stocks are highly desirable in a rising market, although the excess return is not guaranteed due to the possible impact of company-specific factors. A defensive share is BOC Group, with a Beta of 0.76, movements in whose returns tend to understate those of the whole market. The

Table 11.4 Beta values of the constituents of the FT 30 Share Index

Company Name	FTSE-Actuaries Classification	Beta	Variability	Specific Risk	Std Err of Beta	R-Sq'rd
Allied Domecq Holdings	BevDstVn	.65	30	28	.20	9
BAE Systems	Defence	1.13	35	31	.21	19
BG Group	Oil Intg	.71	31	29	.21	10
Blue Circle Industries	BuildMat	.82	31	28	.20	13
BOC Group	ChemCom	.76	24	22	.17	18
Boots Co	Ret Dept	.64	25	24	.18	12
BP Amoco	Oil Intg	.89	25	22	.17	24
British Airways	Air+Tran	1.34	38	33	.22	23
British Telecom	Telcomfx	1.19	36	32	.21	20
Cadbury-Schweppes	FoodProc	.49	24	23	.18	8
Diageo	BevDstVn	.72	24	22	.18	16
EMI Group	PublPrnt	1.07	37	34	.22	16
GKN	AutoPrts	1.17	33	29	.20	23
GlaxoSmithKline	Pharmact	.66	23	21	.17	16
Granada	Broadcst	1.25	30	25	.19	31
Imperial Chemical Industries	ChemSpec	1.29	36	31	.21	24
Invensys	Electrnc	1.37	45	41	.24	17
Lloyds TSB group	Banks	1.39	29	22	.17	42
Logica	Comp Svs	1.17	53	51	.26	9
Marconi	TeleEqpt	1.37	44	40	.24	18
Marks & Spencer	Ret Dept	.67	29	28	.20	10
Peninsular & Oriental 'Dfd'	Shipport	1.21	34	30	.21	23
Prudential	Life Ass	.85	27	25	.19	17
Reuters Group	PublPrnt	1.11	45	42	.24	11
Royal Bank of Scotland	Banks	1.14	31	27	.20	24
Royal & Sun Alliance Ins Grp	InsNonLf	1.18	33	29	.20	23
Scottish Power	Electric	.54	24	23	.18	9
Tate & Lyle	FoodProc	.98	36	33	.22	14
Tesco	FdrugRet	.65	27	25	.19	11
Vodafone Group	Telcomob	.92	33	31	.21	14

Source: Risk Measurement Service, London Business School, April–June 2001

returns on neutral stocks like Tate & Lyle, with its Beta of nearly 1.00, parallel those on the market portfolio.

Notice that the total risk of each security is shown as 'variability', e.g. 33 for GKN. This is a standard deviation. Notice also that this invariably exceeds 'Specific Risk', e.g. 29 for GKN. The difference indicates the market risk that cannot be diversified away. (See the appendix to this chapter for a fuller explanation.)

Self-assessment Activity 11.5

Suggest why the Beta values tend to cluster in a range of roughly 0.8 to 1.2.

(answer at end of chapter)

11.6 Completing the model

The CAPM suggests that only systematic risk is relevant in assessing the required risk premiums for individual securities, and we have established that Beta values reflect the sensitivity of the returns on securities to movements in the market return. However, the size of the risk premium on individual securities (or on efficient portfolios) will depend on the extent to which the return on the investment concerned is correlated with the return on the market. For a security perfectly correlated with the market, the market risk premium would be suitable; otherwise the required return depends on the Beta.

The CAPM concludes that when an efficient capital market is in equilibrium, i.e. all securities are correctly priced, the relationship between risk and return is given by the **security market line (SML)**, as depicted in Figure 11.5.

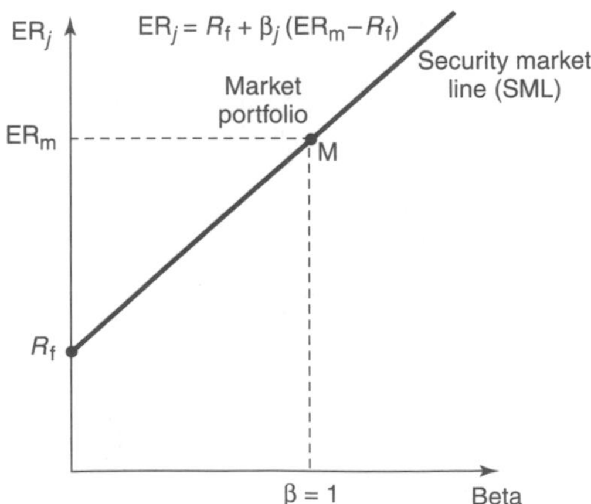

Figure 11.5 The security market line

Self-assessment Activity 11.6

Why is the Beta of the overall market equal to 1.0?

(answer at end of chapter)

The security market line

The equation of the SML states that the required return on a share is made up of the return on a risk-free asset, plus a premium for risk related to the market's own risk premium, but which varies according to the Beta of the share in question:

$$ER_j = R_f + \beta_j(ER_m - R_f)$$

If Beta is 1, the required return is simply the average return for all securities, i.e. the return on the benchmark market portfolio; otherwise, the higher the Beta, the higher are both the risk premium and the total return required. *A relatively high Beta does not, however, guarantee a relatively high return*. The actual return depends partly on the behaviour of the market, which acts as a proxy for general economic factors. Similarly, expected returns for the individual security hinge on the expected return for the market. In a 'bull', or rising, market, it is worth holding high Beta (aggressive) securities. Conversely, defensive securities offer some protection against a 'bear', or falling, market. *However, holding a single high Beta security is foolhardy, even on a rising market. Undiversified investments, whatever their Beta values, are prey to specific risk factors. Portfolio formation is essential to eliminate the risks unique to individual companies.*

11.7 Using the CAPM: assessing the required return

We may now apply the CAPM formula to derive the rate of return required by shareholders in a particular company. To do this, we require information on three components: the risk-free rate, the risk premium on the market portfolio and the Beta coefficient.

Specifying the risk-free rate

No asset is totally risk-free. Even governments default on loans and defer interest payments. However, in a stable political and economic environment, government stock is about the nearest we can get to a risk-free asset. Most governments issue an array of stock. These range from very short-dated securities, such as Treasury Bills in the UK, maturing in 1–3 months, to long-dated stock, maturing in 15 years or more and even, exceptionally, undated stock, such as 3.5 per cent War Loan with no stated redemption date. It is tempting to try to match up the life of the investment project with the corresponding government stock when assessing the risk-free rate. For example, when dealing with a ten-year project, we might look at the yield on ten-year government stock.

This seems unsatisfactory for several reasons. First, although the *nominal* yield to maturity is guaranteed, the *real* yield may well be undermined by inflation at an unknown rate. Second, there is an element of risk in holding even government stock. This is reflected in the 'yield curve', which normally rises over time to reflect the increasing liquidity risk of longer-dated stock. Third, although the yield to maturity is given, a forced seller of the stock might have to take a capital loss during the intervening period, since bond values fluctuate over time with variations in interest rates.

A better way to specify R_f is to take the shortest-dated government stock available, normally three-month Treasury Bills, for which these risks are minimised. The current yield appears in the financial press. This is about the same as LIBOR, the London Interbank Borrowing Rate, the rate of interest at which banks lend to each other overnight.

Finding the risk premium on the market portfolio

The risk premium on the market portfolio, ($ER_m - R_f$), is an expected premium. Therefore, having assessed R_f, we need to specify ER_m by finding a way of capturing the market's expectations about future returns. An approximation can be obtained by looking at past returns, which, taken over lengthy periods, are quite stable. The usual approach with ordinary shares is to analyse the actual total returns on equities as compared with total returns on fixed-interest government stocks over some previous time period. The results are likely to differ according to the period taken and the type of government stock used as the reference level (e.g. short-term securities such as Treasury Bills or long-term gilts). However, studies seem to come up with quite stable results. For example, Dimson and Brealey (1978), Day *et al.* (1987) and Dimson (1993) for the periods 1918–77, 1919–84 and 1919–92, respectively, showed average annual returns above the risk-free rate of 9, 9.1 and 8.7 per cent (before taxes) for the market index in the UK.

Similar estimates have been obtained in the USA. In 1985, Mehra and Prescott found that, after adjusting for inflation, equities delivered average *real* returns of 7 per cent p.a. over a quarter of a century, compared with 1 per cent for Treasury bonds – a real risk premium of 6 per cent. Fama and French (2000) found the equity risk premium averaged 8.3 per cent p.a. over 1950–99, this being well in excess of the 4.1 per cent p.a average for 1872–1949. Ibbotson Associates, a consulting firm, specifies a risk premium above the US Treasury Bill return at 8.8 per cent based on long-term research.

Dimson (1993) reported similar premiums in Japan (9.8 per cent, 1970–92), Sweden (7.7 per cent, 1919–90) and the Netherlands (8.5 per cent, 1947–89), although the last two estimates were in real terms, i.e. relative to domestic inflation.

A rather lower UK risk premium was recorded by Grubb (1993/4), at 6.2 per cent for 1960–92. Grubb suggests that returns to equities in the 1970s and 1980s were exceptional and that under a 'modern scenario of moderate growth and moderate inflation', a much lower premium on equities of only 2 per cent would be reasonable. This view is supported by Wilkie (1994), who, after exhaustive study of past trends in dividend yields and inflation, argues for a risk premium of 3 per cent for longer-term investment and 2 per cent for the short term. The evidence is inconclusive, but it is unlikely that many finance directors would contemplate recommending projects with such low premiums for risk.

However for shorter periods, say five or ten years (more akin to project lifetimes), returns are highly volatile and sometimes negative. Clearly, people neither require nor expect negative returns for holding risky assets! It therefore seems more sensible to take the long-term average, and to accept that, in the short-term, markets exhibit unpredictable variations.

The investment banking arm of Barclays Bank, Barclays Capital (**www.barcap.com**) publishes an annual study of equity and gilt-edged returns for various time periods. Their data show real investment returns on equities and government stock, and also on cash deposits. The long-term (101 years) equity risk premium is 4.4 per cent in real terms, and 4.6 per cent above the return on cash deposits.

Like many observers, Barclays Capital suggests that as the world economy moves from the low growth/high inflation phase of the 1970s and 1980s to the high growth/low inflation experienced more recently, equity returns have been untypically high. One reason for expecting lower future returns is technological progress, in general, and the information revolution, in particular, resulting in shorter competitive advantage periods. Firms typically have less time to exploit a 'first mover's advantage' before competitors arrive i.e. entry barriers are lower. Another likely depressant is the increased openness of the world economy due to the activities of the World Trade Organisation.

The Barclays Capital website has an interactive facility that allows users to calculate average annual returns for specified periods for the UK markets for any period over 1919 to date, and from 1925 to date for the USA. Table 11.5 shows some sample calculations for long periods and a year-by-year analysis over the 1990s for both countries.

In this table, the risk premium is expressed in nominal terms, i.e. before removing inflation. The data suggest that, recently, equity premia have been high in relation to longer-term outcomes. Note the remarkable similarity between UK and US premia. The data are *real* geometric average annualised returns, i.e. they exclude the effect of inflation.

One might conclude that, although 2000 was a poor year, pulling down the rolling average, there is little solid evidence in these data of a sea-change in the equity risk premium. However, to reflect prevailing thought, subsequent analysis will build in a risk premium for equities, i.e. the risk premium of the overall market portfolio, of 6%.

In probably the most thorough analysis to date of the equity risk premium, Dimson, Marsh & Staunton (2002) updated and largely corroborated these figures in a study of the equity risk premium for 16 countries, over a full century (1900–2000). They suggested that some earlier studies (including their own!) might have over-estimated the equity premium by excluding the First World War era,

Table 11.5 Equity-gilts relative returns

	UK			US		
Period	**Equities**	**Gilts**	**Equity Premium**	**Equities**	**Gilts**	**Equity Premium**
1925–2000	6.6	1.9	5.7	7.5	2.2	5.3
1925–1946	6.0	5.7	0.3	5.0	3.5	1.5
1946–91	5.9	−1.2	7.1	7.7	0.7	7.0
92	6.1	−0.8	6.9	7.7	0.8	6.9
93	6.5	−0.3	6.8	7.7	1.1	6.6
94	6.2	−0.6	6.8	7.5	0.9	6.6
95	6.4	−0.3	6.7	8.0	1.3	6.7
96	6.6	0.1	6.7	8.5	1.5	7.0
97	6.8	0.1	6.7	8.5	1.5	7.0
98	6.9	0.5	6.4	8.7	1.6	7.1
99	7.1	0.3	6.8	9.0	1.4	7.6
2000	6.8	0.4	6.4	8.5	1.6	6.9

Source: Barclays Capital (**www.barcap.com**)

when equity returns were poor, and by confining the study to the performance of surviving firms, thus excluding the relatively poor performers that had expired.

They found:

- The average global real return on equity was 4.6 per cent.
- Germany had offered the highest risk premium at 6.7 per cent.
- Denmark offered the lowest risk premium at just 2 per cent.
- In the US, for every 20-year period examined, equities outperformed bonds.
- Only four countries – German, Netherlands, Sweden and Switzerland – exhibited any 20-year periods over which bonds outperformed equities.
- It is reasonable to expect an equity premium of 5–6 per cent in the UK in the future.

Self-assessment Activity 11.7

Visit the Barclays Capital website to conduct your own analysis of risk premia, e.g. update the figures shown on Table 11.5.

Finding Beta

Beta values appear to be fairly stable over time, so we can use Beta values based on past recorded data, such as those provided by the RMS, with a fair degree of confidence. This is acceptable so long as the company is not expected to alter its risk characteristics in the future: for example, by a takeover of a company in an unrelated field or a spin-off of unwanted activities.

The required return

We now demonstrate the calculation of the required return for the 'aggressive' share British Airways, using the equation for the SML:

$$ER_j = R_f + \beta_j (ER_m - R_f)$$

The Beta recorded by the RMS at June 2001 was 1.34. At the same date, the yield on three-month Treasury Bills was about 5 per cent. For British Airways, this results in the following required return, assuming a market risk premium of 6 per cent:

$$ER = 5\% + 1.34(6\%) = 5\% + 8.0\% = 13.0\%$$

Application to investment projects

As British Airways shareholders appear to require a return of 13.0 per cent, it may seem reasonable to use this rate as a cut-off for new investments. However, two warnings are in order.

First, *the discount rate applicable to new projects often depends on the nature of the activity*. For example, if a new project takes British Airways away from its present spheres of activity into, say, telecommunications, its systematic risk will alter, as suggested by the Beta for Vodaphone of 0.92. The relevant premium for risk hinges on the systematic risk of telecommunications rather than of airline operation. This suggests that we 'tailor' risk premiums, and thus discount rates, to particular activities. This aspect is examined in the next chapter.

Self-assessment Activity 11.8

What is the implied discount rate for investment by British Airways into retailing?

(answer at end of chapter)

Second, *the appropriate discount rate may depend upon the method of financing used*. Until now, we have implicitly been dealing with an all-equity financed company whose premium for risk is a reward purely for the business risk inherent in the company's activity. In reality, most firms are partially debt-financed, exposing shareholders to financial risk. Using debt capital increases the risk to shareholders because of the legally-preferred position of creditors. Defaulting on the conditions of the loan (e.g. failing to pay interest) can result in liquidation if creditors apply to have the company placed into receivership. The more volatile the earnings of the firm, the greater the risk of default.

Financial risk raises the Beta of the equity, as shareholders demand additional returns to compensate. The Beta of the equity becomes greater than the Beta of the underlying activity. In Chapter 21, we shall see that observed Betas have two components, one to reflect business risk and one to allow for financial risk. The Betas recorded by the RMS are actually equity Betas, so the required return computed for British Airways (a highly geared company) is the *shareholders'* required return, part of which is to compensate for financial risk. However, when a company borrows, only the method of financing changes; nothing happens to alter the riskiness of the basic activity. The cut-off rate reflecting the basic risk of physical investment projects is often lower than the *shareholders'* own required return.

In the previous sections, we have concentrated on developing the operational aspects of the CAPM, without explaining the underlying theoretical relationships. The underlying theory is explained in Sections 11.8 and 11.9 and brought together in Section 11.10, which you may omit at this stage. Section 11.11 discusses some general issues raised by the CAPM.

11.8 The underpinnings of the CAPM

All theories rely on assumptions in order to simplify the analysis and expose the important relationships between key variables. In economics and related sciences, it is generally accepted that the validity of a theory depends on the empirical accuracy of its predictions rather than on the realism of its assumptions (Friedman 1953). However, if we find that the predictions fail to correspond with reality, and we are satisfied that this is not due to measurement errors or random influences, then it is appropriate to reassess the assumptions. The ensuing analysis, based on an amended set of assumptions, may lead to the generation of alternative predictions that accord more closely with reality.

The assumptions of the CAPM

The most important assumptions are as follows:

1. All investors aim to maximise the utility they expect to enjoy from wealth-holding.
2. All investors operate on a common single-period planning horizon.
3. All investors select from alternative investment opportunities by looking at expected return and risk.
4. All investors are rational and risk-averse.
5. All investors arrive at similar assessments of the probability distributions of returns expected from traded securities.
6. All such distributions of expected returns are normal.
7. All investors can lend or borrow unlimited amounts at a similar common rate of interest.
8. There are no transaction costs entailed in trading securities.
9. Dividends and capital gains are taxed at the same rates.
10. All investors are price-takers: that is, no investor can influence the market price by the scale of his or her own transactions.
11. All securities are highly divisible, i.e. can be traded in small parcels.

Several of these assumptions are patently untrue, but it has been shown that the CAPM stands up well to relaxation of many of them. Incorporation of apparently more realistic assumptions does not materially affect the implications of the analysis. A full discussion of these adjustments is beyond our scope, but van Horne (1986) offers an excellent analysis.

11.9 Portfolios with many components: the capital market line

The theory behind the CAPM revolves around the concept of the 'risk–return trade-off', encountered in Chapter 10. This suggested that investors demand progressively higher returns as compensation for successive increases in risk. The derivation of this relationship, known as the **capital market line (CML)**, relies on the portfolio analysis techniques examined in Chapter 10.

The reader may find it useful to re-read Section 10.7, where we explained the derivation of the efficient set available to an investor who can invest in a large number of assets. One conclusion of this analysis was that the only way to differentiate between the many portfolios in the efficient set was to examine the investor's risk–return preferences, i.e. there was no definable optimal portfolio of equal attractiveness to all investors.

Introducing a risk-free asset

The above conclusion applies only in the absence of a risk-free asset. A major contribution of the CAPM is to introduce the possibility of investing in such an asset. If we allow for risk-free investment the range of opportunities widens much further. For example, on Figure 11.6 which is based on Figure 10.5 which showed an efficient frontier of AE, consider the line from R_f, representing (after

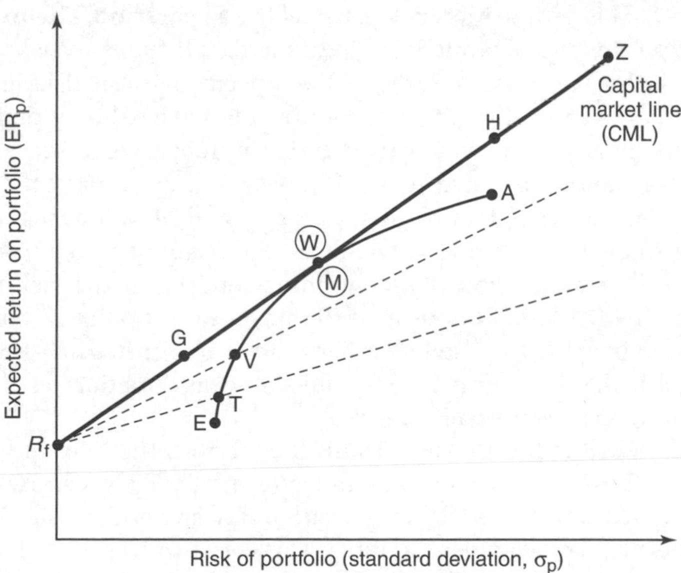

Figure 11.6 The capital market line

investment) the return available on the risk-free asset, passing through point T on the efficient frontier. This represents all possible combinations of the risk-free asset and the portfolio of risky securities represented by T. To the left of T, both portfolio return and risk are less than those for T, and conversely for points to the right of T. This implies that between R_f and T the investor is tempering the risk and return on T with investment in the risk-free asset (i.e. is lending at the rate R_f), while above T the investor is seeking higher returns even at the expense of greater risk (i.e. he borrows in order to make further investment in T).

However, the investor can improve portfolio performance by investing along the line R_fV, representing combinations of the risk-free asset and portfolio V. He or she can do better still by investing along R_fWZ, the tangent to the efficient set. This schedule describes the best of all available risk–return combinations. No other portfolio of risky assets when combined with the risk-free assets allows the investor to achieve higher returns for a given risk. The line R_fWZ becomes the new efficiency boundary.

Portfolio W is the most desirable portfolio of risky securities as it allows access to the line R_fWZ. If the capital market is not already in equilibrium, investors will compete to buy the components of W and tend to discard other investments. As a result, realignment of security prices will occur, the prices of assets in W will rise and hence their returns will fall; and conversely, for assets not contained in W. The readjustment of security prices will continue until all securities traded in the market appear in a portfolio like W, where the line drawn from R_f touches the efficient set. *This adjusted portfolio is the 'market portfolio' (re-labelled as M), which contains all traded securities, weighted according to their market capitalisations. For rational risk-averting investors, this is now the only portfolio of risky securities worth holding.*

There is now a definable optimal portfolio of risky securities, portfolio M, which all investors should seek, and which does not derive from their risk–return preferences. This proposition is known as the **Separation Theorem** – the most preferred portfolio is separate from individuals' attitudes to risk. The beauty of this result is that we need not know all the expected returns, risks and covariances required to derive the efficient set in Figure 11.6. We need only define the market portfolio in terms of some widely used and comprehensive index.

However, having invested in M, if investors wish to vary their risk–return combination, they need only to move along R_fMZ, lending or borrowing according to their risk–return preferences. For example, a relatively risk-averse investor will locate at point G, combining lending at the risk-free rate with investment in M. A less cautious investor may locate at point H, borrowing at the risk-free rate in order to raise his or her returns by further investment in M, but incurring a higher level of risk. We would need information on attitudes to risk to *predict* how specific investors behave.

The line R_fMZ is highly significant. It describes the way in which rational investors – those who wish to maximise returns for a given risk or minimise risk for a given return – seek compensation for any additional risk they incur. In this sense, R_fMZ describes an optimal risk–return trade-off that all investors and thus the whole market will pursue; hence, it is called the **capital market line** (CML).

The capital market line

The CML traces out all optimal risk–return combinations for those investors astute enough to recognise the advantages of constructing a well-diversified portfolio. Its equation is:

$$ER_p = R_f + \left[\frac{(ER_m - R_f)}{\sigma_m}\right]\sigma_p$$

Its slope signifies the rate at which investors travelling up the line will be compensated for each extra unit of risk, i.e. $(ER_m - R_f)/\sigma_m$ units of additional return.

For example, imagine investors expect the following:

$R_f = 10\%$
$ER_m = 20\%$
$\sigma_m = 5\%$

so that

$$\left[\frac{ER_m - R_f}{\sigma_m}\right] = \left[\frac{20\% - 10\%}{5\%}\right] = 2$$

Every additional unit of risk that investors are prepared to incur, as measured by the portfolio's standard deviation, requires compensation of two units of extra return. With a portfolio standard deviation of 2 per cent, the appropriate return is:

$$ER_p = 10\% + (2 \times 2\%) = 14\%$$

for $\sigma_p = 3\%$, $ER_p = 16\%$; for $\sigma_p = 4\%$, $ER_p = 18\%$; and so on.

Anyone requiring greater compensation for these levels of risk will be sorely disappointed.

To summarise, we can now assess the appropriate risk premiums for combinations of the risk-free asset and the market portfolio, and therefore the discount rate to be applied when valuing such portfolio holdings. The final link in the explanation of risk premiums is an explanation of how the discount rates for individual securities are established and hence how these securities are valued. This was provided by the discussion of the SML in Section 11.6.

11.10 How it all fits together: the key relationships

The CAPM on first acquaintance may look complex. However, its essential simplicity can be analysed by reducing it to the three panels of Figure 11.7.

Panel I shows the CML, derived using the principles of portfolio combination developed in Chapter 10. The CML is a tangent to the envelope of efficient portfolios of risky assets, the point of tangency occurring at the market portfolio, M. Any combination along the CML (except M itself) is superior to any combination of risky assets alone. In other words, investors can obtain more desirable risk–return combinations by mixing the risk-free asset and the market portfolio to suit their preferences, i.e. according to whether they wish to lend or borrow.

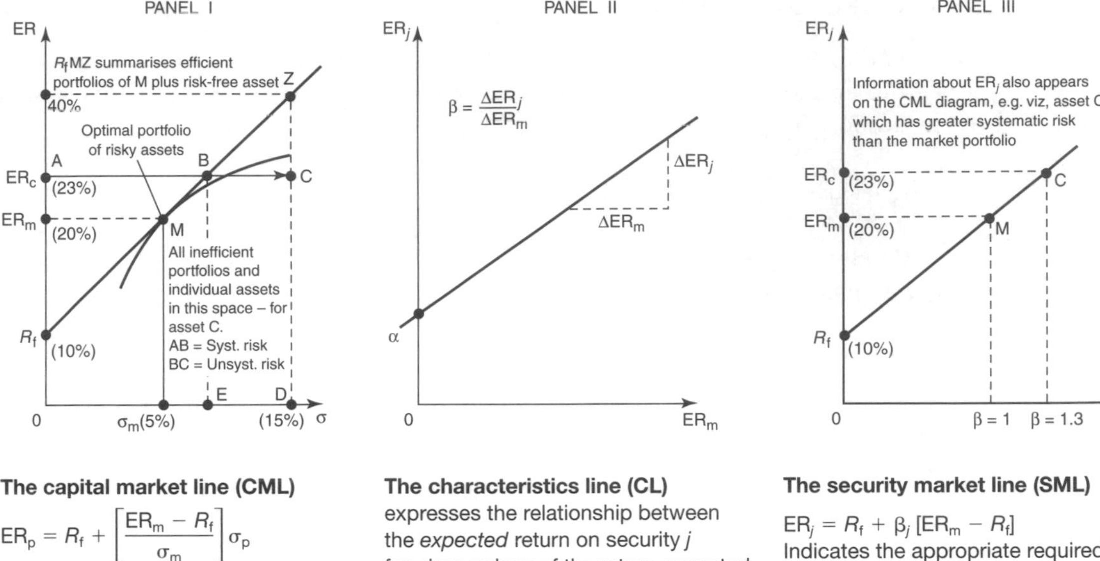

The capital market line (CML)

$$ER_p = R_f + \left[\frac{ER_m - R_f}{\sigma_m}\right]\sigma_p$$

Indicates the required risk premium for any *portfolio* comprising the risk-free asset and the market portfolio of risky assets.

The characteristics line (CL) expresses the relationship between the *expected* return on security *j* for given values of the return expected on the portfolio. (Slope = β, measured from past data by regression analysis).

The security market line (SML)

$$ER_j = R_f + \beta_j\,[ER_m - R_f]$$

Indicates the appropriate required return on *individual assets* (and also inefficient portfolios).

Figure 11.7 The CAPM: the three key relationships

The slope of the CML, given by $[(ER_m - R_f)/\sigma_m]$ defines the best available terms for exchanging risk and return. It is desirable to hold a well-diversified portfolio of securities in order to eliminate the specific risk inherent in individual securities like C. When holding single securities, investors cannot expect to be rewarded for total risk (e.g. 15 per cent for C) because the market rewards investors only for bearing the undiversifiable or systematic risk. The extent to which risk can be eliminated depends on the covariance of the share's return with the return on the overall market. Hence, the degree of correlation with the return on the market influences the reward from holding a security and thus its price.

The characteristics line in Panel II shows how the return on an individual share, such as C, is expected to vary with changes in the return on the overall market. Its slope, the Beta, indicates the degree of systematic risk of the security.

The security market line in Panel III shows the market equilibrium relationship between risk and return, which holds when all securities are 'correctly' priced. Clearly, the higher the Beta, the higher the required return. Although Beta is not a direct measure of systematic risk, it is an important indicator of relevant risk.

The decomposition of the overall variability, or variance, of the share's return into systematic and unsystematic components is explained in the appendix to this chapter. It can be demonstrated by focusing on security C in Panel III of Figure 11.7. Security C lies to the right of the market portfolio because its Beta of 1.3 exceeds that of the overall market. If the market as a whole is expected to generate a return of 20 per cent, and the risk-free rate is 10 per cent, C's expected return is:

$$ER_C = 10\% + 1.3(20\% - 10\%) = 10\% + 13\% = 23\%$$

This reward compensates only for systematic risk, rather than for the share's total risk. Of the total risk of C, represented by distance OD, only OE is relevant.

The risk–return trade-off, given by the slope of the CML, is (20%–10%)/5% = 2, since the risk of the market itself is 5 per cent. For C, with overall risk of 15 per cent, we would not expect to obtain compensation at this rate (i.e. 2 × 15% = 30% giving an overall return of 40 per cent), because much of the total risk can be diversified away.

Observe that a variety of required return figures could have emerged from our calculation – in fact, anything along the perpendicular ZD in Panel I of Figure 11.7, depending on the extent to which security C is correlated with the market portfolio. The nearer C lies to Z, the greater the correlation and the higher the required return, and conversely, should C be nearer to D. This reflects the changing balance between the two risk components along ZD.

If the market rewarded total risk, the return offered on security C would be the risk-free rate of 10 per cent supplemented by the risk–return trade-off (2 × the total security risk of 15 per cent), yielding a total of 40 per cent. However, because the total risk is partly diversifiable, the market offers a return of just 23 per cent for security C. This relationship is indicated on Panel I of Figure 11.7 by the distances AB and BC, representing respectively the systematic and specific risk components of security C's total risk (not to scale).

Self-assessment Activity 11.9

You expect the stock market to rise in the next year on so. Could you beat the market portfolio by holding, say, the five securities with the highest Betas?

(answer at end of chapter)

11.11 Reservations about the CAPM

The CAPM analyses the sources of asset risk and offers key insights into what rewards investors should expect for bearing these risks. However, certain limitations detract from its applicability.

It relies on a battery of 'unrealistic' assumptions

It is often easy to criticise theories for the lack of realism of their assumptions, and certainly, many of those embodied in the CAPM, especially concerning investor behaviour, do not seem to reflect reality. However, if the aim is to provide predictions that can be tested against real world observations, the realism of the underlying assumptions is secondary. Obviously, if the predictions themselves do not accord reasonably closely with reality, then the theory is undoubtedly suspect.

Single time period

A key assumption of the CAPM is that investors adopt a one-period time horizon for holding securities. Whatever the length of the period (which may or may not be one year), the rates of return incorporated in investor expectations are rates of return over the whole holding period, assumed to be common for all investors. This provides obvious problems when we come to use a required return derived from a CAPM exercise in evaluating an investment project. Quite simply, we may not compare like with like. If an investor requires a return of, say, 25 per cent, over a five-year period, this is rather different from saying that the returns from an investment project should be discounted at 25 per cent p.a. Attempts have been made, notably by Mossin (1966), to produce a multi-period version of the CAPM, but its mathematical complexity takes it out of the reach of most practising managers, especially those inclined to scepticism about the CAPM.

11.12 Testing the CAPM

Many writers have observed that, in principle, the CAPM is untestable, since it is based on investors' expectations about future returns, and expectations are inherently awkward to measure. Hence, tests of the CAPM have to examine past returns and take these as proxies for future expected returns, based on a key premise. If a long enough period is examined, mistaken expectations are likely to be corrected, and people will come to rely on past average achieved returns when formulating expectations. Greatly simplified, the essence of the research methods is as follows.

Research usually proceeds in two stages. First, using time series analysis over a lengthy period applied to a large sample of securities (say 750), researchers estimate both the Beta for each security and its average return. Relying heavily on market efficiency, these estimates are taken to be estimates of the *ex ante* expected return, i.e. it is assumed that rational investors will be strongly influenced by past returns and their variability when formulating future expectations.

Second, the researcher tries to locate the SML to investigate whether it is upward sloping, as envisaged by the CAPM. The 750 pairs of estimates for Beta and the average return for each security are used as the input into a cross-section regression model of the form:

$$R_i = a_1 + a_2\beta_i + u_i$$

where R_i is the expected return from security i, a_1 is the intercept term (i.e. the risk-free rate), a_2 is the slope of the SML and u_i is an error term.

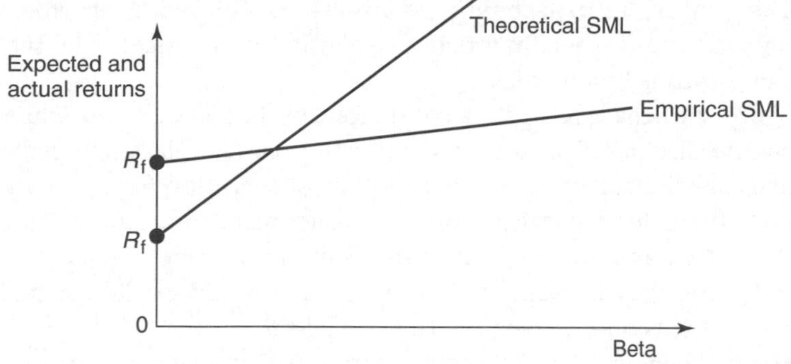

Figure 11.8 Theoretical and empirical SMLs

If the CAPM is valid, the measured SML would appear as in the steeper line on Figure 11.8, with an intercept approximating to recorded data for the risk-free rate: for example, the realised return on Treasury Bills.

Several early studies (e.g. Black *et al.* 1972; Fama and McBeth 1973) did seem to support the positive association between Beta and average stock returns envisaged by the CAPM for long periods up to the late 1960s. However, evidence began to emerge that the empirical SML was much flatter than implied by the theory and that the intercept was considerably higher than achieved returns on 'risk-free' assets.

Some researchers have continued to test the validity of the CAPM, but others, following Ross (1976), have concluded that some of the 'rogue' results stem from intrinsic difficulties concerning the CAPM that make it inherently untestable. In the process, they have developed an alternative theory, based on the Arbitrage Pricing Model (APM), discussed in Section 11.13.

Some of the reasons why the CAPM is thought to be nigh impossible to test adequately are as follows:

1 It relies on specification of a risk-free asset – there is some doubt whether such an asset really exists.
2 It relies on analysing security returns against an efficient benchmark portfolio, the market portfolio, usually proxied by a widely-used index. Because no index captures all stocks, the index portfolio itself could be inefficient, as compared with the full market portfolio, thus distorting empirical results.
3 The model is unduly restrictive in that it includes only securities as depositories of wealth. A full 'capital asset pricing model' would include all forms of asset, such as real estate, oil paintings or rare coins – in fact, any asset that offers a future return. Hence, the CAPM is only a *security* pricing model.

Fama and French (1992) made a thorough test of the CAPM, finding no evidence for the 'correct' relationship between security returns and Beta over the period 1963–90. The cross-section approach supported neither a linear nor a positive relationship. It appeared that average stock returns were explained better by company size as measured by market capitalisation, large firms generally offering lower returns, and by the ratio of book value of equity to market value, returns being positively associated with this variable. They concluded that rather than being explained by a single variable, Beta, security risk was multi-dimensional.

Neither of the UK studies conducted by Beenstock and Chan (1986) and by Poon and Taylor (1991) found significant positive relationships between security returns and Beta. Acting on Levis' (1985) observation for the period 1958–82 that smaller firms tend to outperform larger firms (although erratically), Strong and Xu (1997) attempted to replicate the Fama and French analysis in a UK context. Specifically, they investigated whether Beta could explain security returns and whether it was outweighed by 'the size effect'.

For the period 1960–92, they found a positive risk premium associated with Beta in isolation, but this became insignificant when Beta was combined with other variables in a multiple regression. For the whole period, market value dominated Beta, but over 1973–1992, it was itself insignificant compared with book-to-market value of equity, and gearing. However, the explanatory power of various combinations of variables used was poor, never exceeding an R^2 of 8 per cent. Overall, there appeared to be a size effect, but it did not operate in as clear or as stable a fashion as in the Fama and French study of US data.

11.13 The Arbitrage Pricing Theory

The alternative theory to the CAPM is the **Arbitrage Pricing Theory (APT)**, developed by Ross (1976). Unlike the CAPM, APT does not assume that shareholders evaluate decisions within a mean–variance framework. Rather, it assumes the return on a share depends partly on macroeconomic factors and partly on events specific to the company. Instead of specifying a share's returns as a function of one factor (the return on the market portfolio), it specifies the returns as a function of multiple macroeconomic factors upon which the market portfolio depends.

The expected risk premium of a share would be:

$$\mathrm{ER}_j = R_f + \beta_1(\mathrm{ER}_{\text{factor 1}} - R_f) + \beta_2(\mathrm{ER}_{\text{factor 2}} - R_f) + \cdots + u_j$$

where ER_j is the expected rate of return on security j, $\mathrm{ER}_{\text{factor 1}}$ is the expected return on macroeconomic factor 1, β_1 is the sensitivity of security j to factor 1 and u_j is the random deviation based on unique events impacting on the security's returns.

Diversification can eliminate the specific risk associated with a security, leaving only the macroeconomic risk as the determinant of required security returns.

The APT model does not specify what the explanatory factors are; they could be the stock market index, Gross National Product, oil prices, interest rates and so on. Different companies will be more sensitive to certain factors than others.

In theory, a riskless portfolio could be constructed (i.e. a 'zero Beta' portfolio) which would offer the risk-free rate of interest. If the portfolio gave a higher return, investors could make a profit without incurring any risk by borrowing at the risk-free rate to buy the portfolio. This process of 'arbitrage' (i.e. taking profits for zero risk) would continue until the portfolio's expected risk premium was zero.

The Arbitrage Pricing Theory avoids the CAPM's problem of having to identify the market portfolio. But it replaces this problem with possibly more onerous tasks. First, there is the requirement to identify the macroeconomic variables. American research indicates that the most influential factors in explaining asset returns in the APT framework are changes in industrial production, inflation, personal consumption, money supply and interest rates (McGowan and Francis 1991).

Once the main factors influencing share returns are established, there remain the problems of estimating risk premiums for each factor and measuring the sensitivity of share returns to these factors. For this reason, the APT is currently only in the prototype stage.

Tests of the APT, especially for the UK, are still in their relative infancy. However, Beenstock and Chan (1986) found that, for the period 1977–83, the first few years of the UK's 'monetarist experiment', share returns were largely explained by a set of monetary factors – interest rates, the sterling M3 measure of money supply and two different measures of inflation, all highly interrelated variables. In 1994, Clare and Thomas reported results from analysing 56 portfolios, each containing 15 shares sorted by Beta and by size of company by value. For the Beta-ordered portfolios, the key factors were oil prices, two measures of corporate default risk, the Retail Price Index (RPI), private sector bank lending, current account bank balances and the yield to redemption on UK corporate loan stock. Using portfolios ordered by size, the key factors reduced to one measure of default risk and the RPI. Again, there was much intercorrelation among variables, but the return on the stock market index, although included in the initial tests, appeared in none of these final lists.

11.14 Issues raised by the CAPM: some food for managerial thought

The CAPM raises a number of important issues, which have fundamental implications for the applicability of the model itself and the role of diversification in the armoury of corporate strategic weapons.

Should we trust the market?

Legally, managers are charged with the duty of acting in the best interests of shareholders, i.e. maximising their wealth (although company law does not express it *quite* like this). This involves investing in all projects offering returns above the shareholders' opportunity cost of capital. The CAPM provides a way of assessing the rate of return required by shareholders from their investments, albeit based partly on past returns. If the Beta is known and a view is taken on the future returns on the market, then the apparently required return follows and becomes the cut-off rate for new investment projects, at least for those of similar systematic risk to existing activities. This implies that managers' expectations coincide with those of shareholders or, more generally, with those of the market. If, however, the market as a whole expects a higher return from the market portfolio, some projects deemed acceptable to managers may not be worthwhile for shareholders.

The subsequent fall in share price would provide the mechanism whereby the market communicates to managers that the discount rate applied was too low. The CAPM relies on efficiently-set market prices to reveal to managers the 'correct' hurdle rate and any mistakes caused by misreading the market. The implication that one can trust the market to arrive at correct prices and hence required rates of return is problematic for many practising managers, who are prone to believe that the market persistently undervalues the companies that they operate. Managers who doubt the validity of the EMH are unlikely to accept a CAPM-derived discount rate.

Should companies diversify?

The CAPM is based on the premise that rational shareholders form efficiently diversified portfolios, realising that the market will reward them only for bearing market-related risk. The benefits of diversification can easily be obtained by portfolio formation, i.e. buying securities at relatively low dealing fees. The implication of this is that *corporate diversification is perhaps pointless because companies are seeking to achieve what shareholders can do themselves, probably more efficiently*. Securities are far more divisible than investment projects and can be traded much quicker when conditions alter. So why do managers diversify company activities?

An obvious explanation is that managers have not understood the message of the EMH/CAPM, or doubt its validity, believing instead that shareholders' best interests are enhanced by reduction of the total variability of the firm's earnings. For some shareholders this may indeed be the case, as a large proportion of those investing directly on the stock market hold undiversified portfolios.

Many small shareholders were attracted to equity investment by privatisation issues or by Personal Equity Plans and their successor, ISAs (Individual Savings Accounts). Larger shareholders sometimes tie up major portions of their capital in a single company in order to take, or retain, an active part in its management. In such cases, market risk, based on the covariability of the return on a company's shares with that on the market portfolio, is an inadequate measure of risk. The appropriate measure of risk for capital budgeting decisions probably lies somewhere between total risk, based on the variance, or standard deviation, of a project's returns, and market risk, depending on the degree of diversification of shareholders.

A more subtle explanation of why managers diversify is the divorce of ownership and control. Managers relatively free from the threat of shareholder interference in company operations may pursue their personal interests above those of shareholders. If an inadequate contract has been written between the manager-agents and the shareholder-principals, managers may be inclined to promote their own job security. This is understandable, since shareholders are highly mobile between alternative security holdings, but managerial mobility is often low. *To managers, the distinction between systematic risk and specific risk may be relatively insignificant, since they have a vested interest in minimising total risk to increase their job security*. If the company flounders, it is of little comfort for them to know that their personal catastrophe has only a minimal effect on well-diversified shareholders.

As we will see in Chapter 22, there are many motives for diversification beyond merely reducing risk. However, it is common to justify diversification to shareholders purely on these grounds, at least under certain types of market imperfection. When a company fails, there are liquidation costs to bear as well as the losses entailed in selling assets at 'knock-down' prices. These costs may result in both creditors and shareholders failing to receive full economic value in the asset disposal. Although this will not devastate a well-diversified shareholder, the resulting hole in his or her portfolio will require filling in order to restore balance. Company diversification may reduce these risks and also the costs of portfolio disruption and readjustment.

Another Perspective on the Equity Risk Premium

FT

Euro markets: keeping a close eye on the future of risk

The forward-looking equity risk premium (ERP) is a tempting but elusive analytical tool. It plays a crucial role in, for instance, pension fund long-term asset allocation models, and yet there is no way in which it can be directly observed in the stock market. Now Commerzbank Securities has embarked upon a new attempt to estimate risk premia across Europe equity sectors. Perceived risk, according to investment theory, must be matched by higher expected returns. The equity risk premium can be defined as the additional return expected from stocks over and above the risk-free return from long-term government bonds.

The concept has triggered extensive academic arguments, mainly focusing on the oddly high level of historical premia. At times equities have very strongly outperformed bonds. Over the whole twentieth century the risk premium in the UK averaged 4.7 per cent, according to Barclays Capital. Alternative UK estimates by Credit Suisse First Boston are on a 30-year rolling average basis, showing that the premium peaked at a formidable 9 per cent around 1970 but has since subsided to 4 per cent. In Japan, incidentally, the premium was negative during the 1990s.

It is the future that matters for investors, however, and Commerzbank is measuring a forward-looking ERP estimated across European sectors. It has assembled historical data going back to 1993, and is calculating the premium on the basis of a ten-year forward-looking model.

The average European risk premium is calculated by Commerzbank to be 4.1 per cent, slightly above the long-run average of 3.75 per cent. But it ranges from 5.9 per cent on the basic resources sector to a mere 2.2 per cent for telecoms.

Based on *Financial Times*, December 6 2000

Summary

We have examined the nature of the risks affecting the holders of securities and discussed whether the return required by shareholders, as implied by market valuations, can be used as a cut-off rate for new investment projects.

Key points

- Security risk can be split into two components: risk specific to the company in question, and the variability in return due to general market movements.
- Rational investors form well-diversified portfolios to eliminate specific risk.
- The most efficient portfolio of risky securities is the market portfolio, although investors may mix this with investment in the risk-free asset in order to achieve more preferred risk–return combinations along the capital market line.
- The risk premium built into the required return on securities reflects a reward for systematic risk only.
- The risk premium depends on the risk premium on the overall market and the extent to which the return on the security moves with that of the whole market, as indicated by the Beta coefficient.
- This premium for risk is the second term in the equation for the security market line: $ER_j = R_f + \beta_j(ER_m - R_f)$.
- Practical problems in using the CAPM centre on measurement of Beta, specification of the risk-free asset and measurement of the market's risk premium.
- In an all-equity financed company, the return required by shareholders can be used as a cut-off rate for new investment if the new project has systematic risk similar to the company's other activities.
- There is some debate about whether managers should diversify company activities merely in order to lower risk.
- Empirical studies seem to throw increasing doubt on the CAPM.
- The main proposed alternative, the Arbitrage Pricing Theory (APT), relies on fewer restrictive assumptions but is still in the prototype stage.

Further reading

As with basic portfolio theory, Copeland and Weston (1988) offer a rigorous treatment of the derivation of the formulae used in this chapter. Brealey and Myers (1996) offer an alternative, less mathematical treatment. You should also read the famous critique of the CAPM by Roll (1977). Fama and French's paper (1992), although difficult, is essential reading, as is Strong and Xu (1997), for a UK perspective.

Appendix
Analysis of variance

The total risk of a security (σ_T), comprising both unsystematic risk (σ_{USR}), and systematic risk (σ_{SR}), is measured by the variance of returns, which can be separated into the two elements. Imagine an asset with total risk of $\sigma_T^2 = 500$, of which 80 per cent (400) is explained by systematic risk factors, the remainder resulting from factors specific to the firm:

$$\sigma_T^2 = 500 = \sigma_{SR}^2 + \sigma_{USR}^2 = 100 + 400$$

In terms of standard deviations, $\sigma_{SR} = \sqrt{400} = 20$ and $\sigma_{USR} = \sqrt{100} = 10$. Notice that we cannot express the overall standard deviation by summing the two component standard deviations – only variances are additive, but not standard deviations – the square root of the total risk is $\sqrt{500} = 22.4$, rather than the sum of σ_{SR} and σ_{USR} ($20 + 10 = 30$).

In regression models, the extent to which the overall variability in the dependent variable is explained by the variability in the independent variable is given by the *R*-squared (R^2) statistic, the square of the correlation coefficient. The R^2 is thus a measure of 'goodness of fit' of the regression line to the recorded observations. If all observations lie on the regression line, R^2 equals 1 and the variations in the market return fully explain the variations in the return on security *j*. In this case, all risk is market risk. It follows that the lower is R^2, the greater the proportion of specific risk of the security. For investors wishing to diversify away specific risk, such securities are highly attractive. Notice that an R^2 of 1 does not entail a Beta of 1, as Figure 11.9 illustrates. All three securities have R^2 of 1, but they have different degrees of market risk, as indicated by their Betas.

In the example above, the R^2 of 80 per cent would correspond to a correlation coefficient, r_{jm}, of $\sqrt{0.8} = 0.89$. Looking at the standard deviations, we can infer that 0.89 of the standard deviation is market risk, i.e. $0.89 \times 22.4 = 19.94$, while

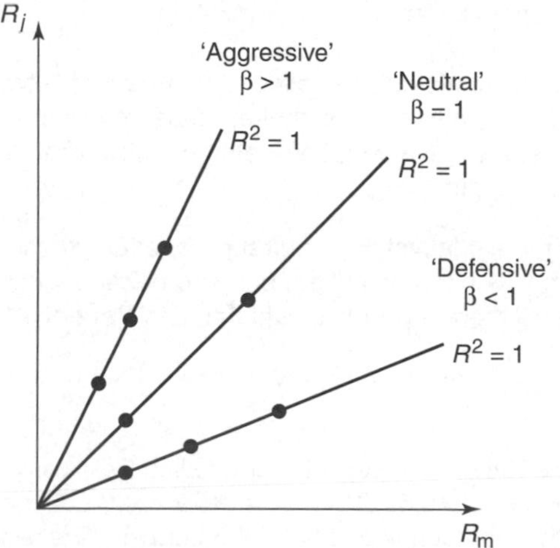

Figure 11.9 Alternative characteristics lines

the specific risk = $(1 - r_{jm}) \times 22.4 = 0.11 \times 22.4 = 2.46$. Let us re-emphasise these relationships:

Market, or systematic risk, is

$R^2 \times$ the overall variance, σ_T^2; or ($r_{jm} \times$ the overall standard deviation, σ_T)
$(0.8 \times 500) = 400$; or $0.89 \times 22.4\% = 19.94\%$

Specific risk is

$(1-R^2) \times$ overall variance, σ_T^2; or $(1-r_{jm}) \times$ overall standard deviation σ_T
$(0.2 \times 500) = 100$; or $(0.11 \times 22.4\%) = 2.46\%$.

The reader may find it useful to test out these relationships using the data provided in Table 11.4 ('Variability' is total risk expressed as a standard deviation). However, not all cases work out neatly owing to rounding errors.

Self-assessment Answers

11.1 TSR = [Dividend + Capital Gain]/Opening share price, expressed as a percentage.
= [£0.01 + £0.17]/£2.20 = £0.27/£2.20 = 0.123 i.e. 12.3%

11.2 To eliminate the specific risk, the investor would have to hold every share quoted on the market i.e. the market portfolio.

11.3 Systematic risk: collapse of the government
exchange rate fluctuation
interest rate changes.
Unique risk: labour relations problems
announcement of a major new contract
discovery of a defect in a key product.

11.4 Variations around the characteristics line reflect the impact of factors unique to the firm. For BA, this could be due to a pilots' strike, pressure to relinquish landing slots at Heathrow, sale of its stake in Qantas, competition authorities blocking its strategic alliance with KLM, etc.

11.5 The Beta values cluster in a relatively narrow range because these are large firms that are, themselves, mostly well diversified, but also because they constitute a major part of the overall market portfolio, which has a Beta of 1.0.

11.6 The market portfolio has a Beta of 1.0 simply because it varies in perfect unison with itself!

11.8 Here, we need surrogate Betas. Two very similar retailing Betas are given: Boots with 0.64, and Marks & Spencer with 0.67. Taking their average 0.655, and using a risk-free rate of 5 per cent and the market risk premium of 6 per cent, the required return is:

5% + 0.655 (6%) = 5% + 3.9% = 8.9%.

This investment would lower the overall Beta of British Airways, depending on the relative size of the two areas of activity.

11.9 An investor might outperform the market with this policy, assuming it did actually rise. However, with such a narrowly-diversified portfolio, he/she would be unduly exposed to risk factors unique to these five firms.

Questions

1 *Solution in Appendix A (page 814).* The ordinary shares of Firm A have a Beta of 1.23. The risk-free rate of interest is 5 per cent, and the risk premium achieved on the market index over the past 20 years has averaged 11.5 per cent p.a. What is the future expected return on A's shares?

If you believe that overall market returns will fall to 8 per cent in future years, how does your answer change?

2 *Solution in Appendix A (page 814).* Supply the missing links in the following:

ER_j	R_f	β	ER_m
(i) 14%	?	1.10	18%
(ii) 17%	5%	?	12%
(iii) ?	4%	0.75	10%
(iv) 15%	7%	0.65	?

3 *Solution in Appendix A (page 814).* Locate the security market line (SML) given the following information: $R_f = 8\%$, $ER_m = 12\%$.

4 *Solution in Appendix A (page 814).* Which of the following shares are over-valued?

	Beta	Current Rate of Return
A	0.7	7%
B	1.3	13%
C	0.9	9%

The risk-free rate is 5 per cent, and the return on the market index is 10 per cent.

5 *Solution in Appendix A (page 814).* The market portfolio has yielded 12 per cent on average over past years. It is expected to offer a risk premium in future years of 7%. The standard deviation of its return is 8 per cent. The risk-free rate is 5 per cent.

(i) What is the expected return from the market portfolio?
(ii) Draw a diagram to show the location of the Capital Market Line.
(iii) What is the expected return on a portfolio comprising 50% invested in the market portfolio and 50% invested in the risk-free asset?
(iv) What is the risk of the portfolio in (iii)?
(v) What is the market trade-off between portfolio risk and return suggested by these figures?

6 *Solution in Appendix A (page 815).* The following figures relate to monthly observations of the return on a widely used stock market index (R_m) and the return on a particular ordinary share (R_j) over a period of six months.

Month	R_m	R_j
1	5	4
2	−10	−8
3	12	9.6
4	3	2.4
5	−4	−3.2
6	7	5.6

(a) Plot these data on a graph and deduce the value of the Beta coefficient.
(b) To what extent are variations in R_m due to specific risk factors?
(c) Calculate the systematic risk of the security. (NB: systematic risk = $\beta^2\sigma_m{}^2$.)

7 Z plc is a long-established company with interests mainly in retailing and property development. Its current market capitalisation is £750 million. The company trades exclusively in the UK, but it is planning to expand overseas either by acquisition or joint venture within the next two years. The company has built up a portfolio of investments in UK equities and corporate and government debt. The aim of developing this investment portfolio is to provide a source of funds for its overseas expansion programme. Summary information on the portfolio is given below.

Type of security	Value £ million	Average % return over the last 12 months
UK equities	23.2	15.0
US equities	9.4	13.5
UK corporate debt	5.3	8.2
Long-term government debt	11.4	7.4
Three-month Treasury bonds	3.2	6.0

Approximately 25 per cent of the UK equities are in small companies' shares, some of them trading on the Alternative Investment Market. The average return on all UK equities, over the past 12 months, has been 12 per cent.

On US equities, it has been 12.5 per cent.

Ignore taxation throughout this question.

Required

Discuss the advantages and disadvantages of holding such a portfolio of investments in the circumstances of Z plc.

(CIMA, November 1997)

12 The required rate of return on investment and Shareholder Value Analysis

Setting the cost of equity

Very few companies are forthcoming about the rate of return they require on investment. The following quotation endures as a remarkably open statement of targets by Quaker Oats Inc. (now part of PepsiCo).

> The cost of equity is a measure of the minimum return Quaker must earn to properly compensate investors in a stock of comparable risk. It is made up of two prime components: the 'risk-free' rate and the 'equity risk premium'. The risk-free rate is the sum of the expected rate of inflation and a 'real' return, above inflation, of 2 to 3 per cent. A commonly used surrogate for the risk-free rate is the rate for US Treasury Bonds, which are unconditional obligations of the government intended to pay a real return of 2 or 3 per cent above long-term inflation expectations. For fiscal 1989, the average risk-free rate on these securities was approximately 9 per cent.
>
> For Quaker, a 'risk premium' of about 5.3 per cent is added to the risk-free rate to compensate investors for holding Quaker's stock, the returns of which depend on the future profitability of the Company. To derive Quaker's cost of equity, the risk premium is added to the risk-free rate. In fiscal 1989, the company's average cost of equity was approximately 14.2 per cent.

Source: Quaker Inc., Annual Report

Learning objectives

This chapter applies the models developed in earlier chapters to measuring the required rate of return on investment projects. After reading it, you should:

- Understand how the Dividend Growth Model is used to set the hurdle rate.
- Understand how the Capital Asset Pricing Model is also used for this purpose.
- Be able to apply the required rate of return to firm valuation.

- Appreciate that different rates of return may be required at different levels of an organisation.
- Be aware of the practical difficulties in specifying discount rates for particular activities.
- Appreciate how taxation may influence discount rates.

12.1 Introduction

The Quaker Annual Report showed the company's keen appreciation of the need to reward its shareholders. No company can expect prolonged existence without achieving returns that at least compensate investors for their opportunity costs. Shareholders who receive a poor rate of return will vote with their wallets, depressing share price. If its share price underperforms the market (allowing for systematic risk), a company is ripe for re-organisation, takeover or both. A management team, motivated if only by job security, must earn acceptable returns for shareholders. This chapter deals with assessing such rates of return and showing how they can be used in valuing firms. Different returns may be required for different activities, according to their riskiness. Multi-division companies, which operate in a range of often unrelated activities, may require tailor-made 'divisional cut-off rates' to reflect the risk of particular activities.

The return that a company should seek on its investment depends not only on its inherent business risk, but also on its capital structure – its particular mix of debt and equity financing. However, because determining this rate for a geared company is complex, we defer treatment of the impact of gearing until Chapters 20 and 21. *Here we focus on the return required by the shareholders in an all-equity company.*

Shareholders seek a return to cover the cost of time, to compensate them for having to wait for their returns at a rate sufficient to safeguard the purchasing power of their money, plus a premium to cover the exposure to risk of their capital, depending on the underlying risk of the business activity.

Two widely-adopted approaches are the Dividend Growth Model (DGM), encountered in Chapter 4, and the Capital Asset Pricing Model (CAPM), developed in the last chapter. Under each approach, we determine the return that shareholders demand on their investment holdings. We then consider whether this return should dictate the hurdle rate on new investment projects.

12.2 The required return in all-equity firms: the DGM

The DGM revisited

In Chapter 4, we discussed the value of shares in an all-equity firm which retained a constant fraction, b, of its earnings in order to finance investment. If retentions are expected to achieve a rate of return, R, thus resulting in a growth rate of $g = bR$. The share price is:

$$P_o = \frac{D_o(1 + g)}{(k_e - g)} = \frac{D_1}{(k_e - g)}$$

where D_o and D_1 represent this year's and next year's dividends per share respectively, and k_e is the rate of return required by shareholders.

The cost of equity

Rearranging the expression, we find the shareholder's required return is:

$$k_e = \frac{D_1}{P_o} + g$$

The shareholder's required return is thus a compound of two elements, the *prospective* dividend yield and the expected rate of growth in dividends.

It is important to appreciate that this formula for k_e is based on the current market value of the shares, and that it incorporates specific expectations about growth, dependent on assumptions about both the retention ratio, b, and the expected rate of return on new investment, R. With b and R constant, the rate of growth, g, is also constant. These are highly restrictive assumptions. Often, the nearest we can get to assessing the likely growth rate is to project the past rate of growth, 'tweaking' it if we believe that a faster or slower rate may occur in future.

For example, assume Arthington plc is valued by the market at £3 per share, having recently paid a dividend of 20p per share, and has recorded dividend growth of 12 per cent p.a. Projecting this past growth rate into the future, we can infer that shareholders require a return of 19.5 per cent, viz:

$$k_e = \frac{20\text{p } (1.12)}{300\text{p}} + 0.12 = (0.075 + 0.12) = 0.195\text{, i.e. } 19.5\%$$

Self-assessment Activity 12.1

What is the required return in the following case:
Share price = £1.80 (ex div)
Past growth = 3%
EPS = £0.36
Dividend cover = 3 times

(answer at end of chapter)

Tomkins plc (www.tomkins.co.uk)

Let us relate this approach to a real company. Table 12.1 shows the dividend payment record and end-of-financial year share prices for Tomkins, a rapidly growing conglomerate, over the financial years 1990–2000.

The dividend per share (DPS) grew by 384% from 4.55p in 1991 to 17.45p by 2000. Using discount tables, we find the average annual compound growth rate

Table 12.1 The return on Tomkins plc shares

Year	Net dividend (p)	Closing share price (p)
1990–91	4.55	148.0
1991–92	5.23	228.5
1992–93	6.35	212.0
1993–94	7.38	254.0
1994–95	8.65	234.0
1995–96	9.95	278.0
1996–97	11.45	268.5
1997–98	13.17	351.8
1998–99	15.15	264.3
1999–2000	17.45	197.3

is about 11 per cent.[1] Applying this result to the share price of 197.3p ruling at Tomkins' latest year end, we find:

$$k_e = \frac{17.45\text{p}\ (1.11)}{197.3\text{p}} + 0.11 = 0.098 + 0.11 = 0.208, \quad \text{i.e. } 20.8\%$$

Some problems

Apart from the restrictive assumptions of the dividend growth model, some further warnings are in order.

1 The dividend growth depends on the time period used

Suppose the growth calculation was conducted over a shorter time period, say, the most recent five year period 1995–2000, during which DPS rose from 8.65p to 17.45p, reflecting average growth of some 15 per cent p.a. The formula for k_e would indicate a return of about 25.2 per cent required by Tomkins' shareholders, well above our first result.

The calculation of g, and hence k_e, should be based on a sufficiently long period to allow random distortions to even out. We may still feel that past growth is an unreliable guide to future performance, especially for a company in a mature industry, growing roughly in line with the economy as a whole. If past growth is considered unrepresentative, we may interpose our own forecast, but this would involve second-guessing the market's growth expectations, which is tantamount to challenging the EMH.

[1] The growth rate, g, is found from the expression:

$4.55\text{p}/(1 + g)^9 = 17.45\text{p}$ or $(1 + g)^9 = 3.8352$

The growth rate can be found directly from compound interest tables, or by inverting the expression from the present value tables, i.e. $1/(1 + g)^9 = 0.2607$, whence g approximates to 11 per cent.

A spanner in the works!

The analysis implies Tomkins' shareholders have been seeking higher returns in recent years. In fact, the picture is more complex than this. Tomkins has adopted a policy of increasing annual dividends at the constant rate of 15 per cent, despite slackening earnings growth, resulting in falling dividend cover. Meanwhile, several of its diverse activities have grown much more slowly than in previous years, and some laggards, e.g. the food products business RHM (RankHovisMcDougall), have been divested. Tomkins is now a more focused but smaller, slower-growing group. Recognising that past dividend policy was unsustainable, it decided in 2001 to cut dividend per share to 12.00p.

In the 2000–01 Annual Report, the Chairman stated:

> This rebases the dividend for the year to a level from which it can be grown in future years on a sustainable and prudent basis taking into account the cyclical nature of some of the businesses, the continuing capital requirements and future prospects of the Group.

In other words, Tomkins paid out too much dividend in the past, inflating shareholders returns and biasing upwards the apparent cost of equity. Thus, what we have measured is not the *cost* of equity but the *return* on equity over an exceptional time period.

This, of course, throws out each of our growth rate calculations, i.e. 11 per cent for 1990–91, and 15 per cent for 1995–2000. Including 2000–01 would sharply lower these averages to probably meaningless figures, given that fast growth is still feasible in future years from the lower base of dividend per share of 12.0p.

2 The calculated k_e depends on the choice of reference date for measuring share price

Our calculation used the price at the end of the accounting period, but this pre-dates the announcement of results and payment of dividend. We should use the ex-dividend price, as this values all future dividends, beginning with those payable in one year's time. This would reduce the distortion to share price caused by the pattern of dividend payment (i.e. the share price drops abruptly when it goes 'ex-dividend', beyond which purchasers of the share will not qualify for the declared dividend). However, the eventual ex-dividend price may well reflect a different set of expectations than those ruling at the company financial year end.

Conversely, in an efficient capital market, share prices gradually increase as the date of dividend payment approaches, so that, especially for companies that pay several dividends each year, some distorting effect is always likely to be present. Our practical advice is to take the ruling share price as the basis of calculation, but to moderate the calculation according to whether a dividend is in the offing. For example, if a 5p dividend is expected in two months' time, a prospective fall in share price of 5p should be allowed for. In our assessment, the error caused by using an out-of-date share price is likely to outweigh that from using a valuation incorporating a forthcoming dividend.

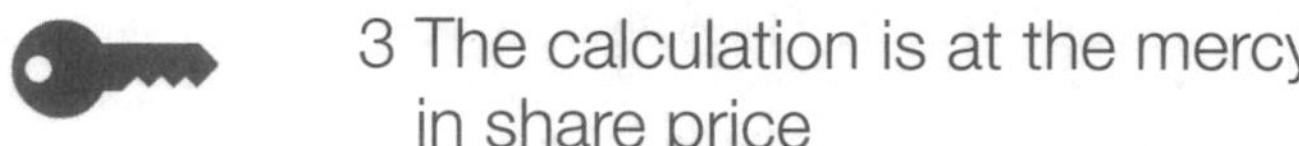

3 The calculation is at the mercy of short-term movements in share price

If, as many observers believe, capital markets are becoming more volatile, possibly undermining their efficiency in valuing companies, the financial manager may feel disinclined to rely on current market prices. Managers are generally reluctant to accept the EMH and commonly assert that the market undervalues 'their companies'. However, there remains a need for a benchmark return to guide managers. One might examine, over a period of years, the actual returns received by shareholders in the form of both dividends and capital gains. One way of conducting such a calculation is to focus on average annual rates of return, based on the analysis adopted in Chapter 11, where such a calculation was applied to Pilkington. This generated an average annual return of 6.7 per cent, based on the rather artificial assumption of a one-year holding period. You are advised to re-examine Table 11.1 and to digest the wild swings in annual returns. These are a clear indication of the risk involved in short-term equity investment.

4 Taxation

In Chapter 6, we argued the importance of allowing for taxation in project appraisal when estimating cash flows. Consistency seems to require discounting post-tax cash flows at a tax-adjusted cost of finance.

A project's NPV can be found on a post-tax or a pre-tax basis. If the NPV model is used on a pre-tax basis, both denominator and numerator must be on a pre-tax basis, and vice versa. If, for example, we wish to work in post-tax terms, the standard NPV expression for a one-off end of year cash flow, X, is:

$$\mathrm{NPV} = \frac{X(1 - T)}{(1 + k_T)}$$

where T is the rate of Corporation Tax and k_T is the required return adjusted for tax. If shareholders seek a return of, say, 10 per cent after tax at 30 per cent, the company has to earn a pre-tax return of 10%/(1–30%) = 14.3 per cent. In principle, computation on a pre-tax basis should generate the same NPV as that produced by a post-tax calculation, so long as the discount rate is suitably adjusted. However, this relationship is complicated by access to capital allowances. As a result, it is usual to compute NPVs on a post-tax basis.

The rate of tax applicable to corporate earnings might appear to be the rate of Corporation Tax. However, the picture is clouded by the prevailing type of tax regime (e.g. whether classical or an imputation tax system), and by the forms in which shareholders receive income (i.e. the balance between dividend income and capital gains, and the relevant rates of tax on these two forms of income). In other words, it is important to consider the interaction between the system of corporate taxation and the system of personal taxation.

Under an imputation tax, a shareholder receives a tax credit for the income tax component incorporated into the profits tax. Shareholders subject to tax at the standard rate face no further tax liability, while higher rate taxpayers face a supplementary tax demand. To add to the complexity, some imputation systems allow investors to reclaim all the tax paid on their behalf (full imputation), while others involve a discrepancy between the rate of corporation tax and the relevant rate of income tax (partial imputation). Since partial imputation applies in the UK, we will consider only this form.

When we calculated k_e using the DGM, the computation was based on the net-of-tax dividend payment, so it may appear that we have met the requirement to allow for taxation. However, the UK tax system imposes two possible tax distortions. First, the relative tax treatment of capital gains and dividend income has differed over time, and second, as we have just seen, different shareholders are subject to tax in different ways.

Regarding the differential tax treatment of dividends and capital gains, a major policy change occurred in 1988. Capital gains achieved after 1982 became taxable at the same rate as dividends (although with a much higher threshold), thus largely removing the tax penalty on dividends, especially as the top rate of income tax was simultaneously lowered to 40 per cent. Many companies reacted by sharply increasing their dividend payouts, which distorted the growth pattern of dividends.

A major problem facing a company is divining the tax status of its shareholders. Inspection of the shareholder register may provide much information, but no easy solution to this problem. The share price is set by the market as a result of the interaction of the supply and demand for its shares as expressed by thousands of investors. Although each may well be in a different tax position, the resulting share price is the result of investors assessing whether the shares represent good value or not. In other words, the market automatically takes into account the average tax positions of its participants.

Under this view, it is not the function of the company to gauge the tax requirements of the investor and to adjust the discount rate accordingly. This is impossible in a capital market with large numbers of investors. The market imposes a required return for particular companies, and then it is up to individual investors to make their own arrangements regarding taxation. The market-determined rate of return can be regarded as the return that the company must make on its investments. This becomes the after-tax return that the company should use to discount the after-tax cash flows from capital projects. (The only adjustment that the company should make is to allow for the tax shield on debt, as explained in Chapter 20.)

To summarise: in principle, we could discount pre-tax cash flows, but the identification of the appropriate pre-tax required return is complicated by the existence and timing of capital allowances. Hence, a post-tax computation is preferable. Theoretically, we ought to allow for investors' personal tax positions as well as Corporation Tax (i.e. discount project cash flows net of both Corporation Tax and investors' personal tax liabilities). But this requires such detailed knowledge of the relevant tax rates applicable to shareholders as to render it impracticable. As a result, it is usual to discount post-Corporation Tax cash flows at the market-expressed required return, assuming that shareholders have made their own tax arrangements. This means that shareholders will gravitate to those companies whose dividend policies most suit their tax positions. This personal **clientèle effect** is discussed further in Chapter 19.

Self-assessment Activity 12.2

Specify the two conditions under which the DGM breaks down completely. (You may have to revisit Chapter 4.)

(answer at end of chapter)

12.3 The required return in all-equity firms: the CAPM

In Chapter 11, we saw how the security market line (SML) traces out the systematic risk–return characteristics of all the securities traded in an efficient capital market. The SML equation is:

$$ER_j = R_f + \beta_j (ER_m - R_f)$$

ER_j is the return required on the shares of company j, and is therefore the same as k_e, R_f is the risk-free rate of return, and ER_m is the expected return on the market portfolio. We saw in Chapter 11 that, in order to utilise the CAPM, we needed either to measure or to make direct assumptions about these items. (Refer back to the discussion of measurement difficulties and the application to British Airways.)

However, despite these problems, the CAPM has major advantages over the DGM. The DGM usually involves extrapolating past rates of growth and accepting the validity of the market's valuation of the equity at any time. If we suspect that past growth rates are unlikely to be replicated and/or that a company's share price is over- or under-valued, we might doubt the validity of an estimate of k_e derived from the DGM.

The CAPM does not require growth projections; nor does it totally depend on the instantaneous efficiency of the market. Recall that the Beta is derived from a regression model relating the returns from holding the shares of company j to the returns on the market over a lengthy period. Taking, say, monthly observations over five years (60 in all) effectively irons out short-term influences. This requires semi-strong market efficiency for the period and a reasonably consistent relationship between security returns and the returns on the market portfolios.

How high a hurdle?

Companies generally make their investment decisions by discounting the net cash-flows a project is estimated to generate to their present value. If that net present value is positive, the project should, in theory, make shareholders better off. But the entire decision rests on the accuracy of both the cash-flow forecasts and the discount rate. Set the rate even a sliver too high, and good projects appear bad; set it too low and bad investments look appealing.

This makes it all the more surprising that some companies pay little attention to the impact on the discount rate of changes in their cost of capital. Steve Hodge, treasurer of Shell, the Anglo-Dutch oil giant, says that a difference of only one percentage point in the discount rate can change the value of, say, an oil refinery with a 15-year life by hundreds of millions of dollars.

In a deal-crazy environment such as America's, the fear of missing out on a spectacular merger wave has encouraged managers to keep their hurdle rates as low as possible. On average they are now down to about 10 per cent from 12 per cent a few years ago.

But many managers remain deeply sceptical about the theory behind discount rates. Even though it spits out percentages to several decimal points, the capital-asset pricing model, as the conceptual framework for calculating the rates is called, is controversial in itself. 'The whole basis of setting hurdle rates is flawed,' says Mr Hodge. 'If you change the hurdle rate you're hiding away a management decision in a piece of spurious arithmetic'.

Spurious or not, that arithmetic should reflect not only interest rates but also the riskiness of each individual project. For instance, Siemens, the German industrial giant, last year started assigning a different hurdle rate to each of its 16 businesses, ranging from household appliances to medical equipment and semiconductors. The hurdle rates – from 8 per cent to 11 per cent – are based on the volatility of shares in rival companies in the relevant industry, and are under constant review.

As scientific as it sounds, however, this approach is not foolproof. 'You find two companies in the same industry, who should be using similar rates, but one uses 10 per cent, the other 30 per cent. One or both must be wrong,' says Mr Milano. That is what brings the manager's decision out of hiding.

Based on *The Economist*, May 8 1999

Applying the CAPM to Tomkins plc

The Risk Measurement Service quoted a Beta of 1.18 for Tomkins shares as at September 2001. In late 2001, the yield on three-month Treasury Bills was

4 per cent. Using a market risk premium of 6 per cent yields the following required return for the ungeared company:

$$ER_j = R_f + \beta(ER_m - R_f) = 0.04 + 1.18(0.06) = 0.4 + 0.071$$
$$= 0.111 \text{ (i.e.) } 11.1\%$$

This is considerably below the DGM result. As the two approaches, in principle, should yield about the same result, some reconciliation is required. At the time of this calculation, market interest rates were historically low, at least in money terms, following the terrorist attacks in the USA, generating expectations of low interest rates for the future. Tomkins grew rapidly over the past decade or so, and it would be prudent to expect lower growth in the future.

It appears that estimates of k_e obtained by either method are susceptible to the date of the calculation and prevailing expectations for the future. More fundamentally, whereas the DGM looks at performance over a number of years, the CAPM is essentially a one-period model, although it is commonly used for long-term purposes.

12.4 Using value drivers – Shareholder Value Analysis (SVA)

Now that we know how required rates of return can be estimated, it is appropriate to show how these can be used in valuation of firms. To achieve this, we draw on the earlier treatment of value drivers and firm valuation in Chapter 4.

As we have observed, in recent years there has been much greater appreciation of the need for managers to optimise the interests of shareholders. In general terms, this can be achieved by generating a rate of return on investment which, at the very least, matches their required return on investment, i.e. the cost of equity. Remember that shareholders incur an opportunity cost when subscribing capital for firms to use and managers are legally obliged to safeguard those funds with all due diligence.

Sometimes, managers feel that 'their' companies are not 'correctly' valued by the stock market – there was a steady trickle of firms de-listing from the main UK market in the late 1990s, largely for this reason. Moreover, share prices can swing quite violently in the short term, which tends to undermine managers' faith in market efficiency. Often nonplussed by such gyrations, both managers and shareholders may require a more objective and reliable measure of value than simply the prevailing market price.

Such a measure can be provided by the shareholder value approach, propounded by Alfred Rappaport, drawing on Michael Porter's ideas. You met the concept of a value driver in Chapter 4 – here we make use of this idea to analyse inherent shareholder value (SV), which may be thought of as the fundamental, or inherent, value of the firm to its owners. The SV figure also provides a cross-check on the market's current valuation of the company. This may be regarded as a more stable and possibly more reliable indicator of the fundamental value of the firm that is unaffected by short-term vagaries of the market.

The following example of Safa plc is the vehicle for investigating the SVA approach. But first, a refresher on value drivers may be useful.

Rappaport developed a simple but powerful model to calculate the fundamental value of a business to its owners by focusing on the key factors that determine firm value. He identified seven value drivers, comprising three cash flow variables and four parameters:

- Sales, and its speed of growth
- Fixed capital investment
- Working capital investment
- Operating profit margin
- Tax rate on profits
- The planning horizon
- The required rate of return

In its simplest form, SVA takes the last four drivers as given, and assumes that the first three, the cash flow variables, change at a constant rate. The key to the analysis, as with any budgeting exercise, is the level of sales and the projected rate of increase. From the sales projections, we can programme the operating profits and cash flows over the planning horizon and discount as appropriate to find their present value.

In the full model, the value of the firm comprises three elements, the value of the equity, the value of the debt and the value of any non-operating assets, such as marketable securities. However, to keep the analysis simple, we focus on an all-equity-financed company with no holdings of marketable assets. In addition, we need to explain the treatment of investment expenditure. Quite simply, to generate value, firms have to invest, i.e. to generate future cash flows requires preliminary cash outflows. These reduce value in the short-term but hopefully, generate a more than compensating increase in value via future cash flows.

Categories of investment

Investment in working capital, especially inventories, is required to support a planned increase in sales. Often, companies attempt to apply a roughly constant ratio of working capital to sales, say 5 per cent, so that a 7 per cent sales increase needs an equivalent increase in working capital investment. This is called *incremental working capital investment*.

Replacement investment is undertaken to make good the wear and tear due to equipment use. However, there are phasing issues to consider. In reality, it is correct to observe that, in relation to particular items, the act of replacement is infrequent, occurring in discrete chunks, whereas depreciation is an annual provision, so that in all but the year of replacement, depreciation will likely exceed replacement expenditure. However, taken in aggregate, and especially for larger firms, replacement may be closely related to depreciation provisions.

New investment in fixed assets. This has two dimensions. First, if the firm wants to expand sales of existing products, then, unless it has spare capacity, it will need to invest in additional capital equipment to support the planned sales increase.

Second, new investment may be undertaken to accompany a major strategic venture such as the development of a new product, which will also generate an increase in sales. Taken together, these may be related to the planned sales increase, although there is likely to be a time lag before strategic investment comes fully 'on stream' and is able to deliver higher sales quantities. Notwithstanding this qualification, we can link the amount of investment in new capacity, for whatever reason and which adds to the firm's stock of assets, to a planned increase in sales. We call the resulting sum the *incremental fixed capital investment*.

In the following demonstration example of Safa plc, replacement investment is assumed to equal depreciation provisions (which are treated as part of operating expenses in accounting terms), and both working capital investment and incremental fixed capital investment are made a percentage of any planned sales increase.

12.5 Worked example: Safa plc

The board of Safa plc is concerned about its current stock market value of £95 million, especially as board members hold 40 per cent of the existing 100 million ordinary shares (par value £1) already issued. They are vaguely aware of the SVA concept and have assembled the following data:

Current sales	£100 million
*Operating profit margin**	20 per cent

(*After depreciation. On average, depreciation provisions match ongoing investment requirements and are fully tax-deductible.)

Estimated rate of sales growth	5 per cent p.a.
Rate of corporation tax	30 per cent (with no delay in payment)
Long-term debt	zero
Net book value of assets	£120 million (net fixed assets plus net current assets)

To support the increase in sales, additional investment is required as follows:

(i) Increased investment in *working capital* will be 8 per cent of any concurrent sales increase.

(ii) Increased investment in *fixed assets* will be 10 per cent of any concurrent sales increase.

The risk-free rate of interest is 7.6 per cent, Safa's Beta coefficient is 0.8 and a consensus view of analyst's expectations regarding the overall return on the market portfolio is 15.6 per cent.

Safa presently pays out 30 per cent of profit after tax as dividend. The board estimate that Safa can continue to enjoy its traditional source of competitive advantage as a low cost provider for a further six years, at the end of which, it estimates, the net book value of its assets will be £140 million.

What is the inherent underlying value of this company?

Answer and comments

First of all, we need to find the return required by the shareholders of Safa, using the CAPM formula. This is:

$$k_e = R_f + \beta[ER_m - R_f]$$
$$= 7.6\% + 0.8\,[15.6\% - 7.6\%]$$
$$= (7.6\% + 6.4\%) = 14\%$$

This becomes the appropriate rate at which to value Safa's future cash flows. There is no debt finance so all operating profits (less tax) are attributable to shareholders. There appears to be no long-term strategic investment programme, and wear and-tear is made good at a rate roughly corresponding to tax-allowable depreciation provisions. This means that free cash flows are equal to operating profits less tax.

The firm enjoys a temporary cost advantage for six years, beyond which cash flows are uncertain. Post-year-six cash flows can be handled in a number of ways:

1 The year six cash flow figure can be assumed to flow indefinitely. This seems quite an optimistic assumption to make both in relation to Safa plc and also more generally.
2 A view can be taken on the firm's efforts to restore competitive advantage and some growth assumption can then be incorporated. Again, this can only be speculative, as there is no information on this issue.

3 Perhaps the most prudent assumption to make is that the expected year six book value of assets will approximate to the value of all future cash flows, i.e. the company has no further supernormal earnings capacity. This implies that any subsequent investment has an NPV of zero.

We adopt the third approach mainly for simplicity.

Table 12.2 shows the cash flows over the competive advantage period, years 1–6 inclusive. The base year (year 0) figures are given to establish a reference line from which future cash flows will grow.

Valuing Safa plc

Taking firstly the value created over the competitive advantage period:

PV of operating cash flows (line 7) = £59.5 m

Second, we add in the estimated residual value, our proxy for all future operating cash flows:

The PV of the residual value = £140 m × $PVIF_{14,6}$
= £140 m × 0.4556 = £63.8
Shareholder Value = (£59.50 m + £63.8 m)
= £123.3 m

Table 12.2 Cash flow profile* for Safa, plc (ungeared)

	£m	0	1	2	3	4	5	6, etc.
1	Sales (5% growth)	100	105	110.25	115.76	121.55	127.63	134.00
2	Operating profit margin @ 20%**	20	21	22.05	23.15	24.31	25.53	26.80
3	Taxation @ 30%	(6)	(6.30)	(6.62)	(6.95)	(7.29)	(7.66)	(8.04)
4	Incremental working capital investment @ 8% of sales increase		(0.40)	(0.42)	(0.44)	(0.46)	(0.49)	(0.51)
5	Incremental fixed capital investment @ 10% of sales increase		(0.50)	(0.53)	(0.55)	(0.58)	(0.61)	(0.64)
6	Free cash flow		13.80	14.48	15.21	15.98	16.77	17.61
7	Present value @ 14%		12.11	11.14	10.27	9.46	8.71	8.02

* Accuracy of figures influenced by rounding errors.
** These can be taken as operating cash flows given the assumption that depreciation = replacement investment.

A note on taxation – two simplifications

You should appreciate how taxation is being handled in this example. All replacement investment is treated as being fully tax-deductible in the year of expenditure. This is a simplification adopted primarily for arithmetic convenience. In reality, the tax relief will be spread out over time as the firm claims the 25 per cent writing down allowance (WDA) each year. In addition, we have ignored the tax saving in relation to the 25 per cent WDA on the incremental fixed capital expenditure.

Correction for the first factor would reduce the valuation simply because delay in taking the tax relief would lower the PV of the stream of tax savings. On the other hand, inclusion of the second set of tax savings would raise the SV figure. If you calculate the 'true' valuation by allowing for these aspects, you will find a net increase in the valuation, although the calculation is a little messy.

We now turn to discuss the actual valuation obtained.

Commentary

Looking at the figures as calculated, we find, rather alarmingly, that a large proportion (52 per cent) of the SV is accounted for by the residual value. Moreover, the SV falls short of market value, which itself is below the current book value of assets. This seems to imply that the company is worth more if it were broken up (although this depends on whether the book value of assets would match the market value). It is thus possible that the market is valuing Safa for its break-up potential rather than as a going concern.

This raises the obvious question of why the market should place such a low value on Safa. We can consider some possible reasons for the apparent market under-valuation of Safa. (Identify which value driver is inherent in each point.)

- The market may currently apply a higher discount rate, for example, seeking a higher reward for risk.
- The growth estimate may be regarded as optimistic.
- The flow of information provided to the market may be inadequate – for example, if it does have plans for future investment, are these generally known and understood, at least in outline?
- Board control – presumably reflecting domination by members of the founding family – may look excessive. Such enterprises rarely enjoy a good stock market rating, because there is often a suspicion that the interests of family members may be allowed to dominate those of 'outside' shareholders.
- The dividend policy may be thought ungenerous – a 30 per cent payout ratio is quite low by UK standards, and there appears to be little scope for worthwhile strategic investment. Retentions may simply be going into cash balances.
- There may be doubts about whether Safa can recover some form of competitive advantage.
- The market may be unimpressed with its present cost advantage-based strategy.
- Its gearing – currently, zero – may be thought to be too low. There is no tax shield to exploit (see Chapter 23).

Whatever the reason(s), there is plenty for the Board to consider!

12.6 Using 'tailored' discount rates

Applying the discount rates derived using the CAPM to investment projects assumes that new projects fall into the same risk category as the company's other operations. This might be a reasonable assumption for minor projects in existing areas and perhaps for replacements, but hardly seems justifiable for major new product developments or acquisitions of companies in unrelated areas. If the expected return is positively related to risk, firms that rely on a single discount rate may tend to over-invest in risky projects to the detriment of less risky, though still attractive projects. Many multi-divisional companies are effectively portfolios of diverse activities of different degrees of risk. The Beta of the firm as a whole is thus the weighted average of its component activity Betas. Each division contributes to the firm's overall business risk in a way similar to that in which individual shares contribute to the systematic risk of a portfolio of securities. The dangers of using a uniform discount rate are shown in Figure 12.1.

Figure 12.1 shows the relationship between the rate of return required on a particular project and that expected on the market portfolio, linked by the Beta. The overall portfolio of company activities may have a Beta of, say, 1.2, but this is only a weighted average of the Betas of component activities.

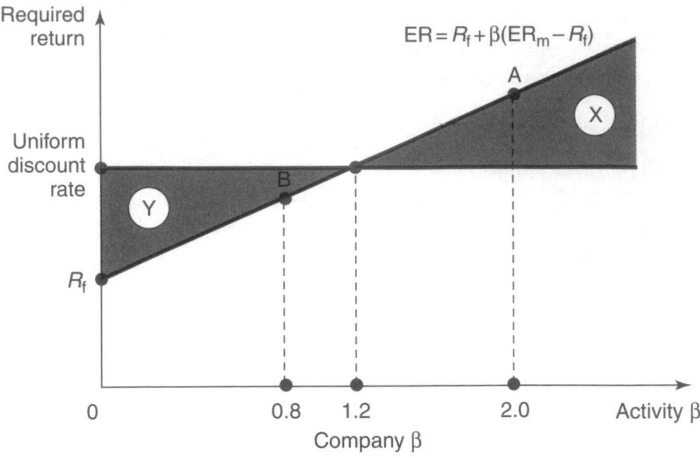

Figure 12.1 Risk premiums for activities of varying risk

For example, activity A has a greater degree of risk, with a Beta of 2.0, and thus a higher-than-average discount rate would be applicable when appraising new projects in this area, while the reverse applies for activity B, which has a Beta of only 0.8. Clearly, to appraise all new projects using a discount rate based on the overall company Beta of 1.2 would invite serious errors. For example, in area X, application of the uniform discount rate would result in accepting some projects that should be rejected because they offer too low a return for their level of risk, while in area Y, some worthwhile low-risk projects would be rejected. Firms should use 'tailor-made' cut-off rates for activities involving a degree of risk different from that of the overall company.

Self-assessment Activity 12.3

What are the discount rates applicable to the firm as a whole and activities A and B on Figure 12.1, assuming a risk-free rate of 5 per cent, and a market risk premium of 6 per cent?

(answer at end of chapter)

Figure 12.2 shows the three levels, or tiers, of risk found in the multi-activity enterprise, each requiring a different rate of return.

In Chapter 21, we will find that there is a fourth tier of risk that uniquely applies to ordinary shareholders. In a geared firm, that faces financial risk, the returns achieved by shareholders are more volatile than the firm's operating cash flows due to the interest payments required. In response to this higher risk, shareholders demand a higher return. In other words, the Beta of the shares exceeds the Beta of the firm's business activities, i.e. it is geared. To arrive at the activity Beta, we would need to 'ungear' the Beta of the shares.

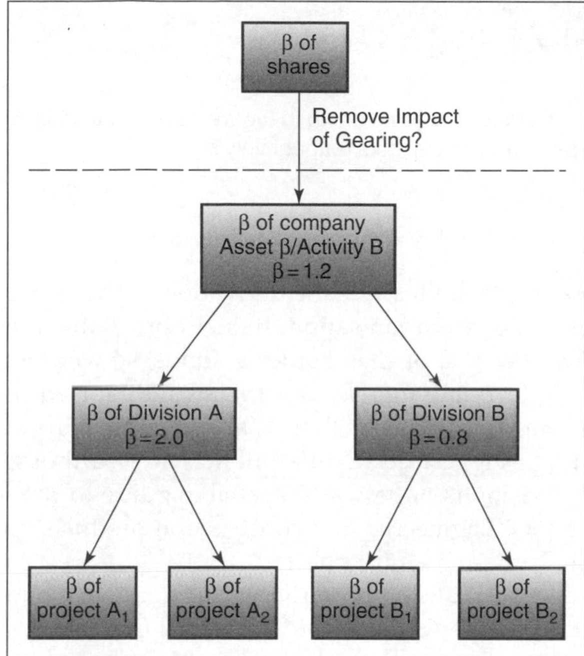

Figure 12.2 The Beta pyramid

If the company is wholly equity-financed, the risks that shareholders incur coincide with those incurred by the company as a whole, i.e. those related to trading and operational factors. In this case, the Beta of the ordinary shares coincides with that of the company itself.

Many companies are structured into separate strategic sub-units or divisions, organised along product or geographical lines. In such companies, it is unlikely that every activity faces identical systematic risk. So differential discount rates should be applied to evaluate 'typical' projects within each division.

However, even within divisions, rarely do two projects have identical risk. Hence, differential discount rates are required when new projects differ in risk from existing divisional activities.

Segmental Betas

The company Beta is a weighted average of component divisional Betas. For a company with two divisions, A and B, the overall Beta is a weighted average by:

$$\text{Company } \beta = \left(\beta_A \times \frac{V_A}{V_A + V_B}\right) + \left(\beta_B \times \frac{V_B}{V_A + V_B}\right)$$

where the weights represent the proportion of company value accounted for by each segment. A similar expression would apply for each division, where the corresponding weights would represent the contribution to divisional value accounted for by each component activity. Figure 12.2 illustrates these concepts as a Beta pyramid.

Self-assessment Activity 12.4

What is the company Beta for the firm shown in Figure 12.1 if activities A and B constitute 65 per cent and 35 per cent of its assets respectively?

(answer at end of chapter)

Let us use Tomkins plc to illustrate the derivation of the appropriate discount rate at different levels of an organisation. Its net borrowing, allowing for cash holdings, was only 2 per cent of shareholder's' funds, so we can treat the parent company as being effectively ungeared[2]. It is also organised into three broad product division lines, as shown in Table 12.2, which lists its seven operating divisions. These titles suggest quite different activities, although a firm's own description of its division is not always a reliable guide to the nature of those activities. For example, 'Engineered and construction products' includes 'wheels and axles' and also 'baths and whirlpools'!

We performed a CAPM calculation earlier in relation to the equity of Tomkins, obtaining a result of 11.1 per cent. Should we apply this rate to all investments undertaken by Tomkins? The answer is 'no', if we believe there are risk differences between the divisions, in which case, we should calculate tailor-made discount rates.

The divisional cut-off rate

We need now to consider what are suitable Betas for the three Tomkins divisions. However, no Betas are recorded for company divisions, simply because no market trades securities representing title to Tomkins' divisional assets. Instead, we need to look for three surrogate companies and use their ungeared Betas as the 'stand-in' estimates for the Betas of the three Tomkins divisions. This involves using what Fuller and Kerr (1981) called the **pure play technique**. It relies on the principle that: 'the risk of a division of a conglomerate company is the same as the risk of an undiversified firm in the same line of business (adjusted for financial risk)'.

Consulting the RMS, we look for suitable surrogate companies whose Betas we can use as proxies for those of the Tomkins divisions. The dangers of doing this should not be understated. Ideally, the surrogate should be a close match for the relevant Tomkins division, i.e. they should conduct the same activity or mix of activities in the same proportions, and should also be ungeared. (If they use debt finance, the gearing effect on their Betas should be stripped out, as explained in Chapter 21.) In principle, the weighted averages of these Beta values will coincide with the overall Beta of Tomkins plc if we have selected good surrogates. The weightings ought to be based on market values, but as these are unknown for company divisions, book values of net operating assets have been used, as

[2] This procedure may not be universally acceptable as Tomkins had a substantial amount of preference shares ('non-equity shareholders' funds') in its capital structure.

Table 12.3 Divisional Betas for Tomkins plc

Division	% of net operating assets	Surrogate company	Surrogate Beta	Weighted Beta
Air Systems Components	11	BTR/Invensys	1.40	0.154
Engineered and Construction Products	20	Wolseley	1.20	0.240
Industrial and Automotive	69	GKN	1.18	0.814
Total	100	–	–	1.21

Source: Tomkins' plc Report and Accounts, Risk Measurement Service (RMS)

presented in Tomkins' annual report. (Not all companies reveal divisional asset values, so a proxy measure such as sales or operating profits may have to be used.)

Table 12.3 shows that the weighted values for Tomkins sum to 1.21, a little above the Beta of 1.18 given in the RMS. How can we explain the discrepancy? Perhaps the surrogates are not close enough matches, or the analysis is distorted by gearing. Although Tomkins is virtually ungeared, the calculation has used equity Beta for the surrogates. BTR/Invensys was highly geared at this time. Removing the effect of gearing (see Chapter 21) would lower the Invensys contribution to the weighted average calculation. Note also that the RMS Beta being based on observations over five years, smooths out not only random fluctuations but also changes in corporate structure. Asset disposals and acquisitions of other companies would affect the overall Tomkins Beta. Yet the full effect will not be recorded by the RMS until several years have elapsed. This exercise clearly demonstrates some of the pitfalls in using Betas.

The project cut-off rate

If any division undertakes a new venture that takes it outside its existing risk parameters, clearly we must look for different rates of return – in effect, we need to obtain estimates for individual project Betas. Without access to internal records, our analysis can only be indicative, but the following principles offer broad guidance.

Essentially, we look for sources of risk that make the individual project more or less chancy relative to existing operations. There are two broad reasons why projects have different risks to the divisions where they are based – different revenue sensitivity and different operating gearing.

Revenue sensitivity

Imagine Tomkins is looking at developing a new automotive product. The sales generated by the projected facility may vary with changes in economic activity to a greater or lesser degree than existing sales in the relevant division.

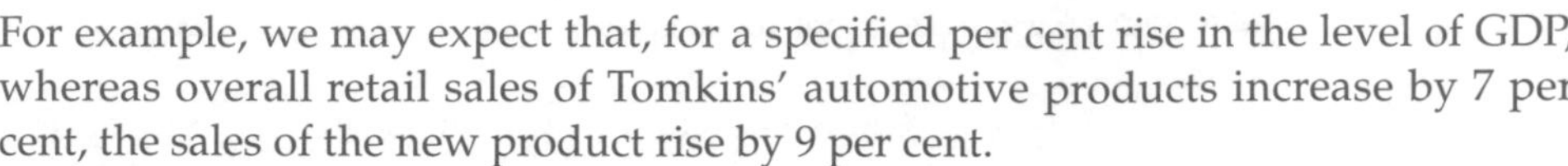

For example, we may expect that, for a specified per cent rise in the level of GDP, whereas overall retail sales of Tomkins' automotive products increase by 7 per cent, the sales of the new product rise by 9 per cent.

The revenue sensitivity factor

This magnifying effect is measured by the **revenue sensitivity factor** (RSF). The RSF is calculated as follows:

$$\text{RSF} = \frac{\text{Sensitivity of project sales to economic changes}}{\text{Sensitivity of divisional sales to economic changes}} = \frac{9\%}{7\%} = 1.29$$

This relationship may stem from the nature of the product – if it is pitched at discretionary spenders (e.g. people who buy 'bolt-on' auto accessories), it may be more closely geared to the economy as a whole.

Operating gearing

This concerns the extent to which the project cost structure comprises fixed charges. The higher the proportion of fixed costs in the cost structure, the greater the impact of a change in economic conditions on the operating cash flow of the project, thus magnifying the revenue sensitivity effect. Again, the project may exhibit a degree of operating gearing different from that of the division as a whole.

To illustrate the impact of operating gearing, consider the figures in Table 12.4, where the firm applies a 50 per cent mark-up on variable cost. An increase in sales revenue of 50 per cent will lead to an increase in net operating cash flow of 67 per cent because of the gearing effect. There is thus a magnifying factor of 1.34. This is called the **project gearing factor** (PGF) and may well differ from the gearing factor(s) found elsewhere in the division.

To measure the relative level of gearing, the **operating gearing factor** (OGF) is used. This is defined as:

$$\text{OGF} = \frac{\text{Project gearing factor}}{\text{Divisional gearing factor}}$$

If the divisional gearing factor is 1.50, for example, the OGF = 1.34/1.50 = 0.89.

The second step in assessing the project discount rate brings together these two sources of relative project risk into a project risk factor (PRF).

Table 12.4 The effect of operating gearing (£m)

Sales revenue	Variable costs	Fixed cash costs	Operating cash flow
90	60	5	25
60	40	5	15

The project risk factor

This is the compound of the revenue sensitivity factor and the operating gearing factor:

Project risk factor = RSF × OGF

In our example, this is equal to (1.29 × 0.89) = 1.15. In this case, the project is considerably more risky than the 'average' project within the division and merits the application of a higher Beta. Based on the Tomkins' automotive Beta, shown in Table 12.3, this is given by:

Project Beta = (1.15 × 1.18) = 1.36

The final step calculates the required return using the basic CAPM equation; based on a 5 per cent risk-free rate and a market risk premium of 6 per cent.

Required return = 0.05 + 1.36(0.06) = 0.131, i.e. 13.1%

Self-assessment Activity 12.5

Determine the required return on a project whose revenue sensitivity is 50 per cent and operating gearing 80 per cent compared to the division where it is located. The divisional Beta is 1.2, the risk-free rate is 5 per cent and the market risk premium 6 per cent.

(answer at end of chapter)

Project discount rates in practice

Considering the informational requirements for obtaining reliable tailor-made discount rates for particular investment projects, few firms go to these lengths. A far more common practice is to seek an overall divisional rate of return, which becomes the average cut-off rate, but is then adjusted for risk on a largely intuitive basis, according to the perceived degree of risk of the project. For example, many firms group projects into 'risk categories' such as the classification in Table 12.5. For each category, a target or required return is established as the cut-off rate.

The divisional required return is 18 per cent, the rate applicable to projects which replicate the firm's existing activities. Around this benchmark are clustered activities of varying degrees of risk, and as the perceived riskiness increases, the target return rises in tandem.

In all these cases, we are discussing a discount rate derived from the ungeared Beta. In other words, we are separating out the inherent profitability of the project from any financing costs and benefits. Analysis of financing complications is deferred to Chapters 20 and 21.

Table 12.5 Subjective risk categories

Project type	Required return (%)
Replacement	12
Cost saving/application of advanced manufacturing technology	15
'Scale' projects, i.e. expansion of existing activities	18
New project development:	
Imitative products	20
Conceptually new products, i.e. no existing competitors	25

12.7 Another problem: taxation and the CAPM

Empirical studies of the risk premium usually reveal gross-of-personal-tax results. To adjust for tax, one might consider the tax status of interest income from the risk-free asset, normally taken as government stock of some form, and the tax status of the return on the market portfolio.

Franks and Broyles (1979) recommend two adjustments. First, adjust the risk-free rate for the shareholders' rate of personal tax (at present, UK basic-rate tax on interest income is 10 per cent), then adjust the risk premium according to the relative proportions of excess return earned in dividends and in capital gain form. Grubb (1993/4) shows that over 1960–92, about half of the return on equities was from dividends and half from capital gain. Two major problems follow. Capital Gains Tax (CGT) was only introduced in 1965, and has been applied at varying rates, while the basic rate of income tax has also changed many times over this period. Moreover, in reality, very few shareholders are liable to CGT. However, taking 20 per cent as an average rate of CGT and 25 per cent as an average rate of tax on dividends yielding a weighted average tax rate (WAT) of $(0.5 \times 0.20) + (0.5 \times 0.25) = 22.5\%$ the calculation of the post-tax required return on Tomkins' ordinary shares (ER_T) would be:

$$\begin{aligned} ER_T &= R_f(1 - \text{present income tax rate}) + \beta[\text{market risk premium}][1 - \text{WAT}] \\ &= 0.05(1 - 0.1) + 1.18[0.06][1 - 0.225] \\ &= 0.045 + 0.0549 = 0.01 \quad \text{i.e. } 10\% \end{aligned}$$

There are obvious problems in taking average rates of tax over periods when tax regimes have altered. Wilkie (1994) argues that such a calculation is conceptually flawed, being based on the assumption that individuals would have invested in a tax-inefficient vehicle (government stock) – although many do! Most personal investors would have been subject to higher rates of income tax and thus would have taken steps anyway to shelter their income from tax. Finally, he points out that the securities market historically has been dominated by tax-exempt investors, in terms of both the percentages of share value held and, more crucially, the flow of new funds to the market, which dictates market prices. He concludes that little accuracy is lost by using the gross-of-tax risk premium, and ignoring any tax effect on the risk-free rate, especially as future tax rates on investment income are likely to be lower than past rates, following widespread tax cuts in the 1990s.

This view is very appealing, both in view of the rapid growth in the popularity of tax breaks like the old TESSAs and PEPs, and now ISAs; and also for simplicity. Difficulties over specifying discount rates may go some way to explaining the continuing popularity of the payback method. Significantly, this is usually used in conjunction with the IRR, which does not require the pre-specification of a discount rate. This combination becomes a convenient means of communicating criteria of investment acceptability throughout a company without requiring continuous updating of the discount rate for the tax position. A survey of over 200 firms conducted for the CBI by Junankar (1994) found that 56 per cent of those which used the IRR method applied it on a pre-tax basis.

12.8 Problems with 'tailored' discount rates

The pure play technique is an appealing device for estimating discount rates for specific activities, but suffers from a number of practical difficulties.

1 *Selecting the proxy*. To select a proxy, the firm needs to examine the range of apparently similar candidates operating in the relevant sector. However, no two companies have the same business risk due to diversity of markets, management skills and other operating characteristics. How one chooses between a range of 'fairly similar' candidates is essentially an issue of judgement.

2 *Divisional interdependencies*. In practice, it is difficult to make a rigid demarcation of divisional costs and incomes, since most divisionalised companies share facilities, ranging from the highest decision-making level to joint research and development, joint distribution channels and joint marketing activities. Indeed, access to shared facilities often provides the initial motive for forming a diversified conglomerate, enabling the elimination of duplicated services and the exploitation of scale economies. If carefully evaluated and implemented, the merging of activities should create value and reduce business risk. Only when a merger has no operating impact across divisional lines can it be suggested that business risk itself is unaffected. Even so, there may well be synergies at the peak decision-making level.

3 *Differential growth opportunities*. Using a cut-off rate based on another firm suggests that the division in question has the same growth prospects as the surrogate. However, opportunities to grow are determined by dividend policy, the extent of capital rationing and the interaction between divisions, e.g. competition for scarce investment capital. In reality, because the firm's own decision processes help to determine the potential for growth, it is not accurate to assume that growth opportunities are externally derived.

4 *Joint ventures*. The use of differential discount rates may destroy the incentive to cooperate on projects that straddle divisional boundaries. For example, a joint venture whose expected return lies between the cut-off rates of the two divisions will be attractive to one and unacceptable to the other. Here, some form of mediation is required at peak level, which reassures the 'loser' of the decision that subsequent performance will be assessed after adjusting for having to operate with a project that it did *not* want, or without a project that it *did* wish to undertake.

12.9 A critique of divisional hurdle rates[3]

Modern strategic planning has moved away from crude portfolio planning devices such as the Boston Consulting Group's market share/market growth matrix towards capital allocation methods that emphasise the creation of shareholder value. Central to value-based approaches is discounting projected cash flows to determine the value to shareholders of business units and their strategies. *A key feature of the DCF approach is the recognition that different business strategies involve different degrees of risk and should be discounted at tailored risk-adjusted rates.*

However, critics such as Reimann (1990) suggest that differential rates will increase the likelihood of internal dissension, whereby a manager of a 'penalised' division may resent the requirement to earn a rate of return significantly higher than some of his colleague-competitors. This resentment may be worsened by the observation that longer-term developments, especially in advanced manufacturing technology and other risky, but potentially high value-added activities, may be 'unfairly' discriminated against. As a result, managers may be reluctant to propose some potentially attractive projects.

As we saw in Chapter 9, risk-adjusted discount rates have the effect of compounding risk differences, making ostensibly riskier projects appear to increase in risk over time. One school of thought contends that in order to avoid this risk penalty, the attempt to tailor discount rates to divisions should be modified, if not abandoned. For example, instead of using differential discount rates, firms might use a more easily understood and acceptable, company-wide discount rate for projects of 'normal' risk, but appraise high-risk/high-return projects using different approaches.

Underlying these arguments is the familiar assertion that diversification by firms differs crucially from shareholder diversification, so that applying the CAPM to the former could be misleading. If an investor adds a new share to an existing portfolio, the market risk of the portfolio will alter according to the Beta of the new security. If its Beta is higher than that of the existing portfolio, then the portfolio Beta increases, and vice versa. With corporate diversification, however, we are not dealing with a basket of shares of unrelated companies, which may be freely traded on the market. A firm that diversifies rarely adds totally unrelated activities to its core operations. It may add value if the new activity possesses synergy, or detract from value if the market views the combination as merely a bundle of disparate, unwieldy activities that are hard to manage.

Market risk can be altered by strategic diversification decisions at two levels. At the corporate level, decisions concerning business and product mixes, and operating and financial gearing can affect market risk. The effect of both types of gearing can be magnified by the business cycle, so that a firm which engages in contra-cyclical diversification may dampen oscillations in shareholder returns and thus reduce market risk. At the business level, market risk can be

[3] This section relies heavily on arguments used by Reimann (1990).

reduced by tying up outlets and supplier sources (i.e. by increasing market power), and by developing business activities that enjoy important interrelationships, such as common skills or technologies (i.e. by exploiting economies of scale).

Many managers feel that the emphasis on hurdle rates is probably misplaced insofar as accurate cash flow forecasts are more important to creating business value than the particular discount rate applied to them. This probably explains the continuing popularity of the payback method, and the reluctance, at least in the UK, to adopt CAPM-based approaches. It may also explain why so many successful firms place great emphasis on post-auditing capital projects in order to sharpen up the cash flow forecasting and project appraisals of subordinate staff. Furthermore, there is evidence (Pruitt and Gitman 1987; Pohlman *et al.* 1988) that senior managers manifest their suspicion of subordinates' cash flow predictions by deflating the figures presented to them when projects are submitted for approval.

In view of these arguments, there may be a case for reconsidering the merits of using certainty equivalents – adjusting the cash flow estimates and then discounting at the risk-free rate. However, this has not been widely adopted. Apart from the difficulty of specifying the risk-free asset, there is the problem of determining the certainty equivalent factors, which involves specifying the probabilities of different possible cash flows as a basis for assessing their utility values. While techniques are available for doing this (Swalm 1966; Chesley 1975), it has not been practicable in most firms.

Reimann (1990) suggests a 'management by exception' approach. The firm should establish and continuously update a corporate cost of capital, based on CAPM principles. This should be applied as a common hurdle rate for the majority of business activities, which, he argues, typically exhibit very similar degrees of risk. At the business level, major emphasis should be given to careful cash flow estimation, based on evaluation of long-term strategic opportunities and competitive advantage. A key element should be a multiple scenario approach, whereby the implications of 'best', 'worst' and 'most likely' states of the world are examined. For projects that, by their very nature, have a demonstrably greater level of risk, other procedures may be appropriate. Rather than adjust the corporate discount rate, Reimann suggests the risk adjustment be made to the cash flow estimates by the business unit executives themselves, i.e. those with closest knowledge both of the market and of competitors' behaviour patterns. Again, a multiple scenario approach should be adopted. This avoids the effect of compounding risk differences over time and thus penalising longer-term projects, which may have a demotivating effect on staff engaged in progressing high-risk activities.

This discussion may seem to downgrade the importance of DCF and CAPM approaches in project appraisal. However, it is really intended to remind you that apparently neat mathematical models rarely hold the whole answer. If the rigid application of a numerical routine leads managers to question the basis of the routine itself (one which we believe offers powerful guidance in many situations) and to exhibit dysfunctional behaviour, it is far better to modify the routine itself to reflect real world practicalities.

12.10 The discount rate for Foreign Direct Investment (FDI)

Opinions differ as to the appropriate discount rate to apply when discounting net cash flows from foreign investment. 'Gut feelings' may suggest that FDI should be evaluated at a higher discount rate than domestic investment 'simply because it involves more risk'. But is this valid?

Assuming all-equity finance, two commonly-suggested possibilities are:

- Use a required return based on the risk of similar activities in the home country. This would be the equity cost for projects in activities similar to existing ones, or a 'tailored' project-specific rate for ventures into new spheres.
- Use a required return comparable to that of local firms.

Before deciding which approach is preferable, there are several issues to consider:

1 Foreign projects generally involve higher levels of risk than domestic ones. However, much of this risk can be dealt with in better ways than simply 'hiking' the discount rate. For example, currency risk can be handled by hedging techniques mentioned in Chapter 17 (if thought necessary), and political risk can be handled in the ways discussed in Chapter 8.

2 Although the total risk of FDI is often very high, the relevant risk is generally much lower, and sometimes lower than for comparable investment at home. FDI involves diversifying into overseas markets in the same way as an investor might diversify shareholdings across international markets. Solnik (1974) showed that the correlation between national stock markets is generally much less than one (although it may have increased in recent years). If investors can lower relevant risk by cross-border portfolio diversification, why should firms not do so? This is especially relevant for firms whose investors cannot diversify internationally, due to exchange controls or transactions costs, or into countries where no organised stock exchange operates.

The relevant Beta value for, say, a UK firm operating abroad may not be the Beta calculated by reference to the UK market portfolio, but the Beta in relation to the local market (if there is one). Consider the following example.

Example: Malaku mining

Malaku Mining is the newly-formed Indonesian subsidiary of Mowmack plc, an all equity-financed UK firm, whose shares have a Beta value of 0.9 relative to the UK market portfolio. The total risk (standard deviation) of the Malaku project is 30 per cent and the risk of the Jakarta Stock Exchange is 20 per cent. The UK stock market has a 50 per cent correlation with the Jakarta market.

Here, the parent Beta of 0.9 is inappropriate. Instead of using this value, it is more appropriate to consider the risk of the proposed activity in relation to the local market and allow for the low correlation between the London and Jakarta exchanges. We can do this by using a variation of the formula found in Section 11.5:

Project Beta = correlation coefficient × (risk of the activity/local market risk)

This yields a project-specific Beta of:

$(0.5 \times 30\%/20\%) = (0.5 \times 1.5) = 0.75$

The cost of equity would be calculated using the UK risk-free rate of, say, 5 per cent and the UK-equity market risk premium of, say, 6 per cent, as the firm has a UK investor base. Hence, the required rate of return for all-equity funding would be found from the usual CAPM formula:

$k_e = R_f + \text{Beta}[ER_m - R_f] = 5\% + 0.75[6\%] = 9.5\%$

Summary

We have considered the relative merits of using the DGM and the CAPM to derive the rate of return required by shareholders. The case for and against using tailor-made discount rates for particular business segments and projects was also discussed.

Key points

- The return required on new investment depends primarily on two factors: degree of risk and the method of financing the project.
- In ungeared companies, the return required by shareholders can be estimated using either the DGM or the CAPM.
- The DGM relies on several critical assumptions: in particular, sustained and constant growth, and the instantaneous reliability of the share price set by the market.
- The CAPM relies on a Beta estimate obtained after smoothing short-term distortions, but the estimated k_e may be affected by random influences on the risk-free rate.
- Application of a uniform company-wide discount rate to all company projects can lead to accepting projects that should be rejected and to rejecting projects that should be accepted.
- To resolve the problem of risk differences between divisions of a company, the Beta of a surrogate firm (adjusted for gearing) can be used to establish divisional cut-off rates.
- If individual projects within the division also differ in risk, the divisional Beta can be adjusted for differences in revenue sensitivity and/or differences in operating gearing.
- Not all academics and business people accept the need to define discount rates so carefully, preferring instead to concentrate on the problems of cash flow estimation.
- Reimann argues that a divisional cut-off rate should be used as a rough benchmark for projects, but alternative methods of risk analysis should be applied to explore more fully the risk characteristics and the acceptability of investment proposals.
- The discount rate for evaluating foreign projects is not necessarily greater than that for evaluating domestic projects.

Further reading

Analyses of the 'tailored' discount rate can be found in Dimson and Marsh (1982) and Andrews and Firer (1987). Gup and Norwood (1982) and Harrington (1983) provide practical illustrations of how US corporations apply divisional discount rates, while Reimann (1990) gives a critique of the whole approach.

Self-assessment Answers

12.1 If EPS = 36p, and the dividend is covered three times, the dividend per share must be 12p (36p/12p = 3).
Hence, the cost of equity is:

$$k_e = \frac{12p(1 + 3\%)}{£1.80} + 3\% = (6.9\% + 3\%) = 9.9\%$$

12.2 Under these two conditions, the DVM breaks down totally:

(i) when the firm pays no dividend
(ii) when the growth rate of dividends exceeds the cost of equity.

12.3 Overall, the required return = 5% + 1.2[6%] = 12.2%
For activity A, it is = 5% + 2.0[6%] = 17%
For activity B, it is = 5% + 0.8[6%] = 9.8%

12.4 Company Beta = (0.65 × Beta of A) + (0.35 × Beta of B)
= (0.65 × 2.0) + (0.35 × 0.8) = 1.58.

12.5 The project Beta = RSF × OGF × divisional Beta
= (0.5 × 0.8 × 1.2) = 0.48
Hence, required return = 5% + 0.48[6%] = 5% + 2.9% = 7.9%.

Questions

1 *Solution in Appendix A (page 815).* The ordinary shares of Rasal plc have a market price of £10.50, following a recent divided payment of £0.80 per share. Dividend growth has averaged 4.5 per cent p.a. over the past five years. What is the rate of return required by shareholders implied by the current share price?

2 *Solution in Appendix A (page 815).* Insert the missing values in the following table:

k_e	P_o	g	D_o
(i) 11%	£8.00	3%	?
(ii) 14%	?	4%	£0.350
(iii) ?	£5.00	6%	£0.155
(iv) 12%	£4.60	?	£0.250

3 *Solution in Appendix A (page 815).* Lofthouse plc has paid out dividends per share over the past few years, as follows:

1996	11.0p
1997	12.5p
1998	14.0p
1999	17.0p
2000	20.0p

In March 2000, the market price per share of Lofthouse is £5.00 ex-dividend. What is the rate of return required by investors in Lofthouse's equity implied by the Dividend Growth Model?

4 *Solution in Appendix A (page 816).* The all-equity financed Lasar plc has a Beta of 0.8. What rate of return should it seek on new investment:

(i) with similar risk to existing activities?
(ii) with 25 per cent greater risk compared to existing activities?
(iii) with 25 per cent lower risk compared to existing activities?

The risk-free rate of interest is 6 per cent, and the expected return on the market portfolio is 11 per cent.

5 *Solution in Appendix A (page 816).* Salas Ltd is an unquoted company that operates four divisions, all focused on single activities as shown in the table below. Salas identifies a proxy quoted company for each activity in order to calculate cut-off rates for new investment.

Division	Proxy Beta	Assets employed (£ m)
Construction (C)	0.7	3.00
Engineering (E)	1.1	8.00
Road Haulage (R)	0.8	4.00
Packaging (P)	0.6	5.00

The risk-free rate is 7 per cent, and the expected return on the market portfolio is 15 per cent.

Required

(i) Calculate the required return at each division.
(ii) Calculate Salas' overall required rate of return.

6 *Solution in Appendix A (page 816).* Megacorp plc, an all-equity financed multinational, is contemplating expansion into an overseas market. It is considering whether to invest directly in the country concerned by building a greenfield site factory. The expected payoff from the project would depend on the future state of the economy of Erewhon, the host country, as shown below:

State of Erewhon economy	Probability	IRR from project (%)
E_1	0.1	10
E_2	0.2	20
E_3	0.5	10
E_4	0.2	20

Megacorp's existing activities are expected to generate an overall return of 30 per cent with a standard deviation of 14 per cent. The correlation coefficient of Megacorp's returns with that of the new project is −0.36, Megacorp's returns have a correlation coefficient of 0.80 with the return on the market portfolio, and the new project has a correlation coefficient of −0.10 with the UK market portfolio.

The Beta coefficient for Megacorp is 1.20.
The risk-free rate is 12 per cent.
The risk premium on the UK market portfolio is 15 per cent.
Assume Megacorp's shares are correctly priced by the market.

Required

(a) Determine the expected rate of return and standard deviation of the return from the new project

(b) If the new project requires capital funding equal to 25 per cent of the value of the existing assets of Megacorp, determine the risk–return characteristics of Megacorp after the investment.

(c) What effect will the adoption of the project have on the Beta of Megacorp?

Ignore all taxes.

7 PFK plc is an undiversified and ungeared company operating in the cardboard packaging industry. The Beta coefficient of its ordinary shares is 1.05. It now contemplates diversification into making plastic containers. After evaluation of the proposed investment, it considers that the expected cash flows can be described by the following probability distribution:

State of economy	Probability	Internal rate of return (%)
Recession	0.2	−5
No growth	0.3	8
Steady growth	0.3	12
Rapid growth	0.2	30

The overall risk (standard deviation) of parent company returns is 20 per cent and the risk of the market return is 12 per cent. The risk-free rate is 5 per cent and the FTSE-100 Index is expected to offer an *overall* return of 10 per cent per annum in the foreseeable future.

The new project will increase the value of PFK's assets by 33 per cent.

Required

(a) Calculate the risk–return characteristics of PFK's proposed diversification.

(b) It is believed that the plastic cartons activity has a covariance value of 40 with the company's existing activity.

- **(i)** Calculate the *total* risk of the company *after* undertaking the diversification.
- **(ii)** Calculate the new Beta value for PFK, given that the diversification lowers its overall covariance with the market portfolio to 120.

(iii) Deduce the Beta value for the new activity.
(iv) What appears to be the required return on this new activity?

(c) Discuss the desirability, from the shareholders' point of view, of the proposed diversification.

You may ignore taxes.

8 *Solution in Appendix A (page 817).* Lancelot plc is a diversified company with three operating divisions – North, South and West. The operating characteristics of North are 50 per cent more risky than South, while West is 25 per cent less risky than South. In terms of financial valuation, South is thought to have a market value twice that of North, which has the same market value as West. Lancelot is all-equity-financed with a Beta of 1.06. The overall return on the FT All-Share Index is 25 per cent, with a standard deviation of 16 per cent.

Recently, South has been under-performing and Lancelot's management plan to sell it and use the entire proceeds to purchase East Ltd, an unquoted company. East is all-equity-financed and Lancelot's financial strategists reckon that while East is operating in broadly similar markets and industries to South, East has a revenue sensitivity of 1.4 times that of South, and an operating gearing ratio of 1.6 compared to the current operating gearing in South of 2.0.

Assume: no synergistic benefits from the divestment and acquisition. You may ignore taxation.

Required

(a) Calculate the asset Betas for the North, South and West divisions of Lancelot. Specify any assumptions which you make.
(b) Calculate the asset Beta for East.
(c) Calculate the asset Beta for Lancelot after the divestment and acquisition.
(d) What discount rate should be applied to any new investment projects in East division?
(e) Indicate the problems in obtaining a 'tailor-made' project discount rate such as that calculated in section (d).

Note: More questions on required rates of return can be found in Chapter 21, where the additional complexities of gearing are discussed.

13 Identifying and valuing options

The marriage (option) contract

'Wilt thou have this woman to be thy lawful wedded wife?' As the minister posed this question, the groom, a highly trained financial analyst, reflected that marriage bore many characteristics of the investment decisions he faced every day. It was clearly a long-term commitment, involving uncertain costs and benefits. What is more, it was largely irreversible; and the abandonment option of divorce was too costly and painful to contemplate. The follow-on option was interesting. How many kids had she mentioned?

But what about the options he would be sacrificing? The option to remain an independent bachelor, or the option to wait another six months to be better informed as to whether the couple were really right for each other. Just how valuable was the marriage option contract, and was now the right expiry date?

After a moment's hesitation, the groom turned and looked into his bride's adoring eyes. All thoughts of rational economic analysis and option theory evaporated as he found himself saying, 'I will'.

Learning objectives

By the end of this chapter, you should possess a clear understanding of the following:

- The basic types of option and how they are employed.
- The main factors determining option values.
- How options can be used to reduce risk.
- How option values can be estimated.
- The various applications of options theory to investment and corporate finance.
- Why conventional net present value analysis is not sufficient for appraising projects.

13.1 Introduction

Business managers like to 'keep their options open'. Options convey the right, but not the obligation, to do something in the future. Like getting married, most business decisions involve closing off certain options while opening up others. Managers seek to create capital projects and financial instruments with valuable options embedded in them. For example, an investment proposal will be worth more if it contains the flexibility to exit relatively cheaply should things go wrong. This is because the 'downside' risk is minimised. Often it is not possible, or too costly, to build in such options. However, the financial manager can achieve much the same effect by creating options in financial markets. Option-like features occur in various aspects of finance, and options theory provides a powerful tool for understanding the value of such options.

This chapter concludes Part Three of this book, on handling risk in investment decisions, by examining the nature and types of options available and how they can reduce risk or add value. It also explains why the conventional net present value approach may not tell the whole story in appraising capital projects.

13.2 Share options

In finance, *options are contractual arrangements giving the owner the right, but not the obligation, to buy or sell something, at a given price, at some time in the future.* Note the two key elements in options: (1) the right to *choose* whether or not to take up the option, and (2) at an *agreed* price. It is not a true option if I am free to buy in the future at the *prevailing* market price, or if I am *compelled* to buy at an agreed price. Many securities have option features: for example, convertible loan stocks and share warrants, where options to convert to, or acquire, equity are given to the owner.

The simplest form of share option is when a company issues them as a way of rewarding employees. If the current share price of HSBC is £8, it might award share options to some of its employees at, say, the same price. If, over the period in which the shares can be exercised, the shares go up, employees could then purchase shares at a price below market price either to sell at a profit or gain an equity interest.

Most options relate to assets which already exist. These are termed **pure options**. To begin with, we will consider pure share options, although much of our analysis could apply equally to currency, oil and commodity markets. But first we need to go back to basics. Figure 13.1(a) depicts the payoff line for investing in ordinary shares in Enigma Drugs plc. If the shares are bought today at 400p, the payoff, or gain, from selling at the same price is zero. If, say, three months later, the share price has risen to 450p, the payoff is +50p; but if it has dropped to 350p, the payoff is −50p. The line is drawn at 45 degrees because a 50p increase in share price from its current level of 400p gives a 50p payoff.

We have all seen the warnings accompanying advertisements for financial products, reminding us that share prices can go up or down. But wouldn't it be nice if, whichever way prices moved, you ended up a winner? This can be done if you also acquire share options. With options you can create a 'no lose' situation

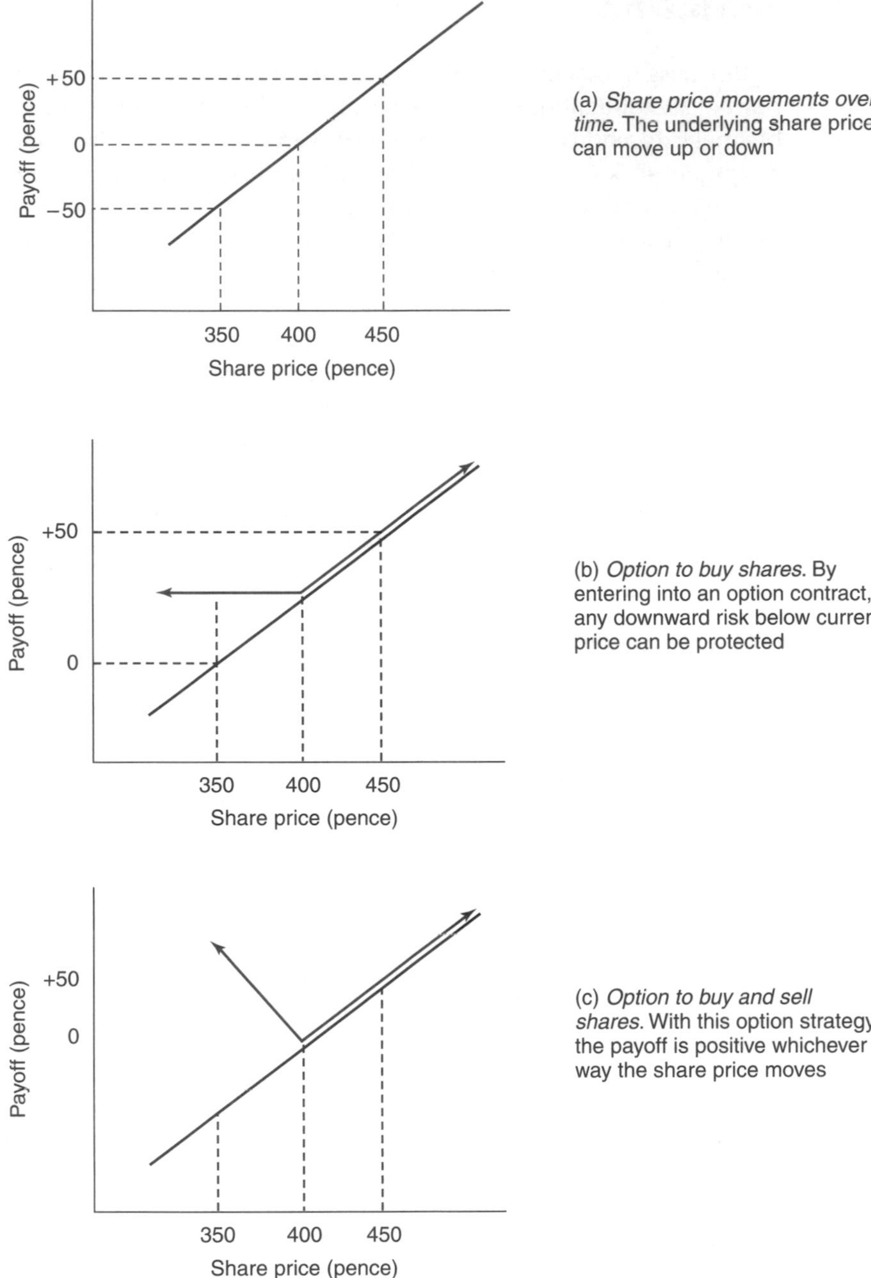

Figure 13.1 Payoff lines for shares and share options in Enigma Drugs plc (underlying share price is black, option contract has arrows)

providing protection from a drop in share price, as shown in Figure 13.1(b). The arrowed line represents the payoff from the option to buy shares. If share price increases, so does the option payoff. But if the share price falls below 400p, the option payoff remains at zero.

By combining different types of option you can even create a 'win–win' situation. For example, Figure 13.1(c) shows the effects of combining options to buy and sell shares at a fixed price. Here, either a rise or a fall in share price gives you a positive payoff. At this stage, however, you do not need to know how this is achieved, simply that it can be done. Of course, few things in life are free and a share option is not one of them (unless they form part of a remuneration package). Later we will show how to value such options.

Considerable interest has developed in recent years in share options, and there is a highly active market on the Stock Exchange for traditional and traded options. **Traditional options** are available on most shares and last for three months. A problem with these is that they are not particularly flexible or negotiable: investors must either exercise their option (i.e. buy or sell the underlying share) or allow it to lapse; they cannot trade their option.

To overcome these difficulties, **Traded Options** markets were established, first in Chicago, then in Amsterdam (the European Options Exchange). In 1978 the London Traded Options Market was established for major companies, now part of the London International Financial Futures and Options Exchange (LIFFE). (See **www.liffe.com**)

Options terminology

This topic has more than its fair share of esoteric jargon, some of the more essential of which are defined below.

- A **call option** gives its owner the right to *buy* specific shares at a fixed price – the **exercise price** or **striking price**.
- A **put option** gives its owner the right to *sell* (put up for sale) shares at a fixed price.
- A **European option** can be exercised only on a particular day (i.e. the end of its life), while an **American option** may be exercised at any time up to the date of expiry. These terms are a little confusing because most options traded in the UK and the rest of Europe are actually American options!
- The **premium** is the price paid for the option. Option prices are quoted for shares and traded in contracts (or units) each containing 1,000 shares.
- **In the money** is where the exercise price for a call option is *below* the current share price. In other words, it makes sense to take up the option.
- **Out of the money** is where the exercise price for a call option is *above* the current share price and it is not profitable to take up the option.

There are two parties to an **option contract**, the buyer (or option holder) and seller (or option writer). The buyer has the right, but not the obligation, to exercise the option. One feature of an option is that, if the share price does not move as expected, it can become completely worthless, regardless of the solvency of the company to which it relates. However, if it does move in line with expectations, very considerable gains can be achieved for very little outlay. Such

Table 13.1 Option on BP shares (current price 397p)

	Call option prices (p)			Put option prices (p)		
Exercise price	April	July	Oct	April	July	Oct
390	17	24½	31½	6½	12	17
420	4½	12	27½	24½	28	33

volatility gives share options a reputation as a highly speculative investment. But, as will be seen later, options can also be used to reduce risk.

In return for the option, the purchaser pays a fee or **premium**. The premium is a small fraction of the share price, and offers holders the opportunity to gain the benefits of investment gearing while limiting their risk to a known amount. The size of the premium depends on the **exercise price** and expected **volatility** of shares, which, in turn, is a function of the state of the market and the underlying risk of the share. The premium might range from as little as 3 per cent for a well-known share in a 'quiet' market to over 20 per cent for shares of smaller companies in a more volatile market. During past stock market collapses, option premiums shot up dramatically.

A **call option** gives the purchaser the right to buy a share at a given price within a set period, usually three months; a **put option** gives the right to sell; a **double** (also called a **straddle**) gives the right to do either (i.e. is a combined put and call option). Payment for the option is not immediate, but takes place when the option is exercised (i.e. taken up) or on expiry, if it is not exercised. The seller of an option must meet his or her obligation to buy or sell shares if the right of the purchaser is so exercised. The reward is, of course, the premium received.

Table 13.1 shows the prices (or premiums) at which options on BP Amoco (BP) are traded on a particular day on the traded options market of the Stock Exchange. The options are traded over a nine-month period with expiry dates every three months. Two exercise prices are given; the first, at 390p, is below the current share price of 397p ('in the money') and the second, at 420p, is above the current price ('out of the money'). Notice that option prices vary both with the agreed **exercise price** (the lower the exercise price for a call option, the higher the premium) and the **exercise date** (the longer the period, the higher the premium). To buy a call option on BP shares, at an exercise price of 390p, cost 17p for expiry in April, but 31½p for expiry six months later in October.

Self-assessment Activity 13.1

By now your head may be spinning with all the terms and concepts introduced. It is therefore a good time to take stock of what you should know.

1 Define a call option and a put option.
2 What is the basic difference between European and American call options?
3 Options are available on what types of asset?

(answer at end of chapter)

Speculative use of options: Kate Casino

Kate Casino thinks that there will be a takeover attempt on BP in the coming months and that the share price will move up sharply from its current level of 397p to a level in April sufficiently above the exercise price of 390p to justify the option price of 17p. Kate instructs her broker to purchase a contract for 1,000 April call options at a cost of (17p × 1,000) = £170. This is termed a **naked option**, held on its own rather than as a hedge against loss.

The current share price of 397p is above the 390p exercise price, so the option is already 'in the money', since Kate could immediately exercise her option to buy shares at 390p to gain 7p, before transaction costs. Of course, she would not do this because the premium to be paid for the option is 17p.

Let us look at three possible share prices arising in April when the option ends. **Best** – if the takeover attempt is made, BP's share price will rise to 460p by April. **Likely** – it will do no better than 415p. **Worst** – it falls as low as 380p. Her profit in each case would be:

Kate Casino's profit on the call option (pence)

	Best	Likely	Worst
Share price in April	460	415	380
Exercise price	390	390	390
Profit on exercise	70	25	Not exercised
Option premium paid	(17)	(17)	(17)
Profit (loss) before transaction costs	53	8	(17)
Profit on contract of 1,000 shares	£530	£80	(£170)

Kate would obviously not exercise her option if the price fell to 380p, so the loss in this case would be restricted to the 17p premium paid. If BP's price on expiry is 415p, the contract profit is a modest £80. But if the share price shoots up to 460p, a large gain of £530 is made on the contract.

It is interesting to compare the option returns with those from investing directly in BP shares. Table 13.2 shows that buying a call option has very different effects from buying the underlying share:

1 The capital outlay for the option contract for 1000 shares is much smaller (£170 compared with £3,970 for the underlying shares).
2 The downside risk on the option contract is far greater in *relative* terms, but not in *absolute* terms. Kate Casino loses all her initial investment on the option contract while the share value declines by only 4 per cent. However, in money terms, the loss is the same for both, £170.

Table 13.2 Returns on BP shares and options

Expiry share price	460p	380p
Buy 1,000 shares	£	£
Cost 397p each	(3,970)	(3,970)
Proceeds from sale	4,600	3,800
Profit (loss)	630	(170)
Return over 3 months on original cost	+15.9%	−4.3%
Call option on 1,000 shares	£	£
Cost of option	(170)	(170)
Cost of exercise at 390p	(3,900)	–
Proceeds on sale	4,600	–
	530	(170)
Return over 3 months	+312%	−100%

3 The return achieved, if the shares reach 460p, is a phenomenal 312 per cent on the options contract compared with 16 per cent on the underlying shares (ignoring dividends).

Figure 13.2 shows that, if the share price does not rise above the exercise price of 390p, the option is worthless. The option breaks even at 407p (390p + 17p premium) and the potential profit to be made thereafter is unlimited.

In general, the value of a call option at expiry (C_1) with a share price (S_1) and exercise price (E) is:

$$C_1 = S_1 - E, \text{ if } S_1 > E$$

At a share price of 415p, therefore, the option value is

$$\begin{aligned} C_1 &= 415\text{p} - 390\text{p} \\ &= 25\text{p} \end{aligned}$$

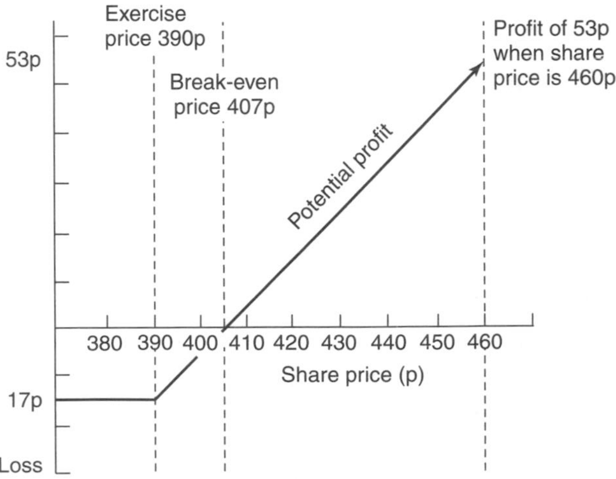

Figure 13.2 BP call option

New options at Marconi

Marconi yesterday sought to put its share option pricing débâcle of the summer behind it, by announcing new plans to award 87 million share options to 600 employees, including 3 million options for Mike Parton, chief executive.

In June, the troubled telecoms equipment group provoked controversy when it sought to reprice share options that were under water – options with exercise prices well above current market prices. It planned, for example, to reprice employee options granted at £16 with ones at £8.

The move, which the company said was needed to incentivise staff, turned out to be a harbinger of its later problems. The company later ditched the repricing scheme amid opposition.

The new plan marks Marconi's latest attempt to retain staff at a time when previous option grants remain under water and the shares show few signs of rebounding. The last round of options were issued last November at a strike price of £6.70. Options issued in June 2000 were priced at £9.47.

The depth of the slide was underlined with details of the new option grant of 35p, the price at the close of trade on November 28. The shares fell 2.06p to 32.6p yesterday.

The option grant is conditional on meeting the target of reducing debt to £2.7 billion–£3.2 billion by the end of March, and on meeting performance targets related to shareholder returns. They become exercisable from November 2002 up to November 2005.

Based on Caroline Daniel, the *Financial Times* November 30 2000

Options as a hedge: Rick Aversion

While options offer an excellent opportunity to speculate, they are equally useful as a means of risk reduction, insurance or **hedging**. Rick Aversion is concerned that the current share price on his BP shareholding will fall over the next two months. Because he wants to keep his shares as a long-term investment, he buys a put option (see Table 13.1), giving the right to sell shares in April at the striking price of 390p. This option costs him 6½p.

By late April, the shares have fallen to 350p, and the option has increased in value to 40p (i.e. 390 – 350). So Rick sells the option and retains the shares, using the profit on the option to offset the loss on the shares. This is administratively cheaper and more convenient than selling his shares and then buying them back. In this way, investors can capture any profits from a rise in share price and hedge against any price fall.

Figure 13.3 shows that when share prices are above the exercise price, the option value of the put is worthless. It should be exercised when prices fall below the 390p exercise price and breaks even at 383½p (exercise price less premium).

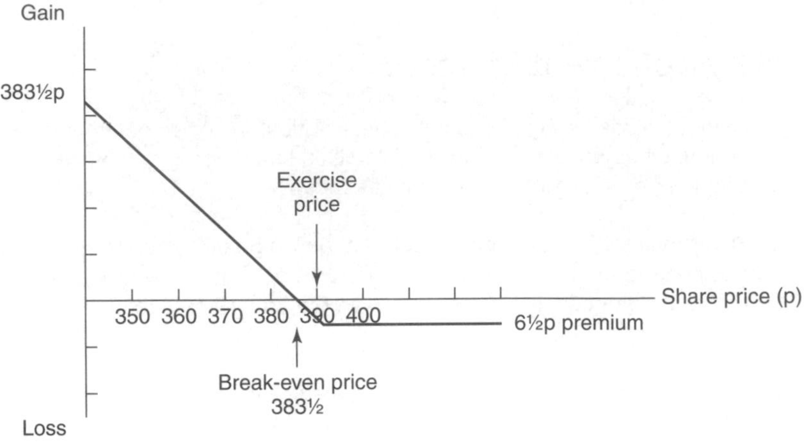

Figure 13.3 BP put option

In general, the value of a put option (P_1) is:

$$P_1 = E - S_1, \text{ if } S_1 < E$$

At a 370p share price, the value of the put option is therefore 20p

$$P_1 = 390\text{p} - 370\text{p}$$
$$= 20\text{p}$$

This is because the holder could buy the shares in the market at 370p and exercise the option to sell at 390p. The profit at this transaction is (20p – 6½p) = 13½p.

Doubles – the option to buy or sell a share – also provide a form of insurance. An investor may buy such an option where a company is about to embark on a major project or product launch, in which successful implementation would strongly enhance shareholder value, but failure could spell disaster for the company. Other option combinations, often with exotic names (e.g. short butterfly, long straddle and bull spread), also enable the treasurer to change the risk–return profile. We need not concern ourselves with the more complex options. Let us recap on the value of the two main forms of option, the call and put.

Option	Share price at expiry date	Option value at expiry
Call	above exercise price	share price – exercise price
	below exercise price	zero
Put	above exercise price	zero
	below exercise price	exercise price – share price

Figure 13.4 illustrates the four main types of option transaction and the relationship between share price movements and wealth created.

Consider the implications of buying a call option (a) and selling a put option (c), where the exercise price is the same for both. From Figure 13.4 we can see

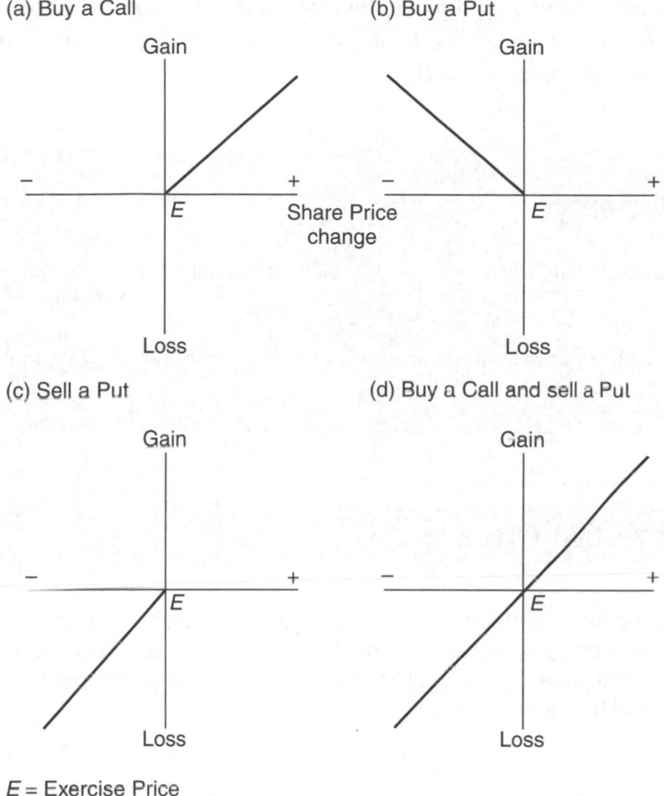

Figure 13.4 Option transactions

that the combined effect is a straight line (d), where the loss moves to profit as the underlying share price increases, achieving the same effects as holding the share itself. In other words, *purchasing a share at today's price is equivalent to buying a call option and selling a put option, while placing the remaining sum on deposit to earn a risk-free return over the option period.*

13.3 Option pricing

We can now focus on what determines the value of options. Option prices comprise two elements: intrinsic value and time-value. **Intrinsic value** is what the option would be worth were it about to expire; it reflects the degree to which an option is 'in the money' – in the case of a call option, the extent to which the exercise price is below the current share price. The **time-value** element depends on the length of time the option has to run – the longer the period, the better the chance of making a gain on the contract.

We showed in the previous section how the combination of buying a call option and selling a put option gave the same payoff as the underlying share price. To find a combination that yields a riskless return, we reverse the options.

By selling a call and buying a put option we create the exact opposite of the underlying share payoff, thereby providing us with a riskless strategy. From this, the *put–call parity relationship* is determined.

Put–call parity

Value of share + Value of put − Value of call = Present value of exercise price

$$S + P - C = E/(1 + R_f)$$

It follows from the above that, given four of the five factors, the fifth can be estimated.

Self-assessment Activity 13.2

You take out options contracts to sell a call and buy a put, both at the exercise price of 55p, exercisable one year hence. The cost of the put is 7p and the cost of the call is 1p. The current share price is 44p and the risk-free interest rate is 10 per cent. What is the present value of the exercise price?

(answer at end of chapter)

Valuing a call

The following notation is employed with respect to valuing call options:

S_0 = Share price today
S_1 = Share price at expiry date
E = Exercise price on the option
C_0 = Value of call option today
C_1 = Value of call option on expiration date
R_f = Risk-free interest rate

A number of formal statements can be made about **call options**:

1 *Option prices cannot be negative.* If the share price ends up below the exercise price on the expiration date, the call option is worthless, but no further loss is created beyond that of the initial premium paid. In mathematical terms:

$$C_1 = 0 \quad \text{if} \quad S_1 \leq E \tag{13.1}$$

This is the case where an option is 'out of the money' on expiry.

2 *An option is worth on expiry the difference between the share price and the exercise price.*

$$C_1 = S_1 - E \quad \text{if} \quad S_1 > E \tag{13.2}$$

This is the case where an option is 'in the money' on expiry.

Thus far we have found the intrinsic values of the option – what it would be worth were it about to expire. We have previously noted that options with some time still to run will generally be worth more than the difference between current share price and exercise price because the share price may rise further.

3 *The maximum value of an option is the share price itself* – it could never sell for more than the underlying share price value.

$$C_0 \leq S_0 \quad (13.3)$$

The minimum value of a call today is equal to or greater than the current share price less the exercise price:

$$C_0 \geq S_0 - E \quad \text{if} \quad S_0 > E \quad (13.4)$$

But the exercise price is payable in the future. It was shown in the previous section that the payoffs from a share are identical to the payoffs from buying a call option, selling a put option and investing the remainder in a risk-free asset that yields the exercise price on the expiry date. In other words, we need to bring the exercise price to its present value by discounting at the risk-free rate of interest. This gives rise to the following revised statement.

4 *The minimum value of an option is the difference between the share price and the present value of the exercise price* (or zero if greater).

$$C_0 \geq S_0 - [E/(1 + R_f)^t] \quad (13.5)$$

The value of a call option can be observed in Figure 13.5. Bradford plc shares are currently priced at 700p. The diagram shows how the value of an option to buy Bradford shares at 1,100p moves with the share price. The upper limit to the option price is the share price itself, and the lower limit is zero for share prices up to 1,100p, and the share price minus exercise price when share price moves above 1,100p. In fact, the actual option prices lie between these two extremes, on the upward-sloping curve. The curve rises slowly at first, but then accelerates rapidly.

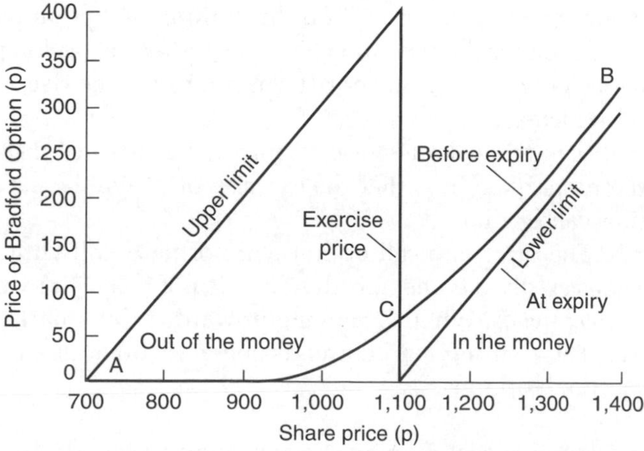

Figure 13.5 Option and share price movements for Bradford plc

At point A on the curve, at the very start, the option is worthless. If the share price for Bradford remained well below the exercise price, the option would remain worthless. At point B, when the share price has rocketed to 1,400p, the option value approximates the share price minus the present value of the exercise price. At point C, the share price exactly equals the exercise price. If exercised today, the option would be worthless. However, there may still be two months for the option to run, in which time the share price could move up or down. In an efficient market, where share prices follow a random walk, there is a 50 per cent chance that it will move higher and an equal probability that it will go lower. If the share price falls, the option will be worthless, but if it rises, the option will have some value. The value placed on the option at point C depends largely on the likelihood of substantial movements in share price. However, we can say that *the higher the share price relative to the exercise price, the safer the option* (i.e. more valuable).

5 *The value of a call option increases over time and as interest rates rise*. Equation (13.4) shows that the value of an option increases as the present value of the exercise price falls. This reduction in present value occurs over time and/or with rises in the interest rate.

6 *The more risky the underlying share, the more valuable the option*. This is because the greater the variance of the underlying share price, the greater is the possibility that prices will exceed the exercise price. But because option values cannot be negative (i.e. the holder would not exercise the option), the 'downside' risk can be ignored.

To summarise, the value of a call option is influenced by the following:

- *The share price*. The higher the price of the share, the greater will be the value of an option written on it.
- *The exercise price of the option*. The lower the exercise price, the greater the value of the call option.
- *The time to expiry of the option*. As long as investors believe that the share price has a chance of yielding a profit on the option, the option will have a positive value. So the longer the time to expiry, the higher the option price.
- *The risk-free interest rate*. As short-term interest rates rise, the value of a call option also increases.
- *The volatility in the underlying share returns*. The greater the volatility in share price, the more likely it is that the exercise price will be exceeded and, hence, the option value will rise.
- *Dividends*. The price of a call option will normally fall with the share price as a share goes ex-div (i.e. the next dividend is not received by the buyer).
- *Strong market trends*. Whether moving upwards ('bull' markets) or downwards ('bear' markets), strong market trends generally offer greater scope for making money through options.

A call option is therefore a **contingent claim security** that depends on the value and riskiness of the underlying share on which it is written.

Self-assessment Activity 13.3

Explain why option value increases with the volatility of the underlying share price.
List the factors that determine option value.

(answer at end of chapter)

A simplified option-price model

Valuing options is a highly complex business, including a lot of mathematics or, for most traders, a user-friendly software package. But we can introduce the valuation of options by using a simple (if somewhat unrealistic) example. We argued earlier that it is possible to replicate the payoffs from buying a share by purchasing a call option, selling a put option and placing the balance on deposit to earn a risk-free return over the option period. This provides us with a method for valuing options.

Valuing a call option in Riskitt plc

In April, the share price of Riskitt plc is 100p. A three-month call option on the shares with a July expiry date has an exercise price of 125p. With the current price well below the exercise price it is clear that, for the option to have value, the share price must stand a chance of increasing by at least 25p over the next quarter.

Assume that by the expiry date there is an equal chance that the share price will have either soared to 200p or plummeted to 50p. There are no other possibilities. Assume also that you can borrow at 12 per cent a year, or about 3 per cent a quarter.

What would be the payoff for a call option on one share in Riskitt?

	Best	**Worst**
Share price	200p	50p
Less exercise price	(125p)	(125p)
Payoff	75p	–

You stand to make 75p if the share price does well, but nothing if it slips below the exercise price. To work out how much you would be willing to pay for such an option, we must replicate an investment in call options by a combination of investing in Riskitt shares and borrowing.

Suppose we buy 200 call options. The payoffs in July will be zero if the share price is only 50p and £150 (i.e. 200 × 75p) if the share price is 200p. This is shown in Table 13.3. Note that the cash flow we are trying to determine is the April premium, represented by the question mark.

To replicate the call option cash flows, you adopt the second strategy in Table 13.3: namely, buying 100 shares and borrowing sufficient cash to give identical

Table 13.3 Valuing a call option in Riskitt plc

Strategy	Cash flow in April	Payoff in July if share price is 200p	Payoff in July if share price is 50p
	£	£	£
1 Buy 200 call options	?	+150	–
2 Buy 100 shares	−100	+200	+50
Borrow	+48.54	−50	−50
	51.46	+150	–

Value of call option = £51.46/200 calls = 25.73p, say 26p

cash flows in July as the call option strategy. This means borrowing £50. The net cash flows for the two strategies are now the same in July whatever the share price. But the £50 loan repayment in July will include three months' interest at 3 per cent for the quarter. The initial sum borrowed in April would therefore be the present value of £50, i.e. £50/1.03 = £48.54. Deducting this from the share price paid gives a net figure of £51.46, which must also be the April cash payment for 200 call options. The price for one call option is therefore about 26p.

Black–Scholes pricing model

The above example took a highly simplified view of uncertainty, using only two possible share price outcomes. Black and Scholes (1973) combined the main determinants of option values to develop a model of option pricing. Although its mathematics are daunting, the model does have practical application. Every day, dealers in options use it in specially programmed calculators to determine option prices.

For those who like a challenge, the complex mathematics of the Black–Scholes pricing model are given in the appendix to this chapter. However, the key message is that option pricing requires evaluation of five of the variables listed earlier: share price, exercise price, risk-free rate of interest, time and share price volatility.

Acorn plc shares are currently worth 28p with a standard deviation of 30 per cent. The risk-free rate of interest is 6 per cent, continuously discounted. What is the value of a call option on Acorn shares expiring in nine months and with an exercise price of 30p?

The fully-worked solution to this problem is given in the appendix to this chapter, but we can identify here the five input variables:

Share price (S) = 28p
Exercise price (E) = 30p
Risk-free rate (k) = 6 per cent p.a.
Time to expiry (t) = nine months
Share price volatility (σ) = 30 per cent

Application of the Black–Scholes formula to the above data (see Appendix) gives a value of the call option of 2.6p.

Black–Scholes option pricing formula

Value of call option (C) is:

$$C = SN(d_1) - EN(d_2)e^{-tk}$$

where

$$d_1 = \frac{\ln (S/E) + tk}{\sigma t^{1/2}} + \frac{\sigma t^{1/2}}{2}$$

$$d_2 = d_1 - \sigma t^{1/2}$$

$N(d)$ is the value of the cumulative distribution function for a standardised normal random variable and e^{-tk} is the present value of the exercise price continuously discounted.

A simplified Black–Scholes formula can be used as an approximation for options less than one year:

$$\frac{C}{S} \approx \frac{1}{\sqrt{2\pi}} \sigma \sqrt{t}$$

This formula emphasises the impact of volatility and time to expiry on the option price.

Applying the above to the previous example we derive a slightly higher option price:

$$C \approx 0.398 \times 0.3 \sqrt{0.75} \times 28 = 2.9\text{p}$$

13.4 Application of option theory to corporate finance

Option theory has implications going far beyond the valuation of traded share options. It offers a powerful tool for understanding various other contractual arrangements in finance. Here are some examples:

1. *Share warrants*, giving the holder the option to buy shares directly from the company at a fixed exercise price for a given period of time.
2. *Convertible loan stock*, giving the holder a combination of a straight loan or bond and a call option. On exercising the option, the holder exchanges the loan for a fixed number of shares in the company.
3. *Loan stock* can have a call option attached, giving the company the right to repurchase the stock before maturity.
4. *Executive share option schemes* are share options issued to company executives as incentives to pursue shareholder goals.
5. *Insurance and loan guarantees* are a form of put option. An insurance claim is the exercise of an option. Government loan guarantees are a form of insurance. The government, in effect, provides a put option to the holders of risky bonds

so that, if the borrowers default, the bond-holders can exercise their option by seeking reimbursement from the government. Underwriting a share issue is a similar type of option.

6 *Currency and interest rate options* are discussed in later chapters as ways of hedging or speculating on currency or interest rate movements.

Two further forms of option discussed in the next sections are **equity options** and **capital investment options**.

Equity as a call option on a company's assets: Reckless Ltd

Option-like features are found in financially geared companies. *Equity is, in effect, a call option on the company's assets.*

Reckless Ltd has a single £1 million debenture in issue, which is due for repayment in one year. The directors, on behalf of the shareholders, can either pay off the loan at the year end, thereby having no prior claim on the firm's assets, or default on the debenture. If they default, the debenture-holders will take charge of the assets or recover the £1 million owing to them.

In such a situation, the shareholders of Reckless have a call option on the company's assets with an exercise price of £1 million. They can exercise the option by repaying the loan, or they can allow the option to lapse by defaulting on the loan. Their choice depends on the value of the company's assets. If they are worth more than £1 million, the option is 'in the money' and the loan should be repaid. If the option is 'out of the money', because the assets are worth less than £1 million, option theory argues that shareholders would prefer the company to default or enter liquidation. This option-like feature arises because companies have limited liability status, effectively protecting shareholders from having to make good any losses.

Options and moral hazard

Moral hazard is the risk that the existence of a contract will change the behaviour of one or both parties to the contract.

Option contracts can have moral hazard implications. For example, an insurance policy (a type of put option) may encourage management to take fewer fire precautions because the loss is carried by the insurer. Similar moral hazard aspects can be found in loan guarantee and underwriting contracts. Perhaps the most significant example was referred to above: that shareholders in highly-geared companies, where asset values are below the level of borrowings, will allow the default, knowing that the loss will be sustained by the loan stock-holders.

13.5 Capital investment options

We can now apply option theory to capital budgeting. Capital investment options (sometimes termed **real** options) are option-like features found in capital budgeting decisions. While discounted cash flow techniques are very useful tools of analysis, they are generally more suited to financial assets, because they assume that assets are held rather than managed. The main difference between evaluating financial assets and real assets is that investors in, say, shares, are generally *passive*. Unless they have a fair degree of control, they can only monitor performance and decide whether to hold or sell their shares.

Corporate managers, on the other hand, play a far more *active* role in achieving the planned net present value on a capital project. When a project is slipping behind forecast they can take action to try to achieve the original NPV target. In other words, they can create options – actions to mitigate losses or exploit new opportunities presented by capital investments. Managerial flexibility to adapt its future actions creates an asymmetry in the NPV probability distribution that increases the investment project's value by improving the upside potential while limiting downside losses.

We will consider three types of option: the abandonment option, the timing option and strategic investment options.

Abandonment option

Major investment decisions involve heavy capital commitments and are largely irreversible: once the initial capital expenditure is incurred, management cannot turn the clock back and do it differently. The costs associated with divestment are usually very high. Most capital projects divested early will realise little more than scrap value. In the case of a nuclear power plant, the decommissioning cost could be phenomenal. Because management is committing large sums of money in pursuit of higher, but uncertain, payoffs, the

option to abandon, without incurring enormous costs if things look grim, can be very valuable. Any project that permits management to extract value when things go bad has an embedded put option. To ignore this is to undervalue the project.

Example: Cardiff Components Ltd

Cardiff Components Ltd is considering building a new plant to produce components for the nuclear defence industry. Proposal A is to build a custom-designed plant using the latest technology, but applicable only to nuclear defence contracts. A less profitable scheme, Proposal B, is to build a plant using standard machine tools, giving greater flexibility in application.

The outcome of a general election to be held one year hence has a major impact on the decision. If the current government is returned to office, its commitment to nuclear defence is likely to give rise to new orders, making Proposal A the better choice. If the current opposition party is elected, its commitment to run down the nuclear defence industry would make Proposal B the better course of action. Proposal B has, in effect, a put option attached to it, giving the flexibility to abandon the proposed operation in favour of some other activity.

Timing option

The Cardiff Components example not only introduces an abandonment option, it also raises the **timing option**. Management may have viewed the investment as a 'now or never' opportunity, arguing that in highly competitive markets there is no scope for delay. However, most project decisions have three possible outcomes – accept, reject or defer until economic and other conditions improve. In effect, this amounts to viewing the decision as a call option that is about to expire on the new plant, the capital investment outlay being the exercise price. If a positive NPV is expected, the option will be exercised; otherwise the option lapses and no investment is made.

The option to defer the decision by one year, until the outcome of the general election is known, makes obvious sense. This may look something like the curved line in Figure 13.6.

An immediate investment would yield either a negative NPV – in which case it would not be taken up – or a positive NPV. Delaying the decision by a year to gain valuable new information (the curved broken line) is a more valuable option. Managements sometimes delay taking up apparently wealth-creating opportunities because they believe that the option to wait and gather new information is sufficiently valuable.

Investment as a call option

The five main variables in pricing a share call option can be applied to capital investment (or real) call options.

Share call option	Real call option
Current value of share	Present value of expected cash flows
Exercise price	Investment cost
Time to expiry	Time until investment opportunity disappears
Share price uncertainty	Project value uncertainty
Risk-free interest rate	Risk-free interest rate

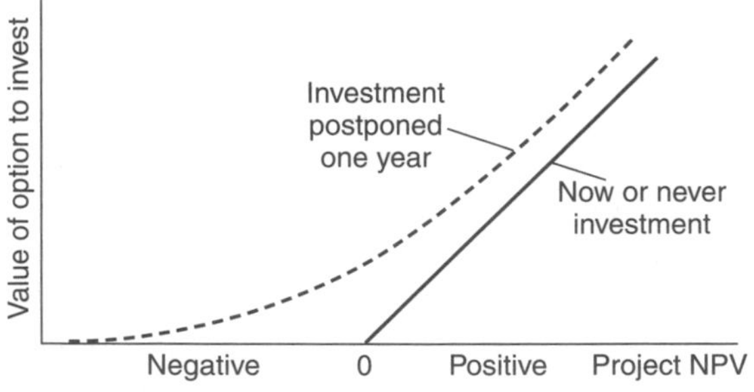

Figure 13.6 The value of the options to delay investments: Cardiff Components Ltd

Mini case

BP's successful options approach to oil exploration

A major reason why BP managed to increase its market value by 167 per cent between 1990 and 1996 is attributed to its successful strategy in making incremental investments in risky oil exploration and production to secure the upside while insuring against the downside.

The first stage in developing an oil field is to acquire a real option in the form of a licence to explore and produce oil over a five-year period. The next stage is to undertake low-cost seismic exploration which, if promising, leads to exploratory drilling. Only if the outcome of this is positive will the heavy investment involved in full development be incurred.

After thirty years of North Sea oil exploration, profitable low-risk investments were long gone. Conventional net present value analysis indicated that new investment opportunities, such as those off the Shetlands, carried large geological and technical risks which made them uneconomic. However, an options approach recognises that holding the licences gave a potentially huge payoff should these risks ever be resolved.

The Andrew Field was discovered in the 1970s, but was not developed because it required heavy investment due to its technical complexity. With the oil price collapse in the 1980s, BP must have questioned whether its options were of any real value. Yet, by the mid-1990s, BP had developed new approaches to drilling, field development and project management. Combined with stronger oil prices, this made exploration and production valuable for shareholders. In effect, BP bought an out-of-the-money option to develop the field and defer the option until it had driven down the exercise price (i.e. the investment cost) until it became in-the-money.

NPV analysis assumed a 'now or never' rather than 'wait and see' approach. It also undervalued volatility – risk has its upside, while the downside can often be resolved by managerial effort. By using an options approach, BP managed to create value from small, high-risk oil fields that conventional investment analysis rejected.

Based on 'The Real Power of Real Options', *Corporate Finance*, January 1998

Question

What does the options approach offer that conventional NPV analysis lacks?

Strategic investment options

Certain investment decisions give rise to **follow-on opportunities** that are wealth-creating. New technology investment, involving large-scale research and development, is particularly difficult to evaluate. Managers refer to the high level of intangible benefits associated with such decisions. What they really mean is that these investments offer further investment opportunities (e.g. greater flexibility), but that, at this stage, the precise form of such opportunities cannot be quantified.

Strategic options in Harlequin plc

Harlequin plc has developed a new form of mobile phone, using the latest technology. It is considering whether to enter this market by investing in equipment costing £400,000 to assemble and then market the product in the north of England during the first four years. (Most of the product parts will be bought in.) The expected net present value from this initial project, however, is −£25,000. The strategic case for such an investment is that by the end of the project's life sufficient expertise would have been developed to launch an improved product on a larger scale to be distributed throughout Europe. The cost of the second project in four years' time is estimated at £1.32 million. Although there is a reasonable chance of fairly high payoffs, the expected net present value suggests this project will do little more than break even.

'Obviously, with the two projects combining to produce a negative NPV, the whole idea should be scrapped', remarked the finance director.

Gary Owen, a recent MBA graduate, was less sure that this was the right course of action. He reckoned that the second project was a kind of call option, the initial cost being the exercise price and the present value of its future stream of benefits being equivalent to the option's underlying share price. The risks for the two projects looked to be in line with the variability of the company's share price, which had a standard deviation of 30 per cent a year.

If, by the end of Year 4, the second project did not suggest a positive NPV, the company could walk away from the decision, the option would lapse and the cost to the company would be the £25,000 negative NPV on the first project (the option premium). But it could be a winner, and only 'upside' risk is considered with call options.

Gary knew that Harlequin's discount rate for such projects was 20 per cent and the risk-free interest rate was 10 per cent. Table 13.4 shows his estimation of the main elements to be considered.

Gary Owen then entered these variables into a computer model. He found that the present value of the four-year call option to invest in the follow-on project, with an exercise price of £1.32 million, was worth around £75,000. This is because there is a chance that the project could be really profitable, but the company will not know whether this is likely until the outcome of the first project is known. The high degree of risk in the second project actually increases the value of the call option. It seems, therefore, that the initial project launch, which creates an option value of £75,000 for a 'premium' of £25,000 (negative NPV) may make economic as well as strategic sense.

Table 13.4 Harlequin plc: call option valuation

Initial project	(£000)
Cost of investment	(400)
PV of cash inflows	375
Net present value	(25)
Follow-on-project in Year 4	
Cost of investment	(1320)
PV of cash inflows	1320
Net present value in Year 4	–
Main factors in valuing the call option:	
1. Asset value	PV of cash flows at Year 4 discounted to Year 0
	= £1.32 m/(1.2)^4
	= £0.636 m
2. Exercise price	= cost of follow-on project
	= £1.32 m
3. Risk-free discount rate	= 10%
4. Time period	= 4 years
5. Asset volatility	= standard deviation of 30%

Such valuation calculations applied to strategic investment options raise as many questions as they answer. For example, how much of the risk for the follow-on project is dependent upon the outcome of the initial project? But option pricing does offer insights into the problem of valuing 'intangibles' in capital budgeting, particularly where they create options not otherwise available to the firm.

13.6 Why conventional NPV may not tell the whole story

Earlier chapters have rehearsed the theoretical argument that capital projects offer positive net present values, when discounted at the risk-adjusted discount rate, should be accepted. In Chapter 7 we raised a number of practical shortcomings with discounted cash flow approaches; here we introduce an important theoretical point.

We have noted that orthodox capital projects analysis adopts a 'now or never' mentality. But the timing option reminds us that a 'wait and see' approach can add value. Whenever a company makes an investment decision it also surrenders a call option – the right to invest in the same asset at some later date. Such waiting may be passive, waiting for the right economic and market conditions, or active, where management seeks to gather project-related information to reduce uncertainty (further product trials, competitor reaction, etc.). Hence, the true NPV of a project being undertaken today should include the values of various options associated with the decision:

$$\text{True NPV} = \begin{matrix}\text{NPV}\\ \text{of basic}\\ \text{project}\end{matrix} + \begin{matrix}\text{NPV}\\ \text{of abandonment}\\ \text{option}\end{matrix} + \begin{matrix}\text{NPV}\\ \text{of follow-on}\\ \text{projects}\end{matrix} - \begin{matrix}\text{NPV}\\ \text{of option}\\ \text{to wait}\end{matrix}$$

If the total is positive, the project creates wealth. This is why firms frequently defer apparently wealth-creating projects or accept apparently uneconomic projects. Senior managers recognise that investment ideas often have wider strategic implications, are irreversible and improve with age.

Real options are particularly important in investment decisions when the conventional NPV analysis suggests that the project is 'marginal', uncertainty is high and there is value in retaining flexibility. In such cases, the conventional NPV will almost always understate the true value.

Mini case

Eurotunnel considers all its options

The idea of a road tunnel under the Channel is a legacy of Baroness Thatcher's 11-year reign as the prime minister who got the first tunnel built.

So keen was she on the idea, she insisted Eurotunnel be contractually obliged to submit a feasibility study by 2000, or lose an exclusive option over the second link.

Eurotunnel asked two consultants to investigate seven options for a second link – over and under the water. The study settled on two options: a two-tier road tunnel or a second rail tunnel.

Both would probably run alongside the existing Chunnel; the main difference being that technological advances would make it possible to build a large single-bore tunnel, rather than the existing two main tunnels sandwiching a third service tunnel.

The rail option – to be reserved exclusively for Eurostars and freight trains – sounds safe. For an estimated £3 billion Eurotunnel could simply extend services it and customers already know.

But the report suggests the road tunnel would be more financially viable. Initial studies suggest that a rail option would not make an adequate return unless there was a very significant shift from road to rail.

Whether there will be the passenger demand for a second tunnel of either type is too early to say. Eurotunnel estimates the existing tunnel will reach capacity use in 2025 – but great changes could happen to travel needs and methods over a quarter of a century.

The company has ten years to make up its mind – the deadline is 2010 and it seems in no hurry to be rushed.

Based on Juliette Jowit, *Financial Times*, January 6 2000

Self-assessment Activity 13.4

What is the type of option available to Eurotunnel and what factors would you consider in assessing its value?

(answer at end of chapter)

Summary

The options literature has developed highly complex models for valuing options, but insufficient attention has been paid to value creation through options.

Options or option-like features permeate virtually every area of financial management. A better understanding of options and the development of option pricing have made the topic an increasingly important part of financial theory. We have sought to increase your awareness of what options are, where they are to be found, and how managers can begin to value them. The topic is still in its infancy, but its study will yield important insights into financial and investment decisions.

Key points

- Option features are to be found in most areas of finance (e.g. convertibles and warrants, insurance, currency and interest rate management, and capital budgeting).
- Pure options are financial instruments created by exchanges (e.g. stock markets) rather than companies.
- The two main types of option are (1) **call options**, giving the holder the right to buy a share (or other asset) at the exercise price at some future time, and (2) **put options**, giving the holder the right to sell shares at a given price at some future time.
- The minimum value of a call option is the difference between the share price and the present value of the exercise price.
- The value of call options increases as:
  The underlying share price increases.
  The exercise price falls.
  The time to expiry lengthens.
  The risk-free interest rate rises.
  The volatility of the underlying share price increases.
- The Black–Scholes Option Pricing Model can be applied to estimate the value of call options.
- Capital investment decisions may have options attached covering the option to (1) abandon, (2) delay or (3) invest in follow-on opportunities.
- Where the value of a company's assets falls below the value of its borrowings, shareholders may not exercise their option to repay the loan, but prefer the company to default on the debt.

Further reading

A more detailed treatment of options is found in Brealey and Myers (2000) and Bodie and Merton (2000). An introduction to options is given by Redhead (1990). Kester (1984) discusses the topic of real options and Dixit and Pindyck (1995) provide an easy-to-read article on the options approach to capital investment. Those who like a mathematical challenge may want to try Black and Scholes' (1973) classic paper or Cox *et al.* (1979). Merton (1998) gives an excellent review of the application of option pricing, particularly to investment decisions.

Useful websites

Futures and Options Word: **www.fow**
Harden International Financial: **www.liffe.com**
International Swaps and Derivatives Association: **www.isda.org**

Appendix

Black–Scholes option pricing formula

The Black–Scholes formula, for valuing a call option (*C*), with no adjustment for dividends, is given by:

$$C = SN(d_1) - EN(d_2)e^{-tk}$$

where:

$$d_1 = \frac{\ln(S/E) + tk}{\sigma t^{1/2}} + \frac{\sigma t^{1/2}}{2}$$

$$d_2 = d_1 - \sigma t^{1/2}$$

We already have described *S* as the underlying share price and *E* as the exercise price. In addition, σ is the standard deviation of the underlying asset, *t* is the time, in years, until the option expires, *k* is the risk-free rate of interest continuously compounded, *N*(*d*) is the value of the cumulative distribution function for a standardised normal random variable and e^{-tk} is the present value of the exercise price continuously discounted.

Example

Acorn plc shares are currently worth 28p each with a standard deviation of 30 per cent. The risk-free interest rate is 6 per cent, continuously compounded. Compute the value of a call option on Acorn shares expiring in nine months and with an exercise price of 30p.

We can list the values for each parameter: $S = 28$, $\sigma = 0.30$, $E = 30$, $K = 0.06$, $t = 0.75$.

$$\sigma t^{1/2} = (0.3)(0.75)^{1/2} = 0.2598$$

$$\begin{aligned} d_1 &= \frac{\ln(S/E) + tk}{\sigma t^{1/2}} + \frac{\sigma t^{1/2}}{2} \\ &= \frac{\ln(28/30) + 0.75(0.06)}{0.2598} + \frac{0.2598}{2} \\ &= -0.2655 + 0.1732 + 0.1299 \\ &= 0.0375, \text{ say } 0.04 \end{aligned}$$

$$\begin{aligned} d_2 = d_1 - \sigma r^{1/2} &= 0.0375 - 0.2598 \\ &= -002223, \text{ say } -0.22 \end{aligned}$$

Using cumulative distribution function tables:

$N(d_1) = N(0.04) = 0.5160$
$N(d_2) = N(-0.22) = 0.4129$

Inserting the above into the original equation:

$$C = SN(d_1) - EN(d_2)e^{-tk}$$
$$= 28(0.5160) - 30(0.4129)e^{-0.045}$$
$$= 2.6\text{p}$$

The value of the call is 2.6p.

Strictly speaking, adjustment for dividends on shares should be made by applying the Merton formula, not dealt with in this text.

Self-assessment Answers

13.1 **(1)** A call option gives the owner the right to buy shares (or whatever) at a fixed price within a set period. A put option is the right to sell at a fixed price.

(2) A European option can only be exercised on the expiry date, while an American option can be exercised any time over the life of the option. Most traded options in Europe are actually the American variety.

(3) A wide range including shares, bonds, currency, interest rates, gold, silver, wool, soya beans etc. Options are also available on interest rates.

13.2 Applying the equation on page 408, we find that the put–call parity relationship holds:

Share price	*+ value of put*	*− value of call*	*= E/(1 + R_f)*
44	*7*	*1*	*= 55/1.10*
PV exercise price			*= 50p*

13.3 Option value increases with the volatility of the underlying share price because the greater the variability in share price, the greater the probability that the share price will exceed the exercise price. Because option values cannot be negative, only the probability of exceeding the exercise price is considered.

13.4 Option values are determined by five main factors:

- share price
- exercise price of the option
- time to expiry of the option
- the risk-free rate of interest
- volatility of the underlying share price

In addition, the payment of dividends and underlying stock market trends have some influence on option values.

Questions

1 *Solution in Appendix A (page 818).* Give two examples where companies can issue call options (or something similar).

2 *Solution in Appendix A (page 818).* On 1 March the ordinary shares of Gaymore plc stood at 469p. The traded options market in the shares quotes April 500p puts at 47p. If the share price falls to 450p, how much, if any, profit would an investor make? What will the option be worth if the share price moves up to 510p?

3 Explain the factors influencing the price of a traded option and whether volatility of a company's share option price is necessarily a sign of financial weakness.

4 Frank purchased a call option on 100 shares in Marmaduke plc six months ago at 10p per share. The share price at the time was 110p and the exercise price was 120p. Just prior to expiry the share price has risen to 135p.

Required

(a) State whether the option should be exercised.
(b) Calculate the profit or loss on the option.
(c) Would Frank have done better by investing the same amount of cash six months ago in a bank offering 10 per cent p.a.?

5 *Solution in Appendix A (page 818).* Find the value of the call option given that the present value of the exercise price is 10p, the value of the put option is 15p and the current value of the share on which the option is based is 25p.

6 *Solution in Appendix A (page 818).* Find the present value of the exercise price given that the value of the call is 19p, the value of the put is 5p and the current market price of the underlying share is 30p.

7 *Spot the options in Enigma Drugs plc.* The mini-case presented below incorporates five options. Can you identify the type of option, its length and exercise price? Recall that American options offer the holder the right to exercise at any time up to a certain date, while a European option is exercised on one particular date.

Enigma Drugs plc is an innovative pharmaceutical company. The management team is considering setting up a separate limited company to develop and produce a new drug.

The project is forecast to incur development costs and new plant expenditure totalling £50 million and to break even over the next five years (by which time its competitors are likely to have found a way round the patent rights). Enigma's management is considering deferring the whole decision by two years, when the outcome of a major court case with important implications for the drug's success will be known.

The risks on the venture are high, but should the project prove unsuccessful and have to be abandoned, the 'know-how' developed from the project can be used inside the group or sold to its competitors for a considerable sum. Enigma's management realises that there is little or no money to be made in the initial five years, but it should allow them to gain vital expertise for the development of a 'wonder drug' costing £120 million, which could be launched in four years' time.

The newly formed company would be largely funded by borrowing £40 million in the first instance, repayable in total after eight years, unless the company prefers to be 'wound up' for defaulting on the loan. Some of the debt raised will be by 9 per cent Convertible Loan Stock, giving holders the right to convert to equity at any time over the next four years at 360p compared with the current price of 297p.

Practical assignment

1 Choose two forms of financial contracting arrangement with option features and show how option pricing theory can help in analysing them.

2 Consider a major capital investment recently undertaken or under review. Does it offer an option? Could an option feature be introduced? What would the rough value of the option be?

PART IV

Short-term financing and policies

The acquisition of every asset has to be financed. Companies obtain two forms of finance, short and long term, although, in practice, it is difficult to make a rigid demarcation between them. Part IV is devoted to analysing short-term financing, while the analysis of long-term financing decisions is postponed to Part V.

Chapter 14 offers an overview of the financing operations of the modern corporation, focusing on balancing the inflows and outflows of funds in the process of treasury management. The chapter examines the importance of working capital management, and how the financial manager may use the derivatives markets.

Chapter 15 looks at managing short-term assets – cash, stocks, debtors – and the financing implications of different working capital policies. Chapter 16 describes the various forms of short- (and medium-) term sources of finance, especially trade credit and the banking system, and also discusses the analysis of leasing decisions and the finance of foreign trade. In Chapter 17, we discuss a major problem faced in the management of foreign debtors and creditors: namely, currency risk. Alternative ways of managing foreign exchange risk are examined and the analysis is widened to include the management of the long-term currency exposures presented by overseas investment projects, an issue deferred from Chapter 8.

429 Treasury management and working capital policy

466 Short-term asset management

500 Short- and medium-term finance

539 Managing currency risk

14 Treasury management and working capital policy

Drowning in the Queens Moat

In March 2002, Queens Moat Houses, a hotel chain, had a stock market capitalisation value of £28 million, just a fraction of the value of its competitors like Stakis and Thistle. The story could have been so very different had the company maintained sound treasury management and financial controls.

Until March 1993, when its shares were suspended, Queens Moat Houses appeared to be a well-run leading European hotel chain with a long and successful history as a publicly-quoted company. Though some investors had become concerned by the group's rapid expansion, funded by high levels of debt and a number of rights issues, no one could have forecast its virtual collapse. The corporate horror story revealed a catalogue of mistakes and breaches of company law, including the unlawful payment of dividends out of capital, overstatement of past profits, and massive over-valuation of properties. The result was losses of more than £1 billion and net borrowing of £1.2 billion.

How did Queens Moat Houses arrive at this sorry position? A report by the new management identifies a few telling factors:

- Lack of the most basic financial controls over its subsidiaries.
- No clearly defined treasury function.
- The company was raising cash expensively with the sale and leaseback of German hotels.

It is all too easy to be wise after the event, but the Queens Moat Houses demise could have been avoided through proper treasury management and financial controls.

Learning objectives

Treasury management and working capital policy are central to the whole of corporate finance. After reading this chapter, you should appreciate the following:

- The purpose and structure of the treasury function.
- Treasury funding issues.
- How to manage banking relationships.
- Risk management, hedging and the use of derivatives.
- Working capital policies.
- The cash operating cycle and overtrading problems.

14.1 Introduction

Treasury management, once viewed as a peripheral activity conducted by back-office boffins, today plays a vital role in corporate management. Most business decisions have implications for cash flow and risk, both of which are of direct relevance to treasury management. Queens Moat Houses is not the only major company that has experienced problems through poor treasury management in recent years. This area has become a major concern in business, particularly the manner in which companies manage exposure to currency and other risks.

Most companies do not have a corporate treasurer; such a person is usually warranted only in larger companies. However, all firms are involved in treasury management to some degree. Treasury management can be defined in many ways. We will adopt the Association of Corporate Treasurers definition: 'the efficient management of liquidity and financial risk in the business'.

This chapter seeks to explain the main functions of treasury management and to provide an overview of working capital management. It also acts as an introduction to many of the succeeding chapters in this book.

14.2 The treasury function

The size, structure and responsibilities of the treasury function will vary greatly among organisations. Key factors will be corporate size, listing status, degree of international business and attitude to risk. For example, BP Amoco is a major multinational company with a strong emphasis on value creation, where currency and oil price movements can have a dramatic impact on corporate earnings. It is not surprising to see that it has a highly developed group treasury function, covering the following:

1. *Global dealing* – foreign exchange, interest rate management, short-term borrowing, short-term deposits.
2. *Treasury services* – cash management, systems, transactional banking.
3. *Corporate finance* – capital markets, banking relationships, trade finance, risk management, liability management.

4 *M&A equity management* – mergers and acquisitions, equity markets, investor relations and divestitures (from *The Treasurer*, February 1992).

For most companies the treasury department is much simpler, typically with a distinction between **funding** (cash and liquidity management, short-term financing and cash forecasting) and **treasury operations** (financial risk management and portfolio management). Treasury departments have come under increasing scrutiny by the financial press. Barely a month passes without some large company announcing hefty losses resulting from some major blunder by its treasury department. In the highly complex, highly volatile world of finance, there are bound to be mistakes; the secret is to set up the treasury function such that mistakes are never catastrophic.

UK TREASURER

INTERNATIONAL CONSUMER PRODUCTS GROUP

WEST LONDON

- UK headquartered consumer products group with wide range of household name brands. Turnover exceeds £3 billion from some 40 countries.
- Will be a member of a small team reporting to the Group Treasurer and will have responsibility for all banking, supported by a team of two.
- Principal activities will cover the dealing area; cash management systems and liaison with the Group's bankers; interest risk management, both forex and interest rate; and *ad hoc* projects including overseas banking reviews

C.£80,000 BENEFITS

- Graduate, part or fully qualified ACT with hands-on dealing room experience. Background is likely to be within a substantial international group. An accountancy qualification would be advantageous.
- Excellent communicator, able to quickly establish credibility and develop sound working relationships across the business. A team-worker with flexibility of approach, committed to technical excellence.
- This is a first-class opportunity within a group which has an excellent reputation for its pro-active approach to treasury management.

A typical job advertisement in the press.

It is the responsibility of the board of directors to set the treasury aims, policies, authorisation levels, risk position and structure. It should establish, for example, the following:

- The degree of treasury centralisation.
- Whether it should be a profit centre or cost centre.
- The extent to which the company should be exposed to financial risk.
- The level of liquidity desired.

We pick up the last two points later, but deal with the structural issues in the following sections.

Degree of centralisation

Even in the most highly decentralised companies, it is common to find a centralised treasury function. The advantages of centralisation are self-evident:

1 The treasurer sees the total picture for cash, borrowings and currencies and is therefore able to influence and control financial movements on a global basis to achieve maximum after-tax benefit. The gains from centralised cash management can be considerable.
2 Centralisation helps the company develop greater expertise and more rapid knowledge transfer.
3 It permits the treasurer to capture any benefits of scale. Dealing with financial and currency markets on a group basis not only saves unnecessary duplication of effort, but should also reduce the cost of funds.

A recent survey found that 76 per cent of responding firms had centralised group treasury functions. However, there are some benefits from decentralising certain treasury activities:

- By delegating financial activities to the same degree as other business activities, the business unit becomes responsible for all operations. Divisional managers in centralised treasury organisations are rightly annoyed at being assessed on profit after financing costs, over which they have little direct control.
- It encourages management to take advantage of local financing opportunities of which group treasury may not be aware and be more receptive to the needs of each division.

Hewlett-Packard is one major firm that has opted for a more decentralised structure, whereby certain treasury management decisions can be made at different levels. However, centralisation is also evident through key linkages in such areas as policy, common objectives and information systems.

Profit or cost centre?

The treasury function, like any other business activity, should be measured in terms of its performance against objectives. An example of a profit centre is Marks & Spencer, which states in its accounts: 'The Group's Treasury operates as a profit centre, but within strict risk limits and with a prohibition on speculative activity.'

The construction company Mowlem, on the other hand, states: 'The Group's Treasury Department is responsible for currency exposures and financing. The policy is for the Group to borrow centrally and to lend to Group companies and divisions on commercial terms. The Treasury Department does not operate as a profit centre' (Annual Report 1994).

A survey by *Euromoney* (August 1994) revealed that three-quarters of major companies operated their treasuries as cost centres. But whichever way treasury functions are structured, they are expected to manage their operations in the most cost-efficient manner.

Self-assessment Activity 14.1

How would you define treasury management?

(answer at end of chapter)

Let us now examine the four pillars of treasury management: funding, banking relationships, risk management, and liquidity and working capital.

14.3 Funding

Corporate finance managers must address the funding issues of: (1) how much should the firm raise this year, and (2) in what form? We devote two later chapters to these questions, examining long-, medium- and short-term funding. For the present, we simply raise the questions that subsequent chapters will pursue in greater depth.

1 *Why do firms prefer internally generated funds?* Internally generated funds, defined as profits after tax plus depreciation, represent easily the major part of corporate funds. In many ways, it is the most convenient source of finance. You could say it is equivalent to a compulsory share issue, because the alternative is to pay it all back to shareholders and then raise equity capital from them as the need arises. Raising equity capital, via the back door of profit retention, saves issuing and other costs. But, at the same time, it avoids the company having to be judged by the capital market as to whether it is willing to fund its future operations in the form of either equity or loans.
2 *How much should companies borrow?* These is no easy solution to this question. But it is a vital question for corporate treasurers. Borrow too much and the business could go bust; borrow too little and you could be losing out on cheap finance.

   The problem is made no easier by the observation that levels of borrowing differ enormously among companies and, indeed, among countries. Levels of borrowing in Italy, Japan, Germany and Sweden are generally higher than in the UK and the USA. One reason is the difference in the strength of relationship between lenders and borrowers. Bankers in Germany and Japan, for example, tend to take a longer-term funding view than UK banks. (Japanese banks may even form part of the same group of companies.) We devote Chapters 20 and 21 to the key question of how much a firm should borrow.

   Here we consider two theories that explain how much of the capital employed by firms should be in the form of borrowing and how much in equity. **Trade-off theory** recognises that firms want to enjoy the benefits of lower costs of borrowing (the after-tax cost of borrowing is normally much less expensive than the cost of equity). But at the same time, firms do not wish to increase the financial risk that entering into contractual commitments to pay interest and repay debt involves. From this we would expect to find that firms enjoying high profits create additional debt-servicing capacity and have more taxable income to shield and therefore should operate on higher borrowing levels.

An alternative explanation of why firms have different debt/equity ratios is provided by the **pecking order theory**. In its simplest form it argues that:

- Firms prefer to employ internal finance (operational cash flow).
- Where external finance is required, firms prefer to raise debt with equity raised as a last resort.

The argument for this pecking order is based on *information asymmetry*. Managers know far more about the firm's performance and prospects than outside shareholders. They are therefore unlikely to issue equity when they believe shares are 'undervalued', but more likely to issue shares when they believe them to be 'overpriced'. Naturally, external shareholders are aware of this likely managerial behaviour and therefore view equity issues with some suspicion. They might well interpret a share issue as a signal that management thinks the shares are overpriced and mark down the shares accordingly, thereby making the cost of equity more expensive. Investors would therefore expect managers to finance the firm's future investment programme first through internal finance, then through debt, up to the appropriate debt/equity mix, and, finally, through issuing equity .

3 *What form of debt is appropriate*? If the strategic issue is to decide upon the level of borrowing, the tactical issue is to decide on the appropriate form of debt, or how to manage the debt portfolio. The two elements comprise the capital structure decisions. The debt mix question considers:
   (a) *form* – loans, leasing or other forms?
   (b) *maturity* – long-, medium- or short-term?
   (c) *interest rate* – fixed or floating?
   (d) *currency mix* – what currencies should the loans be in?

   These issues are discussed in Chapters 16 and 18.

4 *How do you finance asset growth*? Each firm must assess how much of its planned investment is to be financed by short-term finance and how much by long-term finance. This involves a trade-off between risk and return.

   Current assets can be classified into:
   (a) *Permanent current assets* – those current assets held to meet the firm's long-term requirements. For example, a minimum level of cash and stock is required at any given time, and a minimum level of debtors will always be outstanding.
   (b) *Fluctuating current assets* – those current assets that change with seasonal or cyclical variations. For example, most retail stores build up considerable stock levels prior to the Christmas period and run down to minimum levels following the January sales.

Figure 14.1 illustrates the nature of fixed assets and permanent and fluctuating current assets for a growing business. How should such investment be funded? There are several approaches to the funding mix problem.

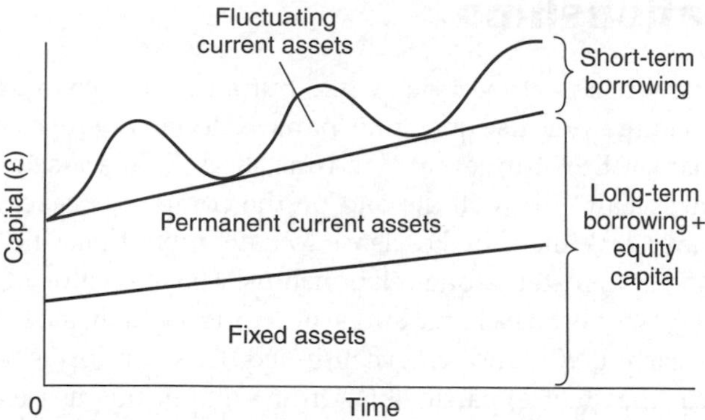

Figure 14.1 Financing working capital: the matching approach

First, there is the **matching approach** (Figure 14.1), where the maturity structure of the company's financing exactly matches the type of asset. Long-term finance is used to fund fixed assets and permanent current assets, while fluctuating current assets are funded by short-term borrowings.

A more **aggressive** and risky approach to financing working capital is seen in Figure 14.2, using a higher proportion of relatively cheaper short-term finance. Such an approach is more risky because the loan is reviewed by lenders more regularly. For example, a bank overdraft is repayable on demand. Finally, a **relaxed** approach would be a safer but more expensive strategy. Here, most if not all the seasonal variation in current assets is financed by long-term funding, any surplus cash being invested in short-term marketable securities or placed in a bank deposit.

Self-assessment Activity 14.2

What do you understand by the matching approach in financing fixed and current assets?

(answer at end of chapter)

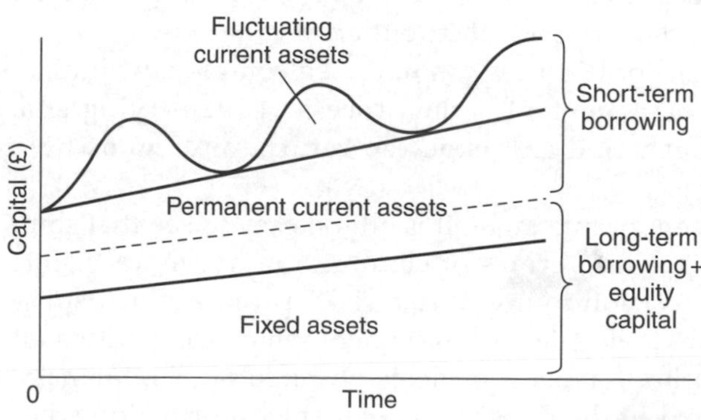

Figure 14.2 Financing working capital needs: an aggressive strategy

14.4 Banking relationships

Every company needs at least one bank, but a recent survey reveals that only 8 per cent of companies use just one bank. Global business may deal with hundreds of banks; Eurotunnel, at one time, had 225 banks to deal with! The number of banks dealt with will depend on the company's size, complexity and geographical spread. While it makes sense to have more than one bank, too many can make it difficult to foster strong relationships. The real value of a good banking relationship is discovered when things get tough (such as in the prolonged recession of the early 1990s) and when continued bank support is required.

We often hear the charge, particularly from smaller businesses, that banks are providing an inadequate service or charging too high interest rates. It seems that the banking relationship is more of a love/hate relationship than a healthy financial partnership.

A flourishing banking relationship requires the company to deal openly, honestly and regularly with the bank, keeping it informed of progress and ensuring there are no nasty surprises.

14.5 Risk management

The financial manager should recognise the many types of risk to be managed:

- *Liquidity risk* – managing corporate liquidity to ensure that funds are in place to meet future debt obligations. We discuss this later in the chapter.
- *Credit risk* – managing the risks that customers will not pay. We discuss this in the next chapter.
- *Market risk* – managing the risk of loss arising from adverse movements in market prices in interest rates, foreign exchange, equity and commodity prices. It is this form of risk that we now consider.

Every business needs to expose itself to risks in order to seek out profit. But there are some risks that a company is in business to take, and others that it is not. A major company, like Ford, is in business to make profits from cars. But is it also in business to make money from taking risks on the currency movements associated with its worldwide distribution of cars?

While the risks of business can never be completely eliminated, they can be *managed*. **Risk management is the process of identifying and evaluating the trade-off between risk and expected return, and choosing the appropriate course of action.**

With the benefit of hindsight, it is all too easy to see that some decisions were 'wrong'. In this sense, errors of commission are more visible than errors of omission; the decision to invest in a risky project which subsequently fails is more obvious than the rejected investment which competitors take up with great success. As with all aspects of decision making, risk management decisions should be judged in the light of the available information when the decision is made. The treasurer plays a vital role in identifying, assessing and managing corporate risk exposure in such a way as to maximise the value of the firm and ensure its long-term survival.

Self-assesment Activity 14.3

Take a look at the latest Annual Report of Cadbury Shweppes (**www.cadburyschweppes.com**). What does the Operating and Financial Review say about its treasury risk management policy?

Stages in the risk management process

Identify risk exposure. Taking risks is all part of business life, but businesses need to be quite sure exactly what risks they are taking. For example, while a firm will probably insure against the risk of fire, it may not consider the risk of loss of profits from the resulting disruption of the fire. The Brazilian coffee farmer could see his whole crop wiped out by a late frost. The UK fashion exporter could see her profit margins disappear because of the strong value of sterling.

Before any attempt is made to cover risks, the treasurer should undertake a complete review of corporate risk exposure, including business and financial risks. Some of these risks will naturally offset each other. For example, exports and imports in the same currency can be netted off, thereby reducing currency exposure.

Evaluate risks. We saw in Chapter 9, that there are various ways in which the risks of investments can be forecast and evaluated. The decision as to whether the risk exposure should be reduced will depend on the corporate attitude to risk (i.e. its degree of risk aversion) and the costs involved. **Hedgers** take positions to reduce exposure to risk. **Speculators** take positions to increase risk exposure.

Manage risks. The treasurer can manage risk exposure in four ways: risk retention, avoidance, reduction and transfer, each of which is considered below.

1 *Risk retention.* Many risks, once identified, can be carried – or absorbed – by the firm. The larger and more diversified the firm's activities, the more likely it is to be able to sustain losses in some areas. There is no need to pay premiums to market institutions when the risk can easily be absorbed by the company. Firms may hold precautionary cash balances, or maintain lower than average borrowing levels, in order to be better able to absorb unanticipated losses. It should, of course, be borne in mind that there are costs associated with such action, particularly the lower return to the firm from holding such large cash balances.
2 *Risk avoidance.* Some businesses prefer to keep well away from high-risk investments. They prefer to stick to conventional technology rather than promising new technology manufacture, and to avoid doing business with countries with volatile exchange rates. Such risk-avoiding behaviour may be acceptable in the short term, but, ultimately, it threatens the firm's competitiveness and survival.

3 *Risk reduction*. We all that know that by having a good diet and taking the right amount of exercise we can reduce our exposure to the risk of catching a cold. Similarly, firms can reduce exposure to failure by doing the right things. Risk of fire can be reduced by an effective sprinkler system; risk of project failure can be reduced by careful planning and management of the implementation process and clear plans for abandonment at minimum cost should the need arise.
4 *Risk transfer*. Where a risk cannot be avoided or reduced and is too big to be absorbed by the firm, it can be turned into someone else's problem or opportunity by 'selling', or transferring, it to a willing buyer. Bear in mind that most risks are two-sided. There may be a speculator willing to acquire the very risk that the hedger firm wishes to lose. It is this area of risk transfer which is of particular importance to corporate finance. Whole markets and industries have developed over the years to cater for the transfer of risk between parties.

Risk can be transferred in three main ways.

- *Diversification*. We saw, in Chapter 10, that risk exposure to the firm or shareholder can be considerably reduced by holding a diversified portfolio of investments. Diversification rarely eliminates all risk because most assets have returns positively correlated with the returns from other assets in the portfolio. It does, however, eliminate sufficient risk for the firm to consider absorbing the remaining risk exposure.
- *Insurance*. This seeks to cover downside risk. A premium is paid to the insurer to transfer losses arising from insured events but to retain any gains. As we saw in Chapter 13, financial options are a form of insurance whereby losses are transferred to others while profits are retained.
- *Hedging*. With hedging, the firm exchanges, for an agreed price, a risky asset for a certain one. It is a means by which the firm's exposure to specific kinds of risk can be reduced or 'covered'. Hence the fashion exporter can now enter into a contract guaranteeing an exchange rate for her exports to be paid in three months' time. Similar hedges can be created for risks in interest rates, commodity prices and many more transactions.
  Hedging has a cost, often in the form of a fee to a financial institution, but this cost may well be worth paying if hedging reduces financial risks. The extent to which an exposure is covered is termed the *hedge efficiency*: eliminating all financial risk is a 'perfect hedge' (i.e. 100 per cent efficiency).

Bako Ltd is a medium-size bakery business. The financial manager has identified that its main risk exposures lie in the following areas:

Risk exposure	Market hedge
Raw material prices – specifically, flour and sugar	Commodity
Currency movements on imports and exports	Currency
Interest rate movements on its variable-rate borrowings	Financial
Loss of profits, e.g. lost production from a possible bakery fire or a bad debt	Insurance

The first three risks can be managed through hedging in the commodity, currency and financial markets, letting the market bear the risks. The last can be covered through various forms of insurance.

Derivatives

The financial instruments employed to conduct hedging are termed **derivatives**, because the instrument derives its value from securities underlying a particular asset, such as a currency, share or commodity. One of the earliest derivatives was money itself, which for centuries derived its value from the gold into which it could be converted. 'Derivative' has today become a generic term that is used to include all types of relatively new financial instruments, such as options and futures.

The esoteric world of derivatives has hardly been out of the news in recent years. Procter & Gamble, Barings Bank, Metallgesellschaft and Kodak are all examples of major businesses whose corporate fingers have been burned through derivative transactions. Although sometimes viewed as instruments of the devil, derivatives are really nothing more than an efficient means of transferring risk from those exposed to it, but who would rather not be (hedgers), to those who are not, but would like to be (speculators).

Derivatives are financial instruments, such as options or futures, which enable investors either to reduce risk or speculate. They offer the treasurer a sophisticated 'tool-box' to manage risk. A risk management programme should reduce a company's exposure to the risks it is *not* in business to take, while reshaping its exposure to those risks it does wish to take. Risk exposure comes mainly in unexpected movements in interest rates, commodity prices and foreign exchange, all of which should be managed.

There are, essentially, four main types of derivative: forwards, futures, swaps and options.

Forward contracts

A **forward contract** is an agreement to sell or buy a commodity (including foreign currency) at a fixed price at some time in the future. In business, buyers and sellers are often subject to exactly opposite risks. The manufacturer of confectionery is concerned that the price of sugar may rise next year, while the sugar cane producer is concerned that the price may fall. In a world where it is extremely difficult to predict future commodity prices, both parties may want to exchange uncertain prices for sugar delivered next year for a fixed price.

By agreeing a price for sugar delivery next year, the confectionery manufacturer hedges against prices escalating, while the sugar cane producer hedges against prices dropping. They do this by entering into a **forward contract**, enabling future transactions and their prices to be agreed today, but not to be paid for until delivery at a specified future date.

Forward markets exist for most of the major commodities (e.g. cocoa, metals and sugar), but even more important is the forward market in foreign exchange.

No future in futures for Barings?

When Nick Leeson was posted by the Barings group to work as a clerk at Simex, the Singapore International Monetary Exchange, who would have thought that he would eventually, apparently single-handedly, bring the famous bank to its knees?

He progressed well and by 1993 had risen to general manager of Barings Futures (Singapore), a 25-person operation that ran the bank's Simex activities. The original role of the operation was to allow clients to buy and sell futures contracts on Simex, but the group decided to focus on trading on its own account as part of its group strategy. In the first seven months of 1994, Leeson's department generated profits of US$30.7 million, one-fifth of the whole of Barings' group profits in the previous year.

The bank set up an integrated Group Treasury and Risk function to try to manage its risk exposure better. Leeson adopted a new strategy of buying and selling options (or 'straddles') on the Nikkei 225 index, paying the premium into a secret trading account. In effect, he was betting on the market not having sharp movements up or down. But on 17 January 1995, an earthquake hit Japan, causing immense damage and loss of life. It also led to a collapse of the Nikkei 225 index, exposing Barings to huge losses.

Leeson's response was to invest heavily in buying Nikkei futures contracts in an apparent attempt to support the market price. Some have suggested he was simply applying the traditional 'wisdom' of trying to salvage an otherwise hopeless position by a 'double-or-quits' approach. If so, the high-risk strategy backfired. The result is well known: Barings Futures (Singapore) lost £860 million for the group, leaving the group with no future and resulting in its acquisition by the Dutch bank Internationale Nederlandes Group (ING) for £1.

Nick Leeson left the following fax for his boss in London: 'Sincere apologies for the predicament that I have left you in.'

Was it the use of futures derivatives that brought Barings down? Derivatives were certainly involved, and it is hardly conceivable that such a disaster could have arisen from, say, share dealing. But it was the strategy and lack of controls – not the instrument – that were the real problems. To ban derivatives on the grounds that they are dangerous instruments would be akin to banning cars because they lead to more accidents than bicycles. But we all know that it is usually the person behind the wheel, not the car, that is at fault. Similarly, it is the derivatives trader and his or her trading strategy that are really the problem when spectacular collapses like that of Barings occur.

A forward currency contract is when a company agrees to buy or sell a specified amount of foreign currency at an agreed future date and at a rate that is agreed in advance.

For example, if you want to pay US$50,000 in six months' time, you can use a forward contract to hedge against adverse currency movements. You can agree a price today that will pay for the dollars by arranging with your bank to buy dollars forward. At the end of six months, you pay the agreed sum and take delivery of the US dollars (see Chapter 17).

Futures contracts

Like a forward contract, a **futures contract** is a commitment to buy or sell an asset at an agreed date and at an agreed price. The difference is that futures are standardised in terms of period, size and quality and are traded on an exchange. In the UK, this is the London International Financial Futures and Options Exchange (LIFFE).

A chemical company plans to buy crude oil in three months' time. The spot price (i.e. current market price) is $20 a barrel and a three month futures contract can be agreed at $22 a barrel. To guard against the possibility of an even higher price rise, the company enters a 'long' futures position (i.e. agrees to buy) at $22 a barrel, thereby reducing its exposure to oil price hikes. If, in three months time, the spot oil price has risen beyond $22, the company will not suffer unforeseen losses.

If, however, just before delivery, the spot price has fallen to $18 a barrel, the company will want to benefit from the lower price. It will buy at the spot price and cancel the long contract by entering into a short contract (i.e. an agreement to sell) at around the $18 spot price. The loss of £4 a barrel on the two contracts is offset by the profit of $4 from buying at the spot rather than the original futures price.

Why might a company prefer a futures contract when a forward contract could be tailor-made to meet its specific requirements? The main reason lies in the obvious benefits from trading through an exchange, not least that the exchange carries the default risk of the other party failing to abide by the contract terms, so-called 'counterparty risk'. For this benefit, both the buyer and seller must pay a deposit to the exchange, termed the 'margin'.

Financial futures have become highly popular among both hedgers and traders, who buy or sell futures in order to profit from a view that the market will go up or down. The main forms of financial futures contracts cover short-term interest futures, bond futures and equity-linked futures using stock market indices.

Swaps

Swaps are arrangements between two firms to exchange a series of future payments. A swap is essentially a long-dated forward contract between two parties through the intermediation of a third party, such as a bank. For example, a company might agree to a currency swap, whereby it makes a series of regular payments in yen in return for receiving a series of payments in US dollars.

Heavy dependence upon short-term borrowing not only increases the risk of insolvency from funding long-term assets with short-term borrowing, but also exposes the company to short-term interest rate increases.

Options

An **option** gives the right, but not the obligation, to buy or sell an asset at an agreed price at, or up to, an agreed time. It is this right not to exercise the option that distinguishes it from a future. We discussed options in Chapter 13.

A farmer has a ripening crop which he plans to sell in September. He would like to benefit from any price movements but also be 'insured' against any fall in price. A put option (i.e. the right to sell at an agreed price) is rather like insurance. If the price falls, the option to sell at an agreed price is exercised. If the price rises, the option is not exercised and the spot price at the date of sale is taken.

Self-assessment Activity 14.4

Consider the following example of a company which plans to buy aluminium. It enters into a call option contract, paying an appropriate premium for the privilege to buy aluminium at $1,500/tonne in three months' time. If, at the end of the period, the spot price is $1,400/tonne, should the company exercise its option or let it lapse?

(answer at end of chapter)

To hedge or not to hedge

Does hedging enhance shareholder value? Some argue that it helps firms achieve competitive advantage over rivals by cost-effectively reducing risks over which it has little experience and exploiting those risks over which it has strong

In every crisis, there's risk and opportunity

The Chinese word for crisis (pronounced 'Wegi') is made from two words: risk ('We') and opportunity ('Gi'). Typical managers in the Western world tend to view a crisis as a major problem, but fail to identify the opportunities that such risks bring. However, the economic collapse in many Eastern economies suggests that they have invested heavily in commercial opportunities with little regard for the risks. Business survival rests on seizing the investment opportunity in risky markets, without jeopardising long-run corporate survival.

Korea's crisis in 1998 was a little matter of virtually the total economy going bust. The IMF had to step in to provide a $58 billion rescue package and help reschedule $22 billion of foreign debt. Korea had debt-burdened industrial companies, insolvent banks, growing unemployment and high interest rates, plus a massive amount of foreign borrowings. Total corporate debt was twice the gross domestic product. Now that's what you call a crisis!

The main reason why so many Korean banks were insolvent was the high level of bad debts. Insufficient credit assessment was undertaken and major companies, with gearing levels well beyond anything found in the UK, were encouraged to borrow even more, often investing their new capital in dubious, high-risk ventures. Getting the balance between risk and opportunity wrong can turn a crisis into economic catastrophe.

levels of competence. Pure theorists, on the other hand, argue that corporate hedging is a costly process doing no favours for shareholders. After all, portfolio diversification by investors is one form of hedging. Corporate hedging does nothing that shareholders could not do themselves, employing derivatives in exactly the same way as corporate treasurers to follow their own risk management strategy. So why do most large companies hedge? All shareholders in a business have a vested interest in its long-run prosperity and hedging risk exposure is an important means of avoiding financial distress.

Whatever the risk management strategy, it is important that the treasurer explains to senior management what has been done and what risk exposure remains.

Interest rate management

Every company is exposed to a degree of interest rate risk. This occurs when changes in the interest rate affect a company's profits and/or the value of its assets and liabilities. The nature of the exposure depends on whether the company is a net borrower or net investor.

The first form of interest rate risk is *basis risk* – the risk that the level of interest rates will change. A second form of risk relates to changes in the yield curve over time. This was discussed in Chapter 3 and refers to differences in short- and long-term interest rates. The normal, positive yield curve arises where interest rates increase as the term lengthens. In practice, however, the curve can be flat or even inverted.

Steps to manage interest rate exposure

The treasurer needs to understand the company's interest rate risk exposure, how it is likely to change over time and, where any of these exposures are compensating, how they can be netted off against each other. The three-step process involves:

1. Identify the expected future cash flows that are exposed to interest rate fluctuations.
2. Specify those rates of interest beyond which steps must be taken to reduce exposure.
3. Reduce exposure by:

   - *Natural hedging* – for example, an exposure to pay a rate of interest on a loan may be partially offset by an investment linked to the same or a similar rate.
   - *Fixing the interest rate* – loans can be taken out at a fixed rate rather than a floating rate.
   - *Interest rate swaps*. This is an arrangement whereby two parties agree to exchange interest payments with each other over an agreed period. In other words, Company A agrees to pay the interest on Company B's loan, while Company B reciprocates by paying the interest on Company A's loan. Of course, what they are really swapping is the different characteristics

of the two loans. The most common characteristic being exchanged is the fixed or variable interest rate, and this swap is termed a *plain vanilla or generic swap*.

- *Hedging contracts*. The corporate treasurer has a variety of techniques available to reduce interest rate risk, many of which have already been discussed. The main methods are forward rate agreements (FRAs), interest rate futures, interest rate options, interest rate swaps and more complex methods, such as options on interest rate swaps ('swaptions'). We are more concerned with the principles of interest rate management than the detailed application. The following example illustrates an approach to managing interest rates.

Managing interest rate risk at MedExpress Ltd

It was Karen Bailey's first day as the financial controller of MedExpress Ltd, a fast-growing business in the medical support industry. A quick look at the balance sheet revealed that the company, although highly profitable, was heavily geared, with large amounts of debt capital repayment due over the coming years. Interest rates have changed little over the past two years, but opinions are divided over whether the Governor of the Bank of England would have to raise interest rates quite steeply in order to keep inflation within prescribed government limits, or whether rates would hold, or even fall, to stimulate exports currently suffering from the strong value of sterling.

To Bailey's surprise, the company had taken no steps to manage its exposure to interest rate movements. Her first step was to identify the exposure to interest rate risk.

1 A £2 million overdraft, with a variable interest rate, would have a significant impact on profits and cash flow were the rate to increase in the near future. If the interest rate rise was dramatic, it could seriously affect cash flows and increase the risk of liquidation.
2 The £5 million fixed-rate long-term loan would become much less attractive were interest rates to fall. Carrying unduly high interest rates adversely affects profitability.
3 £1.8 million of the fixed rate loan matures shortly and will need to be replaced. The company can choose to repay the loan at any time over the next two years. If rates are expected to rise over that period, early redemption would be preferable.

As Bailey sought to get a grip on the interest rate exposure, she considered the following ways of managing interest rate risk:

(a) *Interest rate mix*. A mix of fixed and variable rate debt to reduce the effects of unanticipated rate movements. She would need to give more thought to whether the existing ratio of £2 million variable/£5 million fixed rate was sufficiently well balanced.
(b) *Forward rate agreement (FRA)*. Some risk exposure could be eliminated by entering into a forward rate agreement with the bank. This would lock the

company into borrowing at a future date at an agreed interest rate. Only the difference between the agreed interest that would be paid at the forward rate and the actual loan interest is transferred.

(c) *Interest rate 'cap'*. It is possible to 'cap' the interest rate to remove the risk of a rate rise. If the cap is set at 11 per cent, an upper limit is placed on the rate the company pays for borrowing a specific sum. Unlike the FRA, if the rate falls, the company does not have to compensate the bank.

(d) *Interest rate futures.* These contracts enable large interest rate exposures to be hedged using relatively small outlays. They are similar in effect to FRAs, except that the terms, the amounts and the periods are standardised.

(e) *Interest rate options.* Also termed interest rate guarantees, these contracts grant the buyer the right but not the obligation to deal at a specific interest rate at some future date.

(f) *Interest rate 'swaps'*. These occur where a company (usually very large firms) with predominantly variable rate debt, worried about a rise in rates, 'swaps' or matches its debt with a company with predominantly fixed-rate debt concerned that rates may fall. A bank usually acts as intermediary in the process, but it can be through direct negotiations with another company. Each borrower will still remain responsible for the original loan obligations incurred. Typically, firms continue to pay the interest on their own loan and then, at the end of the agreed period, a cash adjustment will be made between the two parties to the swap agreement. Interest rate swaps can also involve exchanges in different currencies.

Self-assessment Activity 14.5

Define in your own words the main forms of derivatives – forwards, futures, swaps and options.

(answer at end of chapter)

14.6 Working capital management

The last main area of treasury management is the management of working capital, including liquidity management. We devote the remainder of this chapter to working capital policy and the following chapter to short-term asset management. Let us first clarify the basic terms and ratios employed in working capital management.

Net working capital (or simply working capital) refers to current assets less current liabilities – hence its alternative name of net current assets. Current assets include cash, marketable securities, debtors and stock. Current liabilities are obligations that are expected to be repaid within the year.

Working capital management refers to the financing, investment and control of net current assets within policy guidelines. The treasurer acts as a steward of

Mini case

Treasury management in ICI

ICI, Britain's largest chemicals company, operates a small group treasury function. Its main function is to manage risks rather than to speculate on currency and other movements. It seeks to reduce or eliminate financial risk, to ensure sufficient liquidity is available to meet foreseeable needs, and to invest cash assets safely and profitably. Strict controls exist on the use of financial instruments in managing the group's risk and on aggregate credit exposure.

With only 10 per cent of its £11 billion revenues being generated in sterling, currency management is paramount. It has bank accounts denominated in 30 different currencies and regularly deals in over 50 different currency movements between one country and another. In 1997, ICI was responsible for £18.5 billion of foreign exchange transactions, backed up by a variety of hedging operations. Transaction exposure from sales and purchases in other currencies is mainly hedged using forward contracts.

Interest rate management is also an important part of the treasury management function. Interest rate caps and swaps are two of the more commonly-employed risk management techniques. At any one time, the treasury team manages a float of money totalling on average about £1.5 billion, although this is only a fraction of the group's total cash flow. Surplus funds are invested in high-quality liquid marketable instruments including commercial paper, bank deposits, money market instruments and asset-backed securities. ICI has £2.4 billion unutilised committed credit facilities at its disposal with varying maturities up to 2004.

Question

The treasurer of ICI has asked you, as a new recruit to the treasury team, to identify the main financial risks and to suggest risk-reduction methods to deal with them.

corporate resources and needs to devise and operate clear and effective working capital policies.

Liquidity management is the planned acquisition and utilisation of cash – or near cash – resources to ensure that the company is in a position to meet its cash obligations as they fall due. It requires close attention to be devoted to cash forecasting and planning. If the wheels of business are oiled by cash flow, the cash forecast, or cash budget, gauges how much 'oil' is left in the can at any time. Any predicted cash shortfall may require the raising of additional finance, disposal of fixed assets or tighter control over working capital requirements in order to avoid a liquidity crisis.

Various ratios are useful in assessing corporate liquidity, the following being the most commonly employed:

1 The **current ratio** is the ratio of current assets to current liabilities. A high ratio (relative to the industry) would suggest that the firm is in a relatively liquid position. However, if much of the current assets are in the form of raw materials and finished stocks, this may not be the case.
2 The **quick** or **'acid test' ratio** recognises that stocks may take many weeks to realise in cash terms. Accordingly, it is computed by dividing current liabilities into current assets excluding stock.
3 **Days cash-on-hand ratio** is found by dividing the cash and marketable securities by projected daily cash operating expenses. As its name implies, it indicates the number of days the firm could meet its cash obligations, assuming that no further cash is received during the period. Daily cash operating expenses should be based on the projected cash flows from the cash budget, but a somewhat cruder approach is to divide the annual cost of sales plus selling, administrative and financing costs by 365.

Example: The General Eclectic Company (GEC).
The working capital of GEC is as follows:

	£m
Current assets	
Stocks and contracts in progress	1,195
Debtors	1,572
Investments	400
Cash at bank and in hand	1,009
	4,176
Less creditors due within one year	(2,037)
Net current assets	2,139

Notice that current assets are ranked in descending order of liquidity. The liquidity ratios for GEC and the industry are:

		GEC	Industry average
Current ratio	(4,176/2,037)	2.05	1.6
Acid test	(4,176 – 1,195)/2,037	1.46	1.2

GEC's current and acid test ratios are both higher than the industry averages, reflecting the company's healthy liquidity position. But what would the position look like if the £1 billion of cash were already committed, say, for major capital expenditure? If you recalculate the current and acid test ratios, you will find that the liquidity position then falls below the industry average.

Self-assessment Activity 14.6

Which areas of treasury management would you say are most neglected by smaller firms?

(answer at end of chapter)

14.7 Predicting corporate failure

Excessive levels of gearing are often responsible for corporate failure. However, very highly geared companies do survive and, conversely, some low-geared companies fail. This suggests that there are many other clues to the viability of a company, and it is not enough simply to examine a single Balance Sheet ratio when attempting to predict financial failure.

The '**Z-score**' method, developed by Altman (1968), attempts to balance out the relative importance of different financial indicators. This was based on examining the financial characteristics of two samples of failed and surviving US companies to detect which ratios were most important in discriminating between the two groups. For example, were past failures characterised by low liquidity ratios? What other ratios were important discriminators, and what was their relative importance?

Using a technique called discriminant analysis, the relative significance of each critical ratio can be expressed in an equation that generates a 'Z-score', a critical value below which failed firms typically fall, and above which survivors locate. In general terms, the equation is:

$$Z = a + bR_1 + cR_2$$

In this equation, a, b and c are constants derived from past observations and R_1 and R_2 are two identified key discriminatory ratios.

A Z-score model using data for UK firms was developed by Marais (1982), an extension of which is currently used by the Datastream database. For Datastream, Marais examined over 40 ratios before settling on four critical ones in his final model:

$$\text{Profitability: } \frac{\text{Pre-tax profit} + \text{depreciation}}{\text{Current liabilities}}$$

$$\text{Liquidity: } \frac{\text{Current assets less stocks}}{\text{Current liabilities}}$$

$$\text{Gearing: } \frac{\text{All borrowing}}{\text{Total capital employed less intangibles}}$$

$$\text{Stock turnover} = \frac{\text{Stock}}{\text{Sales}}$$

Other analysts, using different samples of firms, employ different ratios and weightings in the equation for Z. In Marais' model, the critical Z-value is zero. This does not prove that an existing company displaying a Z-score of around zero is on the brink of insolvency, merely that the firm is displaying characteristics similar to previous failures. Given that there are accounting policy differences between companies, it may be more useful to look at changes in the Z-score over time. A steadily declining Z-score suggests a worsening financial condition, while an improving Z-score indicates strong corporate financial management.

Corporate failure models, such as Z-scores, have their weaknesses:

(a) 'Failure' is difficult to define. Usually its definition is wider than liquidation, but all sorts of restructuring and rescue operations arise for a variety of reasons.

Amazon spreads its risks

Has Jeff Bezos just made a big mistake?

Last week, the chairman of Amazon.com told securities analysts that the company planned to start selling personal computers in the second half of 2001.

By traditional retailing logic, this is a bizarre mistake. In the past, retailers have more often succeeded by concentrating on a small number of related product lines than by trying to become generalists.

There is a simple reason for this: to sell something effectively, you need to know a lot about the product. Without this knowledge, you risk filling your shelves with items that customers do not want.

In the early days of electronic commerce, it looked as though these rules did not apply to online retailing. Companies such as Amazon kept no inventories of the vast majority of books they sold: only when your order came in did they buy in the book you wanted from a wholesaler.

Thanks to the clever use of software, the process happened so quickly that the book arrived within a few days – just as fast as from a mail order retailer that was a little slower off the mark in shipping its orders. And this way of doing business had a marvellous advantage: what accountants call a negative operating cycle. Because the retailer got credit, it could sell the books to customers and get paid before having to settle up with its suppliers. Instead of sucking a flow of cash out of the business, the products being sold provided working capital for other purposes.

As competition intensified, however, the customers expected more reliable fulfilment. Thus Amazon, along with everybody else, was forced to keep more items in stock. That is why the company has ended up as one of the larger operators of centralised inventory in the US.

The attractions of the negative operating cycle are still in place. Amazon can still receive payment for its sales before paying its suppliers.

Based on Tim Jackson, *Financial Times*, June 12 2001

(b) All models are based on the past, when macroeconomic conditions were different from the present.
(c) Companies employ different accounting policies, making comparison difficult.

Z-scoring is used primarily for credit risk assessment by banks and other financial institutions, industrial companies and credit insurers. While it does not tell the whole story behind the company's prospects, it is widely regarded as an important indicator of a company's financial health and hence its credit status.

14.8 Cash operating cycle

For a typical manufacturing firm, there are three primary activities affecting working capital: purchasing materials, manufacturing the product and selling the product. Because these activities are subject to uncertainty (delivery of materials may come late, manufacturing problems may arise, sales may become sluggish etc.), the cash flows associated with them are also uncertain. If a firm is to maintain liquidity, it needs to invest funds in working capital and to ensure that the operating cycle is properly controlled.

The **cash operating cycle** is the length of time between the firm's cash payment for purchases of material and labour and cash receipts from the sale of goods. In other words, it is the length of time the firm has funds tied up in working capital. This is calculated as follows:

Cash operating cycle

Cash operating cycle = stock period + customer credit period − supplier credit period.

The cash operating cycle: Briggs plc

Briggs plc, a manufacturer of novelty toys, has the following working capital items in its Balance Sheet at the start and end of its financial year:

	1 January	31 December
Stock	£5,500	£6,500
Debtors	£3,200	£4,800
Creditors	£3,000	£4,500

Turnover for the year, all on credit, is £50,000 and cost of sales is £30,000. For how many days is working capital tied up in each item? What is the cash operating cycle period?

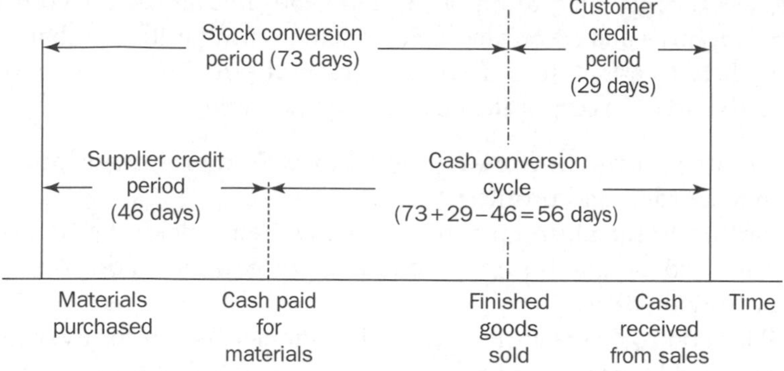

Figure 14.3 Cash conversion cycle

Our first task is to calculate the turnover ratios for each:

$$\text{Stock turnover} = \frac{\text{Cost of sales}}{\text{Average stock}} = \frac{£30{,}000}{£6{,}000} = 5 \text{ times p.a.}$$

$$\text{Debtors' turnover} = \frac{\text{Sales}}{\text{Average debtors}} = \frac{£50{,}000}{£4{,}000} = 12.5 \text{ times p.a.}$$

$$\text{Creditors' turnover} = \frac{\text{Cost of sales}}{\text{Average creditors}} = \frac{£30{,}000}{£3{,}750} = 8 \text{ times p.a.}$$

To find the number of days each item is held in working capital, we divide the turnover calculations into 365 days:

Stock period = 365/5 = 73 days
Debtors' (customer credit) period = 365/12.5 = 29.2 days
Creditors' (supplier credit) period = 365/8 = 45.6 days

The cash operating cycle is therefore:

(73 + 29.2 − 45.6) = 56.6 days

This is illustrated in Figure 14.3.

Self-assessment Activity 14.7

Explain why two firms in the same industry could have very different cash operating cycles. What are the financial implications?

(answer at end of chapter)

14.9 Working capital policy

The treasury manager should ensure that the firm operates sound working capital policies. These policies cover such areas as the levels of cash and stock held, and the credit terms granted to customers and agreed with suppliers.

Successful implementation of these policies influences the company's expected future returns and associated risk, which, in turn, influence shareholder value.

Failure to adopt sound working capital policies may jeopardise long-term growth and even corporate survival. For example:

1 Failure to invest in working capital to expand production and sales may result in lost orders and profits.
2 Failure to maintain current assets that can quickly be turned into cash can affect corporate liquidity, damage the firm's credit rating and increase borrowing costs.

3 Poor control over working capital is a major reason for **overtrading** problems, discussed later in this chapter.

Typical questions arising in the working capital management field include the following:

- What should be the firm's total level of investment in current assets?
- What should be the level of investment for each type of current asset?
- How should working capital be financed?

We now consider how firms establish and finance the levels of working capital appropriate for their businesses, and how they impact on profitability and risk. The level and nature of working capital within any organisation depend on a variety of factors, such as the following:

- The industry within which the firm operates.
- The type of products sold.
- Whether products are manufactured or bought in.
- Level of sales.
- Stock and credit policies.
- The efficiency with which working capital is managed.

We saw in Chapter 1 that the relationship between risk and the required financial return is central to financial management. Investment in working capital is no exception. In establishing the planned level of working capital investment, management should assess the level of liquidity risk it is prepared to accept, risk being defined as the possibility that the firm will not be able to meet its financial obligations as they fall due. This is a further dimension of financial risk.

Working capital strategies: Helsinki plc

Helsinki plc, a dairy produce distributor, is considering which working capital policy it should adopt.

Figure 14.4 shows the two working capital strategies under consideration. Notice that both schedules are curvilinear, suggesting that economies of scale permit working capital to grow more slowly than sales. The firm operates with lower levels of stock, debtors and cash under a more *aggressive* approach than under a more relaxed strategy.

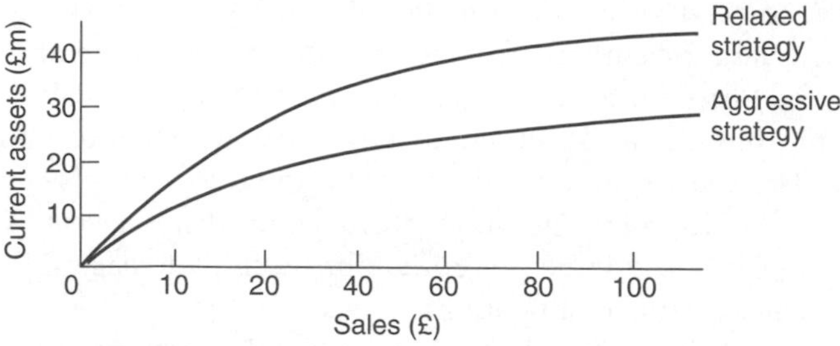

Figure 14.4 Helsinki plc working capital strategies

Suppliers to examine e-commerce

Six of the largest automotive parts suppliers are joining forces to examine potential e-commerce initiatives in an effort to accelerate cost-savings. The six – Delphi Automotive, Dana Eaton, TRW, Motorola and Valeo – are among the biggest 'tier one' suppliers and together have annual revenue of $100 billion.

They said yesterday they had identified several areas of 'mutual interest' involving the use of e-commerce technologies. The main objectives would be better supply-chain management and customer support, and management of after-market activities.

'By working together on joint technology solutions, we can avoid repetitive costs and establish common solutions that ultimately improve effectiveness throughout the supply chain', said Alexander Cutler, Eaton's chief operating officer.

The move comes as e-commerce possibilities are causing turmoil in the industry. The three big US vehicle manufacturers – General Motors, Ford and DaimlerChrysler – have already announced plans for a jointly-owned trade exchange. This, in turn, has caused many suppliers to worry about further pressure from the manufacturers on costs, and wonder whether they will garner the full benefit of technology-driven procurement changes.

Some suppliers have suggested that GM, Ford and DaimlerChrysler, through their ownership of the exchange, would reap most of the benefit of any improvements, and that suppliers could be pawns in the process.

At the same time, suppliers face pressure from Wall Street, where analysts, worried about a potential downturn in the surging US vehicle market, have them trading on low price-earnings multiples. The average multiple for the industry is less than 10 – worse than all other sectors apart from house-building and tobacco.

The suppliers acknowledge that there is scope for improving their own procurement arrangements – by concentrating expenditure and reducing inventory.

Based on Nikki Tait, *Financial Times*, June 4 2000

A *relaxed*, lower-risk and more flexible policy for working capital means maintaining a larger cash balance and investment in marketable securities that can quickly be turned into cash, granting more generous customer credit terms and investing more heavily in stock. This may attract more custom, but will usually lead to a reduction in profitability for the business, given the high cost of tying up capital in relatively low-profit-generating assets. Conversely, an aggressive policy should increase profitability, while increasing the risk of failing to meet the firm's financial obligations.

In Table 14.1, the relaxed working capital strategy involves a further £20 million investment in current assets. The additional stocks and more generous credit facilities enable Helsinki's management to attain an additional £5 million sales with the aggressive policy. This gives a 19.5 per cent return on capital employed and a secure current ratio of 2.7.

A more aggressive working capital strategy would certainly improve the return on capital. In Helsinki's case, the rate increases to 30 per cent. But this is achieved by increasing corporate risk. Net working capital falls to only £5 million and the current ratio to 1.3.

Working capital costs

Managing working capital involves a trade-off not only between risk and required return, but also between costs that increase and costs that fall with the level of investment. Costs that increase with additional investment are termed **carrying costs**, while costs that fall with increases in investment are termed **shortage costs**. These two types of cost may be found in most forms of current assets, but particularly in stocks and cash.

The main form of carrying costs is opportunity costs associated with the cost of financing the investment.

Table 14.1 Helsinki plc: profitability and risk of working capital strategies

	Relaxed (£m)	Aggressive (£m)
Current assets (CA)	40	20
Fixed assets	25	25
Total assets	65	45
Current liabilities (CL)	(15)	(15)
Capital employed (net assets)	50	30
Planned sales	65	60
Planned profit (15% of sales)	9.75	9.0
Return on capital employed	19.5%	30.0%
Net working capital (CA – CL)	£25 m	£5 m
Current ratio (CA/CL)	2.7	1.3

Financing costs: Bedford Auto-Vending Machine Company

The Bedford Auto-Vending Machine Company is considering how much to invest in current assets. Two working capital policies are under investigation.

	Flexible policy (£m)	Aggressive policy (£m)
Stock	32	25
Debtors	28	22
Cash and marketable securities	12	–
	72	47

It will be seen that the flexible policy requires a further £25 million investment in working capital over and above that required for the aggressive policy. What is the cost of carrying this £25 million additional working capital? The main carrying cost is the return that could be earned by investing the additional £25 million in financial assets outside the business. If these could generate 10 per cent p.a., the additional earnings would be £2.5 million (less any interest earned on short-term cash and securities). Other carrying costs include the additional storage and handling costs for stock.

Aggressive or restrictive working capital policies are more susceptible to incurring shortage costs. These costs are usually of two types:

1 **Ordering costs** – costs incurred in placing orders for stock, cash, etc. (in the case of stocks this may also include the production setup costs). Operating a restrictive policy means ordering stock more regularly and in smaller amounts than for more relaxed policies.
2 **Costs of running out of stock or cash** – the most obvious costs here are the loss of business and even the possible liquidation of the firm. Less tangible costs are the loss of customer goodwill, the disruption to the production schedule, and the time and cost of negotiating alternative sources of finance.

The trade-off between carrying costs and shortage costs is shown in Figures 14.5 and 14.6. In Figure 14.5, carrying costs are seen to increase steadily as current

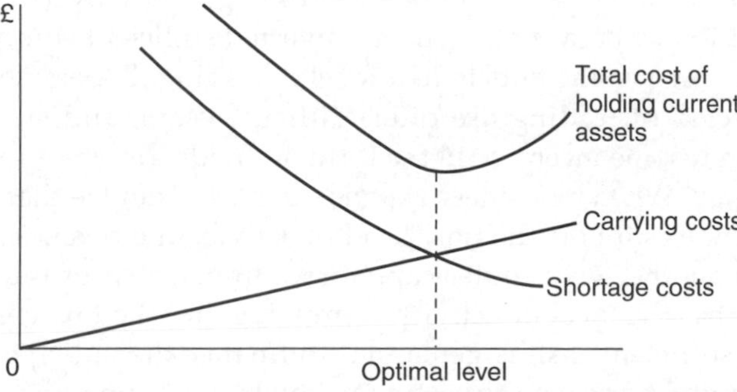

Figure 14.5 Optimal level of working capital for a 'relaxed' strategy

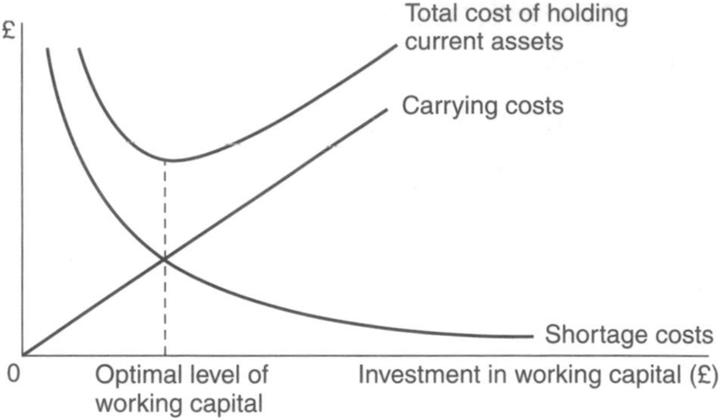

Figure 14.6 Optimal level of working capital for an 'aggressive' strategy

assets grow. Conversely, shortage costs fall with the level of investment in current assets. The cost of holding current assets is the combined cost of the two, *the minimum point being the optimal amount of current assets held*. For simplicity, we have shown current assets in total. Later, we consider each element, such as cash or stock, separately.

Different businesses will be more sensitive to certain types of cost. An aggressive policy is more appropriate when carrying costs are high relative to shortage costs, as in Figure 14.6. For example, a major car manufacturer like Ford will not want to hold excessive quantities of raw material stocks, but will buy in materials and parts just before they are to be used in car production, reflecting the Just-in-Time philosophy. Often there will be penalty clauses for non-delivery of such materials to the manufacturer by agreed dates. A flexible policy tends to be more suited to low carrying costs relative to shortage costs (see Figure 14.5).

14.10 Overtrading problems

Here we address the problems arising from operating a business with an inappropriate capital structure, a phenomenon known as **overtrading**.

Overtrading arises from at least three serious managerial mistakes:

1 *Initial under-capitalisation*. Many businesses experience overtrading problems from the very start because they never invested sufficient equity at the time of formation to finance the anticipated level of trading. Experience suggests that the early years of trading are often difficult years, and shareholders will probably want some incentive in the form of dividends.
2 *Over-expansion*. When a business expands to such a degree that its capital base is insufficient to support the new level of activity, the business is overtrading or, to put it another way, under-capitalised. In many cases the business looks healthy, in that the level of activity is growing and the business is profitable. But unless sufficient cash is generated to finance the anticipated increase in working capital and fixed investment, the business may encounter serious overtrading problems.

3 *Poor utilisation of working capital resources.* Even when a business has been adequately capitalised and is not over-expanding its activity, overtrading can still occur in several ways:

(a) Failure to achieve planned profit and cash flow levels may mean that debt capacity, originally intended for working capital needs, is used to replace lost earnings.

(b) Cost overruns on fixed capital projects and other unanticipated capital investment can swallow up finance intended for working capital needs.

(c) Similarly, strategic decisions, such as a major acquisition, can have adverse effects on working capital finance unless the capital basis is adequately enlarged.

(d) Higher dividends mean reduced profit retentions, often the major source of finance for working capital.

Overtrading problems: Growfast Publishers Ltd

Growfast Publishers Ltd distributes books worldwide. Its most recent accounts reveal:

	£000
Sales	280
Cost of sales (all variable)	(240)
Profit	40

Stock is two months cost of sales. Trade creditors pay within one month, while debtors take three months to pay.

Growfast Publishers has recently gained exclusive rights to publish *Corporate Finance and Investment* in Mongolia and is confident that this will lead to a doubling in total sales. Because all costs are variable, the profit will also double, giving a healthy £80,000 profit.

Cash flow for the year, however, is less impressive:

	£000
Trading profit	80
Increase in stocks (240/6)	(40)
Increase in debtors (280/4)	(70)
Increase in creditors (240/12)	20
Net cash flow from operating activities	(10)
Taxation on trading profit (@35%)	(26)
Consequence	(36)

The consequence of a doubling in sales and profits is actually a reduction in cash by £36,000. If the increased working capital is permanent, it should be funded by longer-term finance.

Consequences of, and remedies for, overtrading

The consequences of overtrading can be extremely serious and possibly fatal. As the pace of activity increases, working capital needs will also increase. Without the necessary capital structure and cash flow, serious liquidity problems will arise. Business life then becomes a matter of crisis management: finding the cash to meet the wage bill, the creditors' claims and the tax charges. Such myopic behaviour takes attention away from the business of creating wealth and will, ultimately, lead to a decline in competitiveness and profitability.

What can management do to remedy the cash flow problems caused by overtrading?

1 The most drastic step is to *reduce the level of business activity*. Profitable orders may be rejected due to insufficient capital to finance additional working capital needs. If the alternative is to accept the order and, in so doing, jeopardise the business by exceeding the overdraft limit, a slower rate of growth is the preferred course of action.
2 The most obvious remedy is to *increase the capital base*. Figure 14.2 showed that an aggressive strategy for financing working capital operates on a lower long-term capital base, thus making overtrading more likely. Movement towards a matching approach is perhaps called for, where permanent increases in current assets are matched by the injection of permanent capital, preferably in the form of equity or long-term loans, perhaps with a moratorium on repayments in the early years.
3 Finally, steps should be taken to maintain tight control over working capital. Constant review of the working capital policy and its cash flow implications can allow the firm to minimise the extra capital resources required to fund expansion.

Self-assessment Activity 14.8

Define overtrading. How does it arise and what are its consequences?

(answer at end of chapter)

14.11 How firms can use the yield curve

In Chapter 3, we examined the term structure of interest rates showing the yields on securities of varying times to maturity. The yield curve offers important information to treasury managers wanting to borrow funds. Although it is based on the structure of yields on government stock, similar principles apply to the market for corporate loans, or bonds. However, corporates have higher default risk than governments so that markets require higher yields on corporate bonds.

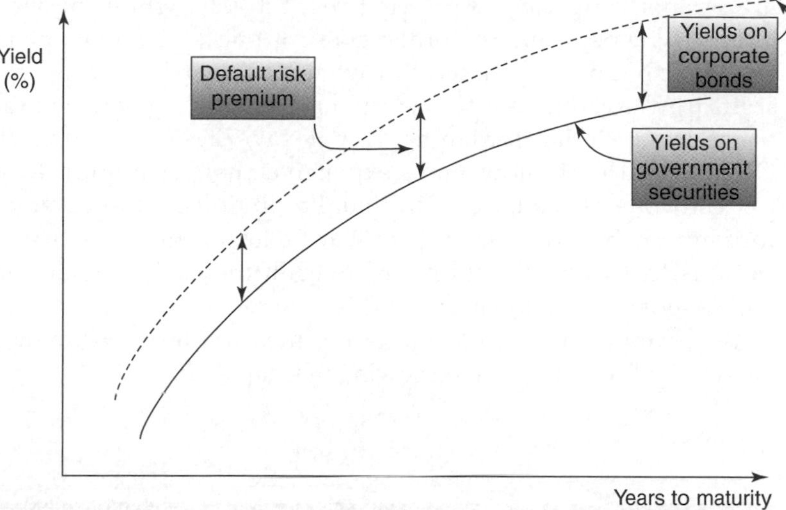

Figure 14.7 Yield curves

The market for government stock provides a benchmark that dictates the general shape of the yield curve with the curve for corporate bonds located above this. Figure 14.7 reproduces Figure 3.3 with an additional yield curve to describe yields in the market for corporate bonds. The distance between the two lines represents the premium required by the market to cover the risk of default by corporate borrowers. For top-grade corporate borrowers, with a very high credit rating, the premium will be relatively narrow, whereas firms considered to be more risky will be subject to higher risk premia. The corporate versus government yield premium would usually widen with time to maturity as corporate insolvency risk probably increases with time.

Today's yield curve incorporates how people expect interest rates to move in the future. An upward-sloping yield curve reflects investors' expectations of higher future interest rates and vice versa. The action points are clear:

- A rising yield curve may be taken to imply that higher future interest rates are expected. This suggests firms might borrow long-term now, and avoid variable interest rate borrowing.
- A falling yield curve may be taken to imply that lower future interest rates are expected. This suggests firms might borrow short-term now, and utilise variable interest rate borrowing.

Words of warning

In some circumstances, managers may be deceived by short-term rates. Say, they follow a policy of borrowing at short-term rates while the yield curve is upward-sloping, planning to switch to long-term borrowing when short-term rates exceed long-term rates.

For example, Jordan plc wants to borrow for six years, and the yield curve currently slopes upwards. The yields on five-year and six-year bonds are 5.5 per cent and 5.8 per cent respectively, while the yield on one-year bonds is 5.0 per cent. So, Jordan goes for one-year bonds, planning to issue a five-year bond a year later. But what if, a year later, the whole yield curve shifts upwards due to macro-economic changes, e.g. a rise in the expected rate of inflation, so that Jordan has to pay say, 7.5 per cent on a five-year bond? Obviously, this is now more expensive than arranging to lock in the 5.8 per cent rate at the base year. Equally obviously, the reverse could apply – Jordan may benefit from a downward shift in the yield curve. However, the point is that firms should not be over-influenced by relatively small differentials along the yield curve.

We examine methods of short- and medium-term borrowing in Chapter 16 and methods of long-term borrowing in Chapter 18.

Summary

Treasury management is central to corporate finance in practice. Even in smaller businesses, where no formalised treasury function exists, the main treasury activities of managing corporate funding, risk, banking relationships, liquidity and working capital will still be conducted. This chapter has introduced the reader to those treasury activities, but most of them receive extensive treatment in subsequent chapters.

Key points

- Treasury management is the efficient management of liquidity and financial risk in the business.
- Each company should establish whether it requires a separate treasury function and whether it should be a cost or profit centre.
- Clear treasury policies are required for funding, banking relationships, risk management and working capital management.
- In general, long-term finance should be used to fund both fixed assets and permanent current assets, fluctuating current assets being funded by short-term borrowing.
- Hedging can take various forms, but derivative instruments, such as futures, forward contracts, options and swaps, are the most common.
- Working capital policy trades off expected profitability and risk. An 'aggressive' working capital policy, which seeks to employ the minimum level of net current assets (including cash and marketable securities), will probably achieve a higher return on investment, but may jeopardise the financial health of the business.
- The cash operating cycle (the length of time between cash payment and cash receipt for goods) should be regularly reviewed and controlled.
- The consequences of overtrading (or under-capitalisation) can be extremely serious, if not fatal, for the firm.

Further reading and website

Treasury management is a practical topic and *The Treasurer* is a useful guide. Collier *et al.* (1988) cover the subject of treasury management, while Smith (1988) is a helpful book of readings and Gentry (1988) a good article on short-term financial management. A pioneer paper on predicting corporate failure is Altman (1968). Risk management and the benefits of hedging are discussed in *Mastering Finance* 1998 (Pitman). A useful website is the Association of Corporate Treasurers: **www.corporate-treasurers.co.uk**.

Self-assessment Answers

14.1 Treasury management involves the efficient management of liquidity and risk in the business. The treasurer usually has primary responsibilities for funding, risk management, working capital management and liquidity, and managing banking relationships.

14.2 The matching approach to funding is where the maturity structure of the company's financing matches the cash flows generated by the assets employed. In simple terms, this means that long-term finance is used to fund fixed assets and permanent current assets, while fluctuating current assets are funded by short-term borrowings.

14.4 It should let it lapse as the spot price is cheaper than the exercise price.

14.5
- *Forward* – commits the user to buying or selling an asset at a specific price on a specific future date.
- *Future* – a forward contract traded on an exchange.
- *Swap* – a contract by which two parties exchange cash flows linked to an asset or liability.
- *Option* – the right to buy or sell at an agreed price.

14.6 Smaller firms will rarely have a separate treasury function, the accountant or managing director having to perform much of this role. There is a real danger that key areas will be neglected. For example, liquidity management or banking relationships may be largely neglected. Funding may be through short-term overdraft facilities when a larger, more secure form of funding may prove beneficial. Other dangers are that small businesses involved in exporting or importing may neglect the need to manage or hedge currency risks, or corporate borrowers may neglect exposure to interest rate fluctuations.

14.7 A company with a simple production process, which makes to order, enjoys generous supplier credit terms and offers cash discounts for early payment could have a much shorter operating cycle than the industry average. A firm with a longer cycle demands more capital and is more exposed to bad debt and stock losses.

14.8 Overtrading arises when businesses operate with inadequate long-term capital. It occurs when firms:

(a) are set up with insufficient capital;
(b) expand too rapidly without a commensurate increase in long-term finance;

(c) utilise net current assets in an inefficient manner. The consequences can be extremely serious and possibly fatal unless the problem is addressed.

Questions

1 Atlas Ltd is a newly formed digital media company with a number of locations in the UK, France and Germany. The board of directors is currently discussing whether the finance function should be centralised or decentralised. What advice would you offer?

2 What are the risks a manufacturing company might encounter as a result of interest rate movements?

Describe two financial instruments the company could use to reduce such risks.

3 ABC plc is a UK-based service company with a number of wholly owned subsidiaries and interests in associated companies throughout the world. In response to the rapid growth in the company, the Managing Director has ordered a review of the company's organisation structure, particularly the finance function. The Managing Director holds the opinion that a separate treasury department should be established. At present, treasury functions are the responsibility of the chief accountant.

Required

(a) Describe the main responsibilities of a treasury department in a company such as ABC plc and explain the benefits that might accrue from the establishment of a separate treasury function.

(b) Describe the advantages and disadvantages which might arise if the company established a separate treasury department as a profit centre rather than a cost centre.

(CIMA, November 1995)

4 **(a)** **(i)** Discuss the theories, or arguments, which suggest that financial analysis can be used to forecast the probability of a given firm's failure; and

(ii) explain why such an analysis, even if properly applied, may not always predict failure.

(b) Discuss the following statement: 'It is always a sound rule to liquidate a company if its liquidation value is above its value as a going concern.'

5 **(a)** Explain, with the use of a numerical example, the meaning of the term 'cash operating cycle' and its significance in relation to working capital management.

(b) Delcars plc own a total of ten franchises, in a variety of United Kingdom locations, for the sale and servicing of new and used cars. Six of the franchises sell just second hand vehicles, with the remaining four operating a car service centre in addition to retailing both new and used vehicles. Delcars operate different systems for banking of sales receipts, depending on the type of sale. All monies from new car sales must be banked by the garage on the day of the sale; receipts from second hand car sales are banked once a week on Mondays, and receipts from car servicing work are banked twice a week on Wednesdays and Fridays. No banking facilities are available at the weekend, i.e. Saturdays and Sundays. The sales mix of the three elements (as a percentage of Delcars' total revenue) is as follows: 60 per cent new vehicles; 25 per cent second hand vehicles; 15 per cent servicing. Total sales for all three business areas amounted to £25 million in 1999. Delcars pays interest at a rate of 8.5 per cent per annum on an average overdraft of £65,000, and the company's finance director has suggested that the company could significantly reduce the interest charge if all sales receipts were banked on the day of sale. All the garages are open every day except Sunday. Assume that the daily sales value (for all three areas of business) is spread evenly across the week.

Required

Calculate the value of the annual interest which could be saved if all ten franchises adopted the finance director's suggestion of daily banking.

(c) Using the example of a car dealership such as Delcars, as given in **(b)** above, outline the advantages and disadvantages of centralisation of the treasury function.

(ACCA)

6 *Solution in Appendix A (page 819).* Hercules Wholesalers Ltd has been particularly concerned with its liquidity position in recent months. The most recent Profit and Loss Account and Balance Sheet of the company are as follows:

Profit and Loss Account for the year ended 31 May 199X

	£	£
Sales		452,000
Less: Cost of sales		
Opening stock	125,000	
Add purchases	341,000	
	466,000	
Less: Closing stock	143,000	323,000
Gross profit		129,000
Expenses		132,000
Net loss for the period		(3,000)

Balance Sheet as at 31 May 199X

	£	£	£
Fixed assets			
Freehold premises at valuation			280,000
Fixtures and fittings at cost less depreciation			25,000
Motor vehicles at cost less depreciation			52,000
			357,000
Current assets			
Stock		143,000	
Debtors		163,000	
		306,000	
Less creditors due within one year			
Trade creditors	145,000		
Bank overdraft	140,000	285,000	
			21,000
			378,000
Less creditors due after more than one year			
Loans			120,000
			258,000

Continued

	£	£	£
Capital and reserves			
Ordinary share capital			100,000
Retained profit			158,000
			258,000

The debtors and creditors were maintained at a constant level throughout the year.

Required

(a) Explain why Hercules Wholesalers Ltd is concerned with its liquidity position.
(b) Explain the term 'operating cash cycle' and state why this concept is important in the financial management of a business.
(c) Calculate the operating cash cycle for Hercules Wholesalers Ltd based on the information above. (Assume a 360 day year.)
(d) State what steps may be taken to improve the operating cash cycle of the company.

(Certified Diploma)

7 Micrex Computers Ltd was established in 1989 to sell a range of computer software to small businesses. Since its incorporation, the business has grown rapidly and demand for its products continues to rise. The most recent financial accounts for the company are set out below:

Balance Sheet as at 31 May 199X

	£	£	£
Fixed assets			
Freehold land and buildings at cost		55,000	
Less: Accumulated depreciation		4,000	51,000
Equipment and fittings at cost		20,000	
Less: Accumulated depreciation		5,000	15,000
Motor vehicles at cost		24,000	
Less: Accumulated depreciation		6,000	18,000
			84,000
Current assets			
Stocks		26,000	
Trade debtors		59,000	
		85,000	
Less creditors: amounts falling due within one year			
Trade creditors	88,000		
Proposed dividend	1,000		
Taxation	6,000		
Bank overdraft	10,000	105,000	(20,000)
			64,000
Less creditors: amounts falling due beyond one year			
14% bank loan (secured on freehold property)			20,000
			44,000
Capital and reserves			
Ordinary £1 shares			25,000
Retained profit			19,000
			44,000

Profit and Loss Account for the year ended 31 May 199X

	£	£
Sales		660,000
Less: Cost of sales		
Opening stock	22,000	
Purchases	426,000	
	448,000	
Less: Closing stock	26,000	422,000
Gross profit		238,000
Less: Selling and distribution expenses	176,000	
Administration expenses	38,000	
Finance expenses	7,000	221,000
Net profit before taxation		17,000
Corporation tax		6,000
Net profit after taxation		11,000
Proposed dividend		1,000
Retained profit for the year		10,000

The company is family-owned and controlled and, since incorporation, has operated without qualified finance staff. However, the managing director recently became concerned with the financial position of the company and therefore decided to appoint a qualified finance director to help manage the financial affairs of the business. Soon after joining the company, the finance director called a meeting of his fellow directors and at this meeting stated that, in his opinion, the company was overtrading.

Required

(a) What do you understand by the term 'overtrading' and what are the possible consequences of this type of activity?

(b) What are the main causes of overtrading and how might the management of a business overcome the problem of overtrading?

(c) Use financial ratios for Micrex Computers Ltd that you believe would be useful in detecting whether the company was overtrading. Explain the significance of each ratio you calculate.

(Certified Diploma)

Practical assignment

Look at the annual reports of two companies in the same industry. What do they say about the treasury function and treasury or risk management policies? How do the two companies differ and what might be the implications of such differences in treasury management?

15 Short-term asset management

Managing the supply chain at Zeneca

Since the de-merger of ICI in 1993, both Zeneca, the bioscience operation comprising pharmaceuticals, chemicals and seeds, and the restructured ICI have taken a close look at the way they manage working capital.

About 70 per cent of Zeneca Agrochemicals' costs lie in the supply chain, which stretches from raw material supplier through to the customer. Its key goal was to reduce the amount of money tied up in working capital – whether in the form of raw materials, stocks or outstanding debts. In its first year, Zeneca reduced this amount by one quarter, and has continued to keep a tight grip on its working capital in the ensuing years. Two initiatives helped achieve this reduction:

1. Supply chain efficiency was improved, focusing on deriving competitive advantage by producing high-quality products that cost less to manufacture and are made available to the customer faster.
2. New systems and procedures were put in place, covering purchasing, manufacturing, forecasting and ordering to provide a consistent supply chain across the agrochemicals business.

ICI has also improved its management of working capital. In its relentless pursuit of operational excellence, it introduced a Value Opportunity Programme, largely through more efficient purchasing and improved customer satisfaction. Under a worldwide initiative, the Group seeks to maximise its purchasing and logistics capability, streamline its list of suppliers and raise the profile of skills of the purchasing function. By 1998, it had achieved its target of annual savings of £400 million and significantly improved its management of working capital.

Learning objectives

Having read this chapter, you should have a general appreciation of the importance of short-term asset management in corporate finance and of the basic control methods involved. Specific attention will be paid to the following:

- Managing trade credit.
- Inventory management.
- Cash management.

15.1 Introduction

It is a simple mistake to assume that financial management concerns only long-term financial decisions, such as capital investment, capital structure and dividend policy decisions. In reality, much of financial management addresses issues of shorter duration, such as short-term financing and working capital management. In this chapter, we examine how short-term assets, such as debtors, inventory and cash, can be managed to maximise shareholder wealth.

15.2 Managing trade credit

Trade credit can be both a source and a use of finance because it can be obtained (via trade creditors or payables) and extended (via trade debtors or receivables). We will concentrate on the extension of trade credit and its management, although many of the issues raised apply also to the receipt of trade credit, discussed in Chapter 16.

Debtors represent the currently unpaid element of credit sales. While the extension of credit is accepted practice in most industries, credit is essentially an unproductive asset (unless it generates additional business) which both ties up scarce financial resources and is exposed to the risk of default, particularly when the credit period taken by customers is lengthy. Effective management of debtors is therefore an essential element of sound financial management practice.

Why offer trade credit?

Approximately one-third of the assets of UK businesses is in the form of trade debt – money to be paid at some future time for goods or services already received. The benefits to the customer are obvious, but why should the seller incur financing and other costs in extending credit to selected customers?

1 *Investment and marketing*. Trade credit should be viewed as an investment forming part of the sales package, the payoff being profitable repeat business. Most companies would lose a significant proportion of their customer base to their competitors were they to demand cash on delivery. As with all investment, there are risks involved. Credit risk exists when the company

offering credit is exposed to the possibility that the debt will not be paid on time or at all.

The decision to grant credit involves a trade-off between the credit risk and the reward from the profit margin. A common mistake is to assume that a credit sale is a 'one-off', ignoring potential repeat business. If a firm loses business from refusing a customer £1,000 credit, what is the effect? It is more than simply the lost profit margin of, say, 40 per cent on the sale. The business from most new customers will grow in time and offer significant repeat business. Assuming they would have entered into a long-term relationship and ordered £10,000 p.a., growing at 3 per cent a year, the present value of the lost business (given a 13 per cent interest rate) could be as much as £40,000:

$$PV = \frac{£10{,}000 \times (1.03)}{0.13 - 0.03} \times 0.4 = £41{,}200$$

2 *Industry and competitive pressures*. It is difficult for firms to offer credit terms that are less generous than their competitors' offerings.
3 *Finance*. Certain types of firm have better access to capital markets and can raise finance more cheaply than others. This competitive advantage can be reflected in offering generous credit to customers who experience greater difficulties in raising finance.
4 *Efficiency*. Information asymmetry exists between buyer and seller. The buyer does not know whether the product delivered is of the quality ordered until it has been thoroughly inspected. The credit period therefore provides a valuable inspection and verification period. Many companies deliver to customers on a daily basis. Trade credit is therefore a convenient means for separating the delivery of goods from the payment of deliveries.

Customer credit mission and goals for Makebelieve Ltd

Mission: To maintain and protect a portfolio of high-quality accounts receivable and to develop sound credit policies and administer credit operations in a manner that increases sales, contributes to profits, aids customer loyalty and improves shareholder value.

Goals:

1 To maintain monthly debtors to 45 days.
2 To achieve agreed monthly cash collection targets.
3 To limit overdue debts to 30 per cent of sales.
4 To limit bad debts to 1 per cent of sales.
5 To resolve credit-related customer queries within 3 days.
6 To improve the relationship between the credit function and major customers through regular contact and visits.
7 To convert 20 per cent of existing customers to direct debit in the year.

The aims of trade credit management are the following:

- To safeguard the firm's investment in debtors.
- To maximise operational cash flows by assessing customer credit risks, agreeing appropriate terms and collecting payments in accordance with these terms.

The level of debtors in a company will depend on its terms of sale, credit screening, cash discounts offered and cash collection procedures.

Effective debtor control policy requires careful consideration of the following:

- Credit period.
- Credit standards.
- Cost of cash discounts.
- Collection policy.

Each of these are discussed in the following section.

While the main responsibility for setting credit policy lies within financial management, other functions should be involved, particularly marketing. However, all too often, this collaboration is lacking. The credit management process is shown in Figure 15.1.

Credit period

The main factors influencing the period of credit granted to customers are:

1. *The normal terms of trade for the industry.* It is difficult to operate a trade credit policy where the period offered is considerably below the normal expectation for the industry unless the company has another clear competitive advantage, such as a recognised better quality product.
2. *The importance of trade credit as a marketing tool.* Determining the optimum credit period requires the finance manager to identify the point where the costs of increased credit are matched by the profits made on the increased sales generated by the additional credit. The more vital the perception of credit as a marketing tool, the longer the likely period of credit offered.
3. *The individual credit ratings of customers.* Most firms operate regular credit terms for good-quality customers and specific credit terms for higher-risk customers. The credit quality of customers is based on the credit standards addressed in the following example.

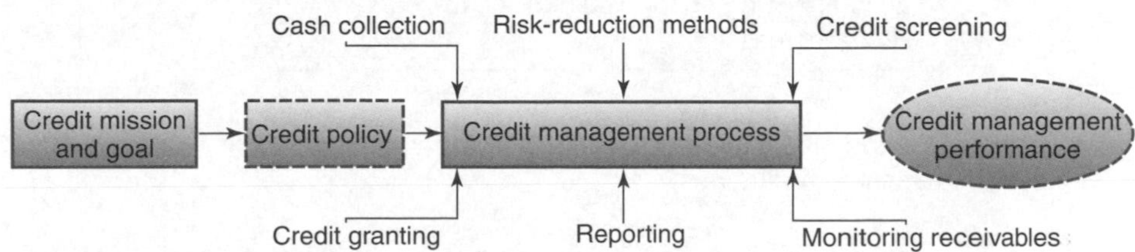

Figure 15.1 The credit management process

Example: change in credit policy at Pickles Ltd

Pickles Ltd produces a single product sold throughout the UK. Its profit analysis is given below:

	Per unit	
	£	£
Selling price		40
Variable costs	(36)	
Fixed cost apportionment	(3)	(39)
Net profit per unit		1

Pickles has an annual turnover of £4.8 million and an average collection period for debtors of one month. It has conducted a study on entering new European markets and believes that this would produce an additional 25 per cent of sales, but the new business would require three months' credit. Stocks and creditors would rise by £400,000 and £200,000 respectively. The cost of financing any increase in working capital is 10 per cent.

Operating profit before finance costs increases as a result of the new business by £120,000:

Sales increase (25% × £4.8 m) = £1.2 m
Contribution/sales ratio (40−36)/40 = 10%
Increase in profit = £120,000

The question of whether profits increase as a result of the expansion into European markets very much rests on whether the existing UK customers also demand more favourable terms.

1 *Assuming only new customers take three months' credit*

	£000
New business (£4.8 m × 25%)	1,200
New debtors (£1.2 m × 3/12)	300
Additional stocks	400
Additional creditors	(200)
Required increase in working capital	500
Increase in profit (£1.2 m × 10%)	120
Less financing cost (£500,000 × 10%)	(50)
Profit increase	70

Thus profits increase by £70,000. But what happens if existing customers demand the same credit terms?

Continued

2 *Assuming existing customers take three months' credit*

	£000
Sales (£4.8 m + £1.2 m)	6,000
New debtors level (3/12 × £6 m)	1,500
Less existing debtors (1/12 × £4.8 m)	(400)
	1,100
Additional stocks	400
Additional creditors	(200)
Additional working capital	1,300
Profit increase (as above)	120
Less financing cost (10% × £1.3 m)	(130)
Profit reduction after financing costs	(10)

After charging the cost of finance on additional debtors, stocks and creditors, the extra business does not increase profits.

Credit limits should be set for each customer based on their credit worthiness. The firm should consider:

1 *Customer payment record*: is the customer a prompt payer?
2 *Financial signals*: is there evidence of the customer running up losses or having liquidity problems?

Very high-risk customers may be reviewed monthly and have to pay, in full or part, with order. Other customers may be granted credit on the basis of percentage of annual purchases.

Commonly quoted trade credit terms

- Cash before delivery (CBD)
- Cash on delivery (COD)
- Invoice terms (e.g. 2/10, net 30). A two-stage payment term giving a 2 per cent cash discount for payment within 10 days, otherwise the net amount is due after 30 days.
- Consignment sales – pay for goods when used or sold.
- Periodic statement – payment by a specific date for all invoices up to a cut-off date.
- Seasonal dating – payments due at specific dates to match the buyer's seasonal income.

Credit standards

We have noted that granting trade credit is partly a marketing exercise designed to increase sales. However, at the individual customer level it is essentially a credit assessment and control exercise. In this sense, extending trade credit is no different from a bank granting a loan to a customer. The risk of granting trade credit can be seen when we consider the effect on profit of customer default. If a company sells a product for £1,000 with a 10 per cent net margin, which subsequently becomes a bad debt, the business must make ten similar sales to good customers simply to recover the £1,000 bad debt incurred.

Credit assessment should involve the following:

1 Prior experience with the particular customer. The credit extended and payment experience in the past is a useful guide, but it may relate to a time when the customer was not experiencing financial difficulty. Even so, it is wise to have more rigorous procedures for assessing new accounts.
2 Analysis of the customer's accounts and credit reports. Profit and Loss accounts and Balance Sheets are available from the company's registered office, but can more easily be taken from computer databases. Credit reports include:
   (a) Bank references
   (b) Trade references expressing the views of other businesses trading with the customer
   (c) Credit bureau reports. Credit-reporting agencies (such as Dun & Bradstreet) provide data and credit ratings that can be used in credit analysis. It is common practice for firms to offer credit agencies full disclosure of financial and trading information in order to gain a good rating. From an assessment of the customer's creditworthiness, it is possible to establish appropriate credit rules covering the terms of sale:
      (i) the maximum period of credit granted;
      (ii) the maximum amount of credit;
      (iii) the payment terms, including any discounts for early payment and interest charges on overdue accounts.

The businesses most vulnerable to late payment are often those that do least to vet their customers. According to the Confederation of British Industry, many small firms fail to chase their late payers with any degree of urgency, partly because their credit management systems are not good enough to support such activity.

In evaluating customer creditworthiness, it is useful to remember the five Cs of credit: capacity, character, capital, collateral and conditions.

1 *Capacity* – does the customer have the capacity to repay the debt within the required period? This may require examination of the past payment record of the customer.
2 *Character* – will the customer make a serious effort to repay the debt in accordance with the terms agreed? Bank and trade references will be useful here.

3 *Capital* – what is the financial health of the customer? Is the firm profitable and liquid? Is it borrowing beyond its means? Financial accounts and credit agency reports will help here.
4 *Collateral* – should some form of security be required in return for extending credit facilities? Alternatively, should part payment in advance or retention of title be specified?
5 *Conditions* – what are the normal terms for the industry? Are our main competitors offering more generous terms?

Cash discounts

The longer a customer's account remains unpaid, the greater the risk that it will never be paid. But the cost of financing late payments is often greater than the cost of bad debts. Surveys suggest that customers, on average, take 30 days' extra credit beyond the payment terms.

Cash discounts are financial inducements for customers to pay accounts promptly. Such discounts can be very costly.

Example: Yorko plc

Yorko plc offers terms of trade which are '2/10 net 30'. This means that a 2 per cent discount is offered for all accounts settled within ten days, otherwise payment in full is to be made in 30 days. A 2 per cent discount may not seem much until one realises that it is given for a payment in advance of just 20 days (i.e. 30 – 10). The annualised cost is actually over 37 per cent, calculated by the formula below:

The cost of a discount

$$\text{Cost of cash discount} = \frac{\text{Discount \%}}{(100 - \text{discount \%})} \times \frac{365}{(\text{Final date} - \text{discount period})}$$

In the Yorko example, the annualised cost of forgoing the cash discount is:

$$\begin{aligned}\text{Cost} &= \frac{2}{(100-2)} \times \frac{365}{(30-10)} \\ &= 0.0204 \times 18.25 \\ &= 37.23\%\end{aligned}$$

A more precise calculation is to find the **effective annual rate of return**. We have already calculated for Yorko the two elements:

Cost of discount = 2/(100 – 2) = 0.0204% per 20-day period
Number of 20-day periods a year = 365/20 = 18.25 periods
Effective annual interest rate = $(1.0204)^{18.25} - 1 = 44\%$

This cost is greater than in the first calculation because it assumes compound rather than simple interest.

Continued

Where such generous terms are available, it probably makes sense for customers to opt for the discount even if it means borrowing, as long as the cost of finance is clearly below the annualised cost of discount. So why should firms offer such inducements? First, early payment can significantly improve cash flow and reduce bad debt risk. Second, cash discounts can encourage new customers who are attracted by the discounts. However, the financial manager should be aware of the true cost of such discounts and be able to justify why terms should be offered costing more than the cost of capital.

Self-assessment Activity 15.1

A survey of large UK companies (Pike *et al*. 1998) found that the normal credit period granted was 30 days, but the average credit period taken by customers was 46 days. Only 20 per cent of firms offered prompt payment cash discounts, with the most common terms being 2½ per cent/net 30 days. For a company offering those terms, what would be the effective interest rate for granting cash discounts assuming that firms would otherwise pay within 46 days?

(answer at end of chapter)

Credit collection policy

A good credit collection policy is one in which procedures are clearly defined and customers know the rules. Debtors who are experiencing financial difficulties will always try to delay payment to companies with poor or relaxed collection procedures. The supplier who insists on payment in accordance with agreed terms, and who is prepared to cut off supplies or take action to recover overdue debts, is most likely to be paid in full and on time.

Figure 15.2 shows the debt collection cycle, starting with the customer order and ending with the cash received. Any speeding up of the order will reduce the required working capital. Late payment by major customers often has a knock-on effect throughout the supply chain. For example, if a customer of company A pays its debts 60 days late, this may force Company A to pay its bills late to Company B, which might create sufficient cash flow pressures for B to go out of business.

It is a sad fact that firms only run out of cash once. Second chances are rare when it comes to cash failure. So getting on top of the credit screening and control process is vital. Smaller businesses often complain that some larger companies take an unduly long time to settle their accounts. There is a real problem in British industry that far too much time and energy has to be devoted to chasing debts, for no real net gain to the business community. The CBI has introduced a Code of Practice, *Prompt Payers – In Good Company*, where firms agree to pay within the agreed payment terms. Businesses have a statutory right to charge larger customers interest on overdue accounts. The interest rate is set high because most firms must finance late payment from bank overdrafts.

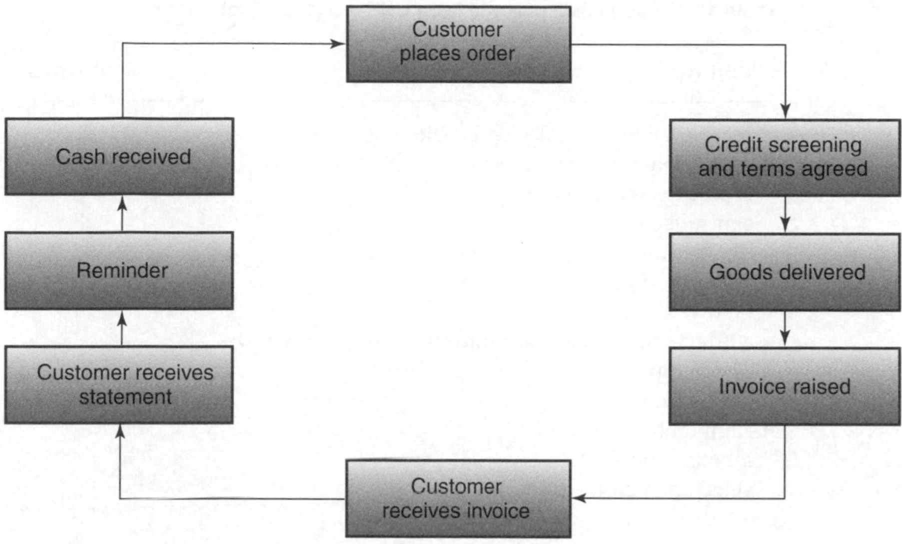

Figure 15.2 Ordering and debt collection cycle

CBI Prompt Payment Code

A responsible company should:

- Have a clear, consistent policy of paying bills in accordance with contract.
- Ensure that the finance and purchasing departments are both aware of this policy and adhere to it.
- Agree payment terms at the outset of a deal and stick to them.
- Not extend or alter payment terms without prior agreement.
- Provide suppliers with clear guidance on payment procedures.
- Ensure that there is a system for dealing quickly with complaints and disputes, and advise suppliers without delay when invoices are contested.

Tables 15.1 and 15.2 show the credit policies and practices of large UK companies.

Using debtors as security

The financing of trade debtors may involve either the assignment of debts (invoice discounting) or the selling of debts (factoring). With invoice discounting, the risk of default on the trade debtors pledged remains with the borrower. Factoring, on the other hand, can be and usually is 'without recourse', i.e. the factor bears the loss in the event of a bad debt. Factors provide a wide range of services, the most common of which are as follows:

1 Advancing cash against invoices. Up to 80 per cent of the value of invoices can typically be obtained; repayments (together with interest on the advances) are paid from the subsequent cash collected from debtors.

Table 15.1 Trade credit policy in large UK firms (145 firms)

Credit management policy	% of firms
Over 90 per cent of sales on credit	81
Credit department structure:	
separate credit company	6
centralised	28
decentralised	66
Normal credit terms	
below 30 days	14
30 days net (or end of month following delivery)	52
31–45 days	31
over 45 days	3
Assign credit limits	
all customers	68
selected customers	90
Cash discounts	20
Interest charged on overdue accounts	47

Source: Pike *et al.* (1998)

Table 15.2 Credit management practices in large UK firms (145 firms)

	% of firms
Risk screening information sources	
Credit agency reports	81
Customers' financial statements	64
Trade references	60
Bank references	48
Competitor trade sources	38
Sales department report	31
Other group companies	32
In-house screening system	16
Risk reduction and financing	
Credit insurance	38
Retention of title	61
Third party guarantees	31
Factoring without recourse	–
Invoice discounting	5
Use of trade debt to secure borrowings	3
Cash collection	
Payment in advance	48
Direct debits	29
Sales staff involved in cash collection	68
Debt collection agents	17

Source: Pike *et al.* (1998)

The subtle art of getting paid: Late Payment

Some small businesses develop creative ways to pursue customers who are paying their bills late.

An antique fireplace shop in north London until recently kept on call a 6ft 3in ex-con who had two fingers missing on his left hand and halitosis. His job was simple: to persuade defaulting customers to pay up by going to their workplace and sitting quietly, but unpleasantly, in the lobby. He seldom had to stay long before the promised cheque appeared.

Another small businessman, this time in advertising, was owed money by a smart furniture shop. He took the afternoon off to stand in the customer's doorway telling people coming in that they would be ripped off. He had his cheque within an hour.

Neither approach would feature in a business school textbook on credit management, but both were effective. One spent money on paying someone to chase the debt, the other judged it an effective use of his time to do it himself. Both related to a simple business problem: staying afloat when customers delay paying invoices as long as possible.

Each year, 10,000 UK businesses fail because their invoices are paid late, according to Dun & Bradstreet, the credit management consultancy. Out of £17 billion owed to UK small businesses last year, £6.8 billion was paid after the due date. Yet few small businesses make use of legislation that penalises late payers, and most believe the law can be of little help when withholding payment appears to be becoming the norm. As an economic downturn approaches the situation is bound to deteriorate.

To address this, the Late Payment of Commercial Debts (Interest) Act 1998 allows creditors to add interest to unpaid invoices without having to go to court. A European Community directive, for which the UK consultation period ends on Friday, would allow companies to claim compensation as well as interest from late paying customers.

Trade credit is a loan to your customer, yet customer/supplier contracts can be surprisingly vague on the terms of payment. There are three steps to managing trade credit:

- Sell the payment terms at the same time as you sell the product, agree those terms and get to know the person who actually signs the cheque.
- Eliminate 'own goals' such as delivering the product late or sending an invoice that does not match the delivery note.
- Be prepared to ask for the money you are owed. Big companies, which are organised, will introduce interest on overdue accounts automatically. Small companies will not have the resources to chase interest payments up. A useful website is **www.payontime.co.uk**

Based on *Financial Times*, April 26 2001

2 Insurance against bad debts.
3 Administration of the credit control functions. This involves sending out invoices, maintaining the sales ledger and collecting payments.

We return to this topic in Chapter 16.

Self-assessment Activity 15.2

What are the main elements in a firm's credit policy?

(answer at end of chapter)

15.3 Inventory management

Inventory, or stock, may be classified into the following:

1 *Pre-production inventory* – stocks of raw materials and bought-in parts.
2 *In-process inventory* – work-in-progress at various stages of the production process.
3 *Finished goods inventory* – manufactured goods ready for sale.

In most cases, finished goods will convert most rapidly into cash; but where customer tastes change rapidly, such as in the fashion trade, this stock can also be the most risky.

Inventory is the least liquid of current assets. It is therefore vital to manage it in such a way that it can be converted from raw material to work-in-progress and finished goods as quickly as possible.

Stock is carried for two reasons:

1 *Business is uncertain*. Consumer demand and production requirements are difficult to forecast, and suppliers may not always be reliable in meeting delivery requirements. The cost of being out-of-stock, in terms of lost sales, profits and goodwill, is generally very high.
2 *Economies in ordering*. Each business needs to determine its economic order quantity for its main stock items.

Inventory control is an important topic for both production management and financial management, which should work closely to establish an inventory policy that meets customers' requirements while operating at optimum stock levels.

Overstocking results in the following:

- An unduly high level of working capital investment.
- Additional storage space requirements and greater handling and insurance costs.
- Possible deterioration and increased obsolescence risk.

Understocking reduces the working capital required, but can lead to out-of-stock situations with orders unfulfilled, idle machines and underemployed workers.

In the past, carrying higher than necessary stocks has been a way of compensating for inefficient production and distribution or poor forecasting. But in today's highly competitive global markets, with Japanese and other overseas businesses operating efficient production schedules and minimal stock levels, European companies have been forced to examine their inventory management processes more closely.

Approaches to inventory management

There is now a whole variety of methods for improving stock control, some simple, others more sophisticated, using computer software. We will limit our discussion to three forms of stock control:

1 'Broad-brush' approaches.
2 Economic order quantity models.
3 Computer-based material requirements and just-in-time methods.

Broad-brush approaches

A simple, but useful, starting point is to consider the total stock position using the number of days' stock ratio:

$$\text{Number of days' stock} = \frac{\text{Average stock}}{\text{Cost of sales}} \times 365$$

Consider the stock levels of two companies, based on latest accounts (Table 15.3). U-Save, a discount supermarket chain, carries only finished stocks. Its generic strategy – to be the lowest-cost grocery retailer – requires tight control over its ordering, deliveries and stocks. Its stockholding period is 22 days, which means that stock will probably be turned into cash before the invoice for the goods is paid. By contrast, a major diversified producer like Unicom has very significant raw material stocks and a stockholding period which is double that of U-Save.

Table 15.3 Total inventory levels and stockholding periods

	U-Save (£m)	Unicom (£m)
Raw materials	–	1,380
Work-in-progress	–	175
Finished goods	148	1,894
Total stock	148	3,449
Cost of sales	2,403	25,926
Days' stock	22.5	48.5

While such cross-industry comparisons are interesting, U-Save will want to compare its stockholding period against Tesco and other competitors to see whether it is more efficient in its inventory control processes.

Major companies may well have thousands of items in stock. How should they determine the appropriate level of inventory control for each item? A simple stock classification, often called the **ABC system**, can help identify how closely stock items should be controlled. It divides a company's inventory into three groups according to importance to sales value, with high-value stocks requiring the highest stock control attention.

ABC stock classification in Boris plc

An analysis of stock items in Boris plc revealed the following:

Short-term financing and policies

Category	Stock items (%)	Stock value (%)
A	12	72
B	38	18
C	50	10
	100	100

Category A stock items have only 12 per cent of the total number of items in stock, but account for 72 per cent of stock value. It was decided that these items required a considerable degree of stock control attention, regular forecasting and monitoring, carefully assessed economic order quantities and an appropriate level of buffer stocks.

Category B stock items cover 38 per cent of total items, but only 18 per cent of stock value. The inventory policy for these items would be less sophisticated; forecasting would be simpler and less frequent.

Category C, which covers half the stock items but only 10 per cent of stock value, requires much simpler treatment, with few stock records and less regular monitoring. For example, stocks of nuts and bolts might simply require that an ample supply is always on hand.

Economic order quantity models

The costs of holding high levels of stocks include the interest lost in tying up capital in such assets, the costs of storing, insuring, managing and protecting stock from pilferage, deterioration, etc., and obsolescence costs. Against this, there are costs involved in holding low levels of stock or running out of stock:

1 Loss of goodwill from failure to deliver by the date specified by customers.
2 Lost production and disruption due to essential items being unavailable.
3 More frequent re-order costs (buyer's and storekeeper's time, telephone, postage, invoice-processing costs, etc.).

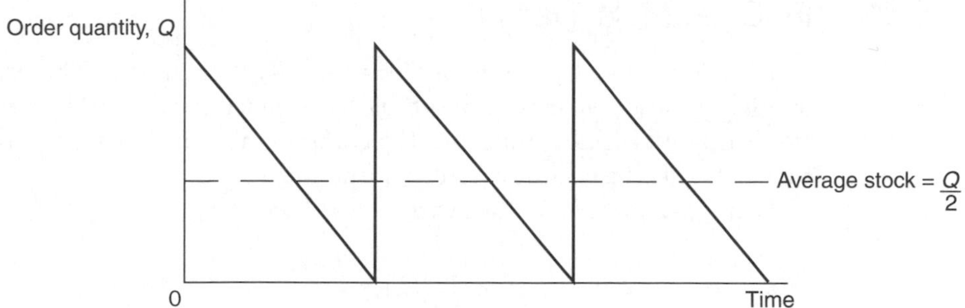

Figure 15.3 The inventory cycle

A variety of stock management models have been developed to help managers determine the optimal level of stock that balances holding costs against shortage costs. One way of addressing the issue is to determine the **economic order quantity (EOQ)** for the stock required.

Every firm should operate a clear stock control policy, which specifies for its main items the timing of stock replenishments, re-order quantities, safety stock levels and the implications of being out of stock. Figure 15.3 depicts the inventory cycle for a simple stock control model. It assumes a single items of stock, immediate stock replenishment, constant usage and certainty.

The total cost is:

Total cost = Ordering costs + Holding costs

Algebraically,

$$\text{Total cost} = \left(\frac{C}{Q} \times A\right) + \frac{Q}{2} \times H$$

where Q is the quantity ordered, C is the cost of placing an order, H is the cost of holding a unit of stock for one year, and A is the annual usage of stock.

The economic order quantity is that quantity (Q) which minimises the total cost function. We examined a similar cost function when we discussed total working capital investment.

At its simplest, the economic order quantity can be calculated as follows:

$$\text{EOQ} = \sqrt{\frac{2AC}{H}}$$

Self-assessment Activity 15.3

What do you understand by carrying costs and ordering costs? How do they fit into the economic order quantity formula?

(answer at end of chapter)

EOQ example: Ivan plc

Ivan plc uses 2,000 units of stock item KPR each year. The cost of holding a single item for a year is £2 and the cost of placing each order is £45. The current order quantity is 200 units, but the company is considering changing to batches of 400. Is this the optimum re-order quantity?

Using the cost equation above:

$$\text{Total cost for 200} = \left(\frac{£45}{200} \times 2{,}000\right) + \left(\frac{200}{2} \times £2\right) = £650$$

$$\text{Total cost for 400} = \left(\frac{£45}{400} \times 2{,}000\right) + \left(\frac{400}{2} \times £2\right) = £625$$

$$\text{Total cost for 300} = \left(\frac{£45}{300} \times 2{,}000\right) + \left(\frac{300}{2} \times £2\right) = £600$$

The minimum total cost is achieved by ordering 300 units.

This is confirmed as the most economic order quantity by the EOQ model:

$$EOQ = \sqrt{\frac{2 \times 2000 \times £45}{£2}} = \sqrt{90{,}000}$$
$$= 300 \text{ units}$$

Each order will be placed for 300 units, which implies that orders will be placed every 55 days (i.e. 300/2,000 × 365).

This simple model has two limitations:

1 Demand, and therefore stock usage, may be seasonal. Hence the constant usage rate for stock assumed here may be unrealistic. Alternatively, demand may be difficult to predict, which necessitates **safety** or **buffer stocks**, and calls for a modification of the model.
2 Only the more easily quantifiable costs are included. Many of the other costs referred to earlier (lost goodwill, lost production, etc.) should also be considered.

We have so far assumed that stocks are used up at a constant rate and are replenished when the old level falls to zero. A **stockout** occurs when a firm is unable to deliver a product due to the lack of a specific inventory item. It is therefore tempting for firms to hold large levels of safety stocks to reduce this risk. In effect, this is a form of just-in-case management, as opposed to Just-in-Time management.

Holding costs will rise through carrying safety stocks, but costs associated with stockouts will fall. The level of safety stock will be affected by management's ability to forecast stock usage and lead time replenishment. Lead time is the delay between ordering and arrival of stock. Each stock item requires a re-order point to be set to cover safety stocks and lead time. The re-order point will be:

$$R = LW + S$$

In words, the re-order point (R) equals the lead time (L) times the weekly stock demand (W) plus the average safety stock (S).

Returning to the example of Ivan plc, if the stock item under consideration has a three week re-order lead time and an average level of safety stocks is set at 40 units, we can determine the re-order point, assuming a 50-week working year.

$$R = LW + S$$
$$= 3 \times \frac{2{,}000}{50} + 40$$
$$= 160 \text{ units}$$

In practice, it is rarely the case that demand is uniform and that usage and lead times are known with certainty. Determining the optimal stock levels and order quantities under conditions of uncertainty requires probabilistic inventory control models, which are beyond the scope of this book. However, the fundamental point remains that determining the optimal stock level involves balancing the expected costs of ordering and stockouts against the cost of holding additional stocks.

Materials Requirement Planning (MRP)

MRP is a computer-based planning system for scheduling stock replenishment, ensuring that adequate materials are always available for production purposes. Raw materials are determined from production schedules and lead times for replenishment. MRP can greatly reduce stockholding costs where the finished product requires a multi-stage production process with a large number of components and sub-assemblies, such as in motor car manufacture.

MRPII is a more comprehensive manufacturing resource planning system, which integrates all resource requirements of the company. In addition to stocks, it also encompasses labour and machine requirements.

Just-In-Time

In recent times, managers in some manufacturing firms have been aiming for 'stockless production' and just-in-time (JIT) deliveries. JIT aims for an 'ideal' level of zero stocks, but with no hold-ups due to stock shortages. Materials and parts are delivered from suppliers just before they are needed, and products are manufactured just before they are needed for sale to customers. Where such an operation is successful, the consequent reduction in inventory and the cash operating cycle can be very considerable. Indeed, trade creditors can virtually match the current asset investment, thus enabling the business to operate with the minimum of working capital.

While it focuses on minimising stock levels, JIT forms part of a total quality production programme and rarely works well in isolation. A number of conditions are necessary for JIT to operate successfully:

- Strong links and shared information with suppliers and customers.
- Satisfied customers.
- A quality production process in a 'right-first-time' culture.
- Computerised ordering and inventory tracking systems.
- Smooth movement of materials from process to process.

Suppliers are typically located close to the manufacturer, making regular (often daily) deliveries in small quantities. They are tightly managed and deliver quality assured components to meet agreed production schedules.

JIT was first introduced in Toyota in 1981, using the famous Kanban (card) system. Cards are attached to component containers to monitor the flow of production through the factory, then are returned to signal the need for more supplies. It is particularly suited to high-volume products where assembly line schedules operate continuously.

The main benefits of JIT, experienced by a growing number of companies, are:

1 Drastically reduced stock levels with commensurate savings in storage space, staff and financing costs.
2 A 'right-first-time' culture.
3 Reduced stock defects.
4 Increased productivity.

15.4 Cash management

Throughout this book, we have emphasised the importance of cash – rather than profit – in financial management. We now consider why cash has such a vital role to play, and how cash flow forecasts are prepared and used to help manage businesses operating in uncertain environments.

Why hold cash?

The word *cash* is something of a misnomer. While some cash will be in the form of notes and coins, or bank accounts giving immediate access, much will be invested in short-term bank deposits giving some kind of return.

Why should a company hold sums of money in cash or short-term deposits when the return is relatively small? There are a number of reasons why companies hold cash balances:

1 *Transactions motive*. Day-to-day cash inflows and outflows do not match perfectly; cash serves as a buffer to ensure that transactions occur at the appropriate time. Cash balances are particularly important where the patterns of cash inflows and outflows differ greatly, e.g. where business is highly seasonal.
2 *Precautionary motive*. Cash flows are often difficult to predict. Cash balances are required to cater for unanticipated cash disbursements.
3 *Speculative motive*. Cash allows the business to be highly flexible and to exploit wealth-creating opportunities more easily. Large cash balances are common among acquisitive companies where a cash alternative to a takeover bid is required.
4 *Compensation balances motive*. Banks provide a range of financial services, many of which are 'free' as long as the company keeps a positive bank balance.

Surplus cash is not always reinvested immediately in the business. The cash – or near cash – balance in some companies can be far greater than that required for normal trading purposes. The financial press publishes the main types of short-term financial investment opportunities available to companies, showing the relationship between maturity and interest rates.

Figure 15.4 illustrates the pivotal role played by cash in a typical firm. The cash balance is the result of the interactions of various activities with stakeholders.

- *Operating activities* – cash from customers less payments to employees and suppliers.
- *Servicing finance* – dividends and interest on loans.
- *Taxation* – Corporation Tax and VAT.
- *Investing activities* – purchase and sale of fixed assets.
- *Financing activities* – new finance from shareholders and bondholders, and loan repayments.

The cash balance is restored to its appropriate level by short-term bank borrowing or repayment and the sale or purchase of marketable securities. The financial manager should therefore project the firm's ability to finance its operations and to manage corporate cash flow.

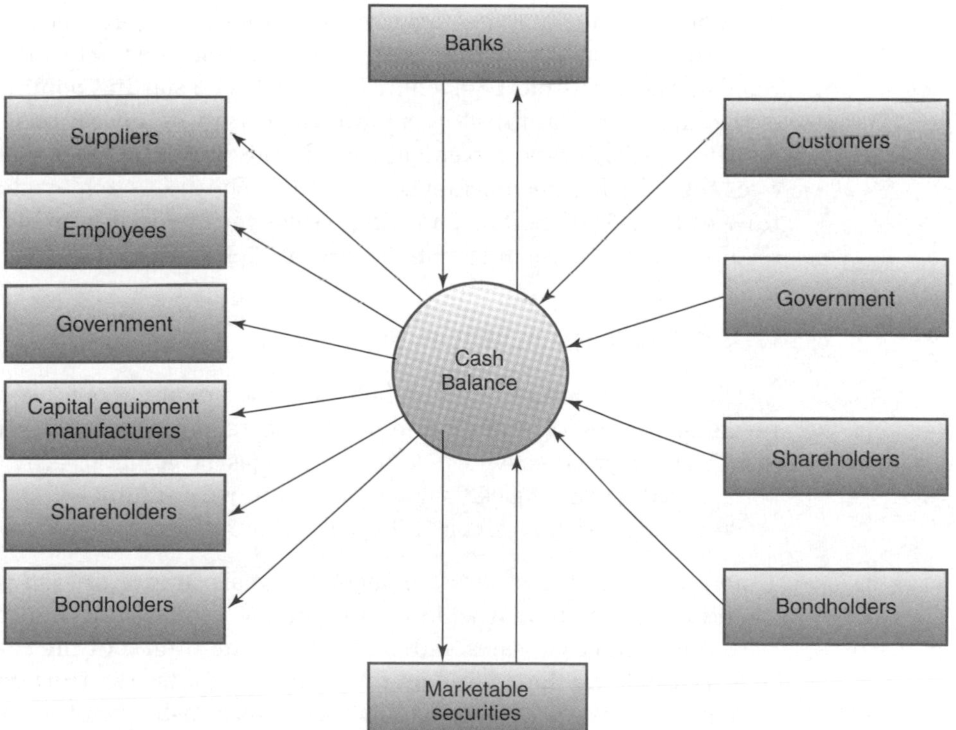

Figure 15.4 Cash flow activity for main stakeholders

Self-assessment Activity 15.4

What are the main motives for holding cash?

(answer at end of chapter)

Even in well-diversified firms, it makes sense to centralise cash management:

1 It allows the treasurer to operate on a larger scale, which should lead to more competitive interest rates and lower staffing costs.
2 Specialist staff can be employed to work in cash management.
3 Negative cash flows from one operating unit may be offset by positive cash flows from others, thus avoiding additional financing and loan-raising costs. This may well mean that the overall level of cash required to cover unanticipated cash shortfalls is reduced.
4 Banking operations become faster and more efficient, giving rise to advantageous banking arrangements.

Cash flow statements

In 1991, the Accounting Standards Board in the UK issued a standard (FRS1) requiring most companies to present a cash flow statement within their published accounts. The intention was to move away from an over-reliance on profits.

A summarised cash flow statement for the chocolate manufacturer and retailer, Thorntons plc, is given in Table 15.4. The starting point in the statement is the company's ability to generate cash from its operations. A shareholder reading the cash flow statement can identify how the change in cash position over the year has been achieved. For 2000, Thorntons achieved a positive cash flow of £2,443,000 before financing. However, the requirement to repay loans resulted in a decrease in cash in the year of £1,379,000.

Cash flow forecasting

The cash flow forecast, or cash budget, is the primary tool in short-term financial planning. It helps identify short-term financial requirements and surpluses based on the firm's budgeted activities. Cash budgeting is a continuous activity with budgets being rolled forward, usually in weeks or months, over time.

Preparation of the cash budget involves four distinct stages:

1 *Forecast the anticipated cash inflows.* The main source of cash is usually sales, and the sales forecast will therefore be the primary data source. Sales can be divided into cash sales and credit sales, the timing of the cash flow arising from the latter depending on the agreed credit terms. Thus, for example, the sales forecast for January would appear as a cash receipt in March if all sales were on credit terms of 60 days. Other cash inflows might be income from investments, cash from disposal of fixed assets, etc.

Table 15.4 Thorntons plc consolidated cash flow statement

	2000	1999
	£000	*£000*
Cash flow from operating activities	16,218	29,693
Returns on investment and servicing of finance	(4,330)	(3,978)
Taxation	(122)	(2,872)
Capital expenditure and financial investment	(4,837)	(37,066)
Equity dividends paid	(4,486)	(4,297)
Cash inflow (outflow) before use of liquid resources and financing	2,443	(18,520)
Management of liquid resources	(264)	11,596
Financing		
Issue of shares	179	569
(Decrease)/increase in debt	(3,737)	10,529
Decrease/increase in cash in the period	(1,379)	4,174

2 *Forecast the anticipated cash outflows.* The principal payment is generally the payment of trade purchases. Once again, the credit period taken must be allowed for. Other cash outflows include wages and salaries, administrative costs, taxation, capital expenditure and dividends.
3 Compare the anticipated cash inflows and outflows to determine the *net cash flow* for each period.
4 Calculate the *cumulative cash flow* for each period by adding the opening cash balance to the net cash flow for the period.

Cash budget: Mangle Ltd

Mangle Ltd produces a single product – a manually operated spindryer. It plans to increase production and sales during the first half of next year; the plans for the next eight months are shown in Table 15.5.

The selling price is £100, with an anticipated price increase to £110 in June. Raw materials cost £20 per unit; wages and other variable costs are £30 per unit. Other fixed costs are £1,800 a month, rising to £2,200 from May onwards. Forty per cent of sales are for cash, the remainder being paid in full 60 days following delivery. Material purchases are paid one month after delivery and are held in stock one month before entering production. Wages and variable and fixed costs are paid in the month of production.

A new machine costing £10,000 is to be purchased in February to cope with the planned expansion of demand. An advertising campaign is also to be launched, involving payments of £2,000 in January and March. The directors

Table 15.5 Mangle Ltd: production and sales

Month	Production	Sales
November	70	70
December	80	80
January	100	80
February	120	100
March	120	120
April	140	130
May	150	140
June	150	160

plan to pay a dividend of £1,000 in May. On 1 January the firm expects to have £2,000 in the bank. How will the cash position appear over the following six months?

Table 15.6 reveals that the first step is to determine the sales revenue each month. Forty per cent of sales are for cash and are therefore received in the month of sales, while the remaining 60 per cent are received two months after the month of sale.

Purchases are made in the month prior to entering production, but because a month's credit is taken, the payment to creditors is in the same month as production.

Table 15.6 Mangle Ltd: cash budget for six months to June (£)

		Jan.	Feb.	Mar.	Apr.	May	June
Inflows							
Receipts from cash sales		3,200	4,000	4,800	5,200	5,600	7,040
Receipts from debtors		4,200	4,800	4,800	6,000	7,200	7,800
	(A)	7,400	8,800	9,600	11,200	12,800	14,840
Outflows							
Payments to creditors		2,000	2,400	2,400	2,800	3,000	3,000
Variable costs		3,000	3,600	3,600	4,200	4,500	4,500
Fixed costs		1,800	1,800	1,800	1,800	2,200	2,200
Advertising		2,000		2,000			
Capital expenditure			10,000				
Dividend						1,000	
	(B)	8,800	17,800	9,800	8,800	10,700	9,700
Net cash surplus (deficit) in month (A – B)		(1,400)	(9,000)	(200)	2,400	2,100	5,140
Opening cash balance		2,000	600	(8,400)	(8,600)	(6,200)	(4,100)
Closing cash balance		600	(8,400)	(8,600)	(6,200)	(4,100)	1,040

After including all cash flows, the net cash flow for each of the six months shows that in the first three months, Mangle Ltd has a negative cash flow, and a negative cash balance for the February to May period. The company may decide that this is a seasonal business and that it is acceptable to operate with such monthly cash flow figures. In this case, the firm should seek to negotiate a loan to cover the shortfall. However, it would do well to consider ways of minimising the monthly deficits. For example, could cash receipts from debtors be collected more quickly? Could payment of creditors be deferred for a few weeks? Could the price increase be brought forward? Could payment terms on the capital equipment be extended over a longer period, possibly by leasing the equipment? The cash budget allows finance managers to consider such questions well ahead of events. Frequently, forward planning avoids the need to raise external finance through astute management of working capital.

Float

The 'cash at bank' position shown in a company's books will not usually be the same as that shown on the bank statement. Float is the money arising from the time lag between posting a cheque and it being cleared by the bank.

Float management in Marcus Ltd

On 1 July, the bank statement and cash account in the ledger of Marcus Ltd both show £40,000. The company pays suppliers £20,000 by cheque and receives cheques from suppliers for £15,000. The net cash balance in the accounts is therefore (£40,000 – £20,000 + £15,000) = £35,000. But the bank position is still £40,000. The cheques from customers will take three days to clear and the cheques paid will take more like 6 8 days to clear, including postal delay and time taken to pay in the cheque.

The cash controller must, therefore, regularly reconcile the two positions, but also manage the float by recognising that the actual cleared bank balance, upon which interest is calculated, is likely to be somewhat higher than the balance in the company's accounts. If Marcus can get its customers to pay by **direct debit**, this will speed up the banking process and further improve the bank position.

Another method of speeding up collections is **concentration banking**, where customers in a geographical area pay a local branch office rather than head office. The cheque is then deposited in the local bank branch. Where both the customer and the company have local banks, this can reduce both postal and clearing time.

Electronic funds transfer has certain benefits over cheque payment by post. Cost savings arise from the reduction in administration effort, time and postage. The transfer is instantaneous, which means that cash can stay in the company's bank account longer. The main disadvantage is that 'the cheque is in the post' excuse can no longer be employed. If payment is made on the same day as the cheque used to be posted, it impacts on the bank account quicker and results in more interest charges. BACS (Bankers' Automated Clearing Services) enables computerised funds transfers between banks. Corporate customers can use BACS, particularly for payment of salaries, by providing details of payments. Payment is made in two days. For large payments, same day clearance can be made through CHAPS (Clearing House Automated Payment System).

15.5 Cash management models

We have already examined inventory control models. Cash is, in many ways, simply a form of inventory, the minimum stock of cash required to enable a business to operate effectively.

William Baumol (1952) recognised the similarity between cash and inventory for control purposes, particularly when the bank balance is simply a draw-down account. This is when a firm has a cash balance upon which it draws steadily, and which it replenishes to the original balance at some point before running out (see the sawtooth diagram for stock in Figure 15.3). Any surplus cash is invested in interest-bearing short-term securities.

In this case, the economic order quantity (EOQ) model can be employed, where EOQ represents the short-term securities to be sold to replenish the balance.

Recall that the equation is:

$$\text{EOQ} = \sqrt{\frac{2CA}{H}}$$

where C now represents the transaction cost for selling securities, H is the holding cost of cash (i.e. the interest rate), and A is the annual cash disbursements.

Cash management model for Bizarre plc

The treasurer of Bizarre plc, a company specialising in unusual gifts for eccentric business managers (a rapidly growing market), has a sizeable sum invested in short-term investments, earning 6 per cent interest. Every time, she sells investments to top up the bank balance, the transaction cost is £25. Monthly cash payments are around £200,000. How often and by how much should she transfer money to the bank account?

The EOQ model gives an indication of the most economic amount of cash to be drawn each time:

$$\text{EOQ} = \sqrt{\left(\frac{2 \times \text{annual cash payments} \times \text{cost of selling securities}}{\text{annual interest rate}}\right)}$$

$$= \sqrt{\left(\frac{2 \times \text{£}2{,}400{,}000 \times \text{£}25}{0.06}\right)} = \text{£}44{,}721\text{, say £}45{,}000$$

The frequency with which the treasurer will transfer cash is £2.4 million/£45,000 = 53 times a year, or approximately weekly.

Self-assessment Activity 15.5

As interest rates increase, it obviously becomes more attractive to transfer smaller quantities. Try reworking the Bizarre problem assuming a doubling of the interest rate to 12 per cent.

The above cash management model works pretty well when daily cash drawings on the bank account are uniform. This is rarely the pattern of actual cash flows in business. Cash flows go up and down in what often appears a fairly random manner. Miller and Orr (1966) suggested that, instead of assuming a constant rate of cash payment, perhaps we should assume that daily balances cannot be predicted – they meander in a random fashion. This is further discussed in the Appendix to this chapter.

Short-term investment

When the cash budget indicates a cash surplus, the financial manager needs to consider opportunities for short-term investment. Any cash surplus beyond the immediate needs should be put to work, even if just invested overnight. The following considerations should be made in assessing how to invest short-term cash surpluses:

1 The length of time for which the funds are available.
2 The amount of funds available.
3 The return offered on the investment in relation to the investment involved.
4 The risks associated with calling in the investment early (e.g. the need to give three months' notice to obtain the interest).
5 The ease of realisation.

Examples of short-term investment opportunities are as follows:

- *Treasury Bills* – issued by the Bank of England and guaranteed by the UK government. No interest as such is paid, but they are issued at a discount and redeemed at par after 91 days. At any time, the bills can be sold on the money market.
- *Bank deposits* – a wide range of financial instruments is available from banks, but the more established investment opportunities are:
  (a) term deposits, where for a fixed period (usually from one month to six years) a fixed rate is given. For shorter periods (typically up to three months) the interest may be at a variable rate based on money market rates
  (b) Certificates of Deposit, issued by the banks at a fixed interest rate for a fixed term (usually between three months and five years), but which can be sold on the money market at any time.
- *Money market accounts* – most major financial institutions offer schemes for investment in the money market at variable rates of interest (e.g. Treasury accounts).

Summary

The management of working capital is a key element in financial management, not least because, for most firms, current assets represent a major proportion of their total investment. Working capital policy is concerned with determining the total amount and the composition of a firm's current assets and current liabilities.

Key points

- An effective debtor control policy should cover the credit period, credit standard, cost of cash discounts and collection policy.
- Credit terms should reflect the customer's credit rating, normal terms of the industry and the extent to which the firm wishes to use credit as a marketing tool.
- In evaluating customer credit worthiness, remember the five Cs: capacity, character, capital, collateral and conditions.
- Trade debtors can be used to raise finance through invoice discounting and factoring.
- Inventory management involves determining the level of stock to be held, when to place orders and how many units to order at a time.
- Inventory costs can be classified into carrying or holding costs, which increase as the level of stock rises, and shortage costs (or stockout costs and ordering costs), which fall as stock levels increase.
- A variety of economic order quantity models is available for determining the order quantity that will minimise total inventory cost. The basic model is:

  $$\text{EOQ} = \sqrt{\frac{2AC}{H}}$$

  where C is the cost of placing an order, A is the annual usage of stock and H is the cost of holding a unit of stock for one year.
- The cash flow forecast, or cash budget, is a vital tool in short-term financial planning.
- Cash management models (e.g. Baumol and Miller–Orr models) are useful in setting limits that trigger cash adjustment.

Further reading

Pike *et al.* (1998, 2001) report findings on trade credit management in large companies.

Brigham and Gapenski (1991) and Brealey and Myers (2000) provide fuller discussions on the issues addressed in this chapter. Sartoris and Hill (1981) provide a present value approach to credit evaluation. The pioneering work on cash management models is found in Baumol (1952) and Miller and Orr (1966).

Useful websites

Better Payments Practice Group: **www.payontime.co.uk**
Credit checks: **www.checkit.co.uk**
Companies House: **www.companieshouse.co.uk**
Dun & Bradstreet: **www.dnb.com**

Appendix
Miller–Orr cash management model

When daily cash flows are very difficult to predict, it may be sensible to assume that the pattern of cash flows is random. This gives rise to the cash position shown in Figure 15.5. Rather than decide how often to transfer cash into the account, the treasurer sets upper and lower limits that trigger cash adjustments, sending the balance back to the return point by selling short-term investments. The diagram prompts two questions:

1 How are the limits set?
2 Why isn't the return point midway between the two?

In general, the limits will be wider apart when daily cash flows are highly variable, transaction costs are high and interest on short-term investments is low. The Miller and Orr formula for setting the limits is:

$$\text{Range between upper and lower limits} = 3\left(\frac{3}{4} \times \frac{\text{transaction cost} \times \text{cash flow variance}}{\text{interest rate}}\right)^{1/3}$$

The cash balance does not return to a point mid-way between the upper and lower limits. The return point is:

$$\text{Return point} = \text{lower limit} + \frac{\text{range}}{3}$$

By having a return point below the mid-point between the two limits, the average cash balance on which interest is charged is reduced.

The Baumol and Miller–Orr models are really two extremes: the former assumes cash flows are constant, while the latter assumes they are unpredictable. In practice, an experienced cash controller, using a detailed cash budget, should perform better than a cash management model and should enable the company to operate on a lower cash balance. The primary value of simple cash management

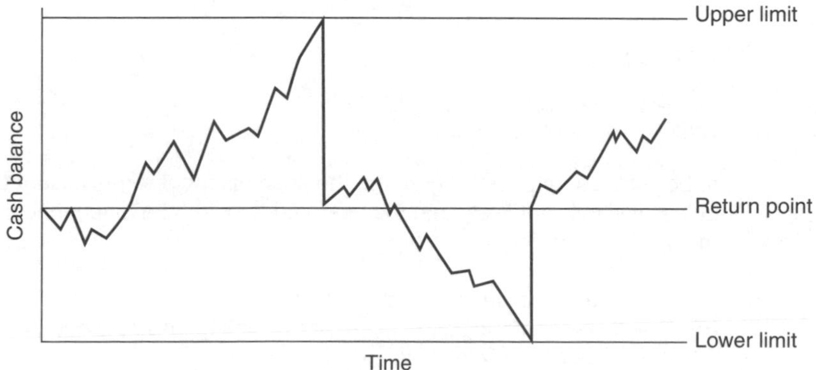

Figure 15.5 Miller–Orr cash management model

Example

The financial manager at Millor Ltd believes that cash flows are almost impossible to predict on a daily basis. She knows that a minimum cash balance of £20,000 is required and transferring money to or from the bank costs £50 per transaction. Inspection of daily cash flows over the past year suggests that the standard deviation is £3,000 a day (i.e. £9 million variance). The interest rate is 0.03 per cent per day.

The Miller–Orr model specifies the range for the cash balance as below:

$$\text{Range} = 3\left(\frac{3}{4} \times \frac{50 \times 9{,}000{,}000}{0.0003}\right)^{0.3333} = £31{,}200 \text{ approx.}$$

The upper limit = lower limit + range = £20,000 + £31,200 = £51,200

$$\text{The return point} = \text{lower limit} + \frac{\text{range}}{3} = £30{,}400$$

The decision rule is: if the cash balance reaches £51,200, buy £20,800 (£51,200 − £30,400) of marketable securities. If the cash balance falls to £20,000, sell £10,400 marketable securities for cash to return it to £30,400.

models may be to evaluate how much better the 'hands-on' expert can perform than the 'hands-off' control model.

Self-assessment Answers

15.1 *Conventional method*

$$\text{Cost of discount} = \frac{\text{Discount \%}}{100 - \text{discount \%}} \times \frac{365}{\text{Final date} - \text{discount date}}$$
$$= \frac{2.5}{100 - 2.5} \times \frac{365}{46 - 30} = 58.5\%$$

APR method

Interest = 2.5/(100 − 2.5) = 2.56%
APR = $1.0256^{365/16} - 1 = 78\%$

In both cases, the cost of granting the cash discount terms is very expensive, unless it is thought likely that the customer would take much longer to pay than most other customers.

15.2 **(a)** Credit terms, including credit period.
(b) Credit standards for offering credit to existing and new customers, including credit risk screening.
(c) Credit collection policy, including use of cash discounts and collection agents.
(d) Credit reporting.

15.3 Carrying costs include the cost of storing, insuring and maintaining stocks as well as the lost interest tied up in holding such assets.

Ordering costs include not only the obvious administrative cost of making regular orders, but also the costs associated with running out of stock (lost orders, goodwill, etc.). These two types of cost are traded off to find the optimum order quantity, given by the formula:

$$\text{EOQ} = \sqrt{\frac{2AC}{H}}$$

where C is the cost of placing an order, A is the annual stock usage and H is the cost of holding a unit of stock.

15.4 The main motives for holding cash are:

(a) to act as a buffer to ensure that transactions can be paid for (transactions motive)
(b) to cater for unanticipated cash outflows (precautionary motive)
(c) to permit companies to take advantage of profitable opportunities (speculative motive)
(d) to take advantage of 'free' banking services for firms with positive cash balances (compensation balances motive)

Questions

1 *Solution in Appendix A (page 820).* Specify the basic formula for calculating the cost of cash discounts.

2 *Solution in Appendix A (page 820).* What are the main differences in the assumptions underlying the Baumol and Miller–Orr cash models?

3 *Solution in Appendix A (page 820).* Hunslett Express Company specifies payment from its customers at the end of the month following delivery. On average, customers take 70 days to pay. Sales total £8 million per year and bad debts total £40,000 per year.

The company plans to offer cash discounts for payment within 30 days. It is estimated that 50 per cent of customers will take up the discount, but that the remaining customers will take 80 days to pay. The company has an overdraft facility costing 13 per cent p.a. If the proposed scheme is introduced, bad debts will fall to £20,000 and savings in credit administration of £12,000 p.a. are expected.

Should the company offer the new credit terms?

4 *Solution in Appendix A (page 821).* Salford Engineers Limited, a medium-sized manufacturing company, has discovered that it is holding 180 days' stock while its main competitors are holding only 90 days' stock.

Required

(a) Discuss what you consider to be the most important factors determining the optimum level of stockholding for the company.
(b) What action would you take if you were asked to investigate the reasons for Salford's high level of stock?

(Certified Diploma)

5 Torrance Ltd was formed in 1988 to produce a new type of golf putter. The company sells the putter to wholesalers and retailers and has an annual turnover of £600,000. The following data relate to each putter produced:

	£	£
Selling price		36
Variable costs	(18)	
Fixed cost apportionment	(6)	(24)
Net profit		12

The cost of capital (before tax) of Torrance Ltd is estimated at 15 per cent.

Torrance Ltd believes it can expand sales of this new putter by offering customers a longer period in which to pay. The average collection period of the company is currently 30 days. The company is considering three options in order to increase sales. These are as follows:

	Option 1	Option 2	Option 3
Increase in average collection period (days)	10	20	30
Increase in sales (£s)	30,000	45,000	50,000

Torrance Ltd is also reconsidering its policy towards trade creditors. In recent months the company has suffered from liquidity problems, which it believes can be alleviated by delaying payment to trade creditors. Suppliers offer a 2.5 per cent discount if they are paid within 10 days of the invoice date. If they are not paid within 10 days, suppliers expect the amount to be paid in full within 30 days. Torrance Ltd currently pays suppliers at the end of the 10-day period in order to take advantage of the discounts. However, it is considering delaying payment until either 30 or 45 days after the invoice date.

Required

(a) Prepare calculations to show which credit policy the company should offer its customers.

(b) Discuss the advantages and disadvantages of using trade credit as a source of finance.

(c) Prepare calculations to show the implicit annual interest cost associated with each proposal to delay payment to creditors. Discuss your findings.

(Certified Diploma)

6 **(a)** Discuss:

(i) The significance of trade creditors in a firm's working capital cycle, and

(ii) the dangers of over-reliance on trade credit as a source of finance.

(b) Keswick plc traditionally follows a highly aggressive working capital policy, with no long-term borrowing. Key details from its recently compiled accounts appear below:

	£m
Sales (all on credit)	10.00
Earnings before interest and tax (EBIT)	2.00
Interest payments for the year	0.50

Shareholders' funds (comprising £1 million issued share capital, par value 25p, and £1 million revenue reserves)	2.00
Debtors	0.40
Stocks	0.70
Trade creditors	1.50
Bank overdraft	3.00

A major supplier which accounts for 50 per cent of Keswick's cost of sales is highly concerned about Keswick's policy of taking extended trade credit. The supplier offers Keswick the opportunity to pay for supplies within 15 days in return for a discount of 5 per cent on the invoiced value.

Keswick holds no cash balances but is able to borrow on overdraft from its bank at 12 per cent. Tax on corporate profit is paid at 33 per cent.

Required

Determine the costs and benefits to Keswick of making this arrangement with its supplier, and recommend whether Keswick should accept the offer.

Your answer should include the effects on:

The working capital cycle
Interest cover
Profits after tax
Earnings per share
Return on equity
Capital gearing

7 International Golf Ltd operates a large warehouse, selling golf equipment direct to the public by mail order and to small retail outlets. The cash position of the company has caused some concern in recent months. At the beginning of December 1993 there was an overdraft at the bank of £56,000. The following data concerning income and expenses has been collected in respect of the forthcoming six months:

	December £000	**January £000**	**February £000**	**March £000**	**April £000**	**May £000**
Expected sales	120	150	170	220	250	280
Purchases	156	180	195	160	150	160
Advertising	15	18	20	25	30	30
Rent	40			40		
Rates		30				
Wages	16	16	18	18	20	20
Sundry expenses	20	24	24	26	26	26

The company also intends to purchase and pay for new motor vans in February at a cost of £24,000 and to pay taxation due on 1 March of £30,000.

Sales to the public are on a cash basis and sales to retailers are on two months' credit. Approximately 40 per cent of sales are made to the public. Debtors at the beginning of December are £110,000, 70 per cent of which are in respect of November sales.

Purchases are on one month's credit and, at the beginning of December, the trade creditors were £140,000. The purchases made in December, January and February are considered necessary to stock up for the sales demand from March onwards.

All other expenses are paid in the month in which they are incurred. Sundry expenses include £8,000 per month for depreciation.

Required

(a) Explain the benefits to a business of preparing a cash flow forecast.
(b) Identify and discuss the costs to a business associated with:
  (i) holding too much cash;
  (ii) holding too little cash.
(c) Prepare a cash flow forecast for International Golf Ltd for the six months to 31 May 1994, which shows the cash balance at the end of each month.
(d) State what problems International Golf Ltd is likely to face during the next six months and how these might be dealt with.

(Certified Diploma)

8 **(a)** The Treasurer of Ripley plc is contemplating a change in financial policy. At present, Ripley's balance sheet shows that fixed assets are of equal magnitude to the amount of long-term debt and equity financing. It is proposed to take advantage of a recent fall in interest rates by replacing the long-term debt capital with an overdraft. In addition, the Treasurer wants to speed up debtor collection by offering early payment discounts to customers and to slow down the rate of payment to creditors.

As his assistant, you are required to write a brief memorandum to other Board members explaining the rationales of the old and new policies and pinpointing the factors to be considered in making such a switch of policy.

(b) Bramham plc, which currently has negligible cash holdings, expects to have to make a series of cash payments (*P*) of £1.5 million over the forthcoming year. These will become due at a steady rate. It has two alternative ways of meeting this liability.

Firstly, it can make periodic sales from existing holdings of short-term securities. According to Bramham's financial advisers, the most likely average percentage rate of return (*i*) on these securities is 12 per cent over the forthcoming year, although this estimate is highly uncertain. Whenever Bramham sells securities, it incurs a transaction fee (*T*) of £25, and places the proceeds on short-term deposit at 5 per cent per annum interest until needed. The following formula specifies the optimal amount of cash raised (*Q*) for each sale of securities:

$$Q = \frac{2 \times P \times T}{i}$$

The second policy involves taking a secured loan for the full £1.5 million over one year at an interest rate of 14 per cent based on the initial balance of the loan. The lender also imposes a flat arrangement fee of £5,000, which could be met out of existing balances. The sum borrowed would be placed in a notice deposit at 9 per cent and drawn down at no cost as and when required.

Bramham's Treasurer believes that cash balances will be run down at an even rate throughout the year.

Required

Advise Bramham as to the most beneficial cash management policy.

Note: ignore tax and the time-value of money in your answer.

(c) Discuss the limitations of the model of cash management used in part (b).

Practical assignments

1 Sound credit management can play an important role in the financial success of a business.

Required

(a) Explain the role of the credit manager within a business.
(b) Discuss the major factors a credit manager would consider when assessing the creditworthiness of a particular customer.
(c) Identify and discuss the major sources of information that may be used to evaluate the creditworthiness of a commercial business.
(d) State the basis upon which any proposed changes in credit policy should be evaluated.

(Certified Diploma)

2 If you are based in a firm where credit management is important, apply the above question to your organisation.

16 Short- and medium-term finance

Banking on the wrong lender?

Despite their attempts to improve relations with the business community, banks are often criticised for their lack of support in difficult times.

During the recession of the early 1990s, many companies faced severe cash flow difficulties, unable to meet their obligations to their bankers. Barclays Bank reportedly cancelled without notice the overdraft facility of a small textile company, Crimpfil, based in South Wales. This forced the company to appoint an Administrator to rescue the company if possible, and to liquidate it if necessary. Crimpfil sought and obtained a High Court ruling against Barclays under which the bank was instructed to pay interim damages. In February 1995, Barclays lost an appeal against the ruling.

At the heart of this case lies the crucial relationship between banks and their clients. Some commercial banks do not always enjoy easy relationships with their clients. In recent years, banks have been criticised by small firm pressure groups over a number of issues:

- Reluctance to advance longer-term finance in the form of loans rather than overdrafts.
- Insisting on 'excessive' levels of security to back their lending.
- Reluctance to make equity investments in small firms.
- The scale and range of their charges.
- Tardiness in passing on interest rate reductions to customers.
- Undue haste in recalling funds when client companies encounter trading difficulties, as in the case of Crimpfil.

Learning objectives

This chapter aims to evaluate the advantages and disadvantages of the following means of short- and medium-term finance:

- Trade credit.
- Bank finance.
- Factoring and invoice discounting.
- Bills of exchange and acceptance credits.
- Hire purchase.
- Leasing.
- Financing foreign trade.

Particular attention is given to leasing in view of its importance as a method of financing the acquisition of a wide range of assets.

16.1 Introduction

While banks have taken a number of steps to address the criticisms raised by the introductory case, many firms still find it difficult to arrange short-term finance, and many remain critical of the banking system. (For news of developments in the field of finance for small firms, see the website of the British Bankers Association: **www.bba.org.uk**.) Despite such problems, the banks remain the most important source of external finance for small- and medium-sized firms, providing approximately 60 per cent of their external finance. However, it is not only smaller firms that tend to rely on shorter-term finance; firms of all sizes use these sources to varying degrees. For example, most large companies arrange access to overdraft finance to tide them over temporary liquidity shortages.

In this chapter, we examine the nature and characteristics of alternative sources of finance, ranging from very short-term facilities (e.g. trade credit) to rather longer-term ones (e.g. bank loans and finance leasing). Generally, we classify these under the heading of short and medium term, although the distinction is somewhat arbitrary. For example, lease finance can be used for varying time periods, ranging from a few weeks (operating leases) to as long as 15 years in the case of some finance leases. In addition, bank overdrafts are essentially short-term in nature, but are often used continuously for lengthy periods.

16.2 Trade credit

Trade credit is finance obtained from suppliers of goods and services over the period between delivery of goods (or provision of a service) and the subsequent settlement of the account by the recipient. During this time, the company can enjoy the goods or benefit from the service provided without having to pay up. Granting customers a credit period is part of normal trading relationships throughout most of UK industry. For this reason, it is sometimes called 'spontaneous finance'.

Additional features of trade credit packages include the amount of credit that a company is allowed to obtain, whether interest is paid on overdue accounts, and whether discounts are offered for early payment.

A common way of expressing credit terms is as follows:

'2/10: net 30'

This means that the supplier will offer a 2 per cent discount for early settlement (in this case, within 10 days); otherwise, it expects payment of the invoice in full within 30 days. As shown below, *not* to take a discount is often an expensive option. Moreover, a very effective way of antagonising suppliers is to delay payment *and* attempt to claim the discount.

A firm's trade credit position is volatile, as it depends on which of its suppliers are awaiting payment and for how much, and these factors change continuously with the flow of business transactions. It is preferable to express the average trade credit period in days calculated as follows:

$$\text{Creditor days} = \frac{\text{Trade creditors}}{\text{Credit purchases}} \times 365$$

However, this figure is only valid at the Balance Sheet date, and could have been 'window-dressed' by accelerated settlements immediately prior to drawing up the accounts. It is sometimes expressed in terms of total purchases and sometimes, when data for purchases is unavailable, in terms of overall cost of sales. The length of the trade credit period offered depends partly on the following factors:

- ***Industry custom and practice***. Terms of trade credit typically reflect traditional norms built up over years of trading. Although these terms often vary between industries, they are quite uniform within industries. Any supplier wanting to depart from the industry norm has to compensate with some other product offering, say, speed of delivery, to avoid losing sales.
- ***Relative bargaining power***. If the supplier has a large range of customers, none of whom are crucial to it, and if the product is essential to buyers, the supplier has great power to impose its own terms. This power is enhanced by lack of strong competitors.
- ***Type of product***. Products that turn over rapidly are often sold on short credit terms because they command small profit margins. Delay in settlement would severely erode the margin.

Self-assessment Activity 16.1

Trade credit is often called 'spontaneous finance' or 'automatic finance'. Can you see why?

(answer at end of chapter)

Because trade credit represents temporary borrowing from suppliers until invoices are paid, it becomes an important method of financing investment in current assets. Firms may be tempted to view trade creditors as a cheap source of finance although statutory rights to claim interest on late payments now exist. Having a debtors' collection period shorter than the trade collection period may be taken as a sign of efficient working capital management. However, trade credit is by no means free – it carries both hidden and overt costs.

Excessive delay in settling invoices can undermine the stability of a business in a number of ways. Existing suppliers may be unwilling to extend more credit until existing accounts are settled. They may start to assign lower priority to future orders placed by the culprit, they may raise prices in the future or they may simply not supply at all. In addition, if the firm acquires a reputation as a bad payer among the business community, its relationships with other suppliers may be soured.

Finally, by delaying payment of accounts due, the company may be passing up valuable discounts, thus effectively increasing the cost of goods sold. This can be shown with a simple example.

Menston plc is offered a discount of 2.5 per cent on an invoice of £100,000 by a major supplier if it settles the account within 10 days, rather than taking the normal credit period of 30 days. Menston, which has at present a zero cash balance, can borrow from its bank at an interest rate of 15 per cent p.a. Should it borrow and exploit the discount, or take the full credit period of 30 days?

If it takes the discount and pays on (but not before!) day 10, it will have to borrow (97.5 per cent × £100,000) = £97,500 for an additional period of 20 days, since it would have to settle anyway after 30 days. If it waits until day 30, the cost of settling the bill is effectively the lost discount of £2,500. By advancing payment, Menston is borrowing £97,500 for 20 days in order to save £2,500, an interest rate over 20 days of 2.56 per cent. Expressed as an annual return interest rate, this approximates to:

$$\frac{\pounds 2{,}500}{\pounds 97{,}500} \times \frac{365}{20} \times 100 = 46.8\%$$

A more accurate solution can be obtained by compounding over the number of 20-day periods in a year (18.25). The true rate is:

$$[(1.0256)^{18.25} - 1] = 58.6\%$$

As this compares very favourably with the 15 per cent cost of borrowing, Menston should borrow in order to advance this payment.

During the recession of the early 1990s, there was widespread concern over the tendency for more firms to delay payment of accounts, resulting in an average payment delay in 1990 of 60 days. Larger firms have allegedly exploited their industrial muscle by simultaneously spinning out their trade credit periods while insisting on prompter payment from small firm customers. This problem led the UK Government in 1998 to introduce legislation for a statutory right to demand interest on overdue accounts, initially for smaller companies only.

Until the passage of the Late Payments of Commercial Debts (Interest) Act in 1998, interest could only be claimed on late debts if it was included in the contract or if awarded by a court. The Act enabled small businesses (50 or fewer employees) to claim interest from large businesses and the public sector. From November 2000, they were entitled to claim interest from other small businesses. From November 2002, any business will have the statutory right to claim interest from any other firm or from the public sector.

Firms that suffer from late payment have to fall back on their banks for supplementary finance, via either overdraft or loan facilities. We now consider bank lending.

Self-assessment Activity 16.2

What is the true annual interest rate paid when a firm delays payment under the following credit terms: '$1\frac{1}{2}$/15: net 40'?

(answer at end of chapter)

16.3 Bank credit facilities

Major commercial banks extend a variety of credit facilities, ranging from short-term overdrafts to long-term loans of varying terms. The interest rate generally increases with the term of the advance, the actual rate being linked to the bank's base rate, which in turn depends on the base rate set by the national monetary authority (in the UK, the Monetary Policy Committee).

Self-assessment Activity 16.3

What do you think are the main considerations a banker makes in assessing an application for a loan or overdraft?

(answer at end of chapter)

Overdrafts

The best-known form of bank finance is the overdraft, a facility available for specified short-term periods such as six months or a year. This facility specifies a maximum amount that the firm can draw upon either via direct cash withdrawals or in payments by cheque to third parties. Interest is paid on the negative balance outstanding at any time rather than the maximum advance agreed. Compared with many other forms of finance, it is relatively inexpensive, with the interest cost set at some two to five percentage points above base rate, although most banks also levy an arrangement fee (perhaps 1 per cent) of the maximum facility.

In principle, overdrafts are repayable at very short notice, even on demand, although unless the company abuses the terms of the facility by exceeding the agreed overdraft limit, the overdraft is unlikely to be called in. Besides, it is rarely in the best interests of a bank to do this suddenly, as it could exert such severe financial pressure on the client as to force it into liquidation.

Nevertheless, the bank retains the right to appoint a receiver if the client defaults on the debt. In practice, well-behaved clients can roll forward overdrafts from period to period. As a result, the overdraft effectively becomes a form of medium-term finance. Even in these cases, it is wise policy not to use an overdraft to invest in long-term assets that would be difficult to liquidate at short notice if the bank suddenly decided to call in the debt.

To protect against risk of loss, the bank will usually demand that the overdraft be secured against company assets, i.e. in the event of default, the receiver will reimburse the bank out of the proceeds of selling these assets. Security can be in two forms: a **fixed charge**, where the overdraft is secured against a specific asset, or a **floating charge**, which offers security over all of the company's assets, i.e. those with a ready and stable second-hand market. For trading companies, overdrafts are often secured against the inventory that the company purchases with the funds borrowed or even against debtors. In this respect, the overdraft is *'self-liquidating'* – it can be reduced as the company sells goods and banks the proceeds.

NatWest deletes overdraft clause

Campaigners for small companies claimed a victory yesterday after NatWest bank abolished its right to remove a customer's overdraft at a moment's notice.

NatWest said it would turn current industry practice on its head by deleting the 'repayable on demand' clause from small business overdrafts.

The bank said it would end the uncertainty faced by SMEs by ensuring that a three-, six- or 12-month overdraft meant exactly that. The conditions will apply to both secured and unsecured overdrafts.

The Federation of Small Businesses suggested that the decision was prompted by the recent Cruickshank report, which criticised the banking sector. 'The banks are trying to make themselves appear to be more business-friendly, because they got a pasting,' said David Hands of the FSB.

However, there were no indications yesterday that NatWest's rivals would follow suit. Barclays said its research had shown the clause was not an issue for its customers.

Based on Jim Packard, *Financial Times*, November 21 2000

Alternatively, and more to the liking of most bankers, overdrafts are secured against property. However, this created problems in the recession of the early 1990s, when the unprecedented collapse of property market prices often reduced the value of assets upon which overdrafts were secured below the balance outstanding. Many banks made major provisions against the increasing likelihood of bad debts. In addition, they incurred much ill-will by allegedly recalling overdrafts prematurely, thus exacerbating the liquidity difficulties of their clients, already seriously affected by falling sales. Many critics accused the banks of forcing many essentially sound companies out of business.

Term loans

Term loans are loans for longer than a year. UK banks have traditionally been reluctant to lend on a long-term basis, mainly because the bulk of their deposit liabilities are short-term. In the event of unexpectedly high demand by the public to withdraw cash, this could leave them vulnerable if they were unable to recall advances quickly from borrowers. This low exposure to default risk is generally regarded as the reason why banking collapses are relatively uncommon in the UK.

However, because of criticism by a series of official reports on the financial system and the advent of intensive competition from London branches of overseas banks, the main UK banks are now far more willing to lend long-term. Term loans can be arranged at variable or fixed rates of interest, although the interest cost is usually higher in the latter case. For variable rate loans, the rate set may be two to five percentage points above the bank's base rate, depending on the credit rating of the client and the quality of the assets offered as security. In addition, an arrangement fee is usually charged.

Self-assessment Activity 16.4

Which are normally more expensive – overdrafts or term loans? Why?

(answer at end of chapter)

Tailor-made facilities are available to some firms, with repayment terms designed to suit their expected cash flow profiles. Sometimes, the bank may grant a 'grace period' at the outset of the loan when no capital is repayable and interest may be charged at a relatively low, but increasing, rate. This is particularly suitable for a small, developing company trying to establish itself. Similarly, a **balloon loan** is where increasing amounts of capital are repaid towards the end of the loan period, while a **bullet loan** is where no capital is repaid until the very end of the loan period.

In its 'Finance for Small Firms' report in 1995, the Bank of England estimated that fixed-term lending had overtaken overdraft finance. The proportion of total lending in the form of term loans was 60 per cent, compared with 40 per cent only two years previously. By 2000, the ratio of overdrafts to term lending had fallen to 28:72. (Finance for Small Firms' is published annually and can be viewed on **www.bankofengland.co.uk**.)

Revolving credit facilities (Revolvers)

A term loan generally specifies an agreed payment profile and the amounts repaid cannot normally be re-borrowed. A revolver allows the borrower to borrow, re-pay and re-borrow over the life of the loan facility, rather like a continuous overdraft. Like an overdraft, it is frequently secured on the borrower's working capital, e.g. using debtors and stocks as collateral, although very large firms may not be asked for any security. The advantage of revolvers is the enhanced flexibility provided, i.e. funds can be re-used in a continuous credit line. The commitment by the bank thus 'revolves' – the borrower can continue to ask for loans, subject to giving suitable notice, so long as the committed total is not exceeded. The fees charged include:

- A front-end or facility fee for setting up the loan.
- A commitment fee to compensate the bank for having to commit some of is loan capacity by setting aside reserve assets to meet capital adequacy rules.
- The interest cost, usually expressed as so many basis points (one bp = 0.01%) above LIBOR, the rate at which London-based banks lend to each other.

Loan Guarantee Scheme (LGS)

The LGS was introduced in 1981 following the Report of the Committee to Review the Functioning of Financial Institutions, set up to investigate the provision of finance to business. The Committee pointed to the difficulty faced by smaller firms with little or no track record in obtaining suitable longer-term finance.

Mini case

In May 2001, the soon-to-be-disgraced electronics and advanced telecoms equipment firm, Marconi plc, announced a new syndicated revolving credit facility of €3 billion. This was designed to consolidate two existing facilities, a €6 billion revolving credit (€1.3 billion drawn down) dating from 1998, and a further €2.5 billion revolver agreed in 1999. The new facility had a 12-month term with a margin of 40 bp above LIBOR with a commitment fee of 12.5 bp. When drawings exceed 50 per cent of the facility, a 5 bp utilisation fee would become payable.

Such firms are reluctant to release control by issuing equity, while investors are reluctant to purchase equity owing to the risks involved, especially the difficulty of liquidating their investment on acceptable terms. They also have difficulty persuading banks of the inherent viability of their businesses, and are frequently unable to offer sufficient and suitable security. Where banks do offer loan finance, it is often on less advantageous terms than those extended to larger firms and less likely to be augmented in times of difficult trading.

The LGS is financed by the Department of Trade and Industry. In its initial form, the scheme was supposed to be self-financing. The government originally guaranteed that, in the event of failure of a business, 80 per cent of the loan would be repaid to the financial institution making the loan. The cost of meeting guarantees would be met by borrowers paying to the government a premium of three percentage points above the normal commercial rate applied by the bank. Loans were available for periods of two to seven years. Losses on the scheme turned out much higher than anticipated, largely, it was alleged, because banks contrived to shift existing shaky clients on to it. After many modifications over the years, it now embodies the following features:

- Firms apply for loans directly to banks and other lenders.
- Applicants must demonstrate they have applied for a conventional loan and have been rejected for lack of security.
- Only firms with less than 200 employees and annual turnovers no more than £1.5 million (£3 million for manufacturers) are eligible.
- 85 per cent of the loan is guaranteed.
- Loans are available for amounts between £5,000 and £250,000.
- Borrowers pay a 'normal commercial' interest rate to the bank, plus a premium of 1.5 per cent p.a. for variable rate loans, or 0.5 per cent for fixed rate loans.
- Term of loan from two to 10 years.

For updates on the LGS, see **www.bba.org.uk**.

16.4 Factoring and invoice discounting

Some companies, which need to extend trade credit to customers for competitive reasons, find that they need payment earlier than agreed in order to assist their own cash flow. Institutions called **factors**, mainly subsidiaries of the major banks and members of the Factors and Discounters Association (**www.factors.org.uk**), exist to help such companies. Factors do not always provide new finance, but accelerate the cash conversion cycle for client companies, allowing them to gain access to debtors more quickly than if they waited for the normal trade credit period to unwind. Factoring has increased greatly in

importance over the past decade or so, but it still only accounts for about 6 per cent of total external finance for small firms, while larger firms rarely use it at all. In 2000, firms with over £5 million turnover accounted for just 10 per cent of factoring business, while firms with turnover of below £500,000 accounted for 45 per cent. In that year, the value of domestic business factoring by client turnover was £20,927 million split roughly 4:1 between domestic and overseas business.

Factors provide two main types of service: factoring proper and invoice discounting.

Factoring

Factoring involves raising immediate cash based on the security of the company's debtors, thus accelerating payment from customers. A factor provides three main services – sales administration, credit protection and provision of finance, usually up to 80 per cent of the value of approved invoices.

Sales administration

A factor assumes the various functions of sales ledger administration, ranging from recording sales details to sending out invoices and reminders and collecting payment. The benefits for the client are the cost savings from reducing in house administration and access to a more efficient, specialist debtor management team. This is particularly valuable to a young fast-growing company, which may outgrow its administration system and otherwise be exposed to the liquidity risks of overtrading. The fee for such an administration service would lie typically in the range of 0.5–2.5 per cent of the value of turnover handled.

Credit protection

The factor may provide a credit evaluation service for clients, analysing customer characteristics before deciding on their creditworthiness. When all risks are borne by the factor, the service is termed *'without recourse'*, i.e. the factor has no 'come-back' on the client if customers default. Where this applies, the factor requires total control of credit approval, monitors customers' payments and attempts to collect payment. This suggests a possible problem with factoring – the intervention of the factor between the factor's client and the debtor company could endanger trading relationships and damage goodwill. For this reason, some clients prefer to retain responsibility for collection of problem debtors. This is known as *'with recourse'* factoring, whereby the factor will call upon its client to reimburse the funds advanced on an invoice relating to a delinquent account.

Provision of finance

A factor will also advance funds to a client, based on a proportion, usually 80 per cent, of approved (i.e. reliable) invoices. For example, a company with sales on 30 day credit terms from reliable customers of £500,000 per month would receive an advance of 80 per cent, i.e. £400,000 each month. The interest rate would be related to bank base rate, probably slightly above the cost of an overdraft. The client would receive the balance of the payment less interest and an administration charge, perhaps equal to 0.5 per cent of turnover.

Although factors provide valuable services, companies are sometimes wary of using them for reasons other than cost. Besides possible difficulties over collection of payment, widespread knowledge that a company is using a factor may arouse fears that the company is beset by cash flow problems. If so, its suppliers may impose more stringent payment terms, thus negating the benefits provided by the factor. Companies concerned by these risks may seek the more widely-used but less comprehensive service of **invoice discounting**.

Self-assessment Activity 16.5

Summarise the benefits of factoring for a small firm.

(answer to end of chapter)

Invoice discounting

Although factors provide a range of services, a company seeking merely to improve its cash flow is likely to use an invoice discounting facility. This involves the purchase of selected invoices, sometimes just one, by the discounter. The discounter will advance immediate cash up to 80 per cent of face value. It assumes no responsibility for the administration of the accounts receivable, or the collection of the debts. The service is totally confidential, the client's debtors being unaware of the existence of the discounter. It is therefore equivalent to the financing service provided by a factor, although restricted to a narrower range of invoices. Invoice discounting business amounted to over £67 billion in 2001.

Administration charges for this service are around 0.5 per cent of a client's turnover. It is more risky than factoring, since the client retains control of its credit policy. Consequently, such facilities are usually confined to established companies with turnovers above £1 million. Interest costs are usually 3–6 per cent above base rate, although larger companies and those that arrange credit insurance may receive keener terms.

How invoice discounting works

At the beginning of February, Menston plc sells goods for a total value of £300,000 to regular customers, but decides that it requires payment earlier than the agreed 30 day credit period for these invoices. A discounter agrees to finance 80 per cent of their face value, i.e. £240,000. Interest is set at 13 per cent p.a. The invoices were due for payment in early March, but were subsequently settled in mid-March, exactly 45 days after the initial transactions. The service charge is set at 1 per cent. As usually applies, a special account is set up with a bank, into which all payments are made. The sequence of cash flows is as follows:

February:

Menston receives cash advance of £240,000

Mid-March:

Customers pay up £300,000
Invoice discounter receives the full £300,000
Menston receives the balance less charges, i.e.

Service fee = 1% × £300,000 = £3,000
Interest = 13% × £240,000 × 45/365 = £3,847
Total charges = £6,847
Net receipts = (20% × £300,000) − £6,847
= £60,000 − £6,847 = £53,153
Total receipts by Menston = £240,000 + £53,153 = £293,153

In effect, Menston has settled for a discount of £6,847/£300,000 = 2.3 per cent over 45 days for early receipt of 80 per cent of the accounts payable. As there are about eight 45 day periods in a year, this corresponds to an annual interest rate of:

$(1.023^8 - 1) = 0.1995$, i.e. 19.95%

16.5 Using the money market: bill finance

A bill is often likened to a post-dated cheque or an IOU, as it represents a commitment to pay out a specific sum of money after a specified period of time. Bills are traded on the money market, which specialises in providing funds repayable over periods of less than a year. The major players in the money market are the commercial banks, which lend to each other, often overnight, to cover temporary cash shortages, at the London Inter-Bank Offered Rate (LIBOR), and to the discount houses. The latter exist primarily to deal in short-term bills issued by the government (Treasury Bills), local governments and companies. They borrow on a very short-term basis from the commercial banks, usually at a very keen interest rate, and use the proceeds to purchase bills, which they may hold to maturity or sell at a profit in the money market.

A company can use two main types of bill to raise finance: a trade bill (Bill of Exchange) or a bank bill (acceptance credit).

Bills of Exchange

Bills of Exchange are generally trade-related, connected to specific trading transactions. The trader purchasing goods draws up a bill stating a promise to repay at some future date, and then conveys the bill to the supplier of the goods.

The supplier may then hold the bill until maturity or sell it in the market to a discount house, if cash is required earlier. The terms of the bill usually include an implicit interest charge, although no interest as such is paid, as the following example indicates.

A trader wishes to acquire goods to the value of £1 million. He draws up a Bill of Exchange, promising to pay £1 million in three months' time. The bill is immediately sold by the seller of the goods to a discount house, which pays out £975,000, i.e. a discount of £25,000. If the discount house holds the bill to its maturity, it earns a profit of £25,000. This is equivalent to an interest rate of £25,000/£975,000 = 2.56% over three months, or in annual terms:

$(1.0256)^4 - 1 = (1.1064 - 1) = 0.1064$, i.e. 10.64%

If the discount house can borrow at less than this rate, it stands to make a profit. If interest rates fall, the discount house's profit margin widens. Alternatively, the discount house may sell the bill on the money market, its value rising as it nears maturity. The ultimate holder will present the bill to the trader, who assumes responsibility for payment and, by this time, has sold the goods at a profit.

Bills of Exchange are drawn up for periods of 60–180 days, for values of at least £75,000, reflecting interest rates based on LIBOR, but dependent on the riskiness of the companies concerned and their respective credit ratings.

Acceptance credits

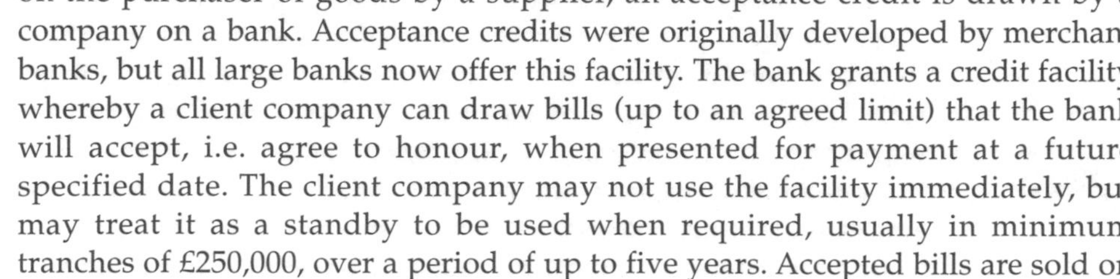

These are often called 'bank bills' – whereas trade Bills of Exchange are drawn on the purchaser of goods by a supplier, an acceptance credit is drawn by a company on a bank. Acceptance credits were originally developed by merchant banks, but all large banks now offer this facility. The bank grants a credit facility whereby a client company can draw bills (up to an agreed limit) that the bank will accept, i.e. agree to honour, when presented for payment at a future specified date. The client company may not use the facility immediately, but may treat it as a standby to be used when required, usually in minimum tranches of £250,000, over a period of up to five years. Accepted bills are sold on the discount market by the bank on behalf of the client company at a relatively 'fine' or low discount. The company thus effectively obtains finance from the purchaser of the discounted bills, using the name and reputation of the accepting bank as security. It is thus a somewhat roundabout way of one company lending to another, using the intermediary services of the bank. Bank bills have a period to maturity of 30, 60, 90 or 180 days. At the maturity date, the bank can either 'accept' a new bill (i.e. effectively roll over the old one) or receive the full value of the bill from the client's account, using the funds to pay the bearer of the bill. The cost to the client is the amount of discount on the bill plus a fee payable to the bank of around 0.6 per cent. It is not unusual for banks to require security for such facilities – the nature and type depending on the size and credit standing of the client.

Acceptance credits have become increasingly popular in recent years. Among their advantages are the following:

1 The 'interest' cost is relatively low, often below that of an overdraft, because the bills are backed by a bank.
2 The cost involved with the bill is known when it is discounted, and is not affected by subsequent interest rate changes, allowing greater accuracy in cash budgeting.
3 Acceptance credits can be negotiated for longer periods than overdrafts, thus offering more security to the borrower.
4 Unlike traditional bills of exchange, they are not tied to specific transactions.

However, they are available only to large companies with sound credit ratings, and they lack the flexibility of overdrafts, which a firm can reduce if it wishes to lower interest costs.

Commercial Paper (CP)

Another financial innovation imported from the USA that UK firms have been allowed to use since 1986, CP is a means whereby the treasurer can circumvent the banking system by issuing promissory notes – effectively IOUs – directly to large financial institutions such as pension funds and insurance companies, or to corporates with temporary excess liquidity.

CP is an example of **dis-intermediation** as it cuts out the banking intermediary as middleman and thus avoids paying the spread on the difference between the bank's lending rate and the rate it pays depositors, i.e. it is cheaper. In addition, CP avoids having to submit to the restrictive covenants that banks often impose on borrowers. However, because it is unsecured, the ability to issue CP is confined to the largest firms with the highest credit ratings.

Specifically, to be allowed to issue CP, a firm must:

- be listed on the London Stock Exchange
- have net assets in excess of £50 million
- issue CP that matures between 7 and 364 days
- issue CP with a minimum denomination of £500,000.

No interest as such is payable on CP – it has a maturity value greater than the amount lent, the difference being the cost to the issuer.

16.6 Hire purchase (HP)

With HP (also known as Asset Purchase), the user of the asset will eventually own it. This method of asset finance accounts for about 12 per cent of all UK fixed capital investment. HP of equipment by firms is very similar to HP by consumers of durables such as washing machines. The equipment is purchased initially by specialist institutions called finance houses, most of which are subsidiaries of commercial banks and members of the Finance and Leasing Association (FLA **www.fla.org.uk**). The hirer usually makes a down-payment and then signs a commitment to a series of (usually) monthly hire charges over a specified period, at the end of which the legal title to the article passes to the user. The hire charge contains two elements: an interest charge to reflect the borrowing of the capital involved; and a capital repayment element.

Two major advantages of HP are the avoidance of a major cash outlay at the outset of the project and the immediate availability of the asset for use, although the user assumes all the responsibilities of maintenance and insurance. However, if the user fails to fulfil the payment schedule, the owner can repossess the asset. The user then loses all title to the asset and obtains no credit for payments already made. HP tends to be used by smaller and riskier firms. Because of the default risk, the contract period is invariably less than the asset lifespan, so that in the event of repossession, the owner knows that it will hold

How HP works

Boston Builders, wishing to obtain an earthmover using HP, contacts a manufacturer, that arranges an HP contract with a finance house. The finance house buys the asset, that has an expected life of four years, for £120,000 and arranges the following contract:

- The asset will be purchased over three years.
- A down-payment of £20,000 is required.
- Interest is charged at 15 per cent on the initial loan of (£120,000 − £20,000) = £100,000.
- Capital will be repaid in three equal instalments.

Note that, even though the balance outstanding declines over the three-year period, interest is applied to the initial loan of £100,000. The payments are thus:

Interest = 15% × £100,000 = £15,000 p.a.
Capital = £100,000/3 = £33,333 p.a.
Total = £48,333 p.a. (or £4,028 monthly)

Because the interest is paid in this way, the true interest rate is roughly double the quoted rate. The annual interest charge of £15,000, applied to the average capital outstanding of £50,000, yields an effective interest rate of (£15,000/£50,000) = 30 per cent, although the precise rate depends on the timing of payments.

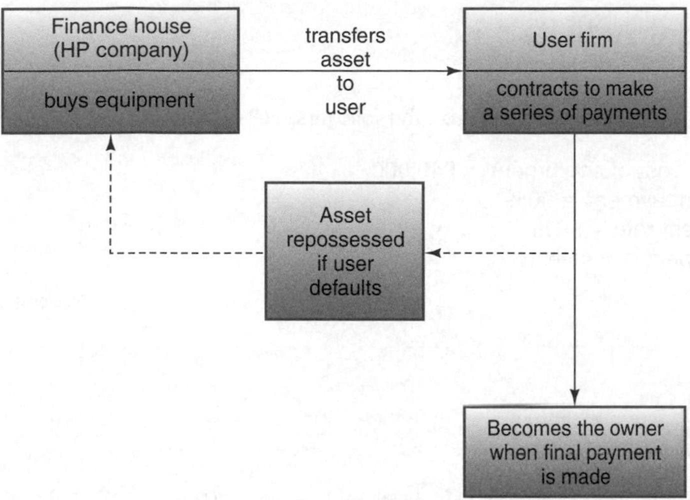

Figure 16.1 How hire purchase works

a saleable asset with some working life. Conversely, over longer-term HP contracts, the owner is exposed to the risk of technological progress outdating the asset and reducing its marketability. As a result of these considerations, HP is expensive.

An advantage of HP is that the user qualifies for tax relief on the interest element in the repayment profile and also a writing-down allowance (WDA) on the capital expenditure component (25 per cent reducing balance), based on the total cash pricc of the asset. Table 16.1 shows the profile of tax reliefs for this example, assuming tax is paid at 30 per cent, with no delay, and that the asset has a sale value of £20,000 after three years, i.e. tax allowable depreciation in £100,000.

Tax relief is of value only to profitable companies with taxable capacity. Many of the smaller and higher-risk companies (often start-ups) that use HP are unable to exploit the tax breaks, making HP a very expensive form of finance.

Table 16.1 Tax relief on an HP contract (£)

Year	Interest	+	WDA	=	Total tax reliefs	Tax saving @ 30%
1	15,000		30,000		45,000	13,500
2	15,000		22,500		37,500	11,250
3	15,000		16,875		31,875	9,562
4	–		30,625		30,625	9,188
Totals	45,000		100,000		145,000	43,500

Self-assessment Activity 16.6

What is the monthly payment on the following HP contract?

- Total cost of equipment = £40,000
- Downpayment = 30%
- Interest rate = 10%
- Hire period = 4 years

(answer at end of chapter)

16.7 Leasing

Leasing resembles both HP and conventional borrowing, but deserves separate and extensive analysis for two reasons. First, it is highly significant as a means of financing fixed capital investment, having grown substantially since the 1970s. It grew to 23 per cent of all UK fixed investment by 1991, but has declined to around 16 per cent due to less advantageous tax benefits and tight accounting regulations for 'off-balance sheet finance' (see later). This compares with about 10 per cent penetration in Japan and about a third in the USA, where leasing originated.

Second, it provides an example of the interaction between investment and financing decisions, and an opportunity to show how DCF principles can be applied to financing as well as investment decisions.

What is leasing?

According to the International Accounting Standards Committee:

> A leasing transaction is a commercial arrangement whereby an equipment owner conveys the right to use the equipment in return for payment by the equipment user of a specified rental over a pre-agreed period of time.

Thus, leasing is a way for companies to obtain the use of equipment when, for varying reasons, they may wish to avoid acquiring it outright using other financing methods. Leasing is a distinctive method of finance because it involves important interactions between the investment and financing decisions.

How a lease works

Most leasing activity is undertaken by banking and similar institutions, such as HSBC Equipment Finance (UK) Ltd. In addition, some manufacturers, such as IBM and John Deere, operate leasing companies to market their own products. A company wishing to obtain the use of an asset (**the lessee**), such as an oil company wishing to lease a tanker, or a Development Corporation wishing to lease property,

will approach the leasing specialist (**the lessor**) with its requirements. The deal will involve the lessor purchasing the tanker, or the site, and renting it out to the lessee in return for a specified series of rental payments over a specific time period.

Types of lease

Where the agreed term of the lease approximates to the expected lifetime of the asset, the lessee is clearly using the lease arrangement as an alternative form of finance to outright acquisition. As a result, it avoids having to incur the perhaps substantial cash outlay required at the outset of the project. Hence, this type of lease is called a **finance lease**, a **capital lease** or a **full payout lease**.

In the UK, it is important that the asset remains the legal property of the lessor, otherwise certain tax advantages may be lost. At the expiration of the lease contract, the two parties may negotiate a **secondary lease**, or the owner may otherwise dispose of the asset. For assets with long lives, the lessor may ignore the potential resale value of the asset when setting the rentals, since it is too distant in time to predict accurately. Instead, the lessor may agree to reimburse the lessee with a proportion, often over 90 per cent (but never 100 per cent) of the resale value, an agreement known as a **rebate clause**. (Rebates are taxable in the hands of the lessee.) Secondary leases are often undertaken at nominal or 'peppercorn' rentals to reflect their bonus nature – the owner will already have received back its outlay plus target profit once the contract has reached its full term.

However, not all forms of lease operate over long time periods. The user may not wish to incur the long-term contractual liability to pay rentals, especially if it wishes to obtain the use of the asset only to perform a specific job, e.g. drilling equipment to bore out a specific oil well. Lessors are willing to rent out equipment to such firms on the basis of an **operating lease**. This is usually job-specific and can be cancelled easily, whereas cancellation of a finance lease usually involves financial penalties so severe that termination is rarely worthwhile. The lessor will hope to arrange a series of such contracts in order to recover its capital outlay and achieve a profit. For this reason, the operating lease is called a **part payout lease**. Unlike the finance lease, where the user bears the full risks both of 'downtime' (inability to use the asset) and obsolescence, in an operating lease, the owner incurs the brunt of these risks. To compensate for the risk of having a yard full of idle and rusting equipment, the lessor will apply a rental that is higher per unit of time than that for a financial lease, thus incorporating a risk premium.

Operating leases have another advantage for lessees. They are usually negotiated on a 'maintenance and insurance' basis, whereby the owner undertakes to insure and service the asset. This is normally the responsibility of the user in the case of the finance lease, although the owner may actually perform the servicing functions for a fee. The suitability of the operating lease for short-term projects explains its popularity in the construction industry under the guise of **plant hire**, and for assets with a rapid rate of technological advance such as photocopiers and computers. To compensate for the risks of leasing out high-technology assets, lessors are sometimes able to protect themselves by using specialist computer leasing insurers, although premium rates are generally high.

The Characteristics of a finance lease

Until 1984, UK companies were able to disguise their true indebtedness by undertaking financial leases. Neither the asset acquired nor the contractual liability incurred had to appear on the Balance Sheet, although the rental payment obligation had to be stated in the notes to the accounts. To ensure that Balance Sheets would give a truer picture of a company's asset/liability position, the Accounting Standards Committee issued SSAP 21, 'Accounting for Leases and Hire Purchase'. This clarified the definition of a finance lease and issued instructions on how to account for leases.

Since the period of a finance lease usually matches the expected lifetime of an asset, SSAP 21 defined a finance lease as one 'that transfers substantially all the risks and rewards of ownership to the lessee'. It assumes that such a transfer takes place if, at the start of the lease, the present value of the lease amounts to 90 per cent or more of the fair value of the asset (normally its cash price). Leases are also treated as financial leases if they meet one or more of the following criteria:

1 At the end of the lease period, the lessee is given the option to buy the asset at a price below its anticipated market value.
2 The lease period is no less than 75 per cent of the estimated working life of the asset.
3 Ownership of the asset can be transferred to the lessee at the end of the lease.

If, at the termination of a finance lease, the ownership of the asset does pass from lessor to lessee, all previously exploited tax benefits will be clawed back by the Inland Revenue.

The rules laid down for the accounting treatment of a finance lease are as follows:

1 The fair value is capitalised as a fixed asset in the Balance Sheet and is depreciated over its useful life (or lease term, if shorter).
2 Rental payments are treated as comprising two elements – a finance charge and a capital repayment. The finance charge is written off over the lease period at a constant periodic rate.
3 The obligation to pay the capital element of the future rentals is recorded as a long-term creditor in the Balance Sheet. At the outset of the lease period, the capital element should equal the cash value of the asset.
4 Every year, the appropriate finance charge is recorded in the Profit and Loss Account.

16.8 Lease evaluation: a simple case

We now formally evaluate the decision of whether to lease or purchase an asset. We begin by establishing the basic principles.

A lease requires a series of fixed rentals. This is a major appeal of a lease – the lessee can predict with certainty its future lease payments, and budget accordingly. Because leasing effectively offers fixed-rate finance, we examine the merits of a lease against the yardstick of the cheapest alternative form of borrowing that would otherwise be used to acquire the asset, normally a bank loan. In other words, *leasing is an alternative to borrowing at the risk-free rate (or, more realistically, the bank's lending rate) in order to buy the asset outright*. Because leasing involves incurring a fixed liability, astute lenders regard leases and debts as substitutes, so that an increase in the former should lead to an exactly compensating decrease in the other. While this 'one-for-one debt displacement hypothesis' is not universally accepted, we will assume that lenders recognise leasing for what it is. The leasing decision then amounts to evaluating the question: 'Is it preferable to lease or borrow-to-buy?'

It follows that the *appropriate rate of discount to use in lease evaluation is the lessee's cost of borrowing*. This is shown in the following example.

Lease evaluation: Hardup plc

Hardup plc wishes to lease an executive jet aircraft from Flush Ltd, the leasing subsidiary of Moneybags Banks plc. The aircraft would otherwise cost £13.75 million to purchase via a bank loan at a 12 per cent interest rate. Flush quotes an annual rental of £5 million over three years, with the first instalment payable immediately, and the rest annually thereafter. Should Hardup lease or borrow-to-buy? With a lease, Hardup avoids the immediate cash outlay of £13.75 million, but loses out on any resale value (ignoring any rebate clause).

We may assess the value of the lease on an incremental basis, by finding the NPV of the decision to lease rather than borrow-to-buy, sometimes called the **net advantage of the lease (NAL)**. Table 16.2 sets out the relevant cash flows. For the purposes of this simple example, tax has been ignored (we will see later that the tax regulations have had an important bearing on the growth of leasing). We also ignore any resale value.

The incremental cash flow profile shows that, by leasing, Hardup effectively obtains net financing of £8.75 million in exchange for debt service costs of £5 million in each of the following two years. (Notice that the timing of rental payments conflicts with our usual assumption of year-end payments. The lease rentals are actually paid at the start of Years 1, 2 and 3, respectively, which has negligible impact on the present value computations, but could have important tax implications.) After allowing for the 12 per cent cost of borrowing, the NPV of

Table 16.2 Hardup plc's leasing analysis

Item of cash flow (£m)	Year 0	Year 1	Year 2
Lease			
Rentals	−5.00	−5.00	−5.00
Buy			
Outlay	−13.75		
Incremental cash flows	+8.75	−5.00	−5.00
Present value at 12%	+8.75	−4.46	−3.99
Net present value = £0.30 m			

+£0.30 million indicates that the optimal form of financing arrangement is to obtain a lease from Flush. The same result could have been obtained by separately discounting the two cash flow streams and choosing the one with the lowest present value. This is simply a comparison between an outlay of £13.75 million and three payments of £5 million p.a. beginning now, with a present value of £13.45 million, discounted at 12 per cent. For many purposes, the incremental layout is easier and clearer: for example, it focuses attention directly on the relative merits of the two options.

An alternative method of evaluation: the equivalent loan

Another approach to lease evaluation is to compare the purchase price of the asset concerned with the **equivalent loan**, defined as the loan that would involve the same schedule of interest and repayments as the profile of rentals required by the lessor. The lease is adjudged worthwhile if the lease rental schedule provides more finance than the loan that would be required to purchase the asset outright. The appeal of this approach is that it emphasises the financing function of a lease. In the Hardup example, the equivalent loan is the maximum loan at 12 per cent that could be supported by a payment of £5 million now and two further payments of £5 million, after one and two years, respectively. To find the equivalent loan, we simply calculate the present value of a two-year annuity of £5 million and add the undiscounted first payment of £5 million, yielding a total of:

$$PV = (£5\text{ m} + £5\text{ m}(PVIFA_{(12,2)})) = (£5\text{ m} + £8.45\text{ m}) = £13.45\text{ m}$$

Table 16.3 shows the behaviour of a loan of this amount, serviced by the same profile of payments as required by the lease itself.

All we have done here is to express the calculation in a different way. We have found that the equivalent loan is £13.45 million, while the lease itself provides the ability to acquire an asset whose price is £13.75 million, i.e. for the same profile of payments, the lease allows the firm to 'borrow' an extra £0.30 million, which is precisely the NAL. We can now see that the lease evaluation effectively involves computing a loan equivalent. A lease is worthwhile if the required payment of cash flows could service a loan higher than the outlay required to undertake the project.

In other words, a lease is worthwhile if the effective financing obtained is higher than the equivalent loan. Many writers and analysts prefer to evaluate

Table 16.3 The behaviour of the equivalent loan (£m)

Year	0	1	2	3
Balance of loan at start of year	13.45	8.45	4.46	0
Interest at 12%	–	1.01	0.54	–
Repayments, of which:	5.00	5.00	5.00	–
interest	–	1.01	0.54	–
capital	5.00	3.99	4.46	–
Balance of loan at end of year	8.45	4.46	0	–

leases in terms of equivalent loans, but, in more realistic cases, the phasing of rental payments, intermingled with tax complications, can make the computation of an equivalent loan highly complex. Generally, we advocate the incremental cash flow approach.

Leasing as a financing decision: the three-stage approach

In this section, we offer a note of warning. In the Hardup example, we found leasing was the optimal form of finance, at least compared to borrowing. However, in many companies, the analysis might not have got this far. For example, had the underlying project (the acquisition of the jet), been revealed as unattractive, the financial manager might not have bothered to undertake a financing analysis. In other words, firms may evaluate decisions in two stages: first, to assess the basic desirability of the activity; and second, if the project is deemed acceptable, to assess the optimal form of financing. The danger in this sequence is that some projects that might be rendered worthwhile by especially favourable financing packages could be rejected. It may make more sense to *evaluate projects as linked investment and financing packages*. To explore further this interaction between investment and financing, we need to explain the *three-stage approach*.

In analysing Hardup's jet acquisition, it was assumed that the investment was inherently worthwhile using the firm's usual financing methods, and that the remaining issue was how best to finance it. Let us now examine the underlying investment decision. Imagine that Hardup is all-equity financed and that its shareholders require a return of 15 per cent. Assume further that acquisition of the jet would result in annual benefits (such as savings in executive time and in travel expenses and fees from hiring) of £6 million p.a. for three years, treated as year-end lump-sum payments, and which, while uncertain to be realised, are no more risky than existing company operations. The NPV of the jet purchase is:

$$\text{NPV} = -£13.75\text{ m} + £6\text{ m}\,(\text{PVIFA}_{(15,3)}) = -£13.75\text{ m} + £13.70\text{ m} = -£0.05\text{ m}$$

The project would be (just) rejected on the NPV criterion and the issue of how best to finance it might never arise (unless there were non-financial motives, such as corporate prestige, to justify it).

However, it could be acceptable using other methods of finance, such as borrowing or leasing. Of these, lease financing is the most attractive because we know the NAL is £0.30 million. In this example, the acquisition should be undertaken, since the NAL exceeds the negative NPV anticipated from all-equity financing. This suggests how and why a three-stage analysis should be applied. The three stages are as follows:

1 Determine whether the project is inherently attractive.
2 Even if the NPV is negative, evaluate the NAL to assess whether to lease or borrow-to-buy.
3 Assess the value of the project with the chosen financing method.

(N.B. Stage 2 could precede Stage 1, of course, but all three should be undertaken.)

To examine stage 3, we compare the benefits anticipated from the project, discounted at the 'risky' rate of 15 per cent, with the costs associated with the cheapest financing method, in this case, the stream of rental payments.

As found earlier, the present value of project benefits is £13.70 million. Now applying the 12 per cent cost of debt finance to the rental stream, we have:

PV of rentals = £5 m + £5 m ($PVIFA_{(12,2)}$) = £13.75 m

Since the project benefits exceed the costs associated with the cheapest financing method, the overall investment-cum-financing package is worthwhile. This is an important result. When judged on its intrinsic merits, and evaluated using 'normal' criteria, the project reduces shareholder wealth by £0.05 million. Yet when evaluated using alternative financing methods, it becomes worthwhile.

Thus we find:

PV of project cash flows = £13.70 m
PV of lease rentals = (£13.45 m)
NPV of project if leased = £0.25 m
This equals the NPV of the basic project (−£0.05 m) + the NAL (+£0.30 m)

Not all marginal investment decisions can be turned around by clever financing decisions, but a three-stage approach can help to avoid rejecting some projects that might be worth undertaking if financed in particular ways. Sometimes, the lease may yield net benefits due to the preferential borrowing ability of the lessor (e.g. a bank), which is passed on to the lessor. Alternatively, it is possible to exploit tax advantages for the mutual benefit of the two parties. Finally, in some cases, the lessor may have bulk-buying advantages not possessed by the lessee.

We will continue to assume that projects are worthwhile in their own right when their benefits are discounted at the appropriate risk-adjusted rate, although it is implicit that a three-stage analysis has been undertaken.

Self-assessment Activity 16.7

What are the main differences between an operating lease (OL) and a finance lease (FL)?

(answer at end of chapter)

16.9 Motives for leasing

Some writers suggest that leasing is undertaken primarily to exploit tax advantages. Large numbers of firms in the 1970s and early 1980s found that their desired capital expenditures exceeded their taxable earnings, and as a result they could not take advantage of the 100 per cent First Year Allowances then available, at least until their profitability had recovered. Under these circumstances, leasing was often a more cost-effective form of asset finance than borrowing-to-buy.

Many firms possessing taxable capacity set up leasing subsidiaries in order to shelter their own profits from tax by purchasing capital equipment on behalf of tax-exhausted firms. As a result, the list of active lessors included such odd-looking bedfellows as Tesco, Mothercare, Ladbrokes and Marks & Spencer, all highly profitable companies during this period. Such companies were able to obtain the tax benefits from equipment purchase considerably earlier than their tax-exhausted clients could expect to. In effect, lessors bought equipment on behalf of clients, took the tax benefits and passed these on to clients in the form of reduced rentals.

The extent to which tax benefits are actually passed on depends on the state of competition in the market for leasing and how near to the end of the lessor's tax year the negotiations take place. Sometimes, very attractive lease terms can be obtained from a lessor anxious to qualify for tax reliefs as soon as possible. In these cases, the lessor can profit from the contract, and the lessee may find leasing more attractive than outright purchase. Therefore, both parties can gain from the arrangement at the expense of the taxpayer.

While tax breaks have been important in explaining the rise of leasing, they do not account for the continuing popularity of leasing after the phased abolition of First Year Allowances between 1984 and 1986. Beyond the tax system, a variety of reasons have been proposed to explain the rise of leasing.

'Leasing offers an attractive alternative source of funds'

For firms subject to capital rationing, leasing may offer an attractive means to access capital markets. This applies especially to small, growing businesses that lack a sufficiently impressive track record to satisfy lenders, or possess inadequate assets upon which to secure a loan. With a lease, no security is required, since if the lessee defaults, the owner simply repossesses the asset and looks for another client. For this reason, it is unusual to find restrictive clauses in lease contracts, in contrast to debt covenants where the lender may stipulate, for example, that the borrower should not exceed a specified gearing ratio. In addition, few lenders will offer 100 per cent debt financing. They prefer instead to see the client inject a significant amount of equity. This is not the case with a lease contract, which may thus be seen as a 'back-door' method of obtaining total debt financing for the equipment needs of a project.

Some organisations, such as local authorities and government departments, persistently suffer from constraints on capital expenditure and may find leasing an appealing device. In such organisations, there is often a rigid distinction between 'revenue' budgets and 'capital' budgets, which can be exploited by managers alert to the leasing alternative. Equipment may be acquired not by using the tightly controlled capital budget, but by undertaking a lease contract where the rentals are paid out of the revenue budget. Indeed, in the short term, leasing may even be presented as a way of 'saving money'. In 1979, the ability of lessors to obtain tax relief on equipment purchase, regardless of the tax status of the lessee, was removed. Since then, tax relief has been available only in cases where the lessee is normally liable for Corporation Tax, even if, perhaps temporarily, tax-exhausted. However, the public sector remains an important source of leasing business.

'Leasing has cash flow planning advantages'

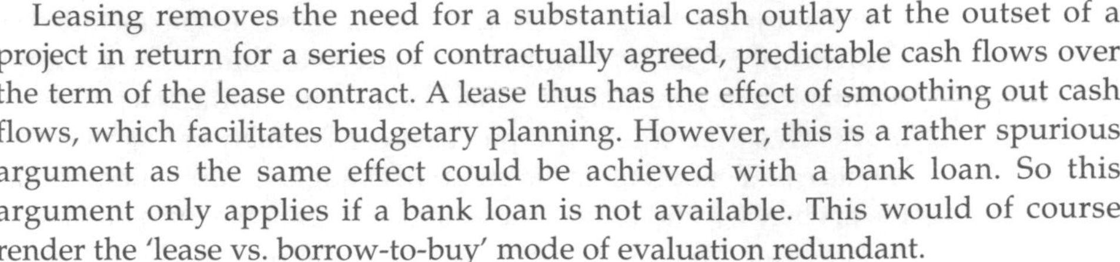

Leasing removes the need for a substantial cash outlay at the outset of a project in return for a series of contractually agreed, predictable cash flows over the term of the lease contract. A lease thus has the effect of smoothing out cash flows, which facilitates budgetary planning. However, this is a rather spurious argument as the same effect could be achieved with a bank loan. So this argument only applies if a bank loan is not available. This would of course render the 'lease vs. borrow-to-buy' mode of evaluation redundant.

'Leasing provided off-Balance Sheet financing'

Until SSAP 21 made capitalisation of leases mandatory, companies were not required to show lease obligations in published accounts. This had the effect of disguising their indebtedness by lowering the recorded gearing ratio, and also raising the return on capital employed. However, lease obligations had to be mentioned in the notes to the accounts, but it may have been fanciful to imagine that lenders (perhaps with their own leasing subsidiaries) were not alert to this form of window-dressing when assessing corporate performance and borrowing levels. However, this argument does apply for operating leases.

'Leasing is cheaper than other forms of finance'

As well as its pragmatic attractions, leasing is often a more cost-effective way of acquiring an asset. We have seen how leasing can be a profitable alternative to bank borrowing under certain conditions. This is equivalent to saying that the effective rate of interest on a lease contract is lower than that on a bank loan. Indeed, many firms evaluate leases by comparing the bank's effective lending rate with the rate of interest implicit in the lease contract, i.e. the internal rate of return on the profile of lease payments, including the 'up-front' financing. Of particular interest is the case of an 'end-year lease', written on or just before the end of the lessor's tax year. At this juncture, the lessor is anxious to get the contract drawn up so as to claim the tax relief in the year just ending, rather than having to wait a further year before reaping the tax advantage. Many lessors have borrowing advantages owing to their size, which they may pass on to lessees in the form of lower rental charges.

A survey of quoted UK companies by Drury and Braund (1990) found that the cost of leasing, Corporation Tax considerations and, to a lesser extent, conservation of working capital were the most important factors in the lease or borrow-to-buy decision.

16.10 Allowing for Corporation Tax in lease evaluation

The Hardup example, while demonstrating the incremental nature of the analysis, omitted the impact of taxation. Lease rentals qualify for tax relief, as do interest payments on loans, while expenditures to purchase capital equipment generally attract capital allowances against Corporation Tax. To include tax is particularly important, since the UK tax system was widely believed to be largely responsible for the upsurge in leasing activity in the UK.

Retaining the figures from the Hardup example, we now assume Corporation Tax is paid at 30 per cent with no delay, and the availability of a 25 per cent writing-down allowance (WDA). A firm with sufficiently high taxable profits can set off 25 per cent of its outlay on capital equipment against profits in the year of expenditure, and in each subsequent year, based on a reducing balance. Consequently, by careful timing of expenditures, a company with sufficient taxable capacity can enjoy significant tax savings.

Assuming that Hardup is not tax-exhausted, it can shelter its profits from tax by acquiring the aircraft. In effect, the taxpayer subsidises the required outlay, making equipment purchase a more attractive proposition for the tax-paying enterprise. Conversely, tax relief on rental payments lowers their effective cost. (For exposition, we assume that all of the rental is wholly tax-allowable as a normal business expense. However, the regulations in this area were changed in 1991, as explained in the next section.) The final tax adjustment is to the discount rate.

The after-tax cost of borrowing

When interest payments qualify for tax relief, the effective rate of interest, r^*, is deflated by the rate of Corporation Tax (T):

$$r^* = r(1 - T)$$

where r is the nominal or quoted pre-tax interest rate.

For Hardup, facing a pre-tax borrowing rate of 12 per cent, this produces a tax-adjusted effective interest rate of about 8.4 per cent, i.e.

$$r^* = 0.12\,(1 - 0.30) = 0.084 = 8.4\%$$

Retaining our previous incremental format, and allowing for the various tax complications, Table 16.4 shows the relevant cash flows.

The figures indicate that the lease is still worthwhile for the lessee. We could have undertaken a parallel analysis from the lessor's standpoint to examine whether it was worthwhile for it to purchase the asset for leasing to Hardup. In fact, the computation has effectively been done for us, because all the cash flows have the same numerical values, except that their signs are reversed. As a result, the NPV of the project to Moneybags is −£0.12 million (assuming that both firms could obtain capital at 12 per cent pre-tax). On this basis, a leasing contract between tax-paying companies is a zero-sum game. In reality, however, the lessor is likely to have special advantages, like access to cheaper finance, reducing its required return to below that of the lessee, and preferential buying terms. Economies of bulk purchase are common for lessors of motor cars, with 40 per cent discounts on list price not unknown.

The relative desirability of leasing and borrowing-to-buy depends largely on the tax regime. If the company is in a non-tax-paying situation (and expects to be so indefinitely), the lease evaluation should be conducted on a pre-tax basis.

Table 16.4 Hardup's leasing decision with tax

Item of cash flow (£m)	0	Year 1	2	3
Lease:				
Rental	−5.00	−5.00	−5.00	–
Tax saving at 30%*		+1.50	+1.50	+1.50
Net lease cash flows (*L*)	−5.00	−3.50	−3.50	+1.50
Borrow-to-buy:				
Outlay	−13.75			
Tax saving**	+1.03	+0.77	+0.58	+1.74
Net purchase cash flows (*B*)	−12.72	+0.77	+0.58	+1.74
Net incremental cash flows (*L* − *B*)	+7.72	−4.27	−4.08	−0.24
Present value at 8.4%	+7.72	−3.94	−3.47	−0.19
Net present value (NAL) =	+0.12			

*Tax savings on the rentals are actually delayed by a year owing to the timing of the rental payments, i.e. on the first day of each of Years 1, 2 and 3.
**The profile of tax savings is based on setting the allowable expenditure against profits in Year 0 and in three subsequent years. The undepreciated balance is set against profits in the last year. No salvage value is assumed. Insurance and maintenance costs are also ignored.

Self-assessment Activity 16.8

What is the tax-adjusted interest rate when the nominal rate is 9 per cent for:

(i) a small firm paying tax at 10 per cent?
(ii) a tax-exhausted firm?

The current tax treatment of lease rentals

In the Hardup example, we treated the rental payment as wholly tax-allowable. In 1991, the UK tax authorities made the rules more complex, to bring the tax treatment of leases into line with SSAP 21. This dictates that finance leases be stated on the Balance Sheet and depreciated accordingly. For leases taken out after April 1991, the Inland Revenue requires a separate treatment for the implicit finance charge and the implicit capital charge. The former depends on the interest rate implicit in the lease contract, and is tax-allowable in full in the relevant accounting period. The capital repayment element is derived by spreading the total capital charge – normally the asset's cash price – over its useful life. In other words, the depreciation charge in the accounts becomes the tax-allowable figure, dependent on the method of depreciation used and its acceptability to the Inland Revenue. An example should clarify this.

Table 16.5 Interest charges on a lease contract (figures in £m)

Year	Opening balance	Interest @ 10%	End of year debt	Repayment	Closing balance
	10.00	1.00	11.00	3.15	7.85
	7.85	0.78	8.63	3.15	5.48
	5.48	0.55	6.03	3.15	2.88
	2.88	0.29	3.17	3.15	0.02[a]

[a]Rounding errors prevent this reducing exactly to zero.

Consider the case of a four-year lease contract, to finance acquisition of an asset costing £10 million. The rental is £3.15 million p.a., paid at each year-end. The effective interest rate is the solution rate in the IRR expression formed by setting the finance raised equal to the sum of discounted payments:

$$£10\text{ m} = \frac{£3.15\text{ m}}{(1+R)} + \frac{£3.15\text{ m}}{(1+R)^2} + \frac{£3.15\text{ m}}{(1+R)^3} + \frac{£3.15\text{ m}}{(1+R)^4}$$

R is exactly 10 per cent. The annual interest charge can now be found by analysing the implicit loan of £10 million as shown in Table 16.5.

Applying straight-line depreciation to the asset cost, the annual charge is £10 m/4=£2.5 m. This is fully allowable against tax in each of the four years. Table 16.6 compares the profiles of tax-allowable expenditures, and thus the impact of the 1991 changes. The present system accelerates the tax relief, and reduces the effective cost of the lease (for the tax-paying company).

Table 16.6 Changes in tax-allowable lease costs (figures in £m)

Year	*Then* Rental	*Now* Interest +	capital charge	= Total
1	3.15	1.00 +	2.50	= 3.50
2	3.15	0.78 +	2.50	= 3.28
3	3.15	0.55 +	2.50	= 3.05
4	3.15	0.29 +	2.50	= 2.79
Totals	12.60	2.62 +	10.00	=12.62[a]

[a]Rounding error.

Policy implications: when should firms lease?

There are two lessons to be drawn from this analysis:

1 Lease evaluation involves analysing a financing decision, as borne out by the three-stage analysis. Sometimes, especially favourable financing arrangements, available via a lease contract, may tip the balance between project rejection and acceptance. But these cases are rare and the margin of acceptance offered by

attractive financing will probably be fairly narrow. If the project is worthwhile only because of the financing package, this should be explicitly recognised and the concessionary finance regarded as a 'one-off', which may not be repeated in other cases. It seems unduly purist to argue that, if the financing deal is all that makes the project acceptable, then it should be rejected. Few financial managers would pass up an attractive financing opportunity. *However, policy is more profitably directed at finding genuinely worthwhile projects, rather than diverting resources to obtaining marginal financing advantages.*

2 The analysis enables us to pinpoint the factors that suggest the relative attractiveness of leasing as compared to other financing arrangements. We now list the factors that impact on the leasing decision, but note that these are mainly 'other things being equal' prognoses. 'Look before you lease' is a sensible motto.

Taxable capacity

Leasing is a means whereby lessors can exploit their own taxable capacity and pass on any tax savings to firms in less favourable tax positions. Hence, the greater the taxable capacity of would-be lessors and the lower that of users of capital equipment, the greater the attractions of leasing.

Competition among lessors

A major factor in the development of the UK leasing market was the entry of new players, eager to exploit their taxable capacity and thus shelter their profits from Corporation Tax. This had the effect of increasing competition for available leasing business and reducing the general level of lease rentals. Therefore, the greater the competition among lessors, the greater is the attractiveness of leasing.

Investment incentives

Another major factor in the growth of the leasing industry was the availability of especially generous inducements to encourage firms to acquire plant, machinery and industrial buildings. Although the present UK incentives are less attractive than those existing prior to 1984, there was no fall-off in leasing after the removal of First Year Allowances, probably owing to the other attractions of leasing. However, it seems reasonable to argue that, the greater the generosity of the tax authorities, the greater the attractiveness of leasing simply because tax-breaks lower the effective cost of equipment purchase for lessors, which may then pass on the benefits to lessees, whether or not they are tax-exhausted.

Corporation Tax

Investment incentives are most valuable when high rates of Corporation Tax raise the value of the tax savings. Until 1984, with 100 per cent First Year Allowances, the total (undiscounted) tax saving with Corporation Tax payable at 52 per cent for a £10 million investment would have been £5.2 million. This falls to £3 million with the present tax rate of 30 per cent and, when discounted, even lower with 25 per cent annual WDAs. The higher the rate of corporate profits tax, the more attractive leasing becomes, because lessors can shelter their profits to a greater extent.

Inflation

Rising price levels reduce the real value of future payments, such as a series of fixed rental payments. Therefore, we suggest that the higher the expected rate of inflation, the greater the appeal of leasing. However, the inflation effect will benefit the lessee only if it correctly anticipates a higher rate of inflation than the lessor. As in all contractual arrangements, unanticipated inflation is what does the damage, and it is by no means certain that the lessee will be more successful than the lessor in forecasting inflation. If lessors feel confident in their ability to predict inflation, if the rentals they set incorporate their expectations, and if they are more or less correct, the benefits expected by lessees will evaporate. In addition, lease contracts may incorporate some form of inflation adjustment.

Interest rates

The relevant rate of discount in lease evaluation is the rate applicable to the best alternative bank loan. The higher the rate of interest, the greater the discounting effect on future payments, including contractual lease obligations. Generally, therefore, the higher the interest rate, the more attractive a lease appears, since the present value of a given set of rentals will become lower. However, this effect may be diluted by the impact of lessors applying higher rentals in order to cover their own increased borrowing costs. If there is any tendency for the spread of interest rates to widen at higher levels of interest rates, this effect may still operate, since lessors usually have access to borrowed capital at more advantageous rates than lessees.

16.11 Financing international trade

Obviously, it takes two parties to trade across country borders, the importer and the exporter, but here, we adopt the perspective of the exporter. Exporting carries particular risks, e.g. the risk of slow (or even non-) payment by customers and the risk of adverse currency movements. Hence, export finance is rather more complex than the finance of domestic trade. The banking system, both domestic and foreign, usually has a pivotal part to play both in arranging contract terms and making arrangements for the exporter to be paid.

The simplest basis of trading is **open account** where the parties simply make a 'gentleman's agreement' about the settlement date, prior to which the goods are shipped, received by the importer and used for production or sale. The exporter thus loses control over the goods and has recourse to the legal system if the importer fails to pay. Open account is thus confined to deals involving established, reliable and highly-credit-worthy customers located in countries that have rapid, fair and reliable payment and legal procedures. Much of the trade involving large UK firms with large EU-based firms is conducted on open account. The advent of the euro as the common currency of the EU is likely to increase the proportion of intra-EU trade conducted on open account.

With less reliable, or new, customers based in other parts of the world, more formal procedures are required. As a first requisite, to overcome the fear of non-payment by a customer in a foreign country, the exporter enlists the help of a well-respected bank to act as intermediary. Using the reputation and good offices of the bank, the trade-cum-financing package typically works as follows:

- the importer secures the promise of the bank to pay on its behalf.
- the bank promises the exporter to pay on behalf of the importer.
- the exporter ships the goods, trusting to the bank's promise to pay.
- the bank pays the exporter at a pre-agreed juncture.
- the bank passes title to goods to the importer.
- the importer pays the bank, often using the sale proceeds of the goods shipped.

Trade documents

Most export deals involve three key documents:

- the bank's promise to pay is called a **Letter of Credit**.
- when the exporter ships the goods to the importer's location, title to the goods is conveyed to the bank by a **Bill of Lading**.
- When the exporter seeks payment from the bank, it presents a '**sight draft**'. When the bank has paid the exporter, title to ownership of the goods passes to the importer which duly pays the bank.

There is obvious potential for delay in these procedures, e.g. in trans-shipment of goods, in inspecting the goods, in acceptance of the documents, etc. Hence the bank plays a key role in 'holding the ring' between importer and exporter and providing a source of short-term finance. The three documents help protect the two parties from the risk of non-completion of the contract.

We now pay particular attention to the Letter of Credit, as this represents the bank's promise to pay.

Letters of Credit (LOC)

An LOC, or documentary letter of credit (DLOC), is a document drawn up by an importer giving its bank detailed instructions as to the circumstances in which the credit can be honoured by the importer's bank (the 'opening bank') in favour of the exporter. It details the nature of the goods, their quality and price and the dates between which the LOC is valid. A DLOC enables the exporter to receive payment for goods in its country of location once shipment has taken place. The burden of financing is thus on the importer who gains the comfort of knowing a definite date by which the exporter must ship the goods. The exporter's risk is reduced insofar as the credit-worthiness of the opening and confirming banks is substituted for that of the buyer.

There are two types of DLOC. An **Irrevocable DLOC** is a written authority from the opening bank to its correspondent bank in the exporter's country (the 'advising bank') to make specified payments provided that the documents specified are presented between the specified dates. If requested, the advising bank will add its own undertaking to that of the opening bank by confirming the DLOC, which becomes a 'Confirmed DLOC.' This type of DLOC is legally binding and thus cannot be modified or cancelled except with the consent of all parties involved.

Conversely, a **Revocable DLOC** can be altered or cancelled at any time without having to give prior notice to the beneficiary, i.e. the exporter. It cannot be confirmed and is not legally binding.

Drawbacks with Letters of Credit

DLOCs are not problem-free:

- They can be expensive. The importer is likely to demand a lower price if it uses a DLOC, as insurance against potential hitches in the transaction, removing the need for the exporter to build these into the price.
- The advising bank has to check that the documents presented exactly conform to the specifications stipulated. If they do not, payment will be refused.
- Banks do not accept responsibility for the goods shipped. A DLOC arrangement is simply about transferring documents at arm's length from the trading activity. If the documents are in order, the credit will be honoured.
- The opening bank bears a credit risk while the credit is open. It may thus demand a cash deposit or lower the importer's other borrowing facilities.

Other methods of financing international trade are: Bills of Exchange, documentary collections, forfaiting and export factoring.

Bills of Exchange in export trade

The use of Bills of Exchange in export trade is similar in essence to their domestic use. An exporter can send a Bill of Exchange for the value of goods shipped through the banking system for payment by a foreign buyer when presented. The exporter usually prepares the bill, drawn on the foreign-based importer, for the amount specified in the export contract.

Using the bill along with the other shipping documents via the banking system, the exporter retains greater control over the goods because, until the bill is paid or accepted by the foreign buyer, they cannot be released. The importer acknowledges his agreement to pay on the due date by writing an acceptance on the bill, but does not have to pay, or agree to pay, until delivery of the goods by the exporter.

The exporter may pass the bill to a domestic bank, which forwards it to a foreign branch of the same bank or to a correspondent bank in the importer's country. The so-called 'collecting bank' presents the bill to whoever it is drawn upon, either for immediate payment, if it is a 'sight draft', or for acceptance, if it is a 'term draft', payable after a specified credit term. Where no shipping documents are required, this is called a 'clean bill collection'.

Where the importer's financial standing is doubtful, the bill may be used in a 'documentary credit collection', The exporter sends the bill to its bank which in turn sends it to its foreign-based correspondent, along with the shipping documents, including the title to the goods, represented by the Bill of Lading. The bank releases the documents to the importer only on payment or acceptance of the bill by the foreign buyer. In this way, greater control of the goods is achieved.

Bills of Exchange have several advantages:

- They are cheaper than Letters of Credit.
- Because the title documents can only be released on payment, the exporter has a stronger position than in open account trades.
- The bills can be discounted via the banking system to release finance for other uses. Effectively, the bank buys the customer's account payable, represented by the proceeds of the export deal at the time that the collection is remitted abroad.
- Banks may also give an advance based on an outward collection of Bills of Exchange, i.e. the anticipated payment.
- Bills of Exchange reduce the risk of non-payment, given that banks do not want to be associated with clients of poor credit standing

Forfaiting

Forfaiting is a form of medium-term export financing that involves the purchase by a bank (the 'forfaiter') of a series of promissory notes, usually due at six-month intervals over perhaps three to four years, signed by an importer in favour of an exporter. The notes are usually guaranteed ('avalised') by the importer's bank and then sold by the exporter to the forfaiting bank at a discount. The bank pays the exporter, allowing it to finance the production of the goods destined for export, and enabling the importer to settle later. The promissory notes are held by the forfaiter for collection as they mature, on a without-recourse basis, thus the exporter is not liable in case of default by the importer.

The rate of discount applied in forfaiting depends on the terms of the notes, the currencies of denomination, the credit ratings of the importer and of the bank that guarantees the notes, as well as the country risk of the importer's base. Because the forfaiting bank will quote a discount rate on demand, the exporter is able to quote a selling price to foreign customers that allows for financing costs.

Export factoring

Export factoring is similar in essence to domestic factoring, with the added bonus that the factor usually assumes the foreign exchange risk. If an export receivable is to be settled on open account, rather than by DLOC or Bill of Exchange, the exporter can offer the receivable to a factor in exchange for domestic currency, thus offering protection against foreign exchange rate movements. The factor provides finance and also absorbs credit risk. Export factoring may therefore be expensive.

Factors may have their own offices abroad where they can investigate directly the credit status of firms' clients locally, or may be a member of a network of independent factoring organisations. The largest of these is Factors Chain International (FCI), founded in 1968. FCI now has around 90 member firms, in about 40 of the world's main commercial centres. Many factoring companies are subsidiaries of banks, e.g. Credit Factoring International is part of Royal Bank of Scotland.

As with domestic factoring, recourse and non-recourse versions are available, the latter being very convenient for export business, although more expensive. As well as a charge for providing finance, the factor applies a service fee of between 0.5 per cent and 2 per cent for running the sales ledger and collecting debts. In 2001, international factoring represented 23% of factoring by UK firms.

Summary

We have described a variety of short- and medium-term methods of financing company operations: trade credit, bank lending, factoring and invoice discounting, money market finance, HP and leasing. The key features of each source were examined, and particular emphasis was given to leasing and HP, where the tax implications were analysed. Several ways of financing foreign trade were also outlined.

Key points

- Companies have access to significant amounts of trade credit through normal trading relationships.
- Abuse of trade credit facilities can lead to severe liquidity problems.
- Companies are using term loans more extensively, even though they are generally more expensive than overdraft facilities.
- The money market can offer significant amounts of credit through bill finance.
- Hire purchase is often used by smaller, less creditworthy, companies to purchase equipment. The asset becomes the property of the user upon completion of the contract as scheduled. Users can exploit capital allowances in relation to assets acquired via HP.
- Leasing is a way of obtaining the use of an asset without incurring the initial 'lump' of capital outlay required for outright purchase.
- Leases may be 'job-specific', contracts applicable for periods less than the lifespan of assets (operating leases), or for periods coinciding with the asset's expected lifetime (financial leases).
- A lease contract normally involves a commitment to pay a series of fixed rental charges, which qualify the lessee for tax relief. A financial or capital lease is an alternative to borrowing in order to purchase an asset, and the firm should expect its ability to borrow to fall by an equivalent amount.
- In the UK, if the ownership of a leased asset passes to the lessee, the tax breaks are clawed back by the Inland Revenue.

- SSAP 21 stipulates that leased assets acquired via finance leases must be included among fixed assets on the firm's Balance Sheet and that future rental obligations be recorded as liabilities.
- Evaluation of a lease, i.e. whether to lease or to borrow-to-buy, may be undertaken in three equivalent ways:
  1. by comparing the present values of the respective cash flow streams;
  2. by assessing what equivalent loan could be raised with the same stream of payments entailed by the lease;
  3. by comparing the effective rate of interest payable on the lease with the costs of raising an equivalent loan.
- Lease evaluation usually assumes that the asset is worth obtaining in its own right, regardless of financing method, but an unattractive investment could be rendered worth-while by leasing. To ascertain this, a three-stage analysis should be undertaken.
- Even though financial criteria may point to a definite preference, consideration of non-financial factors may reverse the lease or borrow-to-buy decision.
- Banks perform a pivotal role in financing international trade.

Further reading

The classic works on leasing are by Clark (1978) and Tomkins *et al.* (1979). Rutterford (1992) gives a more up-to-date treatment, while successive annual reports of the Finance and Leasing Association will keep you abreast of developments. Drury and Braund (1990) survey UK practice. See Bowman (1980) and Narayanaswamy (1994) for empirical work that supports the leasing–debt equivalence view in the USA and the UK respectively, and Ang and Peterson (1984) for an exception. Myers *et al.* (1976) develop the standard lease evaluation model on which the analysis in the chapter is based. Jarvis *et al.* (2000) have conducted a historical appraisal of UK government policy in this area.

Self-assessment Answers

16.1 Trade credit results from the time lag between receiving goods and having to pay for them. For as long as it takes the recipient of the goods to settle the account, the supplier is effectively financing the client. Hence, each order and delivery triggers a 'spontaneous' supply of finance.

16.2 Effective annual interest:
Discount lost/Extra finance = (1.5%/98.5%) = 1.523%
Number of 25 day periods in a year = (365/25) = 14.6
Effective interest rate = $(1 + 0.01523)^{14.6} - 1 = 0.247$, i.e. 24.7%.

16.3 The mnemonic PARTS is sometimes used to help remember this:
Purpose: Is the purpose of the loan acceptable to the bank?
Amount: Has the financial requirement been correctly specified (e.g. will additional working capital be required later)?

Repayment: How will the loan be repaid? Will the funds generate sufficient income to enable repayment?
Term: What is the duration of the loan?
Security: What, if any, is the proposed security?

16.4 Overdrafts are normally cheaper than term loans because:

- They can be recalled at short, or no, notice; term loans are for agreed durations.
- Arrangement fees are higher for a term loan.
- With an overdraft, interest is only paid on the credit used, not the credit available.

16.5

- It receives cash to pay suppliers promptly and take advantage of any early payment discounts available.
- Growth can be financed through revenue from sales rather than through additional capital.
- Management need not devote so much time to chasing debtors and running the sales ledger.
- Finance is directly linked to sales. (Overdrafts are linked to the balance sheet and the security offered by assets.)
- If factoring is 'without recourse', any bad debts are no longer the firm's problem.

16.6 Loan = (70% × £40,000) = £28,000
Total interest = (4 × 10% × £28,000) = £11,200
Total to be repaid = (£28,000 + £11,200) = £39,200
Monthly payment = £39,200/(4 ×12) = £816.67

16.7

- *Purpose* – an OL is undertaken in order to perform a specific job over a short period of time, whereas an FL is usually contracted over a term which matches the expected working life of an asset.
- *Termination* – an OL can be easily terminated whereas cancellation penalties on an FL are prohibitive.
- *Obsolescence risk* – with an OL, this is borne by the lessor, while the lessee bears the risk with an FL.
- *Cost* – OLs are generally more expensive than FLs for the same period.

16.8 **(i)** 9% [1 − 10%] = 8.1%
(ii) The full 9% as the firm cannot use the tax break.

Questions

1 *Solution in Appendix A (page 821)*. A supplier offers you the following trade credit terms: '3/15: net 45'.

If you delay payment until day 45, what effective annual interest rate are you paying for additional trade credit?

2 *Solution in Appendix A (page 821)*. A bank offers a client a choice between two financing options over a one-year period:

Option 1: a bullet loan for the full year of £500,000 to be repaid at end year with interest fixed at 12 per cent p.a.

Option 2: An overdraft, with a quoted rate of 14 per cent p.a, with interest charged quarterly on the average balance.

The firm expects to need finance of £400,000 in the first quarter, £500,000 in quarter 2, £500,000 in quarter 3 and only £200,000 in the final quarter due to the seasonal nature of its business. (These are all quarterly averages).

Unused funds can be invested at 2 per cent per quarter. The bank will not charge interest on accumulated quarterly interest charges.

(a) What advice would you give?

(b) What is the break-even rate on the overdraft, assuming the interest rate on the loan is fixed at 12 per cent?

3 *Solution in Appendix A (page 822).* A trader receives from a customer a Bill of Exchange set to mature in six months, and decides, after two months, to sell it to a bank. The face value is £200,000 and the bank discounts the Bill for £195,500.

What effective annual interest rate is the trader paying to accelerate receipt of his money?

4 *Solution in Appendix A (page 822).* What is the monthly interest payment on the following HP contract?

- Total purchase cost of equipment = £100,000
- Down payment = 15 per cent
- Interest rate = 7.5 per cent
- Equal monthly payments over four years.

5 Haverah plc is a manufacturer and distributor of denim garments. It employs a highly aggressive working capital policy, and uses no long-term borrowing. Highlights from its most recent accounts appear below:

	£ m
Sales	45.00
Purchases	20.00
Earnings before interest and tax	5.00
Interest payments	2.00
Shareholder funds	4.00
(comprising £1 m issued shares, par value 50 p, and £3 m reserves)	
Debtors	2.50
Stocks	1.00
Trade creditors	6.00
Bank overdraft	5.00

Killinghall is a supplier of cloth to Haverah and accounts for 40 per cent of its purchases. It is most anxious about Haverah's policy of taking extended trade credit, so it offers Haverah the opportunity to pay for supplies within 25 days in return for a discount on the invoiced value of 4 per cent.

Haverah is able to borrow on overdraft from its bank at 10 per cent. Tax on corporate profit is paid at 30 per cent.

If Haverah made this arrangement with its supplier, what would be the effect on its working capital cycle and key accounting measures such as interest cover, profit after tax, earnings per share, return on equity and gearing? Should it accept the offer?

6 Raphael Ltd is a small engineering business which has annual credit sales of £2.4 million. In recent years, the company has experienced credit control problems. The average collection period for sales has risen to 50 days even though the stated policy of the business is for payment to be made within 30 days. In addition, 1.5 per cent of sales are written off as bad debts each year.

The company has recently been in talks with a factor who is prepared to make an advance to the company equivalent to 80 per cent of debtors, based on the assumption that customers will, in future, adhere to a 30 day payment period. The interest rate for the advance will be 11 per cent per annum. The trade debtors are currently financed through a bank overdraft which has an interest rate of 12 per cent per annum. The factor will take over credit control procedures of the business and this will result in a saving to the business of £18,000 per annum. However, the factor will make a charge of 2 per cent of sales for this service. The use of the factoring service is expected to eliminate the bad debts incurred by the business.

Raphael Ltd is also considering a change in policy towards payment of its suppliers. The company is given credit terms which allow a 2.5 per cent discount providing the amount due is paid within 15 days. However, Raphael Ltd has not taken advantage of the discount opportunity to date and has, instead, taken a 50 day payment period even though suppliers require payment within 40 days. The company is now considering the payment of suppliers on the fifteenth day of the credit period in order to take advantage of the discount opportunity.

Required

(a) Calculate the net cost of the factor agreement to the company and state whether or not the company should take advantage of the opportunity to factor its trade debts.

(b) Explain the ways in which factoring differs from invoice discounting.

(c) Calculate the approximate annual percentage cost of forgoing trade discounts to suppliers and state what additional financial information the company would need in order to decide whether or not it should change its policy in favour of taking the discounts offered.

(d) Discuss any other factors which may be important when deciding whether or not it should change its policy in favour of taking the discounts offered.

(Certified Diploma, June 1996)

7 *Solution in Appendix A (page 822).* Amalgamated Effluents plc, a chemical company currently in legal difficulties over its pollution record, is considering a proposal to acquire new equipment to improve waste generation. The equipment would cost £500,000 and have a working life of four years. At the end of Year 4, the disposal value of the equipment is expected to be £50,000. The machine is expected to generate incremental cash flows of £200,000 for each of the four years.

Amalgamated can acquire the equipment in two ways:

(a) Outright purchase via a four-year bank loan at a pre-tax interest cost of 7 per cent.

(b) A financial lease with rentals of £70,000 at the end of each of the four years.

Amalgamated is presently ungeared. Its shareholders seek a return of 10 per cent after allowing for all taxes. Corporation Tax is paid at 30 per cent with no tax delay. If the equipment is purchased, a 25 per cent writing-down allowance (reducing balance) is available.

Should Amalgamated acquire the equipment and, if so, how should it be financed?

Practical assignment

Obtain the latest annual report of a leading construction company and examine the structure of its short- and long-term liabilities. Now consult the notes to the accounts, and obtain information on (1) leased assets and (2) obligations in connection with lease contracts.

Consider the extent to which SSAP 21 has influenced the company's Balance Sheet.

17 Managing currency risk

Steeled for the worst

Corus Group plc (**www.corusgroup.com**) (formerly British Steel plc), as a capital intensive manufacturer, is particularly vulnerable to swings in economic activity both in the UK and overseas. In the mature international steel market, producers are relatively easily able to switch sales to other regions to maintain outputs. British Steel has long complained about the widespread and EU-condoned availability of state aid to support weaker, often state-owned, producers. Despite this uneven playing field British Steel achieved remarkable efficiency increases during the 1990s due to high levels of capital expenditure financed from cash flow. In 1995–96, its operating profit more than doubled to £941 million.

However, operating profit in 1996–97 dropped to £376 million, to £265 million in 1997–8, to a loss of £174 million in 1998–9, and following a merger with the Dutch group, Hoogovens, to a loss of £1,152 million in the calendar year 2000. The reason for this slump in profitability was easy to find – British Steel had found a new and more insidious enemy.

Exchange rates, especially the Deutschmark (DM) and now the euro are vital to British Steel's competitiveness and results. Germany is the EU's largest national market for steel. A rise in sterling against the euro/Deutschmark adversely affects British Steel's results in three ways:

1 It directly reduces export revenues from the UK.
2 It improves the relative competitiveness of steel producers in countries with weaker currencies allowing them to discount prices into the UK market.
3 It exposes their UK customers to similar pressures, leading to a reduction in demand for steel in the UK.

Learning objectives

This chapter explains the nature of the special risks incurred by companies that engage in international operations:

- It explains the economic theory underlying the operation of international financial markets.
- It offers an understanding of the three forms of currency risk: translation risk, transaction risk and economic risk.
- It explains how firms can manage these risks by adopting hedging techniques internal to the firms' operations.
- It explains how firms can use the financial markets to hedge these risks externally.

17.1 Introduction

World trade has grown by a factor of three over the last 20 years. Companies increasingly deal, as buyer, seller or investor, in foreign currency, making it a key factor in financial management. For competitive reasons, exporters are commonly obliged to invoice in the customer's currency – in 2001, the Customs and Excise reported that 50 per cent of UK exports were invoiced in foreign currencies (and, surprisingly, 60 per cent of imports).

Foreign currency can change in value relative to the home currency to significant degrees over a short time. For example, during eight months in 1991, sterling fell by 15 per cent against the US dollar, and in 1992 it fell to a similar extent against the other main European currencies. In 1995, sterling fell 5 per cent against the Deutschmark in only three months.

This fall was more than reversed during an eighteen-month period over 1995–7 when sterling rose by 35 per cent against the old German currency to the detriment of exporters like Corus Group. Sterling also rose by nearly 20 per cent against the US dollar, an increase which has now (end-2001) been unwound. Nevertheless, sterling remained high against the euro. Indeed, sterling had risen by over 10 per cent against the euro since the latter's inception in January 1999, despite continuing claims that the euro is undervalued. However sterling is widely expected to fall prior to UK membership of the euro.

Such changes can seriously undermine the profitability of a trader awaiting payment in foreign currency. If sterling appreciates, the sterling value of the deal can evaporate before its eyes, while the likelihood of repeat business diminishes unless it lowers price, i.e. takes a smaller profit margin in sterling terms. It is easy to understand the concern of a major exporter like Corus Group, a great proportion of whose export trade is priced in euros.

In this chapter, we explain the theory of foreign exchange markets and how they work in practice, and how exporters and importers can protect themselves against the risks of foreign exchange rate variations. There are two key issues for the treasurer of a company with significant foreign trading links to address:

1 Whether to seek protection against these variations, i.e. to *'hedge'*, or to ride the risks, on the basis that in the long-term they will even out. Most companies do seek hedges, being risk-averters. Yet some actively seek out foreign exchange risk, and use dealing opportunities as a source of profit by deliberately taking 'positions' in particular currencies. BP Amoco plc (**www.bpamoco.com**) for example, exploits its position as a multinational with a substantial two-way flow in several currencies to operate its currency dealing activity as a separate profit centre. Such companies are called *'speculators'*.

2 The second issue concerns the *extent* to which the firm wants to **hedge** – whether to totally avoid exposure to exchange rate risk or to control the degree of exposure. Corus Group's policy is unequivocal. It states: 'The Group hedges 100 per cent of its contracted currency transaction exposure by way of forward currency exchange contracts and options'. But it acknowledges that '. . . such (hedging) is effective for only the defined time'.

Not all companies are so prudent. In March 1998, Britain's largest maker of caravans, ABI Leisure plc, went into receivership. The trigger was the insolvency of its French distributor in January 1998, yet well before this event, ABI was reeling from foreign currency problems.

In August 1997, several senior ABI managers resigned after an internal investigation revealed major errors in foreign currency management. ABI made more than half of its profits overseas, yet not only had foreign currency exposures not been hedged, excess foreign currency balances had not been converted back into sterling at a time when the pound's upward surge was undermining earnings. As a result, an expected profit for 1997 of £4.5 million was transformed into a reported loss of £5.6 million – a case of a basically sound company brought down by financial mis-management.

Adverse foreign exchange rate movements also damage investors. In 2001, Nissan, which had invested in car assembly plant in Sunderland to establish a European production base, announced that a currency movement of 20 per cent or more would cancel out its gross margin on its small cars. (Sterling had risen 27 per cent against the euro since 1999.)

Self-assessment Activity 17.1

What is the distinction between a foreign exchange 'speculator' and a 'hedger'?

(answer at end of chapter)

The task of this chapter is to explain the various types of exchange risk and how they can be managed.

17.2 The structure of exchange rates: spot and forward rates*

Most currency transactions are conducted between firms and individuals on one hand, and banks which make a market, i.e. quote an exchange rate in a variety of currencies, on the other.

It is misleading to talk of 'the exchange rate' between currencies because there always exists a spectrum of rates according to when delivery of the currency transacted is required.

The simplest rate to understand is the **spot market rate** that the bank quotes for 'immediate' (in practice, within two days) delivery. For example, on November 9 2001, the closing quotation for the spot rate for Swiss Francs (CHF) against sterling (GBP) was

2.3882–2.3897

The first figure is the rate at which the currency can be purchased from the bank and the higher one is the rate at which the bank sells CHF. The difference, (0.15 centimes), or **spread**, provides the bank's profit margin on transactions. At times of great volatility in currency markets, the spread widens to reflect the greater risk in currency trading.

It is also possible to buy and sell currency for delivery and settlement at specified future dates. This can be done via the **forward market**, which sets the rate applicable for advance transactions. On the above day, these terms were quoted for delivery in one month:

39.0 to 27.0 prem

The numbers are referred to as 'points' with each point representing 1 per cent of a centime, or 0.0001 of a CHF. The 'prem' means that the CHF is selling at a *forward premium*, i.e. it is 'predicted' to appreciate versus sterling.

The quotation given is not an exchange rate as such, but a 'prediction' of how the CHF spot exchange rate will change over the relevant period: in this case, appreciate against sterling. The rate itself (called an '*outright*') is found by deducting the expected premium from the spot rate (or adding a discount to it). Subtraction is required because the market expects that one unit of sterling will purchase fewer CHF in the future, i.e.

Spot	2.3882 – 2.3897
F/w premium	(0.0039 – 0.0027)
	2.3843 – 2.3870

Notice that the spread widens from 0.15 centimes (or 15 points) to 0.27 centimes (27 points). This is a reflection of the greater risk associated with more distant transactions. An important point is that, when a forward transaction is entered into, there exists a contractual obligation to deliver the currency that

*Throughout the following sections, we use standard international abbreviations for currencies, e.g. pound sterling = GBP, US dollar = USD, etc. We also frequently use the abbreviation FX to denote foreign exchange (rates).

is legally binding on both parties. The rate of exchange incorporated in the deal is thus fixed. Hence, a forward contract is a way of locking in a specific exchange rate, and is appealing when there is great uncertainty about the future course of exchange rates.

From spot to forward

Spot and forward rates for other currencies against GBP are thus connected as follows:

$$\text{Forward rate} = \text{spot rate}\begin{cases} \textit{plus} \text{ forward discount (denoted by `dis')} \\ \text{OR} \\ \textit{minus} \text{ forward premium (denoted by `prem').} \end{cases}$$

Forward rates, therefore, appear to be an assessment of how the currency market expects two currencies to move in relation to each other over a specified time period, and are sometimes regarded as a prediction of the future spot rate at the end of that period. As we shall see, this is not entirely a correct interpretation.

The reader may wish to visit the website (**www.bis.org**) of the Bank of International Settlements (BIS) for statistics on the volume of trading on these markets. The average *daily* turnover in April 2001 was US$387 billion spot transactions and US$131 billion in outright forward transactions.

Self-assessment Activity 17.2

The closing spot rates and forward quotations on November 9 2001 for GBP versus two currencies were as shown below.
Calculate the forward outrights.

	Closing rates	Forward quotation
Canada	2.3341–2.3356	33.0 to 21.0 prem
Norway	12.86–12.87	274.0 to 395.0 dis

Source: Guardian, November 10 2001.

(answer at end of chapter)

17.3 Foreign exchange exposure

Foreign exchange exposures occur in three forms:

1 Transaction exposure (or short-term cash flow exposure).
2 Translation exposure (or Balance Sheet exposure).
3 Economic exposure (or long-term cash flow exposure).

Transaction exposure

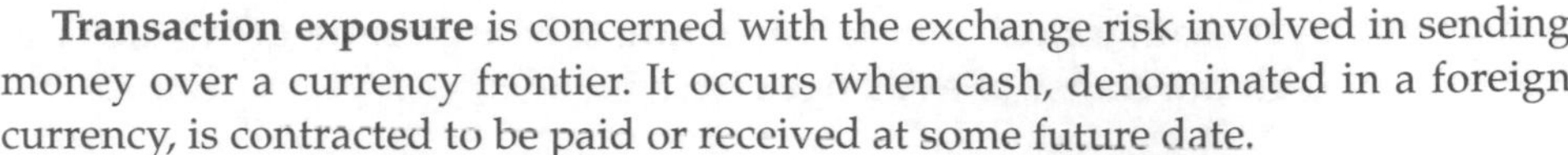

Transaction exposure is concerned with the exchange risk involved in sending money over a currency frontier. It occurs when cash, denominated in a foreign currency, is contracted to be paid or received at some future date.

For example, a UK company might contract to buy US$45 million worth of computer chips from a US company over a three-year period. When the contract is set up, the rate of exchange between the dollar and the pound is US$1.50 to £1, but what will happen in a year or two's time? What if the rate of exchange alters to US$1.25 to £1 in a year's time?

The US$45 million was equivalent to $45/1.50 = £30 m at the beginning of Year 1, but after the fall in the value of the pound against USD the cost of the contract in GBP rises to $45 m/1.25 = £36 m. Such a substantial rise in costs could easily eliminate the UK company's profit margin.

Similar risks apply to expected cash inflows. If the UK company was due to receive 50 million Canadian dollars (CAD) and the CAD actually rose from C$2.2 to £1 to C$2.0 to £1, the UK company would gain £2.28 million on the contract (i.e. the difference between the expected income of £22.72 m (C$50/2.2) and the actual income of £25m (C$50/2.0)).

Thus, as we saw with Corus Group, unexpected changes in exchange rates can inflict substantial losses (and provide unexpected gains) unless action is taken to control the risk.

Translation exposure

Translation exposure is concerned with the value of company assets and liabilities denominated in currencies other than the home one, e.g. the items listed on the Balance Sheet of the Australian subsidiary of a UK parent company.

Translation vs. transaction exposure

Translation exposure is concerned with *values*, while transaction exposure is concerned with *cash flows*. To put it another way, transaction exposure is concerned with items set out in the Profit and Loss Account, while translation exposure is mostly concerned with items set out in the Balance Sheet.

Examples of items that a treasurer might consider to be subject to translation exposure if denominated in foreign currency are debts, loans, inventory, shares in foreign companies, land and buildings, plant and equipment.

If the CAD falls in value by 3 per cent between the date an export contract is signed and the date the dollars are received in the UK, this represents a real loss to the UK company if no action is taken to hedge the exchange risk. But is a real loss sustained by a UK company with a Canadian subsidiary if C$30 million of its inventory or C$10 million of its accounts receivable are being held in Toronto at the time of a devaluation of the CAD against GBP? This question has been much debated during the last 30 years.

It is often argued that because translation risk is a purely accounting issue, i.e. it relates to past transactions, it has no impact on the economic value of the firm and thus there is no need to hedge, i.e. people already know about it in an efficient market. However, this stance tends to overlook possible effects on key performance measures and ratios, especially EPS, in relation to reporting overseas earnings, and gearing, via reported asset and liability values.

A multinational company may have significant borrowings in several currencies. If foreign currencies have been used to acquire assets located overseas, then, should GBP decline in value, any adverse effect on the GBP value of borrowing will be offset by a beneficial effect on the sterling value of overseas assets. In this respect, the overseas borrowing is 'naturally' hedged, and no further action is required.

However, the UK company may face limits on its total borrowing which could be violated by adverse foreign exchange rate movements. For example, a weaker domestic currency, relative to currencies in which debt is denominated, could adversely affect borrowing capacity and the cost of capital.

Say a company has debt expressed in both GBP and USD, as in the following capital structure:

Equity	£350 m
Loan stock: sterling	£50 m
Loan stock: (US$ 80 m)	£50 m
Total	£450 m

The valuation of the USD loan is translated at the exchange rate of $1.60:£1, the rate ruling at the end of the financial year. At this juncture, the gearing ratio (debt-to-equity) is (£100 m/£350 m) = 28.5%. Imagine there is a covenant attaching to the sterling loan which limits the gearing ratio to 30 per cent. If GBP falls to, say, $1.30:£1, the company has a problem. Its USD-denominated debt now represents a liability of $80 m/1.30 = £61.5 m, and the debt-to-equity ratio rises to:

(£50 m + £61.5 m) ÷ £350 m = 32%

The borrowing limit has been breached. To avoid this situation occurring, the company could borrow in a range of currencies that might move in different directions relative to GBP, with adverse movements offset by favourable ones. For example, British Airways, a highly geared company, borrows in euros, yen (JPY) and USD as well as GBP.

Economic exposure

Economic exposure which we met in Chapter 8 is also known as long-term cash flow or operating exposure. Imagine a UK company which buys goods and services from abroad and sells its goods or services into foreign markets. If the exchange rate between sterling and foreign currencies shifts over time, then the value of the stream of foreign cash flows in sterling will alter through time, thus affecting the sterling value of the whole operation.

In general, a UK company should try to buy goods in currencies falling in value against GBP and sell in currencies rising in value against GBP.

Of course, the transactions exposure could be eliminated by denominating all its contracts in GBP, which shifts the risk to the trading partner. However, this tactic cannot remove economic exposure. The foreign company will convert the GBP cost of purchases and sales into its own currency for comparison with purchases or sales from companies in other countries using other currencies. Management of economic exposure involves looking at long-term movements in exchange rates and attempting to hedge long-term exchange risk by shifting out of currencies that are moving to the detriment of the long-term profitability of the company. It is worth noting that many economic exposures are driven by political factors, e.g. changes in overseas governments resulting in different economic policies such as taxation.

Self-assessment Activity 17.3

Distinguish between translation, transaction and economic exposure.

(answer at end of chapter)

17.4 Economic theory and exposure management

The first step in currency management is to identify the transaction, translation and economic exposure to which the company is subject. The second step is to decide how the exposure should be managed. Should the risk be totally hedged, or should some degree of risk be accepted by the company?

The international treasurer must devise a hedging strategy to control exposure to exchange rate changes. The precise strategy adopted is likely to be influenced by certain economic theories that have evolved over the last century, and the extent to which they are considered valid. These theories are as follows:

1 The Purchasing Power Parity Theory (PPP).
2 The Expectations Theory.
3 The Interest Rate Parity Theory (IRP).
4 The Open Fisher Theory.
5 The international version of the Efficient Markets Hypothesis.

We will provide brief sketches of these important contributions to the literature of international economics.

Purchasing Power Parity (PPP)

In Chapter 8, we encountered the Law of One Price and Purchasing Power Parity. You are advised now to re-read Section 8.6 to refresh your understanding of these theories. PPP and The Law of One Price have important implications for the relationship between spot and forward rates of exchange. If people possessed perfect predictive ability, and the rates of inflation were certain, the market could specify with total precision the appropriate exchange rate between USD and GBP for delivery in the future (i.e. the forward rate of exchange).

More specifically, PPP states that foreign exchange rates will adjust in response to international differences in inflation rates and so maintain the Law of One Price. Thus the forward rate should be:

$$\text{Forward rate} = \text{Spot rate} \times \frac{(1 + \text{US inflation rate})}{(1 + \text{UK inflation rate})}$$

If the spot rate between sterling and the US$ is $1.60 vs £1, and people expect UK inflation at 10 per cent and only 3 per cent in the USA, this implies a one-year forward rate of:

$1.6:£1 spot rate × (1.03)/(1.10) = $1.5:£1.

In this example, the forward rate is predicting the spot rate that *should* apply in the future. If buyers and sellers of foreign exchange can rely on the currency markets to operate in this way, the risks presented by differential inflation rates could be removed by using the forward market. Forecasting future spot rates would then be a trivial exercise.

Unfortunately, the forward rate has been shown to be a poor predictor of the future spot rate. However, it has also been shown to be an **unbiased predictor**, in that although the forward rate often underestimates the future spot rate and often overestimates the future spot rate, it does not consisently do either. In the long run, the differences between the forward rate prediction for a given date and the future spot rate on that date sum to zero. If the forward market operates in this way, firms can regard today's forward rate as a reasonable expectation of the future spot rate. This is the **Expectations Theory**.

Levich (1989) found that in the early 1980s the forward rate of GBP vs. USD tended to underestimate the strength of the USD, but during 1985–7, the forward rate overestimated the strength of the dollar. However, taking the 1980s as a whole, the data suggested that the forward rate on average was very close to the future spot rate.

Self-assessment Activity 17.4

Use the Law of One Price and PPP to predict the relative local prices of a cup of coffee and the future sterling/dollar spot rate under the following conditions:

- Price now in New York = $1.50
- Price now in London = £1.00
- Exchange rate for USD vs. GBP = $1.50: £1
- UK inflation is 4 per cent; US inflation is 2 per cent

(answer at end of chapter)

Interest Rate Parity (IRP)

Interest Rate Parity is concerned with the difference between the spot exchange rate (the rate applicable for transactions involving immediate delivery) and the forward exchange rate (the rate applicable for transactions involving delivery at some future specified time) between two currencies. Suppose the spot rate for USD to GBP is $1.6:£1, and the one-year forward rate is $1.5:£1. Here, the USD is selling at a 10 cent premium – it is more expensive in terms of GBP for forward deals. The currency market thus expects the USD to rise in value against GBP during the year by about 6.7%.

IRP converts this expected rise in the value of the USD against GBP into a difference in the rate of interest in the two countries. The rate of interest on one-year bonds denominated in USD will be lower than bonds otherwise identical in risk, but denominated in GBP. The difference will be determined by the premium on the forward exchange rate. If depreciation of GBP against USD is expected, this should be reflected in a comparable interest rate disparity as borrowers in London seek to compensate lenders for exposure to the risk of currency losses. In other words, interest rates offered in different locations tend to become equal, to compensate for expected exchange rate movements.

The equilibrium relationship that operates under IRP is given by:

$$\text{Forward rate} = \text{Spot rate} \times \frac{(1 + \text{US interest rate})}{(1 + \text{UK interest rate})}$$

For example, if the interest rate available in London is 12 per cent p.a., the figures in our example will indicate a US interest rate as follows:

$$(1 + \text{US interest rate}) = 1.12 \times \frac{1.5}{1.6} = 1.05$$

So the US interest rate is (1.05 − 1) − .05 (i.e.) 5% p.a.

This is an interesting result. A New Yorker attracted by high UK interest, who is tempted to place money on deposit for a year in London, will find that what is gained on the interest rate differential will be lost on the adverse movement of GBP against USD over the year. To appreciate this 'swings and roundabouts' argument, consider the following figures, which relate to the two options the investor faces:

1. *Invest in GBP:*

January Convert $1,000 into GBP @ 1.6 = £625.
Invest for one year in London at 12%: £625 (1.12) = £700.

December Convert back to USD @ 1.5 = $1,050.

vs.

2. *Invest in USD*

January Invest $1,000 in New York @ 5% = $1,050 in December.

Clearly, the rational investor should be indifferent between these two alternatives, unless interest rates are expected to fall in New York relative to those in London, or the forward rate is not a good predictor of the spot rate in one year's time.

One reason why this predictive ability is weakened in practice is intervention in foreign exchange markets by governments. In the absence of such intervention, exchange rates seem to operate so as to smooth out interest rate disparities, but with the creation of artificial market inefficiencies, there often exist opportunities to arbitrage: for example, borrowing money at low interest rates in one market, hoping to repay it before IRP fully exerts itself. However, many UK corporate treasurers have been wrong-footed by borrowing apparently cheap money overseas, but having to repay at exchange rates quite different from those envisaged when raising the loan, because market forces have eventually asserted themselves to remove the interest rate discrepancy.

This equalising process is effected by financial operators called **arbitrageurs**, who act upon any short-term disparities. For example, if in the previous example, the interest rate disparity were 3 per cent, it would pay to borrow in GBP and purchase US bonds in London.

Checking the agios: the scope for arbitrage

When currency and money markets are in equilibrium, any difference in interest rates available through investment in two separate locations should correspond to the differential between the spot and forward rates of exchange. The interest rate differential is called the **interest agio**, and the spot/forward differential is called the **exchange agio**. If these are not equal, arbitrageurs have scope to earn profits.

Consider this example. An investor has £1 million to invest for a year. The interest rate is 8 per cent in London and 5 per cent in New York. The current spot rate of exchange (ignoring the spread) is \$1.6:£1 and the dollar sells at a one year forward premium of 5 cents, i.e. the forward outright is \$1.55:£1. What is the best home for the investor's money?

He could invest the £1 million where interest rates are highest, i.e. place the £1 million on deposit in London to earn £80,000 interest over one year. Alternatively, he could engage in **covered interest arbitrage**. This works as follows:

1 Convert £1 m at spot into USD, i.e.

£1 m × 1.60 = \$1.6 m

2 Invest \$1.6 m at 5 per cent for one year, i.e.

\$1.6 m × 1.05 = \$1.68 m

3 Meanwhile, sell this forward over one year, i.e. for delivery in one year:

\$1.68 m/1.55 = £1,083,871

The guaranteed proceeds from arbitrage are greater by £3,871. However, this situation cannot last for very long. As other investors spot the scope for risk-free profits and rush into the market, their actions will quickly eliminate the opportunity. This is why spot/forward relationships almost always reflect prevailing interest rate differentials.

For this reason, the forward rate is the product of a technical relationship linking the spot rate to relative interest rates, rather than a prediction in the true sense (although it might be viewed as such in a perfect market).

Equilibrium requires equality between the exchange agio and the interest agio, i.e. the spot/forward differential should equal the interest rate differential:

$$\frac{F_o - S_o}{S_o} = \frac{i_\$ - i_£}{1 + i_£}$$

where F_o is today's forward quotation, S_o is today's spot quotation, $i_\$$ is the interest rate available by investment in USD, and $i_£$ is the interest rate available by investment in GBP.

Note that the interest agio is found by discounting the interest differential over one year at the UK interest rate. If the period concerned were less than a year – say, three months – the three-monthly interest rate would be used.

In the above example, the two agios are:

$$\frac{1.55 - 1.60}{1.60} \text{ vs. } \frac{0.05 - 0.08}{1.08}$$

i.e.:

-3.125% vs. -2.778%

This inequality signifies the scope for risk-free profit via covered interest arbitrage. **Uncovered arbitrage** is where the arbitrageur does not sell forward, but takes a gamble on how the spot rate changes over the year. In the example, he or she would earn bigger profits if the spot rate in one year turned out to be lower than \$1.55:£1. This distinction highlights the difference between hedging and speculation. However, although differences in agios can persist for a while, transactions cost may preclude profitable arbitrage.

Self-assessment Activity 17.5

If interest rates are higher in London than New York by 2.5 per cent p.a. and today's spot rate is \$1.4455 vs. £1, what would you expect the three-month forward quotation to be if IRP applied?

(answer at end of chapter)

The Open Fisher Theory

The 'Open Fisher' Theory, sometimes called the 'International Fisher' Theory, claims that the difference between the interest rates offered on identical bonds in different currencies represents the market's estimate of the future changes in the exchange rates over the period of the bond. The theory is particularly important in the case of fixed-rate bonds having a long life to maturity, say, five to fifteen years' duration.

Suppose that a firm wishes to raise £50 million for a one-year period. It approaches a bond broker and is offered the following loan alternatives:

1 A loan in GBP at 12 per cent p.a.
2 A USD loan at 5 per cent p.a.

The Open Fisher Theory asserts that the interest rate difference represents the market's 'best estimate' of the likely future change in the exchange rates between the currencies over the next year. In other words, the market expects GBP to depreciate by around 7 per cent against USD over the next year.

To understand this, recall the relationship between 'real' and 'money' interest rates encountered in Chapter 6. The Fisher Effect concerns the relationship between expectations regarding future rates of inflation and domestic interest rates – investors' expectations about future price level changes will be translated directly into nominal market interest rates. In other words, rational lenders will expect compensation not only for waiting for their money, but also for the likely erosion in real purchasing power. For example, if in the UK, the real rate of interest that balances the demand and supply for capital is 5 per cent, and people in general expect inflation of 10 per cent p.a., then the nominal rate of interest will be about 15 per cent (actually 15.5 per cent). Recall that real and nominal interest rates are connected by the Fisher formula:

$$(1 + P)(1 + I) = (1 + M)$$

where P is the real interest rate, I is the expected general inflation rate and M is the market interest rate.

The Open Fisher Theory asserts that all countries will have the same real interest rate, i.e. in real terms, all securities of a given risk will offer the same yield, although nominal or market interest rates may differ due to expected inflation rates. It can be more precisely expressed by amalgamating the PPP and IRP theories:

$$\frac{(1 + \text{US interest rate})}{(1 + \text{UK interest rate})} \times \text{Spot rate} = \text{Forward rate}$$
$$= \frac{(1 + \text{US inflation rate})}{(1 + \text{UK inflation rate})} \times \text{Spot rate}$$

For example, suppose the London and New York interest rates are 12 per cent and 5 per cent, respectively, as quoted by our bond brokers, and the respective expected rates of inflation are 10 per cent and 3 per cent. If the spot rate is \$1.6:£1, then the Open Fisher Theory predicts a depreciation in the pound as expressed by the forward rate thus:

$$\frac{1.05}{1.12} \times 1.6 = 1.5 = \frac{1.03}{1.10} \times 1.6$$

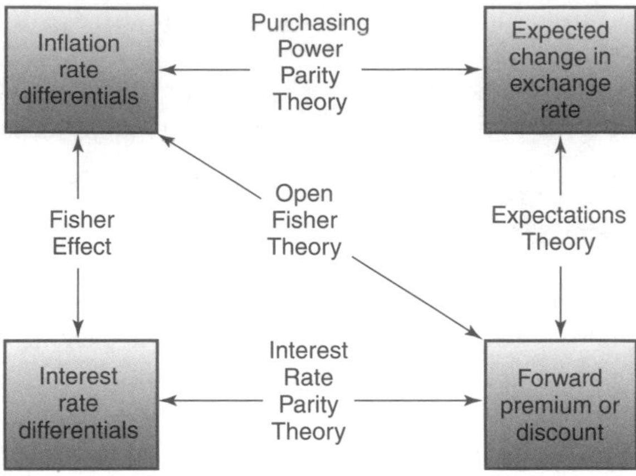

Figure 17.1 Interlocking theories in international economics

In other words, when the spot rate is \$1.6:£1, this combination of inflation rates and interest rates is consistent with a forward rate of \$1.5:£1, as calculated earlier.

These economic theories are interlocking or mutually reinforcing, as shown by the 'equilibrium grid' in Figure 17.1. Several other factors, such as the timing of the change, tax and exchange controls can also affect the relative movement of currencies, but the major factor influencing the movements in exchange rates is claimed to be the expected future movement in inflation rates, which is signalled by current differentials in interest rates.

The international EMH

The EMH claims that, in an efficient market, all publicly available information is very quickly incorporated into the value of any financial instrument. In other words, past information is of no use in valuation. Any change in value is due to future events, which are, by definition, unknowable at the present time. Past trends in exchange rates cannot provide any useful information to assist in predicting future rates.

This theory applies only to information-efficient markets. Currencies operating within a system of fixed average rates (or maximum permitted bands of fluctuation), such as the former European exchange rate mechanism (ERM), are operating within a controlled market, so the EMH will not apply fully. *Where markets are information-efficient, the EMH casts doubt on the ability of treasurers to make profits out of using exchange rate forecasts.*

This section of the chapter has provided a brief sketch of some economic theories relevant to devising a foreign exchange management strategy. We will shortly try to design such a strategy by applying these theories to the various types of foreign exchange exposure outlined earlier. But because these theories may not always apply (and some people think they rarely, if ever, apply), it is helpful to examine approaches to forecasting FX rates.

17.5 Exchange rate forecasting

First of all, consider why firms may want to forecast future exchange rates. There are both short-term and long-term reasons for this:

- To help decide whether to protect outstanding current assets and liabilities from potential foreign exchange losses.
- To assist in quoting prices in foreign currency when constructing an international price list.
- To aid working capital management, e.g. accurate exchange rate forecasts may assist the decision regarding the most efficient timing of transmitting currency in situations where the firm is able to lead and lag payments.
- To evaluate foreign investment projects requiring exchange rate forecasts over several years.

Because FX forecasts are required for both short- and long-term purposes, they may require continuous revision. In addition, long-term forecasts for investment appraisal purposes often require more intensive analysis of a range of different scenarios. In general, the firm's FX forecasting needs hinge on:

- The pattern of its trading and investment activities, i.e. its degree of globalisation.
- The required frequency of forecast revision.
- The internal resources and expertise available for forecasting analysis.

Approaches to FX forecasting

There are two broad approaches to FX prediction: **(a) Fundamental Analysis**, which bases forecasts on the financial and economic theories outlined earlier and **(b) Technical Analysis**, which is based on analysis and projection of time series trends.

(a) Fundamental Analysis

This approach is sub-divided into two analytical perspectives:

(i) The Balance of Payments (BOP) perspective

This regards a country's BOP (more accurately, its balance of payments on current account) as an indicator of likely pressure on its exchange rate. When a country, say, the UK, spends more on foreign-produced goods and services than its export earnings, the resulting deficit on current account increases the probability of depreciation of its currency. Overseas residents accumulate monetary claims on sterling – when they convert into their own currencies, this will exert downward pressure on the GBP (and *vice versa* for a surplus of exports over imports).

Analysts who focus on the BOP try to evaluate not only the country's ongoing BOP performance but also the determinants of international competitiveness, such as prospects for inflation, e.g. a government budget deficit and how it is financed, and underlying productivity movements.

(ii) The asset market approach

This examines the willingness of foreign residents to hold claims on the domestic currency in monetary form. Their willingness depends on relative real interest rates and on a country's prospects for economic growth and the profitability of its industry and commerce. The asset market perspective could explain the continuing strength of the USD during the 'Greenspan Boom' of the 1990s, during which the USA received a massive inflow of overseas funds seeking a home in the stock markets, helping to offset the continuing gaping US current account deficit.

Any factor expected to increase real returns on investment, e.g. technological progress such as the rise of e-commerce, promising higher corporate profitability is thus likely to lead to relative exchange rate appreciation (and *vice versa*).

In practice, it is difficult to disentangle the various fundamental pressures on exchange rates to *identify* the true reasons for their movements. Some argue that short-term movements are largely determined by the relative attractiveness of international asset markets, interest rates and the expectations of market players plus a dose of speculation, while in the long-term, equilibrium exchange rates depend on PPP.

(b) Technical Analysis

Technical analysts conduct intensive scrutiny of charts to identify trends in foreign exchange rate movements. These **Chartists** focus on both price and volume data to ascertain whether past trends are likely to persist into the future. The underlying premise behind Chartism is that future FX rates are based on the current rates. Chartists assert that FX movements can be split into three temporal categories:

- **(i)** day-to-day movements, mainly random 'noise'
- **(ii)** short-term movements, which extend from a few days to periods lasting several months
- **(iii)** long-term movements, characterised by persistent upward and/or downward trends.

The longer the forecasting time horizon, the less accurate the prediction is likely to be. However, for most firms, a major part of their forecasting needs are short-to-medium term, so 'expert' forecasting may have some role to play. Forecasting for the long-term however, depends on the economic fundamentals of exchange rate determination, although some people believe in the existence of long-term waves in currency movements (at least, when they float!). A major flaw of technical analysis is that it is purely mechanical with no attempt to provide supporting theory regarding explanation of causation.

Research by Osler and Chang (1999) suggests that technical analysis is largely a waste of time and money for trades in most currency pairs. They studied the performance of a particular dealing rule, the so-called 'head and shoulders' pattern. This pattern is formed when a market price forms three peaks, a high one (the head) flanked by two lower ones (the shoulders). When the price rises through the second neckline, many technical analysts treat this as a buy signal. During 1973–1994, this rule would not have worked except for JPY–USD and DEM–USD trades, where profits at annualised rates of 19 per cent and 13 per cent would have been made. Possibly, this is because with the widespread use of these techniques, such patterns often become self-fulfilling prophecies. However, even for these trading pairs, much simpler trading rules, such as buying when a price was above its recent trading levels, would have generated superior returns.

Forecasting in practice

Most leading banks offer FX forecasting services and many MNCs employ in-house forecasting staff. The value of these activities is open to question, but this really depends on the motivation for forecasting. A long-term forecast may be needed to underpin an investment decision in a foreign country. A forecast based on long-term fundamentals may not need to be perfectly accurate but may help in analysing more fully the risks surrounding the decision and its implementation.

Conversely, short-term forecasts may be needed to hedge debtors or creditors for settlement in a month or so. In such cases, long-term fundamentals may be less important than market-related technical factors, e.g. closing of positions, political factors or 'sentiment' in the market. The required degree of accuracy increases as the prospect of loss is more immediate and less remedial action is possible. In general, long-term forecasts are based on economic models reflecting fundamentals, while short-term forecasts tend to rely on technical analysis. Chartists often attempt to correlate exchange rate changes with various other factors regardless of the economic rationale for the co-movement.

FX forecasting and market efficiency

The likelihood of forecasts being consistently useful or profitable depends on whether the FX markets are efficient. The more efficient the market, the more likely that FX rates are random walks, with past behaviour having no bearing on future movements. The less efficient the market, the more likely that forecasters will 'get lucky' and stumble on a key relationship that happens to hold for a while. Yet, if such a relationship really exists, others will soon discover and exploit it, and the market will regain its efficiency regarding that item of information.

The role of central banks

A key requirement of market efficiency is that all market players are rational wealth seekers. This is often not the case with a major market participant, the central bank that tries to raise or lower its currency by buying or selling in the open market, often in defiance of market trends and sentiment. Evidence exists that at times when central banks intervene, markets become less efficient and it is possible to make money by betting against them. This happened most notably on 'Black Wednesday' in 1992 when sterling was evicted from the ERM despite the

A forecasting fiasco

During mid-to-late 1999, after an early flurry, the euro fell sharply from its opening value of €1.17 against the USD, reaching €1.05. It was widely felt that the euro had been oversold and would recover rapidly during 2000. Table 17.1 shows a selection of forecasts made by 17 leading banks in November 1999 of the euro's value twelve months ahead, i.e. in November 2000.

Table 17.1 Twelve-month forecasts to November 1 2000

Bank	US$ vs. euro
American Express	1.15
Bank of Montreal	1.09
Barclays Bank	1.10
CCF	1.10
Citibank	1.15
Commerzbank	1.18
Dresdner Kleinwort Benson	1.18
Goldman Soachs	1.22
Hanseatic Bank	1.20
HSBC Midland	1.20
Lloyds TSB	1.18
NatWest Group	1.16
Royal Bank of Scotland	1.15
Societé Générale	1.08
Warburg Dillon Read	1.14
Mean	1.15
Range	1.22–1.08
Spot rate November 1 1999	1.05
Forward rate (one year)	1.08

Source: *Corporate Finance*, December 1999

The actual spot rate on November 1 2000 was €0.86 per USD. Similar shortfalls were recorded against other major currencies. Subsequently, the euro did recover to 0.96 in early 2000, but slipped back to 0.88 in April that year. The forward market was predicting in November 1999 a 3 cents appreciation in the euro. These figures remind us that the 'experts' like the FX markets sometimes get things wrong, but warn us that, at times, all the experts get things badly wrong – and so do the markets.

Bank of England spending billions of GBP worth of foreign exchange. However, these opportunities are likely be only very short-term phenomena.

The jury is still out on FX forecasting – it should not be possible to outguess the market, but sometimes it works: the question is 'when?' Meanwhile, some businesspeople derive comfort from having 'expert' forecasts available, possibly as a focus of blame! The implications for hedging are hazy – if one believes in PPP in the short-term, then hedging is pointless, but PPP seems only to operate in the longer-term and with unclear time lags. So, for peace of mind, most firms try to devise a hedging strategy.

The *Economist* magazine publishes an annual survey (usually in April) on PPP. This is based on the global price of a Big Mac (The Big Mac Index), and purports to identify – in a tongue-in-cheek fashion – cases where PPP does not apply between currencies.

17.6 Devising a foreign exchange management (FEM) strategy

Hedging translation exposure: Balance Sheet items

Total exchange exposure is made up of cash flowing across a national frontier plus the assets and liabilities of the company that are denominated in a foreign currency.

An international treasurer who does not believe the theories outlined in Section 17.4, might decide to hedge all foreign currency transactions plus the total net worth of all foreign subsidiaries. This strategy is over-elaborate and very expensive, but is adopted by many companies, particularly those dealing in currencies that fluctuate widely in value over short periods.

Figure 17.2 illustrates a more systematic approach. The basic strategy is to remove from consideration all items that are self-hedging so far as exchange rate risk is concerned, and to concentrate attention on those cash flows, assets and liabilities that are subject to exchange rate risk in the short term.

We start with a position where all cash flows, assets and liabilities denominated in foreign currency values are assumed to be subject to exposure. Let us now try to eliminate some of these items from the exposure equation. First, we eliminate all non-monetary assets such as land, buildings and inventory. These should float in value with internal inflation. The rate of adjustment in value will vary, internationally traded goods will jump in local value faster than the value of land, but eventually the prices of all of these non-monetary assets will rise to compensate for the fall in value of the local currency. PPP relates inflation differences to changes in exchange rates. In time, the asset or liability denominated in the foreign currency will rise in value sufficiently to compensate for the fall in the foreign currency value. In other words, the owner of the asset could sell it for more foreign currency units, each commanding a lesser value than before. The total in terms of home currency will remain unchanged.

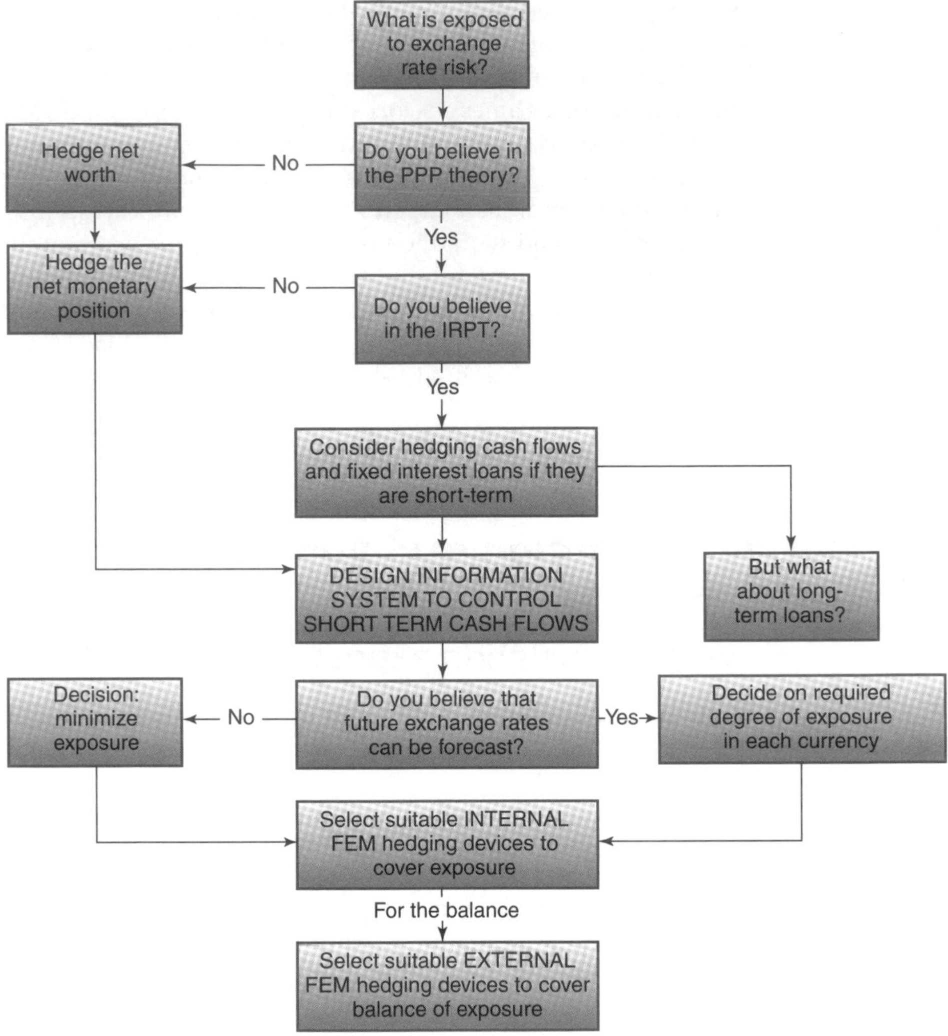

Figure 17.2 Flow chart demonstrating a logical approach towards devising a foreign exchange management strategy (based on McRae (1996))

Self-assessment Activity 17.6

Langer plc is worried about a fall in the Australian dollar by 5 per cent, compared to the present A$2.75 per £1, that might inflict translation losses regarding its A$100 million assets in Adelaide. Why should it not worry?

(UK inflation is 2 per cent. Australian inflation is 7 per cent.)

(answer at end of chapter)

Non-monetary assets are thus self-hedging at least in the long term. If the asset has to be sold in the short term and the foreign cash exchanged into local currency, the amount then becomes a part of transaction exposure. A real loss might be involved.

Short-term loans can, for the most part, also be considered self-hedged. The higher or lower interest rate on the foreign currency loan is a kind of insurance policy against the future fall or rise of the 'away' currency in terms of the 'home' currency. A forward contract could be taken out to cover the risk, but this would be a needless expense (given that spreads are wider on forward transactions), since the forward rate is an unbiased predictor of the future spot rate. On average, the forward contracts would make neither a profit nor a loss.

Long-term loans are more problematic. A fervent believer in the Open Fisher Theory would claim that the long-term loan, like the short, is also self-hedged. The interest rate difference is the market's best guess as to the future changes in the value of the currency. A lower-rate loan suggests a higher capital sum to repay in the home currency. A higher-rate loan suggests a smaller capital sum.

If in doubt about monetary assets or liabilities being self-hedging, one solution is to calculate the 'net monetary asset position' in each currency and make sure it is either in balance or in the 'right' direction. *In other words, if it is predicted that a currency will fall in value against GBP, the firm should owe money in that currency. If it is predicted that a currency will rise in value against GBP, then it should be owed money in that currency*. This might require some juggling with the financing mix of the firm via 'currency swaps', which we discuss later in the chapter.

The key problem in currency risk management is thus to identify the various types of exposure facing the company and then to hedge any unwanted exposure risks. Non-monetary assets and short-term loans in foreign currency are for the most part self-hedged. The exchange risk involved in financing with foreign loans and bonds is less clear. With regard to transaction exposure, a currency information system needs to be designed and installed to identify estimated short-term cash flow exposure in each currency.

Transaction exposure: hedging the cash flows

The first step in identifying and hedging cash flow exposure in foreign currency is to set up a **currency information system**. The control of currency is much simplified if this information system is centralised, but this is not a necessary condition of efficient currency management.

Once this system is in place, the company must decide whether it (1) believes that future exchange rates can be forecast, and (2) will permit speculation in currency. If the answer to either question is 'no', then the company must seek to minimise the exposure position in all currencies. If a profit-maximising strategy is adopted, the company will use currency forecasts to decide on an optimal position in each foreign currency. If the company believes that currency forecasting is impossible, or not profitable, then it has to adopt a **risk-minimising policy**. The aim will be to reduce exposure in all currencies to a minimum unless the cost of this policy is prohibitive.

Once the estimated cash flows in each currency have been identified, the next step is to consolidate the data. The individual flows are netted to arrive at the estimated net balance in each currency for each forward period. Monthly estimates for six months ahead are the most common requirement, but large companies holding or trading in many currencies may require weekly or even daily reports (especially if speculative positions are opened).

If the company believes that currency forecasting is both possible and profitable, it must decide, in the light of current currency forecasts, the degree of imbalance desirable in each currency in which it trades. Even if forecasting is thought to be possible and profitable, the company might decide to prohibit currency speculation as a matter of principle. Many UK multinationals take this position. In the past, US multinationals have been more willing than similar UK companies to speculate in currency, but research by Belk and Glaum (1990) suggests that attitudes among UK treasurers may have changed.

The next step is to convert the 'natural' exposure position arising from normal trading into the 'desired' exposure position. This is done by using various currency hedging devices, some of which are internal to the firm and others external. Prindl (1978), who introduced the distinction between internal and external hedging, also pointed out that internal hedging is almost invariably cheaper than external hedging. The international treasurer should first adjust the 'natural' exposure position using internal techniques and use the more expensive external techniques only once the internal hedging possibilities have been exhausted.

17.7 Internal hedging techniques

Internal hedging techniques exploit characteristics of the company's trading relationships without recourse to the external currency or money markets. Most are simple in concept and operation.

Netting applies where the head office and its foreign subsidiaries net off intra-organisational currency flows at the end of each period, leaving only the balance exposed to risk and hence in need of hedging. Netting is illustrated in the following simple example.

A UK-based multinational has a German operating subsidiary. In a particular month, it transfers components worth €20 million to Germany. In the same month, the subsidiary transfers finished goods worth €40 million to the UK. With netting, the company need only make a net currency transfer of €20 million, rather than making two separate transactions totalling €60 million. As well as reducing exposure, netting saves transfer and commission costs, but it requires a two-way flow in the same currency.

Bilateral netting applies where pairs of companies in the same group net off their own positions regarding payables and receivables, often without the involvement of the central treasury. If the previous company also had a Swiss subsidiary, a bilateral netting arrangement could operate between the German and the Swiss subsidiaries. **Multilateral netting** is performed by the central treasury where several subsidiaries interact with the head office. Subsidiaries are required to notify the treasury of the intra-organisational flows of receivables and

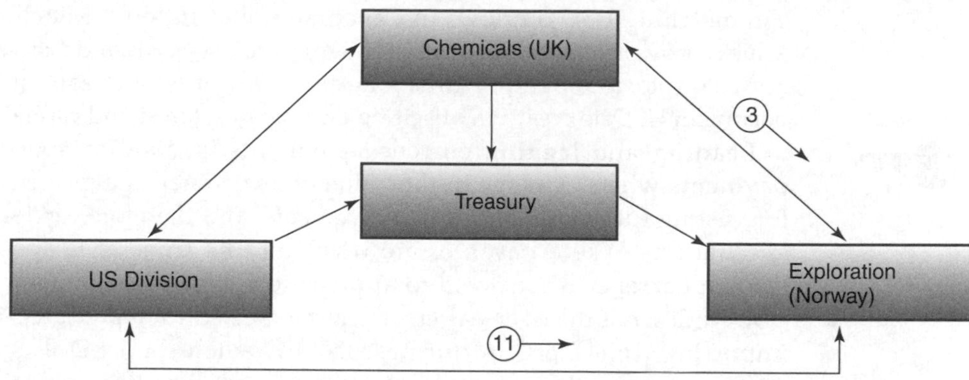

Figure 17.3 Illustration of multilateral netting

payments. Again, a common currency is required. To illustrate this, Oilex is a UK-based oil company with an exploration division based on Norway, major interests in the USA and chemical plants in the UK. The group treasury 'holds the ring' at the centre of this nexus, as shown in Figure 17.3. All intra-group transactions are conducted in USD, which is the operating currency of the oil industry.

Table 17.2 shows transactions expected for one particular month. In total, currency flows of $41 million would be required with no treasury intervention. By multilateral netting, the treasury can reduce the exposed flows by $27 million. Such a system produces greatest benefits when the inter-subsidiary positions are most similar, and where payments are made directly to the relevant subsidiaries, thus avoiding cash transfers into and then out of the treasury. In this case, chemicals would transfer $3 million direct to exploration and the US operation would transfer $11 million likewise, resulting in total flows of only $14 million.

Matching is similar in concept to netting, but involves third parties. A company tries to match its currency inflows by amount and timing with its expected outflows. For example, a company exporting to the USA and thus anticipating USD receipts could match this payable by arranging a USD outflow, perhaps by contracting to import from the same country. Clearly, as with netting, a two-way flow of currency is desirable – **'natural matching'**. However, 'parallel matching' can be achieved by matching in terms of currencies that tend to move closely together over time,

Table 17.2 Oilex's internal currency flows

		Paying subsidiary ($m)				
		UK	**US**	**Norway**	**Total**	**Net**
	UK	–	10	4	+14	−3
Receiving	US	5	–	2	+7	−11
subsidiary ($m)	Norway	12	8	–	+20	+14
	Total	−17	−18	−6	41	
	Net	−3	−11	+14		

e.g. matching USD outflows to Canadian dollar inflows. Matching can also be achieved by offsetting Balance Sheet items against Profit and Loss Account items. For example, a company with a long-term cash inflow stream in USD may also borrow in USD, to create an offsetting outflow of interest and capital payments.

Leading and lagging currency payments is done to speed up or delay payments when a change in the value of a currency is expected. This involves forecasting future exchange rate movements, and therefore carries an element of speculation. Where payables are involved, the transfer is speeded up if the foreign currency is expected to appreciate against the domestic currency and slowed down if the overseas currency is expected to depreciate. A UK company importing from the USA during 2000–01, when the USD was rising against sterling, may well have tried to lead payments. Leading and lagging within a group of companies is relatively easy to arrange, but when dealing with other firms, this can be problematic. A customer buying on credit will advance payment only if offered an inducement such as a discount for early payment. The same applies to delaying payment to an external supplier – the danger is loss of goodwill. Even for intra-firm transactions, there may still be local regulations and currency controls that limit flexibility.

Currency transfers by companies into and out of less-developed countries, whose currencies tend to be weak, are closely scrutinised by the governments of those countries because of the destabilising effect they may have on their currency. In some cases, they are illegal, both for their ability to exacerbate currency weakness and also because of the effect on local minority shareholders of an overseas subsidiary. Leading a payment from the overseas subsidiary to the UK parent will raise the GBP profits of the parent, but lower the overseas currency profits of the subsidiary thus damaging local shareholders' interests which risks alienating local opinion. This is one reason why repatriation of profits from overseas subsidiaries is often closely controlled by foreign governments.

Self-assessment Activity 17.7

Delete as appropriate:

Leading is advancing out payments in a strong/weak currency and advancing inflows in a strong/weak currency. Lagging is delaying inflows in a strong/weak currency and delaying inflows in a strong/weak currency.

(answer at end of chapter)

The UK exporter might also consider a pre-emptive **price variation**. If it expects GBP to strengthen against the currency of an overseas customer, it may raise the contract price. However, this may have adverse consequences for sales, especially if competitors are prepared to shoulder currency risk by accepting payment in the overseas currency. Conversely, the acceptability of this ploy may be greater if the exporter quotes a price based on the forward rate rather than the spot rate when setting the value of the contract. Generally, however, such price variations require a strong competitive position in overseas markets. For this reason, another such device, switching the currency in which the contract is denominated to a third currency, say USD, also has to be used with caution. However, traders in basic commodities have no such flexibility, since most of these are priced in USD.

A Customs and Excise Survey in 2001 revealed that 29 per cent of UK exports and 34 per cent of imports were invoiced in USD.

Risk-sharing is a contractual arrangement whereby the buyer and seller agree in advance to share between them the impact of currency movements. This is recommended when the two parties want to build a long-term relationship. However, if exchange rate variations exceed tolerable limits, the arrangement may have to be re-negotiated.

It might work like this. Firm X supplies Firm B in another country. They may agree that all transactions will be made at the ruling spot rate between the two parties' respective currencies. If, however, the rate at settlement varies by up to, say, 5 per cent either side of the original spot rate, X may accept the transaction exposure. If the rate varies by, say 5–10 per cent of the original spot, they may share the difference equally, but for variations in excess of 10 per cent, the agreement may become void. Harley Davidson is known to operate this policy with foreign importers.

Re-invoicing centres. A re-invoicing centre (RIC) is a separate corporate subsidiary that manages from one location, often off-shore, all the transaction exposure arising from intra-company trading.

For example, a manufacturing unit may sell goods to distribution subsidiaries of its parent firm indirectly by selling first to the re-invoicing centre, which then re-sells the goods to the distribution subsidiary. Title to the goods passes to the RIC but the goods are shipped directly from the manufacturing subsidiary to the distributor. The RIC thus manages the transactions on paper but keeps no physical stocks. All transactions exposure resides with the RIC.

A problem may arise due to allegations of profit-shifting via transfer pricing. To avoid such allegations, the RIC may sell at cost plus a commission for its services. The resale price is commonly the manufacturer's price times the forward exchange rate for the date when settlement by the distributor is expected.

RICs offer the major benefit of concentrating the management of all FX transactions in one location. As a result, the MNC can develop specialist expertise in judging which hedging technique is optimal at any one time. However, it should avoid conducting business with other firms in its country of location in order to establish non-resident status.

17.8 External hedging techniques

The most widely used external hedging technique is the **forward contract**. It involves pre-selling/buying a specific amount of currency at a rate specified now for delivery at a specified time in the future. It is a way of totally removing risk of currency variation by locking in the rate quoted today by the forward market.

However, there remain the risks of the trading partner (**credit risk**) defaulting and that of failure of the bank that arranges the deal (**counterparty risk**).

Consider the case of a UK exporter entering an export contract in February for \$10 million with a company in Denver. The companies agree on payment in three months time, i.e. in May. The current spot rate is \$1.6:£1, valuing the contract at \$10 m/1.6 = £6.25 m. If the exporter is concerned by the possibility of a decline in the USD versus GBP, it will look carefully at the rate quoted for 3-month delivery of USD. Assume the forward market quotes '2c discount'. The forward outright is thus:

Spot \$1.60 plus 2.0 c = \$1.62:£1

If the exporter believes in the predictive accuracy of the forward market, it may decide to sell forward the anticipated \$10 million receipt for \$10 m/1.62 = £6.17 m. This involves taking a discount on the current spot value of the deal. Hedging costs the exporter £80,000, a little over 1 per cent of the original value of the deal (although a higher proportion of his profits), but this may look trivial beside the losses that could materialise if GBP strengthens further than this. Conversely, the exporter is precluded from any gains if the USD appreciates in value.

If the exporter is unsure about the precise payment date by its customer, it may enter a **forward option**. In this case, the bank leaves the currency settlement date open, but books the deal at the most costly forward rate ruling over the period concerned. Say the two companies had agreed on payment 'sometime over the next three months', but the exporter knows that the customer may delay payment for six months. The relevant forward quotations are:

1 month:	0.5c dis	Outright: 1.6050
2 months:	1.0c dis	Outright: 1.6100
3 months:	2.0c dis	Outright: 1.6200
6 months:	3.0c dis	Outright: 1.6300

The worst rate for the exporter is the six-month rate, so the deal will be booked for \$10 m/1.63 = £6.13 m, again a minor increase in cost. If the customer pays up at any other time, the bank is committed to paying the exporter the amount agreed in the forward contract when the \$10 million is handed over.

Another way of covering uncertainty over settlement dates is to undertake a **foreign currency swap**. The Bank of International Settlements (BIS, website: **www.bis.org**) defines a swap as follows:

> 'Foreign exchange swaps commit two counterparties to the exchange of two cash flows and involve the sale of one currency for another in the spot market with the simultaneous repurchase of the first currency in the forward market'.

An exporter can take forward cover to a specified date, but if a later settlement date than this is agreed, it can extend the contract to the newly agreed date. For example, a **forward–forward swap** is needed if our exporter covers ahead from February until May, but if in March, a firm settlement date is agreed for June. Contractually, it has to meet the first contract maturing in May, and then take cover for a further month. This is done in March by buying \$10 million two months forward, i.e. for delivery in May to meet the existing contract, and by selling \$10 million three months forward for delivery in June. In this case, the exporter swaps the maturity date and ends up holding three separate contracts. Instead, it could adopt the riskier alternative of a **spot–forward swap**, fulfilling the May contract by buying the $10 million on the spot market, and also arranging to sell $10 million one month forward, i.e. June. The BIS estimated average daily swap transactions at US$656 billion in April 2001, 56 per cent of total non-derivatives trading.

Money market cover involves the exporter creating a liability in the form of a short-term loan in the same currency that it expects to receive. The amount to borrow will be sufficient to make the amount receivable coincide with the principal of the loan plus interest. Assume the Eurodollar rate of interest, the annual rate payable on loans denominated in USD, is 8 per cent, i.e. 2.67 per cent over three months. The UK exporter would borrow ($10 m/1.0267) = $9.74 m. This would be converted into GBP at the spot rate – in our example, $1.6:£1 – to realise ($9.74 m/1.6) = £6.09 m. This looks like a considerable discount on the spot value of the export deal (£6.25 m), but the GBP proceeds of this operation can be invested for three months to defray the cost. Obviously, if the exporter could invest at a rate in excess of 8 per cent p.a., it would profit from this, but IRP should make this impossible, i.e. if USD sells at a forward discount, interest rates in New York should exceed those in London. If USD should unexpectedly fall in value against GBP, lower than expected receipts from the US contract are offset by the lower GBP payment required to repay the Eurodollar loan.

An alternative to a one-off loan to cover a specific contract is for the exporter to operate an overdraft denominated in one or a set of overseas currencies. The trader will aim to maintain the balance of the overdraft as sales are made, and use the sales proceeds as and when received to reduce the overdraft. This is a convenient technique where a company makes a series of small overseas sales, many with uncertain payment dates. A converse arrangement, i.e. a currency bank deposit account, may be arranged by a company with receivables in excess of payables.

International factoring is a fast-expanding business among UK traders, growing by 12 per cent to £4.8 billion (measured by client turnover factored) in 2000, and more than doubling over the previous five years. The international factor can provide many services to the small company, including absorbing the exchange rate risk. Once a foreign contract is signed, the factor pays, say, 80 per cent of the foreign value to the UK exporter in GBP. If the exchange rate moves against the UK company before receipt of the foreign currency, the factor absorbs the loss. In compensation, the factor also takes any gain arising from a change in rates. Factors make use of overseas correspondent factors, enabling clients to benefit from expert local knowledge of overseas buyers' credit-worthiness. Overseas factoring is usually expensive but offers the benefits of lower administration and credit collection costs.

Export receivables involving settlement via **Bills of Exchange** can also be discounted with a bank in the customer's country and the foreign currency proceeds repatriated at the relevant spot rate. Alternatively, the bill can be discounted in the exporter's home country, enabling the exporter to receive settlement directly in home currency.

The most sophisticated external hedging facilities involve derivatives such as options, futures and swaps. These are treated in more detail below.

Currency options

A currency option confers the right, but (unlike the forward contract) not the obligation, to buy or sell a fixed amount of a particular currency at or between two specified future dates at an agreed exchange rate (**the strike price**).

A **call option** gives the purchaser of the option the right to sell. In each case, the buyer of the option pays the 'writer' of the option a premium. Options traded through exchanges are written in specified contract sizes: for example, on the Philadelphia Stock Exchange (PHLX), GBP is dealt in lot or contract sizes of 31,250 units, i.e. £31,250. Most exchanges offer a limited number of alternative exercise prices and maturity dates. PHLX also trades USD options against the Australian dollar (contract size A$100,000), Canadian dollar (C$100,000), Japanese Yen (12,500,000) and the Swiss Franc (125,000), as well as euro contracts (62,500). Delivery dates are for the quarter months of March, June, September and December plus the two immediately upcoming months. For non-standard options, the would-be purchaser may have to shop around for a customised quotation on the **over-the-counter** (OTC) market. This may be necessary for unusual or 'exotic' currencies.

A '**European option**' can be exercised only at the specified maturity date, while an '**American option**' can be exercised at any time up to the specified expiry date. If an option is not exercised, it lapses and the premium is lost. However, the appeal of an option is that the maximum loss is limited to the cost of the premium, while the purchaser retains the upside potential. The size of the premium depends on the difference between the current exchange rate and the strike price (for an unlikely strike price, premiums will be very low), the volatility of the two currencies, the period to maturity and, for OTC contracts, the size of the contract.

Here is an example of how a trader could use a currency option for hedging purposes. A UK exporter sells goods for $12 million to a customer in Baltimore in June for settlement in September. The contract is worth £8 million when valued at spot of $1.50:£1, but the exporter is concerned that sterling might appreciate before settlement, thus eroding the profit margin. In this case, it might purchase a call option on GBP, i.e. an option to sell USD in exchange for GBP. The following premiums per option unit are available at the Philadelphia exchange:

Sterling September calls	
Exercise price ($/£)	**Premium (US cents)**
1.50	4.0
1.55	3.0
1.60	1.8
1.65	0.7

Clearly, the stronger the position of USD, the more expensive the option. Obviously, there is no point buying an option at a strike price below 1.50, as all exchange rates below 1.50 are advantageous. The exporter can lock in the spot rate, or purchase protection against the rate rising above the current spot by various amounts. This requires it to take a view on the most likely adverse movements. Choosing the 1.55 strike price gives the exporter insurance against the exchange rate going higher than 1.55. The cost of purchasing the option is:

$$\text{Number of lots required} = \frac{\$12\text{ m}}{1.50} \div £31{,}250 = 256$$

$$\text{Cost of option} = £31{,}250 \times \$0.03 \times 256 = \$240{,}000$$

i.e. £160,000 at spot.

If the spot rate in September is less than $1.55, the option is not worth exercising and is said to be 'out of money'; if spot is $1.55, it is 'at the money'; while if spot is over $1.55, say $1.65, the option is 'in the money'. In the last case, export earnings of $12 million can be sold at $1.55 to realise £7.74 million, compared with a spot value of $12 m/1.65 = £7.27 m. Although the option has cost £160,000, it has prevented the exporter from losing (£7.74 m – £7.27 m) = £470,000, i.e. a net benefit of £310,000, allowing for the cost of the option.

Self-assessment Activity 17.8

What is the net cost/benefit of an option that is 'at the money'?

(answer at end of chapter)

It is important to appreciate that options are 'zero-sum games' – what the holder wins, the writer loses, and vice versa. It is relatively unusual to use currency options to hedge ongoing trading exposures – options are complex, they are often expensive compared to using the forward market and it is time-consuming to monitor an American option to judge whether it is worth closing out the position prematurely. Options tend to be used to cover major isolated expenditures, e.g. the cost of completing the acquisition of an overseas company or the phased payments in a major overseas construction project.

The PHLX website (**www.phlx.com**) gives a history of option trading and also a trading guide, and daily quotations on sterling and euros appear in the *Financial Times*.

Currency futures

In principle, a futures contract can be arranged for any product or commodity, including financial instruments and currencies. A currency futures contract is a commitment to deliver a specific amount of a specified currency at a specified future date for an agreed price incorporated in the contract. It performs a similar function to a forward contract, but has some major differences.

Currency futures contracts have the following characteristics:

1 They are marketable instruments traded on organised futures markets.
2 They can be completed (liquidated) before the contracted date, whereas a forward contract has to run to maturity.

3 They are relatively inflexible, being available for a limited range of currencies and for standard maturity dates. The world's largest market for currency futures is the Chicago Mercantile Exchange (CME). It trades futures in eleven different currencies for delivery four times each year: March, June, September and December.
4 They are dealt in standard lot sizes, or contracts.
5 The CME requires a down-payment called a 'performance bond' or 'margin' of about 1.5 per cent of the contract value, whereas forward contracts involve a single payment at maturity.
6 They also involve 'variation payments', essentially the ongoing losses on the contract to be paid to the exchange on which the contract is dealt.
7 They are usually cheaper than forward contracts, requiring a small commission payment rather than a buy/sell spread.

It is difficult to 'tailor make' a currency future to the precise needs of the parties involved, which explains why some exchanges, e.g. LIFFE, have now stopped currency futures trading.

How a currency future works

This is best shown with an example. In June, a UK importer agrees to buy goods worth $10 million from a firm in Detroit. The sterling/dollar spot rate is $1.50:£1, valuing the deal at $10 m/1.50 = £6,666,666. Settlement is agreed for 15 August, but the exporter is concerned that appreciation of USD will undermine its profitability (it will have to find more GBP to meet the import cost). On the CME, the market price (i.e. the exchange rate) for September GBP futures is $1.48, suggesting that the market expects USD to appreciate.

The exporter needs eventually to acquire GBP to pay for its imports, so it should sell (i.e. go short of) GBP by selling GBP futures contracts at $1.48. With the standard contract size of £62,500, the number of whole contracts required is:

[$10 m/(£62,500 × 1.48)] = 108 approx.

Note the indivisibility problem – 108 contracts covers exposure of only (108 × £62,500 × 1.48) = $9,990,000. This makes hedging by futures unattractive to small exporters. There is also a timing problem, as the importer has to supply USD before the expiry of the contract in August. When payment is due, the importer will close out the contract by arranging a reverse trade, i.e. one with exactly opposite features, which means buying 108 September GBP futures at the ruling market price. If USD has strengthened against GBP between June and August, the importer will make a profit on the futures contract.

Imagine this does happen and the spot rate on 15 August is $1.49 and the September futures price is $1.475. As payment for the goods is required, the importer converts GBP for USD on the spot market at a cost of ($10 m/1.49) = $6,711,409. Compared with the cost of the deal at the June spot rate, it has made a loss of £44,743, owing to the feared USD appreciation. However, the importer holds 108 futures contracts, enabling it to sell GBP at $1.48. To close its position, the importer can buy the same number of contracts at an exchange rate of $1.475. It will thus make a profit on the futures market of:

Sells 108 × £62,500 × 1.480	=	$9,990,000
Buys 108 × £62,500 × 1.475	=	$9,956,250
Profit		$33,750

Valued at spot of $1.49, this is worth ($33,750/1.49) = £22,651, leaving a net loss of (£44,743 – £22,651) = £22,088. This demonstrates the difficulty of achieving a perfectly hedged position with currency futures. Moreover, the futures market may not always move to the same degree as the spot market, owing to expectations about future exchange rate movements.

The CME website (**www.cme.com**) provides a beginner's guide to using the futures markets, and prices for USD currency futures are quoted daily in the *Financial Times*.

Currency swaps

The BIS defines currency swaps as follows:

'A currency swap (or cross-currency swap) commits two counterparties to several cash flows, which in most cases involve an initial exchange of principal and a final re-exchange of principal upon maturity of the contract, and in all cases, several streams of interest payments'.

Swaps originated from controls applied by the Bank of England over foreign exchange movements prior to 1979. Firms wishing to obtain foreign currency to invest overseas, say in the USA, found they could avoid these controls by entering an agreement with a US company that operated a subsidiary in the UK. In return for receiving a loan from the US company to finance its own activity in the USA, the UK company would lend to the UK-based subsidiary of the US company. The two firms would agree to repay the loans in the local currency after an agreed period, thereby locking in a particular exchange rate. The interest rate would be based on prevailing local rates. Such arrangements were called **'back-to-back loans'** – from the UK company's perspective, they involved agreeing to make a series of future USD payments in exchange for receiving a flow of GBP income.

After exchange controls were removed in 1979, such loans were replaced by currency swaps. These need not involve two companies directly. In general terms, a currency swap is a contract between two parties (e.g. between a bank and an overseas investor) to exchange payments denominated in one currency for payments denominated in another. A simple example will illustrate this.

How currency swaps work

Currency swaps are complex. In particular, they require matching up two companies' mutual requirements in terms of type and amount of currency required and term of financing. The final agreement will reflect the bargaining power of the parties involved and is most viable when each party has a differential borrowing advantage in one currency which it can transfer to the other. This point is important – a currency swap almost invariably involves an interest rate swap.

To illustrate the process, consider the example of two companies, ABC and XYZ. ABC, which can borrow in Swiss Francs (CHF) at 5.5 per cent, is seeking USD financing of $40 million for three years. The Dutch subsidiary of a US bank is prepared to act as intermediary, which involves finding a suitable matching company which has a borrowing advantage in USD and is seeking CHF finance. Until the match is found, the bank will be exposed to currency and interest rate risk, which it may cover by entering the spot market, or possibly using the options market. Company XYZ emerges as a suitable swap candidate. (More complex swaps might involve several participant companies if a directly corresponding currency requirement cannot be identified.)

XYZ has a borrowing advantage in USD, being able to borrow at 7 per cent, compared to ABC's borrowing rate of 7.75 per cent. Conversely, XYZ would have to borrow in CHF at 6 per cent. XYZ is seeking CHF finance of 52 million. At the ruling exchange rate of 1.3 CHF per USD, this is an exact match. With the bank's intermediation, the two companies now agree to swap currencies and assume each other's interest rate obligations over a three-year term, with transactions conducted via the bank. Figure 17.4 shows the structure of the swap and the sequence of transactions. In reality, the two companies would have to pay rather higher interest rates than those shown in order to yield a profit margin for the bank, sufficient to compensate it for assuming the risks of either company defaulting on interest payments or re-exchange of principal.

There are three legs to such deals:

1 Exchange of principal at spot (either notional or a physical transfer) in order to provide a basis for computing interest.
2 Exchange of interest streams.
3 Re-exchange of principal on terms agreed at the outset.

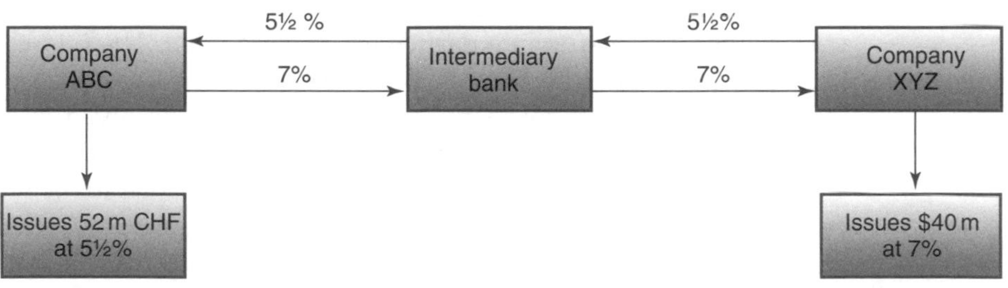

The sequence of Transactions

Time	*ABC*		*XYZ*	
Outset	Pays Receives	52 m CHF $40 m	Pays Receives	$40m 52 m CHF
Years 1–3	Pays Receives	7% on $40 m 5½% on 52 m CHF	Pays Receives	5½% on 52 m CHF 7% on $40 m
End Year 3	Pays Receives	$40 m 52 m CHF	Pays Receives	52 m CHF $40 m

Figure 17.4 Achieving the swap

The principal is fully hedged, unlike the interest rate payments, which may require hedging via the forward market.

In the example, the company benefits from lower interest rates and effectively uses the superior credit rating of the swap specialist to access cheaper finance. Most currency swaps are undertaken to exploit such interest rate disparities, whereby one party can pass on to another the benefit of superior creditworthiness. There are two main forms of currency swap. In a **fixed/fixed swap**, one party swaps a stream of fixed interest payments for a corresponding stream of fixed interest payments in another currency (as in the above example). In a **fixed/floating swap**, or **cross-currency interest swap**, one or both payment streams are on a variable basis, e.g. linked to LIBOR.

17.9 Hedging the risk of foreign projects

This issue has already been addressed in Chapter 8. Operating a foreign investment involves both translation exposure and economic exposure. The translation risk stems from exposure to unexpected exchange rate movements: for example, a fall in the value of the Australian dollar (AUD) against GBP will reduce the GBP value of assets appearing in the Australian subsidiary's Balance Sheet. When consolidated into the parent's accounts, this will require a write-down of the value of assets in GBP terms. This problem can be avoided if the exposed assets are matched by a corresponding liability. For example, if the initial investment is financed by a loan denominated in AUD, the diminution in the sterling value of assets will be matched by the diminution in the GBP value of the loan.

Perfect matching of assets and liabilities is not always possible. Many overseas capital markets are not equipped to supply the required capital. Besides, it is probably politic to provide an input of parent company equity to signal commitment to the project, the government and the country. However, perfect matching is probably unnecessary, since some assets such as machinery can be traded internationally. The cause of the exchange rate depreciation (i.e. higher internal prices) will lead to a rise in prices, and if the Law of One Price holds, this appreciation in the value of locally-held assets will compensate for the reduced GBP value of the currency. As a result, the need to match probably applies only to property assets and items of working capital such as debtors, which cannot readily be traded on international markets. (Note the obvious attraction of operating with a sizeable volume of short-term creditors, especially at the financial year end.)

Economic exposure is the long-term counterpart of transaction exposure – it applies to a stream of cash inflows and outflows. In theory, the problem of variations in the prices of inputs and outputs should also be solved by the operation of the Law of One Price. For example, local price inflation at a rate above that prevailing in the parent company's country will be exactly offset by depreciation in the local currency, thus maintaining intact the GBP value of locally produced goods.

However, in practice, problems arise when PPP does not apply in the short term and when *project* prices alter at different rates from *prices in general*. The movement in the local price index is only an average price change, hiding a wide spread of higher and lower price variations. In principle, the firm could use the forward market to remove this element of unpredictability in the value of cash flows, but in practice, the forward market has a very limited time horizon, or is non-existent for many currencies.

Nevertheless, the parent company with widely spread overseas operations can adopt a number of devices. It can mix the project's expected cash flows and outflows with those of other transactions to take advantage of netting and matching opportunities. It can lead and lag payments when it expects adverse currency movements, although host governments usually object to this. It can also use third-party currencies. For example, if it invests in oil extraction, its output will be priced in USD and the otherwise exposed cost of inputs may be sourced or invoiced in USD or in a currency expected to move in line with USD. A more aggressive policy might involve invoicing sales in currencies expected to be strong and sourcing in currencies expected to be weak, perhaps including the local one.

Another tactic is to use the foreign project's net cash flows to purchase goods produced in the host country that are exportable, or can be used as inputs for the parent's own production requirements. This converts the foreign currency exposure of the project's cash flow into a world price exposure of the goods traded. This may be desirable if the degree of uncertainty surrounding the relevant exchange rate is greater than that attaching to the relevant product price.

Much world trade is conducted on the stipulation that the exporter accepts payment in goods supplied by the trading partner, or otherwise undertakes to purchase goods and services in the country concerned. This linking of export contracts with reciprocal agreements to import is known as **counter-trade**. It is usually found where the importer suffers from a severe shortage of foreign currency or limited access to bank credits.

One form of countertrade is **buy-back**, which is a way of financing and operating foreign investment projects. In a buy-back, suppliers of plant, equipment or technical know-how agree to accept payment in the form of the future output of the investment concerned. This long-term supply contract with the overseas partner raises some interesting principal/agent issues, concerning in particular the quality of the output and the management of the operation. Ideally, the output should be a product for which a ready market is available or that the exporter can use as an input to its own production process. In recent years, Iran has signed buy-back deals with European energy majors Royal Dutch/Shell, TotalFinaElf and ENI to finance the development of oil and gas projects.

The advantage of buy-backs for a Western company is that they secure long-term supplies and obviate any need to worry about exchange rate movements. The effective cost is the cost incurred in financing the original construction, and perhaps an opportunity cost if world prices of the goods received fall. Buy-backs thus offer a way of locking into the present world price for the goods transferred, which has some appeal in markets where prices fluctuate widely, for example, oil.

17.10 Conclusions

The globalisation of world trade has forced financial managers to take a keener interest in managing foreign exchange exposure. There are three types of exposure: transaction exposure, affecting the flow of cash across a currency frontier; translation exposure, affecting the value of assets and liabilities denominated in a foreign currency; and economic exposure, which is the impact on long-term cash flows of possible changes in exchange rates.

Not all transactions, assets and liabilities denominated in foreign currencies are necessarily exposed to exchange rate risk. The essential skills in currency management are to identify the assets and cash flows which are at risk and to devise suitable means of hedging the risks. It is important to differentiate between hedging techniques internal and external to the firm. Several financial markets have been developed that allow the international treasurer to hedge foreign exchange risk, and financial instruments such as swaps, options, futures and forwards can be used for this purpose.

The international treasurer must decide whether or not exchange rates can be forecast with any degree of reliability. With exchange rates floating freely, research suggests that forecasting is not profitable. However, when governments begin to interfere with the free market, forecasting has proved to be a profitable activity. The dogged, but ultimately doomed, commitment by international monetary authorities to support artificially high or low exchange rates may make forecasting worthwhile.

Summary

This chapter examined the nature and sources of a company's exposure to the risk of adverse foreign exchange rate movements. It explained a number of widely used strategies to hedge or safeguard against these risks, applying techniques both internal to the firm and also available on external capital markets.

Key points

- Corporate profitability can be seriously affected by adverse movements in foreign exchange rates.
- Currency can be transacted for immediate payment on the spot market or for future delivery via the forward market.
- The international treasurer is faced with three kinds of foreign exchange exposure: transaction exposure, translation exposure and economic exposure.
- Transaction exposure relates to the likely variability in short-term operating cash flows: for example, the cost of specific imported raw materials and the income from specific exported goods.

- Translation exposure relates to the risk of exchange rate movements altering the sterling value of assets located overseas or the sterling value of liabilities due to be settled overseas.
- Economic exposure refers to the ongoing risks incurred by the company in its choice of long-term contractual arrangements, such as licensing deals or decisions to invest overseas. These risks are the long-term equivalent of transaction exposure.
- Companies that trade internationally should devise a foreign exchange strategy.
- The strategy might depend on the treasurer's belief in the validity of various international trade theories: Purchasing Power Parity (PPP), Interest Rate Parity (IRP), the Expectations Theory and the Open Fisher Theory.
- PPP states that, allowing for the prevailing exchange rate, identical goods must sell for a common price in different locations. If inflation rates differ between locations, exchange rates will adjust to preserve the Law of One Price.
- IRP asserts that any differences in international interest rates are a reflection of expected exchange rate movements, so that the interest rate offered in a location whose currency is expected to depreciate will exceed that in an appreciating currency location by the amount of the expected exchange rate movement.
- The forward premium or discount should equal the expected rate of appreciation or depreciation of a currency.
- The Open Fisher Theory asserts that different countries will offer the same expected real interest rate, so that differences in their nominal rates of interest can be explained by expected differences in their rates of inflation.
- Once the exposure position of the company is identified and measured, the treasurer must devise a hedging strategy to control the foreign exchange risk faced by the firm.
- Many apparent exposures are often self-hedging: for example, holdings of plant and machinery that can be traded internationally.
- Generally, internal hedging techniques are cheaper to apply than using the external markets, which offer various financial instruments for hedging currency risks.
- Hedging cash flows for long-term investment projects is more problematic, but can be handled by internal methods.

Further reading

Extensive treatments of foreign exchange exposure and ways of hedging risks can be found in a variety of textbooks on international finance: for example, McRae (1996), Buckley (1992), Shapiro (1989) and Eiteman *et al.* (1995). For detailed treatments of the mechanics of the various markets for hedging instruments, see Andersen (1987) and Price and Henderson (1988). For the underlying economic theory of the operation of currency and other markets, see Prindl (1978) and Kindleberger (1978).

Articles by Rodriguez (1981), Collier and Davies (1985) and Belk and Glaum (1990) report on the currency management practices of US and UK multinational companies. Giddy (1994) contains several excellent chapters on the use of derivatives in managing foreign exchange exposure. Madura (1995) is highly readable on all these issues.

Self-assessment Answers

17.1 A speculator deliberately risks losing money by taking a long or short 'position' in a particular currency. A hedger tries to minimise exposure to risk.

17.2

	Canada		Norway	
Spot	2.3341 –	2.3356	12.8600 –	12.8700
Forward points	−33	−21	+274	+395
F/ward outright	2.3308 –	2.2235	12.8874 –	12.9095

17.3
- Transaction exposure is the risk of loss associated with short-term contractual obligations.
- Translation exposure is the risk of loss when constructing end-of-year financial statements.
- Economic, or Operating, or Strategic, exposure is the risk of the whole value of the firm falling due to adverse foreign exchange rate changes affecting the PV of future cash flows.

17.4 New York price in one year = \$1.50(1.02) = \$1.53
London price in one year = £1.00(1.04) = £1.04
Exchange rate under PPP = (\$1.53/£1.04) = \$1.47 per £1

17.5 Annual interest rate differential of 2.5% = 2.5%/4 over 3 month = 0.625%. This is the interest *agio*.
Forward rate should be Spot less forward *agio* = (£1.4455 × 99.375%) = \$1.4365.
The USD trades at a premium of 90 points.

17.6 Langer's assets are now worth (A\$100 m/2.75) = £36.36 m. If all prices inflate at 7% in Australia, Langer's assets will appreciate to A\$100 m(1.07) = A\$107 m in one year. The AUD vs. GBP exchange rate should become (2.75 × 1.07/1.02) = A\$2.884 per £1. At this rate, the sterling value of these assets = (A4107 m/2.884) = £37.1. This is the level to which they would have appreciated had they been located in Britain and experienced 2% UK inflation i.e. £36.36(1.02) = £37.1 m.

17.7 Leading is advancing outflows in a strong currency and advancing inflows in a weak one. Lagging is delaying inflows in strong currencies and delaying outflows in a weak one.

17.8 There is no point exercising an option 'at the money'. The purchaser simply loses the premium.

Questions

1 *Solution in Appendix A (page 823).* The Local Bank plc quotes the following rates for the euro versus sterling:

1.6296 – 1.6320

(a) How many euros would a firm receive when selling £10 million?
(b) How much sterling would it receive when selling €12 million?

2 *Solution in Appendix A (page 823).* On November 30, a UK exporter sells goods worth £10 million to a French importer on three months' credit. The customer is billed in euros, for which the spot rate versus sterling is €1.6 vs. £1. The three-month forward rate is €1.62 per £1.

(a) What is the amount invoiced?
(b) If the spot rate is €1.7 vs. £1 at the settlement date, what is the exporter's gain or loss, assuming it does not hedge?
(c) If the spot rate is €1.5 vs. £1 at the settlement date, what is the exporter's gain or loss, assuming it does not hedge?
(d) If the exporter takes forward cover, what is the cost of the hedge
  (i) compared to the current spot rate?
  (ii) compared to case **(b)**?
  (iii) compared to case **(c)**?

3 *Solution in Appendix A (page 824).* Work out the forward outrights from the exchange rates versus sterling given in the table below.

Country/Currency	Closing market rates	One month forward rates
Euro	1.6296 – 1.6320	1.0 to 4.0 dis
Japan	175.16 – 175.28	61.0 to 50.0 prem
USA	1.4571 – 1.4576	22.6 to 20.6 prem

Source: *Guardian*, November 10 2001.

4 A selected bundle of goods costs £100 in the UK, and a similar bundle costs 1200 krona (DKR) in Denmark.

People generally expect the rate of inflation to be 5 per cent in the UK and 3 per cent in Denmark.

(a) Assuming that PPP applies, what is the current exchange between GBP and DKR?
(b) Assuming that PPP will continue to hold, what spot exchange rate would you predict for twelve months hence?
(c) Again assuming PPP, what exchange rate should be quoted for three-month forward transactions?

5 *Solution in Appendix A (page 824).* The respective interest rates in the USA and the UK are 9 per cent and 10 per cent respectively in annual terms. If the spot exchange rate is US$1.6000 to £1, what is the forward rate if IRP applies?

6 *Solution in Appendix A (page 824).* Assume you are the treasurer of a multinational company based in Switzerland. Your company trades extensively with the USA. You have just received US$1 million from a customer in the USA. As the company has no immediate need of capital you decide to invest the money in either US$ or Swiss Francs for 12 months. The following information is relevant:

- The spot rate of exchange is CHF1.3125 to US$1.
- The 12-month forward rate is CHF1.275 to US$1.

- The interest rate on a 1-year Swiss Franc bond is $4\frac{9}{16}$ per cent.
- The interest rate on a 1-year US$ bond is $7\frac{5}{8}$ per cent.

Assume investment in either currency is risk-free and ignore transaction costs.

Required

Calculate the returns under both options (investing in US$ or Swiss Francs) and explain why there is so little difference between the two figures.

Your answer may be expressed either in $US or in Swiss Francs.

(CIMA May 1998)

7 The following situation is observed in the money markets.

Sterling: US dollar exchange rates:

	Spot	$1.6550–1.6600
	Forward (1 Year)	$1.6300–1.6450
Interest rates (fixed):	New York	$5\frac{1}{2}$%–$5\frac{1}{4}$%
	London	$5\frac{3}{4}$%–$5\frac{5}{8}$%

(a) Calculate *both* the interest and the exchange agios.
(b) Using the figures provided, investigate whether an arbitrageur operating in London could profit from covered interest arbitrage.

Notes:

(a) Assume he borrows £100,000.
(b) You may ignore commission and transaction costs other than the spreads.

8 Europa plc is a UK-based import–export company. It is now 15 May and the following transaction has been agreed:

The sale of pine furniture worth $1,250,000 to the USA receivable on 15 August.

$/£ FX rates	
Spot	1.6480–1.6490
2 months forward	0.88–0.76c premium
3 months forward	1.30–1.24c premium
Three-month money market interest rates	
	£10%–8%
	$8%–6%

Required

(a) Hedge Europa's risk exposure on the forward market.
(b) Hedge Europa's risk exposure on the money market.
(c) Which is the more favourable hedge from Europa's point of view?

9 Slade plc is a medium-sized UK company with export and import trade links with US companies. The following transactions are due within the next six months. Transactions will be in the currency specified.

Purchase of components, cash payment due in 3 months:	£116,000
Sale of finished goods, cash receipt due in 3 months:	$197,000

Purchase of finished goods for resale, cash payment due in 6 months:		$447,000
Sale of finished goods, cash receipt due in 6 months:		$154,000
Exchange rates quoted on London market		
		$/£
Spot		1.4106–1.4140
3 months forward		0.82–0.77
6 months forward		1.39–1.34
Interest rates (annual)		
3 months or 6 months	Borrowing	Lending
Sterling	7.5%	4.5%
Dollars	6.0%	3.0%

Required

Calculate the *net* sterling receipts which Slade might expect for both its three and six month transactions if it hedges foreign exchange risk on:

(a) the forward foreign exchange market;
(b) the money market.

10 Exchange-traded foreign currency option prices in Philadelphia for dollar/sterling contracts are shown below:

	Sterling (£12,500) contracts			
	Calls		Puts	
Exercise price ($)	**December**	**September**	**December**	**September**
1.90	5.55	7.95	0.42	1.95
1.95	2.75	3.85	4.15	3.80
2.00	0.25	1.00	9.40	–
2.05	–	0.20	–	–

Option prices are in cents per £. The current spot exchange rate is $1.9405–$1.9425/£.

Required

Assume that you work for a US company that has exported goods to the United Kingdom and is due to receive a payment of £1,625,000 in three months' time. It is now the end of June.

Calculate and explain whether your company should hedge its sterling exposure on the foreign currency option market if the company's treasurer believes the spot rate in three months' time will be:

(a) $1.8950–1.8970/£
(b) $2.0240–2.0260/£ (ACCA)

11 A professional accountancy institute in the UK is evaluating an investment project overseas in Eastasia, a politically stable country. The project involves the establishment of a training school to offer courses on international accounting and management topics. It will cost an initial 2.5 million Eastasian dollars (EA$) and it is expected to earn post-tax cash flows as follows:

Year	1	2	3	4
Cashflow (EA$000)	750	950	1,250	1,350

The following information is available:

- The expected inflation rate in Eastasia is 3 per cent a year.
- Real interest rates in the two countries are the same. They are expected to remain the same for the period of the project.
- The current spot rate is EA$2 per £1 sterling.
- The risk-free rate of interest in Eastasia is 7 per cent and in the UK 9 per cent.
- The company requires a sterling return from this project of 16 per cent.

(CIMA)

Required

Calculate the sterling net present value of the project using *both* the following methods:

(a) by discounting annual cash flows in sterling,
(b) by discounting annual cash flows in Eastasian $.

12 *Solution in Appendix A (page 824).* Hogan plc exports computer components valued at 28 million Australian dollars (AUD) to Dundee Proprietary in Australia on three months credit. The current spot exchange rate is A$2.80 vs. £1. Because of recent volatility in the foreign exchange markets, Hogan's directors are worried that a fall in the AUD could wipe out their profits on the deal. Three alternative hedging strategies have been suggested:

(i) using a forward market hedge
(ii) using a money market hedge
(iii) using an option hedge.

Hogan's treasurer discovers the following information:

- The three-month forward rate is A$2.805 vs. £1
- Hogan could borrow in AUD at 9 per cent interest (annual rate).
- A three-month American put option to sell A$28 million at an exercise rate of A$2.81 vs. £1 could be purchased at a premium of £200,000 on the London OTC option market.

Required

Show how each hedge would operate, assuming the following spot rates apply in three months' time:

(a) A$2.78 vs. £1
(b) A$2.82 vs. £1.

Practical assignment

Many companies experience accounting problems in recording overseas transactions and in translating foreign currency values into their accounts. Select a company involved in international trade. Examine its report and accounts to determine its policy with regard to foreign exchange, and the extent of foreign currency losses or gains for the year concerned. Do you think these were 'real money' losses or gains, or merely accounting entries?

PART V

Strategic financial decisions

Financial managers face two key decisions: which assets to invest in and how to finance them? Earlier in the book, we discussed strategic investment decisions, and we examined short-term finance in Part IV.

Also in Part IV, there was strong emphasis on the 'Golden Rule' of financing – that long-term assets should be financed by long-term sources of finance (although we did encounter alternative stances). It is now appropriate to look at methods of financing long-term investments, i.e. long-term sources of finance. This is done in Chapter 18.

Choices between alternative forms of finance essentially reduce to choices between different mixes of borrowing and equity capital in the firm's capital structure. We therefore examine, in Chapter 19, the factors that determine a firm's dividend policy – a decision to distribute higher dividends has implications for the debt/equity mix, but there are important constraints on dividend policy.

In Chapters 20 and 21, we examine how the use of borrowed funds can affect the value of the company and the return required on new investments. Chapter 20 presents the 'traditional' view on these issues, while Chapter 21 presents the 'modern' theory of capital structure, which emphasises the essential underlying relationships. We will also discover how borrowing affects the Beta coefficient, and how to tackle cases of investment evaluation where a firm alters its gearing and its (systematic) risk. We extend the analysis to cover interactions between investment and financing decisions and develop a decision rule – the adjusted present value – to handle complex interactions.

In Chapter 22, we examine mergers and takeovers – why they occur, how they are financed, and the effects they have on organisational structure and shareholder wealth. Other forms of restructuring are also considered.

583 Long-term finance

626 Returning value to shareholders: the dividend decision

662 Capital structure and the required return

706 Does capital structure really matter?

741 Acquisitions and restructuring

18 Long-term finance

Joining the Jet set

Jet Airways, set up in 1992, is one of the fastest growing airlines in the world, having rapidly eroded the market share of state-run market leader Indian Airlines, a chronic loss-maker. Jet's 42 per cent of the Indian market, by 2001 made it India's second largest airline, operating 215 flights daily to 39 cities.

Jet's strategy involves further expansion within India and, if the government permits, developing overseas destinations in South-East Asia, China and the Arabian Gulf. At present, only state-run airlines are allowed to operate outside India but privatisation is expected to herald more general deregulation. To support its growth plans, Jet is acquiring 13 new aircraft – 10 new Boeing 737s, in a package worth $400 million, financed 85 per cent by debt – plus three smaller turbo-prop. aircraft for flying feeder routes.

In December 2000, Jet borrowed $15 million from the International Finance Corporation, a subsidiary of the World Bank, via cumulative redeemable preference shares, convertible into equity. Counting this as debt, and including Boeing-related borrowings to date, Jet's debt-equity ratio stood at 4:1 at July 2001.

With such rapid past and expected future growth and on a narrow equity base of only $25 million, financing needs careful attention and planning if funding needs are not to become a constraint on growth. To help square the financing circle, Jet announced plans to raise between $150 and $250 million via a private equity placing, aimed at both domestic and foreign financial institutions. Jet denies any firm plans to make a public flotation of shares, but 'did not rule that out in the future to create an exit route for investors buying a stake through the private placement'.

This chapter describes the range of long-term financial avenues which Jet Airways might consider.

Learning objectives

After reading this chapter, you should understand the following:

- The key characteristics of the main forms of long-term finance.
- The benefits and drawbacks of each capital form.
- The factors that influence the choice between the various forms.

18.1 Introduction

The next four chapters analyse the factors which determine a firm's long-term financing decisions. Before we can do this, it is important to present the main sources of finance and their essential characteristics. With an understanding of the pros and cons of different financial instruments, the reader will more fully appreciate the choices open to companies and the pressures that drive their choices.

The basic distinction in long-term financing is that between debt and equity, or, more accurately, between the various forms of debt and the various forms of equity. In recent years, the demarcation line between debt and equity has become increasingly blurred by the development of '**hybrid**' forms of finance, such as warrants and convertibles, as companies and their advisers have sought to exploit the advantages of each form of capital without incurring all the disadvantages.

In 1994, the UK accounting authorities issued a standard, FRS4 Capital Instruments, designed to clarify these differences and to offer guidance to companies in constructing and presenting their Balance Sheets. FRS4 divides capital instruments into debt and shareholder funds. Debt is any instrument that creates a liability, including the right to demand cash or shares at some future date. Shareholder funds are instruments that are not debt. These are split into equity and non-equity interests: broadly, ordinary shares and preference shares respectively.

18.2 Guiding lights: corporate aims and corporate finance

Strategists often divide companies into two categories: niche and global. A **niche company** sells high-quality products at a price that offers healthy profits. Such companies exist by exploiting a product differentiation advantage. A **global company** is able to compete in world markets with leading international firms by exploiting its own products at a competitive cost of production. Global companies thus combine product and cost advantages.

Not all companies aspire to global status; some are run by the proprietor to provide a livelihood for his or her family. Such **proprietorial companies** rarely offer sufficient potential to interest outside investors. Conversely, the **entrepreneurial company** has high growth potential and is driven by the desire of the owners to generate substantial wealth – in crude terms, to be 'seriously rich'.

Yet the predominant motive of many entrepreneurs is not money but the creative urge, the desire to build a thriving company, often for dynastic purposes. However, for the owners of such companies to realise their full potential, most eventually have to offer a share of the action to external participants, thus relinquishing a degree of control. Selling shares of equity involves releasing voting rights (it is possible to issue non-voting shares, but the Stock Exchange bans these for companies seeking a listing), and exposing the company's operations to outside scrutiny. Issuing debt usually involves some form of restrictive covenant over company financial policy, such as limits on subsequent borrowing and on dividend policy.

We now examine a short case showing a firm in roughly the same situation as Jet Airways to give a flavour of the strategic dimension of long-term financing.

Mitre Ltd: strategic financing issues

Mitre is a young, rapidly growing company, operating in the highly competitive computer software market. Its directors are the five founder members, all former employees of a giant US-owned computer manufacturer. All five found that 'working for a master' inhibited their creative energies. The company was set up on a shoestring, using the personal financial resources of the founders, supplemented by small inputs of capital from trusting close friends and relatives. After two years of struggle in rented premises, without paying its owners a salary, it managed to show an operating profit, on the basis of which it persuaded the local bank to extend overdraft facilities.

In subsequent years, Mitre has financed its operations through ploughing back the bulk of its profits, by further borrowing from the bank and by taking as much trade credit as possible from suppliers. It expects further rapid growth in the next few years, but is most concerned to avoid the problems of overtrading. It is, therefore, seeking to obtain long-term funding to support this growth.

Choosing the financing mix of short- and long-term debt and equity that best meets the investment requirements of a business is a key element of financial management. Four strategic issues need to be addressed.

Risk

How uncertain is the environment in which the business operates? How sensitive is it to turbulence in the economy? Mitre Ltd would probably be viewed by potential investors as having relatively high risk, particularly if the existing level of borrowing was high. Such a company will probably have a relatively inflexible cost structure, at least in the short term. As most of its costs will be fixed (unless it subcontracts work), it exhibits a high level of **operating gearing**.

Ownership

A major injection of equity capital by financiers would dilute the control currently exercised by the founder members/directors. The desire to retain control of the company's activities may well make them prefer to borrow.

Duration

The finance should match the use to which it is put. If, for example, Mitre Ltd required finance for an investment in which no returns were anticipated in the early years, it might be desirable to raise capital that has little, if any, further drain on cash flow in these years. Conversely, it would be unwise for Mitre Ltd to raise long-term finance if the projects to be funded have a relatively short life. This could result in the business being over-capitalised, and unable to generate returns sufficient to service and repay the finance.

Debt capacity

If Mitre Ltd has a low level of borrowing at present, it has a greater capacity to raise debt than a similar firm with a higher borrowing level. However, debt capacity is not just a function of current borrowing levels, but also depends on factors such as the type of industry, and the security that the company can offer. An important benefit of borrowing is that the interest paid attracts tax relief and, hence, lowers effective financing charges, although this advantage can only be exploited when the company is profitable.

18.3 How companies raise finance in practice

The financial manager can raise long-term funds internally, from the company's cash flow, or externally, via the capital market – the market for funds of more than a year to maturity. This exists to channel finance from persons and organisations with temporary cash surpluses to those with, or expecting to have, cash deficits. A critical intermediary function is provided by the major institutions such as pension funds, insurance companies and various types of bank. These collect relatively small savings and channel them to companies and other organisations seeking capital. As a result, the institutions are now the major holders of securities, both debt and equity, issued by companies.

The record of business financing patterns over the past 50 years or so shows several clear features:

- The majority of funds comes from internal sources – retained earnings and depreciation provisions (more strictly, cash flow), depending on company profitability and dividend policies.

- Bank borrowing plays a major role but is highly volatile, even negative in some years as firms repay debt. Firms tend to use bank finance as a buffer – borrowing heavily when interest rates are low and repaying when rates rise.
- Sales of shares on the New Issue Market are relatively unimportant, although many firms try to exploit high and rising stock markets by making rights issues.
- Long-term debt issues are also small contributors, as are preference share issues.

We now consider the main forms of raising long-term finance to cast some light on these trends. In Chapters 20 and 21, we will examine several theories that attempt to explain firms' long-term financing decisions.

Self-assessment Activity 18.1

What impact might the events of September 11 2001 have on corporate financing decisions?

(answer at end of chapter)

18.4 Shareholders' funds

Ordinary shares

Share ownership lies at the heart of modern capitalism. By purchasing a portion or 'share' of the ownership of a firm, an investor becomes a shareholder with some degree of control over a company. A share is therefore a 'piece of the action' in a company. When a company is formed, its **Articles of Association** will specify how many ordinary shares it is authorised to issue. This maximum can be varied only with the agreement of ordinary shareholders. Meanwhile, the issued share capital is the cornerstone of a company's capital structure. Ordinary shareholders carry full rights to participate in the business through voting in general meetings. They are entitled to payment of a dividend out of profits and ultimately repayment of capital in the event of liquidation, but only after all other claims have been met. As owners of the company, the ordinary shareholders bear the greatest risk, but also enjoy the fruits of corporate success in the form of higher dividends and/or capital gains.

Authorised and issued share capital

The accounts for Scottish Power plc (**www.scottishpower.com**) as at March 31 2001 showed:

Authorised	**£m**
3,000,000,000 ordinary shares of 50p each	1,500.0
Allotted, called up and fully paid	
1,849,025,792 ordinary shares of 50p each	924.5

Scottish Power thus has scope to issue about a further 1.15 billion shares without seeking amendment to its Articles. Notice that share capital in recorded in the accounts at par value.

When ordinary shares are first issued, they are given nominal or par values. For example, a company could issue £5 million ordinary share capital in a variety of configurations, such as 10 million shares at a nominal value of £0.50 each, or 500,000 shares of £10 each. The main consideration is marketability. Investors tend to view shares with lower nominal values (e.g. 50p) as more easily marketable, particularly when, after a few years, shares often trade well above their nominal value. The most common unit nowadays is 25p. Issued share capital appears on the Balance Sheet at its par value, which explains why it often seems a minor item. For example, Tomkins' issued share capital (it refers to this as 'called-up share capital', i.e. issued and paid for), denominated in 5p units, accounts for only £60 million (8 per cent) of shareholder capital. However, the market value of these shares (August 2002) was considerably higher than the par value, at 220p each.

Once a company is established, its shares usually trade above the basic par value. A company wanting to sell new shares is therefore likely to issue them not at their nominal value, but at a **premium**. Share premium forms an integral part of the share capital, £90 million (4 per cent) in the case of Tomkins. Most companies are limited liability companies incorporated under the Companies Acts. This implies that the owners (or shareholders) have obligations limited to the amount they have invested. If the company were ever wound up or liquidated, leaving outstanding debts, the shareholders would not be liable to meet such claims. Limited liability companies in the UK with a capitalisation over £50,000 and shares held by the public are termed public liability companies and denoted by the letters 'plc'. Public status does not necessarily mean that their shares are quoted on a stock exchange.

Preference shares

According to FRS 4, preference shares also constitute part of shareholders' funds – designated 'non-equity shareholders' funds', as they are hybrids falling between pure equity and pure debt. Holders receive an annual dividend, usually a fixed percentage of the par value. Holders also have preferential rights over ordinary shareholders. Preferred dividends are paid before ordinary share dividends, and preference capital precedes ordinary share capital when assets are sold in a liquidation and the proceeds distributed.

They normally carry no voting rights except in the case of a proposed liquidation or a takeover, or when the company passes the dividend. Preference share dividends do not qualify for tax relief. This lack of a tax shield explains why preference shares are relatively unattractive to companies compared to other forms of fixed rate security. They may have some appeal to risk-averse investors looking for a relatively reliable income stream and a limited degree of participation in company affairs.

Types of preference share

Firms can issue many varieties of preference share. For example, the accounts of Tomkins plc for 2001 showed:

Convertible cumulative preference shares:	£337 million
Redeemable convertible cumulative preference shares:	£427 million

The respective dividend rates on these shares are 5.56 per cent and 4.34 per cent of their par values. Both shares have US dollar-denominated par values ($50), but are expressed on the Balance Sheet at their equivalent sterling values.

The labels have the following meanings:

- **Convertible** means that the preference shares can be converted into ordinary shares at some future date. In this case, both securities can be converted at any time at the holders' option into fully paid ordinary shares on the basis of 9.77 ordinary shares of par value 5p each for every convertible preference share.
- **Cumulative** means that if a dividend is passed (i.e. not paid), it will be carried forward for payment at some future date.
- **Redeemable** means that holders will eventually be repaid their capital, usually at par, and sometimes at a date chosen by the firm. Tomkins' redeemable preference shares that remain unconverted will be redeemed in July 2006.

Some preference shares are **'participating'**. In an exceptionally good year, the directors may decide to declare an extra dividend for preference shareholders above the regular fixed return, i.e. holders participate in the profits otherwise attributable to ordinary shareholders.

Maybe one can now appreciate why these are called hybrids – they can exhibit characteristics of both equity and debt, but the question often arises as to which they *most* resemble, for example, when calculating gearing ratios. The answer really depends on what type of preference share we are dealing with, and the strength of the commitment made to investors:

- If they are cumulative, so that a passed dividend will eventually be paid, they resemble debt more than equity.
- If convertible, and the conversion date is near, they look more like equity than debt.
- If redeemable, they look more like debt.
- If participating, they look more like equity.

At one extreme, non-cumulative, convertible, irredeemable, participating preference shares look very much like equity, while the cumulative, convertible, redeemable, non-participating variety look very much like debt. However, there is plenty of room along the spectrum for preference shares with less clear-cut combinations of features.

Reserves

The share premium account is an example of a reserve. It is a common mistake to assume that reserves represent cash balances. Some reserves may once have had a cash counterpart, but this will almost certainly already have been re-invested in wealth-creating assets such as plant and machinery, stocks and debtors. In addition to share premium, reserves are created to account for profits retained from the recently ended and preceding years. These may be called revenue reserves, retained earnings or, simply, Profit and Loss Account, to indicate their origin. This reserve sets the limit on the amount of dividend that a company can pay.

A **revaluation reserve** is created when a revaluation of assets reveals a surplus – without such a reserve to represent enhanced value of the shareholders' stake, the Balance Sheet would not balance.

Internal finance, including retained profits, provides the main source of new capital for companies in general. This is partly because it is less costly than selling new shares, as it avoids expensive issuing costs. It may seem that retained earnings are a free source of finance and far more attractive to management than, say, raising interest-bearing loans. However, retention of earnings imposes an opportunity cost – if returned to shareholders by way of dividend, the cash could be invested to yield a return. The cost of retained earnings is therefore the return that could be achieved by shareholders on investments of comparable risk to the company: in other words, the usual cost of equity. However, the cost of using retained earnings can be adjusted as follows to reflect the issue costs saved:

$$\text{cost of retained earnings} = k_{RE} = \frac{\text{normal cost of equity}}{(1 + f)}$$

where f is the percentage costs of issue, or flotation, costs that are avoided.

Self-assessment Activity 18.2

Criticise the following statement made by your marketing director:

'Well, we can always finance the new product development from our reserves.'

(answer at end of chapter)

18.5 Methods of raising equity finance

It is useful to make a distinction between companies not quoted on the Stock Exchange and those which are listed. A listing opens up far greater access to capital of all kinds, and to a wider pool of shareholders. This is one reason why many private and other unquoted companies aspire to an eventual listing.

Unquoted companies

The supply of equity to an unquoted company depends partly on its size and partly on its stage of development. Most new companies find it virtually impossible to raise equity finance except of a 'personal' nature, i.e. from supportive friends and relatives. Some venture capitalists (see below) will provide start-up finance for highly promising activities, but most invariably look for a track record on the part of the entrepreneur(s). Until this is established, such companies need to rely on additional supplies of personal finance and retained earnings for further equity.

Having established some sort of record of operating success and potential, further avenues open up. Among these are the following.

Business angels

A business angel is a private equity investor with spare funds to invest who wishes to gamble on the future prospects of young companies, often start-ups, managed by entrepreneurs lacking a track record but possessing a good idea plus enthusiasm. Angels are motivated partly by the prospect of riches and partly out of a desire to nurture the spirit of entrepreneurship. Bank of England data suggests that 20,000 angels invest some £1 billion in 6,000 UK firms each year. Unlike venture capitalists, which typically seek an exit in 3–5 years, angels tend to invest for much longer periods. However, despite attractive tax relief (see below) angel investment is not for the faint-hearted. Mason and Harrison (1999) estimate that angels lose money in 40 per cent of their investments and make returns exceeding 50 per cent in less than a quarter of them.

Several networks or 'marriage bureaux' are designed to bring together prospective investors who seek high returns but are prepared to tolerate a high risk of total loss and entrepreneurs needing capital and prepared to release an equity stake. Many are localised, and some are highly informal, operated by accountants and solicitors; others are more organised. The largest, and most formal, network designed to introduce capital-hungry entrepreneurs to wealthy individuals is the National Business Angels Network (NBAN), claiming to act for over 6,000 firms. It was formed in 1999 by the major high street banks and leading firms of solicitors and accountants. Backed by the Department of Trade and Industry, it grew out of the former Local Investment Networking Company (LINC), that had operated for ten years, and absorbed the NatWest Bank's own scheme, Network Angels, set up in 1996.

Government-backed schemes

In 1981, the **Business Start-up Scheme** (later named the **Business Expansion Scheme** or **BES**) was introduced to assist small, newly-formed and hence high-risk companies to raise equity finance, and extended to include existing companies in 1983. Investors could invest up to £40,000 p.a. in such companies and qualify for relief from income tax and also capital gains tax on disposal of shares if held for five years.

The BES had only modest success in its early years, but grew rapidly in the late 1980s and early 1990s after it was extended to include investment in companies investing in residential property on short leasehold terms. This shift was ostensibly to increase the supply of rented accommodation to encourage greater labour mobility. Whereas orthodox companies were restricted to raising just £0.5 million p.a. under the BES, residential property companies were allowed to raise up to £5 million p.a. This change spawned an upsurge in speculative property schemes, and because it became clear that company sponsors were using the BES primarily as a tax avoidance device, it was abolished as from December 1993.

It was superseded in January 1994 by the **Enterprise Investment Scheme** (EIS) with similar objectives to the original version of the BES, but offering less attractive tax reliefs. Investors may invest up to £150,000 in any tax year in qualifying companies, receive relief from Income Tax at 20 per cent and freedom from Capital Gains Tax if the investment is held for three years. Unlike the old BES, losses realised under the scheme are allowable against Income Tax. Companies cannot raise more than £1 million under the scheme in any one tax year.

Venture Capital Trusts (VCTs) are a form of investment trust set up specifically to provide equity capital to small and growing companies. To attract investors concerned at the high risks of EIS companies, VCTs offer investors a wider spread of investments than is possible under the EIS, thus operating in a similar way to orthodox investment trusts. Tax reliefs are similar to those available under the EIS, although dividends received from VCTs are free from income tax. The VCT can only invest up to £1 million in any one company in any calendar year, no more than 15 per cent of its funds in each company and each company assisted cannot have gross assets of more than £10 million. The VCT itself must be quoted on the Stock Exchange.

According to PriceWaterhouseCoopers, between 1995 and mid-2000, 43 VCTs raised over £950 million from private investors for investment in 517 companies. This included £121 million in 125 AIM companies.

Corporate venturing

The CBI describes corporate venturing as: 'a formal, direct relationship usually between a larger, and an independent smaller company, in which both contribute financial management or technical resources, sharing risks and rewards equally for mutual growth'. The larger partner (e.g. Shell) aims to foster the development of the small firm for a variety of reasons, partly altruistic. The arrangement can take a number of forms. The two parties could simply agree to cooperate in joint distribution or production, they could form a joint venture and/or the major company could take a minority equity stake in the small firm and inject cash into it. Aside from idealistic notions of nurturing the capitalist ethic, there are sound business reasons behind developing such links. For example:

- the large firm can tap into innovative R&D at low cost
- it may be able to use spare managerial capacity for training purposes
- it may develop a new source of supply
- it may gain access to a new market.

The UK government provides fiscal incentives to encourage corporate venturing under the **Corporate Venturing Scheme**, for example, Corporation Tax relief at 20 per cent on corporate venturing investments in new ordinary shares held for at least three years, and tax relief for capital losses on disposals of shares.

Venture capital

Venture capital (VC) is funding mainly for the development of existing companies with sound management and high growth potential, but sometimes for especially attractive start-ups. Funds are usually provided in large packages (typically over £250,000) of debt and equity, split this way partly to offer a degree of security, but mainly to allow the VC company to participate in any major success. VC companies will be hoping for an eventual flotation of the companies they assist, are usually prepared to see their investments 'locked in' for five to ten years, but will anticipate an annualised return of 30 per cent or more. VC companies often provide managerial assistance, and some (e.g. the biggest VC company, 3i, itself a listed company following its own Stock Exchange flotation in 1994) reserve the right to place their own appointee on the Board of Directors, although this is infrequently done.

VC companies fall into two groups: **independent companies** and **captive firms**. Independent funds are set up by private venture capitalists, raising funds from a variety of sources to invest in projects for a specified time and then to liquidate the investments. Captive funds are subsidiaries of major financial institutions, such as banks and insurance companies, set up to channel a portion of their capital into risky enterprises. VC companies are often criticised for their preoccupation with the south-east of England. An exception is the Leeds-based company Capital for Companies Ltd, a captive offshoot of stockbrokers BW Rensburg.

In recent years, VC organisations have devoted more of their energies and funding to large **management buy-out (MBO)** investments, rather than concentrating on smaller and riskier start-up and development capital. In an MBO the existing management of a company undertakes to purchase the firm from the present owners. Most MBOs involve managers buying out an unwanted, often underperforming, subsidiary from a larger parent, which feels that the business unit no longer fits its strategy. Exceptionally, the buy-out may involve taking an existing quoted company off the Stock Exchange, usually financed by large amounts of debt, but with equity provided by the managers, who themselves borrow heavily to provide these funds. There is an element of '**moral hazard**' here – managers wishing to buy out a company or division may be tempted to depress its performance so as to lower the price they need to pay to acquire it.

Moreover, there is a problem of **information asymmetry** – managers are far better able to judge the value of a company or operating unit than an outside analyst or the head office of a larger company.

Nevertheless, given the structure of the funding arrangements, the managers of MBOs are under considerable pressure to perform in order to service debts out of cash flow and to enhance the values of their own equity stake (and that of the venture capitalist). Many VC firms find the risk–return prospects of these deals more appealing than those of orthodox businesses. This is largely because the time taken before the venture capitalist can make an exit is usually much shorter.

In a **management buy-in** (MBI), an outside group of managers buys a stake in an existing company and assumes managerial responsibility for its operation. MBIs are largely financed in the same ways as MBOs, and occur for the same motives.

Private placing (or 'placement')

Private placing is a means whereby well-established companies can widen their shareholder base without going for a Stock Exchange listing. It is arranged through a stockbroker or issuing house, which buys the shares and then 'places' them with (i.e. sells them to) selected clients.

Piercing the jargon

Venture capitalists, suspended between the worlds of heady financiers and down-to-earth businessmen, have developed their own incomprehensible jargon. Here's an introduction to the terms that make their hearts beat faster:

Business plan: needed to apply for financing. A good plan should outline the business opportunity, the management's track record, the company's past and present performance, market demand, competition and trends, the structure of the company and the shareholders, long-term plans and goals, and the proposed role of venture capital (how much and what for). See *Due diligence*.

Control: one of the most hotly debated topics. Even where venture capitalists have a minority share, they want to be able to influence and/or have veto rights over decisions on strategy, like taking out credits, setting up subsidiaries or signing licensing agreements. This issue often creates conflict with entrepreneurs, but venture capitalists disagree among themselves as to whether control requires a majority share or just a good shareholders' agreement, and where the balance lies between supporting and stifling the entrepreneurial spirit. See *Hands on*.

Deal flow: the number and quality of applications for investment that come to the venture capitalist. Deal flow can come from referrals (banks, accountants, advisory services), walk-ins, or from hard work pounding the streets.

Development capital: also known as expansion capital. Venture capital financing used for expansion of an already established company.

Due diligence: several months of scrutiny designed to dig up all the necessary information for evaluating the business plan and establishing whether the entrepreneur is a solid investment.

Exit: the all-important sale of the shareholding in a company which enables the venture capitalist to (at least) recoup his investment and pacify his investors. Most exits in Central Europe will be by trade sale, but some might be by management buy-out or flotation on the stock market – or by write-off, if the investment is a disaster. The usual time-frame for exit is around five years, meaning there has been very little so far in the region.

Continued

Hands on: what most venture capitalists in Central Europe claim to be. It means that they're not interested in a passive shareholding but want to support the management with expertise, usually in marketing, finding export partners, or in financial planning.

Living dead: a company that is not a failure but which is making the sort of insignificant profits that make it almost impossible to sell, and even then would yield low returns.

Management buy-out: the purchase of a business by the existing management. The venture capitalist pays proportionately much more for his stake to recognise the value the management brings to the enterprise. Also used to describe a possible exit route, by which the management buys out the venture capitalist's share. The question is: at what price?

Second-round financing: most companies need more than the initial injection of capital, whether to enable them to expand into new markets, develop more production capacity, or to overcome temporary problems. There can be several rounds of financing.

Seed capital: capital used to turn a good idea into a commercially viable product or service; a very risky form of investment, although it generally involves small sums.

Start-up capital: capital used to establish a company from scratch or within the first few months of its existence. Also risky, but with huge returns for the few successes.

Trade sale: the sale of a company (or part of it) to a larger corporation. This is the main source of exits envisaged for Central Europe, but it means that the entrepreneur may have to become an employee or sell out his share.

Venture capital: equity finance in an unquoted, and usually quite young, company to enable it to start up, expand or restructure its operations entirely. It's cheaper than bank finance initially because paying dividends can be deferred; it also provides a strategic partner – but it implies handing over some control, a share of earnings and decisions over future sales.

Source: *Business Central Europe*, February 1995. Reprinted with permission.

Quoted companies

Seeking a quotation: from unquoted to quoted status

Eventually, the unquoted company may require such a large amount of new capital that it may decide to 'go public' by issuing shares through a Stock Exchange. When a firm obtains a listing on a Stock Exchange by selling shares, this is referred to as an **Initial Public Offering (IPO)**. Such issues are managed by sponsors, such as a merchant bank or a member of the Stock Exchange, which advise on aspects such as the timing and the price of the shares to be issued.

To enhance the prospects of a successful IPO, the company ought to show a record of consistent and increasing profitability, and that it is managed by respected, experienced directors. There are numerous other criteria to qualify on the London market (a 'full listing') that must also be satisfied, principally:

- It must provide fully audited accounts covering at least three years.
- It must be an independent business activity that has earned revenue for at least three years.
- The senior management and key directors should not have changed significantly throughout the three-year period, and should possess appropriate expertise and experience.
- If the company has a controlling shareholder, this must not prevent it from operating and making decisions independently.
- At least 25 per cent of the company's ordinary shares must be in public hands after listing.

The Stock Exchange cites a seven-point list of benefits and possible drawbacks involved in obtaining a quotation:

- *Prestige*. Being seen to comply with the rules of the Stock Exchange may enhance the company's standing in the business community. This may lead to better relationships with suppliers, creditors and customers.
- *Growth*. The initial flotation can be used to raise cash, which can be used to lower gearing. Flotation may also lower the cost of using bank facilities. Access to the wider markets can be exploited if the company wishes to raise more finance in the future. Greater marketability of the shares increases the ability to conduct takeovers by offering equity in exchange for the target company's shares.
- *Access*. As well as giving companies greater access to fresh supplies of capital, flotation gives shareholders access to a wider market, enabling existing owners to convert shares into cash and new ones to buy and sell more readily, i.e. it makes the company's shares more liquid.
- *Visibility*. The initial flotation gives the company publicity and more regular coverage by the media as it announces subsequent results. Greater awareness among the securities industry may enhance the ability to raise further capital on favourable terms.
- *Accountability*. Quotation imposes new responsibilities on directors and increases the need to consult shareholders before taking major decisions, such as a major acquisition.
- *Responsibility*. Directors must ensure that the company meets the listing rules of the Exchange, and that price-sensitive information is released in a timely and orderly way, so that every shareholder has equal access to it.
- *Regulation*. The Stock Exchange, as the only competent authority for listing, rigorously screens applications of companies seeking a listing, monitors companies' ongoing compliance with its rules and deals with breaches of its rules.

Source: London Stock Exchange

Fraport's market debut fails to take off

In June 2001, Fraport AG, the operator of Frankfurt International Airport, made an IPO to raise funds for expansion involving a new runway, a third terminal and new retail facilities. Frankfurt is mainland Europe's largest airport hub. 30 per cent of the equity was sold at a price of €35 per share, raising €914 million.

Although the issue was over-subscribed 8.5 times, the shares opened at just a 1 per cent premium, before slipping back to €33, and were selling at €29 a month later. The managers of the issue had been hoping to float the issue at well over €40, but these ambitions were frustrated by generally depressed stock market conditions, concern about local opposition to the expansion programme and a pilot's strike at Lufthansa, Fraport's largest single customer.

The IPO valued Fraport at €3.15 billion making it the world's second biggest airport operator, after BAA plc, valued at €11 billion. BAA operates more airports and also a vastly more extensive range of retail activities, its primary revenue raiser.

Methods of obtaining a listing

There are three main methods of obtaining a quotation on the Stock Exchange: (1) **Offer for sale by prospectus**. Shares are sold to an issuing house, generally a merchant bank, and then are offered at a fixed price to the public at large, including both institutions and private individuals. Application forms and a prospectus, setting out all relevant details of the company's past performance and future prospects, as stipulated by Stock Exchange regulations laid down in 'The Yellow Book', must be published in the national press. An offer for sale is obligatory for issues involving £30 million or more.

Usually such an issue is underwritten, i.e. the issuing house guarantees to buy up any shares not taken up by the public so as to ensure that the company receives the monies required. To spread the risk of being called upon to buy up possibly substantial blocks of shares, the lead underwriter usually makes sub-underwriting arrangements with other financial institutions.

Offers for sale are usually made at a fixed price, which is determined before the offer period based on the expertise and knowledge of the company's financial advisers. There is a tendency to price prospectus issues conservatively to ensure their success – companies whose shares have to be bought up by the underwriters often find it difficult to raise further capital through the Stock Exchange on attractive terms.

A variant on this method is the **issue by tender**, where no prior issue price is announced, but prospective investors are invited to bid for shares at a price of their choosing. The eventual 'striking price' at which shares are sold is determined by the weight of applications at various prices. Essentially, the final price is set by supply and demand. A tender is often used when there is no comparable company already listed to use as a reference point in valuing the company. However, by underlining the uncertainty in valuation, it may deter investors. In a tender, the shares are underwritten at a certain minimum price. This is the most expensive form of issue, although it may be argued that there is less risk of underpricing.

(2) In a **placing**, shares are 'placed', or sold to, institutional investors, such as pension funds and insurance companies, selected by the merchant bank advising the company and the company's stockbroker. In this case, the general public has to wait until official dealing in the shares begins before it, too, can buy the shares. Placings are geared to smaller companies and involve relatively little publicity and, hence, limited expense. Conversely, although placings should aim at securing a wide distribution of shareholdings to promote liquidity on the secondary market, the resulting spread of holdings is inevitably far narrower than with offers for sale.

An **intermediaries offer** is a placing with financial intermediaries, which allows brokers other than the one advising the issuing company to apply for shares. These brokers are allocated shares that they can subsequently distribute to their clients.

(3) **Stock Exchange introduction**. This is applicable when the shares are already widely held, the proportion in public hands already exceeds 25 per cent, and existing shareholders do not intend to dispose of shares at the time of flotation. No money is actually raised from the public – the purpose of the exercise is merely to create a wider market in the company's shares. Because no underwriting is required, and advertising costs are minimal, this is the cheapest form of issue.

Continuing obligations

Once a company is listed, its directors have to obey a strict set of rules in order to safeguard its continued listing. In particular, it must observe the regulations relating to disclosure and directors' dealings.

1 **Disclosure**. A quotation places considerable demands on directors, especially in the release of price-sensitive information about the company's activities. The main occasions on which announcements are required through the Stock Exchange include:
   - major developments in a company's activities, e.g. new products, contracts or customers
   - decisions to pay or pass a dividend
   - preliminary announcements of profits for the year or half-year
   - an acquisition or disposal of major assets
   - a change in directors, or directors' responsibilities
   - decisions to make major capital issues.

2 **Directors' dealings**. Share dealings by the directors of a listed company are subject to the Criminal Justice Act 1993 and the Exchange's 'Model Code for Directors' Dealings', aimed to prevent insider dealing. Directors are precluded from dealing for a minimum period (normally two months) prior to an

announcement of recurrent information such as trading results, or dealing in advance of the announcement of extraordinary events involving the publication of price-sensitive information. Companies whose directors infringe these rules are likely to jeopardise the continued listing of the company and also to sour relationships with investors, especially the financial institutions.

The Alternative Investment Market (AIM)

The AIM was set up by the Stock Exchange in 1995 to replace the declining Unlisted Securities Market. Its purpose is to provide a market for the shares of companies that are too young or too small to qualify for, or benefit from, a full listing. The Exchange organises a service called SEATS PLUS, which displays information about orders to buy and sell shares, to enable matching of buyers and sellers. To qualify for the AIM, companies have to satisfy certain criteria – in the main, less demanding than those of the full market – and to observe certain 'ongoing obligations' regarding the release of key information at appropriate times and the conduct of directors. In addition, the company must appoint and retain a nominated adviser to assist with continuing compliance with the AIM's rules and a nominated broker to organise share transactions. By July 2001, there were 587 companies with an AIM listing with market capitalisation of £12.4 billion.

Equity issues by quoted companies

Once a company has achieved a quotation, it will find it easier to raise further equity, assuming a successful trading and profit record. The commonest method of raising new equity is by a **rights issue** (see below). The Companies Act of 1985 gives existing shareholders the right to subscribe to new share issues in proportion to their existing holdings. This generally rules out a public issue although these **pre-emption rights** can be waived with the agreement of shareholders at a properly convened meeting. With such agreement, a placing may be arranged whereby shares are sold to participating institutions provided that the price involves no more than a 10 per cent discount to the market price.

Shares can also be issued as full or partial consideration when acquiring another company. In some cases, this may be done via a **vendor placing**, or **placing with clawback**. In a vendor placing, the acquiring company places the new shares with a group of institutions, thus diluting the ownership and earnings of existing shareholders. For sufficiently large issues, existing shareholders have the right to reclaim the shares they would have been entitled to, had there been a rights issue. If they do not, they receive no compensation for the loss in value of their holdings as there are no detachable rights to sell (see below).

In view of their importance, we now give detailed consideration to rights issues.

AIM trickle becomes a torrent

A surge in companies listing on AIM last week suggested the gloom that has been hanging over the new issues market since the beginning of the year may be lifting.

Activity in the new issue market was at its lowest level in more than a decade in the first quarter of 2001, according to statistics from KPMG, and only two new issues made it to the Official List.

AIM bucked the main board trend with a steady trickle of small offerings. Last week, however, that flow of issues grew into a stream with a spurt of offerings in sectors ranging from media to window manufacturing. The Moomins landed on AIM on Monday, with the listing of Maverick Entertainment, which owns the intellectual property of children's characters and toys. It is run by John Howson and Michael Diprose, who were involved in marketing Mr Blobby and Wallace and Gromit at the BBC. Shares were issued at 3p and the company, which had a market capitalisation of £4.3 million at listing, raised £1.96 million.

Proactive Sports, which manages footballers such as Andy Cole and Stuart Pearce, listed on AIM on Thursday at 25p. Shares in the company – 3 per cent of which is owned by Kenny Dalglish who also acts as a consultant – rose 62 per cent on Thursday, valuing the company at £40 million.

Proactive was founded in 1990 by Paul Stretford, chief executive, and manages 150 professional footballers. Kevin Moran, finance director, said the timing for the flotation was right despite the problems of other new issues this year. 'Our industry is very different from those sectors which have suffered on the stock market this year like the dotcoms,' he said.

Based on Sarah Ross, *Financial Times*, May 21 2001

Rights issues

Shareholders are granted the right to subscribe for shares (or less commonly, for other types of security) in proportion to their existing holdings, thus enabling them to retain their existing share of voting rights. Apart from the control factor, rights issues have certain other attractions:

1 They are far cheaper than a public share issue. Provided the issue is for less than 10 per cent of the class of capital, there is no need for a **prospectus**, although a brochure must still be made available.
2 They may be made at the discretion of the directors without consent of the shareholders or the Stock Exchange. At one time, a queuing system for all new issues was operated by the government broker, acting for the Bank of England, in order to ensure a measured flow of new securities on to the market.

Nowadays, lead institutions are merely requested to notify the Bank in advance of new issues to enable the Bank to compile a 'calendar' of all forthcoming new issues proposed for £20 million or more.

3 When stock market prices are generally high, companies have been known to raise cash through rights issues and to place it on deposit while seeking suitable candidates for acquisition. Hanson raised over £500 million in this way, in 1985, specifically to finance its planned acquisition programme. This gives a high degree of flexibility in timing a bid, i.e. the cash is already to hand.

4 The finance is guaranteed, either from existing shareholders or from the underwriters. Existing shareholders are given an incentive either to take up their rights or to sell them. It is not a sensible option to do nothing: this effectively reduces their wealth, as shares are typically offered at a discount of about 20 per cent below the current market price. If, as is usual, they are underwritten, the company is guaranteed to receive the cash, although it is embarrassing to have to call upon the underwriters to fulfil their obligations.

The underwriting controversy

The size of underwriting fees and the allegedly uncompetitive way in which contracts are awarded has generated considerable controversy. Typically, companies 'lose' 2 per cent of the monies raised from a new share issue in fees. The lead underwriter, usually the merchant bank handling the issue, takes 0.5 per cent, and the firm's stockbroker 0.25 per cent, with the remaining 1.25 per cent split among the institutional sub-underwriters (who are in many cases shareholders!). Critics of the system argue that costs are higher than they would be if a system of open tender applied. Indeed, rights issues which have involved tendering for the sub-underwriting business have produced lower fees. For example, the construction company Berkeley plc made a rights issue in 1997 incurring sub-underwriting fees of just 0.2 per cent.

In 1997, the Office of Fair Trading instructed the Monopolies and Mergers Commission (MMC) to investigate the fee structure and system of awarding sub-underwriting contracts. In May 1998, the MMC reported that a 'complex monopoly' existed in these areas and identified 28 ways in which it could operate against the public interest. Following the final report of the MMC in 1999, and instructions issued by the Secretary of State for Trade and Industry, the following measures were implemented:

- LSE listing rules were amended to instruct firms to explain fully to shareholders why a share issue is made with less than two-thirds of the sub-underwriting offered for tender.
- The Bank of England published a 'best practice' guide which focused on the use of tendering for sub-underwriting, and on the circumstances in which deep discounts might be advantageous.
- The SFA was instructed to remind its members that they should give client firms all information necessary to make balanced judgements including the alternatives to underwriting at standard fees.

ICI rights priced at 45 per cent discount

Imperial Chemical Industries, the heavily indebted chemicals company, will today issue more than 440 million new shares at 180p a share, in an attempt to cut its £2.9 billion debt burden.

The issue is underwritten by UBS Warburg Merrill Lynch and Goldman Sachs. It will be at a 45 per cent discount to the prevailing share price and at the bottom of the range of analysts' forecasts. It is expected to involve seven new shares for every 11 held and will raise just over £800 million.

Bankers involved in the deal said they had had strong support from the institutional shareholders and there had been no problems with demand. 'The basis of a deeply discounted rights issue is that you have the momentum to get it away and that's what ICI has done', said one banker. 'It's a good deal. The company did not want to be here but they are and they have had the support of their shareholders.' However, one analyst said US shareholders, who hold 30 per cent of ICI, were lukewarm.

When ICI's shares start to trade 'ex-rights' – that is, without the right to buy the new shares at 180p attached – they should fall sharply. On the basis of Friday's close of 324p, the so-called ex-rights price would be 262p to reflect the dilution of the fund raising.

News that ICI was going to announce a rights issue leaked out last week, but the terms of the deal were not fully decided until the weekend, and were being ratified by the board late last night.

ICI is attempting to pre-empt the credit ratings agencies, which have threatened to downgrade its corporate debt to junk bond status. Any downgrade would mean that the cost of servicing existing and future debt would increase.

However there was some criticism from financial analysts that the issue might be too little too late. Martin Evans, the head of European research at Crédit Lyonnais Securities, said although the issue would definitely succeed the company might have missed an opportunity to make larger inroads into its debt. 'ICI should have gone for a greater amount. In the short term it gets the credit rating agencies off their back but it does not resolve the longer term debt problem'.

Based on Peter John, *Financial Times*, February 4 2002

Shareholders' choices in a rights issue: Grow-up plc

Grow-up plc decides to make a rights issue of one new share for every three held. The share price prior to the issue is 200p and the new shares are to be offered at 160p. In practice, rights issues are made at a discount, partly to make them **look** attractive and thus encourage shareholders to subscribe, and partly to safeguard against the risk of a fall in the market price during the offer period.

The **theoretical ex-rights price (TERP)** *is the price at which shares are expected to trade after the rights issue has been completed.* It is calculated below at 190p:

	Effect of a 1-for-3 rights issue	
Before	3 old shares prior to rights issue at 200p each:	600p
	1 new share at 160p:	160p
After	4 shares worth:	760p
	1 share is therefore worth (760p ÷ 4) = TERP =	190p

The value of the rights is the difference between the pre-rights share price and the TERP. In the case of Grow-up plc this is (200p − 190p) = 10p for every existing share held, or (190p − 160p) = 30p for every new share. This 30p is termed the '**nil paid price of rights**'. The first option for shareholders is to sell their rights, obtaining 10p per share, less any costs. A shareholder with 3,000 shares in the company would have a holding with market value prior to the rights issue of (3,000 × £2) = £6,000. After the issue, the value will fall to (£3,000 × £1.90) = £5,700, a decline of £300, which is the amount he or she would receive for the rights sold (1,000 new shares × 30p).

The second option is to subscribe for the new shares by *taking up the rights.* This should happen only if the shareholder has the resources to acquire the additional shares and believes this is the best way to invest such money. Additional reasons for taking up the rights are the fact that no stamp duty or broker's commission is payable, and the desire to maintain one's existing share of voting power.

A third option is to *sell sufficient of the rights to provide the cash to take up the balance.* This option known as 'tail-swallowing' makes sense for shareholders who want to maintain their existing investment in the company in value terms.

The formula for calculating the number of shares is:

$$\frac{\text{Nil paid price}}{\text{Ex-rights price}} \times \text{Number of shares allotted}$$

As noted the *nil paid price* is the difference between the TERP and the subscription price, i.e. (190p − 160p) = 30p. The number of new shares to which our investor with 3,000 existing shares retains acquisition rights is:

$$\frac{30\text{p}}{190\text{p}} \times 1{,}000 = 157 \text{ shares}$$

To buy 157 shares at 160p will cost £251.20, funded from (843/1,000) rights sold at 30p = £252.90. The total investment is now worth (3,157 × 190p) = £5,998, which (when rounded) is equivalent to the original investment of £6,000.

The final option is to *let the rights lapse* by doing nothing. In this case, the company may sell the new shares in the market and, reimburse the shareholder net of dealing fees. Alternatively, as in the BT issue (see below), the issuer may conduct an auction of rights not taken up to avoid the need to appoint underwriters.

The real message from rights issues is that shareholders cannot expect to receive something for nothing. The apparent gain from the invitation to purchase new shares at a discount on the existing price is more illusory than real.

Self-assessment Activity 18.3

What is the TERP in the following case?

- pre-announcement share price = £5.
- rights issue of 1-for-6 at £3.50 issue price

(answer at end of chapter)

The BT rights issue

In 2000, BT, and other leading European telecoms firms, made massive outlays, estimated at around $100 billion, on licences to develop the new generation of mobile phones. Having also taken a string of strategic, but minority, stakes in joint ventures elsewhere, BT's debt ballooned to around £30 billion. Due to increasing doubts about its 'scattergun' strategy and stratospheric gearing at a time when its core domestic market was restricted by regulatory pressures, BT's share price plummeted. By May 2001, it had fallen over 60 per cent from a peak of 1513p in December 1999, against a general market retreat of under 20 per cent. Desperate measures were called for to meet the obvious need to slash debt.

BT began a programme of asset sales, including de-merging its mobile division, BT Wireless, built around its British, Irish, Dutch and German assets. After reporting the first loss since its 1984 privatisation, worsened by a £3 billion write down of investments in Germany, it axed its dividend to staunch cash outflow. On May 10 2001, it launched the biggest ever UK rights issue. Aimed at raising £5.9 billion by selling nearly two billion new shares, the issue more than tripled the previous record, set by media group Pearson plc.

The offer of 3 shares for every 10 held was deeply discounted at 300p to save 'tens of millions' of pounds in underwriting fees. The 47 per cent discount to the previous day's closing price of 566p implied a TERP of 507p. The market reacted savagely – by the close of the offer period, a month later, the share price had cascaded to 434p. However, despite expectations that many investors, especially private shareholders (holding 18 per cent of the equity), would spurn the offer, it was 89.5 per cent subscribed, realising £5.3 billion. The residual 207 million shares were auctioned by BT's merchant bank to fund managers at an average price of 429p. After adding the rights issue proceeds to cash generated from asset sales, BT had already raised some £15 billion, thus halving its debt mountain.

Scrip issues and bonus issues

Whereas a rights issue raises new finance, a **scrip issue** simply gives shareholders more shares in proportion to their existing holdings. As a result, the value of their total holdings is unchanged, but the share price will fall due to earnings dilution. Scrip issues are often used by companies whose unit share price is 'high' – a high or '**heavyweight**' share price (usually £10 or above) is regarded as a deterrent to trading. This was the reason given by the airport operator, BAA plc, in 1994, when it made a 'one-for-one' scrip issue. For every share held, owners were given a free share. According to BAA, 'this will improve the marketability of the company's shares as the increased number of shares in issue should result in a corresponding reduction in share price'.

Companies like BAA have built up substantial reserves by retention of earnings, making their issued share capital look relatively small. In the case of BAA, the issued share capital was £511 million and the revenue reserve was £1,348 million. The effect of the scrip issue was to double the issued share capital and to reduce the revenue reserve by £511 million to £837 million. In other words, BAA converted, or 'capitalised', its reserves into issued share capital, hence the common use of the synonym '**capitalisation issue**'.

Scrip issues do not always involve such a drastic reorganisation of shareholder funds. They are often given as '**bonus issues**' in addition to cash dividends, and are often taken by the market as a signal of higher future dividends. If a company makes, say, a one-for-ten scrip and maintains the dividend per share, this is tantamount to a future increase in dividends of 10 per cent (the new shares do not normally qualify for the dividend immediately). This signifies the company's expectation of greater capacity to pay dividends in the future, i.e. higher future earnings. In such cases, the share price may not fall quite so far as the simple arithmetic may suggest, i.e. by 1/11th, but may even increase as the market responds to the 'signals' emitted by the company.

Share splits ('stock splits' in the USA)

An alternative way of addressing the heavyweight status of a share is to split the ordinary shares into a larger number with lower par value. This was done in 1998 by GKN plc, the engineering group. Prior to the split, GKN ordinary shares had a par value of £1 each, but had recently been trading at around £15. To 'reduce the weight of the share price and to facilitate a more active market in the shares', each £1 ordinary share was subdivided into two new ordinary shares of 50p each. This had no effect on the total book value of GKN's share capital and, of course, no additional funds were raised, leaving net assets, reserves and shareholders' interests in future profits unchanged. GKN proposed that, for the future, the aggregate amount of dividend in respect of every two new 50p shares would be equivalent to the amount that would have been paid on each of the old £1 shares.

Self-assessment Activity 18.4

In a share split, e.g. '2-for-1', what is the effect on:

- the number of shares issued?
- the shareholders' capital in the balance sheet?
- the firm's assets?
- its market value – per share? in total?

(answer at end of chapter)

Equity capital: checklist of key features

For

- No fixed charges (e.g. interest payments). Dividends are paid if the company generates sufficient cash, the level being decided by the directors.
- No repayment is required. It is truly permanent capital.
- In the case of retained profits and rights issues, directors have greater control over the amount and timing, with minimal paperwork or issuing costs.
- It carries a higher return than loan finance and acts as a better hedge against inflation for investors.
- Shares in most listed companies can be easily disposed of at a fair value.

Against

- Issuing equity finance can be cost-effective (as in the case of retained profits or a rights issue), but it is expensive in the case of a public issue (often 5 per cent or more of the finance raised).
- Issuing ordinary shares to new shareholders dilutes the degree of control of existing members.
- Dividends are not tax-deductible, making equity relatively more expensive than borrowing.
- A higher proportion of equity can increase the overall cost of capital for the company (see Chapter 20).
- Shares in unlisted companies are difficult both to value and to dispose of.

18.6 Debt instruments: debentures, bonds and notes

The array of instruments for raising debt finance is even greater than for equity finance. Firms can raise long-term debt via the banking system, e.g. by a term-loan, or via the money and bond markets, by issuing a security that can be traded rather than held to maturity. The money markets supply short-term borrowing while the bond markets supply medium-to-long term finance.

The word 'bond' is a general term used to describe a variety of longer-term loans to companies. In some markets, they are described as '**loan stock**', or, especially where the interest payable is variable, as '**notes**'. A bond is simply a receipt or promise to repay money on a loan, usually with interest i.e. it binds the borrower to a commitment that can range between one and 30 years.

Characteristics of a bond are:

- the nominal or par value in the currency of denomination.
- the redemption value – usually the par value, but other possibilities include a stated premium or index-linking.
- the rate of interest payable – known as the coupon – expressed as a percentage of the nominal value.
- the redemption date.

For example, BAA plc, the UK airports operator, is committed to the following bond:

BAA plc 7.875% 2007 £200 million

The £200 million will be repaid in full in 2007; and £7.875 interest is payable per £100 of stock each year in two stages.

Debentures

In strict legal terms, a debenture is a document acknowledging that the firm has borrowed money, whether or not any security has been given to back the loan. However, in normal business usage, this term is used to describe a loan which is secured on the assets of the company by mortgage deeds – a secured debenture is often called a **mortgage debenture**. If the issuer goes into liquidation, or defaults on interest or capital payments, the holders can apply for a court ruling to order the sale of either specified assets (called a **fixed charge**) or any of the firm's assets (a **floating charge**). The firm cannot dispose of assets subject to a fixed charge without the permission of the creditors.

As regards priority for payment, debts rank in order of issue – holders of the earliest issued debentures must be paid interest before the later comers. Where a firm has issued a series of bonds, a *pari passu* clause is inserted into the document acknowledging the debt. Debentures that rank lower down the priority list are called 'junior' or 'subordinated' stock.

The BAA stock referred to above is unsecured, and thus ranks behind its secured borrowing, but ahead of a number of subsequently-issued unsecured bonds. Unsecured stock is riskier than secured stock and investors thus require a higher coupon rate.

The pejorative term '**junk bond**' is applied to the unsecured loan stock of a borrower that merits sub-investment grade by a bond-rating agency. Standard & Poor's investment grade is BBB or above – any security rated below this 'is regarded as having predominantly speculative characteristics with respect to capacity to pay interest and repay principal'. Obviously, junk carries much higher than average yields, hence the euphemism 'high yield bonds'.

Loan agreements usually specify **restrictive covenants**. Such conditions might include the following:

1 *Dividend restrictions* – limitations on the level of dividends a company is permitted to pay. This is designed to prevent excessive dividend payments, which may seriously weaken the company's future cash flows and thereby place the lender at greater risk.
2 *Financial ratios* – specified levels below which certain ratios may not fall, e.g. debt-to-net-assets ratio, current ratio.

3 *Financial reports* – regular accounts and financial reports to be provided to the lender to monitor progress.
4 *Issue of further debt* – the amount and type of debt that can be issued may be restricted. Subordinated loan stock (i.e. stock ranking below the existing unsecured loan stock) can usually still be issued.
5 *Asset backing* – a specified minimum level of tangible fixed assets.

Debentures and unsecured loan stock: checklist of key features

For

- Most loan stocks give ten or more years before repayment is due. A 'bullet' loan is where there is just one final repayment, and a 'balloon' loan is where increasing amounts of capital are repaid towards the end of the period of the loan. Bullet and balloon loans give attractive cash flow benefits in the early years, where little or no interest is payable.
- A successful company may eventually be able to redeem the loan stock through a new issue, without drawing upon operating cash flows (although the company is exposed to the risk of higher interest rates).
- Interest is tax-deductible.

Against

- Restrictions are placed on the company in terms of either the charge over assets or the restrictive covenants imposed.
- Unsecured loan stock may impose demanding performance requirements.
- Greater monitoring and control takes place over a public issue such as a debenture than with, say, a term loan with a bank.

Deep-discount bonds

Some debt instruments are sold at a price well below the par value, with a so-called deep-discount. An extreme case of this is Zero-coupon bonds, e.g. a bond issued at £70 with a five-year life to maturity when it will be repaid at par of £100. Such bonds carry no entitlement to interest as such, thus appealing to investors who would normally pay Income or Corporation Tax on interest income, but who may not be liable to Capital Gains Tax, or who wish to defer it. The annualised rate of return from the capital gain if held to maturity for the full five years is represented by the rate r in the following compound interest expression:

$$£70\ (1 + r)^5 = £100$$

This can be written as:

$$\frac{1}{(1 + r)^5} = \frac{£70}{£100} = 0.700$$

The discount tables (PVIF) can be used to find r (about 10.75 per cent p.a.).

Self-assessment Activity 18.5

What is the yield to maturity on a zero-coupon bond issued at £50, repayable at par of £100, in ten years' time?

(answer at end of chapter)

Asset-Backed Securities (ABSs) – a new development

In recent years, some companies – and even certain individuals – have issued a new breed of securities, backed not by physical assets but by a reliable long-term stream of future earnings. A category of assets commonly utilised has been intellectual property represented by patents and copyrights. Like most security issues, ABSs are sold essentially to raise cash for investing in other activities.

Organisations effectively *capitalise* their future income into a single lump sum and sell it on the financial markets to generate immediate cash. The firm's financial advisors set up a **Special Purpose Vehicle (SPV)**, as shown on Figure 18.1. This is effectively a 'bank' which handles the bond issue and into

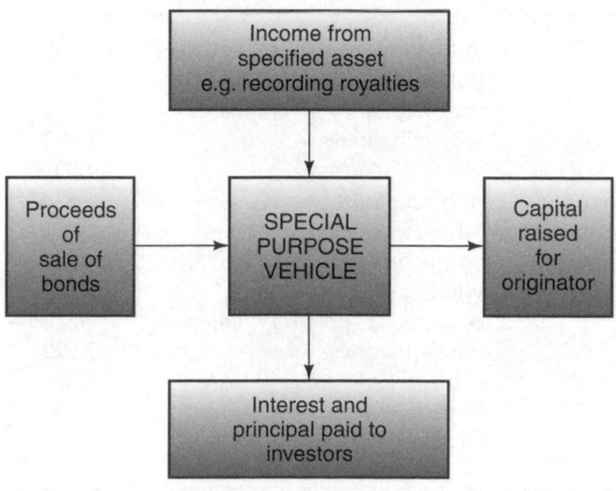

Figure 18.1 How an SPV works

which the designated income stream is paid and from which is paid the stream of interest payments needed to service the borrowing.

This process of converting non-tradable claims into tradable ones is called **securitisation**. Like most financial innovations, securitisation originated in the USA. Banks parcelled up mortgage commitments made by house purchasers into bundles of mortgages to sell as interest-bearing securities, originally known as collateralised mortgage obligations (CMOs). Having both liquidity and a bank's guarantee, these could be offered at a lower interest rate than that charged on the underlying mortgages, the difference representing profit for the bank. This practice is now widespread in Europe, where it is increasingly seen as a cheaper alternative to unsecured bond issues.

The following examples of the ABS principle demonstrate its flexibility and versatility:

- In 1992, the Disney Corporation issued $400 million in seven-year notes with a variable rate of interest to be paid from royalties receivable from its portfolio of film copyrights, a path followed also by News Corporation in 1996.
- Holland's De Nationale Investeringsbank NV (DNIB) is a major player. Its ABS issue in March 1999, worth 290 million Euros, was its fourth inside two years.
- Calvin Klein, GE Capital and Nestle have all issued ABSs secured on trademarks.
- In 1997, David Bowie raised $55 million by selling bonds backed by his music copyright portfolio, with an average bond life of ten years. This tactic was also adopted by Rod Stewart and Michael Jackson, using similar security.

Table 18.1 lists the 14 major ABS issues made in Europe in the first half of 2001.

Table 18.1 European corporate asset-backed deals, Jan.–June 2001

Originator	Asset class	Amount (€m)	Country
Volkswagen Leasing	auto loans and leases	750	Germany
Enterprise Inns	pub revenues	196	UK
Canary Wharf	commercial property leases	189	UK
Eurotunnel	whole business	1,433	UK/France
Foodbrands+	whole business	1,037	UK
Unique Pub Company	pub revenues	528	UK
Sainsbury's Supermarkets	whole business	471	UK
Chantiers de l'Atlantique	whole business	324	France
THPA	whole business	486	UK
ProLogis Trust	commercial property leases	214	Europe
Dwr Cymru	whole business	3,070	UK
Canary Wharf	commercial property leases	1,353	UK
British Land	supermarket leases	935	UK
Telecom Italia	telephone bill receivables	700	Italy

Source: *Euromoney*, July 2001, p. 8.

Convertibles

A convertible begins life as a form of debt, but carries the right, at the holder's option, to convert into ordinary shares at some specified date in the future and on specified terms, e.g. how many new ordinary shares can be obtained on conversion per unit of convertible stock.

Firms which issue convertibles increase their gearing ratios and may be viewed as being more risky. Yet the greater risk is not always reflected in a higher coupon rate. As there is a prospect of making a capital gain should the share price market perform strongly, convertibles can usually be issued at a lower rate of interest than straight or 'plain vanilla' debt. Until the date of conversion, the holder receives a fixed rate of interest and is a long-term creditor of the company.

Convertibles are particularly suitable for companies facing relatively high business risks but strong potential growth because they offer investors the possibility of participating in future prosperity. This explains the ease with which many 'dotcom' companies were able to issue so much convertible debt. The downside for companies is that interest, although tax-deductible, must be paid every year, good or bad, and the principal requires repayment if holders do not convert.

The downside for existing shareholders is the prospect of dilution of their equity, and hence a fall in EPS, as and when conversion occurs. Dilution is especially damaging if the conversion terms are misjudged, e.g. if growth is a lot stronger than expected, the conversion terms may be over-generous to convertible holders. It often makes sense for existing shareholders to hedge against this risk by acquiring the convertibles themselves. Indeed, convertibles may be issued initially to owners in a rights issue.

The language of convertibles

Convertible conversion terms can be complex.

- the **conversion date** (or range of dates) tells you when it can be converted.
- the **conversion rate** tells you the terms on which conversion can be made. This is stated either as a **conversion price** – the nominal value of loan stock that can be converted into one ordinary share – or as a **conversion ratio** – the number of ordinary shares that will be obtained from one unit of loan stock.
- the **conversion value** is the market value of ordinary shares into which a unit of convertible loan stock can be converted. This is equal to the conversion ratio times the current market price per ordinary share.
- the **conversion premium** is the difference between the market price of the convertible and its conversion value.
- the **rights premium** is the difference between the market value of the convertible and its value as straight debt. Each of the last two terms can be expressed as an absolute value or per share.

An example will help clarify this terminology.

Example: Cannon plc

Cannon plc's balance sheet shows 10 per cent convertible loan stock, par value of £100, redeemable at par in seven years. Each unit of stock can be converted at any time in the next three years into 20 ordinary shares. The debenture currently trades at £117, interest has just been paid and the current ordinary share price is £3.60. The ex-interest market price of the debentures of a company of similar risk is £109.

Current conversion value	= (20 × £3.60)	= £72
Current conversion premium	= (£117 − £72)	= £45 (or £2.25 per share)
Current rights premium	= (£117 − £109)	= £8 (or £0.40 per share)

At the initial issue date, the conversion value will be less than the issue price. Investors hope that as the conversion date nears, and as the market price of the underlying shares increases, the conversion value will rise accordingly i.e. conversion becomes more attractive to investors. The conversion premium is proportional to the time remaining before conversion occurs. As conversion approaches, the market value and the conversion value converge until the conversion premium disappears. With no conversion premium, the value of the convertible is simply its value as straight debt with a similar coupon and maturity.

The market value of the convertible thus depends on:

- the current conversion value
- the time remaining to conversion
- the market's expectations regarding the expected returns
- the degree of risk of the underlying ordinary shares.

The 2001 accounts of British Airways plc, disclosed a convertible issue of 9.75 per cent Convertible Capital Bonds with par value £1. Holders of the stock are entitled until 2005 to convert these into ordinary shares on the basis of one ordinary share for each £2.34 of bonds held. At this date, BA can require remaining bondholders to convert their bonds into ordinary shares which would then be sold on their behalf. On August 3rd 2002, the market prices for the bonds and for the ordinary shares were £1.08 and £1.40 respectively.

Convertible loan stock: key features

- Convertible loan stock can be issued more cheaply than a 'straight' loan because it offers an equity incentive.
- Companies perceived as relatively high risk can attract loan finance by offering the possibility of participating in future growth.
- Interest on the loan (while it is a loan) is tax-deductible.
- The bonds can also be traded on the Stock Exchange.

Continued

- Where it is believed that the true worth of the company is not adequately reflected in the share price, convertibles provide a means of raising capital that may eventually become equity without diluting the value of existing equity.
- Convertibles offer the benefits of both equity and loan stock, thereby attracting additional investors.
- If all goes as planned, the conversion to equity will occur, reducing the gearing ratio (but also lowering Earnings Per Share).
- If the conversion price is misjudged, the company is left with unwanted debt. If the equity growth is faster than expected, conversions will take place on over-generous terms at the expense of existing shareholders.

Bond yields

Investors who buy debentures and loan stock will want to know the rate of return, or yield, on their investments. Two ratios are commonly given in this regard. The **flat yield** or **interest yield** is the gross interest receivable, expressed as a percentage of the current market value of the stock. Thus a 7 per cent stock with a market value of £85 and a nominal value of £100 has a flat yield of:

$$\frac{£7}{£85} \times 100 = 8.2\%$$

This represents the gross yield. The net-of-tax yield to the investor depends on his tax position:

$$\text{Net interest yield} = \text{Gross yield} \times (1 - t_p)$$

where t_p is the personal rate of tax incurred by the bondholder.

The **redemption yield** combines the income accruing from interest payments with the capital gain or loss on maturity. It will be greater than the flat yield where the current value is below the redemption value because the investor will also receive a capital gain if the bond is held until maturity.

If the above stock has five years life to maturity, someone who buys it for £85 will receive a capital gain on redemption of £15. Averaged over five years, this represents an additional gain of £3 p.a. Based on the purchase price of £85, this raises the yield to redemption thus:

$$\text{Flat yield} + £3/£85 = 8.2\% + 3.5\% = 11.7\%$$

However, this is only an approximation to the true redemption yield, which depends on the precise timing of the investor's returns. For example, assume he or she buys the stock now, having just missed out on the interest payment, thus anticipating five future annual interest payments plus the redemption payment of £100 at the end of the fifth year. The yield to maturity is the solution R in the following internal rate of return expression:

$$£85 = \frac{£7}{(1 + R)} + \frac{£7}{(1 + R)^2} + \cdots + \frac{(£7 + £100)}{(1 + R)^5}$$

The precise solution is 10.9 per cent. As above, this would be offset by the investor's liability to tax. As this figure is gross-of-tax, it is also called the **gross redemption yield**. Similar principles apply in calculating yields on government securities.

Self-assessment Activity 18.6

A bond with nominal value of £100 and coupon rate of 8.3 per cent has market value of £110. What is:

(a) its flat yield?
(b) its yield to maturity in three years?

(answer at end of chapter)

Warrants

A **warrant** is an option to buy ordinary shares. We include warrants in the section on debt finance because they are more frequently linked to debt issues than to equity issues (although many companies distribute warrants to shareholders as a 'sweetener'). The warrant holder is entitled to buy a stated number of shares at a specific price up to a certain date. Each warrant will state the number of shares the owner may purchase and the time limit (unless a **perpetual warrant**) within which the option to purchase can be exercised.

Companies issue warrants for a number of reasons. They can be attached to loan stock, thus providing loan stock holders with an opportunity to participate in the future growth and prosperity of the company, or, alternatively, used to attract investors by new and expanding companies. They may be also part of the purchase consideration in a takeover. In both cases, they act as a 'sweetener' to the investor. Frequently, such an inducement enables the company to obtain a lower rate of interest or less restrictive conditions in the debenture agreement. Whether or not warrants eventually give rise to additional finance by holders taking up their option to purchase depends, of course, on the future trading success of the company and the exercise price.

How warrants work

In 1998, when its ordinary shares carried a market price of £2.00, XYZ plc issued debenture stock with one warrant attached to each unit of stock giving the right to buy one ordinary share at a price of £2.50 in 2002. If, at the exercise date, the market share price is, say, £4.00, we would expect investors to exercise their rights, thus making a capital gain of £1.50 per share purchased. As a result of their purchases, the earnings of existing shareholders will be diluted – the company is, in effect, giving away £1.50 per share, which is not a problem if the same shareholders also hold the debentures, to which the warrants are attached, although this is rather unusual. The accounting mechanism would involve a reduction in the company's reserves. Warrants are often called 'time bombs' for this reason. This also explains why the issue of warrants may be used as a takeover defence tactic – warrants implant a 'poison pill' for the predator to swallow.

Warrants can be traded separately from the securities to which they were originally attached. In the XYZ example, if the ordinary shares are trading at £3.00, the warrants will be worth 50p each, because they embody the right to buy ordinary shares at a 50p discount. They also possess the attractive property of gearing. If the ordinary shares rise in value by 5 per cent from £3.00 to £3.15, the warrant would also rise by 15p in value, but by the considerably greater proportion of (15p/50p) = 30 per cent. For this reason, they are referred to as 'geared plays'.

Self-assessment Activity 18.7

What is the market value of a warrant that gives the right to buy one new share for every four shares held, given market price per share = £8, and the exercise price is £5?

(answer at end of chapter)

Mezzanine finance

Mezzanine debt is another form of hybrid finance, ranking for payment between straight debt and straight equity. Although it lies nearer the former, it ranks behind more formal borrowing contracts, which is why it is called 'subordinated' or 'intermediate' debt. Because of its low priority for payment, it attracts a relatively high interest rate, usually 3–5 per cent above LIBOR, and usually carries warrants and/or the right to convert into ordinary shares. Mezzanine finance is often used in the financing of management buy-outs (MBOs), since it offers investors exposure to the upside potential of the venture – if the MBO performs well, the warrants offer the prospect of capital gain. However, these are chancy investments – both the company and the instrument carry major risks.

A successful MBO – romping away from the opposition

Adams Childrenswear was an MBO for £90 million in 1999 from the struggling Sears retail empire that had been acquired by dynamic entrepreneur Philip Green. Adams now has 400 stores in the UK and 42 abroad, and is one of the few UK operators that make money from children's clothing.

Continued

Its 8 per cent share of the UK market share now equals that of Marks & Spencer, and it aims to double its size by 2005. The omens are good – in its first two years of independence, it grew profits by over 70 per cent. In 1999, sales rose by 10 per cent to £217 million and trading profits by 34 per cent, its improved margins reflecting success in differentiation and cost control.

A key to Adams' growth so far has been development of concessions and partnerships that contributed 31 per cent to trading profit by 2001, a proportion that Chief Executive Michael Hobbs wished to raise to 50 per cent. In his strategic review, he set out options that included acquisition, merger and flotation in order to fund growth, possibly involving moving into the US, the graveyard of many UK retailers. Although acknowledging the pitfalls, Hobbs said: 'we are a young and hungry team'.

Foreign bonds

These are domestic issues by non-residents, e.g. an issue of stock by a US company in London (a 'bulldog'), or in Tokyo (a 'samurai') or in Australia (a 'kangaroo'). Such bonds are domestic bonds in the local currency – only the issuer is foreign. If British Airways makes a bond issue in New York, this is a 'yankee' bond.

Eurobonds ('International bonds')

The term **Eurobond** is a misnomer – they need not be issued in Europe nor be denominated in a European currency! They are most easily understood as international loans denominated in a currency other than that of the issuer, but technically they are any long-term bonds issued by companies outside the country of the currency in which the bonds are denominated. An example is a Eurodollar issue denominated (and thus repayable) in dollars by a US corporation, issued via the Frankfurt capital market. They are available only to large, credit-worthy companies and state-owned corporations, and are generally unsecured. Corporate Eurobond issuers in 2001 included France Telecom 275 billion yen, Kia Motor Corporation $200 million, Lithuania Gas €30 million, Reed Elsevier, the Anglo-Dutch publishing house, $1.8 billion, brewers San Miguel Corporation A $2.25 billion and Unilever N.V. €1 billion.

Eurobond issues are mainly organised and underwritten by international syndicates of investment banks acting on behalf of such organisations. The market originally developed in response to the desire by US companies to avoid the now defunct withholding tax, which they were obliged to pay to the tax authorities on behalf of investors who purchased bonds sold locally.

Eurobonds are bearer bonds (i.e. they are transferable), with interest paid annually, and gross of tax, which may appeal to investors eager to delay (or evade) tax. Empirical evidence suggests that this feature may allow companies to borrow at rates lower than on their own domestic markets, although any such yield differential would be eliminated by arbitrageurs if the international bond market were efficient and unsegmented.

Lower overseas interest rates are not necessarily good news. Many corporate treasurers who try to take advantage of relatively low overseas interest rates often overlook the reasons why interest rates are lower overseas. Domestic interest rates are linked to future expected inflation rates and to expected exchange rate movements. If the inflation rate in Switzerland is lower than in the UK, the Swiss franc will appreciate against sterling and current interest rates in London will exceed those in Zurich. This is to compensate both domestic investors for inflation and also overseas investors from, say, Switzerland for the prospective reduction in the Swiss franc value of investments in London. If a British corporate treasurer borrows 'cheap' in Zurich, he or she should not be surprised to find that, when it comes to repay the loan in Swiss francs, the sterling cost has increased, following depreciation of sterling. What is won from the interest rate savings will probably be lost from the capital value change. However, for treasurers who believe that exchange rate movements can be predicted in advance, Eurobonds may offer speculative opportunities. For those who simply want to create an overseas liability to offset an exposure in relation to an overseas income flow, Eurobonds may present an attractive way of hedging. (These aspects were examined in more detail in Chapter 17.)

In addition to interest cost advantages, Eurobonds usually involve fewer, if any, restrictive covenants, and usually require less disclosure of information than is required for similar issues on domestic markets. The unregulated nature of the market has probably contributed to its innovativeness in terms of the features attaching to many issues, whereby bonds can be tailored to specific corporate requirements.

Floating rate notes (FRNs)

These are Eurobonds that pay a variable rather than a fixed interest rate. FRNs are especially favoured by financial institutions that conduct a great part of their business at a floating rate and therefore value the protection given by the ability to borrow at a floating rate. As rates of interest rise, banks' income rises, as do their costs – FRNs are thus a way of achieving a neat match between assets and liabilities.

Abbey National plc is very active in the Eurobond market, borrowing in a wide variety of currencies, e.g. yen, dollars, euros, Swiss francs, at both fixed and floating rates. The reason why it borrows in so many currencies and at fixed rates is bound up with the swaps market. Abbey may not want the currency for itself nor even want a variable rate liability. It is borrowing in the currency in which, at prevailing market conditions, it is easiest and cheapest to borrow, say, the Eurodollar market. It can then use the swap market to exchange the US$ for the currency it really requires.

A swap works in two stages. Take the case of Abbey's issue of US$500 million FRNs repayable in 2005. This can be swapped into sterling via another bank (the 'swap bank') at the time of issue, perhaps at a fixed rate. The parties agree to swap back at maturity so that Abbey can repay the bond. The swap bank then passes to Abbey a stream of sterling until 2005 with which to pay the interest, in return for which it receives from Abbey a fluctuating stream of USD with which to pay its own interest liability up to 2005.

In this swap, there is an exchange not only of currencies but also a floating liability for a variable one. This is called a Combined Interest Rate and Currency Swap (CIRCUS). The point of this is to enable the two parties to raise money where the terms are most attractive before swapping it into the currency they really want. At other times, Abbey National itself may borrow at floating rates both in sterling and in other currencies.

A new financial market takes wing

In July 2001, Emirates, the Dubai-based airline (and Chelsea FC sponsor) launched a Floating Rate Note (FRN) issue, amounting to dirhams* 1.5 billion, repayable at par in 2006, and denominated in 100,000 dirhams units. The minimum subscription was 5 million dirhams, targeting the issue at corporate and institutional investors plus (very) high net worth individuals. The issue was over-subscribed two-and-a-half times and taken up by pension funds (7%), corporates (6%), professional investors (14%) and banks (73%).

The finance was needed for Emirates' aggressive expansion plans, including investment of 14.5 billion dirhams in fleet and equipment modernisation. Its growth ambitions involve trebling its fleet size over 2001–10.

This issue was the first bond issue made on the nascent Dubai Financial Market, the largest dirham-denominated bond issue to date and the first made by a United Arab Emirates corporate borrower. Interest on the notes is to be paid semi-annually at 70 basis points (0.7%) above the six-month Emirates Interbank Offered Rate (EBOR), a formula resulting in a rate of 4.675% for the first interest period.

* 3.678 Arab Emirate dirhams = one US dollar

18.7 Leasing and sale-and-leaseback (SAL)

Lease contracts were discussed in Chapter 16. It is possible to arrange long-term leases for certain assets, such as ships and aircraft, or for property.

SAL involves selling assets (usually property) to a financial institution seeking good quality investments with potential for long-term growth in capital value. The seller, while giving up the ownership rights to the property, will then arrange to lease the premises from the new owner. SAL, therefore, is a transfer of ownership with retention of rights to use for a specified period. Its attraction to the vendor is the raising of capital, although its obvious disadvantage is usually the loss of any entitlement to capital appreciation. However, for a company eager to grow, the returns in the early years of strategic growth projects could outweigh the lost capital gains. This was the reasoning behind the

SAL by Tesco, the supermarket chain, of many of its store sites in the 1980s when it was eager to claw back the market share advantage held by Sainsbury (it subsequently grew to number one in the supermarket league by 1996). The finance generated by a series of SALs was used to purchase and develop new sites for stores.

In 1997, Imperial Chemical Industries (ICI) sold its headquarters office building in London's Millbank to the Prudential insurance company for over £100 million. The funds raised were partly to finance ICI's acquisition of Unilever's speciality chemical business.

BT's £2.3 billion UK property sale cheers market

British Telecommunications plc cheered investors yesterday with a £2.3 billion ($3.2 billion) property sale and news that an experienced hand would guide the spin-off of its mobile division.

The group, which has embarked on a radical shake-up to cut its debt by about a third this year, said it had agreed to sell six million square metres (65 million sq feet) of telephone exchanges and offices to property developer Land Securities Trillium and privately-owned William Pears Group.

BT also appointed David Varney, former chief executive of gas and oil producer BG Group plc, as chairman of its Wireless unit that will be hived off this year. At BG, Varney oversaw the successful spin-off of pipeline business Lattice Group Plc.

BT shares climbed as much as four per cent on news of the sale, which had been expected to net nearer £2 billion, and Varney's appointment.

At 1245GMT, they were 3.75 per cent up at 449-1/4p, outperforming the Dow Jones Stoxx pan-European telecoms index, which was up 1.17 per cent.

BT announced plans for the property sale, which excludes London's landmark BT tower, in April as part of its strategy to cut a near £30 billion debt mountain run up in costly auctions for new generation mobile phone licences. Last month, it also launched a record £5.9 billion rights issue to help slash debt. Under the property sale agreement, BT will lease back the exchanges, allowing it to focus on its core telecoms business.

When the transaction was first announced, credit analysts questioned whether a sale and leaseback constituted a reduction in BT's debt, because it tied the former UK telecoms monopoly into future cash payments.

Tim Rees, a fund manager at Clerical Medical, said that regardless of how the transaction was viewed by credit rating agencies, 'it was helpful to underlying sentiment'. Rees was also positive on Varney's appointment.

Continued

The deal also will bring tax benefits, a spokesman for BT told Reuters.

Complex accounting rules mean that BT will book a capital loss on the sale, which can then be used to offset capital gains tax on other disposals, such as the recent £2.14 billion sale of Yell business directories. The spokesman declined to quantify the tax benefit.

'This represents a further step forward in BT's drive for cash and the reduction of the headline debt,' Chairman Christopher Bland said of the property sale.

Based on *Financial Times*, June 14 2001

Self-assessment Activity 18.8

What is the effect of a sale and lease back on a firm's Balance Sheet?

(answer at end of chapter)

Summary

We have discussed the features of the principal forms of long-term finance available to companies, and their benefits and drawbacks.

Key points

- The main factors in considering the appropriate source of finance are risk, ownership, duration and debt capacity.
- Over half of the new finance raised for UK companies is usually through retained profits. This is not a free source of finance as it involves an opportunity cost in terms of the return that shareholders would have obtained had they received the profit as dividends and re-invested it elsewhere.
- New shares are issued through a private placing, stock exchange placing, public issue (prospectus issue, offer for sale or issue by tender) or by a rights issue.
- The enhanced ability to make a rights issue is a major attraction of a Stock Exchange listing.
- Equity capital is an attractive form of finance to companies because there are no interest charges or capital repayments; to investors, it offers a hedge against inflation, and a higher yield than loan stock. On the other hand, equity capital can be expensive to raise, and new issues to the public dilute the control of existing members.

- Debt finance (debentures, loan stock, etc.) is flexible, offering a wide range of financial products to the corporate treasurer. Interest payments are tax-deductible, but restrictions (e.g. charges over assets and monitoring of activities) are common practice.
- Convertible loan stock is a debt instrument that can, at the option of the holder, be converted into equity. It offers investors and firms the benefit of loan stock in the early years and, if all goes to plan, will enable the benefits of equity to be captured when the business is better established.

Further reading

Weston and Copeland (1988) devote considerably more space to this area than we have been able to. A practitioner's guide is found in Rutterford (1992).

Self-assessment Answers

18.1 The events of 9/11 have made people more fearful for the future, and less inclined to invest. Equity would look safer for firms as it carries no interest obligations, although as the authorities used interest rate reductions to support their economies, this might encourage more borrowing, e.g. as firms re-finance existing loans at more favourable rates. So, on balance, probably a shift towards fixed interest financing to lock in historically low interest rates, certainly for as long as it takes fragile equity markets to recover.

18.2 The statement is nonsense. Reserves are a method of financing past investment, i.e. they represent funds already invested. The speaker is probably confused between reserves and 'cash reserves', common parlance for 'cash balances'.

18.3 Pre-issue, a shareholder holds (6 × £5) = £30 in shares plus £3.50 in cash, totalling £33.50. Post-issue this value is spread over 7 shares (6 + 1) so the TERP = £33.50/7 = £4.79.

18.4 In a '2-for-1' split:

- the number of shares doubles, i.e. two new for each old one.
- both capital and assets are unchanged – no further cash is raised.
- the market value of the whole equity is unchanged but the value per share is halved.

18.5 £50 grows to £100 over 10 years, i.e. £50$(1 + g)^{10}$ = £100.
Inverting, $1/(1 + g)^{10}$ = (£50/£100) = 0.5000. From the tables, g = 7.2%.

18.6 **(a)** Flat yield = interest/market price = (£8.30/£110) = 7.5%
(b) Yield to maturity is the interest rate that satisfies:

£110 = (£8.3 × 3-year annuity factor) + (£100 × 3-year discount factor).

The solution is 5.35%.

18.7 The warrant gives the right to buy something worth £8 for £5 – its value is thus £3. The one-for-four terms are irrelevant to the value per warrant. Someone holding 400 shares would have 100 warrants valued at (100 × £3) = £300, etc.

18.8 A SAL generates cash which raises assets, but as the lease is long-term it must be capitalised. It will thus appear (remain as) as a fixed asset, but is offset by the corresponding PV of rental commitments, shown as long-term debt. Overall, it leaves net assets unchanged but increases the calculated gearing ratio. The balance sheet effect is purely cosmetic ('smoke and mirrors'), except that it does increase liquidity.

Questions

1 *Solution in Appendix A (page 825).* The ordinary shares of Anglia Paper Company are currently trading at £3.20. Existing shareholders are offered one new share at £2 for every three held.

(i) What is the theoretical ex-rights price?
(ii) What is the nil-paid rights price?

2 *Solution in Appendix A (page 825).* Cambridge Castings Ltd plans a major expansion to modernise its manufacturing plant, thereby improving productivity and reducing unit costs. The existing capital base is fairly evenly divided between equity and debt, and it is clear that the capital investment programme can only partly be funded through profit retention.

It is suggested that the additional finance could be raised through a preference share issue. You are required to evaluate this source of finance for the company, compared with equity or debt:

(a) from the company's point of view;
(b) from the viewpoint of investors.

3 Shaw Holdings plc has 20 million ordinary shares of 50p in issue. These shares are currently valued on the Stock Exchange at £1.60 per share. The directors of Shaw Holdings believe the company requires additional long-term capital and have decided to make a one-for-four rights issue at £1.30 per share.

An investor with 2,000 shares in Shaw Holdings has contacted you for investment advice. She is undecided whether to take up the rights issue, sell the rights, or allow the rights offer to lapse.

Required

(a) Calculate the theoretical ex-rights price of an ordinary share.
(b) Calculate the value at which the rights are likely to be traded.
(c) Evaluate each of the options being considered by the owner of 2,000 shares.
(d) Explain why rights issues are usually made at a discount.
(e) From the company's viewpoint, how critical is the pricing of a rights issue likely to be?

(ACCA Certified Diploma)

4 *Solution in Appendix A (page 826).* Burnsall plc is a listed company which manufactures and distributes leisurewear under the brand name Paraffin. It made sales of 10 million

units world-wide at an average wholesale price of £10 per unit during its last financial year ending at 30 June 1995. In 1995–96, it is planning to introduce a new brand, Meths, which will be sold at a lower unit price to more price-sensitive market segments. Allowing for negative effects on existing sales of Paraffin, the introduction of the new brand is expected to raise total sales value by 20 per cent

To support greater sales activity, it is expected that additional financing, both capital and working, will be required. Burnsall expects to make capital expenditures of £20 million in 1995–96, partly to replace worn-out equipment but largely to support sales expansion. You may assume that, except for taxation, all current assets and current liabilities will vary directly in line with sales.

Burnsall's summarised Balance Sheet for the financial year ending 30 June 1995 shows the following:

Assets employed	**£m**	**£m**	**£m**
Fixed (net)			120
Current:			
stocks	16		
debtors	23		
cash	6		
		45	
Current liabilities:			
Corporation tax payable	(5)		
Trade creditors	(18)		
		(23)	
Net current assets			22
Long-term debt at 12%			(20)
Net assets			122
Financed by			
Ordinary shares (50p par value)			60
Reserves			62
Shareholders' funds			122

Burnsall's profit before interest and tax in 1994–95 was 16 per cent of sales, after deducting depreciation of £5 million. The depreciation charge for 1995–96 is expected to rise to £9 million. Corporation tax is levied at 33 per cent, paid with a one-year delay. Burnsall has an established distribution policy of raising dividends by 10 per cent p.a. In 1994–95, it paid dividends of £5 million net.

You have been approached to advise on the extra financing required to support the sales expansion. Company policy is to avoid cash balances falling below 6 per cent of sales.

Required

(a) By projecting its financial statements, calculate how much additional *external* finance Burnsall must raise.

Notes:

1 It is not necessary to present your projection in FRS 1 format.

2 You may assume that all depreciation provisions qualify for tax relief.

(b) Offer advice as to the appropriate method of financing for Burnsall's sales expansion.

(ACCA)

5 The managing director of Lavipilon plc wishes to provide an extra return to the company's shareholders and has suggested making either:

(i) a two for five bonus issue (capitalisation issue) in addition to the normal dividend.
(ii) a one for five scrip dividend instead of the normal cash dividend.
(iii) a one for one share (stock) split in addition to the normal dividend.

Summarised Balance Sheet of Lavipilon plc (end of last year)

Fixed assets		65
Current assets	130	
Less: current liabilities	(55)	
Net current assets		75
Total assets less current liabilities		140
Less: Long-term liability		
11% debenture		(25)
Net assets	115	
Capital and reserves:		
Ordinary shares (50 pence par value)	25	
Share premium account	50	
Revenue reserves	40	
Shareholders' funds		115

The company's shares are trading at 300 pence before the dividend is paid, and the company has £50 million of the (post-tax) profit from this year's activities available to ordinary shareholders, of which £30 million will be paid as a dividend if options (i) or (iii) are chosen. None of the £40 million revenue reserves would be distributed. This year's financial accounts have not yet been finalised.

(a) For each of the three proposals, show the likely effect on the company's Balance Sheet at the end of this year, and the likely effect on the company's share price.
(b) Comment on how well these suggestions fulfil the managing director's objective of providing an extra return to the company's shareholders.
(c) Discuss reasons why a company might wish to undertake:
  (i) a scrip dividend,
  (ii) a share (stock) split.

(ACCA)

6 Netherby plc manufactures a range of camping and leisure equipment, including tents. It is currently experiencing severe quality control problems at its existing fully depreciated factory in the south of England. These difficulties threaten to undermine its reputation for producing high-quality products. It has recently been approached by the European Bank for Reconstruction and Development, on behalf of a tent manufacturer in Hungary, which is seeking a UK-based trading partner which will import and distribute its tents. Such a switch would involve shutting down the existing tent manufacturing operation in the United Kingdom and converting it into a distribution depot. The estimated restructuring costs of £5 million would be tax-allowable, but would exert serious strains on cash flow.

Importing, rather than manufacturing, tents appears inherently profitable, as the buying-in price, when converted into sterling, is less than the present production cost. In addition, Netherby considers that the Hungarian product would result in increased sales, as the existing retail distributors seem impressed with the quality of the samples which they have been shown. It is estimated that for a five-year contract, the annual cash flow benefit would be around £2 million p.a. before tax.

However, the financing of the closure and restructuring costs would involve careful consideration of the financing options. Some directors argue that dividends could be reduced, as several competing companies have already done a similar thing, while other directors argue for a rights issue. Alternatively, the project could be financed by an issue of long-term loan stock at a fixed rate of 12 per cent.

The most recent Balance Sheet shows £5 million of issued share capital (par value 50p), while the market price per share is currently £3. A leading security analyst has recently described Netherby's gearing ratio as 'adventurous'. Profit after tax in the year just ended was £15 million and dividends of £10 million were paid.

The rate of Corporation Tax is 33 per cent, payable with a one-year delay. Netherby's reporting year coincides with the calendar year and the factory will be closed at the year end. Closure costs would be incurred shortly before deliveries of the imported product began, and sufficient stocks will be on hand to overcome any initial supply problems. Netherby considers that it should earn a return on new investment of 15 per cent p.a. net of all taxes.

Required

(a) Is the closure of the existing factory financially worthwhile for Netherby?

(b) Explain what is meant when the capital market is said to be information-efficient in a semi-strong form.
If the stock market is semi-strong efficient and without considering the method of finance, calculate the likely impact of acceptance and announcement of the details of this project to the market on Netherby's share price.

(c) Advise the Netherby board as to the relative merits of a rights issue rather than a cut in dividends to finance this project.

(d) Explain why a rights issue generally results in a fall in the market price of shares. If a rights issue is undertaken, calculate the resulting theoretical ex-rights share price of issue prices of £1 per share and £2 per share, respectively. (You may ignore issue costs.)

(e) Assuming the restructuring proposal meets expectations, assess the impact of the project on earnings per share if it is financed by a rights issue at an offer price of £2 per share, and loan stock, respectively. (Again, you may ignore issue costs.)

(f) Briefly consider the main operating risks connected with the investment project, and how Netherby might attempt to allow for these.

Practical assignment

Consider the long-term financing of a company with which you are familiar. Evaluate each of the main sources of finance and suggest, with reasons, two methods of finance that are not currently used, but which may prove attractive to the company.

19 Returning value to shareholders: the dividend decision

Anyone want their money back?

Telecoms operator Cable & Wireless (**www.cableandwireless.com**), managed to avoid becoming embroiled in the scramble for third-generation mobile phone licences. Instead, it sold off overseas assets, mainly in the Far East, e.g. C&W Optus (Australia), to shift its focus from cable and mobile telephony towards providing communications networks and Internet services for firms.

As a result, it was holding cash balances of £4.7 billion by November 2001, when it announced a widely-anticipated share buy-back of £1.4 billion plus a Special Dividend of 11.5 pence per share, amounting to £320 million. This still left liquid balances of over £3 billion to spend. Interestingly, C&W had previously cut its interim dividend by 70 per cent to reflect falling profitability due to its contraction – the Special Dividend simply restored the total distribution to the previous year's level.

However, life being what it is, not everyone was delighted. A typical analyst's comment was that it was a 'half-way house, not going to please everybody', suggesting that C&W should aim to get its core corporate network business into the black or give back all the cash. One suggestion ground out by the rumour mill was that C&W might bid for the smaller British telecoms operator, Colt Telecom, then valued at £1.2 billion, in order to add a European network to complement its other activities.

But the market was happy – C&W's share price rose 6 per cent.

Learning objectives

After reading this chapter, you should:

- Understand the competing views about the role of dividend policy.
- Understand what factors a financial manager should consider when deciding to recommend a change in dividend payouts.

- Understand what is meant by the 'information content' of dividends.
- Appreciate the impact of taxation on dividend decisions.
- Understand why changes in dividend payments usually lag behind changes in company earnings.

19.1 Introduction

This chapter will help you to appreciate the factors that drive dividend decisions.

Most quoted companies pay two dividends to ordinary shareholders each year: an interim, or 'taster', based on half-year results, followed by the main, or final, dividend, based on the full-year reported profits. The amount of dividend is determined by the board of directors, with the advice of financial managers, and presented to the Annual General Meeting of shareholders for approval. The board and their advisers thus face a twice-yearly decision about what percentage of post-tax profits to distribute to shareholders (the 'payout ratio') and hence what percentage to retain (the 'retention ratio').

Until a specified **Record Day**, the shares are traded **cum-dividend**: that is, purchasers will be entitled to receive the dividend. The approved dividends are paid to all shareholders appearing on the share register on the Record Day, after which the shares are quoted **ex-dividend**, i.e. without entitlement to the dividend. In practice, there is a time lag between the shares going ex-dividend and the Record Day to allow the company's Registrar to update the shareholders' register to reflect recent dealings. The Financial Calender of Kelda Group (formerly Yorkshire Water plc) is shown in Table 19.1. People purchasing Kelda shares whose names did not appear on the register by 7th September 2001 would not have received the final dividend payable per share (17.30p).

How should top management approach the dividend decision? Should it be generous and follow a high payout policy, or retain the bulk of earnings? The pure theory of dividend policy shows that, under certain conditions, it makes no difference what they do! One authority argues: 'to the management of a company acting in the best interests of its shareholders, dividend policy is a mere detail' (Miller and Modigliani 1961). However, the conditions required to support this conclusion are highly restrictive and unlikely to apply in real-world capital markets. Indeed, many financial managers and investment analysts take the opposite view, appearing to believe that the dividend payout decision is critical to company valuation and hence a central element of corporate financial strategy. These are the extreme views – an evaluation of the

Table 19.1 Kelda Group plc Financial Calendar

Announcement of results	7 June 2001
Annual general meeting	26 July 2001
Ex-dividend date	5 September 2001
Record date	7 September 2001
Final dividend payment date	1 October 2001

case for and against dividend generosity leads to more pragmatic 'middle-of-the-road' conclusions.

In this chapter, we consider the strategic, theoretical and practical issues surrounding dividend policy, and discuss some of the alternatives to dividend payment. *The basic message for management is: define the dividend policy, make a smooth transition towards it, and think very carefully before changing it.*

Few people doubt that dividend levels influence share prices. Indeed, a common method of valuation, the Dividend Valuation Model (introduced in Chapter 4) relies on discounting the future dividend stream. However, debate centres on what is the most attractive *pattern* of dividend payments, and the effects of changes in dividend policy.

Shareholders can receive returns in the form of dividends now and/or capital appreciation, which is the market's valuation of future expected dividend growth. But are shareholders more impressed by the higher near-in-time dividends than by the capital gain generated by a policy of low current payments, with retentions used to finance worthwhile investment? Graham *et al.* (1962) claimed that $1 of dividend was valued four times more highly by shareholders than $1 of retained earnings. Yet it is not uncommon to observe quite parsimonious (or even zero, e.g. Dell) payout ratios. Conventional wisdom warns companies subject to volatility of earnings to operate relatively high dividend covers to safeguard dividend payments in the event of depressed profitability. Similarly, smaller companies with less easy access to fresh supplies of capital are also advised to conserve cash and liquidity by operating a conservative dividend policy.

Over the past two decades, attitudes in the UK to dividend payouts have appeared to change in favour of higher payouts. Why is this?

1 Companies may be more aware of the threat of takeover, and use high payouts as a pre-emptive defence to buy shareholder loyalty.
2 The tax changes in the 1988 Finance Act largely removed the tax discrimination against dividend payments.
3 Reflecting the short-termist perspective, it may be that companies feel under greater pressure from institutional shareholders to pay out higher dividends.

Whatever the reasons, it has become more difficult to generalise about optimal dividend policy.

In the following sections, we consider strategic and legal issues before examining the theory of dividend policy and, in particular, the 'irrelevance' hypothesis. We then consider the major qualifications to the theory, suggesting reasons why some shareholders may, in practice, prefer dividend income. You will see that dividend policy is an enigma with no obvious optimal strategy. However, it is possible to make some broad recommendations to guide the financial manager.

19.2 The strategic dimension

Formulating corporate strategy requires specification of clear objectives and delineation of the strategic options contributing to the achievement of these objectives. Although maximisation of shareholder wealth may be the paramount aim, there may be various routes to it. For example, diversifying into new industrial sectors involves a choice between internal growth and growth by acquisition. Whichever alternative is selected, the enterprise will need to consider both the level of required financing and the possible sources. The main alternatives for the listed company are short- and long-term debt capital, new share issues (normally rights issues) and internal financing (via retention of profits and depreciation provisions).

This is where we encounter the role of dividend policy. The amount of finance required to support the selected strategic option may exceed the borrowing capacity of the company, necessitating the use of additional equity funding. A capital-hungry firm therefore faces the choice between retention of earnings, i.e. restricting the dividend payout, or paying out high dividends but then clawing back capital via a subsequent rights issue. Neither policy is risk-free, as both may have undesirable repercussions on the ability to exploit strategic options. Retention may offend investors reliant on dividend income, resulting in share sales and lower share price, conflicting with the aim of wealth-maximisation, as well as exposing the company to the threat of takeover. Alternatively, the dividend payment-plus-rights issue policy incurs administrative expenses and the risk of having to sell shares on a flat or falling market. To this extent, the dividend decision is a strategic one, since an ill-judged financial decision could subvert the overall strategic aim. Consequently, financial managers must carefully consider the likely reaction of shareholders, and of the market as a whole, to dividend proposals.

19.3 The legal dimension

Legal factors impose further constraints on managers' freedom of action in deciding dividends. Although shareholders are the main risk-bearers in a company, other stakeholders, such as creditors and employees, carry a measure of risk. Accordingly, shareholders can be paid dividends only if the company has accumulated sufficient profits. They cannot be paid out of capital, except in a liquidation, as to do so would mean they would be paid ahead of prior claims on the business.

Section 264 of the Companies Act 1985 states that, for public companies, the maximum distribution is the net total of accumulated profits, whether realised or unrealised. Private companies are restricted to accumulated realised profits. Furthermore, bondholders may insist on restrictive covenants being written into loan agreements to prevent large dividends being declared.

Of course, paying the maximum legally permitted dividend is rarely likely to make strategic sense. Moreover, dividends are paid *out of profits* but *with* cash (or borrowings). It is quite common for companies to report low or negative profits, yet to maintain the previous year's dividend. If the company had retained sufficient profits in earlier years and its cash position was reasonably healthy, this is fairly acceptable. Indeed, the share prices of some struggling companies actually rise when they pay a maintained dividend out of reserves. This is because a maintained dividend is believed to be a signal to the market of better times ahead.

19.4 The theory: dividend policy and firm value

The critical issue is how, if at all, does dividend policy affect the value of the firm? This section shows that the answer depends on whether or not a firm has external financing opportunities. In the absence of external financing, dividend payment may damage company value if the company has better investment opportunities than its shareholders. Payment of dividends thus prevents access to worthwhile investment. With external financing, however, at least in a perfect market, dividends become totally irrelevant, since payment no longer precludes worthwhile investment, simply because the firm can recoup the required finance by selling shares.

In Chapter 4, we used the Dividend Valuation Model to show that the value of a company[1] ultimately depends on its dividend-paying capacity. For a company with constant and perpetual free cash flows[2] of E_t in any year t, paid wholly as dividend, D_t, the market will discount this stream at the rate of return required by shareholders, k_e, so that:

$$\text{Value of equity} = V_o = \sum_{t=1}^{N} \frac{E_t}{(1 + k_e)^t} = \frac{E_t}{k_e} \left(\text{or } V_o = \frac{D_t}{k_e} \quad \text{since} \quad E_t = D_t \right)$$

If a proportion, b, of earnings is retained each year, beginning in period 1, for example, thus reducing the next dividend payable to $E_1(1 - b)$, company value is given by the forthcoming dividend divided by the cost of equity less the growth rate. The growth rate, g, is given by the retention ratio, b, times the return on reinvested funds, R (as explained in Chapter 4):

$$\text{Value of equity} = V_o = \frac{E_1 (1 - b)}{(k_e - g)} = \frac{D_1}{(k_e - g)} = \frac{D_1}{(k_e - bR)}$$

Self-assessment Activity 19.1

Using the following figures, remind yourself why the growth rate of earnings = ($b \times R$).

- Earnings in latest year = £1,000; b = 60%; R = 15%.

(answer at end of chapter)

---

[1] In this chapter, we assume no company borrowing, hence the value of the company is synonymous with the value of the equity. When referring to the present value of the whole equity, we use the symbol V_o, and when referring to the value of an individual share, P_o.

[2] In this and subsequent chapters, the letter E is used to denote a free cash flow concept of earnings, as explained in Chapter 4. Here, free cash flow is calculated *after* replacement investment but *before* strategic investment. Free cash flow is likely to deviate from accounting earnings, so when the latter accounting concept is intended, the phrases 'accounting profit' or 'reported earnings' are used.

The expressions can cause confusion. In the first case, the market appears to value the stream of earnings, while in the second, the valuation is based upon the stream of dividends. Indeed, in the early stages of the debate about the importance and role of dividend policy, much attention was paid to the issue of whether the market values earnings or dividends. This apparent dichotomy can be easily resolved if we focus on the reasons for earnings retention. Retention may occur for two main reasons.

First, the company may wish to *bolster its holdings of liquid resources*. For example, dividend distribution may run down current assets or perhaps increase borrowings. Many profitable companies borrow to avoid having to reduce or omit (or 'pass') a dividend, for reasons explained later.

However, the primary reason for retention is to *finance investment in fixed and other assets* to generate higher future earnings and, hence, enhance future dividend-paying capacity. The growth rate of earnings depends on the retention ratio b, and also the rate of return achieved on ploughed-back funds, R, i.e. $g = (b \times R)$. By introducing retention and growth, the Dividend Valuation Model becomes the **Dividend Growth Model** (DGM).

It is important to remember that the DGM assumes a constant retention ratio and a constant return on new investment projects. If these assumptions hold, both earnings and dividends grow at the same rate. Whether this rate is acceptable to shareholders depends on the return they require from their investments, k_e. The relationship between k_e and R, the return on reinvested earnings, provides the key to resolving the valuation dispute.

Dividend irrelevance in perfect capital markets

Miller and Modigliani (MM) pointed out in 1961 that earnings retention was simply one way of financing investment. If the company has access to better investment opportunities than its shareholders, under perfect capital market conditions, investors may benefit from retention.

The original MM analysis proves dividend irrelevance in terms of a single dividend cut to finance worthwhile investment. MM envisaged an all-equity-financed company that has previously paid out its entire annual net cash flow as dividend. To illustrate their analysis, let us examine the case of Divicut plc.

One-off dividend cuts: Divicut plc

Divicut currently generates a perpetual free cash flow of £1,000 p.a. Shareholders require a return of 10 per cent. The market will value Divicut at (£1,000/10%) = £10,000 on unchanged policies. If the management now decides to retain the whole of next year's dividend in order to invest in a project offering a single cash flow of £1,200 in the following year, the new market value of Divicut equals the present value of the revised dividend flow, assuming reversion to 100 per cent payouts:

Year	1	2	3	4	etc.
Dividend (£)	0	2,200	1,000	1,000	– – – – – – – – – – – – –

This revised dividend flow is acceptable only if the resulting market value is at least equal to the pre-decision value, i.e. if the NPV of the project is at least zero. This is clearly the case, as the PV of the extra £1,200 in two years is greater than the PV of £1,000 less in one year, i.e.:

$$\frac{£1{,}200}{(1.1)^2} > \frac{£1{,}000}{(1.1)}$$

or, £992 > £909

Divicut's shareholders are better off by £83.

Shareholder wealth is enhanced, since Divicut has used the funds released by the dividend cut to finance a worthwhile project. If these funds had been invested at only 10 per cent, the net effect would have been zero, while if investment had occurred at a rate of return of less than 10 per cent, shareholders would have been worse off. This simple example shows that the impact on company value is attributable to the investment, rather than the dividend, decision.

Self-assessment Activity 19.2

Re-work the Divicut example for the case where the returns on the investment are £1,080 rather than £1,200 in year 2.

(answer at end of chapter)

MM's dividend irrelevance conclusion was obtained in a world of certainty, and then extended to the case of risk/uncertainty, where the same conclusions emerge so long as investor behaviour and attitudes conform to conditions of 'symmetric market rationality'. This requires the following:

1 All investors are maximisers of expected wealth.
2 All investors have similar expectations.
3 All investors behave rationally.
4 All investors believe that other market participants will behave rationally and that other investors expect rational behaviour from them.

These assumptions were spelled out by Brennan (1971) and form part of the battery of conditions required for a perfect capital market. The additional assumptions required to support the 'irrelevance' hypothesis are as follows:

1 No transaction costs or brokerage fees.
2 All investors have equal and costless access to information.
3 All investors can lend or borrow at the same rate of interest.
4 No buyer or seller of securities can influence prices.
5 No personal or corporate income or capital gains taxes.
6 Dividend decisions are not used to convey information.

The full significance of some of these assumptions will be highlighted when we examine some of the reasons why shareholders may have a definite preference for either dividends or retentions.

The kindest cut

Go on, say it: British Telecommunications is going to cut its dividend. The company more or less admitted as much to buyers of yesterday's £6.4 billion bond issue. With BT paying 40 to 50 basis points more than the market price of Deutsche Telekom's debt and facing stiff interest penalties if it does lose its single-A credit rating, it would be senseless not to.

Scrapping the dividend would send a stark message to the market and infuriate legions of retail investors. But a business should not be imprisoned by its old dividend policy when its circumstances have changed. It is far better for BT to stop paying out cash than to sell more assets than it needs when prices are at rock bottom – a certain recipe for value destruction.

Based on Lex Column, *Financial Times*, January 19 2001

Permanent dividend cuts: more Divicut

This argument can also be applied to the case of permanent retentions using the Dividend Growth Model, although the analysis is a little more complex. Retention may lower the dividend payment only temporarily, resulting in a rate of growth yielding higher dividends discounted through time. This is shown in Figure 19.1. At point-in-time t_1, the company, which currently pays out all its earnings, E_o, plans to cut dividends from D_o to $(1 - b)E_1$, where b is the retention ratio.

Dividends do not regain their former level until time t_N, involving a cumulative loss in dividend payments equal to the area XYZ. Beyond time t_N, dividends exceed their original level as a result of continued reinvestment. Clearly, shareholders will be better off if the area of subsequently higher dividends, VZW, exceeds XYZ (allowing for the discounting process). This holds if R, the return on retained funds, exceeds k_e. This contention can be illustrated using the example of Divicut again.

Recall that, prior to alteration in dividend policy, the value of Divicut was £10,000, derived by discounting the perpetual earnings stream. Imagine the company announces its intention to retain 50 per cent of earnings in all future years (i.e. from and including Year 1) to finance a series of projects offering a perpetual yield of 15 per cent. Market value according to the dividend growth model is:

$$\text{Value of equity} = V_o = \frac{E_1(1 - b)}{(k_e - g)} = \frac{E_1(1 - b)}{(k_e - bR)} = \frac{£1{,}000(1 - 0.5)}{0.1 - (0.5 \times 0.15)}$$

$$= \frac{£500}{0.025} = £20{,}000$$

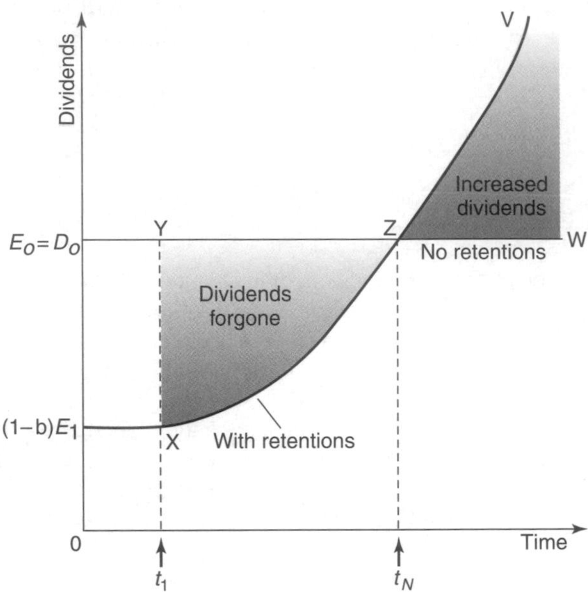

Figure 19.1 The impact of a permanent dividend cut

This may seem a remarkable result. The decision to retain and reinvest doubles company value! Does this mean that dividend payments make shareholders worse off? The answer is simple.

Payment of dividends may make shareholders worse off than they otherwise might be if distribution results in failure to exploit worthwhile investment. In other words, the beneficial impact on Divicut's value is achieved because of the inherent attractions of the projected investments. Conversely, if the funds had been invested to yield only 5 per cent, market value would have fallen to £6,666.

The in-between case, where the return on reinvested funds, $R = k_e = 10$ per cent, leaves company value unchanged. This suggests that, if we strip out the effects of the investment decision, the dividend decision itself has a *neutral* effect. This can be done by assuming retentions are used to finance projects that yield an aggregate NPV of zero, i.e. yielding a return of k_e. With this assumption, dividend decisions are irrelevant to shareholder wealth. If Divicut achieves a return on reinvested funds of 10 per cent, the company's value is:

$$\text{Value of equity} = V_o = \frac{E_1(1-b)}{(k_e - g)} = \frac{£1{,}000\ (1-0.5)}{0.1 - (0.5 \times 0.1)} = \frac{£500}{0.05} = £10{,}000$$

Here we have valued the dividend stream, and the result is equivalent to valuing the steady stream of earnings with no retentions. This equivalence may perhaps be more readily seen by manipulating the expressions for value. If we neutralise the effect of the investment decision so that $k_e = R$, we may write:

$$\text{Value of equity} = V_o = \frac{D_1}{(k_e - g)} = \frac{E_1(1-b)}{(k_e - g)} = \frac{E_1(1-b)}{(k_e - bR)} = \frac{E_1(1-b)}{(k_e - bk_e)} = \frac{E_1(1-b)}{k_e(1-b)} = \frac{E_1}{k_e}$$

There are clear conclusions from this analysis. In the absence of external financing:

1 *If the expected return on reinvested funds exceeds* k_e, it is beneficial to retain. A dividend cut will lead to higher value but only because funds are used to finance worthwhile projects.
2 *If the return on reinvested funds is less than* k_e, retention damages shareholder interests. A dividend cut would lower company value because shareholders have better uses for capital.
3 *If the return on reinvested funds equals* k_e, the impact of a dividend cut to finance investment is neutral.

Investors nervous as companies take axe to dividends

In recent weeks, several high profile FTSE companies have taken a scythe to their dividends. ICI, Reuters and Royal & Sun Alliance cut theirs by up to a half.

Many investors are now unsure whether companies are entering a period of widespread cuts or whether the headlines are just focusing on the bad news.

Certainly, dividend growth has been slowing for many years. But there is little agreement about how the future will pan out. Schroder Salomon Smith Barney says the consensus among strategists is for average dividend growth across the FTSE of 6 per cent.

The market, as ever, is split between the stalwart income-payers such as the banks and the rest that chop and change payouts according to critical circumstances.

'Industrials are the ones at risk', says Gareth Williams at ABN Amro. 'They account for more than half of all dividends, but face pressure on their capacity to pay.'

Analysts say those with large debt burdens and high gearing are particularly exposed. The market as a whole has lower cover ratios than it once had. Compared to a traditional norm of earnings per share of about two times dividend payouts, the average for the FTSE 100 companies is now about 1.66 and for the FTSE Small Cap about 0.99.

One of the most prominent companies to rebase its payout was Reuters, which cut its distribution from 16p to 10p and pledged to pursue 'a progressive dividend policy' from that new base. There are risks with such a strategy as dividends have propped up share prices. Reuters tell us it will grow, but the returns will be mostly as capital. That is lower quality and less secure than paying out income returns and signals increasing risk.

Based on Patrick Jenkins, *Financial Times*, March 13 2002

Self-assessment Activity 19.3

How can dividend policy damage shareholder interests when no external financing is available?

(answer at end of chapter)

Dividends as a residual

The dividend decision is simply the obverse of the investment decision. As observed earlier, we are examining the impact of one of the various ways in which proposed investment may be financed. By implication, we have been looking at a case where the company feels obliged to retain funds through lack of alternative financing options. If we make this assumption more explicit, i.e. that the firm is capital-rationed with access only to internal sources of finance, we can illustrate the **residual theory of dividends**.

This argues that dividends should be paid only when there are no further worthwhile investment opportunities. Having decided on the optimal set of investment projects, and determined the required amount of financing, the firm should distribute to shareholders only those funds not required for investment financing. This idea is shown graphically in Figure 19.2, using the **marginal efficiency of investment (MEI)** model. The MEI traces out the rate of return on the last £1 invested, and thus shows investment opportunities ranked in declining order of attractiveness.

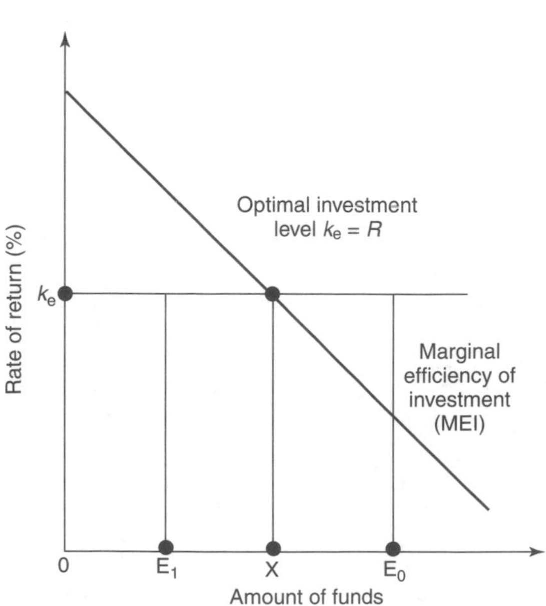

Figure 19.2 Dividends as a residual

With current-year free cash flow of OE_o, there is scope for dividend payments. The limit of worthwhile new investment is at X, where the return on the last unit of investment is equal to the minimum required return k_e. The company can now make residual dividend payments of XE_o. However, if the free cash flow is only OE_1, distribution would impose an opportunity cost on shareholders. The whole cash flow should be reinvested, but it falls short of the finance required to support the optimal programme. The shortfall is E_1X, which could only be plugged by external financing if available.

Self-assessment Activity 19.4

What dividend, if any, should the firm pay in the following situation? Earnings are £100,000; $k_e = 12$ per cent.

Project	Required Outlay	IRR
A	£300,000	18%
B	£400,000	16%
C	£700,000	14%
D	£200,000	10%

(answer at end of chapter)

External equity financing: yet more Divicut

We now consider the case where the firm has access to external financing. Rather than use earnings retention to finance investment, the firm may make a rights issue of shares, i.e. offer existing shareholders the right to buy new shares in proportion to their present holdings. If they all exercise their rights, the existing balance of control is unchanged i.e. everyone ends up holding the same share of the firm. To sustain the irrelevance conclusion, we need to show that shareholder wealth is unaffected by choice of financing method, retention or new issues.

Consider the case where Divicut contemplates a one-off dividend cut to finance a project that requires a cash outlay of £1,000, and offers perpetual earnings of £200 p.a. The shares are not yet quoted ex-dividend. The options are to:

1 Retain the earnings.
2 Pay the dividend out of earnings and then recoup the cash via a rights issue.

The project itself is worthwhile, since its NPV is:

$$\text{NPV} = -£1{,}000 + \frac{£200}{0.1} = -£1{,}000 + £2{,}000 = +£1{,}000$$

The implications for shareholder wealth of each financing alternative are respectively:

1 If the dividend is passed, the value of shareholder wealth (W_o) is:

$$W_o = \text{(dividend in year 0)} + \text{(PV of dividends from existing projects)} + \text{(PV of dividends from new projects)}$$

$$= 0 + \frac{£1,000}{0.1} + \frac{£200}{0.1} = (£10,000 + £2,000) = £12,000$$

Retention therefore benefits Divicut's shareholders, since £1,000 now is exchanged for a dividend stream with present value of £2,000.

2 If a rights issue is used to recoup the required capital, the wealth of shareholders is:

$$W_o = \text{(dividend in year 0)} + \text{(PV of dividends from existing projects)} + \text{(PV of dividends from new projects)} - \text{(amount subscribed for new shares)}$$

$$= £1,000 + \frac{£1,000}{0.1} + \frac{£200}{0.1} - £1,000$$

$$= (£1,000 + £10,000 + £2,000) - £1,000 = £12,000$$

Shareholders' wealth is unaffected if they subscribe for the new shares, anticipating the higher future stream of dividends implied by the new venture. The attraction of the rights issue to some people is that it offers a choice between further investment in the company and an alternative use of capital (although this second option may be irrational if k_e accurately measures the opportunity cost of capital). Either way, in practice, companies often ensure they obtain the required funds by employing specialist financial institutions to underwrite such issues as seen in Chapter 18.

Summary

This section has demonstrated that dividends are relevant to company valuation in the absence of external financing, but only in the sense that, if the company has better investment opportunities than its shareholders, payment of dividends prevents worthwhile investment being undertaken. With external financing, however, in a perfect capital market, dividends become totally irrelevant since dividend payment no longer precludes worthwhile investment. The firm can simply recoup the required finance via a rights issue.

In the next section, we begin to unpick some of the assumptions underpinning the irrelevance theory and consider the implications of doing so.

19.5 Objections to dividend irrelevance

This section examines some of the arguments advanced against the irrelevance theory. Financial managers should weigh up several important considerations before deciding upon the appropriate dividend payout policy:

- To what extent do shareholders rely on dividend income?
- Are nearer-in-time dividends less risky than future dividends?
- Do market imperfections lead companies to adopt policies that attract a particular clientèle of investors?
- Would investors accept a rights issue?
- How does taxation affect dividend policy?

Let us deal with these questions in turn.

Do shareholders rely on dividend income to support expenditure?

Shareholders who require a steady and reliable stream of income from dividends may be concerned by a sudden change in dividend policy, especially a dividend cut, albeit to finance worthwhile projects. Some groups of shareholders may well have a marked preference for current income: for example, the elderly, and institutions such as pension funds, which depend on a stable flow of income to meet their largely predictable liabilities. However, in an efficient capital market, such shareholders should be no worse off after a dividend cut, since the value of their holdings will rise on the news of the new investment. They can realise some or all of their gains, thus converting capital into income. The capital released is called a '**home-made dividend**'. (This is similar to the 'equity release schemes' whereby UK home-owners extract some of the value locked up in their homes.) An example is given in the appendix to this chapter.

There are several criticisms of the validity of the home-made dividends mechanism. Even in the absence of market imperfections, the investor is forced to incur the inconvenience of making the required portfolio adjustments. Allowing for brokerage and other transactions costs, the net benefits of the project for the income-seeking investor are reduced. Also, if capital gains are taxed, the enforced share sale may trigger a tax liability. In the case of only marginally attractive projects, these effects may be sufficient to more than offset the benefits of the project, at least for some investors. Conversely, it can be argued that payment of a dividend to investors who then incur brokerage fees in reinvesting their income is equally disadvantageous.

Are future dividends seen as more risky by shareholders?

The practical limitations on the unfettered ability to home-make dividends were spelt out by Myron Gordon (1963) in a ringing attack on MM's irrelevance conclusion. However, Gordon extended his critique of MM to argue that \$1 of dividend now is valued more highly than \$1 of retained earnings because investors regard the (albeit higher) future stream of dividends stemming from a new project as carrying a higher level of risk. In other words, investors prefer what Gordon called an 'early resolution of uncertainty'. Gordon was, in effect, arguing that shareholders evaluate future expected dividends using a set of rising discount rates. If present dividends are reduced to allow greater investment, thus shifting the dividend pattern into the future, company value will fall.

Keane (1974) refined Gordon's position by suggesting that it is secondary whether, in fact, future dividends are more risky than near ones. If investors perceive them to be riskier, a policy of higher retentions, while not actually increasing risk, may unfavourably alter investor attitudes. In capital markets where full information is not released about investment projects, investors' subjective risk assessments may result in low payout companies being valued at a discount compared to high payout companies: that is, investors' imperfect perceptions of risk may lead them to undervalue the future dividend stream generated by retentions.

The 'bird-in-the-hand fallacy'

If the firm's dividend policy does alter the perceived riskiness of the expected dividend flow, there may be an optimal dividend policy that trades off the beneficial effects of an enhanced growth rate against the adverse impact of increased perceived risk, so as to maximise the market value. However, advocates of dividend irrelevance argue that Gordon's analysis is inherently fallacious. More distant dividends are more risky only if they stem from riskier investment projects. Risk will already have been catered for by discounting cash flows at a suitably risk-adjusted rate. To deflate future dividends for risk further would involve double-counting. There is no reason why risk necessarily increases with time – a model based on this supposition incorporates the **'bird-in-the-hand fallacy'**. According to MM (1961), dividend policy remains a 'mere detail' once a firm's investment policy, and its inherent business risks, is made known.

Self-assessment Activity 19.5

Why is Gordon's 'early resolution of uncertainty' argument in favour of paying early dividends logically flawed?

(answer at end of chapter)

Market imperfections and the clientèle effect

The extent to which investors are willing and able to home-make dividends, and thus adjust the company's actual dividend pattern to suit their own personal desired consumption plans, depends on the degree of imperfection in the capital market. In practice, numerous impediments, especially when aggregated, may significantly offset the benefits of exploiting a profitable project. Some of these have already been mentioned, but the main ones are as follows:

- Brokerage costs incurred when shares are sold.
- Other transaction costs incurred, e.g. the costs of searching out the cheapest brokerage facilities.
- The loss in interest incurred in waiting for settlement.
- The problem of indivisibilities, whereby investors may be unable to sell the precise number of shares required, forcing them to deal in sub-optimal batch sizes.
- The sheer inconvenience of being forced to alter one's portfolio.
- Share sales may trigger a Capital Gains Tax liability.
- If the company is relatively small, its shares may lack marketability, requiring a significant dealing spread and hence a leakage of shareholder capital.
- If the company is unquoted, it may be impossible to find a buyer for the shares.

Under such imperfections, maximising firm value may not be the unique desire of all shareholders; the pattern of receipt of wealth may become equally or more important. Some shareholders may actively prefer companies that offer dividend flows which correspond to their desired consumption, perhaps being prepared to pay a premium to hold these shares. In this way, they avoid having to make their own adjustments. The vehicle for aiding such investors is to provide a stable and known dividend stream. Shareholders can then perceive the nature of the likely future dividend pattern and decide whether or not the company's policy meets their requirements. In other words, the company attracts, and attempts to cater for, a **clientèle** of shareholders.

However, such a policy has costs, including the benefits forgone from projects that have to be passed over, the costs of borrowing if debt finance is used, and/or the issue expenses of a rights issue if external financing is employed. The implications for control if rights are not fully exercised by the existing shareholders may be another problem.

The key difficulty facing the financial manager is lack of knowledge of shareholder preferences, without which it is difficult to balance the two sets of costs.

Self-assessment Activity 19.6

What is meant by a shareholder clientèle? Which shareholders are most likely to prefer near-in-time dividends?

(answer at end of chapter)

Problems with rights issues: Rawdon plc

In addition to the effect of a rights issue on share price, discussed in Chapter 18, the costs of making rights issues can be substantial, and will affect the required return on new investment. Among the costs are the administrative expenses, the costs of printing and circulation to shareholders, and also the underwriters' fees. The impact of these costs is examined using the case of Rawdon plc, whose details are shown in Table 19.2.

Although Rawdon's shareholders require a return of 20 per cent, the new project has to offer a return of *over* 20 per cent. This is because some of the finance raised by the share issue is required to meet the costs of the issue, but the holders of those shares will nevertheless demand a return. Total share capital is now £6 million, and earnings of £1.2 million are now required to generate a 20 per cent return overall. However, the required increase in earnings of £0.2 million must be generated by an investment of £950,000, necessitating a return of (£0.2 m/£0.95 m) = 21.1 per cent. Rawdon's required return on this project is:

$$\frac{\text{Normally required return}}{(1 - \%\ \text{issue costs})} = \frac{k_e}{(1 - c)} = \frac{0.2}{(1 - 0.05)} = 0.211, \text{ i.e. } 21.1\%$$

However, the problem of transactions costs may operate in another direction. Some shareholders, when paid a dividend, may incur some reinvestment costs. The higher the proportion of investors who wish to reinvest, either in the same or in another company, the greater the total saving of brokerage and other fees enjoyed by shareholders when the company retains. Hence, the greater is the attraction of retained earnings to finance investment.

Bearing in mind the impact on share price, the announcement of a rights issue is not always greeted with delight. The shareholder is forced either to take up or sell the rights in order to avoid losing money (even sale of rights will result in brokerage fees), and thus incur the inconvenience involved. If the market takes a dim view of the proposed use of the capital raised (for example, if the funds are required to finance a takeover whose benefits look distinctly speculative), the share price may fall. *But it is important to realise that this would be a consequence of a faulty investment decision rather than of the financing decision itself.*

Table 19.2 Rawdon plc

- 1 m shares have been issued in the past
- Market price per share is £5
- Current company earnings = £1 m (EPS = £1)
- Proposed investment outlay = £950,000
- The project has a perpetual life.
- Terms of rights issue:
  One share for every five held, i.e. 200,000 new shares.
  Purchase price £5: gross proceeds = £1 m
  Issue costs: 5% of gross receipts = (0.05 × £1 m) = £50,000. Net proceeds = £950,000
- k_e = 20%
- Rawdon's value = £5 m

The impact of taxation

In many economies, the tax treatment of dividend income and realised capital gains differs, either via differential tax rates or via different levels of exemption allowed, or both. In such regimes, the theoretical equivalence between dividends and retention becomes further distorted. Typically, tax on capital gains is lower than tax on income from dividends. In some countries, e.g. the Netherlands, there is *no* tax on capital gains. Some shareholders might prefer 'home-made dividends' (i.e. selling shares) when the rate of Capital Gains Tax (CGT) is lower than the marginal rate of Income Tax applied to dividends. Others may prefer dividend payments because their Income Tax liability (plus any reinvestment costs) is lower than CGT payments.

In addition to considerations of personal taxation, where the financial manager has little way of knowing the particular tax positions of shareholders (a major exception to this is the case of institutional investors), complications may also be imposed by the corporate tax system. In an imputation tax system, shareholders receive dividend income net of basic rate tax, while the rate of tax applied to corporate profits is designed to include an element of personal tax, thus making the distribution of dividends tax-neutral.

There are so many different tax regimes operated throughout the world, that it is difficult to generalise about the effect of taxation on dividend policy. However, the following simple example captures the flavour of some of the issues.

Barlow plc is financed entirely by equity and its future cash flows have present value of £500 million at the start of 2001. During 2001, it earns £100 million – for simplicity, we assume that all transactions are in cash, so it now holds cash of £100 m. Profits are taxed at 30 per cent so Barlow must set aside £30 million for tax payments, leaving (70% × £100 m) = £70 m available for distribution. According to the EMH, the firm will be valued at (£500 m + £70 m) = £570 m.

Should Barlow distribute or retain? The answer depends on three factors:

- shareholders' marginal rates of tax.
- the relative rate of tax on dividends vs. tax on capital gains.
- The *nature* of the tax regime.

Under a **classical tax system**, profits are taxed twice if distributed, once simply as profits tax, and secondly, as income tax paid by investors. Imagine the firm makes a full distribution. Consider two rates of investor income tax:

(i) if investors pay tax at 10%, income tax is (10% × £70 m) = £7 m, and the total tax charge is (£30 m + £7 m) = £37 m (or 37% of pre-tax earnings).

(ii) if investors pay tax at 50%, income tax is (50% × £70 m) = £35 m, and the total tax charge is (£30 m + £35 m) = £65 m (or 65% of pre-tax earnings).

It looks better to retain in the second case, but the decision also depends on the rate of capital gains tax (CGT).

Assume the CGT rate is 20 per cent. If we also assume that the firm invests in zero NPV projects (unlikely, but a necessary assumption to strip out the effect of the investment decision), the value of the firm will have risen from £500 million at start-year to £570 million at end-year. The CGT payable is thus (20% × £70 m) = £14 m. Along with the profits tax, the total tax payable is (£30 m + £14 m) = £44 m.

Obviously, shareholders paying income tax at 50 per cent would prefer retention and vice versa.

Under an **imputation tax system**, the relative attractiveness of distribution and retention also depends not only on the relative tax rates, but also on whether there is full or partial imputation.

With full imputation, investors get full credit for corporate profits tax already paid.

In case (i) above, the investor would face no further tax on income and may even get a tax rebate, depending on the tax regime, because the rate of corporate tax exceeds the rate of personal tax.

In case (ii), the investor obtains credit for the corporate tax already paid, and thus faces an additional income tax charge of (50% − 30%) × £70 m = £14 m. With these particular figures, investors would be indifferent between distribution and retention.

With partial imputation, it is less clear-cut – the relative desirability of distribution and retention depends on the degree of imputation, as well as the respective tax rates.

Current UK rates

Under the present UK system of partial imputation, income from dividends and capital gains are taxed at the same rate, depending on the amount involved. *But while there is no apparent discrimination in favour of either form of income, the threshold at which the taxes are payable are different.*

Income tax on dividends

Dividends are paid net of tax, assumed payable at 10 per cent, thus generating a tax credit. Current (2002–3) UK income tax rates applicable to gross dividend income are:

10% for gross (i.e. including the tax credit at 10%)
(dividend income of £1,920 – £29,900),
and at 40% where total income exceeds £29,900.

As the tax is applied to gross incomes, investors in the starting rate band of income pay no further tax, taxpayers in the basic rate bracket pay a further 10 per cent, and those in the higher rate band pay a further 32.5 per cent (to make their overall charge 40 per cent). Income tax becomes payable at incomes above £4,615, but dividends are treated as the top slice of income.

Capital Gains Tax

1 Gains above the threshold £7,700 are taxed as if additional income at the following rates:

- up to the starting rate limit (£1,920) 10%
- between £1,920 and higher rate threshold (£29,900) 20%
- above the higher rate threshold 40%

2 Gains up to 5.4.1998 are inflation-indexed, but indexation is frozen from that date.

3 Tapering relief applies on non-business assets as follows:

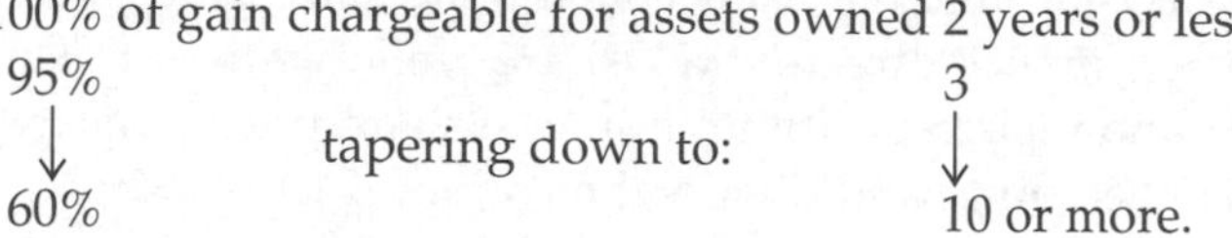

The tax irrelevance thesis

Some argue that, under perfect capital markets, the question of relative tax rates is irrelevant because of arbitrage. Zero/low rate taxpayers prefer to hold shares in firms with high payouts, and those with high marginal rates of tax prefer low payout firms. The process of tax-driven arbitrage would lead each group to bid up the share prices of the firms whose distribution policy suits their own particular tax positions, until in equilibrium, their post-tax rates of return are equalised. This means there is no share price advantage to be obtained from following a particular dividend policy.

Elton and Gruber (1970) noted the importance of marginal tax brackets in determining the return required by shareholders. They defined the cost of using retained earnings as 'that rate which makes a firm's marginal shareholders indifferent between earnings being retained or paid out in the form of dividends'. Under differential tax treatments of dividend income and capital gains, the cost of using retained earnings is a function of the shareholder's marginal tax bracket. We might also expect companies whose shareholders incur high rates of income tax to exhibit low payout rates. Such a relationship between corporate dividend policy and shareholder tax brackets would support the notion of tax 'clientèles', whereby companies seek to tailor their payout policies to the tax situation of particular shareholders. Elton and Gruber's empirical work seemed to indicate that firms attract rational clientèles – *shareholders gravitate to companies whose distribution policy is compatible with their personal tax situations.*

19.6 The information content of dividends: dividend smoothing

Possibly the most important consideration for corporate financial decision-makers when framing dividend policy is the information-processing capacity of the market. Any dividend declaration can be interpreted by the market in a variety of ways. In an uncertain world, information regarding a company's prospects is neither generally available nor costless to acquire. Managers possess more information about the company's trading position than is available to investors as a whole. This so-called **information asymmetry** may mean that the announcement of a new or changed company policy may be interpreted by the market as a signal conveying particular information about a company's prospects.

For example, the decision to pay an unexpectedly high dividend may be seized upon as evidence of greater expected dividend-paying capacity in the future. It may be taken as guaranteeing an ability to sustain at least the higher declared dividend and probably more. As a result, the financial manager should consider carefully how the market is likely to decode the signals contained in the dividend decision, and the likely consequences for share price.

Company finance directors (FDs) are well aware of the signalling power of dividends and their capacity to influence share price. This awareness is implied by the recent earnings and dividend record of BAA plc, shown in Table 19.3.

BAA's EPS figures have increased by 150 per cent over ten years, but erratically, whereas the parallel dividend increase (144 per cent) has been more regular. This 'smoothing' of dividends can be found among many other firms and has been identified empirically. Lintner (1956) showed that companies appear to raise dividends only on the basis of reported earnings increases that they expect to be sustainable in the long term. In a survey of 179 Finance Directors of large quoted companies conducted by 3i (1993), 43 per cent said that the single most important factor influencing dividend policy was prospective long-term profit growth, while 93 per cent agreed with the statement that 'dividend policy should follow the long-term trend in earnings'.

When dividend increases lag behind increases in EPS, the payout ratio falls and *vice versa*. However, average payout ratios have risen in recent years, owing to a number of factors:

1 Increasing corporate profits.
2 Hence, increased confidence in companies' ability to sustain dividends.
3 The increasing pressures exerted by the ever-more powerful institutional investors, especially the tax-exempt funds.

Table 19.3 BAA plc: dividend smoothing

Year	EPS (p)		% increase	DPS (p)		% increase
1992	15.20		–	7.25		–
1993	20.90		13.8	8.00		10.3
1994	23.50		11.2	9.00		11.2
1995	27.20		11.6	10.125		12.5
1996	30.40		11.2	11.25		11.1
1997	28.30		(9.3)	12.40		10.2
1998	26.30		(6.9)	13.65		10.1
1999	37.50		42.6	15.00		9.9
2000	24.20		(35.5)	16.35		9.0
2001	37.70		55.8	17.70		8.3
Average			9.4			10.2
Range		max	55.8		max	12.5
		min	(35.5)		min	8.3
			91.3			4.2

Mini case

CGNU plc

The following example illustrates the poor reaction to a UK firm cutting dividends to provide funds to finance a growth strategy. The firm felt unable to make a rights issue on a weak market, especially as its shares had under-performed the market over the previous year.

In February 2002, the insurance giant, CGNU plc (soon to be re-branded as Aviva), announced that it would slash its dividend by 40 per cent from 38 to 23 pence per share and then grow dividends by 5 per cent annually henceforth. Although the sector had become used to bad news following the huge losses triggered by the attacks on the World Trade Centre, CGNU actually reported an increase in operating profits of 41 per cent, as it began to reap the rewards from a resurgence of insurance premiums and from ***bancassurance*** partnerships in Britain and continental Europe.

CGNU's given reason for the cut was to maintain the momentum of growth in its pensions and savings products, which had grown by 30 per cent since the former CGU and Norwich Union merged in 2000. Investors were not impressed – the share price fell by 9 per cent on a day when the market rose 0.5 per cent. One fund manager was reported as saying that he would sell the shares as he '. . . wanted to make sure that they are making good investments with the money they are not paying to me'.

4 The use of pre-emptive dividend increases to ward off takeover raiders.
5 The tax changes of 1988, which largely removed the tax discrimination for higher-rate taxpayers in favour of retentions.

So do companies ever cut dividends? Obviously, in adversity, dividend cuts are forced on firms in order to preserve cash. In the 3i survey, 55 per cent of FDs agreed with the statement that 'any cut in dividend payout sends adverse signals to the market and should be avoided'. Dividend-cutting is far more common in the USA than in the UK. Empirical work by Ghosh and Woolridge (1989) suggests that even when this was motivated by the need to conserve funds for investment purposes, shareholders suffered significant capital losses, despite the merits claimed for the proposed investments. In the UK, it is almost unheard of for companies to cut dividends to finance investment – the dividend payment-plus-rights issue is invariably the preferred alternative. In the 3i survey, one FD said that 'a dividend cut is a sign of fundamental management failure – when management fails and the Board should change'.

19.7 Alternatives to cash dividends

The motive for cutting a dividend is to save cash outflows. This suggests that liquidity considerations are another influence on the dividend decision. This section discusses how firms that wish to preserve liquidity can still offer 'dividends', and also how firms can cope with excessive liquidity. Alternatives to cash dividends are thus divided into those that preserve liquidity and those that reduce liquidity.

Liquidity saving alternatives

(i) Scrip dividends

Most major companies offer shareholders scrip dividends. This is an opportunity to receive new shares instead of a cash dividend payment. It has certain advantages for both the shareholder and the company.

From the firm's point of view, the scrip alternative preserves liquidity, which may be important at a time of cash shortage and/or high borrowing costs, although it could face a higher level of cash outflows if shareholders revert to preference for cash in the future. With more shares issued, the company's reported financial gearing may fall, possibly enhancing borrowing capacity. In this respect, the scrip dividend resembles a mini-rights issue.

For shareholders wishing to expand their holdings, the scrip is a cheap way into the company as it avoids dealing fees and Stamp Duty. A scrip dividend has no tax advantages for shareholders as it is treated as income for tax purposes.

In an efficient capital market, there is no dilution effect on the share price, which would have fallen anyway because of the 'ex-dividend effect'. However, if the additional capital retained is expected to be used wisely, the share price may be maintained or may even rise, giving shareholders who elect for the scrip dividend access to higher future dividends and capital gains. As a result, there may be a longer-term tax advantage for shareholders. However, most of these effects are marginal. Perhaps the main benefit of a scrip dividend is that, by giving shareholders a choice, it makes the shares more attractive to a wider clientèle.

(ii) Enhanced scrip dividends

To overcome the low take-up rate of scrip dividends, in 1993, several companies with chronic liquidity problems began to offer 'enhanced scrip dividends' (ESDs). The first was BAT Industries (website: **www.bat.com**), which announced a scrip alternative 50 per cent above the equivalent cash dividend, designed to be so generous that shareholders could not refuse. BAT, 88 per cent of whose profits originated overseas, declared a 22.6p final dividend, and then, later that month, offered an ESD alternative of 33.9p. Had all of BAT's shareholders taken up the issue, the cash saving would have been £423 million.

The ESD mechanism is a rights issue in disguise. To the extent that shareholders take the scrip alternative, the company is left with as much cash as if it had paid a cash dividend and then clawed it back from the same shareholders via a rights issue. As with a rights issue, the number of shares issued will rise. Finally, because the scrip is voluntary, the control of shareholders taking cash is diluted. The BAT episode is documented by Millerchip (1993).

Self-assessment Activity 19.7

How many shares would an investor receive in lieu of cash dividends of £1,000 if offered:

(i) a pro rata scrip alternative?
(ii) an ESD of 20%?

Share price is £20.

(answer at end of chapter)

Due to tax changes enacted in 1997, some firms experienced a sharp rise in the take-up rate of scrips – e.g. some 20 per cent of Boots plc's dividend outflow was in scrip form. This was unpalatable to firms that were concerned about the effect on the total number of shares issued by the company, e.g. it reduced the scope for any future rights issue.

In April 1998, GKN plc (website: **www.gkn.plc**) responded to this problem by withdrawing its scrip dividend scheme because 'recent changes in tax legislation affecting institutional shareholders make it more likely that a scrip dividend could lead to the issue of large numbers of new shares which, we believe, is not in shareholders' best interests'. Instead, GKN introduced its Dividend Re-investment Plan (DRIP) as from May 1998, whereby shareholders can purchase existing shares of equivalent value to the cash dividend at a preferential dealing cost (0.5 per cent of the dividend displaced).

Liquidity reducing alternatives

The dividend decision is contorted by the case of companies with too much cash. This phenomenon was encountered in the introductory cameo of Cable & Wireless which decided to mount a share repurchase rather than pay out higher dividends.

The facility to repurchase shares, subject to shareholders' approval, was introduced in the UK by the 1981 Companies Act. It resulted from pressure from the small firms lobby, concerned that low marketability of unquoted firms' equity was hampering their development. Certain conditions were stipulated, designed principally to safeguard the position of creditors, and further restrictions were imposed by the Stock Exchange and the Takeover Panel, aimed at reducing the risk of market-rigging during takeover battles. The first major company to mount a buy-back was GEC in 1984, ostensibly to raise the EPS of the remaining shares. A component of Forte's defence package against the Granada takeover bid in 1995 was share repurchase, designed to raise the cost of the bid.

The Bank of England (1988) cited five possible reasons for repurchases:

- To return surplus cash to shareholders.
- To increase underlying share value.
- To support share price during periods of temporary weakness.
- To achieve or maintain a target capital structure.
- To prevent or inhibit unwelcome takeover bids.

Table 19.4 Analysis of a share repurchase

	Before	After
Trading profit (£m)	200.00	200.00
Interest income at 5% (£m)	5.00	3.20
Pre-tax profit (£m)	205.00	203.20
Tax at 30% (£m)	(61.50)	(60.96)
Profits available for shareholders (£m)	143.50	142.24
Cash balances (£m)	100.00	64.00
Number of shares in issue	500 m	480 m
EPS (p)	28.70	29.63
Required return (%)	16	16
Share price (p)	179	185

The hoped-for increase in share price works through the effect on EPS. A company may attempt a buy-back when it has a cash surplus beyond what it needs to finance normal business operations. This situation is assumed in Table 19.4, which shows the before-and-after situation of a company sitting on a cash pile of £100 million earning interest at 5 per cent. It buys in 20 million shares at 180p, above the market price of 172p, the discrepancy being due to the required premium and the costs of buying the shares. The total buy-back cost is therefore £36 million, on which the company will lose interest income.

In the UK (unlike the USA), when a company buys back shares it has to cancel them. This suggests a problem with buy-backs – directors may buy in shares and might subsequently have to make a rights issue, the costs of which are far higher than those involved in repurchasing shares. US evidence suggests a strong signalling effect, whereby executives can express confidence in their firms by investing in equity. Yet there remains a strong suspicion in the UK that such messages are likely to be decoded adversely. To many observers, buy-backs are tantamount to an admission of managerial failure, signalling lack of confidence in their ability to identify and exploit wealth-creating projects.

However, investment expenditure is rarely a continuous process and small buy-backs may be a useful way of investing temporary cash surpluses, with the beneficial effects on EPS and share price providing a platform for a subsequent rights issue if development funds are needed. In addition, buy-backs may be a useful alternative to paying higher but unsustainable dividends, while preserving choice for investors.

Self-assessment Activity 19.8

Suggest some arguments *against* share repurchases.

(answer at end of chapter)

Mini case

Toyota buys back yet more shares

Buy-backs are not only an Anglo-Saxon phenomenon. The world's third-largest car maker, Toyota, bought back shares every year during 1997–2001, including the biggest ever by a Japanese firm in early 2001, of yen 264 billion (US$2.10 billion). Later in 2001, it announced plans to accelerate the buy-back programme.

Toyota's circumstances were unusual – Japanese banks owned around 15 per cent of Toyota's equity. Until 2001, Japanese banks were able to record investments in marketable securities at cost, rather than the more prudent 'lower of cost or net realisable value' as in the UK and elsewhere. Following the long Japanese bear market, many banks held equity at cost values far higher than market values, thus artificially inflating their asset bases and flattering their capital adequacy ratios.

Under pressure from the central bank to apply 'mark to market' accounting rules before April 1 2000, Japanese banks had to sell equity stakes for cash to bolster their liquidity. Moreover, Sanwa Bank and Tokai Bank, each holding 4.9 per cent of Toyota, needed to offload Toyota stock to comply with competition law ahead of their planned merger in April 2001. Sakura Bank, about to merge with Sumitomo Bank also held 4.9 per cent of Toyota. The huge 'over-hang' of Toyota shares led to Toyota stock under-performing in the first half of 2001. Despite record operating profits in 2000–1,Toyota's share price rose by a relatively pedestrian 20 per cent, whereas Nissan and Honda increased by over 30 per cent. Hence, the need for a buy-back to support the share price to offset potential institutional share dumping

Market reaction was favourable. On a day when the Nikkei index rose by 1.3 per cent, Toyota shares rose 12.8 per cent. A Toyota spokesman stated that the 'buy-back is a kind of contribution to our shareholders', observing that 'it's natural that if the number of stocks is reduced, the value of each share must go up'.

19.8 The dividend puzzle

At a practical level, we encounter a dilemma known as the 'dividend puzzle'. Dividend cuts are undesirable, yet dividend payments may not always be in the best interests of shareholders. For example, under many tax regimes, dividends are immediately taxed, while the tax on capital gains can be deferred indefinitely. Dividend distribution may force a firm subsequently to issue equity or debt instruments which incur issue costs and interfere with gearing ratios (see Chapter 20). However, markets do react favourably to news of unexpectedly high dividend increases despite the acknowledged costs of dividends. The message conveyed by firms when raising dividends seems to be:

Despite the cash flow costs of dividend payments, we are prepared to pay higher dividends because we are confident of our ability to withstand these costs and at least to maintain these higher disbursements.

The case for a stable dividend policy

Astute financial managers appreciate that different shareholders have different needs. A financial institution reliant on a stream of income to match its stream of liabilities will prefer stable dividends, while a 'gross fund' (i.e. one exempt from tax on its income) will prefer shares that offer a high level of dividends. The private individual in the 40 per cent tax bracket will prefer capital gains, at least up to the £7,700 exemption limit (2002–03), while the old-age pensioner with a relatively short time horizon is likely to seek income rather than capital appreciation.

Given the wide diffusion of shareholdings, it is almost impossible for most financial managers to begin to assess the needs of all their shareholders. This is an argument for a stable dividend policy, e.g. the application of a fairly constant dividend increase, implying that dividends rise at the same rate as corporate post-tax earnings, subject perhaps to the proviso that dividends should not be allowed to fall, unless earnings suffer a serious reverse. This will enable shareholders to gravitate towards companies whose payout policies suit their particular income needs and tax positions. In this way, companies can expect to build up a clientèle of shareholders attracted by a particular dividend pattern. Hardly surprising, then, that 75 per cent of FDs in the 3i survey said that 'Companies should aim for a consistent payout ratio.'

Self-assessment Activity 19.9

Rehearse the arguments in favour of a stable dividend policy.

(answer at end of chapter)

Shares without the other bit

'The only thing that gives me pleasure', John D. Rockefeller once said, 'is to see my dividends coming in.' How much fun would Mr Rockefeller have nowadays? If the tycoon invested in the modern equivalents of his own Standard Oil, he would be owning shares in such corporate stars as Microsoft, Cisco, Sun Microsystems, Dell and America Online. But, like most American companies today, none of these has ever paid a dividend, nor has plans to do so.

Continued

In the 1950s, nine out ten of American companies paid dividends. Today only one in five does. Dividends are disappearing so fast in America that Eugene Fama and Kenneth French, professors of finance at the University of Chicago and the Massachusetts Institute of Technology respectively, have looked into the phenomenon. Part of their explanation for it is straightforward: the sorts of companies that are traded on America's stockmarkets have changed radically. Until the early 1970s, an exchange listing was, by and large, the preserve of large, profitable firms – that one would expect to pay dividends.

All this changed after 1971, when the old New York Stock Exchange was joined by an upstart new rival, Nasdaq, which imposed less stringent listing conditions. Naturally, it attracted newer and more innovative companies. These newcomers were different. By 1997, only about half the new listings made any profits at all. Since then, as some cynics on Wall Street joke, making profits, for any self-respecting 'dot.com', has become uncool.

Not only is a company that has no profits to distribute ill-advised to pay a dividend. But even a company with profits should choose to retain them if it thinks that its own investment opportunities are better than those available to shareholders elsewhere. For both reasons, more 'growth' companies will tend to mean fewer dividend-payers.

Even so, there is a puzzle about the disappearing dividend. It is not just growth companies that are opting out of dividends, but all companies, including those enjoying healthy flows of free cash. J.P.Morgan, an investment bank, estimates that the dividend pay-out of America's 500 largest companies has fallen from over half of profits in 1990 to about a third now.

There are several possible explanations for this, but none seems adequate by itself. One is that shareholders do not want dividends. These represent income, which in America is taxed at a top federal rate of 39.6 per cent. By leaving profits in the firm, investors can defer this tax, watch the value of their stake grow and, if need be, cash in a capital gain, which is taxed at only 20 per cent.

Another theory says that dividends have not disappeared, but assumed a new guise: companies' purchases of their own shares. Such 'buy-backs' have risen from 3–5 per cent of annual corporate profits during the 1970s to 26 per cent in the 1980s and 1990s. J.P.Morgan calculates that, counting both dividends and buy-backs, the total pay-out ratio has been quite steady.

There must be more to it than tax or buy-backs. One possibility, though experts might deny this, is mere fashion. Not long ago, bosses were protective of their dividends, because investors saw them as the most potent signal that management could send about the future of its business. To tarry over raising dividends, never mind suspending them, was seen as a confession of failure. Nowadays, the opposite may be true. Mr French says he has friends in investment banking who 'tell their clients that paying dividends is like an admission that you have nothing better to do'.

That does not mean dividends have become completely irrelevant. Companies that trim their dividend still tend to see their share price drop by an average of 6 per cent; those that suspend dividends altogether see prices drop by 25 per cent.

Based on the *Economist*, November 20 1999

19.9 Conclusions

What advice can be offered to practising financial managers? We suggest the following guidelines:

(1) Remember the capacity of ill-advised dividend decisions to inflict damage. In view of the market's often savage reaction to dividend cuts, managers should operate a safe dividend cover, allowing sufficient payout flexibility should earnings decline. This suggests a commitment to a clientèle of shareholders who have come to expect a particular dividend policy from their company. This, in turn, suggests a long-term payout ratio sufficient to satisfy shareholder needs, but also generating sufficient internal funds to finance 'normal' investment requirements. Any 'abnormal' financing needs can be met by selling securities, rather than by dividend cuts. In the long term, it seems prudent to minimise reliance on external finance, but not to the extent of building up a 'cash mountain'. This may merely signal to the financial world that the company has run out of acceptable investment projects. If there is no worthwhile alternative use of capital, then dividends should be paid.

(2) If an alteration in dividend policy is proposed, the firm should minimise the shock effect of an unanticipated dividend cut, e.g. by explaining in advance the firm's investment programme and its financing needs.

(3) In an efficient capital market, the dividend announcement, 'good' or 'bad', will be immediately impounded into share price in an unbiased fashion. News of higher dividends will lead to a higher share price because it conveys the information that management believes there is a strong likelihood of higher future earnings and dividends. In view of this, many observers argue that the primary role of dividend policy should be to communicate information to a security market otherwise starved of hard financial data about future company prospects and intrinsic value, while pursuing a year-by-year distribution rate that does not violate the interests of the existing clientèle of shareholders.

Dividends are likely to be higher:

- The greater the shareholders' reliance on current income.
- The more difficult it is to generate home-made dividends.
- The greater the impact of imperfections, e.g. brokerage fees.
- The lower are income taxes compared to capital gains taxes.
- The lower the costs of a rights issue.
- The greater the ease of reinvestment by shareholders.
- The more often past dividend increases have heralded subsequent earnings and dividend increases.

(4) While it is impossible to be definitive in this area, the box lists the circumstances in which shareholders are likely to prefer dividends to retention and hence, when a dividend increase may raise share price.

(5) Finally, the dividend decision is 'only' a financing decision, in so far as paying a dividend may necessitate alternative arrangements for financing investment projects. There can be few companies (at least, quoted ones) for which dividends have constrained really worthwhile investment. For most companies, it is often sensible to adopt a modest target payout ratio. It is not wise to pay large dividends and then have to incur the costs of raising equity from the very same shareholders.

Summary

We have reviewed the competing arguments regarding the relative desirability of paying out dividends to shareholders and retaining funds to finance investment, resulting in capital gains.

Key points

- The market value of a company ultimately depends on its dividend-paying capacity.
- The irrelevance or residual theory of dividends argues that, under perfect capital market conditions, an alteration in the pattern of dividend payouts has no impact on company value, once the effect of the investment decision is removed.
- If retentions are used to finance worthwhile investment, company value increases, both for one-off retentions and for sustained retention to finance an ongoing investment programme.
- Failure to retain profits can damage shareholder interests if the company has better investment opportunities than shareholders, unless outside capital sources are available and utilised.
- Dividend irrelevance implies that shareholders are indifferent between dividends and capital gains, because the latter can be converted into income.
- In practice, various market imperfections, especially transactions costs and taxes, interfere with this conclusion, although it is difficult to be categoric about the net directional impact.
- Companies are generally unable to detect shareholder preferences, so they should follow a stable dividend policy, designed to suit a particular category, or 'clientèle', of shareholders.
- In practice, companies are reluctant to cut dividends for fear of adverse interpretation by the market of the information conveyed in the announcement.
- Similarly, companies are reluctant to increase dividends too sharply for fear of encouraging over-optimistic expectations about future performance.
- This 'information content' in dividend decisions provides a further argument for dividend stability.

Further reading

A good feel for the dividend policy debate can be obtained from the early articles by Gordon (1959) and Miller and Modigliani (1961), and Gordon's (1963) rejoinder to MM. Bhattacharya (1979) gives a rigorous treatment of the bird-in-the-hand fallacy, while Miller (1986) provides an overview of the debate so far. Copeland and Weston (1988) offer chapters on both the theory of dividend policy and the empirical evidence. Pettit (2001) gives a highly readable assessment of the advantages and dangers of share buybacks.

Appendix

Home-made dividends

Kirkstall plc is financed solely by equity. Its cash flow from existing operations is expected to be £24 million p.a. in perpetuity, all of which has hitherto been paid as dividend. Shareholders require a return of 12 per cent. Kirkstall has previously issued 50 million shares. The value of the dividend stream is:

$$V_o = \frac{£24 \text{ m}}{0.12} = £200 \text{ m, yielding share price of } \frac{£200 \text{ m}}{50 \text{ m}} = £4 \text{ (ex-div)}$$

Imagine you hold 1 per cent of Kirkstall's equity, worth £2 million. This yields an annual dividend income of £240,000, all of which you require to support your lavish lifestyle. Kirkstall proposes to pass the dividend payable in one year's time in order to invest in a project offering a single net cash flow after a further year of £40 million, when the previous 100 per cent payout policy will be resumed. Your new expected dividend flow is:

Year 1	Year 2	Year 3
0	£240,000 + (1% × £40 m) = £640,000	£240,000

The market value of Kirkstall rises to:

$$V_o = 0 = \frac{£64 \text{ m}}{(1.12)^2} + \left[\frac{£24 \text{ m}}{(0.12)} \times \frac{1}{(1.12)^2}\right]$$
$$= (£51.02 \text{ m} + £159.44 \text{ m}) = £210.46 \text{ m}$$

The increase in value reflects the NPV of the project. Share price rises from £4 to £4.21, thus raising the value of your holding from £2 million to £2.104 million. To support your living standards, you could either borrow on the strength of the higher expected dividend in Year 2 or sell part of your share stake in Year 1, when no dividend is proposed.

In Year 1, the value of your holding will be £2.356 million, and each share will be priced at £4.71. To provide sufficient capital to finance expenditure of £240,000, you need to sell £240,000/£4.71 = 50,955 shares, reducing your holding to (500,000 – 50.955) = 449,045 shares. In Year 2, Kirkstall will distribute a dividend of £64 million (£1.28 per share), of which your share will be £574,778. Out of this, you will require £240,000 for immediate consumption, leaving you better off by £334,778. This may be used to restore your previous shareholding, and thus your previous flow of dividends. The ex-dividend share price in Year 2 will settle back to £4, at which price, the repurchase of 50,955 shares will require an outlay of £203,820, leaving you a surplus of (£334,778 – £203,820) = £130,958. The net effect of your transactions is to yield an income flow of:

Year	1	2	3, etc.
Dividend paid by company	0	£574,778	£240,000
Market transaction	£240,000	(£203,820)	
Net income	£240,000	£370,958	£240,000

Overall, your shareholding remains the same, and you earn extra income in Year 2 of £130,958. This has a present value of £104,000, the very amount of your wealth increase when Kirkstall first announced details of the project, i.e.

1% × change in market value = 1% × (£210.41 m – £200 m) = £104,000

(note that rounding errors account for minor deviations).

Self-assessment Answers

19.1 Earnings in year zero = £1,000, of which 60%, i.e. £600 are retained. Returns on new investment = (15% × £600) = £90.
Next year's earnings = (£1,000 + £90) = £1,090.

$$\text{Growth rate} = \frac{(£1{,}090)}{(£1{,}000)} - 1 = 9\% = (60\% \times 15\%),\ (b \times R)$$

19.2 Divicut invests £1,000 in year 1 to return £1,080 in year 2.
The NPV of this is £1,080/ $(1.1)^2$ vs. £1,000/ (1.1)
Or £893 vs. £909, thus a negative NPV of £16, because the return on reinvested earnings falls short of the required 10%.

19.3 Paying out dividends rather than investing in worthwhile projects otherwise inaccessible to shareholders reduces the PV of their future income below what it could have been, i.e. there is an opportunity cost imposed on them.

19.4 Projects A, B and C are all attractive, but C appears unavailable as it would lead to exceeding the budget. However, if C is divisible, the firm should undertake A, B and 3/7 of C; otherwise, it should pay a dividend of £300,000.

19.5 Gordon confuses the risk of the dividends with the risk of the underlying cash flows resulting from new investment. If risk (and any increase in it) is suitably allowed for in the discount rate used to deflate future cash flows, then to discount the more distant future dividend flow would entail double-counting for risk. (If the firm moves into a low risk area, the future dividends could even have lower risk than near-in-time dividends.)

19.6 A clientèle is a set of investors whose interests the firm tries to serve via its particular dividend policy. Investors with short time horizons are likely to include the relatively elderly or infirm, and those with pressing needs for rapid income payments, e.g. to repay debts or to fund a daughter's wedding.

19.7 **(i)** £1,000/£20 = 50 shares
(ii) 50 plus 20% = 60 shares.

19.8 Share repurchases may signal that the firm has exhausted investment opportunities or has become too risk-averse to devoting funds to R and D. They may also trigger CGT liabilities for some investors. It may also cause embarrassment to directors if share prices subsequently fall.

19.9 A stable dividend policy gives reliability and security. Investors can plan their future income and expenditures more easily. Sharp cuts in dividends, as well as causing alarm, may force investors to sell shares on a weak market. Similarly, a sharp increase in dividends may force investors to reconfigure their portfolios, as well as triggering a CGT liability.

Questions

1 *Solution in Appendix A (page 827).* Tom plc follows a residual dividend policy. It has just announced earnings of £10 m and is to pay a dividend of 20p per share. Its nominal issued share capital is £5 m with par value of 50p. What value of capital expenditure is it undertaking? (You may ignore taxes.)

2 *Solution in Appendix A (page 827).* Dick plc faces the following marginal efficiency of investment profile. All projects are indivisible.

Project	IRR (%)	Required outlay (£ m)
A	15	3
B	24	5
C	40	2
D	12	4
E	21	7

Dick's shareholders require a return of 20 per cent. Dick has just reported earnings of £9 m.

What amount of dividend would you recommend if Dick is unable to raise external finance?

3 *Solution in Appendix A (page 828).* Harry plc prides itself on its consistent dividend policy. Past data suggests that its target dividend payout ratio is 50 per cent of earnings. However, when earnings increase, Harry invariably raises its dividend only halfway towards the level that the target dividend payout ratio would indicate. The last dividend was £1 per share and Harry has just announced earnings for the recently ended financial year of £3 per share.

What dividend per share would you expect the Board to recommend?

4 *Solution in Appendix A (page 828)*. Tamas plc, which is ungeared, earned pre-tax accounting profits of £30 million in the financial year just ended. Replacement investment will match last year's depreciation of £2 million. Both are fully tax-allowable.

Corporation tax is payable at 30 per cent. Tamas operates a 50 per cent dividend payout policy, and has previously issued 100 million shares, with par value of 25 pence each. Its shareholders require a return of 15 per cent p.a.

Tamas holds £15 million cash balances.

Required

Determine the market price per ordinary share of Tamas, both cum-dividend and also ex-dividend.

(N.B. Use the perpetuity formula to value Tamas' shares.)

5 *Solution in Appendix A (page 828)*. Galahad plc, a quoted manufacturer of textiles, has followed a policy in recent years of paying out a steadily increasing dividend per share as shown below:

Year	EPS	Dividend (net)	Cover
1986	11.8p	5.0p	2.4
1987	12.5p	5.5p	2.3
1988	14.6p	6.0p	2.4
1989	13.5p	6.5p	2.1
1990	16.0p	7.3p	2.2

Galahad has only just made the 1990 dividend payment, so the shares are quoted ex-dividend. The main board, which is responsible for strategic planning decisions, is considering a major change in strategy whereby greater financing will be provided by internal funds, involving a cut in the 1991 dividend to 5p (net) per share. The investment projects thus funded will increase the growth rate of Galahad's earnings and dividends to 14 per cent. Some operating managers, however, feel that the new growth rate is unlikely to exceed 12 per cent. Galahad's shareholders seek an overall return of 16 per cent.

Required

(a) Calculate the market price per share for Galahad, prior to the change in policy, using the Dividend Growth Model.

(b) Assess the likely impact on Galahad's share price of the proposed policy change.

(c) Determine the break-even growth rate.

(d) Discuss the possible reaction of Galahad's shareholders and of the capital market in general to this proposed dividend cut in the light of Galahad's past dividend policy.

6 Laceby manufactures agricultural equipment and is currently all-equity financed. In previous years, it has paid out a steady 50 per cent of available earnings as dividend and used retentions to finance investment in new projects, which have returned 16 per cent on average.

Its Beta is 0.83, and the return on the market portfolio is expected to be 17 per cent in the future, offering a risk premium of 6 per cent.

Laceby has just made earnings of £8 million before tax and the dividend will be paid in a few weeks' time. Some managers argue in favour of retaining an extra £2 million this year in order to finance the development of a new Common Agricultural Policy (CAP) surplus crop disposal machine. This may offer the following returns under the listed possible scenarios:

	Probability	(£m p.a.) Cash flow (pre-tax)
WTO talks succeed	0.2	0.5
No reform of CAP	0.6	1.5
CAP extended to Eastern Europe	0.2	4.0

The project may be assumed to have an infinite life, and to attract an EU agricultural efficiency grant of £1 million. Corporation Tax is paid at 33 per cent (assume no tax delay).

Required

(a) What is the NPV of the proposed project?

(b) Value the equity of Laceby:

  (i) before undertaking the project,

  (ii) after announcing the acceptance of the project.

(c) Assuming you have found an increase in value in (b)(ii), explain what conditions would be required to support such a conclusion.

7 Pavlon plc has recently obtained a listing on the Stock Exchange. Ninety per cent of the company's shares were previously owned by members of one family, but, since the listing, approximately 60 per cent of the issued shares have been owned by other investors.

Pavlon's earnings and dividends for the five years prior to the listing are detailed below:

Years prior to listing	Profit after tax (£)	Dividend per share (pence)
5	1,800,000	3.60
4	2,400,000	4.80
3	3,850,000	6.16
2	4,100,000	6.56
1	4,450,000	7.12
Current year	5,500,000 (estimate)	

The number of issued ordinary shares was increased by 25 per cent three years prior to the listing and by 50 per cent at the time of the listing. The company's authorised capital is currently £25,000,000 in 25p ordinary shares, of which 40,000,000 shares have been issued. The market value of the company's equity is £78,000,000.

The board of directors is discussing future dividend policy. An interim dividend of 3.16p per share was paid immediately prior to the listing and the finance director has suggested a final dividend of 2.34p per share.

The company's declared objective is to maximise shareholder wealth.

The company's profit after tax is generally expected to increase by 15 per cent p.a. for three years, and 8 per cent per year after that. Pavlon's cost of equity capital is estimated to be 12 per cent per year. Dividends may be assumed to grow at the same rate as profits.

Required

(a) Comment upon the nature of the company's dividend policy prior to the listing and discuss whether such a policy is likely to be suitable for a company listed on the Stock Exchange.

(b) Discuss whether the proposed final dividend of 2.34 pence is likely to be appropriate:
- **(1)** if the majority of shares are owned by wealthy private individuals;
- **(2)** if the majority of shares are owned by institutional investors.

(c) Using the Dividend Valuation Model give calculations to indicate whether Pavlon's shares are currently undervalued or overvalued.

(d) Briefly outline the weaknesses of the Dividend Valuation Model.

(ACCA)

8 Mondrian plc is a newly-formed company which aims to maximise the wealth of its shareholders. The board of directors of the company is currently trying to decide upon the most appropriate dividend policy to adopt for the company's shareholders. However, there is strong disagreement between three of the directors concerning the benefits of declaring cash dividends,

Director A argues that cash dividends would be welcome by investors and that as high a dividend payout ratio as possible would reflect positively on the market value of the company's shares.

Director B argues that whether a cash dividend is paid or not is irrelevant in the context of shareholder wealth maximisation.

Director C takes an opposite view to Director A and argues that dividend payments should be avoided as they would lead to a decrease in shareholder wealth.

Required

(a) Discuss the arguments for and against the position taken by each of the three directors.

(b) Assuming the board of directors decides to pay a dividend to shareholders, what factors should be taken into account when determining the level of dividend payment?

(ACCA Certified Diploma June 1996)

Practical assignment

Obtain the Annual Report and Accounts of any firm of your choice. Look at the five-year record provided, and work out the dividend cover each year and the annual rate of dividend per share increase as compared to the annual increase in EPS. Is there any obvious pattern to the dividend decisions over this period? Does the firm have a clear dividend policy?

20 Capital structure and the required return

Waccing good value

In its Report and Accounts of 1997, the Tomkins plc Chairman answered questions from shareholders. Two such Qs and As are shown below.

Q *What is your weighted average cost of capital (WACC)?*

A Some shareholders may not be familiar with this term. WACC is normally defined as the effective cost, after tax, of all the different sources of capital which fund a business. In order to add value for shareholders, it is necessary for the return on invested capital (including that spent on goodwill) to exceed the WACC.

Calculating WACC is not a precise science as it involves a number of assumptions. However, we believe that gearing of 15 to 20 per cent will achieve a WACC of around 10 per cent.

Q *What level of gearing is planned?*

A In this financial year, we plan to achieve gearing of 15 to 20 per cent of shareholders' funds. We consider a number of factors in determining an appropriate level. They are not static, but dynamic, and will include the extent to which debt is at fixed or protected rates of interest, the trend in interest rates, interest cover, the ratio of debt to total market capitalisation and to shareholders' funds, as well as general market conditions. It will also depend on our immediate acquisition and divestment plans. We are a conservative company when it comes to the use of debt; however, we are committed to an efficient capital structure and to lower progressively our WACC. It will also ensure that we are well financed should there be a recession.

Source: Tomkins plc, Report and Accounts 1997

Learning objectives

This chapter has the following aims:

- To explain some of the ways of measuring gearing.
- To enable you to understand more fully the advantages of debt capital.
- To explain the meaning of, and how to calculate, the WACC.
- To enable you to understand the likely limits on the use of debt, and the nature of 'financial distress' costs.
- To help you understand the issues involved in financing foreign operations.
- To enable you to understand the factors that a finance manager should consider when framing capital structure policy.

20.1 Introduction

Most financing decisions in practice reduce to a choice between debt and equity. The finance manager wishing to fund a new project, but reluctant to cut dividends or to make a rights issue, has to consider the borrowing option. In this chapter, we further examine the arguments for and against using debt to finance company activities and, in particular, consider the impact of gearing on the overall rate of return that the company must achieve.

The main advantages of debt capital centre on its relative cost. Debt capital is usually cheaper than equity because:

1 The pre-tax rate of interest is invariably lower than the return required by shareholders. This is due to the legal position of lenders who, have a prior claim on the distribution of the company's income and who, in a liquidation, precede ordinary shareholders in the queue for the settlement of claims. Debt is usually secured on the firm's assets, which can be sold to pay off lenders in the event of **default**, i.e. failure to pay interest and capital according to the pre-agreed schedule.

2 Debt interest can also be set against profit for tax purposes.
3 The administrative and issuing costs are normally lower, e.g. underwriters are not always required, although legal fees are usually involved.

The downside is that excessively high borrowing levels can lead to inability to meet debt interest payments in years of poor trading conditions. Shareholders are thus exposed to a second tier of risk above the inherent business risk of the trading activity. As a result, rational shareholders seek additional compensation for this extra exposure. In brief, debt is desirable because it is relatively cheap, but there may be limits to the prudent use of debt financing because, although of relatively low risk to the lender, it can be highly risky for the borrower.

In general, larger, well-established companies are likely to have a greater ability to borrow because they generate more reliable streams of income, enhancing their ability to service (make interest payments on) debt capital. Ironically, in practice, we often find that small developing companies that should not over-rely on debt capital are forced to do so through sheer inability to raise equity, while larger enterprises often operate with what appear to be very conservative gearing ratios compared with their borrowing capacities. Against this, we often encounter cases of over-geared enterprises that thought their borrowing levels were safe until they were caught out by adverse trading conditions.

So is there a 'correct' level of debt? Quite how much companies should borrow is another puzzle in the theory of business finance. There are cogent arguments for and against the extensive use of debt capital and academics have developed sophisticated models, which attempt to expose and analyse the key theoretical relationships.

For many years, it was thought advantageous to borrow so long as the company's capacity to service the debt was unquestioned. The result would be higher earnings per share and higher share value, provided the finance raised was invested sensibly. The dangers of excessive levels of borrowing would be forcibly articulated by the stock market by a downrating of the shares of a highly geared company. This prompted the concept of an **optimal capital structure** which maximised company value. However, while the critical gearing ratio is thought to depend on factors such as the steadiness of the company's cash flow and the saleability of its assets, it has proved to be like the Holy Grail, highly desirable but illusory, and difficult to grasp. For some academics, a firmer theoretical underpinning was needed to facilitate the analysis of capital structure decisions and to offer more helpful guidelines to practising managers.

The Modigliani and Miller contribution

When Nobel laureates Modigliani and Miller (MM) published their seminal paper in 1958, finance academics began to examine in depth the relationship between borrowing and company value. MM's work on the pure theory of capital structure initially suggested that company value was unaffected by gearing. This conclusion prompted a furore of critical opposition, leading eventually to a coherent theory of capital structure, the current version of which looks remarkably like the traditional view.

Because this is a complex topic, we have organised the treatment of the impact of gearing into two chapters. This chapter is mainly devoted to the 'traditional' theory of capital structure and the issue of how much a company should borrow. In Chapter 21, we deepen the analysis by discussing the 'modern' theory. However, the present chapter gives a flavour of the main issues involved.

The two chapters together are designed to examine the following issues:

- How is gearing measured?
- Why do companies use debt capital?
- How is the cost of debt capital measured?
- What are the dangers of debt capital? How do shareholders react to 'high' levels of gearing?
- What do the competing theories of capital structure tell us about optimal financing decisions?
- How does taxation affect the analysis?
- What overall return should be achieved by a company using debt?
- What practical guidelines can we offer to financial managers?

20.2 Measures of gearing

There are two basic ways to express the indebtedness of a company. **Capital gearing** indicates the proportion of debt capital in the firm's overall capital structure. **Income gearing** indicates the extent to which the company's income is pre-empted by prior interest charges. Both are indicators of **financial gearing**.

Capital gearing: alternative measures

A widely-used measure of capital gearing is the ratio of all long-term liabilities (LTL), i.e. 'amounts falling due after more than one year', to shareholders' funds, as shown in the Balance Sheet. This purports to indicate how easily the firm can repay debts from selling assets, since shareholder funds measure net assets:

$$\text{Capital gearing} = \frac{\text{LTL}}{\text{Shareholders' funds}}$$

There are several drawbacks to this approach.

First, the market value of equity may be considerably higher than the book value, reflecting higher asset values, so this measure may seem unduly conservative. However, the notion of market value needs to be clarified. When a company is forced to sell assets hurriedly in order to repay debts, it is by no means certain that buyers can be found to pay 'acceptable' prices. The **break-up values** of assets are often lower than those expressed in the accounts, which assume that the enterprise is a going concern. However, using book values does at least have an element of prudence. In addition, the oscillating nature of market values may emphasise the case for conservatism, even for companies with 'safe' gearing ratios.

A second problem is the lack of an upper limit to the ratio, which hinders inter-company comparisons. This is easily remedied by expressing long-term liabilities as a fraction of all forms of long-term finance, thus setting the upper limit at 100 per cent. The gearing measure would become:

$$\frac{\text{LTL}}{\text{LTL} + \text{Shareholders' funds}}$$

A third problem is the treatment of provisions made out of previous years' income. Technically, provisions represent expected future liabilities. Companies provide for contingencies, such as claims under product guarantees, as a matter of prudence. Provisions thus result from a charge against profits and result in lower stated equity. However, some provisions turn out to be unduly pessimistic, and may be written back into profits, and hence equity, in later years. A good example is the provision made for deferred taxation. This is a highly prudent device to provide for possible tax liability if the firm were to sell its fixed assets.

Provisions could thus be treated as either equity or debt according to the degree of certainty of the anticipated contingency. If the liability is 'highly certain', it is reasonable to treat it as debt, but if the provision is the result of ultra-prudence, it may be treated as equity. For example, deferred taxation is a provision against the possibility of incurring a Corporation Tax charge if assets are sold above their written-down value for tax purposes. For most firms, this risk will diminish over time and the provision could safely be treated as equity. In practice, company accounts carry a mixture of provisions of varying degrees of certainty, and it is tempting to delete provisions from liabilities but not to include them in equity when expressing the gearing ratio. However, the nature of provisions should be questioned when the item appears substantial. Adjusted to exclude provisions, the capital gearing ratio becomes:

$$\frac{\text{Long-term borrowings (LTB)}}{\text{Shareholders' funds}} \quad \text{or} \quad \frac{\text{LTB}}{\text{LTB + Shareholders' funds}}$$

Arguably, any borrowing figure should take into account both long-term and short-term borrowing. Many companies depend heavily on short-term borrowing, especially bank overdrafts, and having to repay these debts quickly would place a significant burden on both the cash flow and liquidity of such companies. For this reason, some firms present their gearing ratios inclusive of such liabilities. For example, BP Amoco's measure of gearing focuses on 'market debt', i.e. borrowing via the financial markets from financial institutions:

$$\frac{\text{Market debt}}{\text{Market debt + Shareholders' funds}}$$

There are two objections to this approach. First, since short-term borrowing can be volatile, the year-end figure in the Balance Sheet is not always a reliable guide to short-term debts. However, many companies effectively use their bank overdraft as a long-term form of finance. In other words, the actual bank overdraft figure may include a hard core element of long-term debt and a fluctuating component, although it is not easy to separate these two items from external examination of the accounts.

Second, it may be argued that any holdings of cash and highly liquid, marketable securities ('near cash' assets) should be offset against short-term debt, to yield a measure of 'net debt', i.e.:

$$\text{Net debt} = \frac{\text{(Short- and long-term borrowings) less Cash and marketable securities}}{\text{Shareholders' funds}}$$

In fact, financial commentators increasingly use this measure of gearing, which is shown in the annual reports of many companies, expressed either in absolute terms or in relation to equity.

Self-assessment Activity 20.1

Determine the following gearing ratios using the information supplied.

(i) debt-to-equity ratio
(ii) debt-to-debt plus equity ratio
(iii) net debt

- Equity = £100 m
- Long-term Debt = £50 m
- Short-term Debt = £20 m
- Cash = £10 m

(answer at end of chapter)

All the above measures are commonly used in the UK. In some other countries, a more direct measure of gearing (or leverage) is used. The UK ratios tend to focus on the relationship between debt and equity capital, which is reasonable since equity represents net assets. However, when necessary, debts are repaid by liquidating the assets to which the capital relates. Rather than this roundabout focus on capital, a direct focus on assets available to repay debts may give a clearer picture of ability to repay. For this purpose, many US commentators use an 'American gearing' ratio, such as

$$\frac{\text{Total Liabilities (including short-term liabilities)}}{\text{Total Assets}}$$

Interest cover and income gearing

All the above measures purport to express the ability of the company to repay loans out of capital. However, they are only really helpful if book values and market values of the assets that would have to be sold to repay creditors approximate to each other. Yet, as we have noted, the market value of assets is volatile and difficult to assess. Moreover, capital gearing only indicates the security of creditors' funds in a crisis and may be an unduly cautious way of viewing debt exposure.

The trigger for a debt crisis is usually inability to make interest payments, and the 'front line' is therefore the size and reliability of the company's income in relation to its interest commitments. Although, in reality, cash flow is the more important consideration, the ability of a company to meet its interest obligations is usually measured by the ratio of *profit* before tax and interest, to interest charges, known as **interest cover**, or '**times interest earned**':

$$\text{Interest cover} = \frac{\text{Profit before interest and tax}}{\text{Interest charges}}$$

Strictly, the numerator should include any interest received and the denominator should become interest outgoings. This adjustment is rarely made in practice; net interest charges are commonly used as the denominator (as we do for BAA plc below).

The inverse of interest cover is called **income gearing**, indicating the proportion of pre-tax earnings committed to prior interest charges. If a company earns profit before interest and tax of £20 million, and incurs interest charges of £2 million, then its interest cover is (£20 m/£2 m) = 10 times, and 10 per cent of profit before interest and tax is pre-empted by interest charges.

Arguably, cash flow-to-interest is a better guide to financial security, given that profits are expressed on the accruals basis, i.e., recognised even though cash may not have been received yet for sales. Hence, the formula below is sometimes used:

$$\text{Cash flow cover} = \frac{\text{Operating cash flow}}{\text{Net interest payable}}$$

Self-assessment Activity 20.2

Distinguish between capital gearing and income gearing. How is each measured?

(answer at end of chapter)

Example: BAA plc's borrowings

The figures in Table 20.1 are taken from the Annual Report for BAA plc, the UK airports operator (**www.baa.com**) for the year ended March 31 2001. With these data, we can calculate an array of gearing indicators:

$$\frac{\text{LT borrowing}}{\text{Shareholder's funds}} = \frac{1{,}700}{4{,}839} = 35\%$$

$$\frac{\text{LT borrowing}}{\text{All LT funds}} = \frac{1{,}700}{6{,}539} = 26\%$$

$$\frac{\text{All borrowing}}{\text{Shareholder's funds}} = \frac{1{,}700 + 212}{4{,}839} = 39.5\%$$

$$\text{Net debt} = (1{,}700 + 212 - 385) = £1{,}572\text{ m } (31.6\%\text{ of equity})$$

$$\text{Interest cover} = \frac{615}{85} = 7.2\text{ times}$$

Table 20.1 Financial data for BAA plc

	£m*
Shareholders' funds	4,839
Cash and short-term investments	385
Long-term borrowing (LTD) (including convertible debt of 310)	1,700
Short-term borrowing	212
Group profit before interest and tax	615
Net interest payable by the group	85
Total assets	7,559
Total liabilities	2,720
Operating cash flow	839

*BAA plc has negligible provisions

Income gearing = (1 ÷ 7.2) = 14%

$$\frac{\text{Operating cash flow}}{\text{Net interest payable}} = \frac{879}{85} = 10.3 \text{ times}$$

$$\frac{\text{Total liabilities}}{\text{Total assets}} = \frac{2{,}720}{7{,}559} = 36\%$$

EMI's £1.1 billion debt pile

EMI is considering a sale of non-core assets to address City concerns about its £1.1 billion debt pile and avoid a short-term cash crunch that threatens the dividend.

The world's third-largest music group is understood to be reviewing its £285 million property portfolio and its continued presence in the high-street record retailing business.

There is a new climate at EMI as it seeks to reverse an underperformance that has resulted in two profits warnings in six months. The company has also been distracted by two abandoned merger efforts with Warner Music and then Bertelsmann's BMG.

Alain Levy, appointed chief executive of recorded music last October, believes the underperformance is down to internal shortcomings and not difficult market conditions, according to EMI insiders.

EMI owns freehold property worth £182 million, leasehold property worth £15.4 million and land valued at £86.3 million, according to the company's 2001 annual report. It is believed to be looking for an adviser on property sales.

Mr Levy, preparing to unveil his strategy to the City next month, is believed to be focused on reducing EMI's debt in the short term and raising cashflow from recorded music in the longer term. He is targeting more than £65 million in annual savings after a restructure costing at least £140 million this year.

Analysts are concerned about EMI's debt, two notches above junk, and its interest cover, which stands at about 2.6 times earnings. Furthermore, the dividend is uncovered after exceptional costs this year. 'We do expect EMI to refinance its short-term debt, especially as we consider it is likely it will have the dividend,' said Brett Hucker, media analyst at Merrill Lynch.

Based on Ashling O'Connor, *Financial Times*, February 19 2002

Self-assessment Activity 20.3

Obtain the accounts of a firm of your choice and conduct a similar exercise to the BAA plc calculations.

20.3 Operating and financial gearing

A major reason for using debt is to enhance or 'gear up' shareholder earnings. When a company is financially geared, variations in the level of earnings due to changes in trading conditions generate a more than proportional variation in earnings attributable to shareholders if the interest charges are fixed. This effect is very similar to that exerted by **operating gearing**. We will now examine these two gearing phenomena and illustrate them numerically.

Most businesses operate with a combination of variable and fixed factors of production, giving rise to variable and fixed costs respectively. The particular combination is largely dictated by the nature of the activity and the technology involved. Operating gearing refers to the relative importance of fixed costs in the firm's cost structure, costs that have to be met regardless of output and revenue levels. In general, the higher the proportion of fixed to variable costs, the higher the firm's break-even volume of output. As sales rise above the break-even point, there will be a more than proportional upward effect on profits before interest and tax, and on shareholder earnings.

Firms with high operating gearing, mainly capital-intensive ones, are especially prone to fluctuations in the business cycle. In the downswing, as their sales volumes decrease, their earnings before interest and tax decline by a more than proportional amount; and conversely in the upswing. Hence, such companies are regarded as relatively risky. If such companies borrow, they add a second tier of fixed charges in the form of interest payments, thus increasing overall risk – the higher the interest charges, the greater the risk of inability to pay. Consequently, the risk premium required by investors in such companies is relatively high. It follows that companies that exhibit high operating gearing should use debt finance sparingly.

Operating and financial gearing: Burley plc

Burley plc produces and sells briefcases. It has issued 4 million 50p shares and has £2 million loan finance. Its gearing ratio, measured by the ratio of debt to equity at book values, is one-to-one (i.e. (4 m × 50p)/£2 m). Last year, Burley sold 60,000 units to large retailers at £30 per unit.

Its Profit and Loss Account is:

		£000	£000
Sales			1,800
Less:	Variable costs (VC)	(720)	
	Fixed operating costs (FC)	(480)	(1,200)
	Profit before interest and tax (PBIT)		600
Less:	Interest payable @ 10%		(200)
	Profit before taxation (PBT)		400
Less:	Corporation tax @ 30%		(120)
	Profit after tax (PAT)		280

The earnings per share (EPS) are:

$$\frac{\text{Profit after tax}}{\text{No of ordinary shares}} = \frac{£280{,}000}{4\text{ m}} = 7.0\text{p}$$

Notice that the P and L hides the distinction between gross and net profit. The gross profit is the sales less variable costs, i.e. (£1,800,000 – £720,000) = £1,080,000, also called contribution because the fixed costs are paid from this amount, any surplus over FC is the net or operating profit. Operating profit is thus £600,000 (shown as profit before interest and tax).

Now let us consider the break-even volume, initially ignoring the debt interest obligation. Recall that breaking even means just covering fixed operating costs and variable costs. In Burley's case, this requires an output sufficient to generate a margin of profit high enough to cover the fixed operating costs of £480,000. The unit variable cost was:

(£720,000/60,000) = £12

Were it financed entirely by equity, Burley's break-even output would be found by dividing fixed cost by the gross profit margin of (£30 – £12) = £18:

(£480,000/£18) = 26,667 units

Allowing for the interest commitments of £200,000, Burley has to cover total fixed charges of (£480,000 + £200,000) = £680,000. This requires the higher output of (£680,000/£18 = 37,778) units to break even. Hence, using debt finance raises the break-even volume of production because fixed obligations are higher.

We can use this example to distinguish between operating and financial gearing. **Operating gearing** can be expressed in a variety of ways. Most simply, it is the proportion of total production cost accounted for by fixed costs: (£480,000/£1,200,000) = 40 per cent. Allowing for interest payments, Burley needs to generate a gross margin or contribution of (£480,000 + £200,000)= £680,000 to cover total fixed charges. At present, it is doing this fairly comfortably, since in percentage terms, fixed charges account for (£480,000 + £200,000) ÷ £1,080,000 = 63 per cent of the contribution. Looking at the importance of financial gearing, out of its profit before interest and tax of £600,000, a third (£200,000) is required to cover interest payments, i.e. the interest cover is 3.3 times.

A more sophisticated way of viewing the impact of fixed charges is to calculate **leverage ratios**. **Operating leverage** is the number of times the contribution covers the profit before interest and tax (PBIT), i.e. a multiple of:

$$\frac{\text{Contribution}}{\text{PBIT}} = \frac{(\text{Sales} - \text{VC})}{\text{PBIT}} = \frac{£1{,}080{,}000}{£600{,}000} = 1.8 \text{ times}$$

This indicates the leeway between contribution and the PBIT, and hence, the extent to which the fixed costs can increase without forcing the company into an operating loss. More significantly, the multiplier of 1.8 signifies the relationship between a given increase in sales and the resulting effect on PBIT. As we show below, a 10 per cent increase in sales will result in an increase in PBIT of 18 per cent.

Similarly, **financial leverage** is the number of times the PBIT covers the profit before tax (PBT), i.e. a multiple of:

$$\frac{\text{PBIT}}{\text{PBT}} = \frac{£600{,}000}{£400{,}000} = 1.5 \text{ times}$$

The difference between PBIT and PBT is the interest charge, so this multiple indicates the extent to which interest charges can rise without forcing the company into pre-tax loss. More significantly, the multiplier of 1.5 magnifies the effect of operating leverage – the effect of a sales increase on PBT is greater in a financially geared firm than in one that has no borrowing. Taking the two multipliers together, we obtain a combined leverage effect. In this case, a sales increase of 10 per cent will result in an increase in PBT of (1.8 × 1.5) = 2.7 times as great, i.e. 27 per cent. For a given tax rate, here 30 per cent, the profit after tax and, hence, the EPS, will also rise by the same proportion.

Since these relationships may not be immediately obvious, it is helpful to demonstrate the impact of Burley experiencing a sales increase of 10 per cent. Assuming no change in unit variable costs, the Profit and Loss Account becomes:

		£000	£000	
Sales			1,980	(10% increase)
Less:	Variable costs (VC)	(792)		
	Fixed costs (FC)	(480)	(1,272)	
	Profit before interest and tax (PBIT)		708	(18% increase)
Less:	Interest payable @ 10%		(200)	
	Profit before taxation (PBT)		508	(27% increase)
Less:	Corporation tax @ 30%		(152)	
	Profit after tax (PAT)		356	(27% increase)

The new EPS is:

PAT/No. of shares = (£356,000/4 m) = 8.9p (27% increase)

The increase in EPS of 27 per cent (rounded) is a far greater proportion than the sales increase, illustrating the operation of the combined gearing multiplier. It follows that the higher the proportion of fixed costs in overall costs and the greater the commitment to interest charges, the greater will be the combined gearing effect. This may suggest that using fixed factors of production and using debt capital are both desirable things. However, as the following example demonstrates, financial gearing is double-edged. It is beneficial in favourable economic conditions, but because the gearing effect also works in reverse, it can spell trouble in adverse trading conditions.

Self-assessment Activity 20.4

Show the effect on the combined gearing multiplier in the Burley example if fixed costs are £530,000 and interest charges are £240,000.

(answer at end of chapter)

20.4 Financial gearing and risk: Lindley plc

Lindley plc retains no profit and its shareholders require a 20 per cent return. Issued share capital is £100 million, denominated in £1 units. Lindley's operating profit can vary as shown in Table 20.2, according to trading conditions characterised as bad, indifferent and good. These are denoted by scenarios A, B and C, which have probabilities of 0.25, 0.50 and 0.25, respectively.

After all costs, but before deducting debt interest, earnings are £5 million, £20 million and £35 million under scenarios A, B and C, respectively. This measure of earnings is termed net operating income (NOI). (For simplicity, taxation is ignored.) Let us examine shareholder returns under gearing ratios of zero, 25 per cent and 50 per cent, measured by long-term debt (interest rate 10 per cent) to total long-term finance held constant at £100 million.

For a given increase in income, shareholder earnings rise by a greater proportion: for example, with gearing of 25 per cent, if NOI rises by 300 per cent from £5 million to £20 million, shareholder earnings increase by 600 per cent from £2.5 million to £17.5 million. It is easy to see why adding debt to the capital structure is called gearing – the change in earnings is magnified by a factor of 2.0 in shareholders' favour. Unfortunately, this effect also applies in a downward direction – a given proportionate fall in earnings generates a more pronounced

Table 20.2 How gearing affects shareholder returns in Lindley plc

		Trading conditions	
	Scenario A ($p = 0.25$)	Scenario B ($p = 0.50$)	Scenario C ($p = 0.25$)
Profit before interest (PBIT)[a]	–	–	–
(Net operating income)	£5 m	£20 m	£35 m
Zero gearing			
(100 m equity, £0 m debt)			
Debt interest at 10%	–	–	–
Shareholder earnings	£5 m	£20 m	£35 m
Return on equity (ROE)	5%	20%	35%
25% gearing (Debt/Equity = $\frac{1}{3}$)			
(£75 m equity, £25 m debt, interest 10%)			
Debt interest at 10%	£2.5 m	£2.5 m	£2.5 m
Shareholder earnings	£2.5 m	£17.5 m	£32.5 m
Return on equity (ROE)	3.3%	23.3%	43.3%
50% gearing (Debt/Equity = $\frac{1}{1}$)			
(£50 m equity, £50 m debt, interest 10%)			
Debt interest at 10%	£5 m	£5 m	£5 m
Shareholder earnings	0	£15 m	£30 m
Return on equity (ROE)	0	30%	60%

[a]Taxes are ignored.

decrease in shareholder earnings. Indeed, with 50 per cent gearing, under scenario A, shareholder earnings are entirely wiped out by prior interest charges. The return on equity would be negative at any gearing level higher than this, under this scenario.

Negative returns are not necessarily fatal – companies often survive losses in especially poor trading years – but the likelihood of survival when continued trading losses combine with high fixed interest charges is lowered if the company cannot pay interest charges. In these cases, the enterprise is technically insolvent, although creditors may agree to restructure the company's capital, e.g. by converting debt into preference shares. There is, however, an effective upper limit of gearing for Lindley. Beyond 50 per cent gearing, it may be unable to meet interest charges out of earnings. For practical purposes, the lower limit of earnings will dictate maximum borrowing capacity, although, in reality, this lower earnings limit is highly uncertain. This is why it is usually argued that the more reliable the company's expected cash flow stream, the greater its borrowing capacity.

Our Lindley example demonstrates that, under debt financing, although shareholders may achieve enhanced returns in good years, they stand to receive much lower returns in bad years. In other words, the residual stream of shareholder earnings exhibits greater variability. This can be examined by computing the expected value and the range, or dispersion, of the return on equity (ROE) with each of the three gearing levels.

Self-assessment Activity 20.5

Calculate the expected value of Lindley's ROE under each scenario.

(answer at end of chapter)

Table 20.3 shows that, although the expected value of the return on equity is greater at higher levels of gearing, the dispersion, or range, of possible returns is also wider, which might concern risk-averting shareholders. Notice also that we can decompose the overall risk incurred by shareholders into its underlying

Table 20.3 How gearing affects the risk of ordinary shares

Gearing (%)	Expected ROE (%)	Total dispersion (%)	Due to: Business risk (%)	Financial risk (%)
0	20	30	30	0
25	23.3	40	30	10
50	30	60	30	30

business and financial elements. Business risk refers to the likely variability in returns for an equivalent all-equity financed company, i.e. the dispersion of returns is due to underlying business-related factors. Financial risk is the additional dispersion in net returns to shareholders due to the need to meet interest charges whatever the trading conditions. At every gearing ratio, the range of returns due to business risk is unchanged – nothing has happened to its product range, its customer base or any other aspect of its trading activities. Lindley would simply share out the proceeds of its operations in different ways at different gearing ratios.

It is also helpful to show the effect on ROE graphically. Figure 20.1 shows the data for Lindley's ROE for the three different capital structures. Clearly, the higher the debt-to-equity ratio, the greater the ROE for any level of profit before interest. Figure 20.1 also shows how the break-even value of profit before interest increases as gearing rises. As gearing increases from zero to 1:3 and to 1:1, the break-even earnings increase from 0 to 0X and to 0Y, corresponding to the three interest payment levels of zero, £2.5 m and £5 m respectively. Notice finally that earnings of £10 million would generate the same ROE under all three capital structures.

This discussion of the impact of gearing is incomplete in one important respect. The analysis has been based on book values, despite earlier remarks that gearing ratios may often be better measured in terms of market values. We have yet to consider the effect of gearing on the value of the firm — does gearing actually make shareholders better off?

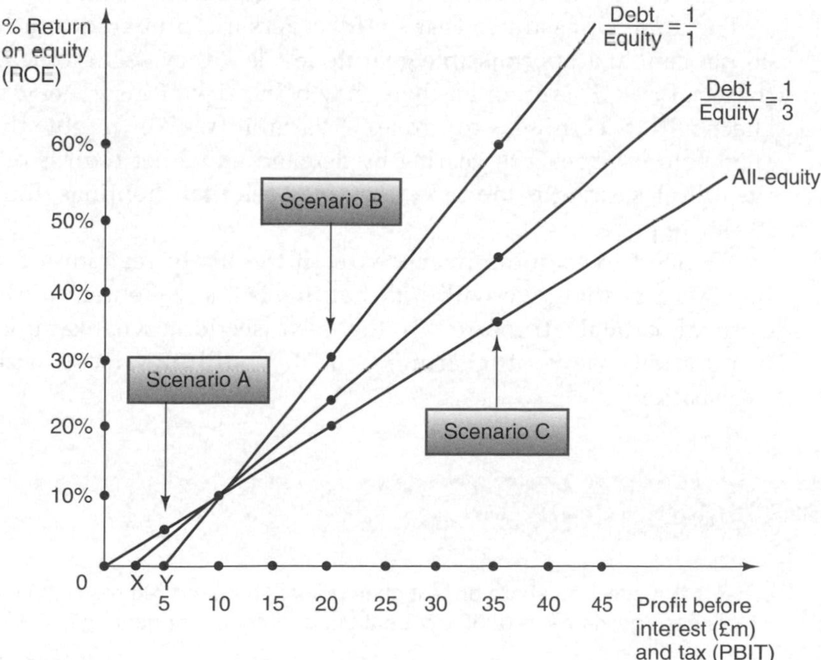

Figure 20.1 How gearing affects the ROE

Table 20.4 How gearing can affect share price

Gearing %	Number of shares	Expected value of shareholder earnings	EPS	Share price[a]
0	100 m	£20 m	20.0p	20.0p/0.2 = £1.00
25	75 m	£17.5 m	23.3p	23.3p/0.2 = £1.17
50	50 m	£15 m	30.0p	30.0p/0.2 = £1.50

[a]Share price is found by discounting the perpetual and constant EPS at 20 per cent

To examine the effect on share price, we need to focus on the expected earnings figure and recall that the value of a share can be found by discounting its stream of earnings, in the simplest case, as a perpetuity. (No distinction is needed between earnings and dividends, as Lindley makes no retentions.) The expected values of shareholder earnings for each of the three gearing ratios are shown in Table 20.4. Recalling that Lindley's shares have a nominal value of £1, we can specify the number of shares corresponding to each gearing ratio and hence the expected value of the EPS. Share prices are found by applying the valuation formula, discounting the perpetual EPS at the 20 per cent return required by Lindley's shareholders.

It appears that, by using debt capital, financial managers can achieve significant increases in shareholder wealth. However, we ought to be suspicious of this effect. Why should shareholders' wealth increase when there have been no changes in trading activity or in expected aggregate income?

The analysis assumes that shareholders are prepared to accept a return of 20 per cent at all permissible gearing levels – they seem to be unconcerned by financial risk. Even though there may be no risk of insolvency, gearing exposes shareholder earnings to greater variability. We might therefore expect shareholders to react to gearing by demanding higher returns on their capital. If they think gearing is too risky, they may sell their holdings, thus driving down the share price.

We need to examine in more detail the likely reaction of shareholders to increased gearing; we will find that this is a key element in the debate about optimal capital structure. In the next section, we examine the so-called 'traditional' view of gearing, probably still the most widely supported explanation.

Self-assessment Activity 20.6

What is the effect on share price if shareholders required returns of 25 per cent under 25 per cent gearing and of 35 per cent under 50 per cent gearing?

(answer at end of chapter)

20.5 The 'traditional' view of gearing and the required return

The traditional view emphasises the benefits of using relatively cheap debt capital as seen in the Lindley example; in particular, the effect on the rate of return required on investment. To analyse this approach in greater depth we first need to make some definitions.

For an ungeared company, market value is found by discounting (or capitalising) its stream of annual earnings, E, at the rate of return required by shareholders, k_e.

Value of an ungeared company

The value of an ungeared company, V_u, is simply the value of the ordinary shares, V_S. For a constant and perpetual stream of annual earnings, E:

$$V_u = V_S = \frac{E}{k_e} \quad \text{so that } k_e = \frac{E}{V_S}$$

Much of the argument about capital structure centres on what happens to the discount rate (or capitalisation rate) as gearing increases. If the analysis is conducted in terms of *substituting* debt for equity, i.e. keeping size of firm constant as we did in the Lindley example, the effect of gearing can be examined while holding E constant. In this case, gearing simply rearranges the share-out of E among the company's stakeholders. We denote the book value of borrowings as B and the interest rate as i, thus involving a prior interest charge of $(i \times B)$. Gearing splits the earnings stream of the company into two components, the prior interest charge and the portion attributable to shareholders, the net income (NI) of $(E - iB)$. The overall value of the company is the value of the shares (V_S) plus the value of the debt, each capitalised at its respective rate of discount. For debt, where there is no discrepancy (as in this example) between book value (B) and market value (V_B), the capitalisation rate is simply the nominal interest rate. The overall value of the geared company, V_g, is the combined value of its shares and its debt:

$$V_g = V_S + V_B = \frac{(E - iB)}{k_e} + \frac{iB}{i} = \frac{(E - iB)}{k_e} + V_B$$

The *overall* capitalisation rate (denoted by k_o) for a company using a mixed capital structure is a weighted average, whose weights reflect the relative importance of each type of finance in the capital structure, i.e. V_S/V_g and V_B/V_g for equity and debt, respectively:

$$k_o = \left(k_e \times \frac{V_S}{V_g}\right) + \left(i \times \frac{V_B}{V_g}\right)$$

Bearing in mind that ($k_e V_S$) and iB (or iV_B, when $V_B = B$) represent the returns to shareholders and lenders respectively, i.e. their respective shares of corporate earnings, E, the weighted average expression simplifies to:

$$k_o = \frac{k_e V_S + iB}{V_g} = \frac{E}{V_g}$$

For both ungeared and geared firms alike, k_o is found by dividing the earnings by the value of the whole firm. k_o is also known as the **weighted average cost of capital (WACC)**, since it expresses the overall return required to satisfy the demands of both groups of stakeholders. The WACC may be interpreted as an average discount rate applied by the market to the company's future operating cash flows to derive the capitalised value of this stream, i.e. the value of the whole company.

It looks as if a company could lower the WACC by adding 'cheap' debt to an equity base. For instance, in the Lindley example, while the required return for the all-equity case is 20 per cent, i.e. the cost of equity, with gearing at 25 per cent, the WACC, using book value weights, becomes:

$$k_o = (0.75 \times 20\%) + (0.25 \times 10\%) = 17.5\%$$

Apparently, gearing can lower the overall cost of capital if both k_e and i remain constant. The effect of this is highly significant. In the traditional view of gearing, shareholders are deemed unlikely to respond adversely (if at all) to minor increases of gearing so long as the prospect of default looks remote. If the cost of equity remains static, substitution of debt for equity will lower the overall cost of capital applied by the market in valuing the company's stream of earnings. This is shown in Figure 20.2 by the decline in the k_o schedule between A and B. Corresponding to this fall in k_o is an increase in the value of the whole geared company, V_g, in relation to that of an equivalent ungeared company, V_u.

This benign impact of gearing has already been shown in the Lindley example. Looking back to Tables 20.3 and 20.4, consider the switch from 0 to 25 per cent gearing. Assuming shareholders continue to seek a return of 20 per cent, the EPS discounted to infinity yields a share price of £1.17. The market value of equity becomes (£1.17 × 75 m) = £88 m, and the overall company value is:

$$V_g = V_S + V_B = (£88\text{ m} + £25\text{ m}) = £113\text{ m}$$

Gearing up to 25 per cent raises market value by £13 million above book value, thus demonstrating the benefits of gearing to shareholders. The market value of the whole company rises because the value per unit of the residual equity increases due to the increase in EPS. Without gearing, each share would sell at £1.

However, sooner or later, shareholders will become concerned by the greater financial risk to which their earnings are exposed and begin to seek higher returns. In addition, providers of additional debt are likely to raise their

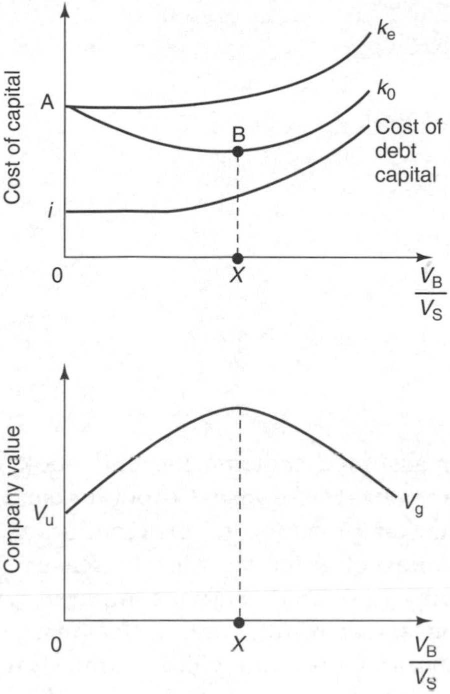

Figure 20.2 The 'traditional' view of capital structure

requirements as they perceive the probability of default increasing. The k_e schedule will probably turn upwards before any upturn in i, given the legally-preferred position of debt holders, although the phasing of these movements is not clear in this model. Whatever the sequence of the upward revisions in required returns, the WACC profile will eventually be forced to rise, and the value of the company will fall. The model clearly involves an optimal debt/equity mix, where company value is maximised and the WACC is minimised. This is gearing ratio $0X$ in Figure 20.2.

To financial managers, a major disappointment of this approach is its failure to pinpoint a specific optimal gearing ratio for all firms in all circumstances. The optimal ratio is likely to depend on the nature of the industry (e.g. whether the activity generates rapid cash flow), the general marketability of the company's assets, expectations about the prospects for the industry, and the general level of interest rates. Clearly, many of these factors vary over time as well as between industries. However, a few pointers are possible.

For example, a supermarket chain, characterised by strong cash flow, can sustain a higher level of gearing than a heavy engineering enterprise, where the working capital cycle is lengthy. Similarly, an airline, for whose assets there is a ready and active second-hand market, might withstand a higher gearing level (especially as flights are often paid for well in advance) than a steel company with both a high level of operating gearing and assets that are highly specific and difficult to sell.

Self-assessment Activity 20.7

What is this firm's WACC? (ignore tax)

- debt to equity ratio = 40%
- cost of equity = 18%
- cost of debt = 8%

(answer at end of chapter)

20.6 The cost of debt

Our analysis has so far assumed that market and book values of debt coincide. This is by no means always the case. Corporate bond values behave in a similar way to the market prices of government stock, or gilt-edged securities. When general market interest rates increase, the returns on previously issued bonds may look unattractive compared with the returns available on newly issued ones. As a result, bond dealers mark down the value of existing stocks until they offer the same yield as investors can obtain by purchasing new issues. In other words, equilibrium in the bond market is achieved when all stocks subject to the same degree of risk and with the same period to redemption offer the same yield.

The simplest case is perpetual (irredeemable) stock such as the UK government's 3.5 per cent War Loan. These were issued, never to be repaid, to support the British war effort between 1939 and 1945. They offer the holder a return of 3.5 per cent (the nominal rate of interest, or '**coupon rate**') on the par value of the stock, i.e. £3.50 per £100 of stock. With higher market rates, say, 7 per cent, War Loan would look unattractive, and its value would fall, e.g. a £100 unit would have to sell at £50 to generate a yield of 7 per cent. An inverse relationship applies between fixed-interest bond prices and interest rates:

The market value of an irredeemable bond is: $\left(\text{nominal value} \times \dfrac{\text{coupon rate}}{\text{market rate}}\right)$

Self-assessment Activity 20.8

What is the market value of 3.5 per cent War Loan when market rates are:

(i) 11%
(ii) 3%

In practice, the calculation is more complex when we consider the far more common case of bonds with limited lifetimes until maturity. In assessing the value of such bonds, the market value will also include the eventual capital repayment.

For example, if the market rate is 10 per cent, a ten-year bond with a coupon rate of 10 per cent, denominated in £100 units, would have the following (present) value:

$$\begin{aligned} PV &= \text{discount interest payments over 10 years} + \text{discounted capital repayment in year 10} \\ &= (10\% \times £100).(PVIFA_{(10,10)}) + (£100).(PVIF_{(10,10)}) \\ &= (£10 \times 6.1446) + (£100 \times 0.3855) \\ &= £61.45 + £38.45 = £100 \end{aligned}$$

The market value coincides with the par value because the coupon rate equals the going market rate. If, however, the market rate were to rise to 12 per cent, all future payments to the bondholder, both capital and interest, would be more heavily discounted, i.e. at 12 per cent, reducing the market value to £88.70.

Values of corporate bonds behave in essentially the same way, although, since companies are more risky than governments, they have to offer investors a rather higher rate of interest. This allows us to identify the cost of debt capital. A company can infer the appropriate rate of interest at which it could raise debt by looking at the market value of its own existing debt or that of a similar company. For example, if the market value of each £100 unit of debenture stock is £95 and has to be repaid in full in two years' time, the cost of debt can be found by solving a simple IRR expression. Someone who decided to purchase the stock in the market would anticipate two interest payments of £10 and a capital repayment of £100. The return expected is denoted by k_d in the following IRR expression:

$$£95 = \frac{£10}{(1 + k_d)} + \frac{(£10 + £100)}{(1 + k_d)^2}$$

The solution for k_d is 13 per cent. The market signals this rate as the cost of raising further debt.

There is another adjustment to make for tax relief on debt interest payments. To allow for tax, we look at the cost of debt from the company's perspective, since it is the company that enjoys the tax break. With a Corporation Tax rate of 30 per cent, each £10 interest payment will generate a tax saving of £3 for the company, reducing the effective interest cost to £10(1 – 30%) = £7.0. The IRR equation becomes:

$$£95 = \frac{£7.0}{(1 + k_d)} + \frac{(£7.0 + £100)}{(1 + k_d)^2}$$

Self-assessment Activity 20.9

Verify that the solution rate is 9.9 per cent.

(answer at end of chapter)

The tax benefits from using debt can be substantial. Take the case of a 10-year bond, issued and redeemable at a price of £100, with a coupon rate of 10 per cent. The value of the tax savings on interest payments, or the '**tax shield**', is:

$$\begin{aligned}\text{Tax shield} &= \text{interest charge} \times (\text{tax rate}) \times \text{PVIFA}_{(10,10)} \\ &= 10\% \times £100) \times (30\%) \times 6.1446 \\ &= £18.43\end{aligned}$$

In practice, this value is reduced by any delay in tax payments, which in turn delays the receipt of tax benefits. It is also assumed that the company always has sufficient taxable profits to benefit from the tax relief on interest payments.

Self-assessment Activity 20.10

What is the value of the tax shield for £10 million debt, coupon rate 6 per cent, tax rate 30 per cent:

(a) if the debt is perpetual?
(b) if it is to be repaid in 20 years?

(answer at end of chapter)

20.7 The overall cost of capital

Section 20.5 discussed the weighted average cost of capital (WACC) concept, illustrated in Figure 20.2. This was interpreted as the overall rate of return required in order to satisfy all stakeholders in the company. It described a U-shaped profile as the firm's level of gearing increased. It fell initially, as cheap debt was added to the capital structure, reached a minimum at the optimal gearing ratio, then rose as gearing came to be regarded as 'excessive'. The behaviour of this schedule provides a clue to the appropriate rate of return required on the company's activities, and, by implication, on new investment projects. We will examine this issue using the Lindley example.

Lindley plc and the cut-off rate for new investment

Lindley's shareholders require a 20 per cent return and its pre-tax cost of debt is 10 per cent. Let us make the simplifying assumptions that Lindley's debt is perpetual and sells at par. Adjusting for tax at 30 per cent, as explained above, this corresponds to an after-tax cost of 7 per cent. What return on investment should Lindley achieve when issuing debt to finance a new project?

It is tempting to argue that the cut-off rate on this new project should be the cost of servicing the finance raised specifically to undertake the project. However, this is probably erroneous because using debt has an opportunity cost. The use of 'cheap' debt now may erode the company's ability to undertake worthwhile projects in the future by the depletion of credit lines. For example, assume that in

2001 Lindley used debt costing 7.0 per cent after tax to finance a project offering a post-tax return of 12 per cent, but this exhausted its credit-raising capacity. As a result, it was unable to exploit a project available in 2002 that offered 14 per cent. This suggests that the 'true' cost of the finance used in 2001 exceeds 7.0 per cent. Hence, to assess the 'correct' cost of capital really requires forecasting all future investment opportunities and capital supplies.

In addition, our previous analysis leads us to expect, at some level of gearing, an adverse reaction by shareholders, who may demand higher returns to compensate for higher financial risk. Consider two possible cases, denoted by points A and B, respectively, on the WACC profile in Figure 20.2. Note that A corresponds to zero gearing and B to the critical ratio.

Case A

Lindley has no debt at present and shareholder capital is £100 million. A new project with perpetual life is to be financed by the issue of £10 million debt at an after-tax cost of 7.0 per cent. No impact on the cost of equity is expected. In this case, the company will have to generate additional post-tax annual returns of (7% × £10 m) = £0.70 million in order to meet the extra financing costs associated with the new project, so that the hurdle rate for the new project is 7.0 per cent. Here, with the explicit assumption that shareholders will not react adversely, it may be reasonable to use the cost of debt as the cut-off rate. In this case, the required return would be simply the interest cost divided by the debt financing provided, i.e. the interest rate:

$$\text{Required return} = iB/B = i$$

However, this position is unlikely to be tenable, except for relatively small projects, and hence small borrowings, since significant changes in gearing (in either direction) are likely to provoke a market reaction.

Case B

We will assume that the optimal gearing ratio involves a capital structure with £50 million of each type of capital. Any further debt financing, even at a constant debt cost, will cause the cost of equity to increase. Assume that the extra £10 million debt financing will provoke shareholders to demand a return of 24 per cent. This would be expressed by downward pressure on share price until the return on holding Lindley's shares became 24 per cent. Now, the project has to meet not only the debt financing costs, but also the additional returns required by shareholders. The total additional required income is:

$$\begin{aligned}\text{Required extra income} &= \text{debt financing costs} + \text{extra return required on equity}\\ &= (7\% \times £10\text{ m}) + (4\% \times £50\text{ m})\\ &= £0.7\text{ m} + £2\text{ m}\\ &= £2.70\text{ m}\end{aligned}$$

Instead of an apparent cost of just 7.0 per cent, the true cost of using debt to finance this project is actually (£2.70 m/£10 m) = 27 per cent.

In the next section, we pinpoint the conditions under which it is acceptable to use the WACC as the cut-off rate for evaluating new investment.

Required conditions for using the WACC

However, some major requirements have to be satisfied before use of the WACC can be justified:

1 The project is a marginal, scalar addition to the company's existing activities, with no overspill or synergistic impact likely to disturb the current valuation relationships.
2 Project financing involves no deviation from the current capital structure (otherwise the MCC should be used).
3 Any new project has the same systematic risk as the company's existing operations. This may be a reasonable assumption for minor projects in existing areas and perhaps for replacements, but hardly for major new product developments.
4 All cash flow streams are level perpetuities (as in the theoretical models).

In the short term, at least, firms are almost certain to deviate from the target structure, especially as market values fluctuate and financial managers perceive and exploit ephemeral financing bargains, e.g. an arbitrage opportunity in an overseas capital market. It is thus unrealistic to expect the hurdle rate for new investment to be adjusted for every minor deviation from the target gearing ratio. To all intents and purposes, the capital structure is given – only for major divergences from the target gearing ratio should the discount rate be altered. Similarly, even where a project is wholly financed by debt or equity, so long as the project is a minor one with no appreciable impact on the overall gearing ratio, then it is appropriate to use the WACC as the cut-off rate.

The preceding discussions suggest that the **marginal cost of capital (MCC)**, rather than the cost of debt or the WACC, should be used as the cut-off rate for new investment. However, the MCC does have operational limitations. In particular, we are required to anticipate *how* the capital market is likely to react to the issue of additional debt. Given that we seem unable to define the WACC profile or pinpoint the optimal gearing ratio at any one time, this presents a problem. We could assume that the present gearing ratio is optimal, but this prompts the question of why different firms in the same industry have different gearing ratios.

The target capital structure: a solution?

A solution commonly adopted in practice is to specify a **target capital structure**. The firm defines what it regards as the optimal long-term gearing ratio, and then attempts to adhere to this ratio in financing future operations. If the optimal ratio is deemed to involve 50 per cent debt and 50 per cent equity (i.e. a debt-to-equity ratio of 100 per cent), any future activities should be financed in these proportions. For example, a £10 million project would be financed by £5 million debt and £5 million equity, via retained earnings or a rights issue. The corollary is to use the WACC as the cut-off rate for new investment. When shareholders require 20% and debt costs 7.0% post-tax, the WACC is:

(cost of equity × equity weighting) + (post-tax cost of debt × debt weighting)
= (20% × 50%) + (7.0% × 50%) = (10% + 3.50%) = 13.50%

The WACC is recommended because it is difficult to anticipate with any precision how shareholders are likely to react to a change in gearing. The somewhat pragmatic solution proposed assumes that the new project will have no appreciable impact on gearing: in other words, that the company already operates at the optimal gearing ratio and does not deviate from it. Obviously, the WACC and the MCC will coincide in this case.

20.8 Worked example: Damstar plc

Damstar plc produces and sells computer modems. The company obtained a market quotation four years ago, since when it has achieved a steady annual return for its shareholders of 14 per cent after tax. It has an issued share capital of 2 million 50p ordinary shares. The ordinary shares sell at a P:E ratio of 11:1. For the year ended 31 March 2002, the company sold 20,000 units.

The profit and loss account for the year to 31 March 2002 is as follows:

	£000	£000
Sales		1,600
Less: Variable expenses	(880)	
Fixed expenses	(350)	(1,230)
Profit before interest and taxation		370
Less: interest payable (10% loan stock)		(150)
Profit before taxation		220
Less: corporation tax (at 30%)		(66)
Profit after taxation		154
Dividend		(120)
Retained profit		34

In recent months, the company has been experiencing labour problems. As a result, it has decided to introduce a new highly automated production process in order to improve efficiency. The production process is expected to increase fixed costs by £140,000 (including depreciation), but will reduce variable costs by £19 per unit.

The new production process will be financed by additional debt in the form of a secured £1,000,000 debenture issue at an interest rate of 12 per cent. If the new production process is introduced immediately, the directors believe that sales for the forthcoming year will be unchanged.

Required

(a) Determine how the proposal affects Damstar's break-even volume.
(b) Assuming no change in P:E ratio, calculate the change in EPS and share price if Damstar introduces its new production process immediately.
(c) What is the effect of the new process on Damstar's weighted average cost of capital using market value weights?

Answer to Damstar example

(a) First, we establish the revenue and cost parameters. Currently, the price is (£1.6 m/20,000) = £80 per unit. The average variable cost (AVC) = (£0.88 m/20,000) = £44. Hence, the operating profit margin (OPM) = (£80 − £44) = £36.

The break-even volume (BEV) can be expressed in operating terms, i.e. before fixed financing charges, and also after allowing for interest. Ignoring interest, the BEV is:

(Fixed costs of £0.35 m)/£36 = 9,722 units

Allowing for interest of £0.15 million, the BEV is:

(£0.35 m + £0.15 m)/£36 = 13,889 units.

With the new process, the AVC becomes (£44 − £19) = £25, and the OPM becomes (£80 − £25) = £55.

The new level of fixed operating costs is £0.49 million.

The BEV ignoring interest = (£0.49 m/£55) = 8,909 units. Allowing for the interest, increased by (12% × £0.12 m) to (£0.15 m + £0.12 m) = £0.27 m, the BEV is:

(£0.49 m + £0.27 m)/£55 = 13,818 units.

Notice that despite the increase in interest charges and the increase in fixed operating costs, the BEV has actually fallen due to the substantial fall in AVC. This warns that higher fixed costs does not always raise the BEV – it depends on what other changes are occurring at the same time.

(b) Currently, the EPS = (£154,000/2 m) = 7.7p. With the 11:1 P:E ratio, the share price is (7.7p × 11) = 85p.

Predicted profit and loss account for year ending 31 March 2003

	£	£
Sales		1,600
Variable Costs (20,000 × £25)	(500)	
Fixed Costs (£0.35 m + £0.14 m)	(490)	(990)
PBIT		610
Interest (£0.15 m + £0.12 m)		(270)
PBT		340
Taxation @ 30%		(102)
PAT		238

EPS now becomes (£238,000/2 m) = 11.9p, and with the same P:E ratio, the new share price would be (11.9p × 11) = £1.31.

(c) Based on market value weights, the WACC is:

		£	Weight
Value of equity	= (£1.31 × 2 m) =	1.7 m	53
Value of debt	= (£150,000/0.1) =	1.5 m	47
(no market value, so book value used)			
Total		3.2 m	100

WACC = (cost of equity × % of equity) + (post-tax debt cost × % of debt)
= (14% × 53%) + (10%[1 − 30%] × 47%)
= (7.4% + 3.3%) = 10.7%

After the issue of £1 million debt at 12 per cent interest, there are now two categories of debt, senior and junior.

		£	Weight
Value of equity	= (£1.31 × 2 m) =	2.60 m	54
Value of senior debt	= (10/12 × £1.5 m) =	1.25 m	26
Value of junior debt	=	1.00 m	20
Total		4.85 m	100

WACC = (14% × 54%) + (10%[1 − 30%] × 26%) + (12%[1 − 30%] × 20%)
= (7.6% + 1.8% + 1.7%) = 11.1%

Comment: In this example, the increase in borrowing hardly affects the WACC, as the equity value increases to compensate. This result, of course, depends on the P:E ratio remaining at 11:1. Note also that the market value of the existing debt falls if interest rates rise.

20.9 International financing

A multinational company (MNC) may have more opportunities to lower the overall cost of capital than a 'domestic'. This is often due to their larger size, and partly due to greater access to international financial markets, allowing them to exploit any temporary disequilibria, as well as receiving host government concessions.

The international financing decision has two elements:

1 In terms of the optimal capital structure, *whether* to borrow and *how much* to borrow?
2 Where to borrow?

Key issues

The issues that determine these decisions are:

- **Gearing ratio**. The debt–equity mix selected for overseas activities is influenced by the gearing of the parent, or by the debt–equity ratios of comparable, competing firms in the location of the FDI. If the parent guarantees the subsidiary's borrowing, so long as the existing gearing of the parent is 'reasonable', the subsidiary's borrowing may be a separate issue, especially if a joint venture is formed and the borrowing of the overseas affiliate can be kept off-Balance Sheet. This enables fuller exploitation of subsidised loans and lower tax rates.

- **Taxation**. MNCs need to examine differences between the treatment of withholding taxes, losses, interest and dividend payments. Tax deductibility of interest provides an incentive to borrow locally.
- **Currency risk**. Local borrowing can also reduce foreign exchange exposure by enabling a match of interest and capital repayments against locally-generated cash inflows denominated in local currency.
- **Political risk**. Expropriation of assets or other interference is less likely if the MNC borrows from local banks or from the international markets. The host government is unlikely to want to offend the international financial community as it would damage its own credit standing. If the MNC borrows via the World Bank, it can include a **cross-default clause**, so that a default to any creditor automatically triggers default on a World Bank loan.

The case for borrowing

- Less risky than equity which puts owners' capital at risk.
- Debt service is based on a strict schedule, helping cash flow planning and currency hedging. Dividends are more erratic.
- Debt service payments are less likely to antagonise host governments. Erratic dividend flows may interfere with a host government's attempts to manage the external value of its currency, especially if the MNC is a major contributor to local GDP.
- Tax relief on interest.
- Opportunity to hedge foreign exchange risk by matching.
- Protection against political risk.
- Access to concessionary local finance.
- Overseas equity markets (if they exist) can be highly inefficient.

The case against borrowing

- The parent's debt–equity ratio may already be high.
- There may be only limited local borrowing facilities.
- Local borrowing may entail more intensive credit risk investigation fees, and higher interest rates if the MNC has no local credit rating.
- The host government may place an upper limit on local borrowing to restrict tax avoidance.

Assessment

The balance of argument usually points to borrowing to finance foreign subsidiaries; indeed braver corporate treasurers may try to exploit perceived disequilibria in global financial markets to access 'cheap' finance. However, the

International Fisher Effect (explained in Chapter 17) should caution against this. The benefit of borrowing at 'low' interest rates should always (eventually at least) be offset by the appreciation in currency in which debts are to be repaid.

Yet global markets often 'overshoot' – the euro seemed undervalued vs. the $US during 1999–2002, and sterling looked overvalued vs. the euro during 1999–2002. Astute treasurers may raise funds denominated in overvalued funds for long maturities and avoid borrowing in undervalued currencies.

Larger MNCs may set up their own financial subsidiaries as **Special Purpose Vehicles**, established largely for the purpose of obtaining the funds required to finance the entire firm's ongoing growth needs. This avoids problems over costs and access to capital in the host country. The SPV simply borrows on world markets using the credit rating of the parent. Firms that use SPVs include General Electric Corporation (via GE Capital), BMW and Ford.

The currency cocktail

There is a strong argument for borrowing in a range or 'cocktail' of currencies to spread the risk over a diversified portfolio of borrowed currencies. By diversifying sources of finance, the MNC may take advantage of what it perceives as unusually low rates in certain financial centres. This requires the MNC to be well-known in international financial markets and to have established sound banking relationships. Thus a firm needing to refinance a medium term loan maturing in London where interest rates are currently 7 per cent may decide to borrow in Japan where interest rates for corporate borrowing are 2–3 per cent.

British Airways borrows in three currencies as shown in Table 20.5. Notice that it also mixes fixed rate borrowing (38 per cent) with floating rate borrowing (62 per cent), based on LIBOR. (It repaid all its French franc borrowing during 2000–1, thus along with the disposal of its French Subsidiary Air Liberté diluting the cocktail.)

Table 20.5 British Airways plc borrowings (£m)

Currency	Fixed rate borrowing	Floating rate borrowing	Total
Sterling	1,518	3,284	4,802
$US	252	1,282	1,534
Japanese Yen	1,065	–	1,065
Total	2,835	4,566	7,401

Source: British Airways Annual Report 2001/2002 (**www.britishairways.com**)

20.10 The WACC for foreign investment projects

In Chapter 12, we explained how a project-specific discount rate could be obtained for a foreign investment. At that point, we were assuming all-equity funding. But what if the project is partly-debt financed? This issue is often highly relevant where foreign governments offer concessionary interest rates, often prompting a level of local debt financing well above the parent's own gearing. The most appropriate solution is to use a tailor-made WACC calculated to reflect the particular financing mix of the project.

To illustrate this, let us revisit the case of Malaku Mining from Chapter 12 (page 392). Recall that it was decided that a local Beta value of 0.75 was appropriate to use, resulting in a project-specific equity cost of 9.5 per cent.

Now assume that Malaku can borrow in Indonesia at the concessionary rate of 3 per cent and that local regulations allow it to offset interest charges against local taxation, paid at 40 per cent. The WACC for the Indonesian mining project is found in the usual way by weighting the cost of each form of finance by its contribution to financial structure, in this case, project financing. Now assume that the project is financed 25 per cent by parental equity and 75 per cent by local borrowing. The WACC is thus:

$$(9.5\% \times \text{equity weight}) + (3\%[1 - 40\%] \times \text{debt weight})$$

$$= (9.5\% \times 25\%) + (1.8\% \times 75\%) = (2.4\% + 1.4\%) = 3.8\%$$

This is an interesting result indeed. The combination of low interest rate and high debt proportion results in a remarkably low required return. These sorts of calculation, although based on sound CAPM logic, can often generate much lower project cut-off rates than for comparable UK investment. To many executives, it is inconceivable that high risk, foreign projects should be evaluated at lower discount rates than UK projects.

Financial managers often have some difficulty in explaining and justifying lower WACCs to sceptical executives whose natural inclination is to use *higher* rates for foreign projects. The response is that although foreign projects often have higher total risks, additional risks are usually project- and country-specific, thus very different from those affecting UK projects. These risks are best handled in more effective ways, e.g. by hedging foreign exchange risk, than by simply hiking the discount rate. Raising the hurdle rate, and possibly excluding an attractive, albeit risky, project is inferior to a considered policy of risk management.

20.11 Financial distress

This is an appropriate stage to clarify our terminology. Up to this point, we have implied that the reason for the upturn in the WACC profile is the threat of 'bankruptcy' resulting in 'liquidation', i.e. a company that fails to meet its debts will be forced by its creditors to liquidate. The term 'bankruptcy' in the UK strictly applies to personal insolvency. Individuals go bankrupt, and firms become insolvent. But what happens to a firm in severe financial distress? Broadly speaking, there are two main forms of treatment. The first is called 'receivership'.

Creditors – and it only takes one of many – may apply to a court to appoint a 'receiver' to recover the debt if the firm defaults on interest on capital repayments.

Burning before earning

Although accountancy firms often do well from insolvencies, they are not immune from failure themselves. Ascot Drummond is a case in point. It pioneered the concept of online accountancy services including company formation, accounts, payroll, book-keeping and taxation accessible on clients' computers. It obtained financing of over £6 million from venture capitalists Mercury Private Equity in October 2001, yet having burnt its way through the first *tranche* of £3 million, it was in receivership less than a year later. After pitching for a client base of over 10,000 by end-2001, it failed to break the 1,000 mark, and was unable to turn this into significant revenues, let alone profit.

Based on an article by L. Meall 'Dot.com dot.gone' *Accountancy*, August 2001

The receiver may sell the business, or parts of it, as a going concern, which continues to trade in a different guise, often involving a reduced scale of operations. However, the receiver's primary duty is to the appointing bank, and once sufficient funds have been realised to repay the loan, the receiver is under no obligation to maximise the proceeds of the sale of the remaining assets, or even to keep them operating. The receiver may choose to liquidate them *in toto* and disburse the net proceeds to remaining creditors and then any residue to shareholders.

The Insolvency Act 1986 introduced a new procedure, **administration**, as an attempt to rescue ailing companies and to protect employment. The company is allowed to continue trading under the overall control of an Administrator, who will attempt to reorganise the company's finances and its operating structure. The Administrator is appointed by a court at the request of the directors and has an equal duty to all creditors. In effect, administration, rather like filing for Chapter 11 bankruptcy under the US Bankruptcy Code, is an attempt to protect the company from its creditors, thus giving the Administrator a breathing space during which it can attempt to secure the company's survival as a reorganised going concern. The main difference compared with the US equivalent is that Chapter 11 bankruptcy allows the incumbent managers and owners to retain control. In addition, Chapter 11 enables the firm to impose a moratorium on interest payments on existing debts for a specified period and also to borrow more funds as money lent after the filing has a prior claim on assets.

During 2001, several well-known firms filed for Chapter 11 bankruptcy. Among these was Polaroid Corporation, pioneer of instant-developing photographic techniques. Threatened by rising competition from digital cameras and one-hour developing shops, it was too slow in marketing its own digital products. After first defaulting on debt interest payments, it found by October 2001, that its total assets of $948 million failed to cover debts of over $600 million to bond-holders and over $300 million to banks. Its share price had peaked at $60.31 in July 1997, but last traded at 28 cents, after dropping 98 per cent during 2001.

The next month, Chiquita Brands International, parent company of the banana traders, also filed for Chapter 11 bankruptcy. It had gained notoriety in its dispute with the European Union over banana imports from former European colonies in the so-called 'banana war'. The 131-year old Chiquita claimed that the dispute had cost it over $1.5 billion over eight years.

It now proposed to swap $700 million of its debt for ordinary shares, leaving existing shareholders with about 1.5 per cent of the equity. Senior bond-holders were to receive 88 per cent of the new equity. However, existing shareholders would also receive warrants allowing them to increase their stake to 17 per cent of the total diluted equity. Chiquita would exchange $861 million in debt and interest for $250 million new loan notes and 96 per cent of the equity. Managers would hold 2.5 per cent of the equity. The debt swap was expected to save Chiquita $60 million in annual interest charges.

Chiquita's subsidiaries, which conduct all its operations, are independent entities that generate their own cash flow and can access their own credit facilities. Subsidiaries will continue to operate normally and without interruption and their creditors will be unaffected. Customers will continue to receive shipments normally and suppliers will continue to be paid in full, according to usual terms.

Any visitor to an auction of bankrupt stock will have no difficulty in appreciating the importance of postponing the break-up decision. Similarly, when repossessed assets, such as consumer durables and houses, are sold by hire-purchase companies and building societies respectively, they rarely fetch 'market values'. This is partly because the vendor often only needs, and expects, to recover an amount less than the market value, having deliberately set the loan itself at less than the market value of the asset upon which it is secured. The vendor is interested in a quick sale to minimise depreciation, interest and other carrying costs. Moreover, when it is generally known that the assets are offered under distressed conditions asset values usually head South! In January 2002, Britain's BG Group plc announced it would pay distressed US energy firm Enron $350 million for its stake in oil and gas fields off the coast of India. The 30 per cent stake in the Tapti and Panna-Mukta fields

Mini cases

Selling up – everything must go!

Case: 1 BT plc

The year 2001 saw widespread asset sales by firms trying to pay down debt and also restructure their activities. Few firms mounted such a massive programme of asset sales as BT during 2001. As a result of over-investment in third-generation mobile telephony

Continued

licences, BT faced debts of some £30 billion, a credit downgrade likely to cost around £300 million p.a. in extra interest, and a plunging share price. It disposed of joint venture stakes in Japan and Spain and also its Yellow Pages subsidiary, Yell, for £2.1 billion.

In November 2001, it sold its property portfolio for £2.4 billion to Telereal, jointly owned by Britain's largest property company Land Securities, and the private firm Pears Group. The deal involved 6,700 properties including telephone exchanges and call centres and warehouses, but excluded the landmark BT tower in London. As BT will lease back these properties, the balance sheet benefit is largely cosmetic as BT is exchanging market debt for longer-term fixed obligations that will still feature on its balance sheet.

Case 2: Rexam plc

Another company troubled by high debts was Rexam, the packaging group. Facing net debt of over £2 billion at the end of 2000, it embarked on a programme of sales of non-core businesses in order to trim this debt by over £800 million. In June 2001, it sold Mitek, its main building and engineering business, to Berkshire Hathaway, the investment vehicle of the renowned private investor, Warren Buffet, for £275 million in cash, bringing its total disposals to date to £615 million.

Case 3: Alcatel

Also in late 2001, Alcatel, the French telecommunications equipment maker, enhanced its balance sheet by selling a stake worth €130 million in Thomson Multi-Media, the French consumer electronics group. Thomson was reported to be facing a loss of €5 billion and had already restructured its debt by raising €1.2 billion from a 5-year bond issue.

Selling the Thomson stake was part of a cash generation programme that included the flotation in June 2001 of Nexans, its cable business, raising €450 million, and selling a stake worth €270 million in Thales, the French defence electronics group. Neither sale was a total disposal as Alcatel wanted to keep a stake sufficient to maintain its Board representation and retain its position as a full strategic partner.

plus 63 per cent of a further untapped field, was valued by Dutch bank ABN AMRO at $450 million, 30 per cent above the agreed price.

The costs incurred at and during liquidation are called the 'direct' costs of financial distress. Empirical studies (e.g. van Horne 1975; Sharpe 1981) have suggested that liquidation costs, including legal and administrative charges, may lower the resale value of distressed companies by 50 per cent or more.

However, a recent US study suggests that distress costs of this magnitude may be an overestimate. In a study of 31 Highly Leveraged Transactions (HLTs) occurring between 1980 and 1989, Andrade and Kaplan (1998) tried to differentiate between the costs of dealing with economic distress, e.g. reacting to loss of contracts, and direct costs of financial distress. Comparing enterprise values at the date of the HLT and at the date of resolution of the distress, they estimated an average loss in firm value of 38 per cent, of which 26 per cent was due to economic distress and 12 per cent due to financial distress.

A more insidious form of financial distress is the impact of increasing gearing on managerial decision-making and the performance of the firm – the so-called 'indirect' costs. As a firm's indebtedness begins to look excessive, it may develop an overriding concern for short-term liquidity. This may be manifested in reduced investment in training and R&D, thus damaging long-term growth capability, and reducing credit periods and stock levels, which may hamper marketing efforts. Supplier power triggered the collapse of US discount retailer, K-Mart in January 2002. Its sole supplier of grocery products suspended payments after K-Mart failed to make a regular weekly payment. More obviously, it may sell established operations at bargain prices, sell or abandon promising new product developments, and, to the extent that it does continue to invest, may express a preference for short-payback, cash-generating projects, rather than strategic activities. Troubled companies often cut their dividends to preserve liquidity, but this often signals to the market the extent of their difficulties. Finally, there may be a pervasive 'corporate gloom effect', which saps morale internally and damages public image externally.

Such costs are likely to be encountered well before the trigger point of cash flow crisis, and, of course, many firms have successfully surmounted them, but not without an often prolonged dip in the value of the company. In other words, both actual and anticipated liquidation costs detract from company value, lowering the effective limit to debt capacity.

The practical importance of the facility to appoint an Administrator before creditors can appoint receivers may now be seen. Administration enhances the probability of survival of a company unable to meet its immediate liabilities and may thus lead to lower costs of financial distress. However, there may be an element of '**moral hazard**' to the extent that financial managers might undertake more dangerous levels of debt, knowing that there is a more relaxed legal procedure in the event of insolvency.

Mini case

Cobra's fangs drawn

The struggling sportswear retailer Cobra Sports went into administration in April 1998. Despite rapid growth in the 1990s to 65 outlets, it was still a minnow compared with the 'Big Four' market leaders: JD Sports, JJB Sports, Blacks Leisure and Sports Division. Cobra was unable to match the discounting power of the market leaders and had been damaged by a price war involving three key brands – Adidas, Nike and Reebok – at the same time as having to finance a move away from the mainstream sportswear market into sports-oriented fashion wear. In March 1998, it issued a profits warning and announced the loss of 1,600 jobs. The next month, Cobra bit the bullet and applied for an administration order, resulting in the appointment of accountants Baker and Tilly, which took over operations.

Self-assessment Activity 20.11

Identify examples of distressed behaviour by highly geared firms from your reading of the financial press.

(see end of chapter)

Capital structure problem at Energis

A number of Energis's bankers are looking to offload their debt in the company at knock-down prices, suggesting that some of them have become resigned to writing off part of the £600 million they have lent the telecommunications operator.

Distressed debt investors reported that several of Energis's lenders have been looking for buyers of the loans they made to Energis at below 70 per cent of their face value. Analysts speculated yesterday that the eagerness of some banks to sell their debt at such low prices indicated they were becoming less confident about a full recovery of their loans.

The future of Energis has largely been in the hands of its 16-bank lending syndicate ever since the carrier admitted that it expected to breach banking covenants agreed with lenders.

Earlier this week, Energis's consortium of bankers agreed to extend the carrier's loan facilities to give it more cash to keep its lossmaking European operations afloat as buyers for the business are found.

But analysts speculated that the low prices being sought by some bankers for the loans indicated that a sale below the value of the telecoms group's entire bank debt, currently estimated at £605 million, was possible.

'A potential equity investor has got to solve the capital structure problem at Energis,' said telecoms analyst research house, Equity Investor.

Based on Robert Budden, *Financial Times*, March 7 2002

20.12 Two more issues: signalling and agency costs

An unexpected reduction in indebtedness is usually greeted with pleasure by the market, whereas a debt increase can be regarded in a favourable or unfavourable light depending on the accompanying arguments. According to Ross (1977), managers naturally have a vested interest in not making the company insolvent, so an increase in gearing might be construed by the market as signalling a greater degree of managerial confidence in the ability of the company to service a higher level of debt. This argument relies on asymmetric information between managers and shareholders, and reflects the pervasive principal/agent problem.

Financial managers, as appointees of the shareholders, are expected to maximise the value of the enterprise, but it is difficult for the owners to devise an effective, but not excessively costly, service contract to constrain managerial behaviour to this goal. In the context of capital structure theory, the financial manager acts as an agent for both shareholders and debt-holders. Although the latter do not offer remuneration, they do attempt to limit managers' freedom of action by including restrictive covenants in the debt contract, such as restrictions on dividend payouts, to protect the asset base of the company.

Such restraints on managerial decision-making may adversely affect the development of the firm and, together with the monitoring costs incurred by the shareholders themselves, may detract from company value. Conversely, it is possible that the close monitoring by a small group of creditors, aiming to protect their capital, may induce managers to pursue more responsible policies likely to enhance the wealth of a widely-diffused group of shareholders.

20.13 Conclusions

What recommendations can we make to the financial manager?

(1) Gearing can lower the overall or weighted average cost of capital that the company is required to achieve on its operations, and can raise the market value of the enterprise. However, this benign effect can be relied upon only at relatively safe gearing levels. Companies can expect the market to react adversely to 'excessive' gearing ratios. The implications for project appraisal are reasonably clear. Strictly, the appropriate cut-off rate for new investment is the marginal cost of capital, but if no change in gearing is caused by the new activity, the WACC can be used.

(2) Considerable care should be taken when prescribing the appropriate use of debt that will enhance shareholder wealth without ever threatening corporate collapse. Levels of gearing that look quite innocuous in calm trading conditions may suddenly appear ominous when conditions worsen. Corporate difficulties do not usually occur singly, and highly geared companies are relatively less well placed to surmount them.

(3) The capital structure decision, like the dividend decision, is a secondary decision – secondary, that is, to the company's primary concern of finding and developing wealth-creating projects. Many people argue that the beneficial impact of debt is largely an illusion. Clever financing cannot create wealth (although it may enable exploitation of projects that would not otherwise have proceeded). It may, however, transfer wealth if some stakeholders are prepared, perhaps due to information asymmetry, to accept too low a return for the risks they incur, or if the government offers a tax subsidy on debt interest.

(4) The decision to borrow should not be over-influenced by tax considerations. There are other ways of obtaining tax subsidies, such as investing in fixed assets, which qualify for tax allowances. A highly geared company could find itself unable to exploit the other tax-breaks offered by governments when a favourable opportunity is uncovered.

(5) Remember that interest rates fluctuate over time. If interest rates move from what seems a 'high' level, financial managers should take advantage of the reduction. For example, if 10 per cent seems like the 'normal' long-term level of interest rates, when rates next fall below 10 per cent, and bankers are offering variable rate loans at, say, 9 per cent, one should not be afraid to take a fixed rate loan at, say, 9.5 per cent. Readiness to work with a slightly higher than minimum rate in the short term could have significant payoffs in the longer term. Anyone who thinks that rates will continue to fall should reserve some borrowing capacity to retain flexibility.

(6) Firms should avoid relying on too many bankers, as with syndicated loans, despite the benefits of access to a variety of banking facilities. If the company hits trading and liquidity problems, it is hard enough to convince one banker that the company should be saved. But if it has to persuade 10 or 20, and their decision has to be unanimous, it is virtually impossible to reach a satisfactory conclusion about capital restructuring. The UK entertainments group Brent-Walker had to negotiate with 47 banks in its efforts to rebuild its capital structure during 1991, while the liquidators of Polly Peck had to deal with 70. Eurotunnel had to deal with 225 at one stage of its troubled existence, later reduced to a mere 200.

(7) The finance manager should question whether debt is the most suitable form of funding in the circumstances. For example, there should be a clear rationale to support the case for debt rather than retentions (i.e. lower dividends) or a rights issue. He or she should recognise the value of retaining reserve borrowing capacity to draw upon under adverse circumstances or when favourable opportunities, like falling interest rates, arise.

(8) These considerations are reflected in two popular theories that attempt to explain how firms address long-term financing decisions. These are:

The Trade-off Theory. This recognises that firms seek to exploit the lower cost benefits of borrowing, especially the tax shield, But at the same time, they are reluctant to increase the financial risk entailed in entering contractual commitments to make ongoing interest and capital repayments. In other words, they trade-off the returns (the cost benefits) against the risks. We might thus expect to find that firms enjoying higher and more stable profit levels, that offer greater scope to shelter profits from tax, should operate at higher borrowing levels.

The Pecking Order Theory. This suggests that firms have an order of priorities in selecting among alternative forms of finance:

- First, they prefer to use the internal finance generated by operating cash flow.
- Second, they prefer to borrow when internal sources are drained.
- Third, they regard selling new shares almost as a last resort

The reason for this order of preference lies in **information asymmetry** – managers know far more about the firm's performance and prospects than outsiders. They are unlikely to issue shares when they believe shares are 'undervalued', but more inclined to issues shares when they believe they are 'overvalued'. Naturally, shareholders are aware of this likely managerial behaviour and thus regard equity issues with suspicion. For example, they may interpret a share issue as a signal that management thinks the shares are overvalued and mark them down accordingly – a very common occurrence – thereby increasing the cost of equity. Investors would expect managers to finance investment programmes, first, using internal resources, second, via borrowing up to an appropriate debt/equity combination, and finally through equity issues. Yet again, signalling considerations are crucial.

Summary

We have explained the meaning of gearing, its likely benefits to shareholders, its dangers and its possible impact on the required return on investment projects.

Key points

- Borrowing often looks more attractive than equity due to its lower cost of servicing, tax-deductibility of interest and low issue costs.
- A company's indebtedness is revealed by its capital gearing and by its income gearing.
- The sum of discounted tax savings conferred by the tax-deductibility of debt interest is called the tax shield.
- In a geared company, variations in earnings before interest and tax generate a magnified impact on shareholder earnings.
- The downside of gearing is the creation of a prior charge against profits, which results in the risk of possible default as well as greater variability of shareholder earnings.
- Default risk is likely to impose further costs on the geared company's shareholders, referred to as the 'costs of financial distress'.
- An insolvent company, i.e. one unable to meet its immediate commitments, is unlikely to achieve full market value in a sale of assets.
- For companies using a mixture of debt and equity, there may be an optimal capital structure at which the overall cost of capital (WACC) is minimised.
- The WACC is found by weighting the cost of each type of finance by its proportionate contribution to overall financing, and may fall as gearing increases.
- The increased risks imposed by gearing are likely to cause lenders and shareholders eventually to demand a higher rate of return, raising the WACC.
- The WACC is the appropriate cut-off rate for new investment so long as the company adheres to the optimal capital proportions.
- When companies deviate from the optimal capital structure, the marginal cost of capital becomes the correct cut-off rate.
- Because the optimal gearing ratio is difficult to identify in practice, many firms aim for a target gearing ratio.
- In view of the risks of gearing, an increase in borrowing may be a way of signalling to the market greater confidence in the future.

Further reading

A good overview of the theoretical ground can be found in Board's contribution to Firth and Keane (1986). Brealey and Myers (2000) devote two chapters to optimal capital structure at a rather less rigorous level than Copeland and Weston (1988).

It would be useful to look at Rutterford (1992) for a treatment of practical issues such as restrictive covenants.

Miller (1991) provides an overview of the capital structure debate in his Nobel lecture.

Appendix
Slipping down the credit ratings

One fallout of European telecoms firms overpaying for third-generation mobile telephony licences was the huge increase in their indebtedness. The credit rating agencies responded in the obvious way. The credit ratings of the two largest operators, BT and Deutsche Telekom, were downgraded within a few weeks of each other. In August 2000, Standard & Poor's reduced BT's status from AA+ , its second highest rating, to A with 'negative implications', i.e. pointing to a further downgrade. In October 2000, S & P cut DT's long-term rating from AA− to A−, again warning of a possible future downgrade if asset sales were not forthcoming to repay debt.

The immediate impact of a credit downgrade is to raise interest rates on borrowings. In BT's case, it faced a 1 per cent (one percentage point) increase in its borrowing rate, which, applied to its £30 billion debt, implies a rise in borrowing costs of £300 million.

Standard & Poor's credit rating system is shown below, together with that of the other main credit rating agency, Moody's.

Credit Risk	S & P	Moody's
Prime	AAA	Aaa
Excellent	AA	Aa
Upper Medium	A	A
Lower Medium	BBB	Baa
Speculative	BB	Ba
Very Speculative	B, CCC, CC	B, Caa
Default	C, D	Ca, C

Source: **www.moodys.com, www.standardpoor.com, www.ratings.com**

Both agencies make further differentiation on the quality of bonds within each category. Moody's uses a numerical system (1,2,3) and S & P uses a plus or minus. For example, a rating of Aa1 from Moody's is a superior rating than Aa3, and an A+ from S & P is a better rating than A−.

Self-assessment Answers

20.1 **(i)** debt/equity = £50 m/£100 m = 50%.
(ii) debt-to-debt plus equity = £50 m/(£50 m + £100 m) = 33.3%.
(iii) net debt = debt less cash = (£70 m − £10 m) = £60 m,
or as a percentage of equity = (£60 m/£100 m) = 60%.

20.2 Both capital and income gearing are forms of financial gearing, i.e. they stem from the firm's financial structure. Capital gearing is obtained from the Balance Sheet and is measured by the amount of borrowing in relation to owner's equity. Income gearing can be gleaned from the P and L, and is measured by interest cover, or its converse, the proportion of EBIT accounted for by interest charges.

20.3 Over to you!

20.4 Contribution is, of course, unaffected, but operating profit or PBIT would fall by £50,000 to £550,000, and PBT would fall a further £40,000 to £310,000. The two multipliers become:

Contribution/PBIT = (£1,080,000/£550,000) = 1.96
PBIT/PBT = (£550,000/£310,000) = 1.77
The combined multiplier = (1.96 × 1.77) = 3.47

20.5 **Scenario A:** EV = (0.25 × 5%) + (0.50 × 20%) + (0.25 × 35%) = 20%

Scenario B: EV = (0.25 × 3.3%) + (0.50 × 23.3%) + (0.25 × 43.3%) = 23.3%

Scenario C: EV = (0.25 × 0%) + (0.50 × 30%) + (0.25 × 60%) = 30%

20.6 With 25% gearing, share price = (23.3p/0.25) = £0.93
With 50% gearing, share price = (30p/0.35) = £0.86
It seems that shareholders' demand for a higher return outweighs the increase in EPS as gearing increases.

20.7 Debt to equity ratio of 40% indicates that debt is 2/7 of the total long-term funds and equity is 5/7. The WACC is thus:

(5/7 × 18%) + (2/7 × 8%) = (12.9% + 2.3%) = 20%

20.8 Over to you!

20.9 **(i)** With 11% interest, market value = (£100 × 3.5%/11%) = £31.82
(ii) With 3% interest, market value = (£100 × 3.5%/3%) = £116.67.

20.10 **(a)** Perpetual debt: (30% × £10 m debt) = £3 m
(b) 20 years to maturity:

(20 year annuity of 6% × £10 m × T) = 11.4699 × £600,000 × 30%)
= £2.06 m

20.11 Over to you again!

Questions

1 *Solution in Appendix A (page 830).* Using the accounting information provided below, calculate the following measures of gearing:

- long-term debt (LTD) to equity
- LTD to LTD plus equity
- total debt to equity
- net debt in absolute terms
- net debt to equity
- total debt to total assets
- interest cover
- income gearing
- total liabilities to total assets

Shareholders' funds	£500 m
Cash	£20 m
Short-term deposits	£40 m
Short-term bank borrowing	£50 m
Debentures and other long-term debts	£200 m
Total assets	£800 m
Total liabilities	£420 m
Profit before interest and tax	£120 m
Net interest payable	£25 m

2 *Solution in Appendix A (page 830).* Calculate the cost of debt facing a firm that issued £50 million in debentures in £100 units two years ago at a nominal interest rate of 8 per cent p.a., in each of the following cases.

(i) market value of debt is £45 million; perpetual life.
(ii) as **(i)**, but allowing for Corporation Tax at 30 per cent.
(iii) as for **(i)**, but life span of debt is 8 years.
(iv) as for **(iii)**, but with tax payable at 30 per cent.

3 *Solution in Appendix A (page 830).* Darnol plc is currently ungeared and is considering a buy-back of ordinary shares via an open market purchase, borrowing in order to do so. You have been commissioned to report on the likely impact of two alternative policies, depending on the level of sales and operating profit for its products. You are given the following information:

Level of sales	PBIT	Probability
Weak	£5 m	0.3
Average	£50 m	0.5
Strong	£150 m	0.2

Equity is currently £200 million at book value. Tax is paid at 30 per cent.
Two alternative share buy-back programmes are under consideration:

(i) Borrowing £40 million at 8 per cent.
(ii) Borrowing £80 million at 8.5 per cent.

Required

(a) Calculate the current, and potential expected annual return on equity (ROE) under each programme.
(b) Calculate the standard deviation of the ROE in each case.
(c) Using the figures you have obtained, explain and illustrate the distinction between business and financial risk.

4 *Solution in Appendix A (page 832).* **(a)** Calculate the value of the tax shield in each of the following cases, all based on borrowing of £100 million at 10 per cent interest p.a., pre-tax.
  (i) Perpetual life debt, tax rate is 30 per cent.
  (ii) Debt repayable in full after five years.
  (iii) Debt repayable in equal tranches over five years, interest paid on the declining balance.
  (b) Specify the factors that determine the value of the tax shield that a firm can exploit.

5 *Solution in Appendix A (page 832).* Calculate the weighted average cost of capital for the following company, using both book value and market value weightings.

	Balance Sheet values	Cost of finance
Ordinary shares: (par value 50p)	£10 m	20%
Reserves:	£20 m	20%
Long-term debt:	£15 m	10%

The debt is permanent and its market value is equal to book value.
The rate of Corporate Tax is 30%.
The ordinary shares are currently trading at £4.50.

6 The directors of Zeus plc are considering opening a new manufacturing facility. The finance director has provided the following information:
Initial capital investment: £2,500,000.
Dividends for the last five years have been:

Year	1993	1994	1995	1996	1997
Net dividend per share (pence)	10.0	10.8	11.4	13.2	13.7

The following is an extract from the Balance Sheet of Zeus plc for the year ended December 31 1997:

Creditors due in more than one year	
8% Debenture	£700,000
Long-term loan (variable rate)	£800,000
Capital and reserves	
2,000,000 shares of 25p each	£500,000

The authorised share capital is 4 million shares, the current market price per share at December 31 1997 is 136p ex-dividend.

The current market price of debentures is £60 (ex-interest) and interest is payable each year on 31 December.

The interest rate on the long-term loan is 1 per cent above LIBOR, which at present stands at 16 per cent.

The debentures are irredeemable.

Ignore taxation.

Required

Calculate the weighted average cost of capital (WACC) for Zeus plc at 31 December 1997.

7 RH plc manufactures machine tools. It has issued two million ordinary shares, quoted at 168 pence each, and £1 million 10 per cent secured debentures quoted at par. To finance expansion, the directors of the company want to raise £1 million for additional working capital.

Cash flow from trading before interest and tax is currently £1 million per annum. It is expected to rise to £1.3 million per annum if the expansion programme goes ahead. To simplify placing a valuation on the company's equity, you should assume that:

- The forecast level of cash flow, and a tax rate of 33 per cent, will continue indefinitely.
- The required rate of return on the market vale of equity, 18 per cent post-tax, will be unaffected by the new financing.
- There is no difference between taxable profits and cash flow.

The company's directors are considering two forms of finance – equity via a rights issue at 15 per cent discount to current share price, or 12 per cent unsecured loan stock at par.

Required

(a) Calculate for both financing options, the expected
  (i) increase in the market value of equity
  (ii) debt/(debt + equity) ratio
  (iii) weighted average cost of capital.

(b) Assume you are the financial manager for RH plc. Write a brief report to the board advising which of the two types of financing is to be preferred. Include in your report brief comments on non-financial factors which should be considered by the directors before deciding how to raise the £1 million finance.

(CIMA)

8 Celtor plc is a property development company operating in the London area. The company has the following capital structure as at 30 November 1993:

	£000
£1 ordinary shares	10,000
Retained profit	20,000
9% debentures	12,000
	42,000

The equity shares have a current market value of £3.90 per share and the current level of dividend is 20 pence per share. The dividend has been growing at a compound rate of 4 per cent per annum in recent years. The debentures of the company are irredeemable and have a current market value of £80 per £100 nominal. Interest due on the debentures at the year end has recently been paid.

The company has obtained planning permission to build a new office block in a redevelopment area. The company wishes to raise the whole of the finance necessary for the project by the issue of more irredeemable 9 per cent debentures at £80 per £100 nominal. This is in line with a target capital structure set by the company where the amount of debt capital will increase to 70 per cent of equity within the next two years.

The rate of corporation tax is 25 per cent.

Required

(a) Explain what is meant by the term 'cost of capital'. Why is it important for a company to calculate its cost of capital correctly?

(b) What are the main factors which determine the cost of capital of a company?

(c) Calculate the weighted average cost of capital of Celtor plc which should be used for future investment decisions.

9 Redley plc, which manufactures building products, experienced a sharp increase in operating profit (i.e. profits before interest and tax) from £27 million in 1995–96 to £42 million in 1996–97 as the company emerged from recession and demand for new houses increased. The increase in profits has been entirely due to volume expansion, with margins remaining static. It still has substantial excess capacity and therefore no pressing need to invest, apart from routine replacements.

In the past, Redley has followed a conservative financial policy, with restricted dividend payouts and relatively low borrowing levels. It now faces the issue of how to utilise an unexpectedly sizeable cash surplus. Directors have made two main suggestions. One is to redeem the £10 million of the secured loan stock issued to finance investment several years previously, the other is to increase the dividend payment by the same amount.

Redley's present capital structure is shown below:

	£m
Issued share capital (par value 50p)	90
Reserves	110
Creditors due after more than one year:	
9% secured loan stock 2004	30

Further information

(i) Redley has no overdraft.

(ii) Redley pays corporate tax at a rate of 33%.

(iii) The last dividend paid by Redley was 1.45 pence per share.

(iv) Sector averages currently stand as follows:

dividend cover	2.5 times
gearing (long-term debt/equity)	48%
interest cover	5.9 times

(v) Redley's P:E ratio is 17:1.

Required

(a) Calculate (i) the dividend cover and (ii) the dividend yield for both 1995–96 and for the reporting year 1996–97, if the dividend is raised as proposed.

(b) You have been hired to work as a financial strategist for Redley, reporting to the Finance Director. Using the information provided, write a report to your superior, which identifies and discusses the issues to be addressed when assessing the relative merits of the two proposals for reducing the cash surplus.

Practical assignment

For a company of your choice, undertake an analysis of gearing similar to that conducted in the text for BAA. Pay particular attention to the treatment of provisions and other components of long-term liabilities. If you decide to include short-term indebtedness in your capital gearing measure, would you include trade and other creditors as well?

Try to form a view as to whether your company is operating with high or low gearing.

21 Does capital structure really matter?

On a different planet – or opening another chapter

In 1990, British former pub owner Robert Earl hit on the idea of an upmarket burger chain, themed around Tinseltown megastars who would grace establishments with their presence, enhancing the dining experience of customers. Planet Hollywood's financial backers included a megastar-studded cast list of shareholders – luminaries like Arnold Schwarzenegger, Demi Moore and Bruce Willis, as well as the world's sixth richest man, the Saudi Prince Al Waleed. Initially, it was successful, growing to 87 outlets, with a flotation on the New York Stock Exchange in 1996 which raised $200 million, and valued the business at $3.5 billion.

Yet by 1999, debts were ballooning, costs soaring and the concept was fading, like some of the stars that had backed it with their money, if not with their physical presence. It filed for Chapter 11 bankruptcy, eventually being rescued by a consortium including Ong Bong Seng, a Singapore property tycoon, and involving more money from Al Waleed, who had earlier played a major financial role in baling out Euro Disney.

After listing on Nasdaq in May 2000, amazingly, it re-appeared before the bankruptcy court as soon as October 2001, again seeking protection from angry creditors. Schwarzenegger himself baled out – a bad omen, for little over a year later, the firm was rocking from the slowdown in the US economy. The 20 per cent loss in sales following the 9/11 attacks on America proved to be the terminating setback.

Can Planet Hollywood repeat its comeback trick? Planet Hollywood III? Space Cowboys II??

Learning objectives

This chapter offers a more theoretically-oriented analysis of capital structure decisions. After reading it, you should:

- Understand the theoretical underpinnings of 'modern' capital structure theory.
- Appreciate the differences between the 'traditional' view of gearing and the Modigliani–Miller versions.
- Be able to identify the extent to which a Beta coefficient incorporates financial risk.
- Assess the required return on an overseas investment

21.1 Introduction

This chapter begins with a question. In the last chapter, we warned that debt could be lethal to company survival, yet here we find an apparently insolvent firm 'rising from the dead' not once but twice. This survival instinct may thus pose a puzzle – how can insolvent firms like Planet Hollywood be worthless one moment but still survive?

The answer lies partly in the non-punitive nature of the US Chapter 11 bankruptcy rules, which many want to see introduced in the UK and elsewhere, and partly in recognising that insolvency does not necessarily mean total loss of enterprise value. Insolvency is the formal acceptance that the business entity cannot meet its financial obligations, whether payment to creditors for supplies, or payments to lenders. Yet it is possible for insolvent firms to retain value as operating entities even though their owners' equity may have been wiped out. A few figures may help.

XYZ owes £10 million to lenders and its assets are only £8 million, so it is technically insolvent, unable to cover its debts with its assets, i.e. its net assets are negative – minus £2 million. However, if its operating activities generate more cash inflows than outflows, then as a debt-free entity it would be viable and have value. Hence, it might look attractive as a restructured going concern to other investors prepared to take responsibility for the debts. Creditors might be prepared to exchange debt for equity or preference shares, or take a discount on their principal, accepting, say, 30p in the pound, just to salvage something from the mess. The equity value has disappeared but the enterprise still has value as a going concern if investors can be found to re-finance it and re-organise it into a viable operation.

One might then conclude that indebtedness does not really matter – a firm that cannot pay its way can be restructured and the jobs of the workers, if not the management, can be preserved.

A few years ago, the former England football manager, Terry Venables, bought Portsmouth FC for £1 – a remarkable bargain, you might think. However, he was buying the club's assets encumbered with debts, which he and his backers were hoping to re-finance or to pay off. The club as a bundle of assets was worth more than £1, and Venables was really paying far more than this. Had he bought the club free of debt, he would have had to pay out more.

So long as assets can be sold at their full economic value, i.e. reflecting operating cash flows, then debt is of most consequence to the hapless owners whose equity is

usually all but obliterated. Meanwhile, the business can proceed, usually under different management, with a new set of backers hoping to do better next time round. This suggests that the sting of insolvency can be drawn and that firms might take on a lot more debt with the sort of protection that Chapter 11 provides.

The traditional theory of gearing says that debt should be handled with great caution but there is a body of analysis that proves that, under certain conditions, debt is truly irrelevant in determining company value and the cost of capital. This is the famous theory developed by Franco Modigliani and Merton Miller (MM), both Nobel prizewinners for Economics. Our next task is to explain this theory.

21.2 The Modigliani–Miller message

To Modigliani and Miller (MM), the traditional perception of the impact and desirability of gearing seemed unsupported by a theoretical framework. In particular, there seemed little reason, apart from some form of market imperfection such as information deficiency, why merely altering the capital structure of a firm should be expected to alter its value. *After all, neither its earnings stream nor its inherent business risk would alter* – it would remain the same enterprise, operating under the same managers and in the same industry.

MM contended that, in a perfect capital market, the value of a company depended simply on its income stream and the degree of business risk attaching to this, regardless of the way in which its income was split between owners and lenders i.e. its capital structure. Therefore, any imbalance between the value of a geared company and an otherwise identical ungeared company could only be a temporary aberration and would be quickly unwound by market forces. The mechanism for equalising the values of companies, identical except for their respective gearing, was the process of 'arbitrage', a feature of all developed financial markets which ensures that assets with the same risk–return characteristics sell at the same prices.

To support these contentions, some algebraic analysis is required, although readers will find that it is much less complex than appears at first sight.

The analytical framework

No distinction is made between short- and long-term debt and we assume that all borrowing is perpetual. The company is expected to deliver constant and perpetual estimated annual earnings, described by a normally distributed range of possible outcomes. Investors are assumed to have homogeneous expectations, i.e. they all formulate similar estimates of company earnings, E, the net operating income (NOI) before interest and tax, or, more simply, revenues less variable costs less fixed operating costs. It is important to note that we are using the **free cash flow** concept of earnings as explained in Chapter 4, i.e. income net of any investment required to rectify wear-and-tear on capital equipment and hence maintain annual earnings at E.

The discount rate applied to the stream of expected earnings depends on the degree of business risk incurred by the enterprise. MM used the concept of 'equivalent risk classes', each one containing firms whose earnings depend on the same risk factors and from which the market expects the same return. In terms of the Capital Asset Pricing Model, this means that the earnings streams from firms in the same risk category are perfectly correlated and that member companies have identical activity Betas.

For consistency, we use the same definitions and notation as in Chapter 20. The key definitions are reproduced in Table 21.1.

The overall rate of return that the company must achieve to satisfy all its investors is the weighted average cost of capital (WACC), denoted by k_o. This can be expressed as:

$$k_o = \left(k_e \times \frac{V_S}{V_o}\right) + \left(k_d \times \frac{V_B}{V_o}\right) = \frac{E}{V_o}$$

The WACC equals E/V_o, since total operating income is composed of payments to shareholders, $k_e V_S$, plus payments to lenders, iB.

Using this set of definitions, we now examine the impact of variations in capital structure on V_o and k_o. The *original* MM analysis did not apply directly to the UK context, being expressed in terms of substituting debt for equity, i.e. using debt to repurchase ordinary shares. This was not generally possible in the UK until the Companies Act 1981, which enabled firms, subject to shareholder approval, to undertake such repurchases. Now this is permitted, the original MM analysis is more readily applicable to the capital structure decisions of UK firms. Using debt-for-equity substitution rather than adding debt to equity has the

Table 21.1 Key definitions in capital structure analysis

V_o	= the overall market value of the whole company
V_S	= the value of the shareholders' stake in the company
V_B	= the market value of the company's outstanding borrowings
B	= the book value of borrowings (generally assumed equal to its market value)
k_e	= the rate of return required by shareholders
k_d	= the rate of return required by providers of debt capital
k_o	= the overall (weighted average) cost of capital
i	= the coupon rate on debt
iB	= annual interest charges (i.e. payments to lenders, based on book value)
$k_e V_S$	= payments to shareholders = $(E - iB)$, so that
E	= annual net operating income (NOI) = $(iB + k_e V_S)$

It should be stressed that we are assuming no retention of earnings, i.e. D (dividends) = E, and hence no growth, and, for the moment, no taxes on corporate profits.

The value of equity in an all-equity firm is:

$$V_S = \frac{D}{k_e} = \frac{E}{k_e}$$

The value of a geared firm making interest payments of iB is:

$$V_S = \frac{(E - iB)}{k_e}$$

The value of the whole firm in either case is:

$$V_o = V_S + V_B$$

major advantage of enabling us to hold constant both the book values of assets and capital employed and also the PBIT, a device used in the Lindley example in Chapter 20. Any gearing change alters only the company's capital structure with no effect on company size or the level and riskiness of operating earnings. As a result, we can focus directly on the relationship between V_o and k_o.

MM's assumptions

The MM thesis did not go unchallenged. Much criticism of MM's analysis stemmed from failure to understand positive scientific methodology. Their analysis attempted to isolate the critical variables affecting firm value under the restrictive conditions of a perfect capital market. This provided a systematic basis for examining how imperfections in real world markets could influence the links between value and risk. The key assumptions are:

- All investors are price-takers, i.e. no individual can influence market prices by the scale of his or her transactions.
- All market participants, firms and investors, can lend or borrow at the same risk-free rate.
- There are neither personal nor corporate income taxes.
- There are no brokerage or other transactions charges.
- Investors are all rational wealth-seekers.
- Firms can be grouped into 'homogeneous risk classes', such that the market seeks the same return from all member firms in each group.
- Investors formulate similar expectations about future company earnings, which are described by a normal probability distribution.
- The assets of an insolvent firm can be sold at full market values.

21.3 MM's propositions

MM's analysis was presented as three propositions, the first being the crucial one.

Proposition I

The central proposition is that *a firm's WACC is independent of its debt/equity ratio and equal to the cost of capital that the firm would have with no gearing in its capital structure.* In other words, the appropriate capitalisation rate for a firm is the rate applied by the market to an ungeared company in the relevant risk category, i.e. that company's cost of equity. The arbitrage mechanism will operate to equalise the values of any two companies whose values are temporarily out of line with each other. The example of Nogear plc and Higear plc will illustrate this.

Nogear plc and Higear plc

Nogear plc is ungeared, financed by 5 million £1 shares, while Higear plc's Balance Sheet shows £1 million debt, interest payable at 10 per cent, and 4 million £1 shares. Higear's debt/equity ratio is thus (£1 m/£4 m) = 25 per cent, at book values. The two firms are identical in every other respect, including their business risks and levels of annual expected earnings (E) of £1 million. The market requires a return of 20 per cent for ungeared streams of equity income of this risk.

Imagine that, temporarily, the market value of Nogear is £4 million and that of Higear is £6 million. Higear's equity is thus valued by the market at (£6 m – £1 m) = £5 m. (Its debt/equity ratio expressed in terms of *market* values is thus £1 m/£5 m = 20 per cent.) These market values correspond to respective share prices of (£4 m/5 m shares) = 80p for Nogear and (£5 m/4 m shares) = £1.25 for Higear.

The different share values conform to the traditional relationship at relatively low gearing ratios. Higear has a greater value presumably due to its gearing. Also, it appears that Nogear is undervalued by the market since, at a required return of 20 per cent, its value should be (£1 m/0.2) = £5 m.

MM argue that such imbalances can only be temporary and the benefit obtained by Higear for its shareholders is largely illusory. It will pay investors to sell their holdings in the overvalued company and buy stakes in the undervalued one. Specifically, shareholders can achieve a higher return by selling holdings in Higear, and simultaneously, replicate its gearing (MM call this 'home-made gearing') and achieve a higher overall return. This process of arbitrage will force up the value of Higear and lower Nogear's value, until their values are equalised. There is thus little point in a firm borrowing to gear-up its capital structure when investors can achieve the same benefits by acting independently.

Home-made gearing

Consider the case of an investor with a 1 per cent equity stake in Higear. At present, this stake is worth (1 per cent of £5 m) = £50,000, attracting an income of 1 per cent of (£1 million less interest payments of 10% × £1 m), i.e. (1% × £900,000) = £9,000. This investor could realise his or her holdings for £50,000 and duplicate Higear's debt/equity ratio of 20 per cent by borrowing £10,000 at 10 per cent and investing the total stake of £60,000 in Nogear shares. This would buy (£60,000/£4 m) = 1.5% of Nogear's equity, to yield a dividend of (1.5% × £1 m) = £15,000. Personal interest commitments amount to (10% × borrowings of £10,000) = £1,000, for a net return of (£15,000 – £1,000) = £14,000. Clearly, it would pay all investors to undertake this arbitrage exercise, thus pushing down the value of Higear and pushing up the value of Nogear until there was no further scope to exploit such gains. This point would be reached when the market values of the two companies were equal and when each offered the appropriate 20 per cent return required by the market:

$$\text{Value of Nogear} = \text{Value of Higear} = \frac{E}{k_e} = \frac{£1\text{ m}}{0.2} = £5\text{ m}$$

At this equilibrium relationship, the price of each company's shares is £1. For Nogear, the calculation is (£5 m/5 m shares) = £1, while for Higear, the relevant figures are (£5 m – £1 m debt) divided by 4 m shares = £1. *In an MM world, there are no prolonged benefits from gearing and any short-term discrepancies between geared and otherwise identical ungeared companies quickly evaporate. As a result, MM* *concluded that both company value and the overall required return, k_o, are independent of capital structure.*

In reality, not all of the conditions required to support the arbitrage process may apply, suggesting that any *observed* benefits may derive from imperfections in the capital market. Moreover, if gearing does result in higher company value, there must have been a wealth transfer, since nothing has occurred to alter the fundamental wealth-creating properties of the company.

Proposition II: the behaviour of the cost of equity

Underpinning Proposition I is a statement about the behaviour of the relevant cost of capital concepts – in particular, the rate of return required by shareholders – which is expressed in MM's second proposition. This states *'the expected yield of a share of equity is equal to the appropriate capitalisation rate, k_e, for a pure equity stream in the class, plus a premium related to the financial risk equal to the debt/equity ratio times the spread between k_e and k_d'*. This proposition can be expressed as follows:

$$k_{eg} = k_{eu} + (k_{eu} - k_d)\frac{V_B}{V_S}$$

where k_{eg} and k_{eu} denote the returns required by the shareholders of a geared company and an equivalent ungeared company, respectively. The expression is easily obtained from Proposition I, as shown in Appendix I to this chapter. It simply tells us that *the rate of return required by shareholders increases linearly as the debt/equity ratio is increased*, i.e. the cost of equity rises exactly in line with any increase in gearing to offset precisely any benefits conferred by the use of apparently cheap debt. The relevant relationships are shown in Figure 21.1.

If you check back to Chapter 20, which covered the traditional view of gearing, and to Figure 20.2 in particular, you will find that the behaviour of k_e is

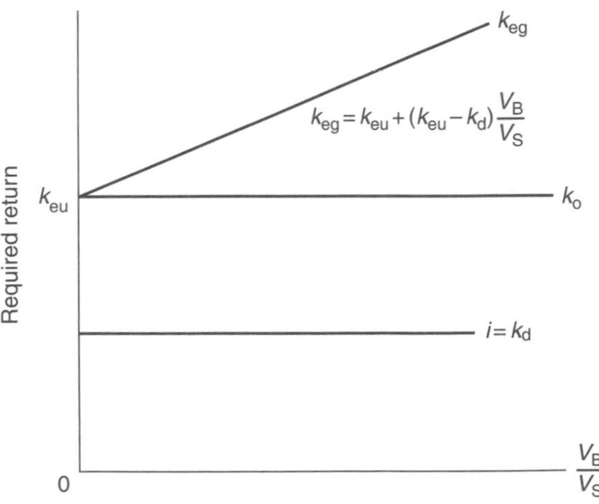

Figure 21.1 MM's Propositions I and II

the critical difference between the MM version and the traditional. In the latter, there is little or no reaction by shareholders to an increase in debt-to-equity ratio over 'modest' levels of gearing. They presumably are not alarmed by the 'judicious' use of debt. By contrast, shareholders, in the MM view, respond immediately when any gearing is undertaken, i.e. to them, any use of debt introduces an element of risk.

It should now be appreciated that in the Nogear/Higear example, Higear shareholders were seeking too low a rate of return, i.e. Higear was overvalued, and the market was temporarily offering Nogear's shareholders too high a return, i.e. Nogear was undervalued. Via the process of arbitrage, their values were brought back into line, and appropriate rates of return on equity established, reflecting their respective levels of gearing. The correct rate of return for Higear's equity, for its particular debt/equity ratio of 25 per cent (at equilibrium market values) is:

$$k_{eg} = k_{eu} + (k_{eu} - k_d)\frac{V_B}{V_S} = 20\% + (20\% - 10\%)\frac{£1\text{ m}}{£4\text{ m}} = 22.5\%$$

Proposition III: the cut-off rate for new investment

MM's third proposition asserts that *'the cut-off rate for new investment will in all cases be k_o and will be unaffected by the type of security used to finance the investment'*.

A proof of this proposition is given in Appendix II to this chapter, but it is quite easy to justify intuitively. Proposition I states that the WACC, k_o, is constant and equal to the cost of equity in an equivalent ungeared company. Since k_o is invariant to capital structure, it follows that however a project is financed, it must yield a return of at least k_o, the overall minimum return required to satisfy stakeholders as a whole.

It is worth illustrating this contention for the case where a company invests to yield a return *above* the cost of the debt used to finance the project, but *below* the cost of equity in an ungeared company.

Nogear: right and wrong investment cut-off rates

Nogear decides to raise £2 million via a debt issue at 10 per cent to finance a new project expected to yield an annual return of 15 per cent for many years into the future. Is this an acceptable project? Proposition I tells us that the initial value of the company, V_o (and the equity, V_{So}) prior to the issue is:

$$V_o = V_{So} = \frac{E}{k_e} = \frac{£1\text{ m}}{0.2} = £5\text{ m}$$

Incorporating the new project's earnings, the post-issue value of the whole company, V_1, is:

$$V_1 = \frac{£1\text{ m} + (15\% \times £2\text{ m})}{20\%} = \frac{£1.30\text{ m}}{0.2} = £6.50\text{ m}$$

Denoting R as the return on the new investment, I, and V_B as the value of the debt issued, the new value of the equity, V_{S1}, is:

$$V_{S1} = V_o + \frac{RI}{k_o} - V_{Bo} - I = £5\text{ m} + \frac{£0.30\text{ m}}{0.2} - 0 - £2\text{ m} = (£6.50\text{ m} - £2\text{ m})$$
$$= £4.50\text{ m}$$

The value of the equity falls because the new project's return, although above the interest rate on the debt used to finance it, is less than the capitalisation rate applicable to companies in this risk category.

Self-assessment Activity 21.1

Why does a geared company have the same value (allowing for size) as an ungeared company of equivalent risk in the 'basic' MM model?

(answer at end of chapter)

21.4 Impediments to arbitrage

The operation of the arbitrage process requires that corporate and personal gearing are perfect substitutes in a perfect capital market. The Nogear/Higear example showed how individual investors could replicate corporate gearing to unwind any transitory premium in the share price of a geared company. Much criticism of MM centres on the perfect capital market assumptions and hence the extent to which the arbitrage process can be expected to operate in practice.

In reality, brokerage fees discriminate against small investors, and other transaction costs limit the gains from arbitrage. Moreover, if companies can borrow at lower rates than individuals, investors may prefer the equity of geared companies as vehicles for obtaining benefits otherwise denied to them. The Wilson Committee (1980) produced evidence that, for reasons of size, security and convenience, large firms could borrow at lower rates than small firms and individuals. In addition, some major UK investors (e.g. the pension funds) face restrictions on their borrowing powers, limiting their scope for home-made gearing. Finally, whereas the shareholders in a geared firm have the protection of limited liability, personal borrowers enjoy no such protection in the event of bankruptcy.

Some authors suggest that such imperfections may foster investor demand for the equity of geared companies. However, to sustain this argument, we would need to produce evidence that relatively (but safely) geared companies are more attractively rated by the market. There is little evidence that such firms sell at relatively high P:E ratios. Indeed, UK investment trust companies, which invest in equities, often using substantial borrowed capital, typically sell at significant *discounts* to their net asset values – discounts far higher than can be explained by the transactions costs that would be incurred in liquidating their portfolios.

Self-assessment Activity 21.2

What factors restrict the ability of investors to arbitrage in the way envisaged by MM?

(answer at end of chapter)

21.5 MM with corporate income tax

The analysis of MM's three propositions in Section 21.3 is a theoretical exercise, designed to isolate the key variables relating company value and gearing. This only becomes operational when 'real-world' complications are introduced. Perhaps the most important of these is corporate taxation. In most economies, corporate interest charges are tax-allowable, providing an incentive for companies to gear their capital structures. In a taxed world, the MM conclusions change significant.

Because Corporation Tax is applied to earnings after deducting interest charges, the value of a geared company's shares is the capitalised value of the after-tax earnings stream (net income), i.e. $(E - iB)(1 - T)$:

$$V_S = \frac{(E - iB)(1 - T)}{k_{eg}}$$

where k_{eg} is the return required by shareholders, allowing for financial risk, and T is the rate of tax on corporate profits.

Assuming that the book and market values of debt capital coincide ($B = V_B$), so that the cost of debt, k_d, equates to the coupon rate, i, the value of debt is the discounted interest stream, i.e. $V_B = iB/i$, so the value of the whole company is

$$V_o = V_S + V_B = \frac{(E - iB)(1 - T)}{k_{eg}} + \frac{iB}{i}$$

It can be shown that geared companies will sell at a premium over equivalent ungeared companies because of the benefits of tax-allowable debt interest. The post-tax annual expected earnings stream, E_T, comprises the earnings attributable to shareholders plus the debt interest:

$$E_T = (E - iB)(1 - T) + iB$$

This simplifies to:

$$E_T = E(1 - T) + TiB$$

This second expression is very useful: the first element is the net income that the shareholders in an equivalent ungeared company would receive, while the second element is the annual tax benefit afforded by debt interest relief. The total value of the geared company, V_g, is found by capitalising the first element at the cost of equity capital applicable to an ungeared company (k_{eu}), while the second is capitalised at the cost of debt, which we have assumed equals the nominal rate of interest, i:

$$V_g = \frac{E(1 - T)}{k_{eu}} + \frac{TiB}{i} = \frac{E(1 - T)}{k_{eu}} + TB = V_u + TB$$

Self-assessment Activity 21.3

What are the respective values of geared and ungeared firms if:

- Earnings = £100 m before tax
- Tax rate = 30%
- k_{eu} = 15%
- The geared firm borrows £200 m?

(answer at end of chapter)

This is a highly significant result. The expression for the value of the geared company comprises the value of an equivalent ungeared company, V_u, plus a premium derived by discounting to perpetuity the stream of tax savings that can be claimed so long as the company has sufficient taxable capacity, i.e. if $E > iB$. The introduction of this second term, TB, the discounted value of future tax savings, or the tax shield, is a major modification of MM's Proposition I, as shown in Figure 21.2.

The company value profile now rises continuously with gearing. Proposition II also needs modification. With no corporate tax, this stated that the shareholders in a geared company require a return, k_{eg}, of:

$$k_{eg} = k_{eu} + (k_{eu} - k_d)\frac{V_B}{V_S}$$

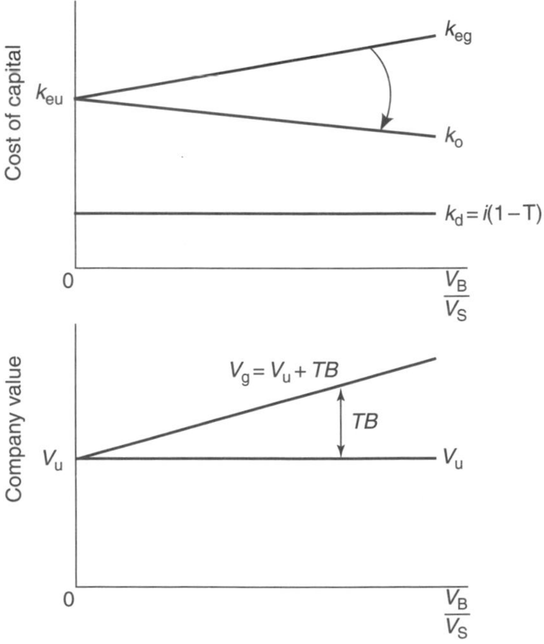

Figure 21.2 The MM thesis with corporate income tax

However, in a taxed world, the return required by shareholders becomes:

$$k_{eg} = k_{eu} + (k_{eu} - k_d)(1 - T)\frac{V_B}{V_S}$$

The return required by the geared company's shareholders is now the cost of equity in an identical ungeared company plus a financial risk premium related to the corporate tax rate and the debt/equity ratio.

The premium for financial risk required by shareholders is lower in this version owing to the tax deductibility of debt interest, making the debt interest burden less onerous. This relationship is also shown by Figure 21.2. It follows that if, at every level of gearing, the cost of equity is lower and also the cost of debt itself is reduced by interest deductibility, the WACC, k_o, is lower at all gearing ratios, and declines as gearing increases. Figure 21.2 shows the resultant pivoting in the k_o profile.

The tax advantage of debt financing is incorporated in the revised equation for the WACC:

$$k_o = \left[k_{eg} \times \frac{V_S}{V_S + V_B}\right] + \left[k_d (1 - T) \times \frac{V_S}{V_S + V_B}\right]$$

This can also be written as:

$$k_o = k_{eu}\left[1 - \frac{T \cdot V_B}{V_S + V_B}\right]$$

Clearly, there are significant advantages from gearing, with the implication that companies should gear up until debt provides almost 100 per cent of its financing. However, this does not seem plausible. Surely there are practical, 'sensible' limits to company gearing, given the risks involved? More of this later!

Self-assessment Activity 21.4

Compare the overall required return in geared and ungeared firms if:

- $k_{eu} = 15\%$
- Tax rate = 30%
- The geared firm has borrowed £200 m at 7% interest, and has issued equity of £400 m.

(answer at end of chapter)

Example of the impact of corporate taxation

It is now helpful to demonstrate 'with-tax' relationships using the examples of Nogear and Higear. Recall that both companies had E of £1 million and their equilibrium market values were £5 million under the 'no-tax' version of the MM thesis. After taxation, shareholder earnings in Nogear fall to £1 m(1 – T). With 30 per cent Corporate Tax, net income is £1 m(1 – 30%) = £0.70 m. Capitalised at 20 per cent, the value of the ungeared company is:

$$V_u = \frac{£1\text{ m}(1 - 30\%)}{k_{eu}} = \frac{£0.70\text{ m}}{0.2} = £3.50\text{ m}$$

In the case of Higear, net income for shareholders is given by taxable earnings of (E – iB) less the tax charge of $T(E - iB)$ to yield net income of:

$$\text{NI} = (E - iB)(1 - T) = [£1\text{ m} - (10\% \times £1\text{ m})](1 - 30\%)$$
$$= (£0.9\text{ m} \times 0.7) = £0.63\text{ m}$$

This might be capitalised at the geared cost of equity and added to the value of debt to yield the overall company value. However, there is a circular problem here, since the calculation of the market value of the shares, V_S, derives from the calculation of k_{eg}, which itself depends on V_S. A remedy for this problem is to use the expression $V_g = V_u + TB$ encountered above. This yields:

$$V_g = V_u + TB = £3.50\text{ m} + (30\% \times £1\text{ m}) = (£3.50\text{ m} + £0.30\text{ m}) = £3.80\text{ m}$$

It is useful also to cross-check on the components of V_g and the return required by Higear's shareholders. If V_g = £3.80 m, and the value of debt is £1 million, the value of Higear's equity must be (£3.80 m – £1 m) = £2.80 m. Using the revised expression for the return required by the shareholders of a geared company, we find:

$$k_{eg} = k_{eu} + (k_{eu} - k_d)(1 - T)\frac{V_B}{V_S}$$
$$= 20\% + (20\% - 10\%)(1 - 30\%)\frac{£1\text{ m}}{£2.8\text{ m}}$$
$$= (20\% + 2.5\%) = 22.5\%$$

The geared company clearly has a greater market value – it is worth more due to the value of the tax shield. The size of this tax shield depends on the gearing ratio, the rate of taxation and the taxable capacity of the enterprise. Since gearing has raised company value, the earlier conclusion, that the benefits of gearing are illusory, must be modified. The reason is that the stakeholders of Higear benefit at the expense of the taxpayer due to the tax deductibility of debt interest. (Whether this is desirable or not in a wider context depends on the value of the forgone tax revenues in their alternative use, which is an issue for welfare economists.)

In its tax-adjusted form, the MM thesis looks rather more like the traditional version, in so far as the WACC declines over some range of gearing. However, the benefits from gearing derive from the tax system, rather than from failure of the shareholders to respond fully to financial risk by seeking higher returns. We will discover that the similarity becomes even closer when we allow for financial distress. Before doing this, we will show how the MM approach can be integrated with the CAPM.

21.6 Capital structure theory and the CAPM

A feature of MM's initial model was the classification of firms into 'homogeneous risk classes' as a way of controlling for inherent operating or business risk. The modern distinction between systematic and specific risk makes this device unnecessary, as relevant business risk is expressed by the Beta. It is a relatively simple task to integrate the MM analysis with the CAPM. This was first performed by Hamada (1969), who demonstrated that the required return on the equity of a geared firm in a CAPM framework is:

$$k_{eg} = R_f + (ER_m - R_f) \cdot \beta_u \cdot \left[1 + \frac{V_B(1-T)}{V_S}\right]$$

where β_u is the Beta applicable to the earnings of an ungeared company, or the pure equity Beta. Multiplying out, we derive:

$$k_{eg} = R_f + \beta_u(ER_m - R_f) + (ER_m - R_f) \cdot \beta_u \cdot \left[\frac{V_B(1-T)}{V_S}\right]$$

This looks unwieldy, but is a useful vehicle for making the distinction between business and financial risk. The Betas recorded by the London Business School, are equity Betas, incorporating elements of both types of risk. From Hamada's revised CAPM expression, it can be seen that the geared Beta, β_g, will be:

$$\beta_g = \beta_u\left[1 + \frac{V_B(1-T)}{V_S}\right]$$

The ungeared equity Beta is therefore:

$$\beta_u = \frac{\beta_g}{\left[1 + \frac{V_B(1-T)}{V_S}\right]}$$

This can also be written as:

$$\beta_u = \beta_g \times \left[\frac{V_S}{V_S + V_B(1-T)}\right]$$

The shareholders of a geared company seek compensation for two separate types of risk – the underlying or basic risk of the business activity, and also for financial risk. The rewards for bearing these two forms of risk are the respective premiums for business risk and for gearing.

Higear and Nogear: separating the risk premiums

To illustrate this distinction, consider again the example of Nogear and Higear. Assume that the ungeared Beta applicable to this risk class is 1.11, the risk-free return is 10 per cent, the return expected on the market portfolio is 19 per cent and the corporate tax rate is 30 per cent. Recall that when we last encountered these companies their respective values were:

Nogear: $V_u = V_S = £3.50$
Higear: $V_g = V_u + \text{TB} = (£3.50\text{ m} + £0.30\text{ m}) = £3.80\text{ m}$
$V_B = £1\text{ m}$
$V_S = (£3.80\text{ m} - £1\text{ m}) = £2.80\text{ m}$

Firstly, we can verify the return required by Nogear's shareholders. This is:

$$k_{eu} = R_f + \beta_u[ER_m - R_f]$$
$$= 10\% + 1.11\,[19\% - 10\%] = (10\% + 10\%) = 20\%$$

Second, we can analyse the composition of the return required by Higear's shareholders. To find the overall return they seek, we need to know the geared Beta. This is given by:

$$\beta_g = \beta_u\left[1 + \frac{V_B(1 - T)}{V_S}\right] = 1.11 \times \left[1 + \frac{£1\text{ m}(1 - 30\%)}{£2.80\text{ m}}\right] = 1.3875$$

For $\beta_g = 1.3875$, the return required by Higear's shareholders is:

$$k_{eg} = R_f + \beta_g\,[ER_m - R_f] = 10\% + 1.3875\,[19\% - 10\%]$$
$$= (10\% + 12.5\%) = 22.5\%$$

Analysing the cost of equity for Higear into its components, we find:

$$k_{eg} = \text{Risk-free rate} + \text{Business risk premium} + \text{Financial risk premium}$$
$$= R_f + \beta_u\,[ER_m - R_f] + [ER_m - R_f]\beta_u \times \frac{V_B(1 - T)}{V_S}$$
$$= 10\% + 1.11\,[19\% - 10\%] + [19\% - 10\%]\,1.11 \times \frac{£1\text{ m}(1 - 30\%)}{£2.80\text{ m}}$$
$$= (10\% + 10\% + 2.5\%) = 22.5\%$$

This corresponds to the result obtained more directly with the CAPM formula. The two separate components of the geared Beta are shown in Figure 21.3. The increase in the geared Beta as the debt/equity ratio increases drives up the additional required premium *pro rata*.

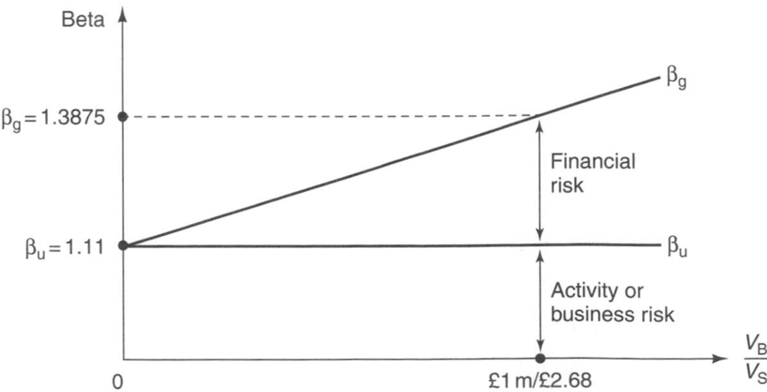

Figure 21.3 The two components of the geared Beta

21.7 MM with financial distress

In Section 21.5, we saw how including corporate taxation in the MM model implied that companies should rely on debt for nearly 100 per cent of their financing. This implication is clearly at odds with observed practice – few companies gear up to extreme levels, through fear of insolvency and its associated costs. MM's omission of liquidation costs from their analysis was a logical consequence of their perfect capital market assumptions. In such a market, where investors are numerous and rational, and have homogeneous expectations and plentiful access to information, the resale value of assets, even those being sold in a liquidation, will reflect their true economic values. Investors will recognise the worth of such assets as measured by the present values of their future income flows, and be prepared to bid up to this value, so that the price realised by a liquidator should not involve any discount.

In effect, liquidation costs and the other **costs of financial distress** introduce a new imperfection into the analysis of capital structure decisions: namely the actual or expected inability to realise 'full value' for assets in a distress sale and the costs of actions taken to forestall this contingency.

Incorporating financial distress

Denoting the 'costs of financial distress' by *FD*, the value of a geared company becomes:

$$V_g = V_u + [TB - FD]$$

From this, we may conclude that the *financial manager should attempt to maximise the gap between tax benefits and financial distress costs, i.e. (TB – FD) and that there exists an optimal capital structure where company value is maximised*. This occurs where the marginal benefit of further tax savings equals the marginal cost of anticipated financial distress. This occurs with debt of X* in Figure 21.4.

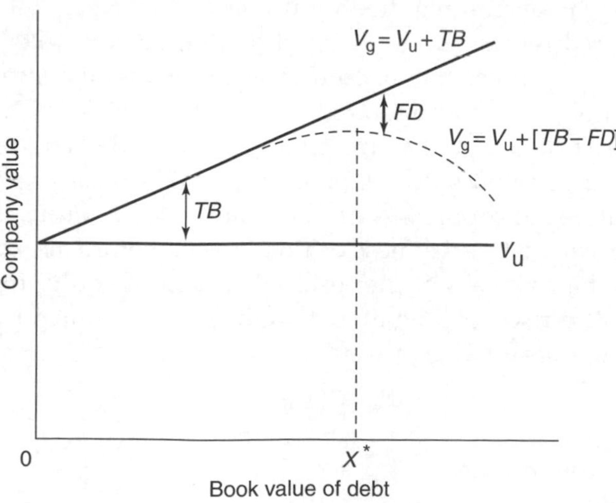

Figure 21.4 Optimal gearing with liquidation costs

The costs of financial distress rise with gearing once the market starts to perceive a substantially increased risk of financial failure. The likelihood of *FD* being non-zero depends on the probability distribution of the firm's earnings profile. For example, in the Lindley example in Chapter 20, for gearing ratios up to 50 per cent the probability of inability to meet interest payments is zero, but it would be 0.25 for any higher gearing ratio. For most companies, the probability, *p*, of financial distress will increase with the book values of debt, *B*, so that the *FD* function increases with gearing. If *d* denotes the expected percentage discount on the pre-liquidation value in the event of a forced sale, the expected costs of financial distress are:

$$FD = (p \times d \times V_g)$$

and the value of the geared firm is:

$$V_g = V_u + (TB - p \times d \times V_g)$$

This suggests that market imperfections can be exploited to raise company value so long as TB exceeds $(p \times d \times V_g)$. Notice that the inverted 'U'-shaped value profile now appears remarkably similar to the traditional version and, of course, is associated with a mirror-image WACC schedule.

You may recall our earlier comment that, after introducing market imperfections such as tax, the MM model begins to look more like the traditional version. With the inclusion of financial distress costs, this resemblance is closer still. However, the discussion of the impact of personal taxation in Appendix III shows that the debate is not yet dead.

21.8 Calculating the WACC

Before progressing, you may find it useful to re-read Chapter 12, where we discussed the hierarchy of discount rates and required rates of return, but deferred consideration of the problems posed by mixed capital structures.

The WACC is the overall required return needed to satisfy all stakeholders. It is also the required return on the assumption that new projects are financed in exactly the same way as existing ones. If the company is all-equity financed, then the WACC is simply the return required by shareholders.

Gearing does not affect the underlying risk of the company's business activities. If a company uses debt capital, it is merely repackaging its operating income into different proportions of debt interest and equity income, but not influencing the size or the riskiness of this income before appropriation. What does change is the riskiness of the residual stream of equity income, which is why the equity Beta rises, pulling up with it the return required by shareholders.

The relevant figures for Higear were:

Value of debt	$= V_B$	$= £1$ m
Value of equity	$= V_S$	$= £2.80$ m
Shareholders' required return	$= k_{eg}$	$= 22.5\%$
Interest cost of debt	$= i$	$= 10\%$
Rate of corporate tax	$= T$	$= 30\%$

The expression for the WACC in the MM case with corporate tax is:

$$k_o = \left(k_{eg} \times \frac{V_S}{V_S + V_B}\right) + \left[i(1 - T) \times \frac{V_B}{V_S + V_B}\right]$$

Using the data for Higear, this expression yields:

$$k_o = \left(22.5\% \times \frac{£2.80\text{ m}}{£2.80\text{ m} + £1\text{ m}}\right) + \left[10\%(1 - 30\%) \times \frac{£1\text{ m}}{£2.80\text{ m} + £1\text{ m}}\right]$$
$$= (22.5\% \times 0.74) + (7\% \times 0.26)$$
$$= 16.6\% + 1.8\% = 18.4\%$$

Alternatively, we can obtain the same result by using the expression:

$$k_o = k_{eu}\left[1 - T \cdot \frac{V_B}{V_S + V_B}\right]$$
$$= 20\%\left[1 - 30\% \frac{£1\text{ m}}{£3.80\text{ m}}\right]$$
$$= 20\% \times 0.92$$
$$= 18.4\%$$

Relaxing critical assumptions

Two important questions now arise. First, what happens to the discount rate if a company diversifies into an activity with a risk profile different from existing operations? Second, what happens if the gearing ratio is altered? The first issue is easier to handle.

Allowing for different risks

Imagine Higear proposes to diversify into a higher risk business. Because the discount rate applicable to evaluating this project should reflect the systematic risk involved, the required return previously calculated is no longer appropriate. To cope with this problem, the following procedure is suggested:

1 Select a company already operating in the target activity, ideally, one with operating characteristics very similar to those exhibited by the project, and obtain its Beta coefficient.
2 If the surrogate company's gearing differs from that of Higear, the Beta must be adjusted by removing the effect of the surrogate's own gearing, and then super-imposing Higear's gearing on the resulting ungeared Beta.
3 Calculate the WACC incorporating the surrogate activity Beta, adjusted for Higear's own gearing.

Assume Higear plans to enter an activity already served by Semigear, whose equity Beta is 1.8, and which has a debt/equity ratio of 1:2. Semigear's Beta is ungeared as follows:

$$\beta_u = \frac{\beta_g}{1 + \frac{V_B}{V_S}(1 - T)} = \frac{1.8}{1 + \frac{1}{2}(1 - 30\%)} = \frac{1.8}{1.35} = 1.33$$

The geared Beta applicable to Higear's capital structure (i.e. £1 million debt and £2.80 million equity) is:

$$\beta_g = \beta_u\left[1 + \frac{V_B}{V_S}\cdot(1 - T)\right]$$
$$= 1.33\left[1 + \frac{£1\text{ m}}{£2.80\text{ m}}\cdot(1 - 30\%)\right]$$
$$= 1.33\,[1.25] = 1.663$$

For this risk, and with a 9 per cent market risk premium, Higear's shareholders require a return of:

$$ER_j = R_f + \beta_g\,[ER_m - R_f] = 10\% + 1.663\,[9\%] = 25\%$$

Finally, the WACC applicable to this activity risk and Higear's gearing is:

$$(25.0\% \times 0.74) + (10\%\,[1 - 30\%] \times 0.26) = 18.5\% + 1.8\% = 20.3\%$$

The second issue, the effect of a change in gearing, poses more of a conundrum.

Allowing for a change of gearing

In the Higear example, no change in gearing was envisaged when financing new projects. However, as we have repeatedly warned, a significant change in gearing affects the market values of both debt and equity capital: for example, shareholders may respond adversely to higher gearing and the higher financial risk. Also, the value of debt may be marked down in the market. To compute the WACC, we would have to assess the new return required by shareholders, k_{eg}, given by:

$$k_{eg} = k_{eu} + (k_{eu} - k_d)\,(1 - T)\,\frac{V_B}{V_S}$$

where

$k_{eu} = R_f + \beta_u\,(ER_m - R_f)$
β_u = the ungeared Beta coefficient

To value the equity, i.e. to derive a measure for V_S, we would need to apply the (perpetuity) expression for valuing a stream of post-tax geared equity income:

$$V_S = \frac{(E - iB)(1 - T)}{k_{eg}}$$

We now encounter a circular problem, since the market value depends on k_{eg}, and to find k_{eg}, we need to know the market value.

A possible solution is to work in terms of a 'tailor-made' WACC based on the project's characteristics (i.e. its systematic risk, allowing for any divergence from existing operations) and on the project's own financing. For example, imagine the project in the previous example were to be financed 20 per cent by debt and

80 per cent by equity. You should verify that with $\beta_u = 1.33$, $\beta_g = 1.56$, and a shareholder would seek a return of 24 per cent and the WACC is:

$$(24\% \times 4/5) + (10\% [1 - T] \times 1/5) = (19.2\% + 1.4\%) = 20.6\%$$

As it happens, use of the WACC in this situation may be inappropriate anyway, since unless the firm is at, and adheres to, the target ratio, the WACC and the marginal cost of capital (MCC) will diverge. If the firm is below the optimal capital structure, the MCC is less than WACC, and the MCC exceeds the WACC when it overshoots the optimal gearing ratio. We found, in Chapter 20, that when the firm departs from the optimal gearing ratio, the appropriate required return is the MCC.

$$\text{MCC} = \frac{\text{Change in total returns required by shareholders and lenders}}{\text{Amount available to invest}}$$

However, to calculate the MCC we again need to know the market values of both equity and debt at the higher level of gearing, i.e. we encounter the circular problem described earlier. It is clear that the WACC is suitable only for small-scale projects that do not materially disturb the gearing ratio, and that the theoretically more correct MCC is also problematic.

Fortunately, as we shall see in the next section, help is at hand.

Self-assessment Activity 21.5

Ungear a Beta of 1.45 if:

- Tax rate = 30%
- The debt-equity ratio = 1:2

(answer at end of chapter)

21.9 The adjusted present value method (APV)

The **adjusted present value** (APV) of a project is simply the 'essential' worth of the project, adjusted for any financing benefits (or costs) attributable to the particular method of financing it. The rationale for the APV method was provided by Myers (1974), using MM's gearing model with corporate tax, but is valid only so long as the WACC profile is declining due to the value of the tax shield. In Section 21.5, we saw that the value of a geared firm, V_g, is the value of an equivalent all-equity-financed company, V_g, plus a tax shield, *TB*, which is the discounted tax savings resulting from the tax-deductibility of debt interest:

$$V_g = V_u + TB$$

This can be translated from the value of a firm to the value of an individual project. However, different projects can probably support different levels of debt. For example, they may involve different inputs of easily resaleable fixed assets and may also have different levels of operational gearing. As a result, it may be more appropriate to evaluate the effects of the financing of each project separately.

The APV is calculated in three steps:

Step 1 Evaluate the 'base case' NPV, discounting at the rate of return that shareholders would require if the project were financed wholly by equity, which is derived by ungearing the company's equity Beta.

Step 2 Evaluate separately the cash flows attributable to the financing decision, discounting at the appropriate risk-adjusted rate.

Step 3 Add the present values derived from the two previous stages to obtain the APV. The project is acceptable if the APV is greater than 0.

A simple example will illustrate the use of the APV.

Using the APV: Rigton plc

Rigton plc has a gearing ratio, measured by debt/equity at market values, of 20 per cent. The equity Beta is 1.30. The risk-free rate is 10 per cent and a return of 16 per cent is expected from the market portfolio. The rate of corporate tax is 30 per cent. Rigton proposes to undertake a project requiring an outlay of £10 million, financed partly by equity and partly by debt. The project, a perpetuity, is thought to be able to support borrowings of £3 million at an interest rate of 12 per cent, thus imposing interest charges of £0.3 million. It is expected to generate pre-tax cash flows of £2.3 million p.a. Using the formula developed earlier for the ungeared Beta:

$$\beta_u = \frac{\beta_g}{\left[1 + \frac{V_B}{V_S} \cdot (1 - T)\right]} = \frac{1.30}{1 + 0.20(1 - 0.30)} = \frac{1.30}{1.14} = 1.14$$

This yields a required return on ungeared equity of:

$$ER_j = R_f + \beta_u (ER_m - R_f) = 0.10 + 1.14\,(0.16 - 0.10) = (0.10 + 0.068)$$
$$= 0.168, \quad \text{i.e. } 16.8\%$$

The base case NPV is:

$$\text{NPV} = -\text{£}10\text{ m} + \frac{\text{£}2.3\text{ m}(1 - 0.30)}{0.168} = -\text{£}10\text{ m} + \frac{\text{£}1.61\text{ m}}{0.168}$$
$$= -\text{£}10\text{ m} + \text{£}9.58\text{ m}$$
$$= -\text{£}0.42\text{ m}$$

The present value of the tax savings, i.e. the tax shield, *TB*, is given by:

$$\frac{TiB}{i} = \frac{(0.30)(0.12)(\text{£}3\text{ m})}{0.12} = \text{£}0.9\text{ m}$$

The adjusted present value is thus:

$$APV = -£0.42\text{ m} + £0.90\text{ m} = +£0.48\text{ m}$$

and the project appears worthwhile. The significance of this result is that, although the base case NPV is negative, the project is rescued by the tax shield of £0.90 million. An essentially unattractive project is rendered worthwhile by the taxation system.

In the Rigton example, the project creates wealth only for Rigton's shareholders. From the perspective of the overall economy, it is wealth-reducing and, unless there are compelling 'social' reasons to justify it, should not be undertaken. This sort of reasoning led the UK government in 1984 to reduce the rate of Corporation Tax in order to lower the tax advantage of debt financing, and hence reduce the extent to which investment decisions were likely to be distorted by the system of tax breaks.

Self-assessment Activity 21.6

What is the APV and how is it calculated?

(answer at end of chapter)

Further aspects

Before leaving the APV, several related issues are worth examining.

(1) The APV in practice is affected by the terms and conditions of a pre-arranged schedule for debt interest and capital repayment. Sometimes, the calculations can be exceptionally tedious. Rather than using the convenient assumption of perpetual debt financing, let us assume that the debt plus interest must be repaid over two years, with interest and two equal capital payments occurring at end-year. Table 21.2 shows the repayment schedule and the resulting tax savings.

With no tax delay assumed, the present value of the tax savings is:

$$\frac{£0.108\text{ m}}{(1.12)} + \frac{£0.054}{(1.12)^2} = (£0.096\text{ m} + £0.043\text{ m}) = £0.139\text{ m}$$

Obviously, the value of the tax shield is much lower with the truncated payments profile.

Table 21.2 The tax shield with finite-life debt

Balance of loan at start of year	Interest at 12%	Tax saving ($T = 30\%$)	Repayment	Balance of loan at end of year
£3.0 m	£0.36 m	(30% × £0.36 m) = £0.108 m	£1.5 m	£1.5 m
£1.5 m	£0.18 m	(30% × £0.18 m) = £0.054 m	£1.5 m	0

(2) Although our example focused on the side-effects of debt financing, the APV routine can be easily applied to any other financing costs and benefits, many of which are awkward to handle with the simple WACC. For example, if equity capital is externally raised, normally there are various issuing and underwriting costs to bear. Including these would alter the APV formula as follows:

APV = Base case NPV + Tax shield – PV of issue costs

A similar treatment would be applied to subsidised borrowing costs, investment grants and tax savings from exploiting investment allowances.

(3) Tax savings are not certain because they depend on the inherent profitability of the company. As this is a random variable, the company's ability to set off interest payments (and other tax reliefs) against income is also random. Our examples assume continuous profitability, but if there are periods during which the company is expected to be tax-exhausted, this should be allowed for in the computation of the APV. If the future pattern of liability to tax is uncertain, then it is not appropriate to use a risk-free rate to discount the tax savings.

(4) Finally, we have glossed over the issues that impact on the debt-supporting capacity of particular projects. In principle, the debt capacity of a project is given by the present value of future expected earnings from the firm as a whole, taking into account any existing borrowings. It might seem obvious that more profitable companies are able to borrow relatively more than unprofitable companies. However, this assumes that there are no costs of financial distress. Enhanced borrowing ability for more profitable companies is not universal, since a would-be lender should still look at the break-up value of the enterprise. In the final analysis, the crucial factor which governs debt capacity is how much can be raised by a distress sale of assets.

Self-assessment Activity 21.7

How would you identify the point beyond which a firm would be unable to borrow?

(answer at end of chapter)

21.10 Applying the APV to foreign direct investment

Discounting at the WACC implies that all the complex interactions involved in the investment can be factored into a single discount rate. In no case is this more difficult than for foreign investment projects that differ from domestic activities in areas such as taxation, foreign exchange rate variability, concessionary financing and numerous additional dimensions of risk. This makes FDI a prime candidate for evaluation by the APV method.

For FDI, the evaluation procedure is:

1 Evaluate the core project assuming it is financed entirely by owners' equity to find the base case, as if the project were undertaken in the home country.

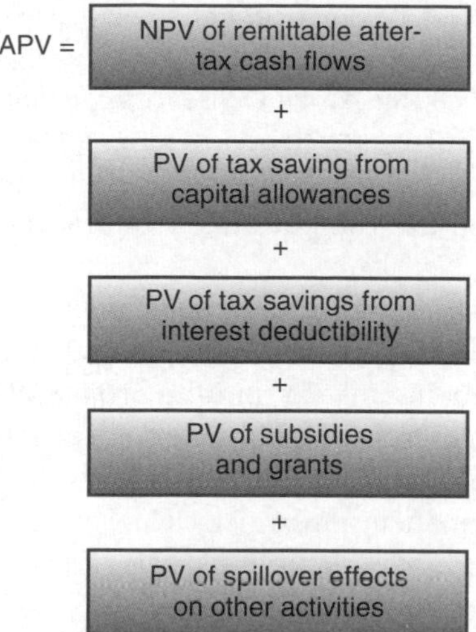

APV = NPV of basic project Plus/Minus PV of financing benefits, etc.

ACCEPT IF APV IS POSITIVE

Figure 21.5 A simple APV model

2 Separately evaluate the 'extras' such as the tax breaks and subsidies offered by the host government, any spill-over effects on other activities, e.g. lost export trade.
3 Calculate APV = [base case NPV – PV of extras]
4 Accept the project if the APV is positive.

A simple APV model is shown in Figure 21.5. The APV is defined as the inherent value of the foreign-located project to the firm's owners, adjusted for all positive and negative side effects. For foreign projects the APV is particularly useful when project financing differs from the parent firm's capital structure, but suffers the limitation that calculation of these side-effects and their associated degrees of risk is difficult in practice. Inevitably, a high degree of judgement is required.

21.11 Which discount rate should we use?

Specifying the correct discount rate to use when a new project involves financing and other differences from parent company activities is something of a puzzle. Now that we have examined the main variations on the discount rate theme, this check-list should help.

Case 1 *New project has same business risk and capital structure as parent company.* Use the parent's WACC.

Case 2 *Higher/lower business risk than the parent but same financing mix.* Adjust the Beta, using a surrogate firm's Beta as a basis but adjust for respective gearing, i.e. ungear the surrogate Beta and gear up the residual equity Beta. Then use the parent's capital structure weights to calculate the WACC.

Case 3 *Same business risk, capital structure different from that of the parent.* Use the parent's equity Beta, gear it for the project financing mix and then use the project's financing mix to find the project WACC.

Case 4 *Higher/lower business risk, different capital structure.* Use the project Beta, and, as in Case 2, gear it for the project financing, and calculate the WACC using the project financing mix.

Case 5 *Complex mixture of risk, financial structure, and side effects.*

Use the APV method.

Summary

Chapters 20 and 21 have covered extensive ground, attempting to isolate the critical variables relating company value to capital structure. In this process, we have moved from the somewhat crude 'traditional' version to the pure and less pure MM analyses, before arriving at the model displayed in Figure 21.4. This closely resembles the traditional theory itself, with its U-shaped cost of capital schedule and optimal capital structure. We have established that *the benefits of debt stem mainly from market imperfections, especially the tax relief on debt interest, but that a different type of imperfection, distress costs, can offset these tax breaks at higher levels of gearing*. In addition, even the tax benefits of gearing may be overstated as they depend on the particular mix of personal and corporate tax rates faced by the company and its stakeholders (see Appendix III).

So in response to the question posed at the start of the chapter, 'Does capital structure matter?', the answer seems to be 'yes', but in a number of complex ways. Debt, or rather, excessive debt, certainly matters to the owners but it may not destroy value. Distressed, but operationally viable, companies can still survive. For non-distressed companies, debt can offer significant tax advantages.

Key points

- MM argue that, as the method of financing a company does not affect its fundamental wealth-creating capacity, the use of debt capital, under perfect market conditions, has no effect on company value.
- Shareholders respond to an increase in the likely variability of earnings, i.e. financial risk, by seeking higher returns to offset exactly the apparent benefits of 'cheap' debt.

- The appropriate cut-off rate for new investment is the rate of return required by shareholders in an equivalent ungeared company.
- When corporate taxation is introduced, the tax deductibility of debt interest creates value for shareholders via the tax shield, but this is a wealth transfer from taxpayers.
- The value of a geared company equals the value of an equivalent ungeared company plus the tax shield:

$$V_g = V_u + TB$$

- With corporate taxation, the rate of return required by the geared company's shareholders is less than that in the all-equity company, reflecting the tax benefits.
- A further effect of corporation taxation is to lower the overall cost of capital, which appears to fall continuously as gearing increases.
- However, this result relies on the absence of default risk and the consequent costs of financial distress incurred as a company reaches or approaches the point of insolvency.
- For geared companies, the required return can be derived by combining k_e with the after-tax debt cost to obtain the WACC.
- However, the WACC is acceptable only under restrictive conditions: in particular, when project financing replicates existing gearing, and when project risk is identical to that of existing activities.
- To resolve the problems of the WACC, the adjusted present value can be used. This is the 'basic' worth of the project, i.e. the NPV assuming all-equity financing, adjusted for any financing benefits such as tax savings on debt interest, or costs such as issue expenses.
- Eventually, the costs of financial distress may begin to outweigh the benefits of the tax shield. A major cost of financial distress is the inability to achieve 'full market value' in a 'distress sale'.
- There is, in theory, an optimal capital structure where the marginal benefit of tax savings equals the marginal cost of financial distress.
- In reality, while companies should balance the benefits of the tax shield against the likelihood of financial stress costs, most finance directors will restrain gearing levels, especially as tax savings are uncertain, depending on fluctuations in corporate earnings.

Further reading

Look at the original articles by Modigliani and Miller (1958, 1963). Other important articles are those by Myers (1974, 1984), which analyse the interactions between financing and investment decisions, and Miller's attempt to resurrect the capital structure irrelevance thesis (1977) and his subsequent Nobel lecture (1991). As ever, Copeland and Weston (1996) offer a more rigorous, mathematical development. A resumé of current thinking on capital structure theory can be found in Barclay *et al.* (1995). Luehrman (1997a,b) offers two articles on the present state of valuation theory and analysis, with strong emphasis on APV and also on strategic options.

Appendix I

Derivation of MM's Proposition II

Given that:

$$\frac{E}{V_S + V_B} = \frac{E}{V_o} = k_o$$

and

$$k_e = \frac{(E - iB)}{V_S}$$

we may write

$$E = k_o V_o = k_o (V_S + V_B)$$

Substituting for E,

$$k_e = \frac{k_o (V_S + V_B) - iB}{V_S} = \frac{k_o V_S + k_o V_B - iB}{V_S} = k_o + (k_o - i) \cdot \frac{V_B}{V_S}$$

Since Proposition I argues that k_o equals the return required by shareholders in an equivalent ungeared company, k_{eu}, and so long as the book and market values of debt capital coincide, ensuring that $i = k_d$, then this expression may be written as:

$$k_{eg} = k_{eu} + (k_{eu} - k_d) \frac{V_B}{V_S}$$

as in the text. In other words, the return required by shareholders is a linear function of the company's debt/equity ratio.

Appendix II

MM's Proposition III: the cut-off rate for new investment

MM's third proposition asserts that 'the cut-off rate for investment will in all cases be k_o and will be unaffected by the type of security used to finance the investment'.

To show this, consider a firm whose initial value, V_o, is:

$$V_o = V_{So} + V_{Bo} = \frac{E_o}{k_o} \qquad \text{(A)}$$

It contemplates an investment project, with outlay £I, involving a perpetual return of R per £ invested. After the investment is accepted, the new value of the firm, V_1, is:

$$V_1 = \frac{E_1}{k_o} = \frac{E_o + RI}{k_o} = V_o + \frac{RI}{k_o}$$

Assuming the project is debt financed, the post-project acceptance value of the shares is:

$$V_{S1} = (V_1 - V_{B1}) = V_1 - (V_{Bo} + 1) \qquad \text{(B)}$$

Substituting Equation (A) into Equation (B) yields:

$$V_{S1} = V_o + \frac{RI}{k_o} - V_{Bo} - I$$

and since

$$V_{So} = (V_o - V_{Bo})$$

the change in V_S equals

$$(V_{S1} - V_{So}) = \frac{RI}{k_o} - I$$

This exceeds zero only if $R > k_o$. Hence, *a firm acting in the best interests of its shareholders should only undertake investments whose returns at least equal* k_o, *the weighted average cost of capital, which itself is invariant to gearing according to Proposition I.*

Appendix III

Allowing for personal taxation: Miller's revision

The MM analysis including corporate earnings taxation still leaves something of a 'puzzle'. The expression for the value of a geared company indicates that the tax shield is equal to the corporate tax rate (*T*) times the book value of corporate debt (*B*), i.e. *TB*. With the present UK rate of Corporation Tax of 30 per cent, for every £1 of corporate debt the value of the company would be increased by £0.30. If such tax benefits can stem from corporate gearing, why do we find widely dispersed gearing ratios even in the same industry? And why are some of these so much lower than the MM theory (even allowing for the costs of financial distress) might suggest? According to Miller (1977), the answers to such questions lie in the interaction of the corporate taxation system with the personal taxation system, an issue omitted from the MM analysis.

Miller's agenda was to re-establish the irrelevance of gearing for company value, thus explaining why US firms did not appear to exploit apparently highly valuable tax shields. Miller argued that if individuals and corporations can borrow at the same rate, and if individuals invest in corporate debt as well as equity, there are no advantages to corporate borrowing because corporations that borrow are simply doing what personal investors can do for themselves. Any temporary premium in the market valuation of a geared company will be quickly unwound by the usual arbitrage process. However, this presupposes that individuals also can obtain tax relief on their personal borrowing (as applies in the USA but not generally in the UK). Intuitively, we may expect to find some benefit to corporate borrowing in the UK because tax breaks on personal borrowing are not available.

Greatly simplifying, the Miller position can be expressed by the simple expression:

Post-tax cost of debt = pre-tax cost $[1 - (T_c - T_p)]$

where T_c is the tax rate at which corporations enjoy relief on debt interest and T_p is the tax rate at which individuals enjoy relief on debt interest.

If $T_c = T_p$, then there is no tax advantage of corporate debt and hence no tax shield to exploit.

Only if T_c and T_p differ is there a tax shield. Note that for $T_c > T_p$ the tax shield is positive, and for $T_c < T_p$, the tax shield appears to be negative, as might apply for shareholders subject to very high rates of tax.

Miller introduced a further mechanism to support the irrelevance of gearing for company value. He argued that if there is a (temporary) tax advantage relating to debt financing, this will lead firms to increase their demand for debt (i.e. increase the supply of debt instruments), thus exerting upward pressure on interest rates until the advantage of issuing further debt disappears. If the effective tax rate on equity income were zero, and personal investors paid tax on debt interest income, companies would have to compensate investors for switching from untaxed equity to taxed debt investments by a higher interest rate. This would stop when the net-of-tax cost of debt to companies equalled the cost of equity. Miller concludes that movement to capital market equilibrium would eliminate any tax advantage of debt, so that $V_g = V_u$.

Self-assessment Answers

21.1 Under MM assumptions, firms identical in all respects apart from capital structure (allowing for size), should have the same value. Value is determined by the stream of operating cash flows and the degree of business risk attaching to these, regardless of how the cash flows are 'packaged' or shared out between different classes of investor.

21.2 Arbitrage in pursuit of 'home-made gearing' is restricted by:

- Taxes on capital gains.
- Differences between the borrowing and lending rates available to all parties.
- Different borrowing rates available to firms and private investors.
- Restrictions on some institutions' ability to borrow.
- Transactions costs.

21.3 Value of ungeared firm $= \dfrac{£100\text{ m}(1 - T)}{0.15} = \dfrac{£70}{0.15} = £466.7\text{ m}$

Value of geared firm $= V_u + TB = £466.7\text{ m} + (30\% \times £200\text{ m})$
$= (£466.7\text{ m} + £60\text{ m}) = £526.7\text{ m}$

21.4 In the ungeared firm, the overall cost of capital is simply the cost of equity, i.e. 15%. In the geared firm, the overall cost of finance is:

$$k_{eu} = 15\%\ (1 - \frac{T \cdot V_B}{V_S + V_B}) = 15\%\ [1 - (30\% \times £200\text{ m}/£600\text{ m})]$$
$$= 15\%\ (1 - 1.5\%) = 13.5\%$$

21.5 Beta ungeared $= \frac{1.45}{[1 + (1 - 30\%) \times \frac{1}{2}]} = \frac{1.45}{1.35} = 1.074$

21.6 The APV is the value of an activity, based on its inherent worth as given by the PV of the stream of operating cash flows, adjusted for any 'special factors' such as tax concessions, financing costs, etc. It is thus the 'basic' NPV plus the PV of non-operating factors.

21.7 In theory, the limit to a firm's taxable capacity is where its interest charge equals the lowest possible level of future cash flows. In reality, it is much less than this. Based on asset-backing, the theoretical limit is where the book value of assets equals the book value of borrowings.

Questions

1 *Solution in Appendix A (page 833).* With the following information about Rushden plc, determine its cost of equity according to the MM no-tax model.

$$k_{eu} = 20\%; \quad k_d = 8\%; \quad \frac{V_B}{V_B + V_S} = 20\%$$

2 *Solution in Appendix A (page 833).* Diamonds plc estimates its costs of debt and equity for different capital structures as follows:

% Debt	% Equity	k_d	k_e	WACC
–	100	–	20%	?
25	75	8%	24%	?
50	50	8%	32%	?
75	25	8%	56%	?

Required

(i) What theory of capital structure is portrayed? (Complete the WACC column.)

(ii) Restate the table allowing for taxation of corporate profits (hence, tax relief on debt) at 30 per cent. Assume Diamonds plc always has sufficient taxable capacity to exploit the tax shield.
Identify the relevant theory of capital structure.

3 *Solution in Appendix A (page 833).* Demonstrate how the process of home-made gearing-cum-arbitrage would operate in an MM world so as to equalise the values of the following two firms. The companies are identical in every respect except their capital structures.

	Geared	Ungeared
Expected earnings	£100	£100
Debt finance (nominal)	£200	–
Interest rate	5%	–
Market value of equity	£900	£950
Market value of company	£1,100	£950

Assume that the market value of geared debt is equal to the nominal value, and the investor holds 10 per cent of Geared's equity.

4 Kipling plc is a food manufacturer which has the following long-term capital structure:

	£
£1 ordinary shares (fully paid)	2,500,000
Share premium account	1,000,000
Retained profit	1,400,000
8% preference shares	1,200,000
10% debentures (secured)	2,600,000
	8,700,000

The directors of the company wish to raise further long-term finance by the issue of either preference shares or debentures. One director, who supports the issue of debentures, believes that, although a debenture issue will increase the company's gearing, it will reduce the overall cost of capital.

Required

(a) Discuss the arguments for and against the view that the company's overall cost of capital can be reduced in this way. The views of Modigliani and Miller should be discussed in answering this part of the question.

(b) Discuss the major factors which the directors should consider when deciding between preference shares and debentures as a means of raising further long-term finance.

(c) Identify and discuss the major factors which will influence the amount of additional debenture finance that Kipling plc will be able to raise.

(ACC Certified Diploma)

5 **(a)** Berlan plc has annual earnings before interest and tax of £15 million. These earnings are expected to remain constant. The market price of the company's ordinary shares is 86 pence per share cum div and of debentures £105.50 per debenture ex-interest. An interim dividend of six pence per share has been declared. Corporate tax is at the rate of 35 per cent and all available earnings are distributed as dividends.
Berlan's long-term capital structure is shown below:

	£000
Ordinary shares (25 pence par value)	12,500
Reserves	24,300
	36,800
16% debenture 31 December 1994 (£100 par value)	23,697
	60,497

Required

Calculate the cost of capital of Berlan plc according to the traditional theory of capital structure. Assume that it is now 31 December 1991.

(b) Canalot plc is an all equity company with an equilibrium market value of £32.5 million and a cost of capital of 18 per cent per year. The company proposes to repurchase £5 million of equity and to replace it with 13 per cent irredeemable loan stock.

Canalot's earnings before interest and tax are expected to be constant for the foreseeable future. Corporate tax is at the rate of 35 per cent. All profits are paid out as dividends.

Required

Using the assumptions of Modigliani and Miller explain and demonstrate how this change in capital structure will affect Canalot's:

(i) market value
(ii) cost of equity
(iii) cost of capital

(c) Explain any weaknesses of both the traditional and Modigliani and Miller theories and discuss how useful they might be in the determination of the appropriate capital structure for a company.

(ACCA)

6 The ordinary shares of Stanley Plc are quoted on the London Stock Exchange. The directors, who are also major shareholders, have been evaluating some new investment opportunities. If they go ahead with these, new capital of £38 million will be required. The directors expect the new projects to earn 15 per cent per annum before tax.

Financial information about the company for 1996 is as follows:

EBIT (existing operations)	£79.50 million
Number of shares in issue (par value £1)	50 million

The company is at present all-equity financed. It has the choice of raising the £38 million new capital by an issue of equity or debt. Equity would be issued by way of a new issue at a 15 per cent discount to current market price. Debt will be raised by an issue at par of 12 per cent unsecured loan stock.

If the finance is raised via equity, the company's P:E ratio is likely to rise from its current level of 9 to 9.5. However, if debt is introduced into the capital structure, the company's financial advisors have warned the two directors that the market is likely to lower the P:E ratio of the company to 8.5.

The company's marginal tax rate is 33 per cent.

Issue costs should be ignored.

(a) Determine the expected share price, total value of equity and value of the firm under the two financing options and comment briefly on which financing option appears the most advantageous.

(b) Assume the company's average cost of equity as an ungeared firm is 14 per cent and it expects to continue to pay tax at 33 per cent. The estimated cost of bankruptcy or financial distress is estimated at £5 million. According to Modigliani and Miller, what would be the value of equity and the firm if the company finances the expansion by (i) equity or (ii) debt.

(c) Explain the basic assumptions underlying MM's theories of capital structure and why, in an efficient market with no taxes, capital structure can have no effect on the value of the firm.

7 You are given the following information about Electronics plc. It has a payout ratio of 0.6, a return on equity of 20 per cent, an equity beta of 1.33 and is expected to pay a dividend next year of £2.00. There are 1 million shares outstanding and it is fairly valued. It also has nominal debt of £20 million issued at 10 per cent and maturing in 5 years. Yields on similar debt have since dropped to 8 per cent. The risk free rate is 6 per cent and the expected market return is 13.5 per cent.

(a) Find Electronics' cost of capital and cost of equity.
(b) The company decides to retire half its debt at current prices. Find the company's cost of capital and equity and explain your results.
(c) The company decides to diversify into a completely different business area and decides to look at Betas of firms currently trading in the new business area. The information is given below.

Company	Beta	Debt/Equity	Market Capitalisation
A	1.5	1:2	£20 million
B	1.8	1:1	£30 million
C	1.2	No debt	£50 million

What discount rate should the company use for the new business?

8 Claxby is an undiversified company operating in light engineering. It is all-equity financed with a Beta of 0.6. Total risk is 40 (standard deviation of annual return). Management want to diversify by acquiring Sloothby Ltd, which operates in an industrial sector where the average equity Beta is 1.2 and the average gearing (debt to total capital) ratio is 1:3. The standard deviation of the return on equity (on a book value basis) for Sloothby is 25. The acquisition would increase Claxby's asset base by 40 per cent. The overall return on the market portfolio is expected to be 18 per cent and the current return on risk-free assets is 11 per cent. The standard deviation of the return on the market portfolio is 10. The rate of Corporation Tax is 33 per cent.

(a) What is the asset Beta for Sloothby?
(b) Analyse both Sloothby's and Claxby's total risk into their respective specific and market risk components.
(c) What would be the Beta for the expanded company?
(d) Using the new Beta, calculate the required return on the expanded firm's equity. Under what conditions could this be taken as the cut-off rate for new investment projects?
(e) In the light of the figures in this example, discuss whether the acquisition of Sloothby may be expected to operate in the best interests of Claxby's shareholders.

9 *Solution in Appendix A (page 834).* The managing director of Wemere, a medium-sized private company, wishes to improve the company's investment decision-making process by using discounted cash flow techniques. He is disappointed to learn that estimates of a company's cost of equity usually require information on share prices which, for a private company, are not available. His deputy suggests that the cost of equity can be estimated by using data for Folten plc, a similar sized company in the same industry whose shares are listed on the USM, and he has produced two suggested discount rates for use in Wemere's future investment appraisal. Both of these estimates are in excess of 17 per cent p.a., which the managing director believes to be very high, especially as the company has

just agreed a fixed rate bank loan at 13 per cent p.a. to finance a small expansion of existing operations. He has checked the calculations, which are numerically correct, but wonders if there are any errors of principle.

Estimate 1: Capital Asset Pricing Model
Date have been purchased from a leading business school
Equity Beta of Folten: 1.4
Market return: 18%
Treasury Bill yield: 12%

The cost of capital is 18% + (18% − 12%)1.4 = 26.4%. This rate must be adjusted to include inflation at the current level of 6 per cent. The recommended discount rate is 32.4 per cent.

Estimate 2: Dividend Growth Model

Folten plc

Year	Average share price (pence)	Dividend per share (pence)
1985	193	9.23
1986	109	10.06
1987	96	10.97
1988	116	11.95
1989	130	13.03

The cost of capital is: $D_1/(P - g)$, where D_1 is the expected dividend, P is the market price and g is the growth rate of dividends (= 14.20p/(138p – 9) = 11.01%).

When inflation is included the discount rate is 17.01 per cent.

Other financial information on the two companies is presented below:

	Wemere £000	Folten £000
Fixed assets	7,200	7,600
Current assets	7,600	7,800
Less: Current liabilities	(3,900)	(3,700)
	10,900	11,700
Financed by:		
Ordinary shares (25 pence)	2,000	1,800
Reserves	6,500	5,500
Term loans	2,400	4,400
	10,900	11,700

Notes

1 The current ex div share price of Folten plc is 138 pence.
2 Wemere's board of directors has recently rejected a takeover bid of £10.6 million.
3 Corporate tax is paid at the rate of 35 per cent.

Required

(a) Explain any errors of principle that have been made in the two estimates of the cost of capital and produce revised estimates using both of the methods.

State clearly any assumptions that you make.

(b) Discuss which of your revised estimates Wemere should use as the discount rate for capital investment appraisal.

Practical assignment

Re-read the exposition in Chapter 12 of how we obtained tailored discount rates for the three Tomkins divisions. How close do you think our surrogates were?

For another divisionalised company of your choice (try to find a two- or three-division company):

1. Consult the Risk Measurement Service for an up-to-date estimate of the equity Beta, and use the CAPM to assess the shareholders' required rate of return.
2. Estimate discount rates for each division. You will need to select surrogate companies, record their Betas, and obtain an indication of their own asset Betas by ungearing their equity Betas.
3. Determine whether the weighted average Beta for the company corresponds to its ungeared Beta. You will probably have to use weights based on earnings or sales as very few companies report book values (let alone market values!) of their segments.

22 Acquisitions and restructuring

Off the map

Running a listed company is supposed to be about maximising the wealth of shareholders. However, it is easy to find examples of ill-fated and apparently, ill thought-out acquisitions that have destroyed value.

In 1999 Emap, a UK specialist publishing company, whose titles include FHM, Kiss FM and Fleet News, the bible of the logistics industry, acquired US publishers Petersen for £860 million, including £200 million of debt. Petersen never prospered in Emap's hands, and as early as May 2001, Emap was obliged to write down its value by £545 million, over 60 per cent of the purchase price. This dragged Emap into the red for the financial year to the tune of £527 million. The Chief Executive of Emap, Kevin Hand, duly swallowed his sword by resigning, taking a year's salary of £425,000 plus share options for what *The Independent* called 'the standard executive reward for failure'.

Learning objectives

A major aim of this chapter is to emphasise the strategic aspects of takeovers. Having read it, you should understand the following:

- Why firms select acquisitions rather than other strategic options.
- How acquisitions can be financed.
- How acquisitions should be integrated.
- How the degree of success of a takeover can be evaluated.
- How corporate restructuring can enhance shareholder value.

22.1 Introduction

Acquisitions of other companies are investment decisions and should be evaluated on essentially the same criteria as say, the purchase of new items of machinery. However, there are two important differences between takeovers and many 'standard' investments.

First, because takeovers are frequently resisted by the target's managers, bidders often have little or no access to intelligence about their targets beyond published financial and market data, and any inside information they may glean. (When the bid process is under way, the defending board is obliged to provide key information to enable the bidder to conduct 'due diligence' examinations. This is essentially a search for 'skeletons in the cupboard'.)

In 1997, Vereinsbank of Germany, in an effort to avoid being taken over by the much larger Deutsche Bank, reportedly cobbled together over a single weekend a merger agreement with Hypobank, a smaller rival. The penalty for undue haste in addressing the financial, legal and human issues involved was the discovery a year later, by the auditors of the new entity (HypoVereinsBank), of huge losses in Hypobank's property portfolio, necessitating loan loss provisions of DM 3.5 billion.

Information from *The Economist*, (2000).

Second, many takeovers are undertaken for longer-term strategic motives, and the benefits are often difficult to quantify. It is common to hear the chairmen of acquiring companies talk about an acquisition opening up a 'strategic window'; what they often do not add is that the window is usually not only shut, but has thick curtains drawn across it! To a large extent, a takeover is a shot in the dark, partly explaining why so many firms that launch giant takeovers come to the sort of grief experienced by Emap.

But there are other reasons. Targets are often too large in relation to bidders, so that excessive borrowings or unexpected integration problems throttle the parent. The demise of Marconi, whose share price fell by 97 per cent during 2000–1, was largely the result of headlong expansion into telecoms equipment manufacturing just before the sector entered recession. Its debt financing proved an albatross which it may never cast off.

There are important lessons to be learned from risk analysis and portfolio theory. When acquisitions have highly uncertain outcomes, the larger they are, the more catastrophic the impact of any adverse outcomes. As a result, it may be rational and less risky to confine takeover activity to small, uncontested bids. Alternatively, a spread of large acquisitions might confer significant portfolio diversification benefits, so long as the components have low cash flow correlation. However, the greater the scale of takeover activity, the greater the resulting financing burden placed on the parent, and the greater the impact of diverting managerial capacity into solving integration problems.

The acquisition decision is thus a complex one. It involves significant uncertainties (except in purely **asset-stripping** takeovers), it often requires substantial funding and it may pose awkward problems of integration. Yet, as some takeover 'kings' have shown, spectacular payoffs can be achieved. These are some of the themes of this chapter – how to evaluate a takeover, how to finance it and how to integrate it. But first, we examine the phenomenon of takeover surges, especially that of the 1980s.

22.2 Takeover waves

Although the terms 'takeover' and 'merger' are used as synonyms, there is a technical difference. A **takeover** is the acquisition by one company of the share capital of another in exchange for cash, ordinary shares, loan stock or some mixture of these. This results in the identity of the acquired company being absorbed into that of the acquirer (although, of course, the expanded company may continue to use the acquired company's brand names and trademarks). A **merger** is a pooling of the interests of two companies into a new enterprise, requiring the agreement of both sets of shareholders. The combination of Daimler–Benz and Chrysler in 1998 was presented (initially, at least) as a merger of friendly partners. In 2001, an unusual three-way merger of leading steel firms Usinor of France, Arbed of Luxembourg and Aceralia of Spain was forged. By definition, mergers involve the friendly (initially, at least) restructuring of assets into a new organisation, whereas many takeovers are hotly resisted. In practice, the vast majority of business amalgamations are takeovers rather than mergers. Table 22.1 shows the upsurge in UK takeover activity in the mid-1980s. Takeover activity often seems to occur in waves, the strongest to date being that of the mid-1980s (number of firms) and the late 1990s (value of acquired firms).

The many explanations for the takeover boom of the late 1980s include the following:

1 The sharp growth in real company profitability in the mid-1980s increased the ability of companies to finance acquisitions. The rising stock market improved their ability to finance takeovers by share exchanges or with cash raised from rights issues.
2 Deregulation of capital markets led to increasing supplies of debt capital accompanied by a greater readiness of institutions to lend in more novel ways.
3 Companies emerging from the recession with lower gearing ratios were more willing and able to borrow.
4 Takeover booms often begin when market values are low in relation to the replacement cost of assets. The high interest rates of the recession years resulted in heavy discounting of future corporate earnings, so that many asset-rich firms appeared to be undervalued. For acquirers wishing to build capacity ahead of an economic upturn, acquisition of 'cheap' targets provided a lower cost alternative than internal growth.
5 Abolition of 100 per cent First Year Allowances in 1984 weakened the incentive to invest in new capacity compared to buying 'off-the-peg'.
6 Apparently contradicting market efficiency arguments, there may have been a tendency for the rising market to overvalue larger firms relative to small ones, making it easier for the former to acquire the latter.
7 The regulatory environment was generally perceived to be more relaxed. In 1983, the UK government famously reversed the Monopolies and Mergers

Table 22.1 The scale and financing of takeover activity of UK firms by UK firms

Year	Number acquired	Outlay (£m)	Cash (%)	Ordinary shares (%)	Fixed interest (%)
1970	793	1,122	22	53	25
1971	884	911	31	48	21
1972	1,210	2,532	19	58	23
1973	1,205	1,304	53	36	11
1974	504	508	68	22	9
1975	315	291	59	32	9
1976	353	448	72	27	2
1977	481	824	62	37	1
1978	567	1,140	57	41	2
1979	534	1,656	56	31	13
1980	469	1,475	52	45	3
1981	452	1,144	68	30	3
1982	463	2,206	58	32	10
1983	477	2,343	44	54	2
1984	568	5,474	54	34	13
1985	474	7,090	40	52	7
1986	842	15,370	26	57	17
1987	**1,528**	**16,539**	**35**	**60**	**5**
1988	1,499	22,839	70	22	8
1989	1,337	27,250	82	13	5
1990	779	8,329	77	18	5
1991	506	10,434	70	29	1
1992	432	5,941	63	36	1
1993	526	7,063	81	16	3
1994	674	8,269	64	34	2
1995	505	32,600	78	20	1
1996	584	30,457	63	36	1
1997	506	26,829	41	58	1
1998	635	29,525	41	58	1
1999	493	26,163	62	37	1
2000	**587**	**106,916**	**37**	**62**	**1**
2001	400	28,391	n/a	n/a	n/a

Sources: Financial Statistics (ONS).

Commission recommendation regarding the takeover bid by Standard Chartered Bank for Anderson Strathclyde, a Scottish engineering firm. In 1984, the Secretary of State for Trade and Industry declared that mergers would henceforth be judged *primarily* on competition grounds, rather than on wider public interest grounds.

The reader will observe that a new wave broke in 1995 peaking in 2000, distinguished by amount of expenditure rather than by number of deals, i.e. these mergers were significantly larger on average. One factor was the strong upward

Table 22.2 Acquisition according to status of acquiree

	Total acquisitions		Independent firms		Inter-company sales of subsidiaries	
Year	Number	Value (£m)	Number	Value (£m)	Number	Value (£m)
1992	432	3,941	232	4,108	200	1,833
1993	526	7,063	337	2,986	189	4,078
1994	674	8,269	465	5,743	209	2,526
1995	505	32,600	299	25,647	206	6,953
1996	584	30,742	336	23,348	248	7,394
1997	506	26,829	384	22,453	122	4,376
1998	635	29,525	485	24,086	150	5,439
1999	493	26,163	400	22,211	93	3,952
2000	587	106,916	466	100,513	121	6,403
2001	400	28,391	253	20,637	147	7,754

Source: National Statistics, 2002

movement in the UK stock market, but the lurch towards the mega-merger was an international phenomenon.

Table 22.2 shows, for the past decade, how the acquisitions by UK firms ('acquirors') of other UK companies ('acquirees') were split into purchases of other independent firms, and acquisitions of subsidiaries of other firms, or 'trade sales'. It can be seen that the trend for bigger mergers is focused in the market for independent firms, where bidding is more public, resistance by incumbent directors is often encountered, competition is more likely and a premium above the market price must be offered to encourage present owners to sell.

According to Peter Doyle, a leading UK marketing academic, the motives for the mega-mergers of recent years differ from those of the 1980s. In the earlier wave, companies like Hanson and BTR were looking to exploit financial economies by restructuring badly-run companies and giving managers incentives to deliver strong cash flows to create value. By contrast, more recent mergers are more likely to be driven by strategic factors. Prominent among these are the increased globalisation of markets, with greater exposure to more aggressive international competition.

Doyle believes that this process has been fuelled by deregulation and privatisation in many countries, which have freed companies in the telecommunications and airline industries, in particular, to seek out global strategic alliances. In addition, technological change has raised the investment expenditures required to research and market new products, meaning that the size of firm confers a major advantage in industries like pharmaceuticals. Moreover, distance is no barrier, given the improvements in transportation and information technology; hence the wave of banking mergers in North America and Europe in the late 1990s.

Table 22.3 Cross-border acquisitions involving UK companies

	UK firms acquired by foreign firms		UK firms' acquisitions of foreign firms	
Year	Number	Value	Number	Value
1992	210	4,139	679	7,264
1993	267	5,187	521	9,213
1994	202	5,213	422	15,164
1995	131	12,817	365	11,967
1996	133	9,513	442	13,377
1997	193	15,717	464	19,176
1998	252	32,413	569	54,917
1999	252	60,860	590	111,193
2000	227	64,618	557	181,285
2001	154	22,493	348	39,901

Source: National Statistics, 2002

The importance of cross-border acquisitions involving UK firms can be seen in Table 22.3, which shows data on acquisitions of UK firms by foreign entities, and acquisitions by UK firms of overseas enterprises. Although it is by no means one-way traffic, in most years, UK firms' involvement in takeover activity as acquirors outweighs their involvement as acquirees. Again, 2000 was the peak year in both categories.

However, the year 2001 might have broken the mould. 2001 saw a substantial drop in world merger activity, falling from $3.5 trillion in 2000 to $1.75 trillion, marking an end to eight straight years of increased activity. Three main reasons were put forward for this:

- Companies whose finances were damaged by the worsening economic recession had insufficient cash resources to hunt prey.
- Stock market volatility made it difficult to assess market values, and hence, bid valuations.
- Increasingly uncertain business conditions increased the difficulty of predicting the future profitability of acquisitions.

2001 was described as 'the year of the broken promise' because many large takeovers failed to come to fruition. Among the jilted partners were German media giant Bertelsmann and EMI, British banks Abbey National and Lloyds TSB, telecom giants Alcatel and Lucent, and, notoriously, Dynergy and Enron. Moreover, the European competition authorities blocked the takeover of Honeywell by GEC on the grounds that competition would be harmed within Europe, thus raising the prospect of more active scrutiny of future amalgamations at a time when European competition regulations were already under review.

Time will tell whether the merger wave of the twentieth century has really broken.

The regulation of takeovers

UK takeovers are regulated in three ways, two of them formal and the third informal.

First, the UK statutory provisions as laid down in the Fair Trading Act 1973 and the Competition Act 1998 give responsibility for dealing with mergers to three entities:

- The Secretary of State for Trade and Industry (the SOS).
- The Director General of Fair Trading (the DGFT).
- The Competition Commission (the CC).

The system relies on flexible interpretation of the regulations, and intervention at the discretion of the authorities. In principle, mergers are judged as to whether they are against the 'public interest'. In practice, this means whether they are likely to reduce competition. The burden of proof lies on the authorities to prove that the merger is harmful, rather than the parties having to prove that it is beneficial. The authorities are heavily dependent on information provided by the parties to the merger.

The role of the DGFT is to:

- assess mergers that come to his attention, e.g. by complaints or by notification by the firms involved.
- consider whether a merger qualifies for reference to the CC for more detailed investigation, i.e. whether worldwide assets taken over exceed £70 million, or whether a UK market share above 25 per cent is to be created.
- hear the view of interested parties relating to qualifying mergers.
- advise the SOS on whether qualifying mergers should be referred to the CC for investigation whether the merger is against the public interest.
- where appropriate, advise the SOS on accepting 'statutory undertakings', e.g. promises to divest assets, in lieu of reference to the CC.
- advise the SOS on action in response to the CC report.
- seek undertakings from the parties involved.
- monitor compliance with undertakings.

The Secretary of State's role is:

- to decide whether a merger should be referred to the CC.
- to decide whether to accept undertakings in lieu of reference.
- to receive and publish the CC report.
- to decide on action in response to the report.

In response to an adverse report, the SOS may decide:

- to block the merger.
- to require the parties to meet certain conditions before approval.

The role of the CC is:

- to hear evidence from all interested parties
- to weigh the evidence to decide whether the merger may operate against the public interest.
- if so, to recommend possible remedies
- to submit the report to the SOS.

The flow chart in Figure 22.1 below shows how these activities interrelate.

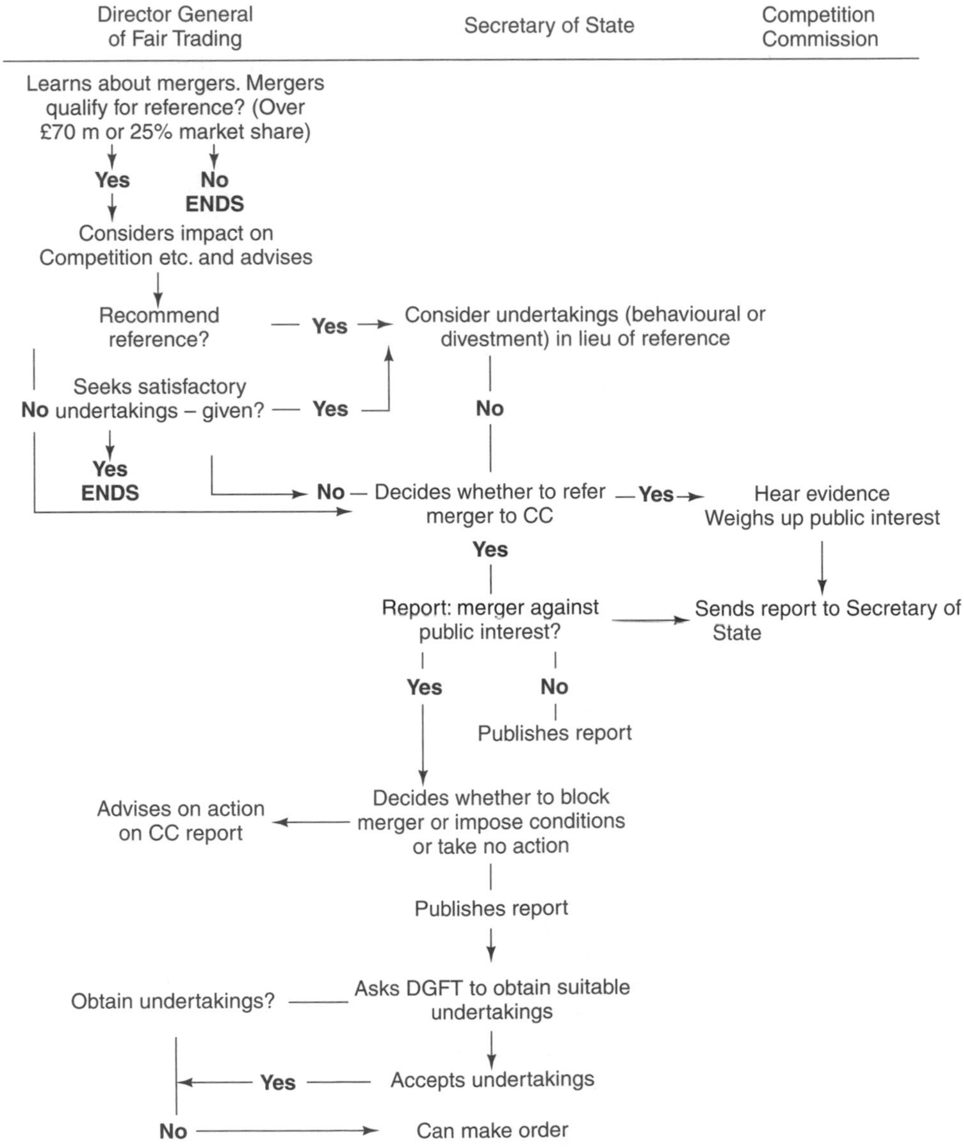

Figure 22.1 Who does what? – merger flow chart.

Source: Department of Trade and Industry. (**www.dti.gov.uk/cp/ukmergerguide.htm**)

The second mode of regulation is under the competition policy of the European Union, set out in Articles 81 (formerly Article 85) and 82 (formerly 86) of the Treaty of Rome. Article 82 prohibits the abuse of a dominant firm position insofar as it may affect trade between member states. The EC Merger Regulation (ECMR) provides that a merger that creates a dominant position, as a result of which competition would be significantly impeded, shall be declared incompatible with the common market. The Regulation applies to all mergers with a 'Community Dimension', defined in terms of turnover levels. The ECMR was designed to provide 'one-stop' merger control to avoid the risk of mergers being investigated under two or more jurisdictions. National authorities may not normally apply their own competition laws to mergers falling within the ECMR.

The current regulations are being reformed at present (2002), but progress has been hampered by lack of agreement on permissible takeover defence behaviour.

The third control on takeovers is operated by the **Takeover Panel**, formed in 1968 to counter the perceived inadequacy of the statutory mechanisms for regulating the conduct of both parties in the takeover process. The Panel consists of representatives from City and other leading business institutions, such as the CBI, the Stock Exchange and the ICAEW accounting body, thus representing the main associations whose members are involved in takeovers, whether as advisers, shareholders or regulators. The Panel promulgates and administers the **Takeover Code**, a set of rules with no force of law, but which reflects what those most closely involved with takeovers regard as best practice. It does, however, have some sanctions to enforce its authority, such as public reprimands, which damage the reputation of violators of the Code, perhaps leading to the collapse of the bid and, for financial advisers, to long-term loss of business. The Panel's ultimate sanction is to request its members to withdraw the facilities of the City from offenders, although this is extremely rare.

The chronology of a hostile bid

The following schedule details the necessary timing of bids and provision of information as required by the Takeover Code.

Day 1: bid announced. Bidder has 28 days in which to make a formal offer to target's shareholders.

Day 14 after formal offer is made: deadline for target company to publish its 'defence document'.

Day 21 after formal offer: first date at which the contest can be ended. Bidder must disclose how many of target's shares have been voted in its favour. If over 50 per cent, bidder has won; if less, it may choose to walk away.

18 days later: last day for defender to produce new arguments to encourage shareholder loyalty.

4 days later: last day for bidder to increase its offer. Beyond this, bidder cannot buy any of target's shares that will take its stake above 30 per cent.

14 days later: by 5 p.m., bidder must declare how many shares have been voted in its favour. If over 50 per cent, the bidder has won. If less, the target remains independent. The bidder is barred from making a further bid within one calendar year.

Normally, the maximum time span allowed for the whole process is 60 days, although the Takeover Panel may 'stop the clock' pending clarification of key points. In the event of a reference to the MMC, the process is halted *sine die* to await its report. This can take upwards of six months, during which the initial 'urge to merge' has been known to evaporate.

The behaviour of defending managers is tightly circumscribed:

1 Shareholders must be given equal access to relevant information to enable them to make an informed decision.
2 Shareholders must be given adequate information to reach a decision, and no relevant information should be withheld.
3 Directors must not act out of personal interest, either to frustrate or to encourage a bidder.
4 Directors are prohibited from taking action to frustrate a *bona fide* offer without the approval of shareholders.
5 The company must not seek to influence the market price of its shares by offering finance or guarantees to others to induce them to buy its shares.

The bidder must also observe certain rules:

1 Any stakeholding above 3 per cent must be openly declared.
2 In the past, bidders and their advisers often made 'dawn raids' on the market to capture a major stake in the target before people realised that a bid was under way. Companies are now prohibited from acquiring, in any seven-day period, shares that would raise their aggregate stake above 15 per cent.
3 If a company accumulates over 30 per cent of the shares, it must make a formal bid to remaining shareholders at a price no less than the highest price paid in the previous twelve months.

22.3 Motives for takeover

Managers seeking to maximise the wealth of shareholders should continually seek to exploit value-creating opportunities. There are two situations when managers feel able to enrich shareholders via takeovers:

1 *When managers believe that the target company can be acquired at less than its 'true value'*. This implies disbelief in the ability of the capital market consistently to value companies correctly. If a company is thought to be undervalued on the market, there may well be opportunities for 'asset-stripping', i.e. selling off the components of the taken-over company for a combined sum greater than the purchase price.

2 *When managers believe that two enterprises will be worth more if merged than if operated as two separate entities*. Thus for two companies, A and B:

$$V_{A+B} > V_A + V_B$$

The principle of **value additivity** would refute this unless the amalgamation resulted in some form of **synergy** or more effective utilisation of the assets of the combined companies.

In practice, it is very difficult to differentiate between these two explanations for merger, especially as many mergers result in only partial disposals, when activities that appear to fit more neatly into existing operations are retained. Companies are valued by the market on the basis of information that their managements release regarding market prospects, value of assets, R&D activity, and so on. Market participants may suspect that an under-performing company could be operated more efficiently by an alternative management team, but until a credible bidder emerges, poor results may simply be reflected in a poor stock market rating.

How different types of acquisition create value

Acquisitions can be split into three types:

1 **Horizontal integration** – where a company takes over another from the same industry and at the same stage of the production process: for example, a hotel chain acquiring a competitor e.g. the Bass acquisition of Posthouse in 2001. The motivation is usually enhancement of market power and/or to obtain production economies.
2 **Vertical integration** – where the target is in the same industry as the acquirer, but operating at a different stage of the production chain, either nearer the source of materials (backward integration) or nearer to the final consumer (forward integration), e.g. Ford's takeover of Kwikfit.
3 **Conglomerate or unrelated diversification** – where the target is in an activity apparently dissimilar to the acquirer although some activities such as marketing may overlap. These takeovers are often said to lack 'industrial logic', but can lead to economies in the provision of company-wide services such as Head Office administration and access to capital markets on improved terms, i.e. financial economies.

In reality, most mergers are difficult to classify into such neat categories, as they are motivated by a complex interplay of factors, which will hopefully enhance the value of the bidder's equity. The more specific reasons cited for launching takeover bids usually reflect the anticipated benefits that a merger is expected to generate:

1 *To exploit scale economies*. Larger size is usually expected to yield production economies if manufacturing operations can be amalgamated, marketing economies if similar distribution channels can be utilised, and financial economies if size confers access to capital markets on more favourable terms.

2 *To obtain synergy*. This term is often used to include any gains from merger, but, strictly, it refers to benefits unrelated to scale. Gains may emerge from a particular way of combining resources. One company's managers may be especially suited to operating another company's distribution systems, or the sales staff of one company may be able to sell another company's, perhaps closely related, product as part of a package.

3 *To enter new markets*. For firms that lack the expertise to develop different products, or do not possess the outlets required to access different market segments, takeover may be a simpler, and certainly a quicker, way of expanding.

The Daimler Benz–Chrysler merger in 1998 was driven by the desire by each firm to 'fill in' its product line – Daimler–Benz was strong in highly-engineered luxury vehicles while Chrysler's expertise lay in volume production of automobiles and the fast-growing market for sports utility vehicles (SUVs). In December 2001, Britain's Compass group, the world's largest catering company, made a £200 million cash acquisition of Seiyo Food Systems, Japan's third-largest contract catering firm, in order to strengthen its presence in Asia.

4 *To provide 'critical mass'*. As many product markets have become more global and the lifespan of products has tended to diminish, greater emphasis has to be placed on R&D activities. In some industries, such as aerospace, telecommunications and pharmaceuticals, small enterprises are simply unable to generate the cash flows required to finance R&D and brand investment. This factor was largely responsible for the sale by Fisons and Boots of their drug-development activities in 1994 to much larger German companies. There is also a credibility effect. For example, companies may be unwilling to use small firms as a source of components when their future survival, and hence ability to supply, is suspect.

5 *To impart or restore growth impetus*. Maturing firms whose growth rate is weakening may look to younger, more dynamic companies both to obtain a quick, short-term growth 'fix', and also for entrepreneurial ideas to achieve higher rates of growth in the longer term. BAT used the substantial cash flows from its mature tobacco business to acquire Allied Dunbar (pensions) and Eagle Star (insurance) in the UK and Farmers in the USA, perceiving the financial services sector as a potential growth area.

6 *To acquire market power*. Obtaining higher earnings is easier if there are fewer competitors. Competition-reducing takeovers are likely to be investigated by the regulatory authorities, but are often justified by the need to enhance ability to compete internationally on the basis of a more secure home market, as in the case of the three-way merger of European steel firms mentioned above. In addition, **backward vertical integration**, mergers undertaken to capture sources of raw materials (e.g. US oil firm Amerada Hess' acquisition of Triton Energy in 2001 to increase its exploration and production capability), and **forward vertical integration** to secure new outlets for the company's products have the effect of increasing the firm's grasp over the whole value chain, and are thus competition-reducing in a wider sense. Many past brewery takeovers were mounted not to obtain

production capacity, but to secure access to the target's estate of tied public houses, and to acquire brands, as in the case of Scottish and Newcastle's purchase of Theakstons.

7 *To reduce dependence on existing, perhaps volatile activities*. In Chapter 11, we concluded that risk reduction *per se* as a motive for diversification may be misguided. There is no reason why two enterprises owned by one company should have greater value unless the amalgamation produces scale economies or some other synergies. If shareholder portfolio formation is a substitute for corporate diversification, there is no point in acquiring other companies to reduce risk – rational shareholders will already have diversified away specific risk, and market risk is undiversifiable. There are two major qualifications to this argument. First, diversification into overseas securities may lower market risk, given that different economies, and hence stock markets, are not perfectly correlated (Madura 1995). Second, it is possible that achieving greater size via conglomerate diversification may lower the costs of financial distress.

The 'market for management control'

Several of the above motives for merger suggest that some companies can be more efficiently operated by alternative managers. A more general motive for merger is thus to weed out inefficient personnel. There are three ways in which the market mechanism can penalise managerial inefficiency:

1 Insolvency, which usually involves significant costs.
2 Shareholder revolt, which is difficult to organise given the diffusion of ownership and the general reluctance of institutional investors to interfere in operational management.
3 The takeover process, which may be regarded as a 'market for managerial control'. The threat of takeover provides a spur to inefficient managers, while removing inefficient managers lowers costs and removes barriers to more effective utilisation of assets. Theory suggests that incompetently managed firms will be acquired at prices that ensure the owners of the acquirer suffer no loss in value. If a bid premium over the market price is payable, this should be recoverable from the higher cash flows generated from more efficient asset utilisation. To this extent, takeover activity is seen by authors such as Jensen (1984) as a perfectly healthy expression of the workings of the market system, potentially benefiting all parties.

Managerial motives for takeover

The motive of diversification to reduce risk suggests a second possible explanation for takeover activity. With the divorce of ownership and control, and the consequent high level of managerial autonomy, managers are relatively free to follow activities and policies, including acquisition of other firms, which enhance their own objectives, both in monetary and non-pecuniary forms.

Managerial salaries and perquisites are usually higher in large and growing firms, and since growth by acquisition is usually easier and swifter than organic growth, managers may view acquisition with some eagerness. If acquisitions are 'managerial' in this sense, then acquirers may be prepared to expend 'excessive' amounts to gain ownership of target companies simply to secure deals that promote managerial well-being, but at the expense of shareholder value. If this explanation is correct, acquisitions may result in a transfer of wealth from shareholders of acquiring firms to shareholders of acquired companies, even when presented as promoting the best interests of the former.

Takeovers may also be related to the way managers are remunerated. In the 1980s, UK managers were increasingly paid by results, with the commonest criterion of performance being growth in EPS. This is a notoriously unreliable measure of performance, as it is not only dependent on accounting conventions, but relatively easy to manipulate. For example, shutting down a loss-making activity can raise reported EPS.

Self-assessment Activity 22.1

Suggest some 'managerial' motives for growth by takeover.

(answer at end of chapter)

How to increase EPS by takeover: Hawk takes over Vole

A common means of increasing EPS has been to acquire other companies with lower P:E ratios than one's own, these being companies out of favour with the market, either through poor performance or because too little was known about them. The acquisition of such companies, in certain conditions, can raise both EPS and share price. Consider the example in Table 22.4. Hawk, with a P:E ratio of 20, reflecting strong growth expectations, contemplates the takeover of Vole, whose P:E ratio is only 10. Hawk proposes to make an all-share offer. If it were able to obtain Vole at the current market price, it would have to issue 5 million shares to Vole's shareholders in exchange for their 20 million shares, i.e. (5 million × £4) = (20 million × £1) = £20 million.

Table 22.4 shows the impact of the exchange if the P:E ratio of the expanded company were to remain at 20. The new EPS is (£22 m/105 m) = 21p, resulting in a post-bid share price of £4.20, and an overall market value of £441 million. This apparently magical effect seems to have generated wealth of £21 million. If it works out this way, the beneficiaries are the two sets of shareholders: Hawk's existing shareholders find their 100 million shares valued at a price higher by 20p, i.e. £20 million in total, and Vole's former shareholders find they now hold

Table 22.4 Hawk and Vole

	Pre-bid		Post-bid
	Hawk	**Vole**	**Hawk + Vole**
Number of shares	100 m	20 m	100 m + 5 m = 105 m
Earnings after tax	£20 m	£2 m	£20 m + £2 m = £22 m
EPS	20p	10p	£22 m ÷ 105 m = 21p
P:E ratio	20:1	10:1	20:1
Share price	£4	£1	20 × 21p = £4.20
Capitalisation (market value)	£400 m	£20 m	105 m × £4.20 = £441 m

shares valued at £21 million, rather than the value of £20 million placed on Vole prior to the bid, i.e.:

Gains to Hawk's shareholders = £20 m
Gains to Vole's shareholders = £1 m
Total gain = £21 m

This so-called **'boot-strapping'** effect may simply be 'financial illusion' because it is unlikely to occur quite like this in reality. First, it assumes the absence of a bid premium. In practice, Hawk would have to offer above the market price to tempt Vole's shareholders into selling, thus altering the balance of gain. Second, it assumes that the market applies the same P:E ratio to the expanded group as the pre-bid ratio for Hawk. If no synergies were expected, then the likely post-bid P:E ratio is the total pre-bid value of the two firms relative to their total pre-bid earnings, i.e.

$$\frac{(£400\text{ m} + £20\text{ m})}{(£20\text{ m} + £2\text{ m})} = \frac{£420\text{ m}}{£22\text{ m}} = 19.09$$

However, if Hawk is expected to reorganise Vole and impart the same growth impetus expected from Hawk itself, the P:E ratio post-bid could exceed this figure, and approach Hawk's pre-bid P:E value of 20. If this occurs, then both groups of shareholders can enjoy the value created by the expectation of a more efficient operation of Vole's assets and higher cash flows thereafter. Conversely, expectations of integration difficulties might offset such gains.

It does not follow that a higher EPS will lead to a higher share price. If the acquisition moved Hawk into riskier areas of operation, its activity Beta should rise accordingly and the higher expected cash flows will be discounted at a higher required return. Similarly, if instead of financing the bid by a share exchange, Hawk had borrowed the required £20 million, then the share price might not rise if the greater gearing and accompanying financial risk resulted in a higher equity Beta. The suspicion remains that many acquisitions, including some of the 'mega-mergers' of the 1980s, ostensibly undertaken to raise the acquirer's share price, were really undertaken for 'managerial' reasons (see Gregory 1997).

Certainly, the subsequent difficulties experienced in post-merger integration and operation do not support the view that mergers are always in the best interests of the bidders' shareholders (see below).

Self-assessment Activity 22.2

Suggest how managerial pay schemes might encourage takeovers against the interests of shareholders.

(answer at end of chapter)

22.4 Financing a bid

Table 22.1 showed data on the three main ways of financing takeovers: cash, issue of ordinary shares and fixed-interest securities (loan stock, convertibles and preference shares). Clearly, the first two methods predominate, although their relative importance varies over time. As a rule of thumb, share exchange is favoured when the stock market is high and rising, while cash offers are used more when interest rates are relatively low or falling, given that many cash offers are themselves financed by the acquirer's borrowing. Increasingly, however, bidders offer their targets a choice of cash or shares, or even a three-way choice between straight cash, cash with shares, or shares alone.

For example, in 1991, when bidding for its main UK competitor, Tootal, the textile company Coats Viyella offered two alternatives. Shareholders of Tootal could either opt for a full cash consideration of 80p per share, which would not qualify them to receive an imminent dividend of 3p per share, or accept 83.3p per share in cash and paper, based on the Coats share price at the date of the offer. The second option involved £51.02 in cash and 23 newly issued Coats shares for every 100 Tootal shares owned.

Such complex offers are designed to appeal to the widest possible body of shareholders. The chosen package depends on the balance of relative advantages and disadvantages of the different methods, from both the bidder's and the target shareholder's viewpoints.

Cash

Everyone understands a cash offer. The amount is certain, there being no exposure to the risk of adverse movement in share price during the course of the bid. The targeted shareholders are more easily able to adjust their portfolio than if they received shares, which involve dealing costs when sold. Because no new shares are issued, there is no dilution of earnings or change in the balance of control of the bidder (unless, in the case of borrowed capital, creditors insist on restrictive covenants). Moreover, if the return expected on the assets of the target exceeds the cost of borrowing, the EPS of the bidder may increase, although perceptions of increased financial risk may mitigate this apparent benefit. A disadvantage from the recipient's viewpoint is possible liability to Capital Gains Tax (CGT).

Share exchanges

Any liability to CGT is delayed with a share offer, and the cash flow cost to the bidder is zero, apart from the administration costs involved. However, equity is more costly to service than debt, especially for a company with taxable capacity, and an issue of new shares may interfere with the firm's gearing ratio. There could be an adverse impact on the balance of control if a major slice of the equity of the bidder came to be held by institutions looking for an opportunity to sell their holdings. The overhanging threat of a substantial share sale may depress the share price of the bidder.

Other methods

The use of other financing instruments is comparatively rare. When fixed-interest securities are used, they are usually offered as alternatives to cash and/or ordinary shares. Convertibles have some appeal because any diluting effect is delayed and the interest cost on the security, which qualifies for tax relief, can usually be pitched below the going market rate on loan stock, due to the expectation of capital gain on conversion. Preference share financing in general is comparatively rare, owing to the lack of tax-deductibility of preferred dividends and to limited voting rights.

Self-assessment Activity 22.3

Why might the shareholders of a target company prefer to be paid in cash rather than shares?

(answer at end of chapter)

22.5 Evaluating a bid: the expected gains from takeovers

Evaluating an acquisition is little different from other investments, assuming the motive of the bid is economic rather than managerial, i.e. designed to maximise the post-bid value of the expanded enterprise. It would be worthwhile Company A taking over Company B so long as the present value of the cash flows of the enlarged company exceeds the present value of the two companies as separate entities:

$$V_{A+B} > V_A + V_B$$

Thus, $[V_{A+B} - (V_A + V_B)]$ measures the increase in value. The net cost to the bidder is the value of the amount expended less the value of the target as it stands:

$$\text{Net cost} = [\text{Outlay} - V_B]$$

so that the net present value of the takeover decision is the gain less the cost, i.e.:

$$\begin{aligned} \text{NPV} &= V_{A+B} - (V_A + V_B) - [\text{Outlay} - V_B] \\ &= V_{A+B} - V_A - \text{Outlay} \end{aligned}$$

The NPV will depend on the method of financing and, of course, the terms of the transaction. Essentially, the bidder is hoping to extract the maximum value of any expected cost savings and synergies from the takeover for its own shareholders. Conversely, the offer must be made attractive to the owners of the target to induce them to sell.

An example will illustrate the way in which the division of the spoils can depend on the method of financing. Fewston plc is launching a cash bid for Dacre plc, both quoted companies and both ungeared. The market value of Fewston is £200 million (100 million 50p shares, market price £2) and that of Dacre is £40 million (10 million 50p shares, market price £4). Fewston hopes to exploit synergies etc. worth £20 million after the takeover. It offers the shareholders of Dacre £50 million in cash. The NPV of the bid to Fewston is thus:

$$\begin{aligned} \text{NPV} &= V_{A+B} - V_A - \text{Outlay} \\ &= (£200\text{ m} + £40\text{ m} + £20\text{ m}) - £200\text{ m} - £50\text{ m} = £10\text{ m} \end{aligned}$$

The overall gain from the takeover (i.e. the synergies of £20 million) is split equally between the two sets of shareholders. The need to make a higher bid or the appearance of another bidder would tilt the balance of gain towards Dacre's shareholders.

If the bid is made in the form of a share-for-share offer to the same value, the arithmetic alters. In this case, Fewston is giving up part of the expanded firm and hence a further share of the gains to Dacre's shareholders. Assuming a bid to the same value, Fewston must offer them (£50 m/£2) = 25 m shares. This would result in a total share issue of 125 million shares, i.e. Fewston is handing over 20 per cent of the expanded company to Dacre's shareholders. In this case, the gain enjoyed by Fewston's shareholders will be lower. The NPV of the takeover is still the gain less the cost; but the cost is greater, i.e. the proportion of the expanded company handed over less the value of Dacre as it stands:

$$\begin{aligned} \text{Cost} &= \left(\frac{25\text{ m}}{100\text{ m} + 25\text{ m}} \times £260\text{ m}\right) - £40\text{ m} \\ &= (£52\text{ m} - £40\text{ m}) = £12\text{ m} \end{aligned}$$

Hence the NPV of the takeover is:

$$\text{NPV} = (\text{gain in value} - \text{cost}) = (£20\text{ m} - £12\text{ m}) = £8\text{ m}$$

Fewston's shareholders are thus left with only £8 million of the net gains from the takeover, 20 per cent lower than in the cash offer case, which is the same proportion as the share of the expanded company handed to Dacre's shareholders.

A share exchange of equivalent value to a cash bid generally leaves the bidder's shareholders worse off because their share of both the company and the gains from the takeover are diluted among the larger number of shares. The post-bid share prices in these two cases are as follows:

Cash bid: (£260 m/100 m) = £2.60
Share exchange: (£260 m/125 m) = £2.08

However, if Fewston has to borrow in order to make the cash bid, the increase in gearing may result in shareholders seeking a higher return, thus lowering the market price. In addition, the analysis hinges on the existence of an efficient capital market whose assessment of the gains from takeover corresponds with that of the two parties.

Self-assessment Activity 22.4

Predator is valued on the market at £1,000 million, and Prey at £200 million. Predator values the expected post-merger synergies at £50 million. If it bids £230 m for Prey what is the NPV of the bid? What is the share of the gains for each firm?

(answer at end of chapter)

22.6 Worked example: ML plc and CO plc

The following question appeared on the CIMA Strategic Financial Management examination paper, May 1999. (It carried 15 of the total 20 marks available).

Question

ML plc is an expanding clothing retailer. It is all-equity financed by ordinary share capital of £10 million in shares of 50p nominal. The company's results to the end of March 1999 have just been announced. Pre-tax profits were £4.6 million. The Chairman's statement included a forecast that earnings might be expected to rise by 5 per cent per annum in the coming year and for the foreseeable future.

CO plc, a children's clothing group, has an issued share capital of £33 million in £1 shares. Pre-tax profits for the year to March 31 were £5.2 million. Because of a recent programme of reorganisation and rationalisation, no growth is forecast for the current year but, subsequently, constant growth in earnings of approximately 6 per cent per annum is predicted. CO plc has had an erratic growth and earnings record in the past and has not always achieved its often ambitious forecasts.

ML plc has approached the shareholders of CO plc with a bid of two new shares in ML plc for every three CO plc shares. There is a cash alternative of 135 pence per share.

Following the announcement of the bid, the market price of ML plc shares fell while the price of shares in CO plc rose. Statistics for ML plc and two other listed companies in the same industry immediately prior to the bid announcement are shown below. All share prices are in pence.

1998		Company	Dividend Yield	PER
High	Low		%	
225	185	ML plc	3.4	15
145	115	CO plc	3.6	13
187	122	HR plc	6.0	12
230	159	SZ plc	2.4	17

Both ML plc and CO plc pay tax at 33 per cent.

ML plc's cost of capital is 12 per cent per annum and CO plc's is 11 per cent per annum.

Required

Assume you are a financial analyst with a major fund manager. You have funds invested in both ML plc and CO plc.

- Assess whether the proposed share-for-share offer is likely to be beneficial to the shareholders in ML plc and CO plc, and recommend an investment strategy based on your calculations.
- Comment on other information that would be useful in your assessment of the bid. Assume that the estimates of growth given above are achieved and that the new company plans no further issues of equity.

State any assumptions that you make.

Answer

First of all, some introductory calculations are needed, before we can analyse the impact of the bid.

Basic information

	ML	CO	combined
Profit after tax (PAT) for each firm is ML: (0.67 × £4.6 m) CO: (0.67 × £5.2 m)	£3.082	£3.484	£9.800
Given respective P:Es, market values are: ML: (15 × £3.082) CO: (13 × (£4.484)	£46.230	£45.290	£91.520

Given the number of shares, share price is:

ML: (£46.230/20,000)	CO: (£45.290/33,000)	£2.31	£1.37
EPS:			
ML: (£3.082/20,000)	CO: (£3.484/33,000)	15.41p	10.56p

Analysis

No. of shares post-bid: 20,000 + (2/3 × 33,000) = 42,000
Expected market prices post-bid = Total market value/No of shares
= (£91.520/42,000) = £2.18
Value of bid at post-issue price = (2 shares × £2.18) = £4.36
Cash value of bid per 3 shares offered: (£1.35 × 3) = £4.05

Assessment

Assuming no changes in the level of market prices, and no re-rating of the sector, ML's share price would fall post-acquisition to £2.18. At this price, the value of the 2-for-3 share offer should attract CO shareholders. They would get shares worth (2 × £2.18) = £4.36 in exchange for shares currently worth (3 × £1.37) = £4.11.

The share-for-share offer is also worth more than the cash alternative: £4.36 vs. £4.05.

This is a 'reverse takeover', where the shareholders of the target end up holding a majority stake in the expanded company – but who gains from this?

Former CO shareholders would hold (22,000/42,000) × £9.520 = £47.939 m of the value of the expanded firm, a gain of (£47.939 m − £45.290 m pre-bid value of CO) = £2.649 m.

ML shareholders would lose £2.649 m, making the share-financed deal distinctly unattractive to them.

Conversely, the cash offer would create wealth for ML shareholders, i.e. they give £4.05 for something worth £4.11 post-bid.

The advice to the fund manager is: 'accept the bid in respect of CO shares and sell ML shares in the market if you can achieve a price above £2.18'.

Commentary on other information required

The advice given above hinges on the behaviour of ML's share price – it has already fallen on the announcement, but by how much? It may already be too late if the market is efficient, as it would already have digested the information contained in the announcement.

Also:

- What benefits are expected from the merger, i.e. cost savings and synergies? To make sense of the bid, ML must be setting the PV of these benefits above £2.649 m to yield a positive NPV for the acquisition.
- How quickly are these benefits likely to show through? Any delay in exploiting these lowers the NPV.

- It is feasible that the market might apply a higher PER to the expanded company – maybe not as high as ML's but possibly at the market average, currently 14.25, compared to the weighted average PER for ML/CO of 14.
- Is ML likely to sell part of CO's operations? And to whom? If ML has already lined up a buyer, it must expect to turn a profit on the deal.
- Is the bid likely to be defended by the target's managers, fearful for their jobs? If so, a higher bid might be expected.
- Is a White Knight likely to appear with a higher bid on more favourable terms?
- Are there competition implications likely to attract the interest of the authorities?

22.7 The importance of strategy

Considerable evidence has emerged that acquisitions have less than an even chance of success. Although definitions of 'success' may vary, any activity that fails to enhance shareholder interests is unlikely to be regarded favourably by the stock market. While it is often difficult to assess what would have happened had a company not embarked on the takeover trail, it is difficult to argue that the acquisition has not been a failure if post-acquisition performance is inferior to pre-acquisition performance, or if the acquisition actually leads to a fall in shareholder wealth.

The McKinsey firm of management consultants studied the 'value-creation performance' of the acquisition programmes of 116 large US and UK companies, using financial measures of performance. The criterion of success used was whether the company earned at least its cost of capital on funds invested in the acquisition process. On this basis, a remarkable 60 per cent of all acquisitions failed, with large unrelated takeovers achieving a failure rate of 86 per cent.

Acquisitions fail for numerous reasons:

1 Acquirers often pay too much for their targets, either as a result of a flawed evaluation process that overestimates the likely benefits or as a result of getting caught up in a competitive bidding situation, where to yield is regarded as a sign of corporate weakness.

   In 1988, the UK television contractor TVS acquired the US TV programme producer MTM Entertainments for £190 million. At the date of purchase, MTM sported a record of stagnant earnings for the three previous years. Within a year, a third of the stock market value of TVS was wiped off as the market reacted to news that MTM had been hit by a slump in the US syndication market, resulting in operating losses of around £15 million for the year. In 1991, TVS wrote down the value of MTM by £21 million, and announced that it had abandoned attempts to sell it. (TVS subsequently lost its UK franchise in 1992 and was shortly afterwards acquired by another media company seeking studio facilities.)

2 'Skeletons' appear in cupboards with alarming frequency. The disastrous takeover by Ferranti of International Signal Corporation (see Chapter 4) is a good example of a badly researched acquisition that ultimately destroyed the acquirer.

3 Acquirers often fail to plan and execute properly the integration of their targets, frequently neglecting the organisational and internal cultural factors. Inadequate

knowledge about the target's business should be corrected in the process of due diligence. Lees (1992) explains how all too often this aspect is overlooked.

Yet many companies have sound acquisition records. Their targets are carefully selected, they rarely get involved in competitive auctions, they often have the sense to walk away from deals when they realise the gravity of the likely integration problems, and they seem able quickly and successfully to integrate acquisitions once deals are completed. What these companies have in common is a strategic approach to acquisitions.

22.8 The strategic approach

Most successful acquirers see their acquisitions as part of a long-term strategic process, designed to contribute towards overall corporate development. This requires acquirers to approach acquisitions only after a careful analysis of their own underlying strengths, and to identify candidates that satisfy chosen criteria and, most importantly, provide 'strategic fit' with the company's existing activities.

Figure 22.2 displays a simple strategic framework within which a thorough-going acquisition programme might be conducted. It begins with a full strategic

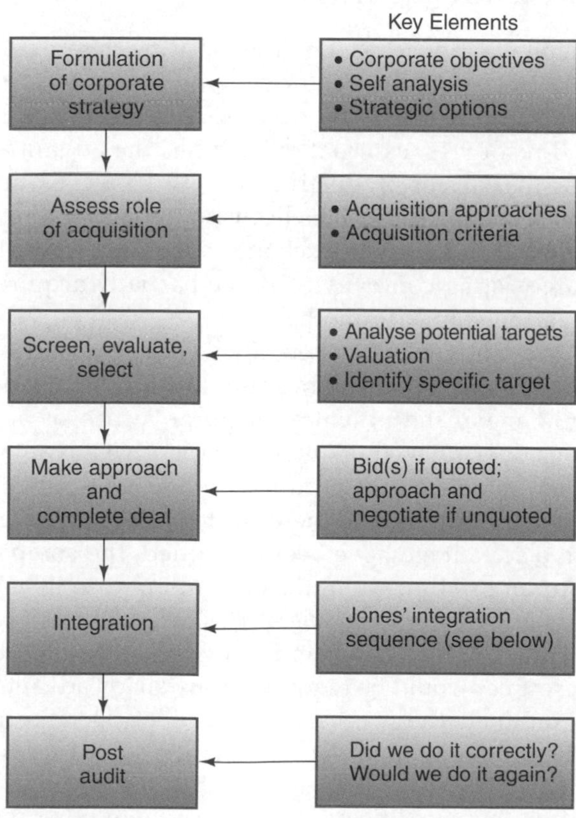

Figure 22.2 A strategic framework (based on Payne (1985))

review of the company as it stands, and its strategic options, followed by a detailed consideration of the role of acquisitions (i.e. the reasons why an acquisition target may be selected), leading to the process of selecting and bidding for the chosen prey, and culminating in the often neglected activities of post-merger integration and post-audit.

Objectives

Formulating strategy should begin with an expression of corporate objectives, concentrating on maximising shareholder wealth. Many firms now publish mission statements, but these are usually somewhat vague expressions of the image that the company would like to portray, often largely for internal consumption in order to motivate staff (Klemm *et al.*, 1991). If, in building the desired image, the company's managers fail to earn at least the cost of equity, they will themselves invite the risk of takeover. Strategy concerns the examination of alternative routes to achieving the ultimate aim, and then the optimal way of executing the chosen path. Achieving long-term goals usually involves expansion of the enterprise, a route often preferred by managers for personal motives.

Internal or external growth?

There are two main ways of achieving growth: (1) by self-development of new products, markets and processes (internal growth) and (2) by acquisition (external growth). Although both of these routes are usually expensive in executive time and resources, external growth has the advantage of securing quick access to new markets or productive capacity. However, firms should not overlook intermediate strategies, such as **licensing**, whereby a royalty is paid to the developer of new technology in exchange for rights to exploit it, or **joint ventures**, where an existing company could be partially acquired, or a totally new one set up in partnership with another firm.

The decision to grow internally or externally will depend partly on an analysis of the strengths, weaknesses, opportunities and threats (SWOTs) of the firm. This self-analysis should make the potential acquirer aware of any competitive advantages it enjoys over rival companies. Competitive advantage stems from two sources: cost advantage, where products are virtually similar, and product differentiation. Exploitation of each of these creates value for shareholders. When areas of competitive advantage have been identified, the company can decide whether to build upon existing strengths or to attempt to develop distinctive competence in areas of perceived weakness. This evaluation may also result in a decision to divest certain activities where no obvious advantage is possessed, or where too many resources would be required to sustain an advantage.

Porter (1987) examined the acquisition record of 33 large diversified US companies. The criterion for judging 'success' was the subsequent divestment rate of earlier acquisitions. The main finding was that successful acquirers almost invariably diversify into related fields, and *vice versa*. In other words, diversifications into activities unrelated to the core business of the acquirer carry much greater risks of failure. Even companies with successful 'related diversification' records achieved poor results when they wandered into unrelated fields. Porter concluded that the corporate portfolio strategy of many diversifying companies had failed because most diversifiers fail 'to think in terms of how they really add value'.

Acquisition criteria

The company should next assess what specific role it hopes the acquisition will perform. Table 22.5, drawn from a publication by the merchant bank 3i (Investors in Industry), which specialises in offering acquisition advice, lists possible strategic reasons for acquisition with suggested routes to achieving the stated aims.

At this stage, the company should reassess the alternatives to merger, in view of the many difficulties involved. Taking over another company is rather like moving to a larger, more expensive house. Mergers involve considerable disruptions during the planning and bidding phase; costs, such as legal advice and the printing and publishing of documents; possible exposure to increased financial risk; and the upheavals of integration. Just as some marriages do not survive the strains of house-moving, some companies often fail to recover after the stress of merger. Having identified the specific role of the acquisition, the company can now consider whether it can be achieved in other, perhaps more cost-effective ways.

Table 22.5 Strategic opportunities

Where you are	► **How to get to where you want to be**
Growing steadily but in a mature market with limited growth prospects	► Acquire a company in a younger market with a higher growth rate
Marketing an incomplete product range, or having the potential to sell other products or services to your existing customers	► Acquire a company with a complementary product range
Operating at maximum productive capacity	► Acquire a company making similar products operating substantially below capacity
Under-utilising management resources	► Acquire a company into which your talents can extend
Needing more control of suppliers or customers	► Acquire a company which is, or gives access to, a significant customer or supplier
Lacking key clients in a targeted sector	► Acquire a company with the right customer profile
Preparing for flotation but needing to improve your Balance Sheet	► Acquire a suitable company which will enhance earnings per share
Needing to increase market share	► Acquire an important competitor
Needing to widen your capability	► Acquire a company with the key talents and/or technology

Source: 3i (Investors in Industry)

Harrison (1987) suggests that for every merger motive there are several alternative ways of achieving the same end. For example, if the aim is sales growth, this can be achieved by internal expansion or by a joint venture. If the aim is to improve earnings per share, a loss-making subsidiary can be shut down or efficiency-enhancing measures can be implemented. If it is wished to use spare cash, this can be invested in marketable securities and trade investments, or even returned to shareholders as dividends or in the form of share repurchases. If an improvement in management skills is sought, appropriately skilled personnel can be bought in to replace existing managers, outside consultants can be used for advice, or incentive and bonus schemes can be introduced. In short, if the decision to grow by acquisition is made, the potential acquirer must be very sure that the stipulated aims are unattainable by alternative measures.

Most firms with corporate planning departments exercise a continuous review of the key members of the industry in which they operate and also of related and, often, unrelated areas. Some firms are known to 'track' several dozen potential takeover candidates, assessing their various strengths and weaknesses, and estimating the likely net value obtainable if they were acquired. Such target companies are cross-checked against a set of possible acquisition criteria.

When the decision to expand by acquisition is taken, the corporate planning staff should be able rapidly to provide a short-list of candidates, expressing the SWOTs of each, especially its vulnerability to takeover at that time. It is common for defending managements to dismiss takeover bids as 'opportunistic' in a pejorative way. For an acquisitive company that adopts the strategic approach, this means 'well-timed', as such companies are continually seeking opportune moments to launch a bid, especially when the stock market rating of the target appears low. The joint takeover by the former GEC and Siemens of Plessey was opportunistic, in the sense that the target's return on capital was relatively low due to a recent substantial investment programme. Whether the market had correctly valued Plessey is arguable, but the bidders undoubtedly spotted a favourable opportunity to acquire Plessey at a time when its performance looked weak in relation to the market, thus eliminating a major competitor for lucrative British Telecom contracts.

Bidding (and defending)

Bidding is an exercise in applied psychology. Readiness to bid implies an assessment that the target is either undervalued as it stands or would be worth more under alternative management. In such cases, the bid itself provides new information about prospective value, and the bidder should expect to have to pay above the market price to secure control. However, it is often unclear before the event how much of a bid premium, if any, is already built into the market price as the market attempts to assess the probability of a bidder emerging and succeeding with its offer. The trick in mounting profitable takeover bids is to promise to use assets more effectively in order to entice existing shareholders to sell, without making such extravagant claims that the target's market price moves up too sharply before the acquisition is completed. Conversely, to accentuate the difficulties of reorganising the target could be regarded as disingenuous or even

call into question the wisdom of the bid itself, leading to a fall in the bidder's own share price. The following box summarises some of the defence tactics which a bidder may encounter.

Choose your weapons! Takeover defence tactics

Takeover strategy is not a one-sided affair. Very few takeovers are recommended at once by the directors of target companies. Even if they expect to lose the fight, the incumbents usually reject the initial bid in the hope of attracting better terms. The first line of defence, therefore, is rejection because the bid is too low, or because the proposed union 'lacks industrial logic'.

Once defenders have had time to marshal their resources and get their public relations act together, more effective defences can be adopted. Some are more credible than others, and some are illegal in the UK but common in the USA. Typical defence ploys by UK firms are:

- Revalue assets – this is often a waste of time, as the market should already have assessed the market value.
- Denigrate the profit and share price record of the bidder, and hence the quality of its management. This invites retaliation in kind.
- Promise a dividend increase – this calls past dividend policy into question, and bidders usually offer this anyway.
- Publish improved profit forecasts – a dangerous ploy, since the forecast has to be plausible yet attractive, and once made, the company has to deliver. Companies that repel raiders but fail to meet profit forecasts are susceptible to further bids.
- Seek a White Knight – an alternative suitor that will acquire the target on more favourable terms (mainly for the management?).
- Lobby the competition authorities.

The following defences mostly originated in the USA and some are difficult to reconcile with the Takeover Code:

- The Crown Jewels defence – selling-off the company's most attractive assets.
- Issuing new shares into friendly hands – this, of course, requires shareholder agreement.
- The Pacman defence – launching a counter-bid for the raider.
- Golden Parachutes – writing such attractive severance terms for managers that the bidder will recoil at the prospective expense.
- Tin Parachutes – offering excessively attractive severance terms for blue collar workers.
- Launching a bid for another company – if successful, this will increase the size of the firm, making it less digestible for the bidder.
- Leveraged buy-out – the purchase of the company by its own management using large amounts of borrowed funds.
- Poison pills – undertaking methods of finance that the bidder will find unattractive to unwind, e.g. large issues of convertibles that the bidder will have to honour.
- Repurchasing of shares to drive up the share price and increase the cost of the takeover (common now in the UK), although not allowed once an informal approach has been made.

22.9 Post-merger activities

Probably the most difficult part of takeover strategy and execution is the integration of the newly acquired company into the parent. In the case of contested bids, the acquirer will normally have only a limited amount of information to guide its integration plans and should not be too shocked to encounter unforeseen problems regarding the quality of the target's assets and personnel. The difficulty of integration depends on the extent to which the acquirer wants to control the operations of the target. If only limited control is required, as in the case of unrelated acquisitions, integration will probably be restricted to meshing the financial reporting systems of the component companies. Conversely, if full integration of common manufacturing activities is required, integration assumes a different order of complexity.

Jones (1982, 1986) points out that the degree of complexity of integration depends on the type of acquisition: for example, whether it is a horizontal takeover of a very similar company, requiring a detailed plan for integrating supply, production and distribution; or, at the other extreme, a purely conglomerate acquisition where there is little or no overlap of functions. The relationship between type of acquisition, overlap of activity (split into financial, manufacturing and marketing) and the resulting degree of integrative complexity is shown in Figure 22.3. Because we believe that integration is perhaps the most important part of the acquisition process, we devote most of the following section to further analysis of this issue.

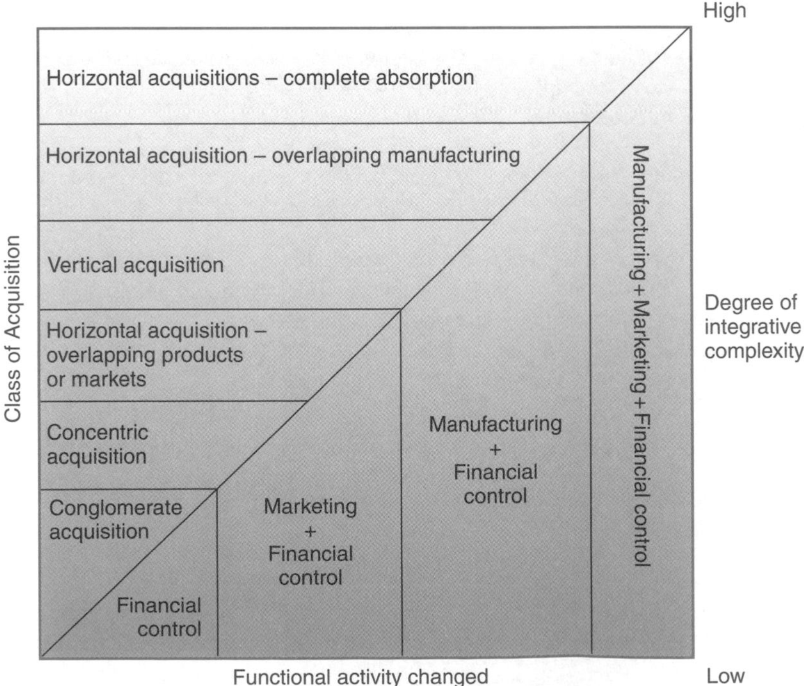

Figure 22.3 Type of acquisition and integrative complexity (Jones 1986)

Finally, the acquisition should be **post-audited**. The post-audit team should review the evaluation phase to assess whether, and to what extent, the appraisal was under- or over-optimistic, and whether appropriate plans were formulated and executed. The review should centre on what lessons can be learned to guide any subsequent acquisition exercise.

Poor planning and poorly-executed integration are two of the commonest reasons for takeover failure. All too often, acquisitive companies focus senior management attention on the next adventure rather than devoting adequate resources to absorbing the newly acquired firm carefully. It is rash to lay down optimal integration procedures in advance, because the appropriate integration procedures are largely situation-specific. The 'right' way to approach integration depends on the nature of the company acquired, its internal culture and its strengths and weaknesses (Lees 1992). However, Drucker (1981) contends that there are Five Golden Rules to follow in the integration process:

1 Ensure that acquired companies have a 'common core of unity' with the parent. In his view, mere financial ties between companies are insufficient to obtain a bond. The companies should have significant overlapping characteristics like shared technology or markets in order to exploit synergies.
2 The acquirer should think through what potential skill contribution it can make to the acquired company. In other words, the takeover should be approached not solely with the attitude of 'what's in it for the parent?', but also with the view 'what can we offer them?'
3 The acquirer must respect the products, markets and customers of the acquired company. Disparaging the record and performance of less senior management is likely to sap morale.
4 Within a year, the acquirer should provide appropriately skilled top management for the acquired company.
5 Again, within a year, the acquirer should make several cross-company promotions.

These are largely common-sense guidelines, with a heavy emphasis on behavioural factors, but many studies have shown that acquirors fail to follow them. A study undertaken by Hunt and Lees of the London Business School with Egon Zehnder Associates (Hunt and Lees, 1987) commented that 'unless the human element is managed carefully, there is a serious risk of losing the financial and business advantages that the acquisition could bring to the parent company'.

Jones' integration sequence

Jones (1986) explains that integration of a new company is a complex mix of corporate strategy, management accounting and applied psychology. Acquirors should follow an 'integration sequence', based on five key steps, the relative weight attaching to each step depending on the type of acquisition. The sequence is as follows:

1 Decide upon and communicate initial reporting relationships.
2 Achieve rapid control of key factors.

3 Review the resource base of the acquired company via a 'resource audit'.
4 Clarify and revise corporate objectives and develop strategic plans.
5 Revise the organisational structure.

Each of these is now briefly examined.

Reporting relationships

Clear reporting relationships have to be established in order to avoid uncertainty. An important issue is whether to impose reporting lines at the outset or whether to await the new organisational structure. In resolving this issue, it is desirable to avoid managers establishing their own informal relationships and to stress that some changes may be temporary.

Control of key factors

Control requires access to plentiful and accurate information. To control key factors, acquirers should rapidly gain control of the information channels that export control messages and import key data about resource deployment. It may sometimes be desirable not to introduce controls identical to those of the parent, first, because group controls may not be appropriate for the acquired company, and second, because those group controls may no longer be appropriate for the revised organisation. If the acquired company's existing control systems are thought to be adequate, it may be worth retaining them. Two important financial controls are the setting of clear borrowing limits and an early review of capital expenditure limits and appraisal procedures.

Jones notes that poor financial controls are often found within newly-acquired companies, and indeed, have often contributed to their acquisition. Examples are over-reliance on financial rather than management accounting systems (MAS), a MAS that provides inappropriate information in an inappropriate format, poor use of the MAS, and distortions in the overhead allocation mechanism, making it difficult to pinpoint unprofitable products and customers. The net result is often poor budgetary control, inadequate costing systems and inability to monitor and control cash movements.

Resource audit

The resource audit should examine both physical and human assets to obtain a clear picture of the quality of management at all levels. The extent of the audit required will depend on how much information is made available prior to the acquisition, but auditors should not be surprised if 'skeletons' are found in cupboards, requiring a reappraisal of the value of the acquired firm and possibly a different way of integrating it into the parent's future strategy and plans. For example, a business that was meant to be absorbed into the parent's operations may be divested if its capital equipment is unexpectedly dilapidated.

Corporate objectives and plans

These should be harmonised with those of the parent, but should also reflect any differences due to industrial sector, such as different 'normal' rates of return or profit margins in different industrial sectors. Managers of acquired firms should have some freedom to formulate their plans to meet the stated aims, but the degree of freedom should depend on the complexity of the merger. For example, in a conglomerate acquisition, where the primary aim is to secure financial control, it may be appropriate to allow executives to develop a system of management control suitable to their own operating patterns, so long as these are consistent with the aims of the takeover. In cases where cash generation is the main spur, all that may be needed is centralised cash management plus control over capital allocations.

Revising the organisational structure

A discussion of organisational design is beyond our scope, but obviously a demoralised labour force is unlikely to offer optimal performance.

Two important factors enhancing the success of a takeover are the thoroughness of the resource audit and the degree of senior management contact in the very early stages of the takeover. Employees of acquired companies seek a rapid resolution of uncertainty, especially regarding how they and their company fit into the future structure and strategy of the acquirer, and how soon the new management team will assume control. Particularly important for morale are the lifting of any previous embargo on capital expenditure and the provision of improved performance incentives, pension schemes and career prospects.

Some of these aspects are illustrated in the following short cases.

Case 1: Post-acquisition integration at GE Capital

According to Ashkenas, DeMonaco & Francis (1998) the process of melding one company into another is frequently badly done because few firms go through the process often enough to develop a pattern. They suggest that many firms see it as a one-off event rather than a replicable process – 'something to get finished, so everyone can get back to business'. Because 'the acquisition event is painful and anxiety-generating, involving change, disruption and job loss, most managers think how to get it over with, not how to do it better next time around'.

They reported on acquisition integration at GE Capital, a subsidiary of General Electric Corporation, founded in 1933 to provide consumers with credit to purchase GEC appliances. GE Capital has grown by acquisition, including over 100 in the five years prior to their report. From interviews with managers and key staff involved in acquisitions, both as former targets and subsequently as acquirors at GE Capital, they devised a framework for acquisition management based on a set of four 'Lessons':

Lesson 1
Acquisition management is not a discrete phase of a deal and does not begin when the documents are signed. Rather, it is a process that begins with due diligence and runs through the ongoing management of the new enterprise.

Lesson 2
Integration management is a full-time job and needs to be recognised as a distinct business function, just like operations, marketing, or finance.

Lesson 3
Decisions about management structure, key roles, reporting relationships, lay-offs, restructuring, and other career-affecting aspects of the integration should be made, announced and implemented as soon as possible after the deal is signed – within days, if possible. Creeping changes, uncertainty, and anxiety that last for months are debilitating and immediately start to drain value from an acquisition.

Lesson 4
A successful integration melds not only the various technical aspects of the businesses but also the different cultures. The best way to do it is to get people working together quickly to solve business problems and accomplish results that could not have been achieved before.

Source: Ashkenas, DeMonaco & Francis (1998)

Case 2: UK bank mergers bear fruit

In early 2002, two British banking groups reported strongly improved performance resulting from the respective mergers that had created them. The source of the benefits was broadly similar – large cost savings combined with buoyant demand for retail financial services.

Royal Bank of Scotland, the UK's second largest by market value after its acquisition of NatWest Bank, was able to shrug off increased bad debt provision and exposure to Enron, the insolvent US energy trader, after exploiting more synergies than originally forecast from the acquisition. Royal Bank shares had out-performed the UK banking sector by 18 per cent as news of rapidly increased revenue growth from NatWest synergies leaked on to the market.

HBOS plc, number five in the banking league table, was formed by the takeover by Halifax of Bank of Scotland. It also achieved strong gains from the merger in the area of savings and mortgage loans. It had achieved a 25 per cent market share in the mortgage market via a policy of interest rate cutting, after years of decline following the de-mutualisation of Halifax Building Society in 1997. It was also threatening the market dominance of the 'Big Four' banks in the small business sector by offering higher interest rates on credit balances (4 per cent against 0.1 per cent!). HBOS had outperformed the banking sector by 27 per cent over the previous year.

Self-assessment Activity 22.5

What are the key elements of an acquisition strategy?

(answer at end of chapter)

22.10 Assessing the impact of mergers

The impact of mergers can be assessed at various levels. At the macroeconomic level, if takeover activity is performing its function of weeding out inefficient managements, we might expect to find takeovers correlated with superior economic performance. However, over the long haul the two economies where takeover activity is most prevalent – the USA and the UK – have underperformed economies where growth by takeover is less common (e.g. until the mould-breaking takeover of Mannesmann by Britains' Vodafone-Airtouch in 2000 there had been only four completed hostile takeovers in Germany since 1945 and never one completed by a foreign bidder). Measures of economic performance such as growth in gross domestic product (GDP) per head and capital formation as a percentage of GDP were, certainly until the 1990s, considerably lower in the UK than in Japan and Germany, as were figures for 'growth drivers' like R&D expenditure as a percentage of GDP.

Although such associations do not prove causation, the presumed link is via the impact of horizontal mergers reducing competition and through the pressures for short-term performance. It is argued that managers in the 'Anglo-Saxon' economies are forced to pay out higher dividends to bolster share price in order to deter prospective raiders. Ever higher payouts represent cash that could have been used to finance investment and growth. However, it seems implausible to argue that the institutions would withhold funds from companies that showed a willingness to perform according to short-termist rules. Nevertheless, after reviewing the evidence, Peacock and Bannock (1991) concluded that mergers and takeovers did not create wealth, but merely transferred ownership of assets. The full explanation of why merger-active economies underperform is probably less simple, as Porter (1992) explains, involving a complex interplay of economic, social and political factors.

Another level of analysis is that of the performance of individual companies. If takeovers are beneficial, we should expect to see merger-active firms improving their performance post-merger.

Investigating the effects of merger activity is one of the busiest areas of contemporary applied finance research. There are two main ways of attempting to assess the impact of mergers.

The first, '**the financial characteristics approach**', is based on examining the key financial characteristics of both acquiring and acquired firms before the takeover, to study whether they are more or less profitable (taking profitability as an indicator of efficiency) than firms not involved in acquisitions, and whether

their profitability improves after the acquisition. The second, **'the capital markets approach'**, is based on examining the impact of the takeover on the share prices of both acquired and acquiring firms, to assess the extent to which expected benefits from merger are impounded in share prices and how these are shared between the two sets of shareholders.

The first method, the **financial characteristics approach**, suffers from severe limitations:

1 Different accounting conventions used by different firms (e.g. treatment of R&D) often make comparisons misleading.
2 Measures of profitability may have been distorted due to the application of acquisition accounting procedures. Prior to the issue of FRS 10 in 1997, firms were allowed to write off goodwill (the excess of purchase price over 'fair value') against reserves. This lowered their equity bases and raised their recorded return on investment. Goodwill now has to be shown on the Balance Sheet as an asset and amortised over its useful life up to 20 years. This abrupt change in the rules of accounting for goodwill means that pre- and post-takeover measurement of performance of firms active in takeovers before and after 1997 is likely to be seriously distorted.
3 To assess properly the impact of the takeover requires an extended analysis ranging over, say, five to ten years. Many acquisitions are undertaken for 'strategic' purposes, the benefits of which may emerge only after several accounting periods, perhaps following lengthy and costly reorganisation. Very frequently, when 'efficient' companies take over 'inefficient' companies, the group's return on net assets and fixed asset turnover ratios automatically fall.
4 Accounting studies are not capable of assessing what the performance of the expanded group would have been in the absence of the merger, and are thus unable to assess what improvement in performance (if any) was due to factors beyond the merger. This problem increases with the time period used for the post-merger investigation.
5 Any improvement in profitability may simply be due to a restriction of competition, rather than more efficient use of resources.
6 The approach does not allow for risk. If the aim of many mergers is to lower total risk (possibly for managerial reasons), or to shift the company into a lower Beta activity, a lower return post-merger is not especially surprising, since according to the EMH/CAPM, relatively low-risk securities offer relatively low returns.

The second method, the **capital markets approach,** caters for many of these difficulties, and is thus the most frequently used mode of analysis. By adopting a CAPM framework, it enables the returns on shares of acquiring firms to be examined prior to and following the merger. As noted in Chapter 11, the market model indicates that the expected return on any security, j, in any time period t, ER_{jt}, is a linear function of the expected return on the market portfolio:

$$ER_{jt} = \alpha_{jt} + \beta_j ER_{mt}$$

However, the actual return in any time period, R_{jt}, results from a compound of market-related and company-specific factors:

$R_{jt} = \alpha_{jt} + \beta_j R_{mt} + u_{jt}$

u_{jt} is an error term with zero expected value, indicating that random company-specific factors are expected to cancel out over several time periods.

If, over a suitable period and allowing for overall movements in the market, we examine the differences between the expected returns and the actual returns, the 'residuals' or 'abnormal returns' should sum to zero, i.e. the expected value of the cumulated differences between ER_{jt} and R_{jt} is zero.

A takeover bid is a company-specific event likely to raise the share price, and hence the return on holding the shares. When a bid occurs, the increase in returns can be attributed to the market's assessment of the impact of the bid, i.e. the evaluation of its likelihood of success, and if successful, its appraisal of the benefits likely to ensue. Therefore, both in the period leading up to the bid, as the potential bidder builds a stake, and also on the day of announcement of the bid, we might expect the residuals to be non-negative. For example, if the market thinks the takeover is a mistake, we may find negative residuals for the bidder but positive residuals for the target, if, as usually happens, the share price of the target rises sharply. Hence, the cumulated residual returns may be taken as an assessment of the value of the takeover to the shareholders of the acquirer and acquired companies, respectively.

To illustrate this use of the market model, consider the data in Table 22.6. This relates to the successful takeover bid for the Kenning Motor Group by the

Table 22.6 Pre- and post-bid returns

Time period (months)	Share price (p)	Actual return (%)	Expected return (%)	Residual	Cumulated residuals
Kenning Motor Group					
−3	140	−3.45	−0.29	−3.16	−3.16
−2	160	14.29	1.67	12.61	9.45
−1	158	1.25	−6.64	−7.89	1.56
0	212	34.18	7.63	26.54	28.10
1	268	26.42	−0.19	26.60	54.70
2	310	15.67	−3.04	18.71	73.41
3	310	0	3.08	−3.08	70.33
Tozer–Kemsley–Milbourn					
−3	66	−2.94	−0.32	−2.62	−2.62
−2	81	22.73	1.87	20.86	18.24
−1	108	33.33	7.42	25.91	44.15
0	136	25.93	8.53	17.39	61.54
1	177	30.15	−0.21	30.36	91.90
2	172	−2.82	−3.40	0.58	92.48
3	180	4.65	3.44	1.21	93.69

Source: Data collected by Krista Bromley.

conglomerate Tozer Kemsley Milbourn (TKM) in 1986. There was a degree of industrial logic in this bid, as both TKM and Kennings retailed motor cars and Kennings operated a substantial car hire business. Kennings had attempted in previous years to diversify, but owing to the haphazard selection of targets and poorly executed integration, its core business was suffering, reflected in declining profitability and weakening cash flow. The data show the residual returns for both companies in the three months prior to, and also following, the bid; month 0 is the day of the bid, eventually completed at a price of £3.10.

The data clearly show positive residuals for Kennings, before the bid, on the day of the bid itself, and also in the following periods as TKM raised its bid. In this case, both sets of shareholders enjoyed substantial returns. After allowing for the movement in the market as a whole, the returns on the shares of both companies were substantially positive, indicating market expectations that this merger would be wealth-creating. This proved to be the case, following very swift and effective reorganisation of Kennings by TKM.

Until recently, the bulk of the empirical evidence (e.g. see surveys by Jensen and Ruback (1983); Department of Trade and Industry (1988); Mathur (1989)) suggested that positive gains from takeovers accrue almost entirely to the shareholders of target firms. While the average abnormal returns (the cumulated residuals for all firms divided by the number of firms examined in the study) recorded in these studies are invariably positive and statistically significant, returns to the shareholders of bidding firms are negative for mergers and not significantly different from zero for takeovers. In other words, on average, takeovers and mergers are not wealth-creating, but the acquisition process transfers wealth from the shareholders of acquirers to those of the acquired. These are very important results as they seem to question the judgement or the motives, or both, of the instigators of takeover bids.

However, a very significant study by Franks and Harris (1989), based on both UK and US data, contradicted much earlier work in an important respect. The study is especially important for two reasons. First, the authors took mergers and takeovers over a much longer period (1955–85) than most other studies; and second, they examined a considerably larger sample than any previous study. For the UK, 1,900 acquisitions involving 1,058 bidders were studied and the US sample was 1,555 acquisitions involving 850 bidders. The targets were all publicly traded, facilitating a capital markets approach. Table 22.7 shows their results in terms of excess stock market returns as compared to the market portfolio, and allowing for systematic risk.

Table 22.7 The gains from mergers

	UK (months)		**US (months)**	
	0	**−4 to +1**	**0**	**−4 to +1**
Targets	+24%	+31%	+16%	+24%
Bidders	+1%	+8%	+1%	+4%

Source: Franks and Harris (1989)

As with earlier studies, these data record a substantial increase in wealth for the shareholders of target firms, but unlike earlier ones, they reveal a relatively smaller, but statistically significant, increase in wealth for the shareholders of acquirers over the whole period leading up to and just after the bid.

A subsequent study by Limmack (1991), using only UK data for the period 1977–86, suggested that 'the gains made by target company shareholders are at the expense of shareholders of bidder companies'. He also suggested that the average wealth decreases suffered by the shareholders of bidding companies are mainly confined to the period 1977–80, and that bids made in the years 1981–86 produce no significant wealth decrease for shareholders of bidding firms.

Limmack's study seemed to imply that bidding firms and the capital market in general might have learned from earlier mistakes, and that some of the gains from merger might be retained by the bidder.

However, Sudarsanam *et al.* (1996), in a study of returns around bid announcement dates over the period 1980–90, found significant negative CARs of around 4 per cent for the announcement period minus 20 days to plus 40 days. In a subsequent study of 398 takeovers during 1984–92 involving bid values of over £10 million, Gregory (1997), found 'the post-takeover performance of UK companies undertaking large domestic acquisitions is unambiguously negative on average, in the longer term'. The results were clearly 'not compatible with shareholder wealth maximisation on the part of acquiring firms' management', Gregory found that acquiring firms underperformed the stock market by 18 per cent on average for two years following a bid. The method of financing the takeover was also discovered to be significant, with share exchanges being especially poor for shareholders. Agreed bids were less successful for acquiring companies than hostile takeovers, and companies making their first takeovers were likely to be poorer performers than more experienced bidders. Finally, companies bidding to diversify their interests were less likely to succeed than takeovers in related business areas (which echoes many previous analyses).

US studies, by both academics and firms of consultants, have found parallel results. Research in 1995 by the Mercer consultancy and *Business Week* of 150 deals valued at $500 million or above during 1990–95 showed that about half destroyed shareholder wealth and only 17 per cent created results that were more than 'marginal'. These and similar studies appear to confirm the view that bidders overpay for their targets (Gregory found an average bid premium of around 30 per cent) and that managers underestimate the work required to make a takeover succeed. Moreover, many managers seem determined to ignore the warning signs.

Some researchers in both the USA and the UK have studied the post-merger behaviour of corporate cash flows. This has the merit of avoiding the problems of accounting measurement and policy when profitability data are used, and also avoids relying on the efficiency of the capital market if share price data is used. For example, Manson *et al.* (1994) studied 38 UK mergers over 1985–87, and found that, on average, takeovers produced significant improvements in operating performance, reflected in cash flow. This supports the view that the market for corporate control provides a discipline for managers, and is consistent with US studies using similar methods.

The value destroyers

In early 1996, Farnell Electronics, a Leeds-based distributor of electronics components, paid £1.8 billion for a US company, Premier Industrial Corporation, an acquisition opposed by two of its main institutional shareholders on the grounds that the price was too high. At the time, the smaller Farnell was valued at around £800 million, giving the combined group a value of around £2 billion, i.e. the market immediately awarded it a valuation penalty.

The whirlwind was duly reaped during 1997–98 when chairman Howard Poulson was forced to make three profit warnings, blaming the effect of the strong pound. When reported, profits for the year 1997–98 were some 15 per cent below analysts' initial forecasts and little changed on the previous year. After the third profit warning, the market value of Premier Farnell was £805 million, more or less where it started from, and in a bull market.

Poulson paid the ultimate price, having to resign when the rest of the Board turned against him in January 1998, although he was probably cheered by receiving a reported £450,000 payoff. Meanwhile, deputy chairman Morton Mandel, the chairman of Premier at the time of the acquisition, took over the helm. The Board was reported as still believing that the acquisition made strategic sense, but that its benefits would take a little longer to filter through – some two to three years.

Franks and Mayer (1996) undertook an explicit test of the disciplinary role of hostile takeovers. They hypothesised that hostile takeovers would have a disciplinary impact, shown by association with, first, a high rate of managerial turnover, second, with substantial internal restructuring (asset sales exceeding 10 per cent of the value of post-acquisition fixed assets) and third, with weak firm performance post-acquisition.

Their study of hostile UK takeovers completed in 1985–6 found:

- 50 per cent of directors resign soon after a friendly bid as compared to 90 per cent after a hostile bid.
- Asset sales exceeded 10 per cent of the total fixed asset value in 26 per cent of friendly bids compared to 53 per cent of hostile bids.
- Bid premia averaged 30 per cent of firm value for hostile bids compared to 18 per cent for friendly bids.
- Bid premia on hostile bids were not correlated with rate of management turnover.
- Using four measures of performance (abnormal share price performance, dividend payments, pre-bid cash flow rates of return and Tobin's Q (the ratio of market value to replacement cost of assets) they found little significant evidence that recipients of hostile bids were poor performers prior to the bid.

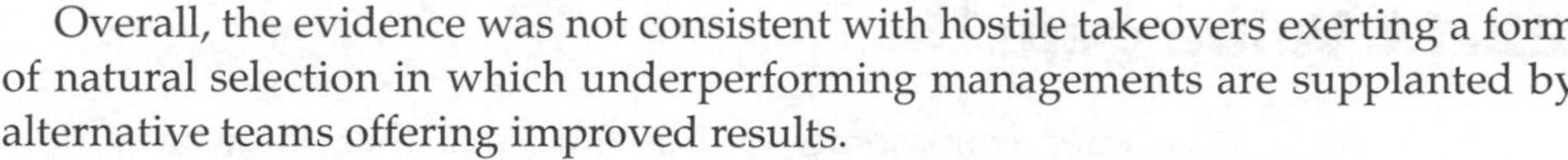

Overall, the evidence was not consistent with hostile takeovers exerting a form of natural selection in which underperforming managements are supplanted by alternative teams offering improved results.

Finally, what about international mergers? In 2000, the accounting firm KPMG reported a study of 700 of the largest cross-border takeovers occurring between 1996 and 1998 in which it attempted to assess the value created. KPMG measured companies' share price performance before and after the deal, and compared the post-deal performance with trends in each of the firm's industries.

The results were:

- 17 per cent of takeovers added value to the combined company.
- 30 per cent produced no significant difference.
- 53 per cent actually destroyed value.

Commenting on why 83 per cent of mergers apparently fail to generate benefits for shareholders, it was suggested that many firms concentrate too heavily on the business and financial mechanics and overlook the personnel-related issues, echoing the earlier study by Lees (1992).

KPMG identified six factors that merit close attention:

- evaluation of synergies.
- integrated project planning.
- due diligence.
- selection of the right management team.
- dealing with culture clashes.
- communication with staff.

Not much new here, readers may think, but it is remarkable how often over-ambitious managers have to be reminded of the ingredients of a successful merger.

In a further survey released in 2002, KPMG claimed that over a third of giant international takeovers completed at the peak of the bull market were being unwound, that 32 per cent of chief executives or Finance Directors responsible for planning the original deals had moved on, and that two-thirds of firms acquired during 1996–98 still needed to be properly integrated. The lesson appears to be that, like Chris Gent of Vodafone, following the acquisition of Mannesmann, top managers should negotiate their bonuses after completion of the mega-deal, but before the problems begin to appear.

In the next section, we return to a recurrent theme in this book: the meaning and reliability of the values placed on companies by the stock market.

Self-assessment Activity 22.6

What are the main causes of 'failure' of takeovers?

(answer at end of chapter)

22.11 Value gaps[1]

Evidence from some studies indicates that there may be net gains from merger, while most surveys indicate that the shareholders of target companies experience a beneficial wealth effect. The near certainty that shareholders of targets will benefit suggests that market values typically fall short of the value that potential or actual bidders would place on them. These disparities in value are called **value gaps**, and there are four main explanations of how they arise.

Poor corporate parenting

Value gaps may arise because some business segments do not make their maximum possible cash or profit contributions to the parent. Ultimately, this is a reflection of poor central management, which is thus failing to add value to the group or actually reducing value. The following are some examples of management deficiencies:

1 Some assets, such as land and premises, may not be fully exploited by either the parent or its subsidiaries.
2 The parent pursues too many ventures of dubious value, perhaps intending to gain entry into other areas of business, but in which it does not possess appropriate expertise.
3 HQ may fail to take sufficiently decisive action to prevent or correct poor profitability in business segments.
4 HQ may indulge in costly central activities or services that are a net burden rather than of benefit to business units.
5 Poor group structure may leave business units at a disadvantage compared with competitors. For example, a business unit may be too small to compete effectively in its main markets, or it may be denied sufficient capital resources to develop its activities. As a result, it may have a greater value under alternative, more perceptive, management.

Poor financial management

The HQ corporate finance department might have followed a gearing policy that fails to exploit its ability fully to borrow and gear up returns to equity; or alternatively, it may be severely over-borrowed. Similarly, its past dividend policy may have been over- or under-generous.

Over-enthusiastic bidding

It has been said that takeover bidders' greatest victims are themselves. Many bids are undoubtedly successful, such as BP's acquisition of Britoil in order to obtain the latter's oil reserves. However, many others, like the Trustee Savings Bank's acquisition of the merchant bank Hill Samuel, are outright failures; and

[1] This section relies on ideas presented in Young and Sutcliffe (1990).

Marrying in haste

Merger and acquisitions continue apace in spite of an alarming failure rate and evidence that they often fail to benefit shareholders. Last week's collapse of the planned Deutsche-Dresdner Bank merger tarnished the reputation of both parties. Deutsche Bank's management was exposed as divided and confused. Dresdner Bank lost its chairman, who resigned. Senior members of Dresdner Kleinwort Benson, its investment banking unit, walked out.

Deutsche-Dresdner was a fiasco that damaged both parties. But even if the takeover had gone ahead, it would probably still have claimed its victims. A long list of studies have all reached the same conclusion: the majority of takeovers damage the interests of the shareholders of the acquiring company. They do, however, often reward the shareholders of the acquired company, who receive more for their shares than they were worth before the takeover was announced. Mark Sirower, visiting professor at New York University, claims that 65 per cent of mergers fail to benefit acquiring companies, whose shares subsequently underperform their sector. Yet the evidence of failure has done nothing to dim senior managers' enthusiasm for takeovers.

Why do so many mergers and acquisitions fail to benefit shareholders? Colin Price, a partner at McKinsey, the management consultants, who specialises in mergers and acquisitions, says the majority of failed mergers suffer from poor implementation. And in about half of those, senior management failed to take account of the different cultures of the companies involved.

Melding corporate cultures takes time, which senior management does not have after a merger. 'Most mergers are based on the idea of "let's increase revenues", but you have to have a functioning management team to manage that process. The nature of the problem is not so much that there's open warfare between the two sides. It's that the cultures don't meld quickly enough to take advantage of the opportunities. In the meantime, the marketplace has moved on.'

Many consultants refer to how little time companies spend before a merger thinking about whether their organisations are compatible. The benefits of mergers are usually couched in financial or commercial terms: cost-savings can be made or the two sides have complementary businesses that will allow them to increase revenues.

Mergers are about compatibility, which means agreeing whose values will prevail and who will be the dominant partner. So it is no accident that managers as well as journalists reach for marriage metaphors in describing them. Merging companies are said to 'tie the knot'. When mergers are called off, as with Deutsche Bank and Dresdner Bank, the two companies fail to 'make it up the aisle' or their relationship remains 'unconsummated'. Yet the metaphors fail to convey the scale of risk companies run when they launch acquisitions or mergers. Even in countries with high divorce rates, marriages have a better success rate than mergers. And in an age of frequent pre-marital cohabitation, the bridal couple usually know one another better than the merging companies do.

Continued

Mr Sirower rejects the view that the principal problem is 'post-merger implementation'. 'Many large acquisitions are dead on arrival, no matter how well they are managed after the deal is done,' he says. He asks why managers should pay a premium to make an acquisition when their shareholders could invest in the target company themselves. How sure are managers that they can extract cost savings or revenue improvements from their acquisition that match the size of the takeover premium?

Perhaps it would help if senior managers abandoned the marriage metaphor in favour of the story of the princess and the toad. Warren Buffett, the US investor, said nearly 20 years ago that many acquisitive managers appeared to see themselves as princesses whose kisses could turn toads into handsome princes. Investors, he observed, could always buy toads at the going price for toads. 'If investors instead bankroll princesses who wish to pay double for the right to kiss the toad, those kisses better pack some real dynamite. We've observed many kisses, but very few miracles. Many managerial princesses remain serenely confident about the future potency of their kisses, even after their corporate backyards are knee-deep in unresponsive toads.'

Based on Michael Skapinker, *Financial Times*, April 12 2000

some, such as British and Commonwealth Holdings' purchase of Atlantic Computers, are totally disastrous. Perhaps, at the time of the bid, the assessment of the bidding management was correct, but they were caught out by changed circumstances. A more likely explanation is that they were buoyed-up with excessive enthusiasm about the bid. Although some bidders have the sense to walk away from a bid (e.g. Meggitts' aborted bid for United Scientific Holdings), in too many cases, bidders delude themselves that the proposed takeover is vital to the development of the group.

Stock market inefficiency

Does the stock market fail to assess the full value of a business, perhaps because it belongs to a sector that is 'out of favour', or because the market adopts too short-term a view of the prospects of the company?

Assessing the relative weights of these arguments is a major challenge for finance and business researchers.

22.12 Corporate restructuring to create value

Corporate restructuring is an important vehicle by which managements can enhance shareholder value by changing the ownership structure of the organisation. It involves three key elements:

1 Concentration of equity ownership in the hands of managers or 'inside' investors well-placed to monitor managers' efforts.
2 Substitution of debt for equity.

3 Redefinition of organisational boundaries through mergers, divestment, management buy-outs etc.

In the dynamic environment within which companies operate, financial managers should be ever-alert to new and better ways of structuring and financing their businesses. The **value-creation process** will involve the following:

- Review the corporate financial structure from the shareholders' viewpoint. Consider whether changes in capital structure, business mix or ownership would enhance value.
- Increase efficiency and reduce the after-tax cost of capital through the judicious use of borrowing.
- Improve operating cash flows through focusing on wealth-creating investment opportunities (i.e. those having positive net present values), profit improvement and overhead reduction programmes and divestiture.
- Pursue financially-driven value creation using various new financing instruments and arrangements (i.e. financial engineering).

Types of restructuring

Recent years have seen the development of new and elaborate methods of corporate restructuring. Restructuring can occur at three different levels:

1 *Corporate restructuring* refers to changing the ownership structure of the **parent company** to enhance shareholder value. Such changes can arise through diversification, forming strategic alliances, leveraged buy-outs and even liquidation.
2 *Business restructuring* considers changing the ownership structure at the strategic **business unit** level. Examples include acquisitions, joint ventures, divestments and management buy-outs.
3 *Asset restructuring* refers to changing the ownership of **assets**. This can be achieved through sale and leaseback arrangements, offering assets as security, factoring debts and asset disposals.

The levels of restructuring are summarised below:

Corporate	Business unit	Asset
Diversification/demerger	Acquisitions	Pledging assets as security
Share issues	Joint ventures	Factoring debts
Share repurchase	Management buy-outs	Leasing and HP
Strategic alliances	Sell-offs	Sale and leaseback
Leveraged buy-outs	Franchising	Divestment
Liquidation	Spin-offs	

Most of these devices have been covered elsewhere in this book. We devote the next section to a brief discussion of share repurchase, divestments and management buy-outs (MBOs), which have so far received only passing mention.

Return to sender at NFC

NFC, the freight distribution and logistics group, announced in June 1998 a £307 million share buy-back, one-quarter of its equity capital. Five years earlier the company had raised £263 million in a rights issue aimed at expanding its transport activity, so why should it now want to give it back? The answer is simple: lack of profitable growth opportunities and a change in management resulted in a three-year turnround and divestment programme which left it with over £50 million net cash on its Balance Sheet, an underperforming share price and no suitable acquisition candidates to pursue.

Rather than sit on a mound of cash, returning excess cash to shareholders was seen as the best way of increasing shareholder value and financially restructuring the business. The scheme would involve payment of 176p in cash or loan notes and three new shares for every four held. At the same time, NFC cut dividends by 2.1p per share on the previous year. Despite this cut, and the fact that gearing would increase to around 80 per cent, the stock market viewed the buy-back as a good move and NFC's share price reacted favourably.

Divestment

A **divestment** is the opposite of an investment or acquisition; it is the sale of part of a company (e.g. assets, product lines, divisions, brands) to a third party. The heavy use of divestment as a means of restructuring reflects the continuing efforts of corporate management to adjust to changing economic and political environments.

One of the motives for acquisition, identified earlier, is the managerial belief that the two businesses are worth more combined than separate. A form of reverse synergy is a major reason for divestment: the two elements of an existing business are worth more separated than combined. Whereas the arithmetic of synergy for acquisitions argues that 2 + 2 = 5, the arithmetic behind divestment, or reverse synergy, argues that 5 – 1 can be worth more than 4. In other words, part of the business can be sold off at a greater value than its current worth to the company. The management team may not relish the prospect of divesting itself of certain business activities, but it is often necessary as the strategic focus changes.

Self-assessment Activity 22.7

Think of a few reasons why a firm may choose to divest part of its business.

(answer at end of chapter)

Two particular forms of divestment are sell-offs and spin-offs. **Sell-offs** involve selling part of a business to a third party, usually for cash. The most

common reason for sell-offs is to divest less profitable, non-core business units to ease cash flow problems. In **spin-offs**, there is no change in ownership. A new company is created with assets transferred to it, and a new management team is usually created to run the spin-off, but the shareholders now have holdings in two companies rather than one.

In theory, the value of the two companies should be no different from that of the single company prior to spin-off. But numerous US studies suggest that spin-offs usually result in strong positive abnormal returns to shareholders. Why should this be the case?

1 It enables investors to value the two parts of the business more easily. Poor-performing business units are more exposed to the stock market, necessitating appropriate managerial action. For example, some high-street retailers have spun-off their properties into separate companies, so that investors can judge performance on retailing and property activities more easily.
2 The creation of a clearer management structure and strategic vision of the two companies should result in greater efficiency and effectiveness.
3 Spin-offs reduce the likelihood of a predatory takeover bid where the bidder recognises underperforming assets in a single company. They also make it easier for the group to sell a clearly defined part of its business at a price better reflecting its true worth.

Divestments enable companies to move their resources to higher-value investment opportunities. They should be evaluated along exactly the same lines as investment decisions, based on the net present value resulting from the divestment.

The motives for a demerger are broadly the same as for divestment discussed earlier. However, with the current vogue to focus on core businesses, it is easy to forget the drawbacks of demerger or divestment:

- Loss of economies of scale where the demerged business shared certain activities, including central overheads.
- A smaller firm may find it harder to raise finance or may incur a more expensive cost of capital.
- Greater vulnerability to takeover.

Management buy-outs

Management buy-outs (MBOs) occur when the management of a company 'buys out' a distinct part of the business that the company is seeking to divest. MBOs usually arise because a parent company decides to divest a subsidiary for strategic reasons. For example, it may decide to exit a certain activity; to sell off an unwanted subsidiary acquired by a takeover of the parent company; to improve the strategic fit of its various business units; or simply to concentrate on its core activities. MBOs can also be purchaser-driven, where the local management recognises that the business has greater potential than the parent company management realises, or where the alternative is closure, with high redundancy and closure costs.

Once a company decides to divest itself of part of its activities, it will usually seek to sell it as an ongoing business rather than selling assets separately. With an MBO, the firm sells the operation to its managers, who put in some of their own capital and obtain the remainder from **venture capitalists**.

The growth of MBO activity has been fuelled by venture capital firms enabling managers to raise large sums of capital through borrowings (leveraged buy-outs), particularly mezzanine finance, which is a cross between debt and equity, offering lenders a high coupon rate and, frequently, the right to convert to equity should the company achieve a quotation. The Finance Act 1981 gave considerable help by allowing finance raised to be secured on the acquired assets.

An MBO typically has three parties: the directors of the group looking to divest, the management team looking to make the buy-out and the financial backers for the buy-out team. A private company may agree to an MBO because the directors wish to retire or because it needs cash for the remaining operations.

It is quite common for the new management team to obtain a better return on the business than the old company. Reasons for this include:

- the greater personal motivation of management.
- flexibility in decision-making.
- lower overheads.
- negotiating a favourable buy-out price.

Tetley tea to float?

It is not too difficult to read the tea-leaves for Tetley, the world's second largest maker of tea-bags. The company planned to make a stock market flotation in the summer of 1998 which, assuming it is capitalised at the P:E for the food sector, would value it at £430 million. Not bad for the small management team and five venture capital groups (including Schroder and Prudential) that paid Allied Domecq £190 million in 1995 for the business.

Its four-fold profit improvement over this period comes from the new management's ability to turn round the US business from a major loss-maker to a profitable operation, to increase sales across all its operations and to reduce overheads. Cost reduction is frequently a benefit from MBO restructuring, where a smaller management team can make the business leaner and fitter. Tetley achieved a 25 per cent reduction in overheads, closing down two plants and improving profit margins. With a large proportion of its workforce being shareholders, Tetley has a strong focus on cash and cost efficiency. Global marketing accounts for 21 per cent of sales – a massive investment in those Tetley tea men.

A stock market listing would provide access to additional capital for product development and acquisitions and to expand into emerging markets. However, in June 1998, a few days prior to the company being floated, it announced that a new opportunity had arisen, suggesting that a takeover bid for the company will soon be tabled. Either way, for Tetley, its future is clearly in the bag!

Checklist for a successful buy-out

The venture capitalist will ask a number of penetrating questions in evaluating whether the MBO is worth backing.

1 Has the management team got the right blend of skill, experience and commitment? The financial backers may require changes in personnel, frequently the introduction of a finance director.
2 What are the motives for the group selling and the management team buying? If the business is currently a loss-maker, how will the new company turn it round? A convincing business plan with fully worked profit and cash flow projections will be required.
3 Is it the assets or the shares of the company that are to be purchased?
4 Will assets require replacement? What are the investment and financing needs?
5 What is an appropriate price?

Buy-out failure is often the result of a wrongly priced bid, lack of expertise in key areas, loss of key staff or lack of finance.

Once the financial backers are satisfied that the MBO is worth backing, a financial package will be agreed. The management team will typically have a minority shareholding, with the financial backers (often more than one) taking the majority stake. While the venture capitalist company views the investment as long-term, it will look for a potential exit route, frequently through a stock market flotation such as the Alternative Investment Market (AIM).

The management team will usually be expected to demonstrate commitment by investing personal borrowings in the business. Redeemable convertible preference shares often form part of the financial arrangements. These shares give voting rights should the preference dividend fall into arrears and enable the holder to redeem shares should the investment fail or to convert to equity if the business performs well.

Venture capitalists make handsome returns from MBOs and similar deals. Average returns from unquoted venture capital funds were around 30 per cent for the five years to 1998 – much higher than the returns on the stock market investments. The question must be asked as to whether large companies are acting in their shareholders' best interests in permitting buy-outs on such favourable terms. It is all very well to say that a particular division is a non-core activity; but firms are constantly changing their definitions as to what exactly is core. Restructuring, whether through MBOs or other forms, is wasteful and non-value-adding if the group selling the business could have achieved the same efficiency and other gains as the new company.

Management buy-ins are the opposite of buy-outs. A group of business managers with the necessary expertise and skills to run a particular type of business search for a business to acquire. The ideal candidate is a business, or part of a business, with strong potential, but which has been underperforming or is in financial difficulty, perhaps because of poor management. The new team rarely has the necessary capital to buy in and often requires the backing of a venture capitalist.

Joint ventures and strategic alliances

Unlike mergers or acquisitions, **joint ventures** and other **strategic alliances** enable both sides to retain their separate identities. They have been employed to good effect to achieve a variety of objectives, but have become a particularly popular way of developing new products and entering new markets, especially overseas. One of the financial benefits is that the strength of two organisations coming together for some specific strategic purpose can often lower capital costs associated with the new investment.

There are two main types of joint venture. An *industrial cooperation* joint venture is for a fixed period of time, where the responsibilities of each of the parties are clearly defined. These are particularly popular in the emerging mixed economies of Central and Eastern Europe. A *joint-equity* venture is where two companies make significant investments in a long-term joint activity. These are more common as a means of investing in countries where foreign ownership is discouraged, such as in Japan and parts of the Middle East.

Like any other investment, the potential partners need to assess the costs and benefits of the joint venture and identify and manage the activities critical to success. One problem can be the inability of the joint venture management team to make decisions without the approval of parent companies. This can be overcome by structuring the alliance with its own board of directors and financial reporting system.

How does restructuring enhance shareholder value? We suggest four ways in which value can be created.

A thirst for joint ventures

The drinks industry has witnessed a number of strategic alliances in recent years.

Unilever, the Anglo-Dutch group, formed a joint venture with PepsiCo, the US soft drinks and snacks group, to sell canned ice tea. The attraction to Unilever was the opportunity to create a new business, building on the complementary strengths of PepsiCo as an industry leader and enabling it to enter the US market.

Scottish & Newcastle, a regional brewer, created a strategic alliance with Coors of the USA, specifically to market and promote Coors' Extra Gold premium lager in the UK. This joint venture offered Coors immediate, low-cost access to the UK market using a proven distribution network. For Scottish & Newcastle, the licensing and distribution agreement added a further brand to its range of premium lagers and a sharing of promotion costs.

Wessex Water, a UK privatised water company, entered a joint venture with Waste Management from the USA. Their objectives were somewhat different. While the US firm looked for access to a new geographical market, Wessex Water was looking to diversify from its price-regulated water business.

1. Business fit and focus

As we saw with divestments, a business unit may 'fit' one company better than another. Management should review its strategy (i.e. business units) and ask whether it operates best under its present ownership or whether it would create more value under some other ownership through an external acquisition or management buy-out. When unrelated activities have been divested, management has a much better focus on its core businesses and can concentrate on pursuing wealth-creating investment opportunities and improving efficiencies.

2. Eliminate sub-standard investment

Managers commonly enter into investments that do not enhance shareholder value:

1 Heavy reliance on a single business may lead to diversification. Quite apart from the additional overheads that may be created from diversification and the lack of managerial expertise, such diversification may have no real benefit for shareholders. As we saw in Chapters 10 and 11, shareholders can often achieve the same, or better, risk-reduction effects by creating diversified portfolios.
2 Pursuit of growth in sales and earnings brings power and, possibly, protection from takeover, but does little for shareholders. Rather than pay out larger dividends, management may be tempted to reinvest in projects or acquisitions that do not add value.
3 While a strategic business unit may be profitable, it is often an amalgamation of profitable and unprofitable projects, the former subsidising the latter. Restructuring the business creates a leaner operation with no room for cross-subsidisation.

3. Judicious use of debt

Cautious managers argue that borrowing should be minimised, as it increases financial risk and leaves little room for errors. Aggressive managers take a very different view.

Debt provides a powerful incentive to improve performance and minimise errors. The consequences of management's successes and mistakes are magnified through gearing, leaving little room for error. Managerial mediocrity is no longer acceptable. Cash flow – not profit – becomes the all-important yardstick, for it is cash flow that must be generated to service the debt and meet repayment schedules. In this respect, incurring debt obligations may provide an important signal to the market concerning the resolve of the management team.

Furthermore, debt is a cheaper source of finance because interest is tax-deductible, while dividends on equity are not. Restructuring the Balance Sheet by substituting debt for equity, within acceptable gearing limits, creates a tax shield and increases the company's market value.

4. Incentives

Raising debt to realise equity can be a powerful incentive to both shareholders and managers. Equity is concentrated in the hands of fewer shareholders, providing a greater incentive to monitor managerial actions. This often leads to the creation of managerial incentives to enhance shareholder value, through executive share options or profit-sharing schemes. Remuneration packages may increase profit-related pay at the expense of salaries and wages. This will also benefit loan stock holders, who have priority ahead of profit-sharing, but after employees' wages and salaries.

A 3-eyed venture capitalist

3i is way out in front as the UK's leading venture capital investment company, accounting for about one-fith of total UK venture capital investment. Its roots go back to 1929, when a report under the chairmanship of Lord Macmillan identified the 'Macmillan gap' – a shortage in the financing of small and medium-sized companies. Little was done, however, until 1945, when the Industrial and Commercial Finance Corporation, backed by the Bank of England, was created to bridge this gap. In 1973, it united with the Finance Corporation for Industry to form Investors in Industry, which later became simply 3i. It was floated on the stock market in 1994 in a £1.6 billion flotation, making it a FTSE Top 100 company.

During its long history, spanning over 50 years, it has provided more than £12 billion venture capital to over 12,000 small and medium-sized businesses, helping to bridge the finance gap experienced by small companies. Its biggest profit on a deal came from its investment in Caledonian Airways, which, when it was eventually acquired by British Airways, netted £100 million. But venture capital is a risky business, and 3i has had its share of failures, the largest of which was its investment in Isosceles, the company set up to mount a contested £2.4 billion management buy-in of the Gateway supermarket chain. The deal backfired, leaving 3i with £83 million debt and equity to write off. Many well known businesses, like Waterstones, Allders, Forte, Geest and Laura Ashley, have benefited from its financial backing.

Summary

We have explored various motives for merger and takeover activity, and have argued the importance of a coherently structured strategic approach to acquisitions, including planned integration that emphasises human and organisational factors. Finally, we briefly discussed other forms of corporate restructuring.

Key points

- The decision to acquire another company is an investment decision and requires evaluation on similar criteria to the purchase of other assets.
- Added complications are the resistance of incumbent managers to hostile bids and the presence of long-term strategic factors.
- The takeovers most likely to succeed are those approached with a strategic focus, incorporating a detailed analysis of the objectives of the takeover, the possible alternatives and how the acquired company can be integrated into the new parent.
- If the takeover mechanism works well, it is an effective and valuable way of clearing out managerial dead wood.
- Many takeovers appear to be launched for 'managerial' motives, such as personal and financial aggrandisement.
- The main reasons for failure of takeovers are poor motivation and evaluation, excessive outlays (often with borrowed capital) and poorly planned and executed integration.
- The complexity of takeover integration is related to the motive for the takeover itself, ranging from cash generation, requiring only a loose control over operations, to economies of scale, requiring highly detailed integration.
- The impact of mergers can be studied by comparing the financial characteristics of merger-active and merger-inactive firms to assess any performance differentials, but this approach suffers from many problems.
- The main alternative is a capital market-based approach to assess how the market judges a merger in terms of share price movements.
- The available evidence suggests that the bulk of the gains from mergers accrue to shareholders of acquired companies, although some evidence suggests that shareholders of acquirers can also share in the benefits, presumably if the takeover is well-considered.
- Corporate restructuring enhances shareholder value through (i) improving the business fit and focus, (ii) judicious use of debt and (iii) providing incentives for management.

Further reading

Cooke (1986) offers a primer on the various steps in takeover strategy from strategic evaluation to post-audit; similar ground is covered by Payne (1997). The two books by Jones (1982, 1983) are useful, both as general reference works and for analyses of the integration process. A treatment of the relative importance of different methods of takeover financing can be found in Franks and Harris (1989), while defences against takeover are examined by Gluck (1988) and Ruback (1988). Jensen (1984) analyses the validity of contemporary criticisms of the takeover mechanism. Gray and McDermott (1989) provide an interesting set of case studies of 'mega'-UK takeover battles: see especially BTR/Pilkington as an example of 'one that got away'.

The advantages of divestment and spin-offs are discussed in *Mastering Finance* (Pitman 1998).

For a summary of corporate restructuring and buy-outs in the UK and the rest of Europe, see Walters (1991) and Wright and Robbie (1991). The impact of corporate restructuring is discussed by Peel (1995).

Sudarsanam (1995) provides discussion of the theory and practice of takeovers and mergers.

The Office of Fair Trading publishes a guide to takeover regulation procedures in the UK.

Gregory's (1997) paper provides an excellent survey of both recent empirical evidence in this field and also of research methods used.

Self-assessment Answers

22.1 Managerial motives reduce to the three Ps – power, pay and prestige, all of which are enhanced by size of firm.

22.2 If managers are paid according to growth in EPS, a takeover that exploits synergies may enhance their bonuses. However, if financed by debt, the value of the firm could actually fall. Takeovers that aim to reduce risk rarely benefit shareholders for whom systematic risk is more relevant than total risk.

22.3 Cash is more certain, whereas the value of shares is volatile – by the time payment is made, the share value might have fallen. Investors wishing to liquidate the shares received will incur dealing fees.

22.4 The NPV of the bid for Predator's shareholders = (£1,000m + £200m + £50m) – (£1,000 + £230m) = £20m.
Prey's shareholders benefit by £30m (60 per cent of gains), and those of Predator by £20m (40 per cent), if the bid is completed at this price.

22.5 The strategic approach to takeover analysis and execution involves the following steps:

- Formulate corporate strategy.
- Assess the role of acquisition candidates in achieving that strategy.
- Screen, value and select from among possible candidates.
- Plan for future integration and/or disposals.
- Make informal approach.
- Announce hostile bid if necessary.
- Complete the deal.
- Integrate the acquisition following a detailed resource audit.
- Post-audit the acquisition and integration processes.

22.6 Takeovers fail to achieve the anticipated benefits due to:

- Managerial motivation rather than shareholder orientation.
- Inadequate evaluation of the target.

- Over-payment for the target.
- Failure to plan the integration process.
- Poor integration, e.g. neglect of the human factor.

22.7 There are many motives for divestment including:

1. Dismantling conglomerates originally created by merger activity through defensive diversification strategies. One result of the unsuccessful takeover attempt for BAT Industries was that this heavily diversified company was obliged to restructure by divesting a number of its activities.
2. A change in strategic focus. This may involve a move away from the core business to new strategic opportunities. Alternatively, a business may decide that it is engaged in too wide a range of activities and seek to concentrate its efforts and resources on a narrow range of core activities. Non-core activities will then be divested.
3. Harvesting past successes, making cash flow available for new opportunities.
4. Selling off unwanted businesses following an acquisition. This is called 'asset-stripping'. Such sell-offs are often planned at the time of the bid.
5. Reversing (or learning from) mistakes.

Questions

1 *Solution in Appendix A (page 835).* As treasurer of Holiday Ltd you are investigating the possible acquisition of Leisure Ltd. You have the following basic data:

	Holiday	**Leisure**
Earnings per share (expected next year)	£5	£1.50
Dividends per share (expected next year)	£3	£0.80
Number of shares	1 million	0.6 million
Share price	£90	£20

You estimate that investors currently expect a steady growth of about 6 per cent in Leisure's earnings and dividends. Under new management, this growth rate would be increased to 8 per cent per year, without any additional capital investment required.

Required

(a) What is the gain from the acquisition?

(b) What is the cost of the acquisition if Holiday pays £25 in cash for each Leisure share? Should it go ahead?

(c) What is the cost of the acquisition if Holiday offers one of its own shares for every three shares of Leisure? Should it go ahead?

(d) How would the cost of the cash offer and the share offer alter if the expected growth rate of Leisure were not changed by the takeover? Does it affect the decision?

2 The directors of Gross plc have made a 850p per share cash bid for Klinsmann plc, a company that is in a similar line of business. The summarised accounts of these two companies are as follows:

		Gross (£m)		Klinsmann (£m)
Sales (all credit)		216		110
Operating costs		(111)		(69)
Operating profit		105		41
Interest		(8)		(10)
Earnings before tax		97		31
Tax		(25)		(10)
Earnings for shareholders		72		21
Fixed assets		76		50
Current assets				
Stock	20		25	
Debtors	40		24	
Cash	8		1	
	68		50	
Current liabilities				
Creditors	(28)		(12)	
Bank overdraft	–		(8)	
	(28)		(20)	
Net current assets		40		30
Total assets less current liabilities		116		80
Long-term liabilities		(60)		(50)
Net assets		56		30
		116		80

Included in the amounts for operating costs for each company are the purchases made during this year – £100 million for Gross and £70 million for Klinsmann.

Details of the amount and market value of each company's shares are as follows:

	Gross	Klinsmann
No. of shares issued	100 m	20 m
Share price	600 p	700p

Required

Analyse this bid to include:

(a) Possible ways in which Gross may hope to recoup the bid premium when operating Klinsmann.

(b) The final and strategic effects on Gross if the bid is accepted by Klinsmann's shareholders.

3 Dangara plc is contemplating a takeover bid for another quoted company, Tefor plc. Both companies are in the leisure sector, operating a string of hotels,

restaurants and motorway service stations. Tefor's most recent Balance Sheet shows the following:

	£m	£m
Fixed assets (net)	800	
Current assets *less*		
Current liabilities	50	
Long-term debt		
(12% debenture 2002)	(200)	
		650
Issued share capital (25p units)	80	
Revenue reserves	420	
Revaluation reserve	150	
		650

Tefor has just reported full-year profits of £200m after tax.

You are provided with the following further information:

(a) Dangara's shareholders require a return of 14 per cent.

(b) Dangara would have to divest certain of Tefor's assets, mainly motorway service stations, to satisfy the competition authorities. These assets have a book value of £100 million, but Dangara thinks they could be sold on to Lucky Break plc for £200 million.

(c) Tefor's assets were last revalued in 1992, at the bottom of the property market slump.

(d) Dangara's P:E ratio is 14:1, Tefor's is 10:1.

(e) Tefor's earnings have risen by only 2 per cent p.a. on average over the previous five years, while Dangara's have risen by 7 per cent p.a. on average.

(f) Takeover premiums (i.e. amount paid in excess of pre-bid market values) have recently averaged 20 per cent across all market sectors.

(g) Many 'experts' believe that a stock market 'correction' is imminent, due to the likelihood of a new government, led by Bony Clair, being elected. The new government would possibly adopt a more stringent policy on competition issues.

(h) If a bid is made, there is a possibility that the Chairman of Tefor will make a counter-offer to its shareholders to attempt to take the company off the Stock Exchange.

(i) If the bid succeeds, Tefor's ex-chairman is expected to offer to repurchase a major part of the hotel portfolio.

(j) Much of Tefor's hotel asset portfolio is rather shabby and requires refurbishments, estimated to cost some £50 million p.a. for the next five years.

Required

As strategic planning analyst, you are instructed to prepare a briefing report for the main board, which:

(i) assesses the appropriate value to place on Tefor, using suitable valuation techniques. (State clearly any assumptions you make.)

(ii) examines the issues to be addressed in deciding whether to bid for Tefor at this juncture.

4 Larkin Conglomerates plc owns a subsidiary company, Hughes Ltd, which sells office equipment. Recently, Larkin Conglomerates plc has been reconsidering its future strategy and has decided that Hughes Ltd should be sold off. The proposed divestment of Hughes Ltd has attracted considerable interest from other companies wishing to acquire this type of business.

The most recent accounts of Hughes Ltd are as follows:

Balance Sheet as at 31 May 1995

	£000	£000	£000
Fixed assets			
Freehold premises at cost		240	
Less Accumulated depreciation		(40)	200
Motor vans at cost		32	
Less Accumulated depreciation		(21)	11
Fixtures and fittings at cost		10	
Less Accumulated depreciation		(2)	8
			219
Current assets		34	
Stock at cost		22	
Debtors		20	
Cash at bank		76	
Creditors: amounts falling due within one year			
Trade creditors	(52)		
Accrued expenses	(14)	(66)	10
			229
Creditors: amounts falling due beyond one year			
12% Loan – Cirencester Bank			(100)
			129
Capital and reserves			
£1 ordinary shares			60
General reserve			14
Retained profit			55
			129

Profit and Loss Account for the year ended 31 May 1995

	£000
Sales turnover	352.0
Profit before interest and taxation	34.8
Interest charges	(12.0)
Profit before taxation	22.8
Corporation tax	(6.4)
Profit after taxation	16.4
Dividend proposed and paid	(4.0)
	12.4
Transfer to general reserve	(3.0)
Retained profit for the year	9.4

The subsidiary has shown a stable level of sales and profits over the past three years. An independent valuer has estimated the current realisable values of the assets of the company as follows:

	£000
Freehold premises	235
Motor vans	8
Fixtures and fittings	5
Stock	36

For the remaining assets, the Balance Sheet values were considered to reflect their current realisable values.

Another company in the same line of business, which is listed on the Stock Exchange, has a gross dividend yield of 5 per cent and a price:earnings ratio of 12.

Assume a standard rate of income tax of 25 per cent.

Required

(a) Calculate the value of an ordinary share in Hughes Ltd using the following methods:
  (i) net assets (liquidation) basis
  (ii) dividend yield
  (iii) price:earnings ratio

(b) Briefly evaluate each of the share valuation methods used above.

(c) Identify and discuss four reasons why a company may undertake divestment of part of its business.

(d) Briefly state what other information, besides the information provided above, would be useful to prospective buyers in deciding on a suitable value to place on the shares of Hughes Ltd.

5 The directors of Fama Industries plc are currently considering the acquisition of Beaver plc as part of its expansion programme. Fama Industries plc has interests in machine tools and light engineering while Beaver plc is involved in magazine publishing. The following financial data concerning each company is available:

Profit and Loss Accounts for the year ended 30 November 1995

	Fama Industries £m	Beaver £m
Sales turnover	465	289
Profit before interest and taxation	114	43
Interest payable	(5)	(9)
Profit before taxation	109	34
Taxation	(26)	9
Net profit after taxation	83	25
Dividends	(8)	(12)
Retained profit for the year	75	13

Balance Sheets as at 30 November 1995

	Fama Industries £m	Beaver £m
Fixed assets	105	84
Net current assets	86	38
	191	122

Continued

	Fama Industries	Beaver
	£m	£m
Less creditors due beyond one year	(38)	(58)
	153	64
Capital and reserves		
Ordinary shares	50	30
Retained profit	103	34
	153	64
Price:earnings ratio prior to bid	16	12

The ordinary share capital of Fama Industries plc consists of 50p shares and the share capital of Beaver plc consists of £1 shares. The directors of Fama Industries plc have made an offer of four shares for every five shares held in Beaver plc.

The directors of Fama Industries plc believe that combining the two businesses will lead to after-tax savings in overheads of £4 million per year.

Required

(a) Calculate:

  (i) the total value of the proposed bid

  (ii) the earnings per share for Fama Industries plc following the successful takeover of Beaver plc

  (iii) the share price of Fama Industries plc following the takeover, assuming that the price:earning ratio is maintained and the savings are achieved.

(b) Comment on the value of the bid from the viewpoint of shareholders of both Fama Industries plc and Beaver plc.

(c) Identify, and briefly discuss, two reasons why the managers of a company may wish to take over another company. The reasons identified should not be related to the objective of maximising shareholder wealth.

6 Europium plc is a large conglomerate which is seeking to acquire other companies. The Business Development division of Europium plc has recently identified an engineering company – Promithium plc – as a possible acquisition target.

Financial information relating to each company is given below:

Profit and Loss Account for the year ended 30 November 1997

	Europium plc	Promithium plc
Turnover	820	260
Profit on ordinary activities before tax	87	33
Taxation on profit on ordinary activities	(27)	(9)
Profit on ordinary activities after tax	60	24
Dividends	(15)	(5)
Retained profit for the year	45	19
Price:earnings ratio	16	10
Capital and reserves		
£1 ordinary shares	80	30
Retained profits	195	124
	275	154

The Business Development division of Europium plc believes that shares of Promithium plc can be acquired by offering its shareholders a premium of 25 per cent above the existing share price. The purchase consideration will be in the form of shares in Europium plc.

Required

(a) Calculate the rate of exchange for the shares and the number of shares of Europium plc which must be issued at the anticipated price in order to acquire all the shares of Promithium plc.

(b) Suggest reasons why Europium plc may be prepared to pay a premium above the current market value to acquire the shares of Promithium plc.

(c) Calculate the market value per share of Europium plc following the successful takeover and assuming the P:E ratio of Europium plc stays at the pre-takeover level. Would you expect the P:E ratio of Europium plc to stay the same?

(d) State what investigations Europium plc should undertake before considering a takeover of Promithium plc.

7 *Solution in Appendix A (page 836)*. As a defence against a possible takeover bid the managing director proposes that Woppit make a bid for Grapper plc, in order to increase Woppit's size and, hence, make a bid for Woppit more difficult. The companies are in the same industry.

Woppit's equity Beta is 1.2 and Grapper's is 1.05. The risk-free rate and market return are estimated to be 10 and 16 per cent p.a. respectively. The growth rate of after-tax earnings of Woppit in recent years has been 15 per cent p.a. and of Grapper 12 per cent p.a. Both companies maintain an approximately constant dividend payout ratio.

Woppit's directors require information about how much premium above the current market price to offer for Grapper's shares. Two suggestions are:

(i) The price should be based upon the Balance Sheet net worth of the company, adjusted for the current value of land and buildings, plus estimated after tax profits for the next five years.

(ii) The price should be based upon a valuation using the Dividend Valuation Model, using existing growth rate estimates.

Summarised financial data for the two companies are shown below:

Most recent Balance Sheets (£m)

		Woppit		Grapper
Land and buildings (net)[a]		560		150
Plant and machinery (net)		720		280
Stock	340		240	
Debtors	300		210	
Bank	20	660	40	490
Less: Trade creditors	(200)		(110)	
Overdraft	(30)		(10)	
Tax payable	(120)		(40)	
Dividends payable	(50)	(400)	(40)	(200)
Total assets *less* current liabilities		1,540		720
Financed by:				
Ordinary shares[b]		200		100

Continued

	Woppit	Grapper
Share premium	420	220
Other reserves	400	300
	1,020	620
Loans due after one year	520	100
	1,540	720

[a]Woppit's land and buildings have been recently revalued. Grapper's have not been revalued for four years, during which time the average value of industrial land and buildings has increased by 25 per cent p.a.
[b]Woppit 10p par value, Grapper 25p par value

Most recent Profit and Loss Accounts (£m)

	Woppit	Grapper
Turnover	3,500	1,540
Operating profit	700	255
Net interest	(120)	(22)
Taxable profit	580	233
Taxation	(203)	(82)
Profit attributable to shareholders	377	151
Dividends	(113)	(76)
Retained profit	264	75

The current share price of Woppit is 310 pence and of Grapper 470 pence.

Required

(a) Calculate the premium per share above Grapper's current share price that would result from the two suggested valuation methods. Discuss which, if either, of these values should be the bid price. State clearly any assumptions that you make.
(b) Assess the managing director's strategy of seeking growth by acquisition in order to make a bid for Woppit more difficult.
(c) Illustrate how Woppit might achieve benefits through improvements in operational efficiency if it acquires Grapper. (ACCA)

Practical assignment

Select one of the merger/takeover situations that has been given prominence recently in the media. Analyse your selected case under the following headings (indicative guidelines are provided).

1 *Strategy* – How does the 'victim' appear to fit into the acquiror's long-term strategy?
2 *Valuation and bid tactics* – Has the acquirer bid or paid 'over the odds'? Should it have done? What were the pros and cons of the financing package?
3 *Defence tactics* – Were the tactics employed sensible ones? Were the managers of the target company genuinely resisting or simply seeking to squeeze out a higher offer?
4 *Impact* – Will the acquired company be difficult to integrate? Are any sell-offs likely?

Appendix A: Solutions to selected questions

Chapter 1

1 The goal of maximising owners' wealth is the normally accepted economic objective for resource allocation decisions. Rather than concentrate on the organisation, it evaluates investments from the viewpoint of the organisation's owners – usually shareholders. Any investment that increases their stock of wealth (the present value of future cash flows) is economically acceptable.

In practice, many of the assumptions underlying this goal do not always hold (e.g. shareholders are only interested in maximising the market value of their shareholdings). In addition, owners are often far removed from managerial decision-making, where capital investment takes place. Accordingly, it is common to find that more easily measurable criteria are used, such as profitability and growth goals. There are also non-economic considerations, such as employee welfare and managerial satisfaction, which can be important for some decisions.

Chapter 2

2 (c) (i) *For the cash offer*

On Day 1, the total value of each firm is:

A: £2 × 2 m shares = £4 m
B: £3 × 6 m shares = £18 m

Company B is making an offer of £6 m for Company A which is apparently worth only £4 million – this will reduce the market value of B by £2 million to £16 million or £16 million/6 = £2.67 per share. Against this, the anticipated savings would raise B's value to (£16 m + £3.2 m) = £19.2 m or £3.20 per share (assuming the market accepts this assessment).

1 Semi-strong form efficiency

Under semi-strong form efficiency, the market prices will only react when the information about the bid enters the public domain. The advent of new information will produce the following share prices:

		Share price	
		A	**B**
Day 2	No new information	£2.00	£3.00
Day 4	Takeover bid announced. B appears to be paying £6m for assets worth £4 m	£3.00	£2.67
Day 10	Information available which revises the market value of B	£3.00	£3.20

2 Strong form efficiency

If the market is strong form efficient, all information is reflected in the share price even if it is not publicly available information. This will mean that on Day 2, when the management of B decides to offer £3.00 for A, the share prices will then react to reflect the full impact of the bid on both shares, perhaps via leakage of information by an informed insider. This will produce the following share prices:

		Share price	
		A	**B**
Day 2	Full impact of decision to bid and make savings reflected in share price	£3.00	£3.20
Day 4	Public announcement of bid, i.e. information of which the market is aware and therefore has no new information content	£3.00	£3.20
Day 10	Public announcement of savings to be derived from bid, i.e. further information of which the market is aware and therefore has no new information content	£3.00	£3.20

(ii) *For the share exchange*

Prior to the bid, the combined value of the two companies is (£4 m + £18 m) = £22 m. If a share-for-share exchange were made on a one-for-one basis, the value per share of the expanded company would become £22 m/8 m = £2.75 m, until further information about prospective savings emerged. Under semi-strong form efficiency, this will not happen until Day 10, but will leak out on to the market immediately under strong form efficiency. Spread over the whole 8 m shares, the savings are worth £3.2/8 m = £0.40 per share.

The sequence of share price movements is thus:

	Level of efficiency			
	Semi-strong		Strong	
	A	B	A	B
Day 2	£2	£3	£3.15	£3.15
Day 4	£2.75	£2.75	£3.15	£3.15
Day 10	£3.15	£3.15	£3.15	£3.15

Notice that the ultimate share price under the share exchange is lower than for the cash offer. This is because the benefits of the merger are spread out over a larger number of shares post-bid. In effect, the shareholders of B will have released part of the benefit they expect to receive from the bid to the former shareholders of A.

Chapter 3

1 Accounting profit is the excess of income over expenditure. Income and expenses relate to a specific period (e.g. the sales and costs for the month of January) based on accounting conventions such as depreciation. Cash flow is the cash receipts and payments from all operations including capital investment.

2 Using the table in Appendix C, the annuity factor for ten years and i = 20% is 4.1925:

PV = £100 × 4.1925 = £419.25

3

Savings:	£500,000 × 3.7908	£18,954
Residual value:	£1,000 × 0.62092	£621
		£19,575
Less: initial cost:		(£20,000)
NPV		£(425)

The NPV is negative. Recommend the project is rejected.

4 **(a)** The firm should invest £6,000 − £4,000 = £2,000.
(b) Market rate of interest = £10,000/£80,000 = 1.25, i.e. 25%
(c) Average return on investment = (£5,000/£2,000) × 100 = 250%.
(d) Present value of an investment of £2,000 = £5,000/1.25 = £4,000.
NPV = £4,000 − £2,000 = £2,000.
(e) Value of firm after investment = £6,000 + £2,000 = £8,000.
(f) If a dividend of £3,000 is paid now, a further £1,000 will be invested on the capital market (there being no internal projects offering a better return). This will give cash next year of £1,000 × 1.25 = £1,250 from external investment plus £5,000 from internal investment, a total dividend of £6,250.

Students should be aware of the assumptions for the two-period investment model:

(i) Only the present and subsequent periods are considered.
(ii) Investors are wealth-maximisers.
(iii) All decision-relevant information is known with certainty.
(iv) Investment projects are entirely independent of each other and are divisible.
(v) No capital markets.
(vi) The firm is owner-managed.

Chapter 4

3 Free cash flow (£) = Revenue less bad debts less operating costs + depreciation less replacement investment less tax (allowing for relief on bad debts)
= (0.98 × 500,000) − (300,000) + (50,000) − (50,000) − (60,000 + [0.3 × 50% × 2% × 500,000])
= (490,000 − 300,000 + 50,000 − 50,000 − 60,000 + 1,500)
= £131,500

(a) valued @ 10% as a perpetuity:

V = (£131,500/0.1) = £1.315 million
i.e. (£1.315 m/2 m) = £0.6575 per share (65.75p)

(b) valued over 10 years:

V = (£131,500 × ten year annuity factor @ 10%)
= (£131,500 × 6.1446) = £808,015 m, or £0.405 per share (40.5p).

4 Free cash flow per share = (£5 m/10 m) = £0.50 or 50p

(i) P_o = (£0.5/0.12) = £4.17

(ii) $P_o = \dfrac{50\% \times 50\text{p}\ (1 + [15\% \times 50\%])}{12\% - [15\% \times 50\%]} = \dfrac{26.88\text{p}}{0.045} = £5.97$

(iii) $P_o = \dfrac{50\% \times 50\text{p}\ (1 + [10\% \times 50\%])}{12\% - [10\% \times 50\%]} = \dfrac{26.25\text{p}}{0.07} = £3.75$

(iv) Present value of dividends over years 1–3:

Year 1 Dividend = 26.88p, as per part (ii) PV @ 12% = £0.239
Year 2 Dividend = 26.88p (1.075) = 28.89p PV @ 12% = £0.230
Year 3 Dividend = 28.89p (1.075) = 31.05p PV @ 12% = £0.221
PV of dividends beyond year 3:

$= \dfrac{31.05\text{p}\ (1.05)}{(12\% - 5\%)} \times \text{(3 year PV factor)}$
= (£4.657 × 0.7118) = £3.315
Share price = Total PV = £4.005

5 **(i)** £0.37955
(ii) (0.6 × 16%) = 9.6%

(iii) £0.65.
(iv) £0.20.
(v) $b = g/R = (2\%/10\%) = 20\%$
(vi) $k_e = (D_1/P_o) + g) = (£0.054/£0.60) + 8\% = 17\%$

As $g = 10.5\%$, and
$b = 0.7$,

$$R = \frac{g}{b} = \frac{0.105}{0.7} = 15\%$$

(vii) 15%

Chapter 5

1 *Microtic Ltd*

	Project A (£)		Project B (£)
1 *Payback period*			
Outlay/annual flow	1,616/500		556/200
	= 3.2 years		= 2.8 years
2 *Net present value (15%)*			
Annual cash flow			
five years			
£500 × 3.352	1,676,000	200 × 3.352	670,400
Scrap value			
£301 × 0.497	149,600	56 × 0.497	27,800
Outlay	(1,616,000)		(556,000)
NPV	209,600		142,200
3 *Internal rate of return*			
(use trial and error to			
obtain NPV of zero)	try 20%		try 25%
Annual cash flow			
500 × 2,991	1,495,500	200 × 2,689	537,800
Scrap value 301 × 0.402	121,000	56 × 0.328	18,400
Outlay	(1,616,000)		(556,000)
NPV	500		200
4 *Accounting rate of return*			
Average profit before			
depreciation	500,000		200,000
Depreciation (1616 – 301)/5	(263,000)	(556 – 56)/5	(100,000)
	237,000		100,000
Average capital employed			
(1616 + 301)/2	958,500	(556 + 56)/2	306,000
Rate	24.7%		32.7%

Investment advice

All appraisal methods apart from the NPV approach recommend acceptance of Project B. This is because it generates a higher return for every £1 invested. The question is, however, which of the two projects creates most wealth for the owners. Clearly, the much larger Project A has the higher NPV.

Unless the firm is experiencing severe capital rationing problems, Project A should be accepted.

2 **Mace Ltd (£000)**

Project	NPV per £ outlay	Ranking	Fraction accepted	Required capital (£)	NPV (£)
1	1.6/60 = 0.027	4	0	–	–
2	1.3/30 = 0.043	3	1/3	10	0.43
3	8.3/40 = 0.207	1	1	40	8.3
4				0	0.9
5	7.9/50 = 0.158	2	1	50	7.9
				100	17.53

Chapter 6

1 The preference for IRR in practice is because:
(a) It is easier to understand (this is debatable).
(b) It is useful in ranking projects (although not always accurate).
(c) Lower-level managers do not need to know the discount rate. Where a risk-adjusted hurdle rate is used, there may be considerable negotiation over the appropriate rate.
(d) Psychological. Managers prefer a percentage.

2 **(a)** Payback = four years. The reciprocal is 25 per cent which is the IRR for a project of infinite life.
(b) For a 20-year life, IRR = 24%. For an eight-year life, IRR = 19%.
(c) The annual cash flows are approximately the same for a long-lived project, the payback reciprocal is a reasonable proxy for the IRR. The actual IRR is always something less than that given by the payback reciprocal.

4 The two basic approaches in handling inflation are:
(a) forecast cash flows in money terms (i.e. including inflation) and discount at the money cost of capital; or
(b) forecast cash flows in current terms and discount at the real cost of capital.

The relationship between the two is given by:

$$(1 + P) = \frac{(1 + M)}{1 + I}$$

where M is the money cost of capital, I is the inflation rate and P is the real cost of capital.

5 **Bramhope Manufacturing**

(i) (a) Additional investment: £123,500 − £15,000 = £108,500. Additional annual inflow = £24,300 (see below). Therefore payback period = £108,500/£24,300 = 4.5 years.

(b)

Time	Cash flow (£)	DF at 15%	PV (£)	DF at 17%	PV (£)
0	(108,500)	1	(108,500)	1	(108,500)
1–8	24,300	4.48732	109,042	4.20716	102,234
8	20,500	0.32690	6,701	0.28478	5,838
			7,243		(428)

(c) NPV AT 15% = £7,243; IRR = approx. 17%.

Workings: Existing project's annual cash inflow
= £200,000 × (0.95 − 0.12 − 0.48) = £70,000.

Net project's annual cash inflow
= £230,000 × (0.95 − 0.08 − 0.46) = £94,300.

Incremental cash flow = £94,300 − £70,000 = £24,300.

(ii) The project appears to offer a positive net present value and should be accepted. However, an NPV of £7,000 on a project costing £123,500 is relatively small, and questions should be asked as to how sensitive the key assumptions are to uncertainty. For example, is it realistic that the additional capacity can be sold at the current price? Will there really be no increase in fixed overheads? If an advanced machine has been developed after just two years, is an eight-year economic life optimistic?

Chapter 7

1 Capital budgeting involves the whole investment process from the original idea to the final post-audit.

The resource allocation process is the main vehicle by which business strategy can be implemented. Investment decisions are not simply the result of applying some evaluation criterion. The investment decision process is essentially one of search: search for ideas, search for information, search for alternatives and search for decision criteria. The prosperity of a firm depends more on its ability to create profitable investment opportunities than on its ability to appraise them.

Once a firm commits itself to a particular project, it must regularly and systematically monitor and control the project through its various stages of implementation. Post-audit reviews – if properly designed – fulfil a useful role in improving the quality of existing and future investment analysis and provide a means of initiating corrective action for existing projects.

2 Aims of post-audits:

(a) improve the quality of existing decisions and underlying assumptions
(b) improve the quality of future decisions
(c) basis for corrective action

3 (a)

	Total automation £ per unit	Partial automation £ per unit
Sales price	75	75
Variable cost	(30)	(55)
Contribution	45	20
Fixed cost (see note 1)	(18)	(5)
Net profit	27	15
Total cost per unit	£48	£60
Annual net profit	£270,000	£150,000
Break-even units (p/a)	4,000	2,500
Net present value:		
	Cash flow £	**Cash flow £**
Outlay	−1,000,000	−250,000
Inflows years 1–5	+450,000	+200,000
Scrap value year 5	+100,000	–
	Present value £	Present value £
Outlay	−1,000,000	−250,000
Inflows at 3.27	+1,471,500	+654,000
Scrap value at 0.48	+48,000	–
Net present value	+519,500	+404,000

Note 1 $\frac{(1{,}000{,}000 - 100{,}000)}{5 \times 10{,}000}$ $\frac{(250{,}000)}{5 \times 10{,}000}$

(b) The total automation option produces a lower product cost. As the sales price and volume are identical for both alternatives a higher annual profit is also reported by this alternative. Partial automation involves lower fixed costs (depreciation), but variable costs are substantially greater. With the cost pattern above, the total automation alternative results in a higher break-even point.

Remember that there is a higher initial capital cost with total automation. The accrual accounting assumptions applied above acknowledge this with an annual charge for depreciation. The net present value technique takes account of the capital cost in a different manner, charging the full cost immediately against discounted future cash flows. In this case, total automation generates a higher NPV but a higher initial outlay.

When the amount of the initial capital investment is considered, the option to undertake partial automation looks attractive. It achieves a net present value of 80 per cent of total automation with only one quarter of the capital expenditure. Partial automation shows a profitability index of 2.62, compared with 1.52 for the total automation, which emphasises the attractiveness of the lower investment. The recommendation of the NPV technique must, however, be interpreted with care and considered in the light of the overall company situation. Investment in total automation is the course of action which will maximise the wealth of the owners (the extra benefit exceeds the extra capital cost at 16 per cent). If the company is not in a capital-constrained situation then total automation should be pursued. If the company has a number of projects, all competing for limited capital, then we would need to know the return from the other investment opportunities and compare them with the incremental investment being directed to total automation.

The data omit certain other factors which may be pertinent to the analysis, for example, quality differences, maximum machine capacities, maximum sales demand, the flexibility and interchangeability of parts and equipment which may be beneficial.

For a lower risk investment with an attractive return, the company should opt for partial automation. If they have extra capital available, electing for total automation of the product line will earn above their extra cost of capital but nothing is known about other projects competing for this extra capital.

Chapter 8

1 In this question, we need to show that the receipts in sterling after adjusting for inflation at both locations remains unchanged.
Current exchange rate = $US 1.50 against £1.
Sterling equivalent of US revenue = $150 m/1.50 = £100 m

Exchange rate	$ revenue	£ revenue	£ revenue (real terms)
(i) 1.05/1.05 × 1.50 = $1.50:£1	$157.5 m	£105 m	£105 m/1.05 = £100 m
(ii) 1.02/1.05 × 1.50 = £1.457:£1	$153 m	£105 m	£105 m/1.05 = £100 m
(iii) 1.05/1.02 × 1.50 = £1.544:£1	$157.5 m	£102 m	£102 m/1.02 = £100 m

2 (a) (i) With exchange controls:

Year	PAT (SA$000)	OJ share (SA$000)	50% div (SA$000)	Sterling (£000)	PV @ 16% (£000)
0	–	–	–	(450)	(450)
1	4,250	2,125	1,062	106	91
2	6,500	3,250	1,625	108	80
3	8,350	4,175	2,088	100	64
			4,775 (balance)	277	146
					NPV = (69)

In this scenario, OJ should reject the project.

(ii) No exchange control:

Year	PAT (SA$000)	OJ share (SA$000)	Sterling (£000)	PV @ 16% (£000)
0	–	–	(450)	(450)
1	4,250	2,125	212	183
2	6,500	3,250	217	161
3	8,350	4,175	199	127
				NPV = +21

In this scenario, the positive NPV indicates acceptance, but the project is marginal e.g. the Profitability Index (NPV/Outlay = 21/450) is only 0.047. Given the risk of exchange controls being imposed, this suggests that OJ should treat the project with great caution.

3 PG plc

Year	0	1	2	3	4
Method 1					
C$ Initial investment	(150,000)				50,000
Other cash flows		60,000	60,000	60,000	45,000
Net cash flows	(150,000)	60,000	60,000	60,000	95,000
C$ per £1	1.700	1.785	1.874	1.968	2.066
Sterling	(88,235)	33,613	32,017	30,488	45,983
DF @ 14%	1.000	0.877	0.769	0.675	0.592
PV	(88,235)	29,479	24,621	20,579	27,222
NPV = £13,666					
Method 2					
C$ net cash flows	(150,000)	60,000	60,000	60,000	95,000
DF @ 19.7%	1.000	0.835	0.698	0.583	0.487
C$	(150,000)	50,100	41,888	34,980	46,265
£ PV @ 1.7	(88,235)	29,479	24,621	20,579	27,222
NPV = 13,666					

For the two approaches to generate the same answer, the discount rate applied to the C$ cash flows must be the combination of the sterling discount rate (14 per cent) and the expected strengthening of sterling, according to PPP. This yields:

$$(1.14 \times 1.05) - 1 = (1.197 - 1) = 0.197, \quad \text{i.e } 19.7\%$$

A forecast 5 per cent appreciation of sterling against the C$ will be associated with UK inflation rates being 5 per cent less than the rate experienced in Canada. In practice, one might inflate the cash flows in C$ to reflect inflation internal to the Canadian economy.

6 Palmerston plc

Forecast Cash Flow Statement (£m)

Euros per £1	1.65	1.60	1.55
Sales			
UK	200	210	220
Germany	**182**	**188**	**194**
Total	382	398	414
Cost of Goods Sold:			
UK	(120)	(120)	(120)
Germany	(121)	(125)	(129)
Total	(241)	(245)	(249)
Gross Profit	141	153	165

Operating Expenses:			
UK – fixed	(50)	(50)	(50)
UK – variable (20% of total sales)	(76)	(80)	(83)
Total	(126)	(130)	(133)
Net Cash Flow	15	23	32
Firm value @ 15%:	(15 × 5.019*)	(23 × 5.019)	(32 × 5.019)
*Annuity factor	= £75.3 m	= £115.4 m	= £160.61

The analysis suggests that Palmerston benefits from a strong euro and *vice versa*. It could further reduce its exposure by shifting its cost base to Germany, or elsewhere in the euro area, preferably to a low cost location, say, Greece or Portugal.

Chapter 9

1 While a capital project may have a high expected return, the risks involved may mean that there is the possibility that the project will be unsuccessful – even to the extent of putting the whole business in jeopardy.

2 Project risk – variability in the projects' cash flows; business risk – variability in operating earnings of the firm; financial risk – risk resulting from the firm's financing decisions, e.g. the level of borrowing.

3 **Woodpulp project**

Year	CE	NCF(£)	ENCF(£)	10% DF	PV(£)
1	0.90	8,000	7,200	0.90	6,480
2	0.85	7,000	5,959	0.83	4,938
3	0.80	7,000	5,600	0.75	4,200
4	0.75	5,000	3,750	0.68	2,550
5	0.70	5,000	3,500	0.62	2,170
6	0.65	5,000	3,250	0.56	1,820
7	0.60	5,000	3,000	0.51	1,530
				PV	23,688

NPV = £23,688 – £13,000 = £10,688. Accept the project. ENCF = Expected net cash flow.

4 **Mystery Enterprises**

Expected value Year (1) (£) $= 0.2(400) + 0.3(500) + 0.3(600) + 0.2(700) = £550$

Variance (£) $= 0.2(400 - 550)^2 + 0.3(500 - 550)^2 + 0.3(600 - 550)^2 + 0.2(700 - 550)^2 = £10,500$

Standard deviation = £102

Expected value Year 2 (£) $= 0.2(300) + 0.3(400) + 0.3(500) + 0.2(600) = £450$

Variance(£) $= 0.2(300 - 450)^2 + 0.3(400 - 450)^2 + 0.3(500 - 450)^2 + 0.2(600 - 450)^2 = £10,500$

Standard deviation = £102

Assuming a discount rate of 10 per cent and independent cash flows:

$$\text{NPV} = \frac{£550}{1.1} + \frac{£450}{(1.1)^2} - £800 = £71$$

$$\text{SD} = \sqrt{\frac{(£102)^2}{(1.1)^2} + \frac{(£102)^2}{(1.1)^4}} = £125$$

$$\text{Coefficient of variation} = \frac{£125}{£71} = 1.76$$

Chapter 10

1 Portfolio standard deviation

$$\begin{aligned} &= \sqrt{[(0.5)^2\sigma_x^2 + (0.5)^2\sigma_y^2 + 2(0.5)(0.5)(r_{xy}\sigma_x\sigma_y)]} \\ &= \sqrt{[(0.5)^2 30^2 + (0.5)^2 45^2 + 2(0.5)(0.5)(0.2)(30)(45)]} \\ &= \sqrt{[225 + 506.25 + 135]} \\ &= \sqrt{866.25} = 29.4 \end{aligned}$$

This portfolio has a risk only slightly below that of investment X, even though the correlation coefficient is quite low. This suggests that the portfolio weighting involves too little of investment X if the intention is to lower portfolio risk.

2 The appropriate formula is:

$$\text{Proportion invested in asset } A = \frac{\sigma_B^2 - \text{cov}_{AB}}{\sigma_B^2 + \sigma_A^2 - 2\text{cov}_{AB}}$$

Also, remember that $\text{cov}_{AB} = r_{AB}\sigma_A\sigma_B$.

- **(i)** The covariance = +21. Note that the 'nonsense' answer appears to give the proportion invested in A in excess of 1. This reflects the indeterminacy of the formula when correlation is perfectly positive.
- **(ii)** The covariance is −36; 29% in A, 71% in B.
- **(iii)** The covariance is −105; 32% in A, 68% in B.
- **(iv)** The covariance is zero; 18% in A, 82% in B.

3 **(a) China**:

Expected value = (0.3 × 50%) + (0.4 × 25%) + (0.3 × 0) = 25%

Growth	Probability	IRR%	Deviation	Squared deviation	Times probability
Rapid	0.3	50	25	625	187.50
Stable	0.4	25	–	–	–
Slow	0.3	0	−25	625	187.50
					Sum = 375.00

Standard deviation = $\sqrt{375.0}$ = 19.4, i.e. 19.4%

Scotland:
Expected value = (0.3 × 10%) + (0.4 × 15%) + (0.3 × 16%) = 13.8%

Growth	Probability	IRR%	Deviation	Squared deviation	Times probability
Rapid	0.3	10	−3.8	14.44	4.33
Stable	0.4	15	1.2	1.44	0.58
Slow	0.3	16	2.2	4.84	1.45
					Sum = 6.36

Standard deviation = $\sqrt{6.36} = 2.5\%$

(b) Covariance calculation:

Covariance = −45

Expected portfolio return
$= (0.75 \times 13.8\%) + (0.25 \times 25\%) = 22.2\%$

Standard deviation

$$= \sqrt{[(0.25^2 \times 19.4^2) + (0.75^2 \times 2.5^2) + (2 \times 0.25 \times 0.75 \times -45)]}$$
$$= \sqrt{[(23.5) + (35.2) + (-16.9)]}$$
$$= \sqrt{41.8} = 6.5, \quad \text{i.e. } 6.5\%$$

4 (a) *Eire*: EV of IRR = $(0.3 \times 20\%) + (0.3 \times 10\%) + (0.4 \times 15\%)$
$= 6\% + 3\% + 6\% = 15\%$

Outcome (%)	Deviation	Sq'd Dev.	p	Sq'd Dev. × p
20	+5	25	0.3	7.5
10	−5	25	0.3	7.5
15	0	0	0.4	0
			Variance = Total	15 σ = 3.87

Humberside: EV of IRR = $(0.3 \times 10\%) + (0.3 \times 30\%) + (0.4 \times 20\%)$
$= 3\% + 9\% + 8\% = 20\%$

Outcome (%)	Deviation	Sq'd Dev.	p	Sq'd Dev. × p
10	−10	100	0.3	30
30	+10	100	0.3	30
20	0	0	0.4	0
			Variance = Total	60 σ = 7.75

(b) (i) For a 50/50 split investment:

EV of IRR = $(0.5 \times 15\%) + (0.5 \times 20\%) = 17.5\%$

$$\sigma = \sqrt{(0.5)^2(15) + (0.5)^2(60) + 2(0.5)(0.5)0.(3.87)(7.75)}$$
$$= \sqrt{[3.75 + 15]} = \sqrt{18.75} = 4.33$$

(ii) 75/25 split:

$$EV = (0.75 \times 15\%) + (0.25 \times 20\%) = 11.25\% + 5\% = 16.25\%$$
$$\sigma = \sqrt{(0.75)^2(15) + (0.25)^2(60)}$$
$$= \sqrt{[8.44 + 3.75]} = \sqrt{12.19} = 3.49\text{, i.e. lower risk than either project}$$

Chapter 11

1 Expected return = 5% + 1.23[11.5% − 5%] = 13%.
With more pessimistic expectations about market returns, this drops to:

ER = 5% + 1.23[8% − 5%] = 8.7%

2 **(i)** R_f = 9%
(ii) Beta = 1.71
(iii) ER_j = 8.5%
(iv) ER_m = 19.3%

3 The intercept of the Security Market Line is the risk-free rate. It passes through the market portfolio which has a Beta of 1.0. In diagrammatic terms:

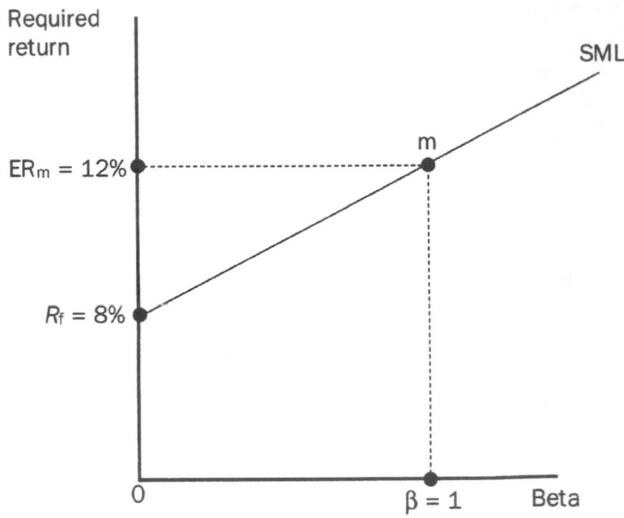

4 ER_A = 5% + 0.7[10% − 5%] = 8.5%
ER_B = 5% + 1.3[5%] = 11.5%
ER_C = 5% + 0.9[5%] = 9.5%

Comparing the expected returns with those currently achieved, A and C generate returns lower than expected, which suggests they are overvalued. (B looks undervalued).

5 **(i)** Projecting past returns into the future, the expected return on the whole market is (5% + 7%) = 12%.
(iii) For a 50/50 portfolio:

ER_p = (0.5 × 12%) + (0.5 × 5%) = 8.5%

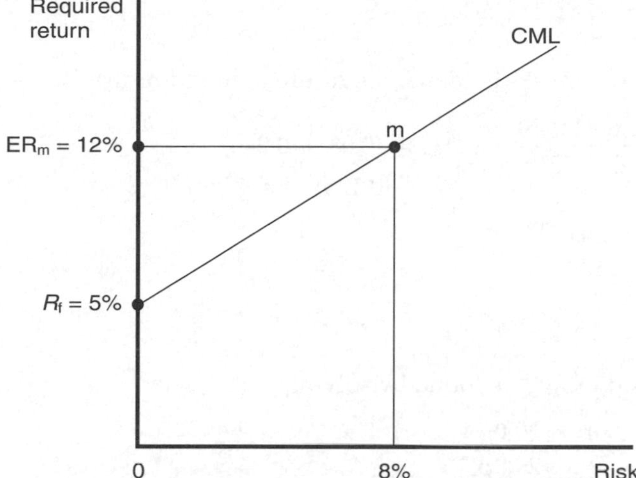

(iv) Bearing in mind there is no correlation between the risk-free rate and the market portfolio, the expression for portfolio risk is;

$$O_p = \sqrt{(0.5)^2(8)^2}$$
$$= \sqrt{16} = 4, \text{ i.e. } 4\%$$

Alternatively, we could use the weighted average expression:

$$(0.5 \times 8\%) + (0.5 \times 0) = 4\%$$

(v) As risk increases from 4% (the 50/50 portfolio) to 8% (the market portfolio), the return required increases from 8.5% to 12%, suggesting a risk–return trade-off (assuming it is linear) of:

$$(3.5\%/4\%) = 0.875$$

Thus, for every one percentage point increase in the portfolio standard deviation, the investor must be compensated by an increase in portfolio return of 0.875%.

6 **(a)** Your graph should show every pair of observations lying along a straight line. This indicates perfect positive correlation between R_j and R_m. The slope of the line, and hence the Beta, is +0.8.

(b) Because all observations lie on the line of best fit, all variation in R_j appears to be explained by variation in R_m, i.e. there is no specific risk.

(c) σ^2_m = variance of the market return. The mean return on the market portfolio = 2.0. Hence

$$\sigma^2_m = (5 - 2)^2 + (-10 - 2)^2 + \cdots + (6 - 2)^2 = 306$$

Thus, systematic risk = $(0.8)^2(306) = 195.84$.

You should expect to find the total risk is also 195.84 because there is no unique risk.

Chapter 12

1 The shares are ex-dividend, the future required return is:

$$k_e = \frac{£\,0.80(1.045)}{£\,10.50} + 0.045 = (0.08 + 0.045)$$
$$= 0.125, \quad \text{i.e. } 12.5\%$$

2 **(i)** D_o = £0.62
(ii) P_o = £3.64
(iii) k_e = 9.3%
(iv) g = 6.2%

3 Dividend growth is found by solving:

$$11\text{p}\,(1 + g)^4 = 20.0\text{p}$$
$$(1 + g)^4 = \frac{20.0\text{p}}{11.0\text{p}} = 1.8182$$

From tables, g = 15.8% approx.

$$\text{Implied } k_e = \frac{20\text{p}(1.158)}{£5.50} + 0.158$$
$$= 0.042 + 0.158 = 0.20, \text{ i.e. } 20\%$$

4 **(i)** $k_e = 6\% + 0.8[11\% - 6\%] = (6\% + 4\%) = 10\%$
(ii) Beta = (0.8 × 1.25) = 1.0

$$k_e = 6\% + 1.0[11\% - 6\%] = (6\% + 5\%) = 11\%$$

(iii) Beta = (0.8 × 0.75) = 0.6

$$k_e = 6\% + 0.6[11\% - 6\%] = (6\% + 3\%) = 9\%$$

5

Division	R_f	Beta	Market Premium	k_e	% of assets
C	7%	0.7	8.00	12.6%	15
E	7%	1.1	8.00	15.8%	40
R	7%	0.8	8.00	13.4%	20
P	7%	0.6	8.00	11.8%	5
Total	/	0.855	/	13.84%	100

Overall Beta = (0.15 × 0.7) + (0.04 × 1.1) + (0.20 × 0.8) + (0.25 × 0.6)
= (0.105 + 0.44 + 0.16 + 0.15) = 0.855

Overall required return = 7% + 0.855[8%] = (7% + 6.84%) = 13.84%

6 **(a)** EV of return = (0.6 × 10%) + (0.4 × 20%) = 14%.

Outcome	Deviation	Squared deviation	Prob.	Sq'd dev. × p	
10%	−4%	16	0.6	9.6	
20%	+6%	36	0.4	14.4	
			Variance = Total	24.0	$\sigma = 4.9$

(b) Megacorp ER = 30% s.d. = 14% proportion = 80%
Erewhon ER = 14% s.d. = 4.9% proportion = 20%

$$ER = (0.8 \times 30\%) + (0.2 \times 14\%) = 24\% + 2.8\% = 26.8\%$$

$$\text{S.d.} = \sqrt{[(0.8)^2(14)^2 + (0.2)^2(4.9)^2 + 2(0.8)(0.2)(-0.36)(14)(4.9)]}$$

(c) The present Beta = 1.20.

$$\text{Beta of project} = \frac{\text{cov}_{jm}}{\sigma^2_m} = \frac{r_{j\,m}\sigma_j\sigma_m}{\sigma^2_m} = \frac{r_{j\,m}\sigma_j}{\sigma_m}$$

What is the risk of the market (σ_m)?
Rearranging:

$$\sigma_m = \frac{\sigma_j r_{j\,m}}{\text{Beta}_j}$$

For Megacorp:

$$\sigma_j = \frac{(14)(0.8)}{1.2} = 9.33$$

$$\text{Project Beta} = \frac{(-0.1)(4.9)}{9.33} = -\frac{0.49}{9.33} = -0.05$$

New Beta for Megacorp = (0.8 × 1.2) + (0.2 × −0.05) = 0.95. Therefore, the new project lowers Megacorp's Beta.

8 (a) Since the asset Beta is a weighted average of the component segment Betas:

$$\beta_A = \left(\frac{1}{4} \times \beta_N\right) + \left(\frac{1}{4} \times \beta_W\right) + \left(\frac{1}{2} \times \beta_S\right) = 1.06$$

where $\beta_N = \beta$ of North, $\beta_W = \beta$ of West, $\beta_S = \beta$ of South.
Since North is 50 per cent more risky than South, and West is 25 per cent less risky than South, it follows that:

$$\frac{(1.5\beta_S)}{4} + \frac{(0.75\beta_S)}{4} + \frac{\beta_S}{2} = 1.06$$

whence $\beta_S = 1.00$, $\beta_N = 1.50$, $\beta_W = 0.75$.

(b) The asset Beta for East (β_E) is:

$$\begin{aligned}\beta_E &= \beta_S \times \text{Relative risk factor}\\ &= \beta_S \times \text{Revenue sensitivity factor} \times \text{Operational gearing factor}\\ &= 1.0 \times 1.4 \times \frac{1.6}{2.0} = 1 \times 1.12 = 1.12\end{aligned}$$

(c) The asset Beta for Lancelot after the divestment and acquisition is again a weighted average of the component asset Betas:

$$\begin{aligned}\beta_A &= \left(\frac{1}{2} \times \beta_E\right) + \left(\frac{1}{4} \times \beta_W\right) + \left(\frac{1}{4} \times \beta_N\right)\\ &= \left(\frac{1}{2} \times 1.12\right) + \left(\frac{1}{4} \times 0.75\right) + \left(\frac{1}{4} \times 1.5\right)\\ &= 0.56 + 0.1875 + 0.375 = 1.12\end{aligned}$$

(d) If we evaluate projects in East on the assumption of all-equity financing, the cut-off rate is

$$R_f + \beta_E(ER_m - R_f) = 10\% + 1.12(15\%) = 26.8\%$$

(e) There are numerous problems involved in obtaining tailor-made project discount rates. First, given that we may have to take the Beta from a surrogate company, ungearing the Beta of its shares requires an accurate assessment of the values of the equity and debt. If the company is quoted, the market valuation of equity can be taken, but not all corporate debt is quoted. Thus the debt:equity ratio used will often be a mixture of market and book values, even for quoted companies. Second, decomposing the ungeared Beta into segmental asset Betas strictly requires weighted average calculations based on market values. Since corporate segments are not generally quoted on stock markets, book values invariably have to be used. Third, to measure project Betas requires consideration of whether the project is of a different order of risk from 'typical' projects in the division. If so, the revenue sensitivity factor requires estimation, mainly based on guesswork for unique projects. In addition, the project gearing factor must also be estimated. Fourth, the general problems relating to specification of the risk-free return and the risk premium on the market portfolio still have to be addressed.

Chapter 13

1 Companies issue a type of call option when issuing share warrants (giving the holder the right to buy shares at a fixed price) and convertible loan stock (giving the holder the right to exchange the loan for a fixed number of shares).

2 **Gaymore plc**

Traded options give the holder the right, but not the obligation, to buy (a call option) or sell (a put option) a quantity of shares at a fixed price on an exercise date in the future. They are usually in contracts of 1,000 shares and for three, six or nine months.

Holders of a put option in Gaymore plc have the right to sell shares in April at 500p. For this right they currently have to pay a premium of 47p, or £470 on a contract of 1,000 shares.

If the share price falls below 453p (i.e. 500p–47p), the shares become profitable and the holder is 'in the money'. So if they fall to 450p, the investor can buy shares at this price and exercise his or her put option to sell shares for 500p, a profit of 50p per share which, after the initial cost of the option, gives a net profit of 3p per share or £30 on the contract.

If the share price moves up to 510p by April, the option becomes worthless, and the investor loses his or her 47p premium.

Options such as this one can be used either to speculate or to hedge on share price changes for a relatively low premium.

5 The put–call parity relationship is:

$S + P - C = E/(1 + R_f)$

From this:

$C = S - (E/(1 + R_f) + P$

where $S = 25$, $P = 15$, $E/(1 + R_f) = 10$.

$C = 25 - 10 + 15 = 30$

The value of the call option is 30p.

6 The put–call parity relationship is:

$S + P - C = E/(1 + R_f)$
$E/(1 + R_f) = 30 + 5 - 19 = 16\text{p}$

Chapter 14

6 **Hercules Wholesalers Ltd**

(a) The liquidity position may be examined by calculating the following ratios:

$$\text{Current ratio} = \frac{\text{Current assets}}{\text{Creditors due for repayment within one year}}$$
$$= \frac{£306,000}{£285,000}$$
$$= 1.1:1$$

$$\text{Acid-test ratio} = \frac{\text{Current assets (less stocks)}}{\text{Creditors due for repayment within one year}}$$
$$= \frac{£163,000}{£285,000}$$
$$= 0.6:1$$

The current ratio reveals that the current assets exceed the short-term liabilities of the company. However, the ratio of 1.1:1 seems rather low. If current assets were to be liquidated, they would only have to be sold off at a small discount on the cost to be insufficient to meet the short-term liabilities. The acid-test ratio excludes stocks from the calculation and represents a more stringent test of liquidity. The ratio of 0.6:1 is also low and suggests the company has insufficient liquid assets to meet its maturing obligations. When interpreting these ratios, it should be borne in mind that they are based on Balance Sheet figures and are therefore representative of only one particular moment in time. It would be useful to monitor the trends in these ratios over time. It would also be useful to prepare a cash flow forecast in order to gain a better understanding of the likely liquidity position of the business in the future. The bank overdraft is the major form of short-term finance and the continuing support of the bank is likely to be of critical importance to the company.

(b) The operating cash cycle of a business represents the time period between the outlay of cash on the purchase of stocks and the receipt of cash from trade debtors. In the case of a wholesale business it can be calculated as follows:

Average holding period for stocks + Average settlement period for debtors − Average settlement period for creditors

The operating cash cycle is important because the longer this period is, the greater the financing requirements of the business and the greater the risks involved.

(c) The operating cash cycle is:

		No. of days
Average period stocks are held	$= \dfrac{\text{average value of stocks held}}{\text{average daily cost of sales}}$	
	$= \dfrac{(£125{,}000 + £143{,}000)/2}{(£323{,}000/360)}$	149
Average settlement period for debtors	$= \dfrac{\text{average level of debtors}}{\text{average daily sales}}$	
	$= \dfrac{£163{,}000}{(£452{,}000/360)}$	130
		279
Less:		
Average settlement period for creditors	$= \dfrac{\text{average level of creditors}}{\text{average daily purchases}}$	
	$= \dfrac{£145{,}000}{(£341{,}000/£360)}$	(153)
		126

(d) The operating cash cycle of the company seems to be quite long. It may be reduced by a reduction in the stocks, improving the collection period from debtors, extending further the average settlement period for creditors or some combination of these measures. The stockholding period and average settlement period for debtors seems high and might be reduced without difficulty. As the average settlement period of creditors appears to be high, it may be difficult to extend this further without incurring problems for the company.

Chapter 15

1 Formula for the cost of cash discounts:

$$\frac{\text{Discount \%}}{(100 - \text{Discount \%})} \times \frac{365}{(\text{Final date} - \text{Discount period})}$$

2 The Baumol cash management model assumes cash is drawn down at an even rate and, at some point, is replenished to its original balance. The Miller–Orr model assumes that short-term cash movements cannot be predicted since they meander in a random fashion.

3 **Hunslett Express Company**

	(£000s)
Average level of debtors – current policy	
70/365 × £8 m	1,534
Average levels of debtors – proposed policy	
50% × 30/365 × £8 m	329
50% × 80/365 × £8 m	876
	1,205
Reduction in debtors under new policy	329
Financing cost savings (13% × £329,000)	43
Bad debt savings	20
Administration cost savings	12
	75
Cost of cash discounts	
50% × £8 m × 2%	(80)
Estimated cost of scheme	(5)

The net cost of the proposed scheme is £5,000.

4 **Salford Engineers Ltd**

(a) The optimum stockholding level is a trade-off between the cost of holding stocks and the cost of not holding stock.

Stockholding costs include:

(i) Storage costs. Where stock is valuable these costs can be large.

(ii) Financing costs. Excessive stock requires unnecessary and expensive working capital.

(iii) Insurance costs against theft or damage.

(iv) Obsolescence costs. Stock held for long periods of time may become obsolete through new products coming to the market.

Costs of holding too little stock include:

(i) Loss of customer goodwill and business through not being able to supply goods on time.

(ii) Production stoppages. A 'stockout' can mean costly and harmful disruptions to the production process.

(iii) Lost flexibility. Shortage of stock makes it difficult for a firm to respond to unexpected demand or to extended production runs.

(b) In investigating the reasons for large stock levels for Salford Engineering, the following action should be taken:

(i) Examine the stock re-order levels for each stock line.

(ii) Examine how the optimum stock level is determined. Is any technique for assessing the optimum level employed?

(iii) Are stock requirements carefully budgeted?

(iv) Are ratios used (e.g. stock turnover) to monitor stock levels in total and by stock lines?

(v) Are stock records reliable and adequate?

Chapter 16

1 Cost of extra trade credit = lost discount of 3 per cent , i.e. £30 on an invoice of face value of £1,000. Over the extra 30 days during which you delay payment, you are paying a cost of roughly:

$$(£30/\text{extra finance}) \times 365/30 = (£30/£970) \times 12.167$$
$$= 3.09 \times 12.167 = 37.6\%$$

More accurately, the annual rate is

$$(1 + £30/£970)^{12.167} - 1 = (1.0309)^{12.167} - 1 = 1.448 - 1 = 0.448, \quad \text{i.e. } 44.8\%$$

2 (a) **Option 1: The net cost of a full-year loan.**

Interest @ 12: £500,000 × 12%	= £60,000
Less interest received on surplus funds	
Q1: (£500,000 − £400,000) × 2% = £2,000	
Compounded for Qs 2–4:	
= £2,000(1.02)^3	= (£2,122)
Q4: (£500,000 − £200,000) × 2%	= (£6,000)
	£51,878

Option 2: The cost of a fluctuating overdraft.

Quarterly interest rate = 14%/4 = 3.5%
Q1: £400,000 × 3.5% = £14,000
Q2: £500,000 × 3.5% = £17,500
Q3: £500,000 × 3.5% = £17,500
Q4: £200,000 × 3.5% = £7,000
Total = £56,000

Even without any interest charges on accumulated quarterly overdraft interest, the loan is the cheaper option. However, the overdraft offers possible access to lower interest rates. (Equally, they could rise!).

(Let I = average monthly overdraft rate

£51,878 = I × [£400,000 + £500,000 + £500,000 + £200,000]
I = [£51,878/£1,600,000]
I = 0.0324, rounded to 0.0325, i.e. 3.25%, or 13% p.a.)

An average annual interest rate of 13% on the overdraft (3.25% per month) is the break-even rate.

3 Cost of early discounting = (£200,000 − £195,500) = £4,500. This corresponds to an effective annual interest cost of roughly:

$$(£4{,}500/£195{,}500) \times 12/4 = 6.9\%$$

More accurately, the annual rate is:

$$(1.023)^3 - 1 = 1.0706 - 1 = 0.0706, \quad \text{i.e. } 7.06\%$$

4

Net amount borrowed = (£100,000 − £15,000)	= £85,000
Total interest cost = (7.5% × £85,000 × 4)	= £25,500
Total required payments	= £110,500

Required monthly payment = £110,500/(4 × 12) = £2,302.

7 Amalgamated Effluents plc

The evaluation should be conducted in three stages.

(i) Is the project inherently worthwhile? The basic project must first be evaluated assuming no change in financing, i.e. using the equity cost of capital. Assuming the outlay can be set against year zero profit, cash flows are:

	Cash flows (marked by *) (£m)				
	0	1	2	3	4
Operating cash inflow*		0.200	0.200	0.200	0.200
Equipment cost*	(0.500)				0.050
WDA	0.125	0.094	0.070	0.053	0.108
WDV	0.375	0.281	0.211	0.158	0.050
Taxable income	(0.125)	0.106	0.130	0.147	0.092
Tax impact @ 30%	0.038	(0.032)	(0.039)	(0.044)	(0.028)
Net cash flows*	(0.462)	0.168	0.161	0.156	0.172
PV @ 10%	(0.462)	0.153	0.133	0.117	0.117

The NPV = + 0.58, i.e. + £58,000, hence the project is worthwhile.

(ii) Should the equipment be leased or purchased? The relevant discount rate is the post-tax cost of borrowing, i.e.
$7\%(1 - 30\%) = 5\%$

The respective cash flow implications of leasing and outright purchase are:

The PV of the rental stream = 0.070($PVIFA_{5/4}$) = 0.070(3.546) = 0.248
The PV of the tax savings = 0.248(0.30) = 0.074, i.e. £74,000

Hence PV of leasing costs = 0.248 − 0.074 = 0.174, i.e. (£0.174).

Purchase via bank loan:

The relevant cash flows are those connected with the purchase itself rather than the operation of the project, i.e. the outlay less tax savings and the residual value.

	Cash flows (marked by *) (£m)				
	0	1	2	3	4
Outlay*	(0.500)				0.050
WDA	0.125	0.094	0.070	0.053	0.108
Tax savings @ 30%	0.041	0.031	0.023	0.017	0.036
Net cash flows*	(0.459)	0.031	0.023	0.017	0.036
PV @ 5%	(0.459)	0.030	0.021	0.015	0.030

PV of cash flow = (0.363), i.e. (£0.363 m)

Hence, leasing is the preferable (least-cost) method of financing (£0.174 m compared to £0.363 m), i.e. the lease has a net advantage of £0.189 m.

(iii) The third stage in the evaluation is now a formality – the optimal decision is to acquire the equipment using lease finance.

Chapter 17

1 Remember the bank always wins, so it sells euros at 1.6296, and buys at 1.6320.
  (a) Selling £10 million, its receipts are (10 × 1.6296) = €16.296 million.
  (b) Selling €10 million, its receipts are (10 m/1.6320) = £6.127 m.

2 (a) Amount invoiced = (£10 m × €1.6) = €16 m.
  (b) With spot at €1.7 vs. £1, proceeds = (€16 m/1.7) = £9.412. Hence, the loss compared to the current spot rate = (£10 m − £9.412) = £0.588 m.
  (c) With spot at €1.5 vs. £1, the sale proceeds are (€16 m/1.5 m) = £10.667. In this case, the exporter gains £0.667 m from the exchange rate change.
  (d) If the exporter sells forward, the contracted proceeds are €16 m/1.62 = £9.877 m.
    (i) The cost of the hedge is thus £0.123 m, i.e. 1.2% of the sterling value of the deal.
    (ii) If sterling falls to €1.5 vs. £1, the forward contract guarantees the exporter £9.877 million, but it could have received £10.667 million had it not hedged. There is thus an opportunity cost of (£10.667 m − £9.877 m) = £0.790 m.
    (iii) If sterling rises to €1.7 vs. £1, the forward contract still guarantees the exporter £9.877 m, but it would have received £9.412 m had it not hedged. The exporter is thus better off by (£9.877 m − £9.412 m) = £0.465 m.

  If the exporter thinks there is an equal chance of a ten per cent variation in the €/£ exchange rate, it must balance an opportunity cost from hedging of £0.75 million if sterling falls against being better off by £0.465 million if sterling rises.

3 The forward outrights are:

EUR:	1.6296 –	1.6320
Plus forward discount	10 –	40
Forward outright	1.6306 –	1.6360
JPY	175.16 –	175.28
Less forward premium	.61	.50
Forward outright	174.55 –	174.78
USD	1.45710 –	1.45760
Less forward premium	226	206
Forward outright	1.45484 –	1.45554

5 According to Interest Rate Parity,

$$\text{Forward rate} = \text{Spot rate} \times \frac{(1 + \text{US interest rate})}{(1 + \text{UK interest rate})}$$

$$= 1.6000 \times \frac{(1.09)}{(1.10)} = 1.5834, \quad \text{i.e. USD stronger on forward market}$$

  The currency of the country in which interest rates are lower (presumably due to lower expected inflation) would be traded at a premium.

6 It is assumed it is desired to hold US$ at the year end. By lending US$ at 7.625 per cent, the end-year balance will be £1 m (1.07625) = $1,076,250.

If wishing to lend in Swiss francs, the treasurer would convert from dollars at spot of 1.3125 to obtain CHF of \$1 m × 1.3125 = SFr1,312,500. Over one year, invested at 4.5625 per cent, this would accumulate to CHF1,372,383.

To cover the risk of adverse exchange rate movements, he will then sell CHF forward at the ruling rate of 1.275 to guarantee US\$ delivery in one year's time of CHF1,372,383/1.275 = \$1,076,379.

The minimal difference of \$129 can be attributed to the operation of IRP. Transactions costs would wipe out any gain from arbitrage.

12 Forward Hedge

The bank contracts to buy A\$28 m for GBP in three months time. Sterling value = (A\$28 m/2.805) = £9.982 m.

(a) with future spot at A\$2.78, Hogan could have received (A\$28 m/2.78) = £10.072 m, involving an opportunity cost of:

(£10.072 m − £9.982 m) = £0.090 m (0.9% of contract value)

(b) with future spot at A\$2.82, Hogan would receive (A\$28 m/2.82) = £9.929 m. The hedge offers a gain of:

(£9.982 m − £9.929 m) = £0.053 m

Money Market Hedge

Three-month interest rate = (9%/4) = 2.25%. Hogan will borrow in AUD sufficient to accumulate at 2.25% to the AUD value of its receipts, i.e.:

(A\$28 m/1.0225) = A\$27.384 m

Exchanged for GBP at today's spot rate, this is worth:

(A\$27.3839 m/2.80) = £9.78 m

(a) At future spot of A\$2.78 vs. £1, unhedged income = £10.072 m. Loss via the money market hedge:

(£10.072 m − £9.78 m) = £0.292 m (2.9% of contract value)

(b) At future spot of A\$2.82 vs. £1, unhedged income = £9.929 m. Hence, value of the hedge is:

(£9.78 m − £9.929 m) = £0.49 m

OTC Option Hedge

(a) At future spot of A\$2.78 vs. £1, the option is 'out of the money', i.e. it is better to sell AUD at spot rather than exercise the option. Hogan's unhedged income is £10.072 m. Net of the option premium, the proceeds are:

(£10.072 m − £0.200 m) = £9.872 m

Hogan's loss through the option hedge is simply the option premium.

(b) At future spot of A\$2.82 vs. £1, the option is 'in the money', i.e. it is better to exercise it than sell GBP at spot to yield (A\$28 m/2.81) = £9.964 m. This nets:

(£9.964 m − £0.200 m) = £9.764 m

Of the three hedging tactics, the most profitable is to enter the forward contract.

Chapter 18

1 (i)

	Pence
3 old shares prior to rights issue at 320 p	960
1 new share at £2	200
4 shares worth	1,160
1 share therefore worth 1,160/4	290

(ii) Value of the rights is the difference between the offer price and the ex-rights price: (290p − 200p) = 90p for every new share issued.

2 Proposed preference share issue

(a) Benefits to the company:

- Dividends are only paid if funds are available.
- No asset security required as with some loans.
- Lower risk than for ordinary share capital, giving a cheaper source of finance.
- Suitable when a company does not want to increase the number of ordinary shares but is concerned that its gearing is already high.

Drawbacks to the company:

- Cost of preference shares is usually higher than for debentures because the risks are greater.
- No tax relief on the dividends (unlike loan interest).

(b) Benefits to the investor:

- Should produce a higher yield than fixed-interest securities.
- Lower risk than ordinary shares.
- Redeemable preference shares provide a means of liquidating the investment where markets are thin or non-existent.

Drawbacks to the investor:

- Unable to participate fully in the profits.
- Not usually secured.
- No guaranteed dividend.

Many of the drawbacks can be overcome where preference shares are cumulative, participating, redeemable and convertible into equity if desired.

4 (a) Burnsall needs additional finance to fund both working and fixed capital needs. As sales are expected to increase by 20 per cent, and since working capital needs are expected to rise in line with sales, the predicted working capital needs will be 20 per cent above the existing working capital level, i.e.

1.2 × [stock + debtors + cash – trade creditors]
= 1.2 × [£16 m + £23 m + £6 m – £18 m]
= £32.4 m, increase of £5.4 m.

Together with the additional capital expenditures of £20 m, the total funding requirement = (£5.4 m + £20 m) = £25.4 m.

This funding requirement can be met partly by internal finance and partly by new external capital. The internal finance available will derive from depreciation provisions and retained earnings, after accounting for anticipated liabilities, such as taxation, that is, from cash flow.

Note that the profit margin on sales of £100 m (£10 × 10 m units) before interest and tax was 16 per cent in 1994–95. If depreciation of £5 m for 1994–95 is added back, this yields a 'cash flow margin' of 21 per cent (ignoring movements in current assets/liabilities).

Using the same margin, and making a simple operating cash flow projection based on the accounts and other information provided:

	£m
Inflows	
Sales in 1995–6 = (£10 × 10 m) + 20%	120.00
Cost of sales before depreciation @ 79%	(94.80)
Operating cash flow	25.20
Outflows	
Tax liability for 1994–5	(5.00)
Interest payments: 12% × £20 m	(2.40)
Dividends: 1.1 × £5 m	(5.50)
	(12.90)
Net internal finance generated	10.30
Funding requirements	
	(25.40)
Net additional external finance required	(13.10)

(b) **(i)** Some new equipment could be leased, via a long-term capital lease. Tax relief is available on rental payments, lowering the effective cost of using the equipment. Lessors may 'tailor' a leasing package to suit Burnsall's specific needs regarding timing of payments and provision of ancillary services. Alternatively, good quality property assets at present owned by Burnsall could be sold to a financial institution and their continued use secured via a leaseback arrangement, although this arrangement involves losing any capital appreciation of the assets.

(ii) If Burnsall's assets are of sufficient quality, i.e. easily saleable, it may be possible to raise a mortgage secured on them. This enables retention of ownership.

(iii) Burnsall could make a debenture issue, interest on which would be tax-allowable. The present level of gearing (long-term debt-to-equity) is relatively low at £20 m/£120 m = 16%, Burnsall has no short-term debt apart from trade creditors and the Inland Revenue, and its interest cover is healthy with profit before tax and interest divided by interest charges = [16% × £100 m]/[12% × £20 m] = 6.6 times. It is likely that Burnsall could make a sizeable debt issue without unnerving the market. Any new debenture would be subordinate to the existing long-term debt and probably carry a higher interest rate.

(iv) An alternative to a debt issue is a rights issue of ordinary shares. Because rights issues are made at a discount to the existing market price, they result in lower EPS and thus market price, although if existing shareholders take up their allocations, neither their wealth nor control is diluted. If the market approves of the intended use of funds, a capital gain may ensue, although the company and its advisers must carefully manage the issue regarding the declared reasons and its timing in order to avoid unsettling the market.

(v) Burnsall could approach a venture capitalist such as 3i, which specialises in extending development capital to small-to-medium-sized firms. However, 3i may require an equity stake, and possibly insist on placing an appointee on the Board to monitor its interests.

(vi) Burnsall could utilise official sources of aid, such as a regional development agency depending on its location, or perhaps the European Investment Bank.

Chapter 19

1 With a residual dividend policy:

Dividends = [Distributable Earnings – Capital Expenditure]

Tom has issued 10 million shares with par value 50 p each, giving total book value of £5 million. Total dividends are (20 p × 10 m) = £2 m. Hence, capex = (£10 m − £2 m) = £8 m.

2 As all projects are indivisible, only whole projects with IRR > 20 per cent can be selected, i.e. B + C + E, with total expenditure of £14 million. As this infringes the capital availability constraint of £9 million, Dick is restricted to only B + C, with joint outlay of £7 million, leaving £2 million as a residual dividend.

3 According to Lintner's target adjustment theory, companies only partially adjust their dividends in line with earnings changes. The change in dividend will be half of the difference between current EPS and the last dividend, i.e.

$$\begin{aligned}\text{Dividend change} &= 0.5 \times [0.5\ \text{EPS}_t - \text{Div}_{t-1}]\\ &= 0.5 \times [0.5 \times (£3.0) - £1]\\ &= 0.5 \times £\,0.5 = £\,0.25\end{aligned}$$

so that the new dividend = (£1.0 + £0.25) = £1.25.

4 Tamas' tax charge = (30% × £30 m) = £9 m
Profit after tax = (£30 − £9 m) = £21 m
Dividend = (50% × £21 m) = £10.5 m
i.e. (£10.5 m/100 m) = 10.5p per share

Net (i.e. post-tax) cash flow = [Pre-tax profit + depreciation − replacement investment − tax]
= [£30 m + £2 m − £2 m − £9 m] = £21 m

Value cum dividend = (£21 m/15%) + £10.5 m
= (£140 m + £10.5 m) = £150.5 m

Per share, this is (£150.5 m/100 m) = £1.505 (cum dividend).

The ex-dividend share price is £1.505 reduced by the dividend per share of 10.5p, i.e. (£1.505 − £0.105) = £1.40.

5 **(a)** The price per share is given by:

$$P_o = \frac{D_1}{(k_e - g)}$$

where D_1 is next year's dividend, k_e is the shareholder's required return and g is the expected rate of growth in dividends.

The growth rate can be found from the expression:

$$5.0\text{p}(1 + g)^4 = 7.3\text{p}$$

where g is the past (compound) growth rate.

$$(1 + g)^4 = \frac{7.3\text{p}}{5.0\text{p}} = 1.46$$

or

$$\frac{1}{(1 + g)^4} = 0.6849$$

From the present value tables, $g = 10\%$, whence:

$$P_o = \frac{7.3\text{p}(1.1)}{(16\% - 10\%)} = \frac{8.03\text{p}}{0.06} = £1.34$$

(b) With D_1 at just 5.0 p, using managerial expectations for the investment:

$$P_o = \frac{5.0\text{p}}{(16\% - 14\%)} = \frac{5.0\text{p}}{0.02} = £2.50$$

(c) To break even, share price must not fall below £1.34, i.e.

$$£1.34 = \frac{5.0\text{p}}{(16\% - g)}$$

Solving for g, we find $g = 12.3\%$, marginally above the assessment of the more pessimistic managers.

(d) Until 1990, Galahad pursued a policy of distributing 40–50 per cent of profit after tax as dividend. Each year, it has offered a steady dividend increase, even in 1989, when its earnings actually fell. This was presumably out of reluctance to lower the dividend, fearing an adverse market reaction, and reflecting a belief that the earnings shortfall was a temporary phenomenon. In 1990 it offered a 12 per cent dividend increase, the highest percentage increase in the time series, possibly to compensate shareholders for the relatively small increase (only 8 per cent) in 1989. It would appear that Galahad has either already built up a clientèle of investors whose interests it is trying to safeguard, or that it is trying to do so.

The proposed dividend cut to 5.0p per share would represent a sharply increased dividend cover of 3.5, on the assumption that EPS also grows at 10 per cent p.a. Such a sharp rise in the dividend safety margin is likely to be construed by the market as implying that Galahad's managers expect earnings to be depressed in the future, especially as it follows a year of record dividend increase. Such an abrupt change in dividend policy is thus likely to offend its clientèle of shareholders at best, and at worst, to alarm the market as to the reliability of future earnings.

In an efficient capital market, with homogeneous investor expectations, the share price would increase by the amount calculated in (b), at least, if the market agreed with the managers' views about the attractions of the projected expenditure. However, in view of the information content of dividends, Galahad's board will have to be very confident of its ability to persuade the market of the inherent desirability of the proposed investment programme. This may well be a difficult task, especially given the stated doubts of some of its managers. The board will have to explain why they feel internal financing is preferable to raising capital externally, either by a rights issue, or by raising further debt finance. While the level of indebtedness of Galahad is not given, the implication is that it is unacceptably high, so as to obviate the issue of additional borrowing instruments. If this is the case, then it seems doubly risky to propose a dividend cut, as it may signal fears regarding Galahad's ability to service a high level of debt.

If the dividend cut is greeted adversely, then the ability of the shareholder clientèle to home-make dividends will be impaired, since, apart from the transactions costs involved, there will perhaps be no capital gain to realise. Any significant selling to convert capital into income will further depress share price.

If the investment programme is truly worthwhile, Galahad's managers perhaps should not shrink from offering a rights issue, since, despite the costs of such issues, shareholders will eventually reap the benefits in the form of higher future earnings and dividends. However, this might suggest a short-term reduction in share price, which may penalise short-term investors, but who still have the option of protecting their interests by selling their rights.

Chapter 20

1
- LTD/Equity = (£200 m/£500 m) = 40%
- LTD/(LTD + Equity) = £200 m/(£200 m + £500 m) = 28%
- Total Debt/Equity = (£200 m + £50 m)/£500 m = 50%
- Net Debt = (£200 m + £50 m) − (£20 m + £40 m) = £190 m.
- Net Debt/Equity = (£190 m/£500 m) = 38%
- Interest Cover = (£120 m/£25 m) = 4.8 times.
- Income Gearing = (1/4.8) × 100 = 21%
- Total Liabilities/Total Assets = (£420 m/£800 m) = 52.5%

2 Market value of debt = £100 × (£45 m/£50 m) = £90

(i) cost of debt = [8% × £100]/£90 = (£8/£90) = 8.9%

(ii) cost of debt = £8 (1 − 30%)/£90 = (£5.6/£90) = 6.2%

(iii) cost of debt is the solution R to:

$$£90 = \frac{£8}{(1+R)} + \frac{£8}{(1+R)^2} + \cdots + \frac{£8 + £100}{(1+R)^6}$$

Solution value for $R = 10.3\%$

(iv) The cost of debt is the solution R to:

$$£90 = \frac{£8\,(1-30\%)}{(1+R)} + \frac{£5.6}{(1+R)^2} + \cdots + \frac{(£5.6 + £100)}{(1+R)^6}$$

Solution value for $R = 8.25\%$.

3 (a)

	£m		
	prob. = 0.3	prob. = 0.5	prob. = 0.2
EBIT	5	50	150
Current Structure – £200 m equity.			
Tax @ 30%	(1.5)	(15)	(45)
PAT	3.5	35	105
ROE	1.8%	17.5%	52.5%
Programme (i) – £40 m debt/£160 m equity.			
Interest @ 8%	(3.2)	(3.2)	(3.2)
Taxable profit	1.8	46.8	146.8
Tax @ 30%	(0.5)	(14.0)	(44.0)
PAT	1.26	32.8	102.8
ROE	0.8%	20.5%	64.3%
Programme (ii) – £80 m debt/£120 m equity.			
Interest @ 8%	(6.8)	(6.8)	(6.8)
Taxable profit	–	43.2	143.2
Tax @ 30%	–	(13.0)	43.0
PAT	–	30.2	100.2
ROE	(1.5%)	25.2%	83.5%

(b) Risk is measured by the standard deviation of the returns on equity (ROE) around the respective expected values (EVs).

Current Capital Structure.
EV of ROE = (0.3 × 1.8) + (0.5 × 17.5) + (0.2 × 52.5) = 19.8%

Outcome	EV	Deviation	Squared	× probability
1.8	19.8	−18.0	324	97.2
17.5	19.8	−2.3	5.3	2.65
52.5	19.8	32.7	1069.3	213.86
			Total = variance =	313.71

Standard deviation = $\sqrt{313.71}$ = 17.7, i.e. 17.7%.

Programme (i)
EV of ROE = (0.3 × 0.8) + (0.5 × 20.5) + (0.2 × 64.3) = 23.4%

Outcome	EV	Deviation	Squared	× probability
0.8	23.4	−22.6	255.38	76.61
20.5	23.4	−2.9	8.41	4.205
64.3	23.4	40.9	1672.81	334.56
			Total = variance =	415.379

Standard deviation = $\sqrt{415.379}$ = 20.4, i.e. 20.4%.

Programme (ii)

EV of ROE = (0.3 × −1.5) + (0.5 × 25.2) + (0.2 × 83.5) = 28.9%

Outcome	EV	Deviation	Squared	× probability
−1.5	28.9	−30.4	924.16	277.248
25.2	28.9	−3.7	13.69	6.845
83.5	28.9	54.6	2981.16	596.23
			Total = variance =	880.32

Standard deviation = $\sqrt{880.32}$ = 29.7, i.e. 29.7%

(c) Business risk, exposure to the risk of fluctuations in business activity, can be measured in different ways, e.g. the variability in sales or in some measure of profitability. This example shows how ROE varies under three scenarios. By abstracting from financial risk, the ROE in the all-equity case shows inherent business risk – the ROE varies from 1.8 per cent to 52.5 per cent, with a standard deviation of 17.7 per cent.

Gearing adds a second layer of risk because it imposes an extra fixed cost, i.e. the prior interest charge – the higher the level of gearing, the higher the financial risk. Consequently, we see that the standard deviation of the ROE rises to 28.9 per cent under the relatively modest level of gearing, programme (i), while programme (ii) raises it to 29.7 per cent.

4 (a) (i) Perpetual debt:

$$\text{PV of Tax Savings} = \frac{(T \times i \times \text{Nominal Debt Value})}{i} = \frac{TiB}{i}$$

$$= (30\% \times 10\% \times £100\text{ m})/10\%$$

$$= (£3\text{ m}/0.1) = £30\text{ m}$$

(ii) When debt is repaid in full after 5 years:

PV = £3 m p.a. over 5 years @ 10% discount rate
= (£3 m × 3.7908) = £11.37 m

(iii) Debt repaid in equal tranches:

Year	Start-year debt	Interest	Tax saving	PV	Repayment
1	100	10	3	2.73	20
2	80	8	2.4	1.98	20
3	60	6	1.8	1.35	20
4	40	4	1.2	0.82	20
5	20	2	0.6	0.37	20
			Total =	£7.25 m	

(b) The value of the tax shield is higher:

- the higher the interest rate
- the higher the tax rate

- the higher the amount of debt
- the longer the term of the loan
- the slower that debt is repaid
- the greater the firm's taxable capacity

5 Book value weights:

		weight	*cost*
Equity [£10 m + £20 m] =	£30 m	i.e. 66.7%	20%
Debt	£15 m	33.3%	10% pre-tax
	£45 m	100%	

WACC = (20% × 66.7%) + (10%[1 − 30%] × 33.3%)
= (13.3% + 2.3%) = 16.6%

Market value of equity = (20 m shares × £4.50) – £90 m. The weights become

Equity: £90 m/£105 m = 85.7%
Debt:£15 m/£105 m = 14.3%

WACC = (20% × 85.7%) + (10%[1 − 30%] × 14.3%)
= (17.1% + 1.0%) = 18.1%

Chapter 21

1 (i) From MM's Proposition 1, the cost of equity is:

$$k_{eg} = k_{eu} + (k_{eu} - k_d)\frac{V_B}{V_S}$$

If the proportion of debt to total finance is 20%, the ratio of debt to equity must be 1:4, i.e. 0.25. Hence,

$$k_{eg} = 20\% + (20\% - 8\%)(0.25) = 23\%.$$

2 (i) Because the WACC is constant at 20% at all gearing levels, the figures correspond to the MM-no tax theory.

(ii) This now illustrates the MM-with tax theory, wherein the WACC falls continuously as gearing increases. The cost of equity becomes:

$$k_{eg} = k_{eu} + (k_{eu} - k_d)(1 - T)\frac{V_B}{V_S}$$

The amended table is:

% Debt	% Equity	k_d	k_e	WACC
–	100	–	20%	20%
25	75	5.6%	22.8%	18.5%
50	50	5.6%	28.4%	17.2%
75	25	5.6%	45.2%	15.5%

3 Assume the investor holds 10 per cent of Geared's equity.

Value of stake = 10% × £900 = £90
Personal income initially = 10% × [£100 − (5% × £200)]
= 10% × £90 = £9
Geared's gearing = £200/£900 = 22.2%

Assume investor sells stake in Geared for £90, borrows £20 at 5 per cent to duplicate Geared's gearing and invests the whole stake in Ungeared's equity.

Now entitled to earnings of (£110/£950) × £100 = £11.58
Personal interest liability = (5% × £20) = (£1.00)
Net income = £10.58

The investor is better off by (£10.58 − £9.00) = £1.58

9 (a) CAPM
The stated Beta is an equity Beta so that the required return on equity is:

$$ER_j = R_f + \beta_j(ER_m - R_f)$$
$$= 12\% + 1.4(18\% - 12\%) = 20.4\%$$

This is unsuitable as a discount rate because:

(i) It is the required return on equity rather than the required return on the overall company.

(ii) The equity Beta of 1.4 reflects the financial risk of Folten's equity. Wemere's gearing differs from that of Folten, hence their equity Betas will differ.

The inflation adjustment is unnecessary since ER_m and R_f already incorporate the expected impact of inflation.

The equity Beta for Wemere can be estimated by ungearing Folten's equity Beta and regearing to reflect the financial risk of Wemere.

The market value-weighted gearing figures are:

Folten
Equity (138p × 7.2 m shares) = £9.936 m, i.e. 69.3% of total
Debt = £4,400 m, i.e. 30.7% of total
Total = £14,336 m

Wemere
Equity (using the takeover bid offer) = £10.6 m, i.e. 81.5% of total
Debt = £2.4 m, i.e. 18.5% of total
Total = £13.0 m

Assuming coporate debt is risk-free, the ungeared equity Beta is

$$\beta_u = \beta_g \times \frac{1}{\left[1 + \frac{V_B}{Vs}\cdot(1 - T)\right]} = 1.4 \times \frac{1}{1 + (0.44)(1 - 35\%)}$$
$$= 1.089$$

Regearing Beta for Wemere,

$$\beta_g = \beta_u\left[1 + \frac{V_B}{V_S}\cdot(1 - T)\right]$$
$$= 1.089\ [1 + 0.23(1 - 35\%)] = 1.25$$

The cost of equity for Wemere is thus:

12% + 1.25[18% − 12%] = 19.5%

Given the cost of debt is 13%:

WACC = [13% (1 − 35%) × 18.5%] + [19.5% × 81.5%]
= 1.56% + 15.89% = 17.5%

However, the WACC is only suitable as a discount rate if the systematic risk of the new investment is similar to that of the company as a whole.

Dividend Growth Model

The expression for this model relates to the cost of equity, not the overall cost of capital, i.e.

$$k_e = \frac{D_1}{P_o} + g = \frac{14.20\text{p}}{138\text{p}} + 9\% = 19.3\%$$

No inflation adjustment is required.
The WACC is: [13%(1 − 35%) × 18.5%] + [19.3% × 81.5%]
= 1.56% + 15.73% = 17.3%

(b) Neither method is problem-free. The surrogate company is unlikely to have identical charactersitics, either at an operating level or in terms of financial characteristics. For example, the cost of equity in the Dividend Growth Model is derived from a different set of data regarding dividend policy, growth and share prices.

Folten's managers may have different capabilities, and the company may face different growth opportunities. Before using the estimated WACC, Wemere must be confident that the two companies are a sufficiently close fit.

Even so, the calculated WACC is inappropriate if the systematic risk of any new project differs from that of the company as a whole, and/or if project financing involves moving to a new capital structure.

Chapter 22

1 (a) Value of target now:

$$P_o = \frac{D_1}{k_e - g}$$
$$20 = \frac{80\text{ p}}{k_e - 6\%}$$

whence $k_e = 10\%$.

Value of target would become

$$P = \frac{80\text{p}}{10\% - 8\%} = £40 \text{ per share}$$

Value of equity = £40 × 0.6 m = £24 m, i.e. an increase of £12 m.

(b) Cost of acquisition: (£25 − £20) = £5 per share. In total, £5 × 0.6 m = £3 m. NPV of acquisition: (£12 m − £3 m) = £9 m. Advise to proceed.

(c) Number of new shares required: 0.6 m/3 = 0.2 m; new total = 1.2 m.

$$\text{Value of new company} = \frac{£90\text{ m} + £12\text{ m} + £12\text{ m}}{1.2\text{ m}}$$
$$= £114/1.2\text{ m} = £95 \text{ per share}$$

Cost of acquisition = (0.2 m × £95 m) − £12 m = £7 m. NPV of acquisition = (£12 m − £7 m) = £5 m. Again, advise to proceed.

(d) **(i)** Cost of cash bid unchanged. Pointless to proceed as there are no gains.
(ii) With the share exchange:

$$\text{Value of new company} = \frac{£90\text{ m} + £12\text{ m}}{1.2\text{ m}} = £85 \text{ per share}$$

NPV of acquisition: (0.2 m × £85) − £12 m = (£5 m). Advise not to proceed on this basis.

7 **(a)** The Balance Sheet net asset value is total assets minus total liabilities, i.e. £620 m. Land and buildings have an estimated value of £150 m × $(1.25)^4$ = £366 m, i.e. £216 m higher than the book value. Hence, the adjusted NAV is £836 m. Applying Grapper's 12 per cent growth rate, estimated PAT for the coming five years is:

£151(1.12) + £151$(1.12)^2$, etc. = £1,074 m

This yields total value of £836 m + £1,074 m = £1,910 m. Grapper's market value is currently (400 m shares × share price 470p) = £1,880 m. The premium is thus £30 m or 7.5p per share.

This is not a sound basis for valuation as it ignores the time-value of money. The premium of 1.6 per cent above the current market price is very small compared with those achieved in many 'real' bids.

Using the Dividend Valuation Model:

$$P_o = \frac{D_1}{k_e - g} = \frac{D_o(1+g)}{k_e - g}$$

$$\text{Current dividend per share} = \frac{£76\text{ m}}{400\text{ m}} = 19\text{p}$$

Hence D_1 = 19p(1.12) = 21.3 p.
From the CAPM:

$$k_e = ER_j = R_f + \beta_j(ER_m - R_f) = 10\% + 1.05\,(16\% - 10\%) = 16.3\%$$

Thus:

$$P_o = \frac{21.3\text{p}}{16.3\% - 12\%} = 495\text{p}$$

i.e. 5.3 per cent above the market price.

Restrictive assumptions underlying such a valuation include a constant growth rate, and an unchanged dividend policy. It is more rational to assess the value of Grapper incorporating post-merger rationalisation.

(b) The post-merger sales revenue of Woppit will be over £5,000 million, a size which could deter other takeover raiders, at least from the United Kingdom. However, bids from US and other European sources should not be ruled out. In addition, debt-financed bids from consortia like Hoylake (which bid for BAT) show that size alone is not an adequate protection against a takeover bid.

(c) An indication of the scope for improving Grapper's efficiency can be obtained by examination of key financial ratios.

	Woppit	**Grapper**
Operating profit margin (PBIT/sales)	20%	16.6%
Asset turnover (sales/total assets)	1.80	1.36
Debtors' collection period	31 days	50 days
Stock turnover	10.3	6.4
Current ratio	1.65:1	2.45:1

There are clear opportunities to improve Grapper's performance by rationalisation and restructuring of activities. For example:

- Grapper's operating profit margin could be brought into line with Woppit's by a price increase and/or cost reduction.
- Grapper's stock level looks high by comparison. There could well be stockholding economics in an expanded operation.
- Grapper's cash holdings look excessive – again, centralised cash management may generate economies.
- Grapper's asset turnover is relatively low. Some assets could well be sold and others worked more intensively.
- Grapper seems to have scope for reducing its investment in debtors.
- Introduction of such economies may well close the gap between Woppit's return on assets of 36 per cent and Grapper's present 22.5 per cent.

Appendix B: Present value interest factor (PVIF) per £1.00 due at the end of *n* years for interest rate of:

n	1%	2%	3%	4%	5%	6%	7%	8%	9%	10%	*n*
1	0.99010	0.98039	0.97007	0.96154	0.95238	0.94340	0.93458	0.92593	0.91743	0.90909	1
2	0.98030	0.96117	0.94260	0.92456	0.90703	0.89000	0.87344	0.85734	0.84168	0.82645	2
3	0.97059	0.94232	0.91514	0.88900	0.86384	0.83962	0.81630	0.79383	0.77218	0.75131	3
4	0.96098	0.92385	0.88849	0.85480	0.82270	0.79209	0.76290	0.73503	0.70843	0.68301	4
5	0.95147	0.90573	0.86261	0.82193	0.78353	0.74726	0.71299	0.68058	0.64993	0.62092	5
6	0.94204	0.88797	0.83748	0.79031	0.74622	0.70496	0.66634	0.63017	0.59627	0.56447	6
7	0.93272	0.87056	0.81309	0.75992	0.71068	0.66506	0.62275	0.58349	0.54703	0.51316	7
8	0.92348	0.85349	0.78941	0.73069	0.67684	0.62741	0.58201	0.54027	0.50187	0.46651	8
9	0.91434	0.83675	0.76642	0.70259	0.64461	0.59190	0.54393	0.50025	0.46043	0.42410	9
10	0.90529	0.82035	0.74409	0.67556	0.61391	0.55839	0.50835	0.46319	0.42241	0.38554	10
11	0.89632	0.80426	0.72242	0.64958	0.58468	0.52679	0.47509	0.42888	0.38753	0.35049	11
12	0.88745	0.78849	0.70138	0.62460	0.55684	0.49697	0.44401	0.39711	0.35553	0.31863	12
13	0.87866	0.77303	0.68095	0.60057	0.53032	0.46884	0.41496	0.36770	0.32618	0.28966	13
14	0.86996	0.75787	0.66112	0.57747	0.50507	0.44230	0.38782	0.34046	0.29925	0.26333	14
15	0.86135	0.74301	0.64186	0.55526	0.48102	0.41726	0.36245	0.31524	0.27454	0.23939	15
16	0.85282	0.72845	0.62317	0.53391	0.45811	0.39365	0.33873	0.29189	0.25187	0.21763	16
17	0.84438	0.71416	0.60502	0.51337	0.43630	0.37136	0.31657	0.27027	0.23107	0.19784	17
18	0.83602	0.70016	0.58739	0.49363	0.41552	0.35034	0.29586	0.25025	0.21199	0.17986	18
19	0.82774	0.68643	0.57029	0.47464	0.39573	0.33051	0.27651	0.23171	0.19449	0.16351	19
20	0.81954	0.67297	0.55367	0.45639	0.37689	0.31180	0.25842	0.21455	0.17843	0.14864	20
21	0.81143	0.65978	0.53755	0.43883	0.35894	0.29415	0.24151	0.19866	0.16370	0.13513	21
22	0.80340	0.64684	0.52189	0.42195	0.34185	0.27750	0.22571	0.18394	0.15018	0.12285	22
23	0.79544	0.63414	0.50669	0.40573	0.32557	0.26180	0.21095	0.17031	0.13778	0.11168	23
24	0.78757	0.62172	0.49193	0.39012	0.31007	0.24698	0.19715	0.15770	0.12640	0.10153	24
25	0.77977	0.60953	0.47760	0.37512	0.29530	0.23300	0.18425	0.14602	0.11597	0.09230	25

continued

continued

n	11%	12%	13%	14%	15%	16%	17%	18%	19%	20%	n
1	0.90090	0.89286	0.88496	0.87719	0.86957	0.86207	0.85470	0.84746	0.84034	0.83333	1
2	0.81162	0.79719	0.78315	0.76947	0.75614	0.74316	0.73051	0.71818	0.70616	0.69444	2
3	0.73119	0.71178	0.69305	0.67497	0.65752	0.64066	0.62437	0.60863	0.59342	0.57870	3
4	0.65873	0.63552	0.61332	0.59208	0.57175	0.55229	0.53365	0.51579	0.49867	0.48225	4
5	0.59345	0.56743	0.54276	0.51937	0.49718	0.47611	0.45611	0.43711	0.41905	0.40188	5
6	0.53464	0.50663	0.48032	0.45559	0.43233	0.41044	0.38984	0.37043	0.35214	0.33490	6
7	0.48166	0.45235	0.42506	0.39964	0.37594	0.35383	0.33320	0.31392	0.29592	0.27908	7
8	0.43393	0.40388	0.37616	0.35056	0.32690	0.30503	0.28487	0.26604	0.24867	0.23257	8
9	0.39092	0.36061	0.33288	0.30751	0.28426	0.26295	0.24340	0.22546	0.20897	0.19381	9
10	0.35218	0.32197	0.29459	0.26974	0.24718	0.22668	0.20804	0.19106	0.17560	0.16151	10
11	0.31728	0.28748	0.26070	0.23662	0.21494	0.19542	0.17781	0.16192	0.14756	0.13459	11
12	0.28584	0.25667	0.23071	0.20756	0.18691	0.16846	0.15197	0.13722	0.12400	0.11216	12
13	0.25751	0.22917	0.20416	0.18207	0.16253	0.14523	0.12989	0.11629	0.10420	0.09346	13
14	0.23199	0.20462	0.18068	0.15971	0.14133	0.12520	0.11102	0.09855	0.08757	0.07789	14
15	0.20900	0.18270	0.15989	0.14010	0.12289	0.10793	0.09489	0.08352	0.07359	0.06491	15
16	0.18829	0.16312	0.14150	0.12289	0.10686	0.09304	0.08110	0.07078	0.06184	0.05409	16
17	0.16963	0.14564	0.12522	0.10780	0.09393	0.08021	0.06932	0.05998	0.05196	0.04507	17
18	0.15282	0.13004	0.11081	0.09456	0.08080	0.06914	0.05925	0.05083	0.04367	0.03756	18
19	0.13768	0.11611	0.09806	0.08295	0.07026	0.05961	0.05064	0.04308	0.03669	0.03130	19
20	0.12403	0.10367	0.08678	0.07276	0.06110	0.05139	0.04328	0.03651	0.03084	0.02608	20
21	0.11174	0.09256	0.07680	0.06383	0.05313	0.04430	0.03699	0.03094	0.02591	0.02174	21
22	0.10067	0.08264	0.06796	0.05599	0.04620	0.03819	0.03162	0.02622	0.02178	0.01811	22
23	0.09069	0.07379	0.06014	0.04911	0.04017	0.03292	0.02702	0.02222	0.01830	0.01509	23
24	0.08170	0.06588	0.05322	0.04308	0.03493	0.02838	0.02310	0.01883	0.01538	0.01258	24
25	0.07361	0.05882	0.04710	0.03779	0.03038	0.02447	0.01974	0.01596	0.01292	0.01048	25

continued

continued

n	21%	22%	23%	24%	25%	26%	27%	28%	29%	30%	n
1	0.82645	0.81967	0.81301	0.80645	0.80000	0.79365	0.78740	0. 78125	0. 77519	0.76923	1
2	0.68301	0.67186	0.66098	0.65036	0.64000	0.62988	0.62000	0.61035	0.60093	0.59172	2
3	0.56447	0.55071	0.53738	0.52449	0.51200	0.49991	0.48819	0.47684	0.46583	0.45517	3
4	0.46651	0.45140	0.43690	0.42297	0.40960	0.39675	0.38440	0.37253	0.36111	0.35013	4
5	0.38554	0.37000	0.35520	0.34111	0.32768	0.31488	0.30268	0.29104	0.27993	0.26933	5
6	0.31863	0.30328	0.28878	0.27509	0.26214	0.24991	0.23833	0.22737	0.21700	0.20718	6
7	0.26333	0.24859	0.23478	0.22184	0.20972	0.19834	0.18766	0.17764	0.16822	0.15937	7
8	0.21763	0.20376	0.19088	0.17891	0.16777	0.15741	0.14776	0.13878	0.13040	0.12259	8
9	0.17986	0.16702	0.15519	0.14428	0.13422	0.12493	0.11635	0.10842	0.10109	0.09430	9
10	0.14864	0.13690	0.12617	0.11635	0.10737	0.09915	0.09161	0.08470	0.07836	0.07254	10
11	0.12285	0.11221	0.10258	0.09383	0.08590	0.07869	0.07214	0.06617	0.06075	0.05580	11
12	0.10153	0.09198	0.08339	0.07567	0.06872	0.06245	0.05680	0.05170	0.04709	0.04292	12
13	0.08391	0.07539	0.06780	0.06103	0.05498	0.04957	0.04472	0.04039	0.03650	0.03302	13
14	0.06934	0.06180	0.05512	0.04921	0.04398	0.03934	0.03522	0.03155	0.02830	0.02540	14
15	0.05731	0.05065	0.04481	0.03969	0.03518	0.03122	0.02773	0.02465	0.02194	0.01954	15
16	0.04736	0.04152	0.03643	0.03201	0.02815	0.02478	0.02183	0.01926	0.01700	0.01503	16
17	0.03914	0.03403	0.02962	0.02581	0.02252	0.01967	0.01719	0.01505	0.01318	0.01156	17
18	0.03235	0.02789	0.02408	0.02082	0.01801	0.01561	0.01354	0.01175	0.01022	0.00889	18
19	0.02673	0.02286	0.01958	0.01679	0.01441	0.01239	0.01066	0.00918	0.00792	0.00684	19
20	0.02209	0.01874	0.01592	0.01354	0.01153	0.00983	0.00839	0.00717	0.00614	0.00526	20
21	0.01826	0.01536	0.01294	0.01092	0.00922	0.00780	0.00661	0.00561	0.00476	0.00405	21
22	0.01509	0.01259	0.01052	0.00880	0.00738	0.00619	0.00520	0.00438	0.00369	0.00311	22
23	0.01247	0.01032	0.00855	0.00710	0.00590	0.00491	0.00410	0.00342	0.00286	0.00239	23
24	0.01031	0.00846	0.00695	0.00573	0.00472	0.00390	0.00323	0.00267	0.00222	0.00184	24
25	0.00852	0.00693	0.00565	0.00462	0.00378	0.00310	0.00254	0.00209	0.00172	0.00152	25

continued

continued

n	31%	32%	33%	34%	35%	36%	37%	38%	39%	40%	n
1	0.76336	0.75758	0.75188	0.74627	0.74074	0.73529	0.72993	0.72464	0.71942	0.71429	1
2	0.58272	0.57392	0.56532	0.55692	0.54870	0.54066	0.53279	0.52510	0.51757	0.51020	2
3	0.44482	0.43479	0.42505	0.41561	0.40644	0.39754	0.38890	0.38051	0.37235	0.36443	3
4	0.33956	0.32939	0.31959	0.31016	0.30107	0.29231	0.28387	0.27573	0.26788	0.26031	4
5	0.25920	0.24953	0.24029	0.23146	0.22301	0.21493	0.20720	0.19980	0.19272	0.18593	5
6	0.19787	0.18904	0.18067	0.17273	0.16520	0.15804	0.15124	0.14479	0.13865	0.13281	6
7	0.15104	0.14321	0.13584	0.12890	0.12237	0.11621	0.11040	0.10492	0.09975	0.09486	7
8	0.11530	0.10849	0.10214	0.09620	0.09064	0.08545	0.08058	0.07603	0.07176	0.06776	8
9	0.08802	0.08219	0.07680	0.07179	0.06714	0.06283	0.05882	0.05509	0.05163	0.04840	9
10	0.06719	0.06227	0.05774	0.05357	0.04973	0.04620	0.04293	0.03992	0.03714	0.03457	10
11	0.05129	0.04717	0.04341	0.03998	0.03684	0.03397	0.03134	0.02893	0.02672	0.02469	11
12	0.03915	0.03574	0.03264	0.02984	0.02729	0.02498	0.02287	0.02096	0.01922	0.01764	12
13	0.02989	0.02707	0.02454	0.02227	0.02021	0.01837	0.01670	0.01519	0.01383	0.01260	13
14	0.02281	0.02051	0.01845	0.01662	0.01497	0.01350	0.01219	0.01101	0.00995	0.00900	14
15	0.01742	0.01554	0.01387	0.01240	0.01109	0.00993	0.00890	0.00798	0.00716	0.00643	15
16	0.01329	0.01177	0.01043	0.00925	0.00822	0.00730	0.00649	0.00578	0.00515	0.00459	16
17	0.01015	0.00892	0.00784	0.00691	0.00609	0.00537	0.00474	0.00419	0.00370	0.00328	17
18	0.00775	0.00676	0.00590	0.00515	0.00451	0.00395	0.00346	0.00304	0.00267	0.00234	18
19	0.00591	0.00512	0.00443	0.00385	0.00334	0.00290	0.00253	0.00220	0.00192	0.00167	19
20	0.00451	0.00388	0.00333	0.00287	0.00247	0.00213	0.00184	0.00159	0.00138	0.00120	20
21	0.00345	0.00294	0.00251	0.00214	0.00183	0.00157	0.00135	0.00115	0.00099	0.00085	21
22	0.00263	0.00223	0.00188	0.00160	0.00136	0.00115	0.00098	0.00084	0.00071	0.00061	22
23	0.00201	0.00169	0.00142	0.00119	0.00101	0.00085	0.00072	0.00061	0.00051	0.00044	23
24	0.00153	0.00128	0.00107	0.00089	0.00074	0.00062	0.00052	0.00044	0.00037	0.00031	24
25	0.00117	0.00097	0.00080	0.00066	0.00055	0.00046	0.00038	0.00032	0.00027	0.00022	25

Appendix C: Present value interest factor for an annuity (PVIFA) of £1.00 for *n* years for interest rate of:

n	1%	2%	3%	4%	5%	6%	7%	8%	9%	10%	*n*
1	0.9901	0.9804	0.9709	0.9615	0.9524	0.9434	0.9346	0.9259	0.9174	0.9091	1
2	1.9704	1.9416	1.9135	1.8861	1.8594	1.8334	1.8080	1.7833	1.7591	1.7355	2
3	2.9410	2.8839	2.8286	2.7751	2.7232	2.6730	2.6243	2.5771	2.5313	2.4868	3
4	3.9020	3.8077	3.7171	3.6299	3.5459	3.4651	3.3872	3.3121	3.2397	3.1699	4
5	4.8535	4.7134	4.5797	4.4518	4.3295	4.2123	4.1002	3.9927	3.8896	3.7908	5
6	5.7955	5.6014	5.4172	5.2421	5.0757	4.9173	4.7665	4.6229	4.4859	4.3553	6
7	6.7282	6.4720	6.2302	6.0020	5.7863	5.5824	5.3893	5.2064	5.0329	4.8684	7
8	7.6517	7.3254	7.0196	6.7327	6.4632	6.2098	5.9713	5.7466	5.5348	5.3349	8
9	8.5661	8.1622	7.7861	7.4353	7.1078	6.8017	6.5152	6.2469	5.9852	5.7590	9
10	9.4714	8.9825	8.5302	8.1109	7.7217	7.3601	7.0236	6.7101	6.4176	6.1446	10
11	10.3677	9.7868	9.2526	8.7604	8.3064	7.8868	7.4987	7.1389	6.8052	6.4951	11
12	11.2552	10.5753	9.9539	9.3850	8.8632	8.3838	7.9427	7.5361	7.1607	6.8137	12
13	12.1338	11.3483	10.6349	9.9856	9.3925	8.8527	8.3576	7.9038	7.4869	7.1034	13
14	13.0038	12.1062	11.2960	10.5631	9.8986	9.2950	8.7454	8.2442	7.7861	7.3667	14
15	13.8651	12.8492	11.9379	11.1183	10.3796	9.7122	9.1079	8.5595	8.0607	7.6061	15
16	14.7180	13.5777	12.5610	11.6522	10.8377	10.1059	9.4466	8.8514	8.3125	7.8237	16
17	15.5624	14.2918	13.1660	12.1656	11.2740	10.4772	9.7632	9.1216	8.5436	8.0215	17
18	16.3984	14.9920	13.7534	12.6592	11.6895	10.8276	10.0591	9.3819	8.7556	8.2014	18
19	17.2261	15.6784	14.3237	13.1339	12.0853	11.1581	10.3356	9.6036	8.9501	8.3649	19
20	17.8571	16.3514	14.8774	13.5903	12.4622	11.4699	10.5940	9.8181	9.1285	8.5136	20
21	18.0457	17.0111	15.4149	14.0291	12.8211	11.7640	10.8355	10.0168	9.2922	8.6487	21
22	19.6605	17.6580	15.9368	14.4511	13.1630	12.0416	11.0612	10.2007	9.4424	8.7715	22
23	20.4559	18.2921	16.4435	14.8568	13.4885	12.3033	11.2722	10.3710	9.5802	8.8832	23
24	21.2435	18.9139	16.9355	15.2469	13.7986	12.5503	11.4693	10.5287	9.7066	8.9847	24
25	22.0233	19.5234	17.4131	15.6220	14.0939	12.7833	11.6536	10.6748	9.8226	9.0770	25

continued

continued

n	11%	12%	13%	14%	15%	16%	17%	18%	19%	20%	n
1	0.9009	0.8929	0.8850	0.8772	0.8696	0.8621	0.8547	0.8475	0.8403	0.8333	1
2	1.7125	1.6901	1.6681	1.6467	1.6257	1.6052	1.5852	1.5656	1.5465	1.5278	2
3	2.4437	2.4018	2.3612	2.3216	2.2832	2.2459	2.2096	2.1743	2.1399	2.1065	3
4	3.1024	3.0373	2.9745	2.9137	2.8550	2.7982	2.7432	2.6901	2.6486	2.5887	4
5	3.6959	3.6048	3.5172	3.4331	3.3522	3.2743	3.1993	3.1272	3.0576	2.9906	5
6	4.2305	4.1114	3.9976	3.8887	3.7845	3.6847	3.5892	3.4976	3.4098	3.3255	6
7	4.7122	4.5638	4.4226	4.2883	4.1604	4.0386	3.9224	3.8115	3.7057	3.6046	7
8	5.1461	4.9676	4.7988	4.6389	4.4873	4.3436	4.2072	4.0776	3.9544	3.8372	8
9	5.5370	5.3282	5.1317	4.9464	4.7716	4.6065	4.4506	4.3030	4.1633	4.0310	9
10	5.8892	5.6502	5.4262	5.2161	5.0188	4.8332	4.6586	4.4941	4.3389	4.1925	10
11	6.2065	5.9377	5.6869	5.4527	5.2337	5.0286	4.8364	4.6560	4.4865	4.3271	11
12	6.4924	6.1944	5.9176	5.6603	5.4206	5.1971	4.9884	4.7932	4.6105	4.4392	12
13	6.7499	6.4235	6.1218	5.8424	5.5931	5.3423	5.1183	4.9095	4.7147	4.5327	13
14	6.9819	6.6282	6.3025	6.0021	5.7245	5.4675	5.2293	5.0081	4.8023	4.6106	14
15	7.1909	6.8109	6.4624	6.1422	5.8474	5.5755	5.3242	5.0916	4.8759	4.6755	15
16	7.3792	6.9740	6.6039	6.2651	5.9542	5.6685	5.4053	5.1624	4.9377	4.7296	16
17	7.5488	7.1196	6.7291	6.3729	6.0472	5.7487	5.4746	5.2223	4.9897	4.7746	17
18	7.7016	7.2497	6.8399	6.4674	6.1280	5.8178	5.5339	5.2732	5.0333	4.8122	18
19	7.8393	7.3658	6.9380	6.5504	6.1982	5.8575	5.5845	5.3162	5.0700	4.8435	19
20	7.9633	7.4694	7.0248	6.6231	6.2593	5.9288	5.6278	5.3527	5.1009	4.8696	20
21	8.0751	7.5620	7.1016	6.6870	6.3125	5.9731	5.6648	5.3837	5.1268	4.8913	21
22	8.1757	7.6446	7.1695	6.7429	6.3587	6.0113	5.6964	5.4099	5.1486	4.9094	22
23	8.2664	7.7184	7.2297	6.7921	6.3988	6.0442	5.7234	5.4321	5.1668	4.9245	23
24	8.3481	7.7843	7.2829	6.8351	6.4338	6.0726	5.7465	5.4509	5.1822	4.9371	24
25	8.4217	7.8431	7.3300	6.8729	6.4641	6.0971	5.7662	5.4669	5.1951	4.9476	25

continued

continued

n	21%	22%	23%	24%	25%	26%	27%	28%	29%	30%	*n*
1	0.8264	0.8197	0.8130	0.8065	0.8000	0.7937	0.7874	0.7813	0.7752	0.7692	1
2	1.5095	1.4915	1.4740	1.4568	1.4400	1.4235	1.4074	1.3916	1.3761	1.3609	2
3	2.0739	2.0422	2.0114	1.9813	1.9520	1.9234	1.8956	1.8684	1.8420	1.8161	3
4	2.5404	2.4936	2.4483	2.4043	2.3616	2.3202	2.2800	2.2410	2.2031	2.1662	4
5	2.9260	2.8636	2.8035	2.7454	2.6893	2.6351	2.5827	2.5320	2.4830	2.4356	5
6	3.2446	3.1669	3.0923	3.0205	2.9514	2.8850	2.8210	2.7594	2.7000	2.6427	6
7	3.5079	3.4155	3.3270	3.2423	3.1611	3.0833	3.0087	2.9370	2.8682	2.8021	7
8	3.7256	3.6193	3.5179	3.4212	3.3289	3.2407	3.1564	3.0758	2.9986	2.9247	8
9	3.9054	3.7863	3.6731	3.5655	3.4631	3.3657	3.2728	3.1842	3.0997	3.0915	9
10	4.0541	3.9232	3.7993	3.6819	3.5705	3.4648	3.3644	3.2689	3.1781	3.1090	10
11	4.1769	4.0354	3.9018	3.7757	3.6564	3.5435	3.4365	3.3351	3.2388	3.1473	11
12	4.2785	4.1274	3.9852	3.8514	3.7251	3.6060	3.4933	3.3868	3.2859	3.1903	12
13	4.3624	4.2028	4.0530	3.9124	3.7801	3.6555	3.6381	3.4272	3.3224	3.2233	13
14	4.4317	4.2646	4.1082	3.9616	3.8241	3.6949	3.5733	3.4587	3.3507	3.2487	14
15	4.4890	4.3152	4.1530	4.0013	3.8593	3.7261	3.6010	3.4834	3.3726	3.2682	15
16	4.5364	4.3567	4.1894	4.0333	3.8874	3.7509	3.6228	3.5026	3.3896	3.2832	16
17	4.5755	4.3908	4.2190	4.0591	3.9099	3.7705	3.6400	3.5177	3.4028	3.2948	17
18	4.6079	4.4187	4.2431	4.0799	3.9279	3.7861	3.6536	3.5294	3.4130	3.3037	18
19	4.6346	4.4415	4.2627	4.0967	3.9424	3.7985	3.6642	3.5386	3.4210	3.3105	19
20	4.6567	4.4603	4.2786	4.1103	3.9539	3.8083	3.6726	3.5458	3.4271	3.3158	20
21	4.6750	4.4756	4.2916	4.1212	3.9631	3.8161	3.6792	3.5514	3.4319	3.3198	21
22	4.6900	4.4882	4.3021	4.1300	3.9705	3.8223	3.6844	3.5558	3.4356	3.3230	22
23	4.7025	4.4985	4.3106	4.1371	3.9764	3.8273	3.6885	3.5592	3.4384	3.3254	23
24	4.7128	4.5070	4.3176	4.1428	3.9811	3.8312	3.6918	3.5619	3.4406	3.3272	24
25	4.7213	4.5139	4.3232	4.1474	3.9849	3.8342	3.6943	3.5640	3.4423	3.3286	25

continued

continued

n	31%	32%	33%	34%	35%	36%	37%	38%	39%	40%	*n*
1	0.7634	0.7576	0.7519	0.7463	0.7407	0.7353	0.7299	0.7246	0.7194	0.7143	1
2	1.3461	1.3315	1.3172	1.3032	1.2894	1.2760	1.2627	1.2497	1.2370	1.2245	2
3	1.7909	1.7663	1.7423	1.7188	1.6959	1.6735	1.6516	1.6302	1.6093	1.5889	3
4	2.1305	2.0957	2.0618	2.0290	1.9969	1.9658	1.9355	1.9060	1.8772	1.8492	4
5	2.3897	2.3452	2.3021	2.2604	2.2200	2.1807	2.1427	2.1058	2.0699	1.9352	5
6	2.5875	2.5342	2.4828	2.4331	2.3852	2.3388	2.2936	2.2506	2.2086	2.1680	6
7	2.7386	2.6775	2.6187	2.5620	2.5075	2.4550	2.4043	2.3555	2.3083	2.2628	7
8	2.8539	2.7860	2.2708	2.6582	2.5982	2.5404	2.4849	2.4315	2.3801	2.3306	8
9	2.9419	2.8681	2.7976	2.7300	2.6653	2.6033	2.5437	2.4866	2.4317	2.3790	9
10	3.0091	2.9304	2.8553	2.7836	2.7150	2.6495	2.5867	2.5265	2.4689	2.4136	10
11	3.0604	2.9776	2.8987	2.8236	2.7519	2.6834	2.6180	2.5555	2.4956	2.4383	11
12	3.0995	3.0133	2.9314	2.8534	2.7792	2.7084	2.6409	2.5764	2.5148	2.4559	12
13	3.1294	3.0404	2.9559	2.8757	2.7994	2.7268	2.6576	2.5916	2.5286	2.4685	13
14	3.1522	3.0609	2.9744	2.8923	2.8144	2.7403	2.6698	2.6026	2.5386	2.4775	14
15	3.1696	3.0764	2.9883	2.9047	2.8255	2.7502	2.6787	2.6106	2.5457	2.4839	15
16	3.1829	3.0882	2.9987	2.9140	2.8337	2.7575	2.6852	2.6164	2.5509	2.4885	16
17	3.1931	3.0971	3.0065	2.9209	2.8398	2.7629	2.6899	2.6202	2.5546	2.4918	17
18	3.2008	3.1039	3.0124	2.9260	2.8443	2.7668	2.6934	2.6236	2.5573	2.4941	18
19	3.2067	3.1090	3.0169	2.9299	2.8476	2.7697	2.6959	2.6288	2.5592	2.4958	19
20	3.2112	3.1129	3.0202	2.9327	2.8501	2.7718	2.6977	2.6274	2.5606	2.4970	20
21	3.2154	3.1158	3.0227	2.9349	2.8519	2.7734	2.6991	2.6285	2.5616	2.4979	21
22	3.2173	3.1180	3.0246	2.9365	2.8533	2.7746	2.7000	2.6294	2.5623	2.4985	22
23	3.2193	3.1197	3.0260	2.9377	2.8543	2.7754	2.7008	2.6300	2.5628	2.4989	23
24	3.2209	3.1210	3.0271	2.9386	2.8550	2.7760	2.7013	2.6304	2.5632	2.4992	24
25	3.2220	3.1220	3.0279	2.9392	2.8556	2.7765	2.7017	2.6307	2.5634	2.4994	25

Glossary

Acceptance Credit: a facility to issue bank-guaranteed bills (**bank bills**) by a firm wanting to raise short-term finance. They can be sold on the money market, but are unrelated to specific trading transactions. The bank accepts the liability to exchange cash for bills when presented at the due date.

Acquirees: taken-over firms. Also, 'targets' or 'victims'.

Acquirors: firms that make takeovers. Also, 'predators'.

Adjusted NAV: the NAV as per the accounts, adjusted for any known or suspected deviations between book values and market, or realisable values.

Adjusted Present Value (APV): the basic NPV of an activity adjusted for 'bolt-on extras' like financing costs and benefits, e.g. the tax shield, costs of issuing new finance.

Agency Costs: costs that owners (principals) have to incur in order to ensure that their agents (managers) make financial decisions consistent with their best interests.

Aggressive Stocks generate returns that vary by a larger proportion than overall market returns. Their betas exceed 1.0.

Alternative Investment Market (AIM): where smaller, younger companies can acquire a stock market listing.

American Options can be exercised at any time up to the maturity date.

Amortisation: repayment of debt by a series of instalments. Also used as a term for depreciation of intangible assets.

Annual Percentage Rate (APR): the true annualised cost of finance.

Annuity: a finite series of cash flows.

Arbitrage: the profitable exploitation of divergences between the prices of goods (or between interest rates), that violate the Law of One Price. Also applied in MM's capital structure analysis to refer to the process of equalising the values of geared and ungeared firms. Hence, **arbitageur**.

The **Arbitrage Pricing Model (APT):** an extension of the CAPM to include more than one factor (hence, an example of a **multi-factor model**) used to explain the returns on securities. Each factor has its own Beta coefficient.

Articles of Association: a document drawn up at the formation of an enterprise, detailing the rights and obligations of shareholders and directors.

Asset or **Activity Beta:** the inherent systematic riskiness of a firm's operations, before allowing for gearing. Also known as **Firm Beta**, **Company Beta**, or **Ungeared Beta**.

Asset-Backed Securities are bonds issued on the security of a stream of highly certain income flows, e.g. mortgage payments to a bank, out of which interest payments are made.

Asset-Stripping: selling off the assets of a taken-over firm, often in order to recoup the initial outlay.

Asymmetric Information: one party to a contract is in possession of more information than the other.

Balloon Repayment: most of the loan repayment is made on maturity.

Bancassurance: a term coined to denote the combination of banking and insurance business within the same organisation.

A **Bank Loan** is usually extended for a fixed term with a pre-agreed schedule of interest and capital repayments. Interest is usually payable on the initial amount borrowed, regardless of the falling balance as repayments are made.

Barter: the simplest form of counter-trade, involving direct exchange of goods with no money being exchanged.

Betas (or Beta Coefficients) relate the responsiveness of the returns on individual securities to variations in the return on the overall market portfolio.

Beta Geared: the Beta attaching to the ordinary shares of a geared firm. These bear a risk higher than the firm's basic activity.

Beta Ungeared: the geared Beta stripped of the effect of gearing. Corresponds to the activity Beta in an equivalent ungeared firm.

Bilateral Netting is operated by pairs of firms in the same group netting off their respective positions regarding payables and receivables.

Bill of Exchange: a promise to pay at a specific time issued to suppliers by purchasers in exchange for goods. Bills may be held to maturity or sold at a discount on the money market if cash is required sooner.

Bill of Lading: a document that transfers title to exported goods to the bank that finances the deal when the goods are shipped.

Bird-in-the-Hand Fallacy: the mistaken belief that dividends paid early in the future are worth more than dividends expected in later time periods, simply because they are nearer in time.

Bonds: any form of borrowing firms can undertake in the form of a medium- or long-term security, that commits them to specific repayment dates, at fixed or variable interest.

Bonus or **Scrip Issues:** issues of free shares to existing shareholders *in lieu* of, or in addition to, cash dividends. Reflected in lower reserves, hence the alternative label, **Capitalisation Issue**.

Book-to-Market Ratio: ratio of the book value of equity to the market value of the shares.

Break-Up Value (BUV): the value that can be obtained by selling off the firm's assets piecemeal to the highest bidders.

Bullet Repayment: where a loan is repaid wholly at the maturity date.

Business Angels: wealthy private investors who take equity stakes in small, high-risk firms.

The **Business Expansion Scheme** was established to enable investors to obtain tax relief when purchasing ordinary shares in unquoted firms seeking 'seed-corn' funds for development.

Buy-back: a method of obtaining payment for building a manufacturing unit overseas by taking the future physical product of the plant in return.

Capital: strictly, the funds invested in a firm by shareholders when they purchase ordinary shares, but often used to indicate all forms of equity, and often to refer to any form of finance, whether equity or debt.

Capital Allowances: tax allowances for capital expenditure.

Capital Asset: any investment that offers a prospective return, with or without risk. However, in finance, the term is usually applied to securities and ordinary shares in particular.

Capital Asset Pricing Model (CAPM): a theory used to explain how efficient capital markets value securities, i.e. capital assets, by discounting future expected returns at risk-adjusted discount rates.

Capital Gains Tax is paid on realising an increase in share value. Capital gains are currently treated as income in the UK.

Capital Gearing: the mixture of debt and equity in a firm's capital structure, which influences variations in shareholders' profits in response to sales and EBIT variations.

Capitalisation: the procedure of converting (by discounting) a series of future cash flows into a single capital sum.

Capitalisation Rate: a discount rate used to convert a series of future cash flows into a single capital sum.

The **Capital Market Line (CML)** traces out the efficient combinations of risk and return available to investors when combining a risk-free asset with the market portfolio.

Capital Structure: the mixture of debt and equity resulting from decisions on financing operations.

Cash Operating Cycle: length of time between cash payment to suppliers and cash received from customers.

The **Characteristics Line (CL)** relates the periodic returns on a security to the returns on the market portfolio. Its slope is the Beta of the security. The regression model used to estimate Betas is called the **market model**.

Chartist: analyst who relies on charts of past share movements to predict future movements.

A **Classical Tax System** initially taxes company profits, and then also taxes any dividend income. This double taxation of dividends thus provides an incentive to retain profits.

Clientèle Effect: the notion that a firm attracts investors by establishing a set dividend policy that suits a particular group of investors.

Commercial Paper: a short-term promissory note or IOU, issued by a highly creditworthy corporate borrower to financial institutions and other cash-rich corporates.

Co-movement or **Co-Variability:** the tendency for two variables, e.g. the returns from two investments, to move in parallel. It can be measured using either:

(i) the **Correlation Coefficient:** a relative measure of co-movement that locates assets on a scale between −1 and +1. Where returns move exactly in unison, perfect positive correlation exists, and where exactly opposite movements occur, perfect negative correlation exists. Most investments fall in between, generally, with positive correlation.

(ii) the **Covariance:** an absolute measure of co-movement with no upper or lower limits.

A **Concentric Acquisition** is undertaken to exploit synergies in marketing of two firms' products, without production economies.

Conglomerate Takeover: the acquisition of a target firm in a field apparently unrelated to the acquiror's existing activities.

Contra-Cyclical: a term applied to an investment whose returns fluctuate in opposite ways to general trends in business activity, i.e. contrary to the cycle.

Convertible Loan Stock: a debenture that can be converted into ordinary shares, often on attractive terms, usually at the option of the holder. Some preference shares are convertible.

Cost of Debt: the yield a firm would have to offer if undertaking further borrowing at current market rates.

Cost of Equity: the minimum rate of return a firm must offer owners to compensate for waiting for their returns, and for bearing risk.

Counter-Party Risk: the risk that the opposite party to a contract defaults on its obligations.

Counter-Trade: a form of trade involving reciprocal obligations with a trading partner, or counter-party, e.g. a commitment to buy from a firm or country that the firm sells to.

Country Risk: the risk of adverse effects on the net cash flows of a MNC due to political and economic factors peculiar to the country of location of FDI.

Coupon Rate of Interest: the fixed rate of interest, as printed on the debt security, that a firm must pay to lenders.

Crest: an electronic mechanism for settling and registering shares sold on the London Stock Exchange.

Critical Mass: the minimum size of firm thought necessary to compete effectively, e.g. to finance R & D.

Currency Futures Contract: a commitment to deliver a specific amount of foreign exchange at a specified future date at an agreed price incorporated in the contract. Contracts can be traded on an exchange in standard sizes.

Currency Option: the right, but not the obligation, to buy or sell a fixed amount of currency at a pre-determined rate at a specified future date.

Currency Swap: a transfer of cash payment obligations denominated in foreign currencies. The two parties initially exchange the principal of their respective borrowings, plus the interest commitments in the currencies over an agreed period, and re-exchange the principal at the end of this period.

Currency Switching: where a firm uses foreign exchange received in the course of operations to settle obligations to a third party, often located in a third country.

Current Cost Accounting (CCA) attempts to capture the effect of inflation on asset values (and liabilities) by recording them at their current replacement cost, i.e. the cost of obtaining an identical replacement.

Current Ratio: ratio of current assets to current liabilities.

Debentures: in law, any form of borrowing that commits a firm to pay interest and repay capital. In practice, usually applied to long-term loans that are secured on a firm's assets.

The **Debt Capacity** of an investment or a whole firm is the maximum amount of debt finance, and hence interest payments that it can support without incurring financial distress.

Default: the failure by a borrower to adhere to a pre-agreed schedule of interest and/or capital payments on a loan.

A **Defensive Stock** generates returns that vary by a smaller proportion than overall market returns. Its Beta is less than one.

Derivative: financial instrument whose value derives from an underlying asset.

Discount Rate: any percentage required return used to convert future expected cash flows into their equivalent present values.

Discounted Cash Flow: future cash flows adjusted for the time-value of money.

Disintermediation: the process whereby firms borrow and lend funds directly without going through a bank or other intermediary.

Diversifiable Risk can be removed by efficient portfolio diversification.

Diversification: extension of a firm's activities into new and unrelated fields. Although this may generate cost savings, e.g. via shared distribution systems, as a by-product, the fundamental motive for diversification is to reduce exposure to fluctuations in economic activity.

Dividend Irrelevance: the theory that, when firms have access to external finance, it is irrelevant to firm value whether they pay a dividend or not.

Dividend Valuation Model: a way of assessing the value of shares by capitalising the future dividends. With growing dividend payments, it becomes the **Dividend Growth Model**.

Dividend Yield: gross dividend per ordinary share (including both interim and final payments) divided by current share price.

Double Tax Agreements (DTAs): reciprocal arrangements between countries whereby tax paid in one location is credited in the second, thus avoiding doubling up the firm's tax bill. Hence, Double Tax Relief (DTR).

Earnings Before Interest, Tax, Depreciation & Amortisation (EBITDA): a rough measure of operating cash flow, effectively, operating profit with depreciation added back. It differs from the 'Net Cash Inflow from Operating Activities' shown in cash flow statements due to working capital movements.

Earnings Dilution: the dampening effect on EPS of issuing further shares at a discount as in a rights issue.

Earnings Yield: EPS divided by current share price. Sometimes, it refers to expected or 'prospective' EPS, becoming the **'Prospective Earnings Yield'**. It is a simple way of expressing the investor's Return on Investment on the share.

EBIT: Earnings (i.e. profits) before Interest and Taxation.

Economic Order Quantity (EOQ): the most economic quantity to be ordered that minimises holding and ordering costs.

Economic Value Added (EVA): post-tax accounting profit generated by a firm reduced by a charge for using the equity (usually, cost of equity times book value of equity).

The **Efficiency Frontier** traces out all the available portfolio combinations that either minimise risk for a stated expected return or maximise expected return for a specified measure of risk.

Efficient Markets: where current share prices fully reflect the information available.

Enhanced Scrip Dividends: scrip alternatives offered to investors that are worth more than the alternative cash payment.

The **Enterprise Investment Scheme** replaced the BES in 1994, incorporating less generous tax breaks.

Enterprise Value: the value of the whole firm.

Entrepreneurial Companies are driven by the growth ambitions and desire of the owners to create significant wealth.

Equity, or **Equity Value:** the value of the owners' stake in a firm, however calculated.

The **Equity Beta** indicates the systematic riskiness attaching to the returns on ordinary shares. It equates to the asset Beta for an ungeared firm, or is adjusted upwards to reflect the extra riskiness of shares in a geared firm, i.e. the '**Geared Beta**'.

Equivalent Loan: the loan that would involve the same schedule of interest and loan repayments as the profile of rentals required by an equipment lessor.

Equivalent Risk Class: a concept used by MM to include all firms subject to the same business risks (i.e. all having the same Activity Betas).

Eurobonds (or **International Bonds**)**:** securities issued by borrowers in a market outside that of their domestic currency.

European Options can only be exercised at the specified maturity date.

Exchange ***Agio***: the percentage difference between the spot and forward rates of exchange between two currencies.

A share is quoted **Ex-Dividend (Ex-Div.**, or **xd)** when subsequent purchasers no longer qualify for the forthcoming dividend payment. Until this point, the shares are quoted **Cum-Dividend.**

Exercise (Strike) Price: the price at which the option to buy or sell can be transacted.

Expectations (or **Unbiased Forward Predictor) Theory:** the postulate that the expected change in the spot rate of exchange is equal to the difference between the current spot rate and the current forward rate for the relevant period.

Externalisation: the transfer of key functions and expertise to an overseas strategic partner.

Factoring: a means of obtaining faster cash inflow, and thus increased funds. A firm appoints the factor to collect outstanding accounts payable and to administer debtors' accounts. It also lends money to the client based on the value of the firm's sales.

Finance Lease: a method of acquiring an asset that involves a series of rental payments extending over the whole expected life-time of the asset.

Financial Distress: in narrow terms, the difficulty that a firm encounters in meeting obligations to creditors. More broadly, it refers to the adverse consequences, e.g. restrictions on behaviour that result, usually from excessive borrowing by a firm.

Financial Gearing includes both capital gearing and income gearing.

Financial Intermediaries: specialist financial institutions which collect funds from savers and lend to corporate and other borrowers.

Financial Services Authority (FSA): a regulatory body for maintaining confidence in the finance markets.

A **Fixed Charge** applies when a lender can force the sale of pre-specified company's assets in order to recover debts in the event of default on interest and/or capital payments.

The **Flat Yield** (or **Running Yield**) on a bond is the ratio of the fixed interest payment to the current market price of the bond.

A **Floating Charge** applies when a lender can force the sale of any (i.e. unspecified) of a company's assets in order to recover debts in the event of default on interest and/or capital payments.

Floating Rate Note (FRN): a bond issue where interest is paid at a variable rate.

Foreign Bonds: issues of loan stock on the domestic market by non-resident firms or organisations. In London, called 'bulldogs', in New York 'Yankees'.

Foreign Currency Swap: a way of extending the delivery date incorporated in a forward contract. A spot/forward swap involves completing the original contract by a spot transaction and entering a new forward contract for the additional of time.

Foreign Direct Investment (FDI): investment in fixed assets located abroad for operating distribution and/or production facilities.

Foreign Exchange Exposure: the risk of loss stemming from exposure to adverse foreign exchange rate movements.

Forfaiting: the practice whereby a bank purchases an exporter's sales invoices or promissory notes, that usually carry the guarantee of the importer's bank.

Forward Contract: a legal obligation to deliver a specified amount of currency at some specified future date. The rate of exchange is fixed at the date of the contract.

Forward Option: a forward currency contract that incorporates an open settlement date between two fixed dates.

Forward Rate of Exchange: the rate is the rate fixed for transactions that involve delivery and settlement at some specified future date.

Free Cash Flow (FCF): a firm's cash flow free of obligatory payments. Strictly, it is cash flow after interest, tax and replacement investment, although it is measured in many other ways in practice, e.g. after all investment.

Fundamental Analysis: estimation of the true value of a share based on expected future returns.

FX: abbreviation for foreign exchange.

Generally Accepted Accounting Principles (GAAP): the set of legal regulations and accounting standards that dictate 'best practice' in constructing company accounts.

Global Companies serve a range of overseas markets both by exporting and direct investment.

Going Concern Value (GCV): the value of the assets as stated in the accounts that assume that the firm will continue as a viable entity as it stands, i.e. as an ongoing activity.

Hedging: attempting to minimise the risk of loss stemming from exposure to adverse foreign exchange rate movements.

Hire Purchase: a means of obtaining the use of an asset before payment is completed. An HP contract involves an initial, or 'down payment', followed by a series of hire charges at the end of which ownership passes to the user.

Home-Made Dividends: cash released when an investor realises part of his/her investment in a firm in order to supplement his/her income.

Home-Made Gearing: personal borrowing undertaken in the process of arbitraging between the ordinary shares of geared and ungeared firms.

Horizontal Integration: the acquisition of a competitor in pursuit of market power and/or scale economies.

Hybrid: a security that embodies features of both equity and debt, and is thus difficult to classify under either category.

Imputation Systems of taxation offer shareholders tax credits (fully or partially) in respect of company tax already paid when assessing their income tax liability on dividends paid out.

Income Gearing: the proportion of EBIT pre-empted by prior interest commitments, i.e. the inverse of interest cover.

The **Incremental Hypothesis** suggests that firms tend to gradually build their degree of involvement in foreign markets, beginning with exporting and culminating in FDI.

Information Asymmetry: the imbalance in access to information about a firm's affairs as between directors and owners.

Information Content: the extra, unstated intelligence that investors deduce from the formal announcement by a firm of any financial news, i.e. what people read 'between the lines', or 'financial body language'.

Initial Public Offering (IPO): the first issue of shares by an existing or a newly-formed firm to the general public.

Insider trading: dealing in shares using information not publicly available.

Interest *Agio*: the percentage difference between interest rates prevailing in the money markets for lending/borrowing in two currencies.

Interest Cover: the number of times the profit before interest exceeds loan interest.

Interest Rate Parity (IRP) asserts that the difference between the spot and forward exchanges is equal to the differential between interest rates prevailing in the money markets for lending/borrowing in the respective currencies.

Internal rate of return the rates that equate the present value of future cash flows with initial investment cost.

Internalisation: the retention by the MNC of key management functions and technology.

The **International** (or **Open**) **Fisher Theory:** the notion that, because real rates of interest are equalised throughout the world, given freedom of capital mobility, any observed differences in nominal rates between different locations must be due to different expectations of inflation between those locations.

Invoice Discounting: a service less comprehensive than factoring, involving the sale for cash of approved invoices to a financial institution.

Joint Venture: a strategic alliance involving the formal establishment of a new marketing and/or production operation involving two or more partners.

Junk Bonds: low-quality, risky bonds with no credit rating.

Lagging: settling as late as possible a payable (receivable) denominated in a currency expected to weaken (strengthen).

Law of One Price: the proposition that any good or service will sell for the same price, adjusting for the relevant exchange rate, throughout the world.

Leading: advancing before the due date a payable denominated in a foreign currency that is expected to strengthen, or advancing a receivable in a currency expected to weaken.

Letter of Credit: a credit drawn up by an importer in favour of an exporter. It is endorsed by a bank that guarantees payment provided the beneficiary delivers the Bill of Lading proving that goods have been shipped.

Licensing involves the assignment of production and selling rights to producers located in foreign locations in return for royalty payments.

Listed Companies: firms whose shares are quoted on the Official List of the Stock Exchange.

Loan Guarantee Scheme: a facility whereby banks are able to lend to firms that would not otherwise qualify for bank finance due to lack of track record, the loan being guaranteed by the Department of Trade and Industry.

Management Buy-In (MBI): acquisition of an equity stake in an existing firm by new management that injects expertise as well as capital into the enterprise.

Management Buy-Out (MBO): acquisition of an existing firm by its existing management usually involving substantial amounts of straight debt and mezzanine finance.

Marginal Cost of Capital (MCC): the additional return required on incremental investment that is financed in a way that alters the firm's capital structure.

Marginal Efficiency of Investment (MEI): a schedule listing available investments, in declining order of attractiveness.

Market Capitalisation: the market value of a firm's equity, i.e. number of ordinary shares issued times market price.

The **Market Portfolio** includes all securities traded on the stock market weighted by their respective capitalisations. Usually, a more limited portfolio such as the FT All Share Index is used as a proxy.

Matching: offsetting a currency inflow in one currency, e.g. a stream of revenues, by a corresponding stream of costs, thus leaving only the profit element unmatched. Firms may also match operating cash flows against financial flows, e.g. a stream of interest and capital payments resulting from overseas borrowing in the same currency.

Mergers: pooling by firms of their separate interests into newly-constituted business, each party participating on roughly equal terms.

Mezzanine Finance covers hybrids such as convertibles that embody both debt and equity features.

Modified Internal Rate of Return (MIRR): the internal rate of return modified for the reinvestment assumption.

Modigliani & Miller's (MM) Capital Structure Theories are:

(i) MM-no tax, which 'proves' that no optimal capital structure exists, and that the WACC is invariant to debt/equity ratio.

(ii) MM-with tax which suggests that the tax shield should be exploited up to the point of almost 100 per cent debt financing.

Monetary Policy Committee: a body whose members are appointed by the Bank of England, responsible for setting UK interest rates at monthly meetings.

Money Market Cover involves an exporter borrowing on the money market (i.e. creating a liability) in the same currency in which it expects to receive a payment.

Moral Hazard: the temptation facing managers to engage in risky activities when they are protected from the consequences of failure, e.g. by guaranteed severance payments.

Multilateral Netting: a central Treasury department operation to minimise net flows of currency throughout an organisation.

Multi-National Company (MNC): one that conducts a significant proportion of its operations abroad.

Natural Hedge: where the adverse impact of FX rate variations on cash inflows are offset by the effect on cash outflows, or *vice versa*.

Net Advantage of a Lease (NAL): the NPV of the acquisition of an asset adjusted for financing benefits.

Net Asset Value (NAV): the value of owners' stake in a firm, found by deducting total liabilities (i.e. debts) from total assets.

Net Debt: a firm's net borrowing including both long-term and also short-term debt, offset by cash holdings. Expressed either in absolute terms, or in relation to owner's equity.

Net Present Value: the value of a stream of cash flows adjusted for the time-value of money. A positive NPV adds value.

Netting: offsetting a firm's internal currency inflows and outflows in the same currency to minimise the net flow in either direction.

Neutral Stocks generate returns that vary by the same proportion as overall market returns. Their Betas equal 1.0. Also called 'market-tracking' investments.

New Issue Market: the market for selling and buying newly-issued securities. It has no physical existence.

Niche Companies serve a limited segment of their markets, usually offering high-quality, differentiated products at a high margin.

Non-Recourse (as distinct from recourse) factoring operates where factors are unable to reclaim bad debts from a client's accounts.

Official List: daily list of securities and prices traded on the London Stock Exchange.

Operating Gearing is the importance of fixed expenses within a firm's overall cost structure. It can be measured in various ways, for example, by looking at the responsiveness of operating profit to sales variations.

Operating Gearing Factor: a ratio that compares the operating gearing of a particular activity, e.g. a product division within a larger firm to that of a larger entity such as the whole firm.

Operating/Strategic Exposure: the risk that adverse foreign exchange rate movements will affect the present value of the firm's future cash flows (effectively, long-term transactions exposure).

Operating Lease: a method of hiring assets over periods less than the expected lifetime of those assets.

Opportunity Cost: the value forgone by opting for a particular course of action.

Optimal Capital Structure: the financing mix that minimises the overall cost of finance and maximises market value.

Optimal Portfolio: the one chosen by an investor to achieve his/her most desired combination of risk and return. This choice depends on the investor's attitude to risk, or risk–return preference, i.e. how he/she rates different combinations of risk and return. If a risk-free asset is available, the optimal portfolio of risky assets is the market portfolio.

Options: the right but not the obligation to buy or sell something at some time in the future at a given price.

Overdraft: short-term finance extended by banks subject to instant recall. A maximum deficit balance is pre-agreed and interest is paid on the actual daily balance outstanding.

Overtrading: where a firm has insufficient long-term capital to finance business growth.

Owner's Equity: in accounting terms, simply the NAV, but can also be expressed in market value terms, i.e. share price times number of ordinary shares issued, or '**capitalisation**'.

Parallel Matching applies where a firm offsets inflows in one currency with outflows denominated in a closely correlated currency.

Perpetuity: an infinite series of cash flows.

Poison Pill: a provision designed to damage the interests of a takeover bidder, e.g. handsome severance terms for departing managers, which is activated on completion of the bid.

Political Risk: the risk of politically-motivated interference by a foreign government in the affairs of a MNC, that adversely affects its net cash flows.

Portfolio: a combination of investments – securities or physical assets – into a single 'bundled' investment. A well-diversified portfolio has the potential capacity to lower the investor's exposure to the risk of fluctuations in the overall economy.

Portfolio Effect: the tendency for the risk on a well-diversified holding of investments to fall below the risk of most and sometimes, all of its individual components.

Portfolio Investment: investment in paper claims such as ordinary shares, without obtaining a voice in management.

Post-completion Audit: audit of a capital project at an agreed time following implementaion.

Preference Shares: hybrid securities that rank ahead of ordinary shares for dividend payment, usually at a fixed rate, and also in distributing the proceeds of a liquidation. Normally, they carry no voting rights.

Price:Earnings Ratio (PER): the current share price divided by the latest reported earnings (i.e. profits after tax) per share.

Profitability index: ratio of the present value of benefits to costs.

Project Risk Factor: the product of the Revenue Sensitivity Factor and the Operating Gearing Factor multiplied together.

Proprietorial Companies are run by founders and their heirs to provide a livelihood for their families. They usually have limited growth aims.

Provision: a notional deduction from profits to allow for some highly likely future financial contingency. In accounting terms, an appropriation of profit after taxation.

A **Proxy Beta** is used when the firm has no market listing and thus no Beta of its own. It is taken from a comparable listed firm, and adjusted as necessary for relative financial gearing levels. Hence, **Proxy Discount Rate**.

Purchasing Power Parity (PPP): the theory that foreign exchange rates are in equilibrium when they can purchase the same amount of goods at the prevailing exchange rate.

Random Walk Theory: share price movements are independent of each other so that tomorrow's share price cannot be predicted by looking at today's.

Real Assets: assets in the business (tangible or intangible).

Real Options: capital investment options rather than financial options.

Record Day: the cut-off date beyond which further entrants to the shareholder register do not qualify for the next dividend.

Relevant Risk: the component of total risk taken into account by the stock market when assessing the appropriate risk premium for determining capital asset values.

Reserves: the funds that shareholders invest in a firm in addition to their initial subscription of capital.

The **Residual Theory of Dividends** asserts that firms should only pay cash dividends when they have financed new investments. It assumes no access to external finance.

Retained Earnings: reserves represented by retention of profits. Sometimes, labelled 'profit & loss account' on the Balance Sheet. Also called **Revenue Reserves**.

Revenue Sensitivity: the extent to which revenue of an activity varies in response to general economic fluctuations.

Revenue Sensitivity Factor: the revenue sensitivity of a particular activity, e.g. a product division, relative to that of a larger entity, such as the whole firm.

A **Revolving Credit Facility** enables a firm to borrow up to a pre-specified amount usually over 1–5 years. As repayments of outstanding balances are made, the loan facility is replenished.

Rights Issues: sales of further ordinary shares at less than market price to existing shareholders who are usually able to sell the rights on the market should they not wish to purchase additional shares.

Risk-free Assets: securities with zero variation in overall returns.

Risk Premium: the additional return demanded by investors above the risk-free rate to compensate for exposure to systematic risk.

Scale Economies: cost efficiencies, e.g. bulk-buying, due to increasing a firm's size of operation.

A **Scrip Dividend** is offered to investors in lieu of the equivalent cash payment. Also called a **scrip alternative**.

SEAQ: a computer-based quotation system on the London Stock Exchange where market makers report bid and offer prices and trading volumes.

Securitisation: the technique of packaging non-tradable claims into a traded security backed by an asset such as a flow of low risk income payments.

Security Market Line (SML): an upward-sloping relationship tracing out all combinations of expected return and systematic risk, available in an efficient market. All traded securities locate on this schedule. In effect, the Capital Market Line adjusted for systematic risk.

Sensitivity Analysis: analysis of the impact of changes in assumptions on investment returns.

Share Buyback: repurchase by a firm of its existing shares, either via the market or by a tender to all shareholders.

Shareholder Value Analysis (SVA): a way of assessing the inherent value of the equity in a company, taking into account the sources of value creation and the time horizon over which the firm enjoys competitive advantages over its rivals.

Share Premium Account: a reserve set up to account for the issue of new shares at a price above their par value.

Share Splits (USA: **Stock Splits**)**:** a way of reducing the share price of 'heavyweight' shares (prices above £10). Achieved by reducing the par value of issued shares, e.g. two shares of par value 50p to replace one share at £1 is a one-for-one split, halving the share price.

Short Selling: selling securities not yet owned in the expectation of being able to buy them later at a lower price.

Signalling: using financial announcements to deliver more information than is actually spelt out in detail.

Specific Risk: the variability in the return on a security due to exposure to risks relating to that security in isolation, e.g. risk of losing market share due to poor marketing decisions.

Spot Rate: the rate of exchange quoted for transactions involving immediate settlement. Hence, **spot market**.

Spread: the difference between the exchange rates (interest rates) at which banks buy and sell foreign exchange (lend and borrow).

Straight, or **Plain Vanilla, Debt:** fixed rate borrowing with no additional features such as convertibility rights or warrants.

Sunk Cost: a cost already incurred, or committed to.

Synergies: gains in revenues or cost savings resulting from takeovers and mergers, not resulting from firm size, i.e. stemming from a 'natural match' between two sets of assets.

Systematic Risk: variability in a security's return due to exposure to risks affecting all firms traded in the market (hence, **market risk**), e.g. the impact of exchange rate changes.

Takeover: acquisition of the share capital of another firm, resulting in its identity being absorbed into that of the acquiror.

Take over Code: the non-statutory rules laid down by the Take-Over Panel to guide the conduct of participants in the take-over process.

Take over Panel: a non-statutory body set up by, and with the participation of, leading financial organisations to oversee the conduct of takeover bids.

Tax Breaks: tax concessions, e.g. relief of interest payments against profits tax.

Tax Credit: see **Imputation System**.

Tax Shield: a method of sheltering profits from corporation tax. It is measured by the discounted value of future tax savings generated by the available tax reliefs.

Theoretical Ex-Rights Price (TERP): the market price to which the ordinary shares should gravitate following the completion of a rights issue.

Time-value of Money: the notion that money received in the future is worth less than the same amount received today.

Total Shareholder Return (TSR): the overall return enjoyed by investors, including dividend and capital appreciation, expressed as a percentage of their initial investment. Related to individual years, or to a lengthier time period, and then converted into an annualised, or equivalent annual return.

Trade Credit: temporary financing extended by suppliers of goods and services pending the customer settlement.

Traditional Theory of Capital Structure: the theory that an optimal capital structure exists, where the WACC is minimised and market value is maximised.

Transaction Exposure: the risk of loss due to adverse foreign exchange rate movements that affect the home currency value of import and export contracts denominated in a foreign currency.

A **Transfer Price:** the cost applied to goods transferred between operating units owned by the same firm.

Translation Exposure: the risk of loss from adverse foreign exchange movements that affect sterling values of Balance Sheet items held overseas and past transactions in foreign currency.

Treasury Bills: short-dated (up to three months) securities issued by the Bank of England on behalf of the UK government to cover short-term financing needs.

Unit Trust: investment business attracting funds from investors by issuing units of shares or bonds to invest in.

Value-based management: a managerial approach where the whole aim, strategies and actions are linked to shareholder value creation.

Venture Capital: finance, usually equity, offered by specialist merchant banks wanting to take a stake in firms with high growth potential, but involving a high risk of loss.

Vertical Integration: extension of a firm's activities further back, or forward, along the supply chain from existing activities.

Warrants: options to buy ordinary shares at a pre-determined 'exercise price'. Usually attached to issues of loan stock.

Weighted Average Cost of Capital (WACC): the overall return a firm must achieve in order to meet the requirements of all its investors.

White Knight: a takeover bidder emerging after a hostile bid has been made, usually offering alternative bid terms that are more favourable to the defending management.

Working Capital: current assets less current liabilities.

Yield: income from a security as a percentage of market price.

Yield Curve: a graph of the relationship between the yield on bonds and their current length of time to maturity.

Z-score: a mathematically-derived critical value below which firms are associated with failure.

Zero Coupon Bond: a bond that does not pay interest but is issued at a discount and redeemed at par (full) value.

References

Altman, E.I. (1968) 'Financial Ratios, Discriminant Analysis and the Prediction of Corporate Bankruptcy', *Journal of Finance*, September.

Andersen, J.A. (1987) *Currency and Interest Rate Hedging* (Prentice Hall).

Andrade, G. and S.N. Kaplan (1998) 'How Costly is Financial (not Economic) Distress? Evidence from Highly-Leveraged Transactions that became Distressed', *Journal of Finance*, Vol. 53, October, pp. 1443–93.

Andrews, G.S. and C. Firer (1987) 'Why Different Divisions Require Different Hurdle Rates', *Long Range Planning*, October.

Ang, J. and P.P. Peterson (1984) 'The Leasing Puzzle', *Journal of Finance*, Vol. 39, No. 4, pp. 1055–65.

Arnold, G. and P. Hatzopoulos (2000) 'The theory-practice gap in capital budgeting: evidence from the United Kingdom', *Journal of Business Finance & Accounting*, June/July, pp. 603–26.

Ashkenas, R., L.J. De Monaco and S.C. Francis (1998) 'Making the Deal Real: How GE Capital Integrates Acquisitions', *Harvard Business Review*, Vol. 76, No. 1, January–February, pp. 165–78.

Ashton, D.J. (1989a) 'The Cost of Capital and the Imputation Tax System', *Journal of Business Finance and Accounting*, Spring.

Ashton, D.J. (1989b) 'Textbook Formulae and UK Taxation: Modigliani and Miller Revisited', *Accounting and Business Research*, Summer.

Ball, J. (1991) 'Short Termism – Myth or Reality', *National Westminster Bank Quarterly Review*, August.

Ball, R. and Brown (1968) 'An empirical evaluation of accounting income numbers', *Journal of Accounting Research*, Autumn, pp. 159–78.

Bank of England (1988) 'Share Repurchase by Quoted Companies', *Quarterly Bulletin*, August.

Bank of England (1994) 'Investment Appraisal Criterion and the Impact of Low Inflation', *Quarterly Bulletin*, August.

Barclay, M.J., C.W. Smith and R.L. Watts (1995) 'The Determinants of Corporate Leverage and Dividend Policies', *Journal of Applied Corporate Finance*, Winter.

Bartlet, C. and S. Ghoshal (1989) *Managing Across Borders* (Harvard Business School Press).

Barwise, P., Marsh, P. and R. Wersley, (1989) 'Must finance and strategy clash?' *Harvard Business Review*, September–October.

Baumol, W. (1952) 'The Transactions Demand for Cash: An Inventory Theoretic Approach', *Quarterly Journal of Economics*, November.

Beenstock, M. and K. Chan (1986) 'Testing the Arbitrage Pricing Theory in the UK', *Oxford Bulletin of Economics and Statistics*, May.

Belk, P.A. and M. Glaum (1990) 'The Management of Foreign Exchange Risk in UK Multinationals: An Empirical Investigation', *Accounting and Business Research*, Winter.

Bennet, N. (2001) 'One day we will go out of business', *Sunday Telegraph*, 9 December.

Bhattacharya, M. (1979) 'Imperfect Information, Dividend Policy and the Bird-in-the-Hand Fallacy', *Bell Journal of Economics and Management Science*, Spring.

Bierman Jr, H. and J.E. Hass (1973) 'Capital Budgeting under Uncertainty: A Reformulation', *Journal of Finance*, March.

Black, F. and M. Scholes (1973) 'The Pricing of Options and Corporate Liabilities', *Journal of Political Economy*, May–June.

Black, F., M.C. Jensen and M. Scholes (1972) 'The Capital Asset Pricing Model: Some Empirical Tests', in M. Jensen (ed.) *Studies in the Theory of Capital Markets* (Praeger).

Bodie, Z. and R. Merton (2000) *Finance* (Prentice-Hall).

Bowman, R.G. (1980) 'The Debt Equivalence of Leases: An Empirical Investigation', *Accounting Review*, Vol. 55, No. 2, pp. 237–53.

Branson, R. (1998) *Losing my Virginity* (Virgin Publishing).

Brealey, R.A. and S.C. Myers (2000) *Principles of Corporate Finance* (McGraw-Hill).

Brennan, M. (1971) 'A Note on Dividend Irrelevance and the Gordon Valuation Model', *Journal of Finance*, December.

Brett, M. (1995) *How to Read the Financial Papers* (4th edn) (Century Press).

Brickley, J., C. Smith and J. Zimmerman (1994) 'Ethics, Incentives, and Organisational Design', *Journal of Applied Corporate Finance*, Summer.

Brigham, E.F. and L.C. Gapenski (1991) *Financial Management Theory and Practice* (Dryden).

Bromwich, M. and A. Bhimani (1991) 'Strategic Investment Appraisal', *Management Accounting*, March.

Brooks, R. and L. Catao (2000) 'The New Economy and Global Stock Returns', *IMF Working Paper 216*, December.

Brown, B. (1986) *The Forward Market in Foreign Exchange* (Croom Helm).

Buckley, A. (1992) *Multinational Finance* (Prentice Hall)

Buckley, A. (1996) *Multinational Capital Budgeting* (Prentice Hall)

Buckley, P.J. and M. Casson (1981) 'The Optimal Timing of a Foreign Direct Investment', *Economic Journal*, Vol. 92, No. 361, March.

Butler, R., L. Davies, R. Pike and J. Sharp (1993) *Strategic Investment Decisions* (Routledge).

BZW (2001) *Equity–Gilt Study*, London.

CBI (1998) *Target Practice: How Companies Approach their Key Capital Investment Decisions* (Confederation of British Industry, London).

Chang, K. and C. Osler (1999) 'Methodical Madness: Technical Analysis and the Irrationality of Exchange Rate Forecasts', *Economic Journal*, Vol. 109, Issue 458, pp. 636–661.

Chesley, G.R. (1975) 'Elicitation of Subjective Probabilities: A Review', *Accounting Review*, April.

Clare, A.D. and S.H. Thomas (1994) 'Macroeconomic Factors, the Arbitrage Pricing Theory and the UK Stockmarket', *Journal of Business Finance and Accounting*, April.

Clark, T.M. (1978) *Leasing* (McGraw-Hill).

Collier, P. and E.W. Davies (1985) 'The Management of Currency Transaction Risk by UK Multinational Companies', *Accounting and Business Research*, Autumn.

Collier, P., T. Cooke and J. Glynn (1988) *Financial and Treasury Management* (Heinemann).

Cooke, T.E. (1986) *Mergers and Acquisitions* (Blackwell).

Cooper, D.J. (1975) 'Rationality and Investment Appraisal', *Accounting and Business Research*, Summer.

Copeland, T.E. and J.F. Weston (1988) *Financial Theory and Corporate Policy*, 3rd edn (Addison-Wesley).

Copeland, T.E., T. Koller and J. Murrin (1994) *Valuation: Measuring and Managing the Value of Companies* (Wiley).

Copeland, T., T. Koller and J. Murrin (1996) *Valuation* (2nd edn) (McKinsey and Co.).

Cox, J., S. Ross and M. Rubinstein (1979) 'Option Pricing: A Simplified Approach', *Journal of Financial Economics*, September.

Daniels, J.D. and L.H. Radebaugh (1989) *International Business: Environments and Operations* (Reading, Mass., Addison-Wesley).

Day, R., D. Allen, I. Hirst and J. Kwiatkowski (1987) 'Equity, Gilts, Treasury Bills and Inflation', *The Investment Analyst*, January, No. 83.

Department of Trade and Industry (1988) *Mergers Policy* (HMSO).

Department of Trade and Industry (1990) *Innovation: City Attitudes and Practices* (HMSO).

Dimson, E. (1993) 'Appraisal Techniques', Proceedings of the Capital Projects Conference, May, Institute of Actuaries and Faculty of Actuaries.

Dimson, E. and R.A. Brealey (1978) 'The Risk Premium on UK Equities', *The Investment Analyst*, December.

Dimson, E. and P. Marsh (1982) 'Calculating the Cost of Capital', *Long Range Planning*, April.

Dimson, E. and P. Marsh (1986) 'Event Study Methodologies and the Size Effect: The Case of UK Press Recommendations', *Journal of Financial Economics*, September.

Dimson, E., P. Marsh and M. Staunton (2002) *Triumph of the Optimists* (Princeton University Press).

Dissanaike, G. (1997) 'Do stock market investors overreact?' *Journal of Business Finance and Accounting*, 24(1), pp. 27–49.

Dixit, A. and R. Pindyck (1995) 'The Options Approach to Capital Investment', *Harvard Business Review*, May–June.

Dobbins, R., S. Witt and J. Fielding (1994) *Portfolio Theory and Investment Management* (Blackwell).

Doyle, P. (1994) 'Setting Business Objectives and Measuring Performance', *Journal of General Management*, Winter.

Drucker, P.F. (1981) 'Five Rules for Successful Acquisition', *Wall Street Journal*, 15 October.

Drury, J.C. and S. Braund (1990) 'The Leasing Decision: A Comparison of Theory and Practice', *Accounting and Business Research*, Summer.

Economist (2001) 'Economics Focus: Double or Nothing', Vol. 361, No. 8252, 15 December, p. 84.

Economist (2000) 'Making Mergers Work' (The Economist Newspaper Ltd, London).

Eiteman, D.K., A.I. Stonehill and M.H. Moffet (1995) *Multinational Business Finance* (Reading, Mass., Addison-Wesley).

Elton, E.J. (1970) 'Capital Rationing and External Discount Rates', *Journal of Finance*, June.

Elton, E.J. and M. Gruber (1970) 'Marginal Stockholder Tax Rates and the Clientele Effect', *Review of Economics and Statistics*, February.

Fairburn, J.A. and J.A. Kay (eds.) (1989) *Mergers & Merger Policy* (Oxford University Press).

Fama, E.F. (1970) 'Efficient Capital Markets: A Review of Theory and Empirical Work', *Journal of Finance*, May.

Fama, E.F. (1992) 'Efficient Capital Markets', *Journal of Finance*, December.

Fama, E.F. and K.R. French (2000) 'The Equity Premium, *MIT working paper*, July.

Fama, E.F. and K.R. French (1992) 'The Cross-Section of Expected Stock Returns' *Journal of Finance*, June.

Fama, E.F. and J. McBeth (1973) 'Risk, Return and Equilibrium: Empirical Tests', *Journal of Political Economy*, Vol. 81.

Fama, E.F. and M.H. Miller (1972) *The Theory of Finance* (Holt, Rinehart and Winston).

Ferguson, A. (1989) 'Hostage to the Short Term', *Management Today*, March.

Finnie, J. (1988) 'The Role of Financial Appraisal in Decisions to Acquire Advanced Manufacturing Technology', *Accounting and Business Research*, Spring.

Firth, M. and S. Keane (1986) *Issues in Finance* (Philip Allan).

Foley, B.J. (1991) *Capital Markets* (Macmillan).

Fosback, N. (1985) *Stock Market Logic* (The Institute for Economic Research, Fort Lauderdale).

Franks, J. and J. Broyles (1979) *Modern Managerial Finance* (Wiley).

Franks, J.R. and R.S. Harris (1989) 'Shareholder Wealth Effects of Corporate Takeovers: The UK Experience 1955–85', *Journal of Financial Economics*, Vol. 23.

Franks, J. and C. Mayer (1996a) 'Do Hostile Take-overs Improve Performance?', *Business Strategy Review*, Vol. 7, No. 4, pp. 1–6.

Franks, J. and C. Mayer (1996b) 'Hostile Take-overs and the Correction of Managerial Failure', *Journal of Financial Economics*, Vol. 40, No. 1, pp. 163–81.

Franks, J.R., R.S. Harris and C. Mayer (1988) 'Means of Payment in Takeovers: Results from the UK and US', in A.J. Auerbach (ed.), *Corporate Takeovers: Causes and Consequences* (National Bureau of Economic Research, Chicago Press).

Friedman, M. (1953) 'The Methodology of Positive Economics', in *Essays in Positive Economics* (The University of Chicago Press).

Fuller, R.J. and H.S. Kerr (1981) 'Estimating the Divisional Cost of Capital: An Analysis of the Pure-Play Technique', *Journal of Finance*, December.

Gale, B.T. and D.J. Swire (1988) 'Business Strategies that Create Wealth', *Planning Review*, March–April.

Gentry, J. (1988) 'State of the Art of Short-Run Financial Management', *Financial Management*, Summer.

Ghosh, C. and J. Woolridge (1989) 'Stock Market Reaction to Growth – Induced Dividend Cuts: Are Investors Myopic?', *Managerial & Decision Economics*, March.

Giddy, I.H. (1994) *Global Financial Markets* (D.C. Heath).

Gluck, F.W. (1988) 'The Real Takeover Defense', *The McKinsey Quarterly*, Winter.

Gordon, M. (1959) 'Dividends, Earnings and Financing Policy', *Review of Economics and Statistics*, May.

Gordon, M. (1963) 'Optimal Investment and Financing Policy', *Journal of Finance*.

Graham, B., D. Dodd and S. Cottle (1962) *Security Analysis: Principles and Techniques* (4th edn) (McGraw-Hill).

Grant, R.M. (1998) *Contemporary Strategic Analysis* (Blackwell Publishers).

Graves, S.B. (1988) 'Institutional Ownership and Corporate R&D in the Computer Industry', *Academy of Management Journal*, Vol. 31.

Gray, S.J. and M.C. McDermott (1989) *Mega-Merger Mayhem* (Paul Chapman Publishing).

Gregory, A. (1985) 'Appraising the Effect of Different Financing Methods', *Management Accounting*, November.

Gregory, A. (1997) 'An Examination of the Long-Run Performance of UK Acquiring Firms', *Journal of Business Finance and Accounting*, Vol. 24, No. 7–8, September, pp. 971–1002.

Gregory, A., J. Rutterford and M. Zaman (1999) *The Cost of Capital in the UK: A Comparison of the Perceptions of Industry and the City* (Chartered Institute of Management Accountants, London).

Grinyer, J.R. (1986) 'An Alternative to Maximisation of Shareholders' Wealth in Capital Budgeting Decisions', *Accounting and Business Research*, Autumn.

Grubb, M. (1993/4) 'A Second Generation of Low Inflation', *Professional Investor*, December/January.

Gup, B.E. and S.W. Norwood (1982) 'Divisional Cost of Capital: A Practical Approach', *Financial Management*, Spring.

Hamada, R.S. (1969) 'Portfolio Analysis: Market Equilibrium and Corporate Finance', *Journal of Finance*, March.

Harrington, D.R. (1983) 'Stock Prices, Beta and Strategic Planning', *Harvard Business Review*, May–June.

Harrington, D. (1987) *Modern Portfolio Theory, The Capital Asset Pricing Model and Arbitrage Pricing Theory: A User's Guide* (Prentice Hall).

Harrison, J.S. (1987) 'Alternatives to Merger – Joint Ventures and Other Strategies', *Long Range Planning*, December.

Harvey-Jones, J. (1989) *Making It Happen – Reflections on Leadership* (Fontana).

Hayes, R.H. and D.A. Garvin (1982) 'Managing as if Tomorrow Mattered', *Harvard Business Review*, May–June.

Hertz, D.B. (1964) 'Risk Analysis in Capital Investment', *Harvard Business Review*, January–February.

Hirshleifer, J. (1958) 'On the Theory of Optimal Investment Decision', *Journal of Political Economy*, Vol. 66.

Hodder, J.E. (1986) 'Evaluation of Manufacturing Investments: A Comparison of US and Japanese Practices', *Financial Management*, Spring.

Hodgkinson, L. (1989) *Taxation and Corporate Investment* (CIMA).

Hunt, J., J. Grumber, S. Lees and P. Vivien (1987) *Acquisition – the Human Factors* (London Business School and Egon Zehnder Associates).

Ibbotson Associates (1999) *Stocks, Bonds, Bills and Inflation, 1999 Yearbook* (Ibbotson Associates).

ICAEW (1989) *Accounting for Brands*, P. Barwise, C. Higson, A. Likierman and P. Marsh (Institute of Chartered Accountants in England and Wales, London Business School).

Jarvis, R., J. Collis and P. Bainbridge (2000) 'The Finance Leasing Market in the 1990s: a Chronological Review', Association of Certified and Corporate Accountants Occasional Paper No. 28.

Jensen, M.C. (1984) 'Takeovers: Folklore and Science', *Harvard Business Review*, November–December.

Jensen, M.C. and W.H. Meckling (1976) 'Theory of the Firm: Managerial Behaviour, Agency Costs and Ownership Structure', *Journal of Financial Economics*, October.

Jensen, M.C. and W.H. Meckling (1994) 'The Nature of Man', *Journal of Applied Corporate Finance*, Summer.

Jensen, M.C. and R.S. Ruback (1983) 'The Market for Corporate Control: The Scientific Evidence', *Journal of Financial Economics*, April.

Johanson, J. and F. Wiedersheim-Paul (1975) 'The Internationalisation of the Firm – Four Swedish Cases', *Journal of Management Studies*, October, pp. 305–22.

Jones, C.S. (1982) *Successful Management of Acquisitions* (Derek Beattie Publishing).

Jones, C.S. (1983) *The Control of Acquired Companies* (Chartered Institute of Cost and Management Accountants).

Jones, C.S. (1986) 'Integrating Acquired Companies', *Management Accounting*, April.

Junankar, S. (1994) 'Realistic Returns: How do Manufacturers Assess New Investment?', Confederation of British Industry, July.

Jupe, R.E. and B.A. Rutherford (1997) 'The Disclosure of "Free Cash Flow" in Published Financial Statements: a Research Note', *British Accounting Review*, Vol. 29, No. 3, September.

Kagona, T. (1985) *Strategic vs Evolutionary Management: A US–Japan Comparison of Strategy and Organisation* (Prentice Hall).

Kaplan, R.S. (1986) 'Must CIM be Justified by Faith Alone?', *Harvard Business Review*, March–April.

Kaplanis, E. (1997) 'Benefits and Costs of International Portfolio Investments' in *Financial Times Mastering Finance* (FT/Pitman Publishing, London).

Keane, S. (1974) 'Dividends and the Resolution of Uncertainty', *Journal of Business Finance and Accountancy*, Autumn.

Keane, S.M. (1983) *Stock Market Efficiency: Theory, Evidence, Implications* (Philip Allan).

Kester, W.C. (1984) 'Today's Options for Tomorrow's Growth', *Harvard Business Review*, March–April.

Kindleberger, C.P. (1978) *International Economics* (Irwin).

King, P. (1975) 'Is the Emphasis of Capital Budgeting Misplaced?', *Journal of Business Finance and Accounting*, Spring.

Klemm, M., S. Sanderson and G. Luffman (1991) 'Mission Statements: Selling Corporate Values to Employees', *Long-Range Planning*, June.

Koziol, J.D. (1990) *Hedging: Principles, Practices and Strategies* (John Wiley).

Lambert, R.A. and D.F. Larcker (1985) 'Executive Compensation, Corporate Decision-making and Shareholder Wealth: A Review of the Evidence', *Midland Corporate Finance Journal*, Winter.

Larcker, D.F. (1983) 'Association between Performance Plan Adoption and Capital Investment', *Journal of Accounting and Economics*, April.

Lees, S. (1992) 'Auditing Mergers and Acquisitions – *Caveat Emptor*', *Managerial Auditing Journal*, Vol. 7, No. 4, pp. 6–11.

Lessard, D.R. (1979) 'Evaluating Foreign Projects: An Adjusted Present Value Approach', in D.R. Lessard, *International Financial Management Theory and Application* (Warren, Gorham and Lamont).

Levich, R.M. (1989) 'Is the Foreign Exchange Market Efficient?', *Oxford Review of Economic Policy*, Vol. 5, No. 3, pp. 40–60.

Levis, M. (1985) 'Are Small Firms Big Performers?', *The Investment Analyst*, No. 76, April, pp. 21–7.

Levy, H. and M. Sarnat (1994) *Portfolio and Investment Selection: Theory and Practice* (Prentice Hall).

Levy, H. and M. Sarnat (1994) *Capital Investment and Financial Decisions* (Prentice Hall).

Limmack, R.J. (1991) 'Corporate Mergers and Shareholder Wealth Effects: 1977–1986', *Accounting and Business Research*, Summer.

Lintner, J. (1956) 'The Distribution of Incomes of Corporations among Dividends, Retained Earnings and Taxes', *American Economic Review*, May.

Lorie, J.H. and L.J. Savage (1955) 'Three Problems in Capital Rationing', *Journal of Business*, October.

Luehrman, T.A. (1997a) 'What's it worth? A General Manager's Guide to Valuation', *Harvard Business Review*, Vol. 75, No. 3, May–June, pp. 132–42.

Luehrman, T.A. (1997b) 'Using APV: A Better Tool for Valuing Operations', *Harvard Business Review*, Vol. 75, No. 3, May–June, pp. 145–54.

Lumby, S. (1994) *Investment Appraisal and Financing Decisions* (Chapman & Hall).

Madura, J. (1995) *International Financial Management* (West Publishing Co.).

Madura, J. and A.M. Whyte (1990) 'Diversification Benefits of Direct Foreign Investment', *Management International Review*, Vol. 30, No. 1.

Malkiel, B. (1985) *A Random Walk Down Wall Street* (Norton & Co.).

Manson, S., A. Stark and M. Thomas (1994) 'A Cash Flow Analysis of the Operational Gains from Takeovers', *ACCA Certified Research Report 35*.

Mao, J.C.T. and J.F. Helliwell (1969) 'Investment Decisions under Uncertainty: Theory and Practice', *Journal of Finance*, May.

Marais, D. (1982) 'Corporate Financial Strength', *Bank of England Quarterly Bulletin*, June.

Markowitz, H.M. (1952) 'Portfolio Selection', *Journal of Finance*, March.

Markowitz, H.M. (1991) 'Foundations of Portfolio Theory', *Journal of Finance*, June.

Marsh, P. (1990) *Short-termism on Trial* (International Fund Managers Association).

Mason, C. and R. Harrison (1999) *Is it Worth it? The Rates of Return for Informal Venture Capital Investments*. Venture Finance Working Paper, No. 16, University of Southampton.

Mathur, I. (1989) 'A Review of the Theories of and Evidence on Returns Related to Mergers and Takeovers', *Managerial Finance*, Vol. 15, No. 4.

McDaniel, W.R., D.E. McCarty and K.A. Jessell (1988) 'Discounted Cash Flow with Explicit Reinvestment Rates: Tutorial and Extension', *The Financial Review*, August.

McGowan, C.B. and J.C. Francis (1991) 'Arbitrage Pricing Theory Factors and their Relationship to Macro-economic Variables', in C.F. Lee, T.J. Frecka and L.O. Scott (eds.), *Advances in Quantitative Analysis of Finance and Accounting* (JAI Press).

McIntyre, A.D. and N.J. Coulthurst (1985) 'Theory and Practice in Capital Budgeting', *British Accounting Review*, Autumn.

McLaney, E.J. (1994) *Business Finance for Decision Makers* (Pitman).

McRae, T.W. (1996) *International Business Finance* (John Wiley and Sons).

Meall, L. (2001) 'Dot.com dot.gone', *Accountancy*, Vol. 128, No. 1296, August, p. 70.

Mehra, R. and E.C. Prescott (1985) 'The Equity Premium: A Puzzle', *Journal of Monetary Economics*, Vol. 15, pp. 145–61.

Merton, R. (1998) 'Applications of option pricing theory: twenty five years later', *American Economic Review*, pp. 323–49.

Miller, M. (1977) 'Debt and Taxes', *American Economic Review*, May.

Miller, M. (1986) Behavioural Rationality in Finance: The Case of Dividends', *Journal of Business*, October.

Miller, M.H. (1991) 'Leverage', *Journal of Finance*, June.

Miller, M.H. and F. Modigliani (1961) 'Dividend Policy and the Valuation of Shares', *Journal of Business*, October.

Miller, M. and D. Orr (1966) 'A Model of the Demand for Money by Firms', *Quarterly Journal of Economics*, August.

Mills, R.W. (1988) 'Capital Budgeting Techniques Used in the UK and USA', *Management Accounting*, January.

Mittra, S. and C. Gassen (1981) *Investment Analysis and Portfolio Management* (Harcourt Brace Jovanovich).

Modigliani, F. and M. Miller (1958) 'The Cost of Capital, Corporation Finance and the Theory of Investment', *American Economic Review*, June.

Modigliani, F. and M.H. Miller (1963) 'Corporate Income Taxes and the Cost of Capital: A Correction', *American Economic Review*, June.

Mossin, J. (1966) 'Equilibrium in a Capital Assets Market', *Econometrica*, October.

Murphy, J. (1989) *Brand Valuation: A True and Fair View* (Hutchinson).

Myers, S.C. (1974) 'Interactions of Corporate Financing and Investment Decisions – Implications for Capital Budgeting', *Journal of Finance*, March.

Myers, S.C. (1984) 'The Capital Structure Puzzle', *Journal of Finance*, July.

Narayanaswamy, V.J. (1994) 'The Debt Equivalence of Leases in the UK: An Empirical Investigation, *British Accounting Review*, Vol. 26, No. 1, pp. 337–51.

Neale, B., A. Milsom, C. Hills and J. Sharples (1998) 'The Hostile Takeover Process: A Case Study of Granada Versus Forte', *European Management Journal*, Vol. 16, No. 2, April, pp. 230–41.

Neale, C.W. and P.J. Buckley (1992) 'Differential British and US Adoption Rates of Investment Project Post-Completion Auditing', *Journal of International Business Studies*.

Neale, C.W. and D.E.A. Holmes (1988) 'Post-Completion Audits: The Costs and Benefits', *Management Accounting*, Vol. 66, No. 3.

Neale, C.W. and D.E.A. Holmes (1991) *Post-Completion Auditing* (Pitman).

O'Shea, D. (1986) *Investing for Beginners*, Financial Times Business Information.

Payne, A.F. (1997) 'Approaching Acquisitions Strategically', *Journal of General Management*, Winter.

Peacock, A. and G. Bannock (1991) *Corporate Takeovers and the Public Interest* (David Hume Institute).

Peel, M.J. (1995) 'The Impact of Corporate Re-structuring: Mergers, Divestments and MBOs', *Long Range Planning*, April.

Peters, E.E. (1991) *Chaos and Order in the Capital Markets* (John Wiley).

Peters, E.E. (1993) *Fractal Market Analysis* (Wiley).

Peters, T. and R. Waterman (1982) *In Search of Excellence* (Harper & Row).

Pettit, J. (2001) 'Is a Share Buyback Right for Your Company?', *Harvard Business Review*, Vol. 79, No. 4, October, pp. 141–7.

Pike, R.H. (1982) *Capital Budgeting in the 1980s* (Chartered Institute of Management Accountants).

Pike, R.H. (1983) 'The Capital Budgeting Behaviour and Corporate Characteristics of Capital-Constrained Firms', *Journal of Business Finance and Accounting*, Summer.

Pike, R.H. (1988) 'An Empirical Study of the Adoption of Sophisticated Capital Budgeting Practices and Decision-Making Effectiveness', *Accounting and Business Research*, Autumn.

Pike, R. (1996) 'A Longitudinal Survey on Capital Budgeting Practices', *Journal of Business Finance and Accounting*, Vol. 23, No. 1.

Pike, R. and N. Cheng (2001) 'Credit Management: An Examination of Policy Choices, Practices and Late Payment in UK Companies', *Journal of Business Finance and Accounting*, Vol. 28, No. 7, pp. 1013–42.

Pike, R.H. and S.M. Ho (1991) 'Risk Analysis Techniques in Capital Budgeting Contexts', *Accounting and Business Research*, Vol. 21, No. 83.

Pike, R.H. and T.S. Ooi (1989) 'The Impact of Corporate Investment Objectives and Constraints on Capital Budgeting Practices', *British Accounting Review*, August.

Pike, R.H. and M. Wolfe (1988) *Capital Budgeting in the 1990s* (Chartered Institute of Management Accountants).

Pike, R., J. Sharp and D. Price (1989) 'AMT Investment in the Larger UK Firm', *International Journal of Operations and Production Management*, Vol. 9, No. 2.

Pike, R.H., J. Meerjanssen and L. Chadwick (1993) 'The Appraisal of Ordinary Shares by Investment Analysis in the UK and Germany', *Accounting and Business Research*, Autumn.

Pike, R., N. Cheng and L. Chadwick (1998) *Managing Trade Credit for Competitive Advantage* (CIMA).

Pinches, G. (1982) 'Myopic Capital Budgeting and Decision-Making', *Financial Management*, Vol. 11, No. 3.

Pohlman, R.A., E.S. Santiago and F.L. Markel (1988) 'Cash Flow Estimation Practices of Large Firms', *Financial Management*, Summer.

Pointon, J. (1980) 'Investment and Risk: The Effect of Capital Allowances', *Accounting and Business Research*, Autumn.

Poon, S. and S.J. Taylor (1991) 'Macroeconomic Factors and the UK Stock Market', *Journal of Business Finance and Accounting*, Vol. 18, September, pp. 619–36.

Porter, M.E. (1980) *Competitive Strategy* (Free Press).

Porter, M.E. (1985) *Competitive Advantage* (Free Press).

Porter, M.E. (1987) 'From Competitive Advantage to Corporate Strategy', *Harvard Business Review*, May–June.

Porter, M.E. (1992) 'Capital Disadvantage – America's Failing Capital Investment System', *Harvard Business Review*, September–October.

Prasad, S.B. (1987) 'American and European Investment Motives in Ireland', *Management International Review* (Third quarter).

Price, J. and S.K. Henderson (1988) *Currency and Interest Rate Swaps* (Butterworths).

Prindl, A. (1978) *Currency Management* (John Wiley).

Pruitt, S.W. and L.J. Gitman (1987) 'Capital Budgeting Forecast Biases: Evidence from the Fortune 500', *Financial Management*, Spring.

Rappaport, A. (1986) *Creating Shareholder Value: The New Standard for Business Performance* (Macmillan).

Rappaport, A. (1987) 'Stock Market Signals to Managers', *Harvard Business Review*, November–December.

Redhead, K. (1990) *Introduction to Financial Futures and Options* (Woodhead-Faulkner).

Reimann, B.C. (1990) 'Why Bother with Risk-Adjusted Hurdle Rates?', *Long Range Planning*, June. *Risk Measurement Service*, London Business School.

Robbins, S. and R. Stobaugh (1973) 'The Bent Measuring Stick for Foreign Subsidiaries', *Harvard Business Review*, September–October.

Robicek, A. and S. Myers (1965) *Optimal Financing Decisions* (Prentice Hall).

Rodriguez, R.M. (1981) 'Corporate Exchange Risk Management: Theme and Aberrations', *Journal of Finance*, May.

Roll, R. (1977) 'A Critique of the Asset Pricing Theory's Tests; Part I: On Past and Potential Testability of the Theory', *Journal of Financial Economics*, March.

Ross, D. (1991) 'Treasury Survey of Internal Controls', *The Treasurer*, November.

Ross, S.A. (1976) 'The Arbitrage Theory of Capital Asset Pricing', *Journal of Economic Theory*, Vol. 13, No. 3.

Ross, S.A. (1977) 'The Determination of Financial Structure: the Incentive Signalling Approach', *Bell Journal of Economics*, Spring.

Ross, S., R. Westerfield and D. Bradford (1991) *Fundamentals of Corporate Finance* (Irwin).

Ruback, R.S. (1988) 'An Overview of Takeover Defenses', in A.J. Auerbach (ed.), *Mergers and Acquisitions* (University of Chicago Press).

Rugman, A.M., D.J. Lecraw and L.D. Booth (1985) *International Business, Firm and Environment* (McGraw-Hill).

Rutterford, J. (1992) *Handbook of UK Corporate Finance* (Butterworths).

Sartoris, W. and N. Hill (1981) 'Evaluating Credit Policy Alternatives: A Present Value Framework', *Journal of Financial Research*, Spring.

Shao, L.P. (1996) 'Capital Budgeting for the Multi-national Enterprise', *Managerial Finance*, Vol. 22, No. 1.

Shapiro, A. (1985) 'Corporate Strategy and the Capital Budgeting Decision', *Midland Corporate Finance Journal*, Spring.

Shapiro, A.C. (1989) *Multinational Financial Management* (Allyn and Bacon).

Sharpe, P. and T. Keelin (1998) 'How SmithKline Beecham Makes Better Resource-Allocation Decisions', *Harvard Business Review*, March and April, pp. 45–57.

Sharpe, W.F. (1963) 'A Simplified Model for Portfolio Analysis', *Management Science*, January.

Sharpe, W.F. (1964) 'Capital Asset Prices – A Theory of Market Equilibrium under Conditions of Risk', *Journal of Finance*, September.

Sharpe, W. (1981) *Investments* (Prentice Hall).

Sharpe, W.F. and G.J. Alexander (1990) *Investments* (Prentice Hall).

Shaw, P. (1996) 'Capital Budgeting for the Multinational Enterprise', *Managerial Finance*, Vol. 22, No. 21, special issue.

Smith, K.V. (1988) *Readings in Short-term Financial Management* (West Publishing).

Solnik, B.H. (1974) 'Why not Diversify Internationally Rather than Domestically?', *Financial Analysts Journal*, July/August pp. 48–54.

Stock Exchange Fact Book (1997) *The International Stock Exchange* (published annually).

Stonham, P. (1995) 'Reuter's Share Re-purchase', *European Management Journal*, Vol. 13, No. 1, pp. 99–109.

Strong, N. and X.G. Xu (1997) 'Explaining the Cross-Section of UK Expected Stock Returns', *British Accounting Review*, March, Vol. 29, No. 1, pp. 1–23.

Sudarsanam, P.S. (1995) *The Essence of Mergers and Acquisitions* (Prentice Hall).

Sudarsanam, P., P. Holl and A. Salami (1996) 'Shareholder Wealth Gains in Mergers: Effect of Synergy and Ownership Structure', *Journal of Business Finance and Accounting*, Vol. 23, No. 5/6, July, pp. 673–98.

Swalm, R.O. (1966) 'Utility Theory – Insights into Risk-taking', *Harvard Business Review*, November–December.

Taffler, R. (1991) 'Z-scores: An Approach to the Recession', *Accountancy*, July.

3i *Making an Acquisition*.

3i (1993), *Dividend Policy*, April.

Tobin, J. (1958) 'Liquidity Preference as Behaviour Towards Risk', *Review of Economic Studies*, February.

Tomkins, C. (1991) *Corporate Resource Allocation* (Blackwells).

Tomkins, C.R., J.F. Lowe and E.J. Morgan (1979) *An Economic Analysis of the Financial Leasing Industry* (Saxon House).

Vaga, T. (1991) 'The Coherent Market Hypothesis', *Financial Analysts Journal*, December.

Van Horne, J. (1975) 'Corporate Liquidity and Bankruptcy Costs', Research Paper 205, Stanford University.

Van Horne, J. (1986) *Financial Management and Policy* (Prentice Hall).

Walters, A. (1991) *Corporate Credit Analysis* (Euromoney Publications).

Wardlow, A. (1994) 'Investment Appraisal Criteria and The Impact of Low Inflation', *Bank of England Quarterly Bulletin*, August.

Wearing, R.T. (1989) 'Cash Flow and the Eurotunnel', *Accounting & Business Research*, Winter.

Weaver, S.C., D. Peters, R. Cason and J. Daleiden (1989) 'Capital Budgeting', *Financial Management*, Spring.

Weingartner, H. (1977) 'Capital Rationing: Authors in Search of a Plot', *Journal of Finance*, December.

Weston, J.F. and T.E. Copeland (1988) *Managerial Finance* (Cassell).

Wilkie, A.D. (1994) 'The Risk Premium on Ordinary Shares', Institute of Actuaries and Faculty of Actuaries, November.

Wilson Committee (1980) 'Report of the Committee to Review the Functioning of Financial Institutions', Cmnd. 7937, HMSO.

Wilson, M. (1990) 'Capital Budgeting for Foreign Direct Investments', *Managerial Finance*, Vol. 16, No. 2.

Wright, M. and K. Robbie (1991) 'Corporate Restructuring, Buy-Outs and Managerial Equity: The European Dimension', *Journal of Applied Corporate Finance*, Winter.

Young, D. (1997) 'Economic Value Added: A Primer for European Managers', *European Management Journal*, Vol. 15, No. 4, August.

Young, D. and B. Sutcliffe (1990) 'Value Gaps – Who is Right? The Raiders, the Market or the Manager?', *Long Range Planning*, Vol. 23, No. 4, August, pp. 20–34.

Index

abandonment option 415
Abbey National plc 617, 745
ABC system of stock management 480
ABI Leisure plc 541
ABN AMRO 635, 693
acceptance credit 512–13, 846
accepting houses 37
accounting rate of return
  in investment decisions 163–5
  in project appraisal 202–3
Aceralia 743
acquirees 745, 846
acquirors 745, 762, 846
activity beta 381, 847
activity ratios 68
Adams Childrenswear 615–16
adjusted NAV 846
adjusted present value (APV) 725–8, 846
  on foreign investment 728–9
administration 691
advanced manufacturing technology (AMT) investment 225–7
agency costs 14, 695–6, 838
agency theory 13–16, 25
  managing 14–16
aggressive stocks 846
Airbus 296–8
Al Waleed Bin Talal Bin AbdulAziz 160, 706
Alcatel 693, 745
Alexander, G.J. 327
Allied Domecq 786
Allied Dunbar 752
allocative efficiency 46
All-Share index 59
alternative investment market (AIM) 41, 42, 599, 600, 787, 846
Altman, E.I. 448, 461
Amazon.com 449
Amerada Hess 752
American option 401, 566, 846
amortisation 66, 846
analysis of variance 342
  in CAPM 363–4
Andersen, J.A. 574
Anderson Strathclyde 744
Andrade, G. 693
Andrews, G.S. 394
Ang, J. 534
annual percentage rate (APR) 83, 846
annual writing-down allowances 198
annuity 86, 90, 846
  present value of 108
  valuing 91
Arbed 743
arbitrage 47, 708, 846
  and currency risk 549
  impediments to 714–15
arbitrage pricing Model (APT) 357, 358–9, 846
Arnold, G. 200, 203, 207, 237, 295
Articles of Association 587, 847
Asea Brown Boveri (ABB) 245
Ashkenas, R. 771–2
asset beta 381, 847
asset market approach to exchange rate forecasting 554
asset restructuring 783
asset value 332–3
asset-backed securities 608, 609–13, 847
asset-stripping 742, 750, 847
asymmetric information 847

BAA 607, 668
Bace Manufacturing 114
backward vertical integration 752
bail-out payback period 162
balance of payments, and exchange rate forecasting 553–4
balance sheet 63–6
balanced scorecard 52
balancing allowances 198
balancing changes 198
Ball, J. 49, 62
balloon repayment 506, 847
bancassurance 647, 847
bank bills 512, 847
bank borrowing for long-term finance 586
bank credit 504–8
  overdraft 504–6
  term loans 506–7
bank loan 506–7, 529, 847
bank mergers 772
Bank of England 44, 207, 649
Bank of International Settlements 543
Bank of Scotland 772
Bannock, G. 773
Barclay, M.J. 731
Barings Bank 10, 440
barter 847
Barwise 144
BAT Industries 648–9, 752
Baumol, William 490, 492
Beenstock, M. 358, 359
Belk, P.A. 560, 574
benchmarks 123
Bennett, N. 224
Bertelsmann 745
beta 342, 847
  finding 348–9
beta coefficient 340
beta geared 384, 847
beta ungeared 384, 847
BG Group 692
Bhattacharya, M. 656
Bierman, H. Jr 299
'Big Bang' 41, 50
bilateral netting 560, 847
bill finance 511–13
bill of lading 530, 847
Bills of Exchange 35, 512, 531–2, 565, 847
bird-in-the-hand fallacy 640, 847

Black, F. 357, 412, 421
Black Monday 55
Black-Scholes pricing model 412–13, 422–3
Bland, Christopher 620
Bodie, Z. 421
bonds 847
  valuing 92–4
  yields 613–14
bonus issues 605, 847
Boo.com 80
book-to-market ratio 847
Boots 752
boot-strapping 755
borrowing 12, 696
  in international finance 688
  and term structure of interest rates 104–6
Bose, Kunal 250
Boston Consulting Group 223
Bowie, David 610
Bowman, R.G. 534
brand valuation 119–22
  brand strength 121–2
  cost-based methods 120
  market observation methods 121
  NAV, role of 122
Branson, Richard 127, 187, 278
Braund, S. 524, 534
break-even sensitivity analysis 289–90
break-up value (BUV) 665, 847
Brealey, R.A. 26, 99, 175, 346, 362, 421, 492, 699
Brennan, M. 632
Brett, M. 62
Brickly, J. 26
Brigham, E.F. 207, 492
Bristol Myers Squibb 206
British Airways 612, 689
British Petroleum 417, 430, 780
British Telecom 117, 604, 619–20, 633, 692–3
Britoil 780
Brooks, R. 339
Brown, 49
Broyles, J. 388
Buckley, A. 270, 574
Buckley, P.J. 249, 251
Budden, Robert 695
buffer stocks 482
Buffett, Warren 782
building societies 38
bullet loan 506
business angels 591, 848
business expansion proposals 234
business expansion scheme 591, 848
business fit and focus 789
business plan 594
business restructuring 783
business risk 281–2
business strategy 19–20
Butler, R. 251
buyback 572, 848
BW Rensburg 593
CAC-40 index 58
Cadbury Schweppes 122
call option 401, 402, 566
  equity as 414
Calvin Klein 610
Canary Wharf 160, 295–6
capital 848
  cost of 682–5
capital allowances 61, 848
  and Corporation tax 198–9
capital asset 848
capital asset pricing model (CAPM) 326, 848
  arbitrage pricing theory 358–9
  assumptions of 350–1
  capital market line 351–3
  different equity markets 338–9
  issues raised by 359–61
  required return, assessing 345–50
  reservations over 355–6
  risk and return 333–7, 709
  security market line 344–5
  security valuation and discount rates 332–3
  and shareholder value analysis 374–6
  systematic risk 339–44
  testing 356–8
  variance analysis in 363–4
capital budgeting 229–30
Capital for Companies Ltd 593
capital gains tax 373, 388, 643, 848
capital gearing 665–7, 848
capital growth 81–4
capital investment option 414–19
capital investment process 229–37
  authorisation 234–5
  budget determination 230–1
  evaluation 233–4
  monitoring and control 237
  project classification 233–4
  project definition 232–3
  project search and development 231–2
  screening 232
capital market 34, 35
  imperfections 106–7
capital market approach to mergers 774–5
capital market line (CML) 351–3, 848
capital rationing 170–4, 229
  hard 170
  and information asymmetry 171–2
  multi-period 174
  one period 172–4
  soft 170–1
  transaction costs 172
capital structure 368, 696, 848
  and CAPM 719–20
  MM on 708–10
  target structure 684–5
capitalisation 848
capitalisation issue 605, 847
capitalisation rate 677
captive venture capital firms 593
carrying costs 454
cash
  financing a takeover 756–7
  sources 8–9
cash discounts 473–4
cash float 489–90
cash flow analysis 154–5
  incremental, in project appraisal 188–92
  in investment decisions 154–5
cash flow return on investment (CFROI) 124
cash flow statement 66–8
cash flows 94
  leasing advantages 524
  multi-period, and risk 299–302
  remittable in foreign investment 251
  single-period 283–6
  timing of 155
  and translation exposure 544–5
  unconventional 167–9
  valuing 125–7
cash management 484–91
  cash flow forecasts 486–9
  cash flow statements 486
  models of 490–1
  reasons for holding cash 484–6
  short term investment 491
cash operating cycle 450–1, 848
Casson, M. 249
Catao, L. 339
central banks 555–7
certainty 278
certainty equivalence 292–3
CGNU 647
Chan, K. 358, 359
Chang, K. 555
chaos theory 55–7
characteristics line (CL) 340, 848
chartist 48, 554, 848
Chesley, G.R. 391
Chiquita Brans International 692
Chrysalis 40
Chrysler 743, 752
Cisco Systems 118
Clare, A.D. 359
Clark, T.M. 534
classical tax system 643, 848
clientele effect 374, 640–1, 848
CNBC 50
Coats Viyella 114, 756
Cobra Sports 694
Coca-Cola 124, 169, 221
coefficient of variation 286
Cohen, Norma 160
Coherent Market Hypothesis (CMH) 56
collaterallised mortgage obligations (CMOs) 610
Collier, P. 461, 574
Commercial Finance Corporation 790
commercial paper 513, 848
co-movement 313, 849
Companies Act (1981) 649, 709

Companies Act (1985) 629
Compaq 135
Compass Group 752
Competition Act (1998) 747
Competition Commission 747, 748
competitive strategy 19–20
compound interest 81–4
concentration banking 489
concentric acquisition 849
Confederation of British Industry 57
conglomerate takeover 751, 849
constant dividend valuation model 137–8
contigent claim security 410
contra-cyclical 849
contra-cyclical returns 310
control 594
convertible loan stock 399, 413, 612–13, 849
convertible shares 589, 611
convertibles 611–13
  conversion terms 611
  in financing a takeover 757
Cooke, T.E. 791
Cooper, D.J. 207
Coors 788
Copeland, T.E. 26, 62, 144, 362, 621, 656, 699, 731
corporate recovery 135
corporate restructuring 782–90
  business fit and focus 789
  debt, use of 789
  divestment 784–5
  incentives 790
  joint ventures 788
  MBOs 785–6
corporate strategy 19
corporate venturing 592–3
Corporation Tax 196
  impact of 717–18
  MM on 715–18, 733–4
correlation coefficient 849
Corus Group plc 539, 540
cost of debt 849
cost of equity 369, 849
cost reduction 37
cost reduction proposals in capital investment 233
costs of running out of stock or cash 455
Coulthurst, N.J. 207
counter-party risk 564, 849
counter-trade 572, 849
country risk 264–8, 849
coupon rate of interest 680, 849
co-variability 313, 849
covariance 314–15, 849
covered interest arbitrage 549
Cox, J. 421
credit collection policy 474–5
credit limits 471
credit risk 436, 564
creditors 691
CREST 849
Criminal Justice Act (1993) 598
critical mass 752, 849
cross-currency interest swap 571
cross-default clause 688
crown jewels defence 767
cum-dividend 627, 851
cumulative shares 589
currency futures contract 567–9, 849
currency information system 559
currency option 414, 566–71, 849
currency risk
  exchange rate forecasting 553–7
  exchange rate structure 542–3
  exposure management 546–52
  external hedging 563–71
  foreign exchange exposure 543–6
  foreign exchange management strategy 557–60
  hedging risk of foreign projects 571–2
  internal hedging 560–3
  in international finance 688
currency swap 441, 569–71, 849
currency switching 263, 849
current assets 65
current cost accounting 117, 850
current ratio 69, 447, 608, 850
Cutler, Alexander 453
cut-off rate for new investment 713–14, 732–3

Daimler-Benz 743, 752
Daniel, Caroline 405
Daniels, J.D. 269
Davies, E.W. 574
Day, R. 346
days cash-on-hand ratio 447
De Nationale Investeringsbank 610
deal flow 594
debentures 850
debt
  cost of 680–2
  and shareholder wealth 696
  tax advantage of 717
debt capacity 850
debt instruments 606–18
  asset-backed securities 609–13
  bond yields 613–14
  convertibles 611–13
  debentures 607–8
  deep discount 608–9
  Eurobonds 616–17
  floating rate notes 617–18
  foreign bonds 616
  mezzanine debt 615
  warrants 614–15
debt/equity ratio 710–12, 732
debtor days 68
debtors 117
deep discount debt instruments 608–9
default 663, 850
defensive stock 850
Dell Computers 135
Delphi techniques 266–7
DeMonaco, L.J. 771–2
deregulation of financial markets 10–11
derivatives 35, 850
  and risk management 439–42
Deutsche Bank 742, 781
development capital 594
Diageo 120
Dimson, E. 54, 346, 394
direct debit 489
Director General of Fair Trading 747
directors' dealings 598–9
disclosure 598
discount factor 85
discount houses 37
discount rate 850
  growth rate exceeding 136–7
  on investment projects 387–8, 729–30
  and required return 349
  and SVA 381–8
  variable 167
discount tables 85–8
  discounting, effect of 88–9
discounted cash flow (DCF) 114, 850
  in project appraisal 200–1
  in valuation 127–31
  in valuing bonds 92
discounted payback 162
discounting 84
  effect of 88–9
disintermediation 40, 513, 850
Disney Corporation 220, 610
Dissanaike 53
diversifiable risk 337, 438, 850
diversification 309, 850
  and required returns 360
  and risk 337
  and risk transfer 438
  by takeovers 753–4
divestment 784–5
dividend cover 68
dividend growth model 128, 133–4, 850
  and firm value 631, 633
  problems with 135–8
  and shareholder value analysis 368–74
dividend irrelvance 631, 850
  objections to 638–45
dividend per share 70
dividend puzzle 651–3
dividend restrictions 608
dividend stream, valuing 132–3
dividend valuation model 131–4, 630, 850
dividend yield 59, 71, 850
dividends 66
  alternatives to 647–51
  clientele effect 640–1
  external equity financing 637–8
  and firm value 630–8
  information content of 646–7
  legal considerations 629–30
  reducing 631–5
  as residual 636–7

dividends *(continued)*
and rights issues 642
shareholders' reliance on 639
shareholders' risk 639–40
stable policy for 652
strategic considerations 628–9
and taxation 643–5
Dixit, A. 421
domestic firms 259
Done, Kevin 298
double 402, 406
double tax agreements (DTAs) 255, 850
Dow, Charles 51
Dow Jones index 58
Dow Theory 51
Doyle, Peter 26, 745
Dresdner Bank 781
Drucker, P.F. 769
Drury, J.C. 524, 534
due diligence 594, 742
Dun & Bradstreet 477
duration of long-term finance 586
Dynergy 745

Eagle Star Insurance 752
Earl, Robert 706
earnings before interest, tax, depreciation & amortisation (EBITDA) 66, 124–5, 850
earnings before interest and taxes (EBIT) 66, 850
earnings dilution 850
earnings per share (EPS) 12, 71
and takeovers 754–6
earnings stream, valuing 122–4
earnings yield 137, 850
EC Merger Regulation 749
Eckert, Robert 229
economic exposure 260, 545–6
economic order quantity 481, 851
economic theory and currency risk 546–52
expectations theory 547
interest rate parity 548–9
international EMH 552
'Open Fisher' theory 550–2
purchasing power parity 546–7
economic value added (EVA) 141, 851
effective rate of interest 525
efficiency frontier 318, 851
Efficient Market Hypothesis (EMH) 47–8
anomalies in 54–5
and CAPM 333
and chaos theory 55–7
criticisms of 53
fundamental and technical analysis 48–51
semi-strong form of 48
strong form of 48
weak form of 47–8
efficient markets 851
Egon Zehnder Associates 769
Eiteman, D.K. 269, 574
electronic funds transfer 489
Ellison, Larry 118
Elton, E.J. 175, 645
Emap 741
EMI 669, 745
Emirates Airline 618
Energis 695
enhanced scrip dividends 648–9, 851
ENI 572
Enron 745
enterprise investment scheme 592, 851
enterprise value 851
entrepreneurial companies 584, 851
equity 726, 851
equity beta 349, 385, 851
equity capital 8
cost of, MM on 712–13
equity finance, raising 590–606
AIM 599
corporate venturing 592–3
equity issues 599–600
obligations 598–9
obtaining a quotation 597–8
quoted companies 595–7
rights issues 600–4
scrip issues 605
stock splits 605
unquoted companies 590–5
venture capital 593–5
equity markets 339
equity option 414
equity value 851
equivalent loan 520–1, 851
equivalent risk class 851
Euro Disney 220
Eurobonds 616–17, 851
Euromoney 432
European option 401, 566, 851
European Union 45–6
Eurotunnel 277, 420
Evron 692
exchange *Agio* 549, 851
exchange controls 252
exchange rate forecasting 553–7
and central banks 555–7
and market efficiency 555
Exchange Rate Mechanism 10, 552
exchange rates
changes 252–4
risk 259–61
structure of 542–3
ex-dividend 627, 851
executive share option schemes 413
exercise date 402
exercise price 401, 402, 851
exit 594
expectations 101, 851
expected net present value (ENPV) 279–80
Export Credit Guarantee Department 268
export factoring 532–3
exporting 246
exporting firms 259
external hedging techniques 563–71
currency option 566–71
currency swap 569–71
futures contracts 567–9
externalisation 246, 851

factoring 508–10, 851
Factors Chain International (FCI) 533
fair game 46
Fair Trading Act (1973) 747
Fama, Eugene 62, 327, 346, 357, 362, 653
Farmers Insurance 752
Farnell Electronics 778
Ferguson, A. 57
Ferranti 118–19
finance, principles of 23–7
corporate behaviour 25
individual behaviour 23–5
market behaviour 25–6
theory and practice 26–7
Finance Act (1981) 786
Finance Act (1988) 628
Finance and Leasing Association (FLA) 514
Finance Corporation for Industry 790
finance department 11
finance function 6–8
investment decisions 7–8
finance lease 517, 518, 852
financial assets 7
financial characteristics approach to mergers 773–4
financial decision 7
financial distress 690–5, 852
costs of 721
MM on 721–2
financial gearing 670–2, 852
and risk 673–4
financial institutions 36–7
financial intermediaries 35, 852
financial management 9–11
financial markets 34–7
efficiency of 46–55
financial objective 12–13
financial pages, reading 58–61
financial ratios 69, 608
financial reports 608
financial risk 282
Financial Services Act (1986) 44
Financial Services Authority 44, 852
financial services sector 37–41
deposit-taking institutions 37–8
savings institutions 38–9
unit and investment trusts 39–41
financial statement analysis 63–72
balance sheet 63–6
cash flow statement 66–7
interpretation of accounts and ratios 71–2
profit and loss account 66
ratios 67–71
Finnie, J. 240
Firer, C. 394

first-year allowances 198, 528
Firth, M. 144, 269, 699
Fisons 752
fixed assets 65
  new investment in 377–8
fixed charge 505, 852
fixed costs 282
fixed interest securities 757
fixed/fixed swap 571
fixed/floating swap 571
flat yield 613, 852
flexible manufacturing system (FMS) 225
floating charge 505, 852
floating rate note (FRN) 617–18, 852
Foley, B.J. 62
foreign bonds 616, 852
foreign currency swap 564, 852
foreign direct investment (FDI) 852
  discount rate for 392–3
  evaluating 255–8
  factors favouring 247–8
foreign exchange exposure 251, 259–61, 263–4, 852
  and currency risk 543–6
foreign exchange management (FEM) strategy 557–60
  hedging translation exposure 557–9
  transaction exposure 559–60
foreign exchange market 34
foreign investment
  complexities of 250–2
  entry modes 247
  entry strategies 246–8
  evaluation of 255–8
  exchange controls 252
  exchange rate changes 252–4
  factors favouring 247–8
  foreign exchange risk 259–61
  hedging risk of 571–2
  incremental hypothesis 248–50
  multinational corporations in 244, 245–6
  operating exposure 263–4
  political and country risk 264–8
  taxation differences 255–8
  WACC for 690
forfaiting 532, 852
Forté's 649
forward buying/selling 34
forward contract 439–40, 563, 852
forward market 542
forward option 564, 852
forward premium 542
forward rate of exchange 260–1, 852
forward vertical integration 752
forward-forward swap 564
Fosback, N. 336
France Telecom 616
Francis, J.C. 359
Francis, S.C. 771–2
Franks, J. 388, 776, 778, 791
free cash flow (FCF) 128–31, 708, 852
French, Kenneth 346, 357, 362, 653
Friedman, M. 350
FT-SE 250 index 59
FTSE 100 index 58
FT-SE Actuaries 350 index 59
FT-SE Fledging index 59
FT-SE index 58–9
FT-SE Small Cap index 59
FT-SE techMARK index 59
full payout lease 517
Fuller, R.J. 384
fundamental analysis 48–51
  exchange rate forecasting 553–4
future value 81–2
futures 35
  currency contract 567–9, 849
  and risk management 441

Gale, B.T. 20
Gapenski, L.C. 207, 492
Garvin, D.A. 227
Gates, Bill 135, 224
Gatorade 124
GE Capital 610, 771–2
gearing 9, 230
  in cash flow statement 67
  measures of 665–8
  MM on 711
  ratio in international finance 687–8
  traditional view of 677–9
  and WACC 696, 724–5
GEC 649, 745, 766
general valuation model (GVM) 126–7
generally accepted accounting principles (GAAP) 65, 117, 852
generic swap 444
Gent, Chris 779
Gentry, J. 461
Ghosh, C. 647
Giddy, I.H. 574
Gitman, L.J. 391
GKN plc 649
Glaum, M. 560, 574
global companies 259, 584, 853
Gluck, F.W. 791
going concern value 853
golden handcuffs 131
golden parachutes 767
Gordon, Myron 639, 656
government stock 100
Graham, B. 628
Granada 649
Grand Metropolitan Hotels 120
Graves, S.B. 57
Gray, S.J. 791
Green, Philip 615
Gregory, A. 755, 777, 792
Grinyer, J.R. 26
Grubb, M. 346, 388
Gruber, M. 645
Gup, B.E. 394

Halifax 772
Hamada, R.S. 719
Hand, Kevin 741
hands on 595
Harrington, D.R. 394
Harris, R.S. 776, 791
Harrison, J.S. 766
Harrison, R. 591
Harry Potter 169
Hass, J.E. 299
Hatzopoulos, P. 200, 203, 207, 237, 295
Hayes, R.H. 227
HBOS 772
hedging 853
  and currency risk 541
  and interest rate risk 444
  and risk exposure 437
  and risk transfer 438
  with share options 405–7
Helliwell, J.F. 299
Henderson, S.K. 574
Hertz, D.B. 291
Hewlett-Packard 432
highly leveraged transactions (HLTs) 693
Hill, N. 492
Hill Samuel 780
hire purchase 514–15, 853
Hirshleifer, J. 99
Ho, S.M. 299
Hobbs, Michael 616
Hodgkinson, L. 207
Holland 269
Holmes, D.E.A. 207, 237
home-made dividends 639, 656–7, 853
home-made gearing 711, 853
Honeywell 745
horizontal integration 751, 853
hostile bid, chronology of 749–50
Hucker, Brett 669
Hunt, J. 769, 779
hurdle rates in SVA 390–1
hybrid 853
Hypobank 742

ICAEW 121
ICI 446, 602, 635
ImClone 206
importing firms 259
improvement proposals in capital investment 234
imputation systems 644, 853
in the money 401, 407
income gearing 667–9, 853
income statement 66
incremental cash flow analysis in project appraisal 188–92
incremental hypothesis 248–50, 853
incrementalism 24
independent venture capital firms 593
industrial cooperation joint venture 788
inflation
  in project appraisal 194–6
  and time-value of money 81

information asymmetry 25, 52, 593, 697, 853
  and capital rationing 171–2
  and corporate funding 434
  and dividend policy 645–7
information content 853
information efficiency of markets 46
information technology 339
inherent shareholder value 376
initial public offering (IPO) 595, 853
Inland Revenue 196
insider trading 853
insolvency 690, 707
Insolvency Act (1986) 691
insurance
  companies 38
  and loan guarantees 413
  and risk transfer 438
insured schemes 38
interest *Agio* 549, 853
interest cover 67, 667–9, 853
interest rate exposure 443–4
interest rate management 443–5
interest rate option 414
interest rate parity (IRP) 548–9, 853
interest rate swap 443–4
interest rates
  calculating 91–2
  change 82, 697
  factors affecting 94
interest yield 613
intermediaries offer 598
internal hedging techniques 560–3
internal rate of return 92, 853
  and investment appraisal 158–61
internalisation 246, 248, 853
international bonds 616–17, 854
international diversification 338–9
international financing 687–9
International Fisher Theory 550–2, 689, 854
International Monetary Fund (IMF) 98
International Signals Corporation 118–19
international trade 529–33
  documents for 530
Internet Bubble 54
intrinsic worth of a share 48, 407
inventory management 478–84
investment categories in SVA 377–8
investment decisions 7–8, 154, 230
  accounting rate of return 163–5
  and capital rationing 170–4
  cash flow analysis 154–5
  constraints 170
  and financing decisions 191
  IRR techniques 158–61
  mutually exclusive projects, ranking 165–70
  NPV techniques 156–8
  payback period 162–3
  profitability index 161
investment portfolio 38, 39, 309
investment risk *see* risk
investment strategy
  advanced manufacturing technology investment 225–7
  capital investment process 229–37
  considerations 221–5
  environmental aspects 228–9
  post-auditing 237–9
investment trusts 39–40
investment-consumption decision 102–7
investor ratios 70
Investors for Industry (3i) 593, 647, 790
invoice discounting 510–11, 854
irredeemables 90, 100, 680
issue by tender 597
Issuing Houses Association 37

Jackson, Michael 610
Jenkins, Patrick 635
Jensen, M.C. 13, 24, 26, 53, 753, 776, 791
Jet airways 583
Johanson, J. 248
John, Peter 602
John Lewis Partnership 17
Johnson, Jo 206
joint ventures 764, 854
  and strategic alliances 788
joint-equity venture 788
Jones, C.S. 768, 769, 791
Jowit, Juliette 420
J.P. Morgan 653
Junankar, S. 389
junk bonds 607, 854
Jupe, R.E. 130
just-in-time planning 483

kanban system 484
Kaplan, R.S. 227, 240
Kaplan, S.N. 693
Kaplanis, E. 338
Keane, S. 144, 269, 640, 699
Keelin, T. 236
Kelda Group 627
Kenning Motor Group 775
Kerr, H.S. 384
Kester, W.C. 421
Keynes, J.M. 54
Kia Motor Corporation 616
Klemm, M. 764
K-Mart 694
KPMG 779

Lafontan, Robert 297
lagging 562, 854
Lambert, R.A. 26
Larcker, D.F. 26, 232
Late Payments of Commercial Debts (Interest) Act (1998) 503–4
Law of One Price 47, 252–3, 854
leading 562, 854
leasing 516–29
  as alternative source of funds 523
  cash flow advantages 524
  and corporation tax 524–9
  cost of 524
  equivalent loan 520–1
  evaluation 518–22
  as financing decision 521–2
  in long-term finance 618–20
  motives for 522–4
  off-balance sheet financing 524
  types 517
Lees, S. 763, 769, 779
Leeson, Nick 440
letter of credit 530–1, 854
  drawbacks to 531
leverage ratio 671
leveraged buy-out 767
Levis, M. 358
Levy, Alain 669
Levy, H. 207, 299, 327
licensing 246, 247, 764, 854
limited liability 4, 5
Limmack, R.J. 777
linear programming 177–81
Lintner, J. 646
liquidation 690
liquidity
  and dividend policy 648–51
  management of 446
  risk to 436
  transformation 36
liquidity preference theory 101
liquidity ratios 69
listed companies 854
Lithuania Gas 616
living dead 595
Lloyds TSB 745
Lloyd-Webber, Andrew 127
Lo, Andrew 51
loan capital 9
loan guarantee scheme 508, 854
loan stock 413, 606
Local Investment Networking Company (LINC) 591
London Inter-Bank Offer Rate (LIBOR) 511, 615
London International Financial Futures and Options Exchange (LIFFE) 11, 34
London Stock Exchange 41–6
  European market 45–6
  history 41–3
  market regulation 43–4
  share ownership 45
long-term finance
  corporate aims 584–6
  debt instruments 606–18
  leasing and sale-and-leaseback 618–20
  raising equity finance 590–606
  raising finance 586–7
  shareholder funds 587–90
Lorie, J.H. 175
Lucent 746
Luehrman, T.A. 731

McBeth, J. 357
McDaniel, W.R. 175
McDermott, M.C. 791
McGowan, C.B. 359
McIntyre, A.D. 207
MacKinlay, Craig 51
McKinsey 781
McKinsey-General Electric portfolio matrix 222
McRae T.W. 574
Madura, J. 269, 270, 574, 753
management buy-in (MBI) 594, 854
management buy-out (MBO) 593, 595, 615–16, 785–6, 854
  successful, checklist for 787
managerialism 13
Manchester United 43
Mandel, Morton 778
Mannesmann 10, 773
Manson, C. 777
Mao, J.C.T. 299
Marais, D. 448
Marconi 405, 507, 742
marginal cost of capital (MCC) 684, 854
marginal efficiency of investment (MEI) 636, 854
market capitalisation 65, 854
market efficiency 46–55
  greater 52–3
  implications of 51–2
market model 340
market portfolio 336, 352, 854
market risk 282–3, 436, 859
market segmentation theory 101
markets, access to 5
Markowitz, H.M. 310, 327
Marsh, P. 54, 57, 62, 394
Mason, C. 591
matching 435, 561, 854
materials resources planning (MRP) 483
Mathur, I. 776
Mattel 229
Mayer, C. 778
Meall, L. 691
mean-variance rule 287
Meckling, W.H. 13, 24, 26
Mehra, R. 346
Mercer Consultancy 777
Merchant, Khozem 250
merchant banks 37
mergers 10, 855
  impact of, assessing 773–9
  integration sequence 769–71
  for management control 753
  post-merger integration 768–73
Merton, R. 421
mezzanine finance 615, 855
Microsoft 135, 224
Miller, M. 327, 491, 492, 627, 631, 639–40, 656, 664, 699, 708–10, 731
Mills, R.W. 207
minimum-risk portfolio 316, 322
Mississippi Bubble 5
modified internal rate of return (MIRR) 176–7, 855
Modigliani, F. 627, 631, 639–40, 656, 664, 708–10, 731
Modigliani & Miller (MM) capital structure theories 855
monetary policy committee 855
money market 34
money market cover 565, 855
Monopolies and Mergers Commission (MMC) 44, 601
Monte Carlo simulation 291
moral hazard 414, 593, 694, 855
Mossin, J. 356
Mowlem 432
Mozambique 98
MTM Entertainments 762
Mulally, Alan 297
multilateral netting 560, 855
multi-national company (MNC) 244, 855
  advantages 245–6
  international financing 687–9
multi-period capital rationing 174, 177–81
multi-period cash flows and risk 299–302
Murphy, J. 144
Muscovy Company 5
mutually exclusive projects, ranking 165–70
Myers, S.C. 26, 99, 175, 362, 421, 492, 534, 699, 725, 731

naked option 403
Nalco 250
Narayanaswamy 534
Nasdaq 706
natural hedge 263, 443, 855
natural matching 561
NatWest 505, 772
Neale, C.W. 207, 237, 251
negative returns 674
Nestlé 119–20, 610
net advantage of a lease (NAL) 519, 521, 847
net asset value (NAV) 114, 115, 855
  in brand valuation 122
  problems with 116–20
net book value 65
net debt 666, 855
net operating income 673
net present value (NPV) 94–8, 855
  adjusting for risk 292–5
  DCF and 156–8
  positive 25
  theoretical case for 102–4
  and unconventional cash flows 168
net working capital 445–7
netting 560, 855
neutral stocks 855
new issue markets 855
new product proposals in capital investment 234
News Corporation 610
NFC 784
niche companies 584, 855
Nikkei index 58
nil paid price of rights 603
Nissan 541
non-financial goals of management 13
non-recourse 855
Norwood, S.W. 394
notes 607

O'Connor, Ashling 669
offer for sale by prospectus 597
Office of Fair Trading 44, 601, 792
official list 44, 856
offset 267
Ong Bong Seng 706
open account 529
'Open Fisher' theory 550–2
operating clause 517
operating efficiency of markets 46
operating exposure 260–1, 856
  managing 263–4
operating gearing 281, 386, 585, 670–2, 856
operating gearing factor 386–7, 856
operating lease 856
operating leverage 671
operating profit 66
operational strategy 20
opportunity costs 24, 856
  in project appraisal 189
opportunity set 317, 322
optimal capital structure 316, 664, 856
optimal portfolio 316, 318, 856
option contract 401
option to abandon 415
option to wait and see 416, 419
option writer 401
options 25, 856
ordering costs 455
ordinary share capital 8, 587–8
Orr, D. 491, 492
O'Shea, D. 62
Osler, C. 555
out of the money 401
outright 542
overdraft 856
over-expansion 456
overreaction hypothesis 53
overstocking 478
over-the-counter (OTC) market 43, 566
overtrading 452, 456–8, 856
  consequences of and remedies for 458
owner's equity 856
ownership
  and long-term finance 585
  transferability of 4
Oxford Biomedica 42

Packard, Jim 505
Pacman defence 767
Panel on Takeovers and Mergers 44

parallel matching 264, 561, 856
part payout lease 517
participating shares 589
patents 247
payback period
in investment decisions 162–3
in project appraisal 203–5
Payne, A.F. 791
pay-out ratio 627
Peacock, A. 773
Pearson plc 308
pecking order theory 434, 697
Peel, M.J. 792
pension funds 38
PepsiCo 251, 788
perfectly correlated cash flows 300–1
perpetual warrant 614
perpetuity 100, 856
present value of 107–8
valuing 90–1
Peters, Edgar 56
Peters, E.E. 62
Petersen Publishers 741
Peterson, P.P. 534
Pettit, J. 656
Pike, R.H. 88, 171, 175, 200, 207, 240, 295, 299, 492
Pilkington 166, 334
Pinches, G. 207
Pindyck, R. 421
placing 598
placing with clawback 599
plain vanilla debt 611, 858
plain vanilla swap 444
Planet Hollywood 706
plant hire 517
Pohlman, R.A. 391
Pointon, J. 207
poison pill 767, 856
Polaroid Corporation 691
political risk 264–8, 856
in international finance 688
Poon, S. 358
Porter, M.E. 19, 764, 773
portfolio 309, 856
portfolio effect 310, 311–12, 856
portfolio investment 857
portfolio risk 282–3
portfolio theory
correlation, degrees of 319–23
with more than two components 323–4
principles 310–12
on project appraisal 325–6
risk, measuring 313–16
risk and return, differing 316–18
post-completion auditing 237–9, 769, 857
Poulson, Howard 778
Prasad, S.B. 269
pre-emption rights 599
preference shares 588–9, 857
in financing a takeover 757
preferential borrowing 522
Premier Industrial Corporation 778
premium 401, 588
Prescott, E.C. 346
present value 84–9
of annuity 108
arithmetic of 89–92
discount tables 85–8
of perpetuity 107–8
present value interest factor for an annuity (PVIFA) 86
present value interest factor (PVIF) 86, 158
Price, Colin 781
Price, J. 574
price variation 562
price:earnings ratio (PER) 59–61, 71, 857
and constant dividend valuation model 137–8
price-to-earnings multiple 114, 122
meaning of 123
pricing efficiency of markets 46
primary capital markets 35
principal-agent relationship 13
Prindl, A. 574
private placing 594
profit after tax (PAT) 66
profit and loss account 66
profit before interest and tax (PBIT) 671, 710
profit margin 67
profit retention 12
profitability index 161, 857
profitability ratios 67
project appraisal
ARR methods 202–3
DCF techniques 200–1
fixed overheads 191
incremental cash flow analysis in 188–92
inflation 194–6
payback period 203–5
portfolio analysis in 325–6
replacement decisions 192
taxation 196–200
project finance 225
project gearing factor 384
project risk factor 387, 857
proprietorial companies 584, 857
prospective earnings yield 850
prospectus 597, 600
provision 857
proxy beta 857
proxy discount rate 857
Pruitt, S.W. 391
purchasing power parity 252–3, 857
pure options 399
pure play technique 384
put option 401, 402
put-call parity 408

quadratic programming 323–4
Quaker Oats Company 12, 124, 367
Queens Moat Hotels 429
quick assets 69
quick ratio 447
quotation, obtaining 597–8
obligations 598–9
quotation, seeking 596–7
benefits and drawbacks 596
quoted companies 595–7

Radebaugh, L.H. 269
random walk theory 48, 857
Rank-Hovis-McDougal 120
Rappaport, A. 62, 138, 377
real assets 7, 857
real options 414, 420, 857
Really Useful Group 127
rebate clause 517
receivership 690
Recognised Investment Exchange (RIE) 44
record day 627, 857
redeemable shares 589
redemption 100
redemption yield 613
Redhead, K. 62, 421
Reed Elsevier 616
Reichmann, Paul 160
Reimann, B.C. 390, 391, 394
re-invoicing centres 563
relevant risk 857
re-packaging finance 36
replacement chain approach 208
replacement cost 117
replacement decisions 192
replacement investment 377
replacement proposals in capital investment 233
required return, assessing 345–50
and beta 349
risk premium, finding 346–8
risk-free rate 345–6
required return, traditional view of 677–9
reserves 589–90, 857
residual income 203
residual theory of dividends 636–7, 857
resourceful, evaluative, maximising model (REMM) 24
restrictive covenants 608
retail banking 37
retained earnings 857
retained profits 9
return on capital employed (ROCE) 12, 68, 163
return on equity 70, 674–5
return on shareholder's funds 70
returns from holding shares 333–4
Reuters 635
revaluation reserve 590
revenue reserves 857
revenue sensitivity 385–6, 857
revolving credit facility 507, 857
Rexam plc 693
rights issues 599, 600–4, 858
and dividends 642
rights lapse 603

risk
adjusted NPV 292–5
attitudes to 280–1
expected net present value (ENPV) 279–80
in factoring 509
in financial decisions 18–19
and financial gearing 673–4
in long-term finance 585
measurement of 283–7
multi-period cash flows 299–302
and return 333–7
and return in portfolio analysis 316–18
scenario analysis 291
sensitivity analysis 288–90
simulation analysis 291–2
techniques employed 295–8
and time-value of money 81
types 281–3
risk aversion 25, 280
in portfolio theory 312
with share options 405–7
risk avoidance 437
risk exposure 437
risk management 436–45
derivatives 439–42
hedging 442
interest rate management 443–5
stages 437–9
risk minimising policy 559
risk premium 18, 344, 858
risk reduction 36, 438
risk retention 437
risk sharing 563
risk transfer 438
risk-adjusted discount rate 293–5
risk-free assets 351–3, 858
R.J. Reynolds Tobacco 153
Robbie, K. 792
Robbins, S. 251
Rockefeller, John D. 652
Rodriguez, R.M. 574
Roll, R. 53, 362
Rolls-Royce 20, 141–3
Rose 792
Ross, S.A. 53, 357, 358, 695
Ross, Sarah 600
Rowntree 119–20
Royal & Sun Alliance 635
Royal Bank of Scotland 772
Royal/Dutch Shell Group 228, 572
Ruback, R.S. 776, 791
Rugman, A.M. 269
running yield 852
Rutherford, B.A. 130
Rutterford, J. 534, 621, 699

safety stocks 482
Saigol, Lina 229
Sainsbury 619
sale-and-leaseback (SAL) 618–20
San Miguel Corporation 616
Sanofi-Synthelabo 206
Sarnat, M. 207, 299, 327
Sartoris, W. 492
Savage, L.J. 175
scale economies 751, 858
scenario analysis 291
Scholes, M. 412, 421
Scottish and Newcastle 753, 788
scrip dividends 648, 858
scrip issues 605, 847
SEAQ 41, 60, 858
secondary capital markets 35
secondary lease 517
second-round financing 595
securities market 34
securitisation 610, 858
security market line (SML) 344, 858
seed capital 595
segmental beta 383
Seiyo Food Systems 752
self-administered schemes 38
sell-offs 784
semi-variance 285–6
sensitivity analysis 288–90, 858
and multi-period capital rationing 177, 180–1
separation theorem 106, 352
Shao, L.P. 269
Shapiro, A.C. 269, 574
share buyback 767, 858
share exchanges in financing takeovers 757
share options 15, 399–407
and corporate finance 413–14
and futures 441
as a hedge 405–7
pricing 407–13
speculative use of 403–5
terminology 401
share premium account 588, 858
share splits 605, 858
share warrants 413
shareholder value, maximising 12
shareholder value analysis (SVA) 138–43, 858
cost of equity 369
discount rate for FDI 392–3
and dividend growth model 368–74
hurdle rates 390–1
investment categories in 377–8
required return 374–6
tailored discount rates 381–8, 389
taxation and CAPM 388–9
value drivers in 376–8
shareholder wealth, and social responsibility 16–17
shareholder's funds 65, 587–90
authorised and issued share capital 587
ordinary shares 587–8
preference shares 588–9
see also under dividends
Sharpe, P. 236
Sharpe, W.F. 323, 327, 332, 693
short- and medium-term finance
bank credit 504–8
bill finance 511–13
factoring 508–10
hire purchase 514–15
for international trade 529–33
invoice discounting 510–11
leasing 516–29
trade credit 501–4
short selling 858
short term investment 491
shortage costs 454
short-term asset management
cash management 484–91
inventory management 478–84
short-term investment 491
trade credit 467–78
short-termism 57–8
Siemens 766
sight draft 530, 531
signalling 695–6, 850
signalling effect 25
simple interest 81–2
simulation analysis 291–2
single-period cash flows 283–6
Sirower, Mark 781–2
Skapinker, Michael 782
Smith, Adam 16
SmithKline Beecham 236
Smith, K.V. 461
social efficiency of markets 46
social responsibility 16–17
Solnik, B.H. 338
South Sea Bubble 5, 54
Special Purpose Vehicle (SPV) 609, 689
specific risk 335–6, 858
speculators 437
spin-offs 784–5
spot buying/selling 34
spot market 542, 858
spot rate 258, 858
spot-forward swap 565
spread 542, 858
Standard Chartered Bank 744
standard deviation 284–5, 335
start-up capital 595
statutory proposals in capital investment 234
Stewart, Rod 610
Stobaugh, R. 251
Stock Exchange Electronic Trading Service (SETS) 42
Stock Exchange introduction 598
stock splits 858
stockholding period 69
stockout 482
straddle 402
straight vanilla debt 611, 858
strategic exposure 260, 856
strategic investment option 417–19
strategic portfolio analysis 221
strategic proposals in capital investment 234
strategy in financial decisions 19–23
and value creation 20–3
strike price 401, 566, 851
Strong, N. 358, 362

Sudarsanam, P.S. 777, 792
sunk costs 24, 858
  in project appraisal 189–90
supplier credit days 69
sustainable competitive advantage 221
Swalm, R.O. 325, 391
swaps 441, 569
Swire, D.J. 20
switchover costs 249
SWOT analysis 762
synergies 752, 859
systematic returns 341–2
systematic risk 335–6, 859
  and security valuation 339–44

tailored discount rates in SVA 381–8, 389
Tait, Nikki 453
take-over code 749, 859
take-over panel 749, 859
takeovers 859
  acquisition criteria 765–6
  bidding 766–7
  creating value 751–3
  defence tactics 767
  evaluating a bid 757–62
  failure of 762–3
  financing a bid 756–7
  hostile 778–9
  hostile bid, chronology of 749–50
  managerial motives 753–4
  motives for 750–6
  regulation of 747–9
  strategy of 762–7
  waves 743–50
taking up rights 603
tangible fixed assets 65
tax breaks 859
tax credit 859
tax irrelevance thesis 645
tax shield 682, 716, 718, 859
taxation 61
  and dividend growth model 372–4
  in foreign investment, differences 255–8
  in international finance 688
  in project appraisal 196–200
Taylor, S.J. 358
technical analysis 48–51
  exchange rate forecasting 554–5
technical efficiency of markets 46
term structure of interest rates 94, 100–1
terms of trade 469
Tesco 60, 619
Tetley 244, 786
Theakstons 753
theoretical ex-rights price (TERP) 603, 859
Thomas, S.H. 359
times interest earned 667
time-value of money 26, 80, 81, 407, 859
timing option 416–17, 419
tin parachutes 767
Tobin, J. 99, 327
Tomkins, C.R. 207, 269, 534
Tomkins plc 309, 369–70, 375–6, 588, 662
Tootal 767
Total Fina Elf Group 572
total shareholder return (TSR) 333–4, 859
Toyota 484, 651
Tozer Kemsley Milbourn 776
Trade and Industry, Department of 57, 508, 747, 776
trade credit 859
trade credit, managing 467–78
  cash discounts 473–4
  collection policy 474–5
  credit period 469–71
  credit standards 472–3
  debtors as security 475–8
  reasons for 467–9
trade credit for short- and medium-term finance 501–4
trade sale 595
trade-off theory 433–4, 697
traditional economic model 24
traditional options 401
traditional theory of capital structure 664, 859
transaction costs
  and capital rationing 172
  in foreign investment 248
transaction exposure 544, 859
transfer price 859
translation exposure 544–5, 859
trans-national organisation (TNO) 859
treasury bills 18, 278, 851
treasury function 430–3
  banking relationships 436
  cash operating cycle 450–1
  centralisation 432
  funding 433–5
  overtrading 456–8
  predicting failure 447–50
  risk management 436–45
  working capital management 445–7
  working capital policy 451–6
  yield curve, use of 458–60
treasury operations 431
Triton Energy, 752
Trustee Savings Bank 780
TVS 762

uncertainty 278–9
undated stocks 100
under-capitalisation 456
understocking 479
under-valuing 750
underwriting 601
Unilever 616, 788
unit trust 39–41, 859
United Nations Conference on Trade and Development (UNCTAD) 244
unquoted companies
  raising equity finance 590–5
  valuation of 131
unsystematic returns 341–2
Usinor 743
utility and risk 280

Vaga, T. 56
valuation 113–14
  of cash flows 125–7
  DCF approach 127–31
  dividend valuation model 131–4
  of earnings stream 122–4
  EBITDA 124–5
  free cash flow 128–31
  of shares 131–4
  of unquoted companies 131
  using published accounts 115–22
value additivity 751
value creation process 783
value drivers 139, 376–8
value gaps 780–2
  bidding 780–2
  and corporate parenting 780
  and financial management 780
  stock market efficiency 782
value-based management 859
Van Horne, J. 351, 693
variable costs 282
Venables, Terry 707
vendor placing 599
venture capital 593–5, 860
  and MBOs 786
Venture Capital Report 591
venture capital trusts 592
Vereinsbank 742
vertical integration 751, 860
Vickers 141
Virgin 127, 187, 278
Vodafone 10, 773
volatility of share prices 402

Waitrose 17
Walters, A. 792
warrants 614–15, 860
Waste Management 788
wealth, measuring 79–80
Weaver, S.C. 237
weighted average cost of capital (WACC) 678–9, 682, 685–7, 860
  calculating 722–5
  and capital structure 709
  and debt/equity ratio 710–12, 732
  for foreign investment 690
  and gearing 696, 724–5
  MM on 710–12
  required conditions for 684
Weingartner, H. 175
welfare proposals in capital investment 234
Wessex Water 788
Weston, J.F. 62, 362, 621, 656, 699, 731
white knight 767, 860
Whyte A.M. 270

Wiedersheim-Paul, F. 248
Wilkie, A.D. 347, 388
Williams, Gareth 635
Wilson, M. 251, 269
Wilson Committee 171, 714
Wolfe, M. 207
Woolridge, J. 647
working capital 65, 860
  changes, in project appraisal 190–1
  investment in 377
  management of 445–7
working capital costs 454
working capital policy 451–6
World Bank 98
World Trade Organisation 347
Wright, M. 792
writing-down allowances 198, 515, 525

Xu, X.G. 358, 362

yield 61, 860
yield curve 100, 860
  explaining 100–1
  use of 458–60
Young, D. 144

Zeneca 466
zero coupon bonds 608, 860
zero-sum game, options as 567
z-score 448–9, 860